Department of Economic and Social Affairs
Statistics Division

NATIONAL ACCOUNTS STATISTICS: MAIN AGGREGATES AND DETAILED TABLES, 2012

PART IV

UNITED NATIONS
NEW YORK, 2013

The Department of Economic and Social Affairs of the United Nations Secretariat is a vital interface between global policies in the economic, social and environmental spheres and national action. The Department works in three main interlinked areas: (i) it compiles, generates and analyses a wide range of economic, social and environmental data and information on which Members States of the United Nations draw to review common problems and to take stock of policy options; (ii) it facilitates the negotiations of Member States in many intergovernmental bodies on joint courses of action to address ongoing or emerging global challenges; and (iii) it advises interested Governments on the ways and means of translating policy frameworks developed in United Nations conferences and summits into programmes at the country level and helps build national capacities through technical assistance.

NOTE

Symbols of United Nations documents are composed of capital letters combined with figures. Mention of such a symbol indicates a reference to a United Nations document. The first 14 editions of the National Accounts Yearbook were issued without series symbols.

The designations used in this publication have been provided by the competent authorities. Those designations and the presentation of material in this publication do not imply the expression of any opinion whatsoever on the part of the Secretariat of the United Nations concerning the legal status of any country, territory, city or area or of its authorities, or concerning the delimitation of its frontiers or boundaries.

Where the designation "country or area" appears in the headings of tables, it covers countries, territories, cities or areas.

ST/ESA/STAT/SER.X/50. PART IV

UNITED NATIONS PUBLICATION
Sales No. E.14.XVII.5 H

ISBN 978-92-1-161574-6
e-ISBN 978-92-1-056273-7

Inquiries should be directed to:
SALES SECTION
UNITED NATIONS
NEW YORK, NY 10017

Printed by the United Nations Reproduction Section, New York

CONTENTS

INTRODUCTION

1. This is the fifty-fourth issue of *National Accounts Statistics: Main Aggregates and Detailed Tables*[1,2] showing detailed national accounts estimates for 204 countries and areas for the reporting years 2001 to 2012. Like the previous issues, it has been prepared by the Statistics Division of the Department for Economic and Social Affairs of the United Nations Secretariat with the generous co-operation of national statistical offices. It is issued in accordance with the recommendation of the Statistical Commission at its first session[3] that the Statistics Division of the United Nations should publish regularly the most recent available data on national accounts for as many countries and areas as possible.

THE NATIONAL ACCOUNTS QUESTIONNAIRE

2. This publication is the fourteenth issue based on the United Nations National Accounts Questionnaire (NAQ) introduced in October 1999, which in turn is based on *the System of National Accounts 1993 (1993 SNA)*[4].

3. The 1993 SNA was unanimously recommended to the United Nations Economic and Social Council by its Statistical Commission at its 24th session in March 1993. Similar to the recommendation made in 1968 for its predecessor, *A System of National Accounts* (1968 SNA)[5], the Council in its resolution 1993/5 of 12 July 1993 recommends that Member States use the 1993 SNA in the international reporting of comparable national accounting data. However, it should be highlighted that the Council went a few steps further in 1993 and also recommends that Member States consider using the 1993 SNA: (a) as the standard for the compilation of their national accounts statistics, (b) to promote the integration of economic and related statistics, and (c) as an analytical tool. In 2003 the United Nations Statistical Commission (UNSC) called for an update of the 1993 SNA. The updated SNA, called The System of National Accounts 2008[6], or in short the 2008 SNA, was finalised during 2009. It is expected that most countries would start submitting national accounts data according to the 2008 SNA from 2015 onwards. So far, only Australia; China, Hong Kong Special Administrative Region; and Timor-Leste have started submitting data according to the 2008 SNA.

4. Taking into account all the above recommendations the United Nations Statistics Division (UNSD), in cooperation with the United Nations Regional Commissions, has designed the United Nations National Accounts Questionnaire (NAQ) based with the following objectives in mind:

(a) The tables included are those that provide a data set most relevant for global and regional analysis carried out by the United Nations Department of Economic and Social Affairs (DESA) and other international and regional organizations. It should be noted that the scope of the 1993 SNA aims at a much more detailed analysis at the national level than what the questionnaire tables represent. The UNSC has agreed that the scope and pace of the implementation of the 1993 SNA must be decided by each country according to its analytical and policy needs, the resources available for implementation, and the current state of basic data.

(b) The tables reflect an equally balanced emphasis between production analysis based on supply and use information by industries on the one hand, and production, income and financial analysis based on integrated accounts for institutional sectors on the other. Thus, the behaviour of economic agents and distributional effects which are very important in explaining differences in economic structures and developments of countries can be identified.

SCOPE OF THE QUESTIONNAIRE

5. The data tables of the questionnaire are divided into five parts. Part I (Tables 1.1 to 1.3) requests summary information on gross domestic product by expenditure in current and constant prices and on the relations among product, income, saving and net lending aggregates.

6. Part II (Tables 2.1 to 2.6) of the questionnaire requests information on kind of activity breakdowns. The data series for this group of tables are requested to be reported according to the International Standard Industrial Classification of all Economic Activities (ISIC[7,8]). Tables 2.1 to 2.3 follow the ISIC Rev. 3 and are equivalent to Tables 2.4 to 2.6, which follow the ISIC Rev. 4, and countries can complete the appropriate tables according to the ISIC version they use for compiling their national accounts. Data can be provided either as a combination of tabulation categories (A+B, G+H, J+K and M+N+O, for the ISIC Rev. 3; or A, B+C+D+E, C, F, G+H+I, J, K, L, M+N, O+P+Q and R+S+T, for the ISIC Rev. 4) or as single tabulation categories (Sections A to P for ISIC Rev. 3; and A to T, for ISIC Rev. 4) (one-digit level of ISIC). In the case of ISIC Section A, information at the two-digit level is requested for divisions 01, 02 (and 03, for the ISIC Rev. 4); whereas for ISIC Rev. 3 Section I information is requested for division 64 and the sum of the divisions 60 to 63. Where appropriate both current and constant prices are specified.

7. Part III (Tables 3.1 and 3.2) of the questionnaire requests information on functional breakdowns in current prices. The data series are requested to be reported according to the Classifications of Expenditure According to Purpose[9]. For the general government final consumption expenditure (including both individual and collective consumption expenditure), data are requested for the 10 divisions of the Classification of the Functions of Government (COFOG). For the individual consumption expenditure by households, data are requested for the first 12 divisions of the Classification of Individual Consumption According to Purpose (COICOP), which is based on the Central Product Classification (CPC)[10,11]. For the individual consumption expenditure by non-profit institutions serving households, data are requested for groups 13.1 through 13.6 of division 13 of COICOP. For the individual consumption expenditure by general government, data are requested for groups 14.1 through 14.5 of division 14 of COICOP.

8. Part IV (Tables 4.1 to 4.9) of the questionnaire requests information on the integrated economic accounts. The data requested in this part includes the sequence of accounts for the total economy, rest of the world and the five institutional sectors of the system, i.e. the non-financial corporations, financial corporations, general government, households, and non-profit institutions serving households. For all of the sectors as well as for the total economy data for the uses and resources as well as balancing items are requested for each of the accounts from the production account through the financial account as specified in Annex V, Part II of the 1993 SNA.

9. Part V (Tables 5.1 and 5.2) of the questionnaire requests information on the cross-classification of gross value added by industries and institutional sectors. Data are requested to be reported for gross value added of the total economy and the five institutional sectors of the system included in Part IV cross-classified by categories of ISIC Rev. 3 (Table 5.1) or ISIC Rev. 4 (Table 5.2) as indicated in Part II above.

10. Countries are requested to update the data tables and complete them as comprehensively as possible. The tables are listed below:

Part I: Main aggregates

Table 1.1 Gross domestic product by expenditures at current prices
Table 1.2 Gross domestic product by expenditures at constant prices
Table 1.3 Relations among product, income, saving and net lending aggregates at current prices

Part II: Domestic production by industries

Table 2.1 Value added by industries at current prices (ISIC Rev. 3)
Table 2.2 Value added by industries at constant prices (ISIC Rev. 3)
Table 2.3 Output, gross value added and fixed assets by industries at current prices (ISIC Rev. 3)
Table 2.4 Value added by industries at current prices (ISIC Rev. 4)
Table 2.5 Value added by industries at constant prices (ISIC Rev. 4)
Table 2.6 Output, gross value added and fixed assets by industries at current prices (ISIC Rev. 4)

Part III: Classifications of expenditure according to purpose

Table 3.1 General government final consumption expenditure by function at current prices
Table 3.2 Individual consumption expenditures at current prices

Part IV: Integrated economic accounts

Table 4.1 Total economy (S.1)
Table 4.2 Rest of the world (S.2)
Table 4.3 Non-financial corporations (S.11)
Table 4.4 Financial corporations (S.12)
Table 4.5 General government (S.13)
Table 4.6 Households (S.14)
Table 4.7 Non-profit institutions serving households (S.15)
Table 4.8 Combined Sectors: Non-Financial and Financial Corporations (S.11 + S.12)
Table 4.9 Combined Sectors: Households and NPISH (S.14 + S.15)

Part V: Cross classification of gross value added by industries and institutional sectors

Table 5.1 Cross classification of gross value added by industries and institutional sectors (ISIC Rev. 3)
Table 5.2 Cross classification of gross value added by industries and institutional sectors (ISIC Rev. 4)

11. It should be noted that the NAQ does not cover the full scope of the accounts and tables that comprise the 1993 SNA since it mainly serves to collect data needed for global and regional analysis rather than national analysis. Also, it is in certain respects less comprehensive than the previous questionnaire based on the 1968 SNA since, for example, it does not include tables for the other changes in assets accounts and the balance sheets of the total economy and institutional sectors; the data requested on stocks of fixed assets is very limited; the tables requested broken down by kind of economic activity are less detailed, showing mainly

the one-digit level of ISIC instead of the two-digit level of ISIC.

COLLECTION OF DATA

12. To collect the large volume of national accounts data, the Statistics Division annually sends a pre-filled NAQ to countries or areas. The recipients are requested to update the questionnaire with the latest available national accounts estimates and to indicate where the scope and coverage of the country estimates differ for conceptual or statistical reasons from the definitions and classifications recommended by the 1993 SNA. Data obtained from these replies are supplemented by information gathered from correspondence with the national statistical offices and from national source publications. Countries are also requested to provide a brief overview of the sources and methods to compile their national accounts.

13. In order to lighten the reporting burden of countries to different international and regional organizations the UNSD receives data from the Statistical Office of the European Commission (EUROSTAT), the Organisation for Economic Co-operation and Development (OECD), the United Nations Economic Commission for Europe (ECE) and the Caribbean Community (CARICOM) on behalf of their constituents. The UNSD, EUROSTAT and the OECD have agreed on an integrated set of national accounts questionnaires. The three organizations exchange data to a maximum extent possible. Thanks to the consistency of the 1993 SNA and the European System of Accounts (ESA 1995), all OECD countries submit data either to EUROSTAT or OECD but need not provide duplicate submissions. Member States of OECD which are not members of the European Community complete a sub-set of the ESA 1995 questionnaire. The ECE provides data for transition economies. CARICOM uses the NAQ to collect data from its Member States and provides it to UNSD. As a result, the United Nations questionnaire based on the 1993 SNA is sent to less than 160 countries, areas, and territories out of the 235 (of which only 204 have provided sufficient data to be published) included in the UNSD National Accounts database.

14. In order to create a comprehensive database based on the 1993 SNA, UNSD made a one-time conversion of data from the 1968 SNA format to the 1993 SNA format for all countries included in the UNSD national accounts database.

CONCEPTUAL REFERENCES AND PRESENTATION OF DATA

15. The form and concepts of the statistical tables in the present publication generally conform to the recommendations by the 1993 SNA. A summary of the conceptual framework and definitions of transactions is provided in chapter I of the present publication.

16. Although the NAQ collects data in the 1993 SNA format, countries may still use the 1968 SNA (or in some rare cases the 1953 SNA) guidelines to compile their national accounts. The UNSD evaluates the status of the conceptual adherence to the 1993 SNA from time to time.

17. The Series note at the top of each table indicates which SNA version is used by the given country to compile their national accounts. Series numbers below 100 relates to data according to the 1968 SNA data and series numbers 100 and above relates to data according to the 1993 SNA. Whenever 1968 SNA data are not replaced backwards for all years by a series of 1993 SNA data, the 1993 SNA data are presented in a new row with one overlapping year in order to allow users to link the two series. When the scope and coverage of the estimates differ for conceptual or statistical reasons from the definitions and classifications recommended by the 1993 SNA, a footnote is attached to the relevant tables.

18. In the tables with constant price data (Tables 1.2, 2.2 and 2.5), the data with a new fixed base year are presented as a new sub-series in a separate row with one overlapping year. The new base year (or reference year) is indicated in the column of the year in which the new sub-series starts. An exception to this rule is chain linked volume series where figures are given at prices of the previous year. Such data are presented as a single series and the respective base year is indicated for every year. For countries, which use chain linked volume series but link the data to a uniform reference year, a respective qualification is made in the country note. It has to be noted that constant price data, which are linked or chained in such a way are not additive, i.e. the total is not equivalent to the sum of its components. Also, constant price data, which are scaled up or down to a certain reference year in order to allow international comparison, are not additive.

19. In the present publication, the data for each country or area are presented in separate chapters, in alphabetical order, under uniform table headings and classifications of the 1993 SNA. Unless otherwise stated, the data in the country tables relate to the calendar year against which they are shown. The Series note at the top of each table indicates the type of fiscal year used for any given series.

COMPARABILITY OF THE NATIONAL ESTIMATES

20. Every effort has been made to present the estimates of the various countries or areas in a form designed to facilitate international comparability. To this

end, important differences in concept, scope, coverage and classification have been described in the notes, which precede and accompany the country tables. Such differences should be taken into account if misleading comparison among countries or areas are to be avoided. It should also be noted that the country notes not only refer to the latest data covered in this publication but to the country in general.

REVISIONS

21. The figures shown are the most recent estimates and revisions available at the time of compilation. In general, figures for the most recent year are to be regarded as provisional.

NOMENCLATURE

22. The information for the countries and areas shown in this publication reflect what is available to the UNSD as of August 2013. Updated national accounts data are usually provided by countries to the UNSD between January and July. Data for the year 2012 are currently available for 118 countries and areas.

23. The data for the countries listed below are represented as follows:

China is published in this yearbook in three sections: China; China, Hong Kong Special Administrative Region; and China, Macao Special Administrative Region. The data for China exclude the special administrative regions of Hong Kong and Macao.

Netherlands Antilles – The Netherlands Antilles as a country was dissolved on 10 October 2010. As of this date, Curaçao and Sint Maarten became countries within the Kingdom of the Netherlands, and the islands Bonaire, Saba and Sint Eustatius became special municipalities of the Netherlands. Data up to 2009 that appear under Netherlands Antilles refer to the former country. Data for Curaçao and Sint Maarten appear separately under the respective country names. Data for the islands Bonaire, Saba and Sint Eustatius, when available, will appear together under the appropriate name.

Sudan and South Sudan – South Sudan seceded from Sudan in July 2011. Data for the former Sudan appear under "Sudan (up to 2011)". Data for Sudan and South Sudan in the new configuration (after July 2011) appear under the respective country names.

Tanzania – The data for Tanzania are published in two parts in this yearbook: mainland Tanzania and Zanzibar. Note that the data listed under Tanzania does not include Zanzibar.

SYMBOLS AND DATA DISPLAY

24. The following symbols have been employed:

Data not available.. [...]

Magnitude nil or less than five percent of the unit employed.. [**0.0**]

Decimal figures are always preceded by a point [.]

25. Each series version is presented in a separate row and identified by a series number in the column of the year in which it starts. A new series version is introduced if the data displayed differs from preceding data in terms of methodology, fiscal-year type or currency. A Series note at the top of each table informs about the SNA version applied, currency denomination, and fiscal-year type used. The scale used to present the data is displayed at the top right of each table.

26. Decimals in tables do not necessarily add to totals shown because of rounding.

GENERAL DISCLAIMER

27. The designations employed and the presentation of material in this publication do not imply the expression of any opinion whatsoever on the part of the Secretariat of the United Nations concerning the legal status of any country, territory, city or area or of its authorities, or concerning the delimitation of its frontiers and boundaries.

28. Where the designation "country or area" appears in the headings of tables, it covers countries, territories, cities or areas. In prior issues of this publication where the designation "country" appears in the headings of tables, it covers countries, territories, cities or areas

---

1/ United Nations, 1957-1981, Yearbook of National Accounts Statistics. 25 editions. New York: United Nations Publications.

2/ United Nations, 1982-2011, National Accounts Statistics: Main Aggregates and Detailed Tables. 28 editions. New York: United Nations Publications.

3/ United Nations, 1947, Official Records of the Economic and Social Council Supplement No. 6 (E/264), chap. VIII, para. 42. New York: United Nations Publications.

4/ Commission of the European Communities, International Monetary Fund, Organisation for Economic Cooperation and Development, United Nations, and World Bank, 1993, System of National Accounts 1993. New York: United Nations Publications.

5/ United Nations, 1968, A System of National Accounts, Studies in Methods, Series F No.2, Rev.3. New York: United Nations Publications.

6/ European Commission, International Monetary Fund, Organisation for Economic Cooperation and Development, United Nations, and World Bank, 2009, System of National Accounts 2008. New York: United Nations Publications.

7/ United Nations, 1990, International Standard Industrial Classification of All Economic Activities (ISIC Revision 3), Statistical Paper, Series M, No.4, Rev.3. New York: United Nations Publications.

8/ United Nations, 2008, International Standard Industrial Classification of All Economic Activities (ISIC Revision 4), Statistical Paper, Series M, No.4, Rev.4. New York: United Nations Publications.

9/ United Nations, 1999, Classifications of Expenditure according to Purpose: Classification of the Functions of Government (COFOG); Classification of Individual Consumption According to Purpose (COICOP); Classification of the Purposes of Non-Profit Institutions Serving Households (COPNI); Classification of the Outlays of Producers According to Purpose (COPP), Statistical Paper, Series M, No. 84. New York: United Nations Publications.

10/ United Nations, 1997, Central Product Classification Version 1.0, Statistical Paper, Series M, No.77, Ver.1.0. New York: United Nations Publications.

11/ United Nations, 2008, Central Product Classification Version 2.0, available at http://unstats.un.org/unsd/cr/registry/docs/CPCv2_structure.pdf.

I. SYSTEM OF NATIONAL ACCOUNTS

1. The origins of the System of National Accounts (SNA) trace back to the 1947 Report of the Sub-Committee on National Income Statistics of the League of Nations Committee of Statistical Experts under the leadership of Richard Stone[1]. At its first session in 1947, the United Nations Statistical Commission emphasized the need for international statistical standards for the compilation and updating of comparable statistics in support of a large array of policy needs. Specifically, the Commission recommended that the United Nations Statistical Office, in consultation with the interested specialized agencies, should work on guidelines for national accounts statistics (national income and expenditure), taking into consideration best practises and international comparability[2]. In view of the emphasis on international statistical standards, the first national accounts standard was produced and published in 1953. The SNA was subsequently revised and updated in 1960, 1964, 1968 and 1993. In 2003 the Statistical Commission called for an update of the 1993 SNA. The System of National Accounts 2008[3], (in short the 2008 SNA) was finalised in 2009. This chapter describes the concepts and definitions of the SNA as recommended by the 1993 SNA.

A. THE SNA AS A SYSTEM

2. The System of National Accounts is a statistical framework that provides a coherent, consistent and integrated set of macroeconomic accounts, balance sheets and tables based on a set of internationally agreed concepts, definitions, classifications and accounting rules. It provides a comprehensive accounting framework within which economic data can be compiled and presented in a format that is designed for purposes of economic analysis, decision-taking and policy-making. The accounts themselves present in a condensed way a great mass of detailed information, organized according to economic principles and perceptions, about the working of an economy. They provide a comprehensive and detailed record of the complex economic activities taking place within an economy and of the interaction between the different economic agents, and groups of agents that takes place on markets or elsewhere. In practice the accounts are compiled for a succession of time periods, thus providing a continuing flow of information that is indispensable for the monitoring, analysis and evaluation of the performance of an economy over time. The SNA provides information not only about economic activities, but also about the levels of an economy's productive assets and the wealth of its inhabitants at particular points of time. Finally, the SNA includes an external account that displays the links between an economy and the rest of the world.

3. The SNA may be implemented at different levels of aggregation: at the level of individual economic agents, or institutional units as they are called in the System; for groups of such units, or institutional sectors; or at the level of the total economy. Although traditionally described as a system of national accounts, for analytical purposes the SNA has to be implemented at lower levels of aggregation. In order to understand the workings of the economy, it is essential to be able to observe and analyse the economic interactions taking place between the different sectors of the economy. Certain key aggregate statistics, such as gross domestic product (GDP), which are widely used as indicators of economic activity at the level of the total economy, are defined within the System, but the calculation of such aggregates has long ceased to be the primary purpose for compiling the accounts.

4. The System is built around a sequence of interconnected flow accounts linked to different types of economic activity taking place within a given period of time, together with balance sheets that record the values of the stocks of assets and liabilities held by institutional units or sectors at the beginning and end of the period. Each flow account relates to a particular kind of activity such as production, or the generation, distribution, redistribution or use of income. Each account is balanced by introducing a balancing item defined residually as the difference between the total resources and uses recorded on the two sides of the account. The balancing item from one account is carried forward as the first item in the following account, thereby making the sequence of accounts an articulated whole. The balancing items typically encapsulate the net result of the activities covered by the accounts in question and are therefore economic constructs of considerable interest and analytical significance - for example, value added, disposable income and saving. There is also a strong link between the flow accounts and the balance sheets, as all the changes occurring over time that affect the assets or liabilities held by institutional units or sectors are systematically recorded in one or another of the flow accounts. The closing balance sheet is fully determined by the opening balance sheet and the transactions or other flows recorded in the sequence of accounts.

B. ACCOUNTS AND THEIR CORRESPONDING ECONOMIC ACTIVITIES

5. The purpose of this section is to give a very brief summary of the main sequence of accounts in order to

describe the main features of the System before discussing other related issues. It is impossible to do justice to the wealth of information contained in the System in a short section of this kind, and reference should be made to chapter II of the 1993 SNA for a comprehensive overview of the System.

1. The sequence of accounts

Current accounts

6. These accounts record the production of goods and services, the generation of incomes by production, the subsequent distribution and redistribution of incomes among institutional units, and the use of incomes for purposes of consumption or saving.

Production account

7. The production account records the activity of producing goods and services as defined within the System. Its balancing item, gross value added, is defined as the value of output less the value of intermediate consumption and is a measure of the contribution to GDP made by an individual producer, industry or sector. Gross value added is the source from which the primary incomes of the System are generated and is therefore carried forward into the primary distribution of income account. Value added may also be measured net by deducting consumption of fixed capital.

Distribution and use of income accounts

8. These consist of a set of articulated accounts showing how incomes are:

> Generated by production
>
> Distributed to institutional units with claims on the value added created by production
>
> Redistributed among institutional units, mainly by government units through social security contributions and benefits and taxes
>
> Eventually used by households, government units or non-profit institutions serving households (NPISHs) for purposes of final consumption or saving.

9. The balancing item emerging from the complete set of income accounts is saving. The income accounts have considerable intrinsic economic interest in themselves. In particular, they are needed to explain the behaviour of institutional units as final consumers - that is, as users of the goods and services emanating from production for the satisfaction of the individual and collective needs and wants of households and the community. The balancing item, saving, is carried forward into the capital account, the first in the System's sequence of accumulation accounts.

Accumulation accounts

10. These are flow accounts that record the acquisition and disposal of financial and non-financial assets and liabilities by institutional units through transactions or as a result of other events:

> The capital account records acquisitions and disposals of non-financial assets as a result of transactions with other units or internal bookkeeping transactions linked to production (changes in inventories and consumption of fixed capital).
>
> The financial account records acquisitions and disposals of financial assets and liabilities, also through transactions.
>
> A third account, the other changes in assets account, consists of two sub-accounts. The first, the other changes in volume of assets account, records changes in the amounts of the assets and liabilities held by institutional units or sectors as a result of factors other than transactions; for example, destruction of fixed assets by natural disasters. The second, the revaluation account, records those changes in the values of assets and liabilities that result from changes in their prices.

11. The link between the accumulation accounts and the income accounts is provided by the fact that saving - that is, disposable income that is not spent on consumption goods or services - must be used to acquire financial or non-financial assets of one kind or another, if only cash, the most liquid financial asset. When saving is negative, the excess of consumption over disposable income must be financed by disposing of assets or incurring liabilities. The financial account shows the way in which funds are channelled from one group of units to another, especially through financial intermediaries. Access to finance is a prerequisite for engaging in many types of economic activities.

Balance sheets

12. The balance sheets show the values of the stocks of assets and liabilities held by institutional units or sectors at the beginning and end of an accounting period. As already noted, the values of the assets and liabilities held at any moment in time vary automatically whenever

any transactions, price changes or other changes affecting the volume of assets or liabilities held take place. These are all recorded in one or another of the accumulation accounts so that the difference between the values in the opening and closing balance sheets is entirely accounted for within the System, provided, of course, that the assets and liabilities recorded in the balance sheets are valued consistently with the transactions and other changes - that is, at current prices.

2. Activities and transactions

13. The accounts of the System are designed to provide analytically useful information about the behaviour of institutional units and the activities in which they engage, such as production, consumption and the accumulation of assets. They usually do this by recording the values of the goods, services or assets involved in the transactions between institutional units that are associated with these activities rather than by trying to record or measure the physical processes directly. For example, the accounts do not record the physical consumption of goods and services by households - the eating of food or the burning of fuel within a given time period. Instead, they record the expenditures that households make on final consumption goods and services or, more generally, the values of the goods and services they acquire through transactions with other units, whether purchased or not. Data on transactions provide the basic source material from which the values of the various elements in the accounts are built up or derived. The use of transactions data has important advantages. First, the prices at which goods and services are exchanged in transactions between buyers and sellers on markets provide the information needed for valuing, directly or indirectly, all the items in the accounts. Secondly, a transaction that takes place between two different institutional units has to be recorded for both parties to the transaction and therefore generally appears twice in a system of macroeconomic accounts. This enables important linkages to be established in the System. For example, output is obtained by summing the amounts sold, bartered or transferred to other units plus the amounts entered into, less the amounts withdrawn from inventories. In effect, the value of output is obtained by recording the various uses of that output by means of data on transactions. In this way, flows of goods and services can be traced through the economic system from their producers to their eventual users. Some transactions are only internal bookkeeping transactions that are needed when a single unit engages in two activities, such as the production and consumption of the same good or service, but the great majority of transactions take place between different units on markets.

C. THE INSTITUTIONAL SECTORS OF THE ECONOMY

14. The purpose of this section is to indicate very briefly the main sectors of the economy for which it is possible to compile the full sequence of accounts summarized in the previous section. Two main kinds of institutional units, or transactors, are distinguished in the System - households and legal entities. The latter are either entities created for purposes of production, mainly corporations and non-profit institutions (NPIs), or government units, including social security funds. Institutional units are essentially units that are capable of owning goods and assets, incurring liabilities and engaging in economic activities and transactions with other units in their own right. For the purposes of the System, institutional units that are resident in the economy are grouped together into five mutually exclusive sectors composed of the following types of units:

Non-financial corporations

Financial corporations

Government units, including social security funds

NPIs serving households (NPISHs)

Households.

The five sectors together make up the total economy. Each sector is also divided into sub-sectors. For example, the non-financial and financial corporations sectors are divided to distinguish corporations subject to control by governments or foreign units from other corporations. The System makes provision for a complete set of flow accounts and balance sheets to be compiled for each sector, and sub-sector if desired, as well as for the total economy. The total number of accounts that may be compiled is therefore potentially quite large, depending upon the level of disaggregation that is required and feasible. Only by disaggregation into sectors and sub-sectors is it possible to observe the interactions between the different parts of the economy that need to be measured and analysed for purposes of policy-making. The complete set of accounts at the level of the five main sectors is shown in annex V of the 1993 SNA.

15. Institutional units that are resident abroad form the rest of the world. The System does not require accounts to be compiled in respect of economic activities taking place in the rest of the world, but all transactions between resident and non-resident units have to be recorded in order to obtain a complete accounting for the

economic behaviour of resident units. Transactions between residents and non-residents are grouped together in a single account, the rest of the world account.

D. OTHER FEATURES OF THE SYSTEM

16. The SNA is a rich and detailed economic accounting system that extends well beyond the main sequence of accounts to encompass other accounts or tables that either contain information that cannot be included in the main accounts or present information in alternative ways, such as matrices, that may be more appropriate for certain types of analysis. It is not proposed to list all these various elements at this point, as they are described in chapter II of the 1993 SNA, but it is useful to draw attention to two specific elements which play a major role in the System.

1. Supply and use tables

17. In addition to the flow accounts and balance sheets described earlier, the central framework of the System also contains detailed supply and use tables in the form of matrices that record how supplies of different kinds of goods and services originate from domestic industries and imports and how those supplies are allocated between various intermediate or final uses, including exports. These tables involve the compilation of a set of integrated production and generation of income accounts for industries - that is, groups of establishments as distinct from institutional units - that are able to draw upon detailed data from industrial censuses or surveys. The supply and use tables provide an accounting framework within which the commodity flow method of compiling national accounts - in which the total supplies and uses of individual types of goods and services have to be balanced with each other - can be systematically exploited. The supply and use tables also provide the basic information for the derivation of detailed input-output tables that are extensively used for purposes of economic analysis and projections.

2. Price and volume measures

18. The System also provides specific guidance about the methodology to be used to compile an integrated set of price and volume indices for flows of goods and services, gross value added and GDP that are consistent with the concepts and accounting principles of the System. It is recommended that annual chain indices should be used where possible, although fixed base indices may also be used when the volume measures for components and aggregates have to be additively consistent for purposes of economic analysis and modelling.

19. Rates of inflation and economic growth appropriately measured by price and volume indices for the main aggregates of the System are key variables both for the evaluation of past economic performance and as targets for the formulation of economic policy-making. They are an essential part of the System, especially given the emergence of inflation as an endemic economic problem in many countries. The System also recognizes that the growth in the volume of GDP and the growth of an economy's real income are not the same because of trading gains or losses resulting from changes in international terms of trade.

E. CONCEPTS

20. The contents of the SNA depend not only on the accounting structure itself - that is, on the type and format of the accounts - but also on the ways in which the items included in the accounts are defined and classified. The issues involved are not simply of a technical nature but raise fundamental questions of economic theory and principles. The concepts and classifications used in the System have a considerable impact on the ways in which the data may be used and the interpretations placed on them.

1. The production boundary

21. The activity of production is fundamental. In the System, production is understood to be a physical process, carried out under the responsibility, control and management of an institutional unit, in which labour and assets are used to transform inputs of goods and services into outputs of other goods and services. All goods and services produced as outputs must be such that they can be sold on markets or at least be capable of being provided by one unit to another, with or without charge. The System includes within the production boundary all production actually destined for the market, whether for sale or barter. It also includes all goods or services produced and provided free to individual households or collectively to the community by government units or NPISHs.

Household production

22. The main problem for defining the range of activities recorded in the production accounts of the System is to decide upon the treatment of activities that produce goods or services that could have been supplied to others on the market but are actually retained by their producers for their own use. These cover a very wide range of productive activities, in particular:

(a) The production of agricultural goods by household enterprises for own final consumption;

(b) The production of other goods for own final use by households: the construction of dwellings, the production of foodstuffs and clothing, etc;

(c) The production of housing services for own final consumption by owner occupiers;

(d) The production of domestic and personal services for consumption within the same household: the preparation of meals, care and training of children, cleaning, repairs, etc.

All of these activities are productive in an economic sense. However, inclusion in the System is not simply a matter of estimating monetary values for the outputs of these activities. If values are assigned to the outputs, values have also to be assigned to the incomes generated by their production and to the consumption of the output. It is clear that the economic significance of these flows is very different from that of monetary flows. For example, the incomes generated are automatically tied to the consumption of the goods and services produced; they have little relevance for the analysis of inflation or deflation or other disequilibria within the economy. The inclusion of large non-monetary flows of this kind in the accounts together with monetary flows can obscure what is happening on markets and reduce the analytic usefulness of the data.

23. The SNA is a multi-purpose system. It is designed to meet wide a range of analytical and policy needs. A balance has to be struck between the desire for the accounts to be as comprehensive as possible and the need to prevent flows used for the analysis of market behaviour and disequilibria from being swamped by non-monetary values. The System therefore includes all production of goods for own use within its production boundary, as goods can be switched between market and non-market use even after they have been produced, but it excludes all production of services for own final consumption within households (except for the services produced by employing paid domestic staff and the own-account production of housing services by owner occupiers). These services are consumed as they are produced and the links between their production and market activities are more tenuous than for goods production, such as agricultural goods which households may produce partly for own final consumption and partly for sale, or barter, on the market. The location of the production boundary in the System is a compromise, but a deliberate one that takes account of the needs of most users. In this context it may be noted that in labour force statistics economically active persons are defined as those engaged in productive activities as defined in the SNA. If the production boundary were extended to include the production of personal and domestic services by members of households for their own final consumption, all persons engaged in such activities would become self-employed, making unemployment virtually impossible by definition. This illustrates the need to confine the production boundary in the SNA and other related statistical systems to market activities or fairly close substitutes for market activities.

Other production boundary problems

24. Certain natural processes may or may not be counted as production depending upon the circumstances in which they occur. A necessary condition for an activity to be treated as productive is that it must be carried out under the instigation, control and responsibility of some institutional unit that exercises ownership rights over whatever is produced. For example, the natural growth of stocks of fish in open seas is not counted as production: the process is not managed by any institutional unit and the fish do not belong to any institutional unit. On the other hand, the growth of fish in fish farms is treated as a process of production in much the same way that rearing livestock is a process of production. Similarly, the natural growth of wild, uncultivated forests or wild fruits or berries is not counted as production, whereas the cultivation of crop-bearing trees, or trees grown for timber or other uses, is counted in the same way as the growing of annual crops. However, the deliberate felling of trees in wild forests, and the gathering of wild fruit or berries, and also firewood, counts as production. Similarly, rainfall and the flow of water down natural watercourses are not processes of production, whereas storing water in reservoirs or dams and the piping, or carrying, of water from one location to another all constitute production.

25. These examples show that many activities or processes that may be of benefit to institutional units, both as producers and consumers, are not processes of production in an economic sense. Rainfall may be vital to the agricultural production of a country but it is not a process of production whose output can be included in GDP.

2. The consumption boundary

26. The coverage of production in the System has ramifications that extend considerably beyond the production account itself. The boundary of production determines the amount of value added recorded and hence the total amount of income generated by production. The range of goods and services that are included in household final consumption expenditures, and actual consumption, is similarly governed by the production boundary; for example, these expenditures include the

estimated values of the agricultural products consumed by households that they have produced themselves and also the values of the housing services consumed by owner occupiers, but not the values of "do-it-yourself" repairs and maintenance to vehicles or household durables, the cleaning of dwellings, the care and training of children, or similar domestic or personal services produced for own final consumption. Only the expenditures on goods utilized for these purposes - e.g., cleaning materials - are included in household final consumption expenditures.

3. The asset boundary

27. Balance sheets are compiled for institutional units, or sectors, and record the values of the assets they own or the liabilities they have incurred. Assets as defined in the System are entities that must be owned by some unit, or units, and from which economic benefits are derived by their owner(s) by holding or using them over a period of time. Financial assets and fixed assets are clearly covered by this definition. However, the ownership criterion is important for determining which naturally occurring - i.e., non-produced - assets are included in the System. Naturally occurring assets such as land, mineral deposits, fuel reserves, uncultivated forests or other vegetation and wild animals are included in the balance sheets provided that institutional units are exercising effective ownership rights over them - that is, are actually in a position to be able to benefit from them. Assets need not be privately owned and could be owned by government units exercising ownership rights on behalf of entire communities. Thus, many environmental assets are included within the System. Assets that are not included are those such as the atmosphere or open seas, over which no ownership rights can be exercised, or mineral or fuel deposits that have not been discovered or that are unworkable - i.e., incapable of bringing any benefits to their owners, given the technology and relative prices existing at the time.

28. Changes in the values of naturally occurring assets owned by institutional units between one balance sheet and the next are recorded in the accumulation accounts of the System. For example, the depletion of a natural asset as a result of its use in production is recorded in the other changes in volume of assets account, together with losses of fixed assets due to their destruction by natural disasters (floods, earthquakes, etc.). Conversely, when deposits or reserves of minerals or fuels are discovered or previously unworkable deposits become workable, their appearance is recorded in this account and they enter the balance sheets in this way.

4. National boundaries

29. The accounts of the System are compiled for resident institutional units grouped into institutional sectors and sub-sectors. The concept of residence is the same as that used in the Balance of Payments Manual of the International Monetary Fund (IMF). An institutional unit is said to be resident within the economic territory of a country when it maintains a centre of economic interest in that territory - that is, when it engages, or intends to engage, in economic activities or transactions on a significant scale either indefinitely or over a long period of time, usually interpreted as one year. As an aggregate measure of production, the GDP of a country is equal to the sum of the gross values added of all resident institutional units engaged in production (plus any taxes, and minus any subsidies, on products not included in the value of their outputs). This is not exactly the same as the sum of the gross values added of all productive activities taking place within the geographical boundaries of the national economy. Some of the production of a resident institutional unit may take place abroad - for example, the installation of some exported machinery or equipment or a consultancy project undertaken by a team of expert advisers working temporarily abroad. Conversely, some of the production taking place within a country may be attributable to foreign institutional units.

F. USES OF THE SNA

30. The SNA is a multi-purpose system, as stated above, designed for economic analysis, decision-taking and policy-making, whatever the industrial structure or stage of economic development reached by a country. The basic concepts and definitions of the System depend upon economic reasoning and principles which should be universally valid and invariant to the particular economic circumstances in which they are applied. Similarly, the classifications and accounting rules are meant to be universally applicable. There is no justification, for example, for seeking to define the components of a production account - output, intermediate consumption and gross value added - differently in less developed than in more developed economies, or in large relatively closed economies than in small open economies, or in high- inflation economies than in low-inflation economies. Certain definitions, or accounting rules, specified in the System may become superfluous in certain circumstances (e.g., when there is no inflation), but it is nevertheless necessary for a general system such as the SNA to include definitions and rules covering as wide a range of circumstances as possible.

31. The fact that data needs and priorities, and also statistical capabilities, may vary considerably between different kinds of countries does not justify the

construction of different systems with different concepts, definitions, classifications or accounting rules. Some countries may be able, at least initially, to calculate only a small number of accounts and tables for the total economy with little or no disaggregation into sectors, but a reduced set of accounts or tables does not constitute an alternative system. It is not appropriate to try to lay down general priorities for data collection when economic circumstances may vary so much from one country to another. In practice, priorities can only be established country by country by economic analysts or policy-makers familiar with the economic situation, needs and problems of the individual countries in question. It is not useful, for example, to try to specify general priorities for developing countries when they constitute a very heterogeneous group of countries at a world level. Data priorities may vary as much between one developing country and another as between a developing and a developed country.

1. Specific uses

32. The main objective of the SNA is to provide a comprehensive conceptual and accounting framework which can be used to create a macroeconomic database suitable for analysing and evaluating the performance of an economy. The existence of such a database is a prerequisite for informed, rational policy-making and decision-taking. Some of the more specific uses of the SNA are described in the following sections.

Monitoring the behaviour of the economy

33. National accounts data provide information covering both different types of economic activities and the different sectors of the economy. It is possible to monitor the movements of major economic flows such as production, household consumption, government consumption, capital formation, exports, imports, wages, profits, taxes, lending, borrowing, etc., the flows of goods and services being recorded at both current and constant prices. Moreover, information is provided about certain key balancing items and ratios which can only be defined and measured within an accounting framework - for example, the budget surplus or deficit, the share of income which is saved, or invested, by individual sectors of the economy or the economy as a whole, the trade balance, etc. National accounts also provide the background against which movements of short-term indicators, such as monthly indices of industrial production or of consumer or producer prices, can be interpreted and evaluated. The monitoring of the behaviour of the economy may be significantly improved if at least some of the main aggregates of the System are compiled quarterly as well as annually, although many of the accounts, tables or balance sheets of the System are not usually compiled more frequently than once a year.

Macroeconomic analysis

34. National accounts are also used to investigate the causal mechanisms at work within an economy. Such analysis usually takes the form of the estimation of the parameters of functional relationships between different economic variables by applying econometric methods to time series data at both current and constant prices which are compiled within a national accounting framework. The types of macroeconomic models used for such investigations may vary according to the school of economic thought of the investigator as well as the objectives of the analysis, but the System is sufficiently flexible to accommodate the requirements of different economic theories or models, provided only that they accept the basic concepts of production, consumption, income, etc. on which the System is based.

35. Advances in computer technology have made it possible for the econometric analysis of large macroeconomic models to be carried out on microcomputers. Many econometric software packages have been developed for this purpose so that this kind of modelling is no longer confined to a few government departments, research institutes or universities with large mainframe computers. It is increasingly being undertaken by private corporations or institutions with only limited resources available for these purposes.

Economic policy-making and decision-taking

36. Economic policy in the short term is formulated on the basis of an assessment of the recent behaviour and current state of the economy and a view, or precise forecast, about likely future developments. Short-term forecasts are typically made using econometric models of the type just described. Over the medium- or long-term, economic policy has to be formulated in the context of a broad economic strategy which may need to be quantified in the form of a plan. Most of the elements which make up a medium- or long-term economic plan consist of national accounts flows, and it may be impossible to draw up such a plan without them. A good macroeconomic model which accurately reflects the past performance of the economy may be indispensable for planning as well as forecasting.

37. Economic policy-making and decision-taking take place at all levels of government and also within public and private corporations. Large corporations such as multinationals have the ability to build their own macroeconomic models tailored to their own requirements, for which they need national accounts data.

The investment programmes of major corporations must be based on long-term expectations about future economic developments that require national accounts data. There are also, of course, specialist agencies that provide forecasts for individual clients in return for fees. Such agencies typically require very detailed national accounts data.

International comparisons

38. The SNA is the system used for reporting to international or supranational organizations national accounts data that conform to standard, internationally accepted concepts, definitions and classifications. The resulting data are widely used for international comparisons of the volumes of major aggregates, such as GDP or GDP per head, and also for comparisons of structural statistics, such as ratios of investment, taxes or government expenditures to GDP. Such comparisons are used by economists, journalists or other analysts to evaluate the performance of one economy against that of other similar economies. They can influence popular and political judgements about the relative success of economic programmes in the same way as developments over time within a single country. Databases consisting of sets of national accounts for groups of countries can also be used for econometric analyses in which time-series and cross-section data are pooled to provide a broader range of observations for the estimation of functional relationships.

39. Levels of GDP or, alternatively, gross national income (GNI) per head in different countries are also used by international organizations to determine eligibility for loans, aid or other funds or to determine the terms or conditions on which such loans, aid or funds are made available. When the objective is to compare the volumes of goods or services produced or consumed per head, data in national currencies must be converted into a common currency by means of purchasing power parities and not exchange rates. It is well known that, in general, neither market nor fixed exchange rates reflect the relative internal purchasing powers of different currencies. When exchange rates are used to convert GDP, or other statistics, into a common currency the prices at which goods and services in high-income countries are valued tend to be higher than in low-income countries, thus exaggerating the differences in real incomes between them. Exchange rate converted data must not, therefore, be interpreted as measures of the relative volumes of goods and services concerned. Levels of GDP, or GDP per head, in different countries are also used to determine, in whole or in part, the size of the contributions which the member countries of an international organization make to finance the operations of the organization.

40. Although international organizations use the SNA in order to be able to collect internationally comparable national accounts data, the SNA has not been created for this purpose. It has become the standard, or universal, system used with little or no modification by most countries in the world for their own national purposes. National statistical offices and government agencies have a strong vested interest in ensuring that the SNA meets their own analytic and policy requirements and have taken an active part in the development of the System for this reason.

2. Flexibility of implementation and use

41. The SNA is designed to be sufficiently comprehensive that individual countries, whatever their economic structures, institutional arrangements or level of development, can select from within it those parts of the System which are considered to be most relevant and useful to implement in the light of their own needs and capabilities. The SNA is meant to be implemented in a flexible manner and the accounts and tables, classifications and sectoring presented in this volume should not be regarded as fixed. In some cases, the System explicitly insists on flexibility. For example, two alternative methods of sub-sectoring the general government sector are proposed in chapter IV of the 1993 SNA without either being assigned priority. Similarly, although the System suggests sub-sectoring the households sector on the basis of the household's principal source of income, it stresses that this is only one possible criterion for sub-sectoring. In some cases, it may be more appropriate to sub-sector on the basis of socio-economic criteria or the type of area in which the household is located or, indeed, to carry the disaggregation of the households sector further by using two or more criteria together in a hierarchical manner.

42. Ways in which the System may be adapted to meet differing circumstances and needs are specifically addressed in chapter XIX of the 1993 SNA. For example, classifications of institutional units, transactions and assets may be implemented flexibly in order to adapt them to the data availability and special circumstances of different countries. The flexible use of classifications does not change the basic concepts and definitions of the System. However, as explained in chapter XXI of the 1993 SNA, flexibility may be taken a stage further by developing satellite accounts that are closely linked to the main System but are not bound to employ exactly the same concepts or restricted to data expressed in monetary terms. Satellite accounts are intended for special purposes such as monitoring the community's health or the state of environment. They may also be used to explore new methodologies and to work out new accounting procedures that, when fully developed and accepted, may

become absorbed into the main System in the course of time, in the way that input-output analysis, for example, has been integrated into the System.

43. Another way in which the System may be implemented flexibly is by rearranging the data in the accounts in the form of a social accounting matrix in order better to serve particular analytical and policy needs. Such matrices should not be construed as constituting different systems but as alternative ways of presenting the mass of information contained in the System which many users and analysts find more informative and powerful for both monitoring and modelling social and economic development.

3. The SNA as a coordinating framework for statistics

44. The System also has a very important statistical function by serving as a coordinating framework for economic statistics in two different senses: first, as the conceptual framework for ensuring the consistency of the definitions and classifications used in different, but related, fields of statistics, and secondly, as an accounting framework for ensuring the numerical consistency of data drawn from different sources, such as industrial inquiries, household surveys, merchandise trade statistics, VAT returns and other administrative sources.

G. HARMONIZATION BETWEEN DIFFERENT STATISTICAL SYSTEMS

45. The SNA and related statistical systems need to be as consistent as possible in respect of their basic concepts, definitions and classifications. National accounts have always occupied a central position in economic statistics because the data from more specialized systems, such as balance of payments or labour force statistics, typically have to be used in conjunction with national accounts data. Consistency between the different systems enhances the analytical usefulness of all the statistics involved. The harmonization of the SNA and related statistical systems, such as financial statistics or balance of payments statistics, has been one of the driving forces behind revisions of the System.

46. Revisions of other statistical systems have been conducted in parallel with, and in close collaboration with, that of the SNA in order to eliminate conceptual differences between them other than a few exceptions that can be specifically justified in terms of the special characteristics of different kinds of data, or the special requirements of different kinds of users. Harmonization between the SNA and other major systems has been largely successful and has been achieved by making changes to the SNA as well as to the other systems.

47. Because of the active involvement of the IMF in the revision of the 1993 SNA, the harmonization process has been particularly effective in respect of balance of payments statistics, government finance statistics and money and banking statistics. Each of these three systems was updated to be consistent with the 1993 SNA to the fullest extent possible.

48. Various other revised international guidelines were issued at about the same time as the 1993 SNA. These include the third revision of the United Nations International Standard Industrial Classification of All Economic Activities (ISIC), the industrial classification that is used in the 1993 SNA. The establishment as described in ISIC is also the statistical unit used to compile the production accounts by industry that make up supply and use tables of the SNA, the concept of the establishment being the same in both the SNA and ISIC. The International Labour Organisation (ILO) has issued revised standards on labour statistics that define employment in a way that is consistent with the boundary of production in the SNA, as summarized earlier in this chapter. An extract from the resolution of the Fifteenth International Conference of Labour Statisticians concerning the distinction between the formal and informal sectors is reproduced as an annex to chapter IV of the 1993 SNA. Another example is provided by the revised Handbook on Agricultural Accounts, prepared by the Food and Agricultural Organization of the United Nations (FAO), which has been brought into line with the treatment of agricultural products and activities in the SNA. It is neither necessary nor feasible to list here all the revisions to international statistical systems and standards that are being undertaken or planned as it is the policy of all the various international agencies involved at a world level to harmonize these systems with each other and with the SNA to the fullest extent possible.

H. IMPLEMENTATION OF CONCEPTS

49. The contents of the accounts are determined not only by the conceptual framework, definitions and classifications of the System but also by the ways in which they are interpreted and implemented in practice. However simple and precise concepts and classifications may appear in principle, there are inevitably difficult borderline cases which cannot easily be fitted into predetermined categories. These points may be illustrated by considering a fundamental distinction in economics and in the System, namely, the distinction between consumption and gross fixed capital formation (or gross fixed investment, as it is often described in other contexts).

1. Final consumption, intermediate consumption and gross fixed capital formation

50. Consumption is an activity in which institutional units use up goods or services. There are two quite different kinds of consumption. Intermediate consumption consists of inputs into processes of production that are used up within the accounting period. Final consumption consists of goods and services used by individual households or the community to satisfy their individual or collective needs or wants. The activity of gross fixed capital formation, on the other hand, is restricted to institutional units in their capacity as producers, being defined as the value of their acquisitions less disposals of fixed assets. Fixed assets are produced assets (mostly machinery, equipment, buildings or other structures but also including some intangible assets) that are used repeatedly or continuously in production over several accounting periods (more than one year).

51. The general nature and purpose of the distinction between gross fixed capital formation and consumption, whether intermediate or final, is clear. The distinction is fundamental for economic analysis and policy-making. Nevertheless, the borderline between consumption and gross fixed capital formation is not always easy to determine in practice. Certain activities contain some elements that appear to be consumption and at the same time others that appear to be capital formation. In order to try to ensure that the System is implemented in a uniform way decisions have to be taken about the ways in which certain difficult, even controversial, items are to be classified. Some examples are given below.

Training, research and development

52. Expenditures by enterprises on activities such as staff training or research and development are not the type of intermediate inputs whose consumption is determined by the level at which production is carried out in the current period but are designed to raise productivity or increase the range of production possibilities in the future, in much the same way as expenditures on machinery, equipment, buildings and other structures. However, expenditures on training and research or development do not lead to the acquisition of assets that can be easily identified, quantified and valued for balance sheet purposes. Such expenditures continue to be classified as intermediate consumption, therefore, even though it is recognized that they may bring future benefits. In fact, many other expenditures undertaken by enterprises may also have impacts in future periods as well as the current period - for example, market research, advertising and expenditures on health and safety that affect the well-being and attitudes of the workforce.

Education

53. It is often proposed that expenditures on education should also be classified as gross fixed capital formation as a form of investment in human capital. The acquisition of knowledge, skills and qualifications increases the productive potential of the individuals concerned and is a source of future economic benefit to them. However, while knowledge, skills and qualifications are clearly assets in a broad sense of the term, they cannot be equated with fixed assets as understood in the System. They are not produced because they are acquired through learning, studying and practising - activities that are not themselves processes of production. The education services produced by schools, colleges, universities, etc. are consumed by students in the process of their acquiring knowledge and skills. Education assets are embodied in individuals as persons. They cannot be transferred to others and cannot be shown in the balance sheets of the enterprises in which the individuals work (except in rare cases when certain highly skilled individuals are under contract to work for particular employers for specified periods). Education assets could possibly be shown in balance sheets for the individuals in which they are embodied, but individuals are not enterprises. They would be difficult to value, bearing in mind that the remuneration received by a skilled worker depends upon the amount of time and effort expended and is not simply a return payable to the owner of an asset.

54. It may also be noted that final consumption consists of the use of goods and services for the direct satisfaction of human needs or wants, individually or collectively. Education services are undoubtedly consumed in this sense. They increase the welfare and improve the general quality of life of those consuming them. Moreover, they are not the only services consumed by individuals to bring long- as well as short-term benefits. For example, the consumption of health services brings long-term benefits and even the consumption of basic items such as food and housing is necessary in order to keep an individual in good health - and good working order.

Repairs, maintenance and gross fixed capital formation

55. Another, less familiar, example of the intrinsic difficulty of trying to draw a dichotomy between consumption and gross fixed capital formation is provided by repairs and maintenance. Ordinary maintenance and repairs undertaken by enterprises to keep fixed assets in good working order are intermediate consumption. However, major improvements, additions or extensions to fixed assets, both machinery and structures, which improve their performance, increase their capacity or

prolong their expected working lives count as gross fixed capital formation. In practice it is not easy to draw the line between ordinary repairs and major improvements, although the System provides certain guidelines for this purpose. Some analysts, however, consider that the distinction between ordinary repairs and maintenance and major improvements and additions is neither operational nor defensible and would favour a more "gross" method of recording in which all such activities are treated as gross fixed capital formation.

2. Interpretation of the distinction between consumption and gross fixed capital formation

56. The examples given above show that a simple dichotomy between consumption and gross fixed capital formation inevitably presents problems when dealing with flows of goods and services that do not fit comfortably under either heading. The issue is not simply how to classify certain flows, but also how to achieve an economically meaningful and feasible set of accounting procedures for the assets acquired through gross fixed capital formation within an integrated, coherent set of accounts encompassing past and future periods as well as the present.

57. Some care and sophistication is needed in using the accounts. For example, goods and services "consumed" by households - i.e., acquired for the satisfaction of their needs or wants - are not suddenly "used up" and do not "vanish" at the moment of acquisition. In particular, households "consuming" services such as health and education may continue to derive benefits over long periods of time. The "consumption" of such services therefore has points of similarity with "investment" in assets. Similarly, enterprises may continue to benefit over long periods of time from the intermediate consumption of services such as maintenance and repairs, training, research and development, market research, etc. Thus, while the acquisition of fixed assets by enterprises - that is, gross fixed capital formation - is undertaken specifically to enhance future production possibilities, they are not the only types of expenditure that may be expected to bring future benefits.

58. The decision whether to classify certain types of expenditure by households or government, such as education or health services, as final consumption expenditures or gross fixed capital formation does not affect the size of GDP, as both are final expenditures. On the other hand, the decision to classify certain expenditures by enterprises as intermediate consumption rather than gross fixed capital formation does reduce the gross value added and operating surplus of the enterprise and hence GDP as a whole. However, treating certain expenditures as intermediate reduces not only gross fixed capital formation but also consumption of fixed capital in subsequent periods. It is therefore an open question as to how net value added and net domestic product (NDP) are affected in the longer term, depending upon the pattern of the relevant expenditures over time.

I. DEFINITIONS OF IMPORTANT TERMS (GLOSSARY)

Acquisitions

Goods and services are acquired by institutional units when they become the new owners of the goods or when the delivery of services to them is completed.

Actual final consumption of general government

Actual final consumption of general government is measured by the value of the collective (as opposed to individual) consumption services provided to the community, or large sections of the community, by general government; it is derived from their final consumption expenditure by subtracting the value of social transfers in kind payable.

Actual final consumption of households

Actual final consumption of households is the value of the consumption goods acquired by households, whether by purchase in general, or by transfer from government units or NPISHs, and used by them for the satisfaction of their needs and wants; it is derived from their final consumption expenditure by adding the value of social transfers in kind receivable.

Actual final consumption of NPISHs

NPISHs have no actual final consumption because most of the services provided by NPISHs are individual in nature and, for simplicity, all services provided by NPISHs are treated by convention as social transfers.

Additivity

Additivity is a property pertaining to a set of interdependent index numbers related by definition or by accounting constraints under which an aggregate is defined as the sum of its components; additivity requires this identity to be preserved when the values of both an aggregate and its components in some reference period are extrapolated over time using a set of volume index numbers.

Base period

The period that provides the weights for an index is described as the base period.

Basic price

The basic price is the amount receivable by the producer from the purchaser for a unit of a good or service produced as output minus any tax payable, and plus any subsidy receivable, on that unit as a consequence of its production or sale; it excludes any transport charges invoiced separately by the producer.

C.i.f. price

The c.i.f. price (i.e. cost, insurance and freight price) is the price of a good delivered at the frontier of the importing country, including any insurance and freight charges incurred to that point, or the price of a service delivered to a resident, before the payment of any import duties or other taxes on imports or trade and transport margins within the country.

Capital transfers

Capital transfers are transactions in which the ownership of an asset (other than cash and inventories) is transferred from one institutional unit to another, in which cash is transferred to enable the recipient to acquire another asset or in which the funds realised by the disposal of another asset are transferred.

Chain indices

Chain indices are obtained by linking price (or volume) indices for consecutive periods by using weighting patterns appropriate to those periods.

Changes in inventories (including work-in-progress)

Changes in inventories (including work-in-progress) are measured by the value of the entries into inventories less the value of withdrawals and the value of any recurrent losses of goods held in inventories.

Compensation of employees

Compensation of employees is the total remuneration, in cash or in kind, payable by enterprises to employees in return for work done by the latter during the accounting period.

Constant prices

Constant prices are obtained by directly factoring changes over time in the values of flows of goods and services into two components reflecting changes in the prices of the goods and services concerned and changes in their volumes (i.e. changes in "constant price terms").

Consumption good or service

A consumption good or service is one that is used (without further transformation in production) by households, NPISHs or government units for the direct satisfaction of individual needs or wants or the collective needs of members of the community.

Consumption of fixed capital

Consumption of fixed capital represents the reduction in the value of the fixed assets used in production during the accounting period resulting from physical deterioration, normal obsolescence or normal accidental damage.

Current transfers

Current transfers consist of all transfers that are not transfers of capital; they directly affect the level of disposable income and should influence the consumption of goods or services.

Deductible VAT

Deductible VAT is the amount of VAT payable on purchases of goods or services intended for intermediate consumption, gross fixed capital formation or for resale which a producer is permitted to deduct from his own VAT liability to the government in respect of VAT invoiced to his customers.

Disposals

Disposals of assets (inventories, fixed assets or land or other non-produced assets) by institutional units occur when one of those units sells any of the assets to another institutional unit.

Export subsidies

Export subsidies consist of all subsidies on goods and services that become payable to resident producers when the goods leave the economic territory or when the services are delivered to non-resident units; they include direct subsidies on exports, losses of government trading enterprises in respect of trade with non-residents, and subsidies resulting from multiple exchange rates.

Export taxes

Export taxes are taxes on goods or services that become payable when the goods leave the economic territory or when the services are delivered to non-residents; they include export duties, profits of export monopolies and taxes resulting from multiple exchange rates.

Exports of goods

Exports of goods consist of exports of the following items from residents to non-residents, generally with a change of ownership being involved: general merchandise, goods for processing, goods procured in domestic ports by non-resident carriers, and non-monetary gold.

Exports of services

Exports of services consist of the following services provided by residents to non-residents: transportation; travel; communications; construction; insurance; financial; computer and information; royalties and licence fees; other business services; personal, cultural, and recreational services; and government services n.i.e.

F.o.b. price

The f.o.b. price (free on board price) is the c.i.f. price less the costs of transportation and insurance charges, between the customs frontier of the exporting (importing) country and that of the importing (exporting) country.

Factor cost

Gross value added at factor cost is not a concept used explicitly in the System but it can easily be derived by subtracting the value of any taxes, less subsidies, on production payable out of gross value added.

Final consumption

Final consumption consists of goods and services used up by individual households or the community to satisfy their individual or collective needs or wants.

Final consumption expenditure of government

Government final consumption expenditure consists of expenditure, including imputed expenditure, incurred by general government on both individual consumption goods and services and collective consumption services.

Final consumption expenditure of households

Household final consumption expenditure consists of the expenditure, including imputed expenditure, incurred by resident households on individual consumption goods and services, including those sold at prices that are not economically significant.

Final consumption expenditure of NPISHs

Final consumption expenditure of NPISHs consists of the expenditure, including imputed expenditure, incurred by resident NPISHs on individual consumption goods and services.

Financial intermediation services indirectly measured (FISIM)

Financial intermediation services indirectly measured (FISIM) is an indirect measure of the value of financial intermediation services provided but for which financial institutions do not charge explicitly.

Fixed assets

Fixed assets are tangible or intangible assets produced as outputs from processes of production that are themselves used repeatedly or continuously in other processes of production for more than one year.

Goods

Goods are physical objects for which a demand exists, over which ownership rights can be established and whose ownership can be transferred from one institutional unit to another by engaging in transactions on markets.

Gross

The term “gross” is a common means of referring to values before deducting consumption of fixed capital (generally used as in “gross capital stock” or “gross domestic product”).

Gross capital formation

Gross capital formation is measured by the total value of the gross fixed capital formation, changes in inventories and acquisitions less disposals of valuables for a unit or sector.

Gross domestic product - expenditure based

Expenditure-based gross domestic product is total final expenditures at purchasers’ prices (including the f.o.b. value of exports of goods and services), less the f.o.b. value of imports of goods and services.

Gross domestic product - income based

Income-based gross domestic product is compensation of employees, plus taxes less subsidies on production and imports, plus gross mixed income, plus gross operating surplus.

Gross domestic product - output based

Output-based gross domestic product is the sum of the gross values added of all resident producers at producers' prices, plus taxes less subsides on imports, plus all non-deductible VAT (or similar taxes).

Gross domestic product at market prices

Gross domestic product at market prices is the sum of the gross values added of all resident producers at producers' prices, plus taxes less subsides on imports, plus all non-deductible VAT (or similar taxes).

Gross fixed capital formation

Gross fixed capital formation is measured by the total value of a producer's acquisitions, less disposals, of fixed assets during the accounting period plus certain additions to the value of non-produced assets (such as subsoil assets or major improvements in the quantity, quality or productivity of land) realised by the productive activity of institutional units.

Gross national disposable income

Gross national disposable income may be derived from gross national income by adding all current transfers in cash or in kind receivable by resident institutional units from non-resident units and subtracting all current transfers in cash or in kind payable by resident institutional units to non-resident units.

Gross national income (GNI)

Gross national income (GNI) is GDP less net taxes on production and imports, less compensation of employees less property income payable to the rest of the world plus the corresponding items receivable from the rest of the world (in other words, GDP less primary incomes payable to non-resident units plus primary incomes receivable from non-resident units); an alternative approach to measuring GNI at market prices is as the aggregate value of the balances of gross primary incomes for all sectors; (note that gross national income is identical to gross national product (GNP) as previously used in national accounts generally).

Gross saving

Gross saving is gross disposable income less final consumption expenditure.

Gross value added

Gross value added is the value of output less the value of intermediate consumption; it is a measure of the contribution to GDP made by an individual producer, industry or sector.

Gross value added at basic prices

Gross value added at basic prices is output valued at basic prices less intermediate consumption valued at purchasers' prices.

Gross value added at producers' prices

Gross value added at producers' prices is output valued at producers' prices less intermediate consumption valued at purchasers' prices.

Import duties

Import duties consist of customs duties, or other import charges, which are payable on goods of a particular type when they enter the economic territory.

Import subsidies

Import subsidies consist of subsidies on goods and services that become payable to resident producers when the goods cross the frontier of the economic territory or when the services are delivered to resident institutional units.

Imports of goods

Imports of goods consist of imports of the following items from non-residents to residents, generally with a change of ownership being involved: general merchandise, goods for processing, goods procured in foreign ports by domestic carriers, and non-monetary gold.

Imports of services

Imports of services consist of the following services purchased by residents from non-residents: transportation; travel; communications; construction; insurance; financial; computer and information; royalties and licence fees; other business services; personal, cultural, and recreational services; and government services n.i.e.

Indirect taxes

As traditionally understood, indirect taxes are taxes that supposedly can be passed on, in whole or in part, to other institutional units by increasing the prices of the goods or services sold but the term "indirect taxes" is not used in 1993 SNA; rather, taxes are specifically identified by their purpose (e.g. taxes on products).

Intermediate consumption

Intermediate consumption consists of the value of the goods and services consumed as inputs by a process of production, excluding fixed assets whose consumption is recorded as consumption of fixed capital; the goods or services may be either transformed or used up by the production process.

Inventories

Inventories consist of stocks of outputs that are still held by the units that produced them prior to their being further processed, sold, delivered to other units or used in other ways and stocks of products acquired from other units that are intended to be used for intermediate consumption or for resale without further processing.

Invoiced VAT

Invoiced VAT is the VAT payable on the sales of a producer; it is shown separately on the invoice which the producer presents to the purchaser.

Market prices

Market prices for transactions are the amounts of money willing buyers pay to acquire something from willing sellers.

Mixed income

Mixed income is the surplus or deficit accruing from production by unincorporated enterprises owned by households; it implicitly contains an element of remuneration for work done by the owner, or other members of the household, that cannot be separately identified from the return to the owner as entrepreneur but it excludes the operating surplus coming from owner-occupied dwellings.

Net

The term "net" is a common means of referring to values after deducting consumption of fixed capital (generally used as in "net capital stock" or "net domestic product"); it should be noted, however, that the term "net" can be used in different contexts in the national accounts, such as "net income from abroad" which is the difference between two income flows.

Net income from abroad

The difference between the total values of the primary incomes receivable from, and payable to, non-residents is often described as net income from abroad.

Net lending

Net lending is the net amount a unit or a sector has available to finance, directly or indirectly, other units or other sectors; it is the balancing item in the capital account and is defined as: (Net saving plus capital transfers receivable minus capital transfers payable) minus (the value of acquisitions less disposals of non-financial assets, less consumption of fixed capital); negative net lending may also be described as "net borrowing".

Net national disposable income

Net national disposable income may be derived from net national income by adding all current transfers in cash or in kind receivable by resident institutional units from non-resident units and subtracting all current transfers in cash or in kind payable by resident institutional units to non-resident units.

Net national income

The aggregate value of the balances of net primary incomes summed over all sectors is described as net national income.

Net saving

Net saving is net disposable income less final consumption expenditure.

Net value added

Net value added is the value of output less the values of both intermediate consumption and consumption of fixed capital.

Non-deductible VAT

Non-deductible VAT is the VAT payable by a purchaser which is not deductible from his own VAT liability, if any.

Non-financial assets

Non-financial assets are entities, over which ownership rights are enforced by institutional units, individually or collectively, and from which economic benefits may be derived by their owners by holding them, or using them over a period of time, that consist of tangible assets, both produced and non-produced, and most intangible assets for which no corresponding liabilities are recorded.

Non-produced assets

Non-produced assets are non-financial assets that come into existence other than through processes of production.

Non-profit institutions serving households (NPISHs)

Non-profit institutions serving households (NPISHs) consist of NPIs which are not financed and controlled by government and which provide goods or services to households free or at prices that are not economically significant.

Non-resident

A unit is non-resident if its centre of economic interest is not in the domestic economic territory.

Operating surplus

The operating surplus measures the surplus or deficit accruing from production before taking account of any interest, rent or similar charges payable on financial or tangible non-produced assets borrowed or rented by the enterprise, or any interest, rent or similar receipts receivable on financial or tangible non-produced assets owned by the enterprise; (note: for unincorporated enterprises owned by households, this component is called "mixed income").

Other subsidies on production

Other subsidies on production consist of subsidies, except subsidies on products, which resident enterprises may receive as a consequence of engaging in production (eg, subsidies on payroll or workforce or subsidies to reduce pollution).

Other subsidies on products

Other subsidies on products consist of subsidies on goods or services produced as the outputs of resident enterprises that become payable as a result of the production, sale, transfer, leasing or delivery of those goods or services, or as a result of their use for own consumption or own capital formation; there are three broad categories: (1) subsidies on products used domestically, (2) losses of government trading organisations, and (3) subsidies to public corporations and quasi-corporations.

Output

Output consists of those goods or services that are produced within an establishment that become available for use outside that establishment, plus any goods and services produced for own final use.

Producer's price

The producer's price is the amount receivable by the producer from the purchaser for a unit of a good or service produced as output minus any VAT, or similar deductible tax, invoiced to the purchaser; it excludes any transport charges invoiced separately by the producer.

Property income

Property income is the income receivable by the owner of a financial asset or a tangible non-produced asset in return for providing funds to or putting the tangible non-produced asset at the disposal of, another institutional unit; it consists of interest, the distributed income of corporations (i.e., dividends and withdrawals from income of quasi-corporations), reinvested earnings on direct foreign investment, property income attributed to insurance policy holders, and rent.

Purchaser's price

The purchaser's price is the amount paid by the purchaser, excluding any deductible VAT or similar deductible tax, in order to take delivery of a unit of a good or service at the time and place required by the purchaser; the purchaser's price of a good includes any transport charges paid separately by the purchaser to take delivery at the required time and place.

Resident

An institutional unit is resident in a country when it has a centre of economic interest in the economic territory of that country.

Services

Services are outputs produced to order and typically consist of changes in the conditions of the consuming units realised by the activities of producers at the demand of the consumers; by the time their production is completed they must have been provided to the consumers.

Stocks

Stocks are a position in, or holdings of, assets and liabilities at a point in time and the System records stocks in accounts, usually referred to as balance sheets, and tables at the beginning and end of the accounting period; stocks result from the accumulation of prior transactions and other flows, and they are changed by transactions and other flows in the period (note that stocks of goods are referred to as "inventories" in the System).

Subsidies

Subsidies are current unrequited payments that government units, including non-resident government units, make to enterprises on the basis of the levels of their production activities or the quantities or values of the goods or services which they produce, sell or import.

Taxes and duties on imports

Taxes and duties on imports, excluding VAT, consist of taxes on goods and services that become payable at the moment when the goods cross the national or customs frontiers of the economic territory or when the services are delivered by non-resident producers to resident institutional units.

Taxes on production and imports

Taxes on production consist of taxes payable on goods and services when they are produced, delivered, sold, transferred or otherwise disposed of by their producers plus other taxes on production, consisting mainly of taxes on the ownership or use of land, buildings or other assets used in production or on the labour employed, or compensation of employees paid.

Taxes on products

Taxes on products, excluding VAT, import and export taxes, consist of taxes on goods and services that become payable as a result of the production, sale, transfer, leasing or delivery of those goods or services, or as a result of their use for own consumption or own capital formation.

Transfer

A transfer is a transaction in which one institutional unit provides a good, service or asset to another unit without receiving from the latter any good, service or asset in return as counterpart.

Valuables

Valuables are produced assets that are not used primarily for production or consumption, that are expected to appreciate or at least not to decline in real value, that do not deteriorate over time under normal conditions and that are acquired and held primarily as stores of value.

Value added - gross

Gross value added is the value of output less the value of intermediate consumption; it is a measure of the contribution to GDP made by an individual producer, industry or sector.

Value added - net

Net value added is the value of output less the values of both intermediate consumption and consumption of fixed capital.

Value added tax (VAT)

A value added tax (VAT) is a tax on products collected in stages by enterprises; it is a wide-ranging tax usually designed to cover most or all goods and services but producers are obliged to pay to government only the difference between the VAT on their sales and the VAT on their purchases for intermediate consumption or capital formation, while VAT is not usually charged on sales to non-residents (i.e., exports).

---

1 United Nations, 1947, Measurement of National Income and the Construction of Social Accounts, Studies and Reports on Statistical Methods No. 7, Geneva: United Nations Publications.

2 United Nations, 1947, Official Records of the Economic and Social Council Supplement No. 6 (E/264), chap. VIII, para. 39. New York: United Nations Publications.

3 European Commission, International Monetary Fund, Organisation for Economic Cooperation and Development, United Nations, and World Bank, 2009, System of National Accounts 2008. New York: United Nations Publications.

II. COUNTRY TABLES

Montenegro

Source

The Statistical Office of Montenegro (MONSTAT) is responsible for the compilation of official national accounts, according to the Statistical Law of Montenegro. Results of this work have been issued in Releases of GDP since 2000, up to 2009. All these publications are available online, on the web site of Statistical Office of Montenegro (www.monstat.org).

MONSTAT has not yet published quarterly national accounts data.

General

The methodology used is harmonized with the System of National Accounts (1993 SNA) and European system of accounts (ESA95). Gross domestic product (GDP) measures the total value of the goods and services produced by resident institutional units. The GDP calculation includes all activities within the production frame defined by 1993 SNA and ESA95 and covers the whole territory of Montenegro. The estimate of non-observed economy is partially included in calculation of GDP. Activities for which non-observed economy is estimated are: agriculture, manufacturing, hotels and restaurants, constructing and real estate, renting and business activities. The following illegal activities: drugs, prostitution, sex-trafficking, illegal selling of CDs, video tapes, illegal use of software, smuggling of weapons, etc. are not included.

The classification of economic units by activity is in line with the national Classification of Activities (CA) that is harmonized with the Classification of Economic Activities in the European Community (NACE Rev.1).

Indices of nominal growth = GDP at current prices in current year / GDP at current prices in previous year.

Real growth rate = GDP at constant prices in current year / GDP at current prices in previous year.

Methodology:

Expenditure Approach

The GDP compilation at current prices by the expenditure approach is based on the data from regular surveys of MONSTAT, Ministry of Finance, Central Bank of Montenegro. Final consumption expenditure of households was calculated on the basis of data from regular statistical surveys of MONSTAT as well as on data from various administrative sources. The main data source is Household Budget Survey (HBS). COICOP classification on 4-digit level is applied. Commodity flow approach is used for estimation of final consumption expenditure of households which represent balance of all goods and services flows that are produced and imported from one side and used and exported on the other side.

Data on Government expenditures were based on data from Ministry of Finance and Budgetary Report of Montenegro. Individual Government final consumption includes expenditures on Education, Health, Social security and welfare and Sport, culture and recreation. Remained expenditures of the government are related to collective consumption (general public services, military and civil defence with ministry, residential and communal services, etc).

Gross fixed capital formation data for corporate enterprises are compiled by commodity flow approach and using data from regular MONSTAT survey: Annual survey on investments in fixed assets. Gross fixed capital formation for the unincorporated sector (construction, trade, agriculture, etc.) was estimated on the basis of available data from regular statistical surveys.

Data on exports and imports of services are based on the Balance of Payment data of Central Bank of Montenegro. Data on exports and imports of goods are based on the MONSTAT data from external trade statistics following special trade system.

GDP calculation by expenditure approach is also done at constant prices. On the basis of available data it is applied extrapolation method for expenditure component: Government final consumption expenditure and for others expenditure categories it is applied deflation method.

Production Approach

The main categories of GDP compilation by production approach are: Gross output is defined as a market value of produced goods and services. It is calculated by activities at approximate basic prices, since all subsidies are treated as subsidies on products and included into calculation on the level of national economy. Intermediate consumption at purchase prices is the value of goods and services, which are transformed, used and consumed in the production process. Gross value added is the value of gross output less the value of intermediate consumption. Gross domestic product at market prices is the value of all goods and services produced by resident units, i.e., the sum of gross value added by activities and taxes on products less subsidies on products. In compilation of intermediate consumption by activates is included the value of financial intermediation services indirectly measured (FISIM) which increase level of harmonisation of GDP compilation in line with European standards. Gross value added calculation at current prices is mostly based on Annual Financial Reports of Enterprises as well as on results of regular statistical surveys.

The data quality of annual Financial Reports was checked and partially corrected on the basis of data from statistical surveys in agriculture, industry, construction, wholesale and retail trade, tourism, transport and other statistics. Additionally, administrative data obtained from Central Bank of Montenegro, Tax authorities, Customs administration and Ministry of Finance was used. Gross value added for activity “Real estate, renting and business activities” is compiled by user-cost approach, which is harmonized with ESA'95 methodology. The used data were adjusted according to the requirements of SNA93 and ESA95 methodologies, while in certain cases particularly estimation were made on the basis of available data. GDP calculation by production approach is also done at constant prices. On the basis of available data it is carried out double deflation method for activity Agriculture and for activities: Financial intermediation and other community, social and personal activities it is applied single deflation method. For all others activities calculation is done by applying single extrapolation method, using appropriate indicators i.e. physical volume indices.

Table 1.1 Gross domestic product by expenditures at current prices

Series 100: 1993 SNA, Euro, Western calendar year — **Data in thousands**

	2001	2002	2003	2004	2005	2006	2007	2008	2009	2010	2011	2012
Series	**100**											
	Expenditures of the gross domestic product											
Final consumption expenditure	1296752.0	1438656.0	1524655.0	1660339.0	1811371.0	2241002.0	2908300.0	3512920.0	3165130.0	3277930.0	3443141.0	
Household final consumption expenditure	970764.0	1100461.0	1120474.0	1221101.0	1267951.0	1660948.0	2368960.0	2814820.0	2503700.0	2550720.0	2728471.0	
NPISHs final consumption expenditure	...	...	...	...	...	...	...	...	...	...	...	
General government final consumption expenditure	325988.0	338195.0	404181.0	439238.0	543420.0	580054.0	539340.0	698103.0	661430.0	727215.0	714670.0	
Individual consumption expenditure	107576.0	129597.0	124801.0	144617.0	146584.0	218357.0	239523.0	292756.0	296815.0	334317.0	326048.0	
Collective consumption expenditure	218412.0	208598.0	279380.0	294621.0	396836.0	361697.0	299817.0	405347.0	364615.0	392898.0	388622.0	
Gross capital formation	303518.0	255217.0	232770.0	277704.0	321735.0	546811.0	906152.0	1255000.0	808478.0	707472.0	631718.0	
Gross fixed capital formation	226683.0	198916.0	200830.0	286072.0	326329.0	469811.0	867109.0	1180000.0	797623.0	655139.0	596453.0	
Changes in inventories	76835.0	56301.0	31940.0	-8368.0	-4594.0	77000.0	39043.0	75000.0	10855.0	52333.0	35265.0	
Acquisitions less disposals of valuables	...	...	...	...	...	...	...	...	...	...	...	
Exports of goods and services	497626.0	480968.0	462269.0	701677.0	790414.0	1061008.0	1189950.0	1219000.0	957498.0	1077390.0	1299326.0	

	2001	2002	2003	2004	2005	2006	2007	2008	2009	2010	2011	2012
Series	**100**											
Exports of goods	327501.0	317460.0	270574.0	452148.0	460648.0	627460.0	515896.0	468000.0	277011.0	330367.0	454381.0	
Exports of services	170125.0	163508.0	191695.0	249529.0	329766.0	433548.0	674056.0	751000.0	680487.0	747024.0	844945.0	
Less: Imports of goods and services	802786.0	814488.0	709566.0	969937.0	1108526.0	1699823.0	2323940.0	2900450.0	1950140.0	1958940.0	2140125.0	
Imports of goods	750276.0	741183.0	629904.0	868584.0	974300.0	1482689.0	2090010.0	2549250.0	1654170.0	1657330.0	1823337.0	
Imports of services	52510.0	73305.0	79662.0	101353.0	134226.0	217134.0	233923.0	351197.0	295965.0	301611.0	316788.0	
Equals: GROSS DOMESTIC PRODUCT	1295110.0	1360353.0	1510128.0	1669783.0	1814994.0	2148998.0	2680470.0	3085620.0	2980970.0	3103860.0	3234060.0	

Table 1.2 Gross domestic product by expenditures at constant prices

Series 100: 1993 SNA, Euro, Western calendar year — **Data in thousands**

	2001	2002	2003	2004	2005	2006	2007	2008	2009	2010	2011	2012
Series								**100**				
Base year								**2007**	**2008**	**2009**	**2010**	
	Expenditures of the gross domestic product											
Final consumption expenditure								3196750.0	3153870.0	3212800.0	3373195.0	
Household final consumption expenditure								2655580.0	2450610.0	2553670.0	2657892.0	
NPISHs final consumption expenditure								...	...	...	...	
General government final consumption expenditure								541165.0	703260.0	659123.0	715303.0	
Individual consumption expenditure								226943.0	293049.0	294143.0	327631.0	
Collective consumption expenditure								314222.0	410211.0	364980.0	387672.0	
Gross capital formation								1182240.0	834613.0	701291.0	621872.0	
Gross fixed capital formation								1103420.0	824622.0	649730.0	587667.0	
Changes in inventories								78822.0	9991.0	51561.0	34205.0	
Acquisitions less disposals of valuables								...	...	...	...	
Exports of goods and services								1165570.0	945916.0	1029240.0	1229502.0	
Exports of goods								456384.0	302734.0	294340.0	417975.0	
Exports of services								709188.0	643182.0	734898.0	811527.0	
Less: Imports of goods and services								2678540.0	2023330.0	1888920.0	2020513.0	
Imports of goods								2338550.0	1728250.0	1592060.0	1712053.0	
Imports of services								339990.0	295079.0	296861.0	308460.0	
Equals: GROSS DOMESTIC PRODUCT								2866030.0	2911070.0	3054410.0	3204056.0	

Table 2.1 Value added by industries at current prices (ISIC Rev. 3)

Series 100: 1993 SNA, Euro, Western calendar year — **Data in thousands**

	2001	2002	2003	2004	2005	2006	2007	2008	2009	2010	2011	2012
Series	**100**											
	Industries											
Agriculture, hunting, forestry; fishing	140017.0	148602.0	149729.0	154654.0	158951.0	178186.0	193969.0	230499.0	246812.0	237886.0		
Agriculture, hunting, forestry	139897.0	148372.0	149245.0	154178.0	158468.0	177021.0	194123.0	230499.0	246812.0	237422.0		
Fishing	120.0	230.0	484.0	476.0	483.0	1165.0	918.0	0.0	561.0	464.0		
Mining and quarrying	24658.0	29935.0	28556.0	25921.0	26049.0	28603.0	31511.0	37438.0	19653.0	38631.0		
Manufacturing	149708.0	141497.0	132265.0	145771.0	148686.0	164695.0	144926.0	166471.0	145791.0	139014.0		
Electricity, gas and water supply	69147.0	72884.0	87565.0	95357.0	85821.0	88496.0	113152.0	129104.0	169538.0	171079.0		
Construction	45482.0	49457.0	43514.0	49758.0	54192.0	76039.0	155108.0	190750.0	161538.0	156969.0		
Wholesale, retail trade, repair of motor vehicles, motorcycles and personal and households goods; hotels and restaurants	175397.0	191972.0	200597.0	219661.0	243909.0	301950.0	474790.0	515167.0	509147.0	541096.0		
Wholesale, retail trade, repair of motor vehicles, motorcycles and personal and household goods	146827.0	160085.0	165175.0	170237.0	190124.0	237872.0	357234.0	382416.0	357070.0	380067.0		
Hotels and restaurants	28570.0	31887.0	35422.0	49424.0	53785.0	64078.0	117556.0	132751.0	152077.0	161029.0		
Transport, storage and communications	156444.0	145769.0	146735.0	163031.0	171327.0	208270.0	238548.0	288887.0	283814.0	299027.0		
Financial intermediation; real estate, renting and business activities	183236.0	195478.0	218257.0	246832.0	254815.0	310123.0	358550.0	371035.0	371511.0	393025.0		
Financial intermediation	29828.0	32538.0	34400.0	38998.0	43854.0	64977.0	102970.0	119590.0	120825.0	124515.0		
Real estate, renting and business activities	153408.0	162940.0	183857.0	207834.0	210961.0	245146.0	255580.0	251445.0	250686.0	268510.0		
Public administration and defence; compulsory social security	91268.0	102819.0	116708.0	130858.0	166421.0	174277.0	195298.0	269118.0	254840.0	255210.0		
Education; health and social work; other community, social and personal services	138360.0	143166.0	168324.0	190989.0	211695.0	226296.0	225098.0	278123.0	309903.0	355300.0		
Education	51238.0	55965.0	61558.0	71569.0	76938.0	87545.0	92009.0	116357.0	125440.0	138545.0		
Health and social work	50221.0	50759.0	62924.0	70715.0	82155.0	84615.0	88926.0	109671.0	118357.0	122653.0		
Other community, social and personal services	36901.0	36442.0	43842.0	48705.0	52602.0	54136.0	44163.0	52095.0	66106.0	94102.0		
Private households with employed persons	5.0	0.0	7.0	10.0	0.0	0.0	0.0	...	0.0	...		
Equals: VALUE ADDED, GROSS, in basic prices	1173722.0	1221579.0	1292257.0	1422842.0	1521866.0	1756935.0	2131262.0	2476592.0	2472547.0	2587237.0		
Less: Financial intermediation services indirectly measured (FISIM)	1885.0	2700.0	2119.0	1353.0	1842.0	4118.0	...	...	...	...		
Plus: Taxes less Subsidies on products	123273.0	141474.0	219990.0	248294.0	294970.0	396181.0	549205.0	609029.0	508420.0	516618.0		
Plus: Taxes on products	...	...	...	...	...	...	562277.0	627621.0	541244.0	555653.0		
Less: Subsidies on products	...	...	...	...	...	...	13072.0	18593.0	32824.0	39035.0		
Equals: GROSS DOMESTIC PRODUCT	1295110.0	1360353.0	1510128.0	1669783.0	1814994.0	2148998.0	2680467.0	3085621.0	2980967.0	3103855.0		
Memorandum Item: FISIM, if distributed to uses	...	...	...	...	...	...	53475.0	87304.0	86800.0	82731.0		

Table 2.2 Value added by industries at constant prices (ISIC Rev. 3)

Series 100: 1993 SNA, Euro, Western calendar year | **Data in thousands**

	2001	2002	2003	2004	2005	2006	2007	2008	2009	2010	2011	2012
Series	**100**											
Base year	**2000**	**2001**	**2002**	**2003**	**2004**	**2005**	**2006**	**2007**	**2008**	**2009**		
Industries												
Agriculture, hunting, forestry; fishing	123532.0	152298.0	147248.0	155881.0	157432.0	166132.0	157378.0	216379.0	234724.0	243492.0		
Agriculture, hunting, forestry	123407.0	152166.0	146979.0	155215.0	156953.0	165441.0	156514.0	216379.0	234724.0	243492.0		
Fishing	...	...	...	666.0	479.0	691.0	864.0	...	...	...		
Mining and quarrying	24195.0	29029.0	30190.0	27080.0	25437.0	26804.0	29032.0	37257.0	13886.0	32444.0		
Manufacturing	100071.0	143061.0	132453.0	139687.0	153733.0	155376.0	180012.0	135678.0	121398.0	140150.0		
Electricity, gas and water supply	54768.0	64583.0	85639.0	100700.0	82579.0	88482.0	64248.0	136026.0	140337.0	206108.0		
Construction	43603.0	43117.0	41841.0	45124.0	58913.0	69366.0	94007.0	187216.0	154126.0	149552.0		
Wholesale, retail trade, repair of motor vehicles, motorcycles and personal and household goods; hotels and restaurants	172123.0	185004.0	199262.0	200716.0	250732.0	291311.0	405754.0	514710.0	442216.0	520690.0		
Wholesale, retail trade, repair of motor vehicles, motorcycles and personal and household goods	140642.0	158720.0	164888.0	163523.0	194240.0	230050.0	327002.0	393637.0	313581.0	360248.0		
Hotels and restaurants	31481.0	26284.0	34374.0	37193.0	56492.0	61261.0	78752.0	121073.0	128635.0	160442.0		
Transport, storage and communications	110672.0	151159.0	144799.0	142389.0	163168.0	200453.0	260439.0	251487.0	323553.0	290625.0		
Financial intermediation, real estate, renting and business activities	128651.0	187403.0	160391.0	224004.0	240335.0	271469.0	359653.0	369206.0	393092.0	377092.0		
Financial intermediation	32016.0	30186.0	27462.0	37393.0	35449.0	45740.0	65562.0	109026.0	122789.0	122395.0		
Real estate, renting and business activities	96635.0	157217.0	132929.0	186611.0	204886.0	225729.0	294091.0	260180.0	270303.0	254697.0		
Public administration and defence; compulsory social security	86964.0	90994.0	106006.0	115424.0	133475.0	168917.0	171284.0	203548.0	272000.0	254942.0		
Education; health and social work; other community, social and personal services	113960.0	131593.0	144146.0	177157.0	180272.0	213453.0	220623.0	223117.0	287916.0	317103.0		
Education	46829.0	53441.0	54230.0	61927.0	70925.0	76938.0	86494.0	91785.0	117288.0	125189.0		
Health and social work	40398.0	43391.0	51470.0	64812.0	68240.0	83387.0	84107.0	88432.0	108575.0	116156.0		
Other community, social and personal services	26733.0	34761.0	38446.0	50418.0	41107.0	53128.0	50022.0	42900.0	62053.0	75758.0		
Private households with employed persons	500.0	500.0	0.0	7.0	10.0	0.0	0.0	0.0	0.0	...		
Equals: VALUE ADDED, GROSS, in basic prices	958544.0	1178246.0	1191975.0	1328170.0	1446090.0	1651760.0	1942430.0	2274624.0	2383595.0	2532198.0		
Less: Financial intermediation services indirectly measured (FISIM)	1626.0	1907.0	2278.0	2516.0	1230.0	1921.0	4155.0	...	...	...		
Plus: Taxes less Subsidies on products	120502.0	143429.0	204429.0	251314.0	294734.0	320632.0	439761.0	591401.0	527475.0	522212.0		
Plus: Taxes on products	...	...	...	...	...	...	...	608910.0	559343.0	561053.0		
Less: Subsidies on products	...	...	...	...	...	...	...	17312.0	31868.0	38841.0		
Equals: GROSS DOMESTIC PRODUCT	1077420.0	1319768.0	1394126.0	1576970.0	1739590.0	1970470.0	2378040.0	2866025.0	2911070.0	3054410.0		
Memorandum Item: FISIM, if distributed to uses	...	...	...	...	...	...	...	81454.0	...	...		

Table 2.4 Value added by industries at current prices (ISIC Rev. 4)

Series 100: 1993 SNA, Euro, Western calendar year | **Data in thousands**

	2001	2002	2003	2004	2005	2006	2007	2008	2009	2010	2011	2012
Series										**100**		
Industries												
Agriculture, forestry and fishing										239494.0	256725.0	
Crop and animal production, hunting and related service activities										237422.0	254918.0	
Forestry and logging										1639.0	1136.0	
Fishing and aquaculture										433.0	671.0	
Manufacturing, mining and quarrying and other industrial activities										382050.0	368638.0	
Mining and quarrying										37702.0	35725.0	
Manufacturing										144512.0	162535.0	
Electricity, gas, steam and air conditioning supply										143115.0	103148.0	
Water supply; sewerage, waste management and remediation activities										56721.0	67230.0	
Construction										151904.0	158080.0	
Wholesale and retail trade, transportation and storage, accommodation and food service activities										648110.0	703736.0	
Wholesale and retail trade; repair of motor vehicles and motorcycles										348770.0	391686.0	
Transportation and storage										144915.0	150880.0	
Accommodation and food service activities										154425.0	161170.0	
Information and communication										176614.0	164957.0	
Financial and insurance activities										124515.0	131839.0	
Real estate activities										183605.0	219875.0	
Professional, scientific, technical, administrative and support service activities										97796.0	114930.0	
Professional, scientific and technical activities										72737.0	88175.0	
Administrative and support service activities										25059.0	26755.0	
Public administration and defence, education, human health and social work activities										529539.0	526441.0	
Public administration and defence; compulsory social security										255073.0	255517.0	
Education										138877.0	139271.0	
Human health and social work activities										135589.0	131653.0	
Other service activities										53609.0	59446.0	
Arts, entertainment and recreation										39710.0	39809.0	
Other service activities										13899.0	19637.0	
Private households with employed persons										...	...	
Equals: VALUE ADDED, GROSS, at basic prices										2587236.0	2704667.0	
Less: Financial intermediation services indirectly measured (FISIM)										...	...	

	2001	2002	2003	2004	2005	2006	2007	2008	2009	2010	2011	2012
Series										**100**		
Plus: Taxes less Subsidies on products										516618.0	529392.0	
Equals: GROSS DOMESTIC PRODUCT										3103854.0	3234059.0	

Table 2.6 Output, gross value added and fixed assets by industries at current prices (ISIC Rev. 4) Total economy

Series 100: 1993 SNA, Euro, Western calendar year

Data in thousands

	2001	2002	2003	2004	2005	2006	2007	2008	2009	2010	2011	2012
Series										**100**		
Output, at basic prices										5159823.0	5239614.0	
Less: Intermediate consumption, at purchaser's prices										2572586.0	2534946.0	
Equals: VALUE ADDED, GROSS, at basic prices										2587237.0	2704668.0	
Compensation of employees										...	...	
Taxes on production and imports, less Subsidies										...	...	
OPERATING SURPLUS, GROSS										...	...	
MIXED INCOME, GROSS										...	...	
Gross capital formation										707472.0	631718.0	
Gross fixed capital formation										655139.0	596453.0	
Changes in inventories										52333.0	35265.0	
Acquisitions less disposals of valuables										...	...	

Table 2.6 Output, gross value added and fixed assets by industries at current prices (ISIC Rev. 4) Agriculture, forestry and fishing (A)

Series 100: 1993 SNA, Euro, Western calendar year

Data in thousands

	2001	2002	2003	2004	2005	2006	2007	2008	2009	2010	2011	2012
Series										**100**		
Output, at basic prices										385320.0	424997.0	
Less: Intermediate consumption, at purchaser's prices										145825.0	168271.0	
Equals: VALUE ADDED, GROSS, at basic prices										239495.0	256726.0	
Compensation of employees										...	...	
Taxes on production and imports, less Subsidies										...	...	
OPERATING SURPLUS, GROSS										...	...	
MIXED INCOME, GROSS										...	...	
Gross capital formation										...	...	

Table 2.6 Output, gross value added and fixed assets by industries at current prices (ISIC Rev. 4) Crop and animal production, hunting and related service activities (01)

Series 100: 1993 SNA, Euro, Western calendar year

Data in thousands

	2001	2002	2003	2004	2005	2006	2007	2008	2009	2010	2011	2012
Series										**100**		
Output, at basic prices										380576.0	418087.0	
Less: Intermediate consumption, at purchaser's prices										143154.0	163169.0	
Equals: VALUE ADDED, GROSS, at basic prices										237422.0	254918.0	
Compensation of employees										...	...	
Taxes on production and imports, less Subsidies										...	...	
OPERATING SURPLUS, GROSS										...	...	
MIXED INCOME, GROSS										...	...	
Gross capital formation										...	...	

Table 2.6 Output, gross value added and fixed assets by industries at current prices (ISIC Rev. 4) Forestry and logging (02)

Series 100: 1993 SNA, Euro, Western calendar year

Data in thousands

	2001	2002	2003	2004	2005	2006	2007	2008	2009	2010	2011	2012
Series										**100**		
Output, at basic prices										3228.0	3376.0	
Less: Intermediate consumption, at purchaser's prices										1589.0	2240.0	
Equals: VALUE ADDED, GROSS, at basic prices										1639.0	1137.0	
Compensation of employees										...	...	
Taxes on production and imports, less Subsidies										...	...	
OPERATING SURPLUS, GROSS										...	...	
MIXED INCOME, GROSS										...	...	
Gross capital formation										...	...	

Table 2.6 Output, gross value added and fixed assets by industries at current prices (ISIC Rev. 4) Fishing and aquaculture (03)

Series 100: 1993 SNA, Euro, Western calendar year

Data in thousands

	2001	2002	2003	2004	2005	2006	2007	2008	2009	2010	2011	2012
Series										**100**		
Output, at basic prices										1516.0	3533.0	
Less: Intermediate consumption, at purchaser's prices										1083.0	2862.0	
Equals: VALUE ADDED, GROSS, at basic prices										433.0	671.0	
Compensation of employees										...	...	

	2001	2002	2003	2004	2005	2006	2007	2008	2009	2010	2011	2012
Series										**100**		
Taxes on production and imports, less Subsidies										...	...	
OPERATING SURPLUS, GROSS										...	...	
MIXED INCOME, GROSS										...	...	
Gross capital formation										...	...	

Table 2.6 Output, gross value added and fixed assets by industries at current prices (ISIC Rev. 4) Manufacturing, mining and quarrying and other industrial activities (B+C+D+E)

Series 100: 1993 SNA, Euro, Western calendar year **Data in thousands**

	2001	2002	2003	2004	2005	2006	2007	2008	2009	2010	2011	2012
Series										**100**		
Output, at basic prices										935485.0	901185.0	
Less: Intermediate consumption, at purchaser's prices										553435.0	532547.0	
Equals: VALUE ADDED, GROSS, at basic prices										382050.0	368638.0	
Compensation of employees										...	...	
Taxes on production and imports, less Subsidies										...	...	
OPERATING SURPLUS, GROSS										...	...	
MIXED INCOME, GROSS										...	...	
Gross capital formation										...	...	

Table 2.6 Output, gross value added and fixed assets by industries at current prices (ISIC Rev. 4) Mining and quarrying (B)

Series 100: 1993 SNA, Euro, Western calendar year **Data in thousands**

	2001	2002	2003	2004	2005	2006	2007	2008	2009	2010	2011	2012
Series										**100**		
Output, at basic prices										66472.0	69729.0	
Less: Intermediate consumption, at purchaser's prices										28770.0	34004.0	
Equals: VALUE ADDED, GROSS, at basic prices										37702.0	35725.0	
Compensation of employees										...	...	
Taxes on production and imports, less Subsidies										...	...	
OPERATING SURPLUS, GROSS										...	...	
MIXED INCOME, GROSS										...	...	
Gross capital formation										...	...	

Table 2.6 Output, gross value added and fixed assets by industries at current prices (ISIC Rev. 4) Manufacturing (C)

Series 100: 1993 SNA, Euro, Western calendar year — **Data in thousands**

	2001	2002	2003	2004	2005	2006	2007	2008	2009	2010	2011	2012
Series										**100**		
Output, at basic prices										545881.0	558502.0	
Less: Intermediate consumption, at purchaser's prices										401369.0	395967.0	
Equals: VALUE ADDED, GROSS, at basic prices										144512.0	162535.0	
Compensation of employees										...	...	
Taxes on production and imports, less Subsidies										...	...	
OPERATING SURPLUS, GROSS										...	...	
MIXED INCOME, GROSS										...	...	
Gross capital formation										...	...	

Table 2.6 Output, gross value added and fixed assets by industries at current prices (ISIC Rev. 4) Electricity, gas, steam and air conditioning supply (D)

Series 100: 1993 SNA, Euro, Western calendar year — **Data in thousands**

	2001	2002	2003	2004	2005	2006	2007	2008	2009	2010	2011	2012
Series										**100**		
Output, at basic prices										244734.0	182682.0	
Less: Intermediate consumption, at purchaser's prices										101619.0	79534.0	
Equals: VALUE ADDED, GROSS, at basic prices										143115.0	103148.0	
Compensation of employees										...	...	
Taxes on production and imports, less Subsidies										...	...	
OPERATING SURPLUS, GROSS										...	...	
MIXED INCOME, GROSS										...	...	
Gross capital formation										...	...	

Table 2.6 Output, gross value added and fixed assets by industries at current prices (ISIC Rev. 4) Water supply; sewerage, waste management and remediation activities (E)

Series 100: 1993 SNA, Euro, Western calendar year — **Data in thousands**

	2001	2002	2003	2004	2005	2006	2007	2008	2009	2010	2011	2012
Series										**100**		
Output, at basic prices										78398.0	90272.0	
Less: Intermediate consumption, at purchaser's prices										21677.0	23042.0	
Equals: VALUE ADDED, GROSS, at basic prices										56721.0	67230.0	
Compensation of employees										...	...	

	2001	2002	2003	2004	2005	2006	2007	2008	2009	2010	2011	2012
Series										**100**		
Taxes on production and imports, less Subsidies										...	...	
OPERATING SURPLUS, GROSS										...	...	
MIXED INCOME, GROSS										...	...	
Gross capital formation										...	...	

Table 2.6 Output, gross value added and fixed assets by industries at current prices (ISIC Rev. 4) Construction (F)

Series 100: 1993 SNA, Euro, Western calendar year **Data in thousands**

	2001	2002	2003	2004	2005	2006	2007	2008	2009	2010	2011	2012
Series										**100**		
Output, at basic prices										566991.0	548109.0	
Less: Intermediate consumption, at purchaser's prices										415086.0	390028.0	
Equals: VALUE ADDED, GROSS, at basic prices										151904.0	158080.0	
Compensation of employees										...	...	
Taxes on production and imports, less Subsidies										...	...	
OPERATING SURPLUS, GROSS										...	...	
MIXED INCOME, GROSS										...	...	
Gross capital formation										...	...	

Table 2.6 Output, gross value added and fixed assets by industries at current prices (ISIC Rev. 4) Wholesale and retail trade, transportation and storage, accommodation and food service activities (G+H+I)

Series 100: 1993 SNA, Euro, Western calendar year **Data in thousands**

	2001	2002	2003	2004	2005	2006	2007	2008	2009	2010	2011	2012
Series										**100**		
Output, at basic prices										1321332.0	1367688.0	
Less: Intermediate consumption, at purchaser's prices										673223.0	663952.0	
Equals: VALUE ADDED, GROSS, at basic prices										648110.0	703744.0	
Compensation of employees										...	...	
Taxes on production and imports, less Subsidies										...	...	
OPERATING SURPLUS, GROSS										...	...	
MIXED INCOME, GROSS										...	...	
Gross capital formation										...	...	

Table 2.6 Output, gross value added and fixed assets by industries at current prices (ISIC Rev. 4) Wholesale and retail trade; repair of motor vehicles and motorcycles (G)

Series 100: 1993 SNA, Euro, Western calendar year — **Data in thousands**

	2001	2002	2003	2004	2005	2006	2007	2008	2009	2010	2011	2012
Series										**100**		
Output, at basic prices										752059.0	771102.0	
Less: Intermediate consumption, at purchaser's prices										403290.0	379416.0	
Equals: VALUE ADDED, GROSS, at basic prices										348770.0	391686.0	
Compensation of employees										...	...	
Taxes on production and imports, less Subsidies										...	...	
OPERATING SURPLUS, GROSS										...	...	
MIXED INCOME, GROSS										...	...	
Gross capital formation										...	...	

Table 2.6 Output, gross value added and fixed assets by industries at current prices (ISIC Rev. 4) Transportation and storage (H)

Series 100: 1993 SNA, Euro, Western calendar year — **Data in thousands**

	2001	2002	2003	2004	2005	2006	2007	2008	2009	2010	2011	2012
Series										**100**		
Output, at basic prices										308344.0	316847.0	
Less: Intermediate consumption, at purchaser's prices										163429.0	165967.0	
Equals: VALUE ADDED, GROSS, at basic prices										144915.0	150880.0	
Compensation of employees										...	...	
Taxes on production and imports, less Subsidies										...	...	
OPERATING SURPLUS, GROSS										...	...	
MIXED INCOME, GROSS										...	...	
Gross capital formation										...	...	

Table 2.6 Output, gross value added and fixed assets by industries at current prices (ISIC Rev. 4) Accommodation and food service activities (I)

Series 100: 1993 SNA, Euro, Western calendar year — **Data in thousands**

	2001	2002	2003	2004	2005	2006	2007	2008	2009	2010	2011	2012
Series										**100**		
Output, at basic prices										260929.0	279739.0	
Less: Intermediate consumption, at purchaser's prices										106504.0	118569.0	
Equals: VALUE ADDED, GROSS, at basic prices										154425.0	161178.0	
Compensation of employees										...	...	

	2001	2002	2003	2004	2005	2006	2007	2008	2009	2010	2011	2012
Series										**100**		
Taxes on production and imports, less Subsidies										...	...	
OPERATING SURPLUS, GROSS										...	...	
MIXED INCOME, GROSS										...	...	
Gross capital formation										...	...	

Table 2.6 Output, gross value added and fixed assets by industries at current prices (ISIC Rev. 4) Information and communication (J)

Series 100: 1993 SNA, Euro, Western calendar year **Data in thousands**

	2001	2002	2003	2004	2005	2006	2007	2008	2009	2010	2011	2012
Series										**100**		
Output, at basic prices										311775.0	298835.0	
Less: Intermediate consumption, at purchaser's prices										135162.0	133878.0	
Equals: VALUE ADDED, GROSS, at basic prices										176614.0	164957.0	
Compensation of employees										...	...	
Taxes on production and imports, less Subsidies										...	...	
OPERATING SURPLUS, GROSS										...	...	
MIXED INCOME, GROSS										...	...	
Gross capital formation										...	...	

Table 2.6 Output, gross value added and fixed assets by industries at current prices (ISIC Rev. 4) Financial and insurance activities (K)

Series 100: 1993 SNA, Euro, Western calendar year **Data in thousands**

	2001	2002	2003	2004	2005	2006	2007	2008	2009	2010	2011	2012
Series										**100**		
Output, at basic prices										195351.0	196551.0	
Less: Intermediate consumption, at purchaser's prices										70836.0	64713.0	
Equals: VALUE ADDED, GROSS, at basic prices										124515.0	131839.0	
Compensation of employees										...	...	
Taxes on production and imports, less Subsidies										...	...	
OPERATING SURPLUS, GROSS										...	...	
MIXED INCOME, GROSS										...	...	
Gross capital formation										...	...	

Table 2.6 Output, gross value added and fixed assets by industries at current prices (ISIC Rev. 4) Real estate activities (L)

Series 100: 1993 SNA, Euro, Western calendar year — **Data in thousands**

	2001	2002	2003	2004	2005	2006	2007	2008	2009	2010	2011	2012
Series										**100**		
Output, at basic prices										250075.0	281281.0	
Less: Intermediate consumption, at purchaser's prices										66470.0	61406.0	
Equals: VALUE ADDED, GROSS, at basic prices										183605.0	219875.0	
Compensation of employees										...	...	
Taxes on production and imports, less Subsidies										...	...	
OPERATING SURPLUS, GROSS										...	...	
MIXED INCOME, GROSS										...	...	
Gross capital formation										...	...	

Table 2.6 Output, gross value added and fixed assets by industries at current prices (ISIC Rev. 4) Professional, scientific, technical, administrative and support service activities (M+N)

Series 100: 1993 SNA, Euro, Western calendar year — **Data in thousands**

	2001	2002	2003	2004	2005	2006	2007	2008	2009	2010	2011	2012
Series										**100**		
Output, at basic prices										295137.0	315559.0	
Less: Intermediate consumption, at purchaser's prices										197341.0	200629.0	
Equals: VALUE ADDED, GROSS, at basic prices										97796.0	114930.0	
Compensation of employees										...	...	
Taxes on production and imports, less Subsidies										...	...	
OPERATING SURPLUS, GROSS										...	...	
MIXED INCOME, GROSS										...	...	
Gross capital formation										...	...	

Table 2.6 Output, gross value added and fixed assets by industries at current prices (ISIC Rev. 4) Professional, scientific and technical activities (M)

Series 100: 1993 SNA, Euro, Western calendar year — **Data in thousands**

	2001	2002	2003	2004	2005	2006	2007	2008	2009	2010	2011	2012
Series										**100**		
Output, at basic prices										232567.0	227888.0	
Less: Intermediate consumption, at purchaser's prices										159830.0	139713.0	
Equals: VALUE ADDED, GROSS, at basic prices										72737.0	88175.0	
Compensation of employees										...	...	

	2001	2002	2003	2004	2005	2006	2007	2008	2009	2010	2011	2012
Series										**100**		
Taxes on production and imports, less Subsidies										...	...	
OPERATING SURPLUS, GROSS										...	...	
MIXED INCOME, GROSS										...	...	
Gross capital formation										...	...	

Table 2.6 Output, gross value added and fixed assets by industries at current prices (ISIC Rev. 4) Administrative and support service activities (N)

Series 100: 1993 SNA, Euro, Western calendar year **Data in thousands**

	2001	2002	2003	2004	2005	2006	2007	2008	2009	2010	2011	2012
Series										**100**		
Output, at basic prices										62570.0	87671.0	
Less: Intermediate consumption, at purchaser's prices										37511.0	60916.0	
Equals: VALUE ADDED, GROSS, at basic prices										25059.0	26755.0	
Compensation of employees										...	...	
Taxes on production and imports, less Subsidies										...	...	
OPERATING SURPLUS, GROSS										...	...	
MIXED INCOME, GROSS										...	...	
Gross capital formation										...	...	

Table 2.6 Output, gross value added and fixed assets by industries at current prices (ISIC Rev. 4) Public administration and defence, education, human health and social work activities (O+P+Q)

Series 100: 1993 SNA, Euro, Western calendar year **Data in thousands**

	2001	2002	2003	2004	2005	2006	2007	2008	2009	2010	2011	2012
Series										**100**		
Output, at basic prices										784037.0	770723.0	
Less: Intermediate consumption, at purchaser's prices										254497.0	244282.0	
Equals: VALUE ADDED, GROSS, at basic prices										529539.0	526441.0	
Compensation of employees										...	...	
Taxes on production and imports, less Subsidies										...	...	
OPERATING SURPLUS, GROSS										...	...	
MIXED INCOME, GROSS										...	...	
Gross capital formation										...	...	

Table 2.6 Output, gross value added and fixed assets by industries at current prices (ISIC Rev. 4) Public administration and defence; compulsory social security (O)

Series 100: 1993 SNA, Euro, Western calendar year — **Data in thousands**

	2001	2002	2003	2004	2005	2006	2007	2008	2009	2010	2011	2012
Series										**100**		
Output, at basic prices										409462.0	401996.0	
Less: Intermediate consumption, at purchaser's prices										154389.0	146479.0	
Equals: VALUE ADDED, GROSS, at basic prices										255073.0	255517.0	
Compensation of employees										...	...	
Taxes on production and imports, less Subsidies										...	...	
OPERATING SURPLUS, GROSS										...	...	
MIXED INCOME, GROSS										...	...	
Gross capital formation										...	...	

Table 2.6 Output, gross value added and fixed assets by industries at current prices (ISIC Rev. 4) Education (P)

Series 100: 1993 SNA, Euro, Western calendar year — **Data in thousands**

	2001	2002	2003	2004	2005	2006	2007	2008	2009	2010	2011	2012
Series										**100**		
Output, at basic prices										153187.0	153518.0	
Less: Intermediate consumption, at purchaser's prices										14309.0	14246.0	
Equals: VALUE ADDED, GROSS, at basic prices										138877.0	139271.0	
Compensation of employees										...	...	
Taxes on production and imports, less Subsidies										...	...	
OPERATING SURPLUS, GROSS										...	...	
MIXED INCOME, GROSS										...	...	
Gross capital formation										...	...	

Table 2.6 Output, gross value added and fixed assets by industries at current prices (ISIC Rev. 4) Human health and social work activities (Q)

Series 100: 1993 SNA, Euro, Western calendar year — **Data in thousands**

	2001	2002	2003	2004	2005	2006	2007	2008	2009	2010	2011	2012
Series										**100**		
Output, at basic prices										221388.0	215209.0	
Less: Intermediate consumption, at purchaser's prices										85799.0	83557.0	
Equals: VALUE ADDED, GROSS, at basic prices										135589.0	131653.0	
Compensation of employees										...	...	

	2001	2002	2003	2004	2005	2006	2007	2008	2009	2010	2011	2012
Series										**100**		
Taxes on production and imports, less Subsidies										...	...	
OPERATING SURPLUS, GROSS										...	...	
MIXED INCOME, GROSS										...	...	
Gross capital formation										...	...	

Table 2.6 Output, gross value added and fixed assets by industries at current prices (ISIC Rev. 4) Other service activities (R+S+T)

Series 100: 1993 SNA, Euro, Western calendar year **Data in thousands**

	2001	2002	2003	2004	2005	2006	2007	2008	2009	2010	2011	2012
Series										**100**		
Output, at basic prices										114320.0	134686.0	
Less: Intermediate consumption, at purchaser's prices										60711.0	75240.0	
Equals: VALUE ADDED, GROSS, at basic prices										53609.0	59446.0	
Compensation of employees										...	...	
Taxes on production and imports, less Subsidies										...	...	
OPERATING SURPLUS, GROSS										...	...	
MIXED INCOME, GROSS										...	...	
Gross capital formation										...	...	

Table 2.6 Output, gross value added and fixed assets by industries at current prices (ISIC Rev. 4) Arts, entertainment and recreation (R)

Series 100: 1993 SNA, Euro, Western calendar year **Data in thousands**

	2001	2002	2003	2004	2005	2006	2007	2008	2009	2010	2011	2012
Series										**100**		
Output, at basic prices										88092.0	93313.0	
Less: Intermediate consumption, at purchaser's prices										48382.0	53504.0	
Equals: VALUE ADDED, GROSS, at basic prices										39710.0	39809.0	
Compensation of employees										...	...	
Taxes on production and imports, less Subsidies										...	...	
OPERATING SURPLUS, GROSS										...	...	
MIXED INCOME, GROSS										...	...	
Gross capital formation										...	...	

Table 2.6 Output, gross value added and fixed assets by industries at current prices (ISIC Rev. 4) Other service activities (S)

Series 100: 1993 SNA, Euro, Western calendar year — Data in thousands

	2001	2002	2003	2004	2005	2006	2007	2008	2009	2010	2011	2012
Series										**100**		
Output, at basic prices										26228.0	41373.0	
Less: Intermediate consumption, at purchaser's prices										12329.0	21736.0	
Equals: VALUE ADDED, GROSS, at basic prices										13899.0	19637.0	
Compensation of employees										...	...	
Taxes on production and imports, less Subsidies										...	...	
OPERATING SURPLUS, GROSS										...	...	
MIXED INCOME, GROSS										...	...	
Gross capital formation										...	...	

Table 3.2 Individual consumption expenditure of households, NPISHs, and general government at current prices

Series 100: 1993 SNA, Euro, Western calendar year — Data in thousands

	2001	2002	2003	2004	2005	2006	2007	2008	2009	2010	2011	2012
Series							**100**					
Individual consumption expenditure of households												
Food and non-alcoholic beverages							719389.0	926002.0				
Alcoholic beverages, tobacco and narcotics							116562.0	136457.0				
Clothing and footwear							105723.0	151602.0				
Housing, water, electricity, gas and other fuels							328354.0	363062.0				
Furnishings, household equipment and routine maintenance of the house							361999.0	417368.0				
Health							60722.0	63512.0				
Transport							392462.0	423730.0				
Communication							170235.0	178966.0				
Recreation and culture							137206.0	160909.0				
Education							26578.0	28262.0				
Restaurants and hotels							301329.0	338327.0				
Miscellaneous goods and services							81014.0	112355.0				
Equals: Household final consumption expenditure in domestic market							2801600.0	3300600.0				
Plus: Direct purchases abroad by residents							26900.0	29500.0				
Less: Direct purchases in domestic market by non-residents							459500.0	515200.0				
Equals: Household final consumption expenditure							2368960.0	2814822.0				
Individual consumption expenditure of non-profit institutions serving households (NPISHs)												
Equals: NPISHs final consumption expenditure							...	...				

	2001	2002	2003	2004	2005	2006	2007	2008	2009	2010	2011	2012
Series							**100**					
Individual consumption expenditure of general government												
Equals: Individual consumption expenditure of general government							239500.0	292800.0				
Equals: Total actual individual consumption							...	...				

Table 4.1 Total Economy (S.1)

Series 100: 1993 SNA, Euro, Western calendar year **Data in thousands**

	2001	2002	2003	2004	2005	2006	2007	2008	2009	2010	2011	2012
Series										**100**		
I. Production account - Resources												
Output, at basic prices (otherwise, please specify)										5159823.0	5239614.0	
Less: Financial intermediation services indirectly measured (only to be deducted if FISIM is not distributed to uses)										...	...	
Plus: Taxes less Subsidies on products										516618.0	529392.0	
Plus: Taxes on products										...	...	
Less: Subsidies on products										...	...	
I. Production account - Uses												
Intermediate consumption, at purchaser's prices										2572586.0	2534946.0	
GROSS DOMESTIC PRODUCT										3103855.0	3234060.0	
Less: Consumption of fixed capital										...	...	
NET DOMESTIC PRODUCT										...	...	

Table 4.3 Non-financial Corporations (S.11)

Series 100: 1993 SNA, Euro, Western calendar year **Data in thousands**

	2001	2002	2003	2004	2005	2006	2007	2008	2009	2010	2011	2012
Series										**100**		
I. Production account - Resources												
Output, at basic prices (otherwise, please specify)										3373965.0	3397587.0	
I. Production account - Uses												
Intermediate consumption, at purchaser's prices										1930587.0	1892600.0	
VALUE ADDED GROSS, in basic prices										1443378.0	1504987.0	
Less: Consumption of fixed capital										...	...	
VALUE ADDED NET, at basic prices										...	...	

Table 4.4 Financial Corporations (S.12)

Series 100: 1993 SNA, Euro, Western calendar year — **Data in thousands**

	2001	2002	2003	2004	2005	2006	2007	2008	2009	2010	2011	2012
Series										**100**		
I. Production account - Resources												
Output, at basic prices (otherwise, please specify)										195351.0	196551.0	
I. Production account - Uses												
Intermediate consumption, at purchaser's prices										70836.0	64713.0	
VALUE ADDED GROSS, at basic prices										124515.0	131839.0	
Less: Consumption of fixed capital										...	...	
VALUE ADDED NET, at basic prices										...	...	

Table 4.5 General Government (S.13)

Series 100: 1993 SNA, Euro, Western calendar year — **Data in thousands**

	2001	2002	2003	2004	2005	2006	2007	2008	2009	2010	2011	2012
Series										**100**		
I. Production account - Resources												
Output, at basic prices (otherwise, please specify)										758008.0	739393.0	
I. Production account - Uses												
Intermediate consumption, at purchaser's prices										247466.0	234557.0	
VALUE ADDED GROSS, at basic prices										510543.0	504836.0	
Less: Consumption of fixed capital										...	...	
VALUE ADDED NET, at basic prices										...	...	

Table 4.6 Households (S.14)

Series 100: 1993 SNA, Euro, Western calendar year — **Data in thousands**

	2001	2002	2003	2004	2005	2006	2007	2008	2009	2010	2011	2012
Series										**100**		
I. Production account - Resources												
Output, at basic prices (otherwise, please specify)										832498.0	906084.0	
I. Production account - Uses												
Intermediate consumption, at purchaser's prices										323698.0	343076.0	
VALUE ADDED GROSS, at basic prices										508800.0	563008.0	
Less: Consumption of fixed capital										...	...	
VALUE ADDED NET, at basic prices										...	...	

Montserrat

Source

Reply to the United Nations national accounts questionnaire from the Statistics Department, Ministry of Finance and Economics Management, Montserrat.

General

The estimates were prepared in accordance with the 1993 United Nations System of National Accounts (1993 SNA) so far as the existing data would permit.

Table 1.1 Gross domestic product by expenditures at current prices

Series 100: 1993 SNA, EC dollar, Western calendar year — **Data in thousands**

	2001	2002	2003	2004	2005	2006	2007	2008	2009	2010	2011	2012
Series	**100**											
	Expenditures of the gross domestic product											
Final consumption expenditure	121520.0	119880.0	129210.0	153850.0	186550.0	182630.0	187540.0	223970.0	196790.0	198670.0	196300.0	
Household final consumption expenditure	71870.0	72390.0	73650.0	91610.0	124070.0	111920.0	109000.0	142720.0	115760.0	124430.0	121470.0	
NPISHs final consumption expenditure	...	...	...	...	...	...	...	...	...	...	...	
General government final consumption expenditure	49650.0	47490.0	55560.0	62240.0	62480.0	70710.0	78540.0	81250.0	81030.0	74240.0	74830.0	
Gross capital formation	39680.0	50210.0	61630.0	48930.0	42530.0	32480.0	33410.0	37660.0	43160.0	40000.0	51490.0	
Gross fixed capital formation	39680.0	50210.0	61630.0	48930.0	42530.0	32480.0	33410.0	37660.0	43160.0	40000.0	51490.0	
Changes in inventories	...	...	...	...	...	...	...	...	...	...	...	
Acquisitions less disposals of valuables	...	...	...	...	...	...	...	...	...	...	...	
Exports of goods and services	42660.0	44190.0	40040.0	54580.0	45030.0	44660.0	48060.0	48520.0	40580.0	33050.0	35540.0	
Exports of goods	3000.0	6610.0	7740.0	14430.0	5060.0	4830.0	8320.0	10990.0	8730.0	2610.0	4740.0	
Exports of services	39660.0	37580.0	32290.0	40160.0	39970.0	39820.0	39740.0	37530.0	31850.0	30440.0	30800.0	
Less: Imports of goods and services	105300.0	104530.0	117560.0	136510.0	140210.0	118490.0	121770.0	153630.0	117900.0	115910.0	115200.0	
Imports of goods	46170.0	60470.0	67520.0	68260.0	70710.0	71750.0	70430.0	90560.0	70390.0	69730.0	69940.0	
Imports of services	59130.0	44060.0	50040.0	68250.0	69500.0	46740.0	51340.0	63070.0	47510.0	46180.0	45260.0	
Equals: GROSS DOMESTIC PRODUCT	98560.0	109760.0	113320.0	120850.0	133910.0	141280.0	147240.0	156520.0	162630.0	155810.0	168130.0	

Table 1.3 Relations among product, income, savings, and net lending aggregates

Series 100: 1993 SNA, EC dollar, Western calendar year — **Data in thousands**

	2001	2002	2003	2004	2005	2006	2007	2008	2009	2010	2011	2012
Series	**100**											
GROSS DOMESTIC PRODUCT	98560.0	109760.0	113320.0	120850.0	133910.0	141280.0	147240.0	156520.0	162630.0	155810.0	168130.0	
Plus: Compensation of employees - from and to the rest of the world, net	...	...	...	...	...	...	...	...	...	...	...	
Plus: Property income - from and to the rest of the world, net	...	...	...	...	...	...	...	...	...	...	...	
Sum of Compensation of employees and property income - from and to the rest of the world, net	-1740.0	-8260.0	-3260.0	-9210.0	-7600.0	-5160.0	-10110.0	-12010.0	-9760.0	-10280.0	-9700.0	

	2001	2002	2003	2004	2005	2006	2007	2008	2009	2010	2011	2012
Series	**100**											
Plus: Taxes less subsidies on production and imports - from and to the rest of the world, net	...	...	...	...	...	...	...	...	...	...	...	
Equals: GROSS NATIONAL INCOME	96810.0	101500.0	110050.0	111650.0	126310.0	136110.0	137130.0	144510.0	152880.0	145530.0	158440.0	
Plus: Current transfers - from and to the rest of the world, net	47980.0	42250.0	59530.0	62670.0	60050.0	58650.0	55700.0	63960.0	52770.0	39810.0	46360.0	
Equals: GROSS NATIONAL DISPOSABLE INCOME	144790.0	143740.0	169580.0	174320.0	186350.0	194760.0	192830.0	208470.0	205650.0	185350.0	204800.0	
Less: Final consumption expenditure / Actual final consumption	121520.0	119880.0	129210.0	153850.0	186550.0	182630.0	187540.0	223970.0	196790.0	198670.0	196300.0	
Equals: SAVING, GROSS	23270.0	23860.0	40380.0	20470.0	-200.0	12130.0	5290.0	-15490.0	8860.0	-13320.0	8500.0	
Plus: Capital transfers - from and to the rest of the world, net	...	...	...	...	...	...	...	...	...	...	...	
Less: Gross capital formation	...	...	...	...	...	...	...	...	...	...	...	
Less: Acquisitions less disposals of non-produced non-financial assets	...	...	...	...	...	...	...	...	...	...	...	
Equals: NET LENDING (+) / NET BORROWING (-) OF THE NATION	...	...	...	...	...	...	...	...	...	...	...	
	Net values: Gross National Income / Gross National Disposable Income / Saving Gross less Consumption of fixed capital											
Less: Consumption of fixed capital	...	...	...	...	...	...	...	...	...	...	...	
Equals: NET NATIONAL INCOME	...	...	...	...	...	...	...	...	...	...	...	
Equals: NET NATIONAL DISPOSABLE INCOME	...	...	...	...	...	...	...	...	...	...	...	
Equals: SAVING, NET	...	...	...	...	...	...	...	...	...	...	...	

Table 2.1 Value added by industries at current prices (ISIC Rev. 3)

Series 100: 1993 SNA, EC dollar, Western calendar year **Data in thousands**

	2001	2002	2003	2004	2005	2006	2007	2008	2009	2010	2011	2012
Series	**100**											
	Industries											
Agriculture, hunting, forestry; fishing	990.0	1320.0	1330.0	1130.0	1020.0	1220.0	1190.0	1320.0	1670.0	1460.0	1960.0	
Agriculture, hunting, forestry	690.0	1020.0	1010.0	830.0	530.0	740.0	850.0	880.0	1130.0	1110.0	1460.0	
Agriculture, hunting and related service activities	630.0	960.0	960.0	760.0	480.0	680.0	790.0	810.0	1070.0	1050.0	1400.0	
Forestry, logging and related service activities	60.0	60.0	60.0	60.0	60.0	60.0	60.0	60.0	60.0	60.0	60.0	
Fishing	300.0	300.0	320.0	300.0	490.0	480.0	340.0	440.0	540.0	350.0	500.0	
Mining and quarrying	70.0	50.0	50.0	90.0	790.0	660.0	1690.0	1620.0	1340.0	340.0	1460.0	
Manufacturing	1120.0	1410.0	1230.0	1200.0	1710.0	2280.0	1630.0	1990.0	2040.0	1900.0	2130.0	
Electricity, gas and water supply	1710.0	2100.0	3020.0	3380.0	3580.0	3380.0	4000.0	4040.0	4140.0	4390.0	4650.0	
Construction	10990.0	14660.0	14890.0	13190.0	13350.0	9190.0	9350.0	10430.0	11950.0	11110.0	12750.0	
Wholesale, retail trade, repair of motor vehicles, motorcycles and personal and households goods; hotels and restaurants	9310.0	10070.0	9570.0	9970.0	11020.0	11460.0	11730.0	13850.0	13380.0	11080.0	11170.0[a]	
Wholesale, retail trade, repair of motor vehicles, motorcycles and personal and household goods	7110.0	7850.0	7660.0	7980.0	8580.0	8760.0	8780.0	10910.0	11080.0	8590.0	9210.0	
Hotels and restaurants	2200.0	2220.0	1910.0	1990.0	2440.0	2700.0	2950.0	2940.0	2300.0	2490.0	2470.0	
Transport, storage and communications	10600.0	11310.0	10970.0	13240.0	12850.0	14000.0	14520.0	13370.0	12470.0	11440.0	14240.0	

	2001	2002	2003	2004	2005	2006	2007	2008	2009	2010	2011	2012
Series	**100**											
Land transport; transport via pipelines, water transport; air transport; Supporting and auxiliary transport activities; activities of travel agencies	5670.0	5900.0	6610.0	6640.0	6170.0	6300.0	5890.0	5860.0	5640.0	4600.0	7260.0	
Post and telecommunications	4930.0	5410.0	4360.0	6600.0	6680.0	7700.0	8630.0	7510.0	6830.0	6840.0	6980.0	
Financial intermediation; real estate, renting and business activities	19770.0	18810.0	23430.0	24990.0	27470.0	29990.0	31300.0	32220.0	32330.0	32580.0	34520.0[a]	
Financial intermediation	9690.0	8360.0	10110.0	11310.0	13380.0	12570.0	13580.0	14300.0	14320.0	14520.0	16530.0	
Real estate, renting and business activities	10080.0	10450.0	13320.0	13680.0	14090.0	17420.0	17720.0	17920.0	18000.0	18060.0	18410.0	
Public administration and defence; compulsory social security	23870.0	25740.0	26120.0	27300.0	31960.0	38920.0	42390.0	45190.0	51530.0	50380.0	50780.0	
Education; health and social work; other community, social and personal services	9260.0	10070.0	10620.0	11170.0	13600.0	15047.0	15340.0	15860.0	15870.0	17210.0	17360.0	
Education	2430.0	2670.0	2850.0	2970.0	4490.0	4590.0	4730.0	5050.0	5060.0	5160.0	5210.0	
Health and social work	4630.0	5210.0	5370.0	5580.0	6130.0	6990.0	7250.0	7490.0	7690.0	7870.0	7970.0	
Other community, social and personal services	2200.0	2190.0	2400.0	2620.0	2980.0	3460.0	3360.0	3320.0	3120.0	4180.0	4180.0	
Private households with employed persons	430.0	450.0	480.0	500.0	530.0	600.0	620.0	630.0	640.0	630.0	640.0	
Equals: VALUE ADDED, GROSS, in basic prices	88130.0	95980.0	101710.0	106160.0	117880.0	126747.0	133760.0	140520.0	147360.0	142520.0	152660.0	
Less: Financial intermediation services indirectly measured (FISIM)	300.0	770.0	870.0	930.0	1180.0	1260.0	1320.0	1430.0	1640.0	2020.0	1860.0	
Plus: Taxes less Subsidies on products	10730.0	14540.0	12470.0	15630.0	17210.0	15780.0	14790.0	17430.0	16940.0	15310.0	17330.0	
Plus: Taxes on products	11500.0	15310.0	13310.0	16470.0	18080.0	16870.0	15820.0	18470.0	17930.0	16260.0	18310.0	
Less: Subsidies on products	770.0	770.0	840.0	840.0	870.0	1090.0	1030.0	1040.0	990.0	950.0	980.0	
Equals: GROSS DOMESTIC PRODUCT	98560.0	109760.0	113320.0	120850.0	133910.0	141280.0	147240.0	156520.0	162630.0	155810.0	168130.0	

[a] Discrepancy between components and total as one or more components have not been revised.

Table 2.2 Value added by industries at constant prices (ISIC Rev. 3)

Series 100: 1993 SNA, EC dollar, Western calendar year

Data in thousands

	2001	2002	2003	2004	2005	2006	2007	2008	2009	2010	2011	2012
Series	**100**											
Base year	**2006**											
	Industries											
Agriculture, hunting, forestry; fishing	1050.0	1230.0	1280.0	1070.0	1070.0	1220.0	1120.0	940.0	1090.0	870.0	1130.0	
Agriculture, hunting, forestry	740.0	920.0	940.0	760.0	580.0	740.0	780.0	640.0	730.0	630.0	840.0	
Agriculture, hunting and related service activities	680.0	860.0	880.0	700.0	520.0	680.0	720.0	580.0	670.0	570.0	780.0	
Forestry, logging and related service activities	60.0	60.0	60.0	60.0	60.0	60.0	60.0	60.0	60.0	60.0	60.0	
Fishing	310.0	310.0	340.0	310.0	490.0	480.0	340.0	300.0	360.0	240.0	290.0	
Mining and quarrying	430.0	320.0	320.0	550.0	1030.0	660.0	1900.0	1230.0	1020.0	260.0	780.0	
Manufacturing	1330.0	1490.0	1560.0	1610.0	2010.0	2280.0	2410.0	2500.0	2250.0	2050.0	2090.0	
Electricity, gas and water supply	2920.0	2880.0	3070.0	3060.0	3310.0	3380.0	3420.0	3450.0	3520.0	3700.0	3800.0	
Construction	12070.0	15900.0	15730.0	13730.0	13870.0	9190.0	8110.0	8420.0	9410.0	8380.0	9340.0	

	2001	2002	2003	2004	2005	2006	2007	2008	2009	2010	2011	2012
Series	**100**											
Base year	**2006**											
Wholesale, retail trade, repair of motor vehicles, motorcycles and personal and household goods; hotels and restaurants	10340.0	10990.0	10280.0	10670.0	11530.0	11460.0	11430.0	13190.0	12640.0	10470.0	9780.0	
Wholesale, retail trade, repair of motor vehicles, motorcycles and personal and household goods	8040.0	8570.0	8270.0	8280.0	8670.0	8760.0	8440.0	10020.0	9950.0	7530.0	7760.0	
Hotels and restaurants	2300.0	2420.0	2010.0	2390.0	2860.0	2700.0	2990.0	3170.0	2690.0	2940.0	2910.0	
Transport, storage and communications	13920.0	12420.0	11670.0	12500.0	12190.0	14000.0	15050.0	15270.0	14380.0	11650.0	13850.0	
Land transport; transport via piplines, water transport; air transport; Supporting and auxiliary transport activities; activities of travel agencies	3870.0	3890.0	4100.0	4890.0	4860.0	6300.0	7780.0	7660.0	6840.0	4250.0	6490.0	
Post and telecommunications	10050.0	8530.0	7570.0	7610.0	7330.0	7700.0	7270.0	7610.0	7540.0	7400.0	7470.0	
Financial intermediation, real estate, renting and business activities	31500.0	26380.0	29380.0	31320.0	30140.0	29990.0	30990.0	30810.0	31000.0	30710.0	32060.0	
Financial intermediation	16000.0	10440.0	13010.0	14720.0	13160.0	12570.0	13410.0	13090.0	13220.0	12940.0	14030.0	
Real estate, renting and business activities	15500.0	15940.0	16370.0	16600.0	16980.0	17420.0	17580.0	17720.0	17780.0	17770.0	18030.0	
Public administration and defence; compulsory social security	30150.0	31460.0	32870.0	34290.0	35580.0	38920.0	41480.0	43490.0	45360.0	45390.0	44850.0	
Education; health and social work; other community, social and personal services	10910.0	11350.0	11750.0	12310.0	13970.0	15040.0	16370.0	16690.0	16820.0	16610.0	16430.0	
Education	2930.0	3070.0	3190.0	3330.0	4220.0	4590.0	5400.0	5400.0	5240.0	5090.0	5040.0	
Health and social work	5250.0	5520.0	5790.0	6100.0	6380.0	6990.0	7380.0	7670.0	7850.0	7830.0	7770.0	
Other community, social and personal services	2730.0	2760.0	2770.0	2880.0	3370.0	3460.0	3590.0	3620.0	3730.0	3690.0	3620.0	
Private households with employed persons	440.0	460.0	490.0	510.0	540.0	600.0	620.0	630.0	690.0	700.0	700.0	
Equals: VALUE ADDED, GROSS, in basic prices	115060.0	114880.0	118400.0	121620.0	125240.0	126740.0	132900.0	136620.0	138180.0	130790.0	134810.0	
Less: Financial intermediation services indirectly measured (FISIM)	1130.0	990.0	1210.0	1350.0	1310.0	1260.0	1210.0	1180.0	1430.0	1650.0	1490.0	
Plus: Taxes less Subsidies on products	...	...	...	...	...	...	...	...	...	...	...	
Equals: GROSS DOMESTIC PRODUCT	...	...	...	...	...	...	...	...	...	...	...	

Table 2.3 Output, gross value added, and fixed assets by industries at current prices (ISIC Rev. 3) Total Economy

Series 100: 1993 SNA, EC dollar, Western calendar year

Data in thousands

	2001	2002	2003	2004	2005	2006	2007	2008	2009	2010	2011	2012
Series	**100**											
Output, at basic prices	188790.0	196950.0	214570.0	220600.0	230840.0	239950.0	254650.0	268950.0	270920.0	264180.0	284750.0	
Less: Intermediate consumption, at purchaser's prices	100660.0	100970.0	112860.0	114430.0	112960.0	113200.0	120880.0	128440.0	123590.0	121660.0	132080.0	
Equals: VALUE ADDED, GROSS, at basic prices	88130.0	95980.0	101710.0	106160.0	117880.0	126760.0	133770.0	140510.0	147320.0	142520.0	152660.0	
Compensation of employees	...	...	...	...	...	...	...	...	...	...	...	
Taxes on production and imports, less Subsidies	...	...	...	...	...	...	...	...	...	...	...	
OPERATING SURPLUS, GROSS	...	...	...	...	...	...	...	...	...	...	...	

	2001	2002	2003	2004	2005	2006	2007	2008	2009	2010	2011	2012
Series	**100**											
MIXED INCOME, GROSS	...	...	...	...	...	...	...	...	...	...	...	
Gross capital formation	...	...	...	...	...	...	...	...	...	...	...	

Table 2.3 Output, gross value added, and fixed assets by industries at current prices (ISIC Rev. 3) Agriculture, hunting, forestry; fishing (A+B)

Series 100: 1993 SNA, EC dollar, Western calendar year — **Data in thousands**

	2001	2002	2003	2004	2005	2006	2007	2008	2009	2010	2011	2012
Series	**100**											
Output, at basic prices	1320.0	1760.0	1790.0	1520.0	1370.0	1600.0	1620.0	1770.0	2230.0	1980.0	2550.0	
Less: Intermediate consumption, at purchaser's prices	340.0	440.0	450.0	390.0	350.0	380.0	430.0	460.0	570.0	520.0	650.0	
Equals: VALUE ADDED, GROSS, at basic prices	990.0	1320.0	1330.0	1130.0	1020.0	1220.0	1190.0	1320.0	1670.0	1460.0	1900.0	
Compensation of employees	...	...	...	...	...	...	...	...	...	...	...	
Taxes on production and imports, less Subsidies	...	...	...	...	...	...	...	...	...	...	...	
OPERATING SURPLUS, GROSS	...	...	...	...	...	...	...	...	...	...	...	
MIXED INCOME, GROSS	...	...	...	...	...	...	...	...	...	...	...	
Gross capital formation	...	...	...	...	...	...	...	...	...	...	...	

Table 2.3 Output, gross value added, and fixed assets by industries at current prices (ISIC Rev. 3) Agriculture, hunting and related service activities (01)

Series 100: 1993 SNA, EC dollar, Western calendar year — **Data in thousands**

	2001	2002	2003	2004	2005	2006	2007	2008	2009	2010	2011	2012
Series	**100**											
Output, at basic prices	830.0	1270.0	1260.0	1030.0	610.0	850.0	1070.0	1080.0	1410.0	1420.0	1860.0	
Less: Intermediate consumption, at purchaser's prices	200.0	310.0	310.0	250.0	130.0	170.0	280.0	270.0	340.0	370.0	460.0	
Equals: VALUE ADDED, GROSS, at basic prices	630.0	960.0	960.0	760.0	480.0	680.0	790.0	810.0	1070.0	1050.0	1400.0	
Compensation of employees	...	...	...	...	...	...	...	...	...	...	...	
Taxes on production and imports, less Subsidies	...	...	...	...	...	...	...	...	...	...	...	
OPERATING SURPLUS, GROSS	...	...	...	...	...	...	...	...	...	...	...	
MIXED INCOME, GROSS	...	...	...	...	...	...	...	...	...	...	...	
Gross capital formation	...	...	...	...	...	...	...	...	...	...	...	

Table 2.3 Output, gross value added, and fixed assets by industries at current prices (ISIC Rev. 3) Forestry, logging and related service activities (02)

Series 100: 1993 SNA, EC dollar, Western calendar year

Data in thousands

	2001	2002	2003	2004	2005	2006	2007	2008	2009	2010	2011	2012
Series	**100**											
Output, at basic prices	60.0	60.0	60.0	60.0	60.0	60.0	60.0	60.0	60.0	60.0	60.0	
Less: Intermediate consumption, at purchaser's prices	0.0	0.0	0.0	0.0	0.0	0.0	0.0	0.0	0.0	0.0	0.0	
Equals: VALUE ADDED, GROSS, at basic prices	60.0	60.0	60.0	60.0	60.0	60.0	60.0	60.0	60.0	60.0	60.0	
Compensation of employees	...	...	...	...	...	...	...	...	...	...	...	
Taxes on production and imports, less Subsidies	...	...	...	...	...	...	...	...	...	...	...	
OPERATING SURPLUS, GROSS	...	...	...	...	...	...	...	...	...	...	...	
MIXED INCOME, GROSS	...	...	...	...	...	...	...	...	...	...	...	
Gross capital formation	...	...	...	...	...	...	...	...	...	...	...	

Table 2.3 Output, gross value added, and fixed assets by industries at current prices (ISIC Rev. 3) Fishing (B)

Series 100: 1993 SNA, EC dollar, Western calendar year

Data in thousands

	2001	2002	2003	2004	2005	2006	2007	2008	2009	2010	2011	2012
Series	**100**											
Output, at basic prices	420.0	430.0	460.0	430.0	700.0	690.0	490.0	630.0	760.0	500.0	630.0	
Less: Intermediate consumption, at purchaser's prices	130.0	130.0	140.0	130.0	210.0	210.0	150.0	190.0	230.0	150.0	190.0	
Equals: VALUE ADDED, GROSS, at basic prices	300.0	300.0	320.0	300.0	490.0	480.0	340.0	440.0	540.0	350.0	440.0	
Compensation of employees	...	...	...	...	...	...	...	...	...	...	...	
Taxes on production and imports, less Subsidies	...	...	...	...	...	...	...	...	...	...	...	
OPERATING SURPLUS, GROSS	...	...	...	...	...	...	...	...	...	...	...	
MIXED INCOME, GROSS	...	...	...	...	...	...	...	...	...	...	...	
Gross capital formation	...	...	...	...	...	...	...	...	...	...	...	

Table 2.3 Output, gross value added, and fixed assets by industries at current prices (ISIC Rev. 3) Mining and quarrying (C)

Series 100: 1993 SNA, EC dollar, Western calendar year

Data in thousands

	2001	2002	2003	2004	2005	2006	2007	2008	2009	2010	2011	2012
Series	**100**											
Output, at basic prices	110.0	80.0	80.0	140.0	1220.0	1020.0	2600.0	2490.0	2060.0	530.0	1560.0	
Less: Intermediate consumption, at purchaser's prices	40.0	30.0	30.0	50.0	430.0	360.0	910.0	870.0	720.0	180.0	550.0	
Equals: VALUE ADDED, GROSS, at basic prices	70.0	50.0	50.0	90.0	790.0	660.0	1690.0	1620.0	1340.0	340.0	1010.0	
Compensation of employees	...	...	...	...	...	...	...	...	...	...	...	

	2001	2002	2003	2004	2005	2006	2007	2008	2009	2010	2011	2012
Series	**100**											
Taxes on production and imports, less Subsidies	...	...	...	...	...	...	...	...	...	...	...	
OPERATING SURPLUS, GROSS	...	...	...	...	...	...	...	...	...	...	...	
MIXED INCOME, GROSS	...	...	...	...	...	...	...	...	...	...	...	
Gross capital formation	...	...	...	...	...	...	...	...	...	...	...	

Table 2.3 Output, gross value added, and fixed assets by industries at current prices (ISIC Rev. 3) Manufacturing (D)

Series 100: 1993 SNA, EC dollar, Western calendar year **Data in thousands**

	2001	2002	2003	2004	2005	2006	2007	2008	2009	2010	2011	2012
Series	**100**											
Output, at basic prices	2750.0	4010.0	3660.0	3990.0	4640.0	5410.0	5810.0	6270.0	6690.0	6160.0	6910.0	
Less: Intermediate consumption, at purchaser's prices	1620.0	2590.0	2430.0	2790.0	2940.0	3130.0	4180.0	4280.0	4650.0	4260.0	4770.0	
Equals: VALUE ADDED, GROSS, at basic prices	1120.0	1410.0	1230.0	1200.0	1710.0	2280.0	1630.0	1990.0	2040.0	1900.0	2130.0	
Compensation of employees	...	...	...	...	...	...	...	...	...	...	...	
Taxes on production and imports, less Subsidies	...	...	...	...	...	...	...	...	...	...	...	
OPERATING SURPLUS, GROSS	...	...	...	...	...	...	...	...	...	...	...	
MIXED INCOME, GROSS	...	...	...	...	...	...	...	...	...	...	...	
Gross capital formation	...	...	...	...	...	...	...	...	...	...	...	

Table 2.3 Output, gross value added, and fixed assets by industries at current prices (ISIC Rev. 3) Electricity, gas and water supply (E)

Series 100: 1993 SNA, EC dollar, Western calendar year **Data in thousands**

	2001	2002	2003	2004	2005	2006	2007	2008	2009	2010	2011	2012
Series	**100**											
Output, at basic prices	9460.0	9720.0	10490.0	11460.0	13720.0	14890.0	15220.0	15350.0	15630.0	16160.0	16980.0	
Less: Intermediate consumption, at purchaser's prices	7740.0	7630.0	7480.0	8080.0	10140.0	11500.0	11220.0	11310.0	11490.0	11770.0	12330.0	
Equals: VALUE ADDED, GROSS, at basic prices	1710.0	2100.0	3020.0	3380.0	3580.0	3380.0	4000.0	4040.0	4140.0	4390.0	4650.0	
Compensation of employees	...	...	...	...	...	...	...	...	...	...	...	
Taxes on production and imports, less Subsidies	...	...	...	...	...	...	...	...	...	...	...	
OPERATING SURPLUS, GROSS	...	...	...	...	...	...	...	...	...	...	...	
MIXED INCOME, GROSS	...	...	...	...	...	...	...	...	...	...	...	
Gross capital formation	...	...	...	...	...	...	...	...	...	...	...	

Table 2.3 Output, gross value added, and fixed assets by industries at current prices (ISIC Rev. 3) Construction (F)

Series 100: 1993 SNA, EC dollar, Western calendar year — **Data in thousands**

	2001	2002	2003	2004	2005	2006	2007	2008	2009	2010	2011	2012
Series	**100**											
Output, at basic prices	31400.0	41900.0	42530.0	37690.0	38160.0	26260.0	26720.0	29790.0	34140.0	31750.0	40870.0	
Less: Intermediate consumption, at purchaser's prices	20410.0	27230.0	27650.0	24500.0	24800.0	17070.0	17360.0	19360.0	22190.0	20640.0	26560.0	
Equals: VALUE ADDED, GROSS, at basic prices	10990.0	14660.0	14890.0	13190.0	13350.0	9190.0	9350.0	10430.0	11950.0	11110.0	14300.0	
Compensation of employees	...	...	...	...	...	...	...	...	...	...	...	
Taxes on production and imports, less Subsidies	...	...	...	...	...	...	...	...	...	...	...	
OPERATING SURPLUS, GROSS	...	...	...	...	...	...	...	...	...	...	...	
MIXED INCOME, GROSS	...	...	...	...	...	...	...	...	...	...	...	
Gross capital formation	...	...	...	...	...	...	...	...	...	...	...	

Table 2.3 Output, gross value added, and fixed assets by industries at current prices (ISIC Rev. 3) Wholesale retail trade, repair of motor vehicles, motorcycles, etc.; hotels and restaurants (G+H)

Series 100: 1993 SNA, EC dollar, Western calendar year — **Data in thousands**

	2001	2002	2003	2004	2005	2006	2007	2008	2009	2010	2011	2012
Series	**100**											
Output, at basic prices	12770.0	13700.0	12920.0	13470.0	15030.0	15720.0	16210.0	18790.0	17850.0	15130.0	16420.0	
Less: Intermediate consumption, at purchaser's prices	3460.0	3630.0	3350.0	3490.0	4010.0	4260.0	4480.0	4940.0	4490.0	4070.0	4300.0	
Equals: VALUE ADDED, GROSS, at basic prices	9310.0	10070.0	9570.0	9970.0	11020.0	11460.0	11730.0	13850.0	13380.0	11080.0	12120.0	
Compensation of employees	...	...	...	...	...	...	...	...	...	...	...	
Taxes on production and imports, less Subsidies	...	...	...	...	...	...	...	...	...	...	...	
OPERATING SURPLUS, GROSS	...	...	...	...	...	...	...	...	...	...	...	
MIXED INCOME, GROSS	...	...	...	...	...	...	...	...	...	...	...	
Gross capital formation	...	...	...	...	...	...	...	...	...	...	...	

Table 2.3 Output, gross value added, and fixed assets by industries at current prices (ISIC Rev. 3) Transport, storage and communications (I)

Series 100: 1993 SNA, EC dollar, Western calendar year — **Data in thousands**

	2001	2002	2003	2004	2005	2006	2007	2008	2009	2010	2011	2012
Series	**100**											
Output, at basic prices	32060.0	28640.0	28310.0	29420.0	27350.0	27590.0	26800.0	27870.0	27250.0	25680.0	29100.0	
Less: Intermediate consumption, at purchaser's prices	21460.0	17340.0	17340.0	16180.0	14500.0	13580.0	12270.0	14480.0	14780.0	14240.0	15860.0	
Equals: VALUE ADDED, GROSS, at basic prices	10600.0	11310.0	10970.0	13240.0	12850.0	14000.0	14520.0	13370.0	12470.0	11440.0	13240.0	
Compensation of employees	...	...	...	...	...	...	...	...	...	...	...	

	2001	2002	2003	2004	2005	2006	2007	2008	2009	2010	2011	2012
Series	**100**											
Taxes on production and imports, less Subsidies	...	...	...	...	...	...	...	...	...	...	...	
OPERATING SURPLUS, GROSS	...	...	...	...	...	...	...	...	...	...	...	
MIXED INCOME, GROSS	...	...	...	...	...	...	...	...	...	...	...	
Gross capital formation	...	...	...	...	...	...	...	...	...	...	...	

Table 2.3 Output, gross value added, and fixed assets by industries at current prices (ISIC Rev. 3) Financial intermediation; real estate, renting and business activities (J+K)

Series 100: 1993 SNA, EC dollar, Western calendar year **Data in thousands**

	2001	2002	2003	2004	2005	2006	2007	2008	2009	2010	2011	2012
Series	**100**											
Output, at basic prices	26520.0	25240.0	31220.0	33330.0	34340.0	39270.0	42010.0	43240.0	43040.0	43660.0	46290.0	
Less: Intermediate consumption, at purchaser's prices	6750.0	6440.0	7790.0	8340.0	6880.0	9270.0	10700.0	11010.0	10710.0	11080.0	11770.0	
Equals: VALUE ADDED, GROSS, at basic prices	19770.0	18810.0	23430.0	24990.0	27470.0	29990.0	31300.0	32220.0	32330.0	32580.0	34520.0	
Compensation of employees	...	...	...	...	...	...	...	...	...	...	...	
Taxes on production and imports, less Subsidies	...	...	...	...	...	...	...	...	...	...	...	
OPERATING SURPLUS, GROSS	...	...	...	...	...	...	...	...	...	...	...	
MIXED INCOME, GROSS	...	...	...	...	...	...	...	...	...	...	...	
Gross capital formation	...	...	...	...	...	...	...	...	...	...	...	

Table 2.3 Output, gross value added, and fixed assets by industries at current prices (ISIC Rev. 3) Public administration and defense; compulsory social security (L)

Series 100: 1993 SNA, EC dollar, Western calendar year **Data in thousands**

	2001	2002	2003	2004	2005	2006	2007	2008	2009	2010	2011	2012
Series	**100**											
Output, at basic prices	53130.0	51410.0	61600.0	66230.0	66780.0	75900.0	85750.0	91050.0	90160.0	84270.0	84940.0	
Less: Intermediate consumption, at purchaser's prices	29260.0	25670.0	35470.0	38930.0	34820.0	36980.0	43360.0	45870.0	38630.0	33890.0	34160.0	
Equals: VALUE ADDED, GROSS, at basic prices	23870.0	25740.0	26120.0	27300.0	31960.0	38920.0	42390.0	45180.0	51530.0	50380.0	50780.0	
Compensation of employees	...	...	...	...	...	...	...	...	...	...	...	
Taxes on production and imports, less Subsidies	...	...	...	...	...	...	...	...	...	...	...	
OPERATING SURPLUS, GROSS	...	...	...	...	...	...	...	...	...	...	...	
MIXED INCOME, GROSS	...	...	...	...	...	...	...	...	...	...	...	
Gross capital formation	...	...	...	...	...	...	...	...	...	...	...	

Table 2.3 Output, gross value added, and fixed assets by industries at current prices (ISIC Rev. 3) Education; health and social work; other community, social and personal services (M+N+O)

Series 100: 1993 SNA, EC dollar, Western calendar year — **Data in thousands**

	2001	2002	2003	2004	2005	2006	2007	2008	2009	2010	2011	2012
Series	**100**											
Output, at basic prices	18840.0	20010.0	21490.0	22850.0	27700.0	31700.0	31290.0	31700.0	31240.0	38220.0	38480.0	
Less: Intermediate consumption, at purchaser's prices	9580.0	9970.0	10870.0	11680.0	14100.0	16660.0	15950.0	15850.0	15370.0	21020.0	21120.0	
Equals: VALUE ADDED, GROSS, at basic prices	9260.0	10070.0	10620.0	11170.0	13600.0	15040.0	15340.0	15860.0	15870.0	17210.0	17360.0	
Compensation of employees	...	...	...	...	...	...	...	...	...	...	...	
Taxes on production and imports, less Subsidies	...	...	...	...	...	...	...	...	...	...	...	
OPERATING SURPLUS, GROSS	...	...	...	...	...	...	...	...	...	...	...	
MIXED INCOME, GROSS	...	...	...	...	...	...	...	...	...	...	...	
Gross capital formation	...	...	...	...	...	...	...	...	...	...	...	

Table 2.3 Output, gross value added, and fixed assets by industries at current prices (ISIC Rev. 3) Private households with employed persons (P)

Series 100: 1993 SNA, EC dollar, Western calendar year — **Data in thousands**

	2001	2002	2003	2004	2005	2006	2007	2008	2009	2010	2011	2012
Series	**100**											
Output, at basic prices	430.0	450.0	480.0	500.0	530.0	600.0	620.0	630.0	640.0	630.0	640.0	
Less: Intermediate consumption, at purchaser's prices	0.0	0.0	0.0	0.0	0.0	0.0	0.0	0.0	0.0	0.0	0.0	
Equals: VALUE ADDED, GROSS, at basic prices	430.0	450.0	480.0	500.0	530.0	600.0	620.0	630.0	640.0	630.0	640.0	
Compensation of employees	...	...	...	...	...	...	...	...	...	...	...	
Taxes on production and imports, less Subsidies	...	...	...	...	...	...	...	...	...	...	...	
OPERATING SURPLUS, GROSS	...	...	...	...	...	...	...	...	...	...	...	
MIXED INCOME, GROSS	...	...	...	...	...	...	...	...	...	...	...	
Gross capital formation	...	...	...	...	...	...	...	...	...	...	...	

Table 4.1 Total Economy (S.1)

Series 100: 1993 SNA, EC dollar, Western calendar year — **Data in thousands**

	2001	2002	2003	2004	2005	2006	2007	2008	2009	2010	2011	2012
Series	**100**											
	I. Production account - Resources											
Output, at basic prices (otherwise, please specify)	188790.0	196950.0	214570.0	220600.0	230840.0	239950.0	254650.0	268950.0	270920.0	264180.0	284750.0	
Less: Financial intermediation services indirectly measured (only to be deducted if FISIM is not distributed to uses)	300.0	770.0	870.0	930.0	1180.0	1260.0	1320.0	1430.0	1640.0	2020.0	1860.0	
Plus: Taxes less Subsidies on products	10730.0	14540.0	12470.0	15630.0	17210.0	15780.0	14790.0	17430.0	16940.0	15310.0	17330.0	

	2001	2002	2003	2004	2005	2006	2007	2008	2009	2010	2011	2012
Series	**100**											
Plus: Taxes on products	11500.0	15310.0	13310.0	16470.0	18080.0	16870.0	15820.0	18470.0	17930.0	16260.0	18310.0	
Less: Subsidies on products	770.0	770.0	840.0	840.0	870.0	1090.0	1030.0	1040.0	990.0	950.0	980.0	
I. Production account - Uses												
Intermediate consumption, at purchaser's prices	100660.0	100970.0	112860.0	114430.0	112960.0	113200.0	120880.0	128440.0	123590.0	121660.0	132080.0	
GROSS DOMESTIC PRODUCT	98560.0	109760.0	113320.0	120850.0	133910.0	141280.0	147240.0	156520.0	162630.0	155810.0	168130.0	
Less: Consumption of fixed capital	...	...	...	...	...	...	...	...	...	...	...	
NET DOMESTIC PRODUCT	...	...	...	...	...	...	...	...	...	...	...	
II.1.1 Generation of income account - Resources												
GROSS DOMESTIC PRODUCT	98560.0	109760.0	113320.0	120850.0	133910.0	141280.0	147240.0	156520.0	162630.0	155810.0	168130.0	
II.1.1 Generation of income account - Uses												
Compensation of employees	...	...	...	...	...	...	...	...	...	...	...	
Taxes on production and imports, less Subsidies	...	...	...	...	...	...	...	...	...	...	...	
Taxes on production and imports	...	...	...	...	...	...	...	...	...	...	...	
Taxes on products	...	...	...	...	...	...	...	...	...	...	...	
Other taxes on production	...	...	...	...	...	...	...	...	...	...	...	
Less: Subsidies	...	...	...	...	...	...	...	...	...	...	...	
Subsidies on products	...	...	...	...	...	...	...	...	...	...	...	
Other subsidies on production	...	...	...	...	...	...	...	...	...	...	...	
OPERATING SURPLUS, GROSS	...	...	...	...	...	...	...	...	...	...	...	
MIXED INCOME, GROSS	...	...	...	...	...	...	...	...	...	...	...	

Morocco

Source
In Morocco, national accounts are compiled by the Department of National Accounts, which comes under the responsibility of the Office of the High Commissioner for Planning. Official annual and quarterly national account statistics are posted on the website www.hcp.ma and are published in the Moroccan statistical yearbook, and in specific national account documents that can be downloaded from the website.

General
Morocco has put in place the System of National Accounts 1993 (1993 SNA) using 1998 as the base year. The compilation of the 1993 SNA accounts involved the following: review of the 1993 SNA and staff training; determination of the statistical data requirements; preparation of the functional classifications; preparation of statistical surveys and organization of data collection and use; installation and implementation of the appropriate information technology (i.e. the "ERETES" software); study and implementation of methodological procedures; and preparation of the accounts and tables.

The compilation of the national accounts involved a number of large-scale statistical operations, including structural surveys such as: structural survey of corporations that keep financial records (1999-2000 but applied to 1998); survey of the informal sector (1999-2000); surveys on standards of living and on household consumption and expenditure (1998 and 2000-2001); investment survey of general government units (2000 but applied to 1998); comprehensive national survey of rural employment (beginning in 1999); and economic census (2001-2002).

A series of accounts for the 1998-2005 fiscal years was published in October 2006. The financial results for the 2004 fiscal year are semi-final, while those for 2005 are provisional. The provisional results for the 2006 fiscal year were published in June 2007.

In Morocco, the accounts and tables, which are compiled on a regular basis include: supply and use balances by product (278 items); production accounts and generation of income accounts by industry (97 items); supply and use tables; institutional sector accounts (from the production account through to the financial account); rest of the world accounts; tables of financial transactions; and tables of integrated economic accounts.

The Moroccan national accounts are compiled on an annual and quarterly basis. The reference period is the calendar year. The volume accounts are compiled using the previous year's prices. Geographic coverage is extensive to the territory of Western Sahara.

Methodology:

Overview of GDP Compilation
GDP is calculated using the production approach and the demand-based approach. The income approach was used to compile the accounts and tables of the 1998 base year but was used only partially in the compilation of the accounts of the current years; this involved calculating wages, taxes, production subsidies and general government consumption of fixed capital. GDP is obtained after conducting a review of the supply and use table, which is prepared annually based on current prices and the previous year's prices. The supply and use table is formulated by cross-classifying industries and products since, in the case of non-agricultural market activities; the basic statistical unit taken into account is the enterprise rather than the institution.

In line with the production and expenditure approaches, GDP is calculated at current prices and at the previous year's prices (in volume). In this regard, all production accounts by industry are compiled at current prices and in volume, as well as supply and use balances by product and supply and use tables. The methods used to compile these accounts and tables in volume depend on the nature of the data available and on the nature of the operations, industries and products concerned.

For example, when data are available in current values, the method consists of deflating the available values by the appropriate price indices. However, if the data are provided in quantities, as in the case of the production of agricultural, mining or energy goods, the volume of the relevant operation is calculated by multiplying the quantities by the average prices of the previous year.

Where the information exists only in the form of volume indices, these are directly applied to the relevant operations of the previous year to determine the volume of the current year. If the data are expressed as values and also as volume indices or quantities, the deflation method is preferred to other methods (when data on prices or appropriate price indices are available).

The different methods used should produce results that correspond to the following equations:
Value = Volume x IP (t/t-1) and IVAL (t/t-1) = IVOL (t/t-1) x IP (t/(t-1), where:
IP (t/t-1) represents the price index between the current year (t) and the previous year (t-1);
IVAL (t/t-1) represents the current value index between the current year (t) and the previous year (t-1); and
IVOL (t/t-1) represents the volume index between the current year (t) and the previous year (t-1).

The volume of value added is obtained by the double deflation method, i.e. the difference between the volume of the product and the volume of intermediate consumption for each industry. This volume is obtained, in particular, from supply and use tables expressed in the previous year's prices. Changes in the prices of different added values (the variation in the value added solely due to changes in the prices of production and intermediate consumption) and changes in GDP (the variation in the general level of prices) are deduced implicitly from the relationship between the value and the volume of these quantities.

Price indices for these studies are compiled by referring to the basic indices used to produce official price indices (the producer price index, the consumer price index, the wholesale price index and the foreign trade index) and data on price levels (the producer price of agricultural products, official prices, regulated prices and average prices). The resulting price indices reflect, for each industry or product classification item, the change in price for the relevant operation. Definitive data, in terms of both volume and prices, are shown in the summary supply and use tables.

Volume and price indices generally correspond to the Laspeyres index. The Fisher index is sometimes used, when permitted by the data. The Paasche index is occasionally used for prices.

Expenditure Approach

Final consumption expenditure of resident households is calculated by product based on data from the survey on household standards of living for the base year 1998 and the survey on household consumption and expenditure for 2001. Final consumption expenditure of non-residents is obtained from balance-of-payments statistics and from the results of the survey on international tourism conducted by the Department of Tourism in 2000 and 2003. The data collected from these surveys are then corrected or adjusted through statistical reconciliation and the compilation of supply and use balances by product. For current years, estimates are made by product classification item (278 items) through direct allocation of resources in goods and services or the compilation of supply and use balances, in the knowledge that an initial estimate is made on the basis of the instantaneous elasticities calculated from the survey on household standards of living. Government final consumption expenditure is represented by the difference between the overall output of this sector, on the one hand, and its non-market output and the partial payments made by households, on the other hand. These different operations are determined from budgetary statistics, the administrative accounts of local governments and the accounting documents of public non-profit institutions.

For the base year, estimates of gross fixed capital formation are calculated using data from structural surveys (surveys of formal and informal sector enterprises, general government and households), accounting documents (budgetary and company), foreign trade statistics, agricultural sector data and data on plantations and livestock farming. Gross fixed capital formation is determined by economic agent and by product according to the product classification selected, which depends on whether these products are local or external (imported) in origin. For current years, foreign trade statistics and data from the annual survey on industrial production are used to obtain indices for the variation in gross fixed capital formation by industrial product according to its origin. Gross fixed capital formation in construction and public works can be determined from accounting data (budgetary and company) and from statistics on construction permits. Agricultural statistics provide information to complement the determination of gross fixed capital formation in agricultural products (plantations and livestock farming). Gross fixed capital formation disaggregated by institutional sector is then deduced. The final figures arrived at correspond to those obtained after balancing and final review. It should be noted that government gross fixed capital formation is determined, for the base year 1998, from the results of the survey on general government investment by subsector and by type of capital asset. For current years, the status of government issues, the status of financial operations of local governments and the accounting documents of different administrative public institutions are used to calculate gross fixed capital formation for the sector.

Changes in inventories are estimated by product, with a distinction made between producer and consumer inventories. For the base year, these two components have been calculated on the basis of data from structural surveys. For current years, changes in producer inventories in industrial products are determined on the basis of the annual survey of processing industries, whereas accounting or administrative statistics are used to calculate inventory changes for other products, such as in the case of mining and energy products. Changes in consumer inventories are also determined, in part, from accounting or administrative data, particularly where agricultural (other than animal farming) and energy products are concerned. For the remaining products, inventory changes are addressed through supply and use balances.

It should be noted, however, that a different approach is used to calculate changes in livestock inventories. The calculation is made, without distinguishing between producer and consumer inventories, on the basis of data from the continuing livestock survey. This makes it possible to distinguish between livestock for fattening (which can be inventoried) and livestock for inclusion in gross fixed capital formation (reproduction, milk production, transport, etc.).

Information on imports and exports of goods and services is obtained directly from foreign trade and balance-of-payments statistics.

Income Approach

This approach has been adopted in full for the base year, through the use of structural surveys and accounting data (company and budgetary). It is carried out only partially for current years by calculating the compensation of employees, other taxes on production net of subsidies, and general government consumption of fixed capital. It is used in its entirety for the financial corporations and general government sectors, on the basis of their accounting documents.

The compensation of employees from other sectors is determined using available annual survey data, particularly the data on processing industries. Annual surveys on other formal market production sectors began in 2005 (for the fiscal year 2004) and have subsequently been conducted on a regular basis for the following fiscal years. This information is supplemented by social security data, annual employment survey data and certain administrative statistics. Finally, other taxes and subsidies on production can be determined from budgetary statistics and the statistics of the relevant public institutions.

Production Approach

The value added by industries is the value of output at base prices less the value of intermediate consumption at purchasers' prices; this does not include the value added by general government, where non-market output is determined by totalling costs.

The agricultural sector is defined using the Moroccan classification of economic activities (NMA), which is in accordance with the third revision of the United Nations International Standard Industrial Classification of All

Economic Activities (ISIC). The data were derived from: statistical surveys (annual surveys conducted by the Ministry of Agriculture on crops production and prices and animal farming); statistics produced by the relevant governmental bodies (such as the departments in charge of agriculture, forestry and fishing); structural household surveys conducted periodically by the Office of the High Commissioner for Planning (e.g. the survey on household consumption and expenditure and the survey on household standards of living); and surveys conducted periodically by the Office of the High Commissioner for Planning on fishing enterprises. Generally, the data available for the agricultural sector refer to aggregate quantities; price data (levels or indices) are then used to convert those quantities into values. Agricultural output may be broken down into plant, animal, forestry and fishing production. For each of these components, calculations are made according to product type. The available statistics are sufficient for most products; where they are not, statistics on demand for agricultural output are used instead.

The mining and energy sector comprises all the activities of mining industries (non-metallic ores, including phosphates, and metallic ores and quarry) and energy industries (oil refining, electricity and water). The output of these industries is determined on the basis of data from: annual reports issued by mining and energy companies or oversight departments; statistics on the mining and energy sector compiled by the Ministry of Energy and Mines; and statistical indices produced by the Statistics Division of the Office of the High Commissioner for Planning. One of the primary sources of statistics used to determine output by industry is the annual survey of processing industries conducted by the Ministry of Industry. This survey primarily covers production, sales and inventory by product, employment, staff costs and a few accounting items, such as operating expenses and some of their components. For the base year 1998, this source was used to supplement the structural survey of this sector. The annual survey does not, however, cover the whole range of processing industries; sole proprietorships and informal enterprises are not included. Their output was estimated directly from the results of the survey on the informal sector for the base year as well as employment statistics (continuing household survey on employment conducted by the Statistics Division) by analysing the annual evolution of output in current years.

For construction and public works at the base year, the statistics used to calculate output were taken directly from structural surveys conducted on formal and informal enterprises in the sector. For current years, output was calculated on the basis of data on household demand for housing and on demand from enterprises for various sector products. This data was used to determine the rates of annual variation of output by value and volume. Estimates of individual and corporate demand for construction are made on the basis of building permit statistics. The figures for the year are based on the matrix of coefficients for the annual implementation of authorized construction projects. As for other demand for construction and public works, statistical sources included accounting data provided by enterprises that are leading consumers of public works products, together with detailed general government budget statistics from both State and local governments.

The transport sector comprises transport by rail, air, sea and roadway, as well as auxiliary transport activities. As in the case of other market activities, the computations for the base year are derived from the results of surveys of both formal and informal sector enterprises. With regard to current years, the output and intermediate consumption of rail and air businesses (passengers and goods) are dealt with directly on the basis of accounting documents provided by entities working in these sectors, particularly the National Railway Office and Royal Air Morocco. Statistics on maritime transport by Moroccan shipping companies are used to analyse changes in that industry, while statistics from the National Transport Office, a government body responsible for regulating road freight transport, are used to estimate the output of such transport. Indirect methods, based on demand factors, are used to analyse the road transport of passengers. The output of auxiliary transport activities is determined using the accounting data of enterprises engaged in managing infrastructure for the various types of transport (ports, airports, road freight transport, haulage depots, highways and gas pipelines) and air and maritime passenger data. Production and operating accounts for the post and telecommunications sector are prepared based on the accounting data of the various enterprises working in this sector.

The finance and insurance sector comprises financial intermediaries, insurance and financial auxiliary businesses. Production and operating accounts were prepared for each type of activity. The output of financial intermediaries (the central bank, Bank Al Maghrib, credit institutions and others) was determined on the basis of these establishments' profit and loss statements and according to the appropriate bridge tables. This output encompasses both invoiced production (e.g. commissions, rental of safe-deposit boxes, account management and income from apartment buildings, i.e. rent) and the production of financial intermediary services, which is indirectly measured as the difference between financial income (excluding capital) and interest accruals. Insurance output, regardless of whether the product concerned is life insurance or property damage insurance, is calculated as the total of effective premiums received plus total premium supplements less total owed in benefits less change in actuarial reserves and in dividend reserves for insured persons. The output of financial auxiliary businesses is estimated on the basis of insurance companies' profit and loss statements (cost of policy acquisition) and accounting documents of the Casablanca stock exchange and of mutual fund companies.

Rent was calculated on the basis of data from the national survey on household standards of living (1998), the national survey on household consumption and expenditure (2001) and the national household survey on employment (a continuing survey). To comply with 1993 SNA principles, two types of residential rent are distinguished: market rent and non-market rent. The first two surveys were used to calculate both types of rent for the 1998 and 2001 base years. Starting from the baseline data, rents were estimated for current years by calculating the variation index for tenant households who benefited either from free housing or from employer-subsidized housing, and the variation index for owner households or home buyers, using the data provided in the annual employment survey. These indices made it possible to calculate changes in rent volume. The cost-of-living index relative to rent was used to calculate price variations. However, the index was adjusted on the basis of the relative difference between the variation in rent from 1998 and 2001 and the implicit variation in rent prices, which was calculated by comparing the results of both aforementioned surveys. Output of the property development sector was calculated on the basis on the results of structural surveys, which were supplemented with information from a study carried out by the Ministry of Housing on production capacity and the operating methods of property developers. Production of other real estate services (e.g. real estate brokerage) is assumed to evolve in parallel to actual rent.

For other market services, production for the base year 1998 was established in the same way as for other market industries, with the exception of agriculture, that is, directly based on the results of structural surveys conducted on formal and informal sector enterprises. Production for current years was computed using variation indices, which were based on data specific to each type of activity. Thus, the variation indices for output of the hotels and restaurants sector were established on the basis of statistics on tourist overnight stays and balance-of-payments data (especially the "travel" item, which provides information on the expenditures of the international tourism industry), as well as data on the evolution of the restaurant sector. Services rendered to enterprises are calculated using the technical coefficients of the previous year and the outputs of the various consumer segments during the year in question, as well as balance-of-payments data, which allow for estimation of the imports and exports of such services. The variation index for the output of cultural and recreational activities is calculated on the basis of the following data: revenue generated by the national film industry; the tax on the promotion of audiovisual media, which is the main component used to calculate the production of Moroccan television stations; the financial statements of Maghreb Arabe Presse; and the revenue of the national cultural activities fund. Lastly, the output of personal and domestic services was calculated on the basis of final consumption.

The output of non-market services was measured on the basis of production costs (intermediate consumption, remuneration of employees, other taxes on production, and consumption of fixed capital). Intermediate consumption, remuneration of employees, and other taxes on production were calculated using accounting documents provided by the State, non-profit institutions, local governments and social security administrative bodies. Fixed capital consumption was estimated, for the base year 1998, on the basis of the results of the survey on general government investment, by calculating the stock of fixed capital held by government entities and the probable life length and replacement value of each type of capital. For current years, the stock of capital for the year in question is equal to that of the previous year, adding in gross fixed capital formation for the current year, less disposals. This output is augmented by the market output of goods and services, calculated on the basis of the revenue of the sector's components.

For the base year, the agricultural sector's intermediate consumption was calculated by product for each branch of the sector. A figure was reached by combining the results of the household standards of living survey with other data relating, in particular, to the production and distribution of products that may be used as inputs in the sector's various activities. The data relating to the household standards of living survey are taken from the section of the questionnaires relating to self-employment in agriculture. This section provides information about output, inputs and capital investment for crops and livestock separately. These data are then combined with, or compared to, the aforementioned other data. The latter data generally relate to the supply and distribution of the products in question and are taken from statistical surveys or administrative statistics. The statistics relate to the production, import and distribution of industrial products that may be consumed by agriculture; cultivated areas by category of crop; and agricultural output for intermediate consumption by agriculture, such as animal feed and seeds. As for fishing, statistics relating to intermediate consumption by product were obtained directly from the structural survey (formal part) and the survey on the informal sector. For current years, with the exception of data relating to the structural survey on household standards of living, which is not conducted annually, data are generally available each year. These data are used to calculate price and volume indices for the various items comprising the intermediate consumption of each branch.

To calculate the intermediate consumption of the various branches of the non-agricultural sector, it was necessary, for the base year, to conduct structural surveys of non financial corporations that keep financial records and a survey of the informal sector involving all non-agricultural producer units that do not keep financial records. Part of the questionnaire used in these surveys was reserved for corporations' purchases and expenditure, by product and type of expenditure, and product stocks at the beginning and end of the fiscal year, by price and volume. The data collected in this part of the questionnaire were used to calculate the intermediate consumption of each branch disaggregated by product classification for each type of activity. Intermediate consumption for current years is calculated by projecting the previous year's technical coefficients, which are adjusted on the basis of accounting data relating to the cost of operating and using subsidiaries, and of "cases fixées" (specific data readily available for certain key items), as well as by aligning the data in the context of supply and use balances and the summary supply and use table. Statistics relating to the intermediate consumption of financial activities were taken directly from their accounting documents (breakdown of income and expenditures) for the base year and for the current year.

Taxes on production can be broken down as follows: import duties; non-deductible VAT; domestic consumption tax; and other taxes on production. Generally speaking, statistics for each category of tax are obtained directly from the budgetary statistics of the State and the administrative accounts of local governments. For the purposes of supply and use balances, such taxes are calculated by product in line with the product classification used in the compilation of national accounts, which comprises 278 items. Import duties are calculated on the basis of customs tariffs, which are updated each year, and external trade data compiled in strict compliance with the Harmonized Commodity Description and Coding System (HS) nomenclature. The total is adjusted in line with the figure reached using budgetary statistics. Non-deductible VAT is estimated by product according to type of use, namely intermediate consumption, final consumption expenditure and gross fixed capital formation. With regard to the intermediate consumption and gross fixed capital formation of corporations, part of the questionnaire used in the structural survey was reserved for questions relating to the amount of VAT invoiced and the amount recovered — hence non-deductible — for each product. For current years, for which the structural survey is not available, the previous year's non-deductibility rates are used, before the alignment of data in the context of supply and use balances and the compilation of the summary supply and use table. For sectors such as the general government and informal sectors, which are not subject to VAT and consequently are not concerned with recovering it, the amount of VAT included in the price of the various products they purchase, whether for intermediate consumption or gross fixed capital formation, is calculated on the basis of the regulations in force; these regulations are updated each year when the new finance law is presented. The final consumption and gross fixed capital formation of households is calculated in exactly the same way. Domestic consumption tax and other taxes on production are calculated by product using the direct allocation method, in line with the heading of the budget or accounting items concerned. Statistics relating to subsidies on production are taken primarily from the accounting or statistical documents provided by the administrative bodies concerned, i.e. the Compensation Fund and the National Interprofessional Cereals and Pulses Board. The latter is responsible for flour subsidies, the former for all other subsidies. Subsidies are calculated by product using the direct allocation method.

Table 1.1 Gross domestic product by expenditures at current prices

Series 100: 1993 SNA, Moroccan dirham, Western calendar year — **Data in millions**

	2001	2002	2003	2004	2005	2006	2007	2008	2009	2010	2011	2012
Series	**100**											
	Expenditures of the gross domestic product											
Final consumption expenditure	325706.0	339329.0	360032.0	382923.0	405282.0	439067.0	472242.0	518527.0	551858.0	571485.0	619270.0	654252.0
Household final consumption expenditure	246292.0	257990.0	273562.0	288602.0	303172.0	331996.0	360008.0	400395.0	418461.0	437547.0	472938.0	495134.0
NPISHs final consumption expenditure	...	...	...	...	...	...	...	...	...	...	...	...
General government final consumption expenditure	79414.0	81339.0	86470.0	94321.0	102110.0	107071.0	112234.0	118132.0	133397.0	133938.0	146332.0	159118.0
Gross capital formation	111487.0	115490.0	130481.0	147109.0	151955.0	169902.0	200187.0	262560.0	261075.0	267658.0	288562.0	291831.0
Gross fixed capital formation	105937.0	112320.0	119802.0	132719.0	145256.0	162456.0	192573.0	227465.0	226177.0	234407.0	246394.0	259680.0
Changes in inventories	5550.0	3170.0	10679.0	14390.0	6699.0	7446.0	7614.0	35095.0	34898.0	33251.0	42168.0	32151.0
Acquisitions less disposals of valuables	...	...	...	...	...	...	...	...	...	...	...	...
Exports of goods and services	125411.0	134303.0	136737.0	148325.0	170513.0	197459.0	220302.0	258165.0	210241.0	253941.0	285530.0	299646.0
Exports of goods	81020.0	87243.0	85705.0	90272.0	99952.0	112713.0	121522.0	157777.0	114658.0	151446.0	176023.0	186831.0
Exports of services	44391.0	47060.0	51032.0	58053.0	70561.0	84746.0	98780.0	100388.0	95583.0	102495.0	109507.0	112815.0
Less: Imports of goods and services	136202.0	143696.0	150229.0	173342.0	200071.0	229084.0	276477.0	350409.0	290725.0	329053.0	390755.0	417471.0
Imports of goods	115080.0	120637.0	126454.0	146775.0	170636.0	195057.0	241789.0	311272.0	248157.0	282812.0	336891.0	362761.0
Imports of services	21122.0	23059.0	23775.0	26567.0	29435.0	34027.0	34688.0	39137.0	42568.0	46241.0	53864.0	54710.0
Equals: GROSS DOMESTIC PRODUCT	426402.0	445426.0	477021.0	505015.0	527679.0	577344.0	616254.0	688843.0	732449.0	764031.0	802607.0	828258.0

Table 1.2 Gross domestic product by expenditures at constant prices

Series 100: 1993 SNA, Moroccan dirham, Western calendar year — **Data in millions**

	2001	2002	2003	2004	2005	2006	2007	2008	2009	2010	2011	2012
Series	**100**											
Base year	**1998**											
	Expenditures of the gross domestic product											
Final consumption expenditure	314753.0	323859.0	343876.0	360192.0	369440.0	391619.0	406783.0	430179.0	456676.0	463608.2	494996.3	517395.8
Household final consumption expenditure	242232.0	250917.0	269340.0	282414.0	288910.0	308785.0	320381.0	339589.0	355161.0	363032.3	389839.1	403887.5
NPISHs final consumption expenditure	...	...	...	...	...	...	...	...	...	...	...	...
General government final consumption expenditure	72521.0	72942.0	74536.0	77778.0	80530.0	82834.0	86401.8	90589.7	101515.0	100575.9	105157.2	113508.3
Gross capital formation	108562.0	114591.0	135908.0	149245.0	147171.0	159916.0	180824.0	204007.0	212862.0	209497.5	216439.4	215743.4
Gross fixed capital formation	102045.0	109528.0	117990.0	127892.0	137369.0	150652.0	172195.0	191928.0	196872.0	195527.1	200329.2	204055.4
Changes in inventories	6517.0	5063.0	17918.0	21353.0	9802.0	9264.0	8629.0	12079.0	15990.0	13970.3	16110.2	11688.0
Acquisitions less disposals of valuables	...	...	...	...	...	...	...	...	...	...	...	...
Exports of goods and services	126637.0	133796.0	134656.0	143104.0	162126.0	180966.0	190357.0	204184.0	174036.0	202963.8	207268.6	212933.6
Less: Imports of goods and services	126173.0	134297.0	143805.0	157985.0	173206.0	187337.0	215488.0	241762.0	227225.0	235314.5	247153.4	252061.0
Equals: GROSS DOMESTIC PRODUCT [a]	422221.0	436222.0	463778.0	486048.0	500525.0	539365.0	553959.2	584909.0	612741.0	635063.3	666724.6	684764.8

[a] Discrepancy between components and total.

Table 1.3 Relations among product, income, savings, and net lending aggregates

Series 100: 1993 SNA, Moroccan dirham, Western calendar year **Data in millions**

	2001	2002	2003	2004	2005	2006	2007	2008	2009	2010	2011	2012
Series	**100**											
GROSS DOMESTIC PRODUCT	426402.0	445426.0	477021.0	505015.0	527679.0	577344.0	616254.0	688843.0	732449.0	764031.0	802607.0	828258.0
Plus: Compensation of employees - from and to the rest of the world, net	...	...	...	...	...	...	...	...	...	...	...	...
Plus: Property income - from and to the rest of the world, net	-11104.0	-10671.0	-9958.0	-8754.0	-6768.0	-8220.0	-8030.0	-11407.0	-19240.0	-20755.0	-25010.0	-28283.0
Plus: Property income - from the rest of the world	4657.0	4970.0	4533.0	5460.0	7180.0	7461.0	8987.0	8676.0	8218.0	7721.0	7269.0	6024.0
Less: Property income - to the rest of the world	15761.0	15641.0	14491.0	14214.0	13948.0	15681.0	17017.0	20083.0	27458.0	28476.0	32279.0	34307.0
Sum of Compensation of employees and property income - from and to the rest of the world, net	-11104.0	-10671.0	-9958.0	-8754.0	-6768.0	-8220.0	-8030.0	-11407.0	-19240.0	-20755.0	-25010.0	-28283.0
Plus: Sum of Compensation of employees and property income - from the rest of the world	4657.0	4970.0	4533.0	5460.0	7180.0	7461.0	8987.0	8676.0	8218.0	7721.0	7269.0	6024.0
Less: Sum of Compensation of employees and property income - to the rest of the world	15761.0	15641.0	14491.0	14214.0	13948.0	15681.0	17017.0	20083.0	27458.0	28476.0	32279.0	34307.0
Plus: Taxes less subsidies on production and imports - from and to the rest of the world, net	...	...	...	...	...	...	...	...	...	...	...	...
Equals: GROSS NATIONAL INCOME	415298.0	434755.0	467063.0	496261.0	520911.0	569124.0	608224.0	677436.0	713209.0	743276.0	777597.0	799975.0
Plus: Current transfers - from and to the rest of the world, net	40204.0	36684.0	39431.0	43325.0	47841.0	55571.0	63397.0	67714.0	59850.0	61545.0	65627.0	63662.0
Plus: Current transfers - from the rest of the world	41720.0	38142.0	40980.0	44952.0	49500.0	57424.0	65278.0	69731.0	62142.0	64225.0	68567.0	66829.0
Less: Current transfers - to the rest of the world	1517.0	1458.0	1549.0	1627.0	1659.0	1853.0	1881.0	2017.0	2292.0	2680.0	2940.0	3167.0
Equals: GROSS NATIONAL DISPOSABLE INCOME	455501.0	471439.0	506494.0	539586.0	568752.0	624695.0	671621.0	745150.0	773059.0	804821.0	843224.0	863637.0
Less: Final consumption expenditure / Actual final consumption	325706.0	339329.0	360032.0	382923.0	405282.0	439067.0	472242.0	518527.0	551858.0	571485.0	619270.0	654252.0
Equals: SAVING, GROSS	129795.0	132110.0	146462.0	156663.0	163470.0	185628.0	199379.0	226623.0	221201.0	233336.0	223954.0	209385.0
Plus: Capital transfers - from and to the rest of the world, net	-101.0	-67.0	-96.6	-71.0	-50.0	-81.0	-26.0	-15.0	-4.0	-1.0	-2.0	-1.0
Plus: Capital transfers - from the rest of the world	0.0	0.0	0.0	0.0	3.0	0.0	0.0	9.0	3.0	0.0	0.0	3.0
Less: Capital transfers - to the rest of the world	101.0	67.0	97.0	71.0	53.0	81.0	26.0	24.0	7.0	1.0	2.0	4.0
Less: Gross capital formation	111487.0	115490.0	130481.0	147109.0	151955.0	169902.0	200187.0	262560.0	261075.0	267658.0	288562.0	291829.0
Less: Acquisitions less disposals of non-produced non-financial assets	...	...	...	...	...	...	...	...	...	...	...	...
Equals: NET LENDING (+) / NET BORROWING (-) OF THE NATION	18207.0	16553.0	15884.0	9483.0	11465.0	15645.0	-834.0	-35952.0	-39878.0	-34323.0	-64610.0	-82445.0
	Net values: Gross National Income / Gross National Disposable Income / Saving Gross less Consumption of fixed capital											
Less: Consumption of fixed capital	...	...	...	...	...	...	...	...	...	...	...	...
Equals: NET NATIONAL INCOME	...	...	...	...	...	...	...	...	...	...	...	...
Equals: NET NATIONAL DISPOSABLE INCOME	...	...	...	...	...	...	...	...	...	...	...	...
Equals: SAVING, NET	...	...	...	...	...	...	...	...	...	...	...	...

Table 2.1 Value added by industries at current prices (ISIC Rev. 3)

Series 100: 1993 SNA, Moroccan dirham, Western calendar year **Data in millions**

	2001	2002	2003	2004	2005	2006	2007	2008	2009	2010	2011	2012
Series	**100**											
Industries												
Agriculture, hunting, forestry; fishing	62677.0	65457.0	73933.0	74131.0	69565.0	87482.0	74928.0	90690.0	107050.0	105534.0	114866.0	110575.0
Agriculture, hunting, forestry	55925.0	59146.0	68759.0	69034.0	62932.0	81147.0	68716.0	82969.0	100757.0	98991.0	106342.0	102572.0
Fishing	6752.0	6311.0	5174.0	5097.0	6633.0	6335.0	6212.0	7721.0	6293.0	6543.0	8524.0	8003.0
Mining and quarrying	8973.0	8501.0	7822.0	8116.0	8994.0	10534.0	13155.0	45121.0	16925.0	29579.0	41355.0	40343.0
Manufacturing	63360.0	66276.0	74026.0	79585.0	78650.0	82498.0	82915.0	87959.0	105088.0	108049.0	116298.0	122386.0
Electricity, gas and water supply	11192.0	11731.0	13191.0	13047.0	14583.0	14687.0	15749.0	16123.0	18953.0	19362.0	18962.0	20044.0
Construction	20875.0	21681.0	24379.0	28822.0	31522.0	32912.0	37233.0	38663.0	45776.0	47085.0	47941.0	50099.0
Wholesale, retail trade, repair of motor vehicles, motorcycles and personal and households goods; hotels and restaurants	60099.0	62759.0	62617.0	65285.0	69417.0	74221.0	81352.0	86875.0	88829.0	92261.0	95829.0	99658.0
Wholesale, retail trade, repair of motor vehicles, motorcycles and personal and household goods	50647.0	53300.0	52701.0	54255.0	56454.0	60956.0	65058.0	70597.0	72054.0	72815.0	76977.0	79824.0
Hotels and restaurants	9452.0	9459.0	9916.0	11030.0	12963.0	13265.0	16294.0	16278.0	16775.0	19446.0	18852.0	19834.0
Transport, storage and communications	27627.0	29865.0	31072.0	34000.0	34522.0	36491.0	43151.0	45262.0	47892.0	50545.0	50897.0	51359.0
Land transport; transport via pipelines, water transport; air transport; Supporting and auxiliary transport activities; activities of travel agencies	16589.0	17470.0	17258.0	18605.0	17961.0	18357.0	23264.0	23897.0	25795.0	27480.0	28424.0	30030.0
Post and telecommunications	11038.0	12395.0	13814.0	15395.0	16561.0	18134.0	19887.0	21365.0	22097.0	23065.0	22473.0	21329.0
Financial intermediation; real estate, renting and business activities	61727.0	66148.0	71378.0	76641.0	86093.0	96167.0	113454.0	119778.0	125276.0	129419.0	137454.0	146593.0
Financial intermediation	21357.0	21672.0	22479.0	23675.0	26859.0	30231.0	36444.0	39133.0	40107.0	40595.0	44030.0	46585.0
Real estate, renting and business activities	40370.0	44476.0	48899.0	52966.0	59234.0	65936.0	77010.0	80645.0	85169.0	88824.0	93424.0	100008.0
Public administration and defence; compulsory social security	37555.0	38215.0	40121.0	44208.0	47917.0	50664.0	51910.0	54000.0	59875.0	62600.0	69611.0	74830.0
Education; health and social work; other community, social and personal services [a]	37028.0	37524.0	41759.0	43673.0	48144.0	49997.0	54271.0	59360.0	62293.0	66604.0	75512.0	79902.0
Private households with employed persons [b]	6087.0	6455.0	6971.0	7855.0	7761.0	8246.0	8664.0	9126.0	9502.0	10566.0	10650.0	10912.0
Equals: VALUE ADDED, GROSS, in basic prices [c]	378698.0	395811.0	427561.0	454278.0	473956.0	517948.0	545693.0	619632.0	653157.0	687722.0	742419.0	768491.0
Less: Financial intermediation services indirectly measured (FISIM)	18502.0	18801.0	19708.0	21085.0	23212.0	25951.0	31089.0	33325.0	34302.0	33882.0	36956.0	38210.0
Plus: Taxes less Subsidies on products	47704.0	49615.0	49460.0	50737.0	53723.0	59396.0	70561.0	69211.0	79292.0	76309.0	60188.0	59767.0
Plus: Taxes on products	54081.0	55280.0	55807.0	59066.0	64992.0	72539.0	86711.0	100661.0	94529.0	106507.0	111385.0	115371.0
Less: Subsidies on products	6377.0	5665.0	6347.0	8329.0	11269.0	13143.0	16150.0	31450.0	15237.0	30198.0	51197.0	55604.0
Equals: GROSS DOMESTIC PRODUCT	426402.0	445426.0	477021.0	505015.0	527679.0	577344.0	616254.0	688843.0	732449.0	764031.0	802607.0	828258.0

[a] Refers to Industries Education and Health and Social Work

[b] Includes other community, social and personal services only and Private households with employed persons.

[c] Excludes financial intermediation services indirectly measured (FISIM), but FISIM is included in industry data.

Table 2.2 Value added by industries at constant prices (ISIC Rev. 3)

Series 100: 1993 SNA, Moroccan dirham, Western calendar year

Data in millions

	2001	2002	2003	2004	2005	2006	2007	2008	2009	2010	2011	2012
Series	**100**											
Base year	**1998**											
Industries												
Agriculture, hunting, forestry; fishing	61722.0	64781.0	78832.0	82581.0	72548.0	89197.0	70982.0	82646.5	107185.0	104883.5	110488.5	101453.2
Agriculture, hunting, forestry	56239.0	60813.0	75469.0	79401.0	68694.0	86085.0	68186.0	79318.1	103450.0	101501.5	107158.5	97666.1
Fishing	5483.0	3968.0	3363.0	3180.0	3854.0	3112.0	2796.0	3328.4	3735.0	3382.0	3330.0	3787.1
Mining and quarrying	9129.0	9074.0	9223.0	10676.0	11466.0	11649.0	12707.0	11960.2	9109.0	12621.0	13371.0	13053.5
Manufacturing	66314.0	68877.0	70690.0	71298.0	73958.0	76291.0	79617.0	81211.1	81324.0	83617.0	86097.7	87349.6
Electricity, gas and water supply	11999.0	12250.0	13500.0	14214.0	15315.0	16366.0	17311.0	18331.3	18978.0	20333.0	21558.6	23045.7
Construction	17412.0	17586.0	18985.0	20511.0	21753.0	23642.0	26398.0	28892.5	29862.0	30646.0	31922.8	32608.0
Wholesale, retail trade, repair of motor vehicles, motorcycles and personal and household goods; hotels and restaurants	58401.0	60149.0	61391.0	64786.0	67726.0	71219.0	73141.0	76023.1	78151.0	78758.0	81672.9	83643.5
Wholesale, retail trade, repair of motor vehicles, motorcycles and personal and household goods	50085.0	51817.0	53094.0	55740.0	57979.0	60627.0	62116.0	64911.8	67174.0	66897.0	70048.1	71669.7
Hotels and restaurants	8316.0	8332.0	8297.0	9046.0	9747.0	10592.0	11025.0	11111.2	10977.0	11861.0	11624.8	11973.8
Transport, storage and communications	39284.0	40430.0	42862.0	47875.0	51386.0	55434.0	60665.0	64218.5	66033.0	69763.0	78835.2	91603.6
Land transport; transport via piplines, water transport; air transport; Supporting and auxiliary transport activities; activities of travel agencies	19832.3	19942.3	20034.7	22598.0	24744.2	26032.3	28206.3	28941.0	29766.0	31907.0	33789.6	35042.6
Post and telecommunications	19451.7	20487.9	22826.8	25277.4	26641.8	29402.4	32458.7	35277.5	36267.0	37855.0	45045.5	56560.9
Financial intermediation, real estate, renting and business activities	56492.0	58983.0	62990.0	66307.0	72598.0	78379.0	87594.0	89094.6	90545.0	92186.0	97282.2	102293.8
Financial intermediation	19431.0	19278.0	20300.0	21131.0	23870.0	25996.0	30859.0	32066.7	32408.0	32560.0	35030.7	36737.3
Real estate, renting and business activities	37061.0	39705.0	42690.0	45176.0	48728.0	52383.0	56735.0	57027.9	58137.0	59626.0	62251.5	65556.5
Public administration and defence; compulsory social security	34543.0	34995.0	36025.0	37713.0	39527.0	40776.0	41765.1	43402.3	47429.0	48789.0	51612.1	55058.3
Education; health and social work; other community, social and personal services [a]	33649.0	33461.0	35285.0	35811.0	38169.0	39151.0	42274.0	45957.7	47436.0	49699.0	53870.1	56517.5
Private households with employed persons [b]	5568.0	5757.0	6028.0	6538.0	6344.0	6537.0	6793.0	6909.6	7069.0	7147.0	7219.1	7299.1
Equals: VALUE ADDED, GROSS, in basic prices [c]	373581.0	384812.0	412192.0	432277.0	445439.0	478457.0	487069.8	514627.9	539191.0	556813.3	585997.1	600687.7
Less: Financial intermediation services indirectly measured (FISIM)	18048.7	17840.9	18479.5	19478.2	21230.6	23120.2	27155.2	28015.6	28438.0	27812.0	30124.9	30869.1
Plus: Taxes less Subsidies on products	48620.0	51428.0	51401.0	53554.0	54833.0	60768.0	67211.0	70575.4	73863.0	78835.0	80948.9	85125.0
Equals: GROSS DOMESTIC PRODUCT	422221.0	436222.0	463778.0	486048.0	500525.0	539365.0	553959.2	584909.0	612741.0	635063.3	666724.6	684764.8

[a] Refers to Industries Education and Health and Social Work

[b] Includes other community, social and personal services only and Private households with employed persons.

[c] Discrepancy between components and total. Excludes financial intermediation services indirectly measured (FISIM), but FISIM is included in industry data.

Table 2.3 Output, gross value added, and fixed assets by industries at current prices (ISIC Rev. 3) Total Economy

Series 100: 1993 SNA, Moroccan dirham, Western calendar year — **Data in millions**

	2001	2002	2003	2004	2005	2006	2007	2008	2009	2010	2011	2012
Series	**100**											
Output, at basic prices	710368.0	731682.0	768386.0	811254.0	870054.0	950000.0	1012034.0	1142714.0	1132059.0[a]	1203273.0	1317182.0	
Less: Intermediate consumption, at purchaser's prices [b]	331670.0	335871.0	340825.0	356976.0	396098.0	432052.0	466341.0	523082.0	478902.0[a]	515551.0	574761.0	
Equals: VALUE ADDED, GROSS, at basic prices [c]	378698.0	395811.0	427561.0	454278.0	473956.0	517948.0	545693.0	619632.0	653157.0[a]	687722.0	742421.0	
Compensation of employees	140916.0	146509.0	154097.0	165239.0	177249.0	187200.0	201061.0	212158.0	224491.0	236333.0	257669.0	
Taxes on production and imports, less Subsidies	3956.0	4092.0	3756.0	3989.0	5205.0	4564.0	4678.0	5306.0	5250.0	5161.0	6039.0	
Taxes on production and imports	4318.0	4743.0	4705.0	4850.0	6127.0	5606.0	5501.0	6086.0	6179.0	6196.0	6431.0	
Taxes on products	...	...	...	...	...	...	...	...	...	...	...	
Other taxes on production	4318.0	4743.0	4705.0	4850.0	6127.0	5606.0	5501.0	6086.0	6179.0	6196.0	6431.0	
Less: Subsidies	362.0	651.0	949.0	861.0	922.0	1042.0	823.0	780.0	929.0	1035.0	392.0	
Subsidies on products	...	...	...	...	...	...	...	...	...	...	...	
Other subsidies on production	362.0	651.0	949.0	861.0	922.0	1042.0	823.0	780.0	929.0	1035.0	392.0	
OPERATING SURPLUS, GROSS [d]	233826.0	245210.0	269708.0	285050.0	291502.0	326184.0	339954.0	402168.0	423416.0	446228.0	478711.0	
MIXED INCOME, GROSS	...	...	...	...	...	...	...	...	...	...	...	
Total Economy only: Adjustment for FISIM (if FISIM is not distributed to uses)	18502.0	18801.0	19708.0	21085.0	23212.0	25951.0	31089.0	33325.0	34302.0	33882.0	...	
Gross capital formation	111487.0	115490.0	130481.0	147109.0	151955.0	169902.0	200187.0	262560.0	261075.0	267658.0	288562.0	
Gross fixed capital formation	105937.0	112320.0	119802.0	132719.0	145256.0	162456.0	192573.0	227465.0	226177.0	234407.0	246394.0	
Changes in inventories	5550.0	3170.0	10679.0	14390.0	6699.0	7446.0	7614.0	35095.0	34898.0	33251.0	42168.0	
Acquisitions less disposals of valuables	...	...	...	...	...	...	...	...	...	...	...	

[a] Account does not balance as one or more components have not been revised.
[b] Includes financial intermediation services indirectly measured (FISIM) but FISIM is excluded in the tables by industry.
[c] Excludes financial intermediation services indirectly measured (FISIM) but FISIM is not distributed to uses (i.e. is included in the tables by industry).
[d] Includes Mixed Income, Gross.

Table 2.3 Output, gross value added, and fixed assets by industries at current prices (ISIC Rev. 3) Agriculture, hunting, forestry; fishing (A+B)

Series 100: 1993 SNA, Moroccan dirham, Western calendar year — **Data in millions**

	2001	2002	2003	2004	2005	2006	2007	2008	2009	2010	2011	2012
Series	**100**											
Output, at basic prices	92004.0	92300.0	100903.0	103014.0	99673.0	120840.0	104079.0	125724.0	137580.0	137881.0	149212.0	
Less: Intermediate consumption, at purchaser's prices	29327.0	26843.0	26970.0	28883.0	30108.0	33358.0	29151.0	35034.0	30530.0	32347.0	34346.0	
Equals: VALUE ADDED, GROSS, at basic prices	62677.0	65457.0	73933.0	74131.0	69565.0	87482.0	74928.0	90690.0	107050.0	105534.0	114866.0	
Compensation of employees	5607.0	6986.0	6651.0	6522.0	6492.0	7547.0	8110.0	8393.0	8294.0	8217.0	...	
Taxes on production and imports, less Subsidies	73.0	74.0	115.0	104.0	149.0	135.0	144.0	165.0	157.0	157.0	...	
Taxes on production and imports	73.0	74.0	115.0	119.0	164.0	150.0	144.0	165.0	157.0	157.0	...	
Taxes on products	...	...	...	...	...	...	...	...	...	...	...	

	2001	2002	2003	2004	2005	2006	2007	2008	2009	2010	2011	2012
Series	**100**											
Other taxes on production	73.0	74.0	115.0	119.0	164.0	150.0	144.0	165.0	157.0	157.0	...	
Less: Subsidies	0.0	0.0	0.0	15.0	15.0	15.0	0.0	...	...	...	...	
Subsidies on products	...	...	...	...	...	...	...	...	...	...	...	
Other subsidies on production	0.0	0.0	0.0	15.0	15.0	15.0	0.0	...	...	...	...	
OPERATING SURPLUS, GROSS [a]	56997.0	58397.0	67167.0	67505.0	62924.0	79800.0	66674.0	82132.0	98599.0	97160.0	...	
MIXED INCOME, GROSS	...	...	...	...	...	...	...	...	...	...	...	
Gross capital formation	...	...	...	...	...	...	...	...	...	...	...	

[a] Includes Mixed Income, Gross.

Table 2.3 Output, gross value added, and fixed assets by industries at current prices (ISIC Rev. 3) Agriculture, hunting and related service activities (01)

Series 100: 1993 SNA, Moroccan dirham, Western calendar year — **Data in millions**

	2001	2002	2003	2004	2005	2006	2007	2008	2009	2010	2011	2012
Series	**100**											
Output, at basic prices	82228.0	83839.0	93881.0	96086.0	90748.0	112448.0	96037.0	115775.0	128945.0	129171.0	138500.0	
Less: Intermediate consumption, at purchaser's prices	26303.0	24693.0	25122.0	27052.0	27816.0	31301.0	27321.0	32806.0	28188.0	30180.0	32158.0	
Equals: VALUE ADDED, GROSS, at basic prices	55925.0	59146.0	68759.0	69034.0	62932.0	81147.0	68716.0	82969.0	100757.0	98991.0	106342.0	
Compensation of employees	3527.0	4607.0	4479.0	4420.0	4268.0	5265.0	5663.0	5751.0	6078.0	5944.0	...	
Taxes on production and imports, less Subsidies	4.0	5.0	6.0	-9.0	21.0	22.0	37.0	44.0	37.0	37.0	...	
Taxes on production and imports	4.0	5.0	6.0	6.0	36.0	37.0	37.0	44.0	37.0	37.0	...	
Taxes on products	...	...	...	...	...	...	...	...	...	...	...	
Other taxes on production	4.0	5.0	6.0	6.0	36.0	37.0	37.0	44.0	37.0	37.0	...	
Less: Subsidies	0.0	0.0	0.0	15.0	15.0	15.0	0.0	0.0	0.0	...	...	
Subsidies on products	...	...	...	...	...	...	...	...	...	...	...	
Other subsidies on production	0.0	0.0	0.0	15.0	15.0	15.0	0.0	0.0	0.0	...	...	
OPERATING SURPLUS, GROSS [a]	52394.0	54534.0	64274.0	64623.0	58643.0	75860.0	63016.0	77174.0	94642.0	93010.0	...	
MIXED INCOME, GROSS	...	...	...	...	...	...	...	...	...	...	...	
Gross capital formation	...	...	...	...	...	...	...	...	...	...	...	

[a] Includes Mixed Income, Gross.

Table 2.3 Output, gross value added, and fixed assets by industries at current prices (ISIC Rev. 3) Fishing (B)

Series 100: 1993 SNA, Moroccan dirham, Western calendar year

Data in millions

	2001	2002	2003	2004	2005	2006	2007	2008	2009	2010	2011	2012
Series	**100**											
Output, at basic prices	9776.0	8461.0	7022.0	6928.0	8925.0	8392.0	8042.0	9949.0	8635.0	8710.0	10712.0	
Less: Intermediate consumption, at purchaser's prices	3024.0	2150.0	1848.0	1831.0	2292.0	2057.0	1830.0	2228.0	2342.0	2167.0	2188.0	
Equals: VALUE ADDED, GROSS, at basic prices	6752.0	6311.0	5174.0	5097.0	6633.0	6335.0	6212.0	7721.0	6293.0	6543.0	8524.0	
Compensation of employees	2080.0	2379.0	2172.0	2102.0	2224.0	2282.0	2447.0	2642.0	2216.0	2273.0	...	
Taxes on production and imports, less Subsidies	69.0	69.0	109.0	113.0	128.0	113.0	107.0	121.0	120.0	120.0	...	
Taxes on production and imports	69.0	69.0	109.0	113.0	128.0	113.0	107.0	121.0	120.0	120.0	...	
Taxes on products	...	...	...	...	...	...	...	...	...	...	...	
Other taxes on production	69.0	69.0	109.0	113.0	128.0	113.0	107.0	121.0	120.0	120.0	...	
Less: Subsidies	...	...	...	...	...	...	...	...	...	...	...	
OPERATING SURPLUS, GROSS [a]	4603.0	3863.0	2893.0	2882.0	4281.0	3940.0	3658.0	4958.0	3957.0	4150.0	...	
MIXED INCOME, GROSS	...	...	...	...	...	...	...	...	...	...	...	
Gross capital formation	...	...	...	...	...	...	...	...	...	...	...	

[a] Includes Mixed Income, Gross.

Table 2.3 Output, gross value added, and fixed assets by industries at current prices (ISIC Rev. 3) Mining and quarrying (C)

Series 100: 1993 SNA, Moroccan dirham, Western calendar year

Data in millions

	2001	2002	2003	2004	2005	2006	2007	2008	2009	2010	2011	2012
Series	**100**											
Output, at basic prices	13005.0	13049.0	11999.0	12699.0	14321.0	16417.0	19688.0	52098.0	22236.0	36756.0	49135.0	
Less: Intermediate consumption, at purchaser's prices	4032.0	4548.0	4177.0	4583.0	5327.0	5883.0	6533.0	6977.0	5311.0	7177.0	7780.0	
Equals: VALUE ADDED, GROSS, at basic prices	8973.0	8501.0	7822.0	8116.0	8994.0	10534.0	13155.0	45121.0	16925.0	29579.0	41355.0	
Compensation of employees	2116.0	2127.0	2132.0	2355.0	2322.0	2710.0	2650.0	3013.0	2580.0	4592.0	...	
Taxes on production and imports, less Subsidies	911.0	880.0	775.0	774.0	959.0	757.0	761.0	769.0	1021.0	900.0	...	
Taxes on production and imports	911.0	880.0	775.0	774.0	959.0	757.0	761.0	769.0	1021.0	900.0	...	
Taxes on products	...	...	...	...	...	...	...	...	...	...	...	
Other taxes on production	911.0	880.0	775.0	774.0	959.0	757.0	761.0	769.0	1021.0	900.0	...	
Less: Subsidies	0.0	0.0	0.0	0.0	0.0	0.0	0.0	0.0	0.0	...	...	
Subsidies on products	...	...	...	...	...	...	...	...	...	...	...	
Other subsidies on production	0.0	0.0	0.0	0.0	0.0	0.0	0.0	0.0	0.0	...	...	
OPERATING SURPLUS, GROSS [a]	5946.0	5494.0	4915.0	4987.0	5713.0	7067.0	9744.0	41339.0	13324.0	24087.0	...	
MIXED INCOME, GROSS	...	...	...	...	...	...	...	...	...	...	...	
Gross capital formation	...	...	...	...	...	...	...	...	...	...	...	

[a] Includes Mixed Income, Gross.

Table 2.3 Output, gross value added, and fixed assets by industries at current prices (ISIC Rev. 3) Manufacturing (D)

Series 100: 1993 SNA, Moroccan dirham, Western calendar year — **Data in millions**

		2001	2002	2003	2004	2005	2006	2007	2008	2009	2010	2011	2012
Series		**100**											
Output, at basic prices		234287.0	239271.0	245770.0	255519.0	275748.0	292349.0	307353.0	345357.0	302566.0	351200.0	393774.0	
Less: Intermediate consumption, at purchaser's prices		170927.0	172995.0	171744.0	175934.0	197098.0	209851.0	224438.0	257398.0	198562.0	243151.0	277476.0	
Equals: VALUE ADDED, GROSS, at basic prices		63360.0	66276.0	74026.0	79585.0	78650.0	82498.0	82915.0	87959.0	104004.0	108049.0	116298.0	
Compensation of employees		25242.0	25839.0	26691.0	27328.0	28140.0	28950.0	29761.0	31271.0	32871.0	34415.0	...	
Taxes on production and imports, less Subsidies		1461.0	1863.0	1053.0	1166.0	1722.0	1589.0	1527.0	1689.0	1637.0	1623.0	...	
Taxes on production and imports		1520.0	2053.0	1389.0	1433.0	2004.0	1859.0	1659.0	1866.0	1789.0	...	...	
Taxes on products		...	...	...	...	...	...	...	...	...	...	...	
Other taxes on production		1520.0	2053.0	1389.0	1433.0	2004.0	1859.0	1659.0	1866.0	1789.0	...	...	
Less: Subsidies		59.0	190.0	336.0	267.0	282.0	270.0	132.0	177.0	152.0	...	...	
Subsidies on products		...	...	...	...	...	...	...	...	...	...	...	
Other subsidies on production		59.0	190.0	336.0	267.0	282.0	270.0	132.0	177.0	152.0	...	...	
OPERATING SURPLUS, GROSS	a	36657.0	38574.0	46282.0	51091.0	48788.0	51959.0	51627.0	54999.0	69496.0	72011.0	...	
MIXED INCOME, GROSS		...	...	...	...	...	...	...	...	...	...	...	
Gross capital formation		...	...	...	...	...	...	...	...	...	...	...	

[a] Includes Mixed Income, Gross.

Table 2.3 Output, gross value added, and fixed assets by industries at current prices (ISIC Rev. 3) Electricity, gas and water supply (E)

Series 100: 1993 SNA, Moroccan dirham, Western calendar year — **Data in millions**

		2001	2002	2003	2004	2005	2006	2007	2008	2009	2010	2011	2012
Series		**100**											
Output, at basic prices		16426.0	17283.0	18954.0	19250.0	21893.0	23415.0	25199.0	25647.0	26505.0	28134.0	29845.0	
Less: Intermediate consumption, at purchaser's prices		5234.0	5552.0	5763.0	6203.0	7310.0	8728.0	9450.0	9524.0	7652.0	8772.0	10883.0	
Equals: VALUE ADDED, GROSS, at basic prices		11192.0	11731.0	13191.0	13047.0	14583.0	14687.0	15749.0	16123.0	18953.0	19362.0	18962.0	
Compensation of employees		3271.0	3438.0	3570.0	3751.0	3916.0	4092.0	4109.0	4191.0	4857.0	4961.0	...	
Taxes on production and imports, less Subsidies		127.0	152.0	200.0	212.0	259.0	229.0	234.0	265.0	263.0	263.0	...	
Taxes on production and imports		127.0	152.0	200.0	212.0	259.0	229.0	234.0	265.0	263.0	...	...	
Taxes on products		...	...	...	...	...	...	...	...	...	...	...	
Other taxes on production		127.0	152.0	200.0	212.0	259.0	229.0	234.0	265.0	263.0	...	...	
Less: Subsidies		...	...	...	...	...	...	...	...	...	...	...	
OPERATING SURPLUS, GROSS	a	7794.0	8141.0	9421.0	9084.0	10408.0	10366.0	11406.0	11667.0	13833.0	14138.0	...	
MIXED INCOME, GROSS		...	...	...	...	...	...	...	...	...	...	...	
Gross capital formation		...	...	...	...	...	...	...	...	...	...	...	

[a] Includes Mixed Income, Gross.

Table 2.3 Output, gross value added, and fixed assets by industries at current prices (ISIC Rev. 3) Construction (F)

Series 100: 1993 SNA, Moroccan dirham, Western calendar year — **Data in millions**

	2001	2002	2003	2004	2005	2006	2007	2008	2009	2010	2011	2012
Series	**100**											
Output, at basic prices	54049.0	54924.0	60357.0	65934.0	71844.0	78253.0	90703.0	101676.0	104499.0	110169.0	117631.0	
Less: Intermediate consumption, at purchaser's prices	33174.0	33243.0	35978.0	37112.0	40322.0	45341.0	53470.0	63013.0	58723.0	63084.0	69690.0	
Equals: VALUE ADDED, GROSS, at basic prices	20875.0	21681.0	24379.0	28822.0	31522.0	32912.0	37233.0	38663.0	45776.0	47085.0	47941.0	
Compensation of employees	6573.0	6314.0	6592.0	7314.0	8089.0	8538.0	10362.0	10569.0	11098.0	11515.0	...	
Taxes on production and imports, less Subsidies	136.0	95.0	327.0	337.0	410.0	398.0	411.0	451.0	439.0	329.0	...	
Taxes on production and imports	136.0	95.0	327.0	337.0	410.0	398.0	411.0	451.0	439.0	...	...	
Taxes on products	...	...	...	...	...	...	...	...	...	...	...	
Other taxes on production	136.0	95.0	327.0	337.0	410.0	398.0	411.0	451.0	439.0	...	...	
Less: Subsidies	...	...	...	...	...	...	...	...	...	...	...	
OPERATING SURPLUS, GROSS [a]	14166.0	15272.0	17460.0	21171.0	23023.0	23976.0	26460.0	27643.0	34239.0	35241.0	...	
MIXED INCOME, GROSS	...	...	...	...	...	...	...	...	...	...	...	
Gross capital formation	...	...	...	...	...	...	...	...	...	...	...	

[a] Includes Mixed Income, Gross.

Table 2.3 Output, gross value added, and fixed assets by industries at current prices (ISIC Rev. 3) Wholesale retail trade, repair of motor vehicles, motorcycles, etc.; hotels and restaurants (G+H)

Series 100: 1993 SNA, Moroccan dirham, Western calendar year — **Data in millions**

	2001	2002	2003	2004	2005	2006	2007	2008	2009	2010	2011	2012
Series	**100**											
Output, at basic prices	83644.0	87211.0	87804.0	92683.0	99608.0	107551.0	116150.0	123841.0	125179.0	130579.0	137048.0	
Less: Intermediate consumption, at purchaser's prices	23545.0	24452.0	25187.0	27398.0	30191.0	33330.0	34798.0	36966.0	36350.0	38318.0	41219.0	
Equals: VALUE ADDED, GROSS, at basic prices	60099.0	62759.0	62617.0	65285.0	69417.0	74221.0	81352.0	86875.0	88829.0	92261.0	95829.0	
Compensation of employees	12505.0	13885.0	14223.0	16022.0	17180.0	18876.0	21273.0	22533.0	22999.0	23824.0	...	
Taxes on production and imports, less Subsidies	379.0	466.0	525.0	545.0	664.0	617.0	582.0	645.0	622.0	512.0	...	
Taxes on production and imports	379.0	466.0	525.0	545.0	664.0	617.0	582.0	645.0	622.0	...	...	
Taxes on products	...	...	...	...	...	...	...	...	...	...	...	
Other taxes on production	379.0	466.0	525.0	545.0	664.0	617.0	582.0	645.0	622.0	...	...	
Less: Subsidies	...	...	...	...	...	...	...	...	...	...	...	
OPERATING SURPLUS, GROSS [a]	47215.0	48408.0	47869.0	48718.0	51573.0	54728.0	59497.0	63697.0	65208.0	67925.0	...	
MIXED INCOME, GROSS	...	...	...	...	...	...	...	...	...	...	...	
Gross capital formation	...	...	...	...	...	...	...	...	...	...	...	

[a] Includes Mixed Income, Gross.

Table 2.3 Output, gross value added, and fixed assets by industries at current prices (ISIC Rev. 3) Transport, storage and communications (I)

Series 100: 1993 SNA, Moroccan dirham, Western calendar year — **Data in millions**

	2001	2002	2003	2004	2005	2006	2007	2008	2009	2010	2011	2012
Series	**100**											
Output, at basic prices	45805.0	48703.0	50897.0	56281.0	61668.0	67161.0	77575.0	81177.0	84140.0	90104.0	95903.0	
Less: Intermediate consumption, at purchaser's prices	18178.0	18838.0	19825.0	22281.0	27146.0	30670.0	34424.0	35915.0	36248.0	39559.0	45006.0	
Equals: VALUE ADDED, GROSS, at basic prices	27627.0	29865.0	31072.0	34000.0	34522.0	36491.0	43151.0	45262.0	47892.0	50545.0	50897.0	
Compensation of employees	8969.0	9139.0	9430.0	10248.0	11203.0	12079.0	12481.0	12988.0	13673.0	14404.0	...	
Taxes on production and imports, less Subsidies	400.0	361.0	509.0	526.0	640.0	563.0	581.0	654.0	631.0	411.0	...	
Taxes on production and imports	400.0	361.0	509.0	526.0	640.0	563.0	581.0	654.0	631.0	...	...	
Taxes on products	...	...	...	...	...	...	...	...	...	...	...	
Other taxes on production	400.0	361.0	509.0	526.0	640.0	563.0	581.0	654.0	631.0	...	...	
Less: Subsidies	0.0	0.0	0.0	0.0	0.0	0.0	0.0	...	...	...	...	
Subsidies on products	...	...	...	...	...	...	...	...	...	...	...	
Other subsidies on production	0.0	0.0	0.0	0.0	0.0	0.0	0.0	...	...	...	...	
OPERATING SURPLUS, GROSS [a]	18258.0	20365.0	21133.0	23226.0	22679.0	23849.0	30089.0	31620.0	33588.0	35730.0	...	
MIXED INCOME, GROSS	...	...	...	...	...	...	...	...	...	...	...	
Gross capital formation	...	...	...	...	...	...	...	...	...	...	...	

[a] Includes Mixed Income, Gross.

Table 2.3 Output, gross value added, and fixed assets by industries at current prices (ISIC Rev. 3) Financial intermediation; real estate, renting and business activities (J+K)

Series 100: 1993 SNA, Moroccan dirham, Western calendar year — **Data in millions**

	2001	2002	2003	2004	2005	2006	2007	2008	2009	2010	2011	2012
Series	**100**											
Output, at basic prices	70314.0	75512.0	82211.0	87381.0	97409.0	108466.0	127730.0	134785.0	141835.0	146255.0	156904.0	
Less: Intermediate consumption, at purchaser's prices	8587.0	9364.0	10833.0	10740.0	11316.0	12299.0	14276.0	15007.0	16559.0	16836.0	19450.0	
Equals: VALUE ADDED, GROSS, at basic prices	61727.0	66148.0	71378.0	76641.0	86093.0	96167.0	113454.0	119778.0	125276.0	129419.0	137454.0	
Compensation of employees	10120.0	10766.0	11320.0	12112.0	13061.0	14045.0	17453.0	18490.0	19702.0	20804.0	...	
Taxes on production and imports, less Subsidies	353.0	200.0	159.0	234.0	298.0	205.0	393.0	569.0	408.0	959.0	...	
Taxes on production and imports	611.0	546.0	650.0	688.0	769.0	785.0	904.0	1012.0	965.0	...	...	
Taxes on products	...	...	...	...	...	...	...	...	...	...	...	
Other taxes on production	611.0	546.0	650.0	688.0	769.0	785.0	904.0	1012.0	965.0	...	...	
Less: Subsidies	258.0	346.0	491.0	454.0	471.0	580.0	511.0	443.0	557.0	...	...	
Subsidies on products	...	...	...	...	...	...	...	...	...	...	...	
Other subsidies on production	258.0	346.0	491.0	454.0	471.0	580.0	511.0	443.0	557.0	...	...	
OPERATING SURPLUS, GROSS [a]	51254.0	55182.0	59899.0	64295.0	72734.0	81917.0	95608.0	100719.0	105166.0	107656.0	...	

	2001	2002	2003	2004	2005	2006	2007	2008	2009	2010	2011	2012
Series	**100**											
MIXED INCOME, GROSS	...	...	...	...	...	...	...	...	...	...	...	
Gross capital formation	...	...	...	...	...	...	...	...	...	...	...	

[a] Includes Mixed Income, Gross.

Table 2.3 Output, gross value added, and fixed assets by industries at current prices (ISIC Rev. 3) Public administration and defense; compulsory social security (L)

Series 100: 1993 SNA, Moroccan dirham, Western calendar year **Data in millions**

	2001	2002	2003	2004	2005	2006	2007	2008	2009	2010	2011	2012
Series	**100**											
Output, at basic prices	53291.0	55207.0	56622.0	62542.0	67615.0	72811.0	75418.0	78127.0	89212.0	87881.0	95212.0	
Less: Intermediate consumption, at purchaser's prices	15736.0	16992.0	16501.0	18334.0	19698.0	22147.0	23508.0	24127.0	29337.0	25281.0	25601.0	
Equals: VALUE ADDED, GROSS, at basic prices	37555.0	38215.0	40121.0	44208.0	47917.0	50664.0	51910.0	54000.0	59875.0	62600.0	69611.0	
Compensation of employees	34227.0	34728.0	36489.0	40405.0	43895.0	46400.0	47310.0	48993.0	54515.0	57212.0	...	
Taxes on production and imports, less Subsidies	40.0	43.0	52.0	48.0	55.0	86.0	55.0	62.0	71.0	93.0	...	
Taxes on production and imports	40.0	43.0	52.0	48.0	55.0	86.0	55.0	62.0	71.0	...	...	
Taxes on products	...	...	...	...	...	...	...	...	...	...	...	
Other taxes on production	40.0	43.0	52.0	48.0	55.0	86.0	55.0	62.0	71.0	...	...	
Less: Subsidies	...	...	...	...	...	...	...	...	...	...	...	
OPERATING SURPLUS, GROSS	3288.0	3444.0	3580.0	3755.0	3967.0	4178.0	4545.0	4945.0	5289.0	5295.0	...	
MIXED INCOME, GROSS	...	...	...	...	...	...	...	...	...	...	...	
Gross capital formation	...	...	...	...	...	...	...	...	...	...	...	

Table 2.3 Output, gross value added, and fixed assets by industries at current prices (ISIC Rev. 3) Education; health and social work; other community, social and personal services (M+N+O)

Series 100: 1993 SNA, Moroccan dirham, Western calendar year **Data in millions**

	2001	2002	2003	2004	2005	2006	2007	2008	2009	2010	2011	2012
Series	**100**											
Output, at basic prices	40146.0	40419.0	44625.0	46723.0	51260.0	53212.0	58131.0	63742.0	68314.0	72307.0	80346.0	
Less: Intermediate consumption, at purchaser's prices	3118.0	2895.0	2866.0	3050.0	3116.0	3215.0	3860.0	4382.0	6021.0	5703.0	4834.0	
Equals: VALUE ADDED, GROSS, at basic prices	37028.0	37524.0	41759.0	43673.0	48144.0	49997.0	54271.0	59360.0	62293.0	66604.0	75512.0	
Compensation of employees	30430.0	31287.0	34939.0	36960.0	40587.0	41987.0	45317.0	49434.0	51493.0	54236.0	...	
Taxes on production and imports, less Subsidies	99.0	51.0	129.0	133.0	160.0	124.0	131.0	147.0	152.0	151.0	...	
Taxes on production and imports	99.0	51.0	129.0	133.0	160.0	124.0	131.0	147.0	152.0	...	...	
Taxes on products	...	...	...	...	...	...	...	...	...	...	...	
Other taxes on production	99.0	51.0	129.0	133.0	160.0	124.0	131.0	147.0	152.0	...	...	
Less: Subsidies	0.0	0.0	0.0	0.0	0.0	0.0	0.0	0.0	0.0	...	...	
Subsidies on products	...	...	...	...	...	...	...	...	...	...	...	

	2001	2002	2003	2004	2005	2006	2007	2008	2009	2010	2011	2012
Series	**100**											
Other subsidies on production	0.0	0.0	0.0	0.0	0.0	0.0	0.0	0.0	0.0	...	...	
OPERATING SURPLUS, GROSS [a]	6499.0	6186.0	6691.0	6580.0	7397.0	7886.0	8823.0	9779.0	10648.0	12217.0	...	
MIXED INCOME, GROSS	...	...	...	...	...	...	...	...	...	...	...	
Gross capital formation	...	...	...	...	...	...	...	...	...	...	...	

[a] Includes Mixed Income, Gross.

Table 2.3 Output, gross value added, and fixed assets by industries at current prices (ISIC Rev. 3) Private households with employed persons (P)

Series 100: 1993 SNA, Moroccan dirham, Western calendar year **Data in millions**

	2001	2002	2003	2004	2005	2006	2007	2008	2009	2010	2011	2012
Series	**100**											
Output, at basic prices	7397.0	7803.0	8244.0	9228.0	9015.0	9525.0	10008.0	10540.0	10905.0	12007.0	12170.0	
Less: Intermediate consumption, at purchaser's prices	1310.0	1348.0	1273.0	1373.0	1254.0	1279.0	1344.0	1414.0	1403.0	1441.0	1520.0	
Equals: VALUE ADDED, GROSS, at basic prices	6087.0	6455.0	6971.0	7855.0	7761.0	8246.0	8664.0	9126.0	9502.0	10566.0	10650.0	
Compensation of employees	1856.0	2000.0	2060.0	2222.0	2364.0	1976.0	2235.0	2283.0	2105.0	2153.0	...	
Taxes on production and imports, less Subsidies	-23.0	-93.0	-88.0	-90.0	-111.0	-139.0	-141.0	-110.0	-137.0	-237.0	...	
Taxes on production and imports	22.0	22.0	34.0	35.0	43.0	38.0	39.0	50.0	43.0	...	...	
Taxes on products	...	...	...	...	...	...	...	...	...	...	...	
Other taxes on production	22.0	22.0	34.0	35.0	43.0	38.0	39.0	50.0	43.0	...	...	
Less: Subsidies	45.0	115.0	122.0	125.0	154.0	177.0	180.0	160.0	180.0	...	...	
Subsidies on products	...	...	...	...	...	...	...	...	...	...	...	
Other subsidies on production	45.0	115.0	122.0	125.0	154.0	177.0	180.0	160.0	180.0	...	...	
OPERATING SURPLUS, GROSS [a]	4254.0	4548.0	4999.0	5723.0	5508.0	6409.0	6570.0	6953.0	7534.0	8650.0	...	
MIXED INCOME, GROSS	...	...	...	...	...	...	...	...	...	...	...	
Gross capital formation	...	...	...	...	...	...	...	...	...	...	...	

[a] Includes Mixed Income, Gross.

Table 4.1 Total Economy (S.1)

Series 100: 1993 SNA, Moroccan dirham, Western calendar year **Data in millions**

	2001	2002	2003	2004	2005	2006	2007	2008	2009	2010	2011	2012
Series	**100**											
	I. Production account - Resources											
Output, at basic prices (otherwise, please specify)	710368.0	731682.0	768386.0	811254.0	870054.0	950000.0	1012034.0	1142714.0	1132059.0	1203273.0	1317180.0	
Less: Financial intermediation services indirectly measured (only to be deducted if FISIM is not distributed to uses)	18502.0	18801.0	19708.0	21085.0	23212.0	25951.0	31089.0	33325.0	34302.0	33882.0	36956.0	
Plus: Taxes less Subsidies on products	47704.0	49615.0	49460.0	50737.0	53723.0	59396.0	70561.0	69211.0	79292.0	76309.0	60188.0	
Plus: Taxes on products	54081.0	55280.0	55807.0	59066.0	64992.0	72539.0	86711.0	100661.0	94529.0	106507.0	111385.0	
Less: Subsidies on products	6377.0	5665.0	6347.0	8329.0	11269.0	13143.0	16150.0	31450.0	15237.0	30198.0	51197.0	

	2001	2002	2003	2004	2005	2006	2007	2008	2009	2010	2011	2012
Series	**100**											
	I. Production account - Uses											
Intermediate consumption, at purchaser's prices [a]	331670.0	335871.0	340825.0	356976.0	396098.0	432052.0	466341.0	523082.0	478902.0	515551.0	574761.0	
GROSS DOMESTIC PRODUCT	426402.0	445426.0	477021.0	505015.0	527679.0	577344.0	616254.0	688843.0	732449.0	764031.0	802607.0	
Less: Consumption of fixed capital	...	...	...	...	...	...	...	...	...	...	...	
NET DOMESTIC PRODUCT	...	...	...	...	...	...	...	...	...	...	...	
	II.1.1 Generation of income account - Resources											
GROSS DOMESTIC PRODUCT	426402.0	445426.0	477021.0	505015.0	527679.0	577344.0	616254.0	688843.0	732449.0	764031.0	802607.0	
	II.1.1 Generation of income account - Uses											
Compensation of employees	140916.0	146509.0	154097.0	165239.0	177249.0	187200.0	201061.0	212158.0	224491.0	236333.0	257669.0	
Taxes on production and imports, less Subsidies	51660.0	53707.0	53216.0	54726.0	58928.0	63960.0	75239.0	74517.0	84542.0	81470.0	66227.0	
Taxes on production and imports	58399.0	60023.0	60512.0	63916.0	71119.0	78145.0	92212.0	106747.0	100708.0	112703.0	117816.0	
Taxes on products	54081.0	55280.0	55807.0	59066.0	64992.0	72539.0	86711.0	100661.0	94529.0	106507.0	111385.0	
Other taxes on production	4318.0	4743.0	4705.0	4850.0	6127.0	5606.0	5501.0	6086.0	6179.0	6196.0	6431.0	
Less: Subsidies	6739.0	6316.0	7296.0	9190.0	12191.0	14185.0	16973.0	32230.0	16166.0	31233.0	51589.0	
Subsidies on products	6377.0	5665.0	6347.0	8329.0	11269.0	13143.0	16150.0	31450.0	15237.0	30198.0	51197.0	
Other subsidies on production	362.0	651.0	949.0	861.0	922.0	1042.0	823.0	780.0	929.0	1035.0	392.0	
OPERATING SURPLUS, GROSS [b]	233826.0	245210.0	269708.0	285050.0	291502.0	326184.0	339954.0	402168.0	423416.0	446228.0	478711.0	
MIXED INCOME, GROSS	...	...	...	...	...	...	...	...	...	...	...	
	II.1.2 Allocation of primary income account - Resources											
OPERATING SURPLUS, GROSS [b]	233826.0	245210.0	269708.0	285050.0	291502.0	326184.0	339954.0	402168.0	423416.0	446228.0	478711.0	
MIXED INCOME, GROSS	...	...	...	...	...	...	...	...	...	...	...	
Compensation of employees	140916.0	146509.0	154097.0	165239.0	177249.0	187200.0	201061.0	212158.0	224491.0	236333.0	257669.0	
Taxes on production and imports, less Subsidies	51660.0	53707.0	53216.0	54726.0	58928.0	63960.0	75239.0	74517.0	84542.0	81470.0	66227.0	
Taxes on production and imports	58399.0	60023.0	60512.0	63916.0	71119.0	78145.0	92212.0	106747.0	100708.0	112703.0	117816.0	
Taxes on products	54081.0	55280.0	55807.0	59066.0	64992.0	72539.0	86711.0	100661.0	94529.0	106507.0	111385.0	
Other taxes on production	4318.0	4743.0	4705.0	4850.0	6127.0	5606.0	5501.0	6086.0	6179.0	6196.0	6431.0	
Less: Subsidies	6739.0	6316.0	7296.0	9190.0	12191.0	14185.0	16973.0	32230.0	16166.0	31233.0	51589.0	
Subsidies on products	6377.0	5665.0	6347.0	8329.0	11269.0	13143.0	16150.0	31450.0	15237.0	30198.0	51197.0	
Other subsidies on production	362.0	651.0	949.0	861.0	922.0	1042.0	823.0	780.0	929.0	1035.0	392.0	
Property income	66291.0	69002.0	71141.0	75413.0	80495.0	94198.0	107713.0	118123.0	127890.0	132123.0	139857.0	
	II.1.2 Allocation of primary income account - Uses											
Property income	77395.0	79673.0	81099.0	84167.0	87263.0	102418.0	115743.0	129530.0	147130.0	152878.0	164867.0	
GROSS NATIONAL INCOME	415298.0	434755.0	467063.0	496261.0	520911.0	569124.0	608224.0	677436.0	713209.0	743276.0	777597.0	
	II.2 Secondary distribution of income account - Resources											
GROSS NATIONAL INCOME	415298.0	434755.0	467063.0	496261.0	520911.0	569124.0	608224.0	677436.0	713209.0	743276.0	777597.0	
Current taxes on income, wealth, etc.	28515.0	30632.0	33693.0	36817.0	43627.0	50080.0	60084.0	81486.0	71359.0	64234.0	70011.0	
Social contributions	24365.0	26285.0	30489.0	32632.0	35169.0	39653.0	41418.0	44305.0	49132.0	52303.0	59303.0	
Social benefits other than social transfers in kind	22068.0	24344.0	27670.0	29855.0	32037.0	37600.0	40025.0	41801.0	47048.0	49891.0	53428.0	
Other current transfers	70032.0	67601.0	69705.0	81050.0	104915.0	112127.0	121334.0	151001.0	129970.0	139208.0	166434.0	

	2001	2002	2003	2004	2005	2006	2007	2008	2009	2010	2011	2012
Series	**100**											
II.2 Secondary distribution of income account - Uses												
Current taxes on income, wealth, etc.	28515.0	30632.0	33693.0	36817.0	43627.0	50080.0	60084.0	81486.0	71359.0	64234.0	70011.0	
Social contributions	24455.0	26377.0	30568.0	32727.0	35276.0	39731.0	41500.0	44374.0	49220.0	52410.0	59429.0	
Social benefits other than social transfers in kind	19027.0	20851.0	24073.0	25661.0	27637.0	33166.0	34941.0	36916.0	41071.0	43609.0	46956.0	
Other current transfers	32780.0	34318.0	33792.0	41824.0	61367.0	60912.0	62939.0	88103.0	76004.0	83838.0	107153.0	
GROSS DISPOSABLE INCOME	455501.0	471439.0	506494.0	539586.0	568752.0	624695.0	671621.0	745150.0	773059.0	804821.0	843224.0	
II.4.1 Use of disposable income account - Resources												
GROSS DISPOSABLE INCOME	455501.0	471439.0	506494.0	539586.0	568752.0	624695.0	671621.0	745150.0	773059.0	804821.0	843224.0	
Adjustment for the change in net equity of households on pension funds	106.0	-65.0	975.0	903.0	957.0	1329.0	1196.0	1598.0	1329.0	1329.0	2619.0	
II.4.1 Use of disposable income account - Uses												
Final consumption expenditure	325706.0	339329.0	360032.0	382923.0	405282.0	439067.0	472242.0	518527.0	551858.0	571485.0	619270.0	
Individual consumption expenditure	325706.0	339329.0	360032.0	382923.0	405282.0	439067.0	472242.0	518527.0	551858.0	571485.0	619270.0	
Collective consumption expenditure	...	...	...	...	...	...	...	...	...	...	...	
Adjustment for the change in net equity of households on pension funds	106.0	-65.0	975.0	903.0	957.0	1329.0	1196.0	1598.0	1329.0	1329.0	2619.0	
SAVING, GROSS	129795.0	132110.0	146462.0	156663.0	163470.0	185628.0	199379.0	226623.0	221201.0	233336.0	223954.0	
III.1 Capital account - Changes in liabilities and net worth												
SAVING, GROSS	129795.0	132110.0	146462.0	156663.0	163470.0	185628.0	199379.0	226623.0	221201.0	233336.0	223954.0	
Capital transfers, receivable less payable	-101.0	-67.0	-97.0	-71.0	-50.0	-81.0	-26.0	-15.0	-4.0	-1.0	-2.0	
Capital transfers, receivable	11411.0	13075.0	14327.0	14429.0	17249.0	19185.0	22834.0	35309.0	32508.0	36460.0	35917.0	
Less: Capital transfers, payable	11512.0	13142.0	14424.0	14500.0	17299.0	19266.0	22860.0	35324.0	32512.0	36461.0	35919.0	
Equals: CHANGES IN NET WORTH DUE TO SAVING AND CAPITAL TRANSFERS [c]	129694.0	132043.0	146365.0	156592.0	163420.0	185547.0	199353.0	226608.0	221197.0	233335.0	223952.0	
III.1 Capital account - Changes in assets												
Gross capital formation	111487.0	115490.0	130481.0	147109.0	151955.0	169902.0	200187.0	262560.0	261075.0	267658.0	288562.0	
Gross fixed capital formation	105937.0	112320.0	119802.0	132719.0	145256.0	162456.0	192573.0	227465.0	226177.0	234407.0	246394.0	
Changes in inventories	5550.0	3170.0	10679.0	14390.0	6699.0	7446.0	7614.0	35095.0	34898.0	33251.0	42168.0	
Acquisitions less disposals of valuables	...	...	...	...	...	...	...	...	...	...	...	
Acquisitions less disposals of non-produced non-financial assets	...	...	...	...	...	...	...	...	...	...	...	
NET LENDING (+) / NET BORROWING (-)	18207.0	16553.0	15884.0	9483.0	11465.0	15645.0	-834.0	-35952.0	-39878.0	-34323.0	-64610.0	
III.2 Financial account - Changes in liabilities and net worth												
Net incurrence of liabilities	85333.0	122130.0	90873.0	121188.0	169444.0	281032.0	294136.0	311963.0	228744.0	331287.0	369840.0	
Currency and deposits	45968.0	45471.0	50283.0	45267.0	66256.0	111559.0	100665.0	83467.0	37362.0	22614.0	95754.0	
Securities other than shares	29404.0	20681.0	13230.0	18798.0	28210.0	15659.0	4048.0	9263.0	29255.0	35887.0	62988.0	
Loans	-8057.0	-9095.0	1363.0	6427.0	25664.0	59463.0	90122.0	111136.0	90482.0	72007.0	88434.0	
Shares and other equity	13755.0	33691.0	13524.0	31476.0	26743.0	70501.0	41030.0	59494.0	57482.0	146686.0	60461.0	
Insurance technical reserves	5831.0	7575.0	4319.0	4519.0	4771.0	8262.0	11688.0	9373.0	9525.0	9522.0	11922.0	
Financial derivatives	...	...	...	...	...	...	...	...	...	...	...	
Other accounts payable	-1568.0	23807.0	8154.0	14701.0	17800.0	15588.0	46583.0	39230.0	4638.0	44571.0	50281.0	

	2001	2002	2003	2004	2005	2006	2007	2008	2009	2010	2011	2012
Series	**100**											
NET LENDING (+) / NET BORROWING (-) [d]	18020.0	16597.0	15659.0	9469.0	11524.0	15388.0	-689.0	-35888.0	-39781.0	-34282.0	-64623.0	
	III.2 Financial account - Changes in assets											
Net acquisition of financial assets	103353.0	138727.0	106532.0	130657.0	180968.0	296420.0	293447.0	276075.0	188963.0	297005.0	305217.0	
Monetary gold and SDRs	160.0	-179.0	-261.0	5.0	370.0	-283.0	565.0	301.0	5844.0	206.0	-920.0	
Currency and deposits	51198.0	53568.0	54218.0	53086.0	55165.0	139162.0	89445.0	54574.0	38299.0	13182.0	69515.0	
Securities other than shares	61474.0	19629.0	26468.0	25586.0	58202.0	12100.0	33078.0	24964.0	20763.0	44615.0	63086.0	
Loans	4812.0	7701.0	19193.0	17870.0	30609.0	65982.0	89114.0	101068.0	62070.0	48941.0	74480.0	
Shares and other equity	-16987.0	28790.0	-8823.0	18675.0	12130.0	51429.0	23858.0	43750.0	45735.0	139713.0	44555.0	
Insurance technical reserves	5831.0	7575.0	4319.0	4519.0	4771.0	8262.0	11688.0	9373.0	9525.0	9522.0	11922.0	
Financial derivatives	...	...	...	...	...	...	...	...	...	...	...	
Other accounts receivable	-3135.0	21643.0	11418.0	10916.0	19721.0	19768.0	45699.0	42045.0	6727.0	40826.0	42579.0	

[a] Includes financial intermediation services indirectly measured (FISIM) but FISIM is excluded in the tables by industry.
[b] Includes Mixed Income, Gross.
[c] Item does not consider consumption of fixed capital.
[d] Net lending in the financial account and Net lending in the capital account have not been reconciled.

Table 4.2 Rest of the world (S.2)

Series 100: 1993 SNA, Moroccan dirham, Western calendar year **Data in millions**

	2001	2002	2003	2004	2005	2006	2007	2008	2009	2010	2011	2012
Series	**100**											
	V.I External account of goods and services - Resources											
Imports of goods and services	136202.0	143696.0	150229.0	173342.0	200071.0	229084.0	276477.0	350409.0	290725.0	329053.0	390755.0	
Imports of goods	115080.0	120637.0	126454.0	146775.0	170636.0	195057.0	241789.0	311272.0	248157.0	282812.0	336891.0	
Imports of services	21122.0	23059.0	23775.0	26567.0	29435.0	34027.0	34688.0	39137.0	42568.0	46241.0	53864.0	
	V.I External account of goods and services - Uses											
Exports of goods and services	125411.0	134303.0	136737.0	148325.0	170513.0	197459.0	220302.0	258165.0	210241.0	253941.0	285530.0	
Exports of goods	81020.0	87243.0	85705.0	90272.0	99952.0	112713.0	121522.0	157777.0	114658.0	151446.0	176023.0	
Exports of services	44391.0	47060.0	51032.0	58053.0	70561.0	84746.0	98780.0	100388.0	95583.0	102495.0	109507.0	
EXTERNAL BALANCE OF GOODS AND SERVICES	10791.0	9393.0	13492.0	25017.0	29558.0	31625.0	56175.0	92244.0	80484.0	75112.0	105225.0	
	V.II External account of primary income and current transfers - Resources											
EXTERNAL BALANCE OF GOODS AND SERVICES	10791.0	9393.0	13492.0	25017.0	29558.0	31625.0	56175.0	92244.0	80484.0	75112.0	105225.0	
Compensation of employees	...	...	...	...	...	...	...	...	...	...	...	
Taxes on production and imports, less Subsidies	...	...	...	...	...	...	...	...	...	...	...	
Taxes on production and imports	...	...	...	...	...	...	...	...	...	...	...	
Taxes on products	...	...	...	...	...	...	...	...	...	...	...	
Other taxes on production	...	...	...	...	...	...	...	...	...	...	...	
Less: Subsidies	...	...	...	...	...	...	...	...	...	...	...	
Subsidies on products	...	...	...	...	...	...	...	...	...	...	...	
Other subsidies on production	...	...	...	...	...	...	...	...	...	...	...	
Property income	15761.0	15641.0	14491.0	14214.0	13948.0	15681.0	17017.0	20083.0	27458.0	28476.0	32279.0	
Current taxes on income, wealth, etc.	...	...	...	...	...	...	...	...	...	...	...	

	2001	2002	2003	2004	2005	2006	2007	2008	2009	2010	2011	2012
Series	**100**											
Social contributions	90.0	92.0	79.0	95.0	107.0	78.0	82.0	69.0	88.0	107.0	126.0	
Social benefits other than social transfers in kind	...	...	...	...	...	...	...	...	...	...	...	
Other current transfers	1427.0	1366.0	1470.0	1532.0	1553.0	1775.0	1799.0	1948.0	2204.0	2573.0	2814.0	
Adjustment for the change in net equity of households on pension funds	...	...	...	...	...	...	...	...	...	...	...	
V.II External account of primary income and current transfers - Uses												
Compensation of employees	...	...	...	...	...	...	...	...	...	...	...	
Taxes on production and imports, less Subsidies	...	...	...	...	...	...	...	...	...	...	...	
Taxes on production and imports	...	...	...	...	...	...	...	...	...	...	...	
Taxes on products	...	...	...	...	...	...	...	...	...	...	...	
Other taxes on production	...	...	...	...	...	...	...	...	...	...	...	
Less: Subsidies	...	...	...	...	...	...	...	...	...	...	...	
Subsidies on products	...	...	...	...	...	...	...	...	...	...	...	
Other subsidies on production	...	...	...	...	...	...	...	...	...	...	...	
Property income	4657.0	4970.0	4533.0	5460.0	7180.0	7461.0	8987.0	8676.0	8218.0	7721.0	7269.0	
Current taxes on income and wealth, etc.	...	...	...	...	...	...	...	...	...	...	...	
Social contributions	...	...	...	...	...	...	...	...	...	...	...	
Social benefits other than social transfers in kind	3041.0	3493.0	3597.0	4194.0	4400.0	4434.0	5084.0	4885.0	5972.0	6282.0	6472.0	
Other current transfers	38679.0	34649.0	37383.0	40758.0	45101.0	52990.0	60194.0	64846.0	56170.0	57943.0	62095.0	
Adjustment for the change in net equity of households on pension funds	...	...	...	...	...	...	...	...	...	...	...	
CURRENT EXTERNAL BALANCE	-18308.0	-16620.0	-15981.0	-9554.0	-11515.0	-15726.0	808.0	35937.0	39874.0	34322.0	64608.0	
V.III.1 Capital account - Changes in liabilities and net worth												
CURRENT EXTERNAL BALANCE	-18308.0	-16620.0	-15981.0	-9554.0	-11515.0	-15726.0	808.0	35937.0	39874.0	34322.0	64608.0	
Capital transfers, receivable less payable	101.0	67.0	97.0	71.0	50.0	81.0	26.0	15.0	4.0	1.0	2.0	
Capital transfers, receivable	101.0	67.0	97.0	71.0	53.0	81.0	26.0	24.0	7.0	1.0	2.0	
Less: Capital transfers, payable	0.0	0.0	0.0	0.0	3.0	0.0	0.0	9.0	3.0	0.0	0.0	
Equals: CHANGES IN NET WORTH DUE TO SAVING AND CAPITAL TRANSFERS	-18207.0	-16553.0	-15884.0	-9483.0	-11465.0	-15645.0	834.0	35952.0	39878.0	34323.0	64610.0	
V.III.1 Capital account - Changes in assets												
Acquisitions less disposals of non-produced non-financial assets	...	...	...	...	...	...	...	...	...	...	...	
NET LENDING (+) / NET BORROWING (-)	-18207.0	-16553.0	-15884.0	-9483.0	-11465.0	-15645.0	834.0	35952.0	39878.0	34323.0	64610.0	
V.III.2 Financial account - Changes in liabilities and net worth												
Net incurrence of liabilities	44989.0	6647.0	27006.0	21338.0	28735.0	35982.0	33203.0	2430.0	13099.0	28554.0	8208.0	
Currency and deposits	11502.0	6668.0	6014.0	10391.0	-7571.0	28980.0	-12266.0	-26933.0	8066.0	5195.0	-11375.0	
Securities other than shares	32077.0	-1053.0	13225.0	6767.0	29999.0	-3559.0	29030.0	15701.0	-8492.0	8728.0	98.0	
Loans	313.0	720.0	4450.0	0.0	949.0	3799.0	2105.0	-106.0	-1455.0	-1446.0	0.0	
Shares and other equity	1097.0	312.0	117.0	274.0	692.0	114.0	3221.0	2803.0	3958.0	5203.0	5853.0	
Insurance technical reserves	...	...	...	...	...	...	...	...	...	...	...	
Financial derivatives	...	...	...	...	...	...	...	...	...	...	...	

	2001	2002	2003	2004	2005	2006	2007	2008	2009	2010	2011	2012
Series	**100**											
Other accounts payable	0.0	0.0	3200.0	3906.0	4666.0	6648.0	11113.0	10965.0	11022.0	10874.0	13632.0	
NET LENDING (+) / NET BORROWING (-) [a]	-18020.0	-16597.0	-15659.0	-9469.0	-11524.0	-15388.0	689.0	35888.0	39781.0	34282.0	64623.0	
	V.III.2 Financial account - Changes in assets											
Net acquisition of financial assets	26969.0	-9950.0	11347.0	11869.0	17211.0	20594.0	33892.0	38318.0	52880.0	62836.0	72831.0	
Monetary gold and SDRs	-160.0	179.0	261.0	-5.0	-370.0	283.0	-565.0	-301.0	-5844.0	-206.0	920.0	
Currency and deposits	6272.0	-1429.0	2079.0	2572.0	3520.0	1377.0	-1046.0	1960.0	7129.0	14627.0	14864.0	
Securities other than shares	7.0	-1.0	-13.0	-21.0	7.0	0.0	0.0	...	0.0	0.0	0.0	
Loans	-12556.0	-16076.0	-13380.0	-11443.0	-3996.0	-2720.0	3113.0	9962.0	26957.0	21620.0	13954.0	
Shares and other equity	31839.0	5213.0	22464.0	13075.0	15305.0	19186.0	20393.0	18547.0	15705.0	12176.0	21759.0	
Insurance technical reserves	...	...	...	...	...	...	...	...	...	...	...	
Financial derivatives	...	...	...	...	...	...	...	...	...	...	...	
Other accounts receivable	1567.0	2164.0	-64.0	7691.0	2745.0	2468.0	11997.0	8150.0	8933.0	14619.0	21334.0	

[a] Net lending in the financial account and Net lending in the capital account have not been reconciled.

Table 4.3 Non-financial Corporations (S.11)

Series 100: 1993 SNA, Moroccan dirham, Western calendar year

Data in millions

	2001	2002	2003	2004	2005	2006	2007	2008	2009	2010	2011	2012
Series	**100**											
	I. Production account - Resources											
Output, at basic prices (otherwise, please specify)	376512.0	386232.0	398265.0	417648.0	466056.0	510312.0	549974.0	626100.0	600646.0	665221.0	738124.0	
	I. Production account - Uses											
Intermediate consumption, at purchaser's prices	217863.0	219975.0	220558.0	227325.0	260141.0	282809.0	307248.0	348908.0	309856.0	346710.0	393466.0	
VALUE ADDED GROSS, in basic prices	158649.0	166257.0	177707.0	190323.0	205915.0	227503.0	242726.0	277192.0	290790.0	318511.0	344658.0	
Less: Consumption of fixed capital	...	...	...	...	...	...	...	...	...	...	...	
VALUE ADDED NET, at basic prices	...	...	...	...	...	...	...	...	...	...	...	
	II.1.1 Generation of income account - Resources											
VALUE ADDED GROSS, at basic prices	158649.0	166257.0	177707.0	190323.0	205915.0	227503.0	242726.0	277192.0	290790.0	318511.0	344658.0	
	II.1.1 Generation of income account - Uses											
Compensation of employees	62645.0	65613.0	68165.0	73083.0	77591.0	82798.0	89534.0	94521.0	98778.0	105039.0	111945.0	
Other taxes less Other subsidies on production	3676.0	3828.0	3603.0	3775.0	4934.0	4124.0	4235.0	4936.0	4696.0	3602.0	4877.0	
Other taxes on production	3780.0	4133.0	4061.0	4167.0	5370.0	4754.0	4547.0	5273.0	5208.0	4647.0	5267.0	
Less: Other subsidies on production	104.0	305.0	458.0	392.0	436.0	630.0	312.0	337.0	512.0	1045.0	390.0	
OPERATING SURPLUS, GROSS	92328.0	96816.0	105939.0	113465.0	123390.0	140581.0	148957.0	177735.0	187316.0	209870.0	227836.0	
	II.1.2 Allocation of primary income account - Resources											
OPERATING SURPLUS, GROSS	92328.0	96816.0	105939.0	113465.0	123390.0	140581.0	148957.0	177735.0	187316.0	209870.0	227836.0	
Property income	6311.0	6948.0	8446.0	9031.0	9845.0	11181.0	12654.0	13890.0	15479.0	16025.0	16964.0	
	II.1.2 Allocation of primary income account - Uses											
Property income	27733.0	29589.0	31535.0	33838.0	36020.0	44770.0	51065.0	60026.0	73828.0	78522.0	86077.0	
BALANCE OF PRIMARY INCOMES	70906.0	74175.0	82850.0	88658.0	97215.0	106992.0	110546.0	131599.0	128967.0	147373.0	158723.0	

	2001	2002	2003	2004	2005	2006	2007	2008	2009	2010	2011	2012
Series	**100**											
II.2 Secondary distribution of income account - Resources												
BALANCE OF PRIMARY INCOMES	70906.0	74175.0	82850.0	88658.0	97215.0	106992.0	110546.0	131599.0	128967.0	147373.0	158723.0	
Social contributions	2091.0	1877.0	1903.0	1618.0	1698.0	1698.0	1698.0	1332.0	1332.0	1012.0	1012.0	
Other current transfers	933.0	2202.0	1273.0	1010.0	1485.0	1995.0	1649.0	4494.0	1717.0	1453.0	1863.0	
II.2 Secondary distribution of income account - Uses												
Current taxes on income, wealth, etc.	10655.0	12399.0	12893.0	14730.0	16334.0	19168.0	21784.0	42286.0	34225.0	35454.0	38642.0	
Social benefits other than social transfers in kind	2462.0	2249.0	2479.0	2303.0	2383.0	2383.0	2160.0	1977.0	1977.0	1049.0	1049.0	
Other current transfers	8294.0	9146.0	9137.0	9839.0	11470.0	13338.0	13053.0	15339.0	16669.0	17837.0	20756.0	
GROSS DISPOSABLE INCOME	52519.0	54460.0	61517.0	64414.0	70211.0	75796.0	76896.0	77823.0	79145.0	95498.0	101151.0	
II.4.1 Use of disposable income account - Resources												
GROSS DISPOSABLE INCOME	52519.0	54460.0	61517.0	64414.0	70211.0	75796.0	76896.0	77823.0	79145.0	95498.0	101151.0	
II.4.1 Use of disposable income account - Uses												
Adjustment for the change in net equity of households on pension funds	...	...	...	...	...	...	...	...	...	...	...	
SAVING, GROSS	52519.0	54460.0	61517.0	64414.0	70211.0	75796.0	76896.0	77823.0	79145.0	95498.0	101151.0	
III.1 Capital account - Changes in liabilities and net worth												
SAVING, GROSS	52519.0	54460.0	61517.0	64414.0	70211.0	75796.0	76896.0	77823.0	79145.0	95498.0	101151.0	
Capital transfers, receivable less payable	1859.0	2789.0	2696.0	2575.0	4487.0	3504.0	5791.0	14866.0	4843.0	7646.0	9232.0	
Capital transfers, receivable	1908.0	2849.0	2781.0	2667.0	4652.0	3707.0	6022.0	15254.0	5165.0	7958.0	9619.0	
Less: Capital transfers, payable	49.0	60.0	85.0	92.0	165.0	203.0	231.0	388.0	322.0	312.0	387.0	
Equals: CHANGES IN NET WORTH DUE TO SAVING AND CAPITAL TRANSFERS [a]	54378.0	57249.0	64213.0	66989.0	74698.0	79300.0	82687.0	92689.0	83988.0	103144.0	110383.0	
III.1 Capital account - Changes in assets												
Gross capital formation	59743.0	61100.0	75327.0	86024.0	86184.0	97727.0	116612.0	171436.0	154904.0	157597.0	172393.0	
Gross fixed capital formation	54886.0	59639.0	65151.0	71770.0	80191.0	91389.0	110107.0	137197.0	127344.0	131696.0	138844.0	
Changes in inventories	4857.0	1461.0	10176.0	14254.0	5993.0	6338.0	6505.0	34239.0	27560.0	25901.0	33549.0	
Acquisitions less disposals of valuables	...	...	...	...	...	...	...	...	...	...	...	
Acquisitions less disposals of non-produced non-financial assets	-326.0	-145.0	-126.0	-383.0	-292.0	-112.0	-254.0	-101.0	-267.0	-276.0	-316.0	
NET LENDING (+) / NET BORROWING (-)	-5039.0	-3706.0	-10988.0	-18652.0	-11194.0	-18315.0	-33671.0	-78646.0	-70649.0	-54177.0	-61694.0	
III.2 Financial account - Changes in liabilities and net worth												
Net incurrence of liabilities	13481.0	28686.0	26674.0	36402.0	48642.0	73577.0	72380.0	100892.0	86804.0	130685.0	123798.0	
Currency and deposits	...	...	...	...	...	...	...	...	...	...	...	
Securities other than shares	-161.0	6152.0	-2169.0	4628.0	1470.0	4177.0	-176.0	7565.0	1109.0	-1894.0	5311.0	
Loans	4336.0	3754.0	1981.0	1908.0	22901.0	30450.0	36721.0	55895.0	56078.0	41540.0	50032.0	
Shares and other equity	8876.0	12982.0	15786.0	17980.0	13724.0	27669.0	30696.0	21670.0	25345.0	74091.0	48046.0	
Insurance technical reserves	...	...	...	...	...	...	...	...	...	...	...	
Financial derivatives	...	...	...	...	...	...	...	...	...	...	...	
Other accounts payable	430.0	5798.0	11076.0	11886.0	10547.0	11281.0	5139.0	15762.0	4272.0	16948.0	20409.0	
NET LENDING (+) / NET BORROWING (-) [b]	-4537.0	-3948.0	-11211.0	-18053.0	-11932.0	-18669.0	-33521.0	-77797.0	-71205.0	-53829.0	-60964.0	

	2001	2002	2003	2004	2005	2006	2007	2008	2009	2010	2011	2012
Series	**100**											
	III.2 Financial account - Changes in assets											
Net acquisition of financial assets	8944.0	24738.0	15463.0	18349.0	36710.0	54908.0	38859.0	23095.0	15599.0	76856.0	62834.0	
Monetary gold and SDRs	...	...	...	...	...	...	...	...	...	...	...	
Currency and deposits	7139.0	15389.0	17729.0	7660.0	10857.0	21897.0	13693.0	-2513.0	2868.0	24026.0	6440.0	
Securities other than shares	1940.0	-6635.0	-285.0	2253.0	7228.0	984.0	-4165.0	7466.0	8434.0	-3683.0	4424.0	
Loans	6.0	0.0	1.0	0.0	0.0	-5.0	0.0	0.0	0.0	0.0	0.0	
Shares and other equity	4485.0	7754.0	-5030.0	2910.0	3663.0	13549.0	-9619.0	-7276.0	7151.0	29876.0	11147.0	
Insurance technical reserves	818.0	1091.0	-87.0	652.0	685.0	1619.0	1073.0	1111.0	1254.0	359.0	308.0	
Financial derivatives	...	...	...	...	...	...	...	...	...	...	...	
Other accounts receivable	-5444.0	7139.0	3135.0	4874.0	14277.0	16864.0	37877.0	24307.0	-4108.0	26278.0	40515.0	

[a] Item does not consider consumption of fixed capital.
[b] Net lending in the financial account and Net lending in the capital account have not been reconciled.

Table 4.4 Financial Corporations (S.12)

Series 100: 1993 SNA, Moroccan dirham, Western calendar year **Data in millions**

	2001	2002	2003	2004	2005	2006	2007	2008	2009	2010	2011	2012
Series	**100**											
	I. Production account - Resources											
Output, at basic prices (otherwise, please specify)	26783.0	27326.0	29163.0	30878.0	34283.0	38354.0	46606.0	49865.0	52331.0	52866.0	58631.0	
	I. Production account - Uses											
Intermediate consumption, at purchaser's prices	5426.0	5654.0	6684.0	7203.0	7424.0	8123.0	10162.0	10732.0	12224.0	12271.0	14601.0	
VALUE ADDED GROSS, at basic prices	21357.0	21672.0	22479.0	23675.0	26859.0	30231.0	36444.0	39133.0	40107.0	40595.0	44030.0	
Less: Consumption of fixed capital	...	...	...	...	...	...	...	...	...	...	...	
VALUE ADDED NET, at basic prices	...	...	...	...	...	...	...	...	...	...	...	
	II.1.1 Generation of income account - Resources											
VALUE ADDED GROSS, at basic prices	21357.0	21672.0	22479.0	23675.0	26859.0	30231.0	36444.0	39133.0	40107.0	40595.0	44030.0	
	II.1.1 Generation of income account - Uses											
Compensation of employees	6426.0	6727.0	6967.0	7180.0	7681.0	8127.0	9487.0	10157.0	10760.0	11449.0	12802.0	
Other taxes less Other subsidies on production	374.0	402.0	406.0	453.0	492.0	539.0	650.0	674.0	702.0	1278.0	906.0	
Other taxes on production	393.0	421.0	437.0	468.0	503.0	551.0	661.0	682.0	711.0	1268.0	908.0	
Less: Other subsidies on production	19.0	19.0	31.0	15.0	11.0	12.0	11.0	8.0	9.0	-10.0	2.0	
OPERATING SURPLUS, GROSS	14557.0	14543.0	15106.0	16042.0	18686.0	21565.0	26307.0	28302.0	28645.0	27868.0	30322.0	
	II.1.2 Allocation of primary income account - Resources											
OPERATING SURPLUS, GROSS	14557.0	14543.0	15106.0	16042.0	18686.0	21565.0	26307.0	28302.0	28645.0	27868.0	30322.0	
Property income	40098.0	41088.0	41012.0	41636.0	45611.0	51025.0	60821.0	68540.0	72448.0	73862.0	79194.0	
Adjustment entry for FISIM (balanced by Nominal Sector)	-18502.0	-18801.0	-19708.0	-21085.0	-23212.0	-25951.0	-31089.0	-33325.0	-34302.0	-33882.0	-36956.0	
	II.1.2 Allocation of primary income account - Uses											
Property income	23589.0	24905.0	24050.0	24130.0	24166.0	28168.0	32851.0	36808.0	40404.0	40540.0	43354.0	
BALANCE OF PRIMARY INCOMES	12564.0	11925.0	12360.0	12463.0	16919.0	18471.0	23188.0	26709.0	26387.0	27308.0	29206.0	

	2001	2002	2003	2004	2005	2006	2007	2008	2009	2010	2011	2012
Series	**100**											
II.2 Secondary distribution of income account - Resources												
BALANCE OF PRIMARY INCOMES	12564.0	11925.0	12360.0	12463.0	16919.0	18471.0	23188.0	26709.0	26387.0	27308.0	29206.0	
Social contributions	3631.0	3875.0	5380.0	5752.0	5408.0	6060.0	6673.0	7567.0	8483.0	8837.0	9719.0	
Other current transfers	3745.0	5089.0	4456.0	4398.0	5104.0	6599.0	6255.0	6963.0	7010.0	6299.0	7084.0	
II.2 Secondary distribution of income account - Uses												
Current taxes on income, wealth, etc.	3031.0	2956.0	3871.0	3724.0	5544.0	7150.0	11103.0	8957.0	8396.0	8114.0	8190.0	
Social benefits other than social transfers in kind	3631.0	3875.0	5380.0	5752.0	5408.0	6060.0	6673.0	7567.0	8483.0	8837.0	9719.0	
Other current transfers	3795.0	5121.0	4546.0	4407.0	5127.0	6676.0	6341.0	8398.0	7003.0	6472.0	7198.0	
GROSS DISPOSABLE INCOME	9483.0	8937.0	8399.0	8730.0	11352.0	11244.0	11999.0	16317.0	17998.0	19021.0	20902.0	
II.4.1 Use of disposable income account - Resources												
GROSS DISPOSABLE INCOME	9483.0	8937.0	8399.0	8730.0	11352.0	11244.0	11999.0	16317.0	17998.0	19021.0	20902.0	
II.4.1 Use of disposable income account - Uses												
Adjustment for the change in net equity of households on pension funds	106.0	-65.0	975.0	903.0	957.0	1329.0	1196.0	1598.0	1329.0	1329.0	2619.0	
SAVING, GROSS	9377.0	9002.0	7424.0	7827.0	10395.0	9915.0	10803.0	14719.0	16669.0	17692.0	18283.0	
III.1 Capital account - Changes in liabilities and net worth												
SAVING, GROSS	9377.0	9002.0	7424.0	7827.0	10395.0	9915.0	10803.0	14719.0	16669.0	17692.0	18283.0	
Capital transfers, receivable less payable	-779.0	-1507.0	-1626.0	-1657.0	-3518.0	-2090.0	-3477.0	-4191.0	-3770.0	-4878.0	-2960.0	
Capital transfers, receivable	49.0	60.0	85.0	92.0	165.0	203.0	231.0	388.0	322.0	312.0	387.0	
Less: Capital transfers, payable	828.0	1567.0	1711.0	1749.0	3683.0	2293.0	3708.0	4579.0	4092.0	5190.0	3347.0	
Equals: CHANGES IN NET WORTH DUE TO SAVING AND CAPITAL TRANSFERS [a]	8598.0	7495.0	5798.0	6170.0	6877.0	7825.0	7326.0	10528.0	12899.0	12814.0	15323.0	
III.1 Capital account - Changes in assets												
Gross capital formation	356.0	1160.0	41.0	260.0	885.0	170.0	1505.0	558.0	1378.0	2393.0	2505.0	
Gross fixed capital formation	356.0	1160.0	41.0	260.0	885.0	170.0	1505.0	558.0	1378.0	2393.0	2505.0	
Changes in inventories	...	...	...	...	...	...	...	...	...	...	...	
Acquisitions less disposals of valuables	...	...	...	...	...	...	...	...	...	...	...	
Acquisitions less disposals of non-produced non-financial assets	95.0	122.0	95.0	314.0	260.0	80.0	222.0	101.0	235.0	244.0	284.0	
NET LENDING (+) / NET BORROWING (-)	8147.0	6213.0	5662.0	5596.0	5732.0	7575.0	5599.0	9869.0	11286.0	10129.0	12534.0	
III.2 Financial account - Changes in liabilities and net worth												
Net incurrence of liabilities	59203.0	69084.0	48469.0	58741.0	83236.0	160540.0	167971.0	157638.0	113597.0	124773.0	149027.0	
Currency and deposits	45115.0	32431.0	45747.0	42354.0	71240.0	107580.0	103305.0	82880.0	39363.0	22254.0	102688.0	
Securities other than shares	875.0	-898.0	-4733.0	-1958.0	-7678.0	4796.0	5847.0	8723.0	18454.0	17902.0	17297.0	
Loans	-1171.0	-3571.0	-777.0	1280.0	984.0	3532.0	14912.0	8666.0	3730.0	1309.0	1228.0	
Shares and other equity	4747.0	20540.0	-2378.0	13314.0	12592.0	42757.0	10228.0	37824.0	32068.0	72023.0	8915.0	
Insurance technical reserves	5831.0	7575.0	4319.0	4519.0	4771.0	8262.0	11688.0	9373.0	9525.0	9522.0	11922.0	
Financial derivatives	...	...	...	...	...	...	...	...	...	...	...	
Other accounts payable	3806.0	13007.0	6291.0	-768.0	1327.0	-6387.0	21991.0	10172.0	10457.0	1763.0	6977.0	
NET LENDING (+) / NET BORROWING (-) [b]	8287.0	6324.0	5383.0	5488.0	6048.0	7643.0	5686.0	9775.0	11071.0	10004.0	12377.0	

	2001	2002	2003	2004	2005	2006	2007	2008	2009	2010	2011	2012
Series	**100**											
	III.2 Financial account - Changes in assets											
Net acquisition of financial assets	67490.0	75408.0	53852.0	64229.0	89284.0	168183.0	173657.0	167413.0	124668.0	134777.0	161404.0	
Monetary gold and SDRs	160.0	-179.0	-261.0	5.0	370.0	-283.0	565.0	301.0	5844.0	206.0	-920.0	
Currency and deposits	10712.0	22937.0	12537.0	25093.0	2476.0	55497.0	17155.0	-8247.0	2387.0	-45253.0	13774.0	
Securities other than shares	51471.0	23738.0	19243.0	13690.0	42664.0	12311.0	31947.0	19312.0	13642.0	31392.0	53270.0	
Loans	4434.0	8291.0	19129.0	18524.0	31047.0	65980.0	89157.0	100843.0	61572.0	48902.0	74485.0	
Shares and other equity	612.0	9852.0	9451.0	5985.0	11883.0	29650.0	26474.0	39128.0	23564.0	90872.0	21049.0	
Insurance technical reserves	638.0	1677.0	-158.0	417.0	83.0	213.0	908.0	601.0	931.0	845.0	1068.0	
Financial derivatives	...	...	...	...	...	...	...	...	...	...	...	
Other accounts receivable	-537.0	9092.0	-6089.0	515.0	761.0	4815.0	7451.0	15475.0	16728.0	7813.0	-1322.0	

[a] Item does not consider consumption of fixed capital.
[b] Net lending in the financial account and Net lending in the capital account have not been reconciled.

Table 4.5 General Government (S.13)

Series 100: 1993 SNA, Moroccan dirham, Western calendar year **Data in millions**

	2001	2002	2003	2004	2005	2006	2007	2008	2009	2010	2011	2012
Series	**100**											
	I. Production account - Resources											
Output, at basic prices (otherwise, please specify)	85778.0	88369.0	93375.0	101086.0	109293.0	115806.0	122137.0	129273.0	143417.0	143628.0	155927.0	
	I. Production account - Uses											
Intermediate consumption, at purchaser's prices	18324.0	19405.0	18837.0	20809.0	22176.0	24652.0	26627.0	27705.0	34401.0	29918.0	29009.0	
VALUE ADDED GROSS, at basic prices	67454.0	68964.0	74538.0	80277.0	87117.0	91154.0	95510.0	101568.0	109016.0	113710.0	126918.0	
Less: Consumption of fixed capital	4476.0	4696.0	4890.0	5087.0	5309.0	5700.0	6102.0	...	...	...	...	
VALUE ADDED NET, at basic prices	62978.0	64268.0	69648.0	75190.0	81808.0	85454.0	89408.0	...	...	...	...	
	II.1.1 Generation of income account - Resources											
VALUE ADDED GROSS, at basic prices	67454.0	68964.0	74538.0	80277.0	87117.0	91154.0	95510.0	101568.0	109016.0	113710.0	126918.0	
	II.1.1 Generation of income account - Uses											
Compensation of employees	62925.0	64211.0	69580.0	75125.0	81706.0	85315.0	89292.0	94887.0	101931.0	106595.0	119273.0	
Other taxes less Other subsidies on production	53.0	57.0	68.0	65.0	102.0	139.0	116.0	131.0	140.0	161.0	131.0	
Other taxes on production	53.0	57.0	68.0	65.0	102.0	139.0	116.0	131.0	140.0	161.0	131.0	
Less: Other subsidies on production	...	...	...	...	...	...	...	...	...	...	...	
OPERATING SURPLUS, GROSS	4476.0	4696.0	4890.0	5087.0	5309.0	5700.0	6102.0	6550.0	6945.0	6954.0	7514.0	
	II.1.2 Allocation of primary income account - Resources											
OPERATING SURPLUS, GROSS	4476.0	4696.0	4890.0	5087.0	5309.0	5700.0	6102.0	6550.0	6945.0	6954.0	7514.0	
Taxes on production and imports, less Subsidies	51660.0	53707.0	53216.0	54726.0	58928.0	63960.0	75239.0	74517.0	84542.0	81470.0	66227.0	
Taxes on production and imports	58399.0	60023.0	60512.0	63916.0	71119.0	78145.0	92212.0	106747.0	100708.0	112703.0	117816.0	
Taxes on products	54081.0	55280.0	55807.0	59066.0	64992.0	72539.0	86711.0	100661.0	94529.0	106507.0	111385.0	
Other taxes on production	4318.0	4743.0	4705.0	4850.0	6127.0	5606.0	5501.0	6086.0	6179.0	6196.0	6431.0	
Less: Subsidies	6739.0	6316.0	7296.0	9190.0	12191.0	14185.0	16973.0	32230.0	16166.0	31233.0	51589.0	

	2001	2002	2003	2004	2005	2006	2007	2008	2009	2010	2011	2012
Series	**100**											
Subsidies on products	6377.0	5665.0	6347.0	8329.0	11269.0	13143.0	16150.0	31450.0	15237.0	30198.0	51197.0	
Other subsidies on production	362.0	651.0	949.0	861.0	922.0	1042.0	823.0	780.0	929.0	1035.0	392.0	
Property income	9548.0	9937.0	10718.0	13066.0	12485.0	17954.0	18646.0	18060.0	20453.0	21827.0	23121.0	
II.1.2 Allocation of primary income account - Uses												
Property income	19758.0	18438.0	18325.0	18488.0	18605.0	19893.0	20749.0	19950.0	19345.0	19718.0	20442.0	
BALANCE OF PRIMARY INCOMES	45926.0	49902.0	50499.0	54391.0	58117.0	67721.0	79238.0	79177.0	92595.0	90533.0	76420.0	
II.2 Secondary distribution of income account - Resources												
BALANCE OF PRIMARY INCOMES	45926.0	49902.0	50499.0	54391.0	58117.0	67721.0	79238.0	79177.0	92595.0	90533.0	76420.0	
Current taxes on income, wealth, etc.	28515.0	30632.0	33693.0	36817.0	43627.0	50080.0	60084.0	81486.0	71359.0	64234.0	70011.0	
Social contributions	18643.0	20533.0	23206.0	25262.0	28063.0	31895.0	33047.0	35406.0	39317.0	42454.0	48572.0	
Other current transfers	12637.0	13125.0	12138.0	17422.0	25457.0	29791.0	33921.0	56323.0	39253.0	47910.0	67607.0	
II.2 Secondary distribution of income account - Uses												
Current taxes on income, wealth, etc.	...	...	...	...	...	...	...	...	...	...	...	
Social benefits other than social transfers in kind	12934.0	14727.0	16214.0	17606.0	19846.0	24723.0	26108.0	27372.0	30616.0	33723.0	36188.0	
Other current transfers	11761.0	11396.0	10341.0	15029.0	31470.0	24910.0	27781.0	48313.0	37154.0	43778.0	62953.0	
GROSS DISPOSABLE INCOME	81026.0	88069.0	92981.0	101257.0	103948.0	129854.0	152401.0	176707.0	174754.0	167630.0	163469.0	
II.4.1 Use of disposable income account - Resources												
GROSS DISPOSABLE INCOME	81026.0	88069.0	92981.0	101257.0	103948.0	129854.0	152401.0	176707.0	174754.0	167630.0	163469.0	
II.4.1 Use of disposable income account - Uses												
Final consumption expenditure	79414.0	81339.0	86470.0	94321.0	102110.0	107071.0	112234.0	118132.0	133397.0	133938.0	146332.0	
Individual consumption expenditure	...	...	...	...	...	...	...	...	...	...	...	
Collective consumption expenditure	...	...	...	...	...	...	...	...	...	...	...	
Adjustment for the change in net equity of households on pension funds	...	...	...	...	...	...	...	...	...	...	...	
SAVING, GROSS	1612.0	6730.0	6511.0	6936.0	1838.0	22783.0	40167.0	58575.0	41357.0	33692.0	17137.0	
III.1 Capital account - Changes in liabilities and net worth												
SAVING, GROSS	1612.0	6730.0	6511.0	6936.0	1838.0	22783.0	40167.0	58575.0	41357.0	33692.0	17137.0	
Capital transfers, receivable less payable	-1142.0	-1349.0	-1151.0	-1099.0	-1279.0	-1811.0	-3128.0	-11613.0	-2707.0	-3954.0	-7640.0	
Capital transfers, receivable	9392.0	10099.0	11380.0	11489.0	12129.0	14933.0	15767.0	18720.0	25384.0	27004.0	24543.0	
Less: Capital transfers, payable	10534.0	11448.0	12531.0	12588.0	13408.0	16744.0	18895.0	30333.0	28091.0	30958.0	32183.0	
Equals: CHANGES IN NET WORTH DUE TO SAVING AND CAPITAL TRANSFERS [a]	470.0	5381.0	5360.0	5837.0	559.0	20972.0	37039.0	46962.0	38650.0	29738.0	9497.0	
III.1 Capital account - Changes in assets												
Gross capital formation	14628.0	14292.0	13757.0	14747.0	14053.0	14204.0	17490.0	20527.0	26888.0	26575.0	28022.0	
Gross fixed capital formation	14628.0	14292.0	13757.0	14747.0	14053.0	14204.0	17490.0	20527.0	26888.0	26575.0	28022.0	
Changes in inventories	...	...	...	...	...	...	...	...	...	...	...	
Acquisitions less disposals of valuables	0.0	0.0	0.0	0.0	0.0	0.0	0.0	0.0	0.0	...	...	
Acquisitions of non-produced non-financial assets	1146.0	531.0	530.0	508.0	402.0	538.0	1008.0	1383.0	1571.0	1288.0	1439.0	
NET LENDING (+) / NET BORROWING (-)	-15304.0	-9442.0	-8927.0	-9418.0	-13896.0	6200.0	18541.0	25052.0	10191.0	1875.0	-19964.0	

	2001	2002	2003	2004	2005	2006	2007	2008	2009	2010	2011	2012
Series	**100**											
	III.2 Financial account - Changes in liabilities and net worth											
Net incurrence of liabilities	10227.0	26848.0	12613.0	18071.0	23322.0	2893.0	-6350.0	-1160.0	9528.0	32211.0	48264.0	
Currency and deposits	853.0	13040.0	4536.0	2913.0	-4984.0	3979.0	-2640.0	587.0	-2001.0	360.0	-6934.0	
Securities other than shares	28690.0	15427.0	20132.0	16128.0	34418.0	6686.0	-1623.0	-7025.0	9692.0	19879.0	40380.0	
Loans	-17246.0	-13232.0	-8745.0	-6649.0	-2798.0	-2669.0	1578.0	9866.0	10758.0	17781.0	8099.0	
Shares and other equity	132.0	169.0	116.0	182.0	427.0	75.0	106.0	0.0	71.0	572.0	3500.0	
Insurance technical reserves	...	...	...	...	...	...	...	...	...	...	...	
Financial derivatives	...	...	...	...	...	...	...	...	...	...	...	
Other accounts payable	-2202.0	11444.0	-3426.0	5497.0	-3741.0	-5178.0	-3771.0	-4588.0	-8992.0	-6381.0	3219.0	
NET LENDING (+) / NET BORROWING (-) [b]	-15511.0	-9795.0	-9181.0	-9358.0	-14136.0	6469.0	18001.0	24800.0	9929.0	1511.0	-20286.0	
	III.2 Financial account - Changes in assets											
Net acquisition of financial assets	-5284.0	17053.0	3432.0	8713.0	9186.0	9362.0	11651.0	23640.0	19457.0	33722.0	27978.0	
Monetary gold and SDRs	...	...	...	...	...	...	...	...	...	...	...	
Currency and deposits	13758.0	8662.0	-1619.0	2270.0	1521.0	1447.0	-3099.0	9383.0	9410.0	-8356.0	6613.0	
Securities other than shares	4491.0	4075.0	7700.0	9135.0	6330.0	-1895.0	5019.0	-1491.0	-1562.0	16105.0	4910.0	
Loans	372.0	-590.0	63.0	-654.0	-438.0	7.0	-43.0	225.0	498.0	39.0	-5.0	
Shares and other equity	-21335.0	3555.0	-9167.0	-4421.0	-4352.0	6270.0	3701.0	14025.0	15122.0	15756.0	11253.0	
Insurance technical reserves	...	...	...	...	...	...	...	...	...	...	...	
Financial derivatives	...	...	...	...	...	...	...	...	...	...	...	
Other accounts receivable	-2570.0	1351.0	6455.0	2383.0	6125.0	3533.0	6073.0	1498.0	-4011.0	10178.0	5207.0	

[a] Item does not consider consumption of fixed capital.
[b] Net lending in the financial account and Net lending in the capital account have not been reconciled.

Table 4.6 Households (S.14)

Series 100: 1993 SNA, Moroccan dirham, Western calendar year — **Data in millions**

	2001	2002	2003	2004	2005	2006	2007	2008	2009	2010	2011	2012
Series	**100**											
	I. Production account - Resources											
Output, at basic prices (otherwise, please specify)	221295.0	229755.0	247583.0	261642.0	260422.0	285528.0	293317.0	337476.0	335665.0	341558.0	364498.0	
	I. Production account - Uses											
Intermediate consumption, at purchaser's prices	71555.0	72036.0	75038.0	80554.0	83145.0	90517.0	91215.0	102412.0	88119.0	92770.0	100729.0	
VALUE ADDED GROSS, at basic prices	149740.0	157719.0	172545.0	181088.0	177277.0	195011.0	202102.0	235064.0	247546.0	248788.0	263769.0	
Less: Consumption of fixed capital	...	...	...	...	...	...	...	...	...	...	...	
VALUE ADDED NET, at basic prices	...	...	...	...	...	...	...	...	...	...	...	
	II.1.1 Generation of income account - Resources											
VALUE ADDED GROSS, at basic prices	149740.0	157719.0	172545.0	181088.0	177277.0	195011.0	202102.0	235064.0	247546.0	248788.0	263769.0	
	II.1.1 Generation of income account - Uses											
Compensation of employees	8920.0	9958.0	9385.0	9851.0	10271.0	10960.0	12748.0	12593.0	13022.0	13250.0	13649.0	
Other taxes less Other subsidies on production	-147.0	-195.0	-321.0	-304.0	-323.0	-238.0	-323.0	-435.0	-288.0	120.0	125.0	

	2001	2002	2003	2004	2005	2006	2007	2008	2009	2010	2011	2012
Series	**100**											
Other taxes on production	92.0	132.0	139.0	150.0	152.0	162.0	177.0	0.0	120.0	120.0	125.0	
Less: Other subsidies on production	239.0	327.0	460.0	454.0	475.0	400.0	500.0	435.0	408.0	0.0	0.0	
OPERATING SURPLUS, GROSS [a]	140967.0	147956.0	163481.0	171541.0	167329.0	184289.0	189677.0	222906.0	234812.0	235418.0	249995.0	
MIXED INCOME, GROSS	...	...	...	...	...	...	...	...	...	...	...	
II.1.2 Allocation of primary income account - Resources												
OPERATING SURPLUS, GROSS [a]	140967.0	147956.0	163481.0	171541.0	167329.0	184289.0	189677.0	222906.0	234812.0	235418.0	249995.0	
MIXED INCOME, GROSS	...	...	...	...	...	...	...	...	...	...	...	
Compensation of employees	140916.0	146509.0	154097.0	165239.0	177249.0	187200.0	201061.0	212158.0	224491.0	236333.0	257669.0	
Property income	10334.0	11029.0	10965.0	11680.0	12554.0	14038.0	15592.0	17633.0	19510.0	20409.0	20578.0	
II.1.2 Allocation of primary income account - Uses												
Property income	6315.0	6741.0	7189.0	7711.0	8472.0	9587.0	11078.0	12746.0	13353.0	14098.0	14994.0	
BALANCE OF PRIMARY INCOMES	285902.0	298753.0	321354.0	340749.0	348660.0	375940.0	395252.0	439951.0	465260.0	478062.0	513248.0	
II.2 Secondary distribution of income account - Resources												
BALANCE OF PRIMARY INCOMES	285902.0	298753.0	321354.0	340749.0	348660.0	375940.0	395252.0	439951.0	465260.0	478062.0	513248.0	
Social contributions	...	...	...	...	...	...	...	...	...	...	...	
Social benefits other than social transfers in kind	22068.0	24344.0	27670.0	29855.0	32037.0	37600.0	40025.0	41801.0	47048.0	49891.0	53428.0	
Other current transfers	52717.0	47185.0	51838.0	58220.0	72869.0	73742.0	79509.0	83221.0	81990.0	83546.0	89880.0	
II.2 Secondary distribution of income account - Uses												
Current taxes on income, wealth, etc.	14829.0	15277.0	16929.0	18363.0	21749.0	23762.0	27197.0	30243.0	28738.0	20666.0	23179.0	
Social contributions	24455.0	26377.0	30568.0	32727.0	35276.0	39731.0	41500.0	44374.0	49220.0	52410.0	59429.0	
Social benefits other than social transfers in kind	...	...	...	...	...	...	...	...	...	...	...	
Other current transfers	8930.0	8655.0	9768.0	12549.0	13300.0	15988.0	15764.0	16053.0	15178.0	15751.0	16246.0	
GROSS DISPOSABLE INCOME	312473.0	319973.0	343597.0	365185.0	383241.0	407801.0	430325.0	474303.0	501162.0	522672.0	557702.0	
II.4.1 Use of disposable income account - Resources												
GROSS DISPOSABLE INCOME	312473.0	319973.0	343597.0	365185.0	383241.0	407801.0	430325.0	474303.0	501162.0	522672.0	557702.0	
Adjustment for the change in net equity of households on pension funds	106.0	-65.0	975.0	903.0	957.0	1329.0	1196.0	1598.0	1329.0	1329.0	2619.0	
II.4.1 Use of disposable income account - Uses												
Final consumption expenditure	246292.0	257990.0	273562.0	288602.0	303172.0	331996.0	360008.0	400395.0	418461.0	437547.0	472938.0	
Individual consumption expenditure	...	...	...	...	...	...	...	...	...	...	...	
SAVING, GROSS	66287.0	61918.0	71010.0	77486.0	81026.0	77134.0	71513.0	75506.0	84030.0	86454.0	87383.0	
III.1 Capital account - Changes in liabilities and net worth												
SAVING, GROSS	66287.0	61918.0	71010.0	77486.0	81026.0	77134.0	71513.0	75506.0	84030.0	86454.0	87383.0	
Capital transfers, receivable less payable	-39.0	0.0	-16.0	110.0	260.0	316.0	788.0	923.0	1630.0	1185.0	1366.0	
Capital transfers, receivable	62.0	67.0	81.0	181.0	303.0	342.0	814.0	947.0	1637.0	1186.0	1368.0	
Less: Capital transfers, payable	101.0	67.0	97.0	71.0	43.0	26.0	26.0	24.0	7.0	1.0	2.0	
Equals: CHANGES IN NET WORTH DUE TO SAVINGS AND CAPITAL TRANSFERS [b]	66248.0	61918.0	70994.0	77596.0	81286.0	77540.0	72301.0	76429.0	85660.0	87639.0	88749.0	
III.1 Capital account - Changes in assets												
Gross capital formation	36760.0	38938.0	41356.0	46078.0	50833.0	57801.0	64580.0	70039.0	77905.0	81093.0	85642.0	

	2001	2002	2003	2004	2005	2006	2007	2008	2009	2010	2011	2012
Series	**100**											
Gross fixed capital formation	36067.0	37229.0	40853.0	45942.0	50127.0	56693.0	63471.0	69183.0	70567.0	73743.0	77023.0	
Changes in inventories	693.0	1709.0	503.0	136.0	706.0	1108.0	1109.0	856.0	7338.0	7350.0	8619.0	
Acquisitions less disposals of valuables	0.0	0.0	0.0	0.0	0.0	0.0	0.0	...	...	...	...	
Acquisitions less disposals of non-produced non-financial assets	-915.0	-508.0	-499.0	-439.0	-370.0	-536.0	-976.0	-1383.0	-1539.0	-1256.0	-1407.0	
NET LENDING (+) / NET BORROWING (-)	30403.0	23488.0	30137.0	31957.0	30823.0	20185.0	8697.0	7773.0	9284.0	7802.0	4514.0	
	III.2 Financial account - Changes in liabilities and net worth											
Net incurrence of liabilities	2422.0	-2488.0	3117.0	7974.0	14244.0	44022.0	60135.0	54593.0	18815.0	43618.0	48751.0	
Currency and deposits	...	...	...	...	...	...	...	...	...	...	...	
Securities other than shares	...	...	...	...	...	...	...	...	...	...	...	
Loans	6024.0	3954.0	8904.0	9888.0	4577.0	28150.0	36911.0	36709.0	19916.0	11377.0	29075.0	
Shares and other equity	...	...	...	...	...	...	...	...	...	...	...	
Insurance technical reserves	...	...	...	...	...	...	...	...	-2.0	...	...	
Financial derivatives	...	...	...	...	...	...	...	...	...	...	...	
Other accounts payable	-3602.0	-6442.0	-5787.0	-1914.0	9667.0	15872.0	23224.0	17884.0	-1099.0	32241.0	19676.0	
NET LENDING (+) / NET BORROWING (-) [c]	29781.0	24016.0	30668.0	31392.0	31544.0	19945.0	9145.0	7334.0	10424.0	8032.0	4250.0	
	III.2 Financial account - Changes in assets											
Net acquisition of financial assets	32203.0	21528.0	33785.0	39366.0	45788.0	63967.0	69280.0	61927.0	29239.0	51650.0	53001.0	
Currency and deposits	19589.0	6580.0	25571.0	18063.0	40311.0	60321.0	61696.0	55951.0	23634.0	42765.0	42688.0	
Securities other than shares	3572.0	-1549.0	-190.0	508.0	1980.0	700.0	277.0	-323.0	249.0	801.0	482.0	
Loans	0.0	0.0	0.0	0.0	0.0	0.0	0.0	...	...	...	...	
Shares and other equity	-749.0	7629.0	-4077.0	14201.0	936.0	1960.0	3302.0	-2127.0	-102.0	3209.0	1106.0	
Insurance technical reserves	4375.0	4807.0	4564.0	3450.0	4003.0	6430.0	9707.0	7661.0	7340.0	8318.0	10546.0	
Financial derivatives	...	...	...	...	...	...	...	...	...	...	...	
Other accounts receivable	5416.0	4061.0	7917.0	3144.0	-1442.0	-5444.0	-5702.0	765.0	-1882.0	-3443.0	-1821.0	

[a] Includes Mixed Income, Gross.
[b] Item does not consider consumption of fixed capital.
[c] Net lending in the financial account and Net lending in the capital account have not been reconciled.

Mozambique

Source

Reply to the United Nations national accounts questionnaire from Instituto Nacional de Estatistica, Departamento de Contas Nacionais e Indicadores Globais, of Mozambique. Previous estimates were published by Instituto Nacional de Estatística in "Anuário Estatístico" and on the Mozambican website, www.ine.gov.mz.

General

The latest estimates, shown in the following tables, are considered to be prepared in accordance with the concepts and definitions of the System of National Accounts 1993 (1993 SNA). Estimates are based on responses to a conceptual questionnaire and other available information. Mozambique implemented the use of a new base year of 2003; previously a base year of 1996 was used. All constant price tables reflect the new base year of 2003. When the scope and coverage of the estimates differ for conceptual or statistical reasons from the definitions and classifications recommended in the SNA, a footnote provides explanation.

Table 1.1 Gross domestic product by expenditures at current prices

Series 300: 1993 SNA, Metical, Western calendar year **Data in millions**

	2001	2002	2003	2004	2005	2006	2007	2008	2009	2010	2011	2012
Series	**300**											
	Expenditures of the gross domestic product											
Final consumption expenditure	72459.9	100003.4	112636.6	127610.6	146017.3	165610.1	191136.6	222204.2	248737.0	285093.4	341521.7	
Household final consumption expenditure [a]	61078.6	87756.8	98480.9	109881.2	126354.4	143381.6	166398.5	192512.8	214369.2	241073.0	292625.4	
NPISHs final consumption expenditure	...	...	...	...	...	...	...	...	...	...	...	
General government final consumption expenditure	11381.3	12246.6	14155.7	17729.4	19662.9	22228.5	24738.1	29691.4	34367.8	44020.4	48896.3	
Individual consumption expenditure	...	4380.4	4868.8	6296.0	7294.0	8747.6	10127.0	12366.1	14523.8	16661.1	18876.2	
Collective consumption expenditure	...	7866.2	9286.9	11433.4	12368.9	13480.8	14611.1	17325.3	19844.0	27359.3	30020.0	
Gross capital formation	21844.0	29435.1	24946.4	23604.5	27173.5	30631.4	31783.7	42290.6	39795.8	57535.2	62314.2	
Gross fixed capital formation	16849.9	29802.2	24720.7	23996.6	28360.7	31818.6	33504.3	39613.8	43959.5	51862.4	64949.4	
Changes in inventories	4994.1	-367.1	225.7	-392.0	-1187.2	-1187.2	-1720.6	2676.9	-4163.7	5672.9	-2635.2	
Acquisitions less disposals of valuables	...	...	...	...	...	...	...	...	...	...	...	
Exports of goods and services	17858.6	24816.0	29136.7	38340.8	46212.6	54861.3	64146.2	72638.3	73799.4	87686.7	99117.7	
Exports of goods	14374.3	17646.0	22911.9	33172.0	40163.9	48470.5	55847.4	61833.7	62973.8	75876.1	87771.9	
Exports of services	3484.3	7169.9	6224.9	5168.9	6048.7	6390.8	8298.7	10804.6	10825.6	11810.6	11345.8	
Less: Imports of goods and services	27794.1	54775.5	55747.0	60887.6	67340.0	70861.1	79422.9	96775.4	96119.1	115354.2	137619.2	
Imports of goods	22057.3	43520.1	43773.5	50209.3	54802.0	57558.4	62267.4	74502.6	73848.9	94051.8	113503.7	
Imports of services	5736.7	11255.4	11973.5	10678.3	12538.1	13302.7	17155.6	22272.7	22270.2	21302.4	24115.5	
Equals: GROSS DOMESTIC PRODUCT	84368.4	99479.0	110972.7	128668.3	151706.9	180241.7	207643.6	240357.7	266213.1	314961.2	365334.4	

[a] Includes NPISH final consumption expenditure.

Table 1.2 Gross domestic product by expenditures at constant prices

Series 300: 1993 SNA, Metical, Western calendar year — **Data in millions**

	2001	2002	2003	2004	2005	2006	2007	2008	2009	2010	2011	2012
Series	**300**											
Base year	**2003**											
	Expenditures of the gross domestic product											
Final consumption expenditure	79646.2	106421.2	112636.6	118133.0	126116.6	132720.0	142658.5	155732.4	163767.5	174206.8	194723.9	
Household final consumption expenditure [a]	69260.0	93400.3	98480.9	102683.6	109843.3	114781.8	123427.6	134123.5	140287.6	147713.2	166157.4	
NPISHs final consumption expenditure	...	...	...	...	...	...	...	...	...	...	...	
General government final consumption expenditure	10386.3	13020.9	14155.7	15449.3	16273.3	17938.2	19230.9	21608.9	23479.9	26493.6	28566.5	
Individual consumption expenditure	...	4510.4	4868.8	5272.4	5721.4	6437.9	7122.6	7828.1	8556.2	9816.0	10793.0	
Collective consumption expenditure	...	8510.5	9286.9	10176.9	10551.9	11500.3	12108.3	13780.8	14923.7	16677.6	17773.5	
Gross capital formation	24095.0	26591.6	24946.4	22943.3	25890.6	26657.4	28005.6	37390.4	39297.2	42580.9	43241.3	
Gross fixed capital formation	20066.2	26808.7	24720.7	23334.3	25704.5	27300.7	28884.7	34023.5	35866.2	38328.8	42131.2	
Changes in inventories	4028.8	-217.1	225.7	-391.0	186.1	-643.3	-879.2	3366.8	3431.0	4252.1	1110.1	
Acquisitions less disposals of valuables	...	...	...	...	...	...	...	...	...	...	...	
Exports of goods and services	17707.5	24493.5	29136.7	35329.0	37543.5	42136.8	48849.5	49011.5	50125.1	53837.2	63642.9	
Exports of goods	15491.5	18753.6	22911.9	30213.4	31683.2	36421.5	41202.7	38663.2	40312.7	44672.7	54965.6	
Exports of services	2216.0	5739.8	6224.9	5115.6	5860.4	5715.3	7646.7	10348.3	9812.4	9164.5	8677.4	
Less: Imports of goods and services	26044.4	53293.9	55747.0	56683.7	59787.2	60483.7	68213.7	80499.3	81316.7	86575.2	104083.7	
Imports of goods	20618.1	42414.0	43773.5	45653.9	47249.3	48168.2	51788.4	60328.1	61102.8	71087.3	84495.8	
Imports of services	5426.3	10879.9	11973.5	11029.9	12537.9	12315.5	16425.2	20171.2	20214.0	15487.9	19587.9	
Equals: GROSS DOMESTIC PRODUCT	95404.3	104212.3	110972.7	119721.6	129763.5	141030.4	151299.9	161635.0	171873.1	184049.7	197524.4	

[a] Includes NPISH final consumption expenditure.

Table 1.3 Relations among product, income, savings, and net lending aggregates

Series 300: 1993 SNA, Metical, Western calendar year — **Data in millions**

	2001	2002	2003	2004	2005	2006	2007	2008	2009	2010	2011	2012
Series	**300**											
GROSS DOMESTIC PRODUCT	84368.4	99479.0	110972.7	128668.3	151706.9	180241.7	207643.6	240357.7	266213.1	314961.2	365334.4	
Plus: Compensation of employees - from and to the rest of the world, net	...	-231.2	712.2	1008.4	872.1	1076.7	1050.1	2221.0	3118.4	3056.0	2826.8	
Plus: Compensation of employees - from the rest of the world	...	547.0	922.2	1216.0	1092.2	1379.9	1470.9	3735.1	4716.1	5549.0	5792.7	
Less: Compensation of employees - to the rest of the world	...	778.2	210.1	207.6	220.1	303.2	420.8	1514.0	1597.7	2493.0	2965.9	
Plus: Property income - from and to the rest of the world, net	...	-13753.9	-4575.2	-7536.9	-8868.0	-15478.6	-14045.4	-16773.5	-14266.2	-5114.1	-9075.4	
Plus: Property income - from the rest of the world	...	662.1	382.7	440.1	1047.9	2086.8	2718.4	2066.2	2353.1	2127.1	1139.6	
Less: Property income - to the rest of the world	...	14415.9	4957.9	7976.9	9916.0	17565.4	16763.8	18839.7	16619.3	7241.2	10215.0	
Sum of Compensation of employees and property income - from and to the rest of the world, net	...	-13985.0	-3863.0	-6528.5	-7995.9	-14401.9	-12995.4	-14552.5	-11147.8	-2058.1	-6248.6	

	2001	2002	2003	2004	2005	2006	2007	2008	2009	2010	2011	2012
Series	**300**											
Plus: Sum of Compensation of employees and property income - from the rest of the world	...	1209.1	1304.9	1656.0	2140.1	3466.6	4189.3	5801.2	7069.2	7676.1	6932.3	
Less: Sum of Compensation of employees and property income - to the rest of the world	...	15194.1	5167.9	8184.5	10136.0	17868.6	17184.7	20353.7	18217.1	9734.2	13180.9	
Plus: Taxes less subsidies on production and imports - from and to the rest of the world, net	...	...	...	...	...	...	...	...	...	...	...	
Equals: GROSS NATIONAL INCOME	...	85494.0	107109.7	122139.8	143711.0	165839.7	194648.2	225805.2	255065.2	312903.1	359085.8	
Plus: Current transfers - from and to the rest of the world, net	...	14862.5	5208.0	6903.1	6222.0	10597.8	12787.5	20848.1	21404.6	21870.6	24076.6	
Plus: Current transfers - from the rest of the world	...	19255.5	6842.7	8155.9	8501.6	12166.9	14134.4	23627.0	25901.0	27091.3	31124.4	
Less: Current transfers - to the rest of the world	...	4393.0	1634.7	1252.7	2279.6	1569.2	1346.9	2778.9	4496.4	5220.6	7047.8	
Equals: GROSS NATIONAL DISPOSABLE INCOME	...	100356.5	112317.8	129043.0	149933.0	176437.5	207435.7	246653.4	276469.9	334773.8	383162.5	
Less: Final consumption expenditure / Actual final consumption	72459.9	100003.4	112636.6	127610.6	146017.3	165610.1	191136.6	222204.2	248737.0	285093.4	341521.7	
Equals: SAVING, GROSS	...	353.1	-318.9	1432.4	3915.8	10827.4	16299.1	24449.2	27732.9	49680.3	41640.8	
Plus: Capital transfers - from and to the rest of the world, net	...	-27077.7	-6629.9	-5591.4	-4311.6	-3981.4	-11830.7	-10187.1	-11792.9	-11523.2	-11224.3	
Plus: Capital transfers - from the rest of the world	...	9.9	11.8	7025.7	85.7	0.0	-21.2	192.3	184.1	180.8	32.6	
Less: Capital transfers - to the rest of the world	7386.6	27087.6	6641.8	12617.1	4397.2	3981.4	11809.5	10379.4	11977.0	11704.0	11256.9	
Less: Gross capital formation	...	29435.1	24946.4	23604.5	27173.5	30631.4	31783.7	42290.6	39795.8	57535.2	62314.2	
Less: Acquisitions less disposals of non-produced non-financial assets	...	...	...	...	...	...	...	...	...	...	...	
Equals: NET LENDING (+) / NET BORROWING (-) OF THE NATION	...	-56159.8	-31895.1	-27763.5	-27569.3	-23785.3	-27315.4	-28028.5	-23855.8	-19378.1	-31897.7	
	Net values: Gross National Income / Gross National Disposable Income / Saving Gross less Consumption of fixed capital											
Less: Consumption of fixed capital	...	...	...	...	...	...	...	...	...	...	...	
Equals: NET NATIONAL INCOME	...	...	...	...	...	...	...	...	...	...	...	
Equals: NET NATIONAL DISPOSABLE INCOME	...	...	...	...	...	...	...	...	...	...	...	
Equals: SAVING, NET	...	...	...	...	...	...	...	...	...	...	...	

Table 2.1 Value added by industries at current prices (ISIC Rev. 3)

Series 300: 1993 SNA, Metical, Western calendar year — **Data in millions**

	2001	2002	2003	2004	2005	2006	2007	2008	2009	2010	2011	2012
Series	**300**											
	Industries											
Agriculture, hunting, forestry; fishing	16911.9	25288.8	28132.0	31878.6	37121.9	45852.9	52829.0	64367.6	71651.4	89229.2	104314.2	
Agriculture, hunting, forestry	15463.3	23507.8	26006.5	29634.5	34837.8	43042.4	49431.0	60108.9	67424.6	83974.3	98599.7	
Agriculture, hunting and related service activities	13309.5	20610.9	22759.0	25871.4	30002.4	37530.1	43059.7	52326.3	59259.3	75312.9	89728.1	
Forestry, logging and related service activities	2153.8	2896.9	3247.5	3763.1	4835.4	5512.3	6371.3	7782.6	8165.3	8661.5	8871.6	
Fishing	1448.6	1780.9	2125.5	2244.2	2284.0	2810.4	3398.0	4258.7	4226.8	5254.8	5714.5	
Mining and quarrying	215.6	522.9	657.2	1160.8	1476.4	2337.1	2967.3	3318.3	3566.4	4074.3	5086.0	

		2001	2002	2003	2004	2005	2006	2007	2008	2009	2010	2011	2012
Series		**300**											
Manufacturing		10438.4	12622.6	16635.9	20528.8	21304.1	26355.2	29369.8	33610.1	34449.3	39880.5	43168.0	
Electricity, gas and water supply		2478.0	4414.8	5071.2	6358.7	7605.6	9578.9	11065.5	10044.4	11585.6	13276.6	14828.1	
Construction		6270.1	3481.9	3826.1	3835.2	4506.8	5213.3	5936.4	6860.0	7533.0	8855.1	10336.8	
Wholesale, retail trade, repair of motor vehicles, motorcycles and personal and households goods; hotels and restaurants		18595.0	12186.5	12645.0	13711.8	20355.1	25579.3	32050.6	37237.6	41638.1	51236.7	62685.8	
Wholesale, retail trade, repair of motor vehicles, motorcycles and personal and household goods		17520.6	10757.4	11023.7	11919.5	18213.4	23071.3	28969.8	33456.8	37734.6	46400.0	56486.0	
Hotels and restaurants		1074.3	1429.1	1621.3	1792.3	2141.7	2508.1	3080.8	3780.8	3903.5	4836.7	6199.8	
Transport, storage and communications		8302.3	9895.9	10421.0	12415.1	14559.6	16458.0	19011.0	22179.9	24913.4	28665.9	33030.2	
Land transport; transport via pipelines, water transport; air transport; Supporting and auxiliary transport activities; activities of travel agencies		6553.1	7650.5	8037.3	9307.5	10978.8	12341.7	14153.3	16328.6	17693.4	20664.5	23681.1	
Post and telecommunications		1749.2	2245.4	2383.8	3107.5	3580.8	4116.3	4857.6	5851.3	7220.0	8001.5	9349.1	
Financial intermediation; real estate, renting and business activities		4531.8	13979.1	14319.5	15720.4	18055.9	19317.8	21313.2	23016.5	24762.1	26917.6	28539.1	
Financial intermediation		2841.4	3385.0	3705.9	4544.4	6748.8	7657.9	9088.1	9521.6	10507.9	12034.4	12812.6	
Real estate, renting and business activities		1690.4	10594.1	10613.6	11176.0	11307.1	11659.9	12225.0	13494.9	14254.2	14883.2	15726.4	
Public administration and defence; compulsory social security		2820.1	3705.7	4134.4	5005.2	5658.9	6639.6	7350.2	8518.9	9848.2	11249.6	13420.5	
Education; health and social work; other community, social and personal services	a	6462.1	6605.2	7364.9	8759.5	10184.8	11983.6	14093.9	16511.8[b]	18777.2	21034.3	22947.7	
Education		1961.4	3149.3	3658.6	4705.8	5613.7	6521.1	7788.8	8518.9	10888.3	12244.0	13356.4	
Health and social work		831.5	1237.4	1326.5	1514.5	1846.0	2396.4	3024.8	3514.0	4014.8	4614.7	5027.5	
Other community, social and personal services		3669.2	2218.4	2379.8	2539.2	2725.1	3066.1	3280.3	3677.3	3874.1	4175.6	4563.8	
Private households with employed persons		...	...	...	...	...	...	...	...	...	...	...	
Equals: VALUE ADDED, GROSS, in basic prices	c	75146.3	90896.9	100340.7	116289.6	137691.6	164584.0	190652.2	219977.3	242321.8	287474.2	330950.9	
Less: Financial intermediation services indirectly measured (FISIM)		1878.9	1806.3	2866.6	3084.5	3137.3	4731.8	5334.6	5687.7	6403.0	6945.6	7405.5	
Plus: Taxes less Subsidies on products		9222.0	8582.1	10632.0	12378.7	14015.3	15657.6	16991.3	20380.4	23891.3	27487.0	34383.5	
Plus: Taxes on products		9222.0	8582.1	10632.0	12378.7	14015.3	15657.6	16991.3	20380.4	23891.3	27487.0	34383.5	
Less: Subsidies on products		...	...	...	...	...	...	...	...	...	...	...	
Equals: GROSS DOMESTIC PRODUCT		84368.4	99479.0	110972.7	128668.3	151706.9	180241.7	207643.6	240357.7	266213.1	314961.2	365334.4	

[a] Includes data for Private households with employed persons.
[b] Discrepancy between components and total.
[c] Excludes financial intermediation services indirectly measured (FISIM) but FISIM is included in the tables by industry.

Table 2.2 Value added by industries at constant prices (ISIC Rev. 3)

Series 300: 1993 SNA, Metical, Western calendar year

Data in millions

	2001	2002	2003	2004	2005	2006	2007	2008	2009	2010	2011	2012
Series	**300**											
Base year	**2003**											
Industries												
Agriculture, hunting, forestry; fishing	24000.8	26685.5	28132.0	29470.5	31377.1	34577.9	37422.6	40823.0	43252.3	46125.7	49228.0	
Agriculture, hunting, forestry	22065.2	24727.8	26006.5	27339.9	29227.4	32263.4	34899.7	38130.5	40825.1	43503.3	46447.1	
Agriculture, hunting and related service activities	19234.7	21555.8	22759.0	23985.8	25759.2	28604.1	31140.6	34280.1	36885.8	39465.7	42312.0	
Forestry, logging and related service activities	2830.5	3172.0	3247.5	3354.1	3468.1	3659.3	3759.1	3850.4	3939.3	4037.6	4135.1	
Fishing	1935.6	1957.7	2125.5	2130.6	2149.7	2314.5	2522.9	2692.5	2427.2	2622.4	2780.9	
Mining and quarrying	439.7	566.0	657.2	1127.6	1135.4	1451.5	1731.0	1855.1	1910.1	2151.4	2498.3	
Manufacturing	13070.5	14213.0	16635.9	18832.0	19235.2	19803.5	20411.6	21402.7	21913.5	22885.8	23573.2	
Electricity, gas and water supply	4173.9	4608.0	5071.2	5896.8	6910.5	7816.6	8486.9	7448.7	8419.9	8894.8	9490.8	
Construction	3149.1	3489.1	3826.1	3559.0	4028.9	4449.8	4973.0	5595.0	5921.4	6238.3	6524.9	
Wholesale, retail trade, repair of motor vehicles, motorcycles and personal and household goods; hotels and restaurants	11341.6	11867.7	12645.0	13475.0	15130.5	18141.6	19853.8	21368.6	22574.0	23513.5	24974.2	
Wholesale, retail trade, repair of motor vehicles, motorcycles and personal and household goods	9886.4	10337.7	11023.7	11804.3	13232.3	16052.0	17447.5	18688.0	19833.9	20611.1	21791.7	
Hotels and restaurants	1455.3	1530.0	1621.3	1670.7	1898.3	2089.6	2406.3	2680.6	2740.1	2902.4	3182.5	
Transport, storage and communications	9342.2	10123.5	10421.0	11426.4	12334.2	13621.8	14943.6	16881.3	18608.1	21305.5	23704.9	
Land transport; transport via piplines, water transport; air transport; Supporting and auxiliary transport activities; activities of travel agencies	7126.3	7722.3	8037.3	8367.2	8839.9	9911.2	10897.0	11976.0	13699.2	15459.7	17482.3	
Post and telecommunications	2215.9	2401.3	2383.8	3059.1	3494.3	3710.7	4046.6	4905.3	4909.0	5845.8	6222.6	
Financial intermediation, real estate, renting and business activities	13321.8	13853.2	14319.5	15879.0	18315.2	18664.2	19294.5	19631.8	20656.4	21986.2	22837.4	
Financial intermediation	2896.4	3352.6	3705.9	4639.5	6928.8	7182.3	7817.6	8073.6	8863.1	9960.1	10604.6	
Real estate, renting and business activities	10425.4	10500.5	10613.6	11239.5	11386.4	11482.0	11476.9	11558.2	11793.4	12026.1	12232.8	
Public administration and defence; compulsory social security	3673.5	3944.7	4134.4	4325.8	4622.6	5139.3	5402.1	5792.7	6228.7	6786.2	7402.2	
Education; health and social work; other community, social and personal services [a]	6661.3	6955.3	7364.9	7949.1	8594.8	9257.7	10238.0	10877.6	11759.5	12729.4	13438.5	
Education	3225.4	3377.0	3658.6	4086.6	4572.7	4954.0	5588.1	6002.0	6659.8	7345.2	7803.3	
Health and social work	1186.6	1254.3	1326.5	1425.6	1526.7	1748.4	2033.2	2196.2	2356.0	2574.7	2758.3	
Other community, social and personal services	2249.4	2324.0	2379.8	2436.9	2495.4	2555.3	2616.6	2679.4	2743.7	2809.5	2877.0	
Private households with employed persons	...	...	...	...	...	...	...	...	...	...	...	
Equals: VALUE ADDED, GROSS, in basic prices [b]	87774.8	94574.0	100340.7	108645.4	118172.4	128437.5	138138.9	146758.6	155868.3	166807.7	177478.7	
Less: Financial intermediation services indirectly measured (FISIM)	1399.8	1731.8	2866.6	3295.7	3512.0	4486.4	4618.2	4917.8	5375.7	5809.1	6194.0	
Plus: Taxes less Subsidies on products	7629.5	9638.3	10632.0	11076.1	11591.1	12592.9	13161.0	14876.4	16004.8	17242.0	20045.8	
Plus: Taxes on products	7629.5	9638.3	10632.0	11076.1	11591.1	12592.9	13161.0	14876.4	16004.8	17242.0	20045.8	

	2001	2002	2003	2004	2005	2006	2007	2008	2009	2010	2011	2012
Series	**300**											
Base year	**2003**											
Less: Subsidies on products	...	...	...	...	...	...	...	...	...	...	...	
Equals: GROSS DOMESTIC PRODUCT	95404.3	104212.3	110972.7	119721.6	129763.5	141030.4	151299.9	161635.0	171873.1	184049.7	197524.4	

[a] Includes data for Private households with employed persons.
[b] Excludes financial intermediation services indirectly measured (FISIM) but FISIM is included in the tables by industry.

Table 2.3 Output, gross value added, and fixed assets by industries at current prices (ISIC Rev. 3) Total Economy

Series 300: 1993 SNA, Metical, Western calendar year **Data in millions**

	2001	2002	2003	2004	2005	2006	2007	2008	2009	2010	2011	2012
Series	**300**											
Output, at basic prices	...	157757.7	181583.5	210387.4	238015.7	279048.6	312250.1	361592.0	396019.7	467481.1	522773.6	
Less: Intermediate consumption, at purchaser's prices	...	65054.5	78376.2	91013.3	97186.8	109732.8	116263.4	135926.9	147294.9	173061.2	184417.2	
Equals: VALUE ADDED, GROSS, at basic prices	...	92703.2	103207.3	119374.1	140828.9	169315.8	195986.8	225665.1	248724.8	294419.8	338356.4	
Compensation of employees	...	26596.4	29425.7	35295.3	39057.9	45727.9	50330.6	59479.8	67893.9	78215.3	89614.8	
Taxes on production and imports, less Subsidies [a]	...	8582.1	10632.0	12378.7	14015.3	15657.6	16991.3	20380.4	23891.3	27487.0	34383.5	
Taxes on production and imports	...	8582.1	10632.0	12378.7	14015.3	15657.6	16991.3	20380.4	23891.3	27487.0	34383.5	
Less: Subsidies	66.6	106.6	145.5	182.2	101.3	312.3	377.6	422.5	438.2	1746.2	0.0	
OPERATING SURPLUS, GROSS	...	...	...	...	...	...	...	...	...	...	...	
MIXED INCOME, GROSS	...	...	...	...	...	...	...	...	...	...	...	
Total Economy only: Adjustment for FISIM (if FISIM is not distributed to uses)	...	1806.3	2866.6	3084.5	3137.3	4731.8	5334.6	5687.7	6403.0	6945.6	7405.5	
Gross capital formation	...	29435.1	24946.4	23604.5	27173.5	30631.4	31783.7	42290.6	39795.8	57535.2	62314.2	
Gross fixed capital formation	...	29802.2	24720.7	23996.6	28360.7	31818.6	33504.3	39613.8	43959.5	51862.4	64949.4	
Changes in inventories	...	-367.1	225.7	-392.0	-1187.2	-1187.2	-1720.6	2676.9	-4163.7	5672.9	-2635.2	
Acquisitions less disposals of valuables	...	...	...	...	...	...	...	...	...	...	...	

[a] Discrepancy between components and total.

Table 2.3 Output, gross value added, and fixed assets by industries at current prices (ISIC Rev. 3) Agriculture, hunting, forestry; fishing (A+B)

Series 300: 1993 SNA, Metical, Western calendar year **Data in millions**

	2001	2002	2003	2004	2005	2006	2007	2008	2009	2010	2011	2012
Series		**300**										
Output, at basic prices		28654.4	32852.4	36422.8	41951.2	51853.2	60085.4	72779.3	80314.3	100149.8	114365.6	
Less: Intermediate consumption, at purchaser's prices		3365.7	4720.4	4544.2	4829.3	6000.4	7256.4	8411.7	8662.9	10920.6	10051.3	
Equals: VALUE ADDED, GROSS, at basic prices		25288.8	28132.0	31878.6	37121.9	45852.9	52829.0	64367.6	71651.4	89229.2	104314.2	
Compensation of employees		1495.6	1529.6	2641.8	1866.7	2333.7	2616.1	2638.0	3002.4	3860.8	3891.4	
Taxes on production and imports, less Subsidies		...	...	...	...	...	...	...	...	...	...	
OPERATING SURPLUS, GROSS		...	...	...	...	...	...	...	...	...	...	

	2001	2002	2003	2004	2005	2006	2007	2008	2009	2010	2011	2012
Series		**300**										
MIXED INCOME, GROSS		...	...	...	...	...	...	...	...	...	...	
Gross capital formation		...	...	...	...	...	...	...	...	...	...	

Table 2.3 Output, gross value added, and fixed assets by industries at current prices (ISIC Rev. 3) Agriculture, hunting and related service activities (01)

Series 300: 1993 SNA, Metical, Western calendar year

Data in millions

	2001	2002	2003	2004	2005	2006	2007	2008	2009	2010	2011	2012
Series		**300**										
Output, at basic prices		22222.6	25699.2	28546.5	32949.6	41243.6	47268.2	57435.4	64687.2	82162.7	95290.5	
Less: Intermediate consumption, at purchaser's prices		1611.7	2940.1	2675.1	2947.2	3713.4	4208.6	5109.1	5427.9	6849.9	5562.4	
Equals: VALUE ADDED, GROSS, at basic prices		20610.9	22759.0	25871.4	30002.4	37530.1	43059.7	52326.3	59259.3	75312.8	89728.1	
Compensation of employees		675.6	704.1	1790.7	991.1	1332.2	1338.8	1630.8	1798.0	2625.1	2308.2	
Taxes on production and imports, less Subsidies		...	...	...	...	...	...	...	...	...	...	
OPERATING SURPLUS, GROSS		...	...	...	...	...	...	...	...	...	...	
MIXED INCOME, GROSS		...	...	...	...	...	...	...	...	...	...	
Gross capital formation		...	...	...	...	...	...	...	...	...	...	

Table 2.3 Output, gross value added, and fixed assets by industries at current prices (ISIC Rev. 3) Forestry, logging and related service activities (02)

Series 300: 1993 SNA, Metical, Western calendar year

Data in millions

	2001	2002	2003	2004	2005	2006	2007	2008	2009	2010	2011	2012
Series		**300**										
Output, at basic prices		2991.6	3349.6	3880.2	4992.0	5700.7	6590.3	8030.1	8421.4	8930.1	9146.8	
Less: Intermediate consumption, at purchaser's prices		94.6	102.2	117.1	156.5	188.4	219.0	247.5	256.1	268.6	275.3	
Equals: VALUE ADDED, GROSS, at basic prices		2896.9	3247.5	3763.1	4835.4	5512.3	6371.3	7782.6	8165.3	8661.5	8871.5	
Compensation of employees		59.6	64.3	73.7	98.5	118.6	137.8	155.8	161.2	169.1	173.3	
Taxes on production and imports, less Subsidies		...	...	...	...	...	...	...	...	...	...	
OPERATING SURPLUS, GROSS		...	...	...	...	...	...	...	...	...	...	
MIXED INCOME, GROSS		...	...	...	...	...	...	...	...	...	...	
Gross capital formation		...	...	...	...	...	...	...	...	...	...	

Table 2.3 Output, gross value added, and fixed assets by industries at current prices (ISIC Rev. 3) Fishing (B)

Series 300: 1993 SNA, Metical, Western calendar year **Data in millions**

	2001	2002	2003	2004	2005	2006	2007	2008	2009	2010	2011	2012
Series		**300**										
Output, at basic prices		3440.3	3803.6	3996.2	4009.6	4908.9	6226.9	7313.7	7205.7	9057.0	9928.2	
Less: Intermediate consumption, at purchaser's prices		1659.4	1678.1	1752.0	1725.6	2098.5	2828.9	3055.1	2978.8	3802.1	4213.7	
Equals: VALUE ADDED, GROSS, at basic prices		1780.9	2125.5	2244.2	2284.0	2810.4	3398.0	4258.7	4226.8	5254.8	5714.5	
Compensation of employees		760.4	761.2	777.5	777.1	882.8	1139.5	851.4	1043.2	1066.6	1409.9	
Taxes on production and imports, less Subsidies		...	...	...	...	...	...	...	...	...	...	
OPERATING SURPLUS, GROSS		...	...	...	...	...	...	...	...	...	...	
MIXED INCOME, GROSS		...	...	...	...	...	...	...	...	...	...	
Gross capital formation		...	...	...	...	...	...	...	...	...	...	

Table 2.3 Output, gross value added, and fixed assets by industries at current prices (ISIC Rev. 3) Mining and quarrying (C)

Series 300: 1993 SNA, Metical, Western calendar year **Data in millions**

	2001	2002	2003	2004	2005	2006	2007	2008	2009	2010	2011	2012
Series		**300**										
Output, at basic prices		903.9	1134.5	2171.5	3093.0	4996.7	5613.5	7072.7	7386.5	8213.4	10003.6	
Less: Intermediate consumption, at purchaser's prices		381.0	477.3	1010.7	1616.7	2659.5	2646.2	3754.4	3820.0	4139.1	4917.5	
Equals: VALUE ADDED, GROSS, at basic prices		522.9	657.2	1160.8	1476.4	2337.1	2967.3	3318.3	3566.4	4074.3	5086.0	
Compensation of employees		20.5	30.4	172.1	473.3	826.3	874.7	1156.6	1077.9	1058.7	1187.5	
Taxes on production and imports, less Subsidies		...	...	...	...	...	...	...	...	...	...	
OPERATING SURPLUS, GROSS		...	...	...	...	...	...	...	...	...	...	
MIXED INCOME, GROSS		...	...	...	...	...	...	...	...	...	...	
Gross capital formation		...	...	...	...	...	...	...	...	...	...	

Table 2.3 Output, gross value added, and fixed assets by industries at current prices (ISIC Rev. 3) Manufacturing (D)

Series 300: 1993 SNA, Metical, Western calendar year **Data in millions**

	2001	2002	2003	2004	2005	2006	2007	2008	2009	2010	2011	2012
Series		**300**										
Output, at basic prices		30471.5	38964.2	48113.1	50172.1	59303.3	65753.0	74537.0	77420.4	89228.9	94327.2	
Less: Intermediate consumption, at purchaser's prices		17849.0	22328.3	27584.3	28868.1	32948.2	36383.2	40926.9	42971.1	49348.4	51159.2	
Equals: VALUE ADDED, GROSS, at basic prices		12622.6	16635.9	20528.8	21304.1	26355.2	29369.8	33610.1	34449.3	39880.5	43168.0	
Compensation of employees		2622.1	2855.1	3854.1	3998.7	4531.0	4724.8	5356.8	5434.5	6222.7	6489.6	

	2001	2002	2003	2004	2005	2006	2007	2008	2009	2010	2011	2012
Series		**300**										
Taxes on production and imports, less Subsidies		...	...	...	...	...	...	...	...	...	...	
OPERATING SURPLUS, GROSS		...	...	...	...	...	...	...	...	...	...	
MIXED INCOME, GROSS		...	...	...	...	...	...	...	...	...	...	
Gross capital formation		...	...	...	...	...	...	...	...	...	...	

Table 2.3 Output, gross value added, and fixed assets by industries at current prices (ISIC Rev. 3) Electricity, gas and water supply (E)

Series 300: 1993 SNA, Metical, Western calendar year

Data in millions

	2001	2002	2003	2004	2005	2006	2007	2008	2009	2010	2011	2012
Series		**300**										
Output, at basic prices		5852.0	6876.4	9142.6	11136.8	13737.2	16154.5	15289.4	17199.6	19905.1	21822.7	
Less: Intermediate consumption, at purchaser's prices		1437.3	1805.1	2783.9	3531.1	4158.3	5089.0	5245.0	5614.0	6628.5	6994.6	
Equals: VALUE ADDED, GROSS, at basic prices		4414.8	5071.2	6358.7	7605.6	9579.0	11065.5	10044.4	11585.6	13276.6	14828.1	
Compensation of employees		800.1	955.4	1026.0	1145.1	1259.4	1416.5	1485.2	1461.3	1623.9	1647.3	
Taxes on production and imports, less Subsidies		...	...	...	...	...	...	...	...	...	...	
OPERATING SURPLUS, GROSS		...	...	...	...	...	...	...	...	...	...	
MIXED INCOME, GROSS		...	...	...	...	...	...	...	...	...	...	
Gross capital formation		...	...	...	...	...	...	...	...	...	...	

Table 2.3 Output, gross value added, and fixed assets by industries at current prices (ISIC Rev. 3) Construction (F)

Series 300: 1993 SNA, Metical, Western calendar year

Data in millions

	2001	2002	2003	2004	2005	2006	2007	2008	2009	2010	2011	2012
Series		**300**										
Output, at basic prices		9848.7	11567.9	10513.1	12371.8	14293.1	16229.0	18983.5	20880.2	24445.1	28077.6	
Less: Intermediate consumption, at purchaser's prices		6366.7	7741.8	6677.9	7865.1	9079.8	10292.5	12123.5	13347.2	15590.0	17740.9	
Equals: VALUE ADDED, GROSS, at basic prices		3481.9	3826.1	3835.2	4506.8	5213.3	5936.4	6860.0	7533.0	8855.1	10336.8	
Compensation of employees		1695.6	1754.0	1776.6	2103.0	2448.0	2802.7	3243.0	3568.2	4217.4	4962.3	
Taxes on production and imports, less Subsidies		...	...	...	...	...	...	...	...	...	...	
OPERATING SURPLUS, GROSS		...	...	...	...	...	...	...	...	...	...	
MIXED INCOME, GROSS		...	...	...	...	...	...	...	...	...	...	
Gross capital formation		...	...	...	...	...	...	...	...	...	...	

Table 2.3 Output, gross value added, and fixed assets by industries at current prices (ISIC Rev. 3) Wholesale retail trade, repair of motor vehicles, motorcycles, etc.; hotels and restaurants (G+H)

Series 300: 1993 SNA, Metical, Western calendar year — **Data in millions**

	2001	2002	2003	2004	2005	2006	2007	2008	2009	2010	2011	2012
Series		**300**										
Output, at basic prices		21757.2	25545.8	29091.0	31673.2	36947.9	39914.3	48112.0	55314.4	64847.3	73916.1	
Less: Intermediate consumption, at purchaser's prices		9570.6	12900.8	15379.2	11318.1	11368.6	7863.7	10874.4	13676.3	13610.6	11230.3	
Equals: VALUE ADDED, GROSS, at basic prices		12186.5	12645.0	13711.8	20355.1	25579.3	32050.6	37237.6	41638.1	51236.7	62685.8	
Compensation of employees		3825.0	4963.0	5551.4	6158.3	7189.2	7758.3	9405.8	10791.7	12607.5	15223.0	
Taxes on production and imports, less Subsidies		...	...	...	...	...	...	...	...	...	...	
OPERATING SURPLUS, GROSS		...	...	...	...	...	10846.0	...	...	...	...	
MIXED INCOME, GROSS		...	...	...	...	...	6130.0	...	...	...	...	
Less: Consumption of fixed capital		...	...	...	...	...	...	...	...	...	...	
OPERATING SURPLUS, NET		...	...	...	...	...	10846.0	...	...	...	...	
MIXED INCOME, NET		...	...	...	...	...	6130.0	...	...	...	...	
Gross capital formation		...	...	...	...	...	...	...	...	...	...	

Table 2.3 Output, gross value added, and fixed assets by industries at current prices (ISIC Rev. 3) Transport, storage and communications (I)

Series 300: 1993 SNA, Metical, Western calendar year — **Data in millions**

	2001	2002	2003	2004	2005	2006	2007	2008	2009	2010	2011	2012
Series		**300**										
Output, at basic prices		21893.8	23199.7	27639.1	32911.5	37152.2	42672.3	49958.5	55802.5	64856.8	75251.8	
Less: Intermediate consumption, at purchaser's prices		11998.0	12778.6	15224.0	18351.9	20694.2	23661.3	27778.6	30889.1	36190.8	42221.6	
Equals: VALUE ADDED, GROSS, at basic prices		9895.8	10421.0	12415.1	14559.6	16458.0	19011.0	22179.9	24913.4	28665.9	33030.2	
Compensation of employees		3166.0	2969.4	4311.7	5096.0	5786.3	6490.5	7657.8	8679.2	9966.8	11551.2	
Taxes on production and imports, less Subsidies		...	...	...	...	...	...	...	...	...	...	
OPERATING SURPLUS, GROSS		...	...	...	...	...	...	...	...	...	...	
MIXED INCOME, GROSS		...	...	...	...	...	...	...	...	...	...	
Gross capital formation		...	...	...	...	...	...	...	...	...	...	

Table 2.3 Output, gross value added, and fixed assets by industries at current prices (ISIC Rev. 3) Financial intermediation; real estate, renting and business activities (J+K)

Series 300: 1993 SNA, Metical, Western calendar year **Data in millions**

	2001	2002	2003	2004	2005	2006	2007	2008	2009	2010	2011	2012
Series		**300**										
Output, at basic prices		18898.7	19406.9	21332.9	25939.9	28338.3	30193.4	32941.7	34555.4	37501.5	40198.4	
Less: Intermediate consumption, at purchaser's prices		4919.6	5087.3	5612.6	7884.0	9020.5	8880.2	9925.2	9793.3	10584.0	11659.4	
Equals: VALUE ADDED, GROSS, at basic prices		4919.6	14319.5	15720.4	18055.9	19317.8	21313.2	23016.5	24762.1	26917.6	28539.1	
Compensation of employees		3075.2	3407.7	2797.7	3890.2	3570.2	4360.5	4578.4	6327.3	7638.8	9470.8	
Taxes on production and imports, less Subsidies		...	...	...	...	...	...	...	...	...	...	
OPERATING SURPLUS, GROSS		...	...	...	...	...	...	...	...	...	...	
MIXED INCOME, GROSS		...	...	...	...	...	...	...	...	...	...	
Gross capital formation		...	...	...	...	...	...	...	...	...	...	

Table 2.3 Output, gross value added, and fixed assets by industries at current prices (ISIC Rev. 3) Public administration and defense; compulsory social security (L)

Series 300: 1993 SNA, Metical, Western calendar year **Data in millions**

	2001	2002	2003	2004	2005	2006	2007	2008	2009	2010	2011	2012
Series		**300**										
Output, at basic prices		8388.8	9977.1	11867.3	13031.5	14166.7	15364.9	18221.7	20918.8	28525.4	31548.7	
Less: Intermediate consumption, at purchaser's prices		4683.1	5842.8	6862.1	7372.6	7527.1	8014.7	9702.8	11070.6	17275.7	18128.2	
Equals: VALUE ADDED, GROSS, at basic prices		3705.7	4134.4	5005.2	5658.9	6639.6	7350.2	8518.9	9848.2	11249.6	13420.5	
Compensation of employees		3680.2	4101.0	4968.7	5618.6	6599.1	7282.4	8449.2	9776.6	11173.1	13338.6	
Taxes on production and imports, less Subsidies		...	...	...	...	...	...	...	...	...	...	
OPERATING SURPLUS, GROSS		...	...	...	...	...	...	...	...	...	...	
MIXED INCOME, GROSS		...	...	...	...	...	...	...	...	...	...	
Gross capital formation		...	...	...	...	...	...	...	...	...	...	

Table 2.3 Output, gross value added, and fixed assets by industries at current prices (ISIC Rev. 3) Education; health and social work; other community, social and personal services (M+N+O)

Series 300: 1993 SNA, Metical, Western calendar year **Data in millions**

	2001	2002	2003	2004	2005	2006	2007	2008	2009	2010	2011	2012
Series		**300**										
Output, at basic prices		10551.9	11508.9	13514.4	15141.2	17608.6	19509.8	22890.3	25378.7	28901.6	32274.6	
Less: Intermediate consumption, at purchaser's prices		4483.5	4693.7	5334.4	5550.0	6276.3	6176.0	7184.5	7450.5	8773.5	10314.2	
Equals: VALUE ADDED, GROSS, at basic prices		6068.4	6815.2	8180.0	9591.3	11332.3	13333.8	15705.8	17928.2	20128.1	21960.4	
Compensation of employees		5679.2	6310.4	7615.7	8114.4	10533.3	11244.1	14703.0	16925.7	18939.4	20865.7	

	2001	2002	2003	2004	2005	2006	2007	2008	2009	2010	2011	2012
Series		**300**										
Taxes on production and imports, less Subsidies		...	...	...	...	...	...	...	...	...	...	
OPERATING SURPLUS, GROSS		...	...	...	...	...	...	...	...	...	...	
MIXED INCOME, GROSS		...	...	...	...	...	...	...	...	...	...	
Gross capital formation		...	...	...	...	...	...	...	...	...	...	

Table 2.3 Output, gross value added, and fixed assets by industries at current prices (ISIC Rev. 3) Private households with employed persons (P)

Series 300: 1993 SNA, Metical, Western calendar year — **Data in millions**

	2001	2002	2003	2004	2005	2006	2007	2008	2009	2010	2011	2012
Series		**300**										
Output, at basic prices		536.8	549.6	579.6	593.5	651.4	760.1	806.0	849.0	906.2	987.4	
Less: Intermediate consumption, at purchaser's prices		...	...	...	...	...	...	...	...	...	...	
Equals: VALUE ADDED, GROSS, at basic prices		536.8	549.6	579.6	593.5	651.4	760.1	806.0	849.0	906.2	987.4	
Compensation of employees		536.8	549.6	579.6	593.5	651.4	760.1	806.0	849.0	906.2	987.4	
Taxes on production and imports, less Subsidies		...	...	...	...	...	...	...	...	...	...	
OPERATING SURPLUS, GROSS		...	...	...	...	...	...	...	...	...	...	
MIXED INCOME, GROSS		...	...	...	...	...	...	...	...	...	...	
Gross capital formation		...	...	...	...	...	...	...	...	...	...	

Table 3.1 Government final consumption expenditure by function at current prices

Series 300: 1993 SNA, Metical, Western calendar year — **Data in millions**

	2001	2002	2003	2004	2005	2006	2007	2008	2009	2010	2011	2012
Series	**300**											
General public services	...	7753.6	9074.7	11200.0	12112.1	13222.3	14179.5	16911.8	19389.4	26872.9	29499.5	
Defence	...	...	...	...	...	...	...	...	...	...	...	
Public order and safety	...	112.5	212.2	233.4	256.8	258.6	431.7	443.1	454.6	486.5	520.5	
Economic affairs	...	...	...	...	...	...	...	...	...	...	...	
Environment protection	...	...	...	...	...	...	...	...	...	...	...	
Housing and community amenities	...	...	...	...	...	...	...	...	...	...	...	
Health	...	1237.2	1225.7	1602.1	1818.9	2121.9	2393.7	3107.8	3655.5	4244.0	4878.0	
Recreation, culture and religion	...	...	...	...	...	...	...	...	...	...	...	
Education	...	3135.6	3635.1	4686.0	5466.8	6616.7	7723.7	9219.6	10857.4	12403.9	13986.3	
Social protection	...	7.7	7.9	7.8	8.3	9.1	9.5	9.1	10.9	13.2	11.9	
Equals: General government final consumption expenditure	11381.3	12246.6	14155.7	17729.4	19662.9	22228.5	24738.1	29691.4	34367.8	44020.4	48896.3	

Table 3.2 Individual consumption expenditure of households, NPISHs, and general government at current prices

Series 300: 1993 SNA, Metical, Western calendar year **Data in millions**

	2001	2002	2003	2004	2005	2006	2007	2008	2009	2010	2011	2012
Series		**300**										
Individual consumption expenditure of households												
Equals: Household final consumption expenditure in domestic market		...	...	...	...	...	...	...	...	...	...	
Plus: Direct purchases abroad by residents		...	...	...	...	...	...	...	...	...	...	
Less: Direct purchases in domestic market by non-residents		...	...	...	...	...	...	...	...	...	...	
Equals: Household final consumption expenditure		...	...	...	...	...	...	...	...	...	...	
Individual consumption expenditure of non-profit institutions serving households (NPISHs)												
Equals: NPISHs final consumption expenditure		4077.1	4428.0	5267.1	5267.1	5967.2	6203.2	7050.2	7221.0	8128.0	9326.7	
Individual consumption expenditure of general government												
Equals: Individual consumption expenditure of general government		4380.4	4868.8	7294.0	7294.0	8747.6	10127.0	12366.1	14523.8	16661.1	18876.2	
Equals: Total actual individual consumption		...	...	...	...	...	...	...	...	...	...	

Table 4.1 Total Economy (S.1)

Series 300: 1993 SNA, Metical, Western calendar year **Data in millions**

	2001	2002	2003	2004	2005	2006	2007	2008	2009	2010	2011	2012
Series		**300**										
I. Production account - Resources												
Output, at basic prices (otherwise, please specify)		157757.7	181583.5	210387.4	238015.7	279048.6	312250.1	361592.0	396019.7	467481.0	522773.6	
Less: Financial intermediation services indirectly measured (only to be deducted if FISIM is not distributed to uses)		1806.3	2866.6	3084.5	3137.3	4731.8	5334.6	5687.7	6403.0	6945.6	7405.5	
Plus: Taxes less Subsidies on products		8582.1	10632.0	12378.7	14015.3	15657.6	16991.3	20380.4	23891.3	27487.0	34383.5	
Plus: Taxes on products		8582.1	10632.0	12378.7	14015.3	15657.6	16991.3	20380.4	23891.3	27487.0	34383.5	
Less: Subsidies on products		...	...	...	...	...	...	...	...	...	...	
I. Production account - Uses												
Intermediate consumption, at purchaser's prices		65054.5	78376.2	91013.3	97186.8	109733.0	116263.4	135926.9	147294.9	173061.2	184417.2	
GROSS DOMESTIC PRODUCT		99479.0	110972.8	128668.3	151706.9	180241.7	207643.6	240357.7	266213.1	314961.2	365334.4	
Less: Consumption of fixed capital		...	...	...	...	...	...	...	...	...	...	
NET DOMESTIC PRODUCT		...	...	...	...	...	...	...	...	...	...	
II.1.1 Generation of income account - Resources												
GROSS DOMESTIC PRODUCT		99479.0	110972.8	128668.3	151706.9	180241.7	207643.6	240357.7	266213.1	314961.2	365334.4	
II.1.1 Generation of income account - Uses												
Compensation of employees		26596.4	29425.7	35295.3	39057.9	45727.9	50330.6	59479.8	67893.9	78215.3	89614.8	
Taxes on production and imports, less Subsidies		...	...	...	...	...	...	...	...	...	...	
Taxes on production and imports		...	...	...	...	...	...	...	...	...	...	

	2001	2002	2003	2004	2005	2006	2007	2008	2009	2010	2011	2012
Series		**300**										
Taxes on products		...	...	...	...	...	...	...	...	...	...	
Other taxes on production		...	...	...	...	...	...	...	...	...	...	
Less: Subsidies		...	...	...	...	...	...	...	...	...	...	
Subsidies on products		...	...	...	...	...	...	...	...	...	...	
Other subsidies on production		...	...	...	...	...	...	...	...	...	...	
OPERATING SURPLUS, GROSS		...	...	...	...	...	...	...	...	...	...	
MIXED INCOME, GROSS		...	...	...	...	...	...	...	...	...	...	

Table 4.2 Rest of the world (S.2)

Series 300: 1993 SNA, Metical, Western calendar year — **Data in millions**

	2001	2002	2003	2004	2005	2006	2007	2008	2009	2010	2011	2012
Series		**300**										
V.I External account of goods and services - Resources												
Imports of goods and services		54775.5	55747.0	60887.6	67340.0	70861.1	79422.9	96775.4	96119.1	115354.2	137619.2	
Imports of goods		43520.1	43773.5	50209.3	54802.0	57558.4	62267.4	74502.6	73848.9	94051.8	113503.7	
Imports of services		11255.4	11973.5	10678.3	12538.1	13302.7	17155.6	22272.7	22270.2	21302.4	24115.5	
V.I External account of goods and services - Uses												
Exports of goods and services		24816.0	29136.7	38340.8	46212.6	54861.3	64146.2	72638.3	73799.4	87686.7	99117.7	
Exports of goods		17646.0	22911.9	33172.0	40163.9	48470.5	55847.4	61833.7	62973.8	75876.1	87771.9	
Exports of services		7169.9	6224.9	5168.9	6048.7	6390.8	8298.7	10804.6	10825.6	11810.6	11345.8	
EXTERNAL BALANCE OF GOODS AND SERVICES		29959.6	26610.2	22546.8	21127.4	15999.8	15276.8	24137.1	22319.7	27667.5	38501.5	
V.II External account of primary income and current transfers - Resources												
EXTERNAL BALANCE OF GOODS AND SERVICES		29959.6	26610.2	22546.8	21127.4	15999.8	15276.8	24137.1	22319.7	27667.5	38501.5	
Compensation of employees		778.2	210.1	207.6	220.1	303.2	420.8	1514.0	1597.7	2493.0	2965.9	
Taxes on production and imports, less Subsidies		...	...	...	...	...	...	...	...	...	...	
Taxes on production and imports		...	...	...	...	...	...	...	...	...	...	
Taxes on products		...	...	...	...	...	...	...	...	...	...	
Other taxes on production		...	...	...	...	...	...	...	...	...	...	
Less: Subsidies		...	...	...	...	...	...	...	...	...	...	
Subsidies on products		...	...	...	...	...	...	...	...	...	...	
Other subsidies on production		...	...	...	...	...	...	...	...	...	...	
Property income		14415.9	4957.9	7976.9	9916.0	17565.4	16763.8	18839.7	16619.3	7241.2	10215.0	
Current taxes on income, wealth, etc.		...	...	...	...	...	...	...	...	...	...	
Social contributions		...	...	...	...	...	...	...	...	...	...	
Social benefits other than social transfers in kind		...	...	...	...	...	...	...	...	...	...	
Other current transfers		4393.0	1634.7	1252.7	2279.6	1569.2	1346.9	2778.9	4496.4	5220.6	7047.8	
Adjustment for the change in net equity of households on pension funds		...	...	...	...	...	...	...	...	...	...	

	2001	2002	2003	2004	2005	2006	2007	2008	2009	2010	2011	2012
Series		**300**										
V.II External account of primary income and current transfers - Uses												
Compensation of employees		547.0	922.2	1216.0	1092.2	1379.9	1470.9	3735.1	4716.1	5549.0	5792.7	
Taxes on production and imports, less Subsidies		...	...	...	...	...	...	...	...	...	...	
Taxes on production and imports		...	...	...	...	...	...	...	...	...	...	
Taxes on products		...	...	...	...	...	...	...	...	...	...	
Other taxes on production		...	...	...	...	...	...	...	...	...	...	
Less: Subsidies		...	...	...	...	...	...	...	...	...	...	
Subsidies on products		...	...	...	...	...	...	...	...	...	...	
Other subsidies on production		...	...	...	...	...	...	...	...	...	...	
Property income		662.1	382.7	440.1	1047.9	2086.8	2718.4	2066.2	2353.1	2127.1	1139.6	
Current taxes on income and wealth, etc.		...	...	...	...	...	...	...	...	...	...	
Social contributions		...	...	...	...	...	...	...	...	...	...	
Social benefits other than social transfers in kind		...	...	...	...	...	...	...	...	...	...	
Other current transfers		...	...	...	...	...	...	...	...	...	...	
Adjustment for the change in net equity of households on pension funds		...	...	...	...	...	...	...	...	...	...	
CURRENT EXTERNAL BALANCE		...	...	...	...	...	...	...	...	...	...	

Table 4.4 Financial Corporations (S.12)

Series 300: 1993 SNA, Metical, Western calendar year

Data in millions

	2001	2002	2003	2004	2005	2006	2007	2008	2009	2010	2011	2012
Series								**300**				
I. Production account - Resources												
Output, at basic prices (otherwise, please specify)								14689.6	15163.1	17139.5	18499.2	
I. Production account - Uses												
Intermediate consumption, at purchaser's prices								4486.7	2986.4	5317.0	6984.3	
VALUE ADDED GROSS, at basic prices								10202.9	12176.7	11822.5	11514.9	
Less: Consumption of fixed capital								862.9	1124.1	1407.0	1224.1	
VALUE ADDED NET, at basic prices								9340.0	11052.6	10415.6	10290.8	
II.1.1 Generation of income account - Resources												
VALUE ADDED GROSS, at basic prices								10202.9	12176.7	11822.5	11514.9	
II.1.1 Generation of income account - Uses												
Compensation of employees								3504.5	5238.4	8346.6	8346.6	
Other taxes less Other subsidies on production								68.9	122.8	132.8	184.9	
Other taxes on production								68.9	122.8	132.8	184.9	
Less: Other subsidies on production								...	...	...	...	
OPERATING SURPLUS, GROSS								6629.5	6815.5	3343.1	2983.4	

	2001	2002	2003	2004	2005	2006	2007	2008	2009	2010	2011	2012
Series								**300**				
II.1.2 Allocation of primary income account - Resources												
OPERATING SURPLUS, GROSS								6629.5	6815.5	3343.1	2983.4	
Property income								5776.7	3067.1	2952.4	2743.9	
Adjustment entry for FISIM (balanced by Nominal Sector)								5687.7	6403.0	6945.6	7405.5	
II.1.2 Allocation of primary income account - Uses												
Property income								...	...	...	...	
BALANCE OF PRIMARY INCOMES								...	...	...	...	

Table 4.5 General Government (S.13)

Series 300: 1993 SNA, Metical, Western calendar year

Data in millions

	2001	2002	2003	2004	2005	2006	2007	2008	2009	2010	2011	2012
Series		**300**										
I. Production account - Resources												
Output, at basic prices (otherwise, please specify)		13014.9	15151.8	18452.5	20631.6	23263.5	25947.9	31062.0	35998.1	45832.6	51196.3	
I. Production account - Uses												
Intermediate consumption, at purchaser's prices		5930.1	7028.3	8411.8	9546.8	9159.3	9562.5	11407.2	12882.8	19727.5	21482.8	
VALUE ADDED GROSS, at basic prices		7084.8	8123.5	10040.7	11084.9	14104.2	16385.4	19654.8	23115.3	26105.1	29713.5	
Less: Consumption of fixed capital		25.0	33.2	36.5	40.1	40.4	67.6	69.7	71.5	76.5	81.8	
VALUE ADDED NET, at basic prices		7059.8	8090.3	10004.3	11044.7	14063.8	16317.8	19585.2	23043.8	26028.6	29631.7	
II.1.1 Generation of income account - Resources												
VALUE ADDED GROSS, at basic prices		7084.8	8123.5	10040.7	11084.9	14104.2	16385.4	19654.8	23115.3	26105.1	29713.5	
II.1.1 Generation of income account - Uses												
Compensation of employees		7059.3	8057.2	10004.2	11044.6	14063.7	16317.7	19585.1	23043.8	26028.6	29631.6	
Other taxes less Other subsidies on production		0.4	33.1	0.0	0.1	0.1	0.1	0.1	0.1	0.1	0.1	
Other taxes on production		0.4	33.1	0.0	0.1	0.1	0.1	0.1	0.1	0.1	0.1	
Less: Other subsidies on production		...	...	...	...	...	...	...	...	...	...	
OPERATING SURPLUS, GROSS		25.0	33.2	36.5	40.1	40.4	67.6	69.7	71.5	76.5	81.8	
II.1.2 Allocation of primary income account - Resources												
OPERATING SURPLUS, GROSS		25.0	33.2	36.5	40.1	40.4	67.6	69.7	71.5	76.5	81.8	
Taxes on production and imports, less Subsidies [a]		10631.7	11976.7	12927.4	14628.5	16745.9	18169.4	21340.0	25874.3	39778.0	47350.9	
Taxes on production and imports		10525.0	11831.3	12736.0	14527.2	16433.6	17791.7	20945.2	25436.1	38031.9	45058.8	
Taxes on products		8582.0	10632.2	12151.5	13977.1	15752.0	17006.5	20144.1	24584.1	35633.2	42362.6	
Other taxes on production		1943.0	1199.1	584.5	550.1	681.7	785.2	801.1	852.1	2398.7	2696.2	
Less: Subsidies		106.6	145.5	191.4	101.3	312.3	377.6	394.8	438.2	1746.2	2292.1	
Subsidies on products		...	...	...	...	...	...	...	...	...	...	
Other subsidies on production		106.6	145.5	191.4	101.3	312.3	377.6	394.8	438.2	1746.2	2292.1	
Property income		995.7	1021.8	1046.0	-68.6	-141.6	-7.1	-789.8	-141.6	821.9	1697.2	

	2001	2002	2003	2004	2005	2006	2007	2008	2009	2010	2011	2012
Series		**300**										
	II.1.2 Allocation of primary income account - Uses											
Property income		...	...	...	...	...	...	...	...	...	...	
BALANCE OF PRIMARY INCOMES		...	...	...	...	...	...	...	...	...	...	

[a] Discrepancy between components and total.

Myanmar

Source

Reply to the United Nations national accounts questionnaire from the Planning Department, Ministry of Planning and Finance, Naypyitaw. The official estimates and descriptions are published annually in "National Income of Myanmar" and "Review of the Financial Economic and Social Conditions", by the same Department.

General

The estimates shown in the following tables have been prepared in accordance with the United Nations System of National Accounts 1968 (1968 SNA) so far as the existing data would permit. When the scope and coverage differ for conceptual or statistical reasons from the definitions and classifications recommended in SNA, a footnote is indicated to the relevant tables.

Table 1.1 Gross domestic product by expenditures at current prices

Series 30: 1968 SNA, Kyat, Fiscal year beginning 1 April — **Data in billions**

	2001	2002	2003	2004	2005	2006	2007	2008	2009	2010	2011	2012
Series	**30**											
Expenditures of the gross domestic product												
Final consumption expenditure	3139.9	5049.9	6865.7	7965.5	10682.3	14291.4	19861.4	24141.3	28543.0	31463.3	34270.8	
Gross capital formation	410.6	570.8	850.5	1108.7	1620.8	2306.4	3455.7	4570.6	6394.6	9221.1	13505.4	
Gross fixed capital formation	413.2	551.7	850.1	1069.0	1563.8	2282.4	3390.5	4599.8	6436.2	9115.1	13499.4	
Changes in inventories	-2.6	19.1	0.4	39.7	57.0	24.0	65.2	-29.2	-41.6	106.1	6.0	
Acquisitions less disposals of valuables	...	...	...	...	...	...	...	...	...	...	...	
Exports of goods and services	16.4	19.4	13.7	16.0	19.8	29.3	34.0	32.2	38.7	46.1	7140.4	
Less: Imports of goods and services	18.4	14.9	13.4	11.3	11.5	16.8	18.4	24.9	22.8	35.5	7300.3	
Plus: Statistical discrepancy	...	...	...	...	-24.6	242.5	3.4	514.1	-1059.4	-848.3	-3337.4	
Equals: GROSS DOMESTIC PRODUCT	3548.5	5625.3	7716.6	9078.9	12286.8	16852.8	23336.1	29233.3	33894.0	39846.7	44278.9	

Table 1.2 Gross domestic product by expenditures at constant prices

Series 30: 1968 SNA, Kyat, Fiscal year beginning 1 April — **Data in billions**

	2001	2002	2003	2004	2005	2006	2007	2008	2009	2010	2011	2012
Series	**30**											
Base year	**2000**					**2005**				**2010**		
Expenditures of the gross domestic product												
Final consumption expenditure	2518.3	2821.1	3175.0	3546.7	4064.6							
						11781.8	13242.7	14169.1	15969.9	16496.2		
										31463.3	32683.8	
Gross capital formation	326.7	359.6	448.6	564.7	732.8							
						1968.1	2523.5	2949.0	3973.2	5346.3		
										9221.1	12880.1	
Gross fixed capital formation	328.7	348.9	449.0	546.5	708.5							
						1947.8	2478.4	2965.2	3997.4	5290.8		
										9115.1	12874.3	
Changes in inventories	-2.0	10.7	-0.4	18.3	24.3							
						20.3	45.0	-16.1	-24.1	55.5		
										106.1	5.7	
Acquisitions less disposals of valuables	...	...	...	...	...							
						...	...	...	...	...		
										...	...	

	2001	2002	2003	2004	2005	2006	2007	2008	2009	2010	2011	2012
Series	**30**											
Base year	**2000**					**2005**				**2010**		
Exports of goods and services	14.0	17.3	12.9	15.0	15.5							
						24.8	24.0	20.3	19.9	22.1		
										46.1	6723.6	
Less: Imports of goods and services	16.7	13.8	11.6	9.7	9.9							
						16.4	17.6	23.1	18.8	28.5		
										35.5	6073.5	
Plus: Statistical discrepancy	...	...	...	...	-127.8							
						135.0	-213.2	39.8	-979.3	-944.8		
										-848.3	-3985.5	
Equals: GROSS DOMESTIC PRODUCT	2842.3	3184.1	3624.9	4116.6	4675.2							
						13893.4	15559.4	17155.1	18964.9	20891.3		
										39846.7	42228.5	

Table 1.3 Relations among product, income, savings, and net lending aggregates

Series 30: 1968 SNA, Kyat, Fiscal year beginning 1 April

Data in billions

	2001	2002	2003	2004	2005	2006	2007	2008	2009	2010	2011	2012
Series	**30**											
GROSS DOMESTIC PRODUCT	3548.5	5625.3	7716.6	9078.9	12286.8	16852.8	23336.1	29233.3	33894.0	39846.7	44278.9	
Plus: Compensation of employees - from and to the rest of the world, net	...	...	...	...	...	...	...	...	...	...	...	
Plus: Property income - from and to the rest of the world, net	-0.2	-0.0	-0.0	-0.1	-0.0	0.3	0.5	0.3	-0.2	-0.2	-7.0	
Sum of Compensation of employees and property income - from and to the rest of the world, net	-0.2	-0.0	-0.0	-0.1	-0.0	0.3	0.5	0.3	-0.2	-0.2	-7.0	
Plus: Taxes less subsidies on production and imports - from and to the rest of the world, net	...	...	...	...	...	...	...	...	...	...	...	
Equals: GROSS NATIONAL INCOME	3548.3	5625.2	7716.6	9078.8	12286.8	16853.0	23336.6	29233.6	33893.8	39846.5	44271.8	
Plus: Current transfers - from and to the rest of the world, net	...	...	...	...	...	...	...	...	...	...	...	
Equals: GROSS NATIONAL DISPOSABLE INCOME	3548.3	5625.2	7716.6	9078.8	12286.8	16853.0	23336.6	29233.6	33893.8	39846.5	44271.8	
Less: Final consumption expenditure / Actual final consumption	3139.9	5049.9	6865.7	7965.5	10682.3	14291.4	19861.4	24141.3	28543.0	31463.3	34270.8	
Equals: SAVING, GROSS	408.3	575.3	850.9	1113.3	1604.5	2561.7	3475.1	5092.4	5350.8	8383.2	10001.1	
Plus: Capital transfers - from and to the rest of the world, net	...	...	...	...	...	...	...	...	...	...	...	
Less: Gross capital formation	410.6	570.8	850.5	1108.7	1620.8	2306.4	3455.7	4570.6	6394.6	9221.1	13505.4	
Less: Acquisitions less disposals of non-produced non-financial assets	...	...	...	...	...	...	...	...	...	...	...	
Equals: NET LENDING (+) / NET BORROWING (-) OF THE NATION	-2.2	4.5	0.3	4.6	-16.3	255.2	19.5	521.8	-1043.8	-837.9	-3504.3	
Net values: Gross National Income / Gross National Disposable Income / Saving Gross less Consumption of fixed capital												
Less: Consumption of fixed capital	49.8	62.7	80.2	103.6	135.4	179.6	242.5	330.0	472.8	663.8	946.7	
Equals: NET NATIONAL INCOME	3498.5	5562.5	7636.4	8975.3	12151.4	16673.4	23094.1	28903.6	33421.0	39182.6	43325.2	
Equals: NET NATIONAL DISPOSABLE INCOME	3498.5	5562.5	7636.4	8975.3	12151.4	16673.4	23094.1	28903.6	33421.0	39182.6	43325.2	
Equals: SAVING, NET	358.5	512.6	770.6	1009.8	1469.1	2382.1	3232.7	4762.4	4878.0	7719.4	9054.4	

Table 2.1 Value added by industries at current prices (ISIC Rev. 3)

Series 30: 1968 SNA, Kyat, Fiscal year beginning 1 April **Data in billions**

		2001	2002	2003	2004	2005	2006	2007	2008	2009	2010	2011	2012
Series		**30**											
Industries													
Agriculture, hunting, forestry; fishing	a	2025.1	3067.4	3906.2	4372.9	5736.4	7401.6	10109.8	11773.7	12916.4	14632.6	15198.8	
Agriculture, hunting, forestry	a	1758.0	2738.5	3489.2	3742.6	4795.3	6157.8	8343.6	9351.8	10089.8	11240.5	11460.5	
Agriculture, hunting and related service activities	a	1740.2	2717.6	3462.0	3714.7	4718.5	6068.0	8246.2	9236.0	9956.2	11082.2	11282.2	
Forestry, logging and related service activities	a	17.8	20.8	27.3	27.9	76.8	89.8	97.4	115.9	133.6	158.3	178.3	
Fishing	a	267.1	328.9	416.9	630.3	941.1	1243.8	1766.2	2421.9	2826.5	3392.0	3738.2	
Mining and quarrying	b	17.3	25.2	34.6	57.5	89.5	121.9	205.3	254.4	331.4	369.7	539.9	
Manufacturing	c	277.8	516.2	756.2	1051.6	1572.9	2358.1	3473.9	4917.3	6127.6	7897.0	9117.1	
Electricity, gas and water supply	d	3.2	4.7	6.0	20.0	27.7	110.0	189.8	218.2	337.7	422.5	479.0	
Construction	a	77.1	185.6	303.5	356.8	461.7	652.0	893.7	1236.1	1518.3	1839.3	2165.8	
Wholesale, retail trade, repair of motor vehicles, motorcycles and personal and households goods; hotels and restaurants	e	858.1	1326.6	1743.6	2021.3	2667.2	3550.8	4915.2	6175.1	6887.3	7959.9	8879.4	
Transport, storage and communications	a	191.8	358.1	776.7	936.6	1412.2	2020.0	2781.7	3731.5	4586.6	5161.3	6165.2	
Land transport; transport via pipelines, water transport; air transport; Supporting and auxiliary transport activities; activities of travel agencies	a	182.6	335.1	726.9	855.4	1283.0	1848.6	2534.9	3476.5	4278.8	4837.7	5766.6	
Post and telecommunications	a	9.2	23.0	49.8	81.2	129.1	171.4	246.8	255.0	307.8	323.5	398.7	
Financial intermediation; real estate, renting and business activities	f	3.3	4.8	5.3	6.7	10.2	14.4	16.9	20.9	27.4	37.7	51.6	
Financial intermediation	a	3.3	4.8	5.3	6.7	10.2	14.4	16.9	20.9	27.4	37.7	51.6	
Real estate, renting and business activities		...	...	...	...	...	...	...	...	...	...	...	
Public administration and defence; compulsory social security	g	44.7	50.7	64.7	103.9	112.6	340.9	371.3	399.7	551.7	788.2	800.4	
Education; health and social work; other community, social and personal services	h	50.1	86.0	119.8	151.6	196.5	283.1	378.5	506.4	609.8	738.5	881.7	
Private households with employed persons		...	...	...	...	...	...	...	...	...	...	...	
Equals: VALUE ADDED, GROSS, in basic prices	i	3548.5	5625.3	7716.6	9078.9	12286.8	16852.8	23336.1	29233.3	33894.0	39846.7	44278.9	
Less: Financial intermediation services indirectly measured (FISIM)		...	...	...	...	...	...	...	...	...	...	...	
Plus: Taxes less Subsidies on products		...	...	...	...	...	...	...	...	...	...	...	
Equals: GROSS DOMESTIC PRODUCT		3548.5	5625.3	7716.6	9078.9	12286.8	16852.8	23336.1	29233.3	33894.0	39846.7	44278.9	

[a] At producers' prices.
[b] At producers' prices. Includes Energy
[c] At producers' prices. Refers to Processing and Manufacturing
[d] At producers' prices. Refers to Electric Power
[e] At producers' prices. Refers to Trade Value
[f] At producers' prices. Refers to Financial Institutions
[g] At producers' prices. Refers to Social and Administrative Services
[h] At producers' prices. Refers to rental and other services
[i] Value Added refers to GDP.

Table 2.2 Value added by industries at constant prices (ISIC Rev. 3)

Series 30: 1968 SNA, Kyat, Fiscal year beginning 1 April

Data in billions

		2001	2002	2003	2004	2005	2006	2007	2008	2009	2010	2011	2012
Series		**30**											
Base year		**2000**					**2005**				**2010**		
Industries													
Agriculture, hunting, forestry; fishing	a	1588.3	1684.1	1881.2	2087.8	2340.0							
	a						6290.3	6789.9	7170.2	7569.8	7923.7		
	a										14632.6	14727.7	
Agriculture, hunting, forestry	b	1361.5	1425.4	1557.1	1713.5	1895.4							
	a						5234.5	5619.3	5881.4	6122.7	6367.6		
	a										11240.5	11086.0	
Agriculture, hunting and related service activities	a	1346.0	1409.0	1539.7	1697.1	1878.3							
	a						5151.3	5535.8	5799.8	6043.6	6288.3		
	a										11082.2	10915.1	
Forestry, logging and related service activities	a	15.4	16.4	17.4	16.4	17.1							
	a						83.2	83.5	81.6	79.1	79.3		
	a										158.3	170.9	
Fishing	a	226.8	258.6	324.1	374.3	444.6							
	a						1055.9	1170.6	1288.8	1447.2	1556.1		
	a										3392.0	3641.8	
Mining and quarrying	c	15.8	20.5	22.3	25.2	33.2							
	c						98.8	104.8	119.6	133.3	143.4		
	c										369.7	403.9	
Manufacturing	d	222.8	286.8	350.0	436.4	532.2							
	d						1919.9	2326.0	2750.7	3269.5	3938.8		
	d										7897.0	8739.2	
Electricity, gas and water supply	e	3.2	3.9	4.5	4.8	5.7							
	e						30.5	31.9	35.5	41.8	53.5		
	e										422.5	441.9	
Construction	a	59.6	95.6	114.5	130.0	144.3							
	a						531.9	623.4	736.3	837.6	942.7		
	a										1839.3	2004.8	
Wholesale, retail trade, repair of motor vehicles, motorcycles and personal and household goods; hotels and restaurants	f	678.9	750.3	849.9	958.7	1074.3							
	f						3009.8	3357.6	3680.2	4043.0	4460.0		
	f										7959.9	8393.9	
Transport, storage and communications	a	184.1	237.4	284.0	337.2	392.4							
	a						1652.8	1922.9	2211.7	2569.9	2879.6		
	a										5161.3	5811.0	
Land transport; transport via piplines, water transport; air transport; Supporting and auxiliary transport activities; activities of travel agencies	a	174.9	220.0	265.9	309.8	359.9							
	a						1488.7	1703.7	1988.6	2304.2	2597.7		
	a										4837.7	5410.5	
Post and telecommunications	a	9.2	17.5	18.1	27.4	32.5							
	a						164.2	219.2	223.1	265.7	281.9		
	a										323.5	400.5	
Financial intermediation, real estate, renting and business activities	g	3.3	4.8	5.3	6.7	10.2							
	g						12.0	14.2	17.6	23.0	31.6		
	g										37.7	54.9	
Financial intermediation	a	3.3	4.8	5.3	6.7	10.2							
	a						12.0	14.2	17.6	23.0	31.6		
	a										37.7	54.9	
Real estate, renting and business activities		...	...	...	...	...							
							...	...	...	...	...		
											...	...	
Public administration and defence; compulsory social security	h	44.7	50.7	56.2	64.5	69.9							
	h						122.7	133.7	143.9	154.3	154.9		
	h										788.2	800.4	
Education; health and social work; other community, social and personal services	i	41.6	50.0	57.0	65.3	73.1							
	i						224.6	255.0	289.5	322.8	363.0		
	i										738.5	850.7	
Private households with employed persons		...	...	...	...	...							
							...	...	...	...	...		
											...	...	
Equals: VALUE ADDED, GROSS, in basic prices	j	2842.3	3184.1	3624.9	4116.6	4675.2							
	j						13893.4	15559.4	17155.1	18964.9	20891.3		
	j										39846.7	42228.5	
Less: Financial intermediation services indirectly measured (FISIM)		...	...	...	...	...							
							...	...	...	...	...		
											...	...	

	2001	2002	2003	2004	2005	2006	2007	2008	2009	2010	2011	2012
Series	**30**											
Base year	**2000**					**2005**				**2010**		
Plus: Taxes less Subsidies on products	...	...	...	...	...	...	...	...	...	... ...	...	
Equals: GROSS DOMESTIC PRODUCT	2842.3	3184.1	3624.9	4116.6	4675.2	13893.4	15559.4	17155.1	18964.9	20891.3 39846.7	42228.5	

[a] At producers' prices.
[b] At producers' prices. Includes livestock.
[c] At producers' prices. Includes Energy
[d] At producers' prices. Refers to Processing and Manufacturing
[e] At producers' prices. Refers to Electric Power
[f] At producers' prices. Refers to Trade Value
[g] At producers' prices. Refers to Financial Institutions
[h] At producers' prices. Refers to Social and Administrative Services
[i] At producers' prices. Refers to rental and other services
[j] Value Added refers to GDP.

Table 2.3 Output, gross value added, and fixed assets by industries at current prices (ISIC Rev. 3) Total Economy

Series 30: 1968 SNA, Kyat, Fiscal year beginning 1 April **Data in billions**

		2001	2002	2003	2004	2005	2006	2007	2008	2009	2010	2011	2012
Series		**30**											
Output, at basic prices	a	6371.4	10659.9	14522.8	18228.4	24055.8	33919.0	48096.2	63121.0	76273.9	92710.9	105091.1	
Less: Intermediate consumption, at purchaser's prices		2823.0	5034.7	6806.2	9149.5	11769.0	17066.3	24760.1	33887.7	42379.8	52864.2	60812.2	
Equals: VALUE ADDED, GROSS, at basic prices	b	3548.5	5625.3	7716.6	9078.9	12286.8	16852.8	23336.1	29233.3	33894.0	39846.7	44278.9	
Compensation of employees		...	...	...	...	...	...	...	...	...	...	...	
Taxes on production and imports, less Subsidies		...	...	...	...	...	...	...	...	...	...	...	
OPERATING SURPLUS, GROSS		...	...	...	...	...	...	...	...	...	...	...	
MIXED INCOME, GROSS		...	...	...	...	...	...	...	...	...	...	...	
Gross capital formation		...	...	...	...	...	...	...	...	...	...	...	

[a] At producers' prices.
[b] Value Added refers to GDP.

Table 2.3 Output, gross value added, and fixed assets by industries at current prices (ISIC Rev. 3) Agriculture, hunting, forestry; fishing (A+B)

Series 30: 1968 SNA, Kyat, Fiscal year beginning 1 April **Data in billions**

		2001	2002	2003	2004	2005	2006	2007	2008	2009	2010	2011	2012
Series		**30**											
Output, at basic prices	a	2571.3	3857.9	4872.8	5476.4	7305.1	9405.8	13038.7	15402.0	16948.2	19368.5	20205.3	
Less: Intermediate consumption, at purchaser's prices		546.3	790.6	966.6	1103.5	1568.8	2004.2	2928.8	3628.3	4031.9	4735.9	5006.6	
Equals: VALUE ADDED, GROSS, at basic prices	a	2025.1	3067.4	3906.2	4372.9	5736.4	7401.6	10109.8	11773.7	12916.4	14632.6	15198.8	
Compensation of employees		...	...	...	...	...	...	...	...	...	...	...	
Taxes on production and imports, less Subsidies		...	...	...	...	...	...	...	...	...	...	...	
OPERATING SURPLUS, GROSS		...	...	...	...	...	...	...	...	...	...	...	

	2001	2002	2003	2004	2005	2006	2007	2008	2009	2010	2011	2012
Series	**30**											
MIXED INCOME, GROSS	...	...	...	...	...	...	...	...	...	...	...	
Gross capital formation	...	...	...	...	...	...	...	...	...	...	...	

[a] At producers' prices.

Table 2.3 Output, gross value added, and fixed assets by industries at current prices (ISIC Rev. 3) Agriculture, hunting and related service activities (01)

Series 30: 1968 SNA, Kyat, Fiscal year beginning 1 April

Data in billions

	2001	2002	2003	2004	2005	2006	2007	2008	2009	2010	2011	2012
Series	**30**											
Output, at basic prices [a]	2113.3	3295.8	4152.4	4422.4	5650.5	7295.6	10010.5	11267.3	12110.9	13518.7	13751.4	
Less: Intermediate consumption, at purchaser's prices	373.1	578.2	690.4	707.7	932.0	1227.6	1764.3	2031.3	2154.7	2436.5	2469.1	
Equals: VALUE ADDED, GROSS, at basic prices [a]	1740.2	2717.6	3462.0	3714.7	4718.5	6068.0	8246.2	9236.0	9956.2	11082.2	11282.2	
Compensation of employees	...	...	...	...	...	...	...	...	...	...	...	
Taxes on production and imports, less Subsidies	...	...	...	...	...	...	...	...	...	...	...	
OPERATING SURPLUS, GROSS	...	...	...	...	...	...	...	...	...	...	...	
MIXED INCOME, GROSS	...	...	...	...	...	...	...	...	...	...	...	
Gross capital formation	...	...	...	...	...	...	...	...	...	...	...	

[a] At producers' prices.

Table 2.3 Output, gross value added, and fixed assets by industries at current prices (ISIC Rev. 3) Forestry, logging and related service activities (02)

Series 30: 1968 SNA, Kyat, Fiscal year beginning 1 April

Data in billions

	2001	2002	2003	2004	2005	2006	2007	2008	2009	2010	2011	2012
Series	**30**											
Output, at basic prices [a]	28.0	32.9	42.0	44.4	122.0	145.1	159.3	189.8	219.0	259.6	292.9	
Less: Intermediate consumption, at purchaser's prices	10.2	12.0	14.7	16.5	45.1	55.4	61.9	73.9	85.4	101.3	114.6	
Equals: VALUE ADDED, GROSS, at basic prices [a]	17.8	20.8	27.3	27.9	76.8	89.8	97.4	115.9	133.6	158.3	178.3	
Compensation of employees	...	...	...	...	...	...	...	...	...	...	...	
Taxes on production and imports, less Subsidies	...	...	...	...	...	...	...	...	...	...	...	
OPERATING SURPLUS, GROSS	...	...	...	...	...	...	...	...	...	...	...	
MIXED INCOME, GROSS	...	...	...	...	...	...	...	...	...	...	...	
Gross capital formation	...	...	...	...	...	...	...	...	...	...	...	

[a] At producers' prices.

Table 2.3 Output, gross value added, and fixed assets by industries at current prices (ISIC Rev. 3) Fishing (B)

Series 30: 1968 SNA, Kyat, Fiscal year beginning 1 April

Data in billions

		2001	2002	2003	2004	2005	2006	2007	2008	2009	2010	2011	2012
Series		**30**											
Output, at basic prices	a	430.0	529.3	678.5	1009.6	1532.7	1965.1	2868.9	3944.9	4618.3	5590.2	6161.0	
Less: Intermediate consumption, at purchaser's prices		163.0	200.4	261.5	379.3	591.7	721.3	1102.7	1523.0	1791.7	2198.2	2422.8	
Equals: VALUE ADDED, GROSS, at basic prices	a	267.1	328.9	416.9	630.3	941.1	1243.8	1766.2	2421.9	2826.5	3392.0	3738.2	
Compensation of employees		...	...	...	...	...	...	...	...	...	...	...	
Taxes on production and imports, less Subsidies		...	...	...	...	...	...	...	...	...	...	...	
OPERATING SURPLUS, GROSS		...	...	...	...	...	...	...	...	...	...	...	
MIXED INCOME, GROSS		...	...	...	...	...	...	...	...	...	...	...	
Gross capital formation		...	...	...	...	...	...	...	...	...	...	...	

[a] At producers' prices.

Table 2.3 Output, gross value added, and fixed assets by industries at current prices (ISIC Rev. 3) Mining and quarrying (C)

Series 30: 1968 SNA, Kyat, Fiscal year beginning 1 April

Data in billions

		2001	2002	2003	2004	2005	2006	2007	2008	2009	2010	2011	2012
Series		**30**											
Output, at basic prices	a	31.0	50.1	62.1	95.3	151.4	213.1	352.9	439.9	579.5	633.4	917.1	
Less: Intermediate consumption, at purchaser's prices		13.7	24.9	27.5	37.8	61.9	91.2	147.6	185.5	248.2	263.7	377.2	
Equals: VALUE ADDED, GROSS, at basic prices	b	17.3	25.2	34.6	57.5	89.5	121.9	205.3	254.4	331.4	369.7	539.9	
Compensation of employees		...	...	...	...	...	...	...	...	...	...	...	
Taxes on production and imports, less Subsidies		...	...	...	...	...	...	...	...	...	...	...	
OPERATING SURPLUS, GROSS		...	...	...	...	...	...	...	...	...	...	...	
MIXED INCOME, GROSS		...	...	...	...	...	...	...	...	...	...	...	
Gross capital formation		...	...	...	...	...	...	...	...	...	...	...	

[a] At producers' prices.
[b] At producers' prices. Includes Energy

Table 2.3 Output, gross value added, and fixed assets by industries at current prices (ISIC Rev. 3) Manufacturing (D)

Series 30: 1968 SNA, Kyat, Fiscal year beginning 1 April

Data in billions

		2001	2002	2003	2004	2005	2006	2007	2008	2009	2010	2011	2012
Series		**30**											
Output, at basic prices	a	1867.2	3574.7	4881.7	7088.7	9125.1	13561.2	19895.3	28151.5	36110.7	46217.9	53572.0	
Less: Intermediate consumption, at purchaser's prices		1589.4	3058.5	4125.5	6037.0	7552.2	11203.1	16421.4	23234.2	29983.2	38320.9	44454.9	
Equals: VALUE ADDED, GROSS, at basic prices	b	277.8	516.2	756.2	1051.6	1572.9	2358.1	3473.9	4917.3	6127.6	7897.0	9117.1	

	2001	2002	2003	2004	2005	2006	2007	2008	2009	2010	2011	2012
Series	**30**											
Compensation of employees	...	...	...	...	...	...	...	...	...	...	...	
Taxes on production and imports, less Subsidies	...	...	...	...	...	...	...	...	...	...	...	
OPERATING SURPLUS, GROSS	...	...	...	...	...	...	...	...	...	...	...	
MIXED INCOME, GROSS	...	...	...	...	...	...	...	...	...	...	...	
Gross capital formation	...	...	...	...	...	...	...	...	...	...	...	

[a] At producers' prices.
[b] At producers' prices. Refers to Processing and Manufacturing

Table 2.3 Output, gross value added, and fixed assets by industries at current prices (ISIC Rev. 3) Electricity, gas and water supply (E)

Series 30: 1968 SNA, Kyat, Fiscal year beginning 1 April **Data in billions**

	2001	2002	2003	2004	2005	2006	2007	2008	2009	2010	2011	2012
Series	**30**											
Output, at basic prices [a]	16.8	24.6	32.3	36.4	48.7	241.2	487.9	560.0	688.1	870.8	965.7	
Less: Intermediate consumption, at purchaser's prices	13.6	20.0	26.3	16.4	21.0	131.2	298.1	341.8	350.4	448.3	486.8	
Equals: VALUE ADDED, GROSS, at basic prices [b]	3.2	4.7	6.0	20.0	27.7	110.0	189.8	218.2	337.7	422.5	479.0	
Compensation of employees	...	...	...	...	...	...	...	...	...	...	...	
Taxes on production and imports, less Subsidies	...	...	...	...	...	...	...	...	...	...	...	
OPERATING SURPLUS, GROSS	...	...	...	...	...	...	...	...	...	...	...	
MIXED INCOME, GROSS	...	...	...	...	...	...	...	...	...	...	...	
Gross capital formation	...	...	...	...	...	...	...	...	...	...	...	

[a] At producers' prices.
[b] At producers' prices. Refers to Electric Power

Table 2.3 Output, gross value added, and fixed assets by industries at current prices (ISIC Rev. 3) Construction (F)

Series 30: 1968 SNA, Kyat, Fiscal year beginning 1 April **Data in billions**

	2001	2002	2003	2004	2005	2006	2007	2008	2009	2010	2011	2012
Series	**30**											
Output, at basic prices [a]	248.9	485.0	748.3	908.3	1179.0	1565.2	2144.0	2958.8	3643.8	4397.6	5197.6	
Less: Intermediate consumption, at purchaser's prices	171.8	299.4	444.8	551.5	717.4	913.3	1250.4	1722.7	2125.5	2558.3	3031.8	
Equals: VALUE ADDED, GROSS, at basic prices [a]	77.1	185.6	303.5	356.8	461.7	652.0	893.7	1236.1	1518.3	1839.3	2165.8	
Compensation of employees	...	...	...	...	...	...	...	...	...	...	...	
Taxes on production and imports, less Subsidies	...	...	...	...	...	...	...	...	...	...	...	
OPERATING SURPLUS, GROSS	...	...	...	...	...	...	...	...	...	...	...	
MIXED INCOME, GROSS	...	...	...	...	...	...	...	...	...	...	...	
Gross capital formation	...	...	...	...	...	...	...	...	...	...	...	

[a] At producers' prices.

Table 2.3 Output, gross value added, and fixed assets by industries at current prices (ISIC Rev. 3) Wholesale retail trade, repair of motor vehicles, motorcycles, etc.; hotels and restaurants (G+H)

Series 30: 1968 SNA, Kyat, Fiscal year beginning 1 April — **Data in billions**

		2001	2002	2003	2004	2005	2006	2007	2008	2009	2010	2011	2012
Series		**30**											
Output, at basic prices	a	1163.3	1868.5	2455.8	2815.0	3716.9	4950.6	6923.7	8740.5	9759.9	11361.8	12691.5	
Less: Intermediate consumption, at purchaser's prices		305.3	541.9	712.2	793.8	1049.7	1399.8	2008.6	2565.4	2872.6	3401.9	3812.1	
Equals: VALUE ADDED, GROSS, at basic prices	b	858.1	1326.6	1743.6	2021.3	2667.2	3550.8	4915.2	6175.1	6887.3	7959.9	8879.4	
Compensation of employees		...	...	...	...	...	...	...	...	...	...	...	
Taxes on production and imports, less Subsidies		...	...	...	...	...	...	...	...	...	...	...	
OPERATING SURPLUS, GROSS		...	...	...	...	...	...	...	...	...	...	...	
MIXED INCOME, GROSS		...	...	...	...	...	...	...	...	...	...	...	
Gross capital formation		...	...	...	...	...	...	...	...	...	...	...	

[a] At producers' prices.
[b] At producers' prices. Refers to Trade Value

Table 2.3 Output, gross value added, and fixed assets by industries at current prices (ISIC Rev. 3) Transport, storage and communications (I)

Series 30: 1968 SNA, Kyat, Fiscal year beginning 1 April — **Data in billions**

		2001	2002	2003	2004	2005	2006	2007	2008	2009	2010	2011	2012
Series		**30**											
Output, at basic prices	a	267.6	510.6	1091.7	1295.6	1919.6	2760.8	3824.0	5174.6	6336.5	7189.8	8575.3	
Less: Intermediate consumption, at purchaser's prices		75.8	152.5	315.0	359.0	507.4	740.8	1042.3	1443.1	1749.9	2028.5	2410.1	
Equals: VALUE ADDED, GROSS, at basic prices	a	191.8	358.1	776.7	936.6	1412.2	2020.0	2781.7	3731.5	4586.6	5161.3	6165.2	
Compensation of employees		...	...	...	...	...	...	...	...	...	...	...	
Taxes on production and imports, less Subsidies		...	...	...	...	...	...	...	...	...	...	...	
OPERATING SURPLUS, GROSS		...	...	...	...	...	...	...	...	...	...	...	
MIXED INCOME, GROSS		...	...	...	...	...	...	...	...	...	...	...	
Gross capital formation		...	...	...	...	...	...	...	...	...	...	...	

[a] At producers' prices.

Table 2.3 Output, gross value added, and fixed assets by industries at current prices (ISIC Rev. 3) Financial intermediation; real estate, renting and business activities (J+K)

Series 30: 1968 SNA, Kyat, Fiscal year beginning 1 April — **Data in billions**

		2001	2002	2003	2004	2005	2006	2007	2008	2009	2010	2011	2012
Series		**30**											
Output, at basic prices	a	21.7	34.0	37.8	47.5	67.2	94.5	111.9	138.6	182.8	250.8	341.5	
Less: Intermediate consumption, at purchaser's prices		18.4	29.2	32.5	40.8	57.0	80.1	94.9	117.6	155.4	213.0	289.9	
Equals: VALUE ADDED, GROSS, at basic prices	b	3.3	4.8	5.3	6.7	10.2	14.4	16.9	20.9	27.4	37.7	51.6	

	2001	2002	2003	2004	2005	2006	2007	2008	2009	2010	2011	2012
Series	**30**											
Compensation of employees	...	...	...	...	...	...	...	...	...	...	...	
Taxes on production and imports, less Subsidies	...	...	...	...	...	...	...	...	...	...	...	
OPERATING SURPLUS, GROSS	...	...	...	...	...	...	...	...	...	...	...	
MIXED INCOME, GROSS	...	...	...	...	...	...	...	...	...	...	...	
Gross capital formation	...	...	...	...	...	...	...	...	...	...	...	

[a] At producers' prices.
[b] At producers' prices. Refers to Financial Institutions

Table 2.3 Output, gross value added, and fixed assets by industries at current prices (ISIC Rev. 3) Public administration and defense; compulsory social security (L)

Series 30: 1968 SNA, Kyat, Fiscal year beginning 1 April — **Data in billions**

	2001	2002	2003	2004	2005	2006	2007	2008	2009	2010	2011	2012
Series	**30**											
Output, at basic prices [a]	111.5	127.1	162.6	261.7	283.9	753.4	819.9	885.7	1217.7	1442.3	1459.8	
Less: Intermediate consumption, at purchaser's prices	66.8	76.4	97.8	157.9	171.3	412.5	448.6	486.0	666.0	654.1	659.5	
Equals: VALUE ADDED, GROSS, at basic prices [b]	44.7	50.7	64.7	103.9	112.6	340.9	371.3	399.7	551.7	788.2	800.4	
Compensation of employees	...	...	...	...	...	...	...	...	...	...	...	
Taxes on production and imports, less Subsidies	...	...	...	...	...	...	...	...	...	...	...	
OPERATING SURPLUS, GROSS	...	...	...	...	...	...	...	...	...	...	...	
MIXED INCOME, GROSS	...	...	...	...	...	...	...	...	...	...	...	
Gross capital formation	...	...	...	...	...	...	...	...	...	...	...	

[a] At producers' prices.
[b] At producers' prices. Refers to Social and Administrative Services

Table 2.3 Output, gross value added, and fixed assets by industries at current prices (ISIC Rev. 3) Education; health and social work; other community, social and personal services (M+N+O)

Series 30: 1968 SNA, Kyat, Fiscal year beginning 1 April — **Data in billions**

	2001	2002	2003	2004	2005	2006	2007	2008	2009	2010	2011	2012
Series	**30**											
Output, at basic prices [a]	72.0	127.3	177.8	203.5	258.7	373.3	497.9	669.5	806.6	978.1	1165.1	
Less: Intermediate consumption, at purchaser's prices	21.9	41.4	58.0	51.8	62.2	90.1	119.4	163.1	196.8	239.6	283.5	
Equals: VALUE ADDED, GROSS, at basic prices [b]	50.1	86.0	119.8	151.6	196.5	283.1	378.5	506.4	609.8	738.5	881.7	
Compensation of employees	...	...	...	...	...	...	...	...	...	...	...	
Taxes on production and imports, less Subsidies	...	...	...	...	...	...	...	...	...	...	...	
OPERATING SURPLUS, GROSS	...	...	...	...	...	...	...	...	...	...	...	
MIXED INCOME, GROSS	...	...	...	...	...	...	...	...	...	...	...	
Gross capital formation	...	...	...	...	...	...	...	...	...	...	...	

[a] At producers' prices.
[b] At producers' prices. Refers to rental and other services

Namibia

Source

The compilation of national accounts statistics in Namibia is undertaken by the Central Bureau of Statistics department at the National Planning Commission Secretariat. Before 1995 and since 1982, the Ministry of Finance compiled the national accounts and published them in the economic review. The Ministry of finance compiled the national accounts according to the 1968 SNA. In 1995 the Central Bureau of Statistics published the national accounts statistics applying the 1993 SNA. These annual estimates are released twice a year in the national accounts publication. The first release is the preliminary estimates which are released in March of each year and the second release is the revised estimates released in August of each year. The latest publication is the national accounts 2000-2007. The national accounts publication is disseminated in hard copies and electronic format posted at the National Planning Commission Secretariat website www.npc.gov.na. Since 2001 the Central Bureau of Statistics has been compiling provisionally quarterly GDP at constant 1995 prices. The provisional quarterly GDP is released with a time lag of 90 days after the reference quarter and is published in the quarterly bulletin of the Bank of Namibia. The quarterly bulletin is available at the Bank of Namibia website www.bon.com.na. The latest national accounts estimates are based on 2004 base year.

General

The estimates provided to UNSD are compiled in accordance with the concepts and definitions of System of National Accounts 1993 (1993 SNA) since 1995. The Central Bureau of Statistics has published a manual which consists three volumes:

Volume I provides an overview of the 1993 SNA, of concepts and definitions pertaining to main areas of the national accounts.

Volume II describes the scope of Namibia's national accounts, the sources and methods used in compiling them as well as concepts and definitions connected to specific areas.

Volume III is a documentation of the comprehensive computerized system used in the compilation of Namibia's national accounts, System of National Accounts on a PC (SNAPC)

National accounts are intended to describe the development and structure of the economy in a changing reality. Hence the sources and methods must be continually upgraded and adapted to these changes. New economic activities may be launched, new statistical data may be available, sources that are presently used may disappear, etc. In summary there are three kinds of revisions of annual estimates:

• More or less major revisions of time series backwards at regular interval. This should be done every five years in connection with the change of base year.
• Revision of the two latest years are revised once or twice a year because of certain data that becomes available only more than a year after the end of the reference period
• Occasional revisions of estimates of certain variables for more than the latest two years. The aim should be avoid this kind of revisions, but cannot be excluded.

Namibia's national accounts is compiled on calendar year basis (January – December) and the current base year is 2004.

Methodology:

Overview of GDP Compilation
In Namibia, GDP is compiled by the production and expenditure approach. The two approach in theory results in exactly the same figure for GDP; however, in practice this is not the case in Namibia. The reason is imperfections and gaps in the data sources. The production approach is considered the more reliable method and determines GDP both at current and constant prices. The discrepancy between the two approaches is shown in the published tables. Part of the discrepancy is due to the fact that the estimates of changes in inventories are incomplete; estimates are made only for livestock and ores and minerals.

Expenditure Approach
Final consumption expenditure by household includes all expenditure in cash and in kind, by households on goods and services for the purpose of consumption. This item is estimated independently. The commodity flow estimates has provided the method for the estimates have provided the method for the estimates of household consumption. A prerequisite for this estimate has been the availability of detailed import statistics classified by end use categories.

The 2003/04 Household Income and Expenditure Survey provide data for a benchmark estimate for 2004 with disaggregating according to COICOP. While the consumer price index is used on a detailed level to calculate constant prices.

Final consumption expenditure by non profit institutions serving households. The output of such institution, defined as the total cost of producing it, is by definition consumed by the NPISH. Output, at both current and constant prices is obtained through a link to the worksheet for community, social and personal services under GDP by activity. No sales and fees or expenditure on social benefits in kind is recorded at present, thus final consumption expenditure is equal to output.

Final consumption expenditure by government, the estimate is based on accounting records of the central government and estimates for local government are from the accounts of the local authorities. Consumption of fixed capital, both at current and constant prices is obtained through links to the workbook on capital for producers of government services. Intermediate consumption and sales and fees at constant prices, both for central and local government, is computed by using the Namibia consumer price index as a deflator. Compensation of employees in central government at constant prices is calculated by projection with volume indicator based on employment data (number of filled posts according to the State Revenue Fund in the budget document). The implicit deflator for central and local government is used to calculate compensation of employees at constant prices for local government.

Gross fixed capital formation (GFCF) is estimated by type of asset, by industry and by ownership in the Namibian national accounts. The estimates are based on state budget book, data of imports of capital goods and surveys. Constant prices are derived at by deflation by appropriate price indices.

Changes in inventories are calculated for Mining and quarrying, Agriculture and Manufacturing industries only and are based on data on quantities produced and sold, and average unit prices.

Import and export of goods and services are based on Trade statistics and Balance of payments.

Production Approach
Agriculture estimates are compiled and disseminated separately for the commercial farming and subsistence farming. Hunting and forestry are minor activities. Agriculture in Namibia is dominated by livestock with crop and vegetable playing a subordinate role due to climatic condition. Most of the market output of live animals and

animal products is calculated within the commodity flow framework. Basic data on production and unit prices are obtained from the Agronomic Board Namibia, Meat Board of Namibia, Karakul Board, Namibia Agricultural Union and crop assessment report from the Ministry of agriculture. Intermediate consumption, is an assumption that is based on constant prices and reflated using the relevant South African Price Index. For none-market output the main source for basic data is the 2003/04 Household budget survey, which is used for the benchmark estimate.

Fishing is calculated within the commodity flow framework. Data of quantities and unit prices are obtained from the Ministry of Fisheries. The ministry also provides data on Intermediate consumption for the calculation of the value added.

Mining and quarrying is calculated within the commodity flow framework. Data of quantities and unit prices obtained form the Ministry of Mines and Energy. Intermediate consumption is obtained through direct surveys of mining companies. A single indicator deflation approach is used to derive constant price value added.

Manufacturing is calculated within the commodity flow framework. Annual survey of establishments is the source data for this sector. South Africa PPI is used as a deflator.

Electricity Data is sourced from local authorities, the electricity generation company (NAMPOWER) and electricity distribution establishments. Volumes of electricity index and the South African production index are used as deflators. (Double deflation is used).

Water supply Data is obtained from the local authorities and a sole parastatal (NAMWATER) responsible for bulk water supply. Quantitative data is used as a volume indicator for estimates at constant prices of both for output and intermediate consumption.

Construction the source of data is the government administrative records, local authorities and annual surveys to establishments. For traditional houses the source is the population census. Intermediate consumption assumptions are based on 1980 input-output tables.

Wholesale and retail trade, repairs, Output is measured as trade margins realized on goods purchased for resale. Intermediate consumption consists of only goods and services needed to run the trading establishments. Annual survey is the source data and CPI used as a deflator.

Hotels and Restaurant is obtained from annual surveys of respective establishments. Information of output and intermediate consumption is extracted from these surveys. CPI for food and accommodation is used to deflate the current prices estimates to constant prices.

Transport and communication Data is obtained from annual surveys from the respective establishments. The constant prices estimates are obtained by deflation with CPI and PPI South Africa manufacturing.

Financial intermediation Data is obtained from the Central bank, Insurance institutions and Postal banking services. Implicit index used as a deflator for FISIM and CPI for other output.

Government services both for Local and Central government (Data is obtained from annual survey of local authorities and government budget book). Implicit price index from central government is used to deflate local government current price estimates.

The Namibia's national accounts also have estimates for industries such as Real estate and business services; community, social and personal activities. The source data is the household budget surveys, population census, annual economic surveys local authorities and central government. The CPI is used as a deflator.

Table 1.1 Gross domestic product by expenditures at current prices

Series 200: 1993 SNA, Namibia dollar, Western calendar year — **Data in millions**

	2001	2002	2003	2004	2005	2006	2007	2008	2009	2010	2011	2012
Series	**200**											
	Expenditures of the gross domestic product											
Final consumption expenditure	26720.5	29409.2	32817.0	34609.3	35639.8	40867.0	48470.0	56797.2	65345.2	72058.0	78839.6	88538.3
Household final consumption expenditure [a]	19750.4	21796.0	24533.8	25916.1	26734.3	30340.5	35636.0	41945.9	48068.6	52470.9	55914.2	62065.2
NPISHs final consumption expenditure	1422.2	1598.7	1792.9	1925.0	1592.1	1581.9	1717.9	2136.0	2544.0	2436.3	2506.0	2818.7
General government final consumption expenditure	6970.1	7613.2	8283.1	8693.2	8905.5	10526.5	12834.0	14851.3	17276.6	19587.1	22925.4	26473.1
Gross capital formation	6815.0	6562.2	7225.5	8137.6	9092.1	12027.6	14728.1	18499.4	16777.1	17074.7	18147.3	22309.7
Gross fixed capital formation	6391.2	7065.9	7120.7	7921.9	8594.4	11685.8	14695.9	17837.5	16608.8	18377.7	19291.4	22153.2
Changes in inventories	423.8	-503.6	104.8	215.7	497.7	341.7	32.1	661.4	168.2	-1303.0	-1144.1	156.5
Acquisitions less disposals of valuables	...	...	...	...	...	...	...	...	...	...	...	...
Exports of goods and services	12574.0	16299.0	16185.0	16991.0	18678.0	24565.6	31496.4	38776.8	35511.4	38476.5	40926.9	44759.1
Exports of goods	10414.0	13453.0	13054.0	13917.0	16048.0	20967.7	27263.2	34326.4	30049.2	31926.2	34482.7	38524.1
Exports of services	2160.0	2845.0	3131.0	3075.0	2631.0	3598.0	4233.0	4450.3	5462.3	6550.3	6444.2	6235.0
Less: Imports of goods and services	14556.0	17032.0	19574.0	17959.0	18615.0	22454.0	32310.2	39849.1	42115.8	44419.5	47327.1	51170.5
Imports of goods	12306.0	14673.0	17712.0	15475.0	16291.0	19530.0	28692.4	34906.8	37295.2	39306.1	42152.0	45911.6
Imports of services	2250.0	2359.0	1862.0	2484.0	2325.0	2924.0	3617.7	4942.4	4820.6	5113.4	5175.1	5258.8
Plus: Statistical discrepancy	-1018.2	191.5	650.0	899.0	1381.9	-978.6	-304.0	-1277.5	-448.0	-2415.1	15.9	708.9
Equals: GROSS DOMESTIC PRODUCT	30535.2	35429.6	37304.0	42678.3	46177.1	54027.7	62080.0	72946.3	75069.9	80774.6	90602.6	105145.6

[a] Includes NPISH final consumption expenditure.

Table 1.2 Gross domestic product by expenditures at constant prices

Series 200: 1993 SNA, Namibia dollar, Western calendar year — **Data in millions**

	2001	2002	2003	2004	2005	2006	2007	2008	2009	2010	2011	2012
Series	**200**											
Base year	**2004**											
	Expenditures of the gross domestic product											
Final consumption expenditure	32073.0	31512.0	33714.0	34609.0	34300.0	37469.2	40346.0	43673.6	47507.7	49469.3	52579.4	56134.6
Household final consumption expenditure [a]	23831.0	23482.0	25433.0	25916.0	26122.0	28392.4	30128.0	32833.1	36009.6	37587.5	39729.9	42232.9
NPISHs final consumption expenditure	1757.3	1769.5	1859.9	1925.0	1554.4	1469.7	1491.8	1674.3	1855.1	1696.2	1662.9	1712.1
General government final consumption expenditure	8242.0	8030.0	8282.0	8693.0	8179.0	9076.8	10218.0	10840.5	11498.1	11881.8	12849.4	13901.7
Gross capital formation	8285.0	7498.0	7527.0	8138.0	8670.0	10879.1	12345.7	12703.1	10903.4	11793.2	12340.4	14062.6
Gross fixed capital formation	7911.0	7850.0	7458.0	7922.0	8207.0	10651.1	11944.7	12808.6	11397.8	12347.9	12614.7	14078.5
Changes in inventories	374.0	-352.0	69.0	216.0	463.0	228.0	401.0	-105.9	-494.4	-554.7	-274.3	-15.9
Acquisitions less disposals of valuables	...	...	...	...	...	...	...	...	...	...	...	...
Exports of goods and services	12744.0	14813.0	16124.0	16991.0	16850.0	19435.8	20675.0	21740.2	19850.2	23163.1	23295.1	21672.2
Exports of goods	9979.0	11703.0	13016.0	13917.0	14246.0	15556.7	16844.0	18211.0	15975.9	18527.4	18911.6	17619.8
Exports of services	2766.0	3110.0	3109.0	3075.0	2604.0	3879.0	3831.0	3529.0	3874.3	4635.6	4383.5	4052.4
Less: Imports of goods and services	17001.0	18046.0	19942.0	17958.0	18125.0	21083.0	27783.7	30440.2	31692.1	32404.6	33046.9	35296.8

	2001	2002	2003	2004	2005	2006	2007	2008	2009	2010	2011	2012
Series	**200**											
Base year	**2004**											
Imports of goods	14474.0	15596.0	18072.0	15475.0	15852.0	18322.0	24587.7	26450.2	28102.6	28593.5	29386.3	31754.3
Imports of services	2527.0	2451.0	1871.0	2484.0	2273.0	2761.0	3196.0	3990.0	3589.6	3811.2	3660.6	3542.5
Plus: Statistical discrepancy	-1300.0	692.0	591.0	899.0	2063.0	151.4	3788.0	3361.4	3912.7	1472.0	962.6	2356.4
Equals: GROSS DOMESTIC PRODUCT	34801.6	36468.1	38014.3	42678.5	43758.0	46853.0	49371.0	51037.6	50481.9	53492.9	56130.6	58929.0

[a] Includes NPISH final consumption expenditure.

Table 1.3 Relations among product, income, savings, and net lending aggregates

Series 200: 1993 SNA, Namibia dollar, Western calendar year — **Data in millions**

	2001	2002	2003	2004	2005	2006	2007	2008	2009	2010	2011	2012
Series	**200**											
GROSS DOMESTIC PRODUCT	30535.2	35429.6	37304.0	42678.3	46177.1	54027.7	62080.6	72946.3	75069.9	80774.6	90602.6	105145.6
Plus: Compensation of employees - from and to the rest of the world, net	-18.0	-13.0	-27.0	-44.0	-39.6	-39.8	-28.8	-258.5	-34.0	-139.1	-118.1	-72.4
Plus: Compensation of employees - from the rest of the world	40.0	46.0	56.0	56.0	67.0	67.0	66.6	66.6	66.6	66.6	66.6	66.6
Less: Compensation of employees - to the rest of the world	58.0	59.0	83.0	100.0	106.0	106.0	95.4	324.3	100.6	205.7	184.7	139.0
Plus: Property income - from and to the rest of the world, net	8.0	369.0	1759.0	582.0	-674.0	-318.0	-1215.4	-1539.2	-1791.0	-2301.7	1004.8	-163.3
Plus: Property income - from the rest of the world	1664.0	1757.0	2067.0	1427.0	889.0	1237.0	1382.3	1803.0	2045.6	1457.1	1730.0	1665.8
Less: Property income - to the rest of the world	1656.0	1388.0	308.0	845.0	1563.0	1555.0	2597.7	3342.2	3836.6	3758.8	725.2	1829.1
Sum of Compensation of employees and property income - from and to the rest of the world, net	-9.7	356.1	1731.7	538.8	-714.4	-357.4	-1244.2	-1796.4	-1825.0	-2440.8	886.6	-235.7
Plus: Sum of Compensation of employees and property income - from the rest of the world	1704.3	1803.0	2123.0	1483.0	955.2	1304.0	1448.9	1869.6	2112.2	1523.7	1796.6	1732.4
Less: Sum of Compensation of employees and property income - to the rest of the world	1714.0	1446.9	391.3	944.2	1669.6	1661.4	2693.1	3666.5	3937.2	3964.5	910.0	1968.1
Plus: Taxes less subsidies on production and imports - from and to the rest of the world, net	...	...	...	...	...	...	...	...	...	...	...	...
Equals: GROSS NATIONAL INCOME	30525.5	35785.7	39035.7	43217.2	45462.6	53670.3	60835.8	71149.4	73244.9	78333.8	91489.2	104909.9
Plus: Current transfers - from and to the rest of the world, net	2984.7	2894.0	3467.2	4303.8	4261.4	6427.6	7051.6	9278.4	10613.8	9018.4	9596.1	15683.0
Plus: Current transfers - from the rest of the world	3297.0	3202.0	3670.2	4529.1	4547.4	6733.4	7420.8	9762.0	11245.5	9658.7	10175.1	16238.6
Less: Current transfers - to the rest of the world	312.3	308.0	203.0	225.3	286.0	305.8	369.2	483.6	631.7	640.3	578.9	555.7
Equals: GROSS NATIONAL DISPOSABLE INCOME	33510.2	38679.7	42502.9	47520.9	49724.1	60097.9	67888.0	80427.9	83858.7	87352.2	101085.3	120592.9
Less: Final consumption expenditure / Actual final consumption	26720.5	29409.2	32817.0	34609.3	35639.8	40867.0	48470.0	56797.2	65345.2	72058.0	78839.6	88538.3
Equals: SAVING, GROSS	6789.7	9270.5	9686.0	12911.7	14084.3	19230.9	19417.0	23630.6	18513.5	15294.1	22245.7	32054.5
Plus: Capital transfers - from and to the rest of the world, net	42.6	437.4	516.9	524.2	531.6	598.9	586.3	629.4	558.2	808.3	1352.7	1218.4
Plus: Capital transfers - from the rest of the world	44.6	440.9	519.5	527.3	535.1	602.3	589.7	632.9	628.0	878.0	1426.2	1293.1
Less: Capital transfers - to the rest of the world	2.0	3.5	2.7	3.1	3.4	3.4	3.4	3.4	69.8	69.8	73.5	74.8
Less: Gross capital formation	6815.0	6562.2	7225.5	8137.6	9092.1	12027.6	14728.1	18499.4	16777.1	17074.7	18147.3	22309.7

	2001	2002	2003	2004	2005	2006	2007	2008	2009	2010	2011	2012
Series	**200**											
Less: Acquisitions less disposals of non-produced non-financial assets	...	...	...	...	...	...	...	...	...	...	...	...
Equals: NET LENDING (+) / NET BORROWING (-) OF THE NATION	17.3	3145.7	2977.4	5298.3	5523.8	7802.1	5275.2	5760.6	2294.7	-972.3	5451.1	10963.2
	Net values: Gross National Income / Gross National Disposable Income / Saving Gross less Consumption of fixed capital											
Less: Consumption of fixed capital	3187.9	3813.3	4374.3	4883.5	5372.9	6020.0	7250.6	8776.3	9712.7	10606.3	11595.5	12698.8
Equals: NET NATIONAL INCOME	27337.7	31972.4	34661.4	38333.7	40089.7	47650.3	53585.3	62373.1	63532.3	67727.4	79893.7	92211.1
Equals: NET NATIONAL DISPOSABLE INCOME	30322.4	34866.4	38128.6	42637.5	44351.1	54077.9	60637.4	71651.6	74146.0	76745.8	89489.8	107894.1
Equals: SAVING, NET	3601.8	5457.2	5311.7	8028.2	8711.3	13210.8	12166.9	14854.3	8800.8	4687.8	10650.2	19355.7

Table 2.1 Value added by industries at current prices (ISIC Rev. 3)

Series 200: 1993 SNA, Namibia dollar, Western calendar year

Data in millions

	2001	2002	2003	2004	2005	2006	2007	2008	2009	2010	2011	2012
Series	**200**											
	Industries											
Agriculture, hunting, forestry; fishing	2963.0	3544.0	3807.0	3817.0	4793.0	5223.0	5375.3	5379.6	5417.1	5878.9	6587.4	7414.1
Agriculture, hunting, forestry	1510.0	1915.0	2032.0	2252.0	2861.0	3275.0	3045.5	2968.8	2988.7	3339.4	3878.0	4258.5
Fishing	1453.0	1630.0	1775.0	1564.0	1932.0	1948.0	2329.8	2410.8	2428.4	2539.5	2709.4	3155.6
Mining and quarrying	3661.0	4793.0	2992.0	4147.0	4257.0	6654.0	6815.7	11771.7	8002.4	6881.9	7470.4	12093.9
Manufacturing	3553.0	4228.0	5149.0	5339.0	5738.0	7792.0	9774.0	9404.6	10141.6	10239.3	10475.3	12223.8
Electricity, gas and water supply	585.0	731.0	740.0	900.0	1091.0	1012.4	1562.0	1590.2	1850.0	1986.9	2327.1	2461.4
Construction	915.0	716.0	983.0	1138.0	1259.0	1825.6	2285.2	2879.9	2464.8	2643.9	3233.8	3805.1
Wholesale, retail trade, repair of motor vehicles, motorcycles and personal and households goods; hotels and restaurants	3569.0	4215.0	4784.0	5408.0	6031.0	6819.0	7883.6	8965.6	10009.5	11177.3	12240.6	14353.7
Wholesale, retail trade, repair of motor vehicles, motorcycles and personal and household goods	3060.0	3630.0	4113.0	4638.0	5202.0	5879.0	6769.0	7682.3	8610.3	9710.5	10537.9	12584.5
Hotels and restaurants	509.0	585.0	671.0	770.0	829.0	940.0	1114.6	1283.2	1399.2	1466.7	1702.7	1769.1
Transport, storage and communications	1245.0	1462.0	1955.0	2403.0	2662.0	2534.9	2955.0	3394.7	3799.9	4514.6	4769.5	5155.8
Land transport; transport via pipelines, water transport; air transport; Supporting and auxiliary transport activities; activities of travel agencies	539.2	482.8	714.9	905.7	959.3	794.2	1146.4	1441.6	1670.8	2261.3	2199.7	2382.1
Post and telecommunications	705.7	978.8	1240.4	1497.6	1703.0	1740.7	1808.6	1953.1	2129.1	2253.3	2569.8	2773.7
Financial intermediation; real estate, renting and business activities	3836.0	4275.0	5123.0	5607.0	6041.0	6679.8	7524.0	8264.4	9634.6	10626.2	11826.7	13309.4
Financial intermediation	1084.0	1269.0	1691.0	1686.0	1823.0	2200.8	2534.0	2849.5	3648.0	4263.2	4662.3	5502.4
Real estate, renting and business activities	2752.0	3006.0	3433.0	3921.0	4218.0	4479.0	4990.0	5414.9	5986.5	6363.0	7164.4	7807.0
Public administration and defence; compulsory social security	2945.0	3254.0	3677.0	3857.0	4115.0	4423.4	5157.0	6143.1	7099.8	8184.0	9285.4	10662.6
Education; health and social work; other community, social and personal services	5109.0	5369.0	5813.0	6686.0	6484.0	7189.3	8408.0	9623.7	10830.7	12096.1	13881.4	15660.0
Education	2391.0	2625.0	2800.0	3331.0	3208.0	3702.8	4569.5	5201.8	5948.4	6852.7	8076.1	9157.4

	2001	2002	2003	2004	2005	2006	2007	2008	2009	2010	2011	2012
Series	**200**											
Health and social work	1490.0	1554.0	1691.0	1806.0	1579.0	1646.6	1859.3	2228.8	2436.6	2721.4	3031.9	3357.0
Other community, social and personal services	1228.0	1189.0	1322.0	1549.0	1697.0	1839.9	1979.0	2193.1	2445.7	2522.1	2773.3	3145.6
Private households with employed persons	258.0	294.0	322.0	343.0	358.0	384.0	424.2	492.4	559.0	597.4	643.4	707.9
Equals: VALUE ADDED, GROSS, in basic prices [a]	28182.0	32391.0	34798.1	39176.0	42313.3	49894.2	57414.0	67069.8	68795.3	73641.5	81475.7	96299.6
Less: Financial intermediation services indirectly measured (FISIM)	455.4	488.1	546.3	468.8	517.1	644.0	750.0	840.1	1014.0	1184.9	1265.1	1548.0
Plus: Taxes less Subsidies on products	2353.2	3038.6	2505.9	3502.3	3863.7	4133.5	4666.0	5876.5	6274.6	7133.1	9126.8	8846.0
Plus: Taxes on products	2353.2	3038.6	2505.9	3502.3	3863.7	4133.5	4666.0	5876.5	6274.6	7133.1	9126.8	8846.0
Less: Subsidies on products	...	...	...	...	...	...	...	...	...	...	...	...
Equals: GROSS DOMESTIC PRODUCT	30535.2	35429.6	37304.0	42678.3	46177.1	54027.7	62080.0	72946.3	75069.9	80774.6	90602.6	105145.6

[a] Excludes financial intermediation services indirectly measured (FISIM) but FISIM is not distributed to uses (i.e. is included in the tables by industry).

Table 2.2 Value added by industries at constant prices (ISIC Rev. 3)

Series 200: 1993 SNA, Namibia dollar, Western calendar year — **Data in millions**

	2001	2002	2003	2004	2005	2006	2007	2008	2009	2010	2011	2012
Series	**200**											
Base year	**2004**											
Industries												
Agriculture, hunting, forestry; fishing	3290.0	3564.0	3774.0	3817.0	4024.0	3995.0	3623.0	3104.1	3161.5	3117.1	3401.4	3469.6
Agriculture, hunting, forestry	1732.0	2036.0	2093.0	2252.0	2590.0	2687.0	2564.0	2101.1	2114.4	2048.3	2266.0	2387.1
Fishing	1558.0	1528.0	1681.0	1564.0	1434.0	1308.0	1059.0	1003.0	1047.1	1068.8	1135.4	1082.5
Mining and quarrying	2290.0	3115.0	2860.0	4147.0	3697.0	4718.0	4742.0	4606.1	2662.9	3532.6	3252.8	3618.4
Manufacturing	4494.0	4672.0	5320.0	5339.0	5742.0	5897.0	6401.0	6537.0	6920.1	7427.4	7385.2	7701.2
Electricity, gas and water supply	853.0	834.0	841.0	900.0	1119.0	1182.0	1234.0	1214.2	1221.1	1251.1	1307.4	1373.7
Construction	1224.0	844.0	1074.0	1138.0	1166.0	1600.0	1833.0	2015.0	1644.3	1737.3	2071.8	2322.4
Wholesale, retail trade, repair of motor vehicles, motorcycles and personal and household goods; hotels and restaurants	4433.0	4717.0	4994.0	5408.0	5875.0	6319.0	6840.0	7033.2	7199.8	7701.3	7952.5	8789.9
Wholesale, retail trade, repair of motor vehicles, motorcycles and personal and household goods	3803.0	4051.0	4284.0	4638.0	5087.0	5473.0	5904.0	6072.4	6258.6	6754.0	6977.0	7820.7
Hotels and restaurants	630.0	666.0	710.0	770.0	788.0	846.0	936.0	960.8	941.2	947.3	975.5	969.2
Transport, storage and communications	1495.6	1650.3	1910.0	2403.3	2627.0	3006.1	3161.0	3243.4	3415.7	3496.6	3619.0	3826.4
Land transport; transport via piplines, water transport; air transport; Supporting and auxiliary transport activities; activities of travel agencies	667.9	622.0	630.0	905.7	931.1	1262.2	1328.0	1497.7	1613.2	1681.7	1756.0	1866.9
Post and telecommunications	827.7	1028.3	1280.0	1497.6	1695.9	1743.9	1833.0	1745.7	1802.5	1814.9	1863.0	1959.5
Financial intermediation, real estate, renting and business activities	4445.0	4599.0	5132.0	5607.0	6129.0	6366.0	6934.0	7361.6	7959.5	8196.5	8455.1	8999.5
Financial intermediation	1098.0	1176.0	1475.0	1686.0	1941.0	2027.0	2267.0	2487.7	2793.4	2942.6	3037.1	3250.6
Real estate, renting and business activities	3347.0	3423.0	3657.0	3921.0	4188.0	4339.0	4667.0	4873.9	5166.2	5254.0	5418.0	5748.9

	2001	2002	2003	2004	2005	2006	2007	2008	2009	2010	2011	2012
Series	**200**											
Base year	**2004**											
Public administration and defence; compulsory social security	3323.0	3479.0	3710.0	3857.0	3673.0	3825.0	4213.0	4667.8	4901.0	5180.8	5343.9	5692.2
Education; health and social work; other community, social and personal services	6335.0	5821.0	5940.0	6686.0	6168.0	6280.0	6626.0	7013.1	7253.3	7440.3	8089.2	8489.9
Education	3000.0	2790.0	2780.0	3331.0	3066.0	3177.0	3365.0	3559.0	3704.9	3906.9	4403.2	4535.1
Health and social work	1813.0	1706.0	1778.0	1806.0	1446.0	1401.0	1545.0	1727.2	1777.3	1819.8	1877.6	2099.4
Other community, social and personal services	1522.0	1325.0	1382.0	1549.0	1656.0	1702.0	1716.0	1726.8	1771.0	1713.6	1808.4	1855.4
Private households with employed persons	320.0	328.0	335.0	343.0	350.0	358.0	370.0	389.2	406.3	415.5	426.0	439.9
Equals: VALUE ADDED, GROSS, in basic prices [a]	32104.0	33290.0	35467.0	39176.0	40051.0	43027.0	45325.0	46514.3	46079.6	48772.7	50538.5	53877.8
Less: Financial intermediation services indirectly measured (FISIM)	398.0	394.0	424.0	469.0	519.0	593.0	652.0	670.2	666.0	723.8	765.7	845.1
Plus: Taxes less Subsidies on products	2697.0	3179.0	2547.0	3502.0	3707.0	3860.0	4047.0	4523.3	4402.2	4720.2	5592.1	5051.2
Plus: Taxes on products	2697.0	3179.0	2547.0	3502.0	3707.0	3860.0	4047.0	4523.3	4402.2	4720.2	5592.1	5051.2
Less: Subsidies on products	...	...	...	...	...	...	...	...	...	...	...	...
Equals: GROSS DOMESTIC PRODUCT	34801.6	36468.1	38014.3	42678.5	43758.0	46853.5	49371.0	51037.6	50481.9	53492.9	56130.6	58929.0

[a] Excludes financial intermediation services indirectly measured (FISIM) but FISIM is not distributed to uses (i.e. is included in the tables by industry).

Table 2.3 Output, gross value added, and fixed assets by industries at current prices (ISIC Rev. 3) Total Economy

Series 200: 1993 SNA, Namibia dollar, Western calendar year **Data in millions**

	2001	2002	2003	2004	2005	2006	2007	2008	2009	2010	2011	2012
Series	**200**											
Output, at basic prices	48863.3	56044.3	60985.4	68464.6	74447.6	87566.1	102204.0	120562.9	121822.0	131471.9	143874.5	167140.6
Less: Intermediate consumption, at purchaser's prices [a]	20681.0	23653.0	26187.0	29289.0	32134.0	37671.3	44789.0	53493.1	53026.7	57830.4	62398.7	70841.0
Equals: VALUE ADDED, GROSS, at basic prices [b]	28182.0	32391.0	34798.1	39176.0	42313.3	49894.2	57415.0	67069.8	68795.3	73641.5	81475.7	96299.6
Compensation of employees	13743.2	15181.3	16880.9	18787.2	19629.8	21508.6	24835.0[c]	28480.7	31064.7	35658.2	38944.5	45019.0
Taxes on production and imports, less Subsidies	411.9	468.0	563.1	603.0	628.4	791.9	861.0	881.9	951.8	1082.5	1203.2	1221.3
Taxes on production and imports	411.9	468.0	563.1	603.0	628.4	791.9	861.0	881.9	951.8	1082.5	1203.2	1221.3
Taxes on products	...	...	...	...	...	...	...	...	...	...	...	...
Other taxes on production	411.9	468.0	563.1	603.0	628.4	791.9	861.0	881.9	951.8	1082.5	1203.2	1221.3
Less: Subsidies	...	...	...	...	...	...	...	...	...	...	...	...
OPERATING SURPLUS, GROSS [d]	14026.9	16741.7	17354.0	19785.7	22055.1	27593.8	31718.4	37707.2	36778.9	36900.8	41328.0	50059.3
MIXED INCOME, GROSS	...	...	...	...	...	...	...	...	...	...	...	...
Total Economy only: Adjustment for FISIM (if FISIM is not distributed to uses)	455.4	488.1	546.3	468.8	517.1	644.0	750.0	840.1	1014.0	1184.9	1265.1	1548.0
Less: Consumption of fixed capital	3187.9	3813.3	4374.3	4883.5	5372.9	6020.0	7251.0[c]	8776.3	9712.7	10606.3	11595.5	12698.8
OPERATING SURPLUS, NET [e]	10839.1	12928.4	12979.7	14902.3	16682.2	21573.8	24468.0	28930.9	27066.2	26294.5	29732.5	37360.5
MIXED INCOME, NET	...	...	...	...	...	...	...	...	...	...	...	...
Gross capital formation	6815.0	6562.2	7225.5	8137.6	9092.1	12027.6	14728.0	18499.4	16777.1	17074.7	18147.3	22309.7

	2001	2002	2003	2004	2005	2006	2007	2008	2009	2010	2011	2012
Series	**200**											
Gross fixed capital formation	6391.2	7065.9	7120.7	7921.9	8594.4	11685.8	14696.0	17837.5	16608.8	18377.7	19291.4	22153.2
Changes in inventories	423.8	-503.6	104.8	215.7	497.7	341.7	32.0	661.4	168.2	-1303.0	-1144.1	156.5
Acquisitions less disposals of valuables	...	...	...	...	...	...	...	...	...	...	...	...
Closing stocks of fixed assets (produced assets)	55912.0	65321.0	72898.0	80229.0	88303.0	98800.0	115229.6	138586.3	128304.9	135107.1	145311.6	158997.4

[a] Includes financial intermediation services indirectly measured (FISIM) of the Total Economy.
[b] Excludes financial intermediation services indirectly measured (FISIM), but FISIM is included in industry data.
[c] Discrepancy between the data for the total economy and the data by industries.
[d] Includes Mixed Income, Gross.
[e] Includes Mixed Income, Net.

Table 2.3 Output, gross value added, and fixed assets by industries at current prices (ISIC Rev. 3) Agriculture, hunting, forestry; fishing (A+B)

Series 200: 1993 SNA, Namibia dollar, Western calendar year **Data in millions**

	2001	2002	2003	2004	2005	2006	2007	2008	2009	2010	2011	2012
Series	**200**											
Output, at basic prices	4546.9	5436.8	5783.4	5697.0	6893.5	7530.7	8172.0	8357.7	8425.5	8878.8	9869.6	11159.2
Less: Intermediate consumption, at purchaser's prices	1584.0	1893.0	1976.0	1880.0	2101.0	2307.0	2797.0	2978.1	3008.4	2999.9	3282.2	3745.1
Equals: VALUE ADDED, GROSS, at basic prices	2963.0	3544.0	3807.0	3817.0	4793.0	5223.0	5375.0	5379.6	5417.1	5878.9	6587.4	7414.1
Compensation of employees	1031.0	1186.0	1321.0	1241.0	1436.0	1497.0	1698.0	1844.1	1880.3	1906.6	2010.0	2654.0
Taxes on production and imports, less Subsidies	118.0	100.0	57.0	89.0	91.0	92.0	147.0	73.0	93.0	108.0	123.0	74.0
Taxes on production and imports	118.0	100.0	57.0	89.0	91.0	92.0	147.0	73.0	93.0	108.0	123.0	74.0
Taxes on products	...	...	...	...	...	...	...	...	...	...	...	...
Other taxes on production	118.0	100.0	57.0	89.0	91.0	92.0	147.0	73.0	93.0	108.0	123.0	74.0
Less: Subsidies	...	...	...	...	...	...	...	...	...	...	...	...
Subsidies on products	...	...	...	...	...	...	...	...	...	...	...	...
Other subsidies on production	...	...	...	...	...	...	0.0	0.0	0.0	...	...	...
OPERATING SURPLUS, GROSS [a]	1814.1	2257.7	2428.4	2486.7	3265.6	3634.8	3530.0	3462.2	3444.1	3864.6	4454.2	4686.2
MIXED INCOME, GROSS	...	...	...	...	...	...	...	...	...	...	...	...
Less: Consumption of fixed capital	427.5	490.2	551.6	595.3	641.9	683.4	747.2	894.0	986.6	1034.9	1077.5	1207.8
OPERATING SURPLUS, NET [b]	1386.5	1767.5	1876.8	1891.4	2623.6	2951.4	2782.8	2568.2	2457.5	2829.7	3376.7	3478.4
MIXED INCOME, NET	...	...	...	...	...	...	...	...	...	...	...	...
Gross capital formation	569.9	452.1	579.7	441.4	783.4	1005.4	1154.0	845.5	940.9	425.6	286.6	1469.7
Gross fixed capital formation	565.9	620.1	627.7	474.4	567.4	565.4	702.6	843.8	953.9	1047.5	855.6	1684.3
Changes in inventories	4.0	-168.0	-48.0	-33.0	216.0	440.0	451.0	1.7	-13.0	-621.9	-569.1	-214.6
Acquisitions less disposals of valuables	...	...	...	...	...	...	...	...	...	...	...	...
Closing stocks of fixed assets (produced assets)	8188.0	9117.0	9857.0	10333.0	10843.0	11168.0	11926.0	13641.0	14369.4	14557.9	14651.7	15738.6

[a] Includes Mixed Income, Gross.
[b] Includes Mixed Income, Net.

Table 2.3 Output, gross value added, and fixed assets by industries at current prices (ISIC Rev. 3) Agriculture, hunting and related service activities (01)

Series 200: 1993 SNA, Namibia dollar, Western calendar year **Data in millions**

	2001	2002	2003	2004	2005	2006	2007	2008	2009	2010	2011	2012
Series	**200**											
Output, at basic prices	2160.0	2764.0	2863.0	3120.0	3709.0	4324.0	4338.0	4383.0	4427.0	4690.0	5410.8	5961.6
Less: Intermediate consumption, at purchaser's prices	650.0	849.0	831.0	868.0	849.0	1049.0	1293.0	1414.2	1438.3	1350.6	1532.8	1703.1
Equals: VALUE ADDED, GROSS, at basic prices	1510.0	1915.0	2032.0	2252.0	2861.0	3275.0	3045.0	2968.8	2988.7	3339.4	3878.0	4258.5
Compensation of employees	369.0	427.0	470.0	510.0	522.0	575.0	613.0	682.3	721.2	699.7	726.5	1122.1
Taxes on production and imports, less Subsidies	...	...	...	...	...	...	1.0	0.0	0.0	...	...	...
Taxes on production and imports	...	...	...	...	...	...	1.0	0.0	0.0	...	...	...
Taxes on products	...	...	...	...	...	...	...	...	...	...	...	...
Other taxes on production	...	...	...	...	...	...	1.0	0.0	0.0	...	...	...
Less: Subsidies	...	...	...	...	...	...	...	...	...	...	...	...
OPERATING SURPLUS, GROSS [a]	1142.0	1487.0	1562.0	1742.0	2339.0	2700.0	2432.0	2286.5	2267.5	2639.7	3151.5	3136.4
MIXED INCOME, GROSS	...	...	...	...	...	...	...	...	...	...	...	...
Less: Consumption of fixed capital	370.0	420.0	471.0	512.0	553.0	590.0	645.0	770.6	844.1	878.1	917.3	1007.5
OPERATING SURPLUS, NET [b]	771.5	1067.1	1091.2	1230.3	1785.4	2110.0	1787.4	1515.9	1423.4	1761.6	2234.2	2128.9
MIXED INCOME, NET	...	...	...	...	...	...	...	...	...	...	...	...
Gross capital formation	332.3	197.8	354.0	399.1	679.6	934.7	991.2	650.6	707.0	135.5	230.6	636.8
Gross fixed capital formation	328.3	365.8	402.0	432.1	463.6	494.7	540.2	648.9	720.1	757.5	799.7	851.4
Changes in inventories	4.0	-168.0	-48.0	-33.0	216.0	440.0	451.0	1.7	-13.0	-621.9	-569.1	-214.6
Acquisitions less disposals of valuables	...	...	...	...	...	...	...	...	...	...	...	...
Closing stocks of fixed assets (produced assets)	7076.0	7771.0	8326.0	8824.0	9299.0	9621.0	10266.0	11687.5	12157.7	12156.2	12331.3	12626.2

[a] Includes Mixed Income, Gross.
[b] Includes Mixed Income, Net.

Table 2.3 Output, gross value added, and fixed assets by industries at current prices (ISIC Rev. 3) Fishing (B)

Series 200: 1993 SNA, Namibia dollar, Western calendar year **Data in millions**

	2001	2002	2003	2004	2005	2006	2007	2008	2009	2010	2011	2012
Series	**200**											
Output, at basic prices	2387.0	2673.0	2921.0	2577.0	3184.0	3206.0	3834.0	3975.0	3998.5	4188.8	4458.7	5197.6
Less: Intermediate consumption, at purchaser's prices	934.0	1044.0	1145.0	1012.0	1252.0	1258.0	1504.3	1564.0	1570.0	1649.3	1749.4	2042.0
Equals: VALUE ADDED, GROSS, at basic prices	1453.0	1630.0	1775.0	1564.0	1932.0	1948.0	2330.0	2411.0	2428.4	2539.5	2709.4	3155.6
Compensation of employees	663.0	759.0	852.0	731.0	914.0	922.0	1085.0	1162.0	1159.1	1206.9	1283.5	1531.9
Taxes on production and imports, less Subsidies	118.0	100.0	57.0	89.0	91.0	92.0	147.0	73.0	93.0	108.0	123.0	74.0
Taxes on production and imports	118.0	100.0	57.0	89.0	91.0	92.0	147.0	73.0	93.0	108.0	123.0	74.0
Taxes on products	...	...	...	...	...	...	...	...	...	...	...	...
Other taxes on production	118.0	100.0	57.0	89.0	91.0	92.0	147.0	73.0	93.0	108.0	123.0	74.0

	2001	2002	2003	2004	2005	2006	2007	2008	2009	2010	2011	2012
Series	**200**											
Less: Subsidies	...	...	...	...	...	...	...	...	...	...	...	...
OPERATING SURPLUS, GROSS [a]	673.0	770.0	867.0	745.0	927.0	935.0	1098.0	1176.0	1176.6	1224.9	1302.7	1549.8
MIXED INCOME, GROSS	...	...	...	...	...	...	...	...	...	...	...	...
Less: Consumption of fixed capital	57.5	70.1	81.1	83.6	88.8	93.0	102.0	123.0	142.5	156.8	160.2	200.3
OPERATING SURPLUS, NET [b]	615.0	700.4	785.6	661.1	838.2	841.4	996.0	1053.0	1034.1	1068.1	1142.5	1349.5
MIXED INCOME, NET	...	...	...	...	...	...	...	...	...	...	...	...
Gross capital formation	237.6	254.3	225.7	42.3	103.8	70.6	162.0	195.0	233.9	290.1	55.9	832.9
Gross fixed capital formation	237.6	254.3	225.7	42.3	103.8	70.6	162.0	195.0	233.9	290.1	55.9	832.9
Changes in inventories	...	...	...	...	...	...	...	...	...	...	...	...
Acquisitions less disposals of valuables	...	...	...	...	...	...	...	...	...	...	...	...
Closing stocks of fixed assets (produced assets)	1112.0	1346.0	1531.0	1509.0	1544.0	1547.0	1660.0	1954.0	2211.7	2401.7	2320.4	3112.5

[a] Includes Mixed Income, Gross.
[b] Includes Mixed Income, Net.

Table 2.3 Output, gross value added, and fixed assets by industries at current prices (ISIC Rev. 3) Mining and quarrying (C)

Series 200: 1993 SNA, Namibia dollar, Western calendar year

Data in millions

	2001	2002	2003	2004	2005	2006	2007	2008	2009	2010	2011	2012
Series	**200**											
Output, at basic prices	5716.8	7429.6	5760.7	7662.5	8496.8	11547.0	13254.3	19182.0	12839.8	13948.7	14786.5	19391.7
Less: Intermediate consumption, at purchaser's prices	2056.0	2637.0	2769.0	3515.0	4239.0	4893.0	6439.0	7410.0	4837.4	7066.8	7316.2	7297.9
Equals: VALUE ADDED, GROSS, at basic prices	3661.0	4793.0	2992.0	4147.0	4257.0	6654.0	6816.0	11772.0	8002.4	6881.9	7470.4	12093.9
Compensation of employees	664.0	840.0	954.0	1175.0	1213.0	1415.0	1639.9	2267.0	1649.3	2785.4	2128.5	2281.4
Taxes on production and imports, less Subsidies	...	...	...	...	...	...	...	...	...	...	...	...
OPERATING SURPLUS, GROSS [a]	2996.8	3953.2	2038.1	2972.2	3044.6	5239.3	5175.7	9505.0	6353.0	4096.5	5341.9	9812.4
MIXED INCOME, GROSS	...	...	...	...	...	...	...	...	...	...	...	...
Less: Consumption of fixed capital	579.3	712.7	829.6	902.7	935.1	1085.4	1359.1	1633.0	1826.0	2006.5	2164.3	2345.9
OPERATING SURPLUS, NET [b]	2417.4	3240.5	1208.5	2069.5	2109.5	4153.9	3817.0	7872.0	4527.0	2090.0	3177.6	7466.6
MIXED INCOME, NET	...	...	...	...	...	...	...	...	...	...	...	...
Gross capital formation	1226.8	1423.2	1864.4	1872.4	2184.8	3648.0	3001.3	4818.0	3767.6	3780.2	2806.5	4121.1
Gross fixed capital formation	922.8	1760.2	1765.4	1738.4	1761.8	3842.0	3367.3	4274.0	3719.6	4380.0	3328.6	3879.1
Changes in inventories	304.0	-337.0	99.0	134.0	423.0	-194.0	-366.0	544.0	48.0	-599.8	-522.1	241.9
Acquisitions less disposals of valuables	...	...	...	...	...	...	...	...	...	...	...	...
Closing stocks of fixed assets (produced assets)	5750.0	7318.0	8681.0	9760.0	10897.0	14131.0	17726.5	22167.0	24774.3	27055.6	28589.0	30524.7

[a] Includes Mixed Income, Gross.
[b] Includes Mixed Income, Net.

Table 2.3 Output, gross value added, and fixed assets by industries at current prices (ISIC Rev. 3) Manufacturing (D)

Series 200: 1993 SNA, Namibia dollar, Western calendar year — **Data in millions**

	2001	2002	2003	2004	2005	2006	2007	2008	2009	2010	2011	2012
Series	**200**											
Output, at basic prices	7811.6	9318.7	10676.7	11723.0	12972.8	15943.8	18911.0	20467.0	21159.4	21245.8	21300.9	24683.3
Less: Intermediate consumption, at purchaser's prices	4259.0	5091.0	5528.0	6384.0	7235.0	8152.0	9137.0	11063.0	11017.8	11006.5	10825.6	12459.6
Equals: VALUE ADDED, GROSS, at basic prices	3553.0	4228.0	5149.0	5339.0	5738.0	7792.0	9774.0	9404.0	10141.6	10239.3	10475.3	12223.8
Compensation of employees	806.0	880.0	1047.0	1205.0	1278.0	1342.0	1506.8	1758.0	2021.2	2182.8	2317.8	2554.6
Taxes on production and imports, less Subsidies	3.1	3.2	3.5	3.5	2.8	4.8	6.8	8.8	10.8	12.8	14.8	16.8
Taxes on production and imports	3.1	3.2	3.5	3.5	2.8	4.8	6.8	8.8	10.8	12.8	14.8	16.8
Taxes on products	...	...	...	...	...	...	...	...	10.8	12.8	14.8	16.8
Other taxes on production	...	...	...	...	...	...	7.0	9.0	10.8	12.8	14.8	16.8
Less: Subsidies	...	...	...	...	...	...	...	...	...	...	...	...
OPERATING SURPLUS, GROSS [a]	2743.9	3344.5	4098.7	4130.3	4457.6	6440.8	8260.0	7637.0	8109.6	8043.6	8142.7	9652.3
MIXED INCOME, GROSS	...	...	...	...	...	...	...	...	...	...	...	...
Less: Consumption of fixed capital	275.6	336.7	357.3	403.8	442.1	503.2	655.5	832.0	982.2	1180.0	1370.3	1586.9
OPERATING SURPLUS, NET [b]	2468.4	3007.8	3741.4	3726.5	4015.5	5937.6	7604.0	6805.0	7127.3	6863.6	6772.4	8065.4
MIXED INCOME, NET	...	...	...	...	...	...	...	...	...	...	...	...
Gross capital formation	902.2	892.0	301.4	947.6	574.2	1164.4	1323.5	2280.1	2806.8	2618.7	2370.0	2760.8
Gross fixed capital formation	787.2	891.0	247.4	832.6	715.2	1068.4	1376.0	2164.0	2673.7	2700.0	2422.9	2631.7
Changes in inventories	115.0	1.0	54.0	115.0	-141.0	96.0	-52.5	116.1	133.1	-81.3	-52.9	129.1
Acquisitions less disposals of valuables	...	...	...	...	...	...	...	...	...	...	...	...
Closing stocks of fixed assets (produced assets)	3345.6	4275.6	4519.2	5150.6	5725.9	6740.5	8391.8	10766.0	12986.3	14631.0	16140.1	17875.8

[a] Includes Mixed Income, Gross.
[b] Includes Mixed Income, Net.

Table 2.3 Output, gross value added, and fixed assets by industries at current prices (ISIC Rev. 3) Electricity, gas and water supply (E)

Series 200: 1993 SNA, Namibia dollar, Western calendar year — **Data in millions**

	2001	2002	2003	2004	2005	2006	2007	2008	2009	2010	2011	2012
Series	**200**											
Output, at basic prices	1062.4	1299.6	1419.3	1626.1	1795.2	1770.6	2536.0	2761.7	3056.7	3514.6	3972.2	4525.5
Less: Intermediate consumption, at purchaser's prices	478.0	569.0	679.0	726.0	704.0	748.0	974.0	1171.6	1206.7	1527.7	1645.1	2064.1
Equals: VALUE ADDED, GROSS, at basic prices	585.0	731.0	740.0	900.0	1091.0	1012.4	1562.0	1590.2	1850.0	1986.9	2327.1	2461.4
Compensation of employees	261.0	302.0	322.0	345.0	344.0	390.0	488.0	580.3	720.1	803.7	842.5	899.0
Taxes on production and imports, less Subsidies	...	...	...	...	...	...	...	...	...	...	...	...
OPERATING SURPLUS, GROSS [a]	324.0	428.0	417.7	555.3	746.7	618.9	1074.0	1009.9	1129.9	1183.2	1484.6	1562.4
MIXED INCOME, GROSS	...	...	...	...	...	...	...	...	...	...	...	...
Less: Consumption of fixed capital	224.5	259.5	320.7	377.1	413.1	441.9	514.0	624.9	657.2	723.8	827.3	857.6

	2001	2002	2003	2004	2005	2006	2007	2008	2009	2010	2011	2012
Series	**200**											
OPERATING SURPLUS, NET [b]	99.5	168.6	97.0	178.2	333.6	177.0	560.0	385.0	472.7	459.4	657.3	704.8
MIXED INCOME, NET	...	...	...	...	...	...	...	...	...	...	...	...
Gross capital formation	1217.3	284.5	795.9	708.9	309.1	364.0	387.0	680.2	762.1	1247.6	2100.8	1172.6
Gross fixed capital formation	1217.3	284.5	795.9	708.9	309.1	364.0	387.2	680.2	762.1	1247.6	2100.8	1172.6
Changes in inventories	...	...	...	...	...	...	...	...	...	...	...	...
Acquisitions less disposals of valuables	...	...	...	...	...	...	...	...	...	...	...	...
Closing stocks of fixed assets (produced assets)	5276.0	5905.0	6711.0	7541.0	8049.0	8235.0	8659.4	9567.7	9832.4	10034.4	11388.2	12366.7

[a] Includes Mixed Income, Gross.
[b] Includes Mixed Income, Net.

Table 2.3 Output, gross value added, and fixed assets by industries at current prices (ISIC Rev. 3) Construction (F)

Series 200: 1993 SNA, Namibia dollar, Western calendar year

Data in millions

	2001	2002	2003	2004	2005	2006	2007	2008	2009	2010	2011	2012
Series	**200**											
Output, at basic prices	3327.7	2675.0	3282.9	3989.7	4475.2	6236.2	7899.0	9870.5	8819.0	9864.7	11716.4	14102.4
Less: Intermediate consumption, at purchaser's prices	2413.0	1959.0	2300.0	2851.0	3216.0	4410.6	5613.0	6990.6	6354.2	7220.8	8482.6	10297.4
Equals: VALUE ADDED, GROSS, at basic prices	915.0	716.0	983.0	1138.0	1259.0	1825.6	2286.0	2879.9	2464.8	2643.9	3233.8	3805.1
Compensation of employees	186.0	202.0	218.0	242.0	263.0	289.0	313.0	348.1	383.8	422.9	471.0	522.1
Taxes on production and imports, less Subsidies	...	...	...	...	...	...	...	...	...	...	...	...
OPERATING SURPLUS, GROSS [a]	729.4	514.1	765.2	896.3	996.7	1540.0	1973.0	2531.9	2081.0	2221.0	2762.8	3283.0
MIXED INCOME, GROSS	...	...	...	...	...	...	...	...	...	...	...	...
Less: Consumption of fixed capital	200.1	224.7	242.5	250.3	258.6	266.8	280.0	309.1	341.9	362.4	416.5	474.3
OPERATING SURPLUS, NET [b]	529.3	289.4	522.7	646.0	738.1	1273.2	1693.0	2222.7	1739.1	1858.6	2346.3	2808.7
MIXED INCOME, NET	...	...	...	...	...	...	...	...	...	...	...	...
Gross capital formation	176.3	214.3	257.8	287.4	297.0	307.2	334.0	600.9	576.6	541.8	829.1	913.9
Gross fixed capital formation	176.3	214.3	257.8	287.4	297.0	307.2	334.0	600.9	576.6	541.8	829.1	913.9
Changes in inventories	...	...	...	...	...	...	...	...	...	...	...	...
Acquisitions less disposals of valuables	...	...	...	...	...	...	...	...	...	...	...	...
Closing stocks of fixed assets (produced assets)	1060.0	1115.0	1172.0	1229.0	1291.0	1365.0	1481.0	1940.4	2296.9	2505.2	2974.0	3509.4

[a] Includes Mixed Income, Gross.
[b] Includes Mixed Income, Net.

Table 2.3 Output, gross value added, and fixed assets by industries at current prices (ISIC Rev. 3) Wholesale retail trade, repair of motor vehicles, motorcycles, etc.; hotels and restaurants (G+H)

Series 200: 1993 SNA, Namibia dollar, Western calendar year — **Data in millions**

	2001	2002	2003	2004	2005	2006	2007	2008	2009	2010	2011	2012
Series	**200**											
Output, at basic prices	6268.9	7425.8	8472.2	9633.2	10606.3	11899.0	13543.9	15605.5	17376.3	19461.0	21090.4	24685.4
Less: Intermediate consumption, at purchaser's prices	2700.0	3211.0	3688.0	4226.0	4576.0	5080.0	5660.7	6640.0	7366.8	8283.8	8849.8	10331.8
Equals: VALUE ADDED, GROSS, at basic prices	3569.0	4215.0	4784.0	5408.0	6031.0	6819.0	7883.1	8965.6	10009.5	11177.3	12240.6	14353.7
Compensation of employees	1631.0	1942.0	2197.0	2481.0	2740.0	2933.0	3308.7	3681.8	4147.1	4681.3	5081.2	5964.1
Taxes on production and imports, less Subsidies	...	...	...	...	...	...	...	...	...	...	...	...
OPERATING SURPLUS, GROSS [a]	1902.9	2232.5	2538.3	2870.5	3232.9	3823.8	4507.2	5200.5	5772.4	6398.5	7054.5	8279.2
MIXED INCOME, GROSS	...	...	...	...	...	...	...	...	...	...	...	...
Less: Consumption of fixed capital	183.0	214.3	236.0	256.8	278.8	307.4	409.5	512.3	610.3	667.0	751.4	788.7
OPERATING SURPLUS, NET [b]	1719.9	2018.2	2302.3	2613.7	2954.1	3516.4	4097.7	4688.2	5162.1	5731.5	6303.1	7490.5
MIXED INCOME, NET	...	...	...	...	...	...	...	...	...	...	...	...
Gross capital formation	307.4	281.1	249.7	326.0	366.6	432.1	1213.4	1147.1	1074.3	1082.5	1171.2	775.2
Gross fixed capital formation	307.4	281.1	249.7	326.0	366.6	432.1	1213.4	1147.1	1074.3	1082.5	1171.2	775.2
Changes in inventories	...	...	...	...	...	...	...	...	...	...	...	...
Acquisitions less disposals of valuables	...	...	...	...	...	...	...	...	...	...	...	...
Closing stocks of fixed assets (produced assets)	2423.0	2766.0	2981.0	3174.0	3435.0	3803.0	4967.9	6214.2	6981.2	7421.3	7989.0	8239.0

[a] Includes Mixed Income, Gross.
[b] Includes Mixed Income, Net.

Table 2.3 Output, gross value added, and fixed assets by industries at current prices (ISIC Rev. 3) Transport, storage and communications (I)

Series 200: 1993 SNA, Namibia dollar, Western calendar year — **Data in millions**

	2001	2002	2003	2004	2005	2006	2007	2008	2009	2010	2011	2012
Series	**200**											
Output, at basic prices	3165.0	4002.2	4769.2	5391.6	6023.1	6518.4	7503.8	8925.6	9889.6	10326.6	10989.0	11895.1
Less: Intermediate consumption, at purchaser's prices	1920.0	2541.0	2814.0	2988.0	3361.0	3982.0	4548.8	5530.9	6089.7	5812.0	6219.5	6739.3
Equals: VALUE ADDED, GROSS, at basic prices	1245.0	1462.0	1955.0	2403.0	2662.0	2535.0	2955.0	3394.7	3799.9	4514.6	4769.5	5155.8
Compensation of employees	725.0	785.0	843.0	903.0	1042.0	1202.0	1407.7	1660.3	1771.5	1931.7	2144.7	2901.2
Taxes on production and imports, less Subsidies	...	...	...	...	...	...	...	...	...	...	...	...
OPERATING SURPLUS, GROSS [a]	519.0	676.9	1113.0	1500.3	1621.0	1335.8	1547.4	1734.4	2028.3	2582.9	2624.8	2254.6
MIXED INCOME, GROSS	...	...	...	...	...	...	...	...	...	...	...	...
Less: Consumption of fixed capital	494.6	637.4	755.0	874.1	1007.1	1104.9	1110.0	1334.1	1498.8	1640.7	1766.9	1929.8
OPERATING SURPLUS, NET [b]	24.4	39.5	358.0	626.2	613.9	231.0	437.0	400.3	529.6	942.2	857.8	324.8
MIXED INCOME, NET	...	...	...	...	...	...	...	...	...	...	...	...
Gross capital formation	594.9	1124.2	997.7	1095.3	1350.9	1497.5	2296.0	2807.6	1301.8	2464.6	2751.2	2948.4
Gross fixed capital formation	594.9	1124.2	997.7	1095.3	1350.9	1497.5	2295.9	2807.6	1301.8	2464.6	2751.2	2948.4

	2001	2002	2003	2004	2005	2006	2007	2008	2009	2010	2011	2012
Series	**200**											
Changes in inventories	...	...	...	...	...	...	...	...	...	...	...	...
Acquisitions less disposals of valuables	...	...	...	...	...	...	...	...	...	...	...	...
Closing stocks of fixed assets (produced assets)	6550.0	7783.0	8654.0	9518.0	10478.0	11317.0	13347.1	16538.2	17140.8	18915.0	20307.7	22213.1

[a] Includes Mixed Income, Gross.
[b] Includes Mixed Income, Net.

Table 2.3 Output, gross value added, and fixed assets by industries at current prices (ISIC Rev. 3) Financial intermediation; real estate, renting and business activities (J+K)

Series 200: 1993 SNA, Namibia dollar, Western calendar year **Data in millions**

	2001	2002	2003	2004	2005	2006	2007	2008	2009	2010	2011	2012
Series	**200**											
Output, at basic prices	5347.4	5944.2	7077.3	7803.5	8378.0	9299.8	10203.0	11606.0	13222.5	14426.6	15851.5	17549.1
Less: Intermediate consumption, at purchaser's prices	1512.0	1669.0	1954.0	2196.0	2336.0	2617.0	2679.0	3341.6	3588.0	3800.4	4024.7	4239.7
Equals: VALUE ADDED, GROSS, at basic prices	3836.0	4275.0	5123.0	5607.0	6042.0	6679.8	7524.0	8264.4	9634.6	10626.2	11826.7	13309.4
Compensation of employees	840.0	948.0	1076.0	1312.0	1388.0	1519.0	1940.0	2201.0	2349.8	2553.4	2760.4	3043.2
Taxes on production and imports, less Subsidies	...	...	...	...	...	...	...	...	...	...	...	...
OPERATING SURPLUS, GROSS [a]	2995.6	3327.6	4047.4	4295.1	4653.3	5151.0	5585.0	6063.4	7284.7	8072.9	9066.4	10266.2
MIXED INCOME, GROSS	...	...	...	...	...	...	...	...	...	...	...	...
Less: Consumption of fixed capital	293.7	347.3	413.0	472.3	549.0	641.9	772.3	935.0	1062.4	1135.0	1218.8	1353.8
OPERATING SURPLUS, NET [b]	2701.9	2980.3	3634.3	3822.8	4104.2	4509.1	4813.0	5128.4	6222.3	6937.9	7847.6	8912.4
MIXED INCOME, NET	...	...	...	...	...	...	...	...	...	...	...	...
Gross capital formation	727.7	811.4	1077.6	1253.1	1683.6	1839.6	2084.2	2456.4	2813.8	2120.9	2347.4	3953.1
Gross fixed capital formation	727.7	811.4	1077.6	1253.1	1683.6	1839.6	2084.2	2456.4	2813.8	2120.9	2347.4	3953.1
Changes in inventories	...	...	...	...	...	...	...	...	...	...	...	...
Acquisitions less disposals of valuables	...	...	...	...	...	...	...	...	...	...	...	...
Closing stocks of fixed assets (produced assets)	9836.0	11632.0	13306.0	14767.0	16912.0	19606.0	23338.8	27963.2	31131.5	32576.4	34945.0	39341.8

[a] Includes Mixed Income, Gross.
[b] Includes Mixed Income, Net.

Table 2.3 Output, gross value added, and fixed assets by industries at current prices (ISIC Rev. 3) Public administration and defense; compulsory social security (L)

Series 200: 1993 SNA, Namibia dollar, Western calendar year **Data in millions**

	2001	2002	2003	2004	2005	2006	2007	2008	2009	2010	2011	2012
Series	**200**											
Output, at basic prices	4469.7	4864.7	5433.0	5613.2	5851.6	6748.3	8258.0	9776.7	11279.4	12458.2	14489.5	16992.4
Less: Intermediate consumption, at purchaser's prices	1525.0	1611.0	1757.0	1756.0	1736.0	2324.9	3093.0	3633.6	4179.6	4274.2	5204.2	6329.8
Equals: VALUE ADDED, GROSS, at basic prices	2945.0	3254.0	3677.0	3857.0	4115.0	4423.4	5157.0	6143.1	7099.8	8184.0	9285.4	10662.6
Compensation of employees	2562.0	2803.0	3160.0	3280.0	3466.0	3789.5	4363.0	4945.9	5768.9	6764.5	7759.5	9000.8

	2001	2002	2003	2004	2005	2006	2007	2008	2009	2010	2011	2012
Series	**200**											
Taxes on production and imports, less Subsidies	...	...	...	...	...	...	...	...	...	...	...	...
OPERATING SURPLUS, GROSS	...	...	...	...	...	...	...	...	...	...	...	...
MIXED INCOME, GROSS	...	...	...	...	...	...	...	...	...	...	...	...
Less: Consumption of fixed capital	524.5	617.1	707.2	790.4	889.0	1028.7	1350.0	1639.6	1822.7	1943.9	2089.7	2275.9
OPERATING SURPLUS, NET	...	...	...	...	...	...	...	...	...	...	...	...
MIXED INCOME, NET	...	...	...	...	...	...	...	...	...	...	...	...
Gross capital formation	1059.1	1042.0	1057.8	1164.8	1496.7	1728.2	2889.0	2820.6	2685.8	2750.3	3437.1	4151.9
Gross fixed capital formation	1059.1	1042.0	1057.8	1164.8	1496.7	1728.2	2889.0	2820.6	2685.8	2750.3	3437.1	4151.9
Changes in inventories	...	...	...	...	...	...	...	...	...	...	...	...
Acquisitions less disposals of valuables	...	...	...	...	...	...	...	...	...	...	...	...
Closing stocks of fixed assets (produced assets)	15365.0	17731.7	19741.1	21846.2	24208.9	26202.1	30167.9	35748.0	38107.3	39241.1	41647.4	45257.0

Table 2.3 Output, gross value added, and fixed assets by industries at current prices (ISIC Rev. 3) Education; health and social work; other community, social and personal services (M+N+O)

Series 200: 1993 SNA, Namibia dollar, Western calendar year **Data in millions**

	2001	2002	2003	2004	2005	2006	2007	2008	2009	2010	2011	2012
Series	**200**											
Output, at basic prices	6889.0	7353.9	7989.1	8982.2	8597.1	9687.2	11505.0	13517.7	15194.8	16749.6	19165.1	21448.4
Less: Intermediate consumption, at purchaser's prices	1780.0	1985.0	2176.0	2296.0	2113.0	2497.9	3097.0	3894.0	4364.1	4653.4	5283.7	5788.4
Equals: VALUE ADDED, GROSS, at basic prices	5109.0	5369.0	5813.0	6686.0	6484.0	7189.3	8408.0	9623.7	10830.7	12096.1	13881.4	15660.0
Compensation of employees	4779.0	5000.0	5421.0	6261.0	6102.0	6736.8	7746.0	8701.8	9813.6	11028.6	12785.6	14490.6
Taxes on production and imports, less Subsidies	...	...	...	...	...	...	...	...	...	...	...	...
OPERATING SURPLUS, GROSS	...	...	...	...	...	...	...	...	...	...	...	...
MIXED INCOME, GROSS	...	...	...	...	...	...	...	...	...	...	...	...
Less: Consumption of fixed capital	35.2	39.5	42.4	44.4	46.9	49.4	53.3	62.3	67.1	68.9	73.1	78.6
OPERATING SURPLUS, NET	...	...	...	...	...	...	...	...	...	...	...	...
MIXED INCOME, NET	...	...	...	...	...	...	...	...	...	...	...	...
Gross capital formation	32.6	36.9	43.7	41.0	46.1	41.5	46.5	42.0	47.0	42.5	47.5	43.0
Gross fixed capital formation	32.6	36.9	43.7	41.0	46.1	41.5	46.5	42.0	47.0	42.5	47.5	43.0
Changes in inventories	...	...	...	...	...	...	...	...	...	...	...	...
Acquisitions less disposals of valuables	...	...	...	...	...	...	...	...	...	...	...	...

Table 2.3 Output, gross value added, and fixed assets by industries at current prices (ISIC Rev. 3) Private households with employed persons (P)

Series 200: 1993 SNA, Namibia dollar, Western calendar year — **Data in millions**

	2001	2002	2003	2004	2005	2006	2007	2008	2009	2010	2011	2012
Series	**200**											
Output, at basic prices	257.8	293.6	321.6	342.6	358.0	384.3	424.2	492.4	559.0	597.4	643.4	707.9
Less: Intermediate consumption, at purchaser's prices	...	...	...	...	...	...	...	...	...	...	...	...
Equals: VALUE ADDED, GROSS, at basic prices	258.0	294.0	322.0	343.0	358.0	384.0	424.1	492.4	559.0	597.4	643.4	707.9
Compensation of employees	258.0	294.0	322.0	343.0	358.0	384.0	424.1	492.4	559.0	597.4	643.4	707.9
Taxes on production and imports, less Subsidies	...	...	...	...	...	...	...	...	...	...	...	...
OPERATING SURPLUS, GROSS	...	...	...	...	...	...	...	...	...	...	...	...
MIXED INCOME, GROSS	...	...	...	...	...	...	...	...	...	...	...	...
Gross capital formation	...	...	...	...	...	...	...	...	...	...	...	...

Table 3.2 Individual consumption expenditure of households, NPISHs, and general government at current prices

Series 200: 1993 SNA, Namibia dollar, Western calendar year — **Data in millions**

		2001	2002	2003	2004	2005	2006	2007	2008	2009	2010	2011	2012
Series		**200**											
		Individual consumption expenditure of households											
Food and non-alcoholic beverages		4478.0	5098.0	5178.0	5925.0	6136.0	7296.0	9365.9	10390.2	11391.5	12444.9	12984.9	15120.5
Alcoholic beverages, tobacco and narcotics		1077.0	1030.0	1237.0	1708.0	1808.0	1907.0	2016.0	2356.6	2592.3	2670.6	2616.8	3142.0
Clothing and footwear		933.0	1229.0	1393.0	1592.0	1670.0	1880.0	2360.8	2294.4	2744.4	2862.8	3113.4	3308.4
Housing, water, electricity, gas and other fuels		4136.0	4770.0	5175.0	3957.0	3964.0	4478.6	5945.0	7501.1	8238.1	9805.9	11122.7	11981.3
Furnishings, household equipment and routine maintenance of the house		...	...	...	...	...	...	...	...	...	...	...	...
Health		1636.0	1674.0	1954.0	2404.0	1885.0	1871.1	2062.5	2974.0	3073.4	3307.7	3742.5	4155.1
Transport		894.0	827.0	1187.0	1223.0	1344.0	1606.0	1006.1	1171.4	2566.9	2579.6	2635.1	2959.4
Communication		...	...	...	...	...	...	...	...	...	...	...	...
Recreation and culture		...	...	...	...	...	...	...	...	...	...	...	...
Education		963.0	970.0	1081.0	1415.0	1329.0	1484.0	1653.7	1999.4	2103.4	2241.3	2453.7	2804.9
Restaurants and hotels		...	...	...	...	...	...	...	...	...	...	...	...
Miscellaneous goods and services		6930.0	7859.0	9492.0	9957.0	10360.0	11821.3	13551.0	15646.2	17935.3	18911.8	19703.9	21524.4
Equals: Household final consumption expenditure in domestic market		21046.9	23557.3	26699.1	28182.0	28494.0	32344.0	37961.0	44333.3	50645.3	54824.6	58373.0	64995.9
Plus: Direct purchases abroad by residents		457.0	609.0	469.0	483.0	606.0	750.0	885.0	885.7	949.9	1004.8	1444.7	1202.4
Less: Direct purchases in domestic market by non-residents		1753.0	2371.0	2634.0	2749.0	2365.0	2753.0	3210.0	3273.1	3526.5	3358.5	3903.5	4133.1
Equals: Household final consumption expenditure	a	19750.4	21796.0	24533.8	25916.1	26734.3	30340.5	35635.9	41945.9	48068.6	52470.9	55914.2	62065.2
		Individual consumption expenditure of non-profit institutions serving households (NPISHs)											
Housing		...	...	...	...	...	...	...	...	...	...	...	...

Series	2001	2002	2003	2004	2005	2006	2007	2008	2009	2010	2011	2012
	200											
Health	465.0	503.0	607.0	667.0	283.0	168.0	181.0	178.3	205.7	193.2	190.0	189.9
Recreation and culture	...	...	...	...	...	...	...	...	...	...	...	...
Education	59.0	66.0	71.0	67.0	70.0	89.0	97.0	273.4	365.4	381.8	449.7	605.9
Social protection	...	...	...	...	...	...	...	...	...	...	...	...
Other services	898.0	1030.0	1115.0	1192.0	1239.0	1325.0	1440.0	1684.3	1983.0	1861.3	1866.2	2022.9
Equals: NPISHs final consumption expenditure	1422.0	1599.0	1793.0	1926.0	1592.0	1582.0	1718.0	2136.1	2554.1	2436.3	2506.0	2818.7
	Individual consumption expenditure of general government											
Equals: Individual consumption expenditure of general government [b]	6970.0	7613.0	8283.0	8693.0	8905.0	10526.5	12834.1	14851.3	17276.6	19587.1	22925.4	26473.1
Equals: Total actual individual consumption	...	...	...	...	...	...	...	...	...	...	...	...

[a] Includes NPISH final consumption expenditure.
[b] Includes Collective Consumption Expenditure.

Table 4.1 Total Economy (S.1)

Series 200: 1993 SNA, Namibia dollar, Western calendar year

Data in millions

Series	2001	2002	2003	2004	2005	2006	2007	2008	2009	2010	2011	2012
	200											
	I. Production account - Resources											
Output, at basic prices (otherwise, please specify)	48863.3	56044.3	60985.4	68464.6	74447.6	87565.3	102203.8	120562.9	121822.0	131471.9	143874.5	167140.6
Less: Financial intermediation services indirectly measured (only to be deducted if FISIM is not distributed to uses)	455.4	488.1	546.3	468.8	517.1	644.0	750.0	840.0	1014.0	1185.0	1265.0	1548.0
Plus: Taxes less Subsidies on products	2353.2	3038.6	2505.9	3502.3	3863.7	4133.5	4665.7	5876.5	6274.6	7133.1	9126.8	8846.0
Plus: Taxes on products	2353.2	3038.6	2505.9	3502.3	3863.7	4133.5	4665.7	5876.5	6274.6	7133.1	9126.8	8846.0
Less: Subsidies on products	...	...	...	...	...	...	...	...	...	...	...	...
	I. Production account - Uses											
Intermediate consumption, at purchaser's prices [a]	20681.0	23653.0	26187.0	29289.0	32134.0	37671.3	44788.9	53493.1	53026.7	57830.4	62398.7	70841.0
GROSS DOMESTIC PRODUCT	30535.2	35429.6	37304.0	42678.3	46177.1	54027.7	62080.6	72946.3	75069.9	80774.6	90602.6	105145.6
Less: Consumption of fixed capital	3187.9	3813.3	4374.3	4883.5	5372.9	6020.0	7250.5	8776.3	9712.7	10606.3	11595.5	12698.8
NET DOMESTIC PRODUCT	27347.4	31616.3	32929.7	37794.9	40804.1	48007.7	54830.1	64170.0	65357.3	70168.3	79007.0	92446.7
	II.1.1 Generation of income account - Resources											
GROSS DOMESTIC PRODUCT	30535.2	35429.6	37304.0	42678.3	46177.1	54027.7	62080.6	72946.3	75069.9	80774.6	90602.6	105145.6
	II.1.1 Generation of income account - Uses											
Compensation of employees	13743.2	15181.3	16880.9	18787.2	19629.8	21508.0	24835.3	28480.7	31064.7	35658.2	38944.5	45019.0
Taxes on production and imports, less Subsidies	2765.1	3506.6	3069.0	4105.4	4492.2	4925.3	5526.2	6758.4	7226.4	8215.6	10330.0	10067.2
Taxes on production and imports	2765.1	3506.6	3069.0	4105.4	4492.2	4925.3	5526.2	6758.4	7226.4	8215.6	10330.0	10067.2
Taxes on products	2353.2	3038.6	2505.9	3502.3	3863.7	4133.5	4665.7	5876.5	6274.6	7133.1	9126.8	8846.0
Other taxes on production	411.9	468.0	563.1	603.0	628.4	791.9	860.5	881.9	951.8	1082.5	1203.2	1221.3
Less: Subsidies	...	...	...	...	...	...	...	...	...	...	...	...
Subsidies on products	...	...	...	...	...	...	...	...	...	...	...	...
Other subsidies on production	...	...	...	...	...	...	...	...	...	...	...	...

	2001	2002	2003	2004	2005	2006	2007	2008	2009	2010	2011	2012
Series	**200**											
OPERATING SURPLUS, GROSS [b]	14026.9	16741.7	17354.0	19785.7	22055.1	27593.8	31719.1	37707.2	36778.9	36900.8	41328.0	50059.3
MIXED INCOME, GROSS	...	...	...	...	...	...	...	...	...	...	...	...
II.1.2 Allocation of primary income account - Resources												
OPERATING SURPLUS, GROSS	14026.9[b]	16741.7[b]	17354.0[b]	19785.7[b]	22055.1[b]	27593.8[b]	31719.1	37707.2	36778.9	36900.8	41328.0	50059.3
MIXED INCOME, GROSS	...	...	...	...	...	...	...	...	...	...	...	...
Compensation of employees	13725.2	15168.3	16853.9	18743.2	19590.8	21469.0	24806.6	28223.0	31030.7	35519.0	38826.3	44946.6
Taxes on production and imports, less Subsidies	2765.1	3506.6	3069.0	4105.4	4492.2	4925.3	5526.2	6758.4	7226.4	8215.6	10330.0	10067.2
Taxes on production and imports	2765.1	3506.6	3069.0	4105.4	4492.2	4925.3	5526.2	6758.4	7226.4	8215.6	10330.0	10067.2
Taxes on products	2353.2	3038.6	2505.9	3502.3	3863.7	4133.5	4665.7	5876.5	6274.6	7133.1	9126.8	8846.0
Other taxes on production	411.9	468.0	563.1	603.0	628.4	791.9	860.5	881.9	951.8	1082.5	1203.2	1221.3
Less: Subsidies	...	...	...	...	...	...	...	...	...	...	...	...
Subsidies on products	...	...	...	...	...	...	...	...	...	...	...	...
Other subsidies on production	...	...	...	...	...	...	...	...	...	...	...	...
Property income [c]	1664.0	1757.0	2067.0	1427.1	889.0	1237.0	1382.3	1803.0	2045.6	1457.1	1730.0	1665.8
II.1.2 Allocation of primary income account - Uses												
Property income [d]	1656.0	1388.0	308.0	845.0	1563.0	1555.0	2597.7	3342.2	3836.6	3758.8	725.2	1829.1
GROSS NATIONAL INCOME	30525.5	35785.7	39035.7	43217.2	45462.6	53670.3	60835.8	71149.4	73244.9	78333.8	91489.2	104909.9
II.2 Secondary distribution of income account - Resources												
GROSS NATIONAL INCOME	30525.5	35785.7	39035.7	43217.2	45462.6	53670.3	60835.8	71149.4	73244.9	78333.8	91489.2	104909.9
Current taxes on income, wealth, etc.	111.0	79.0	25.0	36.0	53.0	67.0	121.9	188.8	168.1	142.6	211.9	185.7
Social contributions	...	...	...	...	...	...	...	...	...	...	...	...
Social benefits other than social transfers in kind	3.6	5.6	7.6	7.6	7.8	7.8	7.8	7.8	7.8	7.8	7.8	7.8
Other current transfers	3182.1	3117.2	3638.0	4485.5	4486.7	6658.4	7291.1	9565.5	11069.6	9508.3	9955.4	16045.2
II.2 Secondary distribution of income account - Uses												
Current taxes on income, wealth, etc.	12.0	14.0	4.0	4.0	4.0	4.0	4.0	4.0	4.0	4.0	4.0	4.0
Social contributions	...	...	...	...	...	...	...	...	...	...	...	...
Social benefits other than social transfers in kind	...	...	...	...	...	...	...	...	...	...	...	...
Other current transfers	300.3	294.0	199.0	221.3	282.0	301.8	365.2	479.6	627.7	636.3	574.9	551.7
GROSS DISPOSABLE INCOME	33510.2	38679.7	42502.9	47520.9	49724.1	60097.9	67888.0	80427.9	83858.7	87352.2	101085.3	120592.9
II.4.1 Use of disposable income account - Resources												
GROSS DISPOSABLE INCOME	33510.2	38679.7	42502.9	47520.9	49724.1	60097.9	67888.0	80427.9	83858.7	87352.2	101085.3	120592.9
Adjustment for the change in net equity of households on pension funds	...	...	...	...	...	...	...	...	...	...	...	...
II.4.1 Use of disposable income account - Uses												
Final consumption expenditure	26720.5	29409.2	32817.0	34609.3	35639.8	40867.0	48470.6	56797.2	65345.2	72058.0	78839.6	88538.3
Individual consumption expenditure	...	...	...	...	...	...	...	...	...	...	...	...
Collective consumption expenditure	...	...	...	...	...	...	...	...	...	...	...	...
Adjustment for the change in net equity of households on pension funds	...	...	...	...	...	...	...	...	...	...	...	...
SAVING, GROSS	6789.7	9270.5	9686.0	12911.7	14084.3	19230.9	19416.4	23630.6	18513.5	15294.1	22245.7	32054.5

	2001	2002	2003	2004	2005	2006	2007	2008	2009	2010	2011	2012
Series	**200**											
	III.1 Capital account - Changes in liabilities and net worth											
SAVING, GROSS	6789.7	9270.5	9686.0	12911.7	14084.3	19230.9	19416.4	23630.6	18513.5	15294.1	22245.7	32054.5
Capital transfers, receivable less payable	42.6	437.4	516.9	524.2	531.6	598.9	586.3	629.4	558.2	808.3	1352.7	1218.4
Capital transfers, receivable	44.6	440.9	519.5	527.3	535.1	602.3	589.7	632.9	628.0	878.0	1426.2	1293.1
Less: Capital transfers, payable	2.0	3.5	2.7	3.1	3.4	3.4	3.4	3.4	69.8	69.8	73.5	74.8
Equals: CHANGES IN NET WORTH DUE TO SAVING AND CAPITAL TRANSFERS	...	...	...	...	...	...	...	...	...	...	...	...
	III.1 Capital account - Changes in assets											
Gross capital formation	6815.0	6562.2	7225.5	8137.6	9092.1	12027.6	14728.0	18498.9	16777.1	17074.7	18147.3	22309.7
Gross fixed capital formation	6391.2	7065.9	7120.7	7921.9	8594.4	11685.8	14695.9	17837.5	16608.8	18377.7	19291.4	22153.2
Changes in inventories	423.8	-503.6	104.8	215.7	497.7	341.7	32.1	661.4	168.2	-1303.0	-1144.1	156.5
Acquisitions less disposals of valuables	...	...	...	...	...	...	...	...	...	...	...	...
Acquisitions less disposals of non-produced non-financial assets	...	...	...	...	...	...	...	...	...	...	...	...
NET LENDING (+) / NET BORROWING (-)	17.3	3145.7	2977.4	5298.3	5523.8	7802.1	5275.7	5761.1	2294.7	-972.3	5451.1	10963.2

[a] Includes financial intermediation services indirectly measured (FISIM) of the Total Economy.
[b] Includes Mixed Income, Gross.
[c] Refers to Property income from the rest of the world.
[d] Refers to Property income to the rest of the world.

Table 4.2 Rest of the world (S.2)

Series 200: 1993 SNA, Namibia dollar, Western calendar year

Data in millions

	2001	2002	2003	2004	2005	2006	2007	2008	2009	2010	2011	2012
Series	**200**											
	V.I External account of goods and services - Resources											
Imports of goods and services	14556.0	17032.0	19574.0	17959.0	18615.0	22454.0	32310.0	39849.1	42115.8	44419.5	47327.1	51170.5
Imports of goods	12306.0	14673.0	17712.0	15475.0	16291.0	19530.0	28692.4	34906.8	37295.2	39306.1	42152.0	45911.6
Imports of services	2250.0	2359.0	1862.0	2484.0	2325.0	2924.0	3617.7	4942.4	4820.6	5113.4	5175.1	5258.8
	V.I External account of goods and services - Uses											
Exports of goods and services	12574.0	16299.0	16185.0	16991.0	18678.0	24565.6	31496.4	38776.8	35511.4	38476.5	40926.9	44759.1
Exports of goods	10414.0	13453.0	13054.0	13917.0	16048.0	20967.7	27263.2	34326.4	30049.2	31926.2	34482.7	38524.1
Exports of services	2160.0	2845.0	3131.0	3075.0	2631.0	3598.0	4233.0	4450.3	5462.3	6550.3	6444.2	6235.0
EXTERNAL BALANCE OF GOODS AND SERVICES	1982.0	733.0	3389.0	968.0	-63.2	-2111.6	813.8	1072.4	6604.3	5943.0	6400.2	6411.4
	V.II External account of primary income and current transfers - Resources											
EXTERNAL BALANCE OF GOODS AND SERVICES	1982.0	733.0	3389.0	968.0	-63.2	-2111.6	813.8[a]	1072.4	6604.3	5943.0	6400.2	6411.4
Compensation of employees	58.0	59.0	83.0	100.0	106.0	106.0	95.4	324.3	100.6	205.7	184.7	139.0
Taxes on production and imports, less Subsidies	...	...	...	...	...	...	...	...	...	...	...	...
Taxes on production and imports	...	...	...	...	...	...	...	...	...	...	...	...
Taxes on products	...	...	...	...	...	...	...	...	...	...	...	...
Other taxes on production	...	...	...	...	...	...	...	...	...	...	...	...
Less: Subsidies	...	...	...	...	...	...	...	...	...	...	...	...

	2001	2002	2003	2004	2005	2006	2007	2008	2009	2010	2011	2012
Series	**200**											
Subsidies on products	...	...	...	...	...	...	...	...	...	...	...	...
Other subsidies on production	...	...	...	...	...	...	...	...	...	...	...	...
Property income	1656.0	1388.0	308.0	845.0	1563.0	1555.0	2597.7	3342.2	3836.6	3758.8	725.2	1829.1
Current taxes on income, wealth, etc.	12.0	14.0	4.0	4.0	4.0	4.0	4.0	4.0	4.0	4.0	4.0	4.0
Social contributions	...	...	...	...	...	...	...	...	...	...	...	...
Social benefits other than social transfers in kind	...	...	...	...	...	...	...	...	...	...	...	...
Other current transfers	300.0	294.0	199.0	221.0	282.0	302.0	338.0	479.6	627.7	636.3	574.9	551.7
Adjustment for the change in net equity of households on pension funds	...	...	...	...	...	...	...	...	...	...	...	...
V.II External account of primary income and current transfers - Uses												
Compensation of employees	40.0	46.0	56.0	56.0	67.0	67.0	67.0	66.6	66.6	66.6	66.6	66.6
Taxes on production and imports, less Subsidies	...	...	...	...	...	...	...	...	...	...	...	...
Taxes on production and imports	...	...	...	...	...	...	...	...	...	...	...	...
Taxes on products	...	...	...	...	...	...	...	...	...	...	...	...
Other taxes on production	...	...	...	...	...	...	...	...	...	...	...	...
Less: Subsidies	...	...	...	...	...	...	...	...	...	...	...	...
Subsidies on products	...	...	...	...	...	...	...	...	...	...	...	...
Other subsidies on production	...	...	...	...	...	...	...	...	...	...	...	...
Property income	1664.0	1757.0	2067.0	1427.1	889.0	1237.0	1382.3	1803.0	2045.6	1457.1	1730.0	1665.8
Current taxes on income and wealth, etc.	111.0	79.0	25.0	36.0	53.0	67.0	122.0	188.8	168.1	142.6	211.9	185.7
Social contributions	...	...	...	...	...	...	...	...	...	...	...	...
Social benefits other than social transfers in kind	4.0	6.0	8.0	8.0	8.0	8.0	8.0	7.8	7.8	7.8	7.8	7.8
Other current transfers	3182.0	3117.0	3638.0	4485.0	4487.0	6658.0	7263.2	9565.5	11069.6	9508.3	9955.4	16045.2
Adjustment for the change in net equity of households on pension funds	...	...	...	...	...	...	...	...	...	...	...	...
CURRENT EXTERNAL BALANCE	-993.0	-2517.0	-1810.0	-3875.0	-3610.0[b]	-8181.8	-4993.6	-6409.2	-2184.4	-634.6	-4082.6	-9035.9
V.III.1 Capital account - Changes in liabilities and net worth												
CURRENT EXTERNAL BALANCE	-993.0	-2517.0	-1810.0	-3875.0	-3610.0	-8181.8	-4993.6	-6409.2	-2184.4	-634.6	-4082.6	-9035.9
Capital transfers, receivable less payable	-42.6	-437.4	-516.9	-524.2	-531.6	-598.9	-587.0	-629.4	-558.2	-808.3	-1352.7	-1218.4
Capital transfers, receivable	2.0	3.5	2.7	3.1	3.4	3.4	3.4	3.4	69.8	69.8	73.5	74.8
Less: Capital transfers, payable	44.6	440.9	519.5	527.3	535.1	602.3	589.7	632.9	628.0	878.0	1426.2	1293.1
Equals: CHANGES IN NET WORTH DUE TO SAVING AND CAPITAL TRANSFERS	...	...	...	...	...	...	...	...	...	...	...	...
V.III.1 Capital account - Changes in assets												
Acquisitions less disposals of non-produced non-financial assets [c]	-1018.2	191.5	650.0	899.0	1381.9	-978.6	-304.0	-1277.5	-448.0	-2415.1	15.9	708.9
NET LENDING (+) / NET BORROWING (-)	-17.3	-3145.7	-2977.4	-5298.3	-5523.8	-7802.1	-5275.7	-5761.1	-2294.7	972.3	-5451.1	-10963.2

[a] Discrepancy between components and total.
[b] Account does not balance.
[c] Refers to statistical discrepancy.

Table 4.5 General Government (S.13)

Series 200: 1993 SNA, Namibia dollar, Western calendar year

Data in millions

	2001	2002	2003	2004	2005	2006	2007	2008	2009	2010	2011	2012
Series	**200**											
I. Production account - Resources												
Output, at basic prices (otherwise, please specify)	7985.3	8886.0	9715.0	10287.0	10517.0	12186.0	14980.0	17295.5	19964.4	22604.3	26632.6	29879.1
I. Production account - Uses												
Intermediate consumption, at purchaser's prices	2313.0	2547.0	2827.0	2872.0	2724.0	3544.4	4689.0	5542.2	6290.1	6708.5	8197.1	9025.5
VALUE ADDED GROSS, at basic prices	5673.0	6338.0	6884.0	7415.0	7792.0	8641.5	10291.0	11753.3	13674.3	15895.9	18435.4	20853.6
Less: Consumption of fixed capital	524.5	617.1	707.2	790.4	889.0	1028.7	1350.0	1639.6	1822.7	1943.9	2089.7	2275.9
VALUE ADDED NET, at basic prices	5148.1	5721.3	6181.5	6624.4	6903.3	7612.9	8941.0	10113.7	11851.6	13951.9	16345.8	18577.7
II.1.1 Generation of income account - Resources												
VALUE ADDED GROSS, at basic prices	5673.0	6338.0	6884.0	7415.0	7792.0	8641.5	10291.0	11753.3	13674.3	15895.9	18435.4	20853.6
II.1.1 Generation of income account - Uses												
Compensation of employees	4726.0	5238.0	5734.0	6136.0	6327.0	7118.9	8412.0	9397.2	10978.2	12989.2	15142.0	17249.7
Other taxes less Other subsidies on production	...	...	...	...	...	...	...	...	...	...	...	...
Other taxes on production	...	...	...	...	...	...	...	...	...	...	...	...
Less: Other subsidies on production	...	...	...	...	...	...	...	...	...	...	...	...
OPERATING SURPLUS, GROSS	946.9	1100.8	1154.6	1278.7	1464.9	1522.6	1879.0	2356.1	2696.1	2906.7	3293.4	3603.9
II.1.2 Allocation of primary income account - Resources												
OPERATING SURPLUS, GROSS	946.9	1100.8	1154.6	1278.7	1464.9	1522.6	1879.0	2356.1	2696.1	2906.7	3293.4	3603.9
Taxes on production and imports, less Subsidies	2765.1	3506.6	3069.0	4105.4	4492.2	4925.3	5526.0	6758.4	7226.4	8215.6	10330.0	10067.2
Taxes on production and imports	2765.1	3506.6	3069.0	4105.4	4492.2	4925.3	5526.0	6758.4	7226.4	8215.6	10330.0	10067.2
Taxes on products	2353.2	3038.6	2505.9	3502.3	3863.7	4133.5	4666.0	5876.5	6274.6	7133.1	9126.8	8846.0
Other taxes on production	411.9	468.0	563.1	603.0	628.4	791.9	861.0	881.9	951.8	1082.5	1203.2	1221.3
Less: Subsidies	...	...	...	...	...	...	...	...	...	...	...	...
Subsidies on products	...	...	...	...	...	...	...	...	...	...	...	...
Other subsidies on production	...	...	...	...	...	...	...	...	...	...	...	...
Property income	101.5	124.6	136.1	93.2	538.7	429.7	285.0	580.4	603.7	1161.1	1118.8	1042.4
II.1.2 Allocation of primary income account - Uses												
Property income	808.7	876.4	1088.3	1237.6	1199.8	1127.7	1175.8	1268.0	1024.2	1090.2	1930.1	2233.8
BALANCE OF PRIMARY INCOMES [a]	2480.2	3238.5	2564.2	3449.3	4407.0	4721.5	5164.9	6787.3	7679.2	9249.3	10722.5	10203.9
II.2 Secondary distribution of income account - Resources												
BALANCE OF PRIMARY INCOMES	2480.2[a]	3238.5[a]	2564.2[a]	3449.3[a]	4407.0[a]	4721.5	5164.9	6787.3	7679.2	9249.3	10722.5	10203.9
Current taxes on income, wealth, etc.	3757.4	4131.9	3966.8	4389.9	5347.5	6388.6	7701.0	8150.6	9336.3	11000.6	12600.2	13530.1
Social contributions	...	...	...	...	...	...	...	...	...	...	...	...
Other current transfers	...	...	...	...	...	...	...	...	...	...	...	...
II.2 Secondary distribution of income account - Uses												
Current taxes on income, wealth, etc.	...	...	...	...	...	...	...	...	...	...	...	...
Social benefits other than social transfers in kind	839.0	1015.5	1106.1	1214.1	1381.5	1478.2	2128.0	2685.5	3433.4	4596.3	5082.0	6680.8

	2001	2002	2003	2004	2005	2006	2007	2008	2009	2010	2011	2012
Series	**200**											
Other current transfers	...	...	...	...	...	...	...	...	...	...	...	...
GROSS DISPOSABLE INCOME	7375.3	8136.3	7908.3	9854.6	11609.4	14749.1	15879.4	19303.2	21507.3	21214.1	23789.6	27775.6
II.4.1 Use of disposable income account - Resources												
GROSS DISPOSABLE INCOME	7375.3	8136.3	7908.3	9854.6	11609.4	14749.1	15879.4	19303.2	21507.3	21214.1	23789.6	27775.6
II.4.1 Use of disposable income account - Uses												
Final consumption expenditure	6970.1	7613.2	8283.1	8693.2	8905.5	10526.5	12834.0	14851.3	17276.6	19587.1	22925.4	26473.1
Individual consumption expenditure	...	...	...	...	...	...	...	...	...	...	...	...
Collective consumption expenditure	...	...	...	...	...	...	...	...	...	...	...	...
Adjustment for the change in net equity of households on pension funds	...	...	...	...	...	...	...	...	...	...	...	...
SAVING, GROSS	405.2[a]	523.1[a]	-374.8[a]	1161.3[a]	2704.0[a]	4222.6	3045.3	4451.9	4230.8	1627.0	864.2	1302.5
III.1 Capital account - Changes in liabilities and net worth												
SAVING, GROSS [a]	405.2	523.1	-374.8	1161.3	2704.0	4222.6	3045.3	4451.9	4230.8	1627.0	864.2	1302.5
Capital transfers, receivable less payable	-29.3	-16.5	-61.5	-43.7	-114.8	-298.2	-365.4	-659.1	-1124.0	-2558.8	-2629.0	-2763.5
Capital transfers, receivable	41.8	43.6	38.5	39.5	39.6	39.7	40.7	40.8	40.9	40.9	41.0	41.1
Less: Capital transfers, payable	71.1	60.1	100.0	83.3	154.4	337.8	406.2	699.9	1164.8	2599.7	2670.0	2804.5
Equals: CHANGES IN NET WORTH DUE TO SAVING AND CAPITAL TRANSFERS	...	...	...	...	...	...	...	...	...	...	...	...
III.1 Capital account - Changes in assets												
Gross capital formation	1059.1	1042.0	1057.8	1164.8	1496.7	1728.2	2889.0	2820.6	2685.8	2750.3	3437.1	4151.9
Gross fixed capital formation	1059.1	1042.0	1057.8	1164.8	1496.7	1728.2	2889.0	2820.6	2685.8	2750.3	3437.1	4151.9
Changes in inventories	...	...	...	...	...	...	...	...	...	...	...	...
Acquisitions less disposals of valuables	...	...	...	...	...	...	...	...	...	...	...	...
Acquisitions of non-produced non-financial assets [b]	71.9	39.3	12.0	43.0	22.4	50.0	57.0	70.8	65.3	62.5	27.5	27.0
NET LENDING (+) / NET BORROWING (-)	-174.4	126.3	-713.3	563.9	2047.2	3205.5	1086.4	2632.6	1993.5	-1960.5	-3236.3	-3595.8

[a] Refers to Net value, i.e. excludes Consumption of fixed capital.
[b] Refers to acquisition of land.
[c] Refers to statistical discrepancy.

Nauru

Source

Reply to the United Nations national accounts questionnaire from the Bureau of Statistics, Ministry of Finance, Yaren district. Official estimates for the years 2004-2009 can be found on the following website: http://www.spc.int/prism/country/nr/stats/index.htm

General

The estimates shown in the following tables have been prepared in accordance with the United Nations System of National Accounts 1993 (1993 SNA) so far as the existing data would permit. When the scope and coverage of the estimates differ for conceptual or statistical reasons from the definitions and classifications recommended in the SNA, a footnote provides explanation.

Table 2.1 Value added by industries at current prices (ISIC Rev. 3)

Series 100: 1993 SNA, Australian dollar, Fiscal year ending 30 June

Data in thousands

	2001	2002	2003	2004	2005	2006	2007	2008	2009	2010	2011	2012
Series				**100**								
Industries												
Agriculture, hunting, forestry; fishing				2710.0	2680.0	2620.0	2560.0	2600.0	2830.0			
Agriculture, hunting, forestry				1490.0	1330.0	1020.0	930.0	940.0	800.0			
Fishing				1220.0	1350.0	1600.0	1630.0	1660.0	2030.0			
Mining and quarrying				340.0	160.0	480.0	1870.0	6440.0	10150.0			
Manufacturing				3020.0	1220.0	-330.0	190.0	7100.0	17290.0			
Electricity, gas and water supply				-5100.0[a]	-4760.0[a]	-2050.0[a]	1530.0	3120.0	5760.0			
Construction				1080.0	1150.0	2610.0	1280.0	2190.0	2340.0			
Wholesale, retail trade, repair of motor vehicles, motorcycles and personal and households goods; hotels and restaurants				7230.0	6720.0	6740.0	8310.0	8690.0	9090.0			
Wholesale, retail trade, repair of motor vehicles, motorcycles and personal and household goods				4650.0	4070.0	4540.0	6030.0	6580.0	6680.0			
Hotels and restaurants				2580.0	2650.0	2200.0	2280.0	2110.0	2410.0			
Transport, storage and communications				9420.0	8190.0	3890.0	-350.0	6110.0	6420.0			
Financial intermediation; real estate, renting and business activities				4800.0	4890.0	5090.0	5040.0	5390.0	6480.0			
Public administration and defence; compulsory social security				11700.0	11690.0	11780.0	4080.0	4090.0	4860.0			
Education; health and social work; other community, social and personal services				2360.0	2480.0	2900.0	3120.0	3790.0	4320.0			
Education				800.0	840.0	990.0	1080.0	1530.0	1920.0			
Health and social work				1040.0	1080.0	1270.0	1390.0	1590.0	1600.0			
Other community, social and personal services				520.0	560.0	640.0	650.0	670.0	800.0			
Private households with employed persons				...	...	...	...	...	...			
Equals: VALUE ADDED, GROSS, in basic prices				...	...	...	...	...	...			
Less: Financial intermediation services indirectly measured (FISIM)				...	...	...	...	...	...			

	2001	2002	2003	2004	2005	2006	2007	2008	2009	2010	2011	2012
Series				**100**								
Plus: Taxes less Subsidies on products				...	...	...	...	...	...			
Equals: GROSS DOMESTIC PRODUCT				37560.0	34430.0	33720.0	27620.0	49530.0	69550.0			

[a] The figure is negative because value added data are provided at producer prices, including subsidies that were necessary to restructure the water and electricity industries and make them independent from the Nauru Phosphate Corporation (NPC).

Table 2.2 Value added by industries at constant prices (ISIC Rev. 3)

Series 100: 1993 SNA, Australian dollar, Fiscal year ending 30 June **Data in thousands**

	2001	2002	2003	2004	2005	2006	2007	2008	2009	2010	2011	2012
Series				**100**								
Base year				**2007**								
	Industries											
Agriculture, hunting, forestry; fishing				2800.0	2780.0	2650.0	2560.0	2610.0	2650.0			
Agriculture, hunting, forestry				1020.0	1010.0	960.0	930.0	950.0	960.0			
Fishing				1780.0	1770.0	1690.0	1630.0	1660.0	1690.0			
Mining and quarrying				1700.0	480.0	570.0	1870.0	12470.0	8890.0			
Manufacturing				1060.0	1210.0	-720.0	190.0	7220.0	-100.0			
Electricity, gas and water supply				2040.0	2280.0	1720.0	1530.0	2820.0	3520.0			
Construction				1180.0	1220.0	2680.0	1280.0	2100.0	2180.0			
Wholesale, retail trade, repair of motor vehicles, motorcycles and personal and household goods; hotels and restaurants				7530.0	6510.0	7010.0	8310.0	8480.0	7920.0			
Wholesale, retail trade, repair of motor vehicles, motorcycles and personal and household goods				6150.0	5010.0	4790.0	6030.0	6480.0	5690.0			
Hotels and restaurants				1380.0	1500.0	2220.0	2280.0	2000.0	2230.0			
Transport, storage and communications				13780.0	11420.0	4370.0	-350.0	5530.0	5290.0			
Financial intermediation, real estate, renting and business activities				5130.0	5130.0	5210.0	5040.0	5160.0	6080.0			
Public administration and defence; compulsory social security				4460.0	4440.0	4230.0	4080.0	4150.0	4220.0			
Education; health and social work; other community, social and personal services				3410.0	3390.0	3240.0	3120.0	3480.0	3570.0			
Education				1180.0	1170.0	1120.0	1080.0	1380.0	1580.0			
Health and social work				1520.0	1510.0	1440.0	1390.0	1440.0	1320.0			
Other community, social and personal services				710.0	710.0	680.0	650.0	660.0	670.0			
Private households with employed persons				...	...	...	...	...	...			
Equals: VALUE ADDED, GROSS, in basic prices				...	...	...	...	...	...			
Less: Financial intermediation services indirectly measured (FISIM)				...	...	...	...	...	...			
Plus: Taxes less Subsidies on products				...	...	...	...	...	...			
Equals: GROSS DOMESTIC PRODUCT				43090.0	38850.0	30950.0	27620.0	54020.0	44210.0			

Table 5.1 Cross classification of Gross value added by industries and institutional sectors (ISIC Rev. 3) Non-financial corporations

Series 100: 1993 SNA, Australian dollar, Fiscal year ending 30 June

Data in thousands

		2001	2002	2003	2004	2005	2006	2007	2008	2009	2010	2011	2012
Series					**100**								
	Industries												
VALUE ADDED GROSS, at basic prices	[a]				14599.5	11358.9	9856.8	11046.7	31522.9	48898.2			

[a] Includes Taxes less subsidies on products.

Table 5.1 Cross classification of Gross value added by industries and institutional sectors (ISIC Rev. 3) General government

Series 100: 1993 SNA, Australian dollar, Fiscal year ending 30 June

Data in thousands

		2001	2002	2003	2004	2005	2006	2007	2008	2009	2010	2011	2012
Series					**100**								
	Industries												
VALUE ADDED GROSS, at basic prices	[a]				14000.0	14000.2	14479.5	7145.7	8034.6	9102.3			

[a] Includes Taxes less subsidies on products.

Table 5.1 Cross classification of Gross value added by industries and institutional sectors (ISIC Rev. 3) Households

Series 100: 1993 SNA, Australian dollar, Fiscal year ending 30 June

Data in thousands

		2001	2002	2003	2004	2005	2006	2007	2008	2009	2010	2011	2012
Series					**100**								
	Industries												
VALUE ADDED GROSS, at basic prices	[a]				8962.2	9073.4	9388.3	9427.9	9972.3	11552.0			

[a] Includes Taxes less subsidies on products. Includes data for the NPISH (Non-profit institutions serving households) sector.

Table 5.1 Cross classification of Gross value added by industries and institutional sectors (ISIC Rev. 3) Total economy

Series 100: 1993 SNA, Australian dollar, Fiscal year ending 30 June

Data in thousands

		2001	2002	2003	2004	2005	2006	2007	2008	2009	2010	2011	2012
Series					**100**								
	Industries												
VALUE ADDED GROSS, at basic prices	[a]				37561.7	34432.6	33724.6	27620.3	49529.8	69552.5			

[a] Value Added refers to GDP.

Nepal

Source

The institution responsible for compiling National Accounts estimates is the Central Bureau of Statistics. The NRB (Central Bank of Nepal) is responsible for compiling BOP (Balance of Payments) accounts. Official national accounts estimates are published in "National Accounts of Nepal", an annual publication.

General

In Nepal, the concept of 1993 SNA is used to the extent possible for the compilation of national accounts. It was adopted from the year 2000/01. The most recent publication on national accounts is "National Accounts of Nepal 2000-2007". National accounts are released each year in June/July. Recently the base year and methodology of SNA 1968 was updated. Full details of the national accounts and national accounts methodology are available at www.cbs.gov.np.

Benchmarking of national accounts estimates has become prime need for improving the quality of national accounts statistics. The levels of transactions of many economic activities were based on old surveys and studies. Because of the outdated benchmarks, the changes in the structure of output, input, value added, and capital formation of such economic activities were not revealed. Moreover, the changes in the economy occurred with newly emerged economic activities were not properly covered in the accounting system due to data gap in these areas. As a result, estimates were becoming less reliable and inconsistent.

Realizing the fact, Central Bureau of Statistics initiated the work on benchmarking the national accounts estimates exploring and using the available data from different sources. Data collected from major statistical operations such as Population Census 2001, Agriculture Census 2001, Manufacturing Census 2002, Nepal Labor Force Survey 1999, Nepal Living Standard Measurement Survey (NLSS) 2003 are used intensively to update the level and structure of the accounts. In addition, some fresh surveys covering different areas of the economy are conducted and their results are used to update and establish new national accounts benchmarks.

As the system of national accounts of Nepal is based on international guidelines, the methodological changes taken place internationally needs to be accommodated accordingly. Therefore, Central Bureau of Statistics carried out different activities for implementing 1993 System of National Accounts. To implement the system, an assessment of the situation in the context from the old system (1968 SNA) to a new system (1993 SNA) was made. The methodology and data sources of the Nepal System of National Accounts (NSNA) compilation have been reviewed and updated to the extent possible following the 1993 SNA. Similarly, concepts, definitions and also classifications recommended by the 1993 SNA have been followed, including the fact that each table has the same fiscal year which starts from the middle of July according to the Nepali Calendar and national accounts aggregates in constant prices are reported in the form of volume measures with a fixed base year 2000/01.

Methodology:

Overview of GDP Compilation

The main approach to compile GDP is the production approach. Valuation of national accounts aggregates with FISIM is used. Values of output, intermediate consumption, compensation of employees and other values are valued at producers' prices and at basic prices. While computing taxation, two types of taxes have been taken into consideration: taxes on products and taxes on production.

Classification of industries is based on NSIC (Nepal Standard Industrial Classification, 2000). These industries follow the ISIC recommendations. Note that since the contribution of NSIC division P & Q are insignificant, estimates are included in division O.

Expenditure Approach

The estimates of GDP at current and constant prices are prepared for the period 2000/01-2005/06. The compilation is based on the general identity model: Y = Cg+Cp+Ig+Ip+(X-M), where, Cg is government consumption; Cp is private consumption; Ig is government investment; Ip is private investment; X is exports; and M is imports.

Overview of the Compilation of the Integrated Economic Accounts

In the case of Nepal, only the production account is prepared by industry and other sequence of accounts is not available so far as the institutional sectors and sub–sectors are concerned.

An institutional unit is defined in the system as an economic entity that is capable, in its own right, of owning assets, incurring liabilities and engaging in economic activities and in transactions with other entities. The institutional units that make up the total economy are grouped into five mutually exclusive institutional sectors: the non-financial corporation sector; the financial corporation sector; the government sector; the household sector, and the non-profit institutions serving household sector.

All resident non-financial corporations and quasi corporations are included in the non-financial corporation sector. Non-financial corporations are further divided into public and private non-financial corporations. The principal activity of non-financial corporations is the production of goods or non-financial services. The estimates of non-financial corporations are obtained by cross classifying the transaction by economic activities and institutional units. While compiling national accounts aggregates at industry level, transactions are identified at the same time also at institutional sector level. Hence, a cross tabulation of the transaction by economic activities and by institutional sectors is prepared for compilation purposes. Since the preparation of estimates at institutional sector level requires data in greater detail, NA aggregates are mainly based on the benchmark surveys conducted in the years 2004 and 2005.

The financial corporations sector consists of all resident corporations or quasi corporations principally engaged in financial intermediation or auxiliary financial activities related to financial intermediation. For the estimates of gross value added and other aggregates, financial sector is further divided into sub-sectors- the central bank, other depository corporations, other financial intermediaries except insurance and pension funds, financial auxiliaries, insurance companies, and pension funds. National accounts aggregates are estimated utilizing the financial statistics compiled by the Nepal Rastra Bank and also processing the financial statements of the respective institutions.

Government units may be described as unique kinds of legal entities established by political processes, which have legislative, judicial, and executive authority. The activities of government units are grouped into two levels- central government and local government. The transaction of central government is derived from the government accounts. Central government expenditures are reclassified and regrouped to derive estimates by main functional categories.

To get national accounts estimates at local government level, data are compiled separately for local government bodies – Village Development Committee (VDCs), District Development Committee (DDCs), and Municipalities. Data on the transactions of VDCs and DDCs are collected annually administering some pre-designed questionnaire in a sample basis. This information is processed and used in the compilation of NA aggregates for these local government bodies. In case of municipalities, the report prepared by Urban Development Through Local Efforts (UDLE), Ministry of Local development is utilized to get information on the transactions – output, intermediate consumption, taxes, capital formation etc.

The household sector is defined as 'group of persons who share the same living accommodation, who pool some or all, of their income and wealth and consume certain types of goods and services collectively, mainly housing and food' SNA para. 4.132. The household sector engages in production activities that are directly controlled and owned by the members of households, either individually or in partnership with others. Producer units within the household sector are all unincorporated enterprises.

The main data source for NA estimates at household sector level is the Nepal Living Standard Measurement Survey (NLSS 2004). Unincorporated household activities (non-agriculture) are identified using the criteria of not registered and without hired labour and grouped them into NSIC two digit level for estimating output, input and compensation of employees. For the estimates of agricultural activities, the value of output is estimated using the production data supplied by MOAC and DOA. Information on price and cost of production is also available from different departments- Department of livestock, Department of Horticulture, Department of Agriculture/ Marketing Development Directorate, District Agriculture Offices, Fish Development Centre, and Department of Forest. Producers of services for own final use- services of owner-occupied dwellings are estimated using NLSS survey data.

Non-profit institutions are legal or social entities created for the purpose of producing goods or services with non-profit motives. By virtue, these institutions are not permitted to generate operating surplus. The estimates of transactions of NPISHs are based on the survey on NGOs and INGOs (CBS 2002). The survey result provides information on economic transactions – output, input capital formation and compensation of employees. The number of NGOs is used as an extrapolator to get the estimates for other years. Since NPISHs operate non-market transactions like the government, estimates are inflated by the same wage index (public sector wage index) that is used for government services to derive estimates at current prices. The national accounts estimates from NPISHs are merged into the household sector, since it does not permit to prepare separate accounts because of the insufficiency and irregularity of input data required for the compilation.

The rest of the world consists of all non-resident institutional units that enter into transactions with resident units, or have other economic links with resident units. The rest of the world account is compiled using balance of payment (BOP) statistics as published by Nepal Rastra Bank. The BOP data is reclassified and used in the compilation of the activities of the rest of the world. Since there is complete concurrence between the 1993 SNA and BOP –V, the relevant portion of the BOP data, e.g., factor income, current transfers, exports and imports of goods and services are received and used in the compilation of NA estimates of GNI, GNDI, GNS.

Table 1.1 Gross domestic product by expenditures at current prices

Series 100: 1993 SNA, Nepalese rupee, Fiscal year ending 15 July — **Data in millions**

	2001	2002	2003	2004	2005	2006	2007	2008	2009	2010	2011	2012
Series	**100**											
	Expenditures of the gross domestic product											
Final consumption expenditure	390017.0	415843.0	450090.0	473685.0	521301.0	595327.0	656374.0	735470.0	895042.0	1056185.0	1176030.0	1359539.0
Household final consumption expenditure	348989.0	371402.0	400468.0	419290.0	459530.0	527814.0	576911.0	641085.0	772762.0	916993.0	1022126.0	1167861.0
NPISHs final consumption expenditure	5243.0	5855.0	6970.0	7998.0	9319.0	10719.0	12515.0	13721.0	15753.0	20002.0	22987.0	27307.0
General government final consumption expenditure	35785.0	38585.8	42652.0	46397.2	52452.7	56794.0	66949.0	80663.0	106527.0	119189.0	130917.0	164370.0
Individual consumption expenditure	10409.0	10729.0	11277.0	12437.0	17828.0	19689.0	23210.0	25667.0	36689.0	41716.0	44845.0	54800.0
Collective consumption expenditure	25376.0	27857.0	31375.0	33960.0	34625.0	37105.0	43739.0	54996.0	69838.0	77473.0	86072.0	109570.0
Gross capital formation	98649.2	93019.7	105384.0	131670.0	155907.0	175633.0	208779.0	247272.0	313029.0	456489.0	527268.0	535545.0
Gross fixed capital formation	84750.6	89889.3	98072.8	109181.0	117539.0	135532.0	153337.0	178446.0	211039.0	264888.0	292730.0	307384.0
Changes in inventories	13898.6	3130.5	7310.9	22489.0	38367.7	40101.0	55442.0	68826.0	101990.0	191602.0	234537.0	228161.0
Acquisitions less disposals of valuables	...	...	...	...	...	...	...	...	...	...	...	...
Exports of goods and services	99610.2	81491.7	77279.6	89544.2	85958.0	87952.0	93567.0	104207.0	122737.0	114298.0	121714.0	153863.0
Exports of goods	69789.0	57984.0	50761.0	55228.0	59956.0	61482.0	61488.0	61971.0	69907.0	63178.0	68702.0	81512.0
Exports of services	29822.0	23508.0	26519.0	34316.0	26002.0	26470.0	32079.0	42236.0	52830.0	51121.0	53013.0	72352.0

	2001	2002	2003	2004	2005	2006	2007	2008	2009	2010	2011	2012
Series	**100**											
Less: Imports of goods and services	146757.0	130912.0	140522.0	158151.0	173754.0	204828.0	230893.0	271291.0	342536.0	434198.0	450058.0	512948.0
Imports of goods	126238.0	111342.0	121053.0	132910.0	145718.0	171540.0	190437.0	217963.0	279228.0	366693.0	388371.0	454653.0
Imports of services	20519.0	19570.0	19469.0	25241.0	28036.0	33288.0	40456.0	53328.0	63308.0	67506.0	61687.0	58295.0
Equals: GROSS DOMESTIC PRODUCT	441519.0	459443.0	492231.0	536749.0	589412.0	654084.0	727827.0	815658.0	988272.0	1192774.0	1374953.0	1536000.0

Table 1.2 Gross domestic product by expenditures at constant prices

Series 100: 1993 SNA, Nepalese rupee, Fiscal year ending 15 July — **Data in millions**

	2001	2002	2003	2004	2005	2006	2007	2008	2009	2010	2011	2012
Series	**100**											
Base year	**2001**											
	Expenditures of the gross domestic product											
Final consumption expenditure	390017.0	405389.0	421043.0	428452.0	446957.0	468921.0	485657.0	492849.0	522911.0	552676.0	563138.0	599628.0
Household final consumption expenditure	348989.0	360947.0	371421.0	374057.0	392219.0	413217.0	425419.0	430763.0	455468.0	482984.0	485249.0	510257.0
NPISHs final consumption expenditure	5243.0	5855.0	6970.0	7998.0	7765.0	8377.0	9519.0	9707.0	9980.0	11473.0	12036.0	13027.0
General government final consumption expenditure	35785.0	38586.0	42652.0	46397.0	46973.0	47328.0	50719.0	52378.0	57462.0	58220.0	65852.0	76343.0
Individual consumption expenditure	10409.0	10729.0	11277.0	12437.0	15965.0	16408.0	17583.0	16667.0	19791.0	20377.0	22557.0	25452.0
Collective consumption expenditure	25376.0	27857.0	31375.0	33960.0	31008.0	30920.0	33136.0	35711.0	37671.0	37843.0	43295.0	50891.0
Gross capital formation	98649.0	84808.0	90298.0	106047.0	116084.0	121233.0	127327.0	165035.0	179205.0	240920.0	241554.0	242746.0
Gross fixed capital formation	84751.0	84863.0	88069.0	90949.0	91427.0	101570.0	106940.0	108922.0	109459.0	127647.0	126723.0	121978.0
Changes in inventories	13898.0	-55.0	2229.0	15098.0	24657.0	19664.0	20386.0	56113.0	69746.0	113273.0	114831.0	120769.0
Acquisitions less disposals of valuables	...	...	...	...	...	...	...	...	...	...	...	...
Exports of goods and services	99611.0	76512.0	72880.0	81828.0	79344.0	78318.0	77578.0	78142.0	81168.0	72695.0	71158.0	72522.0
Exports of goods	69789.0	54440.0	47871.0	50469.0	55343.0	54748.0	50981.0	46470.0	46231.0	38489.0	38477.0	38083.0
Exports of services	29822.0	22072.0	25009.0	31359.0	24001.0	23570.0	26597.0	31672.0	34937.0	34206.0	32682.0	34439.0
Less: Imports of goods and services	146757.0	124660.0	124734.0	135323.0	144646.0	153988.0	158523.0	171509.0	193175.0	247762.0	236156.0	244161.0
Imports of goods	126238.0	106025.0	107452.0	113725.0	121307.0	128962.0	130747.0	137795.0	157472.0	209242.0	203780.0	216413.0
Imports of services	20519.0	18635.0	17282.0	21598.0	23339.0	25026.0	27776.0	33714.0	35703.0	38520.0	32377.0	27748.0
Equals: GROSS DOMESTIC PRODUCT	441519.0	442048.0	459488.0	481004.0	496026.0	514486.0	532038.0	564517.0	590107.0	618529.0	639694.0	670735.0

Table 1.3 Relations among product, income, savings, and net lending aggregates

Series 100: 1993 SNA, Nepalese rupee, Fiscal year ending 15 July — **Data in millions**

	2001	2002	2003	2004	2005	2006	2007	2008	2009	2010	2011	2012
Series	**100**											
GROSS DOMESTIC PRODUCT	441519.0	459443.0	492231.0	536749.0	589412.0	654084.0	727827.0	815663.0	988272.0	1192774.0	1374953.0	1536000.0
Plus: Compensation of employees - from and to the rest of the world, net	1701.0[a]	-605.0[a]	-676.0[a]	-1684.0[a]	1636.5[a]	4955.5[a]	7431.8[a]	7941.8[a]	11749.5[a]	9117.4	7549.4	12291.4
Plus: Compensation of employees - from the rest of the world	...	...	...	...	7751.6	11432.3	14500.8	13447.7	16506.6	14917.9	17504.0	22521.3

	2001	2002	2003	2004	2005	2006	2007	2008	2009	2010	2011	2012
Series	**100**											
Less: Compensation of employees - to the rest of the world	...	...	...	...	6115.1	6476.8	7069.0	5505.9	4757.1	5800.5	9954.6	10230.0
Plus: Property income - from and to the rest of the world, net	...	...	...	...	...	...	...	...	...	...	...	...
Sum of Compensation of employees and property income - from and to the rest of the world, net	1701.0	-604.9	-675.7	-1683.9	1636.5	4956.0	7432.0	7947.0	11750.0	9117.0	7549.0	12291.0
Plus: Taxes less subsidies on production and imports - from and to the rest of the world, net	...	...	...	...	...	...	...	...	...	...	...	...
Equals: GROSS NATIONAL INCOME	443220.0	458838.0	491556.0	535065.0	591048.0	659040.0	735259.0	823605.0	1000021.0	1201891.0	1382503.0	1550785.0
Plus: Current transfers - from and to the rest of the world, net	65595.0	68186.0	75533.0	84889.0	97704.0	126146.0	128992.0	182817.0	249487.0	282648.0	307859.0	422772.0
Plus: Current transfers - from the rest of the world	67027.7	70157.3	77765.1	89161.8	101301.0	130862.0	133197.0	...	...	...	...	...
Less: Current transfers - to the rest of the world	1432.7	1971.2	2232.1	4273.2	3605.7	4716.0	4204.8	...	...	...	...	...
Equals: GROSS NATIONAL DISPOSABLE INCOME	508815.0	527024.0	567089.0	619954.0	688752.0	785185.0	864251.0	1006422.0	1249508.0	1484539.0	1690362.0	1973557.0
Less: Final consumption expenditure / Actual final consumption	390017.0	415843.0	450090.0	473685.0	521301.0	595327.0	656374.0	735470.0	895042.0	1056185.0	1176030.0	1359539.0
Equals: SAVING, GROSS	118798.0	111181.0	116998.0	146268.0	167451.0	189858.0	207876.0	270952.0	354466.0	428354.0	514331.0	614018.0
Plus: Capital transfers - from and to the rest of the world, net	...	...	...	...	...	...	...	...	...	...	...	...
Less: Gross capital formation	98649.2	93019.7	105384.0	131670.0	155907.0	175633.0	208779.0	247272.0	313029.0	456489.0	527268.0	535545.0
Less: Acquisitions less disposals of non-produced non-financial assets	...	...	...	...	...	...	...	...	...	...	...	...
Equals: NET LENDING (+) / NET BORROWING (-) OF THE NATION	20148.8	18161.1	11614.7	14598.0	11544.6	14225.3	-902.0	23680.0	41437.0	-28135.0	-12936.0	78472.0
	Net values: Gross National Income / Gross National Disposable Income / Saving Gross less Consumption of fixed capital											
Less: Consumption of fixed capital	...	...	...	...	...	...	...	...	...	...	...	...
Equals: NET NATIONAL INCOME	...	...	...	...	...	...	...	...	...	...	...	...
Equals: NET NATIONAL DISPOSABLE INCOME	...	...	...	...	...	...	...	...	...	...	...	...
Equals: SAVING, NET	...	...	...	...	...	...	...	...	...	...	...	...

[a] Refers to Net Primary Incomes.

Table 2.1 Value added by industries at current prices (ISIC Rev. 3)

Series 100: 1993 SNA, Nepalese rupee, Fiscal year ending 15 July

Data in millions

	2001	2002	2003	2004	2005	2006	2007	2008	2009	2010	2011	2012
Series	**100**											
	Industries											
Agriculture, hunting, forestry; fishing	155625.0	166090.0	172803.0	186125.0	199368.0	211704.4	226823.0	247191.0	309553.0	395755.0	478149.0	516951.0
Agriculture, hunting, forestry	153781.0	163925.0	170634.0	183621.0	196686.0	208591.0	223536.0	243323.0	305477.0	391519.0	473270.0	511290.0
Fishing	1844.0	2164.9	2168.2	2503.6	2682.2	3113.4	3287.0	3868.0	4076.0	4236.0	4879.0	5661.0
Mining and quarrying	1817.1	2148.9	2310.4	2506.6	2748.2	3134.0	3417.0	4375.0	5084.0	5926.0	6956.0	8166.0
Manufacturing	38409.0	37736.0	38825.6	41673.3	44884.7	47840.3	52172.0	57185.0	65447.0	70924.0	80531.0	90794.0
Electricity, gas and water supply	7749.6	9137.9	11446.7	11974.4	12781.6	13172.0	14841.0	15219.0	14629.0	15244.0	24001.0	17488.0
Construction	25585.4	28837.6	30955.4	33254.3	36644.2	40952.0	45099.0	54134.0	63741.0	77289.0	89356.0	98536.0

	2001	2002	2003	2004	2005	2006	2007	2008	2009	2010	2011	2012
Series	**100**											
Wholesale, retail trade, repair of motor vehicles, motorcycles and personal and households goods; hotels and restaurants	78387.4	71921.0	76234.7	88161.1	88733.2	99582.5	102691.0	116809.0	138064.0	178414.0	200363.0	222153.0
Wholesale, retail trade, repair of motor vehicles, motorcycles and personal and household goods	69928.4	64778.2	68695.0	79218.6	79838.5	90214.5	92648.0	105306.0	124121.0	161067.0	179306.0	197632.0
Hotels and restaurants	8459.0	7142.8	7539.7	8942.5	8894.7	9368.0	10043.0	11503.0	13943.0	17347.0	21057.0	24521.0
Transport, storage and communications	31424.6	34959.2	39361.9	46283.0	51336.4	61250.0	69555.0	76818.0	92618.0	95304.0	105834.0	123990.0
Financial intermediation; real estate, renting and business activities	46722.4	48727.3	51112.4	53718.8	66584.0	82021.0	99258.0	107175.0	120725.0	139830.0	156347.0	185336.0
Financial intermediation	11455.0	12202.0	12861.0	13728.0	17342.0	21979.0	28467.0	33539.0	39100.0	46083.0	50111.0	65345.0
Real estate, renting and business activities	35267.4	36525.3	38251.4	39990.8	49242.0	60042.0	70791.0	73636.0	81625.0	93747.0	106236.0	119991.0
Public administration and defence; compulsory social security	5288.1	7236.5	8070.3	8018.7	9548.2	10967.0	12227.0	14352.0	18556.0	21695.0	24830.0	29329.0
Education; health and social work; other community, social and personal services [a]	34446.4	37257.4	42426.0	46278.2	53950.0	59678.0	71281.0	86185.0	110475.0	118189.0	131773.0	153386.0
Education	17372.4	20823.3	24581.7	26313.3	31670.6	34996.0	40939.0	48722.0	62642.0	61384.0	67739.0	79077.0
Health and social work	4178.4	4626.3	5407.9	5824.5	7017.3	7842.0	8568.0	10963.0	13744.0	15382.0	17087.0	20259.0
Other community, social and personal services	12895.6	11807.8	12436.4	14140.4	15262.1	16840.0	21774.0	26500.0	34089.0	41423.0	46947.0	54050.0
Private households with employed persons	...	...	...	...	...	...	...	...	...	...	...	...
Equals: VALUE ADDED, GROSS, in basic prices [b]	413429.0	430397.0	460325.0	500699.0	548485.0	611089.0	675859.0	755257.0	909528.0	1083415.0[c]	1256482.0	1396139.0
Less: Financial intermediation services indirectly measured (FISIM)	12025.8	13655.4	13220.6	17294.3	18094.0	19212.0	21505.0	24185.0	29362.0	35156.0	41660.0	49992.0
Plus: Taxes less Subsidies on products	28090.3	29046.2	31906.0	36049.8	40926.9	42966.0	51968.0	60401.0	78744.0	109358.0	118472.0	139861.0
Equals: GROSS DOMESTIC PRODUCT	441519.0	459443.0	492231.0	536749.0	589412.0	654055.0	727827.0	815658.0	988272.0	1192774.0	1374953.0	1536000.0

[a] Includes data for Private households with employed persons.
[b] Excludes financial intermediation services indirectly measured (FISIM).
[c] Discrepancy between Total Economy and breakdown by industry.

Table 2.2 Value added by industries at constant prices (ISIC Rev. 3)

Series 100: 1993 SNA, Nepalese rupee, Fiscal year ending 15 July **Data in millions**

	2001	2002	2003	2004	2005	2006	2007	2008	2009	2010	2011	2012
Series	**100**											
Base year	**2001**											
	Industries											
Agriculture, hunting, forestry; fishing	155625.0	160422.0	165761.0	173734.0	179811.0	183015.0	184796.0	195559.0	201464.0	205517.0	214787.0	225487.0
Agriculture, hunting, forestry	153781.0	158417.0	163676.0	171394.0	177304.0	180260.0	181958.0	192514.0	198257.0	202196.0	211271.0	221706.0
Fishing	1844.0	2005.0	2085.0	2340.0	2507.0	2755.0	2838.0	3045.0	3207.0	3321.0	3516.0	3781.0
Mining and quarrying	1817.1	1976.7	2040.0	2031.2	2169.2	2348.0	2383.0	2513.0	2531.0	2585.0	2637.0	2770.0
Manufacturing	38409.0	36364.0	36379.9	37163.2	38135.9	38898.3	39891.0	39545.0	39132.0	40291.0	41923.0	43445.0
Electricity, gas and water supply	7749.6	8630.9	10274.3	10692.5	11116.7	11562.0	13065.0	13204.0	12750.0	12989.0	13564.0	14705.0
Construction	25585.4	27225.1	27798.0	27701.1	28503.4	30690.0	31453.0	33043.0	33371.0	35430.0	37126.0	37207.0
Wholesale, retail trade, repair of motor vehicles, motorcycles and personal and household goods; hotels and restaurants	78387.4	68753.8	70289.1	78021.2	73218.3	76075.2	72570.0	75813.0	79537.0	84883.0	86542.0	89480.0

	2001	2002	2003	2004	2005	2006	2007	2008	2009	2010	2011	2012
Series	**100**											
Base year	**2001**											
Wholesale, retail trade, repair of motor vehicles, motorcycles and personal and household goods	69928.0	61837.0	63233.0	70066.0	65694.0	68099.0	64292.0	66962.0	70481.0	75237.0	76298.0	78625.0
Hotels and restaurants	8459.0	6917.0	7056.0	7955.0	7525.0	8001.0	8278.0	8851.0	9056.0	9646.0	10244.0	10855.0
Transport, storage and communications	31424.6	34055.0	35825.0	38508.5	39272.0	42001.0	43868.0	48226.0	51585.0	54657.0	57504.0	60806.0
Financial intermediation, real estate, renting and business activities	46722.4	45435.4	44301.4	44375.6	50657.2	56743.0	63343.0	69686.0	71044.0	73145.0	75057.0	77417.0
Financial intermediation	11455.0	11892.0	12090.0	12838.0	15957.0	19843.0	22103.0	24142.0	24623.0	25327.0	26163.0	27071.0
Real estate, renting and business activities	35267.0	33543.0	32212.0	31538.0	34700.0	36900.0	41240.0	45544.0	46421.0	47818.0	48894.0	50346.0
Public administration and defence; compulsory social security	5288.1	7236.5	8070.3	8018.7	8551.0	9139.0	9262.0	9319.0	10012.0	10405.0	10806.0	11346.0
Education; health and social work; other community, social and personal services [a]	34446.4	37301.1	41388.1	44580.2	47198.0	49043.0	54285.0	58394.0	64944.0	70185.0	73410.0	77939.0
Education	17372.0	21030.0	23913.0	25138.0	27606.0	28640.0	30738.0	32716.0	36233.0	38638.0	39799.0	41797.0
Health and social work	4178.0	4487.0	5171.0	5487.0	6109.0	6470.0	6904.0	7474.0	8191.0	8581.0	9012.0	9908.0
Other community, social and personal services	12896.0	11785.0	12303.0	13955.0	13483.0	13933.0	16643.0	18204.0	20520.0	22966.0	24599.0	26234.0
Private households with employed persons	...	...	...	...	...	...	...	...	...	...	...	...
Equals: VALUE ADDED, GROSS, in basic prices [b]	413429.0	414091.0	429699.0	448654.0	461452.0	480409.0	493651.0	522260.0	542652.0	565759.0	587534.0	613877.0
Less: Financial intermediation services indirectly measured (FISIM)	12025.8	13308.7	12428.0	16172.6	17180.0	19105.0	21476.0	23043.0	23725.0	24327.0	25821.0	26725.0
Plus: Taxes less Subsidies on products	28090.3	27956.9	29789.1	32349.6	34574.0	34051.0	38388.0	42257.0	47455.0	52770.0	52160.0	56858.0
Equals: GROSS DOMESTIC PRODUCT	441519.0	442048.0	459488.0	481003.0	496026.0	514460.0	532038.0	564517.0	590107.0	618539.0	639694.0	670735.0

[a] Includes data for Private households with employed persons.
[b] Excludes financial intermediation services indirectly measured (FISIM).

Netherlands

Source

The preparation of the national accounts statistics in the Netherlands is undertaken by Statistics Netherlands in Voorburg. The official estimates, together with methodological notes, are presented annually in the publication "Nationale rekeningen". An English version of this publication is also available (National Accounts of the Netherlands). The national accounts figures are also available on the internet in StatLine, the electronic databank of Statistics Netherlands: www.cbs.nl.

A detailed description of the concepts, definitions, data sources and estimation methods is given in the publication "Gross National Income Inventory 2001, The Netherlands". This publication gives numerical results for the reporting year 2001 as well. The inventory can be consulted on the CBS-website. Data sources and estimation methods of price and volume changes are described in the publication National accounts of the Netherlands.

The following tables have been prepared from successive replies to the United Nations national accounts questionnaire. The data was received through the Organization for Economic Co-operation and Development (OECD), Paris.

General

The latest estimates shown in the following tables have been prepared in accordance with the concepts and definitions of System of National Accounts 1993 (1993 SNA). Previously the estimates were prepared in accordance with the United Nations System of National Accounts 1968 (1968 SNA). The first annual publication on input-output tables, covering the years 1948-1957, was issued in 1960. When the scope and coverage of the estimates differ for conceptual or statistical reasons from the definitions and classifications recommended in SNA, a footnote is indicated to the relevant tables. Chain indices are used to measure volume growth and the resulting chained constant prices data are not additive.

On 1 January 1999 the conversion rate of the national currencies to the new currency euro was irrevocably fixed and the euro became the single currency of the 11 member countries of the European Monetary Union (EMU). For these 11 countries all data starting 1999 is in euro. The newly submitted data for the years before 1999 were reported in national currency but were converted to 'euro' using the fixed exchange rates to allow for easy comparison of national time series data. In this publication the currency name of this data consists of the year of accession plus the ISO currency code of the national currency and the word 'euro'. In the case of Netherlands the currency name for the data before 1999 is "1999 NLG euro". For international comparisons, like for example when converting national data into US dollar the data before the euro introduction has first to be converted back into national currency using the fixed 6-digit Euro conversion rate of 1 Euro = 2.20371 Netherlands guilder. The name of the currency of the newly submitted data is "1999 NLG euro" for the data before 1999 and "euro" for the data from 1999 on. In the database this newly submitted data is stored as a new series of data and will be shown in this yearbook as a new row of data if in the same table there is also previously submitted data. Previously submitted data for the Netherlands, like for example all old data following the 1968 SNA is still in "Netherlands guilder", although this is not specifically indicated in the tables.

In July the annual national accounts estimates are available in StatLine, the electronic databank of Statistics Netherlands. It concerns provisional estimates for the two most recent years and "definitive" estimates for earlier years. Provisional data are subsequently adjusted; definitive published data are generally not revised in subsequent publications, they remain unchanged until the next benchmark revision.

From time to time benchmark revisions of national accounts data are carried out. The level estimates are then adjusted in line with the latest insights, concepts, definitions, classifications, estimation methods and the like. A benchmark revision also allows mistakes to be corrected. The most recent benchmark revisions relate to the reporting years 1969, 1977, 1987, 1995 and 2001. After a benchmark revision the existing time series are adjusted so that comparability in time remains possible.

Methodology:

Overview of GDP Compilation
Gross domestic product is estimated mainly through the production approach. The expenditure and income approach are also used. Supply and use tables and input-output tables are compiled annually, both in current prices and in prices of the previous year. The Dutch national accounts refer to the economic territory of the Kingdom of the Netherlands in Europe. The Dutch section of the continental shelf in the North Sea is also regarded as a part of that economic territory. The economies of the countries of the Kingdom of the Netherlands outside Europe (Curaçao, Sint Maarten and Aruba) are not described in the Dutch national accounts. The islands (public bodies) Bonaire, Sint Eustatius and Saba are indeed part of the Netherlands but are also not included in the national accounts.

Expenditure Approach
Expenditure is estimated in the context of the supply and use table, both in current and in constant prices, where independent estimates of output, intermediate consumption and final use are compared and brought into balance. This integrated procedure ensures the consistency and the equality of GDP estimates using the expenditure and production approach.

In estimating household final consumption expenditure, household budget surveys and retail output statistics are used. The commodity flow method plays an important role in estimating household final consumption expenditure. Main sources for the estimates of government consumption expenditure are administrative records. Fixed capital formation estimates for the various industries are largely based on separate surveys of expenditure by tangible fixed-asset type. Administrative records are also an important source; this refers for example to annual reports and balance sheets of banks, insurance companies and government, to data from tax authorities. For software, the output growth minus exports plus imports is used to extrapolate a survey level from a few years back.

Foreign trade statistics are the major source for data on imports and exports of goods. For companies not included in the surveys, estimates are made using the Ministry of Finance VAT tapes. The estimates of the international trade in services is based on a sample statistics, main sources are reports from 300 large enterprises, reports from a sample of 1500 small and medium-sized enterprises, household surveys and surveys of tourist accommodation providers, data from the Ministries of Foreign Affairs and Defence.

Constant price figures are obtained through deflation with price indexes for nearly all final expenditure components. These figures are compiled within the framework of supply and use tables in constant prices.

Income Approach
The compilation of gross domestic product with reference to the income approach involves its estimation as the sum of the different components of value added, namely compensation of employees, the balance of other taxes and subsidies on production and gross operating surplus/mixed income.

From the point of view of income, GDP can be estimated in different ways; for example with reference to: value added components for the entire economy, value added components on an industry level, value added components on the level of institutional sectors and a combination of these options. In the Netherlands the combination option is used. All available information is combined in the matrices describing the relationship between industries and sectors. These matrices are used to divide the results from the supply and use table into the main components of the income approach, compensation of employees and gross operating surplus.

The calculation of domestic product from the income point of view is largely based on direct estimation methods. A great variety of statistical sources can be drawn upon, in many cases the same ones used in the production approach. Estimates of wages and employers' social contributions are largely based on the Social Statistical Database. This database is realised by integration of data on employees from different sources (e.g. tax authorities and institutions responsible for the administration of social security).

Subsidy and tax estimates are based on figures from government registers. Many sources are available for the determination of operating surplus/mixed income. Estimates of the consumption of fixed capital are made with the perpetual inventory method.

Production Approach

The production approach is used to estimate value added of most industries. From the point of view of production, gross domestic product at market prices is estimated with reference to annually compiled supply and use tables both in current prices and in prices of the previous year.

For agriculture sources of information are survey-based production statistics and administrative records for forestry and forestry services. For the growing of crops, market gardening, horticulture and the farming of animals, functional estimates rather than institutional estimates were made by combining exhaustive data from surveys, administrative records and commodity flow models.

Regarding mining and quarrying survey-based production statistics are the main data basis. The information base for manufacturing are survey-based production statistics. For a number of industries corrections are made to make the data from the survey-based production statistic consistent with survey data on produced volumes provided mostly by commodity boards.

For electricity, gas and water supply survey-based production statistics are the basis for the national accounts figures. Information about the turnover of trade activities is also used. For construction survey-based production statistics are available. The basis for the estimates of wholesale and retail trade figures are survey-based production statistics. The same holds for hotels and restaurants.

Estimates for transport, storage and communications are based on survey-based production statistics. Corrections are made to change the gross administration of certain activities in the production statistics into the net administration of national accounts. Annual reports of a state company are used as well.

The main data sources for the estimates of financial intermediation are administrative records, for example annual reports of the Dutch Central Bank and the Insurance Board. For Special Purpose Entities exports and imports are taken from Central Bank's balance of payment data. In some cases (for instance exchange bureaus and mortgage agents) extrapolations are made based on historical data from 1995 using growth rates of closely related industries.

Estimates for real estate activities are based on survey-based production statistics. Exploitation of houses is estimated on the basis of the number of houses per type and the average rent per type. For the exploitation of buildings other than houses extrapolation techniques are used.

The value added of government services is mainly based on administrative records. For ministries data are taken from the State record of Statistics Netherlands, which was obtained from accounts and budgets of the ministries. For, among other things, provinces, district water boards, public corporate organizations, executing bodies of social security schemes data are obtained from annual financial reports. Consumption of fixed capital is calculated using the PIM method.

Administrative records are used for secondary and higher education (colleges and universities). Extrapolation techniques are used for e.g. primary education and 'other education'. The estimates of health and social work activities are based on various surveys. For boarding schools and advisory services extrapolations are used.

For the estimates of other community, social and personal service activities survey-based production statistics and other surveys are used. Administrative records are also utilized, for instance for government environmental services provided by district water boards this refers to their annual financial reports. In addition extrapolations on data from surveys are used.

Supply and use tables are compiled in both current and previous year prices. This means that for all transactions in those tables volume changes can be determined. The estimation procedure applied for value added in previous year prices depends on the type of production.

Value added in constant prices of industries producing market output is estimated with the double deflation method. In case of industries mainly producing non-market individual goods and services (for instance subsidized education) output in constant prices is estimated by multiplying output in the previous year by the volume index of output. Total value added in constant prices is the difference between deflated gross output and deflated intermediate consumption of goods and services. For the majority of the production of non-market individual goods and services volume indicators are available. The main example is educational services.

In the case of industries mainly producing non-market collective services (public administration) value added in constant prices is calculated as the sum of labour costs, other taxes and subsidies on production and consumption of fixed capital in constant prices.

The main sources in the estimation of price and volume changes are producer and consumer price indices. Examples of other data used are: quantity indicators, unit value indices and price and quantity data from agriculture related agencies. The number of passenger kilometres is used as an indicator for passenger transport. The number of pupils is used as indicator for the production of education. Unit-value indices are used for deflation in some specific cases, for instance the exports and imports of certain agricultural products.

Table 1.1 Gross domestic product by expenditures at current prices

Series 300: 1993 SNA, 1999 NLG Euro / Euro, Western calendar year **Data in millions**

	2001	2002	2003	2004	2005	2006	2007	2008	2009	2010	2011	2012
Series	**300**											
	Expenditures of the gross domestic product											
Final consumption expenditure	325629.0	343289.0	354896.0	361723.0	372028.0	390317.0	407971.0	423230.0	427677.0	434875.0	439268.0	443893.0
Household final consumption expenditure	220466.0	228924.0	233912.0	238521.0	245996.0	250269.0	259235.0	265342.0	258471.0	262655.0	265782.0	267890.0
NPISHs final consumption expenditure	3778.0	4119.0	4191.0	4260.0	4347.0	4606.0	4864.0	5075.0	5066.0	5155.0	5329.0	5400.0
General government final consumption expenditure	101385.0	110246.0	116793.0	118942.0	121685.0	135442.0	143872.0	152813.0	164140.0	167065.0	168157.0	170603.0
Individual consumption expenditure	55216.0	61008.0	64819.0	66392.0	68667.0	79842.0	85536.0	90547.0	97315.0	100392.0	102957.0	105113.0
Collective consumption expenditure	46169.0	49238.0	51974.0	52550.0	53018.0	55600.0	58336.0	62266.0	66825.0	66673.0	65200.0	65490.0
Gross capital formation	96191.0	91587.0	92089.0	93244.0	97614.0	108093.0	116807.0	121856.0	105491.0	105859.0	108911.0	103632.0
Gross fixed capital formation	94673.0	92862.0	92848.0	92426.0	97016.0	106373.0	114340.0	121849.0	108774.0	102031.0	106690.0	101133.0
Changes in inventories	1410.0	-1357.0	-795.0	676.0	509.0	1597.0	2456.0	-136.0	-3388.0	3432.0	2106.0	...
Acquisitions less disposals of valuables	108.0	82.0	36.0	142.0	89.0	123.0	11.0	143.0	105.0	396.0	115.0	...
Exports of goods and services	301216.0	298450.0	300498.0	326111.0	357453.0	393475.0	424229.0	453442.0	393050.0	460493.0	499620.0	524719.0
Exports of goods	236721.0	232123.0	233263.0	256089.0	281867.0	316270.0	342311.0	362462.0	300908.0	363026.0	396924.0	420642.0
Exports of services	64495.0	66327.0	67235.0	70022.0	75586.0	77205.0	81918.0	90980.0	92142.0	97467.0	102696.0	104077.0
Less: Imports of goods and services	275305.0	268112.0	270538.0	289894.0	313688.0	351669.0	377234.0	404047.0	352983.0	412487.0	445826.0	471606.0
Imports of goods	209757.0	200904.0	202221.0	220710.0	241157.0	274775.0	298650.0	319259.0	264680.0	318764.0	348131.0	370387.0
Imports of services	65548.0	67208.0	68317.0	69184.0	72531.0	76894.0	78584.0	84788.0	88303.0	93723.0	97695.0	101219.0
Equals: GROSS DOMESTIC PRODUCT	447731.0	465214.0	476945.0	491184.0	513407.0	540216.0	571773.0	594481.0	573235.0	588740.0	601973.0	600638.0

Table 1.2 Gross domestic product by expenditures at constant prices

Series 300: 1993 SNA, 1999 NLG Euro / Euro, Western calendar year — **Data in millions**

	2001	2002	2003	2004	2005	2006	2007	2008	2009	2010	2011	2012
Series	**300**											
Base year	**2005**											
	Expenditures of the gross domestic product											
Final consumption expenditure	357792.0	363717.0	366658.0	368982.0	372028.0	382772.0	391844.0	398967.0	400861.0	402819.0	400482.0	396967.0
Household final consumption expenditure	239432.0	241490.0	241124.0	243549.0	245996.0	244989.0	249147.0	252358.0	247021.0	247881.0	245261.0	241689.0
NPISHs final consumption expenditure	4204.0	4409.0	4325.0	4307.0	4347.0	4493.0	4716.0	4806.0	4845.0	4838.0	4883.0	4886.0
General government final consumption expenditure	114066.0	117794.0	121213.0	121125.0	121685.0	133290.0	137988.0	141808.0	148841.0	149927.0	150111.0	150122.0
Individual consumption expenditure	62974.0	65319.0	67016.0	67475.0	68667.0	78398.0	81494.0	83919.0	88008.0	89737.0	91815.0	93448.0
Collective consumption expenditure	51092.0	52484.0	54206.0	53654.0	53018.0	54892.0	56492.0	57885.0	60829.0	60178.0	58265.0	56640.0
Gross capital formation	102834.0	95214.0	94295.0	94448.0	97614.0	106005.0	112452.0	115433.0	99058.0	98133.0	103143.0	98862.0
Gross fixed capital formation	101143.0	96543.0	95049.0	93553.0	97016.0	104275.0	110035.0	114962.0	101148.0	93906.0	99303.0	94749.0
Changes in inventories	1249.1	-1155.2	-614.6	657.9	509.0	1730.0	2619.4	472.5	9161.0	-9517.9	-9343.2	-11503.8
Acquisitions less disposals of valuables	...	...	...	...	...	...	...	...	...	...	...	...
Exports of goods and services	305044.0	307867.0	312589.0	337223.0	357453.0	383443.0	407966.0	416197.0	383967.0	427032.0	443649.0	458410.0
Exports of goods	235064.0	238057.0	243185.0	265575.0	281867.0	306425.0	326477.0	330377.0	299512.0	338800.0	352524.0	365657.0
Exports of services	70059.0	69813.0	69368.0	71644.0	75586.0	77018.0	81476.0	85922.0	84741.0	88982.0	91915.0	93559.0
Less: Imports of goods and services	275829.0	276541.0	281603.0	297647.0	313688.0	341387.0	360618.0	368988.0	342881.0	377703.0	391398.0	403695.0
Imports of goods	203493.0	204216.0	210645.0	227671.0	241157.0	265356.0	283487.0	288819.0	261614.0	293637.0	305711.0	316615.0
Imports of services	72486.0	72449.0	70920.0	69954.0	72531.0	76031.0	77054.0	80132.0	81536.0	84720.0	86393.0	87798.0
Plus: Statistical discrepancy	244.0	202.0	166.0	105.0	0.0	0.0	1.0	-12.0	-5.0	-467.0	-605.0	-585.0
Equals: GROSS DOMESTIC PRODUCT [a]	490085.0	490459.0	492105.0	503111.0	513407.0	530833.0	551645.0	561597.0	541000.0	549814.0	555271.0	549959.0

[a] Chain-linked volume measures are presented in this table, thus discrepancies between components and total may exist.

Table 1.3 Relations among product, income, savings, and net lending aggregates

Series 300: 1993 SNA, 1999 NLG Euro / Euro, Western calendar year — **Data in millions**

	2001	2002	2003	2004	2005	2006	2007	2008	2009	2010	2011	2012
Series	**300**											
GROSS DOMESTIC PRODUCT	447731.0	465214.0	476945.0	491184.0	513407.0	540216.0	571773.0	594481.0	573235.0	588740.0	601973.0	600638.0
Plus: Compensation of employees - from and to the rest of the world, net	...	...	...	...	...	...	...	...	...	...	...	...
Plus: Property income - from and to the rest of the world, net	...	...	...	...	...	...	...	...	...	...	...	...
Sum of Compensation of employees and property income - from and to the rest of the world, net [a]	3379.0	4254.0	5423.0	13149.0	2478.0	14525.0	9502.0	-12626.0	-13850.0	-9423.0	5207.0	5926.0
Plus: Sum of Compensation of employees and property income - from the rest of the world	136461.0	100608.0	97739.0	126361.0	143260.0	180125.0	225889.0	198213.0	158456.0	193360.0	191112.0	170042.0
Less: Sum of Compensation of employees and property income - to the rest of the world	133082.0	96354.0	92316.0	113212.0	140782.0	165600.0	216387.0	210839.0	172306.0	202783.0	185905.0	164116.0

	2001	2002	2003	2004	2005	2006	2007	2008	2009	2010	2011	2012
Series	**300**											
Plus: Taxes less subsidies on production and imports - from and to the rest of the world, net	...	...	...	...	...	...	...	...	...	...	...	...
Equals: GROSS NATIONAL INCOME	451110.0	469468.0	482368.0	504333.0	515885.0	554741.0	581275.0	581855.0	559385.0	579317.0	607180.0	606564.0
Plus: Current transfers - from and to the rest of the world, net	-6211.0	-6642.0	-6452.0	-7492.0	-8219.0	-8020.0	-8757.0	-8988.0	-8267.0	-8871.0	-9248.0	-9622.0
Plus: Current transfers - from the rest of the world	5037.0	5332.0	6077.0	6548.0	7092.0	7700.0	7485.0	7874.0	8757.0	9375.0	8748.0	8957.0
Less: Current transfers - to the rest of the world	11248.0	11974.0	12529.0	14040.0	15311.0	15720.0	16242.0	16862.0	17024.0	18246.0	17996.0	18579.0
Equals: GROSS NATIONAL DISPOSABLE INCOME	444899.0	462826.0	475916.0	496841.0	507666.0	546721.0	572518.0	572867.0	551118.0	570446.0	597932.0	596942.0
Less: Final consumption expenditure / Actual final consumption	325629.0	343289.0	354896.0	361723.0	372028.0	390317.0	407971.0	423230.0	427677.0	434875.0	439268.0	443893.0
Plus: Statistical discrepancy [b]	266.0	289.0	272.0	293.0	398.0	433.0	347.0	302.0	230.0	154.0	...	...
Equals: SAVING, GROSS	119536.0	119826.0	121292.0	135411.0	136036.0	156837.0	164894.0	149939.0	123671.0	135725.0	158746.0	153058.0
Plus: Capital transfers - from and to the rest of the world, net	-793.0	-967.0	-1022.0	-1320.0	-1751.0	-1888.0	-1186.0	-2104.0	-2531.0	-3259.0	-2058.0	-1624.0
Plus: Capital transfers - from the rest of the world	1757.0	1461.0	1362.0	1631.0	1630.0	1792.0	2711.0	2401.0	2331.0	2436.0	2076.0	1865.0
Less: Capital transfers - to the rest of the world	2550.0	2428.0	2384.0	2951.0	3381.0	3680.0	3897.0	4505.0	4862.0	5695.0	4134.0	3489.0
Less: Gross capital formation	96191.0	91587.0	92089.0	93244.0	97614.0	108093.0	116807.0	121856.0	105491.0	105859.0	108911.0	103632.0
Less: Acquisitions less disposals of non-produced non-financial assets	...	...	...	...	...	...	...	...	...	...	...	...
Equals: NET LENDING (+) / NET BORROWING (-) OF THE NATION	22552.0	27272.0	28181.0	40847.0	36671.0	46856.0	46901.0	25979.0	15649.0	26607.0	47777.0	47802.0
	Net values: Gross National Income / Gross National Disposable Income / Saving Gross less Consumption of fixed capital											
Less: Consumption of fixed capital	65865.0	69427.0	71461.0	73498.0	75709.0	78594.0	82072.0	85412.0	87974.0	89212.0	88726.0	88242.0
Equals: NET NATIONAL INCOME	385245.0	400041.0	410907.0	430835.0	440176.0	476147.0	499203.0	496443.0	471411.0	490105.0	518454.0	518322.0
Equals: NET NATIONAL DISPOSABLE INCOME	379034.0	393399.0	404455.0	423343.0	431957.0	468127.0	490446.0	487455.0	463144.0	481234.0	509206.0	508700.0
Equals: SAVING, NET	53671.0	50399.0	49831.0	61913.0	60327.0	78243.0	82822.0	64527.0	35697.0	46513.0	70020.0	64816.0

[a] Refers to net primary income (i.e. net compensation of employee, net property income and net taxes less subsidies on production from/to the rest of the world).

[b] Refers to Adjustment for the change in net equity of households in pension funds

Table 2.4 Value added by industries at current prices (ISIC Rev. 4)

Series 300: 1993 SNA, 1999 NLG Euro / Euro, Western calendar year

Data in millions

	2001	2002	2003	2004	2005	2006	2007	2008	2009	2010	2011	2012
Series	**300**											
	Industries											
Agriculture, forestry and fishing	9614.0	8988.0	9300.0	8671.0	8826.0	9808.0	9738.0	8837.0	7898.0	9297.0	8663.0	9109.0
Manufacturing, mining and quarrying and other industrial activities	74402.0	75196.0	77222.0	79959.0	84813.0	90763.0	96280.0	103046.0	92840.0	99002.0	105033.0	106940.0
Manufacturing	55228.0	55516.0	56499.0	58850.0	61405.0	62743.0	67416.0	67700.0	60025.0	65086.0	69626.0	69635.0
Construction	23089.0	24159.0	24169.0	24122.0	25264.0	26930.0	28914.0	30956.0	30678.0	27985.0	28727.0	26190.0
Wholesale and retail trade, transportation and storage, accommodation and food service activities	83016.0	87054.0	85865.0	87967.0	90548.0	94644.0	101033.0	102011.0	94259.0	98004.0	101201.0	100660.0
Information and communication	19549.0	21109.0	22338.0	22530.0	23372.0	24482.0	26200.0	26376.0	25022.0	25333.0	25351.0	24656.0
Financial and insurance activities	24345.0	26908.0	30888.0	32221.0	35093.0	32415.0	30014.0	30058.0	38022.0	43423.0	42534.0	46827.0

	2001	2002	2003	2004	2005	2006	2007	2008	2009	2010	2011	2012
Series	**300**											
Real estate activities	31688.0	31192.0	30337.0	31984.0	33212.0	37022.0	41230.0	42434.0	33161.0	32405.0	34975.0	31774.0
Professional, scientific, technical, administrative and support service activities	46207.0	45821.0	45689.0	47061.0	50029.0	54933.0	60868.0	64800.0	61751.0	59625.0	59885.0	59230.0
Public administration and defence, education, human health and social work activities	75671.0	83286.0	88567.0	91230.0	93645.0	96363.0	101224.0	107168.0	114103.0	117736.0	119377.0	120813.0
Other service activities	9975.0	10661.0	10881.0	11129.0	11380.0	11652.0	12149.0	12553.0	13118.0	13366.0	13629.0	13841.0
Equals: VALUE ADDED, GROSS, at basic prices	397556.0	414374.0	425256.0	436874.0	456182.0	479012.0	507650.0	528239.0	510852.0	526176.0	539375.0	540040.0
Less: Financial intermediation services indirectly measured (FISIM)	...	...	...	...	...	...	...	...	...	...	...	...
Plus: Taxes less Subsidies on products	50175.0	50840.0	51689.0	54310.0	57225.0	61204.0	64123.0	66242.0	62383.0	62564.0	62598.0	60598.0
Plus: Taxes on products	54112.0	55020.0	56125.0	58474.0	61331.0	65373.0	67790.0	69741.0	66099.0	66230.0	65976.0	64072.0
Less: Subsidies on products	3937.0	4180.0	4436.0	4164.0	4106.0	4169.0	3667.0	3499.0	3716.0	3666.0	3378.0	3474.0
Equals: GROSS DOMESTIC PRODUCT	447731.0	465214.0	476945.0	491184.0	513407.0	540216.0	571773.0	594481.0	573235.0	588740.0	601973.0	600638.0

Table 2.5 Value added by industries at constant prices (ISIC Rev. 4)

Series 300: 1993 SNA, 1999 NLG Euro / Euro, Western calendar year **Data in millions**

	2001	2002	2003	2004	2005	2006	2007	2008	2009	2010	2011	2012
Series	**300**											
Base year	**2005**											
	Industries											
Agriculture, forestry and fishing	8193.0	8048.0	8401.0	8872.0	8826.0	8747.0	9088.0	9285.0	9700.0	9593.0	9744.0	9683.0
Manufacturing, mining and quarrying and other industrial activities	81151.0	82079.0	81180.0	84552.0	84813.0	86504.0	89899.0	90570.0	84246.0	90579.0	90889.0	90510.0
Manufacturing	58420.0	58442.0	57917.0	60113.0	61405.0	63527.0	67282.0	66292.0	60188.0	64333.0	66605.0	66326.0
Construction	27279.0	26426.0	25127.0	24487.0	25264.0	25860.0	27301.0	28177.0	26636.0	23685.0	24748.0	22659.0
Wholesale and retail trade, transportation and storage, accommodation and food service activities	83667.0	82521.0	83782.0	87083.0	90548.0	95930.0	101209.0	101700.0	94751.0	98095.0	100880.0	99932.0
Information and communication	20684.0	21577.0	22284.0	22424.0	23372.0	24721.0	26253.0	26906.0	25869.0	25959.0	26047.0	25589.0
Financial and insurance activities	29672.0	30185.0	31609.0	34053.0	35093.0	36972.0	38608.0	41116.0	40678.0	41318.0	40735.0	40371.0
Real estate activities	32418.0	32811.0	32997.0	33132.0	33212.0	33234.0	33331.0	33475.0	33365.0	34186.0	34900.0	35235.0
Professional, scientific, technical, administrative and support service activities	52365.0	49802.0	47988.0	48133.0	50029.0	53293.0	56700.0	59009.0	55078.0	53713.0	53682.0	53112.0
Public administration and defence, education, human health and social work activities	87226.0	90027.0	92306.0	93069.0	93645.0	94504.0	96003.0	98740.0	102374.0	104855.0	106251.0	107491.0
Other service activities	11499.0	11631.0	11339.0	11209.0	11380.0	11611.0	11887.0	11930.0	11807.0	11674.0	11622.0	11553.0
Equals: VALUE ADDED, GROSS, at basic prices	433798.0	434620.0	436743.0	446904.0	456182.0	471376.0	490102.0	500273.0	483757.0	492665.0	498419.0	495016.0
Less: Financial intermediation services indirectly measured (FISIM)	...	...	...	...	...	...	...	...	...	...	...	...
Plus: Taxes less Subsidies on products	56351.0	55889.0	55380.0	56209.0	57225.0	59457.0	61547.0	61334.0	57295.0	57232.0	56956.0	55067.0
Plus: Taxes on products	60751.0	60008.0	59611.0	60334.0	61331.0	63614.0	65733.0	65435.0	61554.0	61361.0	60959.0	58987.0
Less: Subsidies on products	4392.0	4112.0	4209.0	4122.0	4106.0	4157.0	4184.0	4085.0	4350.0	4187.0	4036.0	3966.0

	2001	2002	2003	2004	2005	2006	2007	2008	2009	2010	2011	2012
Series	**300**											
Base year	**2005**											
Plus: Statistical discrepancy	-64.0	-50.0	-18.0	-2.0	0.0	0.0	-4.0	-10.0	-52.0	-83.0	-104.0	-124.0
Equals: GROSS DOMESTIC PRODUCT [a]	490085.0	490459.0	492105.0	503111.0	513407.0	530833.0	551645.0	561597.0	541000.0	549814.0	555271.0	549959.0

[a] Chain-linked volume measures are presented in this table, thus discrepancies between components and total may exist.

Table 2.6 Output, gross value added and fixed assets by industries at current prices (ISIC Rev. 4) Total economy

Series 300: 1993 SNA, 1999 NLG Euro / Euro, Western calendar year — **Data in millions**

	2001	2002	2003	2004	2005	2006	2007	2008	2009	2010	2011	2012
Series	**300**											
Output, at basic prices	853164.0	870427.0	883492.0	913856.0	962007.0	1021783.0	1085522.0	1149443.0	1096415.0	1141512.0	1187629.0	...
Less: Intermediate consumption, at purchaser's prices	455608.0	456053.0	458236.0	476982.0	505825.0	542771.0	577872.0	621204.0	585563.0	615336.0	648254.0	...
Equals: VALUE ADDED, GROSS, at basic prices	397556.0	414374.0	425256.0	436874.0	456182.0	479012.0	507650.0	528239.0	510852.0	526176.0	539375.0	540040.0
Compensation of employees	227390.1	238825.0	245752.0	251030.1	254563.1	264925.3	280309.0	294716.0	298488.0	300434.0	306609.0	307686.0
Taxes on production and imports, less Subsidies	-30.0	-109.0	656.0	732.0	1576.0	1984.0	2055.0	1244.0	-2213.0	909.0	-62.0	1750.0
OPERATING SURPLUS, GROSS [a]	170196.0	175658.0	178848.0	185112.0	200043.0	212103.0	225286.0	232279.0	214577.0	224833.0	232828.0	230604.0
MIXED INCOME, GROSS	...	...	...	...	...	...	...	...	...	...	...	...
Less: Consumption of fixed capital	65865.0	69427.0	71461.0	73498.0	75709.0	78594.0	82072.0	85412.0	87974.0	89212.0	88726.0	88242.0
OPERATING SURPLUS, NET [b]	104331.0	106231.0	107387.0	111614.0	124334.0	133509.0	143214.0	146867.0	126603.0	135621.0	144102.0	142362.0
MIXED INCOME, NET	...	...	...	...	...	...	...	...	...	...	...	...
Gross capital formation	96191.0	91587.0	92089.0	93244.0	97614.0	108093.0	116807.0	121856.0	105491.0	105859.0	108911.0	103632.0
Gross fixed capital formation	94673.0	92862.0	92848.0	92426.0	97016.0	106373.0	114340.0	121849.0	108774.0	102031.0	106690.0	101133.0
Changes in inventories	1410.0	-1357.0	-795.0	676.0	509.0	1597.0	2456.0	-136.0	-3388.0	3432.0	2106.0	...
Acquisitions less disposals of valuables	108.0	82.0	36.0	142.0	89.0	123.0	11.0	143.0	105.0	396.0	115.0	...
Employment (average, in 1000 persons)	8282.4	8323.9	8282.9	8211.0	8251.4	8391.7	8605.9	8732.9	8670.6	8636.4	8698.2	8686.4

[a] Includes Mixed Income, Gross.
[b] Includes Mixed Income, Net.

Table 2.6 Output, gross value added and fixed assets by industries at current prices (ISIC Rev. 4) Agriculture, forestry and fishing (A)

Series 300: 1993 SNA, 1999 NLG Euro / Euro, Western calendar year — **Data in millions**

	2001	2002	2003	2004	2005	2006	2007	2008	2009	2010	2011	2012
Series	**300**											
Equals: VALUE ADDED, GROSS, at basic prices	9614.0	8988.0	9300.0	8671.0	8826.0	9808.0	9738.0	8837.0	7898.0	9297.0	8663.0	9109.0
Compensation of employees	2327.5	2510.9	2555.1	2527.0	2522.9	2573.0	2695.0	2763.0	2818.0	2859.0	2934.0	2923.0
Employment (average, in 1000 persons)	263.9	262.7	257.5	250.1	244.6	240.2	237.1	232.6	227.9	226.3	224.9	226.2

Table 2.6 Output, gross value added and fixed assets by industries at current prices (ISIC Rev. 4) Manufacturing, mining and quarrying and other industrial activities (B+C+D+E)

Series 300: 1993 SNA, 1999 NLG Euro / Euro, Western calendar year **Data in millions**

	2001	2002	2003	2004	2005	2006	2007	2008	2009	2010	2011	2012
Series	**300**											
Equals: VALUE ADDED, GROSS, at basic prices	74402.0	75196.0	77222.0	79959.0	84813.0	90763.0	96280.0	103046.0	92840.0	99002.0	105033.0	106940.0
Compensation of employees	37594.2	38922.1	39210.2	39532.7	38959.1	39855.6	41302.5	43113.0	42652.0	42635.0	43451.0	43604.0
Employment (average, in 1000 persons)	1051.1	1031.7	1000.0	973.1	951.9	947.1	952.5	961.5	939.5	915.3	908.8	903.8

Table 2.6 Output, gross value added and fixed assets by industries at current prices (ISIC Rev. 4) Manufacturing (C)

Series 300: 1993 SNA, 1999 NLG Euro / Euro, Western calendar year **Data in millions**

	2001	2002	2003	2004	2005	2006	2007	2008	2009	2010	2011	2012
Series	**300**											
Equals: VALUE ADDED, GROSS, at basic prices	55228.0	55516.0	56499.0	58850.0	61405.0	62743.0	67416.0	67700.0	60025.0	65086.0	69626.0	69635.0
Compensation of employees	34125.8	35154.2	35276.8	35575.0	35118.9	35963.8	37250.5	38839.0	38192.0	38013.0	38636.0	38800.0
Employment (average, in 1000 persons)	979.8	958.3	926.7	901.7	882.8	879.3	883.8	891.6	868.7	843.5	836.0	831.7

Table 2.6 Output, gross value added and fixed assets by industries at current prices (ISIC Rev. 4) Construction (F)

Series 300: 1993 SNA, 1999 NLG Euro / Euro, Western calendar year **Data in millions**

	2001	2002	2003	2004	2005	2006	2007	2008	2009	2010	2011	2012
Series	**300**											
Equals: VALUE ADDED, GROSS, at basic prices	23089.0	24159.0	24169.0	24122.0	25264.0	26930.0	28914.0	30956.0	30678.0	27985.0	28727.0	26190.0
Compensation of employees	15611.3	16231.4	16133.4	16280.0	16359.2	16856.3	17636.9	18569.0	18542.0	18086.0	18095.0	17663.0
Employment (average, in 1000 persons)	511.5	510.1	490.2	481.6	482.3	491.2	497.3	506.4	497.0	484.9	476.3	465.8

Table 2.6 Output, gross value added and fixed assets by industries at current prices (ISIC Rev. 4) Wholesale and retail trade, transportation and storage, accommodation and food service activities (G+H+I)

Series 300: 1993 SNA, 1999 NLG Euro / Euro, Western calendar year **Data in millions**

	2001	2002	2003	2004	2005	2006	2007	2008	2009	2010	2011	2012
Series	**300**											
Equals: VALUE ADDED, GROSS, at basic prices	83016.0	87054.0	85865.0	87967.0	90548.0	94644.0	101033.0	102011.0	94259.0	98004.0	101201.0	100660.0
Compensation of employees	47491.2	49299.2	50473.5	51654.3	51743.9	53638.7	56557.9	59321.0	59471.0	59959.0	61753.0	62360.0
Employment (average, in 1000 persons)	2103.3	2109.6	2097.0	2078.2	2064.6	2086.0	2153.6	2162.4	2137.1	2136.6	2171.2	2173.9

Table 2.6 Output, gross value added and fixed assets by industries at current prices (ISIC Rev. 4) Information and communication (J)

Series 300: 1993 SNA, 1999 NLG Euro / Euro, Western calendar year

Data in millions

	2001	2002	2003	2004	2005	2006	2007	2008	2009	2010	2011	2012
Series	**300**											
Equals: VALUE ADDED, GROSS, at basic prices	19549.0	21109.0	22338.0	22530.0	23372.0	24482.0	26200.0	26376.0	25022.0	25333.0	25351.0	24656.0
Compensation of employees	11118.9	10883.0	10842.0	10848.1	11415.0	12151.4	13061.7	13919.0	14053.0	13709.0	14043.0	14227.0
Employment (average, in 1000 persons)	273.8	256.5	244.7	235.5	242.9	252.6	262.9	271.3	264.2	255.1	260.4	262.2

Table 2.6 Output, gross value added and fixed assets by industries at current prices (ISIC Rev. 4) Financial and insurance activities (K)

Series 300: 1993 SNA, 1999 NLG Euro / Euro, Western calendar year

Data in millions

	2001	2002	2003	2004	2005	2006	2007	2008	2009	2010	2011	2012
Series	**300**											
Equals: VALUE ADDED, GROSS, at basic prices	24345.0	26908.0	30888.0	32221.0	35093.0	32415.0	30014.0	30058.0	38022.0	43423.0	42534.0	46827.0
Compensation of employees	14215.0	15407.0	15753.9	16210.0	16584.6	17604.8	18853.5	18880.0	18794.0	18863.0	19214.0	18957.0
Employment (average, in 1000 persons)	291.6	290.0	284.0	277.2	278.4	287.2	288.3	280.8	278.2	268.7	264.2	256.4

Table 2.6 Output, gross value added and fixed assets by industries at current prices (ISIC Rev. 4) Real estate activities (L)

Series 300: 1993 SNA, 1999 NLG Euro / Euro, Western calendar year

Data in millions

	2001	2002	2003	2004	2005	2006	2007	2008	2009	2010	2011	2012
Series	**300**											
Equals: VALUE ADDED, GROSS, at basic prices	31688.0	31192.0	30337.0	31984.0	33212.0	37022.0	41230.0	42434.0	33161.0	32405.0	34975.0	31774.0
Compensation of employees	2390.7	2603.3	2797.0	2854.0	2915.1	3031.5	3190.6	3377.0	3442.0	3318.0	3330.0	3328.0
Employment (average, in 1000 persons)	67.2	70.9	71.2	71.3	72.4	73.5	75.6	78.2	79.4	74.8	73.0	70.4

Table 2.6 Output, gross value added and fixed assets by industries at current prices (ISIC Rev. 4) Professional, scientific, technical, administrative and support service activities (M+N)

Series 300: 1993 SNA, 1999 NLG Euro / Euro, Western calendar year

Data in millions

	2001	2002	2003	2004	2005	2006	2007	2008	2009	2010	2011	2012
Series	**300**											
Equals: VALUE ADDED, GROSS, at basic prices	46207.0	45821.0	45689.0	47061.0	50029.0	54933.0	60868.0	64800.0	61751.0	59625.0	59885.0	59230.0
Compensation of employees	32252.6	33067.6	33502.8	34453.7	35781.1	38835.6	42683.8	45836.0	44921.0	43952.0	45626.0	45758.0
Employment (average, in 1000 persons)	1243.3	1233.3	1205.0	1204.3	1255.3	1335.1	1417.5	1456.9	1405.9	1346.3	1365.5	1361.6

Table 2.6 Output, gross value added and fixed assets by industries at current prices (ISIC Rev. 4) Public administration and defence, education, human health and social work activities (O+P+Q)

Series 300: 1993 SNA, 1999 NLG Euro / Euro, Western calendar year

Data in millions

	2001	2002	2003	2004	2005	2006	2007	2008	2009	2010	2011	2012
Series	**300**											
Equals: VALUE ADDED, GROSS, at basic prices	75671.0	83286.0	88567.0	91230.0	93645.0	96363.0	101224.0	107168.0	114103.0	117736.0	119377.0	120813.0
Compensation of employees	58587.1	63801.3	68205.6	70242.2	71792.7	73698.1	77302.6	81595.0	86141.0	89186.0	90345.0	91143.0
Employment (average, in 1000 persons)	1911.0	1995.7	2071.2	2077.8	2090.0	2106.5	2139.8	2181.2	2231.0	2310.9	2337.0	2331.1

Table 2.6 Output, gross value added and fixed assets by industries at current prices (ISIC Rev. 4) Other service activities (R+S+T)

Series 300: 1993 SNA, 1999 NLG Euro / Euro, Western calendar year

Data in millions

	2001	2002	2003	2004	2005	2006	2007	2008	2009	2010	2011	2012
Series	**300**											
Equals: VALUE ADDED, GROSS, at basic prices	9975.0	10661.0	10881.0	11129.0	11380.0	11652.0	12149.0	12553.0	13118.0	13366.0	13629.0	13841.0
Compensation of employees	5801.7	6099.2	6278.6	6428.1	6489.5	6680.1	7024.4	7343.0	7654.0	7867.0	7818.0	7723.0
Employment (average, in 1000 persons)	565.8	563.3	562.2	562.1	568.8	572.2	581.4	601.8	610.4	617.7	617.0	634.9

Table 3.1 Government final consumption expenditure by function at current prices

Series 300: 1993 SNA, 1999 NLG Euro / Euro, Western calendar year

Data in millions

	2001	2002	2003	2004	2005	2006	2007	2008	2009	2010	2011	2012
Series	**300**											
General public services	7306.0	8144.0	8456.0	8616.0	8809.0	8759.0	9081.0	9692.0	10810.0	11191.0	10988.0	...
Defence	7204.0	7293.0	7409.0	7217.0	6529.0	7163.0	7638.0	7986.0	8412.0	7947.0	7892.0	...
Public order and safety	6575.0	7336.0	7857.0	8243.0	8447.0	9126.0	9769.0	10588.0	11060.0	10937.0	10909.0	...
Economic affairs	12340.0	12811.0	13589.0	13613.0	13736.0	13960.0	15090.0	15968.0	16857.0	16772.0	16838.0	...
Environment protection	3150.0	3462.0	3786.0	3759.0	3735.0	4298.0	4514.0	4644.0	5012.0	5082.0	4964.0	...
Housing and community amenities	2096.0	2122.0	2408.0	2205.0	2211.0	2120.0	2186.0	2402.0	2638.0	2614.0	2353.0	...
Health	21716.0	24353.0	26335.0	27106.0	28110.0	37727.0	39651.0	41098.0	45024.0	46482.0	48179.0	...
Recreation, culture and religion	4159.0	4473.0	4759.0	4750.0	4811.0	5058.0	5298.0	5622.0	6024.0	6097.0	5996.0	...
Education	19284.0	20750.0	21814.0	22305.0	23253.0	24058.0	25494.0	26851.0	28813.0	29351.0	29345.0	...
Social protection	17555.0	19502.0	20380.0	21128.0	22044.0	23173.0	25151.0	27962.0	29490.0	30592.0	30693.0	...
Equals: General government final consumption expenditure	101385.0	110246.0	116793.0	118942.0	121685.0	135442.0	143872.0	152813.0	164140.0	167065.0	168157.0	170603.0

Table 3.2 Individual consumption expenditure of households, NPISHs, and general government at current prices

Series 300: 1993 SNA, 1999 NLG Euro / Euro, Western calendar year — **Data in millions**

	2001	2002	2003	2004	2005	2006	2007	2008	2009	2010	2011	2012
Series	**300**											
Individual consumption expenditure of households												
Food and non-alcoholic beverages	24488.0	25547.0	26009.0	26211.0	25985.0	27227.0	28308.0	30068.0	30292.0	30833.0	31548.0	...
Alcoholic beverages, tobacco and narcotics	6609.0	6779.0	6899.0	6965.0	6992.0	7212.0	7530.0	7865.0	8130.0	8297.0	8264.0	...
Clothing and footwear	13150.0	13396.0	12827.0	12762.0	12819.0	13599.0	14220.0	14302.0	14198.0	14455.0	14522.0	...
Housing, water, electricity, gas and other fuels	45187.0	46755.0	49304.0	51343.0	53893.0	56242.0	57481.0	59965.0	61558.0	63010.0	63608.0	...
Furnishings, household equipment and routine maintenance of the house	16163.0	16135.0	15793.0	15521.0	15513.0	16273.0	16805.0	16987.0	16224.0	16177.0	16104.0	...
Health	9761.0	10962.0	11580.0	12189.0	12733.0	5742.0	6178.0	7297.0	7079.0	7236.0	7275.0	...
Transport	24134.0	25763.0	26050.0	27189.0	28289.0	30014.0	31218.0	32844.0	30626.0	32179.0	33290.0	...
Communication	9096.0	10228.0	10890.0	11009.0	11366.0	11634.0	11748.0	11375.0	10888.0	10809.0	10967.0	...
Recreation and culture	24139.0	24817.0	24367.0	24427.0	24795.0	25974.0	27533.0	27951.0	26625.0	26795.0	26776.0	...
Education	1216.0	1299.0	1409.0	1491.0	1316.0	1350.0	1420.0	1490.0	1548.0	1639.0	1723.0	...
Restaurants and hotels	12083.0	12447.0	12153.0	12294.0	12540.0	13124.0	13838.0	13881.0	13241.0	13200.0	13758.0	...
Miscellaneous goods and services	32473.0	32862.0	34806.0	36023.0	38903.0	41266.0	42817.0	40969.0	37425.0	38620.0	39521.0	...
Equals: Household final consumption expenditure in domestic market	218499.0	226990.0	232087.0	237424.0	245144.0	249657.0	259096.0	264994.0	257834.0	263250.0	267356.0	...
Plus: Direct purchases abroad by residents	10510.0	11085.0	10983.0	10317.0	10165.0	10606.0	10878.0	11578.0	11652.0	11628.0	11553.0	...
Less: Direct purchases in domestic market by non-residents	8543.0	9151.0	9158.0	9220.0	9313.0	9994.0	10739.0	11230.0	11015.0	12223.0	13127.0	...
Equals: Household final consumption expenditure	220466.0	228924.0	233912.0	238521.0	245996.0	250269.0	259235.0	265342.0	258471.0	262655.0	265782.0	267890.0
Individual consumption expenditure of non-profit institutions serving households (NPISHs)												
Equals: NPISHs final consumption expenditure	3778.0	4119.0	4191.0	4260.0	4347.0	4606.0	4864.0	5075.0	5066.0	5155.0	5329.0	5400.0
Individual consumption expenditure of general government												
Equals: Individual consumption expenditure of general government	55216.0	61008.0	64819.0	66392.0	68667.0	79842.0	85536.0	90547.0	97315.0	100392.0	102957.0	105113.0
Equals: Total actual individual consumption	279460.0	294051.0	302922.0	309173.0	319010.0	334717.0	349635.0	360964.0	360852.0	368202.0	374068.0	378403.0

Table 4.1 Total Economy (S.1)

Series 300: 1993 SNA, 1999 NLG Euro / Euro, Western calendar year — **Data in millions**

	2001	2002	2003	2004	2005	2006	2007	2008	2009	2010	2011	2012
Series	**300**											
I. Production account - Resources												
Output, at basic prices (otherwise, please specify)	853164.0	870427.0	883492.0	913856.0	962007.0	1021783.0	1085522.0	1149443.0	1096415.0	1141512.0	1187629.0	...
Less: Financial intermediation services indirectly measured (only to be deducted if FISIM is not distributed to uses)	...	...	...	...	...	...	...	...	...	...	...	...
Plus: Taxes less Subsidies on products	50175.0	50840.0	51689.0	54310.0	57225.0	61204.0	64123.0	66242.0	62383.0	62564.0	62598.0	60598.0

	2001	2002	2003	2004	2005	2006	2007	2008	2009	2010	2011	2012
Series	**300**											
Plus: Taxes on products	54112.0	55020.0	56125.0	58474.0	61331.0	65373.0	67790.0	69741.0	66099.0	66230.0	65976.0	64072.0
Less: Subsidies on products	3937.0	4180.0	4436.0	4164.0	4106.0	4169.0	3667.0	3499.0	3716.0	3666.0	3378.0	3474.0
I. Production account - Uses												
Intermediate consumption, at purchaser's prices	455608.0	456053.0	458236.0	476982.0	505825.0	542771.0	577872.0	621204.0	585563.0	615336.0	648254.0	...
GROSS DOMESTIC PRODUCT	447731.0	465214.0	476945.0	491184.0	513407.0	540216.0	571773.0	594481.0	573235.0	588740.0	601973.0	...
Less: Consumption of fixed capital	65865.0	69427.0	71461.0	73498.0	75709.0	78594.0	82072.0	85412.0	87974.0	89212.0	88726.0	...
NET DOMESTIC PRODUCT	381866.0	395787.0	405484.0	417686.0	437698.0	461622.0	489701.0	509069.0	485261.0	499528.0	513247.0	...
II.1.1 Generation of income account - Resources												
GROSS DOMESTIC PRODUCT	447731.0	465214.0	476945.0	491184.0	513407.0	540216.0	571773.0	594481.0	573235.0	588740.0	601973.0	...
II.1.1 Generation of income account - Uses												
Compensation of employees	227390.0	238825.0	245752.0	251030.0	254563.0	264925.0	280309.0	294716.0	298488.0	300434.0	306609.0	...
Taxes on production and imports, less Subsidies	50145.0	50731.0	52345.0	55042.0	58801.0	63188.0	66178.0	67486.0	60170.0	63473.0	62536.0	...
Taxes on production and imports	57892.0	58890.0	60464.0	63301.0	66292.0	70859.0	74333.0	75719.0	70147.0	73568.0	72038.0	...
Taxes on products	54112.0	55020.0	56125.0	58474.0	61331.0	65373.0	67790.0	69741.0	66099.0	66230.0	65976.0	...
Other taxes on production	3780.0	3870.0	4339.0	4827.0	4961.0	5486.0	6543.0	5978.0	4048.0	7338.0	6062.0	...
Less: Subsidies	7747.0	8159.0	8119.0	8259.0	7491.0	7671.0	8155.0	8233.0	9977.0	10095.0	9502.0	...
Subsidies on products	3937.0	4180.0	4436.0	4164.0	4106.0	4169.0	3667.0	3499.0	3716.0	3666.0	3378.0	...
Other subsidies on production	3810.0	3979.0	3683.0	4095.0	3385.0	3502.0	4488.0	4734.0	6261.0	6429.0	6124.0	...
OPERATING SURPLUS, GROSS	138151.0	143845.0	146710.0	153542.0	168193.0	176753.0	225286.0[a]	232279.0[a]	214577.0[a]	224833.0[a]	232828.0[a]	...
MIXED INCOME, GROSS	32045.0	31813.0	32138.0	31570.0	31850.0	35350.0	...	...	...	...	...	...
II.1.2 Allocation of primary income account - Resources												
OPERATING SURPLUS, GROSS	138151.0	143845.0	146710.0	153542.0	168193.0	176753.0	225286.0[a]	232279.0[a]	214577.0[a]	224833.0[a]	232828.0[a]	...
MIXED INCOME, GROSS	32045.0	31813.0	32138.0	31570.0	31850.0	35350.0	...	...	...	...	...	...
Compensation of employees	227243.0	238501.0	245075.0	250018.0	253431.0	263652.0	276453.0	289678.0	293678.0	296106.0	301508.0	...
Taxes on production and imports, less Subsidies	48080.0	49446.0	51164.0	54094.0	57675.0	62002.0	64087.0	65307.0	59182.0	62167.0	60904.0	...
Taxes on production and imports	54758.0	56347.0	57913.0	60975.0	63875.0	68151.0	71214.0	72498.0	68073.0	71363.0	69401.0	...
Taxes on products	50996.0	52495.0	53602.0	56182.0	58914.0	62665.0	64791.0	66661.0	64050.0	64052.0	63345.0	...
Other taxes on production	3762.0	3852.0	4311.0	4793.0	4961.0	5486.0	6423.0	5837.0	4023.0	7311.0	6056.0	...
Less: Subsidies	6678.0	6901.0	6749.0	6881.0	6200.0	6149.0	7127.0	7191.0	8891.0	9196.0	8497.0	...
Subsidies on products	3072.0	3049.0	3279.0	3112.0	3135.0	3250.0	3396.0	3313.0	3461.0	3549.0	3351.0	...
Other subsidies on production	3606.0	3852.0	3470.0	3769.0	3065.0	2899.0	3731.0	3878.0	5430.0	5647.0	5146.0	...
Property income	272418.0	227785.0	211433.0	241127.0	264982.0	324158.0	401437.0	389172.0	286290.0	305978.0	319471.0	...
II.1.2 Allocation of primary income account - Uses												
Property income	266827.0	221922.0	204152.0	226018.0	260246.0	307174.0	385988.0	394581.0	294342.0	309767.0	307531.0	...
GROSS NATIONAL INCOME	451110.0	469468.0	482368.0	504333.0	515885.0	554741.0	581275.0	581855.0	559385.0	579317.0	607180.0	...
II.2 Secondary distribution of income account - Resources												
GROSS NATIONAL INCOME	451110.0	469468.0	482368.0	504333.0	515885.0	554741.0	581275.0	581855.0	559385.0	579317.0	607180.0	...
Current taxes on income, wealth, etc.	51216.0	53238.0	50803.0	51173.0	58457.0	62370.0	67944.0	69281.0	67686.0	70128.0	68630.0	...
Social contributions	111428.0	115312.0	122707.0	127666.0	128764.0	134739.0	139056.0	150936.0	140849.0	141214.0	151068.0	...
Social benefits other than social transfers in kind	75832.0	79946.0	82998.0	85479.0	87427.0	89709.0	91991.0	95913.0	100746.0	105665.0	109497.0	...

	2001	2002	2003	2004	2005	2006	2007	2008	2009	2010	2011	2012
Series	**300**											
Other current transfers	41503.0	47808.0	51075.0	53434.0	52428.0	44494.0	44644.0	45146.0	48422.0	49397.0	47630.0	...
II.2 Secondary distribution of income account - Uses												
Current taxes on income, wealth, etc.	50292.0	52346.0	49939.0	50127.0	57037.0	60743.0	66718.0	68062.0	67295.0	69974.0	67893.0	...
Social contributions	111066.0	114892.0	122151.0	126943.0	128017.0	133954.0	138217.0	149970.0	139754.0	139969.0	149645.0	...
Social benefits other than social transfers in kind	77243.0	81456.0	84664.0	87326.0	89513.0	91722.0	93985.0	97973.0	102803.0	107721.0	111553.0	...
Other current transfers	47589.0	54252.0	57281.0	60848.0	60728.0	52913.0	53472.0	54259.0	56118.0	57611.0	56982.0	...
GROSS DISPOSABLE INCOME	444899.0	462826.0	475916.0	496841.0	507666.0	546721.0	572518.0	572867.0	551118.0	570446.0	597932.0	...
II.4.1 Use of disposable income account - Resources												
GROSS DISPOSABLE INCOME	444899.0	462826.0	475916.0	496841.0	507666.0	546721.0	572518.0	572867.0	551118.0	570446.0	597932.0	...
Adjustment for the change in net equity of households on pension funds	18284.0	19686.0	22766.0	23400.0	24380.0	21683.0	22900.0	24345.0	20431.0	15220.0	17959.0	...
II.4.1 Use of disposable income account - Uses												
Final consumption expenditure	325629.0	343289.0	354896.0	361723.0	372028.0	390317.0	407971.0	423230.0	427677.0	434875.0	439268.0	...
Individual consumption expenditure	279460.0	294051.0	302922.0	309173.0	319010.0	334717.0	349635.0	360964.0	360852.0	368202.0	374068.0	...
Collective consumption expenditure	46169.0	49238.0	51974.0	52550.0	53018.0	55600.0	58336.0	62266.0	66825.0	66673.0	65200.0	...
Adjustment for the change in net equity of households on pension funds	18018.0	19397.0	22494.0	23107.0	23982.0	21250.0	22553.0	24043.0	20201.0	15066.0	17877.0	...
SAVING, GROSS	119536.0	119826.0	121292.0	135411.0	136036.0	156837.0	164894.0	149939.0	123671.0	135725.0	158746.0	...
III.1 Capital account - Changes in liabilities and net worth												
SAVING, GROSS	119536.0	119826.0	121292.0	135411.0	136036.0	156837.0	164894.0	149939.0	123671.0	135725.0	158746.0	...
Capital transfers, receivable less payable	-793.0	-967.0	-1022.0	-1320.0	-1751.0	-1888.0	-1186.0	-2104.0	-2531.0	-3259.0	-2058.0	...
Capital transfers, receivable	10864.0	11846.0	10516.0	10430.0	10323.0	10321.0	11883.0	14044.0	18429.0	14681.0	12602.0	...
Less: Capital transfers, payable	11657.0	12813.0	11538.0	11750.0	12074.0	12209.0	13069.0	16148.0	20960.0	17940.0	14660.0	...
Equals: CHANGES IN NET WORTH DUE TO SAVING AND CAPITAL TRANSFERS	52878.0	49432.0	48809.0	60593.0	58576.0	76355.0	81636.0	62423.0	33166.0	43254.0	67962.0	...
III.1 Capital account - Changes in assets												
Gross capital formation	96191.0	91587.0	92089.0	93244.0	97614.0	108093.0	116807.0	121856.0	105491.0	105859.0	108911.0	...
Gross fixed capital formation	94673.0	92862.0	92848.0	92426.0	97016.0	106373.0	114340.0	121849.0	108774.0	102031.0	106690.0	...
Changes in inventories	1410.0	-1357.0	-795.0	676.0	509.0	1597.0	2456.0	-136.0	-3388.0	3432.0	2106.0	...
Acquisitions less disposals of valuables	108.0	82.0	36.0	142.0	89.0	123.0	11.0	143.0	105.0	396.0	115.0	...
Acquisitions less disposals of non-produced non-financial assets	...	...	...	...	...	...	...	...	...	...	...	...
NET LENDING (+) / NET BORROWING (-)	22552.0	27272.0	28181.0	40847.0	36671.0	46856.0	46901.0	25979.0	15649.0	26607.0	47777.0	...
III.2 Financial account - Changes in liabilities and net worth												
Net incurrence of liabilities	480611.0	226162.0	225411.0	127626.0	261687.0	513106.0	534038.0	7103.0	-134710.0	-180983.0	-303888.0	...
Currency and deposits	84511.0	62120.0	61062.0	97799.0	47610.0	163816.0	167848.0	-94925.0	-4275.0	58213.0	51297.0	...
Securities other than shares	98375.0	61862.0	-19782.0	-47934.0	-44103.0	-34445.0	-15292.0	-122074.0	-90392.0	-287978.0	-476554.0	...
Loans	109006.0	74360.0	102329.0	42137.0	148334.0	138723.0	255786.0	99231.0	-143604.0	21980.0	17353.0	...
Shares and other equity	141478.0	-12039.0	35500.0	11296.0	43008.0	209059.0	87896.0	95931.0	33025.0	20576.0	47943.0	...
Insurance technical reserves	29596.0	29746.0	32004.0	32406.0	35829.0	18214.0	22086.0	28887.0	21154.0	13468.0	16839.0	...
Financial derivatives	...	...	...	...	...	...	...	...	...	...	...	...

	2001	2002	2003	2004	2005	2006	2007	2008	2009	2010	2011	2012
Series	**300**											
Other accounts payable	17645.0	10113.0	14298.0	-8078.0	31009.0	17739.0	15714.0	53.0	49382.0	-7242.0	39234.0	...
Adjustment to reconcile Net Lending of Financial Account and Capital Account	2933.0	644.0	-1694.0	404.0	-475.0	-558.0	-1470.0	-660.0	-1707.0	-689.0	1186.0	...
NET LENDING (+) / NET BORROWING (-) [b]	19619.0	26628.0	29875.0	40443.0	37146.0	47414.0	48371.0	26639.0	17356.0	27296.0	46591.0	...
	III.2 Financial account - Changes in assets											
Net acquisition of financial assets	500230.0	252790.0	255286.0	168069.0	298833.0	560520.0	582409.0	33742.0	-117354.0	-153687.0	-257297.0	...
Monetary gold and SDRs	-125.0	-464.0	-777.0	-27.0	-940.0	-793.0	-222.0	-129.0	-92.0	-17.0	-218.0	...
Currency and deposits	96189.0	38848.0	87660.0	62394.0	63402.0	161733.0	171500.0	-86294.0	-40615.0	1796.0	-48680.0	...
Securities other than shares	33402.0	53454.0	-61713.0	-37642.0	-73296.0	-65860.0	-71436.0	-215550.0	-147760.0	-327774.0	-484495.0	...
Loans	148441.0	95377.0	93484.0	60254.0	124001.0	222991.0	321196.0	159537.0	-64248.0	117903.0	218917.0	...
Shares and other equity	178078.0	28353.0	93063.0	65855.0	111534.0	219989.0	120241.0	158722.0	83775.0	47357.0	49946.0	...
Insurance technical reserves	29725.0	29894.0	32132.0	32547.0	36071.0	18375.0	22427.0	29189.0	21917.0	13422.0	17270.0	...
Financial derivatives	...	...	...	...	...	...	...	...	...	...	...	...
Other accounts receivable	14520.0	7328.0	11437.0	-15312.0	38061.0	4085.0	18703.0	-11733.0	29669.0	-6374.0	-10037.0	...

[a] Includes Mixed Income, Gross.
[b] Excludes Adjustment to reconcile Net Lending of the Financial Account and the Capital Account.

Table 4.2 Rest of the world (S.2)

Series 300: 1993 SNA, 1999 NLG Euro / Euro, Western calendar year

Data in millions

	2001	2002	2003	2004	2005	2006	2007	2008	2009	2010	2011	2012
Series	**300**											
	V.I External account of goods and services - Resources											
Imports of goods and services	275305.0	268112.0	270538.0	289894.0	313688.0	351669.0	377234.0	404047.0	352983.0	412487.0	445826.0	
Imports of goods	209757.0	200904.0	202221.0	220710.0	241157.0	274775.0	298650.0	319259.0	264680.0	318764.0	348131.0	
Imports of services	65548.0	67208.0	68317.0	69184.0	72531.0	76894.0	78584.0	84788.0	88303.0	93723.0	97695.0	
	V.I External account of goods and services - Uses											
Exports of goods and services	301216.0	298450.0	300498.0	326111.0	357453.0	393475.0	424229.0	453442.0	393050.0	460493.0	499620.0	
Exports of goods	236721.0	232123.0	233263.0	256089.0	281867.0	316270.0	342311.0	362462.0	300908.0	363026.0	396924.0	
Exports of services	64495.0	66327.0	67235.0	70022.0	75586.0	77205.0	81918.0	90980.0	92142.0	97467.0	102696.0	
EXTERNAL BALANCE OF GOODS AND SERVICES	-25911.0	-30338.0	-29960.0	-36217.0	-43765.0	-41806.0	-46995.0	-49395.0	-40067.0	-48006.0	-53794.0	
	V.II External account of primary income and current transfers - Resources											
EXTERNAL BALANCE OF GOODS AND SERVICES	-25911.0	-30338.0	-29960.0	-36217.0	-43765.0	-41806.0	-46995.0	-49395.0	-40067.0	-48006.0	-53794.0	
Compensation of employees	1436.0	1570.0	1807.0	2056.0	2143.0	2261.0	4818.0	5979.0	5855.0	5427.0	6185.0	
Taxes on production and imports, less Subsidies	2065.0	1285.0	1181.0	948.0	1126.0	1186.0	2091.0	2179.0	988.0	1306.0	1632.0	
Taxes on production and imports	3134.0	2543.0	2551.0	2326.0	2417.0	2708.0	3119.0	3221.0	2074.0	2205.0	2637.0	
Taxes on products	3116.0	2525.0	2523.0	2292.0	2417.0	2708.0	2999.0	3080.0	2049.0	2178.0	2631.0	
Other taxes on production	18.0	18.0	28.0	34.0	0.0	0.0	120.0	141.0	25.0	27.0	6.0	
Less: Subsidies	1069.0	1258.0	1370.0	1378.0	1291.0	1522.0	1028.0	1042.0	1086.0	899.0	1005.0	
Subsidies on products	865.0	1131.0	1157.0	1052.0	971.0	919.0	271.0	186.0	255.0	117.0	27.0	
Other subsidies on production	204.0	127.0	213.0	326.0	320.0	603.0	757.0	856.0	831.0	782.0	978.0	

	2001	2002	2003	2004	2005	2006	2007	2008	2009	2010	2011	2012
Series	**300**											
Property income	128512.0	92241.0	87958.0	108830.0	136222.0	160631.0	208450.0	201639.0	164377.0	195151.0	177083.0	
Current taxes on income, wealth, etc.	260.0	208.0	210.0	190.0	210.0	228.0	312.0	341.0	233.0	689.0	244.0	
Social contributions	330.0	323.0	299.0	278.0	272.0	276.0	281.0	282.0	284.0	284.0	284.0	
Social benefits other than social transfers in kind	1611.0	1727.0	1873.0	2065.0	2316.0	2255.0	2228.0	2308.0	2305.0	2304.0	2304.0	
Other current transfers	9047.0	9716.0	10147.0	11507.0	12513.0	12961.0	13421.0	13931.0	14202.0	14969.0	15164.0	
Adjustment for the change in net equity of households on pension funds	-266.0	-289.0	-272.0	-293.0	-398.0	-433.0	-347.0	-302.0	-230.0	-154.0	-82.0	
V.II External account of primary income and current transfers - Uses												
Compensation of employees	1289.0	1246.0	1130.0	1044.0	1011.0	988.0	962.0	941.0	1045.0	1099.0	1084.0	
Taxes on production and imports, less Subsidies	...	...	...	...	...	...	...	...	...	...	...	
Taxes on production and imports	...	...	...	...	...	...	...	...	...	...	...	
Taxes on products	...	...	...	...	...	...	...	...	...	...	...	
Other taxes on production	...	...	...	...	...	...	...	...	...	...	...	
Less: Subsidies	...	...	...	...	...	...	...	...	...	...	...	
Subsidies on products	...	...	...	...	...	...	...	...	...	...	...	
Other subsidies on production	...	...	...	...	...	...	...	...	...	...	...	
Property income	134103.0	98104.0	95239.0	123939.0	140958.0	177615.0	223899.0	196230.0	156325.0	191362.0	189023.0	
Current taxes on income and wealth, etc.	1184.0	1100.0	1074.0	1236.0	1630.0	1855.0	1538.0	1560.0	624.0	843.0	981.0	
Social contributions	692.0	743.0	855.0	1001.0	1019.0	1061.0	1120.0	1248.0	1379.0	1529.0	1707.0	
Social benefits other than social transfers in kind	200.0	217.0	207.0	218.0	230.0	242.0	234.0	248.0	248.0	248.0	248.0	
Other current transfers	2961.0	3272.0	3941.0	4093.0	4213.0	4542.0	4593.0	4818.0	6506.0	6755.0	5812.0	
Adjustment for the change in net equity of households on pension funds	0.0	0.0	0.0	0.0	0.0	0.0	0.0	0.0	0.0	0.0	0.0	
CURRENT EXTERNAL BALANCE	-23345.0	-28239.0	-29203.0	-42167.0	-38422.0	-48744.0	-48087.0	-28083.0	-18180.0	-29866.0	-49835.0	
V.III.1 Capital account - Changes in liabilities and net worth												
CURRENT EXTERNAL BALANCE	-23345.0	-28239.0	-29203.0	-42167.0	-38422.0	-48744.0	-48087.0	-28083.0	-18180.0	-29866.0	-49835.0	
Capital transfers, receivable less payable	793.0	967.0	1022.0	1320.0	1751.0	1888.0	1186.0	2104.0	2531.0	3259.0	2058.0	
Capital transfers, receivable	2550.0	2428.0	2384.0	2951.0	3381.0	3680.0	3897.0	4505.0	4862.0	5695.0	4134.0	
Less: Capital transfers, payable	1757.0	1461.0	1362.0	1631.0	1630.0	1792.0	2711.0	2401.0	2331.0	2436.0	2076.0	
Equals: CHANGES IN NET WORTH DUE TO SAVING AND CAPITAL TRANSFERS	-22552.0	-27272.0	-28181.0	-40847.0	-36671.0	-46856.0	-46901.0	-25979.0	-15649.0	-26607.0	-47777.0	
V.III.1 Capital account - Changes in assets												
Acquisitions less disposals of non-produced non-financial assets	0.0	0.0	0.0	0.0	0.0	0.0	0.0	0.0	0.0	0.0	0.0	
NET LENDING (+) / NET BORROWING (-)	-22552.0	-27272.0	-28181.0	-40847.0	-36671.0	-46856.0	-46901.0	-25979.0	-15649.0	-26607.0	-47777.0	
V.III.2 Financial account - Changes in liabilities and net worth												
Net incurrence of liabilities	406221.0	170649.0	111322.0	32353.0	125267.0	432473.0	460325.0	-145274.0	-174210.0	-210398.0	-292736.0	
Currency and deposits	65957.0	27877.0	54900.0	26492.0	39262.0	116039.0	135280.0	-110752.0	-68249.0	-7562.0	-53535.0	
Securities other than shares	37577.0	60982.0	-73166.0	-73627.0	-82984.0	-53714.0	-67556.0	-206487.0	-154421.0	-354655.0	-505106.0	
Loans	117093.0	57648.0	36407.0	13877.0	38880.0	145241.0	268236.0	66701.0	-52333.0	88691.0	187712.0	
Shares and other equity	180539.0	36875.0	94375.0	69313.0	120398.0	229595.0	118710.0	117981.0	107437.0	52753.0	68341.0	

	2001	2002	2003	2004	2005	2006	2007	2008	2009	2010	2011	2012
Series	**300**											
Insurance technical reserves	-12.0	-35.0	-34.0	-47.0	-46.0	-180.0	-3.0	0.0	46.0	0.0	0.0	
Financial derivatives	...	...	...	...	...	...	...	...	...	...	...	
Other accounts payable	5067.0	-12698.0	-1160.0	-3655.0	9757.0	-4508.0	5658.0	-12717.0	-6690.0	10375.0	9852.0	
Adjustment to reconcile Net Lending of Financial Account and Capital Account	-2933.0	-644.0	1694.0	-404.0	475.0	558.0	1470.0	660.0	1707.0	689.0	-1186.0	
NET LENDING (+) / NET BORROWING (-) [a]	-19619.0	-26628.0	-29875.0	-40443.0	-37146.0	-47414.0	-48371.0	-26639.0	-17356.0	-27296.0	-46591.0	
	V.III.2 Financial account - Changes in assets											
Net acquisition of financial assets	386602.0	144021.0	81447.0	-8090.0	88121.0	385059.0	411954.0	-171913.0	-191566.0	-237694.0	-339327.0	
Monetary gold and SDRs	125.0	464.0	777.0	27.0	940.0	793.0	222.0	129.0	92.0	17.0	218.0	
Currency and deposits	54279.0	51149.0	28302.0	61897.0	23470.0	118122.0	131628.0	-119383.0	-31909.0	48855.0	46442.0	
Securities other than shares	102550.0	69390.0	-31235.0	-83919.0	-53791.0	-22299.0	-11412.0	-113011.0	-97053.0	-314859.0	-497165.0	
Loans	77658.0	36631.0	45252.0	-4240.0	63213.0	60973.0	202826.0	6395.0	-131689.0	-7232.0	-13852.0	
Shares and other equity	143939.0	-3517.0	36812.0	14754.0	51872.0	218665.0	86365.0	55190.0	56687.0	25972.0	66338.0	
Insurance technical reserves	-141.0	-183.0	-162.0	-188.0	-288.0	-341.0	-344.0	-302.0	-717.0	46.0	-431.0	
Financial derivatives	...	...	...	...	...	...	...	...	...	...	...	
Other accounts receivable	8192.0	-9913.0	1701.0	3579.0	2705.0	9146.0	2669.0	-931.0	13023.0	9507.0	59123.0	

[a] Excludes Adjustment to reconcile Net Lending of the Financial Account and the Capital Account.

Table 4.3 Non-financial Corporations (S.11)

Series 300: 1993 SNA, 1999 NLG Euro / Euro, Western calendar year

Data in millions

	2001	2002	2003	2004	2005	2006	2007	2008	2009	2010	2011	2012
Series	**300**											
	I. Production account - Resources											
Output, at basic prices (otherwise, please specify)	602521.0	609124.0	610236.0	632981.0	671509.0	720081.0	772665.0	821339.0	751950.0	787135.0	832710.0	
	I. Production account - Uses											
Intermediate consumption, at purchaser's prices	350527.0	346100.0	343605.0	359272.0	384347.0	415869.0	447461.0	481467.0	429021.0	456662.0	491342.0	
VALUE ADDED GROSS, in basic prices	251994.0	263024.0	266631.0	273709.0	287162.0	304212.0	325204.0	339872.0	322929.0	330473.0	341368.0	
Less: Consumption of fixed capital	35583.0	37322.0	38081.0	38819.0	40268.0	41499.0	43201.0	44990.0	46025.0	46371.0	46249.0	
VALUE ADDED NET, at basic prices	216411.0	225702.0	228550.0	234890.0	246894.0	262713.0	282003.0	294882.0	276904.0	284102.0	295119.0	
	II.1.1 Generation of income account - Resources											
VALUE ADDED GROSS, at basic prices	251994.0	263024.0	266631.0	273709.0	287162.0	304212.0	325204.0	339872.0	322929.0	330473.0	341368.0	
	II.1.1 Generation of income account - Uses											
Compensation of employees	154574.0	161243.0	164883.0	168539.0	170995.0	179049.0	190018.0	201020.0	201913.0	201695.0	207349.0	
Other taxes less Other subsidies on production	-376.0	-439.0	84.0	-210.0	394.0	901.0	782.0	396.0	-2145.0	-169.0	-726.0	
Other taxes on production	2217.0	2231.0	2371.0	2526.0	2623.0	2993.0	3668.0	3405.0	2194.0	4277.0	3319.0	
Less: Other subsidies on production	2593.0	2670.0	2287.0	2736.0	2229.0	2092.0	2886.0	3009.0	4339.0	4446.0	4045.0	
OPERATING SURPLUS, GROSS	97796.0	102220.0	101664.0	105380.0	115773.0	124262.0	134404.0	138456.0	123161.0	128949.0	134734.0	
	II.1.2 Allocation of primary income account - Resources											
OPERATING SURPLUS, GROSS	97796.0	102220.0	101664.0	105380.0	115773.0	124262.0	134404.0	138456.0	123161.0	128949.0	134734.0	

	2001	2002	2003	2004	2005	2006	2007	2008	2009	2010	2011	2012
Series	**300**											
Property income	20906.0	19513.0	25077.0	35214.0	39631.0	45631.0	55275.0	52344.0	32477.0	49188.0	55249.0	
II.1.2 Allocation of primary income account - Uses												
Property income	48648.0	42328.0	43444.0	48039.0	65121.0	67932.0	77921.0	81793.0	59866.0	70891.0	67339.0	
BALANCE OF PRIMARY INCOMES	70054.0	79405.0	83297.0	92555.0	90283.0	101961.0	111758.0	109007.0	95772.0	107244.0	122655.0	
II.2 Secondary distribution of income account - Resources												
BALANCE OF PRIMARY INCOMES	70054.0	79405.0	83297.0	92555.0	90283.0	101961.0	111758.0	109007.0	95772.0	107244.0	122655.0	
Social contributions	4772.0	4761.0	4479.0	4499.0	4936.0	4597.0	4643.0	5142.0	5149.0	5235.0	5197.0	
Other current transfers	2683.0	3180.0	3493.0	3876.0	3550.0	2606.0	2437.0	2417.0	2647.0	2565.0	2506.0	
II.2 Secondary distribution of income account - Uses												
Current taxes on income, wealth, etc.	13738.0	12603.0	10248.0	10813.0	12084.0	12598.0	13779.0	14957.0	8427.0	10350.0	9715.0	
Social benefits other than social transfers in kind	4772.0	4761.0	4479.0	4499.0	4936.0	4597.0	4643.0	5142.0	5149.0	5235.0	5197.0	
Other current transfers	3324.0	3791.0	4228.0	4437.0	4131.0	3237.0	3313.0	3149.0	3426.0	3381.0	3694.0	
GROSS DISPOSABLE INCOME	55675.0	66191.0	72314.0	81181.0	77618.0	88732.0	97103.0	93318.0	86566.0	96078.0	111752.0	
II.4.1 Use of disposable income account - Resources												
GROSS DISPOSABLE INCOME	55675.0	66191.0	72314.0	81181.0	77618.0	88732.0	97103.0	93318.0	86566.0	96078.0	111752.0	
II.4.1 Use of disposable income account - Uses												
Adjustment for the change in net equity of households on pension funds	...	...	...	...	...	...	...	...	...	...	...	
SAVING, GROSS	55675.0	66191.0	72314.0	81181.0	77618.0	88732.0	97103.0	93318.0	86566.0	96078.0	111752.0	
III.1 Capital account - Changes in liabilities and net worth												
SAVING, GROSS	55675.0	66191.0	72314.0	81181.0	77618.0	88732.0	97103.0	93318.0	86566.0	96078.0	111752.0	
Capital transfers, receivable less payable	2684.0	1691.0	1862.0	1378.0	1086.0	787.0	1431.0	1254.0	-653.0	2220.0	1892.0	
Capital transfers, receivable	2857.0	2043.0	2053.0	1633.0	1242.0	955.0	1535.0	1938.0	2339.0	2459.0	1992.0	
Less: Capital transfers, payable	173.0	352.0	191.0	255.0	156.0	168.0	104.0	684.0	2992.0	239.0	100.0	
Equals: CHANGES IN NET WORTH DUE TO SAVING AND CAPITAL TRANSFERS	22776.0	30560.0	36095.0	43740.0	38436.0	48020.0	55333.0	49582.0	39888.0	51927.0	67395.0	
III.1 Capital account - Changes in assets												
Gross capital formation	45549.0	43115.0	39827.0	42189.0	44222.0	47864.0	53200.0	55745.0	45410.0	50366.0	51457.0	
Gross fixed capital formation	43958.0	44173.0	40567.0	41435.0	43669.0	46385.0	50841.0	55690.0	48734.0	46760.0	49303.0	
Changes in inventories	1529.0	-1084.0	-740.0	662.0	520.0	1411.0	2361.0	-13.0	-3392.0	3336.0	2114.0	
Acquisitions less disposals of valuables	62.0	26.0	0.0	92.0	33.0	68.0	-2.0	68.0	68.0	270.0	40.0	
Acquisitions less disposals of non-produced non-financial assets	539.0	550.0	943.0	755.0	910.0	1123.0	1045.0	1390.0	-140.0	451.0	591.0	
NET LENDING (+) / NET BORROWING (-)	12271.0	24217.0	33406.0	39615.0	33572.0	40532.0	44289.0	37437.0	40643.0	47481.0	61596.0	
III.2 Financial account - Changes in liabilities and net worth												
Net incurrence of liabilities	59304.0	33239.0	6682.0	11178.0	60012.0	26270.0	21586.0	24873.0	9327.0	17058.0	-10467.0	
Currency and deposits	...	...	...	...	...	...	...	...	...	...	...	
Securities other than shares	7289.0	-3950.0	-11503.0	-10194.0	-6668.0	-4534.0	-4299.0	-406.0	3618.0	-2351.0	-13386.0	
Loans	17366.0	22277.0	14574.0	7636.0	27293.0	23158.0	16955.0	11961.0	5918.0	2283.0	6945.0	
Shares and other equity	18751.0	9625.0	6599.0	11516.0	42235.0	3602.0	8612.0	10683.0	5429.0	23675.0	2489.0	
Insurance technical reserves	...	...	...	...	...	...	...	...	...	...	...	

	2001	2002	2003	2004	2005	2006	2007	2008	2009	2010	2011	2012
Series	**300**											
Financial derivatives	...	...	...	...	...	...	...	...	...	...	...	
Other accounts payable	15898.0	5287.0	-2988.0	2220.0	-2848.0	4044.0	318.0	2635.0	-5638.0	-6549.0	-6515.0	
Adjustment to reconcile Net Lending of Financial Account and Capital Account	2115.0	2604.0	-183.0	3854.0	681.0	-524.0	406.0	-477.0	-1198.0	-3003.0	2823.0	
NET LENDING (+) / NET BORROWING (-) [a]	10156.0	21613.0	33589.0	35761.0	32891.0	41056.0	43883.0	37914.0	41841.0	50484.0	58773.0	
	III.2 Financial account - Changes in assets											
Net acquisition of financial assets	69460.0	54852.0	40271.0	46939.0	92903.0	67326.0	65469.0	62787.0	51168.0	67542.0	48306.0	
Monetary gold and SDRs	...	...	...	...	...	...	...	...	...	...	...	
Currency and deposits	16702.0	4786.0	12150.0	17288.0	3054.0	30889.0	14858.0	9853.0	12400.0	2997.0	-5747.0	
Securities other than shares	4658.0	9168.0	-4974.0	2438.0	-1432.0	-2315.0	-1770.0	-6513.0	1005.0	-13731.0	-8698.0	
Loans	36431.0	9546.0	6814.0	-8109.0	27618.0	2909.0	15885.0	14055.0	11911.0	6736.0	6584.0	
Shares and other equity	-7281.0	23241.0	22747.0	29482.0	57007.0	29707.0	19511.0	38749.0	31460.0	62192.0	39977.0	
Insurance technical reserves	219.0	169.0	365.0	331.0	705.0	206.0	-132.0	1246.0	274.0	-184.0	568.0	
Financial derivatives	...	...	...	...	...	...	...	...	...	...	...	
Other accounts receivable	18731.0	7942.0	3169.0	5509.0	5951.0	5930.0	17117.0	5397.0	-5882.0	9532.0	15622.0	

[a] Excludes Adjustment to reconcile Net Lending of the Financial Account and the Capital Account.

Table 4.4 Financial Corporations (S.12)

Series 300: 1993 SNA, 1999 NLG Euro / Euro, Western calendar year

Data in millions

	2001	2002	2003	2004	2005	2006	2007	2008	2009	2010	2011	2012
Series	**300**											
	I. Production account - Resources											
Output, at basic prices (otherwise, please specify)	49192.0	51522.0	56430.0	58960.0	62067.0	61117.0	59672.0	63004.0	75923.0	81526.0	79286.0	
	I. Production account - Uses											
Intermediate consumption, at purchaser's prices	25040.0	25229.0	26073.0	27346.0	28230.0	30040.0	31065.0	33859.0	39247.0	39185.0	38059.0	
VALUE ADDED GROSS, at basic prices	24152.0	26293.0	30357.0	31614.0	33837.0	31077.0	28607.0	29145.0	36676.0	42341.0	41227.0	
Less: Consumption of fixed capital	5010.0	5196.0	5132.0	5182.0	4609.0	4647.0	4736.0	4848.0	4857.0	4598.0	4313.0	
VALUE ADDED NET, at basic prices	19142.0	21097.0	25225.0	26432.0	29228.0	26430.0	23871.0	24297.0	31819.0	37743.0	36914.0	
	II.1.1 Generation of income account - Resources											
VALUE ADDED GROSS, at basic prices	24152.0	26293.0	30357.0	31614.0	33837.0	31077.0	28607.0	29145.0	36676.0	42341.0	41227.0	
	II.1.1 Generation of income account - Uses											
Compensation of employees	13399.0	14446.0	14984.0	15399.0	15617.0	16606.0	17603.0	17542.0	17166.0	17360.0	17511.0	
Other taxes less Other subsidies on production	217.0	215.0	231.0	228.0	283.0	211.0	246.0	244.0	249.0	228.0	264.0	
Other taxes on production	312.0	309.0	329.0	351.0	385.0	292.0	328.0	325.0	330.0	337.0	351.0	
Less: Other subsidies on production	95.0	94.0	98.0	123.0	102.0	81.0	82.0	81.0	81.0	109.0	87.0	
OPERATING SURPLUS, GROSS	10536.0	11632.0	15142.0	15987.0	17937.0	14260.0	10758.0	11359.0	19261.0	24753.0	23450.0	
	II.1.2 Allocation of primary income account - Resources											
OPERATING SURPLUS, GROSS	10536.0	11632.0	15142.0	15987.0	17937.0	14260.0	10758.0	11359.0	19261.0	24753.0	23450.0	
Property income	186470.0	146114.0	128495.0	146879.0	160363.0	208308.0	267322.0	253167.0	190600.0	200586.0	203406.0	

	2001	2002	2003	2004	2005	2006	2007	2008	2009	2010	2011	2012
Series	**300**											
II.1.2 Allocation of primary income account - Uses												
Property income	183129.0	146434.0	130301.0	147500.0	164210.0	203035.0	264012.0	265744.0	202159.0	210702.0	208553.0	
BALANCE OF PRIMARY INCOMES	13877.0	11312.0	13336.0	15366.0	14090.0	19533.0	14068.0	-1218.0	7702.0	14637.0	18305.0	
II.2 Secondary distribution of income account - Resources												
BALANCE OF PRIMARY INCOMES	13877.0	11312.0	13336.0	15366.0	14090.0	19533.0	14068.0	-1218.0	7702.0	14637.0	18305.0	
Social contributions	40269.0	43719.0	47433.0	49516.0	51857.0	49846.0	52513.0	54881.0	51761.0	48260.0	52720.0	
Other current transfers	15574.0	18437.0	19291.0	20135.0	19110.0	14841.0	14404.0	14827.0	15305.0	15410.0	15074.0	
II.2 Secondary distribution of income account - Uses												
Current taxes on income, wealth, etc.	4111.0	3008.0	3363.0	4382.0	5206.0	5546.0	5084.0	4193.0	3425.0	3036.0	2955.0	
Social benefits other than social transfers in kind	22250.0	24329.0	24943.0	26409.0	27875.0	28596.0	29960.0	30838.0	31560.0	33194.0	34843.0	
Other current transfers	15575.0	18436.0	19279.0	20131.0	19102.0	14841.0	14604.0	14827.0	15305.0	15410.0	15074.0	
GROSS DISPOSABLE INCOME	27784.0	27695.0	32475.0	34095.0	32874.0	35237.0	31337.0	18632.0	24478.0	26667.0	33227.0	
II.4.1 Use of disposable income account - Resources												
GROSS DISPOSABLE INCOME	27784.0	27695.0	32475.0	34095.0	32874.0	35237.0	31337.0	18632.0	24478.0	26667.0	33227.0	
II.4.1 Use of disposable income account - Uses												
Adjustment for the change in net equity of households on pension funds	18018.0	19397.0	22494.0	23107.0	23982.0	21250.0	22553.0	24043.0	20201.0	15066.0	17877.0	
SAVING, GROSS	9766.0	8298.0	9981.0	10988.0	8892.0	13987.0	8784.0	-5411.0	4277.0	11601.0	15350.0	
III.1 Capital account - Changes in liabilities and net worth												
SAVING, GROSS	9766.0	8298.0	9981.0	10988.0	8892.0	13987.0	8784.0	-5411.0	4277.0	11601.0	15350.0	
Capital transfers, receivable less payable	26.0	281.0	183.0	224.0	124.0	131.0	34.0	429.0	5123.0	1222.0	-20.0	
Capital transfers, receivable	57.0	1586.0	685.0	344.0	361.0	189.0	93.0	1370.0	5345.0	1365.0	65.0	
Less: Capital transfers, payable	31.0	1305.0	502.0	120.0	237.0	58.0	59.0	941.0	222.0	143.0	85.0	
Equals: CHANGES IN NET WORTH DUE TO SAVING AND CAPITAL TRANSFERS	4782.0	3383.0	5032.0	6030.0	4407.0	9471.0	4082.0	-9830.0	4543.0	8225.0	11017.0	
III.1 Capital account - Changes in assets												
Gross capital formation	5306.0	1498.0	3411.0	3146.0	1203.0	3396.0	2004.0	3929.0	3732.0	1104.0	5054.0	
Gross fixed capital formation	5302.0	1496.0	3409.0	3145.0	1197.0	3392.0	2000.0	3926.0	3729.0	1101.0	5053.0	
Changes in inventories	...	...	...	...	...	...	...	...	...	...	...	
Acquisitions less disposals of valuables	4.0	2.0	2.0	1.0	6.0	4.0	4.0	3.0	3.0	3.0	1.0	
Acquisitions less disposals of non-produced non-financial assets	203.0	-188.0	-103.0	-65.0	14.0	181.0	-278.0	-36.0	191.0	-205.0	-79.0	
NET LENDING (+) / NET BORROWING (-)	4283.0	7269.0	6856.0	8131.0	7799.0	10541.0	7092.0	-8875.0	5477.0	11924.0	10355.0	
III.2 Financial account - Changes in liabilities and net worth												
Net incurrence of liabilities	384224.0	144486.0	158224.0	70625.0	137931.0	444056.0	466882.0	-141532.0	-188796.0	-255384.0	-337903.0	
Currency and deposits	84560.0	62093.0	61030.0	97810.0	47674.0	163828.0	167855.0	-94917.0	-4181.0	58283.0	51259.0	
Securities other than shares	87726.0	57508.0	-22534.0	-49633.0	-42511.0	-20237.0	-8157.0	-196287.0	-81339.0	-311588.0	-478547.0	
Loans	56367.0	13567.0	42693.0	-1351.0	61436.0	68693.0	192303.0	40606.0	-191368.0	-1101.0	-9732.0	
Shares and other equity	122727.0	-21664.0	28901.0	-220.0	773.0	205457.0	79284.0	85248.0	27596.0	-3099.0	45454.0	
Insurance technical reserves	29596.0	29746.0	32004.0	32406.0	35829.0	18214.0	22086.0	28887.0	21154.0	13468.0	16839.0	
Financial derivatives	...	...	...	...	...	...	...	...	...	...	...	

	2001	2002	2003	2004	2005	2006	2007	2008	2009	2010	2011	2012
Series	**300**											
Other accounts payable	3248.0	3236.0	16130.0	-8387.0	34730.0	8101.0	13511.0	-5069.0	39342.0	-11347.0	36824.0	
NET LENDING (+) / NET BORROWING (-)	4283.0	7269.0	6856.0	8131.0	7799.0	10541.0	7092.0	-8875.0	5477.0	11924.0	10355.0	
	III.2 Financial account - Changes in assets											
Net acquisition of financial assets	388507.0	151755.0	165080.0	78756.0	145730.0	454597.0	473974.0	-150407.0	-183319.0	-243460.0	-327548.0	
Monetary gold and SDRs	-125.0	-464.0	-777.0	-27.0	-940.0	-793.0	-222.0	-129.0	-92.0	-17.0	-218.0	
Currency and deposits	60018.0	15334.0	58243.0	27894.0	37369.0	117819.0	123868.0	-118101.0	-71774.0	-10978.0	-61704.0	
Securities other than shares	25000.0	33890.0	-56892.0	-40494.0	-75635.0	-64149.0	-72325.0	-211730.0	-169562.0	-310244.0	-471110.0	
Loans	113330.0	86730.0	89032.0	68704.0	93469.0	219815.0	302247.0	99932.0	-48467.0	112385.0	204450.0	
Shares and other equity	194466.0	16106.0	70785.0	42019.0	61114.0	197563.0	113629.0	85491.0	74600.0	-13491.0	28333.0	
Insurance technical reserves	0.0	0.0	0.0	0.0	0.0	0.0	0.0	0.0	46.0	0.0	0.0	
Financial derivatives	...	...	...	...	...	...	...	...	...	...	...	
Other accounts receivable	-4182.0	159.0	4689.0	-19340.0	30353.0	-15658.0	6777.0	-5870.0	31930.0	-21115.0	-27299.0	

Table 4.5 General Government (S.13)

Series 300: 1993 SNA, 1999 NLG Euro / Euro, Western calendar year

Data in millions

	2001	2002	2003	2004	2005	2006	2007	2008	2009	2010	2011	2012
Series	**300**											
	I. Production account - Resources											
Output, at basic prices (otherwise, please specify)	84361.0	89775.0	94791.0	96515.0	98800.0	102645.0	107424.0	113736.0	120672.0	122128.0	120980.0	121241.0
	I. Production account - Uses											
Intermediate consumption, at purchaser's prices	30969.0	33070.0	34945.0	35292.0	36410.0	39024.0	40961.0	44004.0	47388.0	46879.0	45607.0	46127.0
VALUE ADDED GROSS, at basic prices	53392.0	56705.0	59846.0	61223.0	62390.0	63621.0	66463.0	69732.0	73284.0	75249.0	75373.0	75114.0
Less: Consumption of fixed capital	10767.0	11402.0	12035.0	12427.0	12872.0	13476.0	14251.0	15092.0	15738.0	16254.0	16672.0	16837.0
VALUE ADDED NET, at basic prices	42625.0	45303.0	47811.0	48796.0	49518.0	50145.0	52212.0	54640.0	57546.0	58995.0	58701.0	...
	II.1.1 Generation of income account - Resources											
VALUE ADDED GROSS, at basic prices	53392.0	56705.0	59846.0	61223.0	62390.0	63621.0	66463.0	69732.0	73284.0	75249.0	75373.0	75114.0
	II.1.1 Generation of income account - Uses											
Compensation of employees	42820.0	45599.0	48040.0	48909.0	49543.0	50216.0	52273.0	54691.0	57725.0	59207.0	58877.0	58419.0
Other taxes less Other subsidies on production	-195.0	-296.0	-229.0	-113.0	-25.0	-71.0	-61.0	-51.0	-179.0	-212.0	-176.0	-142.0
Other taxes on production	471.0	505.0	539.0	549.0	559.0	562.0	569.0	594.0	611.0	641.0	674.0	...
Less: Other subsidies on production	666.0	801.0	768.0	662.0	584.0	633.0	630.0	645.0	790.0	853.0	850.0	...
OPERATING SURPLUS, GROSS	10767.0	11402.0	12035.0	12427.0	12872.0	13476.0	14251.0	15092.0	15738.0	16254.0	16672.0	16837.0
	II.1.2 Allocation of primary income account - Resources											
OPERATING SURPLUS, GROSS	10767.0	11402.0	12035.0	12427.0	12872.0	13476.0	14251.0	15092.0	15738.0	16254.0	16672.0	16837.0
Taxes on production and imports, less Subsidies	48080.0	49446.0	51164.0	54094.0	57675.0	62002.0	64087.0	65307.0	59182.0	62167.0	60904.0	60589.0
Taxes on production and imports	54758.0	56347.0	57913.0	60975.0	63875.0	68151.0	71214.0	72498.0	68073.0	71363.0	69401.0	68431.0
Taxes on products	50996.0	52495.0	53602.0	56182.0	58914.0	62665.0	64791.0	66661.0	64050.0	64052.0	63345.0	...
Other taxes on production	3762.0	3852.0	4311.0	4793.0	4961.0	5486.0	6423.0	5837.0	4023.0	7311.0	6056.0	...

	2001	2002	2003	2004	2005	2006	2007	2008	2009	2010	2011	2012
Series	**300**											
Less: Subsidies	6678.0	6901.0	6749.0	6881.0	6200.0	6149.0	7127.0	7191.0	8891.0	9196.0	8497.0	7842.0
Subsidies on products	3072.0	3049.0	3279.0	3112.0	3135.0	3250.0	3396.0	3313.0	3461.0	3549.0	3351.0	...
Other subsidies on production	3606.0	3852.0	3470.0	3769.0	3065.0	2899.0	3731.0	3878.0	5430.0	5647.0	5146.0	...
Property income	10960.0	8991.0	9098.0	10204.0	11507.0	14639.0	14829.0	20317.0	17837.0	16172.0	16019.0	18537.0
II.1.2 Allocation of primary income account - Uses												
Property income	14211.0	13070.0	12406.0	12217.0	12125.0	11896.0	12586.0	13206.0	12442.0	11472.0	11912.0	11106.0
BALANCE OF PRIMARY INCOMES	55596.0	56769.0	59891.0	64508.0	69929.0	78221.0	80581.0	87510.0	80315.0	83121.0	81683.0	84857.0
II.2 Secondary distribution of income account - Resources												
BALANCE OF PRIMARY INCOMES	55596.0	56769.0	59891.0	64508.0	69929.0	78221.0	80581.0	87510.0	80315.0	83121.0	81683.0	84857.0
Current taxes on income, wealth, etc.	51216.0	53238.0	50803.0	51173.0	58457.0	62370.0	67944.0	69281.0	67686.0	70128.0	68630.0	65689.0
Social contributions	65936.0	66349.0	70347.0	73205.0	71486.0	79850.0	81468.0	90442.0	83465.0	87225.0	92668.0	99295.0
Other current transfers	1775.0	1784.0	1922.0	1966.0	2139.0	2160.0	2136.0	2205.0	2281.0	2344.0	2270.0	2406.0
II.2 Secondary distribution of income account - Uses												
Current taxes on income, wealth, etc.	...	...	...	...	...	...	...	...	...	...	...	...
Social benefits other than social transfers in kind	49770.0	51883.0	54794.0	55972.0	56217.0	58083.0	58950.0	61522.0	65620.0	68798.0	71030.0	72871.0
Other current transfers	7878.0	8286.0	8259.0	9122.0	9587.0	10352.0	9903.0	10486.0	8279.0	10228.0	10123.0	10150.0
GROSS DISPOSABLE INCOME	116875.0	117971.0	119910.0	125758.0	136207.0	154166.0	163276.0	177430.0	159848.0	163792.0	164098.0	169226.0
II.4.1 Use of disposable income account - Resources												
GROSS DISPOSABLE INCOME	116875.0	117971.0	119910.0	125758.0	136207.0	154166.0	163276.0	177430.0	159848.0	163792.0	164098.0	169226.0
II.4.1 Use of disposable income account - Uses												
Final consumption expenditure	101385.0	110246.0	116793.0	118942.0	121685.0	135442.0	143872.0	152813.0	164140.0	167065.0	168157.0	170603.0
Individual consumption expenditure	55216.0	61008.0	64819.0	66392.0	68667.0	79842.0	85536.0	90547.0	97315.0	100392.0	102957.0	105113.0
Collective consumption expenditure	46169.0	49238.0	51974.0	52550.0	53018.0	55600.0	58336.0	62266.0	66825.0	66673.0	65200.0	65490.0
Adjustment for the change in net equity of households on pension funds	...	...	...	...	...	...	...	...	...	...	...	...
SAVING, GROSS	15490.0	7725.0	3117.0	6816.0	14522.0	18724.0	19404.0	24617.0	-4292.0	-3273.0	-4059.0	-1377.0
III.1 Capital account - Changes in liabilities and net worth												
SAVING, GROSS	15490.0	7725.0	3117.0	6816.0	14522.0	18724.0	19404.0	24617.0	-4292.0	-3273.0	-4059.0	-1377.0
Capital transfers, receivable less payable	-2501.0	-1358.0	-1592.0	-1370.0	-1090.0	-540.0	-1342.0	-2353.0	-5492.0	-5327.0	-3041.0	-3052.0
Capital transfers, receivable	1667.0	1960.0	1770.0	1838.0	1923.0	2068.0	2112.0	2029.0	2017.0	2059.0	1814.0	1591.0
Less: Capital transfers, payable	4168.0	3318.0	3362.0	3208.0	3013.0	2608.0	3454.0	4382.0	7509.0	7386.0	4855.0	4643.0
Equals: CHANGES IN NET WORTH DUE TO SAVING AND CAPITAL TRANSFERS	2222.0	-5035.0	-10510.0	-6981.0	560.0	4708.0	3811.0	7172.0	-25522.0	-24854.0	-23772.0	...
III.1 Capital account - Changes in assets												
Gross capital formation	14582.0	16444.0	16958.0	15833.0	16916.0	17862.0	18996.0	20548.0	21553.0	21367.0	20257.0	20212.0
Gross fixed capital formation	14563.0	16425.0	16932.0	15816.0	16884.0	17837.0	18986.0	20535.0	21540.0	21337.0	20238.0	20192.0
Changes in inventories	0.0	0.0	0.0	0.0	0.0	0.0	0.0	0.0	0.0	0.0	0.0	20.0
Acquisitions less disposals of valuables	19.0	19.0	26.0	17.0	32.0	25.0	10.0	13.0	13.0	30.0	19.0	...
Acquisitions of non-produced non-financial assets	-452.0	-272.0	-392.0	-1708.0	-2035.0	-2470.0	-1863.0	-1187.0	657.0	-423.0	-747.0	-615.0
NET LENDING (+) / NET BORROWING (-)	-1141.0	-9805.0	-15041.0	-8679.0	-1449.0	2792.0	929.0	2903.0	-31994.0	-29544.0	-26610.0	-24026.0

	2001	2002	2003	2004	2005	2006	2007	2008	2009	2010	2011	2012
Series	**300**											
	III.2 Financial account - Changes in liabilities and net worth											
Net incurrence of liabilities	-61.0	9747.0	14053.0	7873.0	7120.0	-5571.0	5002.0	85538.0	4432.0	28067.0	21380.0	...
Currency and deposits	-49.0	27.0	32.0	-11.0	-64.0	-12.0	-7.0	-8.0	-94.0	-70.0	38.0	...
Securities other than shares	3360.0	8304.0	14306.0	11924.0	5098.0	-9693.0	-2812.0	74628.0	-12658.0	26035.0	15398.0	...
Loans	-1608.0	-71.0	-1274.0	-2172.0	3273.0	-1238.0	6049.0	13619.0	16489.0	-2234.0	7001.0	...
Shares and other equity	...	...	...	...	...	...	...	...	...	...	...	...
Insurance technical reserves	...	...	...	...	...	...	...	...	...	...	...	...
Financial derivatives	...	...	...	...	...	...	...	...	...	...	...	...
Other accounts payable	-1764.0	1487.0	989.0	-1868.0	-1187.0	5372.0	1772.0	-2701.0	695.0	4336.0	-1057.0	...
NET LENDING (+) / NET BORROWING (-)	-1141.0	-9805.0	-15041.0	-8679.0	-1449.0	2792.0	929.0	2903.0	-31994.0	-29544.0	-26610.0	...
	III.2 Financial account - Changes in assets											
Net acquisition of financial assets	-1202.0	-58.0	-988.0	-806.0	5671.0	-2779.0	5931.0	88441.0	-27562.0	-1477.0	-5230.0	...
Monetary gold and SDRs	...	...	...	...	...	...	...	...	...	...	...	...
Currency and deposits	-32.0	-723.0	-92.0	559.0	6063.0	-3843.0	6770.0	85.0	-1813.0	-3490.0	165.0	...
Securities other than shares	-40.0	-304.0	-262.0	-208.0	-107.0	-118.0	271.0	-87.0	22669.0	-973.0	-1103.0	...
Loans	-1168.0	-383.0	-2549.0	-126.0	2566.0	-150.0	2684.0	45217.0	-27583.0	-1330.0	1235.0	...
Shares and other equity	1908.0	-730.0	-2567.0	-764.0	-877.0	-4906.0	-2439.0	37191.0	-24995.0	-781.0	-6324.0	...
Insurance technical reserves	...	...	...	...	...	...	...	...	...	...	...	...
Financial derivatives	...	...	...	...	...	...	...	...	...	...	...	...
Other accounts receivable	-1870.0	2082.0	4482.0	-267.0	-1974.0	6238.0	-1355.0	6035.0	4160.0	5097.0	797.0	...

Table 4.6 Households (S.14)

Series 300: 1993 SNA, 1999 NLG Euro / Euro, Western calendar year

Data in millions

	2001	2002	2003	2004	2005	2006	2007	2008	2009	2010	2011	2012
Series	**300**											
	I. Production account - Resources											
Output, at basic prices (otherwise, please specify)	112514.0	115090.0	116920.0	120198.0	124335.0	132384.0	140047.0	145386.0	141748.0	144468.0	148254.0	
	I. Production account - Uses											
Intermediate consumption, at purchaser's prices	46436.0	48879.0	50664.0	52078.0	53766.0	54521.0	55070.0	58443.0	66519.0	69206.0	69838.0	
VALUE ADDED GROSS, at basic prices	66078.0	66211.0	66256.0	68120.0	70569.0	77863.0	84977.0	86943.0	75229.0	75262.0	78416.0	
Less: Consumption of fixed capital	14315.0	15309.0	16011.0	16865.0	17754.0	18761.0	19667.0	20259.0	21126.0	21759.0	21262.0	
VALUE ADDED NET, at basic prices	51763.0	50902.0	50245.0	51255.0	52815.0	59102.0	65310.0	66684.0	54103.0	53503.0	57154.0	
	II.1.1 Generation of income account - Resources											
VALUE ADDED GROSS, at basic prices	66078.0	66211.0	66256.0	68120.0	70569.0	77863.0	84977.0	86943.0	75229.0	75262.0	78416.0	
	II.1.1 Generation of income account - Uses											
Compensation of employees	14862.0	15600.0	15896.0	16193.0	16397.0	17043.0	18250.0	19156.0	19198.0	19573.0	20135.0	
Other taxes less Other subsidies on production	309.0	405.0	555.0	814.0	917.0	926.0	1071.0	638.0	-158.0	1040.0	552.0	
Other taxes on production	765.0	819.0	1085.0	1388.0	1387.0	1622.0	1961.0	1637.0	893.0	2061.0	1694.0	

	2001	2002	2003	2004	2005	2006	2007	2008	2009	2010	2011	2012
Series	**300**											
Less: Other subsidies on production	456.0	414.0	530.0	574.0	470.0	696.0	890.0	999.0	1051.0	1021.0	1142.0	
OPERATING SURPLUS, GROSS	18862.0	18393.0	17667.0	19543.0	21405.0	24544.0	65656.0[a]	67149.0[a]	56189.0[a]	54647.0[a]	57742.0[a]	
MIXED INCOME, GROSS	32045.0	31813.0	32138.0	31570.0	31850.0	35350.0	...	...	...	...	...	
	II.1.2 Allocation of primary income account - Resources											
OPERATING SURPLUS, GROSS	18862.0	18393.0	17667.0	19543.0	21405.0	24544.0	65656.0[a]	67149.0[a]	56189.0[a]	54647.0[a]	57742.0[a]	
MIXED INCOME, GROSS	32045.0	31813.0	32138.0	31570.0	31850.0	35350.0	...	...	...	...	...	
Compensation of employees	227243.0	238501.0	245075.0	250018.0	253431.0	263652.0	276453.0	289678.0	293678.0	296106.0	301508.0	
Property income	53500.0	52605.0	48339.0	48364.0	52933.0	54825.0	63047.0	62361.0	44715.0	39624.0	44347.0	
	II.1.2 Allocation of primary income account - Uses											
Property income	20818.0	20071.0	17987.0	18247.0	18760.0	24283.0	31427.0	33790.0	19842.0	16688.0	19712.0	
BALANCE OF PRIMARY INCOMES	310832.0	321241.0	325232.0	331248.0	340859.0	354088.0	373729.0	385398.0	374740.0	373691.0	383872.0	
	II.2 Secondary distribution of income account - Resources											
BALANCE OF PRIMARY INCOMES	310832.0	321241.0	325232.0	331248.0	340859.0	354088.0	373729.0	385398.0	374740.0	373691.0	383872.0	
Social contributions	406.0	432.0	402.0	401.0	434.0	401.0	388.0	423.0	422.0	439.0	427.0	
Social benefits other than social transfers in kind	75832.0	79946.0	82998.0	85479.0	87427.0	89709.0	91991.0	95913.0	100746.0	105665.0	109497.0	
Other current transfers	16504.0	19069.0	20770.0	21729.0	21637.0	18823.0	19318.0	19457.0	21853.0	22604.0	21555.0	
	II.2 Secondary distribution of income account - Uses											
Current taxes on income, wealth, etc.	32443.0	36735.0	36328.0	34932.0	39747.0	42599.0	47855.0	48912.0	55443.0	56588.0	55223.0	
Social contributions	111066.0	114892.0	122151.0	126943.0	128017.0	133954.0	138217.0	149970.0	139754.0	139969.0	149645.0	
Social benefits other than social transfers in kind	406.0	432.0	402.0	401.0	434.0	401.0	388.0	423.0	422.0	439.0	427.0	
Other current transfers	18937.0	21785.0	23603.0	25139.0	25543.0	22131.0	23100.0	23197.0	26352.0	25518.0	24867.0	
GROSS DISPOSABLE INCOME	240722.0	246844.0	246918.0	251442.0	256616.0	263936.0	275866.0	278689.0	275790.0	279885.0	285189.0	
	II.4.1 Use of disposable income account - Resources											
GROSS DISPOSABLE INCOME	240722.0	246844.0	246918.0	251442.0	256616.0	263936.0	275866.0	278689.0	275790.0	279885.0	285189.0	
Adjustment for the change in net equity of households on pension funds	18284.0	19686.0	22766.0	23400.0	24380.0	21683.0	22900.0	24345.0	20431.0	15220.0	17959.0	
	II.4.1 Use of disposable income account - Uses											
Final consumption expenditure	220466.0	228924.0	233912.0	238521.0	245996.0	250269.0	259235.0	265342.0	258471.0	262655.0	265782.0	
Individual consumption expenditure	220466.0	228924.0	233912.0	238521.0	245996.0	250269.0	259235.0	265342.0	258471.0	262655.0	265782.0	
SAVING, GROSS	38540.0	37606.0	35772.0	36321.0	35000.0	35350.0	39531.0	37692.0	37750.0	32450.0	37366.0	
	III.1 Capital account - Changes in liabilities and net worth											
SAVING, GROSS	38540.0	37606.0	35772.0	36321.0	35000.0	35350.0	39531.0	37692.0	37750.0	32450.0	37366.0	
Capital transfers, receivable less payable	-1450.0	-2126.0	-1844.0	-1926.0	-2243.0	-2662.0	-1715.0	-1872.0	-2040.0	-1963.0	-1492.0	
Capital transfers, receivable	5835.0	5712.0	5639.0	6241.0	6425.0	6713.0	7737.0	8269.0	8197.0	8209.0	8128.0	
Less: Capital transfers, payable	7285.0	7838.0	7483.0	8167.0	8668.0	9375.0	9452.0	10141.0	10237.0	10172.0	9620.0	
Equals: CHANGES IN NET WORTH DUE TO SAVINGS AND CAPITAL TRANSFERS	22775.0	20171.0	17917.0	17530.0	15003.0	13927.0	18149.0	15561.0	14584.0	8728.0	14612.0	
	III.1 Capital account - Changes in assets											
Gross capital formation	30518.0	30309.0	31678.0	31878.0	35067.0	38739.0	42383.0	41402.0	34583.0	32808.0	31931.0	
Gross fixed capital formation	30614.0	30547.0	31725.0	31838.0	35067.0	38535.0	42289.0	41466.0	34564.0	32627.0	31881.0	

	2001	2002	2003	2004	2005	2006	2007	2008	2009	2010	2011	2012
Series	**300**											
Changes in inventories	-119.0	-273.0	-55.0	14.0	-11.0	186.0	95.0	-123.0	4.0	96.0	-8.0	
Acquisitions less disposals of valuables	23.0	35.0	8.0	26.0	11.0	18.0	-1.0	59.0	15.0	85.0	58.0	
Acquisitions less disposals of non-produced non-financial assets	-294.0	-94.0	-452.0	1014.0	1107.0	1162.0	1092.0	-171.0	-712.0	173.0	231.0	
NET LENDING (+) / NET BORROWING (-)	6866.0	5265.0	2702.0	1503.0	-3417.0	-7213.0	-5659.0	-5411.0	1839.0	-2494.0	3712.0	

[a] Includes Mixed Income, Gross.

Table 4.7 Non-profit institutions serving households (S.15)

Series 300: 1993 SNA, 1999 NLG Euro / Euro, Western calendar year

Data in millions

	2001	2002	2003	2004	2005	2006	2007	2008	2009	2010	2011	2012
Series	**300**											
I. Production account - Resources												
Output, at basic prices (otherwise, please specify)	4576.0	4916.0	5115.0	5202.0	5296.0	5556.0	5714.0	5978.0	6122.0	6255.0	6399.0	
I. Production account - Uses												
Intermediate consumption, at purchaser's prices	2636.0	2775.0	2949.0	2994.0	3072.0	3317.0	3315.0	3431.0	3388.0	3404.0	3408.0	
VALUE ADDED GROSS, at basic prices	1940.0	2141.0	2166.0	2208.0	2224.0	2239.0	2399.0	2547.0	2734.0	2851.0	2991.0	
Less: Consumption of fixed capital	190.0	198.0	202.0	205.0	206.0	211.0	217.0	223.0	228.0	230.0	230.0	
VALUE ADDED NET, at basic prices	1750.0	1943.0	1964.0	2003.0	2018.0	2028.0	2182.0	2324.0	2506.0	2621.0	2761.0	
II.1.1 Generation of income account - Resources												
VALUE ADDED GROSS, at basic prices	1940.0	2141.0	2166.0	2208.0	2224.0	2239.0	2399.0	2547.0	2734.0	2851.0	2991.0	
II.1.1 Generation of income account - Uses												
Compensation of employees	1735.0	1937.0	1949.0	1990.0	2011.0	2011.0	2165.0	2307.0	2486.0	2599.0	2737.0	
Other taxes less Other subsidies on production	15.0	6.0	15.0	13.0	7.0	17.0	17.0	17.0	20.0	22.0	24.0	
Other taxes on production	15.0	6.0	15.0	13.0	7.0	17.0	17.0	17.0	20.0	22.0	24.0	
Less: Other subsidies on production	...	...	...	...	...	...	...	...	...	...	...	
OPERATING SURPLUS, GROSS	190.0	198.0	202.0	205.0	206.0	210.0	217.0	222.0	228.0	230.0	230.0	
II.1.2 Allocation of primary income account - Resources												
OPERATING SURPLUS, GROSS	190.0	198.0	202.0	205.0	206.0	210.0	217.0	222.0	228.0	230.0	230.0	
Property income	582.0	562.0	424.0	466.0	548.0	755.0	964.0	983.0	661.0	408.0	450.0	
II.1.2 Allocation of primary income account - Uses												
Property income	21.0	19.0	14.0	15.0	30.0	28.0	42.0	48.0	33.0	14.0	15.0	
BALANCE OF PRIMARY INCOMES	751.0	741.0	612.0	656.0	724.0	938.0	1139.0	1158.0	856.0	624.0	665.0	
II.2 Secondary distribution of income account - Resources												
BALANCE OF PRIMARY INCOMES	751.0	741.0	612.0	656.0	724.0	938.0	1139.0	1158.0	856.0	624.0	665.0	
Social contributions	45.0	51.0	46.0	45.0	51.0	45.0	44.0	48.0	52.0	55.0	56.0	
Other current transfers	4967.0	5338.0	5599.0	5728.0	5992.0	6064.0	6349.0	6240.0	6336.0	6474.0	6225.0	
II.2 Secondary distribution of income account - Uses												
Current taxes on income, wealth, etc.	...	...	...	...	...	...	...	...	...	...	...	
Social benefits other than social transfers in kind	45.0	51.0	46.0	45.0	51.0	45.0	44.0	48.0	52.0	55.0	56.0	

	2001	2002	2003	2004	2005	2006	2007	2008	2009	2010	2011	2012
Series	**300**											
Other current transfers	1875.0	1954.0	1912.0	2019.0	2365.0	2352.0	2552.0	2600.0	2756.0	3074.0	3224.0	
GROSS DISPOSABLE INCOME	3843.0	4125.0	4299.0	4365.0	4351.0	4650.0	4936.0	4798.0	4436.0	4024.0	3666.0	
	II.4.1 Use of disposable income account - Resources											
GROSS DISPOSABLE INCOME	3843.0	4125.0	4299.0	4365.0	4351.0	4650.0	4936.0	4798.0	4436.0	4024.0	3666.0	
	II.4.1 Use of disposable income account - Uses											
Final consumption expenditure	3778.0	4119.0	4191.0	4260.0	4347.0	4606.0	4864.0	5075.0	5066.0	5155.0	5329.0	
Individual consumption expenditure	3778.0	4119.0	4191.0	4260.0	4347.0	4606.0	4864.0	5075.0	5066.0	5155.0	5329.0	
Adjustment for the change in net equity of households on pension funds	...	...	...	...	...	...	...	...	...	...	...	
SAVING, GROSS	65.0	6.0	108.0	105.0	4.0	44.0	72.0	-277.0	-630.0	-1131.0	-1663.0	
	III.1 Capital account - Changes in liabilities and net worth											
SAVING, GROSS	65.0	6.0	108.0	105.0	4.0	44.0	72.0	-277.0	-630.0	-1131.0	-1663.0	
Capital transfers, receivable less payable	448.0	545.0	369.0	374.0	372.0	396.0	406.0	438.0	531.0	589.0	603.0	
Capital transfers, receivable	448.0	545.0	369.0	374.0	372.0	396.0	406.0	438.0	531.0	589.0	603.0	
Less: Capital transfers, payable	...	...	...	...	...	...	...	...	...	...	...	
Equals: CHANGES IN NET WORTH DUE TO SAVING AND CAPITAL TRANSFERS	323.0	353.0	275.0	274.0	170.0	229.0	261.0	-62.0	-327.0	-772.0	-1290.0	
	III.1 Capital account - Changes in assets											
Gross capital formation	236.0	221.0	215.0	198.0	206.0	232.0	224.0	232.0	213.0	214.0	212.0	
Gross fixed capital formation	236.0	221.0	215.0	192.0	199.0	224.0	224.0	232.0	207.0	206.0	215.0	
Changes in inventories	...	...	...	...	...	...	...	...	...	...	...	
Acquisitions less disposals of valuables	0.0	0.0	0.0	6.0	7.0	8.0	0.0	0.0	6.0	8.0	-3.0	
Acquisitions less disposals of non-produced non-financial assets	4.0	4.0	4.0	4.0	4.0	4.0	4.0	4.0	4.0	4.0	4.0	
NET LENDING (+) / NET BORROWING (-)	273.0	326.0	258.0	277.0	166.0	204.0	250.0	-75.0	-316.0	-760.0	-1276.0	

Table 4.8 Combined Sectors: Non-Financial and Financial Corporations (S.11 + S.12)

Series 300: 1993 SNA, 1999 NLG Euro / Euro, Western calendar year **Data in millions**

	2001	2002	2003	2004	2005	2006	2007	2008	2009	2010	2011	2012
Series	**300**											
	I. Production account - Resources											
Output, at basic prices (otherwise, please specify)	651713.0	660646.0	666666.0	691941.0	733576.0	781198.0	832337.0	884343.0	827873.0	868661.0	911996.0	
	I. Production account - Uses											
Intermediate consumption, at purchaser's prices	375567.0	371329.0	369678.0	386618.0	412577.0	445909.0	478526.0	515326.0	468268.0	495847.0	529401.0	
VALUE ADDED GROSS, at basic prices	276146.0	289317.0	296988.0	305323.0	320999.0	335289.0	353811.0	369017.0	359605.0	372814.0	382595.0	
Less: Consumption of fixed capital	40593.0	42518.0	43213.0	44001.0	44877.0	46146.0	47937.0	49838.0	50882.0	50969.0	50562.0	
VALUE ADDED NET, at basic prices	235553.0	246799.0	253775.0	261322.0	276122.0	289143.0	305874.0	319179.0	308723.0	321845.0	332033.0	
	II.1.1 Generation of income account - Resources											
VALUE ADDED GROSS, at basic prices	276146.0	289317.0	296988.0	305323.0	320999.0	335289.0	353811.0	369017.0	359605.0	372814.0	382595.0	

	2001	2002	2003	2004	2005	2006	2007	2008	2009	2010	2011	2012
Series	**300**											
	II.1.1 Generation of income account - Uses											
Compensation of employees	167973.0	175689.0	179867.0	183938.0	186612.0	195655.0	207621.0	218562.0	219079.0	219055.0	224860.0	
Other taxes less Other subsidies on production	-159.0	-224.0	315.0	18.0	677.0	1112.0	1028.0	640.0	-1896.0	59.0	-462.0	
Other taxes on production	2529.0	2540.0	2700.0	2877.0	3008.0	3285.0	3996.0	3730.0	2524.0	4614.0	3670.0	
Less: Other subsidies on production	2688.0	2764.0	2385.0	2859.0	2331.0	2173.0	2968.0	3090.0	4420.0	4555.0	4132.0	
OPERATING SURPLUS, GROSS	108332.0	113852.0	116806.0	121367.0	133710.0	138522.0	145162.0	149815.0	142422.0	153700.0	158197.0	
	II.1.2 Allocation of primary income account - Resources											
OPERATING SURPLUS, GROSS	108332.0	113852.0	116806.0	121367.0	133710.0	138522.0	145162.0	149815.0	142422.0	153700.0	158197.0	
Property income	207376.0	165627.0	153572.0	182093.0	199994.0	253939.0	322597.0	305511.0	223077.0	249774.0	258655.0	
	II.1.2 Allocation of primary income account - Uses											
Property income	231777.0	188762.0	173745.0	195539.0	229331.0	270967.0	341933.0	347537.0	262025.0	281593.0	275892.0	
BALANCE OF PRIMARY INCOMES	83931.0	90717.0	96633.0	107921.0	104373.0	121494.0	125826.0	107789.0	103474.0	121881.0	140960.0	
	II.2 Secondary distribution of income account - Resources											
BALANCE OF PRIMARY INCOMES	83931.0	90717.0	96633.0	107921.0	104373.0	121494.0	125826.0	107789.0	103474.0	121881.0	140960.0	
Social contributions	45041.0	48480.0	51912.0	54015.0	56793.0	54443.0	57156.0	60023.0	56910.0	53495.0	57917.0	
Other current transfers	18257.0	21617.0	22784.0	24011.0	22660.0	17447.0	16841.0	17244.0	17952.0	17975.0	17580.0	
	II.2 Secondary distribution of income account - Uses											
Current taxes on income, wealth, etc.	17849.0	15611.0	13611.0	15195.0	17290.0	18144.0	18863.0	19150.0	11852.0	13386.0	12670.0	
Social benefits other than social transfers in kind	27022.0	29090.0	29422.0	30908.0	32811.0	33193.0	34603.0	35980.0	36709.0	38429.0	40040.0	
Other current transfers	18899.0	22227.0	23507.0	24568.0	23233.0	18078.0	17917.0	17976.0	18731.0	18791.0	18768.0	
GROSS DISPOSABLE INCOME	83459.0	93886.0	104789.0	115276.0	110492.0	123969.0	128440.0	111950.0	111044.0	122745.0	144979.0	
	II.4.1 Use of disposable income account - Resources											
GROSS DISPOSABLE INCOME	83459.0	93886.0	104789.0	115276.0	110492.0	123969.0	128440.0	111950.0	111044.0	122745.0	144979.0	
	II.4.1 Use of disposable income account - Uses											
Adjustment for the change in net equity of households on pension funds	18018.0	19397.0	22494.0	23107.0	23982.0	21250.0	22553.0	24043.0	20201.0	15066.0	17877.0	
SAVING, GROSS	65441.0	74489.0	82295.0	92169.0	86510.0	102719.0	105887.0	87907.0	90843.0	107679.0	127102.0	
	III.1 Capital account - Changes in liabilities and net worth											
SAVING, GROSS	65441.0	74489.0	82295.0	92169.0	86510.0	102719.0	105887.0	87907.0	90843.0	107679.0	127102.0	
Capital transfers, receivable less payable	2710.0	1972.0	2045.0	1602.0	1210.0	918.0	1465.0	1683.0	4470.0	3442.0	1872.0	
Capital transfers, receivable	2914.0	3629.0	2738.0	1977.0	1603.0	1144.0	1628.0	3308.0	7684.0	3824.0	2057.0	
Less: Capital transfers, payable	204.0	1657.0	693.0	375.0	393.0	226.0	163.0	1625.0	3214.0	382.0	185.0	
Equals: CHANGES IN NET WORTH DUE TO SAVING AND CAPITAL TRANSFERS	27558.0	33943.0	41127.0	49770.0	42843.0	57491.0	59415.0	39752.0	44431.0	60152.0	78412.0	
	III.1 Capital account - Changes in assets											
Gross capital formation	50855.0	44613.0	43238.0	45335.0	45425.0	51260.0	55204.0	59674.0	49142.0	51470.0	56511.0	
Gross fixed capital formation	49260.0	45669.0	43976.0	44580.0	44866.0	49777.0	52841.0	59616.0	52463.0	47861.0	54356.0	
Changes in inventories	1529.0	-1084.0	-740.0	662.0	520.0	1411.0	2361.0	-13.0	-3392.0	3336.0	2114.0	
Acquisitions less disposals of valuables	66.0	28.0	2.0	93.0	39.0	72.0	2.0	71.0	71.0	273.0	41.0	
Acquisitions less disposals of non-produced non-financial assets	742.0	362.0	840.0	690.0	924.0	1304.0	767.0	1354.0	51.0	246.0	512.0	

	2001	2002	2003	2004	2005	2006	2007	2008	2009	2010	2011	2012
Series	**300**											
NET LENDING (+) / NET BORROWING (-)	16554.0	31486.0	40262.0	47746.0	41371.0	51073.0	51381.0	28562.0	46120.0	59405.0	71951.0	
	III.2 Financial account - Changes in liabilities and net worth											
Net incurrence of liabilities	443528.0	177725.0	164906.0	81803.0	197943.0	470326.0	488468.0	-116659.0	-179469.0	-238326.0	-348370.0	
Currency and deposits	84560.0	62093.0	61030.0	97810.0	47674.0	163828.0	167855.0	-94917.0	-4181.0	58283.0	51259.0	
Securities other than shares	95015.0	53558.0	-34037.0	-59827.0	-49179.0	-24771.0	-12456.0	-196693.0	-77721.0	-313939.0	-491933.0	
Loans	73733.0	35844.0	57267.0	6285.0	88729.0	91851.0	209258.0	52567.0	-185450.0	1182.0	-2787.0	
Shares and other equity	141478.0	-12039.0	35500.0	11296.0	43008.0	209059.0	87896.0	95931.0	33025.0	20576.0	47943.0	
Insurance technical reserves	29596.0	29746.0	32004.0	32406.0	35829.0	18214.0	22086.0	28887.0	21154.0	13468.0	16839.0	
Financial derivatives	...	...	...	...	...	...	...	...	...	...	...	
Other accounts payable	19146.0	8523.0	13142.0	-6167.0	31882.0	12145.0	13829.0	-2434.0	33704.0	-17896.0	30309.0	
Adjustment to reconcile Net Lending of Financial Account and Capital Account	2115.0	2604.0	-183.0	3854.0	681.0	-524.0	406.0	-477.0	-1198.0	-3003.0	2823.0	
NET LENDING (+) / NET BORROWING (-) [a]	14439.0	28882.0	40445.0	43892.0	40690.0	51597.0	50975.0	29039.0	47318.0	62408.0	69128.0	
	III.2 Financial account - Changes in assets											
Net acquisition of financial assets	457967.0	206607.0	205351.0	125695.0	238633.0	521923.0	539443.0	-87620.0	-132151.0	-175918.0	-279242.0	
Monetary gold and SDRs	-125.0	-464.0	-777.0	-27.0	-940.0	-793.0	-222.0	-129.0	-92.0	-17.0	-218.0	
Currency and deposits	76720.0	20120.0	70393.0	45182.0	40423.0	148708.0	138726.0	-108248.0	-59374.0	-7981.0	-67451.0	
Securities other than shares	29658.0	43058.0	-61866.0	-38056.0	-77067.0	-66464.0	-74095.0	-218243.0	-168557.0	-323975.0	-479808.0	
Loans	149761.0	96276.0	95846.0	60595.0	121087.0	222724.0	318132.0	113987.0	-36556.0	119121.0	211034.0	
Shares and other equity	187185.0	39347.0	93532.0	71501.0	118121.0	227270.0	133140.0	124240.0	106060.0	48701.0	68310.0	
Insurance technical reserves	219.0	169.0	365.0	331.0	705.0	206.0	-132.0	1246.0	320.0	-184.0	568.0	
Financial derivatives	...	...	...	...	...	...	...	...	...	...	...	
Other accounts receivable	14549.0	8101.0	7858.0	-13831.0	36304.0	-9728.0	23894.0	-473.0	26048.0	-11583.0	-11677.0	

[a] Excludes Adjustment to reconcile Net Lending of the Financial Account and the Capital Account.

Table 4.9 Combined Sectors: Households and NPISH (S.14 + S.15)

Series 300: 1993 SNA, 1999 NLG Euro / Euro, Western calendar year **Data in millions**

	2001	2002	2003	2004	2005	2006	2007	2008	2009	2010	2011	2012
Series	**300**											
	I. Production account - Resources											
Output, at basic prices (otherwise, please specify)	117090.0	120006.0	122035.0	125400.0	129631.0	137940.0	145761.0	151364.0	147870.0	150723.0	154653.0	
	I. Production account - Uses											
Intermediate consumption, at purchaser's prices	49072.0	51654.0	53613.0	55072.0	56838.0	57838.0	58385.0	61874.0	69907.0	72610.0	73246.0	
VALUE ADDED GROSS, at basic prices	68018.0	68352.0	68422.0	70328.0	72793.0	80102.0	87376.0	89490.0	77963.0	78113.0	81407.0	
Less: Consumption of fixed capital	14505.0	15507.0	16213.0	17070.0	17960.0	18972.0	19884.0	20482.0	21354.0	21989.0	21492.0	
VALUE ADDED NET, at basic prices	53513.0	52845.0	52209.0	53258.0	54833.0	61130.0	67492.0	69008.0	56609.0	56124.0	59915.0	
	II.1.1 Generation of income account - Resources											
VALUE ADDED GROSS, at basic prices	68018.0	68352.0	68422.0	70328.0	72793.0	80102.0	87376.0	89490.0	77963.0	78113.0	81407.0	

	2001	2002	2003	2004	2005	2006	2007	2008	2009	2010	2011	2012
Series	**300**											
II.1.1 Generation of income account - Uses												
Compensation of employees	16597.0	17537.0	17845.0	18183.0	18408.0	19054.0	20415.0	21463.0	21684.0	22172.0	22872.0	
Other taxes less Other subsidies on production	324.0	411.0	570.0	827.0	924.0	943.0	1088.0	655.0	-138.0	1062.0	576.0	
Other taxes on production	780.0	825.0	1100.0	1401.0	1394.0	1639.0	1978.0	1654.0	913.0	2083.0	1718.0	
Less: Other subsidies on production	456.0	414.0	530.0	574.0	470.0	696.0	890.0	999.0	1051.0	1021.0	1142.0	
OPERATING SURPLUS, GROSS [a]	51097.0	50404.0	50007.0	51318.0	53461.0	60105.0	65873.0	67372.0	56417.0	54877.0	57972.0	
MIXED INCOME, GROSS	...	...	...	...	...	...	...	...	...	...	...	
II.1.2 Allocation of primary income account - Resources												
OPERATING SURPLUS, GROSS [a]	51097.0	50404.0	50007.0	51318.0	53461.0	60105.0	65873.0	67372.0	56417.0	54877.0	57972.0	
MIXED INCOME, GROSS	...	...	...	...	...	...	...	...	...	...	...	
Compensation of employees	227243.0	238501.0	245075.0	250018.0	253431.0	263652.0	276453.0	289678.0	293678.0	296106.0	301508.0	
Property income	54082.0	53167.0	48763.0	48830.0	53481.0	55580.0	64011.0	63344.0	45376.0	40032.0	44797.0	
II.1.2 Allocation of primary income account - Uses												
Property income	20839.0	20090.0	18001.0	18262.0	18790.0	24311.0	31469.0	33838.0	19875.0	16702.0	19727.0	
BALANCE OF PRIMARY INCOMES	311583.0	321982.0	325844.0	331904.0	341583.0	355026.0	374868.0	386556.0	375596.0	374315.0	384537.0	
II.2 Secondary distribution of income account - Resources												
BALANCE OF PRIMARY INCOMES	311583.0	321982.0	325844.0	331904.0	341583.0	355026.0	374868.0	386556.0	375596.0	374315.0	384537.0	
Social contributions	451.0	483.0	448.0	446.0	485.0	446.0	432.0	471.0	474.0	494.0	483.0	
Social benefits other than social transfers in kind	75832.0	79946.0	82998.0	85479.0	87427.0	89709.0	91991.0	95913.0	100746.0	105665.0	109497.0	
Other current transfers	21471.0	24407.0	26369.0	27457.0	27629.0	24887.0	25667.0	25697.0	28189.0	29078.0	27780.0	
II.2 Secondary distribution of income account - Uses												
Current taxes on income, wealth, etc.	32443.0	36735.0	36328.0	34932.0	39747.0	42599.0	47855.0	48912.0	55443.0	56588.0	55223.0	
Social contributions	111066.0	114892.0	122151.0	126943.0	128017.0	133954.0	138217.0	149970.0	139754.0	139969.0	149645.0	
Social benefits other than social transfers in kind	451.0	483.0	448.0	446.0	485.0	446.0	432.0	471.0	474.0	494.0	483.0	
Other current transfers	20812.0	23739.0	25515.0	27158.0	27908.0	24483.0	25652.0	25797.0	29108.0	28592.0	28091.0	
GROSS DISPOSABLE INCOME	244565.0	250969.0	251217.0	255807.0	260967.0	268586.0	280802.0	283487.0	280226.0	283909.0	288855.0	
II.4.1 Use of disposable income account - Resources												
GROSS DISPOSABLE INCOME	244565.0	250969.0	251217.0	255807.0	260967.0	268586.0	280802.0	283487.0	280226.0	283909.0	288855.0	
Adjustment for the change in net equity of households on pension funds	18284.0	19686.0	22766.0	23400.0	24380.0	21683.0	22900.0	24345.0	20431.0	15220.0	17959.0	
II.4.1 Use of disposable income account - Uses												
Final consumption expenditure	224244.0	233043.0	238103.0	242781.0	250343.0	254875.0	264099.0	270417.0	263537.0	267810.0	271111.0	
Individual consumption expenditure	224244.0	233043.0	238103.0	242781.0	250343.0	254875.0	264099.0	270417.0	263537.0	267810.0	271111.0	
SAVING, GROSS	38605.0	37612.0	35880.0	36426.0	35004.0	35394.0	39603.0	37415.0	37120.0	31319.0	35703.0	
III.1 Capital account - Changes in liabilities and net worth												
SAVING, GROSS	38605.0	37612.0	35880.0	36426.0	35004.0	35394.0	39603.0	37415.0	37120.0	31319.0	35703.0	
Capital transfers, receivable less payable	-1002.0	-1581.0	-1475.0	-1552.0	-1871.0	-2266.0	-1309.0	-1434.0	-1509.0	-1374.0	-889.0	
Capital transfers, receivable	6283.0	6257.0	6008.0	6615.0	6797.0	7109.0	8143.0	8707.0	8728.0	8798.0	8731.0	
Less: Capital transfers, payable	7285.0	7838.0	7483.0	8167.0	8668.0	9375.0	9452.0	10141.0	10237.0	10172.0	9620.0	

	2001	2002	2003	2004	2005	2006	2007	2008	2009	2010	2011	2012
Series	**300**											
Equals: CHANGES IN NET WORTH DUE TO SAVINGS AND CAPITAL TRANSFERS	23098.0	20524.0	18192.0	17804.0	15173.0	14156.0	18410.0	15499.0	14257.0	7956.0	13322.0	
	III.1 Capital account - Changes in assets											
Gross capital formation	30754.0	30530.0	31893.0	32076.0	35273.0	38971.0	42607.0	41634.0	34796.0	33022.0	32143.0	
Gross fixed capital formation	30850.0	30768.0	31940.0	32030.0	35266.0	38759.0	42513.0	41698.0	34771.0	32833.0	32096.0	
Changes in inventories	-119.0	-273.0	-55.0	14.0	-11.0	186.0	95.0	-123.0	4.0	96.0	-8.0	
Acquisitions less disposals of valuables	23.0	35.0	8.0	32.0	18.0	26.0	-1.0	59.0	21.0	93.0	55.0	
Acquisitions less disposals of non-produced non-financial assets	-290.0	-90.0	-448.0	1018.0	1111.0	1166.0	1096.0	-167.0	-708.0	177.0	235.0	
NET LENDING (+) / NET BORROWING (-)	7139.0	5591.0	2960.0	1780.0	-3251.0	-7009.0	-5409.0	-5486.0	1523.0	-3254.0	2436.0	

[a] Includes Mixed Income, Gross.

Netherlands Antilles

Source

The Central Bureau of Statistics (CBS) of the Netherlands Antilles (consisting of Curacao, Bonaire, St. Maarten, St. Eustatius and Saba) was responsible for the official compilation of National Accounts statistics. On October 2010 CBS was transformed from CBS of the Netherlands Antilles to CBS Curacao, as the Netherlands Antilles as a country were dissolved. As of 10 October 2010, Curaçao and Sint Maarten became countries within the Kingdom of the Netherlands, and the islands Bonaire, Saba and St. Eustatius became special municipalities of the Netherlands.

Data up to 2009 that appear under Netherlands Antilles refer to the former country. These statistics were published annually on the internet (www.cbs.an) in the publication "National Accounts Netherlands Antilles", as well as in the annual Statistical Yearbook Netherlands Antilles.

Data for Curaçao and Sint Maarten appear separately under the respective country names.

General

The system of national accounts of the Netherlands Antilles is based on the concepts and definitions recommended in the SNA93 manual as far as the data availability allows it. As recommended by the SNA93, the central framework of the SNA93 in the Netherlands Antilles consists of:

- Integrated economic accounts (IEA) in which the full set of accounts of institutional sectors and the rest of the world are presented. The integrated accounts are presented for the Netherlands Antilles, Bonaire, Curaçao and the Windward Islands. Due to lack of data no separate IEA's can be compiled for St.Maarten, Saba, and St. Eustatius.

- Supply and use tables (SUT) in which the accounts of industries according to kind of economic activity, and the accounts of transactions in goods and services according to type of product are integrated. This publication contains a summarized SUT for the different geographical areas.

- Cross-Classification of Industries and Sectors (CCIS), in which transactions are cross classified by industries and sectors. This is the only table with separate information regarding St. Maarten, Saba and St. Eustatius.

Both the publications "National Accounts Netherlands Antilles 1996-1999" and the "National Accounts Netherlands Antilles 1997 -2004" are based on the SNA 1993. The previous publications are based on SNA 1968. The revision from the SNA68 to the 1993 system was done in close cooperation with the United Nations Statistical Division, Statistics Netherlands and a private Dutch consultancy firm. In these publications data are in ANG (Dutch Antillean guilder) with a fixed US rate of 1.82

Methodology:

Overview of GDP Compilation

Gross domestic product is estimated mainly through the production approach. Expenditure and income approach are also compiled. Supply and Use tables are currently not compiled annually but at a lower frequency. No Input-Output tables are compiled.

2.1.1 General notes regarding the production and income approach

An important data source for especially the Non financial, Financial, Household and Non Profit Institutions Serving Households sector is the yearly national accounts survey. The results of this survey provide information about the profit and loss account and the balance sheet. This survey excludes commercial banks, unincorporated government enterprises, taxis, bus drivers, domestic services and the government sector.

In the survey three different questionnaires are being used namely:
the general enterprise survey excluding commercial banks, unincorporated government enterprises, taxis, bus drivers and domestic services enterprise survey insurance companies and pension funds enterprise survey credit unions

The difference between the questionnaires has to do with the way the output is being calculated. As stated in the SNA manual the output of insurance is equal to premiums earned plus the premium supplements plus/minus the changes in the technical reserves minus the claims/benefits paid. The output of the credit unions is equal to the interest and fees received minus paid. The output of the other industries is calculated as the gross turnover minus changes in inventories and the output for trade as the trade margin.

This survey is an important data source for national accounts. All enterprises, except for the aforementioned exclusion, with 10 or more employees receive a questionnaire. From the enterprises with less than 10 employees a random sample is taken. Once an enterprise is selected in the sample it stays in it for four consecutive years.

The survey covers about 30 percent (=1900) of all enterprises in the Netherlands Antilles. It is conducted separately for the different islands of the Netherlands Antilles namely Curacao, Bonaire and the Windward islands consisting of St. Maarten, Saba and St. Eustatius. The organization of the survey and control and processing of the data takes place in Curaçao.

Part of the survey in Curaçao (about 400 of the 1100 selected businesses on this island) is conducted via mail. Enterprises with 10 or more employees, which responded well each year, were selected for this “mail survey”. The data regarding the other enterprises are collected by a total of 11 interviewers.

The response from this survey is relatively high, about 75 percent, partly due to a law, which stipulates that each company is obligated to cooperate. In case of refusal to cooperate the Central Bureau of Statistics has the means to take the necessary steps to secure cooperation in the future.

Part of the processing includes adding the International Standard Industrial Classification codes (ISIC rev.3) to the different enterprises. The data from corresponding enterprises are then grouped to industries and sectors to arrive at sample totals. These totals are inflated with a three-year average of the number of employees as measured by the labour force sample survey to arrive at the total population. The data from the labour force survey do not have a sector dimension. On the basis of the sector ratios in the 1998 business census total employment by industry and sector is being calculated.

The questionnaire of this survey provides information about the profit and loss account and the balance sheet. The following data by enterprise can be derived from it:
- Output
- Intermediate consumption
- Wages and salaries
- Profit tax
- Gross capital formation
- Depreciation
- Interest, dividends and retained earning

The survey doesn’t include commercial banks, unincorporated government enterprises, taxis, bus drivers and commercial housekeeping activities. The data regarding these activities are derived from other sources e.g. commercial bank activities are derived form central bank data, and data regarding unincorporated government enterprises from the accounts of the government, and the annual reports of those enterprises.

2.1.2 Classification of taxes

The taxes are divided in:

- taxes on products
- other taxes on production.

The taxes on products in the Netherlands Antilles consist of e.g. import duties, export taxes, excise on beer and liquor.

The other taxes on production consist in the case of the Netherlands Antilles mainly of taxes on the ownership or use of land, motor vehicle tax paid for company cars, legal charges and license fees.

A category of taxes that is related to income is the category current taxes on income and wealth divided into taxes on income (wage tax, profit tax, income tax) and the other current taxes on income. In this category the personal use of vehicles is recorded.
The information regarding taxes and subsidies is obtained directly from the records of the various governments.

2.1.3 Classifications
The classification of industries is according to ISIC rev.3.
The classification of sectors is according to the classification of institutional sectors as mentioned in Annex VA of the manual on a two digit level.
The classification of transactions and other flows is according to annex VB. The classification of the goods and services in the Supply and Use tables is based on the Central product Classification (Annex VG of the manual). For government transactions the COFOG (Classification of functions of the government, annex VI) is used.

Expenditure Approach

The estimates of government final consumption expenditure are based on the accounting records of the island and central departments of Finance and the annual reports of government unincorporated enterprises.

Household final consumption is calculated on the basis of a 5-yearly Budget Survey extrapolated for recent years by inflation and change in the number of households. This figure is then adapted for the difference between the use and supply of products.

Gross fixed capital formation of the different sectors and industries is mainly based on the yearly national accounts survey. GFCF on owner occupied dwelling is based on a combination of census data and data from the Department of Public Works. The GFCF of the commercial banks and government are based on the respective annual reports.

The estimates of exports and imports of goods and services are based on foreign trade and balance of payments statistics.

Constant price estimates are calculated by deflation of the consumer price index.

Income Approach

Direct information is available on compensation of employees for the different sectors and industries on the basis of the yearly national accounts survey, and additional data regarding commercial banks, unincorporated government enterprises, taxis, bus drivers, domestic services and the government sector. Operating surplus is basically derived as a residual item.
In the case of the government sector, data are obtained from the accounting records of government bodies. Depreciation data is also derived form the aforementioned sources.

Production Approach

The production approach is used to estimate value added of nearly all industries, as output minus intermediate consumption. The data are mainly derived from the aforementioned yearly national accounts survey. An exception is the estimation of value added of public administration and defence. In this case the income approach is being used.

Output is calculated as the gross turnover minus the changes in inventories for almost all enterprises/production units. The exceptions are mentioned below.

a. The output of financial intermediary services (ISIC 65)
This is basically calculated as the difference between the interest, fees and commissions received and the interest paid. An exception is being made for the international financial enterprises. With regard to the latter the ISIC is adapted in the sense that the following four categories were added:
- Trust companies (ISIC 65950)
- Financial holdings (ISIC 65960)
- Off-shore banks (ISIC 65970)
- Individual offshore companies with employees (ISIC 65980)
The output of these enterprises is calculated as the sum of the costs, consisting of labour costs, depreciation, and intermediate costs, and profit tax paid.
The commercial bank data is derived from the consolidated income statements of commercial banks (administrative data source), while the data regarding the international financial institutions is derived from the general questionnaire. (see income statement commercial banks)

b. Output of Insurance and pension funding, except compulsory social security
The output of insurance companies both life and non-life is calculated as premiums earned plus premium supplements minus claims plus/minus additions to reserves. Data source is the consolidated profit and loss accounts of insurance companies as published by the central bank.

c. Output of the oil refinery
In the former System the oil refinery was treated as being part of the rest of the world. In the present System the refinery is treated as a resident enterprise. The output is equal to the refining fee, which is exported. This is related to the resident concept and production boundary in the SNA93.The value added is then calculated as to be the difference between output and intermediate consumption.

Table 1.1 Gross domestic product by expenditures at current prices

Series 100: 1993 SNA, Netherlands Antillean guilder, Western calendar year — **Data in millions**

	2001	2002	2003	2004	2005	2006	2007	2008	2009	2010	2011	2012
Series	**100**											
	Expenditures of the gross domestic product											
Final consumption expenditure	3694.2	3905.8	4011.9	4291.5	4515.9	4671.4	5319.2	5850.5				
Household final consumption expenditure	2796.3	2980.5	2974.8	3228.1	3490.9	3590.6	4141.2	4621.3				
NPISHs final consumption expenditure	62.6	53.4	61.4	57.0	52.5	51.3	52.2	53.4				
General government final consumption expenditure	835.4	871.9	975.7	1006.3	972.5	1029.6	1125.9	1175.8				
Individual consumption expenditure	366.1	377.8	421.0	452.3	417.2	437.8	484.3	479.6				
Collective consumption expenditure	469.3	494.1	554.7	554.0	555.3	591.8	641.5	696.2				

	2001	2002	2003	2004	2005	2006	2007	2008	2009	2010	2011	2012
Series	**100**											
Gross capital formation	1888.0	1561.7	1588.9	1489.5	1751.1	1984.0	2210.9	2654.7				
Gross fixed capital formation	1575.0	1609.6	1619.9	1636.5	1756.4	1989.1	2324.0	2570.3				
Changes in inventories	313.1	-47.9	-31.0	-147.0	-5.3	-5.2	-113.1	84.4				
Acquisitions less disposals of valuables	...	...	...	...	...	...	...	...				
Exports of goods and services	3807.0	3744.3	3797.4	4155.6	4445.0	4807.9	4967.2	5626.5				
Exports of goods	899.3	879.3	768.7	933.2	1088.4	1243.6	1210.8	1948.4				
Exports of services	2907.7	2865.0	3028.7	3222.4	3356.6	3564.3	3756.4	3678.1				
Less: Imports of goods and services	4200.0	3959.9	3993.0	4381.2	4845.9	5312.4	5989.4	7071.5				
Imports of goods	2927.0	2669.8	2635.0	3084.0	3491.0	3955.0	4562.2	5511.5				
Imports of services	1273.0	1290.1	1358.0	1297.2	1354.9	1357.4	1427.2	1560.0				
Equals: GROSS DOMESTIC PRODUCT	5189.3	5251.9	5405.2	5555.4	5866.2	6150.9	6507.9	7060.3				

Table 1.3 Relations among product, income, savings, and net lending aggregates

Series 100: 1993 SNA, Netherlands Antillean guilder, Western calendar year

Data in millions

	2001	2002	2003	2004	2005	2006	2007	2008	2009	2010	2011	2012
Series	**100**											
GROSS DOMESTIC PRODUCT	5189.3	5251.9	5405.2	5555.4	5866.2	6150.9	6507.9	7060.3				
Plus: Compensation of employees - from and to the rest of the world, net	-42.7	-51.1	-51.3	-55.8	-58.3	-36.7	-39.6	-35.7				
Plus: Compensation of employees - from the rest of the world	14.3	9.9	10.0	7.0	17.0	31.3	38.5	49.2				
Less: Compensation of employees - to the rest of the world	57.0	61.0	61.3	62.8	75.3	68.0	78.1	84.9				
Plus: Property income - from and to the rest of the world, net	79.8	50.6	38.7	26.0	31.5	34.7	44.8	-38.3				
Plus: Property income - from the rest of the world	172.7	153.5	151.2	151.4	173.3	214.1	266.1	200.7				
Less: Property income - to the rest of the world	92.9	102.9	112.5	125.4	141.8	179.4	221.3	239.0				
Sum of Compensation of employees and property income - from and to the rest of the world, net	37.1	-0.5	-12.6	-29.8	-26.8	-2.0	5.2	-74.0				
Plus: Sum of Compensation of employees and property income - from the rest of the world	187.0	163.4	161.2	158.4	190.3	245.4	304.6	249.9				
Less: Sum of Compensation of employees and property income - to the rest of the world	149.9	163.9	173.8	188.2	217.1	247.4	299.4	323.9				
Plus: Taxes less subsidies on production and imports - from and to the rest of the world, net	...	...	...	...	...	...	...	...				
Equals: GROSS NATIONAL INCOME	5226.4	5251.3	5392.6	5525.6	5839.4	6148.9	6513.1	6986.2				
Plus: Current transfers - from and to the rest of the world, net	37.5	226.3	225.7	106.2	242.6	78.4	2.9	11.5				
Plus: Current transfers - from the rest of the world	424.5	685.6	722.8	586.8	788.2	626.0	587.7	723.1				
Less: Current transfers - to the rest of the world	387.0	459.3	497.1	480.6	545.6	547.6	584.8	711.6				
Equals: GROSS NATIONAL DISPOSABLE INCOME	5263.9	5477.6	5618.3	5631.8	6081.9	6227.3	6516.0	6997.7				

	2001	2002	2003	2004	2005	2006	2007	2008	2009	2010	2011	2012
Series	**100**											
Less: Final consumption expenditure / Actual final consumption	3694.2	3905.8	4011.9	4291.5	4515.9	4671.4	5319.2	5850.5				
Equals: SAVING, GROSS	1569.7	1571.8	1606.4	1340.3	1566.0	1555.8	1196.8	1147.2				
Plus: Capital transfers - from and to the rest of the world, net	54.1	54.6	62.6	143.1	173.0	183.3	219.3	218.3				
Plus: Capital transfers - from the rest of the world	61.5	55.0	66.2	144.1	173.0	185.4	227.2	232.8				
Less: Capital transfers - to the rest of the world	7.4	0.4	3.6	1.0	0.0	2.2	7.9	14.5				
Less: Gross capital formation	1888.0	1561.7	1588.9	1489.5	1751.1	1984.0	2210.9	2654.7				
Less: Acquisitions less disposals of non-produced non-financial assets	...	...	...	...	...	...	...	...				
Equals: NET LENDING (+) / NET BORROWING (-) OF THE NATION	-264.3	64.8	80.1	-6.1	-12.1	-244.9	-794.8	-1289.2				
	Net values: Gross National Income / Gross National Disposable Income / Saving Gross less Consumption of fixed capital											
Less: Consumption of fixed capital	658.8	669.0	695.9	699.1	692.7	693.3	733.7	786.9				
Equals: NET NATIONAL INCOME	4567.6	4582.3	4696.7	4826.5	5146.7	5455.6	5779.5	6199.4				
Equals: NET NATIONAL DISPOSABLE INCOME	4605.1	4808.6	4922.4	4932.7	5389.3	5534.0	5782.3	6210.8				
Equals: SAVING, NET	910.9	902.8	910.5	641.2	873.4	862.5	463.1	360.3				

Table 2.1 Value added by industries at current prices (ISIC Rev. 3)

Series 100: 1993 SNA, Netherlands Antillean guilder, Western calendar year **Data in millions**

	2001	2002	2003	2004	2005	2006	2007	2008	2009	2010	2011	2012
Series	**100**											
	Industries											
Agriculture, hunting, forestry; fishing	49.8	39.4	36.7	37.3	42.9	36.7	38.6	42.7				
Mining and quarrying	...	...	...	...	...	...	...	...				
Manufacturing	346.8	325.0	309.0	323.8	283.9	366.9	356.3	435.9				
Electricity, gas and water supply	245.9	225.0	231.8	214.1	233.9	228.6	233.0	202.6				
Construction	274.8	281.8	278.2	262.5	337.6	309.4	337.4	394.7				
Wholesale, retail trade, repair of motor vehicles, motorcycles and personal and households goods; hotels and restaurants	893.1	842.3	852.6	869.8	938.5	1001.5	1007.9	1277.7				
Wholesale, retail trade, repair of motor vehicles, motorcycles and personal and household goods	675.4	657.4	641.7	639.7	695.3	724.7	723.0	925.6				
Hotels and restaurants	217.7	184.9	210.9	230.1	243.2	276.8	284.9	352.0				
Transport, storage and communications	497.2	540.8	561.3	495.4	521.1	581.1	570.8	729.5				
Financial intermediation; real estate, renting and business activities	1546.5	1624.9	1704.4	1893.1	1976.2	1977.1	2234.5	2063.0				
Financial intermediation	730.3	800.0	886.4	902.9	1067.6	982.7	1183.5	924.2				
Real estate, renting and business activities	816.2	824.9	818.0	990.2	908.6	994.4	1051.0	1138.8				
Public administration and defence; compulsory social security	352.8	362.3	396.0	405.7	458.3	467.5	494.1	524.0				
Education; health and social work; other community, social and personal services	620.7	625.8	646.3	678.0	689.0	718.5	711.2	827.9				

	2001	2002	2003	2004	2005	2006	2007	2008	2009	2010	2011	2012
Series	**100**											
Education	73.6	81.7	97.1	102.6	102.6	113.0	115.9	121.2				
Health and social work	272.5	272.3	273.1	262.4	281.3	297.6	303.2	364.5				
Other community, social and personal services	274.5	271.8	276.0	313.0	305.0	308.0	292.0	342.3				
Private households with employed persons	22.9	20.8	21.6	21.8	19.0	16.8	15.0	13.5				
Equals: VALUE ADDED, GROSS, in basic prices [a]	4850.6	4888.2	5038.0	5201.5	5500.5	5704.1	5998.7	6511.5				
Less: Financial intermediation services indirectly measured (FISIM)	127.9	111.2	110.2	123.1	133.2	142.0	144.9	173.9				
Plus: Taxes less Subsidies on products	466.6	474.8	477.4	477.0	498.8	588.8	654.1	722.7				
Plus: Taxes on products	530.9	541.3	548.1	584.2	618.4	665.4	733.3	806.4				
Less: Subsidies on products	64.3	66.5	70.8	107.2	119.6	76.5	79.2	83.7				
Equals: GROSS DOMESTIC PRODUCT	5189.3	5251.9	5405.2	5555.4	5866.2	6150.9	6507.9	7060.3				

[a] Includes financial intermediation services indirectly measured (FISIM) of the Total Economy.

Table 2.3 Output, gross value added, and fixed assets by industries at current prices (ISIC Rev. 3) Total Economy

Series 100: 1993 SNA, Netherlands Antillean guilder, Western calendar year — **Data in millions**

	2001	2002	2003	2004	2005	2006	2007	2008	2009	2010	2011	2012
Series	**100**											
Output, at basic prices	8798.0	9147.4	9348.2	9658.2	10430.5	11018.3	11869.1	13229.0				
Less: Intermediate consumption, at purchaser's prices [a]	3947.4	4259.1	4310.2	4456.7	4929.9	5314.2	5870.4	6717.6				
Equals: VALUE ADDED, GROSS, at basic prices [b]	4850.6	4888.2	5038.0	5201.5	5500.5	5704.1	5998.7	6511.5				
Compensation of employees	2953.6	2895.0	3079.2	3113.7	3168.8	3530.2	3727.9	4119.2				
Taxes on production and imports, less Subsidies [c]	512.1	514.0	525.0	514.8	532.8	636.8	732.3	792.5				
Taxes on production and imports	594.4	598.9	613.8	647.0	679.3	738.4	836.5	901.2				
Taxes on products	530.9	541.3	548.1	584.2	618.4	665.4	733.3	806.4				
Other taxes on production	63.5	57.7	65.6	62.8	61.0	73.0	103.2	94.8				
Less: Subsidies	82.3	84.9	88.8	132.2	146.5	101.5	104.2	108.7				
Subsidies on products	64.3	66.5	70.8	107.2	119.6	76.5	79.2	83.7				
Other subsidies on production	18.0	18.5	18.0	25.0	26.9	25.0	25.0	25.0				
OPERATING SURPLUS, GROSS [d]	1723.6	1842.9	1800.9	1926.9	2164.5	1983.8	2047.7	2148.5				
MIXED INCOME, GROSS	...	...	...	...	...	...	...	...				
Total Economy only: Adjustment for FISIM (if FISIM is not distributed to uses)	127.9	111.2	110.2	123.1	133.2	142.0	144.9	173.9				
Less: Consumption of fixed capital	658.8	669.0	695.9	699.1	692.7	693.3	733.7	786.9				
OPERATING SURPLUS, NET [e]	1064.8	1173.9	1105.1	1227.8	1471.8	1290.5	1314.1	1361.6				
MIXED INCOME, NET	...	...	...	...	...	...	...	...				
Gross capital formation	1888.0	1561.6	1588.9	1489.5	1751.1	1984.0	2210.8	2654.7				
Gross fixed capital formation	1575.0	1609.6	1619.9	1636.5	1756.4	1989.1	2323.9	2570.3				
Changes in inventories	313.1	-47.9	-31.0	-147.0	-5.3	-5.2	-113.1	84.4				

	2001	2002	2003	2004	2005	2006	2007	2008	2009	2010	2011	2012
Series	**100**											
Acquisitions less disposals of valuables	...	...	...	...	...	...	...	...				
Employment (average, in 1000 persons)	59.4	60.1	62.6	63.1	63.8	67.2	...	...				

[a] Excludes financial intermediation services indirectly measured (FISIM).
[b] Includes financial intermediation services indirectly measured (FISIM) of the Total Economy.
[c] Refers to taxes less subsidies on production and imports.
[d] Includes Mixed Income, Gross.
[e] Includes Mixed Income, Net.

Table 2.3 Output, gross value added, and fixed assets by industries at current prices (ISIC Rev. 3) Agriculture, hunting, forestry; fishing (A+B)

Series 100: 1993 SNA, Netherlands Antillean guilder, Western calendar year **Data in millions**

	2001	2002	2003	2004	2005	2006	2007	2008	2009	2010	2011	2012
Series	**100**											
Output, at basic prices	136.4	104.0	100.9	100.8	97.2	102.3	91.1	103.7				
Less: Intermediate consumption, at purchaser's prices	86.6	64.5	64.2	63.5	54.3	65.6	52.4	61.0				
Equals: VALUE ADDED, GROSS, at basic prices	49.8	39.4	36.7	37.3	42.9	36.7	38.6	42.7				
Compensation of employees	20.4	17.2	17.3	18.5	21.7	24.3	25.5	28.9				
Taxes on production and imports, less Subsidies	...	...	...	...	...	...	...	...				
OPERATING SURPLUS, GROSS [a]	29.3	22.3	19.4	18.8	21.2	12.3	13.1	13.8				
MIXED INCOME, GROSS	...	...	...	...	...	...	...	...				
Less: Consumption of fixed capital	9.2	7.0	6.9	7.5	5.8	6.7	6.3	5.8				
OPERATING SURPLUS, NET [b]	20.1	15.3	12.5	11.3	15.4	5.6	6.9	8.0				
MIXED INCOME, NET	...	...	...	...	...	...	...	...				
Gross capital formation	18.4	10.1	15.3	12.6	13.6	18.0	23.8	27.6				
Gross fixed capital formation	11.3	6.3	6.2	11.4	1.2	2.7	2.5	4.2				
Changes in inventories	7.1	3.9	9.1	1.1	12.4	15.3	21.3	23.4				
Acquisitions less disposals of valuables	...	...	...	...	...	...	...	...				
Employment (average, in 1000 persons)	0.8	0.8	0.8	0.8	0.1	0.9	1.0	1.0				

[a] Includes Mixed Income, Gross.
[b] Includes Mixed Income, Net.

Table 2.3 Output, gross value added, and fixed assets by industries at current prices (ISIC Rev. 3) Manufacturing (D)

Series 100: 1993 SNA, Netherlands Antillean guilder, Western calendar year **Data in millions**

	2001	2002	2003	2004	2005	2006	2007	2008	2009	2010	2011	2012
Series	**100**											
Output, at basic prices	928.3	916.3	850.2	853.1	805.9	914.0	962.8	1106.5				
Less: Intermediate consumption, at purchaser's prices	581.4	591.3	541.2	529.3	522.0	547.0	606.5	670.6				
Equals: VALUE ADDED, GROSS, at basic prices	346.8	325.0	309.0	323.8	283.9	366.9	356.3	435.9				
Compensation of employees	272.5	254.2	252.4	256.7	230.6	241.4	256.6	273.2				

		2001	2002	2003	2004	2005	2006	2007	2008	2009	2010	2011	2012
Series		**100**											
Taxes on production and imports, less Subsidies		...	...	...	...	...	...	...	...				
OPERATING SURPLUS, GROSS	a	74.3	70.8	56.6	67.1	53.3	125.5	99.7	162.7				
MIXED INCOME, GROSS		...	...	...	...	...	...	...	...				
Less: Consumption of fixed capital		30.0	28.2	32.1	30.5	22.9	17.1	18.5	20.0				
OPERATING SURPLUS, NET	b	44.3	42.6	24.5	36.6	30.4	108.4	81.2	142.7				
MIXED INCOME, NET		...	...	...	...	...	...	...	...				
Gross capital formation		8.4	52.9	56.5	62.3	2.2	26.9	36.1	50.6				
Gross fixed capital formation		34.0	20.4	38.2	40.9	6.8	9.5	30.7	30.4				
Changes in inventories		-25.6	32.5	18.2	21.5	-4.6	17.4	5.4	20.3				
Acquisitions less disposals of valuables		...	...	...	...	...	...	...	...				
Employment (average, in 1000 persons)		3.8	3.7	3.8	3.6	3.2	3.4	3.5	3.8				

[a] Includes Mixed Income, Gross.
[b] Includes Mixed Income, Net.

Table 2.3 Output, gross value added, and fixed assets by industries at current prices (ISIC Rev. 3) Electricity, gas and water supply (E)

Series 100: 1993 SNA, Netherlands Antillean guilder, Western calendar year — **Data in millions**

		2001	2002	2003	2004	2005	2006	2007	2008	2009	2010	2011	2012
Series		**100**											
Output, at basic prices		479.9	507.5	527.9	554.8	592.5	678.6	683.8	794.3				
Less: Intermediate consumption, at purchaser's prices		234.0	282.5	296.1	340.7	358.6	450.0	450.8	591.7				
Equals: VALUE ADDED, GROSS, at basic prices		245.9	225.0	231.8	214.1	233.9	228.6	233.0	202.6				
Compensation of employees		111.4	90.3	103.2	103.5	101.9	118.4	104.8	123.6				
Taxes on production and imports, less Subsidies		...	...	...	...	...	...	...	...				
OPERATING SURPLUS, GROSS	a	134.5	134.7	128.6	110.6	132.0	110.2	128.2	79.0				
MIXED INCOME, GROSS		...	...	...	...	...	...	...	...				
Less: Consumption of fixed capital		60.8	61.1	63.7	60.9	53.4	58.7	60.9	62.8				
OPERATING SURPLUS, NET	b	73.7	73.6	64.9	49.7	78.6	51.5	67.2	16.2				
MIXED INCOME, NET		...	...	...	...	...	...	...	...				
Gross capital formation		32.4	169.5	284.1	247.2	399.9	401.5	536.8	524.4				
Gross fixed capital formation		51.7	172.4	288.1	231.9	398.8	407.9	541.6	535.4				
Changes in inventories		-19.3	-2.9	-4.0	15.3	1.1	-6.3	-4.9	-11.0				
Acquisitions less disposals of valuables		...	...	...	...	...	...	...	...				
Employment (average, in 1000 persons)		1.2	1.2	1.1	1.1	1.1	1.1	1.1	1.1				

[a] Includes Mixed Income, Gross.
[b] Includes Mixed Income, Net.

Table 2.3 Output, gross value added, and fixed assets by industries at current prices (ISIC Rev. 3) Construction (F)

Series 100: 1993 SNA, Netherlands Antillean guilder, Western calendar year

Data in millions

	2001	2002	2003	2004	2005	2006	2007	2008	2009	2010	2011	2012
Series	**100**											
Output, at basic prices	870.3	812.3	848.9	863.4	1058.6	1057.6	1104.6	1404.1				
Less: Intermediate consumption, at purchaser's prices	595.5	530.5	570.7	600.9	721.0	748.2	767.2	1009.5				
Equals: VALUE ADDED, GROSS, at basic prices	274.8	281.8	278.2	262.5	337.6	309.4	337.4	394.7				
Compensation of employees	205.5	220.2	212.3	217.3	226.2	276.7	312.0	344.7				
Taxes on production and imports, less Subsidies	6.7	6.9	6.9	7.1	11.0	13.7	16.0	8.4				
Taxes on production and imports	6.7	6.9	6.9	7.1	11.0	13.7	16.0	8.4				
Taxes on products	...	...	...	...	...	...	...	...				
Other taxes on production	6.7	6.9	6.9	7.1	11.0	13.7	16.0	8.4				
Less: Subsidies	...	...	...	...	...	...	...	...				
OPERATING SURPLUS, GROSS [a]	62.5	54.7	59.0	38.1	100.4	19.0	9.4	41.5				
MIXED INCOME, GROSS	...	...	...	...	...	...	...	...				
Less: Consumption of fixed capital	16.0	17.8	16.8	15.9	16.7	15.8	23.3	21.7				
OPERATING SURPLUS, NET [b]	46.5	36.9	42.2	22.3	83.7	3.3	-13.9	19.9				
MIXED INCOME, NET	...	...	...	...	...	...	...	...				
Gross capital formation	126.8	93.1	13.4	-28.5	13.1	57.1	109.5	87.3				
Gross fixed capital formation	18.9	12.5	43.5	22.9	23.0	21.1	59.5	42.2				
Changes in inventories	107.8	80.6	-30.1	-51.4	-9.9	36.0	50.1	45.2				
Acquisitions less disposals of valuables	...	...	...	...	...	...	...	...				
Employment (average, in 1000 persons)	5.4	5.7	5.8	5.8	6.2	6.8	7.7	8.1				

[a] Includes Mixed Income, Gross.
[b] Includes Mixed Income, Net.

Table 2.3 Output, gross value added, and fixed assets by industries at current prices (ISIC Rev. 3) Wholesale retail trade, repair of motor vehicles, motorcycles, etc.; hotels and restaurants (G+H)

Series 100: 1993 SNA, Netherlands Antillean guilder, Western calendar year

Data in millions

	2001	2002	2003	2004	2005	2006	2007	2008	2009	2010	2011	2012
Series	**100**											
Output, at basic prices	1640.9	1677.9	1702.6	1856.6	1987.2	2093.7	2172.8	2521.8				
Less: Intermediate consumption, at purchaser's prices	747.8	835.6	850.0	986.8	1048.7	1092.2	1164.9	1244.1				
Equals: VALUE ADDED, GROSS, at basic prices	893.1	842.3	852.6	869.8	938.5	1001.5	1007.9	1277.7				
Compensation of employees	568.7	564.9	584.6	628.8	659.6	715.3	734.0	819.6				
Taxes on production and imports, less Subsidies	2.0	1.9	2.0	1.9	3.0	4.6	5.7	5.5				
Taxes on production and imports	2.0	1.9	2.0	1.9	3.0	4.6	5.7	5.5				
Taxes on products	...	...	...	...	...	...	...	...				
Other taxes on production	2.0	1.9	2.0	1.9	3.0	4.6	5.7	5.5				

	2001	2002	2003	2004	2005	2006	2007	2008	2009	2010	2011	2012
Series	**100**											
Less: Subsidies	...	...	...	...	...	...	...	...				
OPERATING SURPLUS, GROSS [a]	322.5	275.5	266.1	239.1	275.9	281.6	268.2	452.5				
MIXED INCOME, GROSS	...	...	...	...	...	...	...	...				
Less: Consumption of fixed capital	114.7	117.5	108.4	128.3	126.3	117.9	117.3	135.8				
OPERATING SURPLUS, NET [b]	207.8	158.0	157.7	110.8	149.6	163.8	150.9	316.7				
MIXED INCOME, NET	...	...	...	...	...	...	...	...				
Gross capital formation	313.3	57.4	146.1	-2.1	199.4	199.3	205.3	474.3				
Gross fixed capital formation	95.7	131.9	146.0	176.9	121.9	124.5	203.0	292.5				
Changes in inventories	217.6	-74.5	0.1	-178.9	77.5	74.9	2.3	181.8				
Acquisitions less disposals of valuables	...	...	...	...	...	...	...	...				
Employment (average, in 1000 persons)	18.3	18.8	19.7	19.9	20.5	21.3	22.5	23.3				

[a] Includes Mixed Income, Gross.
[b] Includes Mixed Income, Net.

Table 2.3 Output, gross value added, and fixed assets by industries at current prices (ISIC Rev. 3) Transport, storage and communications (I)

Series 100: 1993 SNA, Netherlands Antillean guilder, Western calendar year — **Data in millions**

	2001	2002	2003	2004	2005	2006	2007	2008	2009	2010	2011	2012
Series	**100**											
Output, at basic prices	870.8	1016.6	1063.5	963.8	975.2	1147.2	1265.0	1489.7				
Less: Intermediate consumption, at purchaser's prices	373.6	475.8	502.2	468.4	454.1	566.1	694.3	760.2				
Equals: VALUE ADDED, GROSS, at basic prices	497.2	540.8	561.3	495.4	521.1	581.1	570.8	729.5				
Compensation of employees	287.1	273.2	298.1	282.1	310.6	322.0	331.6	410.1				
Taxes on production and imports, less Subsidies	28.9	32.8	40.1	39.1	38.1	42.0	44.8	47.8				
Taxes on production and imports	28.9	32.8	40.1	39.1	38.1	42.0	44.8	47.8				
Taxes on products	...	...	...	...	...	...	...	...				
Other taxes on production	28.9	32.8	40.1	39.1	38.1	42.0	44.8	47.8				
Less: Subsidies	...	...	...	...	...	...	...	...				
OPERATING SURPLUS, GROSS [a]	181.1	234.9	223.1	174.2	172.5	217.1	194.4	271.5				
MIXED INCOME, GROSS	...	...	...	...	...	...	...	...				
Less: Consumption of fixed capital	140.6	153.9	164.9	144.9	131.8	126.5	137.7	139.1				
OPERATING SURPLUS, NET [b]	40.6	81.1	58.3	29.3	40.8	90.7	56.8	132.6				
MIXED INCOME, NET	...	...	...	...	...	...	...	...				
Gross capital formation	250.4	375.9	185.1	206.6	360.6	437.0	559.7	542.7				
Gross fixed capital formation	277.4	418.8	254.2	276.5	430.9	478.6	616.6	588.3				
Changes in inventories	-27.0	-42.9	-69.2	-69.9	-70.3	-41.6	-56.9	-45.5				
Acquisitions less disposals of valuables	...	...	...	...	...	...	...	...				
Employment (average, in 1000 persons)	4.0	4.0	4.1	4.0	4.1	4.3	4.8	5.1				

[a] Includes Mixed Income, Gross.
[b] Includes Mixed Income, Net.

Table 2.3 Output, gross value added, and fixed assets by industries at current prices (ISIC Rev. 3) Financial intermediation; real estate, renting and business activities (J+K)

Series 100: 1993 SNA, Netherlands Antillean guilder, Western calendar year

Data in millions

Series		2001	2002	2003	2004	2005	2006	2007	2008	2009	2010	2011	2012
		100											
Output, at basic prices		2285.2	2450.9	2455.9	2590.5	2922.4	2965.7	3401.7	3410.5				
Less: Intermediate consumption, at purchaser's prices		738.6	826.0	751.4	697.4	946.2	988.6	1167.2	1347.5				
Equals: VALUE ADDED, GROSS, at basic prices		1546.5	1624.9	1704.4	1893.1	1976.2	1977.1	2234.5	2063.0				
Compensation of employees		594.5	597.1	662.7	532.8	575.1	676.8	744.8	808.6				
Taxes on production and imports, less Subsidies		7.8	-2.4	-1.3	-10.3	-18.1	-12.2	11.7	8.1				
Taxes on production and imports		25.8	16.1	16.7	14.7	8.9	12.8	36.7	33.1				
Taxes on products		...	...	...	...	...	...	...	...				
Other taxes on production		25.8	16.1	16.7	14.7	8.9	12.8	36.7	33.1				
Less: Subsidies		18.0	18.5	18.0	25.0	26.9	25.0	25.0	25.0				
Subsidies on products		...	...	...	...	...	...	...	...				
Other subsidies on production		18.0	18.5	18.0	25.0	26.9	25.0	25.0	25.0				
OPERATING SURPLUS, GROSS	a	944.2	1030.2	1043.1	1370.6	1419.2	1312.5	1478.0	1246.2				
MIXED INCOME, GROSS		...	...	...	...	...	...	...	...				
Less: Consumption of fixed capital		230.0	233.3	229.5	250.8	249.4	260.8	275.8	293.0				
OPERATING SURPLUS, NET	b	714.2	796.9	813.6	1119.8	1169.8	1051.7	1202.2	953.2				
MIXED INCOME, NET		...	...	...	...	...	...	...	...				
Gross capital formation		827.1	708.4	737.8	877.0	627.4	649.7	549.5	666.7				
Gross fixed capital formation		808.1	733.1	694.8	722.9	643.2	738.7	668.4	794.4				
Changes in inventories		19.0	-24.8	43.0	154.1	-15.8	-89.0	-118.9	-127.7				
Acquisitions less disposals of valuables		...	...	...	...	...	...	...	...				
Employment (average, in 1000 persons)		7.9	8.0	8.5	9.1	9.6	10.2	11.2	12.1				

[a] Includes Mixed Income, Gross.
[b] Includes Mixed Income, Net.

Table 2.3 Output, gross value added, and fixed assets by industries at current prices (ISIC Rev. 3) Public administration and defense; compulsory social security (L)

Series 100: 1993 SNA, Netherlands Antillean guilder, Western calendar year

Data in millions

Series	2001	2002	2003	2004	2005	2006	2007	2008	2009	2010	2011	2012
	100											
Output, at basic prices	487.0	513.0	566.3	582.1	640.7	649.7	682.9	754.7				
Less: Intermediate consumption, at purchaser's prices	134.2	150.7	170.3	176.4	182.4	182.2	188.9	230.7				
Equals: VALUE ADDED, GROSS, at basic prices	352.8	362.3	396.0	405.7	458.3	467.5	494.1	524.0				
Compensation of employees	333.3	344.8	364.5	389.1	425.6	434.4	456.4	474.4				
Taxes on production and imports, less Subsidies	...	...	...	...	...	...	...	...				
OPERATING SURPLUS, GROSS	19.5	17.5	31.5	16.7	32.8	33.0	37.6	49.6				

	2001	2002	2003	2004	2005	2006	2007	2008	2009	2010	2011	2012
Series	**100**											
MIXED INCOME, GROSS	...	...	...	...	...	...	...	...				
Less: Consumption of fixed capital	19.5	17.5	31.5	16.7	32.7	33.0	37.6	49.6				
OPERATING SURPLUS, NET	0.0	0.0	0.0	0.0	0.0	0.1	0.1	0.1				
MIXED INCOME, NET	...	...	...	...	...	...	...	...				
Gross capital formation	35.3	18.7	24.8	20.7	14.5	26.1	26.7	29.1				
Gross fixed capital formation	35.3	18.7	24.8	20.7	14.5	26.1	26.7	29.1				
Changes in inventories	...	...	...	...	...	...	...	...				
Acquisitions less disposals of valuables	...	...	...	...	...	...	...	...				
Employment (average, in 1000 persons)	7.1	6.8	6.6	6.6	6.7	6.9	7.0	7.0				

Table 2.3 Output, gross value added, and fixed assets by industries at current prices (ISIC Rev. 3) Education; health and social work; other community, social and personal services (M+N+O)

Series 100: 1993 SNA, Netherlands Antillean guilder, Western calendar year

Data in millions

	2001	2002	2003	2004	2005	2006	2007	2008	2009	2010	2011	2012
Series	**100**											
Output, at basic prices	1076.4	1128.0	1210.4	1271.2	1331.8	1392.8	1489.4	1630.2				
Less: Intermediate consumption, at purchaser's prices	455.7	502.3	564.2	593.3	642.8	674.3	778.2	802.3				
Equals: VALUE ADDED, GROSS, at basic prices	620.7	625.8	646.3	678.0	689.0	718.5	711.2	827.9				
Compensation of employees	560.1	533.2	584.1	684.9	617.6	720.8	762.1	836.0				
Taxes on production and imports, less Subsidies	...	...	...	...	...	...	...	...				
OPERATING SURPLUS, GROSS [a]	60.6	92.6	62.2	-6.9	71.4	-2.3	-51.0	-8.1				
MIXED INCOME, GROSS	...	...	...	...	...	...	...	...				
Less: Consumption of fixed capital	38.0	32.7	42.1	43.6	53.6	56.8	56.3	59.0				
OPERATING SURPLUS, NET [b]	22.6	59.8	20.0	-50.6	17.8	-59.1	-107.3	-67.1				
MIXED INCOME, NET	...	...	...	...	...	...	...	...				
Gross capital formation	275.9	75.7	125.9	93.8	120.3	168.2	163.3	252.0				
Gross fixed capital formation	242.5	95.5	124.0	132.5	116.0	179.9	174.9	254.0				
Changes in inventories	33.5	-19.8	1.8	-38.7	4.3	-11.7	-11.6	-2.0				
Acquisitions less disposals of valuables	...	...	...	...	...	...	...	...				
Employment (average, in 1000 persons) [c]	10.8	11.2	12.2	12.2	12.3	12.4	12.4	13.0				

[a] Includes Mixed Income, Gross.
[b] Includes Mixed Income, Net.
[c] Includes employment for Private households with employed persons (P).

Table 2.3 Output, gross value added, and fixed assets by industries at current prices (ISIC Rev. 3) Private households with employed persons (P)

Series 100: 1993 SNA, Netherlands Antillean guilder, Western calendar year — **Data in millions**

	2001	2002	2003	2004	2005	2006	2007	2008	2009	2010	2011	2012
Series	**100**											
Output, at basic prices	22.9	20.8	21.6	21.8	19.0	16.8	15.0	13.5				
Less: Intermediate consumption, at purchaser's prices	...	...	...	...	...	...	...	...				
Equals: VALUE ADDED, GROSS, at basic prices	22.9	20.8	21.6	21.8	19.0	16.8	15.0	13.5				
Compensation of employees	...	...	...	...	...	...	...	...				
Taxes on production and imports, less Subsidies	...	...	...	...	...	...	...	...				
OPERATING SURPLUS, GROSS [a]	16.6	20.8	18.8	21.8	19.0	18.9	...	...				
MIXED INCOME, GROSS	...	...	...	...	...	...	...	...				
Less: Consumption of fixed capital	...	...	...	...	...	...	...	...				
OPERATING SURPLUS, NET [b]	22.9	20.8	21.6	21.8	19.0	16.8	15.0	13.5				
MIXED INCOME, NET	...	...	...	...	...	...	...	...				
Gross capital formation	...	...	...	...	...	...	...	...				
Employment (average, in 1000 persons)	3.5	3.2	3.5	3.3	3.2	3.2	...	...				

[a] Includes Mixed Income, Gross.
[b] Includes Mixed Income, Net.

Table 3.1 Government final consumption expenditure by function at current prices

Series 100: 1993 SNA, Netherlands Antillean guilder, Western calendar year — **Data in millions**

	2001	2002	2003	2004	2005	2006	2007	2008	2009	2010	2011	2012
Series	**100**											
General public services	138.9	146.0	159.1	163.5	164.8	160.9	170.6	183.6				
Defence	15.1	16.0	14.1	18.1	21.5	24.2	26.1	23.4				
Public order and safety	137.1	150.6	168.6	178.7	192.6	197.9	224.5	218.2				
Economic affairs	23.4	23.5	25.9	27.6	20.6	37.9	22.7	26.8				
Environment protection	24.2	19.7	22.5	23.6	6.3	12.2	12.4	9.8				
Housing and community amenities	...	...	...	...	...	...	...	...				
Health	56.9	58.0	57.3	61.6	50.0	68.2	79.0	78.2				
Recreation, culture and religion	11.4	11.1	10.9	10.9	6.8	46.2	49.4	7.8				
Education	81.0	83.2	94.5	98.1	89.7	98.0	107.3	109.5				
Social protection	97.1	91.4	98.4	103.9	101.9	57.1	64.5	111.0				
Plus: (Other functions) [a]	250.3	272.3	324.5	320.3	318.4	327.0	369.3	407.5				
Equals: General government final consumption expenditure	835.4	871.9	975.7	1006.3	972.5	1029.6	1125.9	1175.8				

[a] Refers to other community, social and personal service activities.

Table 3.2 Individual consumption expenditure of households, NPISHs, and general government at current prices

Series 100: 1993 SNA, Netherlands Antillean guilder, Western calendar year

Data in millions

	2001	2002	2003	2004	2005	2006	2007	2008	2009	2010	2011	2012
Series	**100**											
	Individual consumption expenditure of households											
Food and non-alcoholic beverages	377.0	401.8	401.3	362.4	391.6	402.5	464.0	517.6				
Alcoholic beverages, tobacco and narcotics	58.0	61.7	61.5	44.3	47.9	49.0	56.6	63.2				
Clothing and footwear	324.8	346.3	346.1	290.1	313.4	320.4	370.8	414.7				
Housing, water, electricity, gas and other fuels	817.6	871.5	869.6	1110.0	1202.1	1234.2	1426.9	1594.5				
Furnishings, household equipment and routine maintenance of the house	130.7	139.4	139.4	108.3	117.0	120.5	138.8	154.7				
Health	145.3	154.9	154.7	145.2	156.6	160.3	185.5	207.5				
Transport	309.6	329.7	328.0	329.5	356.6	368.3	423.5	471.7				
Communication	94.7	101.0	101.1	153.6	165.6	168.5	195.7	219.3				
Recreation and culture	...	...	...	...	...	...	...	...				
Education	22.8	24.2	24.1	30.7	33.3	34.4	39.5	44.0				
Restaurants and hotels	71.9	76.6	76.5	96.6	104.2	108.9	124.1	137.4				
Miscellaneous goods and services	444.0	473.3	472.4	557.4	602.7	623.4	715.8	796.6				
Equals: Household final consumption expenditure in domestic market	...	...	...	...	...	...	...	...				
Plus: Direct purchases abroad by residents	...	...	...	...	...	...	...	...				
Less: Direct purchases in domestic market by non-residents	...	...	...	...	...	...	...	...				
Equals: Household final consumption expenditure	2796.3	2980.5	2974.8	3228.1	3490.9	3590.6	4141.2	4621.3				
	Individual consumption expenditure of non-profit institutions serving households (NPISHs)											
Housing	...	...	...	...	...	...	...	...				
Health	...	...	...	...	...	...	...	...				
Recreation and culture	...	...	...	...	...	...	...	...				
Education	...	...	...	...	...	...	...	...				
Social protection	...	...	...	...	...	...	...	...				
Other services	62.6	53.4	61.4	57.0	52.5	51.3	52.2	53.4				
Equals: NPISHs final consumption expenditure	62.6	53.4	61.4	57.0	52.5	51.3	52.2	53.4				
	Individual consumption expenditure of general government											
Housing	...	...	...	...	...	...	...	...				
Health	56.9	58.0	57.3	61.6	50.0	68.2	79.0	78.2				
Recreation and culture	11.4	11.1	10.9	10.9	6.8	46.2	49.4	7.8				
Education	81.0	83.2	94.5	98.1	89.7	98.0	107.3	109.5				
Social protection	73.2	69.3	75.1	78.7	74.3	28.2	33.6	77.1				
Plus:	143.6	156.2	183.2	203.0	196.4	197.2	215.1	207.0				
Equals: Individual consumption expenditure of general government	366.1	377.8	421.0	452.3	417.2	437.8	484.3	479.6				
Equals: Total actual individual consumption	3225.0	3411.8	3457.2	3737.4	3960.6	4079.7	4677.7	5154.3				

Table 4.1 Total Economy (S.1)

Series 100: 1993 SNA, Netherlands Antillean guilder, Western calendar year — **Data in millions**

		2001	2002	2003	2004	2005	2006	2007	2008	2009	2010	2011	2012
Series		**100**											
I. Production account - Resources													
Output, at basic prices (otherwise, please specify)		8798.0	9147.4	9348.2	9658.2	10430.5	11018.3	11869.1	13229.0				
Less: Financial intermediation services indirectly measured (only to be deducted if FISIM is not distributed to uses)		127.9	111.2	110.2	123.1	133.2	142.0	144.9	173.9				
Plus: Taxes less Subsidies on products		466.6	474.8	477.4	477.0	498.8	588.8	654.1	722.7				
Plus: Taxes on products		530.9	541.3	548.1	584.2	618.4	665.4	733.3	806.4				
Less: Subsidies on products		64.3	66.5	70.8	107.2	119.6	76.5	79.2	83.7				
I. Production account - Uses													
Intermediate consumption, at purchaser's prices	a	3947.4	4259.1	4310.2	4456.7	4929.9	5314.2	5870.4	6717.6				
GROSS DOMESTIC PRODUCT		5189.3	5251.9	5405.2	5555.4	5866.2	6150.9	6507.9	7060.3				
Less: Consumption of fixed capital		658.8	669.0	695.9	699.1	692.7	693.3	733.7	786.9				
NET DOMESTIC PRODUCT		4530.5	4582.9	4709.3	4856.3	5173.5	5457.6	5774.3	6273.4				
II.1.1 Generation of income account - Resources													
GROSS DOMESTIC PRODUCT		5189.3	5251.9	5405.2	5555.4	5866.2	6150.9	6507.9	7060.3				
II.1.1 Generation of income account - Uses													
Compensation of employees		2953.6	2895.0	3079.2	3113.7	3168.8	3530.2	3727.9	4119.3				
Taxes on production and imports, less Subsidies		512.1	514.0	525.0	514.8	532.8	636.8	732.3	792.5				
Taxes on production and imports		594.4	598.9	613.8	647.0	679.3	738.4	836.5	901.2				
Taxes on products		530.9	541.3	548.1	584.2	618.4	665.4	733.3	806.4				
Other taxes on production		63.5	57.7	65.6	62.8	61.0	73.0	103.2	94.8				
Less: Subsidies		82.3	84.9	88.8	132.2	146.5	101.5	104.2	108.7				
Subsidies on products		64.3	66.5	70.8	107.2	119.6	76.5	79.2	83.7				
Other subsidies on production		18.0	18.5	18.0	25.0	26.9	25.0	25.0	25.0				
OPERATING SURPLUS, GROSS	b	1723.6	1842.9	1800.9	1926.9	2164.5	1983.8	2047.7	2148.4				
MIXED INCOME, GROSS		450.7	485.7	470.1	496.9	503.9	530.8	...	...				
II.1.2 Allocation of primary income account - Resources													
OPERATING SURPLUS, GROSS	b	1723.6	1842.9	1800.9	1926.9	2164.5	1983.8	2047.7	2148.4				
MIXED INCOME, GROSS		450.7	485.7	470.1	496.9	503.9	530.8	...	...				
Compensation of employees		2910.9	2843.9	3027.9	3057.9	3110.5	3493.5	3688.3	4083.6				
Taxes on production and imports, less Subsidies		512.1	514.0	525.0	514.8	532.8	636.8	732.3	792.5				
Taxes on production and imports		594.4	598.9	613.8	647.0	679.3	738.4	836.5	901.2				
Taxes on products		530.9	541.3	548.1	584.2	618.4	665.4	733.3	806.4				
Other taxes on production		63.5	57.7	65.6	62.8	61.0	73.0	103.2	94.8				
Less: Subsidies		82.3	84.9	88.8	132.2	146.5	101.5	104.2	108.7				
Subsidies on products		64.3	66.5	70.8	107.2	119.6	76.5	79.2	83.7				
Other subsidies on production		18.0	18.5	18.0	25.0	26.9	25.0	25.0	25.0				
Property income		1254.6	1224.9	1194.6	1381.2	1532.9	1704.9	1874.7	770.9				

	2001	2002	2003	2004	2005	2006	2007	2008	2009	2010	2011	2012
Series	**100**											
II.1.2 Allocation of primary income account - Uses												
Property income	1174.8	1174.3	1155.9	1355.2	1501.4	1670.2	1829.8	809.1				
GROSS NATIONAL INCOME	5226.4	5251.3	5392.6	5525.6	5839.4	6148.9	6513.2	6986.4				
II.2 Secondary distribution of income account - Resources												
GROSS NATIONAL INCOME	5226.4	5251.3	5392.6	5525.6	5839.4	6148.9	6513.2	6986.4				
Current taxes on income, wealth, etc.	765.5	734.1	766.7	786.2	938.7	872.3	875.8	937.1				
Social contributions	317.0	362.5	364.2	365.4	394.5	423.6	498.8	607.8				
Social benefits other than social transfers in kind	315.0	331.7	348.4	365.6	380.5	411.0	488.1	533.6				
Other current transfers	742.9	1034.8	1164.7	876.1	923.7	1030.3	1026.8	1188.2				
II.2 Secondary distribution of income account - Uses												
Current taxes on income, wealth, etc.	678.1	650.4	644.8	686.1	647.2	745.0	809.7	827.4				
Social contributions	317.0	362.5	364.2	365.4	394.5	423.6	498.8	607.8				
Social benefits other than social transfers in kind	315.0	331.7	348.4	365.6	380.5	411.0	488.1	533.6				
Other current transfers	792.8	892.2	1060.9	870.0	972.7	1079.2	1090.0	1286.4				
GROSS DISPOSABLE INCOME	5263.9	5477.6	5618.3	5631.8	6081.9	6227.3	6516.1	6997.8				
II.4.1 Use of disposable income account - Resources												
GROSS DISPOSABLE INCOME	5263.9	5477.6	5618.3	5631.8	6081.9	6227.3	6516.1	6997.8				
Adjustment for the change in net equity of households on pension funds	-19.6	-10.7	14.3	-179.1	-110.3	-94.7	-114.7	-257.2				
II.4.1 Use of disposable income account - Uses												
Final consumption expenditure	3694.2	3905.8	4011.9	4291.5	4515.9	4671.4	5319.2	5850.5				
Individual consumption expenditure	3225.0	3411.8	3457.2	3737.4	3960.6	4079.7	4677.7	5154.3				
Collective consumption expenditure	469.3	494.1	554.7	554.0	555.3	591.8	641.5	696.2				
Adjustment for the change in net equity of households on pension funds	-19.6	-10.7	14.3	-179.1	-110.3	-94.7	-114.7	-257.2				
SAVING, GROSS	1569.7	1571.8	1606.4	1340.3	1566.0	1555.8	1196.9	1147.3				
III.1 Capital account - Changes in liabilities and net worth												
SAVING, GROSS	1569.7	1571.8	1606.4	1340.3	1566.0	1555.8	1196.9	1147.3				
Capital transfers, receivable less payable	54.1	54.6	62.6	143.1	173.0	183.2	219.3	218.3				
Capital transfers, receivable	320.2	295.3	322.7	361.3	402.6	432.0	489.8	491.4				
Less: Capital transfers, payable	266.1	240.7	260.1	218.2	229.6	248.8	270.5	273.1				
Equals: CHANGES IN NET WORTH DUE TO SAVING AND CAPITAL TRANSFERS	965.0	957.4	973.1	784.3	1046.4	1045.7	682.5	578.7				
III.1 Capital account - Changes in assets												
Gross capital formation	1888.0	1561.7	1588.9	1489.5	1751.1	1984.0	2210.9	2654.7				
Gross fixed capital formation	1575.0	1609.6	1619.9	1636.5	1756.4	1989.1	2324.0	2570.3				
Changes in inventories	313.1	-47.9	-31.0	-147.0	-5.3	-5.2	-113.1	84.4				
Acquisitions less disposals of valuables	...	...	...	...	...	...	...	...				

	2001	2002	2003	2004	2005	2006	2007	2008	2009	2010	2011	2012
Series	**100**											
Acquisitions less disposals of non-produced non-financial assets	2.0	3.0	4.0	5.0	6.0	7.0	8.0	9.0				
NET LENDING (+) / NET BORROWING (-)	-266.3	61.8	76.1	-11.1	-18.1	-251.9	-802.7	-1298.1				

[a] Excludes financial intermediation services indirectly measured (FISIM).
[b] Includes Mixed Income, Gross.

Table 4.2 Rest of the world (S.2)

Series 100: 1993 SNA, Netherlands Antillean guilder, Western calendar year — **Data in millions**

	2001	2002	2003	2004	2005	2006	2007	2008	2009	2010	2011	2012
Series	**100**											
	V.I External account of goods and services - Resources											
Imports of goods and services	4200.0	3959.9	3993.0	4381.2	4845.9	5312.4	5989.4	7071.5				
Imports of goods	2927.0	2669.8	2635.0	3084.0	3491.0	3955.0	4562.2	5511.5				
Imports of services	1273.0	1290.1	1358.0	1297.2	1354.9	1357.4	1427.2	1560.0				
	V.I External account of goods and services - Uses											
Exports of goods and services	3807.0	3744.3	3797.4	4155.6	4445.0	4807.9	4967.2	5626.5				
Exports of goods	899.3	879.3	768.7	933.2	1088.4	1243.6	1210.8	1948.4				
Exports of services	2907.7	2865.0	3028.7	3222.4	3356.6	3564.3	3756.4	3678.1				
EXTERNAL BALANCE OF GOODS AND SERVICES	393.0	215.6	195.6	225.6	400.9	504.5	1022.2	1445.0				
	V.II External account of primary income and current transfers - Resources											
EXTERNAL BALANCE OF GOODS AND SERVICES	393.0	215.6	195.6	225.6	400.9	504.5	1022.2	1445.0				
Compensation of employees	57.0	61.0	61.3	62.8	75.3	68.0	78.1	84.9				
Taxes on production and imports, less Subsidies	...	...	...	...	...	...	...	...				
Taxes on production and imports	...	...	...	...	...	...	...	...				
Taxes on products	...	...	...	...	...	...	...	...				
Other taxes on production	...	...	...	...	...	...	...	...				
Less: Subsidies	...	...	...	...	...	...	...	...				
Subsidies on products	...	...	...	...	...	...	...	...				
Other subsidies on production	...	...	...	...	...	...	...	...				
Property income	92.9	102.9	112.5	125.4	141.8	179.4	221.3	239.0				
Current taxes on income, wealth, etc.	...	...	...	...	...	...	...	...				
Social contributions	...	...	...	...	...	...	...	...				
Social benefits other than social transfers in kind	...	...	...	...	...	...	...	...				
Other current transfers	387.0	459.3	497.1	480.6	545.6	547.6	584.8	711.6				
Adjustment for the change in net equity of households on pension funds	...	...	...	...	...	...	...	...				
	V.II External account of primary income and current transfers - Uses											
Compensation of employees	14.3	9.9	10.0	7.0	17.0	31.3	38.5	49.2				
Taxes on production and imports, less Subsidies	...	...	...	...	...	...	...	...				
Taxes on production and imports	...	...	...	...	...	...	...	...				

	2001	2002	2003	2004	2005	2006	2007	2008	2009	2010	2011	2012
Series	**100**											
Taxes on products	...	...	...	...	...	...	...	...				
Other taxes on production	...	...	...	...	...	...	...	...				
Less: Subsidies	...	...	...	...	...	...	...	...				
Subsidies on products	...	...	...	...	...	...	...	...				
Other subsidies on production	...	...	...	...	...	...	...	...				
Property income	172.7	153.5	151.2	151.4	173.3	214.1	266.1	200.7				
Current taxes on income and wealth, etc.	87.4	83.7	121.9	100.1	291.5	127.3	66.1	109.7				
Social contributions	...	...	...	...	...	...	...	...				
Social benefits other than social transfers in kind	...	...	...	...	...	...	...	...				
Other current transfers	337.1	601.9	600.9	486.7	496.7	498.7	521.6	613.4				
Adjustment for the change in net equity of households on pension funds	...	...	...	...	...	...	...	...				
CURRENT EXTERNAL BALANCE	318.4	-10.2	-17.5	149.2	185.1	428.1	1014.1	1507.5				
	V.III.1 Capital account - Changes in liabilities and net worth											
CURRENT EXTERNAL BALANCE	318.4	-10.2	-17.5	149.2	185.1	428.1	1014.1	1507.5				
Capital transfers, receivable less payable	-54.1	-54.6	-62.6	-143.1	-173.0	-183.2	-219.3	-218.3				
Capital transfers, receivable	7.4	0.4	3.6	1.0	0.0	2.2	7.9	14.5				
Less: Capital transfers, payable	61.5	55.0	66.2	144.1	173.0	185.4	227.2	232.8				
Equals: CHANGES IN NET WORTH DUE TO SAVING AND CAPITAL TRANSFERS	264.3	-64.8	-80.1	6.1	12.1	244.9	794.8	1289.2				
	V.III.1 Capital account - Changes in assets											
Acquisitions less disposals of non-produced non-financial assets	...	...	...	...	...	...	...	...				
NET LENDING (+) / NET BORROWING (-)	264.3	-64.8	-80.1	6.1	12.1	244.9	794.8	1289.2				

Table 4.3 Non-financial Corporations (S.11)

Series 100: 1993 SNA, Netherlands Antillean guilder, Western calendar year — **Data in millions**

	2001	2002	2003	2004	2005	2006	2007	2008	2009	2010	2011	2012
Series	**100**											
	I. Production account - Resources											
Output, at basic prices (otherwise, please specify)	6143.1	6312.8	6399.2	6552.2	7016.6	7563.6	7987.5	9381.5				
	I. Production account - Uses											
Intermediate consumption, at purchaser's prices	3109.7	3325.3	3395.8	3445.1	3862.5	4173.3	4539.9	5226.5				
VALUE ADDED GROSS, in basic prices	3033.4	2987.5	3003.4	3107.1	3154.0	3390.4	3447.6	4155.0				
Less: Consumption of fixed capital	457.6	463.2	477.6	481.9	454.5	443.5	465.1	489.2				
VALUE ADDED NET, at basic prices	2575.8	2524.3	2525.8	2625.2	2699.5	2946.9	2982.5	3665.8				
	II.1.1 Generation of income account - Resources											
VALUE ADDED GROSS, at basic prices	3033.4	2987.5	3003.4	3107.1	3154.0	3390.4	3447.6	4155.0				

	2001	2002	2003	2004	2005	2006	2007	2008	2009	2010	2011	2012
Series	**100**											
	II.1.1 Generation of income account - Uses											
Compensation of employees	2041.3	1969.0	2082.0	2076.8	2049.8	2343.4	2457.9	2793.3				
Other taxes less Other subsidies on production	33.8	31.5	39.6	30.3	29.6	41.6	60.7	54.7				
Other taxes on production	51.8	49.9	57.6	55.3	56.5	66.6	85.7	79.7				
Less: Other subsidies on production	18.0	18.5	18.0	25.0	26.9	25.0	25.0	25.0				
OPERATING SURPLUS, GROSS	958.3	987.0	881.8	999.9	1074.7	1005.4	928.9	1307.0				
	II.1.2 Allocation of primary income account - Resources											
OPERATING SURPLUS, GROSS	958.3	987.0	881.8	999.9	1074.7	1005.4	928.9	1307.0				
Property income	58.8	64.2	43.4	77.1	46.6	56.2	80.5	58.3				
	II.1.2 Allocation of primary income account - Uses											
Property income	246.7	243.4	230.7	297.0	300.1	304.3	351.8	390.7				
BALANCE OF PRIMARY INCOMES	770.4	807.8	694.5	780.0	821.2	757.3	657.6	974.6				
	II.2 Secondary distribution of income account - Resources											
BALANCE OF PRIMARY INCOMES	770.4	807.8	694.5	780.0	821.2	757.3	657.6	974.6				
Social contributions	...	...	...	...	...	...	...	...				
Other current transfers	...	...	...	...	...	...	...	...				
	II.2 Secondary distribution of income account - Uses											
Current taxes on income, wealth, etc.	92.1	69.5	57.8	72.5	50.0	87.1	111.9	96.8				
Social benefits other than social transfers in kind	...	...	...	...	...	...	...	...				
Other current transfers	5.9	4.8	3.8	4.6	3.1	3.8	4.4	3.2				
GROSS DISPOSABLE INCOME	672.5	733.5	632.9	702.9	768.2	666.4	541.4	874.6				
	II.4.1 Use of disposable income account - Resources											
GROSS DISPOSABLE INCOME	672.5	733.5	632.9	702.9	768.2	666.4	541.4	874.6				
	II.4.1 Use of disposable income account - Uses											
Adjustment for the change in net equity of households on pension funds	...	...	...	...	...	...	...	...				
SAVING, GROSS	672.5	733.5	632.9	702.9	768.2	666.4	541.4	874.6				
	III.1 Capital account - Changes in liabilities and net worth											
SAVING, GROSS	672.5	733.5	632.9	702.9	768.2	666.4	541.4	874.6				
Capital transfers, receivable less payable	...	...	...	...	...	...	...	...				
Capital transfers, receivable	...	...	...	...	...	...	...	...				
Less: Capital transfers, payable	...	...	...	...	...	...	...	...				
Equals: CHANGES IN NET WORTH DUE TO SAVING AND CAPITAL TRANSFERS	214.9	270.3	155.3	221.0	313.7	222.9	76.3	385.4				
	III.1 Capital account - Changes in assets											
Gross capital formation	1176.2	827.8	897.7	747.7	1070.3	1229.7	1551.8	1856.3				
Gross fixed capital formation	863.5	875.6	929.1	895.0	1076.1	1234.9	1666.2	1774.1				
Changes in inventories	312.7	-47.8	-31.3	-147.4	-5.8	-5.1	-114.4	82.2				
Acquisitions less disposals of valuables	...	...	...	...	...	...	...	...				

	2001	2002	2003	2004	2005	2006	2007	2008	2009	2010	2011	2012
Series	**100**											
Acquisitions less disposals of non-produced non-financial assets	36.3	3.8	12.7	-7.7	28.1	36.0	11.8	6.4				
NET LENDING (+) / NET BORROWING (-)	-540.0	-98.1	-277.5	-37.0	-330.2	-599.4	-1022.2	-988.1				

Table 4.4 Financial Corporations (S.12)

Series 100: 1993 SNA, Netherlands Antillean guilder, Western calendar year

Data in millions

		2001	2002	2003	2004	2005	2006	2007	2008	2009	2010	2011	2012
Series		**100**											
		I. Production account - Resources											
Output, at basic prices (otherwise, please specify)		1098.1	1215.1	1238.8	1311.0	1544.6	1525.8	1851.3	1713.6				
		I. Production account - Uses											
Intermediate consumption, at purchaser's prices		367.8	415.1	352.4	408.2	477.1	543.1	667.8	789.4				
VALUE ADDED GROSS, at basic prices	a	730.3	800.0	886.4	902.9	1067.6	982.7	1183.5	924.2				
Less: Consumption of fixed capital		57.7	59.8	59.9	64.4	65.6	71.2	79.0	90.5				
VALUE ADDED NET, at basic prices		672.7	740.2	826.5	838.5	1002.0	911.5	1104.5	833.6				
		II.1.1 Generation of income account - Resources											
VALUE ADDED GROSS, at basic prices	a	730.3	800.0	886.4	902.9	1067.6	982.7	1183.5	924.2				
		II.1.1 Generation of income account - Uses											
Compensation of employees		338.4	347.6	373.3	397.1	431.0	484.2	533.8	569.5				
Other taxes less Other subsidies on production		...	...	...	...	...	...	...	...				
Other taxes on production		...	...	...	...	...	...	...	...				
Less: Other subsidies on production		...	...	...	...	...	...	...	...				
OPERATING SURPLUS, GROSS	a	391.9	452.3	513.1	505.7	636.6	498.5	649.7	354.7				
		II.1.2 Allocation of primary income account - Resources											
OPERATING SURPLUS, GROSS	a	391.9	452.3	513.1	505.7	636.6	498.5	649.7	354.7				
Property income		723.1	701.6	741.9	823.1	812.9	908.9	1006.6	968.1				
		II.1.2 Allocation of primary income account - Uses											
Property income		517.3	515.7	469.1	537.3	697.9	815.5	888.8	-194.2				
BALANCE OF PRIMARY INCOMES	a	597.7	638.3	785.9	791.5	751.6	591.9	767.5	1516.9				
		II.2 Secondary distribution of income account - Resources											
BALANCE OF PRIMARY INCOMES	a	597.7	638.3	785.9	791.5	751.6	591.9	767.5	1516.9				
Social contributions		...	...	...	...	...	...	...	...				
Other current transfers		137.3	166.6	234.9	175.1	158.7	235.8	204.8	206.9				
		II.2 Secondary distribution of income account - Uses											
Current taxes on income, wealth, etc.		55.2	48.5	40.0	44.1	29.5	56.2	71.6	61.4				
Social benefits other than social transfers in kind		...	...	...	...	...	...	...	...				
Other current transfers		112.8	140.9	199.6	103.8	139.6	151.6	163.4	202.3				
GROSS DISPOSABLE INCOME		567.1	615.5	781.2	818.7	741.2	619.9	737.3	1460.2				

	2001	2002	2003	2004	2005	2006	2007	2008	2009	2010	2011	2012
Series	**100**											
	II.4.1 Use of disposable income account - Resources											
GROSS DISPOSABLE INCOME	567.1	615.5	781.2	818.7	741.2	619.9	737.3	1460.2				
	II.4.1 Use of disposable income account - Uses											
Adjustment for the change in net equity of households on pension funds	-19.6	-10.7	14.3	-179.1	-110.3	-94.7	-114.7	-257.2				
SAVING, GROSS	586.7	626.2	766.9	997.9	851.5	714.7	852.0	1717.4				
	III.1 Capital account - Changes in liabilities and net worth											
SAVING, GROSS	586.7	626.2	766.9	997.9	851.5	714.7	852.0	1717.4				
Capital transfers, receivable less payable	182.0	188.7	203.6	215.4	227.6	242.8	261.3	257.5				
Capital transfers, receivable	182.0	188.7	203.6	215.4	227.6	242.8	261.3	257.5				
Less: Capital transfers, payable	...	...	...	...	...	...	...	...				
Equals: CHANGES IN NET WORTH DUE TO SAVING AND CAPITAL TRANSFERS	711.0	755.1	910.6	1148.8	1013.5	886.3	1034.3	1884.3				
	III.1 Capital account - Changes in assets											
Gross capital formation	386.3	430.7	366.7	421.5	409.9	428.7	415.1	491.5				
Gross fixed capital formation	386.3	430.4	366.6	421.5	409.9	428.7	415.1	491.5				
Changes in inventories	0.0	0.3	0.1	0.0	0.0	0.0	0.0	0.0				
Acquisitions less disposals of valuables	...	...	...	...	...	...	...	...				
Acquisitions less disposals of non-produced non-financial assets	0.0	0.0	0.2	-0.6	0.1	6.9	0.3	-6.2				
NET LENDING (+) / NET BORROWING (-)	382.4	384.2	603.6	792.3	669.1	521.9	697.9	1489.5				

[a] Includes financial intermediation services indirectly measured (FISIM) of the Total Economy.

Table 4.5 General Government (S.13)

Series 100: 1993 SNA, Netherlands Antillean guilder, Western calendar year

Data in millions

	2001	2002	2003	2004	2005	2006	2007	2008	2009	2010	2011	2012
Series	**100**											
	I. Production account - Resources											
Output, at basic prices (otherwise, please specify)	862.4	896.6	995.3	1019.5	1065.9	1094.2	1170.2	1242.0				
	I. Production account - Uses											
Intermediate consumption, at purchaser's prices	296.0	323.0	364.2	387.6	376.9	394.6	435.4	475.3				
VALUE ADDED GROSS, at basic prices	566.4	573.6	631.0	631.9	689.1	699.7	734.8	766.8				
Less: Consumption of fixed capital	26.0	24.5	38.8	22.2	39.4	39.7	44.1	55.6				
VALUE ADDED NET, at basic prices	540.4	549.1	592.2	609.7	649.7	659.9	690.7	711.2				
	II.1.1 Generation of income account - Resources											
VALUE ADDED GROSS, at basic prices	566.4	573.6	631.0	631.9	689.1	699.7	734.8	766.8				
	II.1.1 Generation of income account - Uses											
Compensation of employees	540.6	550.7	592.3	609.8	649.7	660.1	690.6	711.2				
Other taxes less Other subsidies on production	0.1	0.1	0.1	0.1	0.1	0.1	0.1	0.1				
Other taxes on production	0.1	0.1	0.1	0.1	0.1	0.1	0.1	0.1				

	2001	2002	2003	2004	2005	2006	2007	2008	2009	2010	2011	2012
Series	**100**											
Less: Other subsidies on production	...	...	...	...	...	...	...	...				
OPERATING SURPLUS, GROSS	25.8	22.9	38.7	22.0	39.3	39.4	44.1	55.4				
	II.1.2 Allocation of primary income account - Resources											
OPERATING SURPLUS, GROSS	25.8	22.9	38.7	22.0	39.3	39.4	44.1	55.4				
Taxes on production and imports, less Subsidies	512.1	514.0	525.0	514.8	532.8	636.8	732.3	792.5				
Taxes on production and imports	594.4	598.9	613.8	647.0	679.3	738.4	836.5	901.2				
Taxes on products	530.9	541.3	548.1	584.2	618.4	665.4	733.3	806.4				
Other taxes on production	63.5	57.7	65.6	62.8	61.0	73.0	103.2	94.8				
Less: Subsidies	82.3	84.9	88.8	132.2	146.5	101.5	104.2	108.7				
Subsidies on products	64.3	66.5	70.8	107.2	119.6	76.5	79.2	83.7				
Other subsidies on production	18.0	18.5	18.0	25.0	26.9	25.0	25.0	25.0				
Property income	101.0	92.1	106.7	121.1	173.2	150.7	162.9	201.2				
	II.1.2 Allocation of primary income account - Uses											
Property income	246.1	263.3	302.2	357.7	353.4	368.2	384.6	388.1				
BALANCE OF PRIMARY INCOMES	392.7	365.7	368.1	300.2	391.9	458.8	554.7	661.0				
	II.2 Secondary distribution of income account - Resources											
BALANCE OF PRIMARY INCOMES	392.7	365.7	368.1	300.2	391.9	458.8	554.7	661.0				
Current taxes on income, wealth, etc.	765.5	734.1	766.7	786.2	938.7	872.3	875.8	937.1				
Social contributions	317.0	362.5	364.2	365.4	394.5	423.6	498.8	607.8				
Other current transfers	80.8	85.4	62.5	51.5	86.8	81.7	96.4	124.2				
	II.2 Secondary distribution of income account - Uses											
Current taxes on income, wealth, etc.	...	...	...	...	...	...	...	...				
Social benefits other than social transfers in kind	315.0	331.7	348.4	365.6	380.5	411.0	488.1	533.6				
Other current transfers	147.6	125.9	133.0	109.7	146.8	147.9	143.4	176.5				
GROSS DISPOSABLE INCOME	1093.3	1090.0	1080.1	1028.0	1284.6	1277.4	1394.2	1620.1				
	II.4.1 Use of disposable income account - Resources											
GROSS DISPOSABLE INCOME	1093.3	1090.0	1080.1	1028.0	1284.6	1277.4	1394.2	1620.1				
	II.4.1 Use of disposable income account - Uses											
Final consumption expenditure	835.4	871.9	975.7	1006.3	972.5	1029.6	1125.9	1175.8				
Individual consumption expenditure	366.1	377.8	421.0	452.3	417.2	437.8	484.3	479.6				
Collective consumption expenditure	469.3	494.1	554.7	554.0	555.3	591.8	641.5	696.2				
Adjustment for the change in net equity of households on pension funds	...	...	...	...	...	...	...	...				
SAVING, GROSS	257.9	218.1	104.4	21.7	312.0	247.8	268.4	444.3				
	III.1 Capital account - Changes in liabilities and net worth											
SAVING, GROSS	257.9	218.1	104.4	21.7	312.0	247.8	268.4	444.3				
Capital transfers, receivable less payable	-51.1	-82.6	-88.0	-70.5	-52.6	-55.8	-40.6	-38.0				
Capital transfers, receivable	138.3	106.5	119.2	145.9	175.0	189.2	228.5	233.9				
Less: Capital transfers, payable	189.4	189.1	207.2	216.4	227.6	245.0	269.2	272.0				

	2001	2002	2003	2004	2005	2006	2007	2008	2009	2010	2011	2012
Series	**100**											
Equals: CHANGES IN NET WORTH DUE TO SAVING AND CAPITAL TRANSFERS	180.8	111.0	-22.4	-71.1	220.0	152.2	183.6	350.6				
	III.1 Capital account - Changes in assets											
Gross capital formation	74.5	75.5	96.4	82.7	67.0	87.9	85.7	91.1				
Gross fixed capital formation	74.5	75.5	96.3	82.7	67.1	91.0	87.2	91.5				
Changes in inventories	-0.0	0.0	0.1	0.0	-0.1	-3.1	-1.5	-0.4				
Acquisitions less disposals of valuables	...	...	...	...	...	...	...	...				
Acquisitions of non-produced non-financial assets	11.6	2.9	3.1	4.0	2.0	1.4	3.5	3.3				
NET LENDING (+) / NET BORROWING (-)	120.7	57.1	-83.1	-135.6	190.4	102.7	138.5	311.8				

Table 4.9 Combined Sectors: Households and NPISH (S.14 + S.15)

Series 100: 1993 SNA, Netherlands Antillean guilder, Western calendar year — **Data in millions**

	2001	2002	2003	2004	2005	2006	2007	2008	2009	2010	2011	2012
Series	**100**											
	I. Production account - Resources											
Output, at basic prices (otherwise, please specify)	695.0	723.0	715.0	775.0	803.0	835.0	860.0	892.0				
	I. Production account - Uses											
Intermediate consumption, at purchaser's prices	174.0	196.0	198.0	216.0	213.0	203.0	227.0	226.0				
VALUE ADDED GROSS, at basic prices	520.0	527.0	517.0	560.0	590.0	631.0	633.0	665.0				
Less: Consumption of fixed capital	117.0	122.0	120.0	131.0	133.0	139.0	145.0	152.0				
VALUE ADDED NET, at basic prices	403.0	406.0	398.0	429.0	457.0	492.0	487.0	514.0				
	II.1.1 Generation of income account - Resources											
VALUE ADDED GROSS, at basic prices	520.0	527.0	517.0	560.0	590.0	631.0	633.0	665.0				
	II.1.1 Generation of income account - Uses											
Compensation of employees	33.0	28.0	32.0	30.0	38.0	42.0	46.0	45.0				
Other taxes less Other subsidies on production	12.0	8.0	8.0	7.0	4.0	6.0	17.0	15.0				
Other taxes on production	12.0	8.0	8.0	7.0	4.0	6.0	17.0	15.0				
Less: Other subsidies on production	...	...	...	...	...	...	...	...				
OPERATING SURPLUS, GROSS [a]	476.0	492.0	478.0	522.0	547.0	583.0	570.0	605.0				
MIXED INCOME, GROSS	...	...	...	...	...	...	...	...				
	II.1.2 Allocation of primary income account - Resources											
OPERATING SURPLUS, GROSS [a]	476.0	492.0	478.0	522.0	547.0	583.0	570.0	605.0				
MIXED INCOME, GROSS	...	...	...	...	...	...	...	...				
Compensation of employees	2910.9	2843.9	3027.9	3057.9	3110.5	3493.5	3688.3	4083.6				
Property income	372.0	367.0	303.0	360.0	500.0	589.0	625.0	-457.0				
	II.1.2 Allocation of primary income account - Uses											
Property income	165.0	152.0	154.0	163.0	150.0	182.0	205.0	224.0				
BALANCE OF PRIMARY INCOMES	3593.4	3550.7	3654.2	3777.1	4007.8	4482.9	4678.2	4007.7				

	2001	2002	2003	2004	2005	2006	2007	2008	2009	2010	2011	2012
Series	**100**											
	II.2 Secondary distribution of income account - Resources											
BALANCE OF PRIMARY INCOMES	3593.4	3550.7	3654.2	3777.1	4007.8	4482.9	4678.2	4007.7				
Social contributions	...	...	...	...	...	...	...	...				
Social benefits other than social transfers in kind	315.0	331.7	348.4	365.6	380.5	411.0	488.0	534.0				
Other current transfers	524.8	783.0	867.5	649.0	678.0	713.0	726.0	857.0				
	II.2 Secondary distribution of income account - Uses											
Current taxes on income, wealth, etc.	530.8	532.3	547.0	569.5	568.0	602.0	626.0	669.0				
Social contributions	317.0	362.5	364.2	365.4	394.5	423.6	499.0	608.0				
Social benefits other than social transfers in kind	...	...	...	...	...	...	...	...				
Other current transfers	526.5	621.1	724.7	652.0	683.0	776.0	779.0	905.0				
GROSS DISPOSABLE INCOME	3059.0	3149.8	3234.2	3205.3	3421.2	3805.6	3988.0	3216.8				
	II.4.1 Use of disposable income account - Resources											
GROSS DISPOSABLE INCOME	3059.0	3149.8	3234.2	3205.3	3421.2	3805.6	3988.0	3216.8				
Adjustment for the change in net equity of households on pension funds	-19.6	-10.7	14.3	-179.1	-110.3	-94.7	-114.7	-257.2				
	II.4.1 Use of disposable income account - Uses											
Final consumption expenditure	2858.9	3033.9	3036.2	3285.1	3543.4	3641.8	4193.4	4674.7				
Individual consumption expenditure	2742.9	3033.9	3036.2	3285.1	3543.4	3641.8	4193.4	4674.7				
SAVING, GROSS	180.5	105.2	212.3	-259.0	-232.5	69.0	-320.0	-1715.0				
	III.1 Capital account - Changes in liabilities and net worth											
SAVING, GROSS	180.5	105.2	212.3	-259.0	-232.5	69.0	-320.0	-1715.0				
Capital transfers, receivable less payable	-76.8	-51.5	-52.9	-1.8	-2.0	-3.8	-1.3	-1.1				
Capital transfers, receivable	...	...	...	...	...	...	...	...				
Less: Capital transfers, payable	76.8	51.5	52.9	1.8	2.0	3.8	1.3	1.1				
Equals: CHANGES IN NET WORTH DUE TO SAVINGS AND CAPITAL TRANSFERS	-14.0	-68.0	40.0	-391.0	-368.0	-74.0	-467.0	-1868.0				
	III.1 Capital account - Changes in assets											
Gross capital formation	251.0	228.0	228.0	238.0	204.0	238.0	158.0	216.0				
Gross fixed capital formation	251.0	228.0	228.0	237.0	203.0	235.0	156.0	213.0				
Changes in inventories	0.4	-0.4	0.1	0.4	1.0	3.0	3.0	3.0				
Acquisitions less disposals of valuables	...	...	...	...	...	...	...	...				
Acquisitions less disposals of non-produced non-financial assets	-47.9	-6.7	-16.0	4.0	-30.0	-44.0	-16.0	-4.0				
NET LENDING (+) / NET BORROWING (-)	-99.0	-167.0	-53.0	-503.0	-408.0	-128.0	-464.0	-1928.0				

[a] Includes Mixed Income, Gross.

Table 5.1 Cross classification of Gross value added by industries and institutional sectors (ISIC Rev. 3) Non-financial corporations

Series 100: 1993 SNA, Netherlands Antillean guilder, Western calendar year

Data in millions

	2001	2002	2003	2004	2005	2006	2007	2008	2009	2010	2011	2012
Series	**100**											
	Industries											
Agriculture, hunting, forestry; fishing	48.3	37.8	34.8	36.3	41.4	34.4	36.1	40.5				
Mining and quarrying	...	...	...	...	...	...	...	...				
Manufacturing	346.2	324.3	308.5	323.5	283.6	366.3	355.9	435.1				
Electricity, gas and water supply	245.9	225.0	231.8	214.1	233.9	228.6	233.0	202.6				
Construction	273.4	280.5	276.8	261.6	335.8	307.1	335.9	393.2				
Wholesale and retail trade; repair of motor vehicles, motorcycles and personal and household goods; hotels and restaurants	880.2	829.4	842.3	859.5	919.5	980.5	995.4	1262.1				
Transport, storage and communications	453.7	499.2	517.4	451.8	475.1	536.0	528.4	689.7				
Financial intermediation; real estate renting and business activities	394.0	385.8	390.8	516.7	413.5	459.0	491.9	555.5				
Public administration and defence; compulsory social security	...	...	...	...	...	...	...	...				
Education; health and social work; other community, social and personal services	391.5	405.5	401.0	443.6	451.2	478.5	471.1	576.2				
Private households with employed persons	...	...	...	...	...	...	...	...				
VALUE ADDED GROSS, at basic prices	3033.4	2987.5	3003.4	3107.1	3154.0	3390.4	3447.6	4155.0				

Table 5.1 Cross classification of Gross value added by industries and institutional sectors (ISIC Rev. 3) Financial corporations

Series 100: 1993 SNA, Netherlands Antillean guilder, Western calendar year

Data in millions

	2001	2002	2003	2004	2005	2006	2007	2008	2009	2010	2011	2012
Series	**100**											
	Industries											
Agriculture, hunting, forestry; fishing	...	...	...	...	...	...	...	...				
Mining and quarrying	...	...	...	...	...	...	...	...				
Manufacturing	...	...	...	...	...	...	...	...				
Electricity, gas and water supply	...	...	...	...	...	...	...	...				
Construction	...	...	...	...	...	...	...	...				
Wholesale and retail trade; repair of motor vehicles, motorcycles and personal and household goods; hotels and restaurants	...	...	...	...	...	...	...	...				
Transport, storage and communications	...	...	...	...	...	...	...	...				
Financial intermediation; real estate renting and business activities	730.3	800.0	886.4	902.9	1067.6	982.7	1183.5	924.2				
Public administration and defence; compulsory social security	...	...	...	...	...	...	...	...				

	2001	2002	2003	2004	2005	2006	2007	2008	2009	2010	2011	2012
Series	**100**											
Education; health and social work; other community, social and personal services	...	...	...	...	...	...	...	...				
Private households with employed persons	...	...	...	...	...	...	...	...				
VALUE ADDED GROSS, at basic prices	730.3	800.0	886.4	902.9	1067.6	982.7	1183.5	924.2				

Table 5.1 Cross classification of Gross value added by industries and institutional sectors (ISIC Rev. 3) General government

Series 100: 1993 SNA, Netherlands Antillean guilder, Western calendar year

Data in millions

	2001	2002	2003	2004	2005	2006	2007	2008	2009	2010	2011	2012
Series	**100**											
Industries												
Agriculture, hunting, forestry; fishing	0.5	0.6	0.8	0.6	0.8	0.9	1.7	1.1				
Mining and quarrying	...	...	...	...	...	...	...	...				
Manufacturing	...	...	...	...	...	...	...	...				
Electricity, gas and water supply	...	...	...	...	...	...	...	...				
Construction	...	...	...	...	...	...	...	...				
Wholesale and retail trade; repair of motor vehicles, motorcycles and personal and household goods; hotels and restaurants	...	...	...	...	...	...	...	...				
Transport, storage and communications	16.9	15.0	16.7	16.3	16.5	15.1	13.8	12.0				
Financial intermediation; real estate renting and business activities	2.1	3.4	4.7	3.6	4.7	4.7	4.5	3.6				
Public administration and defence; compulsory social security	352.8	362.3	396.0	405.7	458.3	467.5	494.1	524.0				
Education; health and social work; other community, social and personal services	194.1	192.4	212.8	205.7	208.8	211.5	220.8	226.1				
Private households with employed persons	...	...	...	...	...	...	...	...				
VALUE ADDED GROSS, at basic prices	566.4	573.6	631.0	631.9	689.1	699.7	734.8	766.8				

Table 5.1 Cross classification of Gross value added by industries and institutional sectors (ISIC Rev. 3) Households

Series 100: 1993 SNA, Netherlands Antillean guilder, Western calendar year

Data in millions

	2001	2002	2003	2004	2005	2006	2007	2008	2009	2010	2011	2012
Series	**100**											
Industries												
Agriculture, hunting, forestry; fishing	1.0	1.1	1.1	0.5	0.7	1.4	0.8	1.1				
Mining and quarrying	...	...	...	...	...	...	...	...				
Manufacturing	0.7	0.7	0.5	0.3	0.3	0.6	0.4	0.8				
Electricity, gas and water supply	...	...	...	...	...	...	...	...				

	2001	2002	2003	2004	2005	2006	2007	2008	2009	2010	2011	2012
Series	**100**											
Construction	1.3	1.3	1.4	0.9	1.8	2.4	1.5	1.4				
Wholesale and retail trade; repair of motor vehicles, motorcycles and personal and household goods; hotels and restaurants	12.9	12.9	10.4	10.4	19.0	21.0	12.4	15.6				
Transport, storage and communications	26.6	26.7	27.2	27.3	29.5	29.9	28.6	27.7				
Financial intermediation; real estate renting and business activities	420.1	435.7	422.5	469.8	490.4	530.8	554.7	579.7				
Public administration and defence; compulsory social security	...	...	...	...	...	...	...	...				
Education; health and social work; other community, social and personal services	35.0	27.9	32.5	28.7	29.0	28.5	19.3	25.7				
Private households with employed persons	22.9	20.8	21.6	21.8	19.0	16.8	15.0	13.5				
VALUE ADDED GROSS, at basic prices [a]	520.5	527.1	517.1	559.6	589.8	631.4	632.8	665.5				

[a] Includes data for the NPISH (Non-profit institutions serving households) sector.

Table 5.1 Cross classification of Gross value added by industries and institutional sectors (ISIC Rev. 3) Total economy

Series 100: 1993 SNA, Netherlands Antillean guilder, Western calendar year **Data in millions**

	2001	2002	2003	2004	2005	2006	2007	2008	2009	2010	2011	2012
Series	**100**											
Industries												
Agriculture, hunting, forestry; fishing	49.8	39.4	36.7	37.3	42.9	36.7	38.6	42.7				
Mining and quarrying	...	...	...	...	...	...	...	...				
Manufacturing	346.8	325.0	309.0	323.8	283.9	366.9	356.3	435.9				
Electricity, gas and water supply	245.9	225.0	231.8	214.1	233.9	228.6	233.0	202.6				
Construction	274.8	281.8	278.2	262.5	337.6	309.4	337.4	394.7				
Wholesale and retail trade; repair of motor vehicles, motorcycles and personal and household goods; hotels and restaurants	893.1	842.3	852.6	869.8	938.5	1001.5	1007.9	1277.7				
Transport, storage and communications	497.2	540.8	561.3	495.4	521.1	581.1	570.8	729.5				
Financial intermediation; real estate renting and business activities	1546.5	1624.9	1704.4	1893.1	1976.2	1977.1	2234.5	2063.0				
Public administration and defence; compulsory social security	352.8	362.3	396.0	405.7	458.3	467.5	494.1	524.0				
Education; health and social work; other community, social and personal services	620.7	625.8	646.3	678.0	689.0	718.5	711.2	827.9				
Private households with employed persons	22.9	20.8	21.6	21.8	19.0	16.8	15.0	13.5				
VALUE ADDED GROSS, at basic prices [a]	4850.6	4888.2	5038.0	5201.5	5500.5	5704.1	5998.7	6511.5				

[a] Includes financial intermediation services indirectly measured (FISIM) of the Total Economy.

New Caledonia

Source

Reply to the United Nations national accounts questionnaire from the Institut de la Statistique et des Etudes Economiques (ISEE), Nouméa, Nouvelle-Calédonie.

General

The estimates shown in the tables below have been adjusted by the Institut de la Statistique et des Etudes Economiques (ISEE) Nouméa, Nouvelle-Calédonie in accordance with the United Nations System of National Accounts 1993 (1993 SNA), so far as the existing data would permit. When the scope and coverage differ for conceptual or statistical reasons from the definitions and classifications recommended in SNA, a footnote is indicated to the relevant tables.

Table 1.1 Gross domestic product by expenditures at current prices

Series 100: 1993 SNA, CFP franc, Western calendar year — **Data in millions**

	2001	2002	2003	2004	2005	2006	2007	2008	2009	2010	2011	2012
Series	**100**											
	Expenditures of the gross domestic product											
Final consumption expenditure	429925.0	450865.0	473093.0	497615.0	533351.0	572831.0	613092.0	658509.0				
Household final consumption expenditure	305614.0	316819.0	332089.0	352690.0	380406.0	407503.0	437020.0	474570.0				
NPISHs final consumption expenditure	...	...	...	...	...	...	...	...				
General government final consumption expenditure	124311.0	134046.0	141004.0	144925.0	152945.0	165328.0	176072.0	183939.0				
Gross capital formation	100704.0	115630.0	152602.0	150446.0	178604.0	224679.0	288551.0	303871.0				
Gross fixed capital formation	101387.0	116664.0	149647.0	142166.0	170219.0	231521.0	277146.0	303824.0				
Changes in inventories	-682.7	-1033.9	2954.2	8280.0	8385.0	-6842.0	11405.0	47.0				
Acquisitions less disposals of valuables	...	...	...	...	...	...	...	...				
Exports of goods and services	82203.3	85223.9	106884.0	124380.0	128460.0	158482.0	210308.0	136506.0				
Less: Imports of goods and services	173449.0	179722.0	214033.0	206913.0	242013.0	292695.0	343974.0	363172.0				
Equals: GROSS DOMESTIC PRODUCT	439383.0	471996.0	518545.0	565528.0	598402.0	663297.0	767977.0	735714.0				

Table 2.1 Value added by industries at current prices (ISIC Rev. 3)

Series 100: 1993 SNA, CFP franc, Western calendar year — **Data in millions**

	2001	2002	2003	2004	2005	2006	2007	2008	2009	2010	2011	2012
Series	**100**											
	Industries											
Agriculture, hunting, forestry; fishing	10370.3	8922.4	9040.6	10105.2	9267.0	11456.0	9769.0	10209.0				
Mining and quarrying	...	...	...	...	...	...	...	...				
Manufacturing [a]	44327.7	52686.1	68478.7	84865.9	88035.0	112374.0	167394.0	86399.0				
Electricity, gas and water supply	8351.4	8116.4	8331.9	9391.6	9789.0	10640.0	11405.0	10322.0				
Construction	38001.7	40722.5	44345.8	46495.7	48779.0	62137.0	65799.0	79343.0				

	2001	2002	2003	2004	2005	2006	2007	2008	2009	2010	2011	2012
Series	**100**											
Wholesale, retail trade, repair of motor vehicles, motorcycles and personal and households goods; hotels and restaurants	54015.2[b]	58334.5[b]	62141.1[b]	66120.4[b]	68392.0[b]	72592.0[b]	82131.0[b]	87655.0				
Wholesale, retail trade, repair of motor vehicles, motorcycles and personal and household goods	54015.2	58334.6	62141.1	66120.4	68392.0	72592.0	82131.0	87655.0[b]				
Hotels and restaurants	...	...	...	...	...	...	...	...				
Transport, storage and communications	29528.3	31667.7	35270.0	39517.2	41242.0	43036.0	48218.0	50374.0				
Financial intermediation; real estate, renting and business activities [c]	46003.9	48941.2	50359.4	56666.0	58213.0	65118.0	69578.0	77944.0				
Financial intermediation	20196.9	20238.9	17785.9	21155.4	21660.0	23664.0	25653.0	27774.0				
Real estate, renting and business activities	25807.0	28702.3	32573.5	35510.6	36553.0	41453.0	43925.0	50170.0				
Public administration and defence; compulsory social security	86629.8	92184.4	98448.7	99253.1	105893.0	114390.0	119937.0	124743.0				
Education; health and social work; other community, social and personal services [d]	90587.5	94137.3	101239.0	107644.0	121284.0	124098.0	138946.0	148466.0				
Private households with employed persons	...	...	...	...	...	...	...	...				
Equals: VALUE ADDED, GROSS, in basic prices	407816.0	435713.0	477656.0	520059.0	550893.0	615842.0	713176.0	675455.0				
Less: Financial intermediation services indirectly measured (FISIM)	15301.1	14422.3	15001.9	15876.0	16506.0	17740.0	18915.0	18857.0				
Plus: Taxes less Subsidies on products	46868.2	50706.0	55891.4	61345.1	64015.0	65194.0	73715.0	79116.0				
Plus: Taxes on products	47643.4	51515.4	56723.2	62172.6	65148.0	66294.0	75075.0	80549.0				
Less: Subsidies on products	775.2	809.4	831.8	827.5	1133.0	1099.0	1360.0	1433.0				
Equals: GROSS DOMESTIC PRODUCT	439383.0	471996.0	518545.0	565528.0	598402.0	663297.0	767977.0	735714.0				

[a] Includes Mining and quarrying.
[b] Excludes Hotels and restaurants.
[c] Excludes Real estate.
[d] Includes hotels and restaurants, real estate, and private households with employed persons.

Table 2.3 Output, gross value added, and fixed assets by industries at current prices (ISIC Rev. 3) Total Economy

Series 100: 1993 SNA, CFP franc, Western calendar year

Data in millions

	2001	2002	2003	2004	2005	2006	2007	2008	2009	2010	2011	2012
Series	**100**											
Output, at basic prices	732644.8	784982.4	839651.9	919488.4	1001141.0	1134157.0	1308693.0	1332468.0				
Less: Intermediate consumption, at purchaser's prices	324828.9	349269.7	361996.5	399429.6	450248.0	518315.0	595516.0	657013.0				
Equals: VALUE ADDED, GROSS, at basic prices	407816.0	435713.0	477656.0	520059.0	550893.0	615842.0	713176.0	675455.0				
Compensation of employees	...	...	...	...	...	...	...	...				
Taxes on production and imports, less Subsidies	...	...	...	...	...	...	...	...				
OPERATING SURPLUS, GROSS	...	...	...	...	...	...	...	...				
MIXED INCOME, GROSS	...	...	...	...	...	...	...	...				
Total Economy only: Adjustment for FISIM (if FISIM is not distributed to uses)	15301.1	14422.3	15001.9	15876.0	16506.0	17740.0	18915.0	18857.0				
Gross capital formation	100704.0	115630.0	152602.0	150446.0	178604.0	224679.0	288551.0	303871.0				

	2001	2002	2003	2004	2005	2006	2007	2008	2009	2010	2011	2012
Series	**100**											
Gross fixed capital formation	101387.0	116664.0	149647.0	142166.0	170219.0	231521.0	277146.0	303824.0				
Changes in inventories	-682.7	-1033.9	2954.2	8280.0	8385.0	-6842.0	11405.0	47.0				
Acquisitions less disposals of valuables	...	...	...	...	...	...	...	...				

Table 2.3 Output, gross value added, and fixed assets by industries at current prices (ISIC Rev. 3) Agriculture, hunting, forestry; fishing (A+B)

Series 100: 1993 SNA, CFP franc, Western calendar year — **Data in millions**

	2001	2002	2003	2004	2005	2006	2007	2008	2009	2010	2011	2012
Series	**100**											
Output, at basic prices	17863.3	17750.9	18663.1	20443.2	19861.0	23813.0	22943.0	23332.0				
Less: Intermediate consumption, at purchaser's prices	7492.9	8828.5	9622.5	10338.0	10594.0	12357.0	13174.0	13123.0				
Equals: VALUE ADDED, GROSS, at basic prices	10370.4	8922.4	9040.6	10105.2	9267.0	11456.0	9769.0	10209.0				
Compensation of employees	...	...	...	...	...	...	...	...				
Taxes on production and imports, less Subsidies	...	...	...	...	...	...	...	...				
OPERATING SURPLUS, GROSS	...	...	...	...	...	...	...	...				
MIXED INCOME, GROSS	...	...	...	...	...	...	...	...				
Gross capital formation	...	...	...	...	...	...	...	...				

Table 2.3 Output, gross value added, and fixed assets by industries at current prices (ISIC Rev. 3) Manufacturing (D)

Series 100: 1993 SNA, CFP franc, Western calendar year — **Data in millions**

	2001	2002	2003	2004	2005	2006	2007	2008	2009	2010	2011	2012
Series	**100**											
Output, at basic prices [a]	132332.0	142018.0	162858.0	193523.0	212765.0	263193.0	352929.0	252545.0				
Less: Intermediate consumption, at purchaser's prices [a]	88004.2	89332.0	94379.4	108657.0	124730.0	150819.0	185535.0	166146.0				
Equals: VALUE ADDED, GROSS, at basic prices [a]	44327.8	52686.0	68478.6	84865.9	88035.0	112374.0	167394.0	86399.0				
Compensation of employees	...	...	...	...	...	...	...	...				
Taxes on production and imports, less Subsidies	...	...	...	...	...	...	...	...				
OPERATING SURPLUS, GROSS	...	...	...	...	...	...	...	...				
MIXED INCOME, GROSS	...	...	...	...	...	...	...	...				
Gross capital formation	...	...	...	...	...	...	...	...				

[a] Includes Mining and quarrying.

Table 2.3 Output, gross value added, and fixed assets by industries at current prices (ISIC Rev. 3) Electricity, gas and water supply (E)

Series 100: 1993 SNA, CFP franc, Western calendar year **Data in millions**

	2001	2002	2003	2004	2005	2006	2007	2008	2009	2010	2011	2012
Series	**100**											
Output, at basic prices	29140.8	31027.4	31750.8	32307.3	37181.0	42327.0	44308.0	49627.0				
Less: Intermediate consumption, at purchaser's prices	20789.4	22911.0	23418.9	22915.7	27392.0	31686.0	32903.0	39305.0				
Equals: VALUE ADDED, GROSS, at basic prices	8351.4	8116.4	8331.9	9391.6	9789.0	10640.0	11405.0	10322.0				
Compensation of employees	...	...	...	...	...	...	...	...				
Taxes on production and imports, less Subsidies	...	...	...	...	...	...	...	...				
OPERATING SURPLUS, GROSS	...	...	...	...	...	...	...	...				
MIXED INCOME, GROSS	...	...	...	...	...	...	...	...				
Gross capital formation	...	...	...	...	...	...	...	...				

Table 2.3 Output, gross value added, and fixed assets by industries at current prices (ISIC Rev. 3) Construction (F)

Series 100: 1993 SNA, CFP franc, Western calendar year **Data in millions**

	2001	2002	2003	2004	2005	2006	2007	2008	2009	2010	2011	2012
Series	**100**											
Output, at basic prices	90193.0	96774.2	103181.0	110621.0	127811.0	152892.0	171143.0	216903.0				
Less: Intermediate consumption, at purchaser's prices	52191.2	56051.6	58835.3	64125.2	79032.0	90755.0	105343.0	137560.0				
Equals: VALUE ADDED, GROSS, at basic prices	38001.8	40722.6	44345.8	46495.7	48779.0	62137.0	65799.0	79343.0				
Compensation of employees	...	...	...	...	...	...	...	...				
Taxes on production and imports, less Subsidies	...	...	...	...	...	...	...	...				
OPERATING SURPLUS, GROSS	...	...	...	...	...	...	...	...				
MIXED INCOME, GROSS	...	...	...	...	...	...	...	...				
Gross capital formation	...	...	...	...	...	...	...	...				

Table 2.3 Output, gross value added, and fixed assets by industries at current prices (ISIC Rev. 3) Wholesale retail trade, repair of motor vehicles, motorcycles, etc.; hotels and restaurants (G+H)

Series 100: 1993 SNA, CFP franc, Western calendar year **Data in millions**

	2001	2002	2003	2004	2005	2006	2007	2008	2009	2010	2011	2012
Series	**100**											
Output, at basic prices [a]	89128.4	94550.8	99294.4	106387.0	112212.0	118289.0	135708.0	142203.0				
Less: Intermediate consumption, at purchaser's prices [a]	35113.2	36216.3	37153.3	40266.7	43820.0	45698.0	53577.0	54548.0				
Equals: VALUE ADDED, GROSS, at basic prices [a]	54015.2	58334.5	62141.1	66120.4	68392.0	72592.0	82131.0	87655.0				
Compensation of employees	...	...	...	...	...	...	...	...				

	2001	2002	2003	2004	2005	2006	2007	2008	2009	2010	2011	2012
Series	**100**											
Taxes on production and imports, less Subsidies	...	...	...	...	...	...	...	...				
OPERATING SURPLUS, GROSS	...	...	...	...	...	...	...	...				
MIXED INCOME, GROSS	...	...	...	...	...	...	...	...				
Gross capital formation	...	...	...	...	...	...	...	...				

[a] Excludes Hotels and restaurants.

Table 2.3 Output, gross value added, and fixed assets by industries at current prices (ISIC Rev. 3) Transport, storage and communications (I)

Series 100: 1993 SNA, CFP franc, Western calendar year

Data in millions

	2001	2002	2003	2004	2005	2006	2007	2008	2009	2010	2011	2012
Series	**100**											
Output, at basic prices	58000.4	62452.2	67382.6	75362.5	80856.0	85011.0	92183.0	102707.0				
Less: Intermediate consumption, at purchaser's prices	28472.2	30784.5	32112.6	35845.3	39613.0	41975.0	43965.0	52333.0				
Equals: VALUE ADDED, GROSS, at basic prices	29528.2	31667.7	35270.0	39517.2	41242.0	43036.0	48218.0	50374.0				
Compensation of employees	...	...	...	...	...	...	...	...				
Taxes on production and imports, less Subsidies	...	...	...	...	...	...	...	...				
OPERATING SURPLUS, GROSS	...	...	...	...	...	...	...	...				
MIXED INCOME, GROSS	...	...	...	...	...	...	...	...				
Gross capital formation	...	...	...	...	...	...	...	...				

Table 2.3 Output, gross value added, and fixed assets by industries at current prices (ISIC Rev. 3) Financial intermediation; real estate, renting and business activities (J+K)

Series 100: 1993 SNA, CFP franc, Western calendar year

Data in millions

		2001	2002	2003	2004	2005	2006	2007	2008	2009	2010	2011	2012
Series		**100**											
Output, at basic prices	a	67665.6	81470.3	81607.0	85787.9	89608.0	104627.0	116680.0	137482.0				
Less: Intermediate consumption, at purchaser's prices	a	21661.7	32529.0	31247.5	29121.9	31395.0	39509.0	47102.0	59538.0				
Equals: VALUE ADDED, GROSS, at basic prices	a	46003.9	48941.3	50359.5	56666.0	58213.0	65118.0	69578.0	77944.0				
Compensation of employees		...	...	...	...	...	...	...	...				
Taxes on production and imports, less Subsidies		...	...	...	...	...	...	...	...				
OPERATING SURPLUS, GROSS		...	...	...	...	...	...	...	...				
MIXED INCOME, GROSS		...	...	...	...	...	...	...	...				
Gross capital formation		...	...	...	...	...	...	...	...				

[a] Excludes Real estate.

Table 2.3 Output, gross value added, and fixed assets by industries at current prices (ISIC Rev. 3) Public administration and defense; compulsory social security (L)

Series 100: 1993 SNA, CFP franc, Western calendar year **Data in millions**

	2001	2002	2003	2004	2005	2006	2007	2008	2009	2010	2011	2012
Series	**100**											
Output, at basic prices	107671.0	115845.0	122525.0	125371.0	132096.0	142289.0	151544.0	158525.0				
Less: Intermediate consumption, at purchaser's prices	21041.5	23661.0	24076.0	26118.2	26203.0	27898.0	31607.0	33782.0				
Equals: VALUE ADDED, GROSS, at basic prices	86629.8	92184.3	98448.7	99253.1	105893.0	114390.0	119937.0	124743.0				
Compensation of employees	...	...	...	...	...	...	...	...				
Taxes on production and imports, less Subsidies	...	...	...	...	...	...	...	...				
OPERATING SURPLUS, GROSS	...	...	...	...	...	...	...	...				
MIXED INCOME, GROSS	...	...	...	...	...	...	...	...				
Gross capital formation	...	...	...	...	...	...	...	...				

Table 2.3 Output, gross value added, and fixed assets by industries at current prices (ISIC Rev. 3) Education; health and social work; other community, social and personal services (M+N+O)

Series 100: 1993 SNA, CFP franc, Western calendar year **Data in millions**

	2001	2002	2003	2004	2005	2006	2007	2008	2009	2010	2011	2012
Series	**100**											
Output, at basic prices [a]	140650.0	143094.0	152390.0	169685.0	188751.0	201716.0	221255.0	249144.0				
Less: Intermediate consumption, at purchaser's prices [a]	50062.6	48956.3	51150.9	62041.2	67467.0	77617.0	82310.0	100678.0				
Equals: VALUE ADDED, GROSS, at basic prices [a]	90587.5	94137.4	101239.0	107644.0	121284.0	124098.0	138946.0	148466.0				
Compensation of employees	...	...	...	...	...	...	...	...				
Taxes on production and imports, less Subsidies	...	...	...	...	...	...	...	...				
OPERATING SURPLUS, GROSS	...	...	...	...	...	...	...	...				
MIXED INCOME, GROSS	...	...	...	...	...	...	...	...				
Gross capital formation	...	...	...	...	...	...	...	...				

[a] Includes hotels and restaurants, real estate, and private households with employed persons.

New Zealand

Source

New Zealand's national accounts statistics are prepared annually by the National Accounts business unit of Statistics New Zealand, the National Statistical Office, located in Wellington. The official estimates are published on the internet (www.stats.govt.nz), and featured in publications including Hot Off the Press Bulletins, QuickStats and the Statistical Yearbook. The data provided to UNSD is received through the Organization for Economic Co-operation and Development (OECD), Paris.

General

The latest estimates shown in the following tables have been prepared in accordance with the concepts and definitions of the System of National Accounts 1993 (SNA93). Data is disseminated in New Zealand dollars with industry statistics classified according to the Australian and New Zealand Standard Industrial Classification 1996 (ANZSIC96). The fiscal year utilized is 1 April–31 March with the base year for constant price estimates being 1995-96.

The annual production and expenditure GDP accounts are released twice annually. The release includes the provisional accounts for the latest March year and the revisions to earlier years. The industry analysis of GDP (the production accounts), on which the constant price industry value added series are based, are normally available up to year n-3.

Revisions to the previously published series may be made each quarter. The frequency and cause of these revisions are as follows:

• Quarterly: additional data becoming available for the latest quarters, which is used to replace existing estimates; revisions to quarterly data (e.g. revisions to the Balance of Payments or Retail Trade Survey), which will be incorporated as soon as possible to maintain consistency between published macro-economic statistics.

• Annual: introduction of annual data following the release of the latest annual national accounts each year; annual updating of the weights used to combine component series to totals and subsequent chaining.

• Irregular: for example methodological changes. However, note that revisions of this nature are, as far as possible, incorporated to coincide with the annual cycle of revisions outlined above.

In addition, each of the above causes for revision, and/or the addition of a new point in the actual quarterly series, has the potential to alter seasonal factors and therefore may lead to a revision in the seasonally adjusted series.

Methodology:

Overview of GDP Compilation

In the New Zealand System of National Accounts, the items making up GDP and expenditure on GDP are estimated independently using diverse data sources. Annual supply-use analyses (for the years 1987 to n-3) result in balanced GDP and expenditure accounts which are published as final estimates. The results for the most recent 2 years are published as provisional estimates at the total economy level. The income and expenditure measures of GDP are used in the calculation of provisional estimates.

Expenditure Approach

The expenditure-based measure of GDP is obtained by summing the components of final demand comprising:

• Government final consumption expenditure – estimates are derived from production accounts compiled mostly from data obtained through the Central Government Financial System (CFIS) and the Local Authority Survey.

• Household consumption expenditure of goods and services – predominantly obtained from quarterly Retail Trade Surveys and the Household Economic Survey. Expenditure overseas by New Zealand resident households and expenditure in New Zealand by foreign tourists is obtained from Balance of Payments (BoP) statistics.

• Gross fixed capital formation by industry – estimates are derived by reconciling supply-side economy-wide totals by asset type and demand-side industry estimates. The Annual Enterprise Survey (AES) is the key data source used to compile industry statistics, supplemented with data from annual reports, central and local government surveys and the Agriculture Production Survey. For residential and non-residential building investment, the all-sector totals are derived using work put in place from the quarterly Building Activity Survey. In terms of transport equipment, some of the components are valued as the number of new vehicle registrations multiplied by an average price, with the remainder calculated as the value of imports plus domestic production. The plant, machinery and equipment all-sector total is calculated as the value of imports plus domestic production.

• Changes in inventories – estimates are based mostly on quarterly wholesale and retail trade stock surveys. Other sources used include the Agriculture Production Survey, statistics from the Ministry of Agriculture and Forestry (MAF), and the AES.

• Exports and imports of goods and services – estimates are based on overseas trade data and BoP statistics.

Income Approach

The income-based measure of GDP represents the income earned from production in New Zealand, whether that is carried out by New Zealanders or foreign firms operating in New Zealand. This is comprised of:

• Compensation of employees – estimates are obtained from labour market statistics, tax data, AES results, annual report analysis, central and local government surveys.

• Operating surplus – derived as a residual item. Taxes on production and imports, and subsidies are obtained from CFIS.

• Consumption of fixed capital at replacement cost – estimates are obtained from the capital stock perpetual inventory method.

Production Approach

The production-based measure of GDP is calculated as the total market value of goods and services produced in New Zealand after deducting the cost of goods and services utilised in this process, but before the deduction of consumption of fixed capital allowances.

Most industry production accounts are compiled from income and expenditure data sourced from the AES. These may be supplemented by data derived from other sources including annual reports, the Quarterly Manufacturing Survey, the Quarterly Employment Survey, the Labour Cost Index and the Producers Price Index. There are some exceptions:

• Agriculture value added - obtained by deducting the cost of inputs from the gross value of production. Output is calculated as the sum of sales and stock change by product. Volumes data is derived from a number of sources including the Agriculture Production survey, livestock slaughter statistics and annual reports, whilst prices data is collected from organizations including MAF and Meat and Wool New Zealand.

• Government value added – compiled from data obtained through the CFIS and the Local Authority Survey.

• Industry value added – industry value added for the following is calculated using a number of sources other than AES: water supply, owner builders, superannuation operation, residential and commercial property operators and developers, owner-occupied dwellings, private households employing staff and religious organizations.

For constant prices estimates, the industry 'elemental series' that make up the production-based GDP, in most cases, are calculated by extrapolating value added, using indicator series that represent the quantities of output produced. Double deflation is not widely used with the only exceptions being for the agriculture and electricity industries on a quarterly basis, and for water transport and business services on an annual basis.

The chain-volume measures of GDP and expenditure on GDP are constructed by:

• compiling a Laspeyres volume index of the component in question, using the previous year's prices as weights; and then

• chaining the sequence of annual movements to produce a continuous time series.

This procedure is used at different levels within the accounts. For example, GDP is compiled by weighting together the individual industry value-added components to produce a Laspeyres volume index for each quarter, and then linking the resulting indexes to produce the GDP time series. Each industry component, such as transport and communication, is also a chained-volume series. At this lowest level, the 'elemental series' are not chained and are either single series in their own right or fixed-weight series comprising a number of components.

Table 1.1 Gross domestic product by expenditures at current prices

Series 200: 1993 SNA, New Zealand dollar, Fiscal year beginning 1 April — **Data in millions**

	2001	2002	2003	2004	2005	2006	2007	2008	2009	2010	2011	2012
Series	**200**											
	Expenditures of the gross domestic product											
Final consumption expenditure	96283.3	102101.1	109506.6	117036.3	125431.4	133265.8	141504.9	147181.3	151314.5	157432.6	165042.6	
Household final consumption expenditure	72610.7	77552.7	83067.5	88331.3	94365.8	99691.3	104840.6	106985.0	109984.7	114533.3	120303.2	
NPISHs final consumption expenditure	1764.3	1763.9	1810.1	1945.8	1989.6	2090.8	2352.6	2767.8	2893.1	3037.7	3189.6	
General government final consumption expenditure	21908.2	22784.6	24628.9	26759.2	29076.0	31483.7	34311.7	37428.4	38436.8	39861.5	41549.8	
Individual consumption expenditure	12924.1	13644.0	14709.7	16041.1	17535.0	18632.7	20403.0	22597.4	23583.4	24231.5	24204.3	
Collective consumption expenditure	8984.1	9140.6	9919.3	10718.1	11541.0	12851.0	13908.7	14831.1	14853.3	15630.0	17344.5	
Gross capital formation	27921.0	29130.9	32949.8	37004.1	39661.7	38863.3	44026.1	40564.3	35349.3	38055.5	39133.8	
Gross fixed capital formation	26034.8	28037.2	31690.5	35359.7	38561.4	39128.0	42415.0	40513.5	36246.1	37018.7	37280.7	
Changes in inventories	1886.2	1093.6	1259.3	1644.4	1100.4	-264.7	1611.1	50.9	-896.8	1036.8	1853.1	
Acquisitions less disposals of valuables	...	...	...	...	...	...	...	...	...	...	...	
Exports of goods and services	43967.4	42886.8	41033.4	43784.7	44215.6	48667.1	52176.0	58247.5	53770.4	59331.1	62521.4	
Exports of goods	32867.0	30648.3	29053.8	31113.9	31582.0	35635.8	38721.1	44255.2	40103.4	45599.8	48357.7	
Exports of services	11100.4	12238.5	11979.6	12670.8	12633.6	13031.3	13454.8	13992.3	13667.0	13731.3	14163.7	
Less: Imports of goods and services	40890.1	40212.5	40351.4	44636.7	47663.9	50927.4	53710.0	60438.4	50716.3	56317.9	60633.0	
Imports of goods	30533.2	29981.5	30245.7	33343.6	35685.4	38464.1	40596.3	45767.8	37471.1	42092.9	45634.4	
Imports of services	10357.0	10231.0	10105.7	11293.1	11978.4	12463.3	13113.6	14670.7	13245.2	14225.0	14998.5	
Plus: Statistical discrepancy	-0.0	0.4	0.3	0.0	-0.0	-0.0	0.0	-0.1	-0.0	588.0	487.9	
Equals: GROSS DOMESTIC PRODUCT	127281.6	133906.7	143138.7	153188.4	161644.9	169868.8	183997.0	185554.6	189718.0	199089.2	206552.7	

Table 1.2 Gross domestic product by expenditures at constant prices

Series 200: 1993 SNA, New Zealand dollar, Fiscal year beginning 1 April — **Data in millions**

	2001	2002	2003	2004	2005	2006	2007	2008	2009	2010	2011	2012
Series	**200**											
Base year	**1995**											
	Expenditures of the gross domestic product											
Final consumption expenditure	86683.7	90120.0	95697.4	100186.4	104893.7	107968.2	112056.5	111914.0	112443.0	114556.8	117204.7	
Household final consumption expenditure	65709.5	68968.6	73525.9	76927.7	80568.0	82889.6	85676.1	84043.0	84376.4	86033.0	88081.8	
NPISHs final consumption expenditure	1666.6	1721.2	1770.7	1909.8	1962.0	1913.5	2062.1	2297.2	2453.1	2565.3	2717.9	
General government final consumption expenditure	19316.4	19455.5	20432.1	21387.3	22399.0	23174.3	24302.4	25400.3	25456.9	25823.1	26296.5	
Gross capital formation	26136.0	27984.0	31610.0	34602.0	36194.0	33372.0	37382.0	34148.0	28997.0	30445.0	32524.0	
Gross fixed capital formation	24826.0	26816.0	30318.0	32882.0	35030.0	34050.0	36484.0	33561.0	29649.0	30535.0	31238.0	
Changes in inventories	1266.7	1164.1	1363.9	1785.8	1143.4	-344.9	1257.5	583.4	-1023.9	649.7	1387.1	
Acquisitions less disposals of valuables	...	...	...	...	...	...	...	...	...	...	...	
Exports of goods and services	36017.6	38891.2	39254.5	41117.7	41061.1	42389.4	43905.4	42729.5	44845.3	46063.1	47239.0	
Less: Imports of goods and services	33676.8	36080.4	40639.2	45650.4	47668.7	46998.5	51994.0	49982.8	45477.1	50674.9	53742.4	
Equals: GROSS DOMESTIC PRODUCT [a]	114980.8	120726.9	125628.1	130229.0	134616.1	136837.6	141657.5	139162.7	141249.8	141464.2	144556.5	

[a] Chain-linked volume measures are presented in this table, thus discrepancies between components and total may exist.

Table 1.3 Relations among product, income, savings, and net lending aggregates

Series 100: 1993 SNA, New Zealand dollar, Fiscal year beginning 1 April — **Data in millions**

	2001	2002	2003	2004	2005	2006	2007	2008	2009	2010	2011	2012
Series	**100**											
GROSS DOMESTIC PRODUCT	126324.1	132819.8	142024.3	152037.9	160573.5	168663.3	182260.5	185561.1	187802.1	...		
Plus: Compensation of employees - from and to the rest of the world, net	...	...	...	...	...	...	...	...	...	...		
Plus: Property income - from and to the rest of the world, net	...	...	...	...	...	...	...	...	...	...		
Sum of Compensation of employees and property income - from and to the rest of the world, net	-6587.3	-6747.2	-6874.5	-8639.3	-10501.2	-11615.9	-13544.0	-13176.3	-7773.4	...		
Plus: Sum of Compensation of employees and property income - from the rest of the world	4078.7	4710.8	4956.5	5559.7	5109.8	6140.1	6929.0	5538.8	4847.6	...		
Less: Sum of Compensation of employees and property income - to the rest of the world	10666.0	11458.0	11831.0	14199.0	15611.0	17756.0	20473.0	18715.0	12621.0	...		
Plus: Taxes less subsidies on production and imports - from and to the rest of the world, net	...	...	...	...	...	...	...	...	...	...		
Equals: GROSS NATIONAL INCOME	119737.4	126072.7	135148.5	143399.1	150072.0	157047.4	168716.6	172384.9	180028.7	...		
Plus: Current transfers - from and to the rest of the world, net	240.8	124.3	242.0	304.7	140.9	643.7	698.6	853.3	581.1	...		
Plus: Current transfers - from the rest of the world	1331.8	1376.2	1431.1	1555.6	1665.0	1957.1	2094.1	2336.7	2002.9	...		
Less: Current transfers - to the rest of the world	1091.1	1252.0	1189.1	1250.9	1524.1	1313.3	1395.5	1483.4	1421.8	...		
Equals: GROSS NATIONAL DISPOSABLE INCOME	119978.2	126196.9	135390.6	143703.7	150212.9	157691.2	169415.2	173238.2	180609.7	...		

	2001	2002	2003	2004	2005	2006	2007	2008	2009	2010	2011	2012
Series	**100**											
Less: Final consumption expenditure / Actual final consumption	95464.9	101194.2	108572.7	116041.8	124474.1	131995.2	139972.3	145867.8	149046.4	...		
Equals: SAVING, GROSS	24513.3	25002.8	26817.9	27661.9	25738.9	25696.0	29442.9[a]	27370.4[a]	31563.3[a]	...		
Plus: Capital transfers - from and to the rest of the world, net	1508.2	1538.1	726.3	102.4	-325.0	-456.8	-760.0	-717.8	-345.4	...		
Plus: Capital transfers - from the rest of the world	2277.6	2337.1	1773.6	1346.7	997.1	957.2	912.3	887.9	1038.0	...		
Less: Capital transfers - to the rest of the world	769.4	799.0	1047.3	1244.3	1322.1	1414.0	1672.3	1605.6	1383.4	...		
Less: Gross capital formation	27921.0	29130.9	32949.8	37004.1	39661.7	39045.4	43487.0	41511.0	35521.0	...		
Less: Acquisitions less disposals of non-produced non-financial assets	-7.4	-46.7	3.4	-5.7	1.8	0.9	-1.7	-1122.1	-7.9	...		
Equals: NET LENDING (+) / NET BORROWING (-) OF THE NATION	-1892.1	-2543.3	-5409.4	-9234.1	-14249.6	-13807.0	-15142.5	-14319.1	-4795.6	...		
	Net values: Gross National Income / Gross National Disposable Income / Saving Gross less Consumption of fixed capital											
Less: Consumption of fixed capital	17255.4	17900.1	18914.7	20240.2	21881.2	23611.1	25383.8	27363.2	28390.6	29458.0		
Equals: NET NATIONAL INCOME	102482.0	108172.6	116233.8	123158.9	128190.8	133436.4	143332.8	145021.7	151638.0	159233.0		
Equals: NET NATIONAL DISPOSABLE INCOME	102722.8	108296.9	116475.8	123463.6	128331.8	134080.1	144031.4	145875.0	152219.1	...		
Equals: SAVING, NET	7258.0	7102.7	7903.2	7421.8	3857.7	2084.9	4059.1	7.2	3172.7	...		

[a] Discrepancy between components and total as one or more components have not been revised.

Table 2.4 Value added by industries at current prices (ISIC Rev. 4)

Series 200: 1993 SNA, New Zealand dollar, Fiscal year beginning 1 April — **Data in millions**

	2001	2002	2003	2004	2005	2006	2007	2008	2009	2010	2011	2012
Series	**200**											
	Industries											
Agriculture, forestry and fishing	10283.9	7924.6	8297.0	8321.1	7394.1	8590.0	11576.1	9019.5	11550.1	...	...	
Manufacturing, mining and quarrying and other industrial activities	24004.2	25938.2	26530.4	28238.4	30128.3	30037.7	31949.6	34093.1	31978.9	...	...	
Manufacturing	19274.8	20741.3	20962.6	22304.9	23457.4	22998.1	22651.9	23938.8	21734.9	...	...	
Construction	5494.7	6065.3	6825.6	8035.7	8732.2	9645.9	10692.8	10396.7	10380.7	...	...	
Wholesale and retail trade, transportation and storage, accommodation and food service activities	21636.7	22820.9	24683.2	26030.8	27083.1	27703.2	29674.1	28458.5	29122.3	...	...	
Information and communication	4988.9	5452.1	5750.7	5880.8	6030.6	5785.5	6151.2	5668.6	5705.7	...	...	
Financial and insurance activities	5751.0	6218.3	6921.7	7335.8	7490.1	7759.6	8201.4	9276.6	11059.7	...	...	
Real estate activities	15911.4	17105.2	18534.3	20020.3	21718.9	22714.6	23315.4	23293.9	22519.9	...	...	
Professional, scientific, technical, administrative and support service activities	10337.5	11227.2	11989.9	12939.5	14075.8	15283.0	16623.8	17283.6	17495.7	...	...	
Public administration and defence, education, human health and social work activities	15643.0	16667.0	18043.3	19713.0	21443.4	23259.4	25361.8	27621.5	29073.0	...	...	
Other service activities	4490.5	4895.1	5272.1	5530.6	5709.3	5837.0	6281.9	6386.5	6533.0	...	...	
Equals: VALUE ADDED, GROSS, at basic prices	118541.9	124313.9	132848.2	142046.0	149805.9	156616.0	169828.0	171498.4	175419.0	...	...	
Less: Financial intermediation services indirectly measured (FISIM)	...	...	...	...	...	...	...	...	...	...	...	

	2001	2002	2003	2004	2005	2006	2007	2008	2009	2010	2011	2012
Series	**200**											
Plus: Taxes less Subsidies on products	8739.7	9592.8	10290.5	11142.4	11839.0	13252.9	14169.0	14056.2	14298.9	...	...	
Equals: GROSS DOMESTIC PRODUCT	127281.6	133906.7	143138.7	153188.4	161644.9	169868.8	183997.0	185554.6	189718.0	199089.2	206552.7	

Table 2.5 Value added by industries at constant prices (ISIC Rev. 4)

Series 100: 1993 SNA, New Zealand dollar, Fiscal year beginning 1 April — **Data in millions**

	2001	2002	2003	2004	2005	2006	2007	2008	2009	2010	2011	2012
Series	**100**											
Base year	**1995**											
	Industries											
Equals: VALUE ADDED, GROSS, at basic prices	108093.4	113292.0	117936.8	122508.9	126702.4	127773.7	131863.2	130382.3	129911.8			
Less: Financial intermediation services indirectly measured (FISIM)	...	...	...	...	...	...	...	...	...			
Plus: Taxes less Subsidies on products	...	...	...	...	...	...	...	...	...			
Equals: GROSS DOMESTIC PRODUCT [a]	111920.6	117419.1	122521.1	127125.2	131323.7	132335.3	136278.4	134178.5	133546.9			

[a] Discrepancy with equivalent item in Table 1.2 (Gross domestic product by expenditures at constant prices).

Table 2.6 Output, gross value added and fixed assets by industries at current prices (ISIC Rev. 4) Total economy

Series 200: 1993 SNA, New Zealand dollar, Fiscal year beginning 1 April — **Data in millions**

	2001	2002	2003	2004	2005	2006	2007	2008	2009	2010	2011	2012
Series	**200**											
Output, at basic prices	...	...	...	...	...	...	...	...	...	...	...	
Less: Intermediate consumption, at purchaser's prices	...	...	...	...	...	...	...	...	...	...	...	
Equals: VALUE ADDED, GROSS, at basic prices	118541.9	124313.9	132848.2	142046.0	149805.9	156616.0	169828.0	171498.4	175419.0	...	...	
Compensation of employees	51736.8	55146.6	59382.0	64348.0	69682.3	74431.1	80619.1	84848.1	85388.2	...	...	
Taxes on production and imports, less Subsidies	6314.4	6838.8	7200.1	7564.8	7963.8	7782.5	7985.0	8004.9	8660.2	...	...	
OPERATING SURPLUS, GROSS	60490.7	62328.5	66266.1	70133.2	72159.8	74402.4	81223.9	78645.4	81370.7	85939.0	87410.0	
MIXED INCOME, GROSS	...	...	...	...	...	...	...	...	...	...	...	
Gross capital formation	27921.0	29130.9	32949.8	37004.1	39661.7	38863.3	44026.1	40564.3	35349.3	38055.5	39133.8	
Gross fixed capital formation	26034.8	28037.2	31690.5	35359.7	38561.4	39128.0	42415.0	40513.5	36246.1	37018.7	37280.7	
Changes in inventories	1886.2	1093.6	1259.3	1644.4	1100.4	-264.7	1611.1	50.9	-896.8	1036.8	1853.1	
Acquisitions less disposals of valuables	...	...	...	...	...	...	...	...	...	...	...	

Table 2.6 Output, gross value added and fixed assets by industries at current prices (ISIC Rev. 4) Agriculture, forestry and fishing (A)

Series 200: 1993 SNA, New Zealand dollar, Fiscal year beginning 1 April — **Data in millions**

	2001	2002	2003	2004	2005	2006	2007	2008	2009	2010	2011	2012
Series	**200**											
Equals: VALUE ADDED, GROSS, at basic prices	10283.9	7924.6	8297.0	8321.1	7394.1	8590.0	11576.1	9019.5	11550.1			
Compensation of employees	1966.4	2122.8	2225.5	2308.1	2304.8	2392.5	2694.0	2804.6	2931.6			

Table 2.6 Output, gross value added and fixed assets by industries at current prices (ISIC Rev. 4) Manufacturing, mining and quarrying and other industrial activities (B+C+D+E)

Series 200: 1993 SNA, New Zealand dollar, Fiscal year beginning 1 April — **Data in millions**

	2001	2002	2003	2004	2005	2006	2007	2008	2009	2010	2011	2012
Series	**200**											
Equals: VALUE ADDED, GROSS, at basic prices	24004.2	25938.2	26530.4	28238.4	30128.3	30037.7	31949.6	34093.1	31978.9			
Compensation of employees	9934.9	10563.1	11198.7	12004.2	12602.1	12832.3	13532.7	14040.1	13792.1			

Table 2.6 Output, gross value added and fixed assets by industries at current prices (ISIC Rev. 4) Manufacturing (C)

Series 200: 1993 SNA, New Zealand dollar, Fiscal year beginning 1 April — **Data in millions**

	2001	2002	2003	2004	2005	2006	2007	2008	2009	2010	2011	2012
Series	**200**											
Equals: VALUE ADDED, GROSS, at basic prices	19274.8	20741.3	20962.6	22304.9	23457.4	22998.1	22651.9	23938.8	21734.9			
Compensation of employees	9168.0	9732.0	10312.0	10992.0	11445.0	11598.0	12078.0	12418.0	12101.0			

Table 2.6 Output, gross value added and fixed assets by industries at current prices (ISIC Rev. 4) Construction (F)

Series 200: 1993 SNA, New Zealand dollar, Fiscal year beginning 1 April — **Data in millions**

	2001	2002	2003	2004	2005	2006	2007	2008	2009	2010	2011	2012
Series	**200**											
Equals: VALUE ADDED, GROSS, at basic prices	5494.7	6065.3	6825.6	8035.7	8732.2	9645.9	10692.8	10396.7	10380.7			
Compensation of employees	2716.8	3017.0	3422.8	4023.6	4697.2	5303.4	5908.0	6090.4	5841.3			

Table 2.6 Output, gross value added and fixed assets by industries at current prices (ISIC Rev. 4) Wholesale and retail trade, transportation and storage, accommodation and food service activities (G+H+I)

Series 200: 1993 SNA, New Zealand dollar, Fiscal year beginning 1 April — **Data in millions**

	2001	2002	2003	2004	2005	2006	2007	2008	2009	2010	2011	2012
Series	**200**											
Equals: VALUE ADDED, GROSS, at basic prices	21636.7	22820.9	24683.2	26030.8	27083.1	27703.2	29674.1	28458.5	29122.3			
Compensation of employees	11220.0	11838.2	12844.0	13749.3	14763.0	15817.7	17025.2	17571.5	17292.0			

Table 2.6 Output, gross value added and fixed assets by industries at current prices (ISIC Rev. 4) Information and communication (J)

Series 200: 1993 SNA, New Zealand dollar, Fiscal year beginning 1 April — **Data in millions**

	2001	2002	2003	2004	2005	2006	2007	2008	2009	2010	2011	2012
Series	**200**											
Equals: VALUE ADDED, GROSS, at basic prices	4988.9	5452.1	5750.7	5880.8	6030.6	5785.5	6151.2	5668.6	5705.7			
Compensation of employees	1823.4	1809.8	1898.9	2092.2	2157.1	2057.3	2217.6	2360.2	2388.4			

Table 2.6 Output, gross value added and fixed assets by industries at current prices (ISIC Rev. 4) Financial and insurance activities (K)

Series 200: 1993 SNA, New Zealand dollar, Fiscal year beginning 1 April — **Data in millions**

	2001	2002	2003	2004	2005	2006	2007	2008	2009	2010	2011	2012
Series	**200**											
Equals: VALUE ADDED, GROSS, at basic prices	5751.0	6218.3	6921.7	7335.8	7490.1	7759.6	8201.4	9276.6	11059.7			
Compensation of employees	2668.3	2860.0	3099.6	3278.8	3735.3	4090.9	4372.0	4441.1	4454.6			

Table 2.6 Output, gross value added and fixed assets by industries at current prices (ISIC Rev. 4) Real estate activities (L)

Series 200: 1993 SNA, New Zealand dollar, Fiscal year beginning 1 April — **Data in millions**

	2001	2002	2003	2004	2005	2006	2007	2008	2009	2010	2011	2012
Series	**200**											
Equals: VALUE ADDED, GROSS, at basic prices	15911.4	17105.2	18534.3	20020.3	21718.9	22714.6	23315.4	23293.9	22519.9			
Compensation of employees	681.0	734.6	800.3	902.8	1053.1	1082.2	1201.9	1158.4	1099.0			

Table 2.6 Output, gross value added and fixed assets by industries at current prices (ISIC Rev. 4) Professional, scientific, technical, administrative and support service activities (M+N)

Series 200: 1993 SNA, New Zealand dollar, Fiscal year beginning 1 April **Data in millions**

	2001	2002	2003	2004	2005	2006	2007	2008	2009	2010	2011	2012
Series	**200**											
Equals: VALUE ADDED, GROSS, at basic prices	10337.5	11227.2	11989.9	12939.5	14075.8	15283.0	16623.8	17283.6	17495.7			
Compensation of employees	5718.0	6101.4	6481.3	7100.4	7826.7	8587.1	9400.5	9951.8	9818.1			

Table 2.6 Output, gross value added and fixed assets by industries at current prices (ISIC Rev. 4) Public administration and defence, education, human health and social work activities (O+P+Q)

Series 200: 1993 SNA, New Zealand dollar, Fiscal year beginning 1 April **Data in millions**

	2001	2002	2003	2004	2005	2006	2007	2008	2009	2010	2011	2012
Series	**200**											
Equals: VALUE ADDED, GROSS, at basic prices	15643.0	16667.0	18043.3	19713.0	21443.4	23259.4	25361.8	27621.5	29073.0			
Compensation of employees	12623.6	13550.1	14672.5	15982.0	17469.3	18970.8	20735.3	22722.3	24029.5			

Table 2.6 Output, gross value added and fixed assets by industries at current prices (ISIC Rev. 4) Other service activities (R+S+T)

Series 200: 1993 SNA, New Zealand dollar, Fiscal year beginning 1 April **Data in millions**

	2001	2002	2003	2004	2005	2006	2007	2008	2009	2010	2011	2012
Series	**200**											
Equals: VALUE ADDED, GROSS, at basic prices	4490.5	4895.1	5272.1	5530.6	5709.3	5837.0	6281.9	6386.5	6533.0			
Compensation of employees	2384.3	2549.6	2738.3	2906.7	3073.7	3296.9	3531.9	3707.8	3741.5			

Table 3.2 Individual consumption expenditure of households, NPISHs, and general government at current prices

Series 200: 1993 SNA, New Zealand dollar, Fiscal year beginning 1 April **Data in millions**

	2001	2002	2003	2004	2005	2006	2007	2008	2009	2010	2011	2012
Series	**200**											
	Individual consumption expenditure of households											
Equals: Household final consumption expenditure in domestic market	...	...	...	...	...	...	...	...	...	...	...	
Plus: Direct purchases abroad by residents	...	...	...	...	...	...	...	...	...	...	...	
Less: Direct purchases in domestic market by non-residents	...	...	...	...	...	...	...	...	...	...	...	
Equals: Household final consumption expenditure	72610.7	77552.7	83067.5	88331.3	94365.8	99691.3	104840.6	106985.0	109984.7	114533.3	120303.2	
	Individual consumption expenditure of non-profit institutions serving households (NPISHs)											
Equals: NPISHs final consumption expenditure	1764.3	1763.9	1810.1	1945.8	1989.6	2090.8	2352.6	2767.8	2893.1	3037.7	3189.6	

	2001	2002	2003	2004	2005	2006	2007	2008	2009	2010	2011	2012
Series	**200**											
	Individual consumption expenditure of general government											
Equals: Individual consumption expenditure of general government	12924.1	13644.0	14709.7	16041.1	17535.0	18632.7	20403.0	22597.4	23583.4	24231.5	24204.3	
Equals: Total actual individual consumption	87299.1	92960.5	99587.3	106318.2	113890.4	120414.8	127596.2	132350.2	136461.2	141802.5	147697.2	

Table 4.2 Rest of the world (S.2)

Series 200: 1993 SNA, New Zealand dollar, Fiscal year beginning 1 April

Data in millions

	2001	2002	2003	2004	2005	2006	2007	2008	2009	2010	2011	2012
Series							**200**					
	V.III.2 Financial account - Changes in liabilities and net worth											
Net incurrence of liabilities							23370.0	26416.0	-14993.0	13137.8		
Currency and deposits							2762.0	-612.0	-610.0	2977.3		
Securities other than shares							5096.0	14412.0	-19155.0	11993.0		
Loans							6603.0	8901.0	-144.0	-2655.8		
Shares and other equity							4237.0	1609.0	2253.0	1463.0		
Insurance technical reserves							...	...	...	...		
Financial derivatives							...	...	...	...		
Other accounts payable							4671.0	2107.0	2663.0	-639.7		
Adjustment to reconcile Net Lending of Financial Account and Capital Account							1735.0	1963.0	12717.0	3415.8		
NET LENDING (+) / NET BORROWING (-)							-12251.0	-13179.0	-1602.0	-1379.7		
	V.III.2 Financial account - Changes in assets											
Net acquisition of financial assets							11119.0	13237.0	-16595.0	11758.1		
Monetary gold and SDRs							-6.0	-9.0	-6.0	1903.6		
Currency and deposits							-1962.0	-623.0	325.0	1314.8		
Securities other than shares							9777.0	7365.0	-10795.0	8944.0		
Loans							-365.0	1254.0	-3593.0	-1418.4		
Shares and other equity							4535.0	5655.0	82.0	3403.2		
Insurance technical reserves							...	...	...	...		
Financial derivatives							...	...	...	...		
Other accounts receivable							-859.0	-406.0	-2608.0	-2389.2		

Table 4.5 General Government (S.13)

Series 100: 1993 SNA, New Zealand dollar, Fiscal year beginning 1 April | **Data in millions**

	2001	2002	2003	2004	2005	2006	2007	2008	2009	2010	2011	2012
Series	**100**											
	I. Production account - Resources											
Output, at basic prices (otherwise, please specify)	21318.9	22227.2	24062.7	25764.3	27635.2	29732.9	31966.8	34532.7	35411.0			
	I. Production account - Uses											
Intermediate consumption, at purchaser's prices	8412.9	8527.2	9371.7	9863.3	10385.2	11042.9	11717.8	12675.7	12643.0			
VALUE ADDED GROSS, at basic prices	12906.0	13700.0	14691.0	15901.0	17250.0	18690.0	20249.0	21857.0	22768.0			
Less: Consumption of fixed capital	2017.0	2074.0	2161.0	2325.0	2541.0	2746.0	2957.0	3167.0	3274.0			
VALUE ADDED NET, at basic prices	...	...	...	...	...	...	...	...	...			
	II.1.1 Generation of income account - Resources											
VALUE ADDED GROSS, at basic prices	12906.0	13700.0	14691.0	15901.0	17250.0	18690.0	20249.0	21857.0	22768.0			
	II.1.1 Generation of income account - Uses											
Compensation of employees	10680.0	11436.0	12312.0	13317.0	14506.0	15672.0	16992.0	18445.0	19260.0			
Other taxes less Other subsidies on production	150.0	148.0	152.0	172.0	190.0	232.0	248.0	230.0	239.0			
Other taxes on production	...	...	...	...	...	...	...	...	...			
Less: Other subsidies on production	...	...	...	...	...	...	...	...	...			
OPERATING SURPLUS, GROSS	2077.0	2115.0	2228.0	2412.0	2554.0	2785.0	3009.0	3183.0	3268.0			
	II.1.2 Allocation of primary income account - Resources											
OPERATING SURPLUS, GROSS	2077.0	2115.0	2228.0	2412.0	2554.0	2785.0	3009.0	3183.0	3268.0			
Taxes on production and imports, less Subsidies	15054.0	16432.0	17490.0	18707.0	19803.0	20948.0	22100.0[a]	22138.0	23121.0			
Taxes on production and imports	15430.0	16845.0	17932.0	19197.0	20384.0	21544.0	22704.0[a]	23171.0	23776.0			
Taxes on products	...	...	...	...	...	...	...	...	...			
Other taxes on production	...	...	...	...	...	...	...	...	...			
Less: Subsidies	376.0	413.0	442.0	490.0	581.0	596.0	604.0[a]	1033.0	655.0			
Subsidies on products	...	...	...	...	...	...	...	...	...			
Other subsidies on production	...	...	...	...	...	...	...	...	...			
Property income	2551.0	2447.0	2400.0	2841.0	3090.0	4965.0	4145.0	4036.0	4656.0			
	II.1.2 Allocation of primary income account - Uses											
Property income	2864.0	2746.0	2667.0	2645.0	2664.0	2622.0	2524.0	2651.0	2802.0			
BALANCE OF PRIMARY INCOMES	16817.0	18247.0	19452.0	21316.0	22783.0	26077.0	26731.0	26705.0	28245.0			
	II.2 Secondary distribution of income account - Resources											
BALANCE OF PRIMARY INCOMES	16817.0	18247.0	19452.0	21316.0	22783.0	26077.0	26731.0	26705.0	28245.0			
Current taxes on income, wealth, etc.	23933.0	26243.0	28606.0	30680.0	34618.0	37359.0	40262.0	39312.0	34238.0			
Social contributions	1380.0	1575.0	1542.0	1568.0	1672.0	1946.0	2181.0	2170.0	2424.0			
Other current transfers	1204.0	1324.0	1448.0	1593.0	1656.0	1748.0	1879.0	1981.0	2125.0			
	II.2 Secondary distribution of income account - Uses											
Current taxes on income, wealth, etc.	8.0	5.0	5.0	228.0	446.0	502.0	325.0	63.0	99.0			
Social benefits other than social transfers in kind	13453.0	13546.0	14078.0	14035.0	14773.0	16583.0	18236.0	19782.0	21422.0			

	2001	2002	2003	2004	2005	2006	2007	2008	2009	2010	2011	2012
Series	**100**											
Other current transfers	2516.0	2759.0	2885.0	3471.0	3899.0	4214.0	4562.0	5243.0	5129.0			
GROSS DISPOSABLE INCOME	27359.0	31079.0	34079.0	37422.0	41610.0	45832.0	47930.0	45079.0	40380.0			
	II.4.1 Use of disposable income account - Resources											
GROSS DISPOSABLE INCOME	27359.0	31079.0	34079.0	37422.0	41610.0	45832.0	47930.0	45079.0	40380.0			
	II.4.1 Use of disposable income account - Uses											
Final consumption expenditure	21819.0	22687.0	24531.0	26633.0	28969.0	31373.0	34202.0	37265.0	38213.0			
Individual consumption expenditure	12923.0	13640.0	14700.0	16065.0	17551.0	18643.0	20303.0	21918.0	22990.0			
Collective consumption expenditure	8897.0	9048.0	9831.0	10568.0	11418.0	12730.0	13899.0	15348.0	15223.0			
Adjustment for the change in net equity of households on pension funds	...	...	...	...	...	...	...	...	...			
SAVING, GROSS	5540.0	8392.0	9548.0	10789.0	12641.0	14459.0	13727.0	7814.0	2168.0			
	III.1 Capital account - Changes in liabilities and net worth											
SAVING, GROSS	5540.0	8392.0	9548.0	10789.0	12641.0	14459.0	13727.0	7814.0	2168.0			
Capital transfers, receivable less payable	-141.0	122.5	205.1	353.2	507.3	391.8	798.5	161.9	451.3			
Capital transfers, receivable	343.6	604.9	959.2	1230.7	1570.6	1599.0	2021.6	1391.2	1153.1			
Less: Capital transfers, payable	484.6	482.3	754.1	877.5	1063.3	1207.2	1223.1	1229.3	701.8			
Equals: CHANGES IN NET WORTH DUE TO SAVING AND CAPITAL TRANSFERS	...	...	...	...	...	...	...	...	...			
	III.1 Capital account - Changes in assets											
Gross capital formation	3533.0	3716.0	4429.0	4851.0	5642.0	5962.0	6267.0	7089.0	7147.0			
Gross fixed capital formation	3588.0	3635.0	4409.0	4820.0	5643.0	5934.0	6223.0	7024.0	7132.0			
Changes in inventories	-55.0	81.0	20.0	31.0	-1.0	28.0	44.0	65.0	15.0			
Acquisitions less disposals of valuables	...	...	...	...	...	...	...	...	...			
Acquisitions of non-produced non-financial assets	-2.0	34.0	98.0	102.0	70.0	115.0	270.0	67.0	243.0			
NET LENDING (+) / NET BORROWING (-)	1868.0	4767.0	5227.0	6190.0	7436.0	8773.0	7987.0	820.0	-4770.0			

[a] Discrepancy with equivalent item in Table 4.1 (Total Economy).

Table 4.9 Combined Sectors: Households and NPISH (S.14 + S.15)

Series 100: 1993 SNA, New Zealand dollar, Fiscal year beginning 1 April — **Data in millions**

	2001	2002	2003	2004	2005	2006	2007	2008	2009	2010	2011	2012
Series	**100**											
	II.1.2 Allocation of primary income account - Resources											
OPERATING SURPLUS, GROSS	...	...	...	...	...	...	...					
MIXED INCOME, GROSS	...	...	...	...	...	...	...					
Compensation of employees	51653.0	55074.0	59306.0	64268.0	69206.0	73258.0	...					
Property income	7358.0	7947.0	8909.0	11023.0	12875.0	14528.0	...					
	II.1.2 Allocation of primary income account - Uses											
Property income	4366.0	4841.0	5299.0	6209.0	7291.0	8472.0	...					
BALANCE OF PRIMARY INCOMES	...	...	...	...	...	...	...					

	2001	2002	2003	2004	2005	2006	2007	2008	2009	2010	2011	2012
Series	**100**											
	II.2 Secondary distribution of income account - Resources											
BALANCE OF PRIMARY INCOMES	...	...	...	...	...	...	...					
Social contributions	13453.0	13546.0	14078.0	14035.0	14773.0	16583.0	...					
Social benefits other than social transfers in kind	...	...	...	...	...	...	...					
Other current transfers	4442.0	4853.0	5141.0	5659.0	6294.0	6778.0	...					
	II.2 Secondary distribution of income account - Uses											
Current taxes on income, wealth, etc.	17995.0	19613.0	20508.0	21283.0	23852.0	25778.0	...					
Social contributions	1292.0	1490.0	1469.0	1501.0	1608.0	1892.0	...					
Social benefits other than social transfers in kind	...	...	...	...	...	...	...					
Other current transfers	3379.0	3749.0	3994.0	4273.0	4697.0	5070.0	...					
GROSS DISPOSABLE INCOME	73281.0	74364.0	81250.0	87605.0	91876.0	96555.0	...					
	II.4.1 Use of disposable income account - Resources											
GROSS DISPOSABLE INCOME	73281.0	74364.0	81250.0	87605.0	91876.0	96555.0	...					
Adjustment for the change in net equity of households on pension funds	236.0	-352.0	-517.0	165.0	734.0	667.0	508.0					
	II.4.1 Use of disposable income account - Uses											
Final consumption expenditure	73646.0	78507.0	84042.0	89409.0	95504.0	100621.0	106072.6[a]					
Individual consumption expenditure	...	...	...	...	...	...	...					
SAVING, GROSS	...	...	...	...	...	...	...					
	III.1 Capital account - Changes in liabilities and net worth											
SAVING, GROSS	...	...	...	...	...	...	...					
Capital transfers, receivable less payable	...	...	...	...	...	...	...					
Capital transfers, receivable	...	...	...	...	...	...	...					
Less: Capital transfers, payable	...	...	...	...	...	...	...					
Equals: CHANGES IN NET WORTH DUE TO SAVINGS AND CAPITAL TRANSFERS	...	...	...	...	...	...	...					
	III.1 Capital account - Changes in assets											
Gross capital formation	...	...	...	...	...	...	...					
Gross fixed capital formation	4523.0	5732.0	7067.0	7824.0	7953.0	8267.0	...					
Changes in inventories	...	...	...	...	...	...	...					
Acquisitions less disposals of valuables	...	...	...	...	...	...	...					
Acquisitions less disposals of non-produced non-financial assets	...	...	...	...	...	...	...					
NET LENDING (+) / NET BORROWING (-)	-3831.0	-9004.0	-9980.0	-10362.0	-12869.0	-13687.0	...					

[a] Discrepancy with equivalent items in Table 4.1 (Total Economy) and Table 4.5 (General Government).

Nicaragua

Source

The compilation of national accounts in Nicaragua is the responsibility of the National Accounts Department, which is part of the Office of Economic Studies of the Central Bank of Nicaragua (CBN). Estimates are made annually and are published in current and constant terms three months after the end of the reference year. Final figures are published two years later, mainly because many companies close accounts at the end of the fiscal year. In the particular case of Nicaragua, the fiscal year is from July to June of the following year, which delays the submission of financial statements and the completion of annual survey forms. For example, final figures for 2004, preliminary figures for 2005 and estimated figures for 2006 were contained in the 2006 annual report, published in March 2007.

Official figures are contained in two documents compiled by the CBN: the annual report and the Yearbook of Economic Statistics, 2001-2006. These documents are available to the public in hard copy and are also published online on the CBN website: www.bcn.gob.ni. The concepts, definitions, basic statistical sources and estimation methodologies for the different sectors of the economy are available in the document entitled "System of National Accounts of Nicaragua, Base Year 1994", published in May 2003 (and posted in digital form on the CBN website). This document describes the methodology used in the process of calculating the 1994 base year for each and every sector of the economy, and the results obtained from this process.

General

Until May 2003, the compilation of national accounts in Nicaragua was based on the methodological recommendations of the 1968 United Nations System of National Accounts. Estimates at constant prices had 1980 as the base year and gross domestic product (GDP) was calculated using the production and expenditure approaches alone. The CBN National Accounts Department is presently once again implementing a programme to change the base year from 1994 to 2005. This will make it possible to update Nicaragua's productive structure by economic activity; to move forward with the adoption of the recommendations in SNA93, mainly with regard to the compilation of accounts by institutional sector; and to incorporate methodological improvements and new statistical sources (2005 Living Standards Measurement Survey, 2005 Eighth Population Census and Fourth Housing Census, 2006 National Survey of Household Incomes and Expenditure, etc.).

Methodology:

Overview of GDP Compilation

GDP is calculated using the production approach (economic activities), the expenditure approach (types of use) and the income approach (types of income). In the case of Nicaragua, a national classifier of activities and products (CNIC) was set up. This is fully harmonized with the International Standard Industrial Classification of All Economic Activities (ISIC) and the Central Product Classification (CPC), which ensures international comparability between Nicaragua and the other countries that have adopted these classifiers.

Expenditure Approach

This approach consists of the following concepts: household consumption, government consumption, non-profit institutions serving households, fixed capital formation, changes in inventories and exports and imports of goods and services.

Household consumption

A final consumption vector for the year 1999 was calculated using the 1999 Survey of Household Incomes and Expenditure (CBN/National Institute of Information for Development (INIDE)), which covered 17 urban departmental capitals. The remaining urban and rural areas were covered by the 1998 Living Standards Measurement Survey (INIDE). Extrapolations were made back to 1994 using this vector, to allow for comparison and reconciliation with the base year vector, elaborated on the basis of the 1993 Living Standards Measurement

Survey. The vector for 1999 was extrapolated for the subsequent years.

Government consumption
Data sources for the calculation of public consumption are the same as for government activity.

Non-profit institutions serving households
Data sources for the production account of non-profit institutions serving households are the following: list of non-profit institutions registered with the Ministry of the Interior, with details of income and expenditure, and financial statements from non-profit institutions registered with the Ministry of the Interior.

Fixed capital formation
Public fixed capital formation is obtained from data on public sector investments (both central government and autonomous entities). This data is broken down into the following components: construction, machinery and equipment, and other investments. The "machinery and equipment" component for private fixed capital formation is obtained from the difference between total imports of capital assets (from customs records) and the public equipment and machinery component. For its part, private construction is obtained from the quarterly survey of private construction, where the value of the square metres obtained is determined by their economic use.

Finally, the "other private investments" component is an aggregate of the estimates investments made in each branch of economic activity. This component is calculated based on data provided by the Ministry of Agriculture and Forestry, which includes the value of new plantations, such as coffee, sugar cane, bananas and pastures. The component also includes the value of heifers, stallions and egg-laying hens, data on which is obtained from customs records, and the value of new forest plantations, such as pine, data on which is supplied by the Ministry of Natural Resources and Environment.

Changes in inventories
Inventories for some industrial products are obtained from the CBN annual survey of the different economic sectors, while inventories for the remainder are obtained from adjustments to the supply and use table.

Exports and imports of goods and services
The Customs Department (DGSA) database is used to calculate foreign trade in current and constant prices. Constant values of exports and imports are calculated by volume and value and by the unit value of a basket of goods, with unit value indices being calculated by CNIC based on a fixed base year (1994) and on a sliding year.

Income Approach

Compensation of employees
Two methods are used to calculate the compensation of employees:

Direct method: This method consists in using data on remunerations obtained directly from financial statements in the following areas: electricity, drinking water, financial intermediation, general government, insurance companies and post and telecommunications services. Data from annual surveys is used to obtain remunerations for industry, services and mining activities.

Indirect method: This method consists in calculating remunerations for agricultural activities and private construction activities based on the labour requirements per planted and harvested manzana (1 manzana = 0.7 hectare) and per square metre of construction, respectively. The basic data used to calculate remunerations for coffee, sugar cane, basic grains, bananas and oilseed crops are the harvested manzanas of each crop, the unit cost, and the technical requirements of permanent and contracted labour. This data is obtained from the 1994 technological maps of the National Development Bank and from the technological maps of the Ministry of Agriculture and Forestry. Remunerations for other agricultural crops are calculated using data from the production accounts for each crop, since data on harvested areas is not available for every year.

Operating surplus and mixed income

These comprise the accounting balance of the income generation account and are separated in each economic activity, based on responses to the annual survey of the manufacturing and service industries on the legal status of companies and the classification of their accounting records:

(1) Companies which are not legally constituted (and instead have the status of natural persons) and which do not record their transactions with other sectors of the economy, or their assets and liabilities, in financial statements, are considered to be household companies, and the balance is classified as mixed income;

(2) Companies which are not legally constituted (and instead have the status of natural persons) and which record their transactions with other sectors of the economy, and their assets and liabilities in financial statements, are considered to be quasi-corporations, and the balance is classified as gross operating surplus;

(3) Those companies which are legally constituted and have formal accounting are considered to be corporations, and the balance is classified as gross operating surplus. In the case of agricultural, pastoral, fishing and forestry activities, the mixed income and the surplus are separated using the structure of household and business output, as reported in the sectoral surveys.

Taxes less subsidies on production and imports
The main sources of data used to calculate taxes less subsidies are the Revenue Department (DGI) database on collection by tax type and economic activity; the Customs Department (DGSA) database by tax type and tariff heading; revenues of the Municipality of Managua and other local governments; and revenues of the National Institute of Technology. Taxes on domestic and imported products are obtained from databases provided by the Revenue Department and the Customs Department and are classified in accordance with the Central Product Classification and the national classifier of activities and products for inclusion in the supply and use balances.

Production Approach

Agriculture, animal husbandry, fishing and forestry
The following data sources are used to compile production accounts on activities and on the supply and use balances for these products:
(1) Annual agricultural production survey (first, second and third seasons), conducted since 1994 by the Ministry of Agriculture and Forestry in coordination with CBN; and the 1998 survey on non-traditional crop production;
(2) Export crop cost survey: coffee, 1996/1997 cycle; sugar cane and bananas for export, 1997; livestock cost survey, 1997; and the 2000 survey of oilseed crop costs and logging and fuel wood production costs;
(3) Ministry of Agriculture and Forestry price and market bulletins, and technological charts for various crops from the defunct National Development Bank;
(4) Third National Farm Census, 2001, conducted by the National Institute of Statistics and Censuses (NISC);
(5) The vector of final household consumption accounts, compiled from the 1993 and 1998 Living Standards Measurement Survey (INIDE) and from the 1999 National Survey of Household Incomes and Expenditure (CBN/INIDE);
(6) CBN model for estimating herd growth and milk output;
(7) Municipal and industrial slaughterhouse statistics, Ministry of Agriculture and Forestry;
(8) Annual bulletin and first national census of fishing and aquaculture, 1995 (both provided by the Nicaraguan Institute of Fisheries (INPESCA));
(9) Annual survey of production costs for fishing, 1997;
(10) DGSA and DGI databases, which are processed to obtain figures for exports, imports and taxes for products in accordance with the national classifier of activities and products (CNIC);
(11) Data from other institutions, companies and producers' associations.

In the case of primary sector commodities, annual volumes and prices are maintained in order to obtain current values. The volume and price index is then calculated for each of these in order to obtain values in constant prices for each product.

Manufacturing

The following data sources are used to compile production accounts on activities and on the supply and use balances for these products:
(1) Annual manufacturing survey (since 1992): used to collect data on legal status, production, prices, employment, inputs, changes in inventories and fixed capital movement, among other things;
(2) Quarterly survey of economic sectors: used to supplement data on companies not covered in the annual survey;
(3) Monthly manufacturing survey: used to supplement data on companies not covered in the annual or quarterly surveys; and used to compile the producer price index and physical production (or volume) indices;
(4) Free Zones Corporation: data on exports, imports, remunerations and employment for companies under the free-trade zone regime;
(5) DGSA and DGI databases, which are processed to obtain figures for exports, imports and taxes for products according to CNIC;
(6) The vector of final household consumption accounts, compiled from the 1993 and 1998 Living Standards Measurement Survey (NISC) and from the 1999 CBN National Survey of Household Incomes and Expenditure;
(7) The 1996 and 2001 urban economic censuses, which are the basis for the sampling frame and for the compilation of expansion factors;
(8) Municipal and industrial slaughterhouse statistics, Ministry of Agriculture and Forestry;
(9) CBN monthly economic indicators;
(10) Specific research and field visits to leading industrial companies.

Where data is available on output volumes and/or physical units, the gross output value in constant prices is obtained by extrapolating from the volume and/or quantity indices. Where no such data is available, the gross output value is obtained by deflation based on the corresponding price indices.

Mining
The annual mining sector report of the National Administration of Geological Resources (AdGeo) provides the data sources used to compile production accounts on activities and on the supply and use balances for these products.

Construction
The data used to calculate the construction of private residential and non residential buildings is obtained from the quarterly survey of private construction. The survey covers square metres of new construction, which are valued by price per square metre and classified according to their economic use. Annual figures are obtained by adding together the values from the four quarters. Public construction is calculated based on public sector construction data. A composite index is used to calculate public construction in constant prices. This index is calculated by weighting an index for construction material prices representative of public construction, and an index of remuneration for the same activity.

Electricity supply
Gross output values and intermediate consumption for this activity are obtained through the analysis and classification of accounting entries from financial statements. Gross output value comprises the value of sales, output for own consumption and the profit margin from sales of imported energy. To estimate values in constant prices, the prices and quantities (kWh) of consumption are classified by economic sector (residential, commercial, industrial, government, irrigation and pumping).

Capture, purification and distribution of drinking water
Drinking water supply and sewerage systems are the responsibility of the Nicaraguan Water and Sewerage Corporation (ENACAL, previously the Nicaraguan Water and Sewage Institute (INAA)). The gross output value is the value of sales. Gross output values and intermediate consumption figures for this activity are obtained through the analysis and classification of accounting entries in the financial statements provided by the Corporation. For values in constant prices, the prices and quantities (square metres) of consumption are classified by economic sector (household, industrial, commercial and government).

Wholesale and retail trade, repair of vehicles, and personal and household goods

The value of trade output is estimated based on the annual trade survey. The results of the survey of market outlets and gross margins, annexed to the 1997 annual trade survey, were used to distribute the trade margin between the various groups of products. The distribution margins for each product group were obtained from this survey and subsequently separated into transport and trade margins. This research provided a structure for trade margins, which was applied to the basic price for each demand component in each year.

Gross output values and intermediate consumption for the repair of vehicles and for personal and household goods are calculated based on the annual survey of services. Constant values are calculated from price or volume indices for the products, to which margins are applied. The sum of these comprises the gross output value of total trade. In addition, the vehicle stock provided by the national police was used to calculate constant values for the repair of motor vehicles.

Hotels and restaurants
The gross value of production and intermediate consumption in these sectors is calculated from the annual survey of services and reconciled with the data on tourism compiled by the Nicaraguan Tourism Institute (INTUR), which provides a breakdown of spending by foreign tourists in Nicaragua. The figures provided by INTUR (volume index) on the number of nights spent by national and foreign tourists and a rate of use index for service activities are used to establish constant values.

Communications
Current levels of production and demand for inputs in this sector are obtained from analysis and classification of the accounting entries in the financial statements. The gross value of production corresponds to the value of sales. In the case of imports and exports, data on trade with the rest of the world is also available in the balance of payments. Constant values are obtained by deflation of the transport and communications entries by the consumer price index. Depending on availability or reliability, a volume index of conventional telephone service may also be used.

Transport
Data provided by the Ministry of Transport and Infrastructure on the number of passengers transported annually and the corresponding tariff by route is used to calculate the gross value of production. Similarly, in the taxi subsector, figures are provided by a taxi cooperative on the number of passengers, average fares and cost structure and by the Ministry of Transport and Infrastructure on the number of licensed taxis. The 1997 annual trade survey yielded data on the distribution margins for each group of products, which were subsequently separated into transport and trade margins. This survey provided a structure for transport margins, which was applied each year to the base price of each demand component in order to obtain the level of production of the freight transportation sector. The consumer price index for the transportation sector is used to deflate current values.

Financial intermediation and auxiliary activities
The financial statements of each of the institutions in a given sector are used to prepare the production accounts of that sector. Total production comprises the fixed commissions charged by financial intermediaries and the implicit charges known as financial intermediation services indirectly measured(FISIM), which are calculated as the value of the asset income earned by financial intermediaries less interest payable, with the production assigned to a fictitious sector, which is one of the options recommended by the System.

The exchange rate variation is used as a deflator in order to establish constant values. In the case of deposit companies, the necessary indices are obtained from the movement of assets and liabilities. If the latter are denominated in the national currency, they are deflated by the consumer price index. Assets and liabilities denominated in foreign currency (but converted into córdobas) are divided by the current year's rate of exchange deflated by the producer price index (PPI) of the United States of America and expressed in córdobas of the base year using the exchange rate for that year. Total assets and liabilities at base year prices are divided by the base year value in order to obtain the volume index for income and expenditures, respectively.

Real estate and rental activities
Actual and estimated residential leases are calculated from the following data sources: 1993 and 1998 Living Standards Measurement Surveys, 1995 Seventh Population Census and 1995 Third Housing Census, 1999 Household Income and Expenditure Survey, and, since 1998, the quarterly survey of private construction. Data on non-residential rentals is obtained indirectly, in other words, from what is reported in production statements under this head by other economic sectors. Constant values are obtained by using construction price indices.

Private social and health services
The gross value of production and intermediate consumption is calculated from the annual survey of services. Additional data used to cross-check the value of production in this branch included the national health accounts of the Ministry of Health.

Other community, social and personal services
The gross value of production and intermediate consumption is estimated from the annual survey of services, from the financial statements of the lottery, from the Ministry of the Interior in the case of non-profit institutions serving households (NPISH) (for these institutions the gross value of production is equal to final consumption, as recommended by the System), from the 1993 and 1998 Living Standards Measurement Surveys and from the 1999 National Survey of Household Incomes and Expenditure. Variations in the consumer price index (CPI) of the corresponding year and/or the rate of population growth are used to estimate constant values.

Government
The data sources used to prepare the production accounts for the various sectors are: the national budget, with the budget implementation of expenditures for each institution presented by chapter, section and subsection; revenue by type of tax and collecting agency; details of transfers; the report on the implementation of the national budget submitted to the National Assembly; details of the financing of the deficit; implementation of the public investment programme; general balance and statement of results broken down by accounts and sub-accounts and notes appended to financial statements; and budget implementation of expenditures by type of taxes of the Municipality of Managua and other local governments.

The gross production of the central government was distributed among the following categories: public administration and defence, public education, public health services and services provided by associations, and recreational and other services. The calculation of the government at constant prices is done using the double deflation method recommended by the United Nations in the national accounts handbook at constant prices. This method consists in deflating intermediate consumption with price indices and extrapolating the value added with employment volume indices. The value added (remuneration at constant wages) is calculated by extrapolation of the figures recorded in the base year, using a labour index in which variations in the number of workers in each category (or "job sector") are weighted with the total share of the remuneration corresponding to this category in the base year.

Table 1.1 Gross domestic product by expenditures at current prices

Series 200: 1993 SNA, córdoba, Western calendar year
Series 300: 1993 SNA, córdoba, Western calendar year

Data in millions

	2001	2002	2003	2004	2005	2006	2007	2008	2009	2010	2011	2012
Series	**200**					**300**						
Expenditures of the gross domestic product												
Final consumption expenditure	53744.1	57508.8	62576.1	70688.8	81192.1	90804.5 114724.4	130602.7	153853.1	152964.0	170067.9	199851.0	228237.4
Household final consumption expenditure	43173.5	46545.7	50245.2	56714.3	64666.5	72454.0 93361.9	107813.6	...	...	...	...	...
NPISHs final consumption expenditure	747.0	885.1	976.9	1087.5	1226.3	1376.9 3340.1	3613.2	...	...	...	...	...
General government final consumption expenditure	9823.6	10078.0	11354.0	12887.1	15299.3	16973.6 18022.3	19175.9	...	...	...	...	...

	2001	2002	2003	2004	2005	2006	2007	2008	2009	2010	2011	2012
Series	**200**					**300**						
Individual consumption expenditure	3304.9	3956.0	4313.1	4879.5	5721.1	6805.4 6957.4	8613.9	...	...	...	...	...
Collective consumption expenditure	6518.7	6122.0	7041.0	8007.5	9578.2	10168.3 11064.9	10562.0	12413.2	13891.9	15203.6	18464.3	21771.7
Gross capital formation	15580.2	14957.6	16021.3	19937.9	24524.2	28262.8 31554.7	40584.0	47443.3	38078.3	40194.7	50480.0	62940.5
Gross fixed capital formation	14757.6	14261.8	15402.2	18897.9	23193.7	26727.6 28016.6	33903.8	39217.3	35678.9	37851.2	48725.5	63184.7
Changes in inventories	822.6	695.8	619.1	1040.0	1330.5	1535.3 3538.1	6680.2	8226.1	2399.5	2343.4	1754.5	-244.2
Acquisitions less disposals of valuables	...	...	...	...	...	... ...	...	...	...	...	...	...
Exports of goods and services	12476.7	12846.4	15239.8	19492.5	23613.6	29518.4 32239.8	39944.5	51591.7	52462.0	68926.9	90529.4	108962.5
Exports of goods	9483.6	9636.4	11348.5	14937.1	18451.8	23526.8 26584.6	33577.4	42267.4	42382.4	57879.9	77193.0	92910.6
Exports of services	2993.1	3210.0	3891.3	4555.4	5161.8	5991.5 5655.3	6367.2	9324.3	10079.6	11047.0	13336.4	16051.8
Less: Imports of goods and services	26645.7	27936.4	31878.6	38963.7	47805.5	56688.6 59283.7	73752.0	92985.8	77608.7	95808.5	124776.2	152719.4
Imports of goods	21727.8	22836.4	26144.7	32412.0	40271.1	48272.1 50494.0	63375.8	80884.8	67000.4	83941.7	110528.9	135920.3
Imports of services	4917.9	5100.0	5733.9	6551.7	7534.4	8416.5 8789.7	10376.2	12101.0	10608.2	11866.9	14247.3	16799.1
Equals: GROSS DOMESTIC PRODUCT	55155.3	57376.3	61958.6	71155.6	81524.4	91897.0 119235.2	137379.3	159902.3	165895.7	183380.9	216084.2	247421.0

Table 1.2 Gross domestic product by expenditures at constant prices

Series 200: 1993 SNA, córdoba, Western calendar year
Series 300: 1993 SNA, córdoba, Western calendar year

Data in millions

	2001	2002	2003	2004	2005	2006	2007	2008	2009	2010	2011	2012
Series	**200**					**300**						
Base year	**1994**					**2006**						
Expenditures of the gross domestic product												
Final consumption expenditure	26179.6	27127.1	27698.0	28293.2	29305.8	30102.9 114724.4	118553.0	122535.8	123329.2	128879.4	136041.1	142808.5
Household final consumption expenditure	22220.3	23109.6	23529.7	23992.9	24764.0	25470.1 93361.9	97598.5	...	...	...	...	...
NPISHs final consumption expenditure	323.5	369.5	379.2	389.2	401.4	413.0 3340.1	3124.4	...	...	...	...	...
General government final consumption expenditure	3635.7	3648.0	3789.1	3911.2	4140.4	4219.8 18022.3	17830.1	...	...	...	...	...
Individual consumption expenditure	1188.2	1314.1	1320.5	1364.5	1419.1	1512.7 6957.4	7452.3	...	...	...	...	...
Collective consumption expenditure	2447.6	2333.9	2468.6	2546.6	2721.4	2707.1 11064.9	10377.8	11580.1	12621.9	13217.2	14843.7	16036.6
Gross capital formation	7036.4	6537.1	6469.6	7160.8	7971.4	7960.1 31554.7	36979.7	37823.4	28956.0	28954.2	34546.4	41649.1
Gross fixed capital formation	6578.4	6165.5	6202.3	6619.7	7277.4	7415.6 28016.6	30953.1	31360.5	27209.4	27538.3	33756.7	43849.5
Changes in inventories	457.9	371.6	267.3	541.1	693.9	544.5 3538.1	6026.6	6459.4	1801.7	1476.0	982.3	-1363.4
Acquisitions less disposals of valuables	...	...	...	...	...	... ...	...	...	...	...	...	...
Exports of goods and services	7275.0	7019.5	7663.7	8974.6	9662.9	10870.2 32239.8	36409.8	41050.0	42523.4	50471.1	55091.8	59915.3
Exports of goods	5717.5	5446.9	5865.7	6985.0	7517.9	8503.6 26584.6	30515.4	33140.2	34275.0	41858.7	45398.2	47871.3
Exports of services	1557.5	1572.6	1798.0	1989.6	2145.0	2366.6 5655.3	5894.4	7933.3	8277.4	8628.7	9734.8	12451.0
Less: Imports of goods and services	12613.5	12596.2	13035.7	14103.4	15316.2	15996.2 59283.7	66710.9	71157.1	67490.7	76775.6	87619.5	99556.9
Imports of goods	10155.0	10218.0	10513.3	11382.4	12350.0	12845.1 50494.0	56868.4	60304.7	57507.5	66008.7	75297.6	86440.2
Imports of services	2458.5	2378.2	2522.4	2720.9	2966.2	3151.1 8789.7	9842.6	10872.6	9938.8	10662.4	12207.5	12759.0

	2001	2002	2003	2004	2005	2006	2007	2008	2009	2010	2011	2012
Series	**200**					**300**						
Base year	**1994**					**2006**						
Plus: Statistical discrepancy	...	...	...	...	...	... ...	...	-17.1	79.8	483.9	1146.2	1635.4
Equals: GROSS DOMESTIC PRODUCT	27877.4	28087.5	28795.5	30325.2	31623.9	32936.9 119235.2	125231.5	130235.0	127397.7	132012.9	139206.0	146451.3

Table 1.3 Relations among product, income, savings, and net lending aggregates

Series 200: 1993 SNA, córdoba, Western calendar year
Series 300: 1993 SNA, córdoba, Western calendar year

Data in millions

	2001	2002	2003	2004	2005	2006	2007	2008	2009	2010	2011	2012
Series	**200**					**300**						
GROSS DOMESTIC PRODUCT	55155.3	57376.3	61958.6	71155.6	81524.4	91897.0 119235.2	137379.3	159902.3	165895.7	183380.9	216084.2	247421.0
Plus: Compensation of employees - from and to the rest of the world, net	...	...	...	...	...	... -116.5	-0.1	11.6	14.2	17.1	15.7	14.1
Plus: Compensation of employees - from the rest of the world	...	...	...	...	...	... 0.0	0.0	34.9	38.6	42.7	44.8	49.4
Less: Compensation of employees - to the rest of the world	...	...	...	...	...	... 116.5	0.1	23.2	24.4	25.6	29.2	35.3
Plus: Property income - from and to the rest of the world, net	-3230.7	-2810.4	-2994.1	-3061.6	-2510.0	-3278.6 -4520.7	-4123.2	-4347.0	-5204.9	-5196.0	-5715.9	-6877.9
Plus: Property income - from the rest of the world	197.6	131.1	102.7	149.8	379.8	727.4 774.1	964.4	751.6	260.3	279.8	379.0	482.7
Less: Property income - to the rest of the world	3428.4	2941.5	3096.8	3211.4	2889.8	4594.6 5294.8	5087.6	5098.7	5465.2	5475.8	6094.9	7360.6
Sum of Compensation of employees and property income - from and to the rest of the world, net	-3230.7	-2810.4	-2994.1	-3061.6	-2510.0	-3867.2 -4637.1	-4123.3	-4335.4	-5190.6	-5178.9	-5700.3	-6863.8
Plus: Sum of Compensation of employees and property income - from the rest of the world	197.6	131.1	102.7	149.8	379.8	727.4 774.1	964.4	786.5	299.0	322.5	423.8	532.2
Less: Sum of Compensation of employees and property income - to the rest of the world	3428.4	2941.5	3096.8	3211.4	2889.8	4594.6 5411.3	5087.7	5121.9	5489.6	5501.4	6124.1	7396.0
Plus: Taxes less subsidies on production and imports - from and to the rest of the world, net	...	...	...	...	...	... 2.0	2.8	3.2	3.3	3.7	4.3	4.9
Plus: Taxes less subsidies on production and imports - from the rest of the world	...	...	...	...	...	... 2.0	2.8	...	...	...	...	...
Less: Taxes less subsidies on production and imports - to the rest of the world	...	...	...	...	...	... 0.0	0.0	...	...	...	...	...
Equals: GROSS NATIONAL INCOME	51924.6	54566.0	58964.5	68094.0	79014.4	88029.9 114600.1	133258.8	155570.1	160708.4	178205.6	210388.2	240562.1
Plus: Current transfers - from and to the rest of the world, net	6530.1	7557.5	9447.5	12032.7	14347.2	17628.0 18617.5	21228.6	22081.9	22747.7	24786.3	27572.9	30841.3
Plus: Current transfers - from the rest of the world	6530.1	7557.5	9447.5	12032.7	14347.2	17628.0 18857.6	21476.8	...	...	...	...	...
Less: Current transfers - to the rest of the world	...	...	...	...	...	... 240.1	248.2	...	...	...	...	...
Equals: GROSS NATIONAL DISPOSABLE INCOME	58454.6	62123.4	68412.0	80126.7	93361.5	105657.9 133251.4	154530.7	177702.2	183508.2	203049.6	238029.1	271481.1
Less: Final consumption expenditure / Actual final consumption	53744.1	57508.8	62576.1	70688.8	81192.1	90804.5 114724.4	130602.7	153853.1	152964.0	170067.9	199851.0	228237.4
Equals: SAVING, GROSS	4710.5	4614.6	5835.9	9437.8	12169.4	14853.4 18527.0	23928.0	23849.2	30544.2	32981.7	38178.0	43243.7
Plus: Capital transfers - from and to the rest of the world, net	5004.1	5757.5	5572.8	6258.6	5366.4	7907.2 26302.4	51516.4	8463.5	11333.2	6033.2	6038.9	5606.4
Plus: Capital transfers - from the rest of the world	5004.1	5757.5	5572.8	6258.6	5366.4	7907.2 26305.5	51516.4	...	...	...	...	...

	2001	2002	2003	2004	2005	2006	2007	2008	2009	2010	2011	2012
Series	**200**					**300**						
Less: Capital transfers - to the rest of the world	...	...	...	...	...	... 3.1	0.0	...	...	...	...	...
Less: Gross capital formation	15580.2	14957.6	16021.3	19937.9	24524.2	28262.8 31554.7	40584.0	47443.3	38078.3	40194.7	50480.0	62940.5
Less: Acquisitions less disposals of non-produced non-financial assets	...	...	...	...	...	... ...	...	...	...	...	...	...
Equals: NET LENDING (+) / NET BORROWING (-) OF THE NATION	-5865.6	-4585.4	-4612.6	-4241.5	-6988.4	-5502.2 13274.8	34860.3	-15130.6	3799.0	-1179.8	-6263.1	-14090.4
	Net values: Gross National Income / Gross National Disposable Income / Saving Gross less Consumption of fixed capital											
Less: Consumption of fixed capital	...	...	...	...	...	... 4453.0	4967.6	5540.3	5040.5	5347.3	6883.6	8926.3
Equals: NET NATIONAL INCOME	...	...	...	...	...	... 110147.1	128291.2	150029.8	155667.9	172858.3	203504.7	231635.8
Equals: NET NATIONAL DISPOSABLE INCOME	...	...	...	...	...	... 128798.4	149563.1	172161.9	178467.8	197702.2	231145.5	262554.8
Equals: SAVING, NET	...	...	...	...	...	... 14074.0	18960.4	18308.8	25503.8	27634.3	31294.4	34317.4

Table 2.1 Value added by industries at current prices (ISIC Rev. 3)

Series 200: 1993 SNA, córdoba, Western calendar year
Series 300: 1993 SNA, córdoba, Western calendar year

Data in millions

	2001	2002	2003	2004	2005	2006	2007	2008	2009	2010	2011	2012
Series	**200**					**300**						
	Industries											
Agriculture, hunting, forestry; fishing	9650.2	9809.9	10074.9	11824.3	13690.8	15141.4 18878.9	21719.2	26035.9	26674.0	32198.9	38800.9	45035.6
Agriculture, hunting, forestry	9046.6	9137.8	9431.6	11148.4	12904.7	14287.5 17987.7	20682.7	25052.4	25429.4	30784.9	37289.4	42435.3
Agriculture, hunting and related service activities	8435.0	8537.0	8878.1	10544.6	12209.1	13545.9 16547.3	18993.2	22988.6	23358.0	28756.9	34964.9	39817.9
Forestry, logging and related service activities	611.6	600.7	553.5	603.8	695.6	741.7 1440.4	1689.5	2063.8	2071.3	2028.0	2324.5	2617.4
Fishing	603.6	672.2	643.3	675.8	786.1	853.9 891.2	1036.5	983.4	1244.7	1414.0	1511.5	2600.4
Mining and quarrying	584.7	603.3	702.0	902.8	900.1	1141.0 1089.1	1222.4	1685.2	1801.1	3060.1	5009.2	6062.8
Manufacturing	9096.3	10279.2	10448.6	12070.0	13361.5	15289.3 16420.0	19827.1	22274.9	23937.5	26202.1	32843.4	37006.8
Electricity, gas and water supply	1254.6	1307.8	1533.6	2027.9	2254.9	2501.4 1774.2	1531.7	2487.8	2617.8	3008.0	3641.8	4035.1
Construction	3613.3	2977.1	3100.5	3893.2	4654.2	5020.0 5791.7	6349.3	7135.5	7036.8	7375.2	9760.9	13144.2
Wholesale, retail trade, repair of motor vehicles, motorcycles and personal and households goods; hotels and restaurants	7653.9	8029.9	8303.3	9530.9	11254.3	12781.0 17262.4	20709.0	25365.6	26511.5	28183.5	32343.9	37163.8
Wholesale, retail trade, repair of motor vehicles, motorcycles and personal and household goods	6656.4	6900.7	7179.2	8281.9	9775.6	10925.2 13815.6	16309.9	20314.0	20263.2	21686.3	25425.9	29616.2
Hotels and restaurants	997.5	1129.3	1124.0	1249.0	1478.7	1855.8 3446.9	4399.2	5051.6	6248.3	6497.1	6918.0	7547.5
Transport, storage and communications	3032.4	3085.4	3816.1	4168.5	4424.2	5036.8 7310.8	8765.2	9622.6	9296.6	10470.2	12638.0	14603.8
Land transport; transport via pipelines, water transport; air transport; Supporting and auxiliary transport activities; activities of travel agencies	1911.0	2059.8	2623.3	2729.2	2857.3	3096.3 4742.5	5253.8	5534.8	4958.4	5600.8	7178.5	8520.8
Post and telecommunications	1121.4	1025.6	1192.8	1439.3	1566.9	1940.4 2568.3	3511.4	4087.7	4338.2	4869.4	5459.6	6083.0
Financial intermediation; real estate, renting and business activities	7194.9	7877.0	8872.1	10104.0	11188.0	12417.2 21003.7	24111.1	27129.0	29738.6	30724.8	32409.5	35171.3
Financial intermediation	1827.9	2144.9	2480.4	3323.1	3568.7	4173.8 5796.7	7051.6	8297.8	9168.4	8741.8	8850.8	9702.4

	2001	2002	2003	2004	2005	2006	2007	2008	2009	2010	2011	2012
Series	**200**					**300**						
Real estate, renting and business activities	5367.1	5732.1	6391.7	6780.9	7619.3	8243.4 15207.0	17059.6	18831.2	20570.2	21982.9	23558.6	25469.0
Public administration and defence; compulsory social security	3650.5	3432.4	3899.1	4437.5	5236.9	5629.6 6081.4	6156.7	6935.8	7390.9	7880.7	8943.1	10502.6
Education; health and social work; other community, social and personal services	4865.6	5183.1	5882.9	6570.2	7472.0	8554.3 10527.7	12249.3	14776.1	14965.7	15497.6	17427.8	19596.3
Education	2156.9	2355.4	2649.5	3077.8	3476.0	4147.9 5329.9	6205.8	7259.4	7425.3	7565.5	8682.4	9875.1
Health and social work	1697.1	1732.7	1945.0	2087.3	2419.5	2725.0 2817.5	3351.3	3812.0	3957.6	4163.5	4872.0	5588.2
Other community, social and personal services	1011.6	1095.0	1288.4	1405.1	1576.4	1681.4 2380.2	2692.2	3704.7	3582.8	3768.6	3873.4	4133.0
Private households with employed persons	709.2	754.9	811.0	882.0	965.2	1066.1 1847.3	1974.7	2111.1	2366.0	2546.9	2764.7	3004.1
Equals: VALUE ADDED, GROSS, in basic prices [a]	51305.5	53340.1	57443.9	66411.4	75402.0	84578.2 107987.2	124615.7	145559.5	152336.6	167147.8	196583.3	225326.5
Less: Financial intermediation services indirectly measured (FISIM)	1888.0	2105.2	2476.6	3312.7	3639.6	4134.8 ...	...	...	...	...	...	...
Plus: Taxes less Subsidies on products	5737.8	6141.4	6991.1	8056.8	9762.0	11453.7 11248.0	12763.6	14342.8	13559.1	16233.1	19500.9	22094.5
Plus: Taxes on products	5737.8	6141.4	6991.1	8056.8	9762.0	11453.7 11783.5	13600.3	...	...	...	...	...
Less: Subsidies on products	...	...	...	...	...	... 535.5	836.8	...	...	...	...	...
Equals: GROSS DOMESTIC PRODUCT	55155.3	57376.3	61958.5	71155.6	81524.4	91897.0 119235.2	137379.3	159902.3	165895.7	183380.9	216084.2	247421.0

[a] Includes financial intermediation services indirectly measured (FISIM) of the Total Economy.

Table 2.2 Value added by industries at constant prices (ISIC Rev. 3)

Series 200: 1993 SNA, córdoba, Western calendar year
Series 300: 1993 SNA, córdoba, Western calendar year

Data in millions

	2001	2002	2003	2004	2005	2006	2007	2008	2009	2010	2011	2012
Series	**200**					**300**						
Base year	**1994**					**2006**						
	Industries											
Agriculture, hunting, forestry; fishing	5688.7	5674.1	5784.6	6114.8	6397.4	6555.4 18878.9	19917.1	20785.4	20500.1	22513.9	23488.2	23732.6
Agriculture, hunting, forestry	5267.2	5215.4	5327.7	5644.6	5883.5	6061.2 17987.7	18846.8	19673.3	19335.2	21339.5	22301.9	22401.9
Agriculture, hunting and related service activities	4872.7	4812.7	4952.8	5253.4	5476.7	5645.4 16547.3	17391.9	18196.9	17874.0	19937.9	20837.2	20859.1
Forestry, logging and related service activities	394.5	402.7	374.8	391.2	406.9	415.8 1440.4	1454.9	1478.9	1462.7	1419.6	1483.5	1566.8
Fishing	421.5	458.7	456.9	470.2	513.9	494.2 891.2	1070.3	1111.5	1194.2	1178.9	1183.2	1368.3
Mining and quarrying	312.9	330.3	295.5	354.6	317.5	326.0 1089.1	1033.3	1095.6	942.4	1290.2	1587.9	1718.4
Manufacturing	4907.7	5009.4	5131.7	5594.3	5908.3	6287.1 16420.0	17802.2	17296.1	16886.4	17920.6	19112.8	20063.3
Electricity, gas and water supply	606.7	615.1	646.2	674.4	698.6	709.0 1774.2	1685.1	2611.3	2838.2	3120.9	3339.6	3528.9
Construction	1266.3	1098.1	1127.9	1264.1	1356.4	1312.7 5791.7	5501.6	5126.8	4224.7	3611.5	4372.3	5773.5
Wholesale, retail trade, repair of motor vehicles, motorcycles and personal and household goods; hotels and restaurants	4676.7	4830.4	4897.2	5121.2	5236.8	5491.0 17262.4	17738.6	18333.9	18075.1	18777.7	19508.4	20287.4
Wholesale, retail trade, repair of motor vehicles, motorcycles and personal and household goods	3863.0	3958.2	4017.0	4181.5	4263.5	4512.9 13815.6	14120.5	14534.5	14145.4	14693.8	15240.7	15778.4
Hotels and restaurants	813.8	872.2	880.2	939.7	973.3	978.2 3446.9	3618.1	3796.4	3936.1	4090.3	4272.7	4516.2
Transport, storage and communications	1827.5	1877.2	2059.6	2159.1	2303.8	2468.7 7310.8	8732.4	10132.6[a]	9439.1	10132.6	11056.3	11815.6

	2001	2002	2003	2004	2005	2006	2007	2008	2009	2010	2011	2012
Series	**200**					**300**						
Base year	**1994**					**2006**						
Land transport; transport via piplines, water transport; air transport; Supporting and auxiliary transport activities; activities of travel agencies	1139.4	1175.5	1214.6	1276.1	1326.2	1380.9						
						4742.5	5199.7	5288.3	5351.9	5618.0	5974.9	6382.4
Post and telecommunications	688.2	701.7	845.0	883.1	977.6	1087.8						
						2568.3	3532.7	4039.4	4091.7	4503.4	5057.1	5407.6
Financial intermediation, real estate, renting and business activities	3020.7	3092.3	3281.8	3491.2	3657.2	3818.9						
						21003.7	21801.9	22946.0[a]	22055.6[a]	21605.2[a]	21313.1[a]	21736.5[a]
Financial intermediation	706.3	759.6	816.2	1009.3	1044.3	1144.2						
						5796.7	5874.4	6265.6	5363.1	4780.3	4298.6	4358.0
Real estate, renting and business activities	2314.4	2332.7	2465.6	2481.9	2612.9	2674.6						
						15207.0	15927.5	12372.4	12466.0	12701.8	12970.9	13257.9
Public administration and defence; compulsory social security	952.8	949.7	971.6	991.6	1030.0	1069.8						
						6081.4	6332.7	7215.1	7511.3	7844.1	8235.5	8600.0
Education; health and social work; other community, social and personal services	2161.1	2222.4	2275.0	2326.1	2399.4	2524.2						
						10527.7	10712.5	11124.2[a]	11003.2[a]	11065.2[a]	11395.4[a]	11813.2[a]
Education	904.6	918.6	954.0	949.9	1000.0	1100.5						
						5329.9	5418.5	4642.0	4673.1	4657.6	4815.3	4960.9
Health and social work	755.7	757.0	764.5	797.8	809.4	808.6						
						2817.5	2985.7	6564.8	6382.0	6474.2	6642.5	6928.4
Other community, social and personal services	500.7	546.8	556.6	578.3	589.9	615.2						
						2380.2	2308.2	3219.2	3005.5	3103.7	3225.3	3379.5
Private households with employed persons	344.2	353.2	362.3	371.8	381.4	391.3						
						1847.3	1880.7	1914.8	1934.2	1953.7	1973.5	1994.9
Equals: VALUE ADDED, GROSS, in basic prices [b]	25765.4	26052.4	26833.4	28463.1	29686.8	30954.3						
						107987.2	113137.9	118023.6	115343.3	119532.1	125342.1	131495.7
Less: Financial intermediation services indirectly measured (FISIM)	564.8	602.7	684.0	865.3	885.4	993.1						
						...	...	...	...	...	...	...
Plus: Taxes less Subsidies on products	2676.8	2637.8	2646.2	2727.3	2822.4	2975.7						
						11248.0	12093.6	12195.5	12044.1	12468.3	13903.1	15040.4
Plus: Taxes on products	2676.8	2637.8	2646.2	2727.3	2822.4	2975.7						
						11783.5	12655.7	...	...	...	...	...
Less: Subsidies on products	...	...	...	...	...	...						
						535.5	562.1	...	...	...	...	...
Equals: GROSS DOMESTIC PRODUCT	27877.4	28087.5	28795.5	30325.2	31623.9	32936.9						
						119235.2	125231.5	130235.0	127397.7	132012.9	139206.3	146451.3

[a] Discrepancy between components and total.
[b] Includes financial intermediation services indirectly measured (FISIM) of the Total Economy.

Table 2.3 Output, gross value added, and fixed assets by industries at current prices (ISIC Rev. 3) Total Economy

Series 200: 1993 SNA, córdoba, Western calendar year
Series 300: 1993 SNA, córdoba, Western calendar year

Data in millions

	2001	2002	2003	2004	2005	2006	2007	2008	2009	2010	2011	2012
Series	**200**					**300**						
Output, at basic prices	92540.4	96548.7	106570.5	125960.3	146714.9	170028.4						
						210129.4	241687.1	287061.5	291191.6	331093.7	402689.3	460000.8
Less: Intermediate consumption, at purchaser's prices [a]	43122.9	45313.8	51603.1	62861.5	74952.5	89585.0						
						102142.1	117071.4	141502.0	138855.0	163945.9	206105.9	234674.3
Equals: VALUE ADDED, GROSS, at basic prices [b]	49417.6	51234.9	54967.4	63098.7	71762.4	80443.4						
						107987.2	124615.7	145559.5	152336.6	167147.8	196583.3	225326.5
Compensation of employees	20067.1	20266.2	21363.3	25436.0	29152.6	34671.7						
						43857.1	51454.0	...	...	...	...	...
Taxes on production and imports, less Subsidies	565.0	867.5	950.3	1007.9	1246.2	1680.5						
						2143.8	2456.6	...	...	...	...	...
Taxes on production and imports	565.0	867.5	950.3	1007.9	1246.2	1680.5						
						2149.6	2464.1	...	...	...	...	...
Taxes on products	...	...	...	...	...	...						
						...	...	...	...	...	...	...
Other taxes on production	565.0	867.5	950.3	1007.9	1246.2	1680.5						
						2149.6	2464.1	...	...	...	...	...

	2001	2002	2003	2004	2005	2006	2007	2008	2009	2010	2011	2012
Series	**200**					**300**						
Less: Subsidies	...	...	...	...	...	... 5.8	7.5	...	...	...	...	...
Subsidies on products	...	...	...	...	...	... ...	...	...	...	...	...	...
Other subsidies on production	...	...	...	...	...	... 5.8	7.5	...	...	...	...	...
OPERATING SURPLUS, GROSS [c]	15900.5	16825.3	19501.3	22578.5	26079.6	29002.7 34178.2	40092.8	...	...	...	...	...
MIXED INCOME, GROSS [c]	14772.9	15381.1	15628.9	17389.0	18923.6	19223.2 27808.2	30612.3	...	...	...	...	...
Total Economy only: Adjustment for FISIM (if FISIM is not distributed to uses)	1888.0	2105.2	2476.6	3312.7	3639.6	4134.8 ...	...	...	...	...	...	...
Less: Consumption of fixed capital	...	...	...	...	...	... 4453.0	4967.6	5540.3	5040.5	5347.3	6883.6	8926.3
OPERATING SURPLUS, NET	...	...	...	...	...	... 30428.3	35904.1	...	...	...	...	...
MIXED INCOME, NET	...	...	...	...	...	... 27105.1	29833.4	...	...	...	...	...
Gross capital formation	15580.2	14957.6	16021.3	19937.9	24524.2	28262.8 31554.7	40584.0	47443.3	38078.3	40194.7	50480.0	62940.5
Gross fixed capital formation	14757.6	14261.8	15402.2	18897.9	23193.7	26727.6 28016.6	33903.8	39217.3	35678.9	37851.2	48725.5	63184.7
Changes in inventories	822.6	695.8	619.1	1040.0	1330.5	1535.3 3538.1	6680.2	8226.1	2399.5	2343.4	1754.5	-244.2
Acquisitions less disposals of valuables	...	...	...	...	...	... ...	...	...	...	...	...	...

[a] Includes financial intermediation services indirectly measured (FISIM) but FISIM is excluded in the tables by industry.
[b] Excludes financial intermediation services indirectly measured (FISIM) but FISIM is included in the tables by industry.
[c] Includes financial intermediation services indirectly measured (FISIM) of the Total Economy.

Table 2.3 Output, gross value added, and fixed assets by industries at current prices (ISIC Rev. 3) Agriculture, hunting, forestry; fishing (A+B)

Series 200: 1993 SNA, córdoba, Western calendar year
Series 300: 1993 SNA, córdoba, Western calendar year

Data in millions

	2001	2002	2003	2004	2005	2006	2007	2008	2009	2010	2011	2012
Series	**200**					**300**						
Output, at basic prices	13960.0	14303.9	15228.5	17904.5	21081.4	23865.6 29229.6	34194.9	41793.3	42341.9	50781.1	61912.5	72721.4
Less: Intermediate consumption, at purchaser's prices	4309.8	4494.0	5153.6	6080.2	7390.6	8724.2 10350.7	12475.6	15757.5	15667.9	18582.2	23111.6	27685.8
Equals: VALUE ADDED, GROSS, at basic prices	9650.2	9809.9	10074.9	11824.3	13690.8	15141.4 18878.9	21719.2	26035.9	26674.0	32198.9	38800.9	45035.6
Compensation of employees	1792.3	1880.7	2023.9	2627.1	2740.2	3425.7 7254.7	8838.3	...	...	...	...	...
Taxes on production and imports, less Subsidies	0.0	0.0	0.0	0.0	1.6	1.8 308.2	438.3	...	...	...	...	...
Taxes on production and imports	0.0	0.0	0.0	0.0	1.6	1.8 308.2	438.3	...	...	...	...	...
Taxes on products	...	...	...	...	...	... ...	...	...	...	...	...	...
Other taxes on production	0.0	0.0	0.0	0.0	1.6	1.8 308.2	438.3	...	...	...	...	...
Less: Subsidies	...	...	...	...	...	... ...	...	...	...	...	...	...
OPERATING SURPLUS, GROSS	1811.4	1757.2	1914.0	2068.2	2922.6	3092.8 2865.1	2731.9	...	...	...	...	...
MIXED INCOME, GROSS	6046.5	6172.1	6137.0	7129.0	8026.4	8621.1 8450.9	9710.7	...	...	...	...	...
Less: Consumption of fixed capital	...	...	...	...	...	... 137.4	180.9	...	...	...	...	...
OPERATING SURPLUS, NET	...	...	...	...	...	... 2743.3	2570.2	...	...	...	...	...
MIXED INCOME, NET	...	...	...	...	...	... 8435.3	9691.5	...	...	...	...	...
Gross capital formation	...	...	...	...	...	... ...	...	...	...	...	...	...

Table 2.3 Output, gross value added, and fixed assets by industries at current prices (ISIC Rev. 3) Agriculture, hunting and related service activities (01)

Series 200: 1993 SNA, córdoba, Western calendar year
Series 300: 1993 SNA, córdoba, Western calendar year

Data in millions

	2001	2002	2003	2004	2005	2006	2007	2008	2009	2010	2011	2012
Series	**200**					**300**						
Output, at basic prices	11992.3	12265.6	13253.9	15767.5	18558.0	20918.2						
						25538.9	29934.7	36769.8	37061.9	45168.2	55491.1	63522.2
Less: Intermediate consumption, at purchaser's prices	3557.2	3728.5	4375.8	5222.9	6348.9	7372.3						
						8991.6	10941.5	13781.2	13703.9	16411.3	20526.1	23704.3
Equals: VALUE ADDED, GROSS, at basic prices	8435.0	8537.0	8878.1	10544.6	12209.1	13545.9						
						16547.3	18993.2	22988.6	23358.0	28756.9	34964.9	39817.9
Compensation of employees	1493.2	1582.8	1747.0	2324.6	2381.3	3026.1						
						6787.1	8190.9	...	...	...	...	...
Taxes on production and imports, less Subsidies	0.0	0.0	0.0	0.0	1.6	1.8						
						112.9	213.8	...	...	...	...	...
Taxes on production and imports	0.0	0.0	0.0	0.0	1.6	1.8						
						112.9	213.8	...	...	...	...	...
Taxes on products	...	...	...	...	...	...						
						...	...	...	...	...	...	...
Other taxes on production	0.0	0.0	0.0	0.0	1.6	1.8						
						112.9	213.8	...	...	...	...	...
Less: Subsidies	...	...	...	...	...	...						
						...	...	...	...	...	...	...
OPERATING SURPLUS, GROSS	1339.1	1242.3	1404.8	1520.3	2288.4	2284.8						
						2521.4	2447.1	...	...	...	...	...
MIXED INCOME, GROSS	5602.7	5712.0	5726.4	6699.7	7537.8	8233.2						
						7125.9	8141.3	...	...	...	...	...
Less: Consumption of fixed capital	...	...	...	...	...	...						
						130.1	164.4	...	...	...	...	...
OPERATING SURPLUS, NET	...	...	...	...	...	...						
						2406.8	2302.0	...	...	...	...	...
MIXED INCOME, NET	...	...	...	...	...	...						
						7110.3	8122.1	...	...	...	...	...
Gross capital formation	...	...	...	...	...	...						
						...	...	...	...	...	...	...

Table 2.3 Output, gross value added, and fixed assets by industries at current prices (ISIC Rev. 3) Forestry, logging and related service activities (02)

Series 200: 1993 SNA, córdoba, Western calendar year
Series 300: 1993 SNA, córdoba, Western calendar year

Data in millions

	2001	2002	2003	2004	2005	2006	2007	2008	2009	2010	2011	2012
Series	**200**					**300**						
Output, at basic prices	1035.0	1003.9	953.5	1058.4	1250.5	1529.3						
						1879.7	2175.5	2687.2	2655.2	2663.3	3109.3	3501.2
Less: Intermediate consumption, at purchaser's prices	423.4	403.1	400.1	454.6	554.9	787.6						
						439.3	486.0	623.4	583.8	635.3	784.9	883.8
Equals: VALUE ADDED, GROSS, at basic prices	611.6	600.7	553.5	603.8	695.6	741.7						
						1440.4	1689.5	2063.8	2071.3	2028.0	2324.5	2617.4
Compensation of employees	252.0	245.8	229.3	254.0	301.1	335.2						
						283.4	343.6	...	...	...	...	...
Taxes on production and imports, less Subsidies	0.0	0.0	0.0	0.0	0.0	0.0						
						172.9	197.9	...	...	...	...	...
Taxes on production and imports	0.0	0.0	0.0	0.0	0.0	0.0						
						172.9	197.9	...	...	...	...	...
Taxes on products	...	...	...	...	...	...						
						...	...	...	...	...	...	...
Other taxes on production	0.0	0.0	0.0	0.0	0.0	0.0						
						172.9	197.9	...	...	...	...	...
Less: Subsidies	...	...	...	...	...	...						
						...	...	...	...	...	...	...
OPERATING SURPLUS, GROSS	87.9	86.8	85.2	92.4	105.7	235.9						
						...	...	...	...	...	...	...
MIXED INCOME, GROSS	271.7	268.2	239.0	257.5	288.8	170.7						
						984.1	1148.0	...	...	...	...	...

	2001	2002	2003	2004	2005	2006	2007	2008	2009	2010	2011	2012
Series	**200**					**300**						
Less: Consumption of fixed capital	...	...	...	...	...	... ...	...	...	...	...	...	...
OPERATING SURPLUS, NET	...	...	...	...	...	... ...	...	...	...	...	...	...
MIXED INCOME, NET	...	...	...	...	...	... 984.1	1148.0	...	...	...	...	...
Gross capital formation	...	...	...	...	...	... ...	...	...	...	...	...	...

Table 2.3 Output, gross value added, and fixed assets by industries at current prices (ISIC Rev. 3) Fishing (B)

Series 200: 1993 SNA, córdoba, Western calendar year
Series 300: 1993 SNA, córdoba, Western calendar year

Data in millions

	2001	2002	2003	2004	2005	2006	2007	2008	2009	2010	2011	2012
Series	**200**					**300**						
Output, at basic prices	932.8	1034.5	1021.0	1078.6	1272.9	1418.2 1811.0	2084.7	2336.4	2624.8	2949.6	3312.1	5698.1
Less: Intermediate consumption, at purchaser's prices	329.2	362.3	377.7	402.7	486.8	564.3 919.8	1048.2	1353.0	1380.2	1535.6	1800.6	3097.7
Equals: VALUE ADDED, GROSS, at basic prices	603.6	672.2	643.3	675.8	786.1	853.9 891.2	1036.5	983.4	1244.7	1414.0	1511.5	2600.4
Compensation of employees	47.0	52.1	47.7	48.5	57.8	64.5 184.2	303.8	...	...	...	...	...
Taxes on production and imports, less Subsidies	0.0	0.0	0.0	0.0	0.0	0.0 22.4	26.5	...	...	...	...	...
Taxes on production and imports	0.0	0.0	0.0	0.0	0.0	0.0 22.4	26.5	...	...	...	...	...
Taxes on products	...	...	...	...	...	... ...	...	...	...	...	...	...
Other taxes on production	0.0	0.0	0.0	0.0	0.0	0.0 22.4	26.5	...	...	...	...	...
Less: Subsidies	...	...	...	...	...	... ...	...	...	...	...	...	...
OPERATING SURPLUS, GROSS	384.4	428.1	424.0	455.5	528.5	572.1 343.7	284.8	...	...	...	...	...
MIXED INCOME, GROSS	172.1	191.9	171.6	171.9	199.8	217.3 340.9	421.4	...	...	...	...	...
Less: Consumption of fixed capital	...	...	...	...	...	... 7.3	16.5	...	...	...	...	...
OPERATING SURPLUS, NET	...	...	...	...	...	... 336.5	268.2	...	...	...	...	...
MIXED INCOME, NET	...	...	...	...	...	... 340.9	421.4	...	...	...	...	...
Gross capital formation	...	...	...	...	...	... ...	...	...	...	...	...	...

Table 2.3 Output, gross value added, and fixed assets by industries at current prices (ISIC Rev. 3) Mining and quarrying (C)

Series 200: 1993 SNA, córdoba, Western calendar year
Series 300: 1993 SNA, córdoba, Western calendar year

Data in millions

	2001	2002	2003	2004	2005	2006	2007	2008	2009	2010	2011	2012
Series	**200**					**300**						
Output, at basic prices	1032.1	1160.1	1311.3	1773.5	1835.1	2423.8 2399.6	2644.5	3373.6	3173.7	...	...	...
Less: Intermediate consumption, at purchaser's prices	447.3	556.8	609.3	870.7	935.0	1282.8 1310.5	1422.1	1688.4	1372.6	...	...	...
Equals: VALUE ADDED, GROSS, at basic prices	584.7	603.3	702.0	902.8	900.1	1141.0 1089.1	1222.4	1685.2	1801.1	3060.1	5009.2	6062.8
Compensation of employees	265.4	268.8	306.9	415.3	431.5	567.6 552.2	638.1	...	...	...	...	...

	2001	2002	2003	2004	2005	2006	2007	2008	2009	2010	2011	2012
Series	**200**					**300**						
Taxes on production and imports, less Subsidies	0.0	0.0	0.0	0.0	0.0	0.0						
						73.5	84.5	...	...	...	...	...
Taxes on production and imports	0.0	0.0	0.0	0.0	0.0	0.0						
						73.5	84.5	...	...	...	...	...
Taxes on products	...	...	...	...	...	...						
						...	...	...	...	...	...	...
Other taxes on production	0.0	0.0	0.0	0.0	0.0	0.0						
						73.5	84.5	...	...	...	...	...
Less: Subsidies	...	...	...	...	...	...						
						...	...	...	...	...	...	...
OPERATING SURPLUS, GROSS	228.6	239.4	282.8	348.1	334.3	409.4						
						323.5	344.0	...	...	...	...	...
MIXED INCOME, GROSS	90.8	95.0	112.3	139.4	134.2	164.1						
						140.0	155.8	...	...	...	...	...
Less: Consumption of fixed capital	...	...	...	...	...	...						
						...	...	...	...	...	...	...
OPERATING SURPLUS, NET	...	...	...	...	...	...						
						323.5	344.0	...	...	...	...	...
MIXED INCOME, NET	...	...	...	...	...	...						
						140.0	155.8	...	...	...	...	...
Gross capital formation	...	...	...	...	...	...						
						...	...	...	...	...	...	...

Table 2.3 Output, gross value added, and fixed assets by industries at current prices (ISIC Rev. 3) Manufacturing (D)

Series 200: 1993 SNA, córdoba, Western calendar year
Series 300: 1993 SNA, córdoba, Western calendar year

Data in millions

	2001	2002	2003	2004	2005	2006	2007	2008	2009	2010	2011	2012
Series	**200**					**300**						
Output, at basic prices	25016.9	26809.7	29102.1	34787.9	40232.6	48541.4						
						52267.8	62428.2	74842.1	76128.3	87017.5	109444.6	118599.7
Less: Intermediate consumption, at purchaser's prices	15920.6	16530.5	18653.5	22717.9	26871.0	33252.1						
						35847.8	42601.1	52567.2	52190.8	60815.5	76601.2	81592.8
Equals: VALUE ADDED, GROSS, at basic prices	9096.3	10279.2	10448.6	12070.0	13361.5	15289.3						
						16420.0	19827.1	22274.9	23937.5	26202.1	32843.4	37006.8
Compensation of employees	3558.9	3889.6	3283.6	4078.6	4854.1	5869.3						
						7473.4	9342.7	...	...	...	...	...
Taxes on production and imports, less Subsidies	205.6	259.6	250.4	276.9	306.0	383.9						
						424.6	484.0	...	...	...	...	...
Taxes on production and imports	205.6	259.6	250.4	276.9	306.0	383.9						
						424.6	484.0	...	...	...	...	...
Taxes on products	...	...	...	...	...	...						
						...	...	...	...	...	...	...
Other taxes on production	205.6	259.6	250.4	276.9	306.0	383.9						
						424.6	484.0	...	...	...	...	...
Less: Subsidies	...	...	...	...	...	...						
						...	...	...	...	...	...	...
OPERATING SURPLUS, GROSS	4090.2	4755.3	5793.4	6292.5	6742.7	7480.3						
						6508.2	7956.0	...	...	...	...	...
MIXED INCOME, GROSS	1241.5	1374.8	1121.2	1422.1	1458.8	1555.7						
						2013.9	2044.4	...	...	...	...	...
Less: Consumption of fixed capital	...	...	...	...	...	...						
						549.8	532.8	...	...	...	...	...
OPERATING SURPLUS, NET	...	...	...	...	...	...						
						5958.3	7423.2	...	...	...	...	...
MIXED INCOME, NET	...	...	...	...	...	...						
						2013.9	2044.4	...	...	...	...	...
Gross capital formation	...	...	...	...	...	...						
						...	...	...	...	...	...	...

Table 2.3 Output, gross value added, and fixed assets by industries at current prices (ISIC Rev. 3) Electricity, gas and water supply (E)

Series 200: 1993 SNA, córdoba, Western calendar year
Series 300: 1993 SNA, córdoba, Western calendar year

Data in millions

	Series	2001	2002	2003	2004	2005	2006	2007	2008	2009	2010	2011	2012
Output, at basic prices	200	3283.0	3625.0	4203.9	4917.2	5608.8	6347.7						
	300						6555.4	7711.8	9896.3	10014.3	...	...	...
Less: Intermediate consumption, at purchaser's prices	200	2028.4	2317.2	2670.3	2889.2	3354.0	3846.3						
	300						4781.3	6180.1	7408.5	7396.4	...	...	...
Equals: VALUE ADDED, GROSS, at basic prices	200	1254.6	1307.8	1533.6	2027.9	2254.9	2501.4						
	300						1774.2	1531.7	2487.8	2617.8	3008.0	3641.8	4035.1
Compensation of employees	200	526.3	519.3	608.2	581.1	699.4	773.3						
	300						836.3	889.7	...	...	...	...	...
Taxes on production and imports, less Subsidies	200	64.2	71.4	103.4	76.8	72.1	82.2						
	300						74.3	81.1	...	...	...	...	...
Taxes on production and imports	200	64.2	71.4	103.4	76.8	72.1	82.2						
	300						74.3	81.1	...	...	...	...	...
Taxes on products	200	...	...	...	...	...	...						
	300						...	...	...	...	...	...	...
Other taxes on production	200	64.2	71.4	103.4	76.8	72.1	82.2						
	300						74.3	81.1	...	...	...	...	...
Less: Subsidies	200	...	...	...	...	...	...						
	300						...	...	...	...	...	...	...
OPERATING SURPLUS, GROSS	200	664.2	717.2	822.0	1370.0	1483.4	1645.8						
	300						738.5	339.4	...	...	...	...	...
MIXED INCOME, GROSS	200	0.0	0.0	0.0	0.0	0.0	0.0						
	300						125.0	221.5	...	...	...	...	...
Less: Consumption of fixed capital	200	...	...	...	...	...	...						
	300						708.7	845.4	...	...	...	...	...
OPERATING SURPLUS, NET	200	...	...	...	...	...	...						
	300						29.8	-505.9	...	...	...	...	...
MIXED INCOME, NET	200	...	...	...	...	...	...						
	300						125.0	221.5	...	...	...	...	...
Gross capital formation	200	...	...	...	...	...	...						
	300						...	...	...	...	...	...	...

Table 2.3 Output, gross value added, and fixed assets by industries at current prices (ISIC Rev. 3) Construction (F)

Series 200: 1993 SNA, córdoba, Western calendar year
Series 300: 1993 SNA, córdoba, Western calendar year

Data in millions

	Series	2001	2002	2003	2004	2005	2006	2007	2008	2009	2010	2011	2012
Output, at basic prices	200	8624.2	7704.9	8441.6	11322.7	13813.6	15150.0						
	300						19599.5	21927.8	25839.4	23812.5	...	...	...
Less: Intermediate consumption, at purchaser's prices	200	5011.0	4727.8	5341.1	7429.5	9159.4	10130.0						
	300						13807.9	15578.4	18703.9	16775.7	...	...	...
Equals: VALUE ADDED, GROSS, at basic prices	200	3613.3	2977.1	3100.5	3893.2	4654.2	5020.0						
	300						5791.7	6349.3	7135.5	7036.8	7375.2	9760.9	13144.2
Compensation of employees	200	2061.1	1623.3	1703.3	2187.6	2871.4	3090.3						
	300						3686.8	4084.7	...	...	...	...	...
Taxes on production and imports, less Subsidies	200	86.2	93.7	103.1	136.9	181.7	201.1						
	300						49.3	55.4	...	...	...	...	...
Taxes on production and imports	200	86.2	93.7	103.1	136.9	181.7	201.1						
	300						49.3	55.4	...	...	...	...	...
Taxes on products	200	...	...	...	...	...	...						
	300						...	...	...	...	...	...	...
Other taxes on production	200	86.2	93.7	103.1	136.9	181.7	201.1						
	300						49.3	55.4	...	...	...	...	...
Less: Subsidies	200	...	...	...	...	...	...						
	300						...	...	...	...	...	...	...
OPERATING SURPLUS, GROSS	200	1446.4	1239.2	1275.5	1543.1	1579.9	1702.5						
	300						483.2	1002.2	...	...	...	...	...
MIXED INCOME, GROSS	200	19.5	21.0	18.4	25.7	21.1	26.1						
	300						1572.3	1207.1	...	...	...	...	...

	2001	2002	2003	2004	2005	2006	2007	2008	2009	2010	2011	2012
Series	**200**					**300**						
Less: Consumption of fixed capital	...	...	...	...	...	... ...	...	...	...	...	...	...
OPERATING SURPLUS, NET	...	...	...	...	...	... 483.2	1002.2	...	...	...	...	...
MIXED INCOME, NET	...	...	...	...	...	... 1572.3	1207.1	...	...	...	...	...
Gross capital formation	...	...	...	...	...	... ...	...	...	...	...	...	...

Table 2.3 Output, gross value added, and fixed assets by industries at current prices (ISIC Rev. 3) Wholesale retail trade, repair of motor vehicles, motorcycles, etc.; hotels and restaurants (G+H)

Series 200: 1993 SNA, córdoba, Western calendar year
Series 300: 1993 SNA, córdoba, Western calendar year

Data in millions

	2001	2002	2003	2004	2005	2006	2007	2008	2009	2010	2011	2012
Series	**200**					**300**						
Output, at basic prices	11508.8	12262.3	13233.5	15247.8	17971.1	21307.1 28399.7	32176.3	37887.7	38211.1	...	...	...
Less: Intermediate consumption, at purchaser's prices	3855.0	4232.4	4930.2	5716.9	6716.8	8526.1 11137.3	11467.2	12522.1	11699.7	...	...	...
Equals: VALUE ADDED, GROSS, at basic prices	7653.9	8029.9	8303.3	9530.9	11254.3	12781.0 17262.4	20709.0	25365.6	26511.5	28183.5	32343.9	37163.8
Compensation of employees	1975.2	2051.5	2057.9	2524.9	2870.0	4030.5 4652.1	5475.0	...	...	...	...	...
Taxes on production and imports, less Subsidies	114.6	224.1	345.3	323.4	399.8	621.4 661.0	727.0	...	...	...	...	...
Taxes on production and imports	114.6	224.1	345.3	323.4	399.8	621.4 661.0	727.0	...	...	...	...	...
Taxes on products	...	...	...	...	...	... ...	...	...	...	...	...	...
Other taxes on production	114.6	224.1	345.3	323.4	399.8	621.4 661.0	727.0	...	...	...	...	...
Less: Subsidies	...	...	...	...	...	... ...	...	...	...	...	...	...
OPERATING SURPLUS, GROSS	1371.2	1473.9	1669.9	1936.0	2839.5	3508.3 4700.0	6419.2	...	...	...	...	...
MIXED INCOME, GROSS	4192.9	4280.4	4230.2	4746.6	5144.9	4620.9 7249.4	8087.8	...	...	...	...	...
Less: Consumption of fixed capital	...	...	...	...	...	... 547.0	561.8	...	...	...	...	...
OPERATING SURPLUS, NET	...	...	...	...	...	... 4269.6	5948.6	...	...	...	...	...
MIXED INCOME, NET	...	...	...	...	...	... 7132.7	7996.6	...	...	...	...	...
Gross capital formation	...	...	...	...	...	... ...	...	...	...	...	...	...

Table 2.3 Output, gross value added, and fixed assets by industries at current prices (ISIC Rev. 3) Transport, storage and communications (I)

Series 200: 1993 SNA, córdoba, Western calendar year
Series 300: 1993 SNA, córdoba, Western calendar year

Data in millions

	2001	2002	2003	2004	2005	2006	2007	2008	2009	2010	2011	2012
Series	**200**					**300**						
Output, at basic prices	6087.8	6421.0	7630.2	8597.3	10142.0	11896.1 15965.3	18406.3	21270.0	20168.1	24106.6	30124.3	34945.3
Less: Intermediate consumption, at purchaser's prices	3055.4	3335.6	3814.0	4428.8	5717.9	6859.4 8654.5	9641.1	11647.5	10871.5	13636.4	17486.3	20341.5
Equals: VALUE ADDED, GROSS, at basic prices	3032.4	3085.4	3816.1	4168.5	4424.2	5036.8 7310.8	8765.2	9622.6	9296.6	10470.2	12638.0	14603.8
Compensation of employees	893.8	874.0	1074.1	1170.9	1079.7	1250.2 939.0	953.3	...	...	...	...	...

	Series	2001	2002	2003	2004	2005	2006	2007	2008	2009	2010	2011	2012
Taxes on production and imports, less Subsidies	200	30.2	135.5	44.8	75.3	114.6	139.8						
	300						198.8	278.3	...	...	...	...	...
Taxes on production and imports	200	30.2	135.5	44.8	75.3	114.6	139.8						
	300						198.8	278.3	...	...	...	...	...
Taxes on products	200	...	...	...	...	...	...						
	300						...	...	...	...	...	...	...
Other taxes on production	200	30.2	135.5	44.8	75.3	114.6	139.8						
	300						198.8	278.3	...	...	...	...	...
Less: Subsidies	200	...	...	...	...	...	...						
	300						...	...	...	...	...	...	...
OPERATING SURPLUS, GROSS	200	924.0	775.7	974.2	1221.6	1484.5	1800.3						
	300						2764.8	3840.2	...	...	...	...	...
MIXED INCOME, GROSS	200	1184.4	1300.2	1723.0	1700.8	1745.4	1846.4						
	300						3408.3	3693.3	...	...	...	...	...
Less: Consumption of fixed capital	200	...	...	...	...	...	...						
	300						1850.1	2034.3	...	...	...	...	...
OPERATING SURPLUS, NET	200	...	...	...	...	...	...						
	300						1474.8	2462.2	...	...	...	...	...
MIXED INCOME, NET	200	...	...	...	...	...	...						
	300						2848.2	3037.0	...	...	...	...	...
Gross capital formation	200	...	...	...	...	...	...						
	300						...	...	...	...	...	...	...

Table 2.3 Output, gross value added, and fixed assets by industries at current prices (ISIC Rev. 3) Financial intermediation; real estate, renting and business activities (J+K)

Series 200: 1993 SNA, córdoba, Western calendar year
Series 300: 1993 SNA, córdoba, Western calendar year

Data in millions

	Series	2001	2002	2003	2004	2005	2006	2007	2008	2009	2010	2011	2012
Output, at basic prices	200	9241.4	9979.7	11292.6	13119.0	14778.7	16803.5						
	300						26225.5	30442.0	34512.3	37199.7	38609.1	40844.9	44413.5
Less: Intermediate consumption, at purchaser's prices	200	2046.4	2102.7	2420.5	3015.1	3590.7	4386.3						
	300						5221.8	6330.9	7383.3	7461.1	7884.3	8435.4	9242.2
Equals: VALUE ADDED, GROSS, at basic prices	200	7194.9	7877.0	8872.1	10104.0	11188.0	12417.2						
	300						21003.7	24111.1	27129.0	29738.6	30724.8	32409.5	35171.3
Compensation of employees	200	1016.8	1046.9	1244.0	1515.9	1684.5	2140.1						
	300						2882.5	3633.8	...	...	...	...	...
Taxes on production and imports, less Subsidies	200	40.1	43.9	58.3	65.5	76.2	97.5						
	300						122.2	142.1	...	...	...	...	...
Taxes on production and imports	200	40.1	43.9	58.3	65.5	76.2	97.5						
	300						122.4	142.1	...	...	...	...	...
Taxes on products	200	...	...	...	...	...	...						
	300						...	...	...	...	...	...	...
Other taxes on production	200	40.1	43.9	58.3	65.5	76.2	97.5						
	300						122.4	142.1	...	...	...	...	...
Less: Subsidies	200	...	...	...	...	...	...						
	300						0.2	0.0	...	...	...	...	...
OPERATING SURPLUS, GROSS	200	4704.9	5208.9	5947.9	6809.8	7588.7	8237.7						
	300						13797.0	15535.0	...	...	...	...	...
MIXED INCOME, GROSS	200	1433.1	1577.3	1621.9	1712.8	1838.5	1941.8						
	300						4202.1	4800.2	...	...	...	...	...
Less: Consumption of fixed capital	200	...	...	...	...	...	...						
	300						400.5	488.8	...	...	...	...	...
OPERATING SURPLUS, NET	200	...	...	...	...	...	...						
	300						13401.1	15051.7	...	...	...	...	...
MIXED INCOME, NET	200	...	...	...	...	...	...						
	300						4197.4	4794.8	...	...	...	...	...
Gross capital formation	200	...	...	...	...	...	...						
	300						...	...	...	...	...	...	...

Table 2.3 Output, gross value added, and fixed assets by industries at current prices (ISIC Rev. 3) Public administration and defense; compulsory social security (L)

Series 200: 1993 SNA, córdoba, Western calendar year
Series 300: 1993 SNA, córdoba, Western calendar year

Data in millions

	2001	2002	2003	2004	2005	2006	2007	2008	2009	2010	2011	2012
Series	**200**					**300**						
Output, at basic prices	6594.5	6204.3	7135.6	8126.3	9712.9	10416.1						
						11384.2	10950.1	12823.8	14437.9	15868.6	19401.8	22785.0
Less: Intermediate consumption, at purchaser's prices	2944.0	2771.9	3236.6	3688.8	4476.0	4786.5						
						5302.7	4793.4	5887.9	7047.0	7987.9	10458.6	12282.3
Equals: VALUE ADDED, GROSS, at basic prices	3650.5	3432.4	3899.1	4437.5	5236.9	5629.6						
						6081.4	6156.7	6935.8	7390.9	7880.7	8943.1	10502.6
Compensation of employees	3603.5	3365.8	3849.0	4378.2	5157.6	5575.5						
						5972.7	6061.6	...	...	...	...	...
Taxes on production and imports, less Subsidies	4.8	23.3	14.7	22.6	62.3	51.7						
						57.6	43.3	...	...	...	...	...
Taxes on production and imports	4.8	23.3	14.7	22.6	62.3	51.7						
						57.6	43.3	...	...	...	...	...
Taxes on products	...	...	...	...	...	...						
						...	...	...	...	...	...	...
Other taxes on production	4.8	23.3	14.7	22.6	62.3	51.7						
						57.6	43.3	...	...	...	...	...
Less: Subsidies	...	...	...	...	...	...						
						...	...	...	...	...	...	...
OPERATING SURPLUS, GROSS	42.2	43.3	35.4	36.8	17.1	2.3						
						51.1	51.8	...	...	...	...	...
MIXED INCOME, GROSS	...	...	...	...	...	...						
						...	...	...	...	...	...	...
Less: Consumption of fixed capital	...	...	...	...	...	...						
						51.1	51.8	...	...	...	...	...
OPERATING SURPLUS, NET	...	...	...	...	...	...						
						...	...	...	...	...	...	...
MIXED INCOME, NET	...	...	...	...	...	...						
						...	...	...	...	...	...	...
Gross capital formation	...	...	...	...	...	...						
						...	...	...	...	...	...	...

Table 2.3 Output, gross value added, and fixed assets by industries at current prices (ISIC Rev. 3) Education; health and social work; other community, social and personal services (M+N+O)

Series 200: 1993 SNA, córdoba, Western calendar year
Series 300: 1993 SNA, córdoba, Western calendar year

Data in millions

	2001	2002	2003	2004	2005	2006	2007	2008	2009	2010	2011	2012
Series	**200**					**300**						
Output, at basic prices	6482.6	7322.8	8180.3	9281.9	10573.6	12211.0						
						16255.4	18830.7	22711.9	23338.2	24588.4	28338.9	31726.5
Less: Intermediate consumption, at purchaser's prices	1617.0	2139.6	2297.3	2711.7	3101.6	3656.7						
						5727.8	6581.4	7935.8	8372.5	9090.8	10911.1	12130.3
Equals: VALUE ADDED, GROSS, at basic prices	4865.6	5183.1	5882.9	6570.2	7472.0	8554.3						
						10527.7	12249.3	14776.1	14965.7	15497.6	17427.8	19596.3
Compensation of employees	3664.7	3991.3	4401.4	5074.4	5799.1	6882.9						
						7760.0	9562.1	...	...	...	...	...
Taxes on production and imports, less Subsidies	19.4	16.1	30.2	30.7	31.8	100.9						
						174.4	122.7	...	...	...	...	...
Taxes on production and imports	19.4	16.1	30.2	30.7	31.8	100.9						
						180.0	130.2	...	...	...	...	...
Taxes on products	...	...	...	...	...	...						
						...	...	...	...	...	...	...
Other taxes on production	19.4	16.1	30.2	30.7	31.8	100.9						
						180.0	130.2	...	...	...	...	...
Less: Subsidies	...	...	...	...	...	...						
						5.6	7.5	...	...	...	...	...
OPERATING SURPLUS, GROSS	617.3	615.4	786.3	952.4	1086.9	1123.3						
						1946.9	1873.0	...	...	...	...	...
MIXED INCOME, GROSS	564.2	560.4	665.0	512.7	554.2	447.2						
						646.4	691.5	...	...	...	...	...

	2001	2002	2003	2004	2005	2006	2007	2008	2009	2010	2011	2012
Series	**200**					**300**						
Less: Consumption of fixed capital	...	...	...	...	...	... 208.5	271.8	...	...	...	...	...
OPERATING SURPLUS, NET	...	...	...	...	...	... 1744.5	1607.9	...	...	...	...	...
MIXED INCOME, NET	...	...	...	...	...	... 640.3	684.7	...	...	...	...	...
Gross capital formation	...	...	...	...	...	... ...	...	...	...	...	...	...

Table 2.3 Output, gross value added, and fixed assets by industries at current prices (ISIC Rev. 3) Private households with employed persons (P)

Series 200: 1993 SNA, córdoba, Western calendar year
Series 300: 1993 SNA, córdoba, Western calendar year

Data in millions

	2001	2002	2003	2004	2005	2006	2007	2008	2009	2010	2011	2012
Series	**200**					**300**						
Output, at basic prices	709.2	754.9	811.0	882.0	965.2	1066.1 1847.3	1974.7	2111.1	2366.0	2546.9	2764.7	3004.1
Less: Intermediate consumption, at purchaser's prices	0.0	0.0	0.0	0.0	0.0	0.0 ...	...	...	...	...	...	...
Equals: VALUE ADDED, GROSS, at basic prices	709.2	754.9	811.0	882.0	965.2	1066.1 1847.3	1974.7	2111.1	2366.0	2546.9	2764.7	3004.1
Compensation of employees	709.2	754.9	811.0	882.0	965.2	1066.1 1847.3	1974.7	...	...	...	...	...
Taxes on production and imports, less Subsidies	0.0	0.0	0.0	0.0	0.0	0.0 ...	...	...	...	...	...	...
Taxes on production and imports	0.0	0.0	0.0	0.0	0.0	0.0 ...	...	...	...	...	...	...
Taxes on products	...	...	...	...	...	... ...	...	...	...	...	...	...
Other taxes on production	0.0	0.0	0.0	0.0	0.0	0.0 ...	...	...	...	...	...	...
Less: Subsidies	...	...	...	...	...	... ...	...	...	...	...	...	...
OPERATING SURPLUS, GROSS	0.0	0.0	0.0	0.0	0.0	0.0 ...	...	...	...	...	...	...
MIXED INCOME, GROSS	0.0	0.0	0.0	0.0	0.0	0.0 ...	...	...	...	...	...	...
Gross capital formation	...	...	...	...	...	... ...	...	...	...	...	...	...

Table 3.1 Government final consumption expenditure by function at current prices

Series 200: 1993 SNA, córdoba, Western calendar year

Data in millions

	2001	2002	2003	2004	2005	2006	2007	2008	2009	2010	2011	2012
Series	**200**											
General public services	2243.4	1979.4	2112.1	2555.2	2940.8	3847.1	3681.8					
Defence	336.2	418.6	472.7	457.1	510.3	596.6	661.4					
Public order and safety	863.6	994.1	1146.1	1232.4	1442.5	1806.8	2067.3					
Economic affairs	2106.3	1906.9	2439.5	2839.4	3678.4	2804.2	3025.2					
Environment protection	232.1	156.8	203.1	201.3	225.2	254.6	326.5					
Housing and community amenities	49.1	43.9	53.2	57.5	86.4	107.8	67.7					
Health	1509.5	1717.7	1850.9	1904.1	2276.7	2732.1	3353.5					
Recreation, culture and religion	34.9	36.3	39.5	50.4	45.8	57.3	65.9					
Education	1798.7	2243.0	2467.6	2979.9	3450.6	4080.1	5040.2					

	2001	2002	2003	2004	2005	2006	2007	2008	2009	2010	2011	2012
Series	**200**											
Social protection	468.0	360.7	332.9	349.1	363.1	384.2	416.3					
Plus: (Other functions)	181.9	220.5	236.3	260.8	279.5	302.9	541.2					
Equals: General government final consumption expenditure	9823.6	10078.0	11354.0	12887.1	15299.3	16973.6	19246.9					

Table 3.2 Individual consumption expenditure of households, NPISHs, and general government at current prices

Series 200: 1993 SNA, córdoba, Western calendar year
Series 300: 1993 SNA, córdoba, Western calendar year

Data in millions

	2001	2002	2003	2004	2005	2006	2007	2008	2009	2010	2011	2012
Series	**200**					**300**						
	Individual consumption expenditure of households											
Food and non-alcoholic beverages	16328.8	17280.5	18076.4	20598.6	23207.1	25456.7						
						27205.9	32093.2					
Alcoholic beverages, tobacco and narcotics	1874.0	1945.1	2092.4	2300.6	2508.9	2698.4						
						2917.0	3278.0					
Clothing and footwear	1886.5	2042.4	2101.7	2184.3	2463.3	2614.2						
						3000.2	3430.7					
Housing, water, electricity, gas and other fuels	6307.3	6865.4	7614.3	8354.6	9461.6	10464.9						
						13902.9	15373.9					
Furnishings, household equipment and routine maintenance of the house	2814.9	3030.8	3174.6	3515.9	3906.4	4416.5						
						5692.9	6298.8					
Health	3466.0	3879.4	4270.8	4831.0	5611.1	6529.9						
						5507.2	6200.5					
Transport	5097.3	5566.4	6254.4	7284.5	8689.7	10210.9						
						12691.2	14929.3					
Communication	1070.4	1344.0	1749.4	1928.7	2307.0	2790.0						
						3642.4	4472.1					
Recreation and culture	1265.2	1210.9	1374.0	1661.2	1890.7	2173.1						
						4035.8	4419.7					
Education	761.5	818.9	924.0	1013.8	1100.4	1283.3						
						2209.9	2508.9					
Restaurants and hotels	2754.9	3009.8	3348.1	3989.8	4665.6	5305.7						
						6269.2	7440.4					
Miscellaneous goods and services	707.3	860.2	950.9	1133.4	1259.0	1457.3						
						7361.4	8502.6					
Equals: Household final consumption expenditure in domestic market	44334.0	47853.8	51930.8	58796.2	67070.9	75401.0						
						94436.0	108948.1					
Plus: Direct purchases abroad by residents	1097.5	1072.1	1238.9	1517.1	1616.3	1816.2						
						20.9	28.1					
Less: Direct purchases in domestic market by non-residents	2258.0	2380.1	2924.5	3599.1	4020.6	4666.1						
						1094.9	1162.5					
Equals: Household final consumption expenditure	43173.5	46545.7	50245.2	56714.3	64666.5	72454.0						
						93361.9	107813.6					
	Individual consumption expenditure of non-profit institutions serving households (NPISHs)											
Equals: NPISHs final consumption expenditure	747.0	885.1	976.9	1087.5	1226.3	1376.9						
						3340.1	3613.2					
	Individual consumption expenditure of general government											
Housing	...	...	...	...	...	...						
						...	...					
Health	1284.0	1508.9	1542.7	1512.1	1936.0	2295.9						
						...	...					
Recreation and culture	...	...	...	...	...	...						
						...	...					
Education	1798.7	2136.1	2422.4	2938.0	3425.7	4053.6						
						...	...					
Social protection	...	...	...	...	...	...						
						...	...					
Plus:	225.5[a]	315.7[b]	353.5[b]	433.9[b]	365.6[b]	462.8[b]						
						...	...					

		2001	2002	2003	2004	2005	2006	2007	2008	2009	2010	2011	2012
Series		**200**					**300**						
Equals: Individual consumption expenditure of general government	c	3308.2	3960.7	4318.5	4884.0	5727.3	6812.3 6957.4	8613.9					
Equals: Total actual individual consumption		47228.7	51391.5	55540.6	62685.7	71620.1	80643.1 103659.5	120040.8					

[a] Includes individual consumption on medicines.
[b] Includes individual consumption on medicines and textbooks.
[c] Statistical discrepancy with equivalent item in Table 1.1 (Gross domestic product by expenditures at current prices) for years 1996-1997 since an institution was included in the category education but not in individual government consumption as presented in Table 1.1. A similar situation occurred with another institution during the period 2000-2007.

Table 4.1 Total Economy (S.1)

Series 300: 1993 SNA, córdoba, Western calendar year

Data in millions

	2001	2002	2003	2004	2005	2006	2007	2008	2009	2010	2011	2012
Series						**300**						
	I. Production account - Resources											
Output, at basic prices (otherwise, please specify)						210129.4	241687.1[a]					
Less: Financial intermediation services indirectly measured (only to be deducted if FISIM is not distributed to uses)						...	...					
Plus: Taxes less Subsidies on products						11248.0	12763.6[a]					
Plus: Taxes on products						11783.5	13600.3					
Less: Subsidies on products						535.5	836.8					
	I. Production account - Uses											
Intermediate consumption, at purchaser's prices						102142.1	117071.4					
GROSS DOMESTIC PRODUCT						119235.2	137379.3					
Less: Consumption of fixed capital						4453.0	4967.6					
NET DOMESTIC PRODUCT						114782.2	132411.7					
	II.1.1 Generation of income account - Resources											
GROSS DOMESTIC PRODUCT						119235.2	137379.3					
	II.1.1 Generation of income account - Uses											
Compensation of employees						43857.1	51454.0					
Taxes on production and imports, less Subsidies						13391.8	15220.2					
Taxes on production and imports						13933.1	16064.4					
Taxes on products						11783.5	13600.3					
Other taxes on production						2149.6	2464.1					
Less: Subsidies						541.3	844.2					
Subsidies on products						535.5	836.8					
Other subsidies on production						5.8	7.5					
OPERATING SURPLUS, GROSS						34178.2	40092.8					
MIXED INCOME, GROSS						27808.2	30612.3					
	II.1.2 Allocation of primary income account - Resources											
OPERATING SURPLUS, GROSS						34178.2	40092.8					
MIXED INCOME, GROSS						27808.2	30612.3					

	2001	2002	2003	2004	2005	2006	2007	2008	2009	2010	2011	2012
Series						**300**						
Compensation of employees						43740.6	51453.9					
Taxes on production and imports, less Subsidies						13393.8	15223.0					
Taxes on production and imports						13935.1	16067.2					
Taxes on products						11783.5	13600.3					
Other taxes on production						2151.7	2466.9					
Less: Subsidies						541.3	844.2					
Subsidies on products						535.5	836.8					
Other subsidies on production						5.8	7.5					
Property income						14051.3	17821.8					
II.1.2 Allocation of primary income account - Uses												
Property income						18572.0	21944.9					
GROSS NATIONAL INCOME						114600.1	133258.8					
II.2 Secondary distribution of income account - Resources												
GROSS NATIONAL INCOME						114600.1	133258.8					
Current taxes on income, wealth, etc.						4907.7	6158.1					
Social contributions						5214.9	6295.8					
Social benefits other than social transfers in kind						3880.0	4839.4					
Other current transfers						27675.0	32963.9					
II.2 Secondary distribution of income account - Uses												
Current taxes on income, wealth, etc.						4873.9	6114.8					
Social contributions						5213.8	6295.8					
Social benefits other than social transfers in kind						3881.0	4839.4					
Other current transfers						9057.5	11735.3					
GROSS DISPOSABLE INCOME						133251.4	154530.7					
II.4.1 Use of disposable income account - Resources												
GROSS DISPOSABLE INCOME						133251.4	154530.7					
Adjustment for the change in net equity of households on pension funds						11.0	18.0					
II.4.1 Use of disposable income account - Uses												
Final consumption expenditure						114724.4	130602.7					
Individual consumption expenditure						103659.5	120040.8					
Collective consumption expenditure						11064.9	10562.0					
Adjustment for the change in net equity of households on pension funds						11.0	18.0					
SAVING, GROSS						18527.0	23928.0					
III.1 Capital account - Changes in liabilities and net worth												
SAVING, GROSS						18527.0	23928.0					
Capital transfers, receivable less payable						26302.4	51516.4					
Capital transfers, receivable						32359.7	55862.3					
Less: Capital transfers, payable						6057.3	4345.9					

	2001	2002	2003	2004	2005	2006	2007	2008	2009	2010	2011	2012
Series						**300**						
Equals: CHANGES IN NET WORTH DUE TO SAVING AND CAPITAL TRANSFERS [b]						44829.4	75444.4					
III.1 Capital account - Changes in assets												
Gross capital formation						31554.7	40584.0					
Gross fixed capital formation						28016.6	33903.8					
Changes in inventories						3538.1	6680.2					
Acquisitions less disposals of valuables						...	...					
Acquisitions less disposals of non-produced non-financial assets						...	...					
NET LENDING (+) / NET BORROWING (-)						13274.8	34860.3					
III.2 Financial account - Changes in liabilities and net worth												
Net incurrence of liabilities						11457.1	3359.8					
Currency and deposits						5193.3	6252.2					
Securities other than shares						-3145.4	-499.3					
Loans						-3497.9	-26940.6					
Shares and other equity						7043.1	7115.2					
Insurance technical reserves						160.6	4069.2					
Financial derivatives						...	...					
Other accounts payable						5703.4	13363.2					
NET LENDING (+) / NET BORROWING (-) [c]						6376.2	30959.9					
III.2 Financial account - Changes in assets												
Net acquisition of financial assets						17833.2	34320.7					
Monetary gold and SDRs						1.0	-5.3					
Currency and deposits						8174.7	12686.9					
Securities other than shares						-3287.2	-579.9					
Loans						7596.3	10260.0					
Shares and other equity						2019.3	449.7					
Insurance technical reserves						160.6	4070.1					
Financial derivatives						...	...					
Other accounts receivable						3168.4	7439.2					

[a] Discrepancy between the total economy and the domestic sector accounts.
[b] Item does not consider consumption of fixed capital.
[c] Statistical discrepancy between net lending (+)/net borrowing (-) in the financial account and net lending (+)/net borrowing (-) in the capital account.

Table 4.2 Rest of the world (S.2)

Series 200: 1993 SNA, córdoba, Western calendar year
Series 300: 1993 SNA, córdoba, Western calendar year

Data in millions

	2001	2002	2003	2004	2005	2006	2007	2008	2009	2010	2011	2012
Series	**200**					**300**						
V.I External account of goods and services - Resources												
Imports of goods and services	26645.7	27936.4	31878.6	38963.7	47805.5	56688.6			79187.5	98063.2	127839.7	
						59283.7	73752.0					
Imports of goods	21727.8	22836.4	26144.7	32412.0	40271.1	48272.1			65678.1	82441.4	109059.4	
						50494.0	63375.8					
Imports of services	4917.9	5100.0	5733.9	6551.7	7534.4	8416.5			13509.5	15621.8	18780.3	
						8789.7	10376.2					
V.I External account of goods and services - Uses												
Exports of goods and services	12476.7	12846.4	15239.8	19492.5	23613.6	29518.4			45752.0	60009.3	75031.4	
						32239.8	39944.5					
Exports of goods	9483.6	9636.4	11348.5	14937.1	18451.8	23526.8			34365.9	47772.1	60242.6	
						26584.6	33577.4					
Exports of services	2993.1	3210.0	3891.3	4555.4	5161.8	5991.5			11386.0	12237.3	14788.8	
						5655.3	6367.2					
EXTERNAL BALANCE OF GOODS AND SERVICES	14169.0	15090.1	16638.8	19471.2	24191.9	27170.2			33435.6	38053.9	52808.3	
						27043.9	33807.5					
V.II External account of primary income and current transfers - Resources												
EXTERNAL BALANCE OF GOODS AND SERVICES	...	...	...	...	...	...			...	...	...	
						27043.9	33807.5					
Compensation of employees	...	...	...	...	...	...			...	...	...	
						116.5	0.1					
Taxes on production and imports, less Subsidies	...	...	...	...	...	...			...	...	...	
						...	...					
Taxes on production and imports	...	...	...	...	...	...			...	...	...	
						...	...					
Taxes on products	...	...	...	...	...	...			...	...	...	
						...	...					
Other taxes on production	...	...	...	...	...	...			...	...	...	
						...	...					
Less: Subsidies	...	...	...	...	...	...			...	...	...	
						...	...					
Subsidies on products	...	...	...	...	...	...			...	...	...	
						...	...					
Other subsidies on production	...	...	...	...	...	...			...	...	...	
						...	...					
Property income	...	...	...	...	...	...			...	...	...	
						5294.8	5087.6					
Current taxes on income, wealth, etc.	...	...	...	...	...	...			...	...	...	
						...	...					
Social contributions	...	...	...	...	...	...			...	...	...	
						...	...					
Social benefits other than social transfers in kind	...	...	...	...	...	...			...	...	...	
						1.0	0.0					
Other current transfers	...	...	...	...	...	...			...	...	...	
						240.1	248.2					
Adjustment for the change in net equity of households on pension funds	...	...	...	...	...	...			...	...	...	
						...	...					
V.II External account of primary income and current transfers - Uses												
Compensation of employees	...	...	...	...	...	...			...	...	...	
						...	...					
Taxes on production and imports, less Subsidies	...	...	...	...	...	...			...	...	...	
						2.0	2.8					
Taxes on production and imports	...	...	...	...	...	...			...	...	...	
						2.0	2.8					
Taxes on products	...	...	...	...	...	...			...	...	...	
						...	...					
Other taxes on production	...	...	...	...	...	...			...	...	...	
						2.0	2.8					
Less: Subsidies	...	...	...	...	...	...			...	...	...	
						...	...					
Subsidies on products	...	...	...	...	...	...			...	...	...	
						...	...					
Other subsidies on production	...	...	...	...	...	...			...	...	...	
						...	...					
Property income	...	...	...	...	...	...			...	...	...	
						774.1	964.4					

	2001	2002	2003	2004	2005	2006	2007	2008	2009	2010	2011	2012
Series	**200**					**300**						
Current taxes on income and wealth, etc.	...	...	...	...	...	... 33.8	43.3		...	...	...	
Social contributions	...	...	...	...	...	... 1.0	0.0		...	...	...	
Social benefits other than social transfers in kind	...	...	...	...	...	... ...	...		...	...	...	
Other current transfers	...	...	...	...	...	... 18857.6	21476.8		...	...	...	
Adjustment for the change in net equity of households on pension funds	...	...	...	...	...	... ...	...		...	...	...	
CURRENT EXTERNAL BALANCE	...	...	...	...	...	... 13027.7	16656.1		...	...	...	
V.III.1 Capital account - Changes in liabilities and net worth												
CURRENT EXTERNAL BALANCE	...	...	...	...	...	... 13027.7	16656.1		...	...	...	
Capital transfers, receivable less payable	...	...	...	...	...	... -26302.4	-51516.4		...	...	...	
Capital transfers, receivable	...	...	...	...	...	... 3.1	0.0		...	...	...	
Less: Capital transfers, payable	...	...	...	...	...	... 26305.5	51516.4		...	...	...	
Equals: CHANGES IN NET WORTH DUE TO SAVING AND CAPITAL TRANSFERS	...	...	...	...	...	... -13274.8	-34860.3		...	...	...	
V.III.1 Capital account - Changes in assets												
Acquisitions less disposals of non-produced non-financial assets	...	...	...	...	...	... ...	...		...	...	...	
NET LENDING (+) / NET BORROWING (-)	...	...	...	...	...	... -13274.8	-34860.3		...	...	...	
V.III.2 Financial account - Changes in liabilities and net worth												
Net incurrence of liabilities	...	...	...	...	...	... 3314.7	6786.3		...	...	...	
Currency and deposits	...	...	...	...	...	... 3121.2	6443.3		...	...	...	
Securities other than shares	...	...	...	...	...	... -141.8	-80.6		...	...	...	
Loans	...	...	...	...	...	... 4.8	-9.8		...	...	...	
Shares and other equity	...	...	...	...	...	... 21.5	389.9		...	...	...	
Insurance technical reserves	...	...	...	...	...	... ...	...		...	...	...	
Financial derivatives	...	...	...	...	...	... ...	...		...	...	...	
Other accounts payable	...	...	...	...	...	... 309.0	43.5		...	...	...	
NET LENDING (+) / NET BORROWING (-) [a]	...	...	...	...	...	... -6376.2	-30959.9		...	...	...	
V.III.2 Financial account - Changes in assets												
Net acquisition of financial assets	...	...	...	...	...	... -3061.5	-24173.6		...	...	...	
Monetary gold and SDRs	...	...	...	...	...	... -1.0	5.3		...	...	...	
Currency and deposits	...	...	...	...	...	... 139.7	8.6		...	...	...	
Securities other than shares	...	...	...	...	...	... ...	...		...	...	...	
Loans	...	...	...	...	...	... -11089.5	-37210.4		...	...	...	
Shares and other equity	...	...	...	...	...	... 5045.3	7055.4		...	...	...	
Insurance technical reserves	...	...	...	...	...	... ...	...		...	...	...	
Financial derivatives	...	...	...	...	...	... ...	...		...	...	...	
Other accounts receivable	...	...	...	...	...	... 2844.0	5967.5		...	...	...	

[a] Statistical discrepancy between net lending (+)/net borrowing (-) in the financial account and net lending (+)/net borrowing (-) in the capital account.

Table 4.3 Non-financial Corporations (S.11)

Series 300: 1993 SNA, córdoba, Western calendar year | **Data in millions**

	2001	2002	2003	2004	2005	2006	2007	2008	2009	2010	2011	2012
Series						**300**						
I. Production account - Resources												
Output, at basic prices (otherwise, please specify)						103977.1	124004.7					
I. Production account - Uses												
Intermediate consumption, at purchaser's prices						61873.9	73482.6					
VALUE ADDED GROSS, in basic prices						42103.2	50522.1					
Less: Consumption of fixed capital						3298.4	3643.1					
VALUE ADDED NET, at basic prices						38804.8	46879.1					
II.1.1 Generation of income account - Resources												
VALUE ADDED GROSS, at basic prices						42103.2	50522.1					
II.1.1 Generation of income account - Uses												
Compensation of employees						18258.9	22077.8					
Other taxes less Other subsidies on production						1358.1	1616.8					
Other taxes on production						1363.7	1624.3					
Less: Other subsidies on production						5.6	7.5					
OPERATING SURPLUS, GROSS						22486.2	26827.5					
II.1.2 Allocation of primary income account - Resources												
OPERATING SURPLUS, GROSS						22486.2	26827.5					
Property income						651.9	1876.8					
II.1.2 Allocation of primary income account - Uses												
Property income						8557.2	10359.8					
BALANCE OF PRIMARY INCOMES						14580.9	18344.6					
II.2 Secondary distribution of income account - Resources												
BALANCE OF PRIMARY INCOMES						14580.9	18344.6					
Social contributions						381.8	505.5					
Other current transfers						416.1	552.1					
II.2 Secondary distribution of income account - Uses												
Current taxes on income, wealth, etc.						3592.4	5431.2					
Social benefits other than social transfers in kind						381.8	505.5					
Other current transfers						1026.3	1615.9					
GROSS DISPOSABLE INCOME						10378.3	11849.6					
II.4.1 Use of disposable income account - Resources												
GROSS DISPOSABLE INCOME						10378.3	11849.6					
II.4.1 Use of disposable income account - Uses												
Adjustment for the change in net equity of households on pension funds						...	...					
SAVING, GROSS						10378.3	11849.6					

	2001	2002	2003	2004	2005	2006	2007	2008	2009	2010	2011	2012
Series						**300**						
III.1 Capital account - Changes in liabilities and net worth												
SAVING, GROSS						10378.3	11849.6					
Capital transfers, receivable less payable						800.7	1430.6					
Capital transfers, receivable						848.7	1480.4					
Less: Capital transfers, payable						48.0	49.9					
Equals: CHANGES IN NET WORTH DUE TO SAVING AND CAPITAL TRANSFERS [a]						11179.0	13280.1					
III.1 Capital account - Changes in assets												
Gross capital formation						18247.7	24512.8					
Gross fixed capital formation						16305.8	19064.6					
Changes in inventories						1940.7	5449.0					
Acquisitions less disposals of valuables						1.1	-0.8					
Acquisitions less disposals of non-produced non-financial assets						24.9	15.1					
NET LENDING (+) / NET BORROWING (-) [b]						-7093.6	-11247.7					
III.2 Financial account - Changes in liabilities and net worth												
Net incurrence of liabilities						17544.7	25594.9					
Currency and deposits						...	...					
Securities other than shares						331.7	297.1					
Loans						6020.1	8633.9					
Shares and other equity						5771.9	7504.8					
Insurance technical reserves						...	...					
Financial derivatives						...	...					
Other accounts payable						5421.1	9159.0					
NET LENDING (+) / NET BORROWING (-)						-11711.5	-13522.6					
III.2 Financial account - Changes in assets												
Net acquisition of financial assets						5833.2	12072.3					
Monetary gold and SDRs						...	...					
Currency and deposits						366.5	4001.1					
Securities other than shares						-800.9	-821.0					
Loans						-80.6	59.1					
Shares and other equity						2149.5	245.4					
Insurance technical reserves						61.0	4016.1					
Financial derivatives						...	...					
Other accounts receivable						4137.8	4571.6					

[a] Item does not consider consumption of fixed capital.
[b] Statistical discrepancy between net lending (+)/net borrowing (-) in the financial account and net lending (+)/net borrowing (-) in the capital account.

Table 4.4 Financial Corporations (S.12)

Series 300: 1993 SNA, córdoba, Western calendar year **Data in millions**

	2001	2002	2003	2004	2005	2006	2007	2008	2009	2010	2011	2012
Series						**300**						
	I. Production account - Resources											
Output, at basic prices (otherwise, please specify)						8726.7	10617.2					
	I. Production account - Uses											
Intermediate consumption, at purchaser's prices						3220.2	3957.3					
VALUE ADDED GROSS, at basic prices						5506.5	6659.9					
Less: Consumption of fixed capital						321.7	375.5					
VALUE ADDED NET, at basic prices						5184.7	6284.4					
	II.1.1 Generation of income account - Resources											
VALUE ADDED GROSS, at basic prices						5506.5	6659.9					
	II.1.1 Generation of income account - Uses											
Compensation of employees						1895.0	2404.9					
Other taxes less Other subsidies on production						65.5	76.6					
Other taxes on production						65.8	76.6					
Less: Other subsidies on production						0.2	0.0					
OPERATING SURPLUS, GROSS						3545.9	4178.4					
	II.1.2 Allocation of primary income account - Resources											
OPERATING SURPLUS, GROSS						3545.9	4178.4					
Property income						4948.1	6320.0					
	II.1.2 Allocation of primary income account - Uses											
Property income						6759.4	7351.8					
BALANCE OF PRIMARY INCOMES						1734.6	3146.6					
	II.2 Secondary distribution of income account - Resources											
BALANCE OF PRIMARY INCOMES						1734.6	3146.6					
Social contributions						142.5	214.4					
Other current transfers						517.8	549.3					
	II.2 Secondary distribution of income account - Uses											
Current taxes on income, wealth, etc.						408.5	517.5					
Social benefits other than social transfers in kind						132.0	196.3					
Other current transfers						919.8	974.1					
GROSS DISPOSABLE INCOME						934.6	2222.5					
	II.4.1 Use of disposable income account - Resources											
GROSS DISPOSABLE INCOME						934.6	2222.5					
	II.4.1 Use of disposable income account - Uses											
Adjustment for the change in net equity of households on pension funds						10.5	18.1					
SAVING, GROSS						924.1	2204.3					

	2001	2002	2003	2004	2005	2006	2007	2008	2009	2010	2011	2012
Series						**300**						
III.1 Capital account - Changes in liabilities and net worth												
SAVING, GROSS						924.1	2204.3					
Capital transfers, receivable less payable						544.3	352.1					
Capital transfers, receivable						3590.2	572.3					
Less: Capital transfers, payable						3045.9	220.2					
Equals: CHANGES IN NET WORTH DUE TO SAVING AND CAPITAL TRANSFERS [a]						1468.5	2556.4					
III.1 Capital account - Changes in assets												
Gross capital formation						258.3	685.7					
Gross fixed capital formation						250.5	636.6					
Changes in inventories						9.1	49.9					
Acquisitions less disposals of valuables						-1.3	-0.9					
Acquisitions less disposals of non-produced non-financial assets						-21.9	-18.1					
NET LENDING (+) / NET BORROWING (-)						1232.0	1888.8					
III.2 Financial account - Changes in liabilities and net worth												
Net incurrence of liabilities						7366.1	10656.4					
Currency and deposits						5193.3	6251.5					
Securities other than shares						-1617.2	1189.5					
Loans						1492.4	1765.4					
Shares and other equity						1271.2	-389.7					
Insurance technical reserves						114.1	199.1					
Financial derivatives						...	...					
Other accounts payable						912.3	1640.7					
NET LENDING (+) / NET BORROWING (-) [b]						947.6	3034.2					
III.2 Financial account - Changes in assets												
Net acquisition of financial assets						8313.7	13690.6					
Monetary gold and SDRs						1.0	-5.3					
Currency and deposits						5681.6	4078.4					
Securities other than shares						-2741.0	-1147.2					
Loans						7001.5	9380.5					
Shares and other equity						51.1	38.9					
Insurance technical reserves						33.2	-5.7					
Financial derivatives						...	...					
Other accounts receivable						-1713.6	1351.0					

[a] Item does not consider consumption of fixed capital.
[b] Statistical discrepancy between net lending (+)/net borrowing (-) in the financial account and net lending (+)/net borrowing (-) in the capital account.

Table 4.5 General Government (S.13)

Series 300: 1993 SNA, córdoba, Western calendar year — **Data in millions**

	2001	2002	2003	2004	2005	2006	2007	2008	2009	2010	2011	2012
Series						**300**						
I. Production account - Resources												
Output, at basic prices (otherwise, please specify)						18030.7	19068.8					
I. Production account - Uses												
Intermediate consumption, at purchaser's prices						6894.5	6841.0					
VALUE ADDED GROSS, at basic prices						11136.2	12227.8					
Less: Consumption of fixed capital						78.7	88.0					
VALUE ADDED NET, at basic prices						11057.5	12139.8					
II.1.1 Generation of income account - Resources												
VALUE ADDED GROSS, at basic prices						11136.2	12227.8					
II.1.1 Generation of income account - Uses												
Compensation of employees						10824.0	11973.6					
Other taxes less Other subsidies on production						116.9	45.7					
Other taxes on production						116.9	45.7					
Less: Other subsidies on production						...	...					
OPERATING SURPLUS, GROSS						195.2	208.5					
II.1.2 Allocation of primary income account - Resources												
OPERATING SURPLUS, GROSS						195.2	208.5					
Taxes on production and imports, less Subsidies						13393.8	15223.0					
Taxes on production and imports						13935.1	16067.2					
Taxes on products						11783.5	13600.3					
Other taxes on production						2151.7	2466.9					
Less: Subsidies						541.3	844.2					
Subsidies on products						535.5	836.8					
Other subsidies on production						5.8	7.5					
Property income						1244.9	1573.7					
II.1.2 Allocation of primary income account - Uses												
Property income						2837.2	3020.6					
BALANCE OF PRIMARY INCOMES						11996.7	13984.6					
II.2 Secondary distribution of income account - Resources												
BALANCE OF PRIMARY INCOMES						11996.7	13984.6					
Current taxes on income, wealth, etc.						4907.7	6158.1					
Social contributions						4613.6	5502.6					
Other current transfers						5528.7	6764.6					
II.2 Secondary distribution of income account - Uses												
Current taxes on income, wealth, etc.						1.5	3.0					
Social benefits other than social transfers in kind						3290.2	4064.3					

	2001	2002	2003	2004	2005	2006	2007	2008	2009	2010	2011	2012
Series						**300**						
Other current transfers						4739.6	5281.2					
GROSS DISPOSABLE INCOME						19015.4	23061.4					
II.4.1 Use of disposable income account - Resources												
GROSS DISPOSABLE INCOME						19015.4	23061.4					
II.4.1 Use of disposable income account - Uses												
Final consumption expenditure						18022.3	19175.9					
Individual consumption expenditure						6957.4	8613.9					
Collective consumption expenditure						11064.9	10562.0					
Adjustment for the change in net equity of households on pension funds						0.6	-0.2					
SAVING, GROSS						992.5	3885.7					
III.1 Capital account - Changes in liabilities and net worth												
SAVING, GROSS						992.5	3885.7					
Capital transfers, receivable less payable						24520.6	49415.6					
Capital transfers, receivable						27389.2	53263.5					
Less: Capital transfers, payable						2868.6	3847.9					
Equals: CHANGES IN NET WORTH DUE TO SAVING AND CAPITAL TRANSFERS [a]						25513.2	53301.3					
III.1 Capital account - Changes in assets												
Gross capital formation						3587.8	5324.9					
Gross fixed capital formation						3454.7	5169.6					
Changes in inventories						132.9	154.2					
Acquisitions less disposals of valuables						0.1	1.0					
Acquisitions of non-produced non-financial assets						84.6	1.0					
NET LENDING (+) / NET BORROWING (-)						21840.8	47975.5					
III.2 Financial account - Changes in liabilities and net worth												
Net incurrence of liabilities						-17194.8	-37850.2					
Currency and deposits						0.0	0.8					
Securities other than shares						-1859.9	-1986.0					
Loans						-14537.1	-42649.6					
Shares and other equity						...	...					
Insurance technical reserves						46.5	3870.1					
Financial derivatives						...	...					
Other accounts payable						-844.3	2914.6					
NET LENDING (+) / NET BORROWING (-) [b]						20776.5	43299.7					
III.2 Financial account - Changes in assets												
Net acquisition of financial assets						3581.7	5450.5					
Monetary gold and SDRs						...	...					
Currency and deposits						2218.2	2386.1					
Securities other than shares						254.6	1384.8					
Loans						559.5	473.3					

	2001	2002	2003	2004	2005	2006	2007	2008	2009	2010	2011	2012
Series						**300**						
Shares and other equity						-223.8	-0.7					
Insurance technical reserves						2.3	0.0					
Financial derivatives						...	...					
Other accounts receivable						771.0	1207.1					

[a] Item does not consider consumption of fixed capital.
[b] Statistical discrepancy between net lending (+)/net borrowing (-) in the financial account and net lending (+)/net borrowing (-) in the capital account.

Table 4.6 Households (S.14)

Series 300: 1993 SNA, córdoba, Western calendar year **Data in millions**

	2001	2002	2003	2004	2005	2006	2007	2008	2009	2010	2011	2012
Series						**300**						
I. Production account - Resources												
Output, at basic prices (otherwise, please specify)						75896.9	85807.8					
I. Production account - Uses												
Intermediate consumption, at purchaser's prices						27900.2	32132.3					
VALUE ADDED GROSS, at basic prices						47996.7	53675.5					
Less: Consumption of fixed capital						703.1	778.9					
VALUE ADDED NET, at basic prices						47293.7	52896.6					
II.1.1 Generation of income account - Resources												
VALUE ADDED GROSS, at basic prices						47996.7	53675.5					
II.1.1 Generation of income account - Uses												
Compensation of employees						11709.1	13570.6					
Other taxes less Other subsidies on production						590.2	704.5					
Other taxes on production						590.2	704.5					
Less: Other subsidies on production						...	...					
OPERATING SURPLUS, GROSS						7889.3	8788.1					
MIXED INCOME, GROSS						27808.2	30612.3					
II.1.2 Allocation of primary income account - Resources												
OPERATING SURPLUS, GROSS						7889.3	8788.1					
MIXED INCOME, GROSS						27808.2	30612.3					
Compensation of employees						43740.6	51453.9					
Property income						7139.6	7962.8					
II.1.2 Allocation of primary income account - Uses												
Property income						390.1	1198.5					
BALANCE OF PRIMARY INCOMES						86187.6	97618.5					
II.2 Secondary distribution of income account - Resources												
BALANCE OF PRIMARY INCOMES						86187.6	97618.5					
Social contributions						17.8	15.8					
Social benefits other than social transfers in kind						3880.0	4839.4					

	2001	2002	2003	2004	2005	2006	2007	2008	2009	2010	2011	2012
Series						**300**						
Other current transfers						15034.2	19428.4					
II.2 Secondary distribution of income account - Uses												
Current taxes on income, wealth, etc.						871.3	163.0					
Social contributions						5213.8	6295.8					
Social benefits other than social transfers in kind						17.8	15.8					
Other current transfers						1395.5	2838.4					
GROSS DISPOSABLE INCOME						97621.1	112589.1					
II.4.1 Use of disposable income account - Resources												
GROSS DISPOSABLE INCOME						97621.1	112589.1					
Adjustment for the change in net equity of households on pension funds						11.0	18.0					
II.4.1 Use of disposable income account - Uses												
Final consumption expenditure						93361.9	107813.6					
Individual consumption expenditure						93361.9	107813.6					
SAVING, GROSS						4270.2	4793.5					
III.1 Capital account - Changes in liabilities and net worth												
SAVING, GROSS						4270.2	4793.5					
Capital transfers, receivable less payable						132.2	219.2					
Capital transfers, receivable						168.6	404.0					
Less: Capital transfers, payable						36.4	184.8					
Equals: CHANGES IN NET WORTH DUE TO SAVINGS AND CAPITAL TRANSFERS [a]						4402.4	5012.7					
III.1 Capital account - Changes in assets												
Gross capital formation						9418.9	10049.5					
Gross fixed capital formation						7964.5	9019.8					
Changes in inventories						1454.4	1029.1					
Acquisitions less disposals of valuables						0.0	0.7					
Acquisitions less disposals of non-produced non-financial assets						-83.8	0.0					
NET LENDING (+) / NET BORROWING (-)						-4932.6	-5036.8					
III.2 Financial account - Changes in liabilities and net worth												
Net incurrence of liabilities						3725.5	4964.0					
Currency and deposits						...	...					
Securities other than shares						...	...					
Loans						3528.0	5300.1					
Shares and other equity						...	...					
Insurance technical reserves						...	...					
Financial derivatives						...	...					
Other accounts payable						197.5	-336.1					
NET LENDING (+) / NET BORROWING (-) [b]						-3644.6	-1861.5					

	2001	2002	2003	2004	2005	2006	2007	2008	2009	2010	2011	2012
Series						**300**						
	III.2 Financial account - Changes in assets											
Net acquisition of financial assets						80.9	3102.6					
Currency and deposits						-58.5	2232.8					
Securities other than shares						-0.8	5.3					
Loans						112.5	348.8					
Shares and other equity						42.6	166.2					
Insurance technical reserves						64.1	59.4					
Financial derivatives						...	...					
Other accounts receivable						-79.0	290.1					

[a] Item does not consider consumption of fixed capital.
[b] Statistical discrepancy between net lending (+)/net borrowing (-) in the financial account and net lending (+)/net borrowing (-) in the capital account.

Table 4.7 Non-profit institutions serving households (S.15)

Series 300: 1993 SNA, córdoba, Western calendar year **Data in millions**

	2001	2002	2003	2004	2005	2006	2007	2008	2009	2010	2011	2012
Series						**300**						
	I. Production account - Resources											
Output, at basic prices (otherwise, please specify)						3497.9	3958.7					
	I. Production account - Uses											
Intermediate consumption, at purchaser's prices						2253.3	2428.3					
VALUE ADDED GROSS, at basic prices						1244.6	1530.4					
Less: Consumption of fixed capital						51.1	82.2					
VALUE ADDED NET, at basic prices						1193.5	1448.2					
	II.1.1 Generation of income account - Resources											
VALUE ADDED GROSS, at basic prices						1244.6	1530.4					
	II.1.1 Generation of income account - Uses											
Compensation of employees						1170.0	1427.1					
Other taxes less Other subsidies on production						13.1	13.1					
Other taxes on production						13.1	13.1					
Less: Other subsidies on production						...	...					
OPERATING SURPLUS, GROSS						61.6	90.1					
	II.1.2 Allocation of primary income account - Resources											
OPERATING SURPLUS, GROSS						61.6	90.1					
Property income						66.8	88.6					
	II.1.2 Allocation of primary income account - Uses											
Property income						28.1	14.3					
BALANCE OF PRIMARY INCOMES						100.3	164.4					
	II.2 Secondary distribution of income account - Resources											
BALANCE OF PRIMARY INCOMES						100.3	164.4					

	2001	2002	2003	2004	2005	2006	2007	2008	2009	2010	2011	2012
Series						**300**						
Social contributions						59.2	57.5					
Other current transfers						6178.1	5669.4					
II.2 Secondary distribution of income account - Uses												
Current taxes on income, wealth, etc.						0.2	0.1					
Social benefits other than social transfers in kind						59.2	57.5					
Other current transfers						976.3	1025.7					
GROSS DISPOSABLE INCOME						5302.0	4808.1					
II.4.1 Use of disposable income account - Resources												
GROSS DISPOSABLE INCOME						5302.0	4808.1					
II.4.1 Use of disposable income account - Uses												
Final consumption expenditure						3340.1	3613.2					
Individual consumption expenditure						3340.1	3613.2					
Adjustment for the change in net equity of households on pension funds						...	...					
SAVING, GROSS						1961.8	1194.9					
III.1 Capital account - Changes in liabilities and net worth												
SAVING, GROSS						1961.8	1194.9					
Capital transfers, receivable less payable						304.5	99.0					
Capital transfers, receivable						363.0	142.1					
Less: Capital transfers, payable						58.5	43.2					
Equals: CHANGES IN NET WORTH DUE TO SAVING AND CAPITAL TRANSFERS [a]						2266.4	1293.9					
III.1 Capital account - Changes in assets												
Gross capital formation						42.0	11.2					
Gross fixed capital formation						41.2	13.3					
Changes in inventories						0.9	-2.1					
Acquisitions less disposals of valuables						...	...					
Acquisitions less disposals of non-produced non-financial assets						-3.8	2.0					
NET LENDING (+) / NET BORROWING (-)						2228.1	1280.6					
III.2 Financial account - Changes in liabilities and net worth												
Net incurrence of liabilities						15.5	-5.4					
Currency and deposits						...	...					
Securities other than shares						...	...					
Loans						-1.3	9.6					
Shares and other equity						...	...					
Insurance technical reserves						...	...					
Financial derivatives						...	...					
Other accounts payable						16.8	-15.0					
NET LENDING (+) / NET BORROWING (-) [b]						8.2	10.1					

	2001	2002	2003	2004	2005	2006	2007	2008	2009	2010	2011	2012
Series						**300**						
	III.2 Financial account - Changes in assets											
Net acquisition of financial assets						23.7	4.7					
Currency and deposits						-33.0	-11.4					
Securities other than shares						0.9	-1.9					
Loans						3.5	-1.7					
Shares and other equity						...	...					
Insurance technical reserves						-0.0	0.3					
Financial derivatives						...	...					
Other accounts receivable						52.3	19.3					

[a] Item does not consider consumption of fixed capital.
[b] Statistical discrepancy between net lending (+)/net borrowing (-) in the financial account and net lending (+)/net borrowing (-) in the capital account.

Table 5.2 Cross classification of Gross value added by industries and institutional sectors (ISIC Rev. 4) Non-financial corporations

Series 300: 1993 SNA, córdoba, Western calendar year **Data in millions**

	2001	2002	2003	2004	2005	2006	2007	2008	2009	2010	2011	2012
Series						**300**						
	Industries											
Agriculture, forestry and fishing						3959.0	4151.0					
Manufacturing, mining and quarrying and other industrial activities						16298.0	19372.0					
Of which: manufacturing						13904.1	17225.1					
Construction						2389.5	3148.0					
Wholesale and retail trade, transportation and storage, accommodation and food service activities						9551.8	12136.3					
Information and communication						2568.3	3511.4					
Financial and insurance activities						150.3	227.7					
Real estate activities						1301.6	1308.3					
Professional, scientific, technical, administrative and support service activities						1804.0	2145.6					
Public administration and defence, education, human health and social work activities						2784.0	3130.1					
Other service activities						1296.7	1391.7					
VALUE ADDED GROSS, at basic prices						42103.2	50522.1					

Table 5.2 Cross classification of Gross value added by industries and institutional sectors (ISIC Rev. 4) Financial corporations

Series 300: 1993 SNA, córdoba, Western calendar year

Data in millions

	2001	2002	2003	2004	2005	2006	2007	2008	2009	2010	2011	2012
Series						**300**						
Industries												
Agriculture, forestry and fishing						...	...					
Manufacturing, mining and quarrying and other industrial activities						...	...					
Of which: manufacturing						...	...					
Construction						...	...					
Wholesale and retail trade, transportation and storage, accommodation and food service activities						1.3	1.4					
Information and communication						...	...					
Financial and insurance activities						5505.0	6658.4					
Real estate activities						...	...					
Professional, scientific, technical, administrative and support service activities						...	...					
Public administration and defence, education, human health and social work activities						...	...					
Other service activities						0.2	0.2					
Plus: Statistical discrepancy (otherwise, please specify)						0.0	-0.0					
VALUE ADDED GROSS, at basic prices						5506.5	6659.9					

Table 5.2 Cross classification of Gross value added by industries and institutional sectors (ISIC Rev. 4) General government

Series 300: 1993 SNA, córdoba, Western calendar year

Data in millions

	2001	2002	2003	2004	2005	2006	2007	2008	2009	2010	2011	2012
Series						**300**						
Industries												
Agriculture, forestry and fishing						...	...					
Manufacturing, mining and quarrying and other industrial activities						...	...					
Of which: manufacturing						...	...					
Construction						...	...					
Wholesale and retail trade, transportation and storage, accommodation and food service activities						...	...					
Information and communication						...	...					
Financial and insurance activities						...	...					
Real estate activities						...	...					
Professional, scientific, technical, administrative and support service activities						...	...					

	2001	2002	2003	2004	2005	2006	2007	2008	2009	2010	2011	2012
Series						**300**						
Public administration and defence, education, human health and social work activities						11136.2	12227.8					
Other service activities						...	...					
VALUE ADDED GROSS, at basic prices						11136.2	12227.8					

Table 5.2 Cross classification of Gross value added by industries and institutional sectors (ISIC Rev. 4) Households

Series 300: 1993 SNA, córdoba, Western calendar year

Data in millions

	2001	2002	2003	2004	2005	2006	2007	2008	2009	2010	2011	2012
Series						**300**						
Industries												
Agriculture, forestry and fishing						14920.0	17568.3					
Manufacturing, mining and quarrying and other industrial activities						2985.3	3209.1					
Of which: manufacturing						2515.9	2602.0					
Construction						3386.3	3142.5					
Wholesale and retail trade, transportation and storage, accommodation and food service activities						11249.4	12412.4					
Information and communication						...	...					
Financial and insurance activities						141.5	165.5					
Real estate activities						8580.0	9536.5					
Professional, scientific, technical, administrative and support service activities						3459.6	4005.2					
Public administration and defence, education, human health and social work activities						110.9	120.4					
Other service activities						3163.7	3515.6					
VALUE ADDED GROSS, at basic prices						47996.7	53675.5					

Table 5.2 Cross classification of Gross value added by industries and institutional sectors (ISIC Rev. 4) Non-profit institutions serving households

Series 300: 1993 SNA, córdoba, Western calendar year

Data in millions

	2001	2002	2003	2004	2005	2006	2007	2008	2009	2010	2011	2012
Series						**300**						
Industries												
Agriculture, forestry and fishing						...	...					
Manufacturing, mining and quarrying and other industrial activities						...	...					
Of which: manufacturing						...	...					
Construction						15.8	58.8					

	2001	2002	2003	2004	2005	2006	2007	2008	2009	2010	2011	2012
Series						300						
Wholesale and retail trade, transportation and storage, accommodation and food service activities						...	...					
Information and communication						...	...					
Financial and insurance activities						...	...					
Real estate activities						...	...					
Professional, scientific, technical, administrative and support service activities						61.7	63.9					
Public administration and defence, education, human health and social work activities						197.7	235.5					
Other service activities						969.4	1172.2					
VALUE ADDED GROSS, at basic prices						1244.6	1530.4					

Table 5.2 Cross classification of Gross value added by industries and institutional sectors (ISIC Rev. 4) Total economy

Series 300: 1993 SNA, córdoba, Western calendar year **Data in millions**

	2001	2002	2003	2004	2005	2006	2007	2008	2009	2010	2011	2012
Series						300						
Industries												
Agriculture, forestry and fishing						18878.9	21719.2					
Manufacturing, mining and quarrying and other industrial activities						19283.3	22581.2					
Of which: manufacturing						16420.0	19827.1					
Construction						5791.7	6349.3					
Wholesale and retail trade, transportation and storage, accommodation and food service activities						20802.5	24550.1					
Information and communication						2568.3	3511.4					
Financial and insurance activities						5796.7	7051.6					
Real estate activities						9881.6	10844.8					
Professional, scientific, technical, administrative and support service activities						5325.3	6214.7					
Public administration and defence, education, human health and social work activities						14228.9	15713.7					
Other service activities						5430.0	6079.7					
VALUE ADDED GROSS, at basic prices						107987.2	124615.7					

Niger

Source

The responsibility for compiling the complete national accounts (the macroeconomic aggregates useful for analysis, economic forecasting and planning) is granted to the National Institute of Statistics (INS - Institut National de la Statistique) by the decree N° 2004-264/PRM/ME/F of 14 September 2004, which transformed the former Directorate of Statistics and National Accounts (Direction de la Statistique et des Comptes Nationaux) into the National Institute of Statistics (INS).

Two national accounts publications are issued during the year: the first is titled "Flash estimates of year n-1" ("Comptes rapides de l'année n-1") and is issued at the end of March of year n; whereas the second is titled "Estimates of year n" ("Estimations de l'année n"), being issued in November of the year n and also publishing the provisional accounts of year n-1 and the final accounts of year n-2. These publications are available from INS's website: www.ins.ne

More detailed information can be obtained upon request from INS's National Accounts Division, Directorate of Statistics and Economic Studies (Division des comptes nationaux, Direction des statistiques et des études économiques).

General

National accounting in Niger is guided largely by the 1993 System of National Accounts (1993 SNA). The establishment of national accounts according to the 1993 SNA dates back to the year 2000. The reporting period for national accounts is the calendar year.

The national accounts publications are divided in four parts: the first describing the methodological notes; the second offering a brief analysis of the recent evolution of the economic situation; the third provides the national accounts main aggregates, as well as summary tables; and the fourth part presents diverse economic information in the form of annexes.

The publications provide:
- GDP by institutional sector;
- GDP by industry and sector (current and constant prices, the latter at 2006 prices);
- GDP and its uses (current and constant prices, the latter at 2006 prices);
- Production, compensation of employees, indirect taxes and gross fixed capital formation (GFCF) by industry;
- Tables with integrated economic accounts;
- Resource and use table;
- Assorted tables (decomposition of GDP by main uses; GFCF by industry; deflators and growth rates; government financial statistics; balance of payments; monetary situation and convergence indicators in the area of the West African Economic and Monetary Union (WAEMU)).

Methodology:

Overview of GDP Compilation

The process of GDP compilation follows the steps below:

- Inventory of available sources: to ensure that the main basic data are available in order to allow the elaboration of the national accounts. These sources include mainly data on agriculture and husbandry; large companies in the formal sector, the general government budget and financial statistics, international trade and balance of payments, and results from household consumption surveys.
- Translation of source data into national accounts language: this step allows allocating each operation to a national accounts aggregate. For doing so, bridge tables are established that allow the translation of the basic

data into the nomenclature of economic activities, products, transactions, institutional sectors and etc. It is worth noting that the nomenclature used follows the conventions adopted by the Member States of AFRISTAT (NAEMA and NOPEMA). The aggregated classifications include 24 branches of activity and 39 products.
- Balancing of resources and uses and of the accounts of branches.
- Elaboration of the Resource and use tables and the integrated economic accounts.

It is worthwhile mentioning that the value added does not take into account the financial intermediation services indirectly measured (FISIM) because of the difficulties in distributing it to uses, and that value added is measured at producers' prices.

The GDP estimation is done according to the three approaches: the production approach, the expenditure approach and the income approach. The principle used consists in confronting the first two approaches, which are generally favoured by the Nigerien national accountants, to arrive at a reconciled GDP figure.

Expenditure Approach

The Gross Domestic Product is calculated by summing up the expenditures on final consumption, the gross capital formation and the exports minus imports of goods and services. The methods used to estimate the GDP by the expenditure approach are summarised as follows:

Final consumption expenditure of the general government
By convention, it represents the value of non-market services produced by the non-market branches of government and government agencies less the partial payments made by households for the provision of these services. It is calculated based on administrative documents.

Final consumption expenditure of households
It is valued based on the results of household expenditure surveys (QUIBB 2005, and then ENBC 2007/2008), factoring in the rural and urban population growth rates. These surveys provide a detailed household consumption structure in the rural and urban environments.

Gross fixed capital formation (GFCF)
- Non-financial and financial corporations sectors: the GFCF of these institutional units is determined on the basis of their accounting documents by calculating the variations in fixed assets appearing in the balances for years N and N-1.
- General government sector: the translation of public accounting terms into national accounts terms allows the direct calculation of general government GFCF by using the allocation of capital contained in the investment budget.
- Household sector: the GFCF for livestock products is determined by using the following formula: GFCF = 2/3 (births − infant mortality − slaughter + imports − exports). The GFCF of informal sector enterprises not in the primary sector follows the evolution of the value added of this subsector.

Changes in stocks:
At the level of the branches of activity Agriculture (crop and animal production), Forestry and Fishing, there is no direct method to estimate the stocks. However, for each of these branches, the balancing of resources and uses by product allow the calculation of stocks. For the general government sector, the assumption is that there are no changes in stocks. In general, it is at the time of balancing the resources and uses of goods and services that this item is determined or adjusted.

External trade
Foreign trade data is extracted from the balance of payments calculated by the Central Bank of West African States (BCEAO).

Income Approach

In this approach, the GDP is equal to the sum of the compensation of employees, gross operating surplus/mixed income, taxes on production and imports, less subsidies. Each of these elements should be evaluated. It is not an easy method to use directly due to difficulties in obtaining certain basic statistics. In effect, only the wages of public administration are more or less well known. Wages of non-financial and financial corporations are not known in an exhaustive manner, as well as income/ operating surplus. Thus, for the determination of the elements of GDP above, generally trade offs are made that involve households.

Production Approach

This approach consists in estimating the GDP by the calculation of value added obtained by deducting from the value of goods and services produced the intermediary consumption of goods and services used in the above-mentioned production.

The main data sources used are as follows:
- For the non-financial corporations, the fiscal and statistical declarations annually produced by these corporations;
- For the financial corporations, the annual balances;
- For the households: Informal sector: the estimation of the informal sector is based on the informal sector survey conducted in 1995; a new survey is currently being carried out and will be used for future estimations of the informal sector accounts; Crops and animal production – the main sources are: Ministry of Agriculture (MAG/EL), Office of Live Products of Niger (OPVN), Market Information System (SIM), External trade statistics, Activity report of the ONAHA, Early Warning System (SAP), Fund for stabilisation and equalisation of prices in Niger (CSPPN), Data obtained from certain projects of rural development, Information Bulletin on the food situation in Niger; Forestry and hunting: basic data within this domain are hard to get, and available information are usually not of good quality. The main sources are: Directorate of Fishing and Aquaculture, FAO report on consumption of wood in Niger, The Energy Project, IHPC. Fishing: production in weight and average prices are provided by the Directorate of Fishing and Aquaculture. When fish prices are not available, projections are made for the producer price using the average annual variation in the Consumer Price Index (CPI). One fishing survey was carried out, which allowed improving the estimation of fishing production.

- For the general government, the main sources are the National Treasury for the receipts; the General Directorate of Budget for the expenditure; the Interior Ministry for the budgets of the municipalities; The General Directorate of the Economy for the government financial statistics; the National Social Security Fund (CNSS); and the UNDP for external aid.

The estimation methods according to the production approach are as follows:

- Non-financial corporations: data are gathered from accounting documents, and data are entered by branch of activity. For the sake of exhaustiveness, the National Accounts Division estimates the data for the missing institutional units by applying growth indicators calculated from a sample of units that provided data for the years n-1 and n.

- Financial corporations: these include bank and insurance activities. The production of bank services called financial intermediation services indirectly measured (FISIM) is taken as the difference between the property income received (interest on loans) and the property income paid (interest on deposits). The value added is calculated as the difference between the production of these services and the expenses from the production process other than compensation of employees. The production of insurance services is calculated by the sum of premiums earned for the year, net income investments of reserves less losses claims incurred and changes in reserves of life insurance.

- General Government: this sector includes the central government, local public administration and the public administration of the social security. In Niger, the treatment varies according to the data source. In general, public administration is considered as non-market production and valued at production costs identified according to a nomenclature that allows the passage from budget accounts to national accounts; namely, intermediary consumption, compensation of employees, other costs (operating expenses, cultural actions, public ceremonies, topographic works), and other taxes (less subsidies) on production. To that, it remains to be added the production of market goods and services. According to the recommendations of the 1993 SNA, external aid (reimbursable or not) follows a specific treatment, that consists in allocating the parts relative to financing investments, operating expenses and compensation of employees. In the absence of detailed statistics, ratios are used instead. The method of calculating output, intermediary consumption and value added is the same as exposed above.

- Households: the institutional sector of households includes the following subsectors (or branches of economy activity): agriculture, divided in crop production and animal production; fishing; forestry; and the non-agricultural branches of informal economic activity.
- Calculation of the value added of crop production: first, net production and producer prices are determined. The former is achieved by applying the corresponding loss/waste ratio to the gross production of each crop. The latter depends on whether the crop is produced during the Winter season or in the other season.
- For Winter crops, the producer price corresponds to the average price weighted by volume, observed in 16 markets during the months of October, November and December of each year.
- For products for which only consumer prices are available, recourse is had to the average marginal rate, which is arrived at on the basis of the prices of Winter crops.
- Where no price information on a product is available, the variation rate in consumer price indices or the average variation in the price of cereal products is used.

The intermediary consumption is arrived at by calculating the value of agricultural inputs (seeds, manure, light equipment and fertilizers) or by applying an intermediary-consumption ratio.
- Calculation of the value added of animal production: After calculating the number of livestock by applying the rate of gain per animal species, the production quantity is determined as follows: Production (P) = Births (B) – IM – 1/3 AM where B = total (T) x birth rate (BR); IM = infant mortality = B x Infant mortality rate (IMR); and AM = adult mortality = T x Adult mortality rate (AMR). To determine the producer prices, an average price is calculated which is weighted by the number of animals sold or slaughtered by district and animal type. The prices are collected in the various markets.

When no producer prices are available, there are two cases:
- For products for which only consumer prices are available, the annual variation of average producer prices follows the evolution of consumer prices.
- Where no price information on a product is available, an annual average rate is calculated on the basis on the variation of the meat price index.

The intermediary consumption is arrived at by calculating the value of inputs, mainly dry stock feed, bran, vaccines and other phytosanitary and petroleum products or by applying an intermediary-consumption ratio.
- Calculation of the value added of forestry and fishing: Fishing Tonnages and average prices per kg charged by fishermen are provided by the Directorate of Fishing and Aquaculture. Where the price of fish is not available, producer prices are determined in accordance with the average annual variation of fish prices in the Niamey market. The production of fuelwood is determined by using the average annual consumption per capita provided by the FAO. Prices are provided by the Energy Project or based on consumer price trends of "housing, electricity, gas and other fuels." The production of timber, tanning and other products is determined on the basis of informal construction production. As for prices, it is used the change in the price index relative to "housing, electricity, gas and other fuels." The intermediary consumption for these two branches is arrived at by applying an intermediary-consumption ratio to the value of production.
- Calculation of the value added of non-agricultural informal economic activity: production exercised by households without the legal obligation of filing accounting documents. Output and intermediary consumption are estimated for each branch with the help of price and volume indices, having as a basis the national survey on the informal sector conducted in 1995.

Overview of the Compilation of the Integrated Economic Accounts

The integrated economic accounts (IEA) in Niger have been elaborated and published regularly for a number of years. They are, in fact, a summary table providing an overview of a given economy (constrained by what is recommended in the new SNA) that allows the three methodological approaches to GDP calculation to be made coherent between themselves.

The data sources for this table are basically those used for the three GDP approaches. The aggregates not covered by those three approaches are calculated favouring the institutional sectors for which information is more readily available, namely the financial and non-financial corporations and the general government; whereas data for the households are generally derived as a balancing item.

The IEA cover the households, general government, non-financial corporations and financial corporations; to these institutional sectors it remains to be added a fictional sector (FISIM) and the rest of the world. It presents six accounts: the production account and of external trade of goods and services; the generation of income account; the allocation of primary income account; the secondary distribution of income account; the use of disposable income account; and the capital account. The financial account is not yet compiled.

The number of transaction types compiled is around 30 and the main difficulty lies at the level of the household sector, since the transactions are not very well know.

Table 1.1 Gross domestic product by expenditures at current prices

Series 100: 1993 SNA, CFA franc, Western calendar year — **Data in millions**

	2001	2002	2003	2004	2005	2006	2007	2008	2009	2010	2011	2012
Series	**100**											
	Expenditures of the gross domestic product											
Final consumption expenditure	1261901.0	1370495.0	1417644.0	1474392.0	1586806.0	1675494.0	1838927.0	2077649.0	2339388.0	2462448.0	2677821.0	2935454.0
Household final consumption expenditure	1012766.0	1109876.0	1148836.0	1194333.0	1287922.0	1369387.0	1495310.0	1689986.0	1898625.0	2044606.0	2206191.0	2420570.0
NPISHs final consumption expenditure	14732.0	15203.0	16129.0	17372.0	18734.0	19921.0	21752.0	24584.0	27785.0	31402.0	35490.0	40110.0
General government final consumption expenditure	234403.0	245417.0	252679.0	262687.0	280150.0	286186.0	321865.0	363080.0	412978.0	386440.0	436140.0	474774.0
Individual consumption expenditure	36770.0	38498.0	48902.0	50839.0	54350.0	55521.0	62443.0	70439.0	79548.0	73399.0	85516.0	91259.0
Collective consumption expenditure	197633.0	206919.0	203777.0	211848.0	225800.0	230665.0	259422.0	292641.0	333430.0	313041.0	350624.0	383515.0
Gross capital formation	226121.0	259106.0	250600.0	223339.0	410372.0	449700.0	470965.0	776509.0	885288.0	1131543.0	1160766.0	1175503.0
Gross fixed capital formation	210453.0	229894.0	231797.0	258139.0	384618.0	430199.0	467984.0	746513.0	883824.0	1101631.0	1158727.0	1168147.0
Changes in inventories	15668.0	29212.0	18803.0	-34800.0	25754.0	19501.0	2981.0	29996.0	1464.0	29912.0	2039.0	7356.0
Acquisitions less disposals of valuables	...	...	...	...	...	...	...	...	...	...	...	...
Exports of goods and services	241321.0	230006.0	261276.0	282791.0	333068.0	344704.0	358453.0	429008.0	517883.0	628718.0	632144.0	856980.0
Exports of goods	199721.0	194806.0	224481.0	233451.0	286900.0	297353.0	317891.0	370418.0	470701.0	570131.0	599454.0	791947.0
Exports of services	41600.0	35200.0	36795.0	49340.0	46168.0	47351.0	40562.0	58590.0	47182.0	58587.0	32690.0	65033.0
Less: Imports of goods and services	350722.0	364821.0	394796.0	450078.0	553202.0	563059.0	615383.0	863512.0	1194112.0	1390424.0	1445203.0	1510043.0
Imports of goods	242823.0	258721.0	283903.0	311551.0	405862.0	391276.0	438354.0	594410.0	847188.0	972943.0	1034500.0	1039302.0
Imports of services	107900.0	106100.0	111893.0	138527.0	147340.0	171783.0	177029.0	269102.0	346924.0	417481.0	410703.0	470741.0
Equals: GROSS DOMESTIC PRODUCT	1378621.0	1494786.0	1534724.0	1530444.0	1777044.0	1906839.0	2052962.0	2419654.0	2548447.0	2832285.0	3025528.0	3457894.0

Table 1.2 Gross domestic product by expenditures at constant prices

Series 100: 1993 SNA, CFA franc, Western calendar year — **Data in millions**

	2001	2002	2003	2004	2005	2006	2007	2008	2009	2010	2011	2012
Series	**100**											
Base year	**2006**											
	Expenditures of the gross domestic product											
Final consumption expenditure	1441868.8	1516723.3	1594197.1	1610708.3	1615980.5	1675494.0	1753645.0	1844034.0	1966280.0	2023040.0	2149173.0	2258613.0
Household final consumption expenditure	1157608.0	1223446.0	1293683.0	1334181.0	1326523.0	1369387.0	1436501.0	1498855.0	1585413.0	1666532.0	1754539.0	1835299.0
NPISHs final consumption expenditure	16335.0	17262.0	18254.0	18825.0	18720.0	19921.0	20415.0	21804.0	23201.0	25595.0	27732.0	30412.0
General government final consumption expenditure	267926.0	276015.0	282260.0	257702.0	270738.0	286186.0	296729.0	323374.0	357666.0	330913.0	366902.0	392902.0
Individual consumption expenditure	42029.0	43298.0	44277.0	40425.0	42470.0	55521.0	45418.0	48506.0	53357.0	48021.0	53159.0	59013.0
Collective consumption expenditure	225897.0	232717.0	237983.0	217277.0	228268.0	230665.0	251311.0	274868.0	304309.0	282892.0	313743.0	333889.0
Gross capital formation	292122.0	328316.0	303310.0	292901.0	427587.0	449701.0	449820.0	690818.0	733508.0	880680.0	849660.0	863079.0
Gross fixed capital formation	278372.0	301921.0	283792.0	303189.0	399951.0	430199.0	448193.0	670990.0	735451.0	861569.0	868906.0	856659.0
Changes in inventories	13750.0	26395.0	19518.0	-10288.0	27636.0	19502.0	1627.0	19828.0	-1943.0	19111.0	-19246.0	6420.0
Acquisitions less disposals of valuables	0.0	0.0	0.0	0.0	0.0	0.0	0.0	0.0	0.0	0.0	0.0	0.0
Exports of goods and services	315480.0	290364.0	293487.0	306465.0	326625.0	344704.0	354011.0	407550.0	480852.0	575721.0	570510.0	725752.0
Exports of goods	261096.1	245926.8	252155.8	252994.5	281350.1	47351.0	313951.7	351573.0	437044.0	522073.0	539093.0	670677.0
Exports of services	54383.9	44437.2	41331.2	53470.5	45274.9	47351.0	40059.3	55977.0	43808.0	53648.0	31417.0	55075.0
Less: Imports of goods and services	495054.0	498960.0	498921.0	531902.0	567484.0	563059.0	590639.0	786990.0	1040590.0	1160284.0	1196581.0	1217770.0
Imports of goods	342751.5	353848.7	357874.2	368190.8	416340.1	391276.0	420728.2	541735.0	738269.0	811904.0	849941.0	838142.0
Imports of services	152302.5	145111.3	141046.8	163711.2	151143.9	171783.0	169910.8	245255.0	302321.0	348380.0	346640.0	379628.0
Equals: GROSS DOMESTIC PRODUCT	1554416.8	1636443.3	1692073.1	1678172.3	1802708.5	1906838.0	1966837.0	2155412.0	2140051.0	2319157.0	2372762.0	2629674.0

Table 1.3 Relations among product, income, savings, and net lending aggregates

Series 100: 1993 SNA, CFA franc, Western calendar year — **Data in millions**

	2001	2002	2003	2004	2005	2006	2007	2008	2009	2010	2011	2012
Series	**100**											
GROSS DOMESTIC PRODUCT	1378621.0	1494786.0	1534724.0	1530444.0	1777044.0	1906839.0	2052962.0	2419654.0	2548447.0	2832285.0	3025528.0	3457894.0
Plus: Compensation of employees - from and to the rest of the world, net	4873.0	6065.0	6995.0	7184.0	9709.0	14120.0	14564.0	14835.0	15085.0	15572.0	12059.0	12860.0
Plus: Compensation of employees - from the rest of the world	6016.0	7143.0	8114.0	8896.0	11000.0	15187.0	17573.0	18191.0	19540.0	23572.0	34864.0	37945.0
Less: Compensation of employees - to the rest of the world	1143.0	1078.0	1119.0	1712.0	1291.0	1067.0	3009.0	3356.0	4455.0	8000.0	22805.0	25085.0
Plus: Property income - from and to the rest of the world, net	-15857.0	-22936.0	-22181.0	-13994.0	-14721.0	-13486.0	-14775.0	-23317.0	-31409.0	-37409.0	-36159.0	-36374.0
Plus: Property income - from the rest of the world	7817.0	4794.0	2453.0	5090.0	8550.0	15277.0	16698.0	24318.0	22457.0	6982.0	9364.0	37945.0
Less: Property income - to the rest of the world	23674.0	27730.0	24634.0	19084.0	23271.0	28763.0	31473.0	47635.0	53866.0	44391.0	45523.0	74319.0
Sum of Compensation of employees and property income - from and to the rest of the world, net	-10984.0	-16871.0	-15186.0	-6810.0	-5012.0	634.0	-211.0	-8482.0	-16324.0	-21837.0	-24100.0	-23514.0

	2001	2002	2003	2004	2005	2006	2007	2008	2009	2010	2011	2012
Series	**100**											
Plus: Sum of Compensation of employees and property income - from the rest of the world	13833.0	11937.0	10567.0	13986.0	19550.0	30464.0	34271.0	42509.0	41997.0	30554.0	44228.0	75890.0
Less: Sum of Compensation of employees and property income - to the rest of the world	24817.0	28808.0	25753.0	20796.0	24562.0	29830.0	34482.0	50991.0	58321.0	52391.0	68328.0	99404.0
Plus: Taxes less subsidies on production and imports - from and to the rest of the world, net	...	...	...	...	...	...	...	...	...	...	...	...
Equals: GROSS NATIONAL INCOME	1367637.0	1477915.0	1519538.0	1523634.0	1772032.0	1907473.0	2052751.0	2411172.0	2532123.0	2810448.0	3001428.0	3434380.0
Plus: Current transfers - from and to the rest of the world, net	52689.0	36801.0	54108.0	54875.0	95834.0	85421.0	88758.0	103147.0	71193.0	222076.0	161891.0	188106.0
Plus: Current transfers - from the rest of the world	64448.0	45391.0	59657.0	67927.0	114494.0	104294.0	99635.0	113697.0	80347.0	250957.0	222877.0	196906.0
Less: Current transfers - to the rest of the world	11759.0	8590.0	5549.0	13052.0	18660.0	18873.0	10877.0	10550.0	9154.0	28881.0	60986.0	8800.0
Equals: GROSS NATIONAL DISPOSABLE INCOME	1420326.0	1514716.0	1573646.0	1578509.0	1867866.0	1992894.0	2141509.0	2514319.0	2603316.0	3032524.0	3163319.0	3622486.0
Less: Final consumption expenditure / Actual final consumption	1261901.0	1370496.0	1417644.0	1474392.0	1586805.0	1675494.0	1838927.0	2077649.0	2339388.0	2462448.0	2677821.0	2935454.0
Equals: SAVING, GROSS	158425.0	144221.0	156002.0	104117.0	281060.0	317400.0	302582.0	436670.0	263928.0	570076.0	485498.0	687032.0
Plus: Capital transfers - from and to the rest of the world, net	29885.0	64387.0	42564.0	203143.0	99329.0	909444.0	128847.0	114897.0	120396.0	97025.0	71844.0	139237.0
Plus: Capital transfers - from the rest of the world	29885.0	64387.0	42564.0	203143.0	99329.0	909444.0	128847.0	114897.0	120396.0	97025.0	71844.0	139237.0
Less: Capital transfers - to the rest of the world	...	...	...	...	...	...	...	...	...	...	...	...
Less: Gross capital formation	226121.0	259106.0	250600.0	223339.0	410372.0	449700.0	470965.0	776509.0	885288.0	1131543.0	1160766.0	1175503.0
Less: Acquisitions less disposals of non-produced non-financial assets	...	...	...	...	...	...	...	...	...	...	...	...
Equals: NET LENDING (+) / NET BORROWING (-) OF THE NATION	-37811.0	-50498.0	-53034.0	83921.0	-29983.0	777144.0	-39536.0	-224942.0	-500964.0	-464442.0	-603424.0	-349234.0
	Net values: Gross National Income / Gross National Disposable Income / Saving Gross less Consumption of fixed capital											
Less: Consumption of fixed capital	65990.0	66460.0	65440.0	54590.0	44282.0	62580.0	72190.0	72540.0	84860.0	87860.0	94134.0	109957.0
Equals: NET NATIONAL INCOME	1301647.0	1411455.0	1454098.0	1469044.0	1727750.0	1844893.0	1980561.0	2338632.0	2447263.0	2722588.0	2907294.0	3324423.0
Equals: NET NATIONAL DISPOSABLE INCOME	1354336.0	1448256.0	1508206.0	1523919.0	1823584.0	1930314.0	2069319.0	2441779.0	2518456.0	2944664.0	3069185.0	3512529.0
Equals: SAVING, NET	92435.0	77761.0	90562.0	49527.0	236778.0	254820.0	230392.0	364130.0	179068.0	482216.0	391364.0	577075.0

Table 2.1 Value added by industries at current prices (ISIC Rev. 3)

Series 100: 1993 SNA, CFA franc, Western calendar year **Data in millions**

	2001	2002	2003	2004	2005	2006	2007	2008	2009	2010	2011	2012
Series	**100**											
	Industries											
Agriculture, hunting, forestry; fishing	593627.0	658069.0	676833.0	615991.0	754411.0	817662.0	842593.0	1045424.0	999357.0	1158359.0	1156805.0	1320036.0
Agriculture, hunting, forestry	579778.0	641784.0	632458.0	580897.0	716012.0	786733.0	810469.0	1008753.0	951167.0	1098014.0	1092717.0	1252281.0
Agriculture, hunting and related service activities	538485.0	597053.0	586522.0	532876.0	665497.0	733795.0	755295.0	949032.0	886822.0	1031328.0	1022343.0	1179609.0
Forestry, logging and related service activities	41293.0	44731.0	45936.0	48021.0	50515.0	52938.0	55174.0	59721.0	64345.0	66686.0	70374.0	72672.0
Fishing	13849.0	16285.0	44375.0	35094.0	38399.0	30929.0	32124.0	36671.0	48190.0	60345.0	64088.0	67755.0
Mining and quarrying	30997.0	29067.0	29668.0	31428.0	35659.0	40096.0	90775.0	144399.0	162627.0	203462.0	226029.0	372830.0

	2001	2002	2003	2004	2005	2006	2007	2008	2009	2010	2011	2012
Series	**100**											
Manufacturing	81946.0	87467.0	90753.0	94107.0	98349.0	102635.0	106578.0	117559.0	128256.0	134918.0	143942.0	209146.0
Electricity, gas and water supply	15458.0	15042.0	19174.0	17969.0	19576.0	24590.0	22158.0	24289.0	28600.0	32293.0	40498.0	38918.0
Construction	31459.0	33978.0	36635.0	38697.0	41622.0	47471.0	51584.0	58096.0	64096.0	71643.0	76173.0	83448.0
Wholesale, retail trade, repair of motor vehicles, motorcycles and personal and households goods; hotels and restaurants	208716.0	218820.0	218110.0	222405.0	260404.0	273887.0	290831.0	323339.0	384236.0	403338.0	435528.0	460419.0
Wholesale, retail trade, repair of motor vehicles, motorcycles and personal and household goods	190571.0	199972.0	197209.0	199340.0	235441.0	247234.0	262022.0	292350.0	350606.0	367787.0	397703.0	420446.0
Hotels and restaurants	18145.0	18848.0	20900.0	23065.0	24963.0	26653.0	28809.0	30958.0	33630.0	35551.0	37825.0	39973.0
Transport, storage and communications	82411.0	87299.0	93980.0	106495.0	115068.0	124105.0	134886.0	147359.0	156493.0	171911.0	193196.0	209863.0
Land transport; transport via pipelines, water transport; air transport; Supporting and auxiliary transport activities; activities of travel agencies	70787.0	75327.0	78139.0	88063.0	90796.0	94727.0	102538.0	109864.0	116219.0	117892.0	130146.0	142722.0
Post and telecommunications	11624.0	11972.0	15841.0	18432.0	24272.0	29378.0	32348.0	37495.0	40274.0	54019.0	63050.0	67141.0
Financial intermediation; real estate, renting and business activities	57565.0	60841.0	63667.0	70488.0	78931.0	78406.0	93854.0	101528.0	108673.0	115564.0	124844.0	129214.0
Financial intermediation	10858.0	9694.0	13465.0	17863.0	20884.0	21611.0	26131.0	27464.0	31082.0	35349.0	42637.0	45473.0
Real estate, renting and business activities	46707.0	51147.0	50202.0	52625.0	58047.0	56795.0	67723.0	74064.0	77591.0	80215.0	82207.0	83741.0
Public administration and defence; compulsory social security	119731.0	120022.0	143403.0	139496.0	153027.0	166930.0	181111.0	193665.0	225082.0	215784.0	248325.0	280804.0
Education; health and social work; other community, social and personal services	70930.0	80152.0	74590.0	79979.0	88336.0	95934.0	99782.0	104144.0	114196.0	122247.0	134175.0	147010.0
Education	22329.0	25135.0	23546.0	25430.0	29658.0	32689.0	32845.0	34242.0	37082.0	40197.0	43413.0	47233.0
Health and social work	27294.0	32577.0	28144.0	30542.0	32192.0	36266.0	35978.0	37160.0	39390.0	42620.0	43243.0	46220.0
Other community, social and personal services	21307.0	22440.0	22900.0	24007.0	26486.0	26979.0	30959.0	32742.0	37724.0	39430.0	47519.0	53557.0
Private households with employed persons	9169.0	9167.0	10275.0	10349.0	11736.0	12006.0	12306.0	12613.0	12991.0	13355.0	13769.0	14196.0
Plus: Statistical discrepancy	0.0	...	...	...	...	...	...	...	...	...	...	...
Equals: VALUE ADDED, GROSS, in basic prices	1302009.0[a]	1399923.0[a]	1457088.0[a]	1427403.0[a]	1657118.0[a]	1783723.0[a]	1926458.0	2272384.0[a]	2384607.0	2642874.0	2793284.0	3265884.0
Less: Financial intermediation services indirectly measured (FISIM)	7884.0	8025.0	10448.0	12719.0	14599.0	15081.0	18235.0	19165.0	21690.0	22668.0	24341.0	26960.0
Plus: Taxes less Subsidies on products	84496.0	102888.0	97667.0	115759.0	134524.0	138196.0	144737.0	166435.0	185530.0	212080.0	256588.0	218971.0
Plus: Taxes on products	84496.0	102888.0	97667.0	115759.0	134524.0	138196.0	144737.0	166435.0	185530.0	212080.0	256588.0	218971.0
Less: Subsidies on products	0.0	0.0	0.0	0.0	0.0	0.0	0.0	0.0	0.0	0.0	0.0	0.0
Plus: Statistical discrepancy	0.0	0.0	0.0	0.0	0.0	0.0	0.0	0.0	0.0	0.0	0.0	0.0
Equals: GROSS DOMESTIC PRODUCT	1378621.0	1494786.0	1544307.0	1530443.0	1777043.0	1906838.0	2052962.0	2419654.0	2548447.0	2832286.0	3025531.0	3457895.0

[a] Includes financial intermediation services indirectly measured (FISIM).

Table 2.2 Value added by industries at constant prices (ISIC Rev. 3)

Series 100: 1993 SNA, CFA franc, Western calendar year — **Data in millions**

	2001	2002	2003	2004	2005	2006	2007	2008	2009	2010	2011	2012
Series	**100**											
Base year	**2006**											
Industries												
Agriculture, hunting, forestry; fishing	628501.0	675016.0	710137.0	652893.0	741568.0	817662.0	855579.0	994179.0	899393.0	1041398.0	1010544.0	1139813.0
Agriculture, hunting, forestry	587677.0	632553.0	666040.0	612234.0	702052.0	786733.0	823833.0	961131.0	859922.0	994257.0	961753.0	1089558.0
Agriculture, hunting and related service activities	544189.0	587319.0	619065.0	563643.0	651795.0	733795.0	768974.0	904488.0	801435.0	933758.0	899716.0	1026489.0
Forestry, logging and related service activities	43488.0	45234.0	46975.0	48591.0	50257.0	52938.0	54859.0	56643.0	58487.0	60499.0	62037.0	63069.0
Fishing	40824.0	42463.0	44097.0	40659.0	39516.0	30929.0	31746.0	33048.0	39471.0	47141.0	48791.0	50255.0
Mining and quarrying	36924.0	38336.0	38924.0	41309.0	39830.0	40096.0	37762.0	36976.0	51598.0	60490.0	72462.0	142653.0
Manufacturing	90128.0	92393.0	93914.0	99857.0	100244.0	102635.0	102946.0	106924.0	111654.0	115322.0	119930.0	156638.0
Electricity, gas and water supply	26276.0	26289.0	26343.0	24537.0	24865.0	24590.0	21271.0	23135.0	25074.0	27515.0	24183.0	25561.0
Construction	34519.0	36681.0	40538.0	42572.0	45187.0	47471.0	49177.0	51628.0	55705.0	61017.0	63644.0	68417.0
Wholesale, retail trade, repair of motor vehicles, motorcycles and personal and household goods; hotels and restaurants	230718.0	235358.0	245733.0	258304.0	268459.0	273887.0	277060.0	290335.0	307138.0	311906.0	326463.0	338940.0
Wholesale, retail trade, repair of motor vehicles, motorcycles and personal and household goods	208337.0	212071.0	222038.0	233586.0	243040.0	247234.0	249805.0	259114.0	274439.0	278333.0	291539.0	302881.0
Hotels and restaurants	22381.0	23287.0	23695.0	24718.0	25419.0	26653.0	27255.0	31223.0	32699.0	33573.0	34924.0	36059.0
Transport, storage and communications	108957.0	112956.0	115441.0	121424.0	123857.0	124105.0	127006.0	133066.0	139658.0	145700.0	155644.0	168179.0
Land transport; transport via piplines, water transport; air transport; Supporting and auxiliary transport activities; activities of travel agencies	91065.1	95003.5	92037.8	96009.4	90747.0	94727.0	95621.0	100012.0	103944.0	102950.0	110116.0	119964.0
Post and telecommunications	17891.9	17952.5	23403.2	25414.6	33110.0	29378.0	31385.0	33054.0	35714.0	42750.0	45528.0	48215.0
Financial intermediation, real estate, renting and business activities	71732.0	72674.0	78259.0	81594.0	90147.0	92205.0	104122.0	108322.0	115458.0	120702.0	128489.0	134229.0
Financial intermediation	16942.0	17221.0	17175.0	19380.0	21504.0	21611.0	22922.0	23930.0	28926.0	30401.0	35093.0	37023.0
Real estate, renting and business activities	54790.0	55453.0	61084.0	62214.0	68643.0	70594.0	81200.0	84392.0	86532.0	90301.0	93396.0	97206.0
Public administration and defence; compulsory social security	158522.0	156765.0	158203.0	151887.0	158985.0	166930.0	172215.0	175891.0	190360.0	184121.0	193927.0	207436.0
Education; health and social work; other community, social and personal services	76036.1	81147.7	76629.0	81038.0	76968.1	82136.0	82873.0	84912.0	85116.0	87392.0	94492.0	97728.0
Education	29563.3	32829.7	29587.0	31554.0	30812.7	32689.0	32782.0	33247.0	32796.0	34321.0	37833.0	39384.0
Health and social work	36136.8	37389.0	35365.0	37898.0	33445.4	36266.0	34366.0	35010.0	35535.0	36141.0	39839.0	41849.0
Other community, social and personal services	10336.0	10929.0	11677.0	11586.0	12710.0	13181.0	15725.0	16655.0	16785.0	16930.0	16820.0	16495.0
Private households with employed persons	9169.0	9167.0	10275.0	10349.0	11736.0	12006.0	12306.0	12613.0	12991.0	13355.0	13769.0	14196.0
Equals: VALUE ADDED, GROSS, in basic prices	1471482.1[a]	1536782.7[a]	1594396.0	1565764.0	1681846.1[a]	1783723.0[a]	1842316.0[a]	2017982.0[a]	1994144.0	2168918.0	2203547.0	2493790.0
Less: Financial intermediation services indirectly measured (FISIM)	10068.0	10598.0	10251.0	13293.0	15006.0	15081.0	18076.0	19998.0	22633.0	24709.0	28786.0	28968.0
Plus: Taxes less Subsidies on products	93003.0	110258.0	107927.0	125701.0	135869.0	138196.0	142598.0	157428.0	168539.0	174948.0	198001.0	164852.0
Plus: Taxes on products	93003.0	110258.0	107927.0	125701.0	135869.0	138196.0	142598.0	157428.0	168539.0	174948.0	198001.0	164852.0

	2001	2002	2003	2004	2005	2006	2007	2008	2009	2010	2011	2012
Series	**100**											
Base year	**2006**											
Less: Subsidies on products	...	...	...	...	...	...	...	...	...	...	...	...
Equals: GROSS DOMESTIC PRODUCT	1554417.1	1636442.7	1692072.0	1678172.0	1802709.1	1906838.0	1966838.0	2155412.0	2140050.0	2319157.0	2372762.0	2629674.0

[a] Includes financial intermediation services indirectly measured (FISIM).

Table 2.4 Value added by industries at current prices (ISIC Rev. 4)

Series 100: 1993 SNA, CFA franc, Western calendar year — **Data in millions**

	2001	2002	2003	2004	2005	2006	2007	2008	2009	2010	2011	2012
Series	**100**											
Industries												
Agriculture, forestry and fishing	593627.0	658069.0	676833.0	615991.0	754411.0	817662.0	842593.0	1045424.0	999357.0	1158359.0	1156805.0	1320036.0
Crop and animal production, hunting and related service activities	538485.0	597053.0	586522.0	532876.0	665497.0	733795.0	755295.0	949032.0	886822.0	1031328.0	1022343.0	1179609.0
Forestry and logging	41293.0	44731.0	45936.0	48021.0	50515.0	52938.0	55174.0	59721.0	64345.0	66686.0	70374.0	72672.0
Fishing and aquaculture	13849.0	16285.0	44375.0	35094.0	38399.0	30929.0	32124.0	36671.0	48190.0	60345.0	64088.0	67755.0
Manufacturing, mining and quarrying and other industrial activities	128401.0	131576.0	139595.0	143504.0	153584.0	167321.0	219511.0	286247.0	319483.0	370673.0	410469.0	620894.0
Mining and quarrying	30997.0	29067.0	29668.0	31428.0	35659.0	40096.0	90775.0	144399.0	162627.0	203462.0	226029.0	372830.0
Manufacturing	81946.0	87467.0	90753.0	94107.0	98349.0	102635.0	106578.0	117559.0	128256.0	134918.0	143942.0	209146.0
Electricity, gas, steam and air conditioning supply	15458.0	15042.0	19174.0	17969.0	19576.0	24590.0	22158.0	24289.0	28600.0	32293.0	40498.0	38918.0
Water supply; sewerage, waste management and remediation activities	...	...	...	...	...	...	...	...	...	...	...	...
Construction	31459.0	33978.0	36635.0	38697.0	41622.0	47471.0	51584.0	58096.0	64096.0	71643.0	76173.0	83448.0
Wholesale and retail trade, transportation and storage, accommodation and food service activities	279503.0	294147.0	296248.0	310468.0	351200.0	368614.0	393369.0	433173.0	500455.0	521230.0	565674.0	603141.0
Wholesale and retail trade; repair of motor vehicles and motorcycles	190571.0	199972.0	197209.0	199340.0	235441.0	247234.0	262022.0	292351.0	350606.0	367787.0	397703.0	420446.0
Transportation and storage	70787.0	75327.0	78139.0	88063.0	90796.0	94727.0	102538.0	109864.0	116219.0	117892.0	130146.0	142722.0
Accommodation and food service activities	18145.0	18848.0	20900.0	23065.0	24963.0	26653.0	28809.0	30958.0	33630.0	35551.0	37825.0	39973.0
Information and communication	11624.0	11972.0	15841.0	18432.0	24272.0	29378.0	32348.0	37495.0	40274.0	54019.0	63050.0	67141.0
Financial and insurance activities	10858.0	9694.0	13465.0	17863.0	20884.0	21611.0	26131.0	27464.0	31082.0	35349.0	42637.0	45473.0
Real estate activities	46707.0	51147.0	50202.0	52625.0	58047.0	56795.0	67723.0	74064.0	77591.0	80215.0	82207.0	83741.0
Professional, scientific, technical, administrative and support service activities	...	...	...	...	...	...	...	...	...	...	...	...
Public administration and defence, education, human health and social work activities	169354.0	177734.0	195093.0	195468.0	214877.0	235885.0	249934.0	265067.0	301554.0	298601.0	334981.0	374257.0
Public administration and defence; compulsory social security	119731.0	120022.0	143403.0	139496.0	153027.0	166930.0	181111.0	193665.0	225082.0	215784.0	248325.0	280804.0
Education	22329.0	25135.0	23546.0	25430.0	29658.0	32689.0	32845.0	34242.0	37082.0	40197.0	43413.0	47233.0
Human health and social work activities	27294.0	32577.0	28144.0	30542.0	32192.0	36266.0	35978.0	37160.0	39390.0	42620.0	43243.0	46220.0
Other service activities	30476.0	31607.0	33175.0	34356.0	38222.0	38985.0	43265.0	45355.0	50715.0	52785.0	61288.0	67753.0
Arts, entertainment and recreation	...	...	...	...	...	...	...	...	...	...	...	...

	2001	2002	2003	2004	2005	2006	2007	2008	2009	2010	2011	2012
Series	**100**											
Other service activities	21307.0	22440.0	22900.0	24007.0	26486.0	26979.0	30959.0	32742.0	37724.0	39430.0	47519.0	53557.0
Private households with employed persons	9169.0	9167.0	10275.0	10349.0	11736.0	12006.0	12306.0	12613.0	12991.0	13355.0	13769.0	14196.0
Equals: VALUE ADDED, GROSS, at basic prices	1302009.0	1399924.0	1457088.0	1427404.0	1657118.0	1783723.0	1926458.0	2272385.0	2384607.0	2642874.0	2793284.0	3265884.0
Less: Financial intermediation services indirectly measured (FISIM)	7884.0	8025.0	10448.0	12719.0	14599.0	15081.0	18235.0	19166.0	21690.0	22668.0	24341.0	26960.0
Plus: Taxes less Subsidies on products	84496.0	102888.0	97667.0	115759.0	134524.0	138196.0	144737.0	166435.0	185530.0	212080.0	256588.0	218971.0
Plus: Taxes on products	84496.0	102888.0	97667.0	115759.0	134524.0	138196.0	144737.0	166435.0	185530.0	212080.0	256588.0	218971.0
Less: Subsidies on products	...	...	...	...	...	...	...	...	...	...	...	...
Equals: GROSS DOMESTIC PRODUCT	1378621.0	1494787.0	1544307.0	1530444.0	1777043.0	1906838.0	2052960.0	2419654.0	2548447.0	2832286.0	3025531.0	3457895.0

Table 2.5 Value added by industries at constant prices (ISIC Rev. 4)

Series 100: 1993 SNA, CFA franc, Western calendar year — **Data in millions**

	2001	2002	2003	2004	2005	2006	2007	2008	2009	2010	2011	2012
Series	**100**											
Base year	**2006**											
Industries												
Agriculture, forestry and fishing	628501.0	675016.0	710137.0	652893.0	741568.0	817662.0	855579.0	994178.0	899393.0	1041398.0	1010544.0	1139813.0
Crop and animal production, hunting and related service activities	544189.0	587319.0	619065.0	563643.0	651795.0	733795.0	768974.0	904487.0	801435.0	933758.0	899716.0	1026489.0
Forestry and logging	43488.0	45234.0	46975.0	48591.0	50257.0	52938.0	54859.0	56643.0	58487.0	60499.0	62037.0	63069.0
Fishing and aquaculture	40824.0	42463.0	44097.0	40659.0	39516.0	30929.0	31746.0	33048.0	39471.0	47141.0	48791.0	50255.0
Manufacturing, mining and quarrying and other industrial activities	153328.0	157018.0	159181.0	165703.0	164939.0	167321.0	161979.0	167035.0	188326.0	203327.0	216575.0	324852.0
Mining and quarrying	36924.0	38336.0	38924.0	41309.0	39830.0	40096.0	37762.0	36976.0	51598.0	60490.0	72462.0	142653.0
Manufacturing	90128.0	92393.0	93914.0	99857.0	100244.0	102635.0	102946.0	106924.0	111654.0	115322.0	119930.0	156638.0
Electricity, gas, steam and air conditioning supply	26276.0	26289.0	26343.0	24537.0	24865.0	24590.0	21271.0	23135.0	25074.0	27515.0	24183.0	25561.0
Water supply; sewerage, waste management and remediation activities	...	...	...	...	...	...	...	...	...	...	...	...
Construction	34519.0	36681.0	40538.0	42572.0	45187.0	47471.0	49176.0	51628.0	55705.0	61017.0	63644.0	68417.0
Wholesale and retail trade, transportation and storage, accommodation and food service activities	321783.1	330361.5	337770.8	354313.4	359206.0	368614.0	372681.0	390349.0	411082.0	414856.0	436579.0	458904.0
Wholesale and retail trade; repair of motor vehicles and motorcycles	208337.0	212071.0	222038.0	233586.0	243040.0	247234.0	249805.0	259114.0	274439.0	278333.0	291539.0	302881.0
Transportation and storage	91065.1	95003.5	92037.8	96009.4	90747.0	94727.0	95621.0	100012.0	103944.0	102950.0	110116.0	119964.0
Accommodation and food service activities	22381.0	23287.0	23695.0	24718.0	25419.0	26653.0	27255.0	31223.0	32699.0	33573.0	34924.0	36059.0
Information and communication	17891.9	17952.5	23403.2	25414.6	33110.0	29378.0	31385.0	33054.0	35714.0	42750.0	45528.0	48215.0
Financial and insurance activities	16942.0	17221.0	17175.0	19380.0	21504.0	21611.0	22922.0	23930.0	28926.0	30401.0	35093.0	37023.0
Real estate activities	54790.0	55453.0	61084.0	62214.0	68643.0	70594.0	81200.0	84392.0	86532.0	90301.0	93396.0	97206.0
Professional, scientific, technical, administrative and support service activities	...	...	...	...	...	...	...	...	...	...	...	...

	2001	2002	2003	2004	2005	2006	2007	2008	2009	2010	2011	2012
Series	**100**											
Base year	**2006**											
Public administration and defence, education, human health and social work activities	224222.1	226983.7	223155.0	221339.0	223243.1	235885.0	239363.0	244148.0	258691.0	254583.0	271599.0	288669.0
Public administration and defence; compulsory social security	158522.0	156765.0	158203.0	151887.0	158985.0	166930.0	172215.0	175891.0	190360.0	184121.0	193927.0	207436.0
Education	29563.3	32829.7	29587.0	31554.0	30812.7	32689.0	32782.0	33247.0	32796.0	34321.0	37833.0	39384.0
Human health and social work activities	36136.8	37389.0	35365.0	37898.0	33445.4	36266.0	34366.0	35010.0	35535.0	36141.0	39839.0	41849.0
Other service activities	19505.0	20096.0	21952.0	21935.0	24446.0	25187.0	28031.0	29268.0	29776.0	30285.0	30589.0	30691.0
Arts, entertainment and recreation	...	...	...	...	...	...	...	...	...	...	...	...
Other service activities	10336.0	10929.0	11677.0	11586.0	12710.0	13181.0	15725.0	16655.0	16785.0	16930.0	16820.0	16495.0
Private households with employed persons	9169.0	9167.0	10275.0	10349.0	11736.0	12006.0	12306.0	12613.0	12991.0	13355.0	13769.0	14196.0
Equals: VALUE ADDED, GROSS, at basic prices	1471482.1	1536782.7	1594396.0	1565764.0	1681846.1	1783723.0	1842316.0	2017982.0	1994144.0	2168918.0	2203547.0	2493790.0
Less: Financial intermediation services indirectly measured (FISIM)	10068.0	10598.0	10251.0	13293.0	15006.0	15081.0	18076.0	19998.0	22633.0	24709.0	28786.0	28968.0
Plus: Taxes less Subsidies on products	93003.0	110258.0	107927.0	125701.0	135869.0	138196.0	142598.0	157428.0	168539.0	174948.0	198001.0	164852.0
Plus: Taxes on products	93003.0	110258.0	107927.0	125701.0	135869.0	138196.0	142598.0	157428.0	168539.0	174948.0	198001.0	164852.0
Less: Subsidies on products	...	...	...	...	...	...	...	...	...	...	...	...
Equals: GROSS DOMESTIC PRODUCT	1554417.1	1636442.7	1692072.0	1678172.0	1802709.1	1906838.0	1966838.0	2155412.0	2140050.0	2319157.0	2372762.0	2629674.0

Table 2.6 Output, gross value added and fixed assets by industries at current prices (ISIC Rev. 4) Total economy

Series 100: 1993 SNA, CFA franc, Western calendar year

Data in millions

	2001	2002	2003	2004	2005	2006	2007	2008	2009	2010	2011	2012
Series	**100**											
Output, at basic prices	1943560.0	2083417.0	2194567.0	2233649.0	2554626.0	2760992.0	2926045.0	3474035.0	3705356.0	4059410.0	4326454.0	4998093.0
Less: Intermediate consumption, at purchaser's prices	641551.0	683493.0	737479.0	806245.0	897508.0	977269.0	999585.0	1201650.0	1320749.0	1416537.0	1533171.0	1732209.0
Equals: VALUE ADDED, GROSS, at basic prices	1302009.0	1399926.0	1457091.0	1427404.0	1657122.0	1783721.0	1926465.0	2272385.0	2384607.0	2642873.0	2793283.0	3265884.0
Compensation of employees	196590.0	208791.0	222973.0	239349.0	282260.0	316059.0	332471.0	362883.0	405550.0	406230.0	466680.0	523880.0
Taxes on production and imports, less Subsidies	21181.0	24512.0	26089.0	25660.0	15377.0	25122.0	39763.0	47019.0	55206.0	62785.0	132869.0	160196.0
Taxes on production and imports	21181.0	24512.0	26089.0	25660.0	15377.0	25122.0	39763.0	47019.0	55206.0	62785.0	132869.0	160196.0
Taxes on products	...	...	...	...	...	...	...	...	...	...	...	...
Other taxes on production	21181.0	24512.0	26089.0	25660.0	15377.0	25122.0	39763.0	47019.0	55206.0	62785.0	132869.0	160196.0
Less: Subsidies	...	...	...	...	...	...	...	...	...	...	...	...
OPERATING SURPLUS, GROSS	110449.0	107316.0	112699.0	99693.0	129095.0	131991.0	193845.0	244753.0	312815.0	384382.0	345157.0	525928.0
MIXED INCOME, GROSS	965904.0	1051278.0	1084879.0	1050071.0	1215789.0	1295470.0	1342146.0	1598564.0	1589346.0	1766808.0	1824236.0	2028920.0
Total Economy only: Adjustment for FISIM (if FISIM is not distributed to uses)	7884.0	8026.0	10448.0	12719.0	14599.0	15081.0	18235.0	19165.0	21690.0	22668.0	24341.0	26960.0
Less: Consumption of fixed capital	65990.0	66460.0	65440.0	54590.0	44282.0	62580.0	72190.0	72540.0	84860.0	87860.0	94134.0	109957.0
OPERATING SURPLUS, NET	44459.0	40856.0	47259.0	45103.0	84813.0	69411.0	121655.0	172213.0	227955.0	296522.0	251023.0	415971.0
MIXED INCOME, NET	965904.0	1051278.0	1084879.0	1050071.0	1215789.0	1295470.0	1342146.0	1598564.0	1572964.0	1787301.0	1843397.0	...

	2001	2002	2003	2004	2005	2006	2007	2008	2009	2010	2011	2012
Series	**100**											
Gross capital formation	226121.0	259106.0	250600.0	223339.0	410372.0	449700.0	470965.0	776509.0	885288.0	1131543.0	1160766.0	1175503.0
Gross fixed capital formation	210453.0	229894.0	231797.0	258139.0	384618.0	430199.0	467984.0	746513.0	883824.0	1101631.0	1158727.0	1168147.0
Changes in inventories	15668.0	29212.0	18803.0	-34800.0	25754.0	19501.0	2981.0	29996.0	1464.0	29912.0	2039.0	7356.0
Acquisitions less disposals of valuables	...	...	...	...	...	...	...	...	...	...	...	...

Table 2.6 Output, gross value added and fixed assets by industries at current prices (ISIC Rev. 4) Agriculture, forestry and fishing (A)

Series 100: 1993 SNA, CFA franc, Western calendar year **Data in millions**

	2001	2002	2003	2004	2005	2006	2007	2008	2009	2010	2011	2012
Series	**100**											
Output, at basic prices	623906.0	685807.0	776936.0	712150.0	864214.0	936344.0	965374.0	1194551.0	1130722.0	1321937.0	1321955.0	1532945.0
Less: Intermediate consumption, at purchaser's prices	30279.0	27738.0	100103.0	96159.0	109803.0	118682.0	122781.0	149127.0	131365.0	163578.0	165150.0	212909.0
Equals: VALUE ADDED, GROSS, at basic prices	593627.0	658069.0	676833.0	615991.0	754411.0	817662.0	842593.0	1045424.0	999357.0	1158359.0	1156805.0	1320036.0
Compensation of employees	16825.0	19065.0	18758.0	17705.0	18653.0	20188.0	20555.0	25870.0	24428.0	27749.0	29137.0	30098.0
Taxes on production and imports, less Subsidies	25.0	29.0	31.0	29.0	17.0	18.0	18.0	23.0	29.0	36.0	45.0	66.0
Taxes on production and imports	25.0	29.0	31.0	29.0	17.0	18.0	18.0	23.0	29.0	36.0	45.0	66.0
Taxes on products	...	...	...	...	...	...	...	...	...	...	...	...
Other taxes on production	25.0	29.0	31.0	29.0	17.0	18.0	18.0	23.0	29.0	36.0	45.0	66.0
Less: Subsidies	...	...	...	...	...	...	...	...	...	...	...	...
OPERATING SURPLUS, GROSS	...	...	...	...	...	...	...	...	...	...	...	...
MIXED INCOME, GROSS	576777.0	638975.0	658044.0	598257.0	735741.0	797456.0	822020.0	1019531.0	974900.0	1130574.0	1127623.0	1289872.0
Gross capital formation	18882.0	20294.0	25072.0	24559.0	34881.0	51988.0	40313.0	68037.0	38876.0	75044.0	28269.0	83798.0
Gross fixed capital formation	18882.0	20294.0	25072.0	24559.0	34881.0	37130.0	39012.0	47208.0	48888.0	51224.0	55300.0	59892.0
Changes in inventories	0.0	0.0	0.0	0.0	0.0	14858.0	1301.0	20829.0	-10012.0	23820.0	-27031.0	23906.0
Acquisitions less disposals of valuables	...	...	...	...	...	...	...	...	...	...	...	...

Table 2.6 Output, gross value added and fixed assets by industries at current prices (ISIC Rev. 4) Crop and animal production, hunting and related service activities (01)

Series 100: 1993 SNA, CFA franc, Western calendar year **Data in millions**

	2001	2002	2003	2004	2005	2006	2007	2008	2009	2010	2011	2012
Series	**100**											
Output, at basic prices	561590.0	616876.0	674997.0	618363.0	764120.0	841806.0	866967.0	1085922.0	1004028.0	1178744.0	1170729.0	1375028.0
Less: Intermediate consumption, at purchaser's prices	23105.0	19823.0	88475.0	85487.0	98623.0	108011.0	111672.0	137474.0	117815.0	148030.0	149023.0	196110.0
Equals: VALUE ADDED, GROSS, at basic prices	538485.0	597053.0	586522.0	532876.0	665497.0	733795.0	755295.0	948448.0	886213.0	1030714.0	1021706.0	1178918.0
Compensation of employees	14298.0	16139.0	15405.0	14112.0	14849.0	16104.0	16388.0	20625.0	19476.0	22320.0	23269.0	24069.0
Taxes on production and imports, less Subsidies	0.0	0.0	0.0	0.0	0.0	0.0	0.0	0.0	0.0	0.0	0.0	0.0

	2001	2002	2003	2004	2005	2006	2007	2008	2009	2010	2011	2012
Series	**100**											
Taxes on production and imports	0.0	0.0	0.0	0.0	0.0	0.0	0.0	0.0	0.0	0.0	0.0	0.0
Taxes on products	...	...	...	...	...	...	...	...	...	...	...	...
Other taxes on production	0.0	0.0	0.0	0.0	0.0	0.0	0.0	0.0	0.0	0.0	0.0	0.0
Less: Subsidies	...	...	...	...	...	...	...	...	...	...	...	...
OPERATING SURPLUS, GROSS	...	...	...	...	...	...	...	...	...	...	...	...
MIXED INCOME, GROSS	524187.0	580914.0	571117.0	518764.0	650648.0	717691.0	738907.0	927823.0	866737.0	1008394.0	998437.0	1154849.0
Gross capital formation	14293.0	15117.0	23793.0	25078.0	25569.0	42012.0	34164.0	59685.0	30398.0	65443.0	18387.0	73817.0
Gross fixed capital formation	14293.0	15117.0	23793.0	25078.0	25569.0	27154.0	32863.0	38856.0	40410.0	41623.0	45418.0	49911.0
Changes in inventories	0.0	0.0	0.0	0.0	0.0	14858.0	1301.0	20829.0	-10012.0	23820.0	-27031.0	23906.0
Acquisitions less disposals of valuables	...	...	...	...	...	...	...	...	...	...	...	...

Table 2.6 Output, gross value added and fixed assets by industries at current prices (ISIC Rev. 4) Forestry and logging (02)

Series 100: 1993 SNA, CFA franc, Western calendar year

Data in millions

	2001	2002	2003	2004	2005	2006	2007	2008	2009	2010	2011	2012
Series	**100**											
Output, at basic prices	47111.0	51106.0	53729.0	55566.0	58531.0	60843.0	63407.0	68733.0	74517.0	77782.0	82105.0	84871.0
Less: Intermediate consumption, at purchaser's prices	5818.0	6375.0	7793.0	7545.0	8016.0	7905.0	8233.0	9012.0	10172.0	11096.0	11731.0	12199.0
Equals: VALUE ADDED, GROSS, at basic prices	41293.0	44731.0	45936.0	48021.0	50515.0	52938.0	55174.0	59721.0	64345.0	66686.0	70374.0	72672.0
Compensation of employees	500.0	542.0	557.0	582.0	599.0	649.0	660.0	830.0	784.0	939.0	937.0	975.0
Taxes on production and imports, less Subsidies	8.0	9.0	10.0	9.0	5.0	6.0	13.0	7.0	9.0	11.0	14.0	21.0
Taxes on production and imports	8.0	9.0	10.0	9.0	5.0	6.0	13.0	7.0	9.0	11.0	14.0	21.0
Taxes on products	...	...	...	...	...	...	...	...	...	...	...	...
Other taxes on production	8.0	9.0	10.0	9.0	5.0	6.0	13.0	7.0	9.0	11.0	14.0	21.0
Less: Subsidies	...	...	...	...	...	...	...	...	...	...	...	...
OPERATING SURPLUS, GROSS	...	...	...	...	...	...	...	...	...	...	...	...
MIXED INCOME, GROSS	40785.0	44180.0	45369.0	47430.0	49911.0	52283.0	54501.0	58884.0	63552.0	65736.0	69423.0	71676.0
Gross capital formation	2308.0	2504.0	2633.0	2723.0	2823.0	2981.0	3107.0	4984.0	5161.0	5764.0	6130.0	6243.0
Gross fixed capital formation	2308.0	2504.0	2633.0	2723.0	2823.0	2981.0	3107.0	4984.0	5161.0	5764.0	6130.0	6243.0
Changes in inventories	...	...	...	...	...	...	...	...	...	...	...	...
Acquisitions less disposals of valuables	...	...	...	...	...	...	...	...	...	...	...	...

Table 2.6 Output, gross value added and fixed assets by industries at current prices (ISIC Rev. 4) Fishing and aquaculture (03)

Series 100: 1993 SNA, CFA franc, Western calendar year — **Data in millions**

	2001	2002	2003	2004	2005	2006	2007	2008	2009	2010	2011	2012
Series	**100**											
Output, at basic prices	15205.0	17825.0	48210.0	38221.0	41563.0	33695.0	34999.0	39896.0	52177.0	65092.0	69121.0	73046.0
Less: Intermediate consumption, at purchaser's prices	1356.0	1540.0	3835.0	3127.0	3164.0	2766.0	2875.0	3225.0	3987.0	4747.0	5033.0	5291.0
Equals: VALUE ADDED, GROSS, at basic prices	13849.0	16285.0	44375.0	35094.0	38399.0	30929.0	32124.0	36671.0	48190.0	60345.0	64088.0	67755.0
Compensation of employees	2027.0	2384.0	2796.0	3011.0	3205.0	3435.0	3507.0	4415.0	4168.0	4490.0	4931.0	5054.0
Taxes on production and imports, less Subsidies	17.0	20.0	22.0	20.0	13.0	12.0	6.0	16.0	20.0	25.0	31.0	45.0
Taxes on production and imports	17.0	20.0	22.0	20.0	13.0	12.0	6.0	16.0	20.0	25.0	31.0	45.0
Taxes on products	...	...	...	...	...	...	...	...	...	...	...	...
Other taxes on production	17.0	20.0	22.0	20.0	13.0	12.0	6.0	16.0	20.0	25.0	31.0	45.0
Less: Subsidies	...	...	...	...	...	...	...	...	...	...	...	...
OPERATING SURPLUS, GROSS	...	...	...	...	...	...	...	...	...	...	...	...
MIXED INCOME, GROSS	11805.0	13881.0	41557.0	32063.0	35181.0	27482.0	28611.0	32240.0	44002.0	55830.0	59126.0	62656.0
Gross capital formation	2281.0	2674.0	7172.0	5703.0	6489.0	6978.0	8250.0	3368.0	3317.0	3837.0	3752.0	3738.0
Gross fixed capital formation	2281.0	2674.0	7172.0	5703.0	6489.0	6978.0	8250.0	3368.0	3317.0	3837.0	3752.0	3738.0
Changes in inventories	...	...	...	...	...	...	...	...	...	...	...	...
Acquisitions less disposals of valuables	...	...	...	...	...	...	...	...	...	...	...	...

Table 2.6 Output, gross value added and fixed assets by industries at current prices (ISIC Rev. 4) Manufacturing, mining and quarrying and other industrial activities (B+C+D+E)

Series 100: 1993 SNA, CFA franc, Western calendar year — **Data in millions**

	2001	2002	2003	2004	2005	2006	2007	2008	2009	2010	2011	2012
Series	**100**											
Output, at basic prices	358497.0	376933.0	385591.0	404341.0	445717.0	485304.0	557965.0	654608.0	781871.0	865140.0	930364.0	1185691.0
Less: Intermediate consumption, at purchaser's prices	230096.0	245357.0	245996.0	260837.0	292133.0	317983.0	338454.0	368361.0	462388.0	494467.0	519895.0	564797.0
Equals: VALUE ADDED, GROSS, at basic prices	128401.0	131576.0	139595.0	143504.0	153584.0	167321.0	219511.0	286247.0	319483.0	370673.0	410469.0	620894.0
Compensation of employees	33990.0	33946.0	36553.0	38362.0	39578.0	43482.0	48317.0	51988.0	58148.0	58331.0	65745.0	91801.0
Taxes on production and imports, less Subsidies	7473.0	8167.0	8302.0	8560.0	5766.0	10282.0	14597.0	18768.0	21917.0	25992.0	37622.0	44631.0
Taxes on production and imports	7473.0	8167.0	8302.0	8560.0	5766.0	10282.0	14597.0	18768.0	21917.0	25992.0	37622.0	44631.0
Taxes on products	...	...	...	...	...	...	...	...	...	...	...	...
Other taxes on production	7473.0	8167.0	8302.0	8560.0	5766.0	10282.0	14597.0	18768.0	21917.0	25992.0	37622.0	44631.0
Less: Subsidies	...	...	...	...	...	...	...	...	...	...	...	...
OPERATING SURPLUS, GROSS	14267.0	11774.0	15613.0	14456.0	21470.0	23115.0	63283.0	110193.0	126754.0	170766.0	188274.0	354757.0
MIXED INCOME, GROSS	72671.0	77689.0	79127.0	82126.0	86770.0	90442.0	93314.0	105298.0	112664.0	115584.0	118828.0	129705.0
Gross capital formation	35657.0	32108.0	38897.0	50948.0	62652.0	80477.0	83206.0	199954.0	282163.0	401672.0	571832.0	445820.0
Gross fixed capital formation	35657.0	32108.0	38897.0	50948.0	62652.0	80477.0	81526.0	191821.0	279908.0	396582.0	557173.0	445820.0

	2001	2002	2003	2004	2005	2006	2007	2008	2009	2010	2011	2012
Series	**100**											
Changes in inventories	0.0	0.0	0.0	0.0	0.0	0.0	1680.0	8133.0	2255.0	5090.0	14659.0	0.0
Acquisitions less disposals of valuables	...	...	...	...	...	...	...	...	...	...	...	...

Table 2.6 Output, gross value added and fixed assets by industries at current prices (ISIC Rev. 4) Mining and quarrying (B)

Series 100: 1993 SNA, CFA franc, Western calendar year **Data in millions**

	2001	2002	2003	2004	2005	2006	2007	2008	2009	2010	2011	2012
Series	**100**											
Output, at basic prices	71409.0	71552.0	73218.0	80512.0	101452.0	116199.0	179990.0	260280.0	337483.0	380447.0	450752.0	651444.0
Less: Intermediate consumption, at purchaser's prices	40412.0	42485.0	43550.0	49084.0	65793.0	76103.0	89215.0	115881.0	174856.0	176985.0	224723.0	278614.0
Equals: VALUE ADDED, GROSS, at basic prices	30997.0	29067.0	29668.0	31428.0	35659.0	40096.0	90775.0	144399.0	162627.0	203462.0	226029.0	372830.0
Compensation of employees	13626.0	12665.0	13222.0	13388.0	15364.0	18566.0	20610.0	25410.0	27769.0	28160.0	32563.0	57325.0
Taxes on production and imports, less Subsidies	3735.0	3890.0	3979.0	4426.0	2480.0	5563.0	8145.0	11618.0	13919.0	15793.0	21740.0	24852.0
Taxes on production and imports	3735.0	3890.0	3979.0	4426.0	2480.0	5563.0	8145.0	11618.0	13919.0	15793.0	21740.0	24852.0
Taxes on products	...	...	...	...	...	...	...	...	...	...	...	...
Other taxes on production	3735.0	3890.0	3979.0	4426.0	2480.0	5563.0	8145.0	11618.0	13919.0	15793.0	21740.0	24852.0
Less: Subsidies	...	...	...	...	...	...	...	...	...	...	...	...
OPERATING SURPLUS, GROSS	6937.0	5240.0	5006.0	5718.0	9639.0	7410.0	52354.0	96930.0	109959.0	147947.0	159395.0	277431.0
MIXED INCOME, GROSS	6699.0	7272.0	7461.0	7896.0	8176.0	8557.0	9666.0	10441.0	10980.0	11562.0	12331.0	13222.0
Gross capital formation	3958.0	5481.0	9465.0	17563.0	15385.0	20937.0	28838.0	138584.0	210631.0	337800.0	401970.0	384128.0
Gross fixed capital formation	3958.0	5481.0	9465.0	17563.0	15385.0	20937.0	27158.0	130451.0	208376.0	332710.0	387311.0	384128.0
Changes in inventories	...	...	...	...	...	...	1680.0	8133.0	2255.0	5090.0	14659.0	0.0
Acquisitions less disposals of valuables	...	...	...	...	...	...	...	...	...	...	...	...

Table 2.6 Output, gross value added and fixed assets by industries at current prices (ISIC Rev. 4) Manufacturing (C)

Series 100: 1993 SNA, CFA franc, Western calendar year **Data in millions**

	2001	2002	2003	2004	2005	2006	2007	2008	2009	2010	2011	2012
Series	**100**											
Output, at basic prices	248792.0	266043.0	267302.0	277793.0	295485.0	313907.0	324806.0	336045.0	374193.0	390592.0	393804.0	451787.0
Less: Intermediate consumption, at purchaser's prices	166846.0	178576.0	176549.0	183686.0	197136.0	211272.0	218228.0	218486.0	245937.0	255674.0	249862.0	242641.0
Equals: VALUE ADDED, GROSS, at basic prices	81946.0	87467.0	90753.0	94107.0	98349.0	102635.0	106578.0	117559.0	128256.0	134918.0	143942.0	209146.0
Compensation of employees	12710.0	13443.0	15027.0	16003.0	15175.0	14706.0	16713.0	16507.0	17668.0	16787.0	19192.0	20362.0
Taxes on production and imports, less Subsidies	2541.0	2948.0	3222.0	3120.0	2301.0	3280.0	4878.0	4366.0	4730.0	5488.0	11152.0	13826.0
Taxes on production and imports	2541.0	2948.0	3222.0	3120.0	2301.0	3280.0	4878.0	4366.0	4730.0	5488.0	11152.0	13826.0
Taxes on products	...	...	...	...	...	...	...	...	...	...	...	...

	2001	2002	2003	2004	2005	2006	2007	2008	2009	2010	2011	2012
Series	**100**											
Other taxes on production	2541.0	2948.0	3222.0	3120.0	2301.0	3280.0	4878.0	4366.0	4730.0	5488.0	11152.0	13826.0
Less: Subsidies	...	...	...	...	...	...	...	...	...	...	...	...
OPERATING SURPLUS, GROSS	723.0	659.0	838.0	754.0	2279.0	2764.0	1339.0	1829.0	4174.0	8621.0	7101.0	58475.0
MIXED INCOME, GROSS	65972.0	70417.0	71666.0	74230.0	78594.0	81885.0	83648.0	94857.0	101684.0	104022.0	106497.0	116483.0
Gross capital formation	8785.0	10248.0	12024.0	12624.0	18551.0	19709.0	21090.0	25954.0	33120.0	31209.0	149732.0	36529.0
Gross fixed capital formation	8785.0	10248.0	12024.0	12624.0	18551.0	19709.0	21090.0	25954.0	33120.0	31209.0	149732.0	36529.0
Changes in inventories	0.0	0.0	0.0	0.0	0.0	0.0	0.0	0.0	0.0	0.0	0.0	0.0
Acquisitions less disposals of valuables	...	...	...	...	...	...	...	...	...	...	...	...

Table 2.6 Output, gross value added and fixed assets by industries at current prices (ISIC Rev. 4) Electricity, gas, steam and air conditioning supply (D)

Series 100: 1993 SNA, CFA franc, Western calendar year

Data in millions

	2001	2002	2003	2004	2005	2006	2007	2008	2009	2010	2011	2012
Series	**100**											
Output, at basic prices	38296.0	39338.0	45071.0	46036.0	48780.0	55198.0	53169.0	58283.0	70195.0	94101.0	85808.0	82460.0
Less: Intermediate consumption, at purchaser's prices	22838.0	24296.0	25897.0	28067.0	29204.0	30608.0	31011.0	33994.0	41595.0	61808.0	45310.0	43542.0
Equals: VALUE ADDED, GROSS, at basic prices	15458.0	15042.0	19174.0	17969.0	19576.0	24590.0	22158.0	24289.0	28600.0	32293.0	40498.0	38918.0
Compensation of employees	7654.0	7838.0	8304.0	8971.0	9039.0	10210.0	10994.0	10071.0	12711.0	13384.0	13990.0	14114.0
Taxes on production and imports, less Subsidies	1197.0	1329.0	1101.0	1014.0	985.0	1439.0	1574.0	2784.0	3268.0	4711.0	4730.0	5953.0
Taxes on production and imports	1197.0	1329.0	1101.0	1014.0	985.0	1439.0	1574.0	2784.0	3268.0	4711.0	4730.0	5953.0
Taxes on products	...	...	...	...	...	...	...	...	...	...	...	...
Other taxes on production	1197.0	1329.0	1101.0	1014.0	985.0	1439.0	1574.0	2784.0	3268.0	4711.0	4730.0	5953.0
Less: Subsidies	...	...	...	...	...	...	...	...	...	...	...	...
OPERATING SURPLUS, GROSS	6607.0	5875.0	9769.0	7984.0	9552.0	12941.0	9590.0	11434.0	12621.0	14198.0	21778.0	18851.0
MIXED INCOME, GROSS	...	...	...	...	...	...	...	...	...	...	...	...
Gross capital formation	22914.0	16379.0	17408.0	20761.0	28716.0	39831.0	33278.0	35416.0	38412.0	32663.0	20130.0	25163.0
Gross fixed capital formation	22914.0	16379.0	17408.0	20761.0	28716.0	39831.0	33278.0	35416.0	38412.0	32663.0	20130.0	25163.0
Changes in inventories	...	...	...	...	...	...	...	...	...	...	...	...
Acquisitions less disposals of valuables	...	...	...	...	...	...	...	...	...	...	...	...

Table 2.6 Output, gross value added and fixed assets by industries at current prices (ISIC Rev. 4) Construction (F)

Series 100: 1993 SNA, CFA franc, Western calendar year — **Data in millions**

	2001	2002	2003	2004	2005	2006	2007	2008	2009	2010	2011	2012
Series	**100**											
Output, at basic prices	112316.0	122187.0	118969.0	127770.0	144700.0	138202.0	168232.0	250206.0	296171.0	332857.0	407248.0	445741.0
Less: Intermediate consumption, at purchaser's prices	80857.0	88209.0	82334.0	89073.0	103078.0	90731.0	116648.0	192110.0	232075.0	261214.0	331075.0	362293.0
Equals: VALUE ADDED, GROSS, at basic prices	31459.0	33978.0	36635.0	38697.0	41622.0	47471.0	51584.0	58096.0	64096.0	71643.0	76173.0	83448.0
Compensation of employees	13778.0	14832.0	16107.0	17767.0	18376.0	19171.0	20065.0	20139.0	22753.0	21898.0	25746.0	27205.0
Taxes on production and imports, less Subsidies	1372.0	1711.0	2001.0	2161.0	1075.0	1271.0	5003.0	3857.0	3519.0	4075.0	14608.0	17357.0
Taxes on production and imports	1372.0	1711.0	2001.0	2161.0	1075.0	1271.0	5003.0	3857.0	3519.0	4075.0	14608.0	17357.0
Taxes on products	...	...	...	...	...	...	...	...	...	...	...	...
Other taxes on production	1372.0	1711.0	2001.0	2161.0	1075.0	1271.0	5003.0	3857.0	3519.0	4075.0	14608.0	17357.0
Less: Subsidies	...	...	...	...	...	...	...	...	...	...	...	...
OPERATING SURPLUS, GROSS	7432.0	7975.0	7880.0	7612.0	9800.0	12683.0	12246.0	16611.0	18166.0	23208.0	10483.0	11381.0
MIXED INCOME, GROSS	8877.0	9460.0	10647.0	11157.0	12371.0	14346.0	14270.0	17489.0	19658.0	22462.0	25336.0	27505.0
Gross capital formation	48662.0	59938.0	58513.0	41441.0	59011.0	62795.0	77089.0	53151.0	88296.0	251962.0	147119.0	113239.0
Gross fixed capital formation	48662.0	59938.0	58513.0	41441.0	59011.0	62795.0	77089.0	53151.0	88296.0	251962.0	147119.0	113239.0
Changes in inventories	...	...	...	...	...	...	...	...	...	...	...	...
Acquisitions less disposals of valuables	...	...	...	...	...	...	...	...	...	...	...	...

Table 2.6 Output, gross value added and fixed assets by industries at current prices (ISIC Rev. 4) Wholesale and retail trade, transportation and storage, accommodation and food service activities (G+H+I)

Series 100: 1993 SNA, CFA franc, Western calendar year — **Data in millions**

	2001	2002	2003	2004	2005	2006	2007	2008	2009	2010	2011	2012
Series	**100**											
Output, at basic prices	411280.0	435607.0	435274.0	465565.0	498000.0	575307.0	614166.0	626183.0	675476.0	720990.0	765650.0	852262.0
Less: Intermediate consumption, at purchaser's prices	131777.0	141459.0	139025.0	155097.0	146800.0	205872.0	220797.0	193010.0	175021.0	199760.0	199976.0	249121.0
Equals: VALUE ADDED, GROSS, at basic prices	279503.0	294148.0	296249.0	310468.0	351200.0	369435.0	393369.0	433173.0	500455.0	521230.0	565674.0	603141.0
Compensation of employees	21725.0	21252.0	24665.0	29463.0	32533.0	37354.0	36957.0	39409.0	45482.0	43765.0	49609.0	52975.0
Taxes on production and imports, less Subsidies	7809.0	9263.0	10098.0	10833.0	5430.0	7625.0	11180.0	12991.0	16224.0	18303.0	37722.0	50099.0
Taxes on production and imports	7809.0	9263.0	10098.0	10833.0	5430.0	7625.0	11180.0	12991.0	16224.0	18303.0	37722.0	50099.0
Taxes on products	...	...	...	...	...	...	...	...	...	...	...	...
Other taxes on production	7809.0	9263.0	10098.0	10833.0	5430.0	7625.0	11180.0	12991.0	16224.0	18303.0	37722.0	50099.0
Less: Subsidies	...	...	...	...	...	...	...	...	...	...	...	...
OPERATING SURPLUS, GROSS	18750.0	20511.0	22162.0	22234.0	28740.0	29946.0	37158.0	63880.0	78403.0	87014.0	87509.0	86370.6
MIXED INCOME, GROSS	231219.0	243122.0	239324.0	247938.0	284497.0	294510.0	308074.0	316893.0	360346.0	371457.0	397053.0	413696.4
Gross capital formation	19378.0	20818.0	23972.0	17198.0	42926.0	47385.0	52049.0	64379.0	70555.0	63708.0	72771.0	82620.0
Gross fixed capital formation	19378.0	20818.0	23972.0	17198.0	42926.0	47385.0	52049.0	64379.0	70555.0	63708.0	72771.0	82620.0

	2001	2002	2003	2004	2005	2006	2007	2008	2009	2010	2011	2012
Series	**100**											
Changes in inventories	0.0	0.0	0.0	0.0	0.0	0.0	0.0	0.0	0.0	0.0	0.0	0.0
Acquisitions less disposals of valuables	...	...	...	...	...	...	...	...	...	...	...	...

Table 2.6 Output, gross value added and fixed assets by industries at current prices (ISIC Rev. 4) Wholesale and retail trade; repair of motor vehicles and motorcycles (G)

Series 100: 1993 SNA, CFA franc, Western calendar year **Data in millions**

	2001	2002	2003	2004	2005	2006	2007	2008	2009	2010	2011	2012
Series	**100**											
Output, at basic prices	223411.0	233988.0	226490.0	238094.0	260706.0	324156.0	347337.0	365902.0	393515.0	413057.0	439291.0	490198.0
Less: Intermediate consumption, at purchaser's prices	32840.0	34015.0	29281.0	38754.0	25265.0	76922.0	85315.0	73551.0	42909.0	45270.0	41588.0	69752.0
Equals: VALUE ADDED, GROSS, at basic prices	190571.0	199973.0	197209.0	199340.0	235441.0	247234.0	262022.0	292351.0	350606.0	367787.0	397703.0	420446.0
Compensation of employees	11597.0	11763.0	12131.0	14872.0	15577.0	20244.0	17821.0	19617.0	23118.0	21809.0	24746.0	25096.0
Taxes on production and imports, less Subsidies	6415.0	7141.0	7230.0	7404.0	3518.0	4948.0	7714.0	7051.0	8235.0	9109.0	16322.0	23536.0
Taxes on production and imports	6415.0	7141.0	7230.0	7404.0	3518.0	4948.0	7714.0	7051.0	8235.0	9109.0	16322.0	23536.0
Taxes on products	...	...	...	...	...	...	...	...	...	...	...	...
Other taxes on production	6415.0	7141.0	7230.0	7404.0	3518.0	4948.0	7714.0	7051.0	8235.0	9109.0	16322.0	23536.0
Less: Subsidies	...	...	...	...	...	...	...	...	...	...	...	...
OPERATING SURPLUS, GROSS	10264.5	10771.7	10522.0	8461.0	12869.2	13208.0	17769.0	45115.0	61566.0	71066.0	70245.0	69046.5
MIXED INCOME, GROSS	162294.5	170297.3	167326.0	168603.0	203476.8	208834.0	218718.0	220568.0	257687.0	265803.0	286390.0	302767.5
Gross capital formation	8044.0	8939.0	2124.0	8860.0	15437.0	18845.0	19219.0	23740.0	28767.0	27982.0	30836.0	36286.0
Gross fixed capital formation	8044.0	8939.0	2124.0	8860.0	15437.0	18845.0	19219.0	23740.0	28767.0	27982.0	30836.0	36286.0
Changes in inventories	...	...	...	...	...	...	...	...	...	...	...	...
Acquisitions less disposals of valuables	...	...	...	...	...	...	...	...	...	...	...	...

Table 2.6 Output, gross value added and fixed assets by industries at current prices (ISIC Rev. 4) Transportation and storage (H)

Series 100: 1993 SNA, CFA franc, Western calendar year **Data in millions**

	2001	2002	2003	2004	2005	2006	2007	2008	2009	2010	2011	2012
Series	**100**											
Output, at basic prices	121685.0	132089.0	135570.0	149040.0	155062.0	165337.0	176106.0	162915.0	180328.0	200988.0	212263.0	244556.0
Less: Intermediate consumption, at purchaser's prices	50898.0	56762.0	57431.0	60977.0	64266.0	69789.0	73568.0	53051.0	64109.0	83096.0	82117.0	101834.0
Equals: VALUE ADDED, GROSS, at basic prices	70787.0	75327.0	78139.0	88063.0	90796.0	94727.0	102538.0	109864.0	116219.0	117892.0	130146.0	142722.0
Compensation of employees	6601.0	5797.0	8640.0	11686.0	13907.0	12555.0	15352.0	14954.0	17046.0	16927.0	17300.0	19410.0
Taxes on production and imports, less Subsidies	926.0	1652.0	2147.0	2517.0	1292.0	1883.0	2403.0	3481.0	5101.0	6050.0	13236.0	15553.0
Taxes on production and imports	926.0	1652.0	2147.0	2517.0	1292.0	1883.0	2403.0	3481.0	5101.0	6050.0	13236.0	15553.0
Taxes on products	...	...	...	...	...	...	...	...	...	...	...	...

	2001	2002	2003	2004	2005	2006	2007	2008	2009	2010	2011	2012
Series	**100**											
Other taxes on production	926.0	1652.0	2147.0	2517.0	1292.0	1883.0	2403.0	3481.0	5101.0	6050.0	13236.0	15553.0
Less: Subsidies	...	...	...	...	...	...	...	...	...	...	...	...
OPERATING SURPLUS, GROSS	8368.0	9594.0	10838.0	11533.0	12248.0	13387.0	14337.0	15666.0	13919.0	13006.0	13954.0	13826.1
MIXED INCOME, GROSS	54892.0	58284.0	56514.0	62327.0	63349.0	67723.0	70446.0	75763.0	80153.0	81909.0	85656.0	93932.9
Gross capital formation	10055.0	10437.0	14211.0	6611.0	19830.0	20828.0	23144.0	28972.0	31146.0	27723.0	35083.0	41054.0
Gross fixed capital formation	10055.0	10437.0	14211.0	6611.0	19830.0	20828.0	23144.0	28972.0	31146.0	27723.0	35083.0	41054.0
Changes in inventories	...	...	...	...	...	...	...	...	...	...	...	...
Acquisitions less disposals of valuables	...	...	...	...	...	...	...	...	...	...	...	...

Table 2.6 Output, gross value added and fixed assets by industries at current prices (ISIC Rev. 4) Accommodation and food service activities (I)

Series 100: 1993 SNA, CFA franc, Western calendar year **Data in millions**

	2001	2002	2003	2004	2005	2006	2007	2008	2009	2010	2011	2012
Series	**100**											
Output, at basic prices	66184.0	69530.0	73214.0	78431.0	82232.0	85814.0	90723.0	97366.0	101633.0	106945.0	114096.0	117508.0
Less: Intermediate consumption, at purchaser's prices	48039.0	50682.0	52313.0	55366.0	57269.0	59161.0	61914.0	66408.0	68003.0	71394.0	76271.0	77535.0
Equals: VALUE ADDED, GROSS, at basic prices	18145.0	18848.0	20901.0	23065.0	24963.0	26653.0	28809.0	30958.0	33630.0	35551.0	37825.0	39973.0
Compensation of employees	3527.0	3692.0	3894.0	2905.0	3049.0	4555.0	3784.0	4838.0	5318.0	5029.0	7563.0	8469.0
Taxes on production and imports, less Subsidies	468.0	470.0	721.0	912.0	620.0	794.0	1063.0	2459.0	2888.0	3144.0	8164.0	11010.0
Taxes on production and imports	468.0	470.0	721.0	912.0	620.0	794.0	1063.0	2459.0	2888.0	3144.0	8164.0	11010.0
Taxes on products	...	...	...	...	...	...	...	...	...	...	...	...
Other taxes on production	468.0	470.0	721.0	912.0	620.0	794.0	1063.0	2459.0	2888.0	3144.0	8164.0	11010.0
Less: Subsidies	...	...	...	...	...	...	...	...	...	...	...	...
OPERATING SURPLUS, GROSS	117.0	145.0	802.0	2240.0	3623.0	3351.0	5052.0	3099.0	2918.0	3633.0	3310.0	3498.0
MIXED INCOME, GROSS	14033.0	14541.0	15484.0	17008.0	17671.0	17953.0	18910.0	20562.0	22506.0	23745.0	18788.0	16996.0
Gross capital formation	1279.0	1442.0	7637.0	1727.0	7659.0	7712.0	9686.0	11667.0	10642.0	8003.0	6852.0	5280.0
Gross fixed capital formation	1279.0	1442.0	7637.0	1727.0	7659.0	7712.0	9686.0	11667.0	10642.0	8003.0	6852.0	5280.0
Changes in inventories	...	...	...	...	...	...	...	...	...	...	...	...
Acquisitions less disposals of valuables	...	...	...	...	...	...	...	...	...	...	...	...

Table 2.6 Output, gross value added and fixed assets by industries at current prices (ISIC Rev. 4) Information and communication (J)

Series 100: 1993 SNA, CFA franc, Western calendar year — **Data in millions**

	2001	2002	2003	2004	2005	2006	2007	2008	2009	2010	2011	2012
Series	**100**											
Output, at basic prices	19866.0	23038.0	25969.0	38733.0	40755.0	55574.0	66744.0	76806.0	90159.0	112636.0	118974.0	148640.0
Less: Intermediate consumption, at purchaser's prices	8242.0	11066.0	10128.0	20301.0	16483.0	26196.0	34396.0	39311.0	49885.0	58617.0	55924.0	81499.0
Equals: VALUE ADDED, GROSS, at basic prices	11624.0	11972.0	15841.0	18432.0	24272.0	29378.0	32348.0	37495.0	40274.0	54019.0	63050.0	67141.0
Compensation of employees	8174.0	9608.0	8582.0	9508.0	10288.0	14370.0	11407.0	10177.0	12928.0	13720.0	16542.0	17577.0
Taxes on production and imports, less Subsidies	1012.0	994.0	1526.0	1006.0	595.0	1927.0	1115.0	4067.0	4775.0	5528.0	12910.0	15698.0
Taxes on production and imports	1012.0	994.0	1526.0	1006.0	595.0	1927.0	1115.0	4067.0	4775.0	5528.0	12910.0	15698.0
Taxes on products	...	...	...	...	...	...	...	...	...	...	...	...
Other taxes on production	1012.0	994.0	1526.0	1006.0	595.0	1927.0	1115.0	4067.0	4775.0	5528.0	12910.0	15698.0
Less: Subsidies	...	...	...	...	...	...	...	...	...	...	...	...
OPERATING SURPLUS, GROSS	2438.0	1370.0	5733.0	7918.0	13389.0	13081.0	19826.0	23251.0	22571.0	34771.0	33598.0	33866.0
MIXED INCOME, GROSS	...	...	...	...	...	...	...	...	...	...	...	...
Gross capital formation	1505.0	1746.0	2025.0	23216.0	30742.0	32264.0	35827.0	39560.0	59442.0	36046.0	52013.0	45061.0
Gross fixed capital formation	1505.0	1746.0	2025.0	23216.0	30742.0	32264.0	35827.0	39560.0	59442.0	36046.0	52013.0	45061.0
Changes in inventories	...	...	...	...	...	...	...	...	...	...	...	...
Acquisitions less disposals of valuables	...	...	...	...	...	...	...	...	...	...	...	...

Table 2.6 Output, gross value added and fixed assets by industries at current prices (ISIC Rev. 4) Financial and insurance activities (K)

Series 100: 1993 SNA, CFA franc, Western calendar year — **Data in millions**

	2001	2002	2003	2004	2005	2006	2007	2008	2009	2010	2011	2012
Series	**100**											
Output, at basic prices	19425.0	19949.0	23137.0	28232.0	32372.0	34879.0	42281.0	55779.0	58773.0	65469.0	70905.0	71355.0
Less: Intermediate consumption, at purchaser's prices	8567.0	10255.0	9672.0	10369.0	11488.0	13268.0	16150.0	28315.0	27691.0	30120.0	28268.0	25882.0
Equals: VALUE ADDED, GROSS, at basic prices	10858.0	9694.0	13465.0	17863.0	20884.0	21611.0	26131.0	27464.0	31082.0	35349.0	42637.0	45473.0
Compensation of employees	4326.0	4266.0	5458.0	5919.0	6122.0	6333.0	7989.0	10778.0	11070.0	12753.0	13075.0	14720.0
Taxes on production and imports, less Subsidies	244.0	796.0	825.0	1089.0	1413.0	1721.0	2327.0	2369.0	2782.0	2142.0	6648.0	7680.0
Taxes on production and imports	244.0	796.0	825.0	1089.0	1413.0	1721.0	2327.0	2369.0	2782.0	2142.0	6648.0	7680.0
Taxes on products	...	...	...	...	...	...	...	...	...	...	...	...
Other taxes on production	244.0	796.0	825.0	1089.0	1413.0	1721.0	2327.0	2369.0	2782.0	2142.0	6648.0	7680.0
Less: Subsidies	...	...	...	...	...	...	...	...	...	...	...	...
OPERATING SURPLUS, GROSS	6288.0	4632.0	7182.0	10855.0	13349.0	13557.0	15815.0	14317.0	17230.0	20454.0	22914.0	23073.0
MIXED INCOME, GROSS	...	...	...	...	...	...	...	...	...	...	...	...
Gross capital formation	1773.0	1950.0	1980.0	1853.0	6654.0	7523.0	7346.0	12972.0	13340.0	10665.0	12069.0	11010.0
Gross fixed capital formation	1773.0	1950.0	1980.0	1853.0	6654.0	7523.0	7346.0	12972.0	13340.0	10665.0	12069.0	11010.0

	2001	2002	2003	2004	2005	2006	2007	2008	2009	2010	2011	2012
Series	**100**											
Changes in inventories	...	...	...	...	...	...	...	...	...	...	...	...
Acquisitions less disposals of valuables	...	...	...	...	...	...	...	...	...	...	...	...

Table 2.6 Output, gross value added and fixed assets by industries at current prices (ISIC Rev. 4) Real estate activities (L)

Series 100: 1993 SNA, CFA franc, Western calendar year — **Data in millions**

	2001	2002	2003	2004	2005	2006	2007	2008	2009	2010	2011	2012
Series	**100**											
Output, at basic prices	80804.0	85984.0	87716.5	94497.8	105058.3	101637.2	121132.5	120996.0	125862.0	135269.0	143784.0	149994.0
Less: Intermediate consumption, at purchaser's prices	34097.0	34837.0	37514.5	41872.8	47011.3	44842.2	53409.5	46932.0	48271.0	55054.0	61577.0	66253.0
Equals: VALUE ADDED, GROSS, at basic prices	46707.0	51147.0	50202.0	52625.0	58047.0	56795.0	67723.0	74064.0	77591.0	80215.0	82207.0	83741.0
Compensation of employees	11129.7	12037.2	15742.9	16571.0	16067.1	27761.9	21846.7	19376.0	20590.0	21734.0	23654.0	24726.0
Taxes on production and imports, less Subsidies	1975.5	1908.6	1717.4	740.9	137.2	819.4	2807.3	2340.0	2768.0	3129.0	9927.0	10716.0
Taxes on production and imports	1975.5	1908.6	1717.4	740.9	137.2	819.4	2807.3	2340.0	2768.0	3129.0	9927.0	10716.0
Taxes on products	...	...	...	...	...	...	...	...	...	...	...	...
Other taxes on production	1975.5	1908.6	1717.4	740.9	137.2	819.4	2807.3	2340.0	2768.0	3129.0	9927.0	10716.0
Less: Subsidies	...	...	...	...	...	...	...	...	...	...	...	...
OPERATING SURPLUS, GROSS	4569.3	6754.2	3684.5	1711.1	1673.2	-2187.8	212.2	3828.0	3018.0	4098.0	3360.0	2090.0
MIXED INCOME, GROSS	29032.5	30447.0	29057.2	33602.0	40169.5	30401.5	42856.9	48520.0	51215.0	51254.0	45266.0	46209.0
Gross capital formation	349.0	347.0	1176.0	1166.0	3466.0	5429.0	10004.0	152872.0	97824.0	85140.0	58038.0	14906.0
Gross fixed capital formation	349.0	347.0	1176.0	1166.0	3466.0	5429.0	10004.0	152872.0	97824.0	85140.0	58038.0	14906.0
Changes in inventories	...	...	...	...	...	...	...	...	...	...	...	...
Acquisitions less disposals of valuables	...	...	...	...	...	...	...	...	...	...	...	...

Table 2.6 Output, gross value added and fixed assets by industries at current prices (ISIC Rev. 4) Public administration and defence, education, human health and social work activities (O+P+Q)

Series 100: 1993 SNA, CFA franc, Western calendar year — **Data in millions**

	2001	2002	2003	2004	2005	2006	2007	2008	2009	2010	2011	2012
Series	**100**											
Output, at basic prices	277606.7	300919.9	291728.8	312281.3	334452.6	368523.5	402452.5	424401.0	477892.0	445472.0	497081.0	540999.0
Less: Intermediate consumption, at purchaser's prices	108252.7	123185.9	96635.8	116813.3	119575.6	132638.5	152518.5	159334.0	176338.0	146871.0	162100.0	166742.0
Equals: VALUE ADDED, GROSS, at basic prices	169354.0	177734.0	195093.0	195468.0	214877.0	235885.0	249934.0	265067.0	301554.0	298601.0	334981.0	374257.0
Compensation of employees	104583.1	109328.6	120706.4	120827.4	133380.5	146272.2	155122.7	166720.0	188963.0	183982.0	214739.0	235367.0
Taxes on production and imports, less Subsidies	0.0	0.0	0.0	0.0	0.0	0.0	0.0	384.0	563.0	654.0	1128.0	1346.0
Taxes on production and imports	0.0	0.0	0.0	0.0	0.0	0.0	0.0	384.0	563.0	654.0	1128.0	1346.0
Taxes on products	...	...	...	...	...	...	...	...	...	...	...	...

	2001	2002	2003	2004	2005	2006	2007	2008	2009	2010	2011	2012
Series	**100**											
Other taxes on production	0.0	0.0	0.0	0.0	0.0	0.0	0.0	384.0	563.0	654.0	1128.0	1346.0
Less: Subsidies	...	...	...	...	...	...	...	...	...	...	...	...
OPERATING SURPLUS, GROSS	64664.9	68282.4	74256.6	74512.6	81419.5	89486.8	94612.3	96785.0	110586.0	112365.0	114800.0	132974.0
MIXED INCOME, GROSS	...	...	...	...	...	...	...	...	...	...	...	...
Less: Consumption of fixed capital	65990.0	66460.0	65440.0	54590.0	44282.0	62603.0	67858.0	72540.0	84860.0	82350.0	94134.0	109957.0
OPERATING SURPLUS, NET	-1325.1	1822.4	8816.6	19922.6	37137.5	26883.8	26754.3	24245.0	25726.0	30015.0	20666.0	23017.0
MIXED INCOME, NET	...	...	...	...	...	...	...	...	...	...	...	...
Gross capital formation	60334.0	65996.0	65323.0	83327.0	124047.0	128698.0	130164.0	161376.0	193746.0	165069.0	159959.0	349430.0
Gross fixed capital formation	60334.0	65996.0	65323.0	83327.0	124047.0	128698.0	130164.0	161376.0	193746.0	165069.0	159959.0	349430.0
Changes in inventories	...	...	...	...	...	...	...	...	...	...	...	...
Acquisitions less disposals of valuables	...	...	...	...	...	...	...	...	...	...	...	...

Table 2.6 Output, gross value added and fixed assets by industries at current prices (ISIC Rev. 4) Public administration and defence; compulsory social security (O)

Series 100: 1993 SNA, CFA franc, Western calendar year — **Data in millions**

	2001	2002	2003	2004	2005	2006	2007	2008	2009	2010	2011	2012
Series	**100**											
Output, at basic prices	184104.9	192657.0	194167.1	206675.8	216859.6	237638.6	271692.2	286645.0	330260.0	298712.0	343189.0	378441.0
Less: Intermediate consumption, at purchaser's prices	64373.9	72635.0	50764.1	67179.8	63832.6	70708.6	90581.2	92980.0	105178.0	82928.0	94864.0	97637.0
Equals: VALUE ADDED, GROSS, at basic prices	119731.0	120022.0	143403.0	139496.0	153027.0	166930.0	181111.0	193665.0	225082.0	215784.0	248325.0	280804.0
Compensation of employees	74738.8	74920.4	89515.3	87076.5	95522.9	104201.4	113053.5	120890.0	139946.0	133081.0	153800.0	170413.0
Taxes on production and imports, less Subsidies	106.0	123.0	130.0	128.0	77.0	126.0	199.0	235.0	276.0	353.0	391.0	434.0
Taxes on production and imports	106.0	123.0	130.0	128.0	77.0	126.0	199.0	235.0	276.0	353.0	391.0	434.0
Taxes on products	...	...	...	...	...	...	...	...	...	...	...	...
Other taxes on production	106.0	123.0	130.0	128.0	77.0	126.0	199.0	235.0	276.0	353.0	391.0	434.0
Less: Subsidies	...	...	...	...	...	...	...	...	...	...	...	...
OPERATING SURPLUS, GROSS	44886.2	44978.6	53757.7	52291.5	57427.1	62602.6	67858.5	72540.0	84860.0	82350.0	94134.0	109957.0
MIXED INCOME, GROSS	...	...	...	...	...	...	...	...	...	...	...	...
Less: Consumption of fixed capital	65990.0	66460.0	65440.0	54590.0	44282.0	62603.0	67858.0	72540.0	84860.0	82350.0	94134.0	109957.0
OPERATING SURPLUS, NET	-21103.8	-21481.4	-11682.3	-2298.5	13145.1	-0.4	0.5	0.0	0.0	0.0	0.0	0.0
MIXED INCOME, NET	...	...	...	...	...	...	...	...	...	...	...	...
Gross capital formation	60334.0	65996.0	65323.0	83327.0	124047.0	128698.0	130164.0	161376.0	193746.0	165069.0	159959.0	349430.0
Gross fixed capital formation	60334.0	65996.0	65323.0	83327.0	124047.0	128698.0	130164.0	161376.0	193746.0	165069.0	159959.0	349430.0
Changes in inventories	...	...	...	...	...	...	...	...	...	...	...	...
Acquisitions less disposals of valuables	...	...	...	...	...	...	...	...	...	...	...	...

Table 2.6 Output, gross value added and fixed assets by industries at current prices (ISIC Rev. 4) Education (P)

Series 100: 1993 SNA, CFA franc, Western calendar year | **Data in millions**

	2001	2002	2003	2004	2005	2006	2007	2008	2009	2010	2011	2012
Series	**100**											
Output, at basic prices	49149.0	55325.3	51827.7	55974.7	65281.0	71952.6	72296.0	75371.0	81623.0	79708.0	83867.0	88511.0
Less: Intermediate consumption, at purchaser's prices	26820.0	30190.3	28281.7	30544.7	35623.0	39263.6	39451.0	41129.0	44541.0	39511.0	40454.0	41278.0
Equals: VALUE ADDED, GROSS, at basic prices	22329.0	25135.0	23546.0	25430.0	29658.0	32689.0	32845.0	34242.0	37082.0	40197.0	43413.0	47233.0
Compensation of employees	17863.2	20108.0	18836.8	20344.0	23726.4	26151.2	26276.0	29518.0	31603.0	32794.0	37364.0	39716.0
Taxes on production and imports, less Subsidies	0.0	0.0	0.0	0.0	0.0	0.0	0.0	384.0	563.0	654.0	1128.0	1346.0
Taxes on production and imports	0.0	0.0	0.0	0.0	0.0	0.0	0.0	384.0	563.0	654.0	1128.0	1346.0
Taxes on products	...	...	...	...	...	...	...	...	...	...	...	...
Other taxes on production	0.0	0.0	0.0	0.0	0.0	0.0	0.0	384.0	563.0	654.0	1128.0	1346.0
Less: Subsidies	...	...	...	...	...	...	...	...	...	...	...	...
OPERATING SURPLUS, GROSS	4465.8	5027.0	4709.2	5086.0	5931.6	6537.8	6569.0	4340.0	4916.0	6749.0	4921.0	6171.0
MIXED INCOME, GROSS	...	...	...	...	...	...	...	...	...	...	...	...
Gross capital formation	...	...	...	...	...	...	...	...	...	...	...	...

Table 2.6 Output, gross value added and fixed assets by industries at current prices (ISIC Rev. 4) Human health and social work activities (Q)

Series 100: 1993 SNA, CFA franc, Western calendar year | **Data in millions**

	2001	2002	2003	2004	2005	2006	2007	2008	2009	2010	2011	2012
Series	**100**											
Output, at basic prices	44352.8	52937.6	45734.0	49630.8	52312.0	58932.3	58464.3	62385.0	66009.0	67052.0	70025.0	74047.0
Less: Intermediate consumption, at purchaser's prices	17058.8	20360.6	17590.0	19088.8	20120.0	22666.3	22486.3	25225.0	26619.0	24432.0	26782.0	27827.0
Equals: VALUE ADDED, GROSS, at basic prices	27294.0	32577.0	28144.0	30542.0	32192.0	36266.0	35978.0	37160.0	39390.0	42620.0	43243.0	46220.0
Compensation of employees	11981.2	14300.2	12354.3	13406.9	14131.2	15919.6	15793.1	16312.0	17414.0	18107.0	23575.0	25238.0
Taxes on production and imports, less Subsidies	...	...	...	...	...	...	...	...	...	...	...	...
Taxes on production and imports	...	...	...	...	...	...	...	943.0	1166.0	1247.0	3923.0	4136.0
Taxes on products	...	...	...	...	...	...	...	...	...	...	...	...
Other taxes on production	...	...	...	...	...	...	...	943.0	1166.0	1247.0	3923.0	4136.0
Less: Subsidies	...	...	...	...	...	...	...	...	...	...	...	...
OPERATING SURPLUS, GROSS	15312.8	18276.8	15789.7	17135.1	18060.8	20346.4	20184.9	19905.0	20810.0	23266.0	15745.0	16846.0
MIXED INCOME, GROSS	...	...	...	...	...	...	...	...	...	...	...	...
Gross capital formation	...	...	...	...	...	...	...	...	...	...	...	...

Table 2.6 Output, gross value added and fixed assets by industries at current prices (ISIC Rev. 4) Other service activities (S)

Series 100: 1993 SNA, CFA franc, Western calendar year **Data in millions**

	2001	2002	2003	2004	2005	2006	2007	2008	2009	2010	2011	2012
Series	**100**											
Output, at basic prices	34617.4	34801.6	37203.5	39004.1	43036.2	45817.0	50426.2	52185.0	55439.0	56285.0	56725.0	56270.0
Less: Intermediate consumption, at purchaser's prices	13310.4	12361.6	14303.5	14997.1	16550.2	18838.0	19467.2	19443.0	17715.0	16855.0	9206.0	2713.0
Equals: VALUE ADDED, GROSS, at basic prices	21307.0	22440.0	22900.0	24007.0	26486.0	26979.0	30959.0	32742.0	37724.0	39430.0	47519.0	53557.0
Compensation of employees	6509.5	6544.2	6995.8	7334.4	8092.6	8615.5	9482.3	9813.0	12196.0	11943.0	14664.0	15215.0
Taxes on production and imports, less Subsidies	691.2	694.9	742.9	778.8	859.3	914.8	1006.9	1042.0	1187.0	1253.0	7945.0	8033.0
Taxes on production and imports	691.2	694.9	742.9	778.8	859.3	914.8	1006.9	1042.0	1187.0	1253.0	7945.0	8033.0
Taxes on products	...	...	...	...	...	...	...	...	...	...	...	...
Other taxes on production	691.2	694.9	742.9	778.8	859.3	914.8	1006.9	1042.0	1187.0	1253.0	7945.0	8033.0
Less: Subsidies	...	...	...	...	...	...	...	...	...	...	...	...
OPERATING SURPLUS, GROSS	1805.7	1815.3	1940.6	2034.5	2244.8	2389.8	2630.3	2722.0	2651.0	3566.0	569.0	3349.0
MIXED INCOME, GROSS	...	...	...	...	...	...	...	...	...	...	...	...
Gross capital formation	...	...	...	...	...	...	...	...	...	...	...	...

Table 2.6 Output, gross value added and fixed assets by industries at current prices (ISIC Rev. 4) Private households with employed persons (T)

Series 100: 1993 SNA, CFA franc, Western calendar year **Data in millions**

	2001	2002	2003	2004	2005	2006	2007	2008	2009	2010	2011	2012
Series	**100**											
Output, at basic prices	9169.0	9167.0	10275.0	10349.0	11736.0	12006.0	12306.0	12613.0	12991.0	13355.0	13769.0	14196.0
Less: Intermediate consumption, at purchaser's prices	...	...	...	...	...	...	...	...	...	...	...	...
Equals: VALUE ADDED, GROSS, at basic prices	9169.0	9167.0	10275.0	10349.0	11736.0	12006.0	12306.0	12613.0	12991.0	13355.0	13769.0	14196.0
Compensation of employees	9169.0	9167.0	10275.0	10349.0	11736.0	12006.0	12306.0	12613.0	12991.0	13355.0	13769.0	14196.0
Taxes on production and imports, less Subsidies	...	...	...	...	...	...	...	...	...	...	...	...
OPERATING SURPLUS, GROSS	0.0	0.0	0.0	0.0	0.0	0.0	0.0	0.0	0.0	0.0	0.0	0.0
MIXED INCOME, GROSS	...	...	...	...	...	...	...	...	...	...	...	...
Gross capital formation	...	...	...	...	...	...	...	...	...	...	...	...

Table 3.1 Government final consumption expenditure by function at current prices

Series 100: 1993 SNA, CFA franc, Western calendar year

Data in millions

	2001	2002	2003	2004	2005	2006	2007	2008	2009	2010	2011	2012
Series	**100**											
General public services	96974.5	101531.1	104535.4	108675.8	115900.0	120165.0	138569.0	147682.0	140455.0	131429.4	148332.5	151472.0
Defence	16200.0	14400.0	14300.0	16700.0	20300.0	22486.0	25505.0	32705.0	25843.0	22270.6	25134.8	47361.0
Public order and safety	10900.0	8600.0	8500.0	13200.0	14700.0	15988.0	18135.0	20254.0	18392.0	17404.8	19643.2	31383.0
Economic affairs	10600.0	7000.0	3900.0	41300.0	43700.0	49756.0	56437.0	72367.0	80200.0	103118.5	116380.6	120690.0
Environment protection	...	...	...	...	...	...	...	...	...	...	...	...
Housing and community amenities	...	...	...	...	...	...	...	...	...	...	...	...
Health	20594.3	21562.0	22200.0	18000.0	21890.0	22800.0	23251.0	24774.0	20300.0	26367.9	29759.1	32395.2
Recreation, culture and religion	...	...	...	...	...	...	...	...	...	...	...	...
Education	44658.1	46756.5	48140.0	55530.0	56870.0	52290.0	52557.0	61458.0	69904.2	62413.9	70440.9	76680.7
Social protection	340.6	356.6	367.1	381.6	407.0	415.8	467.6	527.5	600.0	561.4	633.7	689.8
Plus: (Other functions)	34135.6	45210.9	50736.5	8899.5	6382.0	2285.2	6943.4	3312.5	57283.8	22873.5	25815.3	14102.4
Equals: General government final consumption expenditure	234403.0	245417.0	252679.0	262687.0	280149.0	286186.0	321865.0	363080.0	412978.0	386440.0	436140.0	474774.0

Table 3.2 Individual consumption expenditure of households, NPISHs, and general government at current prices

Series 100: 1993 SNA, CFA franc, Western calendar year

Data in millions

	2001	2002	2003	2004	2005	2006	2007	2008	2009	2010	2011	2012
Series	**100**											
	Individual consumption expenditure of households											
Food and non-alcoholic beverages	453525.4	496277.1	529480.0	540271.0	586996.0	621596.0	678222.0	766630.0	852544.0	920368.0	1014501.0	1089060.0
Alcoholic beverages, tobacco and narcotics	23689.6	25922.7	27657.0	29199.0	30814.0	32863.0	35885.0	39557.0	45112.0	49109.0	54286.0	58100.0
Clothing and footwear	79717.4	87231.9	93068.0	97161.0	108996.0	115892.0	126549.0	142224.0	159093.0	169832.0	187493.0	202327.0
Housing, water, electricity, gas and other fuels	101786.3	111381.6	118833.0	125296.0	130186.0	137580.0	150231.0	168790.0	188864.0	204648.0	226191.0	242088.0
Furnishings, household equipment and routine maintenance of the house	48472.1	53041.4	56590.0	59792.0	64875.0	69032.0	75445.0	85819.0	95939.0	106326.0	117359.0	125435.0
Health	37989.6	41570.7	44352.0	46549.0	49655.0	52957.0	57827.0	65355.0	63491.0	63859.0	70118.0	74945.0
Transport	84581.1	92554.2	98746.0	102244.0	107547.0	113699.0	124154.0	140318.0	156082.0	166816.0	181709.0	195687.0
Communication	23917.5	26172.1	27923.0	29653.0	32076.0	34124.0	37262.0	42113.0	46845.0	51154.0	56547.0	60522.0
Recreation and culture	46416.4	50792.0	54190.0	64611.0	70619.0	75323.0	82448.0	93880.0	106986.0	116633.0	131190.0	140409.0
Education	8184.3	8955.8	9555.0	10101.0	11690.5	12430.0	13573.0	15340.0	19961.0	20491.0	22619.0	24209.0
Restaurants and hotels	54267.6	59383.2	63356.0	64693.0	69655.0	74287.0	80661.0	91643.0	99109.0	108448.0	119882.0	128042.0
Miscellaneous goods and services	33567.3	36731.5	39189.0	39530.0	40957.0	46778.0	50790.0	58831.0	67707.0	70196.0	79915.0	83443.0
Equals: Household final consumption expenditure in domestic market	1027498.0[a]	1125078.0[a]	1160792.0	1206742.0	1301304.0[b]	1383615.0[b]	1510848.0[a]	1707546.0	1898625.0	2044606.0	2258190.0	2420570.0
Plus: Direct purchases abroad by residents	10586.0	11279.0	14211.0	15112.0	16028.0	17094.0	19345.0	21578.0	23411.0	25536.0	28237.0	28837.0
Less: Direct purchases in domestic market by non-residents	19884.0	7493.0	16378.0	17471.0	18791.0	20041.0	21543.0	24532.0	26519.0	28810.0	31857.0	32533.0

	2001	2002	2003	2004	2005	2006	2007	2008	2009	2010	2011	2012
Series	**100**											
Equals: Household final consumption expenditure	[a] 1012766.0	1109876.0	1148836.0	1194333.0	1287922.0	1369387.0	1495310.0	1689986.0	1898625.0	2044606.0	2206191.0	2420570.0
	Individual consumption expenditure of non-profit institutions serving households (NPISHs)											
Equals: NPISHs final consumption expenditure	14732.0	15203.0	16129.0	17372.0	18734.0	19921.0	21752.0	24584.0	27785.0	31402.0	35490.0	40110.0
	Individual consumption expenditure of general government											
Housing	673.7	705.4	896.0	931.0	995.0	1016.0	1143.0	1275.0	1455.0	1329.0	1543.0	1759.0
Health	6670.2	6983.7	8871.0	9223.0	9860.0	10072.0	11328.0	12778.0	15070.0	13315.0	16493.0	16555.0
Recreation and culture	...	...	...	...	...	...	...	...	...	...	...	...
Education	23061.1	24144.9	30670.0	31885.0	34087.0	34821.0	39162.0	44177.0	49329.0	46033.0	52916.0	57234.0
Social protection	6364.9	6664.1	8465.0	8800.0	9408.0	9611.0	10809.0	12209.0	13695.0	12722.0	14564.0	15712.0
Equals: Individual consumption expenditure of general government	36770.0	38498.0	48902.0	50839.0	54350.0	55520.0	62442.0	70439.0	79549.0	73399.0	85516.0	91260.0
Equals: Total actual individual consumption	[b] 1049536.0	1148374.0	1197738.0	1245172.0	1342272.0	1424908.0	1557753.0	1760425.0	1978173.0	2118005.0	2291707.0	2511829.0

[a] Discrepancy between components and total.
[b] Discrepancy between total and components since data by components include NPISHs final consumption expenditure.

Table 4.1 Total Economy (S.1)

Series 100: 1993 SNA, CFA franc, Western calendar year **Data in millions**

	2001	2002	2003	2004	2005	2006	2007	2008	2009	2010	2011	2012
Series	**100**											
	I. Production account - Resources											
Output, at basic prices (otherwise, please specify)	1943560.0	2083417.0	2194567.0	2233649.0	2554626.0	2760992.0	2926045.0	3474035.0	3705356.0	4059410.0	4326454.0	4998093.0
Less: Financial intermediation services indirectly measured (only to be deducted if FISIM is not distributed to uses)	7884.0	8025.0	10448.0	12719.0	14599.0	15081.0	18235.0	19165.0	21690.0	22668.0	24341.0	26960.0
Plus: Taxes less Subsidies on products	84496.0	102888.0	97667.0	115759.0	134524.0	138196.0	144737.0	166435.0	185530.0	212080.0	256588.0	218971.0
Plus: Taxes on products	84496.0	102888.0	97667.0	115759.0	134524.0	138196.0	144737.0	166435.0	185530.0	212080.0	256588.0	218971.0
Less: Subsidies on products	...	...	...	...	...	...	...	...	...	...	...	...
	I. Production account - Uses											
Intermediate consumption, at purchaser's prices	641551.0	683494.0	737479.0	806246.3	897508.0	977269.0[a]	999585.0[a]	1201650.0	1320749.0	1416537.0	1533171.0	1732209.0
GROSS DOMESTIC PRODUCT	1378621.0	1494789.0	1544310.0	1530444.0	1777047.0	1906837.0	2052967.0	2419654.0	2548447.0	2832285.0	3025530.0	3457895.0
Less: Consumption of fixed capital	65990.0	66460.0	65440.0	54590.0	44282.0	62580.0	72190.0	72540.0	84860.0	87860.0	94134.0	109957.0
NET DOMESTIC PRODUCT	1312631.0	1428329.0	1478870.0	1475854.0	1732765.0	1844257.0	1980771.0	2347114.0	2463587.0	2744425.0	2931396.0	3347938.0
	II.1.1 Generation of income account - Resources											
GROSS DOMESTIC PRODUCT	1378621.0	1494789.0	1544310.0	1530444.0	1777047.0	1906837.0	2052967.0	2419654.0	2548447.0	2832285.0	3025530.0	3457895.0
	II.1.1 Generation of income account - Uses											
Compensation of employees	196590.0	208791.0	222973.0	239349.0	282260.0	316059.0	332471.0	362883.0	405550.0	406230.0	466680.0	523880.0
Taxes on production and imports, less Subsidies	105677.0	127401.0	123756.0	141419.0	149901.0	163317.0	184500.0	213454.0	240736.0	274856.0	389457.0	379167.0
Taxes on production and imports	105677.0	127401.0	123756.0	141419.0	149901.0	163317.0	184500.0	213454.0	240736.0	274865.0	389457.0	379167.0
Taxes on products	84496.0	102888.0	97667.0	115759.0	134524.0	138196.0	144737.0	166435.0	185530.0	212080.0	256588.0	218971.0
Other taxes on production	21181.0	24513.0	26089.0	25660.0	15377.0	25121.0	39763.0	47019.0	55206.0	62785.0	132869.0	160196.0
Less: Subsidies	...	...	...	...	...	...	...	...	...	...	...	...

	2001	2002	2003	2004	2005	2006	2007	2008	2009	2010	2011	2012
Series	**100**											
Subsidies on products	...	...	...	...	...	...	...	...	...	...	...	...
Other subsidies on production	...	...	...	...	...	...	...	...	...	...	...	...
OPERATING SURPLUS, GROSS	110450.0	107316.0	112699.0	99693.0	129095.0	131991.0	193845.0	244753.0	312815.0	384382.0	345157.0	525928.0
MIXED INCOME, GROSS	965904.0	1051278.0	1084879.0	1050071.0	1215789.0	1295470.0	1342146.0	1598564.0	1589346.0	1766808.0	1824236.0	2028920.0
	II.1.2 Allocation of primary income account - Resources											
OPERATING SURPLUS, GROSS	110449.0	107316.0	112699.0	99603.0	129095.0	131991.0	193845.0	244753.0	312815.0	384382.0	345157.0	525928.0
MIXED INCOME, GROSS	965904.0	1051278.0	1084879.0	1050071.0	1215789.0	1295470.0	1342146.0	1598564.0	1589346.0	1766808.0	1824236.0	2028920.0
Compensation of employees	201463.0	214856.0	229968.0	246533.0	291969.0	330179.0	347035.0	377718.0	420635.0	421802.0	478739.0	536740.0
Taxes on production and imports, less Subsidies	105677.0	127401.0	123756.0	141419.0	149900.0	163317.0	184500.0	213454.0	240736.0	274856.0	389457.0	379167.0
Taxes on production and imports	105677.0	127401.0	123756.0	141419.0	149901.0	163317.0	184500.0	213454.0	240736.0	274865.0	389457.0	379167.0
Taxes on products	84496.0	102888.0	97667.0	115759.0	134524.0	138196.0	144737.0	166435.0	185530.0	212080.0	256588.0	218971.0
Other taxes on production	21181.0	24513.0	26089.0	25660.0	15377.0	25121.0	39763.0	47019.0	55206.0	62785.0	132869.0	160196.0
Less: Subsidies	...	...	...	...	...	...	...	...	...	...	...	...
Subsidies on products	...	...	...	...	...	...	...	...	...	...	...	...
Other subsidies on production	...	...	...	...	...	...	...	...	...	...	...	...
Property income	21070.0[b]	15202.0[b]	17641.0[b]	21789.0[b]	28449.0[b]	34765.0[b]	36306.0	33950.0[b]	52035.0	60292.0	84836.0	87791.0
	II.1.2 Allocation of primary income account - Uses											
Property income	36927.0	38138.0	39822.0	35783.0	43170.0	48251.0	51081.0	57267.0	83444.0	97701.0	120995.0	149551.0
GROSS NATIONAL INCOME	1367637.0	1477915.0	1519120.0	1523632.0	1772032.0	1907471.0	2052751.0	2411172.0	2532123.0	2810448.0	3001430.0	3408995.0
	II.2 Secondary distribution of income account - Resources											
GROSS NATIONAL INCOME	1367637.0	1477915.0	1519120.0	1523632.0	1772032.0	1907471.0	2052751.0	2411172.0	2532123.0	2810448.0	3001430.0	3408995.0
Current taxes on income, wealth, etc.	22600.0	23200.0	28300.0	31400.0	36400.0	42803.0	48700.0	67800.0	79600.0	84900.0	96577.0	96577.0
Social contributions	11959.0	11951.0	11271.0	11337.0	11986.0	12671.0	13396.0	14163.0	14973.0	15830.0	16736.0	17693.0
Social benefits other than social transfers in kind	10732.0	9689.0	9593.0	9499.0	10070.0	10675.0	11317.0	11997.0	12718.0	13482.0	14292.0	15151.0
Other current transfers	100516.0	86028.0	101135.0	110309.0	164293.0	158926.0	178556.0	240719.0	220953.0	442575.0	406552.0	486515.0
	II.2 Secondary distribution of income account - Uses											
Current taxes on income, wealth, etc.	22600.0	23200.0	28300.0	31400.0	36400.0	42803.0	48700.0	67800.0	79600.0	84900.0	96577.0	96577.0
Social contributions	11959.0	11951.0	11271.0	11337.0	11986.0	12671.0	13396.0	14163.0	14973.0	15830.0	16736.0	17693.0
Social benefits other than social transfers in kind	10732.0	9689.0	9593.0	9499.0	10070.0	10675.0	11317.0	11997.0	12718.0	13482.0	14292.0	15151.0
Other current transfers	47827.0	49227.0	47027.0	55432.0	68459.0	73505.0	89798.0	137572.0	149760.0	220499.0	244661.0	196906.0
GROSS DISPOSABLE INCOME	1420326.0	1514716.0	1573228.0	1578509.0	1867866.0	1992892.0	2141509.0	2514319.0	2603316.0	3032524.0	3163321.0	3597101.0
	II.4.1 Use of disposable income account - Resources											
GROSS DISPOSABLE INCOME	1420326.0	1514716.0	1573228.0	1578509.0	1867866.0	1992892.0	2141509.0	2514319.0	2603316.0	3032524.0	3163321.0	3622486.0
Adjustment for the change in net equity of households on pension funds	...	...	...	...	...	...	...	...	...	...	...	...
	II.4.1 Use of disposable income account - Uses											
Final consumption expenditure	1261901.0	1370495.0	1417644.0	1474392.0	1586806.0	1675494.0	1838926.0	2077649.0	2339388.0	2462448.0	2677821.0	2935454.0
Individual consumption expenditure	1049536.0	1148374.0	1197738.0	1245172.0	1342272.0	1424908.0	1557753.0	1760425.0	1978173.0	2118005.0	2291707.0	2511829.0
Collective consumption expenditure	212365.0	222122.0	219906.0	229220.0	244533.0	250586.0	281174.0	317225.0	361215.0	344443.0	386114.0	423625.0

	2001	2002	2003	2004	2005	2006	2007	2008	2009	2010	2011	2012
Series	**100**											
Adjustment for the change in net equity of households on pension funds	...	...	...	...	...	...	...	...	...	...	...	...
SAVING, GROSS	158425.0	144221.0	155002.0	104117.0	281060.0	317400.0	302582.0	436670.0	263928.0	570076.0	675268.0	661646.0
	III.1 Capital account - Changes in liabilities and net worth											
SAVING, GROSS	158425.0	144221.0	155002.0	104117.0	281060.0	317400.0	302582.0	436670.0	263928.0	570076.0	675268.0	661646.0
Capital transfers, receivable less payable	29855.0	64387.0	42564.0	203143.0	99329.0	909444.0	128847.0	114897.0	120396.0	97025.0	71844.0	139237.0
Capital transfers, receivable	...	...	...	...	...	...	...	...	...	...	...	...
Less: Capital transfers, payable	...	...	...	...	...	...	...	...	...	...	...	...
Equals: CHANGES IN NET WORTH DUE TO SAVING AND CAPITAL TRANSFERS	...	...	...	...	...	...	...	...	...	...	...	...
	III.1 Capital account - Changes in assets											
Gross capital formation	226121.0	259106.0	250600.0	223339.0	410372.0	449700.0	470965.0	776509.0	885288.0	1131543.0	1160766.0	1175503.0
Gross fixed capital formation	210453.0	229894.0	231797.0	258139.0	384618.0	430199.0	467984.0	746513.0	883824.0	1101631.0	1158727.0	1168147.0
Changes in inventories	15668.0	29212.0	18803.0	-34800.0	25754.0	19501.0	2981.0	29996.0	1464.0	29912.0	2039.0	7356.0
Acquisitions less disposals of valuables	...	...	...	...	...	...	...	...	...	...	...	...
Acquisitions less disposals of non-produced non-financial assets	...	...	...	...	...	...	...	...	...	...	...	...
NET LENDING (+) / NET BORROWING (-)	-37811.0	-50498.0	-53034.0	83921.0	-29983.0	777144.0	-39536.0	-224942.0	-500964.0	-464442.0	-603423.0	-374619.0

[a] Excludes financial intermediation services indirectly measured (FISIM).
[b] Includes financial intermediation services indirectly measured (FISIM).

Table 4.2 Rest of the world (S.2)

Series 100: 1993 SNA, CFA franc, Western calendar year **Data in millions**

	2001	2002	2003	2004	2005	2006	2007	2008	2009	2010	2011	2012
Series	**100**											
	V.I External account of goods and services - Resources											
Imports of goods and services	350723.0	364821.0	394796.0	450078.0	553202.0	563059.0	615383.0	863512.0	1194112.0	1390424.0	1445203.0	1510043.0
Imports of goods	242823.0	258721.0	282903.0	311551.0	405862.0	391276.0	438354.0	594410.0	847188.0	972943.0	1034500.0	1039302.0
Imports of services	107900.0	106100.0	111893.0	138527.0	147340.0	171783.0	177029.0	269102.0	346924.0	417481.0	410703.0	470741.0
	V.I External account of goods and services - Uses											
Exports of goods and services	241321.0	230006.0	261276.0	282791.0	333068.0	344704.0	358453.0	429008.0	517883.0	628718.0	632144.0	856980.0
Exports of goods	199721.0	194806.0	224481.0	233451.0	286900.0	297353.0	317891.0	370418.0	470701.0	570131.0	599454.0	791947.0
Exports of services	41600.0	35200.0	36795.0	49340.0	46168.0	47351.0	40562.0	58590.0	47182.0	58587.0	32690.0	65033.0
EXTERNAL BALANCE OF GOODS AND SERVICES	109402.0	134815.0	134520.0	167287.0	220134.0	218355.0	256930.0	434504.0	676229.0	761706.0	813059.0	653063.0
	V.II External account of primary income and current transfers - Resources											
EXTERNAL BALANCE OF GOODS AND SERVICES	109402.0	134815.0	134520.0	167287.0	220134.0	218355.0	256930.0	434504.0	676229.0	761706.0	813059.0	653063.0
Compensation of employees	1143.0	1078.0	1119.0	1712.0	1291.0	1067.0	3009.0	3356.0	4455.0	8000.0	22805.0	25085.0
Taxes on production and imports, less Subsidies	105677.0	127401.0	123756.0	141419.0	149901.0	163317.0	184500.0	213454.0	240736.0	274865.0	389457.0	379167.0
Taxes on production and imports	105677.0	127401.0	123756.0	141419.0	149901.0	163317.0	184500.0	213454.0	240736.0	274865.0	389457.0	379167.0
Taxes on products	84496.0	102888.0	97667.0	115759.0	134524.0	138196.0	144737.0	166435.0	185530.0	212080.0	256588.0	218971.0
Other taxes on production	21181.0	24513.0	26089.0	25660.0	15377.0	25121.0	39763.0	47019.0	55206.0	62785.0	132869.0	160196.0

	2001	2002	2003	2004	2005	2006	2007	2008	2009	2010	2011	2012
Series	**100**											
Less: Subsidies	...	...	...	...	...	...	...	...	...	...	...	...
Subsidies on products	...	...	...	...	...	...	...	...	...	...	...	...
Other subsidies on production	...	...	...	...	...	...	...	...	...	...	...	...
Property income	23674.0	27730.0	24634.0	19084.0	23271.0	28763.0	31473.0	47635.0	53866.0	44391.0	45523.0	74319.0
Current taxes on income, wealth, etc.	22600.0	23200.0	28300.0	31400.0	36400.0	42803.0	48700.0	67800.0	79600.0	84900.0	96577.0	96577.0
Social contributions	11959.0	11951.0	11271.0	11337.0	11986.0	12671.0	13396.0	14163.0	14973.0	15830.0	16736.0	17693.0
Social benefits other than social transfers in kind	10732.0	9689.0	9593.0	9499.0	10070.0	10675.0	11317.0	11997.0	12718.0	13482.0	14292.0	15151.0
Other current transfers	11759.0	8590.0	5549.0	13052.0	18660.0	18873.0	10877.0	10550.0	9154.0	28881.0	60986.0	8800.0
Adjustment for the change in net equity of households on pension funds	...	...	...	...	...	...	...	...	...	...	...	...
V.II External account of primary income and current transfers - Uses												
Compensation of employees	6016.0	7143.0	8114.0	8896.0	11000.0	15187.0	17573.0	18191.0	19540.0	23572.0	34864.0	37945.0
Taxes on production and imports, less Subsidies	...	...	...	...	...	...	...	...	...	...	...	...
Taxes on production and imports	...	...	...	...	...	...	...	...	...	...	...	...
Taxes on products	...	...	...	...	...	...	...	...	...	...	...	...
Other taxes on production	...	...	...	...	...	...	...	...	...	...	...	...
Less: Subsidies	...	...	...	...	...	...	...	...	...	...	...	...
Subsidies on products	...	...	...	...	...	...	...	...	...	...	...	...
Other subsidies on production	...	...	...	...	...	...	...	...	...	...	...	...
Property income	7817.0	4794.0	2453.0	5090.0	8550.0	15277.0	16698.0	24318.0	22457.0	6982.0	9364.0	12559.0
Current taxes on income and wealth, etc.	...	...	...	...	...	...	...	...	...	...	...	...
Social contributions	...	...	...	...	...	...	...	...	...	...	...	...
Social benefits other than social transfers in kind	...	...	...	...	...	...	...	...	...	...	...	...
Other current transfers	64448.0	45391.0	59657.0	67929.0	114494.0	104294.0	99635.0	113697.0	80347.0	250957.0	222877.0	196906.0
Adjustment for the change in net equity of households on pension funds	...	...	...	...	...	...	...	...	...	...	...	...
CURRENT EXTERNAL BALANCE	67697.0	114885.0	95598.0	119220.0	129312.0	132300.0	168383.0	339839.0	621360.0	561467.0	675268.0	513857.0
V.III.1 Capital account - Changes in liabilities and net worth												
CURRENT EXTERNAL BALANCE	67697.0	114885.0	95598.0	119220.0	129312.0	132300.0	168383.0	339839.0	621360.0	561467.0	675268.0	513857.0
Capital transfers, receivable less payable	-29855.0	-64387.0	-42564.0	-203143.0	-99329.0	-909444.0	-128847.0	-114897.0	-120396.0	-97025.0	-71844.0	-139237.0
Capital transfers, receivable	0.0	0.0	0.0	0.0	0.0	0.0	0.0	0.0	0.0	0.0	0.0	0.0
Less: Capital transfers, payable	29855.0	64387.0	42564.0	203143.0	99329.0	909444.0	128847.0	114897.0	120396.0	97025.0	71844.0	139237.0
Equals: CHANGES IN NET WORTH DUE TO SAVING AND CAPITAL TRANSFERS	...	...	...	...	...	...	...	...	...	...	...	...
V.III.1 Capital account - Changes in assets												
Acquisitions less disposals of non-produced non-financial assets	...	...	...	...	...	...	...	...	...	...	...	...
NET LENDING (+) / NET BORROWING (-)	37811.0	50498.0	53034.0	-83921.0	29983.0	-777144.0	39536.0	224942.0	500964.0	464442.0	603423.0	374619.0

Table 4.3 Non-financial Corporations (S.11)

Series 100: 1993 SNA, CFA franc, Western calendar year — **Data in millions**

	2001	2002	2003	2004	2005	2006	2007	2008	2009	2010	2011	2012
Series	**100**											
	I. Production account - Resources											
Output, at basic prices (otherwise, please specify)	332180.0	351317.0	342034.0	374366.0	418301.0	484281.0	571443.0	768414.0	904537.0	1046615.0	1150125.0	1458294.0
	I. Production account - Uses											
Intermediate consumption, at purchaser's prices	211623.0	229725.0	213681.0	233305.0	253306.0	295006.0	317450.0	413909.0	494644.0	559942.0	610971.0	695573.0
VALUE ADDED GROSS, in basic prices	120557.0	121592.0	128353.0	141061.0	164995.0	189275.0	253993.0	354505.0	409893.0	486673.0	539154.0	762721.0
Less: Consumption of fixed capital	...	...	...	...	...	...	...	...	...	...	...	...
VALUE ADDED NET, at basic prices	...	...	...	...	...	...	...	...	...	...	...	...
	II.1.1 Generation of income account - Resources											
VALUE ADDED GROSS, at basic prices	120557.0	121592.0	128353.0	141061.0	164995.0	189275.0	253993.0	354505.0	409893.0	486673.0	539154.0	762721.0
	II.1.1 Generation of income account - Uses											
Compensation of employees	57868.0	58703.0	68055.0	74736.0	79656.0	97805.0	99074.0	114232.0	134018.0	139015.0	172480.0	204896.0
Other taxes less Other subsidies on production	16054.0	18579.0	19774.0	19449.0	11012.0	18578.0	30125.0	39931.0	47884.0	53422.0	119125.0	142967.0
Other taxes on production	16054.0	18579.0	19774.0	19449.0	11012.0	18578.0	30125.0	39931.0	47884.0	53422.0	119125.0	142967.0
Less: Other subsidies on production	...	...	...	...	...	...	...	...	...	...	...	...
OPERATING SURPLUS, GROSS	46635.0	44310.0	40524.0	46876.0	74327.0	72892.0	124794.0	173061.0	228356.0	294236.0	247549.0	414858.0
	II.1.2 Allocation of primary income account - Resources											
OPERATING SURPLUS, GROSS	46635.0	44310.0	40524.0	46876.0	74327.0	72892.0	124794.0	173061.0	228356.0	294236.0	247549.0	414858.0
Property income	2216.0	2825.0	1714.0	1140.0	5409.0	9933.0	10490.0	7045.0	10213.0	17400.0	23687.0	25897.0
	II.1.2 Allocation of primary income account - Uses											
Property income	7415.0	8857.0	15542.0	19617.0	23936.0	30196.0	30312.0	32998.0	60774.0	74105.0	91139.0	108116.0
BALANCE OF PRIMARY INCOMES	41436.0	38278.0	26696.0	28399.0	55800.0	52629.0	104972.0	147108.0	177795.0	237531.0	180097.0	332639.0
	II.2 Secondary distribution of income account - Resources											
BALANCE OF PRIMARY INCOMES	41436.0	38278.0	26696.0	28399.0	55800.0	52629.0	104972.0	147108.0	177795.0	237531.0	180097.0	332639.0
Social contributions	...	...	...	...	...	...	...	...	...	...	...	...
Other current transfers	3778.0	3449.0	6376.0	6172.0	6473.0	6731.0	20509.0	19304.0	13304.0	37181.0	33021.0	35687.0
	II.2 Secondary distribution of income account - Uses											
Current taxes on income, wealth, etc.	9205.0	9450.0	11527.0	12790.0	14826.0	19190.0	24267.0	33784.0	51239.0	52798.0	61596.0	55838.0
Social benefits other than social transfers in kind	...	...	...	...	...	...	...	...	...	...	...	...
Other current transfers	5922.0	4790.0	4758.0	4382.0	9053.0	14394.0	10708.0	13826.0	29976.0	40913.0	42762.0	60138.0
GROSS DISPOSABLE INCOME	30087.0	27487.0	16787.0	17399.0	38394.0	25776.0	90506.0	118803.0	111884.0	181001.0	108760.0	252350.0
	II.4.1 Use of disposable income account - Resources											
GROSS DISPOSABLE INCOME	30087.0	27487.0	16787.0	17399.0	38394.0	25776.0	90506.0	118803.0	111884.0	181001.0	108760.0	252350.0
	II.4.1 Use of disposable income account - Uses											
Adjustment for the change in net equity of households on pension funds	...	...	...	...	...	...	...	...	...	...	...	...
SAVING, GROSS	30087.0	27487.0	16787.0	17399.0	38394.0	25776.0	90506.0	118803.0	111884.0	181001.0	108760.0	252350.0

	2001	2002	2003	2004	2005	2006	2007	2008	2009	2010	2011	2012
Series	**100**											
	III.1 Capital account - Changes in liabilities and net worth											
SAVING, GROSS	30087.0	27487.0	16787.0	17399.0	38394.0	25776.0	90506.0	118803.0	111884.0	181001.0	108760.0	252350.0
Capital transfers, receivable less payable	...	...	...	...	...	...	...	...	16550.0	6797.0	11673.0	...
Capital transfers, receivable	0.0	0.0	0.0	0.0	0.0	0.0	0.0	0.0	16550.0	14030.0	14700.0	15837.0
Less: Capital transfers, payable	...	...	...	...	...	...	...	...	...	...	...	...
Equals: CHANGES IN NET WORTH DUE TO SAVING AND CAPITAL TRANSFERS	...	...	...	...	...	...	...	...	...	...	...	...
	III.1 Capital account - Changes in assets											
Gross capital formation	87457.0	96913.0	108396.0	97792.0	162831.0	186984.0	207713.0	476261.0	574368.0	834322.0	898316.0	694339.0
Gross fixed capital formation	80581.0	89028.0	98969.0	96600.0	151763.0	182341.0	205712.0	465462.0	568607.0	814863.0	873699.0	692363.0
Changes in inventories	6876.0	7885.0	9427.0	1192.0	11068.0	4643.0	2001.0	10799.0	5761.0	19459.0	24617.0	1976.0
Acquisitions less disposals of valuables	...	...	...	...	...	...	...	...	...	...	...	...
Acquisitions less disposals of non-produced non-financial assets	0.0	0.0	0.0	0.0	0.0	...	...	...	...	...	...	...
NET LENDING (+) / NET BORROWING (-)	-57370.0	-69426.0	-91609.0	-80393.0	-124437.0	-161208.0	-117207.0	-357459.0	-445934.0	-639291.0	-774856.0	-426152.0

Table 4.4 Financial Corporations (S.12)

Series 100: 1993 SNA, CFA franc, Western calendar year

Data in millions

	2001	2002	2003	2004	2005	2006	2007	2008	2009	2010	2011	2012
Series	**100**											
	I. Production account - Resources											
Output, at basic prices (otherwise, please specify)	19425.0	19949.0	23137.0	28231.0	32372.0	34879.0	42281.0	45779.0	48773.0	55469.0	66905.0	71355.0
	I. Production account - Uses											
Intermediate consumption, at purchaser's prices	8567.0	10255.0	9672.0	10368.0	11488.0	13268.0	16150.0	18315.0	17691.0	20120.0	24268.0	25882.0
VALUE ADDED GROSS, at basic prices	10858.0	9694.0	13465.0	17863.0	20884.0	21611.0	26131.0	27464.0	31082.0	35349.0	42637.0	45473.0
Less: Consumption of fixed capital	...	...	...	...	...	...	...	...	...	...	...	...
VALUE ADDED NET, at basic prices	10858.0	9694.0	13465.0	17863.0	20884.0	21611.0	26131.0	27464.0	31082.0	35349.0	42637.0	45473.0
	II.1.1 Generation of income account - Resources											
VALUE ADDED GROSS, at basic prices	10858.0	9694.0	13465.0	17863.0	20884.0	21611.0	26131.0	27464.0	31082.0	35349.0	42637.0	45473.0
	II.1.1 Generation of income account - Uses											
Compensation of employees	4326.0	4266.0	5458.0	5918.0	6122.0	6333.0	6552.0	6778.0	7011.0	7253.0	8174.0	8720.0
Other taxes less Other subsidies on production	779.0	796.0	825.0	1089.0	1413.0	1721.0	2235.0	2369.0	2782.0	3142.0	6648.0	8680.0
Other taxes on production	779.0	796.0	825.0	1089.0	1413.0	1721.0	2235.0	2369.0	2782.0	3142.0	6648.0	8680.0
Less: Other subsidies on production	...	...	...	...	...	...	...	...	...	...	...	...
OPERATING SURPLUS, GROSS	5753.0	4632.0	7182.0	10856.0	13349.0	13557.0	17344.0	18317.0	21289.0	24954.0	27815.0	28073.0
	II.1.2 Allocation of primary income account - Resources											
OPERATING SURPLUS, GROSS	5753.0	4632.0	7182.0	10856.0	13349.0	13557.0	17344.0	18317.0	21289.0	24954.0	27815.0	28073.0
Property income	2713.0	2557.0	3639.0	4260.0	5442.0	6059.0	3506.0	2992.0	3122.0	4117.0	4620.0	4202.0

	2001	2002	2003	2004	2005	2006	2007	2008	2009	2010	2011	2012
Series	**100**											
	II.1.2 Allocation of primary income account - Uses											
Property income	2513.0	3372.0	2478.0	2787.0	3205.0	4043.0	4398.0	4788.0	5212.0	6674.0	8546.0	10943.0
BALANCE OF PRIMARY INCOMES	5953.0	3817.0	8343.0	12329.0	15586.0	15573.0	16452.0	16521.0	19199.0	22397.0	23889.0	21332.0
	II.2 Secondary distribution of income account - Resources											
BALANCE OF PRIMARY INCOMES	5953.0	3817.0	8343.0	12329.0	15586.0	15573.0	16452.0	16521.0	19199.0	22397.0	23889.0	21332.0
Social contributions	...	...	...	...	...	...	...	...	...	...	...	...
Other current transfers	7614.0	7829.0	6254.0	8860.0	10156.0	10392.0	13862.0	19304.0	27363.0	38750.0	37219.0	40187.0
	II.2 Secondary distribution of income account - Uses											
Current taxes on income, wealth, etc.	592.0	1057.0	844.0	994.0	1383.0	1840.0	2446.0	3257.0	4333.0	3221.0	7670.0	10204.0
Social benefits other than social transfers in kind	...	...	...	...	...	...	...	...	...	...	...	...
Other current transfers	7091.0	6906.0	6435.0	7974.0	9826.0	10287.0	13007.0	14194.0	18283.0	34640.0	30302.0	34076.0
GROSS DISPOSABLE INCOME	5884.0	3683.0	7318.0	12221.0	14533.0	13838.0	14859.0	15754.0	23946.0	20742.0	23136.0	17239.0
	II.4.1 Use of disposable income account - Resources											
GROSS DISPOSABLE INCOME	5884.0	3683.0	7318.0	12221.0	14533.0	13838.0	14859.0	15754.0	23946.0	20742.0	23136.0	17239.0
	II.4.1 Use of disposable income account - Uses											
Adjustment for the change in net equity of households on pension funds	...	...	...	...	...	...	...	...	...	...	...	...
SAVING, GROSS	5884.0	3683.0	7318.0	12221.0	14533.0	13838.0	14859.0	15754.0	23946.0	20742.0	23136.0	17239.0
	III.1 Capital account - Changes in liabilities and net worth											
SAVING, GROSS	5884.0	3683.0	7318.0	12221.0	14533.0	13838.0	14859.0	15754.0	23946.0	20742.0	23136.0	17239.0
Capital transfers, receivable less payable	...	...	...	...	...	...	...	...	...	...	...	...
Capital transfers, receivable	...	...	...	...	...	...	...	...	...	...	...	...
Less: Capital transfers, payable	...	...	...	...	...	...	...	...	...	...	...	...
Equals: CHANGES IN NET WORTH DUE TO SAVING AND CAPITAL TRANSFERS	...	...	...	...	...	...	...	...	...	...	...	...
	III.1 Capital account - Changes in assets											
Gross capital formation	1773.0	1950.0	1980.0	2154.0	6892.0	7523.0	9371.0	12970.0	13340.0	10665.0	12069.0	11010.0
Gross fixed capital formation	1773.0	1950.0	1980.0	2154.0	6892.0	7523.0	9371.0	12970.0	13340.0	10665.0	12069.0	11010.0
Changes in inventories	...	...	...	...	...	...	...	...	...	...	...	...
Acquisitions less disposals of valuables	...	...	...	...	...	...	...	...	...	...	...	...
Acquisitions less disposals of non-produced non-financial assets	...	...	...	...	...	...	...	...	...	...	...	...
NET LENDING (+) / NET BORROWING (-)	4111.0	1733.0	5338.0	10067.0	7641.0	6315.0	5488.0	2784.0	10606.0	10077.0	11067.0	6229.0

Table 4.5 General Government (S.13)

Series 100: 1993 SNA, CFA franc, Western calendar year

Data in millions

	2001	2002	2003	2004	2005	2006	2007	2008	2009	2010	2011	2012
Series	**100**											
I. Production account - Resources												
Output, at basic prices (otherwise, please specify)	234464.0	245460.0	247384.0	263321.0	276296.0	302770.0	346157.0	365208.0	434714.0	406779.0	459095.0	527528.0
I. Production account - Uses												
Intermediate consumption, at purchaser's prices	93156.0	96658.0	98036.0	118139.0	94797.0	104782.0	127266.0	132224.0	167088.0	144902.0	160923.0	192519.0
VALUE ADDED GROSS, at basic prices	141308.0	148802.0	149348.0	145182.0	181499.0	197988.0	218891.0	232984.0	267626.0	261877.0	298172.0	335009.0
Less: Consumption of fixed capital	65990.0[a]	66460.0[a]	65440.0[a]	54590.0[a]	44282.0[a]	62580.0[a]	72190.0[a]	72540.0[a]	84860.0	87860.0	94134.0	109957.0
VALUE ADDED NET, at basic prices	75318.0	82342.0	83908.0	90592.0	137217.0	135408.0	146701.0	160444.0	182766.0	174017.0	204038.0	225052.0
II.1.1 Generation of income account - Resources												
VALUE ADDED GROSS, at basic prices	141308.0	148802.0	149348.0	145182.0	181499.0	197988.0	218891.0	232984.0	267626.0	261877.0	298172.0	335009.0
II.1.1 Generation of income account - Uses												
Compensation of employees	75257.0	82280.0	83778.0	90463.0	125404.0	137239.0	148750.0	160209.0	182125.0	173664.0	203647.0	224618.0
Other taxes less Other subsidies on production	106.0	123.0	130.0	128.0	77.0	126.0	199.0	235.0	276.0	353.0	391.0	434.0
Other taxes on production	106.0	123.0	130.0	128.0	77.0	126.0	199.0	235.0	276.0	353.0	391.0	434.0
Less: Other subsidies on production	...	...	...	...	...	...	...	...	...	...	...	...
OPERATING SURPLUS, GROSS	65945.0	66399.0	65440.0	54591.0	56018.0	60623.0	69942.0	72540.0	84860.0	87860.0	94134.0	109957.0
II.1.2 Allocation of primary income account - Resources												
OPERATING SURPLUS, GROSS	65945.0	66399.0	65440.0	54590.0	56018.0	60623.0	69942.0	72540.0	84860.0	87860.0	94134.0	109957.0
Taxes on production and imports, less Subsidies	105677.0	127401.0	123756.0	141419.0	149900.0	163317.0	184500.0	213454.0	240736.0	274865.0	389457.0	379167.0
Taxes on production and imports	105677.0	127401.0	123756.0	141419.0	149901.0	163317.0	184500.0	213454.0	240736.0	274865.0	389457.0	379167.0
Taxes on products	...	...	...	...	...	...	...	...	...	...	...	...
Other taxes on production	...	...	...	...	...	...	...	...	...	...	...	...
Less: Subsidies	...	...	...	...	...	...	...	...	...	...	...	...
Subsidies on products	...	...	...	...	...	...	...	...	...	...	...	...
Other subsidies on production	...	...	...	...	...	...	...	...	...	...	...	...
Property income	345.0	218.0	479.0	450.0	525.0	540.0	555.0	570.0	585.0	601.0	617.0	634.0
II.1.2 Allocation of primary income account - Uses												
Property income	25400.0	22600.0	17400.0	8100.0	10400.0	4900.0	7100.0	9786.0	10320.0	6321.0	10226.0	18900.0
BALANCE OF PRIMARY INCOMES	146567.0	171418.0	172275.0	188359.0	196043.0	219580.0	247897.0	276778.0	315861.0	357005.0	473982.0	470858.0
II.2 Secondary distribution of income account - Resources												
BALANCE OF PRIMARY INCOMES	146567.0	171418.0	172275.0	188359.0	196043.0	219580.0	247897.0	276778.0	315861.0	357005.0	473982.0	470858.0
Current taxes on income, wealth, etc.	22600.0	23200.0	28300.0	31400.0	36400.0	42803.0	48700.0	67800.0	79600.0	84900.0	96577.0	96577.0
Social contributions	11959.0	11951.0	11271.0	11337.0	11986.0	12671.0	13396.0	14163.0	14973.0	15830.0	16736.0	17693.0
Other current transfers	74789.0	63449.0	77719.0	81649.0	139833.0	132853.0	127517.0	186715.0	139384.0	320232.0	279462.0	361438.0
II.2 Secondary distribution of income account - Uses												
Current taxes on income, wealth, etc.	...	...	...	...	...	...	...	...	...	...	...	...
Social benefits other than social transfers in kind	10732.0	9689.0	9593.0	9499.0	10070.0	10675.0	11317.0	11997.0	12718.0	13482.0	14292.0	15151.0

	2001	2002	2003	2004	2005	2006	2007	2008	2009	2010	2011	2012
Series	**100**											
Other current transfers	33066.0	35104.0	34160.0	40587.0	45433.0	46358.0	63049.0	106233.0	98892.0	137569.0	164709.0	197047.0
GROSS DISPOSABLE INCOME	212117.0	225225.0	245812.0	262659.0	328759.0	350874.0	363144.0	427226.0	437208.0	626916.0	687756.0	734368.0
II.4.1 Use of disposable income account - Resources												
GROSS DISPOSABLE INCOME	212117.0	225225.0	245812.0	262660.0	328759.0	350874.0	363144.0	427226.0	437208.0	626916.0	687756.0	734368.0
II.4.1 Use of disposable income account - Uses												
Final consumption expenditure	234403.0	245417.0	252679.0	262687.0	280149.0	286186.0	321865.0	363080.0	412978.0	386440.0	436140.0	474774.0
Individual consumption expenditure	36770.0	38498.0	48902.0	50839.0	54350.0	55521.0	62442.0	70439.0	79548.0	73399.0	85516.0	91259.0
Collective consumption expenditure	197633.0	206919.0	203777.0	211848.0	225799.0	230665.0	259422.0	292641.0	333430.0	313041.0	350624.0	383515.0
Adjustment for the change in net equity of households on pension funds	...	...	...	...	...	...	...	...	...	...	...	...
SAVING, GROSS	-22286.0	-20192.0	-1542.0	-640.0	48609.0	64688.0	41280.0	64146.0	24230.0	240476.0	251616.0	259593.0
III.1 Capital account - Changes in liabilities and net worth												
SAVING, GROSS	-22286.0	-20192.0	-1542.0	-640.0	48609.0	64688.0	41280.0	64146.0	24230.0	240476.0	251616.0	259593.0
Capital transfers, receivable less payable	29885.0	64387.0	42564.0	203143.0	99329.0	909444.0	128847.0	114897.0	103846.0	82995.0	57144.0	123400.0
Capital transfers, receivable	29885.0	64387.0	42564.0	203143.0	99329.0	909444.0	128847.0	114897.0	103846.0	82995.0	57144.0	123400.0
Less: Capital transfers, payable	...	...	...	...	...	...	...	...	...	...	...	...
Equals: CHANGES IN NET WORTH DUE TO SAVING AND CAPITAL TRANSFERS	...	...	...	...	...	...	...	...	...	...	...	...
III.1 Capital account - Changes in assets												
Gross capital formation	60334.0	65996.0	65323.0	83327.0	124047.0	128698.0	130164.0	161376.0	193746.0	165069.0	159959.0	349430.0
Gross fixed capital formation	60334.0	65996.0	65323.0	83327.0	124047.0	128698.0	130164.0	161376.0	193746.0	165069.0	159959.0	349430.0
Changes in inventories	...	...	...	...	...	...	...	...	...	...	...	...
Acquisitions less disposals of valuables	...	...	...	...	...	...	...	...	...	...	...	...
Acquisitions of non-produced non-financial assets	0.0	0.0	0.0	0.0	0.0	0.0	0.0	0.0	0.0	...	...	...
NET LENDING (+) / NET BORROWING (-)	-52735.0	-21801.0	-24301.0	119176.0	23891.0	845434.0	39962.0	17667.0	-65670.0	158402.0	148801.0	33563.0

[a] Refers to consumption of fixed capital for total economy

Table 4.6 Households (S.14)

Series 100: 1993 SNA, CFA franc, Western calendar year

Data in millions

	2001	2002	2003	2004	2005	2006	2007	2008	2009	2010	2011	2012
Series	**100**											
I. Production account - Resources												
Output, at basic prices (otherwise, please specify)	1359490.0	1466697.0	1582012.0	1567731.0	1827657.0	1939082.0	1966164.0	2294634.0	2317332.0	2550547.0	2650332.0	2940916.0
I. Production account - Uses												
Intermediate consumption, at purchaser's prices	330200.0	346861.0	426091.0	444430.0	537920.0	564230.0	538710.0	637202.0	641326.0	691573.0	737012.0	818235.0
VALUE ADDED GROSS, at basic prices	1029285.0	1119836.0	1155921.0	1123297.0	1289740.0	1374848.0	1427445.0	1657432.0	1676006.0	1858974.0	1913320.0	2122681.0
Less: Consumption of fixed capital	...	...	...	...	...	...	...	...	...	...	...	...
VALUE ADDED NET, at basic prices	1029285.0	1119836.0	1155921.0	1123297.0	1289740.0	1374848.0	1427445.0	1657432.0	1676006.0	1858974.0	1913320.0	2122681.0

	2001	2002	2003	2004	2005	2006	2007	2008	2009	2010	2011	2012
Series	**100**											
	II.1.1 Generation of income account - Resources											
VALUE ADDED GROSS, at basic prices	1029285.0	1119836.0	1155921.0	1123297.0	1289740.0	1374848.0	1427445.0	1657432.0	1676006.0	1858974.0	1913320.0	2122681.0
	II.1.1 Generation of income account - Uses											
Compensation of employees	59139.0	63543.0	65682.0	68232.0	71078.0	74682.0	78095.0	81664.0	82396.0	86298.0	82379.0	85646.0
Other taxes less Other subsidies on production	4242.0	5015.0	5360.0	4994.0	2874.0	4696.0	7204.0	4484.0	4264.0	5868.0	6705.0	8115.0
Other taxes on production	4242.0	5015.0	5360.0	4994.0	2874.0	4696.0	7204.0	4484.0	4264.0	5868.0	6705.0	8115.0
Less: Other subsidies on production	...	...	...	...	...	...	...	...	...	...	...	...
OPERATING SURPLUS, GROSS	...	...	...	...	...	...	...	...	...	...	...	...
MIXED INCOME, GROSS	965904.0	1051278.0	1084879.0	1050071.0	1215788.0	1295470.0	1342146.0	1598564.0	1589346.0	1766808.0	1824236.0	2028920.0
	II.1.2 Allocation of primary income account - Resources											
OPERATING SURPLUS, GROSS	...	...	...	...	...	...	...	...	...	...	...	...
MIXED INCOME, GROSS	965904.0	1051278.0	1084879.0	1050071.0	1215788.0	1295470.0	1342146.0	1598564.0	1589346.0	1766808.0	1824236.0	2028920.0
Compensation of employees	201463.0	214856.0	229968.0	246533.0	291969.0	330179.0	347035.0	377718.0	420635.0	421802.0	478739.0	536740.0
Property income	7912.0	1576.0	1361.0	3220.0	2474.0	3152.0	3520.0	4178.0	16421.0	15506.0	31571.0	30098.0
	II.1.2 Allocation of primary income account - Uses											
Property income	1599.0	3309.0	4402.0	5279.0	5629.0	9112.0	9271.0	9695.0	7138.0	10601.0	11084.0	11592.0
BALANCE OF PRIMARY INCOMES	1173680.0	1264401.0	1311806.0	1294545.0	1504602.0	1619689.0	1683430.0	1970765.0	2019268.0	2193515.0	2323462.0	2584166.0
	II.2 Secondary distribution of income account - Resources											
BALANCE OF PRIMARY INCOMES	1173680.0	1264401.0	1311806.0	1294545.0	1504602.0	1619689.0	1683430.0	1970765.0	2019268.0	2193515.0	2323462.0	2584166.0
Social contributions	...	...	...	...	...	...	...	...	...	...	...	...
Social benefits other than social transfers in kind	10732.0	9689.0	9593.0	9499.0	10070.0	10675.0	11317.0	11997.0	12718.0	13482.0	14292.0	15151.0
Other current transfers	14336.0	11301.0	10786.0	13626.0	7831.0	8950.0	16668.0	18016.0	40902.0	46412.0	56850.0	49203.0
	II.2 Secondary distribution of income account - Uses											
Current taxes on income, wealth, etc.	12803.0	12693.0	15929.0	17616.0	20191.0	21773.0	21985.0	30759.0	24028.0	26337.0	27311.0	30535.0
Social contributions	11959.0	11951.0	11271.0	11337.0	11986.0	12671.0	13396.0	14163.0	14973.0	15830.0	16736.0	17693.0
Social benefits other than social transfers in kind	...	...	...	...	...	...	...	...	...	...	...	...
Other current transfers	1749.0	2427.0	1674.0	2429.0	4147.0	2466.0	3034.0	3319.0	3609.0	7377.0	6888.0	7148.0
GROSS DISPOSABLE INCOME	1172238.0	1258321.0	1303311.0	1286230.0	1486179.0	1602404.0	1673000.0	1952537.0	2030278.0	2203865.0	2343669.0	2593144.0
	II.4.1 Use of disposable income account - Resources											
GROSS DISPOSABLE INCOME	1172238.0	1258321.0	1303311.0	1286230.0	1486179.0	1602404.0	1673000.0	1952537.0	2030278.0	2203865.0	2343669.0	2593144.0
Adjustment for the change in net equity of households on pension funds	...	...	...	...	...	...	...	...	...	...	...	...
	II.4.1 Use of disposable income account - Uses											
Final consumption expenditure	1027498.0	1125078.0	1164965.0	1211705.0	1306656.0	1389308.0	1517062.0	1714569.0	1926410.0	2076008.0	2241681.0	2460680.0
Individual consumption expenditure	1012766.0	1109876.0	1148836.0	1194333.0	1287922.0	1369387.0	1495310.0	1689986.0	1898625.0	2044606.0	2206191.0	2420570.0
SAVING, GROSS	144740.0	133243.0	132439.0	75138.0	179523.0	213098.0	155937.0	237968.0	103868.0	127857.0	101989.0	132464.0
	III.1 Capital account - Changes in liabilities and net worth											
SAVING, GROSS	144740.0	133243.0	132439.0	75138.0	179523.0	213098.0	155937.0	237968.0	103868.0	127857.0	101989.0	132464.0
Capital transfers, receivable less payable	...	...	...	...	...	...	...	...	...	...	...	...
Capital transfers, receivable	...	...	...	...	...	...	...	...	...	...	...	...

	2001	2002	2003	2004	2005	2006	2007	2008	2009	2010	2011	2012
Series	**100**											
Less: Capital transfers, payable	...	...	...	...	...	...	...	...	...	...	...	...
Equals: CHANGES IN NET WORTH DUE TO SAVINGS AND CAPITAL TRANSFERS	...	...	...	...	...	...	...	...	...	...	...	...
III.1 Capital account - Changes in assets												
Gross capital formation	76557.0	94247.0	74901.0	40066.0	116582.0	126495.0	123717.0	125902.0	103834.0	121487.0	90424.0	120723.0
Gross fixed capital formation	67765.0	72920.0	65525.0	76058.0	101916.0	111637.0	122737.0	106705.0	108131.0	111034.0	112999.0	115343.0
Changes in inventories	8792.0	21327.0	9376.0	-35992.0	14666.0	14858.0	980.0	19197.0	-4296.0	10453.0	-22575.0	5380.0
Acquisitions less disposals of valuables	...	...	...	...	...	...	...	...	...	...	...	...
Acquisitions less disposals of non-produced non-financial assets	0.0	0.0	0.0	0.0	0.0	0.0	0.0	0.0	0.0	...	...	...
NET LENDING (+) / NET BORROWING (-)	68183.0	38996.0	57538.0	35071.0	62941.0	86603.0	32221.0	112066.0	34.0	6370.0	11565.0	11741.0

Table 5.2 Cross classification of Gross value added by industries and institutional sectors (ISIC Rev. 4) Non-financial corporations

Series 100: 1993 SNA, CFA franc, Western calendar year — **Data in millions**

	2001	2002	2003	2004	2005	2006	2007	2008	2009	2010	2011	2012
Series	**100**											
Industries												
Agriculture, forestry and fishing	0.0	0.0	82.0	75.0	91.0	460.0	551.0	584.0	609.0	614.0	637.0	691.0
Manufacturing, mining and quarrying and other industrial activities	48371.0	45855.0	52132.0	52793.0	58807.0	67964.0	115992.0	171942.0	196844.0	241146.0	270367.0	474839.0
Of which: manufacturing	8873.0	9298.0	11109.0	11596.0	12061.0	12162.0	13072.0	14030.0	16962.0	17310.0	16277.0	76065.0
Construction	12982.0	14280.0	15092.0	15727.0	17413.0	20989.0	24475.0	28171.0	30847.0	35927.0	37066.0	40839.0
Wholesale and retail trade, transportation and storage, accommodation and food service activities	47528.0	48124.0	45625.0	54999.0	64513.0	72725.0	80877.0	87116.0	107965.0	119907.0	129393.0	138229.0
Information and communication	11624.0	11972.0	15841.0	18432.0	24272.0	28557.0	32348.0	37495.0	40274.0	54019.0	63050.0	67141.0
Financial and insurance activities	...	...	...	...	...	...	...	...	...	...	...	...
Real estate activities	2991.0	3260.0	2660.0	3102.0	3976.0	4148.0	4807.0	5431.0	5531.0	5935.0	6570.0	7596.0
Professional, scientific, technical, administrative and support service activities	8973.0	9779.0	7980.0	9307.0	11929.0	12443.0	14423.0	16294.0	20243.0	19492.0	22069.0	23046.0
Public administration and defence, education, human health and social work activities	...	...	...	...	...	...	...	...	...	...	...	...
Other service activities	3670.0	3999.0	3263.0	3805.0	4877.0	5087.0	5896.0	7471.0	7580.0	9633.0	10002.0	10340.0
VALUE ADDED GROSS, at basic prices	136139.0[a]	137269.0[a]	142675.0[a]	158240.0[a]	185878.0[a]	212373.0[a]	279369.0[a]	354504.0[a]	409893.0	486673.0	539154.0	762721.0

[a] Discrepancy with equivalent item in table 4.3.

Table 5.2 Cross classification of Gross value added by industries and institutional sectors (ISIC Rev. 4) Financial corporations

Series 100: 1993 SNA, CFA franc, Western calendar year

Data in millions

	2001	2002	2003	2004	2005	2006	2007	2008	2009	2010	2011	2012
Series	**100**											
Industries												
Agriculture, forestry and fishing	...	...	...	...	...	...	...	...	...	...	...	...
Manufacturing, mining and quarrying and other industrial activities	...	...	...	...	...	...	...	...	...	...	...	...
Of which: manufacturing	...	...	...	...	...	...	...	...	...	...	...	...
Construction	...	...	...	...	...	...	...	...	...	...	...	...
Wholesale and retail trade, transportation and storage, accommodation and food service activities	...	...	...	...	...	...	...	...	...	...	...	...
Information and communication	...	...	...	...	...	...	...	...	...	...	...	...
Financial and insurance activities	10858.0	9694.0	13465.0	17864.0	20883.0	21611.0	26131.0	27464.0	31082.0	35349.0	42637.0	45473.0
Real estate activities	...	...	...	...	...	...	...	...	...	...	...	...
Professional, scientific, technical, administrative and support service activities	...	...	...	...	...	...	...	...	...	...	...	...
Public administration and defence, education, human health and social work activities	...	...	...	...	...	...	...	...	...	...	...	...
Other service activities	...	...	...	...	...	...	...	...	...	...	...	...
VALUE ADDED GROSS, at basic prices	10858.0	9694.0	13465.0	17864.0	20883.0	21611.0	26131.0	27464.0	31082.0	35349.0	42637.0	45473.0

Table 5.2 Cross classification of Gross value added by industries and institutional sectors (ISIC Rev. 4) General government

Series 100: 1993 SNA, CFA franc, Western calendar year

Data in millions

	2001	2002	2003	2004	2005	2006	2007	2008	2009	2010	2011	2012
Series	**100**											
Industries												
Agriculture, forestry and fishing	...	...	...	...	...	...	...	...	...	...	...	...
Manufacturing, mining and quarrying and other industrial activities	...	...	...	...	...	...	...	...	...	...	...	...
Of which: manufacturing	...	...	...	...	...	...	...	...	...	...	...	...
Construction	...	...	...	...	...	...	...	...	...	...	...	...
Wholesale and retail trade, transportation and storage, accommodation and food service activities	...	...	...	...	...	...	...	...	...	...	...	...
Information and communication	...	...	...	...	...	...	...	...	...	...	...	...
Financial and insurance activities	...	...	...	...	...	...	...	...	...	...	...	...
Real estate activities	...	...	...	...	...	...	...	...	...	...	...	...
Professional, scientific, technical, administrative and support service activities	...	...	...	...	...	...	...	...	...	...	...	...

	2001	2002	2003	2004	2005	2006	2007	2008	2009	2010	2011	2012
Series	**100**											
Public administration and defence, education, human health and social work activities	141099.0	148589.0	166591.0	161944.0	181499.0	197988.0	218891.0	232984.0	267626.0	261877.0	298172.0	335009.0
Other service activities	...	...	...	...	...	...	...	...	...	...	...	...
VALUE ADDED GROSS, at basic prices	141099.0	148589.0	166591.0[a]	161944.0[a]	181499.0	197988.0	218891.0	232984.0	267626.0	261877.0	298172.0	335009.0

[a] Discrepancy with equivalent item in Table 4.5 (General Government).

Table 5.2 Cross classification of Gross value added by industries and institutional sectors (ISIC Rev. 4) Households

Series 100: 1993 SNA, CFA franc, Western calendar year **Data in millions**

	2001	2002	2003	2004	2005	2006	2007	2008	2009	2010	2011	2012
Series	**100**											
	Industries											
Agriculture, forestry and fishing	593627.0	658069.0	676751.0	615916.0	754320.0	817202.0	842042.0	1044840.0	986366.0	1181464.0	1188966.0	
Manufacturing, mining and quarrying and other industrial activities	80030.0	85721.0	87463.0	90711.0	94778.0	99357.0	103519.0	114304.0	122639.0	129528.0	138776.0	
Of which: manufacturing	73073.0	78169.0	79644.0	82511.0	86289.0	90473.0	93506.0	103529.0	111294.0	117609.0	126096.0	
Construction	18477.0	19698.0	21543.0	22970.0	24209.0	26482.0	27109.0	29925.0	33249.0	35716.0	39263.0	
Wholesale and retail trade, transportation and storage, accommodation and food service activities	231976.0	246025.0	250624.0	255469.0	286688.0	296709.0	312492.0	346056.0	392490.0	401323.0	434028.0	
Information and communication	...	...	...	...	...	...	...	...	...	...	...	
Financial and insurance activities	...	...	...	...	...	...	...	...	...	...	...	
Real estate activities	43889.0	46777.0	47584.0	51315.0	53149.0	54602.0	57561.0	60913.0	64569.0	67639.0	70638.0	
Professional, scientific, technical, administrative and support service activities	2082.0	2219.0	2257.0	2434.0	2521.0	2590.0	2731.0	2890.0	3063.0	3209.0	3351.0	
Public administration and defence, education, human health and social work activities	...	...	...	...	...	...	...	...	...	...	...	
Other service activities	43832.0	45862.0	48133.0	50541.0	53194.0	54807.0	56616.0	58504.0	61248.0	63816.0	67581.0	
VALUE ADDED GROSS, at basic prices	1013913.0[a]	1104371.0[a]	1134355.0[a]	1089356.0[a]	1268859.0[a]	1351749.0[a]	1402070.0[a]	1657432.0[a]	1663624.0	1882695.0	1942603.0	

[a] Discrepancy with equivalent item in Table 4.6 (Households).

Table 5.2 Cross classification of Gross value added by industries and institutional sectors (ISIC Rev. 4) Total economy

Series 100: 1993 SNA, CFA franc, Western calendar year **Data in millions**

	2001	2002	2003	2004	2005	2006	2007	2008	2009	2010	2011	2012
Series	**100**											
	Industries											
Agriculture, forestry and fishing	593627.0	658069.0	676833.0	615991.0	754411.0	817662.0	842593.0	1045424.0	999357.0	1158359.0	1156805.0	1320036.0
Manufacturing, mining and quarrying and other industrial activities	128401.0	131576.0	139595.0	143504.0	153585.0	167321.0	219511.0	286246.0	319483.0	370673.0	410469.0	620894.0
Of which: manufacturing	81946.0	87467.0	90753.0	94107.0	98350.0	102635.0	106578.0	117559.0	128256.0	134918.0	143942.0	209146.0

	2001	2002	2003	2004	2005	2006	2007	2008	2009	2010	2011	2012
Series	**100**											
Construction	31459.0	33978.0	36635.0	38697.0	41622.0	47471.0	51584.0	58096.0	64096.0	71469.0	76173.0	83448.0
Wholesale and retail trade, transportation and storage, accommodation and food service activities	279504.0	294149.0	296249.0	310468.0	351201.0	368614.0	393369.0	433173.0	500455.0	521230.0	565674.0	603141.0
Information and communication	11624.0	11972.0	15841.0	18432.0	24272.0	29378.0	32348.0	37495.0	40274.0	54019.0	63050.0	67141.0
Financial and insurance activities	10858.0	9694.0	13465.0	17864.0	20883.0	21611.0	26131.0	27464.0	31082.0	35349.0	42637.0	45473.0
Real estate activities	51880.0	55037.0	55244.0	59417.0	62125.0	63750.0	67368.0	70053.0	72435.0	74262.0	75533.0	77498.0
Professional, scientific, technical, administrative and support service activities	11055.0	11998.0	10237.0	11741.0	14450.0	15033.0	17154.0	19184.0	23306.0	22701.0	25420.0	26545.0
Public administration and defence, education, human health and social work activities	141099.0[a]	148589.0[a]	166591.0[a]	161944.0[a]	181499.0[a]	197988.0[a]	218891.0[a]	232984.0[a]	267626.0[a]	261877.0	298172.0	335009.0
Other service activities	42502.0	44861.0	46396.0	49346.0	53071.0	54894.0	57512.0	62265.0	66493.0	72761.0	79351.0	86699.0
VALUE ADDED GROSS, at basic prices	1302008.0	1399921.0	1457085.0	1427403.0	1657118.0	1783722.0	1926461.0	2272385.0	2384607.0	2642874.0	2793284.0	3265884.0

[a] Discrepancy with the sum of equivalent items in table 2.4.

Nigeria

Source
The following tables have been prepared from successive replies to the United Nations national accounts questionnaire. Data under series 100 were received from the National Bureau of Statistics - Nigeria.

General
The official estimates together with methodological notes on sources and methods are published in "Gross Domestic Product of Nigeria". Another publication "National Accounts of Nigeria" with estimates dating back to 1958/59, was published in 1978. Input-output tables have been published for the year 1959/60 in "An Input-Output Analysis of the Nigerian Economy". When the scope and coverage of the estimates differ for conceptual or statistical reasons from the definitions and classifications recommended in SNA, a footnote is indicated to the relevant tables. The estimates shown in the following tables are deemed to have been prepared in accordance with the concepts and definitions of the System of National Accounts 1993 (1993 SNA).

Methodology:

Overview of GDP Compilation
Gross domestic product is estimated mainly through the production approach.

Expenditure Approach
The expenditure approach is used to estimate government final consumption expenditure, exports and imports of goods and services and buildings and other construction of gross fixed capital formation. This approach, in combination with the commodity-flow approach is used to estimate investment in machinery and equipment. Private final consumption expenditure, which includes increase in stocks, is estimated as a residual. Government consumption expenditure is estimated from the annual economic analysis of the accounts of the public authorities. Useful information on private consumption expenditure will become available when the urban consumer survey and the rural consumption inquiry for 1974/75 are completed. The estimates of gross fixed capital formation for machinery, transport and other equipment are based on foreign trade statistics supplemented by information on import duties. A mark-up for trade, transport and installation charges of 33.3 per cent and 10 per cent is added to the import values of machinery and transport equipment respectively. The values of small concrete buildings are based on the value of cement used and of mud-walled houses on the estimated population in need of such houses. For the oil sector, the estimates of gross capital formation are compiled from the returns obtained from the oil companies. Sources for other sectors include the accounts of the Nigerian Coal Corporation, the reports of the Nigerian Steel Development Authority, the Nigerian Railway Corporation and the Nigerian Shipping Line Ltd., and the accounts of the government. The main sources of information for exports and imports of goods and services are the balance of payments accounts.

Income Approach
Compensation of employees, operating surplus, and consumption of fixed capital are obtained as a residual by deducting net indirect taxes from the gross domestic product. For indirect taxes and subsidies, the annual government accounts are used.

Production Approach
The table of gross domestic product by kind of economic activity is prepared in factor values. The production approach is used to estimate the value added of most industries. The income approach is used for producers of government services. Production estimates for 13 harvested agricultural crops are obtained from the national agriculture sample census in 1974/75 and the annual rural economic surveys. Estimates of output for green vegetables, tomatoes, oranges, bananas, sugar cane, coconut, pawpaw and pineapple are based on the average expenditure per household contained in the reports on inquiries into the income and expenditure patterns of lower

and middle income households supplemented by export data. The values are reduced by 50 per cent for trade and transport charges. Foreign trade statistics provide the information for all other crops, except cocoa and tobacco which is estimated from information supplied by the Nigerian Produce Marketing Company, and from manufacturing companies. For livestock and its products, estimates are based on such data as foreign trade statistics, number of animals slaughtered, number of cattle that are milked, Lagos retail prices, etc. Non-monetary activities are covered in the estimates. The output of timber is estimated from the data on logs exported or used locally. Data on the production of fish are obtained from the Federal Fisheries Department.

The annual reports of the Petroleum Division in the Federal Ministry of Mines and Power furnish information on production and f.o.b. values of crude oil and the quantity of gas sold. The same Ministry also furnishes data on production of metalliferious ores. This output is valued at f.o.b. prices. Information on the values of manufacturing output and intermediate consumption are obtained from the annual surveys of large establishments. Adjustment is made of value added by 20 per cent to cover small establishments. The estimates of electricity are based on annual reports of the concerned companies. The sources of information on water supply are the actual expenditure of the government bodies and annual accounts of water boards of corporations. Data for estimating value added in construction are obtained from accounts of public authorities and corporations government enterprises and the survey of large establishments engaged in mining, manufacturing and distributive activities. For smaller construction activities, sources such as the value of cement used, questionnaire and actual of approved expenditure of public authorities are used.

Trade is assumed to be 12.5 per cent of GDP in the base year 1958/59. For other years, value added is extrapolated by indexes. The benchmark value added of road transport is based on the number of commercial vehicles. Other years' estimates are made by projecting the 1958/59 figure by the estimated number of tractors and commercial vehicles and using the CPI of transport services for five urban centres. The value added of railways, harbours, water and air transports are estimated from annual reports of concerned enterprises. The sources of information for estimating the value added of government services are the accountant-general's reports and budget of the public authorities. For education, estimates are based on information obtained from the Federal Ministry of Education and the National Universities Commission for private institutions and on the number of teachers and an assumed average salary per teacher for other institutions. For private health institutions, the expenditure on personal emoluments is regarded as value added and assumed to grow at the same rate as for government institutions. The value added of other services, which includes the financial sector, is assumed to grow at an average annual rate of 13.8 per cent.

For the constant price estimates, price deflation is used for the manufacturing, construction, part of transport and services sectors. For agriculture, the production of crops is either revalued at 1962/63 prices or deflated by retail prices. Value added of mining, electricity, trade and transport relating to passenger-miles and ton-miles is extrapolated by appropriate indicators.

Table 1.1 Gross domestic product by expenditures at current prices

Series 100: 1993 SNA, Naira, Western calendar year — **Data in billions**

	2001	2002	2003	2004	2005	2006	2007	2008	2009	2010	2011	2012
Series	**100**											
	Expenditures of the gross domestic product											
Final consumption expenditure	4090.8	6018.5	7495.0	9423.6	12078.2	12573.1	18375.5	18961.9	22250.9	26869.9	27820.7	29199.1
Household final consumption expenditure	3687.7	5540.2	7044.5	8637.7	11075.1	11289.7	16243.7	16090.5	18981.0	22713.8	22840.8	24248.3
NPISHs final consumption expenditure	...	...	...	...	...	...	...	...	...	...	...	...
General government final consumption expenditure	403.1	478.3	450.5	785.8	1003.1	1283.4	2131.8	2871.4	3269.9	4156.1	4979.9	4950.8
Individual consumption expenditure	...	...	...	...	...	...	...	...	...	...	...	...

	2001	2002	2003	2004	2005	2006	2007	2008	2009	2010	2011	2012
Series	**100**											
Collective consumption expenditure [a]	403.1	478.3	450.5	785.8	1003.1	1283.4	2131.8	2871.4	3269.9	4156.1	4979.9	4950.8
Gross capital formation	372.8	500.4	866.7	864.0	805.6	1548.0	1938.4	2054.6	3052.2	4016.1	3910.6	2803.0
Gross fixed capital formation	372.1	499.7	865.9	863.1	804.4	1546.5	1937.0	2053.0	3050.6	4014.1	3908.3	2800.5
Changes in inventories	0.7	0.7	0.8	0.9	1.2	1.5	1.4	1.6	1.6	2.0	2.3	2.5
Acquisitions less disposals of valuables	...	...	...	...	...	...	...	...	...	...	...	...
Exports of goods and services	2231.3	2563.7	3478.5	3520.8	4664.8	8599.3	7063.1	9837.3	7764.8	13472.3	19961.3	22824.4
Exports of goods	...	...	...	...	...	...	6881.5	9568.9	7434.5	13009.9	19440.4	22446.3
Exports of services	...	...	...	...	...	...	181.6	268.3	330.2	462.4	520.9	378.1
Less: Imports of goods and services	1785.3	1954.4	3097.6	2134.8	2813.2	4010.6	6436.1	6188.5	7831.8	9866.0	13675.6	9395.4
Imports of goods	...	...	...	...	...	...	4127.7	3299.1	5047.9	6648.5	9892.6	5624.9
Imports of services	...	...	...	...	...	...	2308.4	2889.4	2783.9	3217.5	3783.0	3770.5
Equals: GROSS DOMESTIC PRODUCT	4909.5	7128.2	8742.6	11673.6	14735.3	18709.8	20940.9	24665.2	25236.1	34494.6	38017.0	41177.8[b]

[a] Includes individual consumption expenditure of government

[b] Discrepancy between components and total.

Table 1.2 Gross domestic product by expenditures at constant prices

Series 100: 1993 SNA, Naira, Western calendar year **Data in billions**

	2001	2002	2003	2004	2005	2006	2007	2008	2009	2010	2011	2012
Series	**100**											
Base year	**1990**											
Expenditures of the gross domestic product												
Final consumption expenditure	360.0	367.8	427.9	463.2	460.5	407.7	672.6	622.4	748.8	725.3	790.9	762.7
Household final consumption expenditure	345.3	352.3	416.1	384.7	373.8	290.0	488.0	393.4	518.2	467.2	514.0	516.0
NPISHs final consumption expenditure	...	...	...	...	...	...	...	...	...	...	...	...
General government final consumption expenditure	14.7	15.5	11.8	78.5	86.7	117.7	184.6	229.0	230.6	258.1	277.0	246.7
Gross capital formation	32.4[a]	39.0[a]	58.5[a]	44.5[a]	39.9[a]	75.1[a]	90.0	89.3	120.4	142.5	127.1	86.3
Gross fixed capital formation	6.3	7.9	13.0	72.4	92.3	117.9	89.9	89.2	120.3	142.4	126.9	86.2
Changes in inventories	0.1	0.1	0.1	0.1	0.1	0.1	0.1	0.1	0.1	0.1	0.1	0.1
Acquisitions less disposals of valuables	...	...	...	...	...	...	...	...	...	...	...	...
Exports of goods and services	91.1	101.6	133.5	132.2	148.6	253.2	196.1	252.5	175.0	268.7	355.6	273.8
Less: Imports of goods and services	103.9	110.5	169.6	113.2	151.3	205.7	311.1	276.1	308.3	342.9	426.2	219.7
Equals: GROSS DOMESTIC PRODUCT	353.5[a]	366.9[a]	404.9[a]	541.5[a]	560.2[a]	602.3[a]	647.5	688.1	735.9	793.6	847.4	903.1

[a] Discrepancy between components and total.

Table 1.3 Relations among product, income, savings, and net lending aggregates

Series 100: 1993 SNA, Naira, Western calendar year **Data in billions**

	2001	2002	2003	2004	2005	2006	2007	2008	2009	2010	2011	2012
Series	**100**											
GROSS DOMESTIC PRODUCT	4909.5	7128.2	8742.6	11673.6	14735.3	18709.8	20940.9	24665.2	25236.1	34494.6	38017.0	41167.2
Plus: Compensation of employees - from and to the rest of the world, net	-3.1	-3.2	-3.3	-3.5	-3.5	-3.4	23.9	10.9	17.8	22.3	21.1	28.2
Plus: Compensation of employees - from the rest of the world	0.6	0.6	0.6	0.7	0.7	0.7	27.4	15.1	20.6	25.1	27.8	30.5
Less: Compensation of employees - to the rest of the world	3.7	3.8	3.9	4.2	4.2	4.1	3.5	4.2	2.8	2.8	6.7	2.3
Plus: Property income - from and to the rest of the world, net	-343.9	-382.7	-424.0	-436.8	-575.1	-306.4	-1502.1	-1795.9	-2162.5	-2954.5	-3526.8	-3443.7
Plus: Property income - from the rest of the world	40.3	20.0	10.5	20.9	92.5	215.1	295.2	263.7	118.7	125.3	110.3	119.0
Less: Property income - to the rest of the world	384.2	402.7	434.5	457.7	667.6	521.4	1797.3	2059.6	2281.2	3079.8	3637.1	3562.7
Sum of Compensation of employees and property income - from and to the rest of the world, net	-347.0	-385.9	-427.3	-440.3	-578.5	-309.8	-1478.2	-1784.9	-2144.7	-2932.2	-3505.7	-3415.5
Plus: Sum of Compensation of employees and property income - from the rest of the world	40.9	20.6	11.2	21.6	93.2	215.7	322.6	278.8	139.3	150.4	138.1	149.5
Less: Sum of Compensation of employees and property income - to the rest of the world	387.9	406.6	438.5	461.9	671.8	525.6	1800.8	2063.7	2283.9	3082.6	3643.8	3565.1
Plus: Taxes less subsidies on production and imports - from and to the rest of the world, net	...	...	...	...	...	...	...	...	...	...	...	...
Equals: GROSS NATIONAL INCOME	4562.5	6742.3	8315.3	11233.3	14156.8	18400.0	19462.7	22880.3	23091.4	31562.4	34511.3	37751.7
Plus: Current transfers - from and to the rest of the world, net	152.0	170.4[a]	200.8[a]	359.3	447.5	177.0[a]	2333.5	2295.4	2783.5	3123.3	3356.0	3419.4
Plus: Current transfers - from the rest of the world	152.2	167.7	185.1	365.5	455.2	1359.2	2352.4	2358.3	2852.6	3195.4	3428.6	3510.9
Less: Current transfers - to the rest of the world	0.2	2.8	15.8	6.2	7.7	23.1	18.9	62.9	69.0	72.1	72.6	91.5
Equals: GROSS NATIONAL DISPOSABLE INCOME	4714.5	6912.7	8516.2	11592.5	14604.2	18577.0	21796.2	25175.7	25874.9	34685.7	37867.3	41171.1
Less: Final consumption expenditure / Actual final consumption	4090.8	6018.5	7495.0	9423.6	12078.2	12573.1	18375.5	18961.9	22250.9	26869.9	27820.7	29199.1
Equals: SAVING, GROSS	623.8	894.2	1021.1	2169.0	2526.1	6003.8	3420.7	6213.9	3624.0	7815.8	10046.5	11972.0
Plus: Capital transfers - from and to the rest of the world, net	0.0	6.6	2.6	4.7	3.0	4.5	0.0	0.0	0.0	0.0	0.0	0.0
Plus: Capital transfers - from the rest of the world	...	...	...	...	...	...	0.0	0.0	0.0	0.0	0.0	0.0
Less: Capital transfers - to the rest of the world	...	...	...	...	...	...	...	...	...	...	...	...
Less: Gross capital formation	372.8	500.4	866.7	864.0	805.6	1548.0	1938.4	2054.6	3052.2	4016.1	3910.6	2803.0
Less: Acquisitions less disposals of non-produced non-financial assets	...	...	...	...	...	...	...	...	...	...	...	...
Equals: NET LENDING (+) / NET BORROWING (-) OF THE NATION	251.0	400.3	157.1	1309.7	1723.5	4460.4	1482.3	4159.3	571.8	3799.7	6136.0	9168.9
	Net values: Gross National Income / Gross National Disposable Income / Saving Gross less Consumption of fixed capital											
Less: Consumption of fixed capital	42.1	47.7	53.5	374.1	302.0	246.5	460.5	453.7	445.1	587.7	654.4	717.4
Equals: NET NATIONAL INCOME	4520.5	6694.6	8261.8	10859.1	13854.8	18153.4	19002.2	22426.6	22646.3	30974.7	33856.8	37034.2

	2001	2002	2003	2004	2005	2006	2007	2008	2009	2010	2011	2012
Series	**100**											
Equals: NET NATIONAL DISPOSABLE INCOME	4672.5	6865.0	8462.6	11218.4	14302.3	18330.4	21335.7	24722.0	25429.8	34098.0	37212.8	40453.6
Equals: SAVING, NET	581.7	846.5	967.6	1794.8	2224.1	5757.3	2960.1	5760.1	3178.9	7228.1	9392.1	11254.5

[a] Discrepancy between components and total.

Table 2.1 Value added by industries at current prices (ISIC Rev. 3)

Series 100: 1993 SNA, Naira, Western calendar year

Data in billions

	2001	2002	2003	2004	2005	2006	2007	2008	2009	2010	2011	2012
Series	**100**											
Industries												
Agriculture, hunting, forestry; fishing	1594.9	3357.1	3624.6	3903.8	4773.2	5940.2	6757.9	7981.4	9186.3	10310.7	11593.4	13413.8
Agriculture, hunting, forestry	1519.7	3266.6	3518.1	3773.6	4603.3	5743.8	6542.3	7726.8	8895.6	9982.5	11219.9	12985.6
Agriculture, hunting and related service activities	1492.3	3233.4	3477.7	3722.0	4541.5	5670.3	6458.5	7627.7	8784.5	9858.1	11079.7	12829.1
Forestry, logging and related service activities	27.5	33.2	40.4	51.7	61.8	73.5	83.8	99.0	111.1	124.3	140.2	156.6
Fishing	75.2	90.4	106.5	130.1	169.9	196.5	215.5	254.6	290.7	328.2	373.6	428.2
Mining and quarrying	1675.0	1805.9	2750.0	4260.8	5682.2	7010.2	7564.5	9133.9	7458.8	14551.5	15337.5	15064.0
Manufacturing	199.1	236.8	287.7	349.3	412.7	478.5	520.9	585.6	612.3	643.1	694.8	761.5
Electricity, gas and water supply	16.4	18.8	22.4	26.8	29.4	42.6	45.8	52.7	62.1	70.3	80.7	91.3
Construction	40.7	48.0	58.9	166.1	215.8	250.3	266.5	306.6	347.7	394.7	456.3	539.7
Wholesale, retail trade, repair of motor vehicles, motorcycles and personal and households goods; hotels and restaurants	650.7	782.1	933.6	1519.7	1914.3	2799.4	3117.6	3589.2	4181.3	4762.5	5516.6	6436.7
Wholesale, retail trade, repair of motor vehicles, motorcycles and personal and household goods	642.7	772.4	922.1	1484.4	1868.3	2741.8	3044.8	3503.2	4082.4	4648.7	5385.8	6284.9
Hotels and restaurants	8.0	9.7	11.4	35.2	46.1	57.6	72.8	86.1	99.0	113.8	130.8	151.8
Transport, storage and communications	152.3	189.5	239.2	388.7	426.7	609.5	719.7	731.8	765.6	794.5	863.5	1001.0
Land transport; transport via pipelines, water transport; air transport; Supporting and auxiliary transport activities; activities of travel agencies	144.6	178.8	224.9	365.7	385.5	441.8	473.4	479.1	506.7	529.0	565.8	663.8
Post and telecommunications	7.7	10.7	14.3	23.0	41.3	167.7	246.2	252.6	258.9	265.6	297.7	337.2
Financial intermediation; real estate, renting and business activities	243.4	302.2	376.0	566.2	843.6	1105.3	1266.5	1456.5	1657.2	1856.0	2183.5	2449.4
Financial intermediation	54.4	79.4	81.1	103.0	130.7	296.7	340.9	392.0	444.2	507.8	668.2	636.0
Real estate, renting and business activities	189.0	222.8	295.0	463.2	712.8	808.6	925.6	1064.4	1213.0	1348.2	1515.3	1813.3
Public administration and defence; compulsory social security	78.1	82.0	90.2	101.0	115.2	131.3	151.3	174.0	197.3	224.2	253.3	288.1
Education; health and social work; other community, social and personal services [a]	74.5	90.0	104.4	128.7	159.1	197.2	246.7	284.7	325.6	377.3	430.2	498.6
Education	17.7	18.5	20.4	22.8	26.0	29.7	33.4	39.4	47.1	56.1	65.5	76.9
Health and social work	4.6	4.9	5.3	6.0	6.8	7.8	8.7	10.0	11.1	12.5	14.2	16.1
Other community, social and personal services	52.2	66.6	78.7	99.8	126.3	159.7	204.6	235.3	267.4	308.8	350.4	405.7
Private households with employed persons	0.1	0.1	0.1	0.1	0.2	0.2	0.2	0.2	...	...	...	...

	2001	2002	2003	2004	2005	2006	2007	2008	2009	2010	2011	2012
Series	**100**											
Equals: VALUE ADDED, GROSS, in basic prices	4725.1	6912.4	8487.0	11411.1	14572.2	18564.8	20657.3	24296.3	24794.2	33984.8	37409.9	40544.1
Less: Financial intermediation services indirectly measured (FISIM)	...	...	...	...	...	...	...	...	...	...	...	...
Plus: Taxes less Subsidies on products	184.4	215.8	255.6	262.5	163.1	145.0	283.6	368.9	441.8	509.8	607.1	625.6
Plus: Taxes on products	186.6	219.1	259.2	268.1	169.7	173.2	314.5	404.5	479.3	549.3	649.6	672.2
Less: Subsidies on products	2.2	3.3	3.6	5.6	6.6	28.2	31.0	35.6	37.5	39.4	42.5	46.6
Equals: GROSS DOMESTIC PRODUCT	4909.5	7128.2	8742.6	11673.6	14735.3	18709.8	20940.9	24665.2	25236.1	34494.6	38017.0	41169.6

[a] Includes data for Private households with employed persons.

Table 2.2 Value added by industries at constant prices (ISIC Rev. 3)

Series 100: 1993 SNA, Naira, Western calendar year — **Data in billions**

	2001	2002	2003	2004	2005	2006	2007	2008	2009	2010	2011	2012
Series	**100**											
Base year	**1990**											
	Industries											
Agriculture, hunting, forestry; fishing	122.5	190.1	203.4	216.2	231.5	248.6	266.5	283.2	299.8	317.3	335.2	348.5
Agriculture, hunting, forestry	116.5	183.8	196.8	209.0	223.8	240.5	257.8	273.9	290.0	306.9	324.2	336.8
Agriculture, hunting and related service activities	113.9	181.1	194.1	206.2	220.8	237.3	254.4	270.3	286.2	302.9	319.9	332.3
Forestry, logging and related service activities	2.6	2.6	2.7	2.8	3.0	3.2	3.4	3.6	3.8	4.0	4.2	4.5
Fishing	6.0	6.4	6.6	7.2	7.6	8.1	8.7	9.2	9.8	10.4	11.0	11.7
Mining and quarrying	113.5	107.1	132.5	137.1	137.9	131.9	126.2	118.7	119.5	125.9	126.4	125.7
Manufacturing	14.9	16.4	17.4	19.4	21.3	23.3	25.5	27.8	30.0	32.3	34.7	37.3
Electricity, gas and water supply	12.2	13.8	16.2	18.9	20.1	21.1	22.2	23.0	23.7	24.5	25.3	26.2
Construction	7.2	7.5	8.2	7.6	8.5	9.7	10.9	12.3	13.8	15.5	17.3	19.5
Wholesale, retail trade, repair of motor vehicles, motorcycles and personal and household goods; hotels and restaurants	45.0	47.9	50.6	70.0	79.4	91.5	105.4	120.1	133.9	149.0	165.9	181.9
Wholesale, retail trade, repair of motor vehicles, motorcycles and personal and household goods	44.2	47.1	49.8	68.1	77.3	89.1	102.6	117.0	130.4	145.1	161.5	177.0
Hotels and restaurants	0.7	0.8	0.8	2.0	2.2	2.4	2.7	3.1	3.5	3.9	4.4	4.9
Transport, storage and communications	10.7	12.8	13.7	20.7	23.5	27.3	32.1	38.3	46.3	56.7	70.4	87.1
Land transport; transport via piplines, water transport; air transport; Supporting and auxiliary transport activities; activities of travel agencies	7.9	9.2	9.3	14.0	14.9	15.9	17.0	18.2	19.4	20.8	22.2	23.7
Post and telecommunications	2.6	3.3	4.0	6.3	8.2	10.9	15.1	20.1	26.9	36.0	48.2	63.4
Financial intermediation, real estate, renting and business activities	24.5	30.0	28.0	29.2	30.7	32.7	35.0	37.4	39.6	42.0	44.6	47.4
Financial intermediation	17.9	23.2	21.0	21.5	22.1	23.2	24.4	25.6	26.6	27.7	28.8	29.9
Real estate, renting and business activities	6.6	6.8	7.0	7.7	8.5	9.5	10.6	11.8	13.0	14.4	15.9	17.5
Public administration and defence; compulsory social security	3.0	3.6	3.6	3.9	4.1	4.3	4.5	4.7	4.9	5.1	5.3	5.5

	2001	2002	2003	2004	2005	2006	2007	2008	2009	2010	2011	2012
Series	**100**											
Base year	**1990**											
Education; health and social work; other community, social and personal services [a]	3.5	3.9	4.0	4.5	4.9	5.5	6.0	6.7	7.4	8.1	8.9	9.8
Education	0.7	0.7	0.8	0.9	1.0	1.1	1.2	1.3	1.4	1.6	1.7	1.9
Health and social work	0.2	0.2	0.2	0.2	0.2	0.2	0.3	0.3	0.3	0.4	0.4	0.4
Other community, social and personal services	2.6	3.0	3.1	3.4	3.8	4.2	4.6	5.1	5.6	6.1	6.7	7.4
Private households with employed persons	0.0	0.0	0.0	0.0	0.0	0.0	0.0	0.0	...	...	...	...
Equals: VALUE ADDED, GROSS, in basic prices	357.0	433.2	477.5	527.6	561.9	595.8	634.3	672.2	719.0	776.3	834.0	888.9
Less: Financial intermediation services indirectly measured (FISIM)	...	...	...	...	...	...	...	...	...	...	...	...
Plus: Taxes less Subsidies on products	...	...	...	...	...	...	13.3	15.9	16.9	17.2	13.5	13.9
Plus: Taxes on products	...	...	...	...	...	...	14.7	17.5	18.3	18.5	19.6	18.2
Less: Subsidies on products	...	...	...	...	...	...	1.5	1.5	1.4	1.3	6.0	4.2
Equals: GROSS DOMESTIC PRODUCT	...	...	...	...	...	...	647.5	688.1	735.9	793.6	847.5	902.8

[a] Includes data for Private households with employed persons.

Table 2.3 Output, gross value added, and fixed assets by industries at current prices (ISIC Rev. 3) Total Economy

Series 100: 1993 SNA, Naira, Western calendar year **Data in billions**

	2001	2002	2003	2004	2005	2006	2007	2008	2009	2010	2011	2012
Series	**100**											
Output, at basic prices [a]	6326.5	8854.6	10816.9	14253.6	18137.3	22890.7	24654.6	28594.8	29501.8	39242.8	43437.1	47205.6
Less: Intermediate consumption, at purchaser's prices	1417.0	1726.4	2074.3	2667.3	3401.9	4180.9	3997.3	4298.5	4707.5	5258.1	6027.3	6664.0
Equals: VALUE ADDED, GROSS, at basic prices	4909.5[b]	7128.2[b]	8742.6[b]	11673.6[b]	14735.3[b]	18709.8[b]	20657.3[c]	24296.3[c]	24794.2[c]	33984.8[c]	37409.9[c]	40541.6[c]
Compensation of employees	256.5	271.7	296.0	1203.6	770.5	1639.6	5104.1[c]	5654.3[c]	5118.4[c]	8706.3[c]	9361.0[c]	9800.1[c]
Taxes on production and imports, less Subsidies [d]	184.4	215.8	255.6	262.5	163.1	145.0	283.6	368.9	441.8	509.8	607.1	625.6
Taxes on production and imports	186.6	219.1	259.2	268.1	169.7	173.2	314.5	404.5	479.3	549.3	649.6	672.2
Taxes on products	186.6	219.1	259.2	268.1	169.7	173.2	314.5	404.5	479.3	549.3	649.6	672.2
Other taxes on production	...	...	...	...	...	...	...	...	...	...	...	...
Less: Subsidies	2.2	3.3	3.6	5.6	6.6	28.2	31.0	35.6	37.5	39.4	42.5	46.6
Subsidies on products	2.2	3.3	3.6	5.6	6.6	28.2	31.0	35.6	37.5	39.4	42.5	46.6
Other subsidies on production	...	...	...	...	...	...	...	...	...	...	...	...
OPERATING SURPLUS, GROSS [e]	4468.6	6640.7	8191.0	10207.4	13801.8	16925.2	15092.7	18188.3	19230.7	24690.8	27394.4	30024.3
MIXED INCOME, GROSS	...	...	...	...	...	...	...	...	...	...	...	...
Less: Consumption of fixed capital	42.1	47.7	53.5	374.1	302.0	246.5	460.5	453.7	445.1	587.7	654.4	717.2
OPERATING SURPLUS, NET [f]	4426.5	6593.0	8137.5	9833.3	13499.8	16678.7	14632.1	17734.6	18785.7	24103.1	26740.0	29307.1
MIXED INCOME, NET	...	...	...	...	...	...	...	...	...	...	...	...
Gross capital formation	372.8	500.4	866.7	864.0	805.6	1548.0	1938.4	2054.6	3052.2	4016.1	3910.6	2803.0
Gross fixed capital formation	372.1	499.7	865.9	863.1	804.4	1546.5	1937.0	2053.0	3050.6	4014.1	3908.3	2800.5

	2001	2002	2003	2004	2005	2006	2007	2008	2009	2010	2011	2012
Series	**100**											
Changes in inventories	0.7	0.7	0.8	0.9	1.2	1.5	1.4	1.6	1.6	2.0	2.3	2.5
Acquisitions less disposals of valuables	...	...	...	...	...	...	...	...	...	...	...	...

[a] At producers' prices.
[b] Value Added refers to GDP.
[c] Discrepancy between components and total.
[d] Refers to Taxes less Subsidies on products.
[e] Includes Mixed Income, Gross.
[f] Includes Mixed Income, Net.

Table 2.3 Output, gross value added, and fixed assets by industries at current prices (ISIC Rev. 3) Agriculture, hunting, forestry; fishing (A+B)

Series 100: 1993 SNA, Naira, Western calendar year **Data in billions**

	2001	2002	2003	2004	2005	2006	2007	2008	2009	2010	2011	2012
Series	**100**											
Output, at basic prices	1922.5[a]	3808.2[a]	4115.2[a]	4437.5[a]	5525.8[a]	6757.6[a]	7655.4	8826.2	10158.1	11403.3	12825.1	14206.6
Less: Intermediate consumption, at purchaser's prices	324.5	448.1	486.7	528.6	746.3	809.6	897.5	844.8	971.8	1092.6	1231.7	1366.4
Equals: VALUE ADDED, GROSS, at basic prices	1598.0[b]	3360.1[b]	3628.6[b]	3908.9[b]	4779.4[b]	5948.0[b]	6757.9[c]	7981.4[c]	9186.3[c]	10310.7[c]	11593.4[c]	12840.2[c]
Compensation of employees	51.0	52.9	56.6	61.8	66.0	70.8	77.9	71.9	82.7	92.9	104.6	116.4
Taxes on production and imports, less Subsidies	3.1	3.0	4.0	5.2	6.2	7.5	-4.7	-4.0	-4.6	-5.5	-5.8	-6.1
Taxes on production and imports	4.6	5.6	6.7	8.1	9.9	12.2	0.3	0.4	0.5	0.3	0.7	1.0
Taxes on products	4.6	5.6	6.7	8.1	9.9	12.2	0.3	0.4	0.5	0.3	0.7	1.0
Other taxes on production	...	...	...	...	...	...	...	...	...	...	...	...
Less: Subsidies	1.5	2.5	2.7	2.9	3.7	4.7	5.1	4.4	5.1	5.7	6.4	7.1
Subsidies on products	1.5	2.5	2.7	2.9	3.7	4.7	5.1	4.4	5.1	5.7	6.4	7.1
Other subsidies on production	...	...	...	...	...	...	...	...	...	...	...	...
OPERATING SURPLUS, GROSS [d]	1543.9	3304.1	3568.0	3842.0	4707.2	5869.7	6666.2	7900.7	9093.5	10206.4	11476.0	12709.6
MIXED INCOME, GROSS	...	...	...	...	...	...	...	...	...	...	...	...
Less: Consumption of fixed capital	7.0	8.2	8.9	9.5	10.7	12.2	13.7	8.8	10.1	11.4	12.8	14.2
OPERATING SURPLUS, NET [e]	1536.9	3295.9	3559.1	3832.5	4696.4	5857.5	6652.5	7891.9	9083.4	10195.1	11463.3	12695.5
MIXED INCOME, NET	...	...	...	...	...	...	...	...	...	...	...	...
Gross capital formation	...	...	...	...	...	...	...	...	...	...	...	...

[a] At producers' prices.
[b] Value Added refers to GDP.
[c] Discrepancy between components and total.
[d] Includes Mixed Income, Gross.
[e] Includes Mixed Income, Net.

Table 2.3 Output, gross value added, and fixed assets by industries at current prices (ISIC Rev. 3) Agriculture, hunting and related service activities (01)

Series 100: 1993 SNA, Naira, Western calendar year — **Data in billions**

	2001	2002	2003	2004	2005	2006	2007	2008	2009	2010	2011	2012
Series	**100**											
Output, at basic prices	1778.9[a]	3635.2[a]	3910.1[a]	4184.4[a]	5204.0[a]	6391.7[a]	7255.2	8359.0	9626.9	10804.9	12145.7	13439.0
Less: Intermediate consumption, at purchaser's prices	284.9	400.5	430.6	459.9	659.6	718.2	796.6	731.3	842.3	946.8	1066.0	1178.6
Equals: VALUE ADDED, GROSS, at basic prices	1494.0[b]	3234.7[b]	3479.5[b]	3724.5[b]	4544.4[b]	5673.5[b]	6458.5[c]	7627.7[c]	8784.5[c]	9858.1[c]	11079.7[c]	12260.3[c]
Compensation of employees	41.1	42.6	45.7	48.5	52.2	56.2	62.7	56.0	64.5	72.3	81.2	89.8
Taxes on production and imports, less Subsidies	1.7	1.3	1.8	2.5	2.8	3.2	-4.8	-4.1	-4.7	-5.5	-5.8	-6.3
Taxes on production and imports	3.2	3.8	4.5	5.4	6.5	7.9	0.3	0.4	0.4	0.3	0.7	0.9
Taxes on products	3.2	3.8	4.5	5.4	6.5	7.9	0.3	0.4	0.4	0.3	0.7	0.9
Other taxes on production	...	...	...	...	...	...	...	...	...	...	...	...
Less: Subsidies	1.5	2.5	2.7	2.9	3.7	4.7	5.1	4.4	5.1	5.7	6.4	7.1
Subsidies on products	1.5	2.5	2.7	2.9	3.7	4.7	5.1	4.4	5.1	5.7	6.4	7.1
Other subsidies on production	...	...	...	...	...	...	...	...	...	...	...	...
OPERATING SURPLUS, GROSS [d]	1451.1	3190.8	3432.0	3673.4	4489.3	5614.1	6383.1	7564.1	8711.2	9775.9	10987.3	12158.2
MIXED INCOME, GROSS	...	...	...	...	...	...	...	...	...	...	...	...
Less: Consumption of fixed capital	6.7	8.0	8.6	9.1	10.1	11.3	12.8	7.7	8.8	9.9	11.1	12.3
OPERATING SURPLUS, NET [e]	1444.4	3182.9	3423.4	3664.3	4479.2	5602.8	6370.3	7556.4	8702.4	9766.0	10976.2	12145.9
MIXED INCOME, NET	...	...	...	...	...	...	...	...	...	...	...	...
Gross capital formation	...	...	...	...	...	...	...	...	...	...	...	...

[a] At producers' prices.
[b] Value Added refers to GDP.
[c] Discrepancy between components and total.
[d] Includes Mixed Income, Gross.
[e] Includes Mixed Income, Net.

Table 2.3 Output, gross value added, and fixed assets by industries at current prices (ISIC Rev. 3) Forestry, logging and related service activities (02)

Series 100: 1993 SNA, Naira, Western calendar year — **Data in billions**

	2001	2002	2003	2004	2005	2006	2007	2008	2009	2010	2011	2012
Series	**100**											
Output, at basic prices	29.9[a]	36.2[a]	44.1[a]	56.3[a]	68.5[a]	83.5[a]	94.3	108.8	122.0	136.6	154.0	171.2
Less: Intermediate consumption, at purchaser's prices	1.2	1.4	1.7	2.2	3.7	6.2	10.5	9.8	11.0	12.3	13.8	15.4
Equals: VALUE ADDED, GROSS, at basic prices	28.8[b]	34.8[b]	42.4[b]	54.1[b]	64.9[b]	77.3[b]	83.8[c]	99.0[c]	111.1[c]	124.3[c]	140.2[c]	155.9[c]
Compensation of employees	0.1	0.1	0.1	0.1	0.3	0.6	0.6	0.6	0.7	0.8	0.9	1.0
Taxes on production and imports, less Subsidies	1.3	1.6	2.0	2.5	3.1	3.8	0.0	0.0	0.0	0.0	0.0	0.0
Taxes on production and imports	1.3	1.6	2.0	2.5	3.1	3.8	0.0	0.0	0.0	0.0	0.0	0.0
Taxes on products	1.3	1.6	2.0	2.5	3.1	3.8	0.0	0.0	0.0	0.0	0.0	0.0
Other taxes on production	...	...	...	...	...	...	...	...	...	...	...	...

	2001	2002	2003	2004	2005	2006	2007	2008	2009	2010	2011	2012
Series	**100**											
Less: Subsidies	...	...	...	...	...	...	0.0	0.0	0.0	0.0	0.0	0.0
Subsidies on products	0.0	0.0	0.0	0.0	0.0	0.0	0.0	0.0	0.0	0.0	0.0	0.0
Other subsidies on production	...	...	...	...	...	...	...	...	...	...	...	...
OPERATING SURPLUS, GROSS [d]	27.3	33.1	40.3	51.5	61.5	72.8	83.1	98.4	110.4	123.5	139.3	154.9
MIXED INCOME, GROSS	...	...	...	...	...	...	...	...	...	...	...	...
Less: Consumption of fixed capital	0.0	0.0	0.0	0.0	0.0	0.0	0.0	0.0	0.0	0.0	0.0	0.0
OPERATING SURPLUS, NET [e]	27.3	33.0	40.3	51.5	61.5	72.8	83.1	98.4	110.3	123.5	139.3	154.8
MIXED INCOME, NET	...	...	...	...	...	...	...	...	...	...	...	...
Gross capital formation	...	...	...	...	...	...	...	...	...	...	...	...

[a] At producers' prices.
[b] Value Added refers to GDP.
[c] Discrepancy between components and total.
[d] Includes Mixed Income, Gross.
[e] Includes Mixed Income, Net.

Table 2.3 Output, gross value added, and fixed assets by industries at current prices (ISIC Rev. 3) Fishing (B)

Series 100: 1993 SNA, Naira, Western calendar year — **Data in billions**

	2001	2002	2003	2004	2005	2006	2007	2008	2009	2010	2011	2012
Series	**100**											
Output, at basic prices	113.7[a]	136.7[a]	161.0[a]	196.8[a]	253.3[a]	282.4[a]	305.9	358.4	409.2	461.8	525.4	596.4
Less: Intermediate consumption, at purchaser's prices	38.4	46.2	54.4	66.4	83.1	85.2	90.3	103.8	118.5	133.6	151.9	172.4
Equals: VALUE ADDED, GROSS, at basic prices	75.3[b]	90.6[b]	106.6[b]	130.3[b]	170.2[b]	197.2[b]	215.5[c]	254.6[c]	290.7[c]	328.2[c]	373.6[c]	424.0[c]
Compensation of employees	9.7	10.2	10.7	13.1	13.5	13.9	14.6	15.4	17.5	19.8	22.5	25.6
Taxes on production and imports, less Subsidies	0.1	0.1	0.2	0.2	0.3	0.5	0.0	0.0	0.0	0.0	0.0	0.1
Taxes on production and imports	0.1	0.1	0.2	0.2	0.3	0.5	0.0	0.0	0.0	0.0	0.0	0.1
Taxes on products	0.1	0.1	0.2	0.2	0.3	0.5	0.0	0.0	0.0	0.0	0.0	0.1
Other taxes on production	...	...	...	...	...	...	...	...	...	...	...	...
Less: Subsidies	...	...	...	...	...	...	0.0	0.0	0.0	0.0	0.0	0.0
Subsidies on products	0.0	0.0	0.0	0.0	0.0	0.0	0.0	0.0	0.0	0.0	0.0	0.0
Other subsidies on production	...	...	...	...	...	...	...	...	...	...	...	...
OPERATING SURPLUS, GROSS [d]	65.5	80.2	95.7	117.0	156.4	182.7	200.0	238.2	271.9	307.0	349.4	396.6
MIXED INCOME, GROSS	...	...	...	...	...	...	...	...	...	...	...	...
Less: Consumption of fixed capital	0.2	0.3	0.3	0.3	0.5	0.9	0.9	1.1	1.3	1.4	1.6	1.8
OPERATING SURPLUS, NET [e]	65.2	80.0	95.5	116.7	155.8	181.9	199.1	237.1	270.7	305.6	347.8	394.8
MIXED INCOME, NET	...	...	...	...	...	...	...	...	...	...	...	...
Gross capital formation	...	...	...	...	...	...	...	...	...	...	...	...

[a] At producers' prices.
[b] Value Added refers to GDP.
[c] Discrepancy between components and total.
[d] Includes Mixed Income, Gross.
[e] Includes Mixed Income, Net.

Table 2.3 Output, gross value added, and fixed assets by industries at current prices (ISIC Rev. 3) Mining and quarrying (C)

Series 100: 1993 SNA, Naira, Western calendar year | **Data in billions**

	2001	2002	2003	2004	2005	2006	2007	2008	2009	2010	2011	2012
Series	**100**											
Output, at basic prices	1830.5[a]	1974.1[a]	3000.8[a]	4643.7[a]	6190.2[a]	7630.0[a]	8272.8	9267.4	7570.2	14761.4	15559.7	15984.3
Less: Intermediate consumption, at purchaser's prices	147.1	158.9	240.6	371.7	495.6	607.3	708.3	133.5	111.5	209.9	222.3	229.6
Equals: VALUE ADDED, GROSS, at basic prices	1683.4[b]	1815.2[b]	2760.2[b]	4272.0[b]	5694.6[b]	7022.8[b]	7564.5[c]	9133.9[c]	7458.8[c]	14551.5[c]	15337.5[c]	15754.8[c]
Compensation of employees	13.2	14.5	16.0	17.6	19.3	21.6	3656.8	4415.9	3601.5	7039.8	7418.3	7618.1
Taxes on production and imports, less Subsidies	8.4	9.3	10.2	11.3	12.4	12.5	53.9	69.3	80.3	111.8	140.6	147.0
Taxes on production and imports	8.4	9.3	10.2	11.3	12.4	12.5	53.9	69.3	80.3	111.8	140.6	147.0
Taxes on products	8.4	9.3	10.2	11.3	12.4	12.5	53.9	69.3	80.3	111.8	140.6	147.0
Other taxes on production	...	...	...	...	...	...	...	...	...	...	...	...
Less: Subsidies	...	...	...	...	...	...	0.0	0.0	0.0	0.0	0.0	0.0
Subsidies on products	0.0	0.0	0.0	0.0	0.0	0.0	0.0	0.0	0.0	0.0	0.0	0.0
Other subsidies on production	...	...	...	...	...	...	...	...	...	...	...	...
OPERATING SURPLUS, GROSS [d]	1661.8	1791.4	2734.0	4243.2	5662.8	6988.6	3794.6	4581.6	3745.8	7294.2	7689.9	7901.2
MIXED INCOME, GROSS	...	...	...	...	...	...	...	...	...	...	...	...
Less: Consumption of fixed capital	8.5	9.4	10.3	13.3	14.5	14.0	113.1	136.5	111.4	217.5	229.2	235.5
OPERATING SURPLUS, NET [e]	1653.3	1782.0	2723.7	4229.9	5648.4	6974.5	3681.5	4445.1	3634.3	7076.7	7460.7	7665.8
MIXED INCOME, NET	...	...	...	...	...	...	...	...	...	...	...	...
Gross capital formation	...	...	...	...	...	...	...	...	...	...	...	...

[a] At producers' prices.
[b] Value Added refers to GDP.
[c] Discrepancy between components and total.
[d] Includes Mixed Income, Gross.
[e] Includes Mixed Income, Net.

Table 2.3 Output, gross value added, and fixed assets by industries at current prices (ISIC Rev. 3) Manufacturing (D)

Series 100: 1993 SNA, Naira, Western calendar year | **Data in billions**

	2001	2002	2003	2004	2005	2006	2007	2008	2009	2010	2011	2012
Series	**100**											
Output, at basic prices	661.6[a]	775.7[a]	932.1[a]	1184.6[a]	1448.3[a]	1608.9[a]	892.7	1006.9	1072.6	1156.8	1274.2	1413.3
Less: Intermediate consumption, at purchaser's prices	381.2	444.8	535.3	705.5	1022.2	1115.5	371.8	421.4	460.3	513.8	579.4	649.2
Equals: VALUE ADDED, GROSS, at basic prices	280.5[b]	331.0[b]	396.8[b]	479.1[b]	426.1[b]	493.4[b]	520.9[c]	585.6[c]	612.3[c]	643.1[c]	694.8[c]	764.1[c]
Compensation of employees	11.1	11.7	12.3	876.3	403.8	861.2	284.3	34.6	37.1	39.8	43.9	49.4
Taxes on production and imports, less Subsidies	81.4	94.1	109.1	129.8	13.4	14.8	17.2	25.2	32.7	39.3	45.7	64.6
Taxes on production and imports	81.4	94.1	109.1	131.5	15.1	37.1	41.7	53.7	62.1	69.9	78.3	100.2
Taxes on products	81.4	94.1	109.1	131.5	15.1	37.1	41.7	53.7	62.1	69.9	78.3	100.2
Other taxes on production	...	...	...	...	...	...	...	...	...	...	...	...

	2001	2002	2003	2004	2005	2006	2007	2008	2009	2010	2011	2012
Series	**100**											
Less: Subsidies	...	...	...	1.7	1.8	22.3	24.5	28.4	29.4	30.5	32.6	35.7
Subsidies on products	0.0	0.0	0.0	1.7	1.8	22.3	24.5	28.4	29.4	30.5	32.6	35.7
Other subsidies on production	...	...	...	...	...	...	...	...	...	...	...	...
OPERATING SURPLUS, GROSS [d]	188.0	225.2	275.5	-527.0	8.9	-382.6	154.4	533.9	557.1	583.9	629.6	690.9
MIXED INCOME, GROSS	...	...	...	...	...	...	...	...	...	...	...	...
Less: Consumption of fixed capital	4.8	5.5	6.2	319.9	233.2	111.4	82.2	17.0	18.1	19.4	21.3	23.8
OPERATING SURPLUS, NET [e]	183.2	219.7	269.2	-846.9	-224.3	-494.0	72.2	516.9	539.0	564.5	608.3	667.1
MIXED INCOME, NET	...	...	...	...	...	...	...	...	...	...	...	...
Gross capital formation	...	...	...	...	...	...	...	...	...	...	...	...

[a] At producers' prices.
[b] Value Added refers to GDP.
[c] Discrepancy between components and total.
[d] Includes Mixed Income, Gross.
[e] Includes Mixed Income, Net.

Table 2.3 Output, gross value added, and fixed assets by industries at current prices (ISIC Rev. 3) Electricity, gas and water supply (E)

Series 100: 1993 SNA, Naira, Western calendar year **Data in billions**

	2001	2002	2003	2004	2005	2006	2007	2008	2009	2010	2011	2012
Series	**100**											
Output, at basic prices	105.4[a]	121.3[a]	144.8[a]	173.8[a]	189.2[a]	129.9[a]	136.4	165.4	195.3	221.7	254.9	287.5
Less: Intermediate consumption, at purchaser's prices	61.0	70.2	83.9	100.7	109.3	68.6	90.6	112.7	133.2	151.4	174.2	196.2
Equals: VALUE ADDED, GROSS, at basic prices	44.4[b]	51.1[b]	60.9[b]	73.0[b]	79.9[b]	61.4[b]	45.8[c]	52.7[c]	62.1[c]	70.3[c]	80.7[c]	91.3[c]
Compensation of employees	20.9	24.0	28.6	34.3	37.6	158.8	165.7	179.5	212.2	240.0	275.6	311.1
Taxes on production and imports, less Subsidies	28.0	32.2	38.5	46.2	50.5	18.7	4.2	5.9	7.0	11.8	12.3	8.9
Taxes on production and imports	28.4	32.7	39.0	46.8	51.1	19.4	5.0	6.4	7.6	12.5	13.1	9.8
Taxes on products	28.4	32.7	39.0	46.8	51.1	19.4	5.0	6.4	7.6	12.5	13.1	9.8
Other taxes on production	...	...	...	...	...	...	...	...	...	...	...	...
Less: Subsidies	0.4	0.5	0.5	0.6	0.6	0.7	0.8	0.5	0.6	0.7	0.8	0.9
Subsidies on products	0.4	0.5	0.5	0.6	0.6	0.7	0.8	0.5	0.6	0.7	0.8	0.9
Other subsidies on production	...	...	...	...	...	...	...	...	...	...	...	...
OPERATING SURPLUS, GROSS [d]	-4.5	-5.2	-6.2	-7.4	-8.2	-116.2	-133.3	-146.1	-172.8	-195.5	-224.5	-253.2
MIXED INCOME, GROSS	...	...	...	...	...	...	...	...	...	...	...	...
Less: Consumption of fixed capital	5.7	6.5	7.8	9.3	10.2	12.2	13.4	19.3	22.8	25.8	29.6	33.5
OPERATING SURPLUS, NET [e]	-10.2	-11.7	-13.9	-16.7	-18.3	-128.5	-146.7	-165.4	-195.6	-221.2	-254.1	-286.7
MIXED INCOME, NET	...	...	...	...	...	...	...	...	...	...	...	...
Gross capital formation	...	...	...	...	...	...	...	...	...	...	...	...

[a] At producers' prices.
[b] Value Added refers to GDP.
[c] Discrepancy between components and total.
[d] Includes Mixed Income, Gross.
[e] Includes Mixed Income, Net.

Table 2.3 Output, gross value added, and fixed assets by industries at current prices (ISIC Rev. 3) Construction (F)

Series 100: 1993 SNA, Naira, Western calendar year **Data in billions**

	2001	2002	2003	2004	2005	2006	2007	2008	2009	2010	2011	2012
Series	**100**											
Output, at basic prices	79.8[a]	94.5[a]	116.6[a]	175.3[a]	225.8[a]	300.9[a]	427.7	444.7	504.4	572.5	661.5	781.1
Less: Intermediate consumption, at purchaser's prices	38.2	45.2	55.8	91.3	3.5	42.3	161.3	138.1	156.7	177.8	205.2	242.6
Equals: VALUE ADDED, GROSS, at basic prices	41.6[b]	49.2[b]	60.8[b]	171.3[b]	222.3[b]	258.6[b]	266.5[c]	306.6[c]	347.7[c]	394.7[c]	456.3[c]	538.4[c]
Compensation of employees	6.8	7.1	7.5	1.2	4.2	5.4	22.5	28.6	32.4	36.8	42.6	50.2
Taxes on production and imports, less Subsidies	0.8	1.2	1.8	5.2	6.6	8.3	12.3	15.9	18.4	15.6	16.8	20.5
Taxes on production and imports	0.8	1.2	1.8	5.2	6.6	8.3	12.3	15.9	18.4	15.6	16.8	20.5
Taxes on products	0.8	1.2	1.8	5.2	6.6	8.3	12.3	15.9	18.4	15.6	16.8	20.5
Other taxes on production	...	...	...	...	...	...	...	...	...	...	...	...
Less: Subsidies	...	...	...	...	...	...	0.0	0.0	0.0	0.0	0.0	0.0
Subsidies on products	0.0	0.0	0.0	0.0	0.0	0.0	0.0	0.0	0.0	0.0	0.0	0.0
Other subsidies on production	...	...	...	...	...	...	...	...	...	...	...	...
OPERATING SURPLUS, GROSS [d]	34.0	40.9	51.5	164.9	211.6	244.9	224.9	259.7	294.5	334.3	386.5	456.1
MIXED INCOME, GROSS	...	...	...	...	...	...	...	...	...	...	...	...
Less: Consumption of fixed capital	0.0	0.0	0.0	0.2	0.3	7.6	19.1	18.3	20.7	23.5	27.2	32.1
OPERATING SURPLUS, NET [e]	34.0	40.9	51.4	164.7	211.4	237.3	205.8	241.4	273.8	310.8	359.3	424.0
MIXED INCOME, NET	...	...	...	...	...	...	...	...	...	...	...	...
Gross capital formation	...	...	...	...	...	...	...	...	...	...	...	...

[a] At producers' prices.
[b] Value Added refers to GDP.
[c] Discrepancy between components and total.
[d] Includes Mixed Income, Gross.
[e] Includes Mixed Income, Net.

Table 2.3 Output, gross value added, and fixed assets by industries at current prices (ISIC Rev. 3) Wholesale retail trade, repair of motor vehicles, motorcycles, etc.; hotels and restaurants (G+H)

Series 100: 1993 SNA, Naira, Western calendar year **Data in billions**

	2001	2002	2003	2004	2005	2006	2007	2008	2009	2010	2011	2012
Series	**100**											
Output, at basic prices	959.8[a]	1154.3[a]	1379.4[a]	2010.9[a]	2449.2[a]	3409.9[a]	3765.7	4170.4	4857.6	5533.3	6408.7	7354.1
Less: Intermediate consumption, at purchaser's prices	269.7	324.4	387.6	455.0	495.1	608.6	648.1	581.2	676.3	770.8	892.0	1024.6
Equals: VALUE ADDED, GROSS, at basic prices	690.1[b]	830.0[b]	991.8[b]	1555.9[b]	1954.1[b]	2801.4[b]	3117.6[c]	3589.2[c]	4181.3[c]	4762.5[c]	5516.6[c]	6329.5[c]
Compensation of employees	35.5	37.2	39.1	54.5	58.8	29.4	59.3	70.1	81.3	92.9	107.4	123.7
Taxes on production and imports, less Subsidies	39.3	47.9	58.2	36.2	39.7	2.0	88.8	114.2	182.2	137.8	190.2	169.5
Taxes on production and imports	39.3	47.9	58.2	36.2	39.7	2.0	88.8	114.2	182.2	137.8	190.2	169.5
Taxes on products	39.3	47.9	58.2	36.2	39.7	2.0	88.8	114.2	182.2	137.8	190.2	169.5
Other taxes on production	...	...	...	...	...	...	...	...	...	...	...	...

	2001	2002	2003	2004	2005	2006	2007	2008	2009	2010	2011	2012
Series	**100**											
Less: Subsidies	...	...	...	...	...	...	0.0	0.0	0.0	0.0	0.0	0.0
Subsidies on products	0.0	0.0	0.0	0.0	0.0	0.0	0.0	0.0	0.0	0.0	0.0	0.0
Other subsidies on production	...	...	...	...	...	...	...	...	...	...	...	...
OPERATING SURPLUS, GROSS [d]	615.3	744.9	894.5	1465.2	1855.5	2770.0	3049.2	3509.3	4088.6	4656.6	5394.3	6188.5
MIXED INCOME, GROSS	...	...	...	...	...	...	...	...	...	...	...	...
Less: Consumption of fixed capital	3.2	3.3	3.4	3.6	4.4	0.9	9.1	9.8	11.4	13.0	15.0	17.3
OPERATING SURPLUS, NET [e]	612.1	741.6	891.1	1461.6	1851.1	2769.1	3040.2	3499.5	4077.3	4643.6	5379.3	6171.2
MIXED INCOME, NET	...	...	...	...	...	...	...	...	...	...	...	...
Gross capital formation	...	...	...	...	...	...	...	...	...	...	...	...

[a] At producers' prices.
[b] Value Added refers to GDP.
[c] Discrepancy between components and total.
[d] Includes Mixed Income, Gross.
[e] Includes Mixed Income, Net.

Table 2.3 Output, gross value added, and fixed assets by industries at current prices (ISIC Rev. 3) Transport, storage and communications (I)

Series 100: 1993 SNA, Naira, Western calendar year

Data in billions

	2001	2002	2003	2004	2005	2006	2007	2008	2009	2010	2011	2012
Series	**100**											
Output, at basic prices	271.7[a]	337.5[a]	425.1[a]	680.8[a]	803.3[a]	1113.7[a]	1254.4	2201.3	2285.2	2363.4	2604.6	2967.3
Less: Intermediate consumption, at purchaser's prices	114.2	141.9	178.6	283.5	366.1	458.8	534.7	1469.6	1519.6	1568.9	1741.1	1972.2
Equals: VALUE ADDED, GROSS, at basic prices	157.5[b]	195.7[b]	246.5[b]	397.3[b]	437.1[b]	654.9[b]	719.7[c]	731.8[c]	765.6[c]	794.5[c]	863.5[c]	995.0[c]
Compensation of employees	6.9	7.5	8.2	13.1	16.4	199.8	313.4	293.2	306.3	317.3	345.1	397.1
Taxes on production and imports, less Subsidies	5.2	6.1	7.3	8.6	10.4	45.4	27.4	33.8	38.9	52.8	54.6	42.3
Taxes on production and imports	5.4	6.4	7.7	9.0	10.9	46.0	28.0	36.0	41.2	55.2	57.2	45.1
Taxes on products	5.4	6.4	7.7	9.0	10.9	46.0	28.0	36.0	41.2	55.2	57.2	45.1
Other taxes on production	...	...	...	...	...	...	...	...	...	...	...	...
Less: Subsidies	0.3	0.3	0.4	0.4	0.5	0.5	0.6	2.2	2.3	2.4	2.6	2.8
Subsidies on products	0.3	0.3	0.4	0.4	0.5	0.5	0.6	2.2	2.3	2.4	2.6	2.8
Other subsidies on production	...	...	...	...	...	...	...	...	...	...	...	...
OPERATING SURPLUS, GROSS [d]	145.4	182.0	231.0	375.6	410.4	409.7	345.8	387.3	406.3	422.7	457.7	529.2
MIXED INCOME, GROSS	...	...	...	...	...	...	...	...	...	...	...	...
Less: Consumption of fixed capital	5.1	6.1	7.4	7.4	16.4	59.4	60.5	51.3	53.0	54.6	60.6	68.7
OPERATING SURPLUS, NET [e]	140.2	175.9	223.5	368.2	394.0	350.4	285.3	336.0	353.3	368.1	397.0	460.5
MIXED INCOME, NET	...	...	...	...	...	...	...	...	...	...	...	...
Gross capital formation	...	...	...	...	...	...	...	...	...	...	...	...

[a] At producers' prices.
[b] Value Added refers to GDP.
[c] Discrepancy between components and total.
[d] Includes Mixed Income, Gross.
[e] Includes Mixed Income, Net.

Table 2.3 Output, gross value added, and fixed assets by industries at current prices (ISIC Rev. 3) Financial intermediation; real estate, renting and business activities (J+K)

Series 100: 1993 SNA, Naira, Western calendar year — **Data in billions**

	2001	2002	2003	2004	2005	2006	2007	2008	2009	2010	2011	2012
Series	**100**											
Output, at basic prices	286.9[a]	356.5[a]	441.0[a]	639.8[a]	940.8[a]	1505.6[a]	1742.9	1942.6	2208.6	2483.4	2999.7	3238.1
Less: Intermediate consumption, at purchaser's prices	25.3	32.4	38.4	53.5	73.3	364.7	476.4	486.1	551.4	627.4	816.1	794.0
Equals: VALUE ADDED, GROSS, at basic prices	261.5[b]	324.1[b]	402.5[b]	586.3[b]	867.5[b]	1140.9[b]	1266.5[c]	1456.5[c]	1657.2[c]	1856.0[c]	2183.5[c]	2444.1[c]
Compensation of employees	9.2	9.6	10.1	13.0	14.3	121.6	351.0	385.9	565.2	617.9	762.9	836.2
Taxes on production and imports, less Subsidies	18.1	21.9	26.5	20.1	23.9	35.7	42.3	54.4	24.5	39.7	42.1	109.2
Taxes on production and imports	18.1	21.9	26.5	20.1	23.9	35.7	42.3	54.4	24.5	39.7	42.1	109.2
Taxes on products	18.1	21.9	26.5	20.1	23.9	35.7	42.3	54.4	24.5	39.7	42.1	109.2
Other taxes on production	...	...	...	...	...	...	...	...	...	...	...	...
Less: Subsidies	...	...	...	...	...	...	0.0	0.0	0.0	0.0	0.0	0.0
Subsidies on products	0.0	0.0	0.0	0.0	0.0	0.0	0.0	0.0	0.0	0.0	0.0	0.0
Other subsidies on production	...	...	...	...	...	...	...	...	...	...	...	...
OPERATING SURPLUS, GROSS [d]	234.2	292.5	365.9	553.2	829.3	983.6	788.9	929.5	953.4	1083.1	1238.7	1403.4
MIXED INCOME, GROSS	...	...	...	...	...	...	...	...	...	...	...	...
Less: Consumption of fixed capital	7.7	8.4	9.3	10.8	12.0	28.5	126.6	141.1	138.6	155.0	182.0	204.5
OPERATING SURPLUS, NET [e]	226.5	284.1	356.7	542.4	817.3	955.2	662.4	788.4	814.8	928.1	1056.7	1198.9
MIXED INCOME, NET	...	...	...	...	...	...	...	...	...	...	...	...
Gross capital formation	...	...	...	...	...	...	...	...	...	...	...	...

[a] At producers' prices.
[b] Value Added refers to GDP.
[c] Discrepancy between components and total.
[d] Includes Mixed Income, Gross.
[e] Includes Mixed Income, Net.

Table 2.3 Output, gross value added, and fixed assets by industries at current prices (ISIC Rev. 3) Public administration and defense; compulsory social security (L)

Series 100: 1993 SNA, Naira, Western calendar year — **Data in billions**

	2001	2002	2003	2004	2005	2006	2007	2008	2009	2010	2011	2012
Series	**100**											
Output, at basic prices	114.8[a]	120.5[a]	132.6[a]	148.5[a]	169.3[a]	193.1[a]	214.3	238.2	270.1	306.9	346.8	394.3
Less: Intermediate consumption, at purchaser's prices	36.7	38.5	42.4	47.5	54.1	61.7	63.0	64.2	72.8	82.7	93.5	106.3
Equals: VALUE ADDED, GROSS, at basic prices	78.1[b]	82.0[b]	90.2[b]	101.0[b]	115.2[b]	131.3[b]	151.3[c]	174.0[c]	197.3[c]	224.2[c]	253.3[c]	288.0[c]
Compensation of employees	78.0	81.9	90.1	100.9	115.0	131.1	131.4	131.6	149.1	169.5	191.5	217.7
Taxes on production and imports, less Subsidies	...	...	...	...	...	...	15.9	20.4	23.6	39.8	41.1	30.6
Taxes on production and imports	...	...	...	...	...	...	15.9	20.4	23.6	39.8	41.1	30.6
Taxes on products	0.0	0.0	0.0	0.0	0.0	0.0	15.9	20.4	23.6	39.8	41.1	30.6
Other taxes on production	...	...	...	...	...	...	...	...	...	...	...	...

	2001	2002	2003	2004	2005	2006	2007	2008	2009	2010	2011	2012
Series	**100**											
Less: Subsidies	...	...	...	...	...	...	0.0	0.0	0.0	0.0	0.0	0.0
Subsidies on products	0.0	0.0	0.0	0.0	0.0	0.0	0.0	0.0	0.0	0.0	0.0	0.0
Other subsidies on production	...	...	...	...	...	...	...	...	...	...	...	...
OPERATING SURPLUS, GROSS	0.1	0.1	0.1	0.1	0.2	0.2	0.0	0.0	0.0	0.0	0.0	0.0
MIXED INCOME, GROSS	...	...	...	...	...	...	...	...	...	...	...	...
Less: Consumption of fixed capital	0.1	0.1	0.1	0.1	0.2	0.2	20.0	42.5	48.1	54.7	61.8	70.3
OPERATING SURPLUS, NET	0.0	0.0	0.0	0.0	0.0	0.0	-20.0	-42.5	-48.1	-54.7	-61.8	-70.3
MIXED INCOME, NET	...	...	...	...	...	...	...	...	...	...	...	...
Gross capital formation	...	...	...	...	...	...	...	...	...	...	...	...

[a] At producers' prices.
[b] Value Added refers to GDP.
[c] Discrepancy between components and total.

Table 2.3 Output, gross value added, and fixed assets by industries at current prices (ISIC Rev. 3) Education; health and social work; other community, social and personal services (M+N+O)

Series 100: 1993 SNA, Naira, Western calendar year **Data in billions**

		2001	2002	2003	2004	2005	2006	2007	2008	2009	2010	2011	2012
Series		**100**											
Output, at basic prices		93.5[a]	112.0[a]	129.5[a]	158.7[a]	195.4[a]	241.1[a]	292.3	331.5	379.7	440.0	501.9	579.1
Less: Intermediate consumption, at purchaser's prices		19.1	22.0	25.1	30.0	36.3	43.9	45.6	46.9	54.1	62.7	71.8	82.8
Equals: VALUE ADDED, GROSS, at basic prices	a	74.5[b]	90.0[b]	104.4[b]	128.7[b]	159.1[b]	197.2[b]	246.7[c]	284.7[c]	325.6[c]	377.3[c]	430.2[c]	496.3[c]
Compensation of employees		24.0	25.2	27.7	30.9	35.1	39.9	41.8	43.0	50.5	59.4	69.0	80.3
Taxes on production and imports, less Subsidies		-0.0	-0.0	-0.0	-0.0	-0.0	-0.0	26.2	33.7	38.9	66.7	69.6	39.1
Taxes on production and imports		...	...	...	...	...	...	26.2	33.7	38.9	66.7	69.6	39.2
Taxes on products		0.0	0.0	0.0	0.0	0.0	0.0	26.2	33.7	38.9	66.7	69.6	39.2
Other taxes on production		...	...	...	...	...	...	...	...	...	...	...	...
Less: Subsidies		0.0	0.0	0.0	0.0	0.0	0.0	0.0[d]	0.0[d]	0.0[d]	0.0	0.0	0.0
Subsidies on products		0.0	0.0	0.0	0.0	0.0	0.0	0.4[e]	0.4[e]	0.5[e]	...	...	...
Other subsidies on production		...	...	...	...	...	...	...	...	...	...	...	...
OPERATING SURPLUS, GROSS	f	50.5	64.8	76.7	97.7	124.0	157.3	202.0	232.5	264.2	305.1	346.3	398.5
MIXED INCOME, GROSS		...	...	...	...	...	...	...	...	...	...	...	...
Less: Consumption of fixed capital		0.1	0.1	0.1	0.1	0.1	0.1	2.9	9.2	10.9	12.8	14.9	17.5
OPERATING SURPLUS, NET	g	50.4	64.7	76.6	97.6	123.9	157.2	199.1	223.3	253.3	292.2	331.3	381.0
MIXED INCOME, NET		...	...	...	...	...	...	...	...	...	...	...	...
Gross capital formation		...	...	...	...	...	...	...	...	...	...	...	...

[a] Includes data for Private households with employed persons.
[b] Value Added refers to GDP.
[c] Discrepancy between components and total.
[d] Account does not balance as one or more components have not been revised.
[e] Data for this item are not updated.
[f] Includes Mixed Income, Gross.
[g] Includes Mixed Income, Net.

Table 2.3 Output, gross value added, and fixed assets by industries at current prices (ISIC Rev. 3) Private households with employed persons (P)

Series 100: 1993 SNA, Naira, Western calendar year — **Data in billions**

	2001	2002	2003	2004	2005	2006	2007	2008	2009	2010	2011	2012
Series	**100**											
Output, at basic prices	0.1	0.1	0.1	0.1	0.2	0.2	0.2	0.2	0.2	0.3	0.3	0.3
Less: Intermediate consumption, at purchaser's prices	0.0	0.0	0.0	0.0	0.0	0.0	0.0	0.0	0.0	0.0	0.0	0.0
Equals: VALUE ADDED, GROSS, at basic prices	0.1	0.1	0.1	0.1	0.1	0.2	0.2	0.2	0.2	0.2	0.3	0.3
Compensation of employees	0.1	0.1	0.1	0.1	0.2	0.2	0.2	0.2	0.2	0.2	0.3	0.3
Taxes on production and imports, less Subsidies	-0.0	-0.0	-0.0	-0.0	-0.0	-0.0	-0.0	-0.0	-0.0	-0.0	-0.0	-0.0
Taxes on production and imports	...	...	...	...	...	...	...	...	...	...	...	...
Less: Subsidies	0.0	0.0	0.0	0.0	0.0	0.0	0.0	0.0	0.0	0.0	0.0	0.0
Subsidies on products	0.0	0.0	0.0	0.0	0.0	0.0	0.0	0.0	0.0	0.0	0.0	0.0
Other subsidies on production	...	...	...	...	...	...	...	...	...	...	...	...
OPERATING SURPLUS, GROSS	...	...	...	...	...	-0.0	...	...	...	...	...	...
MIXED INCOME, GROSS	...	...	...	...	...	...	...	...	...	...	...	...
Less: Consumption of fixed capital	...	...	...	...	...	...	...	...	...	...	...	...
OPERATING SURPLUS, NET	...	...	...	...	...	-0.0	...	...	...	...	...	...
MIXED INCOME, NET	...	...	...	...	...	...	...	...	...	...	...	...
Gross capital formation	...	...	...	...	...	...	...	...	...	...	...	...

Table 3.2 Individual consumption expenditure of households, NPISHs, and general government at current prices

Series 100: 1993 SNA, Naira, Western calendar year — **Data in billions**

	2001	2002	2003	2004	2005	2006	2007	2008	2009	2010	2011	2012
Series	**100**											
Individual consumption expenditure of households												
Food and non-alcoholic beverages	...	...	...	...	6043.0	6623.5	7413.3	8731.8	8930.0			
Alcoholic beverages, tobacco and narcotics	...	...	...	...	109.0	119.4	133.7	157.5	161.0			
Clothing and footwear	...	...	...	...	623.5	683.4	764.9	900.9	921.4			
Housing, water, electricity, gas and other fuels	...	...	...	...	1199.4	1314.6	1471.4	1733.1	1772.4			
Furnishings, household equipment and routine maintenance of the house	...	...	...	...	749.7	821.7	919.7	1083.3	1107.9			
Health	...	...	...	...	209.1	229.2	256.5	302.1	309.0			
Transport	...	...	...	...	502.7	551.0	616.7	726.4	742.9			
Communication	...	...	...	...	35.4	38.8	43.5	51.2	52.4			
Recreation and culture	...	...	...	...	134.4	147.4	164.9	194.3	198.7			
Education	...	...	...	...	278.5	305.2	341.6	402.4	411.5			
Restaurants and hotels	...	...	...	...	75.2	82.5	92.3	108.7	111.2			
Miscellaneous goods and services	...	...	...	...	339.0	371.6	415.9	489.8	501.0			

	2001	2002	2003	2004	2005	2006	2007	2008	2009	2010	2011	2012
Series	**100**											
Equals: Household final consumption expenditure in domestic market	...	...	...	...	10300.1	11289.6	12635.8	14883.1	15221.0			
Plus: Direct purchases abroad by residents	...	...	...	...	2.2	2.4	2.7	3.2	3.2			
Less: Direct purchases in domestic market by non-residents	...	...	...	...	1.1	1.2	1.3	1.6	1.6			
Equals: Household final consumption expenditure	3687.7	5540.2	7044.5	8637.7	10300.1[a]	11289.6[a]	12635.8[a]	14883.1[a]	15221.0[a]			
	Individual consumption expenditure of non-profit institutions serving households (NPISHs)											
Equals: NPISHs final consumption expenditure	...	...	...	...	1.4	0.2	0.2	0.2	0.2			
	Individual consumption expenditure of general government											
Housing	...	...	...	...	10.5	14.1	15.8	18.6	19.0			
Health	...	...	...	...	114.5	152.9	171.2	201.6	206.2			
Recreation and culture	...	...	...	...	5.0	6.6	7.4	8.7	8.9			
Education	...	...	...	...	179.6	239.9	268.6	316.3	323.5			
Social protection	...	...	...	...	54.1	72.3	80.9	95.3	97.5			
Equals: Individual consumption expenditure of general government	...	...	...	...	363.7	485.9	543.8	640.6	655.1			
Equals: Total actual individual consumption	...	...	...	...	...	...	...	...	...			

[a] Discrepancy with equivalent item in Table 1.1 (Gross domestic product by expenditures at current prices).

Table 4.1 Total Economy (S.1)

Series 100: 1993 SNA, Naira, Western calendar year

Data in billions

	2001	2002	2003	2004	2005	2006	2007	2008	2009	2010	2011	2012
Series	**100**											
	I. Production account - Resources											
Output, at basic prices (otherwise, please specify)	6326.5[a]	8854.6[a]	10816.9[a]	14253.6[a]	18137.3[a]	22890.7[a]	24654.6	28594.8	29485.4			
Less: Financial intermediation services indirectly measured (only to be deducted if FISIM is not distributed to uses)	...	...	...	...	...	...	...	...	...			
Plus: Taxes less Subsidies on products	184.4	215.8	255.6	262.5	163.1	145.0	283.6	368.9	432.0			
Plus: Taxes on products	186.6	219.1	259.2	268.1	169.7	173.2	314.5	404.5	468.4			
Less: Subsidies on products	2.2	3.3	3.6	5.6	6.6	28.2	31.0	35.6	36.3			
	I. Production account - Uses											
Intermediate consumption, at purchaser's prices	1417.0	1726.4	2074.3	2667.3	3401.9	4180.9	3997.3	4298.5	4691.2			
GROSS DOMESTIC PRODUCT	4909.5	7128.2	8742.6	11673.6	14735.3	18709.8	20940.9	24665.2	25226.3			
Less: Consumption of fixed capital	42.1	47.7	53.5	374.1	302.0	246.5	276.6	221.1	242.0			
NET DOMESTIC PRODUCT	...	...	...	...	...	...	...	...	...			
	II.1.1 Generation of income account - Resources											
GROSS DOMESTIC PRODUCT	4909.5	7128.2	8742.6	11673.6	14735.3	18709.8	20940.9	24665.2	25226.3			
	II.1.1 Generation of income account - Uses											
Compensation of employees	256.5	271.7	296.0	1203.6	770.5	1639.6	1143.9	911.8	1023.4			
Taxes on production and imports, less Subsidies	184.4	215.8	255.6	262.5	163.1	145.0	283.6	368.9	432.0			

	2001	2002	2003	2004	2005	2006	2007	2008	2009	2010	2011	2012
Series	**100**											
Taxes on production and imports	186.6	219.1	259.2	268.1	169.7	173.2	314.5	404.5	468.4			
Taxes on products	186.6	219.1	259.2	268.1	169.7	173.2	314.5	404.5	468.4			
Other taxes on production	...	...	...	...	...	...	...	...	...			
Less: Subsidies	2.2	3.3	3.6	5.6	6.6	28.2	31.0	35.6	36.3			
Subsidies on products	2.2	3.3	3.6	5.6	6.6	28.2	31.0	35.6	36.3			
Other subsidies on production	...	...	...	...	...	...	...	...	...			
OPERATING SURPLUS, GROSS	4468.6	6640.7	8191.0	10207.4	13801.8	16925.2	19513.4	23384.5	23770.8			
MIXED INCOME, GROSS	...	...	...	...	...	...	...	...	...			
II.1.2 Allocation of primary income account - Resources												
OPERATING SURPLUS, GROSS	4468.6	6640.7	8191.0	10207.4	13801.8	16925.2	19513.4	23384.5	23770.8			
MIXED INCOME, GROSS	...	...	...	...	...	...	...	...	...			
Compensation of employees	253.4	268.5	292.7	1200.1	767.0	1636.2	1167.8	922.7	1038.5			
Taxes on production and imports, less Subsidies	184.4	215.8	255.6	262.5	163.1	145.0	283.6	368.9	432.0			
Taxes on production and imports	186.6	219.1	259.2	268.1	169.7	173.2	314.5	404.5	468.4			
Taxes on products	186.6	219.1	259.2	268.1	169.7	173.2	314.5	404.5	468.4			
Other taxes on production	...	...	...	...	...	...	...	...	...			
Less: Subsidies	2.2	3.3	3.6	5.6	6.6	28.2	31.0	35.6	36.3			
Subsidies on products	2.2	3.3	3.6	5.6	6.6	28.2	31.0	35.6	36.3			
Other subsidies on production	...	...	...	...	...	...	...	...	...			
Property income	-343.9	-382.7	-424.0	-436.8	-575.1	-306.4	-1502.1	-1474.7	-1506.9			
II.1.2 Allocation of primary income account - Uses												
Property income	...	...	...	...	...	...	...	...	...			
GROSS NATIONAL INCOME	4562.5	6742.3	8315.3	11233.3	14156.8	18400.0	19462.7	23201.4	23734.4			
II.2 Secondary distribution of income account - Resources												
GROSS NATIONAL INCOME	4562.5	6742.3	8315.3	11233.3	14156.8	18400.0	19462.7	23201.4	23734.4			
Current taxes on income, wealth, etc.	...	...	...	...	...	...	...	...	...			
Social contributions	...	...	...	...	...	...	...	...	...			
Social benefits other than social transfers in kind	...	...	...	...	...	...	...	...	...			
Other current transfers	152.0	170.4	200.8	359.3	447.5	177.0	2247.7	2221.7	2676.7			
II.2 Secondary distribution of income account - Uses												
Current taxes on income, wealth, etc.	...	...	...	...	...	...	...	...	...			
Social contributions	...	...	...	...	...	...	...	...	...			
Social benefits other than social transfers in kind	...	...	...	...	...	...	...	...	...			
Other current transfers	...	...	...	...	...	...	...	...	...			
GROSS DISPOSABLE INCOME	4714.5	6912.7	8516.2	11592.5	14604.2	18577.0	21710.4	25423.1	26411.1			
II.4.1 Use of disposable income account - Resources												
GROSS DISPOSABLE INCOME	4714.5	6912.7	8516.2	11592.5	14604.2	18577.0	21710.4	25423.1	26411.1			
Adjustment for the change in net equity of households on pension funds	...	...	...	...	...	...	...	...	...			

	2001	2002	2003	2004	2005	2006	2007	2008	2009	2010	2011	2012
Series	**100**											
	II.4.1 Use of disposable income account - Uses											
Final consumption expenditure	4090.8	6018.5	7495.0	9423.6	12078.2	12573.1	18291.5	18890.3	22074.2			
Individual consumption expenditure	3687.7	5540.2	7044.5	8637.7	11075.1	11289.7	15682.9	15756.2	18861.0			
Collective consumption expenditure	403.1	478.3	450.5	785.8	1003.1	1283.4	2608.6	3134.2	3213.2			
Adjustment for the change in net equity of households on pension funds	...	...	...	...	...	...	...	...	...			
SAVING, GROSS	623.8	894.2	1021.1	2169.0	2526.1	6003.8	3418.9	6532.8	4336.9			
	III.1 Capital account - Changes in liabilities and net worth											
SAVING, GROSS	623.8	894.2	1021.1	2169.0	2526.1	6003.8	3418.9	6532.8	4336.9			
Capital transfers, receivable less payable	0.0	6.6	2.6	4.7	3.0	4.5	0.0	0.0	0.0			
Capital transfers, receivable	...	...	...	...	...	...	...	...	...			
Less: Capital transfers, payable	...	...	...	...	...	...	...	...	...			
Equals: CHANGES IN NET WORTH DUE TO SAVING AND CAPITAL TRANSFERS	...	...	...	...	...	...	...	...	...			
	III.1 Capital account - Changes in assets											
Gross capital formation	372.8	500.4	866.7	864.0	805.6	1548.0	1936.6	2052.4	3049.5			
Gross fixed capital formation	372.1	499.7	865.9	863.1	804.4	1546.5	1935.0	2050.8	3047.7			
Changes in inventories	0.7	0.7	0.8	0.9	1.2	1.5	1.6	1.7	1.8			
Acquisitions less disposals of valuables	...	...	...	...	...	...	...	...	...			
Acquisitions less disposals of non-produced non-financial assets	...	...	...	...	...	...	...	...	...			
NET LENDING (+) / NET BORROWING (-)	251.0	400.3	157.1	1309.7	1723.5	4460.4	1482.3	4480.4	1287.5			

[a] At producers' prices.

Table 4.2 Rest of the world (S.2)

Series 100: 1993 SNA, Naira, Western calendar year

Data in billions

	2001	2002	2003	2004	2005	2006	2007	2008	2009	2010	2011	2012
Series	**100**											
	V.I External account of goods and services - Resources											
Imports of goods and services	1785.3	1954.4	3097.6	2134.8	2813.2	4010.6	6350.3	6114.8	7663.6			
Imports of goods	...	...	...	...	...	...	4127.7	3299.1	5047.9			
Imports of services	...	...	...	...	...	...	2222.6	2815.7	2615.7			
	V.I External account of goods and services - Uses											
Exports of goods and services	2231.3	2563.7	3478.5	3520.8	4664.8	8599.3	7063.1	9837.3	7766.2			
Exports of goods	...	...	...	...	...	...	6881.5	9568.9	7434.5			
Exports of services	...	...	...	...	...	...	181.6	268.3	331.7			
EXTERNAL BALANCE OF GOODS AND SERVICES	-445.9	-609.3	-380.9	-1386.1	-1851.6	-4588.7	-712.8	-3722.5	-102.6			
	V.II External account of primary income and current transfers - Resources											
EXTERNAL BALANCE OF GOODS AND SERVICES	-445.9	-609.3	-380.9	-1386.1	-1851.6	-4588.7	-712.8	-3722.5	-102.6			
Compensation of employees	3.7	3.8	3.9	4.2	4.2	4.1	3.5	4.2	5.5			

	2001	2002	2003	2004	2005	2006	2007	2008	2009	2010	2011	2012
Series	**100**											
Taxes on production and imports, less Subsidies	...	...	...	...	...	...	...	...	...			
Taxes on production and imports	...	...	...	...	...	...	...	...	...			
Taxes on products	...	...	...	...	...	...	...	...	...			
Other taxes on production	...	...	...	...	...	...	...	...	...			
Less: Subsidies	...	...	...	...	...	...	...	...	...			
Subsidies on products	...	...	...	...	...	...	...	...	...			
Other subsidies on production	...	...	...	...	...	...	...	...	...			
Property income	384.2	402.7	434.5	457.7	667.6	521.4	1797.3	1738.4	1640.6			
Current taxes on income, wealth, etc.	...	...	...	...	...	...	...	...	...			
Social contributions	...	...	...	...	...	...	...	...	...			
Social benefits other than social transfers in kind	...	...	...	...	...	...	...	...	...			
Other current transfers	0.2	2.8	15.8	6.2	7.7	23.1	18.9	62.9	69.0			
Adjustment for the change in net equity of households on pension funds	...	...	...	...	...	...	...	...	...			
V.II External account of primary income and current transfers - Uses												
Compensation of employees	0.6	0.6	0.6	0.7	0.7	0.7	27.4	15.1	20.6			
Taxes on production and imports, less Subsidies	...	...	...	...	...	...	...	...	...			
Taxes on production and imports	...	...	...	...	...	...	...	...	...			
Taxes on products	...	...	...	...	...	...	...	...	...			
Other taxes on production	...	...	...	...	...	...	...	...	...			
Less: Subsidies	...	...	...	...	...	...	...	...	...			
Subsidies on products	...	...	...	...	...	...	...	...	...			
Other subsidies on production	...	...	...	...	...	...	...	...	...			
Property income	40.3	20.0	10.5	20.9	92.5	215.1	295.2	263.7	133.6			
Current taxes on income and wealth, etc.	...	...	...	...	...	...	...	...	...			
Social contributions	...	...	...	...	...	...	...	...	...			
Social benefits other than social transfers in kind	...	...	...	...	...	...	...	...	...			
Other current transfers	152.2	167.7	185.1	365.5	455.2	1359.2	2266.6	2284.6	2745.8			
Adjustment for the change in net equity of households on pension funds	...	...	...	...	...	...	...	...	...			
CURRENT EXTERNAL BALANCE	-251.0	-388.3	-122.9	-1305.0	-1720.5	-5614.9	-1482.3	-4480.4	-1287.5			
V.III.1 Capital account - Changes in liabilities and net worth												
CURRENT EXTERNAL BALANCE	-251.0	-388.3	-122.9	-1305.0	-1720.5	-5614.9	-1482.3	-4480.4	-1287.5			
Capital transfers, receivable less payable	0.0	-6.6	-2.6	-4.7	-3.0	-4.5	0.0	0.0	...			
Capital transfers, receivable	...	...	...	...	...	...	...	...	...			
Less: Capital transfers, payable	...	...	...	...	...	...	...	...	...			
Equals: CHANGES IN NET WORTH DUE TO SAVING AND CAPITAL TRANSFERS [a]	623.8	900.8	1023.8	2173.7	2529.0	6008.4	6315.4	6264.0	...			

	2001	2002	2003	2004	2005	2006	2007	2008	2009	2010	2011	2012
Series	**100**											
	V.III.1 Capital account - Changes in assets											
Acquisitions less disposals of non-produced non-financial assets	...	...	...	...	...	...	...	...	...			
NET LENDING (+) / NET BORROWING (-)	-251.0	-400.3	-157.1	-1309.7	-1723.5	-4460.4	-1482.3	-4480.4	-1287.5			

[a] Data for this item has not been revised.

Niue

Source

Data were provided to the United Nations by Statistics Niue.

General

The estimates shown in the following tables have been prepared in accordance with the United Nations System of National Accounts 1968 (1968 SNA) so far as the existing data would permit. When the scope and coverage of the estimates differ for conceptual or statistical reasons from the definitions and classifications recommended in the SNA, a footnote provides explanation.

Table 2.1 Value added by industries at current prices (ISIC Rev. 3)

Series 10: 1968 SNA, New Zealand Dollar, Fiscal year ending 30 June — **Data in thousands**

	2001	2002	2003	2004	2005	2006	2007	2008	2009	2010	2011	2012
Series	**10**											
Industries												
Agriculture, hunting, forestry; fishing	3723.0	3910.0	4157.0	3962.0	4326.0	4913.0	5316.0	5746.0	6088.0			
Mining and quarrying	3.0	-24.0	-12.0	30.0	42.0	47.0	65.0	66.0	78.0			
Manufacturing	273.0	243.0	268.0	279.0	273.0	282.0	299.0	310.0	340.0			
Electricity, gas and water supply	-45.0	-9.0	201.0	139.0	467.0	494.0	495.0	501.0	539.0			
Construction	97.0	43.0	36.0	7.0	49.0	196.0	204.0	208.0	229.0			
Wholesale, retail trade, repair of motor vehicles, motorcycles and personal and households goods; hotels and restaurants	2399.0	2375.0	2747.0	3055.0	3275.0	3163.0	3496.0	3632.0	3816.0			
Wholesale, retail trade, repair of motor vehicles, motorcycles and personal and household goods	1912.0	1840.0	2181.0	2433.0	2653.0	2344.0	2798.0	2879.0	3047.0			
Hotels and restaurants	487.0	535.0	566.0	622.0	622.0	819.0	698.0	753.0	769.0			
Transport, storage and communications	1932.0	993.0	1623.0	1088.0	1273.0	1057.0	1256.0	1328.0	1458.0			
Financial intermediation; real estate, renting and business activities	1443.0	1461.0	1434.0	1547.0	1334.0	1596.0	1648.0	1771.0	1919.0			
Public administration and defence; compulsory social security	6591.0	7519.0	6817.0	7031.0	7006.0	6941.0	7358.0	7512.0	8596.0			
Education; health and social work; other community, social and personal services	519.0	549.0	519.0	506.0	514.0	534.0	602.0	688.0	787.0			
Private households with employed persons	...	...	...	...	...	...	...	...	...			
Equals: VALUE ADDED, GROSS, in basic prices	16935.0	17060.0	17790.0	17644.0	18559.0	19223.0	20739.0	21762.0	23850.0			
Less: Financial intermediation services indirectly measured (FISIM)	315.0	281.0	215.0	336.0	256.0	334.0	338.0	341.0	344.0			
Plus: Taxes less Subsidies on products	91.0	-533.0	245.0	462.0	1139.0	1654.0	1068.0	1352.0	1955.0			
Plus: Taxes on products	1131.0	1173.0	970.0	1007.0	1823.0	960.0	1351.0	1720.0	2372.0			
Less: Subsidies on products	1040.0	1706.0	725.0	545.0	684.0	-694.0	283.0	368.0	417.0			
Equals: GROSS DOMESTIC PRODUCT	16711.0	16245.0	17821.0	17771.0	19441.0	20541.0	21468.0	22771.0	25460.0			

Table 2.2 Value added by industries at constant prices (ISIC Rev. 3)

Series 10: 1968 SNA, New Zealand Dollar, Fiscal year ending 30 June — **Data in thousands**

	2001	2002	2003	2004	2005	2006	2007	2008	2009	2010	2011	2012
Series			**10**									
Base year			**2003**									
Industries												
Agriculture, hunting, forestry; fishing			4157.0	3825.0	4155.0	4618.0	4681.0	4639.0	4402.0			
Mining and quarrying			-12.0	29.0	40.0	44.0	57.0	53.0	56.0			
Manufacturing			268.0	270.0	262.0	265.0	263.0	250.0	246.0			
Electricity, gas and water supply			201.0	134.0	449.0	464.0	436.0	405.0	390.0			
Construction			36.0	7.0	47.0	184.0	180.0	168.0	166.0			
Wholesale, retail trade, repair of motor vehicles, motorcycles and personal and household goods; hotels and restaurants			2747.0	2949.0	3145.0	2973.0	3079.0	2932.0	2759.0			
Wholesale, retail trade, repair of motor vehicles, motorcycles and personal and household goods			2181.0	2348.0	2548.0	2203.0	2464.0	2324.0	2203.0			
Hotels and restaurants			566.0	601.0	597.0	770.0	615.0	608.0	556.0			
Transport, storage and communications			1623.0	1050.0	1223.0	993.0	1106.0	1072.0	1054.0			
Financial intermediation, real estate, renting and business activities			1434.0	1493.0	1281.0	1500.0	1451.0	1430.0	1388.0			
Public administration and defence; compulsory social security			6817.0	6787.0	6730.0	6523.0	6480.0	6066.0	6216.0			
Education; health and social work; other community, social and personal services			519.0	489.0	494.0	502.0	530.0	555.0	569.0			
Private households with employed persons			...	...	...	...	...	...	...			
Equals: VALUE ADDED, GROSS, in basic prices			17790.0	17033.0	17826.0	18066.0	18263.0	17570.0	17246.0			
Less: Financial intermediation services indirectly measured (FISIM)			215.0	324.0	246.0	314.0	297.0	275.0	249.0			
Plus: Taxes less Subsidies on products			245.0	446.0	1094.0	1555.0	940.0	1092.0	1413.0			
Plus: Taxes on products			970.0	972.0	1751.0	902.0	1190.0	1389.0	1715.0			
Less: Subsidies on products			725.0	526.0	657.0	-653.0	250.0	297.0	302.0			
Equals: GROSS DOMESTIC PRODUCT			17821.0	17153.0	18675.0	19306.0	18906.0	18386.0	18410.0			

Table 5.1 Cross classification of Gross value added by industries and institutional sectors (ISIC Rev. 3) Non-financial corporations

Series 10: 1968 SNA, New Zealand Dollar, Fiscal year ending 30 June — **Data in thousands**

	2001	2002	2003	2004	2005	2006	2007	2008	2009	2010	2011	2012
Series	**10**											
Industries												
VALUE ADDED GROSS, at basic prices	2175.0	1335.0	2470.0	2037.0	2919.0	2697.0	3013.4	3042.9	3307.4			

Table 5.1 Cross classification of Gross value added by industries and institutional sectors (ISIC Rev. 3) Financial corporations

Series 10: 1968 SNA, New Zealand Dollar, Fiscal year ending 30 June — **Data in thousands**

	2001	2002	2003	2004	2005	2006	2007	2008	2009	2010	2011	2012
Series	**10**											
	Industries											
VALUE ADDED GROSS, at basic prices	4396.0	4276.0	4317.0	4566.0	4234.0	4870.0	5164.6	5527.7	5873.6			

Table 5.1 Cross classification of Gross value added by industries and institutional sectors (ISIC Rev. 3) General government

Series 10: 1968 SNA, New Zealand Dollar, Fiscal year ending 30 June — **Data in thousands**

	2001	2002	2003	2004	2005	2006	2007	2008	2009	2010	2011	2012
Series	**10**											
	Industries											
VALUE ADDED GROSS, at basic prices	6591.0	7519.0	6817.0	7031.0	7006.0	6941.0	7358.1	7512.2	8596.4			

Table 5.1 Cross classification of Gross value added by industries and institutional sectors (ISIC Rev. 3) Households

Series 10: 1968 SNA, New Zealand Dollar, Fiscal year ending 30 June — **Data in thousands**

	2001	2002	2003	2004	2005	2006	2007	2008	2009	2010	2011	2012
Series	**10**											
	Industries											
VALUE ADDED GROSS, at basic prices	3511.0	3660.0	3936.0	3755.0	4140.0	4445.0	4897.8	5331.2	5675.6			

Table 5.1 Cross classification of Gross value added by industries and institutional sectors (ISIC Rev. 3) Non-profit institutions serving households

Series 10: 1968 SNA, New Zealand Dollar, Fiscal year ending 30 June — **Data in thousands**

	2001	2002	2003	2004	2005	2006	2007	2008	2009	2010	2011	2012
Series	**10**											
	Industries											
VALUE ADDED GROSS, at basic prices	262.0	270.0	251.0	255.0	259.0	269.0	303.3	346.6	396.7			

Table 5.1 Cross classification of Gross value added by industries and institutional sectors (ISIC Rev. 3) Total economy

Series 10: 1968 SNA, New Zealand Dollar, Fiscal year ending 30 June **Data in thousands**

	2001	2002	2003	2004	2005	2006	2007	2008	2009	2010	2011	2012
Series	**10**											
	Industries											
VALUE ADDED GROSS, at basic prices	16935.0	17059.0	17791.0	17645.0	18558.0	19221.0	20737.5	21760.2	23849.4			

Norway

Source

The preparation of national accounts statistics in Norway is undertaken by Division of National Accounts at Statistics Norway, located in Oslo. The official annual estimates are published on the Internet (www.ssb.no), in "National Accounts" in two separate volumes: Production, Uses and Employment; Institutional Sector Accounts (latest for 1995-2002, since 2003 to be published every five years or so), as well as in the annual Statistical Yearbook. All together 36 tables containing annual national accounts estimates are available on the Internet, and also Supply and Use tables (presently for 2004) and Input-Output tables (1992-2002).

General

The latest estimates have been prepared in accordance with the concepts and definitions recommended in the System of National Accounts 1993 (1993 SNA). Previously the estimates were prepared in accordance with the United Nations System of National Accounts 1968 (1968 SNA). When the scope and coverage of the estimates differ for conceptual or statistical reasons from the definitions and classifications recommended in SNA, a footnote is indicated to the relevant tables.

1993 SNA was adopted already when the first results from the main revision were released by summer 1995. Statistics Norway has published revised national accounts estimates in 2002, this time without any major definitional changes to the system. Latest main revision was undertaken in December 2006, including new treatment (allocation) of FISIM. Chain indices are used to measure volume growth (annual chaining), and the resulting chained constant prices data, 2005 reference year, are not additive.

A complete methodological inventory on GDP compilation in current prices in the context of 1995 ESA has been submitted by Statistics Norway to Eurostat in several updated versions, the 2006 version being the latest following the previous 2004, 2001 and 1996 versions. The earliest one was made available in print by Statistics Norway (as Documents 96/5 and 96/6), while the latest 2006 version has been made available to users electronically by Eurostat on the Circa website. A shorter inventory on GDP compilation in constant prices has also been prepared and made available by Eurostat.

Methodology:

Overview of GDP Compilation

Approaches used to calculate gross domestic product (GDP) in the Norwegian National Accounts are multidimensional. The production approach is regarded as the main approach through the strong emphasis on industrial breakdown. The expenditure approach is also much used through the supporting use of the commodity-flow method. The income approach has played a minor, although now increasing, role. The product dimension is a very strong element in the Norwegian approach, due to the long presence of annual Supply and Use Tables (SUT) being integrated in the national accounts.

Expenditure Approach

The expenditure approach is used to estimate all components of gross domestic product by expenditure type. Changes in inventories, however, are primarily calculated as the difference between supply and other uses for each commodity, since structural business statistics so far have been less suitable for changes in inventories.

Government final consumption expenditure is mainly based on government accounts. Central government accounts and local government accounts are used as for output, also for fees. In a few cases, government purchases from non-government producers, recorded as government final consumption expenditure, mean that government output is lower than government consumption on particular products. From 2001, a new statistical system for the collection of information about the activity in local government (KOSTRA) has been implemented and utilized.

Household final consumption expenditure is estimated from household consumer surveys (HBS); retail trade statistics, and a third group consisting of output figures, selected indicators and the commodity-flow method. It is interplay between these three source elements, and since the 1995 revision more use than before has been made of HBS data in current estimations (taking into account averages for smoother time series).

For NPISH final consumption expenditure, mainly central government accounts and local government accounts are used (thus as indirect sources since grants or transfers to NPISHs are recorded here), while supplemented by HBS in particular for deducting fees from households.

Gross fixed capital formation has two main dimensions in terms of breakdowns, one by type of assets, and one by kind of activity (industries). The estimation of gross fixed capital formation is first directed at the use of industry-related sources, such as the SBS-based statistics, and the expenditure approach, while the commodity flow approach takes a substantive role in the next phases. Exports and imports of goods are based on external trade statistics.

Exports and imports of services were previously based on foreign exchange statistics from the Bank of Norway, maritime transport statistics, oil and gas activity statistics and tourist/travel statistics. An important new source to replace the foreign exchange statistics from 2005 is the UT-statistics, i.e. reporting of balance of payments data from non-financial enterprises through quarterly and annual surveys.

For the constant price estimates, double deflation and the commodity-flow approach are used within the framework of detailed annual supply and use tables for all expenditure components. Current values are deflated by appropriate price indices. Household final consumption expenditure is adjusted to reflect the change in the CPI for the product in question. This will lead to adjustments of the current price values for trade margins and the basic prices of household consumption. Exports and imports of goods are mainly base don unit value indices from the external trade statistics, to which a thorough price fluctuation analysis is carried out in order to determine price-homogeneous goods.

Income Approach

Compensation of employees is estimated mainly from structural business statistics, government accounts, and sometimes from an indicator-based approach using wages and employment data. Register of Wages and Salaries has also become a most useful source. The estimation of compensation of employees is closely linked to the estimation of employment. Mixed income is estimated from the accounting statistics of self-employed. Operating surplus is arrived at as a residual, sometimes though being evaluated to have repercussions back on output, intermediate consumption and thus value added in industries involved. Consumption of fixed capital is estimated by using the perpetual inventory method. Time series of gross investment at constant prices and parameters needed provide the basis for calculating consumption of fixed capital. Taxes and subsidies on production are estimated from government accounts.

Production Approach

The production approach is used to estimate value added of almost all industries. This is done within the framework of detailed supply and use tables and using the commodity-flow method. More emphasis has been taken in utilizing accounting data. With the structural business statistics – a main source now for the NA compilation according to the production approach – use is made of a complete set of statements from large enterprises to the tax authorities. For the other enterprises, sales figures and other essential accounting data have been obtained from annual accounts in the Norwegian Register of Company Accounts.

Agricultural production is estimated from data prepared by the Budgeting Committee for Agriculture. A similar but less comprehensive source is used for forestry. Sources for fishing are catch statistics, annual census data for fish farming and cost surveys. For mining and quarrying, most important are oil and gas activity statistics (census-type), which include crude oil and natural gas production in the North Sea. For manufacturing, the annual industrial statistics have been replaced by the enterprise-based Structural Business Statistics, but supplemented also with connected establishment data. For electricity and water, sources are electricity statistics and local government accounts, respectively. The annual statistics of construction (SBS-based source from 1996) give information on the value of production, cost of materials and gross fixed capital formation.

The estimates for wholesale and retail trade are based on annual wholesale and retail statistics (SBS-based), while two sets of sample surveys on trade margins have also been useful. SBS data are now used also for hotels and restaurants, and for all parts of transport and communication. Summary accounts for financial institutions including insurance exist in the annual credit market statistics. The production of rental services is distributed among production of paid rent (market output) and imputed rent by owner-occupiers (production for own use). Housing statistics of various kinds, also HBS and quarterly surveys of actual rents are used for dwelling services. Business services are estimated from annual production statistics, now a SBS-type source. For government services, data are obtained from the local government accounts and central government accounts including social insurance administration, and the reporting system KOSTRA. Private services are partly estimated from SBS-based statistics, partly from other accounting statistics and other sources. In several instances, household budget surveys have been taken into account, used directly for paid services in households.

For the estimation of constant prices, double deflation and the commodity-flow approach are used within the framework of detailed annual supply and use tables. Output and intermediate consumption is deflated by appropriate price indices. Different kinds of price indices are used, such as producer price indices, consumer price indices, price indices for exports and imports, etc. In the production approach, for each of about 1000 products, three price indices are developed, one for output to the domestic market, one for output for exports and one for imports. These different price indices (at different valuations) are stored in the "Price Relative Catalogue", which is used to compare the various price indices at the detailed product level. Balancing is carried out after conversion of all flows to basic prices. Non-market output is deflated by input methods, but research into output measures is ongoing. Hedonic indices are used for lorries, tractors, washing machines, computers and new dwellings.

Table 1.1 Gross domestic product by expenditures at current prices

Series 300: 1993 SNA, Norwegian krone, Western calendar year **Data in millions**

	2001	2002	2003	2004	2005	2006	2007	2008	2009	2010	2011	2012
Series	**300**											
	Expenditures of the gross domestic product											
Final consumption expenditure	984536.0	1037405.0	1098310.0	1161966.0	1220319.0	1303796.0	1396360.0	1491088.0	1558396.0	1648422.0	1722515.0	1794476.0
Household final consumption expenditure	640826.0	669722.0	709860.0	757368.0	798211.0	853328.0	911319.0	958086.0	979235.0	1040627.0	1079392.0	1119843.0
NPISHs final consumption expenditure	26738.0	28304.0	30909.0	33025.0	36413.0	38686.0	40737.0	44561.0	48479.0	49326.0	52340.0	55149.0
General government final consumption expenditure	316972.0	339379.0	357541.0	371573.0	385695.0	411782.0	444304.0	488441.0	530682.0	558469.0	590783.0	619484.0
Individual consumption expenditure	194937.0	210304.0	228282.0	240797.0	256349.0	274472.0	292861.0	320887.0	346461.0	365633.0	388072.0	408703.0
Collective consumption expenditure	122035.0	129075.0	129259.0	130776.0	129346.0	137310.0	151443.0	167554.0	184221.0	192836.0	202712.0	210782.0
Gross capital formation	291970.0	289848.0	287983.0	355968.0	420359.0	501710.0	594863.0	627079.0	530472.0	592192.0	662627.0	728150.0
Gross fixed capital formation	278849.0	273940.0	276727.0	319520.0	376107.0	433103.0	513771.0	542277.0	515580.0	481985.0	536754.0	598017.0
Changes in inventories	13121.0	15908.0	11256.0	36448.0	44252.0	68607.0	81092.0	84802.0	14892.0	110207.0	125872.0	130133.0
Acquisitions less disposals of valuables	...	...	...	...	...	...	...	...	...	...	...	...
Exports of goods and services	703348.0	630235.0	642153.0	732659.0	863705.0	989465.0	1017589.0	1197090.0	953870.0	1029969.0	1140919.0	1182974.0
Exports of goods	531174.0	468735.0	481779.0	555141.0	666751.0	780308.0	792648.0	955641.0	729867.0	779027.0	892429.0	923640.0
Exports of services	172174.0	161500.0	160374.0	177518.0	196954.0	209157.0	224941.0	241449.0	224003.0	250942.0	248490.0	259334.0
Less: Imports of goods and services	442967.0	425181.0	436245.0	497781.0	545476.0	614170.0	702367.0	755343.0	660408.0	726317.0	776098.0	798785.0
Imports of goods	294576.0	278941.0	288635.0	334951.0	364539.0	420844.0	479533.0	514603.0	444043.0	477213.0	520974.0	526041.0

	2001	2002	2003	2004	2005	2006	2007	2008	2009	2010	2011	2012
Series	**300**											
Imports of services	148391.0	146240.0	147610.0	162830.0	180937.0	193326.0	222834.0	240740.0	216365.0	249104.0	255124.0	272744.0
Equals: GROSS DOMESTIC PRODUCT	1536887.0	1532307.0	1592201.0	1752812.0	1958907.0	2180801.0	2306445.0	2559914.0	2382330.0	2544266.0	2749963.0	2906814.0

Table 1.2 Gross domestic product by expenditures at constant prices

Series 300: 1993 SNA, Norwegian krone, Western calendar year

Data in millions

	2001	2002	2003	2004	2005	2006	2007	2008	2009	2010	2011	2012
Series	**300**											
Base year	**2005**											
	Expenditures of the gross domestic product											
Final consumption expenditure	1071743.0	1105355.0	1133779.0	1179730.0	1220319.0	1269193.0	1326956.0	1354661.0	1374021.0	1414042.0	1446106.0	1483678.0
Household final consumption expenditure	682322.0	703771.0	725489.0	764992.0	798211.0	839139.0	887033.0	902627.0	901211.0	937608.0	960977.0	990335.0
NPISHs final consumption expenditure	29973.0	30865.0	32627.0	34428.0	36413.0	36957.0	36460.0	37589.0	39210.0	38434.0	39376.0	40120.0
General government final consumption expenditure	359928.0	371210.0	376016.0	380386.0	385695.0	393097.0	403745.0	414533.0	432263.0	437804.0	445826.0	453871.0
Individual consumption expenditure	223050.0	231490.0	239322.0	245677.0	256349.0	261345.0	265646.0	270749.0	279806.0	283620.0	289996.0	295648.0
Collective consumption expenditure	136875.0	139746.0	136800.0	134782.0	129346.0	131752.0	138120.0	143817.0	152535.0	154258.0	155868.0	158249.0
Gross capital formation	324634.0	322996.0	316649.0	376482.0	420359.0	472985.0	516913.0	515317.0	427705.0	445191.0	475066.0	502235.0
Gross fixed capital formation	299242.0	295851.0	298124.0	331362.0	376107.0	413061.0	460113.0	460910.0	426161.0	391949.0	421569.0	455419.0
Changes in inventories	26058.0	29409.0	14987.0	46364.0	44252.0	59924.0	57532.0	55597.0	12504.0	65469.0	67438.0	64180.0
Acquisitions less disposals of valuables	...	...	...	...	...	...	...	...	...	...	...	...
Exports of goods and services	854350.0	852023.0	851057.0	859812.0	863705.0	856744.0	868401.0	869550.0	832663.0	836161.0	821111.0	835495.0
Exports of goods	659967.0	664592.0	673512.0	671840.0	666751.0	654367.0	663540.0	667670.0	638775.0	618587.0	599482.0	604918.0
Exports of services	194730.0	188352.0	180182.0	188948.0	196954.0	202377.0	204820.0	201553.0	193686.0	217096.0	221874.0	231279.0
Less: Imports of goods and services	450543.0	455021.0	460624.0	505466.0	545476.0	594984.0	654602.0	679862.0	595048.0	648834.0	673485.0	689610.0
Imports of goods	283042.0	288031.0	298603.0	337439.0	364539.0	404106.0	442770.0	454836.0	398710.0	427969.0	447559.0	448603.0
Imports of services	169266.0	168366.0	162607.0	168035.0	180937.0	190878.0	211884.0	225230.0	196480.0	221096.0	226201.0	241188.0
Equals: GROSS DOMESTIC PRODUCT	1791961.0	1818878.0	1836719.0	1909472.0	1958907.0	2003938.0	2057103.0	2058493.0	2024839.0	2034520.0	2059297.0	2122956.0

Table 1.3 Relations among product, income, savings, and net lending aggregates

Series 300: 1993 SNA, Norwegian krone, Western calendar year

Data in millions

	2001	2002	2003	2004	2005	2006	2007	2008	2009	2010	2011	2012
Series	**300**											
GROSS DOMESTIC PRODUCT	1536887.0	1532307.0	1592201.0	1752812.0	1958907.0	2180801.0	2306445.0	2559914.0	2382330.0	2544266.0	2749963.0	2906814.0
Plus: Compensation of employees - from and to the rest of the world, net	...	...	...	...	...	...	...	...	...	...	...	...
Plus: Property income - from and to the rest of the world, net	...	...	...	...	...	...	...	...	...	...	...	...
Sum of Compensation of employees and property income - from and to the rest of the world, net	1370.0	4701.0	9905.0	3356.0	21772.0	1565.0	-7271.0	-11813.0	13467.0	29956.0	15383.0	58429.0

	2001	2002	2003	2004	2005	2006	2007	2008	2009	2010	2011	2012
Series	**300**											
Plus: Sum of Compensation of employees and property income - from the rest of the world	86984.0	82089.0	99604.0	115143.0	168867.0	197849.0	247318.0	249161.0	172230.0	212052.0	209321.0	270049.0
Less: Sum of Compensation of employees and property income - to the rest of the world	85614.0	77388.0	89699.0	111787.0	147095.0	196284.0	254589.0	260974.0	158763.0	182096.0	193938.0	211620.0
Plus: Taxes less subsidies on production and imports - from and to the rest of the world, net	...	...	...	...	...	...	...	...	...	...	...	...
Equals: GROSS NATIONAL INCOME	1538257.0	1537008.0	1602106.0	1756168.0	1980679.0	2182366.0	2299174.0	2548101.0	2395797.0	2574222.0	2765346.0	2965243.0
Plus: Current transfers - from and to the rest of the world, net	-14222.0	-17427.0	-20594.0	-17625.0	-17157.0	-19116.0	-20515.0	-21648.0	-27645.0	-30430.0	-28768.0	-29442.0
Plus: Current transfers - from the rest of the world	16312.0	14934.0	14511.0	17194.0	22233.0	16963.0	18931.0	19693.0	20245.0	20270.0	20977.0	22711.0
Less: Current transfers - to the rest of the world	30534.0	32361.0	35105.0	34819.0	39390.0	36079.0	39446.0	41341.0	47890.0	50700.0	49745.0	52153.0
Equals: GROSS NATIONAL DISPOSABLE INCOME	1524035.0	1519581.0	1581512.0	1738543.0	1963522.0	2163250.0	2278659.0	2526453.0	2368152.0	2543792.0	2736578.0	2935801.0
Less: Final consumption expenditure / Actual final consumption	984536.0	1037405.0	1098310.0	1161966.0	1220319.0	1303796.0	1396360.0	1491088.0	1558396.0	1648422.0	1722515.0	1794476.0
Equals: SAVING, GROSS	539499.0	482176.0	483202.0	576577.0	743203.0	859454.0	882299.0	1035365.0	809756.0	895370.0	1014063.0	1141325.0
Plus: Capital transfers - from and to the rest of the world, net	-840.0	-1490.0	4717.0	-1021.0	-1878.0	-919.0	-971.0	-1138.0	-1120.0	-1268.0	-1499.0	-1279.0
Plus: Capital transfers - from the rest of the world	934.0	310.0	6739.0	720.0	0.0	0.0	0.0	0.0	0.0	0.0	0.0	0.0
Less: Capital transfers - to the rest of the world	1774.0	1800.0	2022.0	1741.0	1878.0	919.0	971.0	1138.0	1120.0	1268.0	1499.0	1279.0
Less: Gross capital formation	291970.0	289848.0	287983.0	355968.0	420359.0	501710.0	594863.0	627079.0	530472.0	592192.0	662627.0	728150.0
Less: Acquisitions less disposals of non-produced non-financial assets	-25.0	-27.0	5.0	7.0	70.0	80.0	29.0	25.0	294.0	293.0	275.0	280.0
Equals: NET LENDING (+) / NET BORROWING (-) OF THE NATION	246714.0	190865.0	199931.0	219581.0	320896.0	356745.0	286436.0	407123.0	277870.0	301617.0	349662.0	411617.0
	Net values: Gross National Income / Gross National Disposable Income / Saving Gross less Consumption of fixed capital											
Less: Consumption of fixed capital	213687.0	217781.0	221731.0	230785.0	245179.0	265258.0	293245.0	325080.0	350172.0	363567.0	380777.0	400197.0
Equals: NET NATIONAL INCOME	1324570.0	1319227.0	1380375.0	1525383.0	1735500.0	1917108.0	2005929.0	2223021.0	2045625.0	2210655.0	2384569.0	2565046.0
Equals: NET NATIONAL DISPOSABLE INCOME	1310348.0	1301800.0	1359781.0	1507758.0	1718343.0	1897992.0	1985414.0	2201373.0	2017980.0	2180225.0	2355801.0	2535604.0
Equals: SAVING, NET	325812.0	264395.0	261471.0	345792.0	498024.0	594196.0	589054.0	710285.0	459584.0	531803.0	633286.0	741128.0

Table 2.4 Value added by industries at current prices (ISIC Rev. 4)

Series 300: 1993 SNA, Norwegian krone, Western calendar year **Data in millions**

	2001	2002	2003	2004	2005	2006	2007	2008	2009	2010	2011	2012
Series	**300**											
	Industries											
Agriculture, forestry and fishing	24625.0	23570.0	21086.0	24600.0	27275.0	29770.0	26918.0	27371.0	29083.0	37865.0	34716.0	30034.0
Manufacturing, mining and quarrying and other industrial activities	485775.0	448450.0	467834.0	541274.0	662881.0	771966.0	747332.0	915883.0	700925.0	766060.0	896575.0	951910.0
Manufacturing	133810.0	132933.0	137283.0	146216.0	156675.0	177882.0	187513.0	194508.0	170973.0	179091.0	189854.0	199132.0
Construction	56588.0	61685.0	65253.0	74608.0	84088.0	98528.0	116106.0	123812.0	121389.0	122932.0	135144.0	152582.0
Wholesale and retail trade, transportation and storage, accommodation and food service activities	240490.0	234783.0	235263.0	250112.0	266099.0	290082.0	318608.0	334230.0	316822.0	332614.0	322905.0	324657.0

	2001	2002	2003	2004	2005	2006	2007	2008	2009	2010	2011	2012
Series	**300**											
Information and communication	50682.0	55847.0	58703.0	64366.0	69201.0	71316.0	76612.0	78213.0	81875.0	86939.0	89998.0	93487.0
Financial and insurance activities	40737.0	41612.0	55774.0	66699.0	68379.0	65545.0	77941.0	83421.0	97194.0	101344.0	101473.0	113763.0
Real estate activities	101540.0	109330.0	112424.0	117559.0	124044.0	134454.0	143132.0	149363.0	156934.0	164321.0	172692.0	180433.0
Professional, scientific, technical, administrative and support service activities	73082.0	75399.0	77990.0	83706.0	95215.0	110218.0	133372.0	148441.0	148868.0	156073.0	174474.0	194671.0
Public administration and defence, education, human health and social work activities	250606.0	264955.0	280268.0	295268.0	311372.0	332044.0	363217.0	398909.0	426796.0	449778.0	481936.0	508574.0
Other service activities	30057.0	33014.0	33095.0	34913.0	35844.0	37961.0	38395.0	39637.0	41161.0	42694.0	45006.0	47873.0
Equals: VALUE ADDED, GROSS, at basic prices	1354182.0	1348645.0	1407690.0	1553105.0	1744398.0	1941884.0	2041633.0	2299280.0	2121047.0	2260620.0	2454918.0	2597984.0
Less: Financial intermediation services indirectly measured (FISIM)	...	...	...	...	...	...	...	...	...	...	...	...
Plus: Taxes less Subsidies on products	182705.0	183662.0	184511.0	199707.0	214509.0	238917.0	264812.0	260634.0	261283.0	283646.0	295079.0	308890.0
Plus: Taxes on products	189964.0	190693.0	192285.0	206870.0	222787.0	246904.0	268257.0	264481.0	265362.0	287420.0	298712.0	312406.0
Less: Subsidies on products	7259.0	7031.0	7774.0	7163.0	8278.0	7987.0	3445.0	3847.0	4079.0	3774.0	3632.0	3515.0
Plus: Statistical discrepancy	0.0	0.0	0.0	0.0	0.0	0.0	0.0	0.0	0.0	0.0	-34.0	-60.0
Equals: GROSS DOMESTIC PRODUCT	1536887.0	1532307.0	1592201.0	1752812.0	1958907.0	2180801.0	2306445.0	2559914.0	2382330.0	2544266.0	2749963.0	2906814.0

Table 2.5 Value added by industries at constant prices (ISIC Rev. 4)

Series 300: 1993 SNA, Norwegian krone, Western calendar year

Data in millions

	2001	2002	2003	2004	2005	2006	2007	2008	2009	2010	2011	2012
Series	**300**											
Base year	**2005**											
Industries												
Agriculture, forestry and fishing	22854.0	24908.0	24511.0	27295.0	27275.0	27672.0	29011.0	30582.0	30116.0	32479.0	32417.0	34975.0
Manufacturing, mining and quarrying and other industrial activities	638250.0	643495.0	643613.0	663463.0	662881.0	640100.0	623853.0	616681.0	597851.0	580217.0	569507.0	583780.0
Manufacturing	139811.0	138670.0	143185.0	150487.0	156675.0	160543.0	165812.0	170668.0	158850.0	162145.0	165328.0	169344.0
Construction	73749.0	74971.0	77876.0	80627.0	84088.0	90467.0	99755.0	101134.0	94072.0	91404.0	94229.0	101077.0
Wholesale and retail trade, transportation and storage, accommodation and food service activities	244495.0	246204.0	249072.0	259192.0	266099.0	281740.0	290649.0	281408.0	274420.0	283004.0	290108.0	299011.0
Information and communication	50541.0	53308.0	55866.0	64373.0	69201.0	71724.0	76724.0	78260.0	82277.0	88253.0	91421.0	94045.0
Financial and insurance activities	51981.0	52689.0	58628.0	63412.0	68379.0	75317.0	81669.0	81446.0	81314.0	80958.0	81063.0	84607.0
Real estate activities	116389.0	119421.0	118513.0	122331.0	124044.0	129581.0	136011.0	137882.0	141962.0	143749.0	145212.0	147162.0
Professional, scientific, technical, administrative and support service activities	83549.0	82538.0	82116.0	86390.0	95215.0	108026.0	117825.0	122778.0	118674.0	120638.0	129076.0	137974.0
Public administration and defence, education, human health and social work activities	294782.0	295683.0	298916.0	303599.0	311372.0	315083.0	328449.0	338671.0	343022.0	347714.0	356186.0	362918.0
Other service activities	36421.0	38047.0	36202.0	35503.0	35844.0	36288.0	34976.0	35276.0	34715.0	34473.0	34976.0	36048.0
Equals: VALUE ADDED, GROSS, at basic prices	1606944.0	1625958.0	1640763.0	1703252.0	1744398.0	1775998.0	1813513.0	1817837.0	1788193.0	1791216.0	1811310.0	1868596.0
Less: Financial intermediation services indirectly measured (FISIM)	...	...	...	...	...	...	...	...	...	...	...	...

	2001	2002	2003	2004	2005	2006	2007	2008	2009	2010	2011	2012
Series	**300**											
Base year	**2005**											
Plus: Taxes less Subsidies on products	186230.0	193429.0	196325.0	206386.0	214509.0	227940.0	244880.0	241820.0	237778.0	244881.0	249737.0	256048.0
Plus: Taxes on products	193094.0	200222.0	203274.0	214623.0	222787.0	236256.0	249269.0	246318.0	242353.0	249961.0	254861.0	261314.0
Less: Subsidies on products	6992.0	6945.0	7099.0	8268.0	8278.0	8316.0	3988.0	4143.0	4249.0	4797.0	4809.0	4949.0
Plus: Statistical discrepancy	0.0	0.0	0.0	0.0	0.0	0.0	-844.0	0.0	0.0	0.0	...	0.0
Equals: GROSS DOMESTIC PRODUCT	1791961.0	1818878.0	1836719.0	1909472.0	1958907.0	2003938.0	2057103.0	2058493.0	2024839.0	2034520.0	2059297.0	2122956.0

Table 2.6 Output, gross value added and fixed assets by industries at current prices (ISIC Rev. 4) Total economy

Series 300: 1993 SNA, Norwegian krone, Western calendar year **Data in millions**

	2001	2002	2003	2004	2005	2006	2007	2008	2009	2010	2011	2012
Series	**300**											
Output, at basic prices	2540106.0	2542660.0	2630471.0	2870617.0	3182537.0	3578160.0	3902125.0	4337764.0	4050121.0	4241588.0	4577950.0	4851190.0
Less: Intermediate consumption, at purchaser's prices	1185924.0	1194015.0	1222781.0	1317512.0	1438139.0	1636276.0	1860492.0	2038484.0	1929074.0	1980968.0	2123032.0	2245034.0
Equals: VALUE ADDED, GROSS, at basic prices	1354182.0	1348645.0	1407690.0	1553105.0	1744398.0	1941884.0	2041633.0	2299280.0	2121047.0	2260620.0	2454918.0	2597984.0
Compensation of employees	678191.0	710181.0	730049.0	765896.0	813424.0	888629.0	986652.0	1085627.0	1117374.0	1148379.0	1223483.0	1303193.0
Taxes on production and imports, less Subsidies	-10991.0	-13578.0	-15661.0	-15520.0	-15413.0	-13767.0	-16402.0	-19215.0	-23360.0	-27519.0	-27843.0	-30132.0
OPERATING SURPLUS, GROSS [a]	686982.0	652042.0	693302.0	802729.0	946387.0	1067022.0	1071383.0	1232868.0	1027033.0	1139760.0	1259278.0	1324923.0
MIXED INCOME, GROSS	...	...	...	...	...	...	...	...	...	...	...	...
Less: Consumption of fixed capital	213687.0	217781.0	221731.0	230785.0	245179.0	265258.0	293245.0	325080.0	350172.0	363567.0	380777.0	400197.0
OPERATING SURPLUS, NET	473295.0	434261.0	471571.0	571944.0	701208.0	801764.0	778138.0	907788.0	676861.0	776193.0	878501.0	924726.0
MIXED INCOME, NET	...	...	...	...	...	...	...	...	...	...	...	...
Gross capital formation	291970.0	289848.0	287983.0	355968.0	420359.0	501710.0	594863.0	627079.0	530472.0	592192.0	662627.0	728150.0
Gross fixed capital formation	278849.0	273940.0	276727.0	319520.0	376107.0	433103.0	513771.0	542277.0	515580.0	481985.0	536754.0	598017.0
Changes in inventories	13121.0	15908.0	11256.0	36448.0	44252.0	68607.0	81092.0	84802.0	14892.0	110207.0	125872.0	130133.0
Acquisitions less disposals of valuables	...	...	...	...	...	...	...	...	...	...	...	...
Employment (average, in 1000 persons)	2328.0	2337.0	2309.0	2320.0	2350.0	2432.0	2532.0	2615.0	2604.0	2590.0	2625.0	2682.0

[a] Includes Mixed Income, Gross.

Table 2.6 Output, gross value added and fixed assets by industries at current prices (ISIC Rev. 4) Agriculture, forestry and fishing (A)

Series 300: 1993 SNA, Norwegian krone, Western calendar year **Data in millions**

	2001	2002	2003	2004	2005	2006	2007	2008	2009	2010	2011	2012
Series	**300**											
Equals: VALUE ADDED, GROSS, at basic prices	24625.0	23570.0	21086.0	24600.0	27275.0	29770.0	26918.0	27371.0	29083.0	37865.0	34716.0	30034.0
Compensation of employees	5960.0	6047.0	6011.0	6013.0	6177.0	6620.0	7066.0	7680.0	7841.0	8592.0	9112.0	9162.0
Employment (average, in 1000 persons)	91.0	88.0	84.0	81.0	77.0	75.0	73.0	72.0	70.0	69.0	68.0	66.0

Table 2.6 Output, gross value added and fixed assets by industries at current prices (ISIC Rev. 4) Manufacturing, mining and quarrying and other industrial activities (B+C+D+E)

Series 300: 1993 SNA, Norwegian krone, Western calendar year **Data in millions**

	2001	2002	2003	2004	2005	2006	2007	2008	2009	2010	2011	2012
Series	**300**											
Equals: VALUE ADDED, GROSS, at basic prices	485775.0	448450.0	467834.0	541274.0	662881.0	771966.0	747332.0	915883.0	700925.0	766060.0	896575.0	951910.0
Compensation of employees	121993.0	127359.0	127173.0	132125.0	142500.0	159112.0	176294.0	193587.0	194818.0	195184.0	206829.0	220933.0
Employment (average, in 1000 persons)	325.0	322.0	311.0	302.0	308.0	327.0	341.0	350.0	340.0	331.0	334.0	340.0

Table 2.6 Output, gross value added and fixed assets by industries at current prices (ISIC Rev. 4) Manufacturing (C)

Series 300: 1993 SNA, Norwegian krone, Western calendar year **Data in millions**

	2001	2002	2003	2004	2005	2006	2007	2008	2009	2010	2011	2012
Series	**300**											
Equals: VALUE ADDED, GROSS, at basic prices	133810.0	132933.0	137283.0	146216.0	156675.0	177882.0	187513.0	194508.0	170973.0	179091.0	189854.0	199132.0
Compensation of employees	91414.0	94189.0	92694.0	95397.0	101833.0	114998.0	123636.0	131243.0	125827.0	123504.0	128297.0	134173.0
Employment (average, in 1000 persons)	267.0	262.0	251.0	241.0	245.0	259.0	265.0	270.0	258.0	247.0	246.0	248.0

Table 2.6 Output, gross value added and fixed assets by industries at current prices (ISIC Rev. 4) Construction (F)

Series 300: 1993 SNA, Norwegian krone, Western calendar year **Data in millions**

	2001	2002	2003	2004	2005	2006	2007	2008	2009	2010	2011	2012
Series	**300**											
Equals: VALUE ADDED, GROSS, at basic prices	56588.0	61685.0	65253.0	74608.0	84088.0	98528.0	116106.0	123812.0	121389.0	122932.0	135144.0	152582.0
Compensation of employees	41386.0	44152.0	47908.0	50361.0	54993.0	62365.0	72593.0	81153.0	80135.0	81008.0	86964.0	94331.0
Employment (average, in 1000 persons)	138.0	142.0	152.0	155.0	163.0	177.0	193.0	199.0	190.0	187.0	193.0	201.0

Table 2.6 Output, gross value added and fixed assets by industries at current prices (ISIC Rev. 4) Wholesale and retail trade, transportation and storage, accommodation and food service activities (G+H+I)

Series 300: 1993 SNA, Norwegian krone, Western calendar year **Data in millions**

	2001	2002	2003	2004	2005	2006	2007	2008	2009	2010	2011	2012
Series	**300**											
Equals: VALUE ADDED, GROSS, at basic prices	240490.0	234783.0	235263.0	250112.0	266099.0	290082.0	318608.0	334230.0	316822.0	332614.0	322905.0	324657.0
Compensation of employees	156136.0	161713.0	164763.0	172546.0	180318.0	191125.0	209223.0	227401.0	229033.0	234082.0	245656.0	258294.0
Employment (average, in 1000 persons)	583.0	586.0	577.0	583.0	591.0	596.0	621.0	642.0	633.0	625.0	627.0	637.0

Table 2.6 Output, gross value added and fixed assets by industries at current prices (ISIC Rev. 4) Information and communication (J)

Series 300: 1993 SNA, Norwegian krone, Western calendar year **Data in millions**

	2001	2002	2003	2004	2005	2006	2007	2008	2009	2010	2011	2012
Series	**300**											
Equals: VALUE ADDED, GROSS, at basic prices	50682.0	55847.0	58703.0	64366.0	69201.0	71316.0	76612.0	78213.0	81875.0	86939.0	89998.0	93487.0
Compensation of employees	38181.0	38708.0	36996.0	38409.0	40960.0	44208.0	49478.0	54393.0	55571.0	56635.0	60796.0	65787.0
Employment (average, in 1000 persons)	92.0	91.0	83.0	83.0	83.0	84.0	84.0	85.0	86.0	86.0	87.0	89.0

Table 2.6 Output, gross value added and fixed assets by industries at current prices (ISIC Rev. 4) Financial and insurance activities (K)

Series 300: 1993 SNA, Norwegian krone, Western calendar year **Data in millions**

	2001	2002	2003	2004	2005	2006	2007	2008	2009	2010	2011	2012
Series	**300**											
Equals: VALUE ADDED, GROSS, at basic prices	40737.0	41612.0	55774.0	66699.0	68379.0	65545.0	77941.0	83421.0	97194.0	101344.0	101473.0	113763.0
Compensation of employees	22300.0	23400.0	24056.0	25833.0	27440.0	29822.0	33733.0	37392.0	39146.0	39555.0	42343.0	44409.0
Employment (average, in 1000 persons)	50.0	50.0	49.0	49.0	47.0	48.0	49.0	50.0	53.0	52.0	52.0	52.0

Table 2.6 Output, gross value added and fixed assets by industries at current prices (ISIC Rev. 4) Real estate activities (L)

Series 300: 1993 SNA, Norwegian krone, Western calendar year **Data in millions**

	2001	2002	2003	2004	2005	2006	2007	2008	2009	2010	2011	2012
Series	**300**											
Equals: VALUE ADDED, GROSS, at basic prices	101540.0	109330.0	112424.0	117559.0	124044.0	134454.0	143132.0	149363.0	156934.0	164321.0	172692.0	180433.0
Compensation of employees	5634.0	5869.0	5965.0	6396.0	6967.0	7803.0	9371.0	10629.0	10582.0	10932.0	11842.0	12922.0
Employment (average, in 1000 persons)	16.0	17.0	17.0	18.0	18.0	19.0	22.0	24.0	23.0	23.0	23.0	24.0

Table 2.6 Output, gross value added and fixed assets by industries at current prices (ISIC Rev. 4) Professional, scientific, technical, administrative and support service activities (M+N)

Series 300: 1993 SNA, Norwegian krone, Western calendar year **Data in millions**

	2001	2002	2003	2004	2005	2006	2007	2008	2009	2010	2011	2012
Series	**300**											
Equals: VALUE ADDED, GROSS, at basic prices	73082.0	75399.0	77990.0	83706.0	95215.0	110218.0	133372.0	148441.0	148868.0	156073.0	174474.0	194671.0
Compensation of employees	53758.0	56303.0	57312.0	60901.0	67356.0	81430.0	94849.0	107206.0	107934.0	110893.0	119656.0	131601.0
Employment (average, in 1000 persons)	170.0	173.0	171.0	171.0	181.0	204.0	224.0	240.0	233.0	229.0	236.0	248.0

Table 2.6 Output, gross value added and fixed assets by industries at current prices (ISIC Rev. 4) Public administration and defence, education, human health and social work activities (O+P+Q)

Series 300: 1993 SNA, Norwegian krone, Western calendar year **Data in millions**

	2001	2002	2003	2004	2005	2006	2007	2008	2009	2010	2011	2012
Series	**300**											
Equals: VALUE ADDED, GROSS, at basic prices	250606.0	264955.0	280268.0	295268.0	311372.0	332044.0	363217.0	398909.0	426796.0	449778.0	481936.0	508574.0
Compensation of employees	215179.0	227869.0	240994.0	254005.0	266270.0	284783.0	311430.0	341099.0	365401.0	383808.0	411016.0	434714.0
Employment (average, in 1000 persons)	787.0	790.0	792.0	802.0	804.0	826.0	848.0	869.0	890.0	902.0	918.0	935.0

Table 2.6 Output, gross value added and fixed assets by industries at current prices (ISIC Rev. 4) Other service activities (R+S+T)

Series 300: 1993 SNA, Norwegian krone, Western calendar year **Data in millions**

	2001	2002	2003	2004	2005	2006	2007	2008	2009	2010	2011	2012
Series	**300**											
Equals: VALUE ADDED, GROSS, at basic prices	30057.0	33014.0	33095.0	34913.0	35844.0	37961.0	38395.0	39637.0	41161.0	42694.0	45006.0	47873.0
Compensation of employees	17664.0	18761.0	18871.0	19307.0	20443.0	21361.0	22615.0	25087.0	26913.0	27690.0	29268.0	31041.0
Employment (average, in 1000 persons)	77.0	78.0	74.0	76.0	77.0	76.0	78.0	84.0	87.0	87.0	88.0	89.0

Table 3.1 Government final consumption expenditure by function at current prices

Series 300: 1993 SNA, Norwegian krone, Western calendar year **Data in millions**

	2001	2002	2003	2004	2005	2006	2007	2008	2009	2010	2011	2012
Series	**300**											
General public services	33301.0	32364.1	32033.2	32335.0	32850.9	35696.4	39426.2	43150.0	48848.1	48138.6	50443.5	...
Defence	28544.4	30230.9	29861.8	30211.1	28101.6	28808.0	31593.7	33505.1	35761.8	36923.4	38211.4	...
Public order and safety	13232.7	15461.2	14862.2	15110.9	14272.6	15097.0	16463.6	18360.4	19854.6	22126.1	24026.5	...
Economic affairs	26209.1	27381.9	28236.1	29221.9	29979.8	31685.6	32429.4	37017.0	41109.1	45030.0	48027.3	...
Environment protection	1312.7	1285.0	1178.8	1201.2	1258.6	1373.9	1539.5	1823.8	2369.1	2378.9	2711.2	...
Housing and community amenities	1029.4	1267.5	1175.9	882.1	695.6	789.1	1033.3	1404.6	1663.1	1715.5	2077.4	...
Health	90137.0	100961.4	107944.8	112239.9	118051.5	124670.1	134488.6	144870.4	154530.2	163157.1	173041.9	...
Recreation, culture and religion	8969.9	9605.5	9527.2	9893.5	10342.9	10962.4	12032.9	13444.5	14641.4	15167.6	16425.4	...
Education	71087.8	75342.1	82751.1	84966.7	88903.1	93905.4	98313.6	106494.2	114660.9	120739.8	124388.4	...
Social protection	43148.4	45488.8	50027.5	55513.5	61254.0	68824.2	76921.7	88475.9	97585.9	103041.3	111208.2	...
Equals: General government final consumption expenditure	316972.4	339388.4	357598.6	371575.8	385710.6	411812.1	444242.5	488545.9	531024.2	558418.3	590561.2	619484.0

Table 3.2 Individual consumption expenditure of households, NPISHs, and general government at current prices

Series 300: 1993 SNA, Norwegian krone, Western calendar year — **Data in millions**

	2001	2002	2003	2004	2005	2006	2007	2008	2009	2010	2011	2012
Series	**300**											
	Individual consumption expenditure of households											
Food and non-alcoholic beverages	90541.0	92695.0	97001.0	99702.0	103588.0	107628.0	113819.0	121814.0	128752.0	132504.0	137621.0	...
Alcoholic beverages, tobacco and narcotics	29166.0	29863.0	31811.0	33893.0	34597.0	35703.0	37568.0	40695.0	42394.0	43132.0	44294.0	...
Clothing and footwear	36113.0	36995.0	38021.0	40380.0	42874.0	45567.0	50106.0	50921.0	52912.0	54854.0	55299.0	...
Housing, water, electricity, gas and other fuels	131341.0	139820.0	152051.0	155558.0	162728.0	175588.0	177747.0	192313.0	201155.0	222434.0	224812.0	...
Furnishings, household equipment and routine maintenance of the house	39550.0	41353.0	42071.0	43826.0	46404.0	49761.0	53636.0	55468.0	55374.0	58061.0	59215.0	...
Health	17650.0	18850.0	20305.0	21570.0	23041.0	23517.0	24565.0	26258.0	26929.0	27925.0	29115.0	...
Transport	92293.0	95300.0	97057.0	107862.0	113782.0	121926.0	137322.0	137513.0	132854.0	147167.0	155686.0	...
Communication	17208.0	18208.0	19673.0	23827.0	24817.0	25794.0	25843.0	26373.0	26801.0	27402.0	27177.0	...
Recreation and culture	81389.0	84803.0	90082.0	95489.0	99840.0	106681.0	114519.0	117551.0	119178.0	124469.0	128954.0	...
Education	3588.0	3784.0	2717.0	2737.0	2870.0	3093.0	3651.0	3657.0	4070.0	4449.0	4679.0	...
Restaurants and hotels	39271.0	40486.0	41003.0	41752.0	43497.0	48342.0	52378.0	57015.0	56834.0	58731.0	62711.0	...
Miscellaneous goods and services	54077.0	57956.0	64053.0	70635.0	76434.0	81749.0	92358.0	97293.0	100778.0	105303.0	107994.0	...
Equals: Household final consumption expenditure in domestic market	632187.0	660113.0	695845.0	737231.0	774472.0	825349.0	883512.0	926871.0	948031.0	1006431.0	1037555.0	...
Plus: Direct purchases abroad by residents	27258.0	27882.0	32790.0	41275.0	46255.0	52185.0	54059.0	58123.0	57328.0	62545.0	...	...
Less: Direct purchases in domestic market by non-residents	18619.0	18273.0	18775.0	21138.0	22516.0	24206.0	26252.0	26908.0	26124.0	28449.0	...	...
Equals: Household final consumption expenditure	640826.0	669722.0	709860.0	757368.0	798211.0	853328.0	911319.0	958086.0	979235.0	1040627.0	1079392.0	1119843.0
	Individual consumption expenditure of non-profit institutions serving households (NPISHs)											
Equals: NPISHs final consumption expenditure	26738.0	28304.0	30909.0	33025.0	36413.0	38686.0	40737.0	44561.0	48479.0	49326.0	52340.0	55149.0
	Individual consumption expenditure of general government											
Equals: Individual consumption expenditure of general government	194937.0	210304.0	228282.0	240797.0	256349.0	274472.0	292861.0	320887.0	346461.0	365633.0	388072.0	408703.0
Equals: Total actual individual consumption	862501.0	908330.0	969051.0	1031190.0	1090973.0	1166486.0	1244917.0	1323534.0	1374175.0	1455586.0	1519803.0	1583694.0

Table 4.1 Total Economy (S.1)

Series 300: 1993 SNA, Norwegian krone, Western calendar year — **Data in millions**

	2001	2002	2003	2004	2005	2006	2007	2008	2009	2010	2011	2012
Series	**300**											
	I. Production account - Resources											
Output, at basic prices (otherwise, please specify)	2540106.0	2542661.0	2630471.0	2870617.0	3182537.0	3578160.0	3902125.0	4337764.0	4050121.0	4241588.0	4577950.0	4851190.0
Less: Financial intermediation services indirectly measured (only to be deducted if FISIM is not distributed to uses)	...	...	...	...	...	...	...	...	...	...	...	...
Plus: Taxes less Subsidies on products	182705.0	183662.0	184511.0	199707.0	214509.0	238917.0	264812.0	260634.0	261283.0	283646.0	295079.0	308890.0

	2001	2002	2003	2004	2005	2006	2007	2008	2009	2010	2011	2012
Series	**300**											
Plus: Taxes on products	189964.0	190693.0	192285.0	206870.0	222787.0	246904.0	268257.0	264481.0	265362.0	287420.0	298712.0	312406.0
Less: Subsidies on products	7259.0	7031.0	7774.0	7163.0	8278.0	7987.0	3445.0	3847.0	4079.0	3774.0	3632.0	3515.0
I. Production account - Uses												
Intermediate consumption, at purchaser's prices	1185924.0	1194015.0	1222781.0	1317512.0	1438139.0	1636276.0	1860492.0	2038484.0	1929074.0	1980968.0	2123032.0	2245034.0
GROSS DOMESTIC PRODUCT	1536887.0	1532308.0	1592201.0	1752812.0	1958907.0	2180801.0	2306445.0	2559914.0	2382330.0	2544266.0	2749963.0	2915354.0
Less: Consumption of fixed capital	213687.0	217781.0	221731.0	230785.0	245179.0	265258.0	293245.0	325080.0	350172.0	363567.0	380776.0	399886.0
NET DOMESTIC PRODUCT	1323200.0	1314527.0	1370470.0	1522027.0	1713728.0	1915543.0	2013200.0	2234834.0	2032158.0	2180699.0	2369187.0	2515468.0
II.1.1 Generation of income account - Resources												
GROSS DOMESTIC PRODUCT	1536887.0	1532308.0	1592201.0	1752812.0	1958907.0	2180801.0	2306445.0	2559914.0	2382330.0	2544266.0	2749963.0	2915354.0
II.1.1 Generation of income account - Uses												
Compensation of employees	678191.0	710181.0	730049.0	765896.0	813424.0	888629.0	986652.0	1085627.0	1117374.0	1148379.0	1223483.0	1308069.0
Taxes on production and imports, less Subsidies	171714.0	170084.0	168850.0	184187.0	199096.0	225150.0	248410.0	241419.0	237923.0	256127.0	267203.0	279203.0
Taxes on production and imports	205893.0	205769.0	207439.0	222560.0	238999.0	265741.0	287916.0	285052.0	284920.0	306105.0	318180.0	333043.0
Taxes on products	189964.0	190693.0	192285.0	206870.0	222787.0	246904.0	268257.0	264481.0	265362.0	287420.0	298678.0	312797.0
Other taxes on production	15929.0	15076.0	15154.0	15690.0	16212.0	18837.0	19659.0	20571.0	19558.0	18685.0	19502.0	20246.0
Less: Subsidies	34179.0	35685.0	38589.0	38373.0	39903.0	40591.0	39506.0	43633.0	46997.0	49978.0	50977.0	53840.0
Subsidies on products	7259.0	7031.0	7774.0	7163.0	8278.0	7987.0	3445.0	3847.0	4079.0	3774.0	3632.0	3599.0
Other subsidies on production	26920.0	28654.0	30815.0	31210.0	31625.0	32604.0	36061.0	39786.0	42918.0	46204.0	47345.0	50241.0
OPERATING SURPLUS, GROSS	624267.0	586564.0	622243.0	734400.0	875247.0	994901.0	993938.0	1152311.0	945777.0	1052618.0	1166860.0	1232648.0
MIXED INCOME, GROSS	62715.0	65479.0	71059.0	68329.0	71140.0	72121.0	77445.0	80557.0	81256.0	87142.0	92418.0	95434.0
II.1.2 Allocation of primary income account - Resources												
OPERATING SURPLUS, GROSS	624267.0	586564.0	622243.0	734400.0	875247.0	994901.0	993938.0	1152311.0	945777.0	1052618.0	1166860.0	1232648.0
MIXED INCOME, GROSS	62715.0	65479.0	71059.0	68329.0	71140.0	72121.0	77445.0	80557.0	81256.0	87142.0	92418.0	95434.0
Compensation of employees	671506.0	705489.0	722700.0	757260.0	802678.0	875374.0	969408.0	1062960.0	1095188.0	1127614.0	1202963.0	1284277.0
Taxes on production and imports, less Subsidies	171714.0	170084.0	168850.0	184187.0	199096.0	225150.0	248410.0	241419.0	237923.0	256127.0	267203.0	279203.0
Taxes on production and imports	205893.0	205769.0	207439.0	222560.0	238999.0	265741.0	287916.0	285052.0	284920.0	306105.0	318180.0	333043.0
Taxes on products	189964.0	190693.0	192285.0	206870.0	222787.0	246904.0	268257.0	264481.0	265362.0	287420.0	298678.0	312797.0
Other taxes on production	15929.0	15076.0	15154.0	15690.0	16212.0	18837.0	19659.0	20571.0	19558.0	18685.0	19502.0	20246.0
Less: Subsidies	34179.0	35685.0	38589.0	38373.0	39903.0	40591.0	39506.0	43633.0	46997.0	49978.0	50977.0	53840.0
Subsidies on products	7259.0	7031.0	7774.0	7163.0	8278.0	7987.0	3445.0	3847.0	4079.0	3774.0	3632.0	3599.0
Other subsidies on production	26920.0	28654.0	30815.0	31210.0	31625.0	32604.0	36061.0	39786.0	42918.0	46204.0	47345.0	50241.0
Property income	553758.0	553986.0	559189.0	527565.0	702588.0	736961.0	877435.0	1088328.0	758570.0	776591.0	854848.0	912789.0
II.1.2 Allocation of primary income account - Uses												
Property income	545703.0	544593.0	541935.0	515573.0	670070.0	722142.0	867462.0	1077474.0	722917.0	725870.0	818945.0	830568.0
GROSS NATIONAL INCOME	1538257.0	1537008.0	1602106.0	1756168.0	1980679.0	2182366.0	2299174.0	2548101.0	2395797.0	2574222.0	2765346.0	2973783.0
II.2 Secondary distribution of income account - Resources												
GROSS NATIONAL INCOME	1538257.0	1537008.0	1602106.0	1756168.0	1980679.0	2182366.0	2299174.0	2548101.0	2395797.0	2574222.0	2765346.0	2973783.0
Current taxes on income, wealth, etc.	309732.0	302181.0	309318.0	366155.0	433169.0	492368.0	493759.0	564952.0	478476.0	532391.0	588226.0	614591.0
Social contributions	180195.0	192647.0	196692.0	207172.0	218215.0	241136.0	267138.0	308170.0	311750.0	318080.0	340500.0	367556.0
Social benefits other than social transfers in kind	235134.0	247140.0	272511.0	281112.0	287143.0	296311.0	309694.0	340719.0	367953.0	386430.0	411175.0	432508.0

	2001	2002	2003	2004	2005	2006	2007	2008	2009	2010	2011	2012
Series	**300**											
Other current transfers	148670.0	149372.0	140660.0	145949.0	156694.0	159336.0	212611.0	210397.0	216455.0	207085.0	229422.0	217453.0
	II.2 Secondary distribution of income account - Uses											
Current taxes on income, wealth, etc.	309051.0	301931.0	309262.0	366067.0	431473.0	491063.0	491577.0	561565.0	477138.0	530768.0	586063.0	611853.0
Social contributions	180195.0	192647.0	196692.0	207172.0	217649.0	240375.0	266088.0	306721.0	310295.0	317008.0	339311.0	366154.0
Social benefits other than social transfers in kind	234996.0	247049.0	272338.0	281145.0	287140.0	296304.0	309689.0	340710.0	367944.0	386441.0	411171.0	432496.0
Other current transfers	163708.0	167140.0	161483.0	163629.0	176116.0	180526.0	236363.0	236890.0	246902.0	240199.0	261546.0	251048.0
GROSS DISPOSABLE INCOME	1524038.0	1519581.0	1581512.0	1738543.0	1963522.0	2163249.0	2278659.0	2526453.0	2368152.0	2543792.0	2736578.0	2944340.0
	II.4.1 Use of disposable income account - Resources											
GROSS DISPOSABLE INCOME	1524038.0	1519581.0	1581512.0	1738543.0	1963522.0	2163249.0	2278659.0	2526453.0	2368152.0	2543792.0	2736578.0	2944340.0
Adjustment for the change in net equity of households on pension funds	12269.0	19426.0	15276.0	16336.0	15399.0	21713.0	27685.0	37342.0	33979.0	31450.0	33858.0	41568.0
	II.4.1 Use of disposable income account - Uses											
Final consumption expenditure	984536.0	1037405.0	1098310.0	1161966.0	1220319.0	1303796.0	1396360.0	1491088.0	1558396.0	1648422.0	1722516.0	1800843.0
Individual consumption expenditure	862501.0	908330.0	969051.0	1031190.0	1090973.0	1166486.0	1244917.0	1323534.0	1374175.0	1455586.0	1519804.0	1587769.0
Collective consumption expenditure	122035.0	129075.0	129259.0	130776.0	129346.0	137310.0	151443.0	167554.0	184221.0	192836.0	202712.0	213074.0
Adjustment for the change in net equity of households on pension funds	12269.0	19426.0	15276.0	16336.0	15399.0	21713.0	27685.0	37342.0	33979.0	31450.0	33858.0	41568.0
SAVING, GROSS	539502.0	482176.0	483202.0	576577.0	743203.0	859453.0	882299.0	1035365.0	809756.0	895370.0	1014062.0	1143497.0
	III.1 Capital account - Changes in liabilities and net worth											
SAVING, GROSS	539502.0	482176.0	483202.0	576577.0	743203.0	859453.0	882299.0	1035365.0	809756.0	895370.0	1014062.0	1143497.0
Capital transfers, receivable less payable	-840.0	-1490.0	4717.0	-1021.0	-1878.0	-919.0	-971.0	-1138.0	-1120.0	-1268.0	-1499.0	-1279.0
Capital transfers, receivable	6745.0	4661.0	11400.0	4605.0	3513.0	4747.0	4716.0	4946.0	4960.0	4960.0	5448.0	5013.0
Less: Capital transfers, payable	7585.0	6151.0	6683.0	5626.0	5391.0	5666.0	5687.0	6084.0	6080.0	6228.0	6947.0	6292.0
Equals: CHANGES IN NET WORTH DUE TO SAVING AND CAPITAL TRANSFERS	324975.0	262905.0	266188.0	344771.0	496146.0	593276.0	588083.0	709147.0	458464.0	530535.0	631787.0	742332.0
	III.1 Capital account - Changes in assets											
Gross capital formation	291970.0	289848.0	287983.0	355968.0	420359.0	501710.0	594863.0	627079.0	530472.0	592192.0	662626.0	729496.0
Gross fixed capital formation	278849.0	273940.0	276727.0	319520.0	376107.0	433103.0	513771.0	542277.0	515580.0	481985.0	528736.0	589688.0
Changes in inventories	13121.0	15908.0	11256.0	36448.0	44252.0	68607.0	81092.0	84802.0	14892.0	110207.0	133890.0	139808.0
Acquisitions less disposals of valuables	...	...	...	...	...	...	...	...	...	...	...	...
Acquisitions less disposals of non-produced non-financial assets	-25.0	-27.0	5.0	7.0	70.0	80.0	29.0	25.0	294.0	288.0	275.0	280.0
NET LENDING (+) / NET BORROWING (-)	246717.0	190865.0	199931.0	219581.0	320896.0	356744.0	286436.0	407123.0	277870.0	301622.0	349662.0	412442.0
	III.2 Financial account - Changes in liabilities and net worth											
Net incurrence of liabilities	253252.5	603401.0	585889.8	668869.8	987126.7	1482505.6	1404827.5	711808.8	167258.1	848372.5	225583.5	...
Currency and deposits	61669.6	115631.1	81909.2	74603.4	209376.0	334501.5	281866.3	277106.7	75768.4	12505.2	226830.7	...
Securities other than shares	12672.6	60746.7	125110.7	20813.7	139568.0	198636.2	177621.9	198232.9	268351.5	164955.6	9415.5	...
Loans	191152.6	327958.3	199609.3	396352.7	363201.2	703459.4	563220.7	247091.4	-280711.1	404098.5	-131141.8	...
Shares and other equity	-3565.2	24417.7	57555.0	31834.9	193904.7	74875.3	71184.9	-15563.0	69592.6	122972.4	13697.4	...
Insurance technical reserves	38539.0	30635.6	55837.7	62654.5	58357.6	59344.5	53128.8	50438.7	64029.8	62611.0	63601.3	...
Financial derivatives	...	...	...	...	...	...	...	...	...	...	...	...

	2001	2002	2003	2004	2005	2006	2007	2008	2009	2010	2011	2012
Series	**300**											
Other accounts payable	-47216.1	44011.5	65868.0	82610.6	22719.1	111688.7	257804.9	-45497.8	-29773.2	81229.8	43180.4	...
Adjustment to reconcile Net Lending of Financial Account and Capital Account	5.0	0.0	0.0	0.0	0.0	-1.0	0.0	1.0	0.0	-1.0	-1.0	...
NET LENDING (+) / NET BORROWING (-)	246712.0	190865.0	199931.0	219581.0	312644.0[a]	356825.0	286465.0	407147.0	253410.0[a]	312292.0[a]	394439.0[a]	...
	III.2 Financial account - Changes in assets											
Net acquisition of financial assets	499964.5	794266.0	785820.8	888450.8	1299770.7	1839330.6	1691292.5	1118955.8	420668.1	1160664.5	620022.5	...
Monetary gold and SDRs	558.0	-590.0	-109.0	-3254.0	-106.0	752.0	-827.0	1060.0	-1214.0	-31.0	-470.0	...
Currency and deposits	13829.6	21593.9	122893.6	39491.9	144343.0	296673.8	214531.9	198238.9	-67137.3	64893.7	230374.7	...
Securities other than shares	117848.5	158580.5	112732.2	212904.3	144915.1	632442.3	63497.2	293927.2	-152417.9	182571.7	22633.2	...
Loans	209212.0	309873.1	221660.7	330173.3	538122.2	410910.4	583824.7	-151704.7	170708.9	283187.5	17121.2	...
Shares and other equity	118281.0	116686.7	135436.6	116208.6	310242.7	239872.3	418425.9	601111.0	453436.6	286086.4	303481.4	...
Insurance technical reserves	43824.4	31289.0	55339.1	53680.6	61146.6	57981.5	51529.8	51508.7	64599.8	64759.0	60508.3	...
Financial derivatives	...	...	...	...	...	...	...	...	...	...	...	...
Other accounts receivable	-3589.0	156832.9	137867.6	139246.2	101107.0	200698.3	360310.1	124814.8	-47308.0	279197.2	-13626.3	...

[a] Statistical discrepancy between net lending (+)/net borrowing (-) in the financial account and net lending (+)/net borrowing (-) in the capital account.

Table 4.2 Rest of the world (S.2)

Series 300: 1993 SNA, Norwegian krone, Western calendar year — **Data in millions**

	2001	2002	2003	2004	2005	2006	2007	2008	2009	2010	2011	2012
Series	**300**											
	V.I External account of goods and services - Resources											
Imports of goods and services	442967.0	425181.0	436245.0	497781.0	545476.0	614170.0	702367.0	755343.0	660408.0	726317.0	776098.0	804119.0
Imports of goods	294576.0	278941.0	288635.0	334951.0	364539.0	420844.0	479533.0	514603.0	444043.0	477213.0	520974.0	523192.0
Imports of services	148391.0	146240.0	147610.0	162830.0	180937.0	193326.0	222834.0	240740.0	216365.0	249104.0	255124.0	280927.0
	V.I External account of goods and services - Uses											
Exports of goods and services	703348.0	630235.0	642153.0	732659.0	863705.0	989465.0	1017589.0	1197090.0	953869.0	1029969.0	1140919.0	1189134.0
Exports of goods	531174.0	468735.0	481779.0	555141.0	666751.0	780308.0	792648.0	955641.0	729867.0	779027.0	892429.0	923632.0
Exports of services	172174.0	161500.0	160374.0	177518.0	196954.0	209157.0	224941.0	241449.0	224003.0	250942.0	248490.0	265501.0
EXTERNAL BALANCE OF GOODS AND SERVICES	-260381.0	-205054.0	-205908.0	-234878.0	-318229.0	-375295.0	-315222.0	-441747.0	-293461.0	-303652.0	-364821.0	-385015.0
	V.II External account of primary income and current transfers - Resources											
EXTERNAL BALANCE OF GOODS AND SERVICES	-260381.0	-205054.0	-205908.0	-234878.0	-318229.0	-375295.0	-315222.0	-441747.0	-293461.0	-303652.0	-364821.0	-385015.0
Compensation of employees	9193.0	7332.0	10121.0	11766.0	14000.0	16644.0	20850.0	26481.0	26138.0	24872.0	24805.0	28249.0
Taxes on production and imports, less Subsidies	...	...	...	...	...	...	...	...	...	...	...	...
Taxes on production and imports	...	...	...	...	...	...	...	...	...	...	...	...
Taxes on products	...	...	...	...	...	...	...	...	...	...	...	...
Other taxes on production	...	...	...	...	...	...	...	...	...	...	...	...
Less: Subsidies	...	...	...	...	...	...	...	...	...	...	...	...
Subsidies on products	...	...	...	...	...	...	...	...	...	...	...	...
Other subsidies on production	...	...	...	...	...	...	...	...	...	...	...	...

	2001	2002	2003	2004	2005	2006	2007	2008	2009	2010	2011	2012
Series	**300**											
Property income	80255.0	74763.0	85014.0	105154.0	136539.0	180291.0	233782.0	236835.0	136712.0	155024.0	166379.0	180291.0
Current taxes on income, wealth, etc.	322.0	190.0	96.0	73.0	94.0	0.0	0.0	0.0	0.0	0.0	0.0	0.0
Social contributions	0.0	0.0	0.0	0.0	241.0	251.0	264.0	260.0	288.0	396.0	293.0	304.0
Social benefits other than social transfers in kind	57.0	39.0	18.0	76.0	40.0	40.0	44.0	44.0	48.0	59.0	54.0	52.0
Other current transfers	30152.0	32132.0	34991.0	34670.0	39015.0	35789.0	39138.0	41037.0	47554.0	50245.0	49398.0	51798.0
Adjustment for the change in net equity of households on pension funds	...	...	...	...	...	...	...	...	...	...	...	...
	V.II External account of primary income and current transfers - Uses											
Compensation of employees	2508.0	2640.0	2772.0	3130.0	3254.0	3389.0	3606.0	3814.0	3952.0	4107.0	4285.0	4457.0
Taxes on production and imports, less Subsidies	...	...	...	...	...	...	...	...	...	...	...	...
Taxes on production and imports	...	...	...	...	...	...	...	...	...	...	...	...
Taxes on products	...	...	...	...	...	...	...	...	...	...	...	...
Other taxes on production	...	...	...	...	...	...	...	...	...	...	...	...
Less: Subsidies	...	...	...	...	...	...	...	...	...	...	...	...
Subsidies on products	...	...	...	...	...	...	...	...	...	...	...	...
Other subsidies on production	...	...	...	...	...	...	...	...	...	...	...	...
Property income	88310.0	84156.0	102268.0	117146.0	169057.0	195111.0	243755.0	247689.0	172366.0	205745.0	202282.0	262512.0
Current taxes on income and wealth, etc.	1003.0	440.0	152.0	161.0	1790.0	1305.0	2182.0	3387.0	1338.0	1623.0	2163.0	2738.0
Social contributions	0.0	0.0	0.0	0.0	807.0	1012.0	1314.0	1709.0	1743.0	1468.0	1482.0	1706.0
Social benefits other than social transfers in kind	195.0	130.0	191.0	43.0	43.0	47.0	49.0	53.0	57.0	48.0	58.0	64.0
Other current transfers	15114.0	14364.0	14168.0	16990.0	19593.0	14599.0	15386.0	14544.0	17107.0	17131.0	17274.0	18203.0
Adjustment for the change in net equity of households on pension funds	...	...	...	...	...	...	...	...	...	...	...	...
CURRENT EXTERNAL BALANCE	-247532.0	-192328.0	-195219.0	-220609.0	-322844.0	-357743.0	-287436.0	-408286.0	-279284.0	-303178.0	-351436.0	-414001.0
	V.III.1 Capital account - Changes in liabilities and net worth											
CURRENT EXTERNAL BALANCE	-247532.0	-192328.0	-195219.0	-220609.0	-322844.0	-357743.0	-287436.0	-408286.0	-279284.0	-303178.0	-351436.0	-414001.0
Capital transfers, receivable less payable	840.0	1490.0	-4717.0	1021.0	1878.0	919.0	971.0	1138.0	1120.0	1268.0	1499.0	1279.0
Capital transfers, receivable	1774.0	1800.0	2022.0	1741.0	1878.0	919.0	971.0	1138.0	1120.0	1268.0	1499.0	1279.0
Less: Capital transfers, payable	934.0	310.0	6739.0	720.0	0.0	0.0	0.0	0.0	0.0	0.0	0.0	0.0
Equals: CHANGES IN NET WORTH DUE TO SAVING AND CAPITAL TRANSFERS	-246692.0	-190838.0	-199936.0	-219588.0	-320966.0	-356824.0	-286465.0	-407148.0	-278164.0	-301910.0	-349937.0	-412722.0
	V.III.1 Capital account - Changes in assets											
Acquisitions less disposals of non-produced non-financial assets	25.0	27.0	-5.0	-7.0	-70.0	-80.0	-29.0	-25.0	-294.0	-288.0	-275.0	-280.0
NET LENDING (+) / NET BORROWING (-)	-246717.0	-190865.0	-199931.0	-219581.0	-320896.0	-356744.0	-286436.0	-407123.0	-277870.0	-301622.0	-349662.0	-412442.0
	V.III.2 Financial account - Changes in liabilities and net worth											
Net incurrence of liabilities	320788.5	475668.4	411561.8	500844.8	730270.0	1166272.9	953102.8	765735.3	-220647.4	690588.6	400092.6	...
Currency and deposits	-33524.1	-22059.7	41055.1	-4541.5	42885.0	72329.3	70290.6	149481.2	-92981.7	-19576.5	201244.0	...
Securities other than shares	104939.0	127724.0	73335.0	228979.0	136941.0	633257.0	99774.0	260702.0	-390008.0	214067.0	79625.0	...
Loans	47820.0	158456.4	95247.4	139123.5	245951.0	101152.0	203011.0	-506082.0	-108125.0	94692.0	-168881.0	...
Shares and other equity	160985.3	97280.0	106852.6	106356.7	231786.0	245020.0	404158.0	575529.0	406201.0	227529.0	297812.0	...

	2001	2002	2003	2004	2005	2006	2007	2008	2009	2010	2011	2012
Series	**300**											
Insurance technical reserves	2045.5	382.3	-1.5	-9544.4	0.0	0.0	5641.0	3408.0	-1245.0	-32.0	-1809.0	...
Financial derivatives	...	...	...	...	...	...	...	...	...	...	...	...
Other accounts payable	38522.8	113885.5	95073.2	40471.3	72707.0	114514.6	170228.1	282697.2	-34488.7	173909.1	-7898.4	...
Adjustment to reconcile Net Lending of Financial Account and Capital Account	-5.0	0.0	0.0	0.0	0.0	1.0	0.0	-1.0	0.0	1.0	1.0	...
NET LENDING (+) / NET BORROWING (-)	-246712.0	-190865.0	-199931.0	-219581.0	-312644.0[a]	-356825.0	-286465.0	-407147.0	-253410.0[a]	-312292.0[a]	-394439.0[a]	...
	V.III.2 Financial account - Changes in assets											
Net acquisition of financial assets	74076.5	284803.4	211630.8	281263.8	417626.0	809447.9	666637.8	358588.3	-474057.4	378296.6	5653.6	...
Monetary gold and SDRs	-558.0	590.0	109.0	3254.0	106.0	-752.0	827.0	-1060.0	1214.0	31.0	470.0	...
Currency and deposits	14315.8	71977.5	70.6	30570.0	107918.0	110157.0	137625.0	228349.0	49924.0	-71965.0	197700.0	...
Securities other than shares	-236.8	29890.3	85713.5	36888.4	131594.0	199450.9	213898.8	165007.7	30761.4	196450.8	66407.2	...
Loans	29760.6	176541.7	73196.0	205303.0	71030.0	393701.0	182407.0	-107286.0	-559545.0	215603.0	-317144.0	...
Shares and other equity	39139.0	5011.0	28971.0	21983.1	115448.0	80023.0	56917.0	-41145.0	22357.0	64415.0	8028.0	...
Insurance technical reserves	-3239.9	-271.1	497.1	-570.5	-2789.0	1363.0	7240.0	2338.0	-1815.0	-2180.0	1284.0	...
Financial derivatives	...	...	...	...	...	...	...	...	...	...	...	...
Other accounts receivable	-5104.2	1064.1	23073.6	-16164.2	-5681.0	25505.0	67723.0	112384.6	-16953.8	-24058.2	48908.4	...

[a] Statistical discrepancy between net lending (+)/net borrowing (-) in the financial account and net lending (+)/net borrowing (-) in the capital account.

Table 4.3 Non-financial Corporations (S.11)

Series 300: 1993 SNA, Norwegian krone, Western calendar year **Data in millions**

	2001	2002	2003	2004	2005	2006	2007	2008	2009	2010	2011	2012
Series	**300**											
	I. Production account - Resources											
Output, at basic prices (otherwise, please specify)	1862502.0	1832482.0	1885587.0	2080440.0	2331712.0	2684382.0	2936094.0	3305036.0	2957513.0	3097042.0	3375894.0	3573695.0
	I. Production account - Uses											
Intermediate consumption, at purchaser's prices	939520.0	936551.0	961426.0	1034438.0	1117756.0	1298824.0	1503107.0	1653916.0	1523382.0	1561432.0	1687360.0	1783056.0
VALUE ADDED GROSS, in basic prices	922982.0	895931.0	924161.0	1046002.0	1213956.0	1385558.0	1432987.0	1651120.0	1434131.0	1535610.0	1688534.0	1790639.0
Less: Consumption of fixed capital	141835.0	143919.0	144985.0	148782.0	157065.0	170289.0	187807.0	209182.0	228031.0	235128.0	244545.0	256433.0
VALUE ADDED NET, at basic prices	781147.0	752012.0	779176.0	897220.0	1056891.0	1215269.0	1245180.0	1441938.0	1206100.0	1300482.0	1443989.0	1534206.0
	II.1.1 Generation of income account - Resources											
VALUE ADDED GROSS, at basic prices	922982.0	895931.0	924161.0	1046002.0	1213956.0	1385558.0	1432987.0	1651120.0	1434131.0	1535610.0	1688534.0	1790639.0
	II.1.1 Generation of income account - Uses											
Compensation of employees	421429.0	438844.0	447458.0	467487.0	501288.0	556954.0	625842.0	693723.0	702340.0	714346.0	758524.0	812534.0
Other taxes less Other subsidies on production	-1326.0	-3170.0	-5225.0	-4538.0	-4078.0	-2118.0	-5123.0	-4251.0	-8469.0	-11674.0	-11205.0	-12398.0
Other taxes on production	14517.0	13619.0	13565.0	13961.0	14121.0	16508.0	16639.0	16957.0	15799.0	14597.0	15718.0	16320.0
Less: Other subsidies on production	15843.0	16789.0	18790.0	18499.0	18199.0	18626.0	21762.0	21208.0	24268.0	26271.0	26923.0	28718.0
OPERATING SURPLUS, GROSS	502879.0	460257.0	481928.0	583053.0	716746.0	830722.0	812268.0	961648.0	740260.0	832938.0	941215.0	990503.0
	II.1.2 Allocation of primary income account - Resources											
OPERATING SURPLUS, GROSS	502879.0	460257.0	481928.0	583053.0	716746.0	830722.0	812268.0	961648.0	740260.0	832938.0	941215.0	990503.0

	2001	2002	2003	2004	2005	2006	2007	2008	2009	2010	2011	2012
Series	**300**											
Property income	143925.0	128404.0	138526.0	115830.0	206968.0	227097.0	257677.0	290130.0	160701.0	153963.0	162804.0	210299.0
	II.1.2 Allocation of primary income account - Uses											
Property income	282389.0	280777.0	297303.0	323313.0	459687.0	444209.0	507185.0	604834.0	396333.0	399784.0	463827.0	493010.0
BALANCE OF PRIMARY INCOMES	364414.0	307884.0	323151.0	375570.0	464027.0	613610.0	562760.0	646944.0	504628.0	587117.0	640192.0	707792.0
	II.2 Secondary distribution of income account - Resources											
BALANCE OF PRIMARY INCOMES	364414.0	307884.0	323151.0	375570.0	464027.0	613610.0	562760.0	646944.0	504628.0	587117.0	640192.0	707792.0
Social contributions	6827.0	3524.0	3410.0	3480.0	4550.0	5306.0	6634.0	16065.0	15362.0	12751.0	13220.0	14279.0
Other current transfers	60234.0	68094.0	51109.0	53316.0	63177.0	66140.0	108208.0	96009.0	93380.0	82658.0	95456.0	84057.0
	II.2 Secondary distribution of income account - Uses											
Current taxes on income, wealth, etc.	132061.0	120366.0	125485.0	167646.0	224656.0	269761.0	246877.0	307341.0	200976.0	242699.0	277849.0	290597.0
Social benefits other than social transfers in kind	6827.0	3524.0	3410.0	3481.0	3967.0	4525.0	5565.0	14616.0	13889.0	11563.0	12031.0	12877.0
Other current transfers	64374.0	73078.0	62328.0	61941.0	70839.0	71777.0	120219.0	106650.0	106594.0	93828.0	113145.0	102552.0
GROSS DISPOSABLE INCOME	228213.0	182534.0	186447.0	199298.0	232292.0	338993.0	304941.0	330411.0	291911.0	334436.0	345843.0	400102.0
	II.4.1 Use of disposable income account - Resources											
GROSS DISPOSABLE INCOME	228213.0	182534.0	186447.0	199298.0	232292.0	338993.0	304941.0	330411.0	291911.0	334436.0	345843.0	400102.0
	II.4.1 Use of disposable income account - Uses											
Adjustment for the change in net equity of households on pension funds	...	...	...	...	...	...	...	...	...	...	...	...
SAVING, GROSS	228213.0	182534.0	186447.0	199298.0	232292.0	338993.0	304941.0	330411.0	291911.0	334436.0	345843.0	400102.0
	III.1 Capital account - Changes in liabilities and net worth											
SAVING, GROSS	228213.0	182534.0	186447.0	199298.0	232292.0	338993.0	304941.0	330411.0	291911.0	334436.0	345843.0	400102.0
Capital transfers, receivable less payable	2414.0	2076.0	7641.0	2178.0	1743.0	2684.0	2140.0	2973.0	2529.0	2583.0	3694.0	3126.0
Capital transfers, receivable	3779.0	2579.0	7807.0	2671.0	1743.0	2684.0	2140.0	2973.0	2529.0	2583.0	3694.0	3126.0
Less: Capital transfers, payable	1365.0	503.0	166.0	493.0	0.0	0.0	0.0	0.0	0.0	0.0	0.0	0.0
Equals: CHANGES IN NET WORTH DUE TO SAVING AND CAPITAL TRANSFERS	88792.0	40691.0	49103.0	52694.0	76970.0	171388.0	119274.0	124202.0	66409.0	101891.0	104992.0	146795.0
	III.1 Capital account - Changes in assets											
Gross capital formation	172387.0	172513.0	166747.0	210164.0	260734.0	317726.0	388132.0	416152.0	325922.0	389730.0	425666.0	474052.0
Gross fixed capital formation	159380.0	157080.0	155921.0	173614.0	216069.0	248800.0	307025.0	331350.0	311030.0	279523.0	291776.0	334244.0
Changes in inventories	13121.0	15908.0	11256.0	36448.0	44252.0	68607.0	81092.0	84802.0	14892.0	110207.0	133890.0	139808.0
Acquisitions less disposals of valuables	-114.0	-475.0	-430.0	102.0	413.0	319.0	15.0	0.0	0.0	0.0	0.0	...
Acquisitions less disposals of non-produced non-financial assets	1770.0	582.0	1641.0	3084.0	3370.0	3037.0	2226.0	1381.0	2586.0	2298.0	2577.0	2893.0
NET LENDING (+) / NET BORROWING (-)	56470.0	11515.0	25700.0	-11772.0	-30069.0	20914.0	-83277.0	-84149.0	-34068.0	-55009.0	-78706.0	-73717.0
	III.2 Financial account - Changes in liabilities and net worth											
Net incurrence of liabilities	13408.7	128327.2	52994.6	158958.3	324982.2	310738.3	462103.9	216950.2	25962.7	347124.1	7202.3	...
Currency and deposits	...	...	...	...	...	...	...	...	...	...	...	...
Securities other than shares	-8245.9	24735.0	-12246.5	-297.7	18429.2	25621.9	25292.2	7766.0	50321.0	8351.3	2911.6	...
Loans	66531.4	66864.5	13680.1	75981.6	140970.3	153335.6	292459.7	330624.1	-116168.8	199251.0	21467.6	...
Shares and other equity	-3314.0	20907.9	42159.7	24335.0	141027.7	55702.7	12000.9	-3551.2	11218.5	89197.1	15687.2	...
Insurance technical reserves	...	...	...	...	...	...	...	...	...	...	...	...

	2001	2002	2003	2004	2005	2006	2007	2008	2009	2010	2011	2012
Series	**300**											
Financial derivatives	...	...	...	...	...	...	...	...	...	...	...	...
Other accounts payable	-41562.8	15819.8	9401.3	58939.4	24555.0	76078.1	132351.1	-117888.7	80592.0	50324.8	-32864.0	...
Adjustment to reconcile Net Lending of Financial Account and Capital Account	17420.6	-32.5	-34975.9	1774.5	-94.5	7443.2	-22980.5	-17310.9	-78995.6	-51376.8	-30817.1	...
NET LENDING (+) / NET BORROWING (-)	39049.4[a]	11547.5[a]	60675.9[a]	-13546.5[a]	-38226.5[b]	13550.8[a]	-60267.5[a]	-64063.1[a]	24288.6[b]	22113.8[b]	-11872.9[b]	...
	III.2 Financial account - Changes in assets											
Net acquisition of financial assets	52458.1	139874.7	113670.5	145411.9	286755.7	324289.1	401836.4	152887.1	50251.3	369237.9	-4670.6	...
Monetary gold and SDRs	...	...	...	...	...	...	...	...	...	...	...	...
Currency and deposits	23100.7	-5642.7	13468.3	60309.5	48389.2	96646.3	90847.9	-30383.1	14999.9	41687.3	17089.3	...
Securities other than shares	-2748.3	-6203.1	-35.7	-7606.0	-3206.7	-8737.6	5639.7	-10398.1	325.6	12726.6	8603.1	...
Loans	709.9	16501.5	1983.1	18924.8	56847.5	13918.8	20905.8	51095.9	21260.0	-8169.0	20671.0	...
Shares and other equity	21330.0	35500.2	15673.5	17065.0	122928.3	125507.9	108898.9	76161.5	37669.8	129917.6	47050.9	...
Insurance technical reserves	2813.7	-515.6	1298.9	1067.9	1721.8	2051.2	2233.0	1501.2	894.3	1559.7	2016.0	...
Financial derivatives	...	...	...	...	...	...	...	...	...	...	...	...
Other accounts receivable	7252.1	100234.4	81282.4	55650.6	60075.6	94902.5	173311.1	64909.7	-24898.5	191515.8	-100100.9	...

[a] Excludes Adjustment to reconcile net lending (+)/net borrowing (-) of the Financial Account and the Capital Account.
[b] Statistical discrepancy between net lending (+)/net borrowing (-) in the financial account and net lending (+)/net borrowing (-) in the capital account.

Table 4.4 Financial Corporations (S.12)

Series 300: 1993 SNA, Norwegian krone, Western calendar year — **Data in millions**

	2001	2002	2003	2004	2005	2006	2007	2008	2009	2010	2011	2012
Series	**300**											
	I. Production account - Resources											
Output, at basic prices (otherwise, please specify)	70578.0	73729.0	88176.0	101202.0	110581.0	118311.0	139404.0	139635.0	153524.0	158847.0	160201.0	179741.0
	I. Production account - Uses											
Intermediate consumption, at purchaser's prices	29841.0	32117.0	32402.0	34503.0	42202.0	52766.0	61463.0	56214.0	56330.0	57503.0	58728.0	65785.0
VALUE ADDED GROSS, at basic prices	40737.0	41612.0	55774.0	66699.0	68379.0	65545.0	77941.0	83421.0	97194.0	101344.0	101473.0	113956.0
Less: Consumption of fixed capital	4326.0	4241.0	4341.0	3975.0	3256.0	3539.0	4538.0	7224.0	7941.0	7898.0	7156.0	6969.0
VALUE ADDED NET, at basic prices	36411.0	37371.0	51433.0	62724.0	65123.0	62006.0	73403.0	76197.0	89253.0	93446.0	94317.0	106987.0
	II.1.1 Generation of income account - Resources											
VALUE ADDED GROSS, at basic prices	40737.0	41612.0	55774.0	66699.0	68379.0	65545.0	77941.0	83421.0	97194.0	101344.0	101473.0	113956.0
	II.1.1 Generation of income account - Uses											
Compensation of employees	22300.0	23400.0	24056.0	25833.0	27440.0	29822.0	33733.0	37392.0	39146.0	39555.0	42343.0	44471.0
Other taxes less Other subsidies on production	-1170.0	-1395.0	-1565.0	-2015.0	-1989.0	-2150.0	-1757.0	-1873.0	-2201.0	-2457.0	-2781.0	-3163.0
Other taxes on production	185.0	196.0	199.0	82.0	94.0	36.0	343.0	394.0	420.0	428.0	195.0	201.0
Less: Other subsidies on production	1355.0	1591.0	1764.0	2097.0	2083.0	2186.0	2100.0	2267.0	2621.0	2885.0	2976.0	3364.0
OPERATING SURPLUS, GROSS	19607.0	19607.0	33283.0	42881.0	42928.0	37873.0	45965.0	47902.0	60249.0	64246.0	61911.0	72648.0
	II.1.2 Allocation of primary income account - Resources											
OPERATING SURPLUS, GROSS	19607.0	19607.0	33283.0	42881.0	42928.0	37873.0	45965.0	47902.0	60249.0	64246.0	61911.0	72648.0

	2001	2002	2003	2004	2005	2006	2007	2008	2009	2010	2011	2012
Series	**300**											
Property income	183070.0	179038.0	163085.0	138484.0	150398.0	195515.0	258688.0	332626.0	239365.0	265188.0	278160.0	260937.0
II.1.2 Allocation of primary income account - Uses												
Property income	179915.0	177888.0	173761.0	147664.0	163806.0	208367.0	258618.0	333415.0	245339.0	252599.0	274721.0	257121.0
BALANCE OF PRIMARY INCOMES	22763.0	20757.0	22607.0	33701.0	29520.0	25021.0	46035.0	47113.0	54275.0	76835.0	65350.0	76464.0
II.2 Secondary distribution of income account - Resources												
BALANCE OF PRIMARY INCOMES	22763.0	20757.0	22607.0	33701.0	29520.0	25021.0	46035.0	47113.0	54275.0	76835.0	65350.0	76464.0
Social contributions	29760.0	37106.0	34894.0	37057.0	37400.0	44226.0	51042.0	64800.0	61156.0	60510.0	65675.0	74213.0
Other current transfers	27743.0	28594.0	32598.0	34365.0	30560.0	29881.0	35736.0	37864.0	40823.0	40165.0	43690.0	41195.0
II.2 Secondary distribution of income account - Uses												
Current taxes on income, wealth, etc.	4399.0	4850.0	2480.0	5513.0	4056.0	9581.0	7373.0	4722.0	15717.0	11822.0	15810.0	11796.0
Social benefits other than social transfers in kind	17490.0	17680.0	19618.0	20720.0	22001.0	22513.0	23375.0	27458.0	27194.0	29176.0	31817.0	32644.0
Other current transfers	41634.0	32578.0	35601.0	34379.0	32320.0	34808.0	33490.0	36979.0	38381.0	39991.0	39124.0	35019.0
GROSS DISPOSABLE INCOME	16743.0	31349.0	32400.0	44511.0	39103.0	32226.0	68575.0	80618.0	74962.0	96521.0	87964.0	112413.0
II.4.1 Use of disposable income account - Resources												
GROSS DISPOSABLE INCOME	16743.0	31349.0	32400.0	44511.0	39103.0	32226.0	68575.0	80618.0	74962.0	96521.0	87964.0	112413.0
II.4.1 Use of disposable income account - Uses												
Adjustment for the change in net equity of households on pension funds	12269.0	19426.0	15276.0	16336.0	15399.0	21713.0	27685.0	37342.0	33979.0	31450.0	33858.0	41568.0
SAVING, GROSS	4474.0	11923.0	17124.0	28175.0	23704.0	10513.0	40890.0	43276.0	40983.0	65071.0	54106.0	70845.0
III.1 Capital account - Changes in liabilities and net worth												
SAVING, GROSS	4474.0	11923.0	17124.0	28175.0	23704.0	10513.0	40890.0	43276.0	40983.0	65071.0	54106.0	70845.0
Capital transfers, receivable less payable	0.0	-14.0	448.0	0.0	0.0	0.0	0.0	0.0	0.0	0.0	0.0	0.0
Capital transfers, receivable	0.0	0.0	1107.0	0.0	0.0	0.0	0.0	0.0	0.0	0.0	0.0	0.0
Less: Capital transfers, payable	0.0	14.0	659.0	0.0	0.0	0.0	0.0	0.0	0.0	0.0	0.0	0.0
Equals: CHANGES IN NET WORTH DUE TO SAVING AND CAPITAL TRANSFERS	148.0	7668.0	13231.0	24200.0	20448.0	6974.0	36352.0	36052.0	33042.0	57173.0	46950.0	63876.0
III.1 Capital account - Changes in assets												
Gross capital formation	7721.0	5426.0	2639.0	6405.0	3780.0	8635.0	8163.0	9852.0	5745.0	4262.0	4408.0	4455.0
Gross fixed capital formation	7607.0	4951.0	2209.0	6507.0	4193.0	8954.0	8178.0	9852.0	5745.0	4262.0	4408.0	4455.0
Changes in inventories	...	...	...	...	...	...	...	...	...	...	...	...
Acquisitions less disposals of valuables	114.0	475.0	430.0	-102.0	-413.0	-319.0	-15.0	0.0	0.0	0.0	0.0	...
Acquisitions less disposals of non-produced non-financial assets	...	...	...	...	...	...	...	...	...	...	...	...
NET LENDING (+) / NET BORROWING (-)	-3247.0	6483.0	14933.0	21770.0	19924.0	1878.0	32727.0	33424.0	35238.0	60809.0	49698.0	66390.0
III.2 Financial account - Changes in liabilities and net worth												
Net incurrence of liabilities	133620.9	232829.3	278249.0	210099.7	459595.4	625581.1	648759.2	584138.1	208545.5	259445.8	387382.8	...
Currency and deposits	61669.6	115631.1	81909.2	74603.4	209376.0	334501.5	281866.3	277106.7	75768.4	12505.2	226830.7	...
Securities other than shares	36048.7	20315.9	80386.3	54305.0	114124.3	151669.4	166553.7	121574.9	9532.4	133762.9	87505.8	...
Loans	13276.2	37738.8	409.9	25901.2	11229.6	54930.5	12655.4	67792.8	73850.6	18647.4	-78874.1	...
Shares and other equity	-251.2	3509.8	15395.2	7499.9	52877.0	19172.6	59183.9	-12011.7	58374.2	33775.3	-1989.7	...
Insurance technical reserves	38539.0	30635.6	55837.7	62654.5	58357.6	59344.5	53128.8	50438.7	64029.8	62611.0	63601.3	...

	2001	2002	2003	2004	2005	2006	2007	2008	2009	2010	2011	2012
Series	**300**											
Financial derivatives	...	...	...	...	...	...	...	...	...	...	...	...
Other accounts payable	-15661.4	24998.1	44310.7	-14864.3	13630.9	5962.6	75371.0	79236.7	-73009.9	-1856.0	90308.9	...
Adjustment to reconcile Net Lending of Financial Account and Capital Account	-22231.1	-20456.9	15344.9	-13989.4	1862.8	-18247.5	902.6	11822.1	67265.9	3305.8	-28329.0	...
NET LENDING (+) / NET BORROWING (-)	18984.1[a]	26939.9[a]	-411.9[a]	35759.4[a]	18061.2[a]	20125.5[a]	31824.4[a]	21601.9[a]	-32029.9[a]	35511.2[b]	68515.0[b]	...
	III.2 Financial account - Changes in assets											
Net acquisition of financial assets	152605.0	259769.2	277837.0	245859.0	477656.6	645706.6	680583.5	605740.0	176515.6	294957.0	455897.8	...
Monetary gold and SDRs	558.0	-590.0	-109.0	-3254.0	-106.0	752.0	-827.0	1060.0	-1214.0	-31.0	-470.0	...
Currency and deposits	-24791.6	2829.5	20604.8	-14265.2	31780.0	86598.3	58554.7	183555.2	-89085.7	-30228.5	197099.0	...
Securities other than shares	-3550.2	69354.6	62003.0	68654.3	93886.8	110179.0	5826.4	109850.3	182592.6	-6691.2	1306.5	...
Loans	150895.2	174168.3	114425.7	162059.0	304209.3	338163.6	425085.0	317892.9	45755.6	231009.1	210204.0	...
Shares and other equity	33725.6	-22139.5	32739.4	45860.7	45816.4	53243.4	52198.0	-18195.5	60996.8	65975.8	10430.2	...
Insurance technical reserves	0.0	0.0	0.0	0.0	0.0	0.0	5641.0	3408.0	-1245.0	-32.0	-1809.0	...
Financial derivatives	...	...	...	...	...	...	...	...	...	...	...	...
Other accounts receivable	-4231.9	36146.3	48173.2	-13195.7	2070.1	56770.4	134105.5	8169.1	-21284.8	34954.8	39137.2	...

[a] Excludes Adjustment to reconcile net lending (+)/net borrowing (-) of the Financial Account and the Capital Account.
[b] Statistical discrepancy between net lending (+)/net borrowing (-) in the financial account and net lending (+)/net borrowing (-) in the capital account.

Table 4.5 General Government (S.13)

Series 300: 1993 SNA, Norwegian krone, Western calendar year — **Data in millions**

	2001	2002	2003	2004	2005	2006	2007	2008	2009	2010	2011	2012
Series	**300**											
	I. Production account - Resources											
Output, at basic prices (otherwise, please specify)	340703.0	358761.0	369426.0	384008.0	397878.0	422420.0	458712.0	501349.0	543209.0	570360.0	603838.0	639269.0
	I. Production account - Uses											
Intermediate consumption, at purchaser's prices	108348.0	114164.0	112761.0	116711.0	117793.0	124119.0	133970.0	145950.0	163095.0	169933.0	174226.0	180792.0
VALUE ADDED GROSS, at basic prices	232355.0	244597.0	256665.0	267297.0	280085.0	298301.0	324742.0	355399.0	380114.0	400427.0	429612.0	458477.0
Less: Consumption of fixed capital	29207.0	29988.0	30683.0	32455.0	34516.0	37461.0	41502.0	46005.0	49524.0	53195.0	57086.0	60184.0
VALUE ADDED NET, at basic prices	203148.0	214609.0	225982.0	234842.0	245569.0	260840.0	283240.0	309394.0	330590.0	347232.0	372526.0	398293.0
	II.1.1 Generation of income account - Resources											
VALUE ADDED GROSS, at basic prices	232355.0	244597.0	256665.0	267297.0	280085.0	298301.0	324742.0	355399.0	380114.0	400427.0	429612.0	458477.0
	II.1.1 Generation of income account - Uses											
Compensation of employees	199739.0	211275.0	223147.0	233456.0	244503.0	260215.0	282380.0	309069.0	330278.0	347201.0	372678.0	398407.0
Other taxes less Other subsidies on production	18.0	9.0	9.0	9.0	9.0	9.0	106.0	125.0	108.0	109.0	51.0	51.0
Other taxes on production	18.0	9.0	9.0	9.0	9.0	9.0	106.0	125.0	108.0	109.0	51.0	51.0
Less: Other subsidies on production	...	...	...	...	...	...	...	...	...	...	...	...
OPERATING SURPLUS, GROSS	32598.0	33313.0	33509.0	33832.0	35573.0	38077.0	42256.0	46205.0	49728.0	53117.0	56883.0	60019.0
	II.1.2 Allocation of primary income account - Resources											
OPERATING SURPLUS, GROSS	32598.0	33313.0	33509.0	33832.0	35573.0	38077.0	42256.0	46205.0	49728.0	53117.0	56883.0	60019.0

	2001	2002	2003	2004	2005	2006	2007	2008	2009	2010	2011	2012
Series	**300**											
Taxes on production and imports, less Subsidies	171714.0	170083.0	168850.0	184187.0	199096.0	225150.0	248410.0	241419.0	237923.0	256127.0	267203.0	279203.0
Taxes on production and imports	205893.0	205769.0	207439.0	222560.0	238999.0	265741.0	287916.0	285052.0	284920.0	306105.0	318180.0	333043.0
Taxes on products	189964.0	190693.0	192285.0	206870.0	222787.0	246904.0	268257.0	264481.0	265362.0	287420.0	298678.0	312797.0
Other taxes on production	15929.0	15076.0	15154.0	15690.0	16212.0	18837.0	19659.0	20571.0	19558.0	18685.0	19502.0	20246.0
Less: Subsidies	34179.0	35686.0	38589.0	38373.0	39903.0	40591.0	39506.0	43633.0	46997.0	49978.0	50977.0	53840.0
Subsidies on products	7259.0	7031.0	7774.0	7163.0	8278.0	7987.0	3445.0	3847.0	4079.0	3774.0	3632.0	3599.0
Other subsidies on production	26920.0	28654.0	30815.0	31210.0	31625.0	32604.0	36061.0	39786.0	42918.0	46204.0	47345.0	50241.0
Property income	155345.0	142421.0	149434.0	168562.0	201802.0	258693.0	269833.0	349762.0	273773.0	263499.0	318986.0	342868.0
	II.1.2 Allocation of primary income account - Uses											
Property income	26429.0	24788.0	23955.0	19695.0	20609.0	31522.0	28031.0	35361.0	28916.0	26665.0	24538.0	18584.0
BALANCE OF PRIMARY INCOMES	333228.0	321029.0	327838.0	366886.0	415862.0	490398.0	532468.0	602025.0	532508.0	546078.0	618533.0	663506.0
	II.2 Secondary distribution of income account - Resources											
BALANCE OF PRIMARY INCOMES	333228.0	321029.0	327838.0	366886.0	415862.0	490398.0	532468.0	602025.0	532508.0	546078.0	618533.0	663506.0
Current taxes on income, wealth, etc.	309732.0	302181.0	309318.0	366155.0	433169.0	492368.0	493759.0	564952.0	478476.0	532391.0	588226.0	614591.0
Social contributions	143355.0	151888.0	158232.0	166468.0	176068.0	191405.0	209223.0	226871.0	234865.0	244330.0	261077.0	278508.0
Other current transfers	14993.0	5334.0	9409.0	7287.0	8316.0	8489.0	7526.0	7220.0	7904.0	8491.0	10044.0	9593.0
	II.2 Secondary distribution of income account - Uses											
Current taxes on income, wealth, etc.	...	...	...	...	...	...	...	...	...	...	...	...
Social benefits other than social transfers in kind	210426.0	225716.0	249154.0	256777.0	260975.0	269067.0	280510.0	298202.0	326494.0	345213.0	366795.0	386419.0
Other current transfers	26708.0	29671.0	31675.0	33507.0	38750.0	41285.0	49052.0	53490.0	60642.0	64113.0	64902.0	66142.0
GROSS DISPOSABLE INCOME	564174.0	525045.0	523968.0	616512.0	733690.0	872308.0	913414.0	1049376.0	866617.0	921964.0	1046183.0	1113637.0
	II.4.1 Use of disposable income account - Resources											
GROSS DISPOSABLE INCOME	564174.0	525045.0	523968.0	616512.0	733690.0	872308.0	913414.0	1049376.0	866617.0	921964.0	1046183.0	1113637.0
	II.4.1 Use of disposable income account - Uses											
Final consumption expenditure	316972.0	339379.0	357541.0	371573.0	385695.0	411782.0	444304.0	488441.0	530682.0	558469.0	590784.0	625939.0
Individual consumption expenditure	194937.0	210304.0	228282.0	240797.0	256349.0	274472.0	292861.0	320887.0	346461.0	365633.0	388072.0	412865.0
Collective consumption expenditure	122035.0	129075.0	129259.0	130776.0	129346.0	137310.0	151443.0	167554.0	184221.0	192836.0	202712.0	213074.0
Adjustment for the change in net equity of households on pension funds	...	...	...	...	...	...	...	...	...	...	...	...
SAVING, GROSS	247202.0	185666.0	166427.0	244939.0	347995.0	460526.0	469110.0	560935.0	335935.0	363495.0	455399.0	487698.0
	III.1 Capital account - Changes in liabilities and net worth											
SAVING, GROSS	247202.0	185666.0	166427.0	244939.0	347995.0	460526.0	469110.0	560935.0	335935.0	363495.0	455399.0	487698.0
Capital transfers, receivable less payable	-2960.0	-2612.0	-2324.0	-1336.0	-1856.0	-1540.0	-535.0	-2138.0	-1218.0	-1474.0	-2816.0	-2518.0
Capital transfers, receivable	1328.0	1243.0	1532.0	1663.0	1768.0	2063.0	2576.0	1973.0	2431.0	2377.0	1754.0	1887.0
Less: Capital transfers, payable	4288.0	3855.0	3856.0	2999.0	3624.0	3603.0	3111.0	4111.0	3649.0	3851.0	4570.0	4405.0
Equals: CHANGES IN NET WORTH DUE TO SAVING AND CAPITAL TRANSFERS	215035.0	153066.0	133420.0	211148.0	311623.0	421525.0	427073.0	512792.0	285193.0	308826.0	395497.0	424996.0
	III.1 Capital account - Changes in assets											
Gross capital formation	41294.0	42502.0	48221.0	52038.0	54834.0	62871.0	71656.0	78929.0	85759.0	81529.0	86798.0	90990.0
Gross fixed capital formation	41294.0	42502.0	48221.0	52038.0	54834.0	62871.0	71656.0	78929.0	85759.0	81529.0	86798.0	90990.0

	2001	2002	2003	2004	2005	2006	2007	2008	2009	2010	2011	2012
Series	**300**											
Changes in inventories	...	...	...	...	...	...	...	...	...	...	...	...
Acquisitions less disposals of valuables	...	...	...	...	...	...	...	...	...	...	...	...
Acquisitions of non-produced non-financial assets	-1795.0	-609.0	-1636.0	-3077.0	-3300.0	-2957.0	-2197.0	-1356.0	-2292.0	-2010.0	-2302.0	-2613.0
NET LENDING (+) / NET BORROWING (-)	204743.0	141161.0	117518.0	194642.0	294605.0	399072.0	399116.0	481224.0	251250.0	282502.0	368087.0	396803.0
	III.2 Financial account - Changes in liabilities and net worth											
Net incurrence of liabilities	4017.8	138326.8	143897.3	159868.8	34090.0	361400.5	84077.5	-214201.1	-178200.5	96696.2	-334815.2	...
Currency and deposits	...	...	...	...	...	...	...	...	...	...	...	...
Securities other than shares	-15127.2	15672.9	56870.9	-33082.6	6821.5	21342.0	-14732.0	68711.0	208549.0	22841.3	-81001.9	...
Loans	16853.4	123366.8	74806.1	162481.7	46952.2	318661.8	67317.8	-281622.5	-364182.8	52321.8	-228333.8	...
Shares and other equity	...	...	...	...	...	...	...	...	...	...	...	...
Insurance technical reserves	...	...	...	...	...	...	...	...	...	...	...	...
Financial derivatives	...	...	...	...	...	...	...	...	...	...	...	...
Other accounts payable	2291.5	-712.9	12220.2	30469.7	-19683.7	21396.8	31491.6	-1289.6	-22566.8	21533.0	-25479.5	...
Adjustment to reconcile Net Lending of Financial Account and Capital Account	9535.4	307.7	11399.8	4108.2	16342.5	8719.9	7108.5	-7473.1	-2510.8	6317.1	9985.3	...
NET LENDING (+) / NET BORROWING (-)	195207.6[a]	140853.3[a]	106118.2[a]	190533.8[a]	278262.5[a]	390352.1[a]	392015.5[a]	488706.1[a]	253760.8[a]	275748.9[b]	362766.7[b]	...
	III.2 Financial account - Changes in assets											
Net acquisition of financial assets	199225.4	279180.1	250015.5	350402.6	312352.6	751752.6	476093.0	274505.0	75560.3	372445.0	27951.5	...
Monetary gold and SDRs	...	...	...	...	...	...	...	...	...	...	...	...
Currency and deposits	-15973.7	-23504.5	62505.6	-35134.9	27489.7	56812.9	409.5	-15992.0	-15254.4	9944.0	-50246.1	...
Securities other than shares	117467.0	93604.0	47256.0	148682.0	50624.0	533111.0	57995.0	200668.0	-333496.2	178385.3	13777.7	...
Loans	58569.8	111620.1	93426.2	135178.3	151863.6	65218.1	139972.3	-514290.7	106776.2	65312.8	-212078.8	...
Shares and other equity	51677.5	88727.3	54807.7	15782.1	62232.0	74404.0	259133.0	558785.0	341605.0	87798.0	250664.4	...
Insurance technical reserves	...	...	...	...	...	...	...	...	...	...	...	...
Financial derivatives	...	...	...	...	...	...	...	...	...	...	...	...
Other accounts receivable	-12515.2	8733.2	-7979.9	85895.2	20143.3	22206.7	18583.1	45334.6	-24070.3	31004.9	25834.3	...

[a] Excludes Adjustment to reconcile net lending (+)/net borrowing (-) of the Financial Account and the Capital Account.
[b] Statistical discrepancy between net lending (+)/net borrowing (-) in the financial account and net lending (+)/net borrowing (-) in the capital account.

Table 4.6 Households (S.14)

Series 300: 1993 SNA, Norwegian krone, Western calendar year **Data in millions**

	2001	2002	2003	2004	2005	2006	2007	2008	2009	2010	2011	2012
Series	**300**											
	I. Production account - Resources											
Output, at basic prices (otherwise, please specify)	235192.0	244462.0	251417.0	266601.0	300674.0	308595.0	319204.0	338651.0	338334.0	356384.0	375420.0	392798.0
	I. Production account - Uses											
Intermediate consumption, at purchaser's prices	93559.0	95577.0	98710.0	114103.0	140776.0	139774.0	139566.0	158072.0	159932.0	165215.0	174061.0	185608.0
VALUE ADDED GROSS, at basic prices	141633.0	148885.0	152707.0	152498.0	159898.0	168821.0	179638.0	180579.0	178402.0	191169.0	201359.0	207190.0
Less: Consumption of fixed capital	36367.0	37645.0	39713.0	43417.0	48052.0	51457.0	56685.0	59727.0	61574.0	64007.0	68293.0	72358.0

	2001	2002	2003	2004	2005	2006	2007	2008	2009	2010	2011	2012
Series	**300**											
VALUE ADDED NET, at basic prices	105266.0	111240.0	112994.0	109081.0	111846.0	117364.0	122953.0	120852.0	116828.0	127162.0	133066.0	134832.0
II.1.1 Generation of income account - Resources												
VALUE ADDED GROSS, at basic prices	141633.0	148885.0	152707.0	152498.0	159898.0	168821.0	179638.0	180579.0	178402.0	191169.0	201359.0	207190.0
II.1.1 Generation of income account - Uses												
Compensation of employees	20200.0	21034.0	19019.0	20672.0	20403.0	20491.0	21095.0	19635.0	17521.0	18561.0	19701.0	20712.0
Other taxes less Other subsidies on production	-8513.0	-9027.0	-8885.0	-8981.0	-9355.0	-9508.0	-9638.0	-13229.0	-12812.0	-13512.0	-13915.0	-14492.0
Other taxes on production	1209.0	1247.0	1376.0	1633.0	1988.0	2284.0	2561.0	3082.0	3217.0	3536.0	3531.0	3667.0
Less: Other subsidies on production	9722.0	10274.0	10261.0	10614.0	11343.0	11792.0	12199.0	16311.0	16029.0	17048.0	17446.0	18159.0
OPERATING SURPLUS, GROSS	67231.0	71399.0	71514.0	72478.0	77710.0	85717.0	90736.0	93616.0	92437.0	98978.0	103155.0	105536.0
MIXED INCOME, GROSS	62715.0	65479.0	71059.0	68329.0	71140.0	72121.0	77445.0	80557.0	81256.0	87142.0	92418.0	95434.0
II.1.2 Allocation of primary income account - Resources												
OPERATING SURPLUS, GROSS	67231.0	71399.0	71514.0	72478.0	77710.0	85717.0	90736.0	93616.0	92437.0	98978.0	103155.0	105536.0
MIXED INCOME, GROSS	62715.0	65479.0	71059.0	68329.0	71140.0	72121.0	77445.0	80557.0	81256.0	87142.0	92418.0	95434.0
Compensation of employees	671506.0	705489.0	722700.0	757260.0	802678.0	875374.0	969408.0	1062960.0	1095188.0	1127614.0	1202963.0	1284277.0
Property income	68643.0	101135.0	105906.0	103095.0	141564.0	54120.0	88018.0	111547.0	82239.0	91190.0	91874.0	95451.0
II.1.2 Allocation of primary income account - Uses												
Property income	56506.0	60657.0	46569.0	24747.0	25801.0	37765.0	72505.0	103040.0	52022.0	46433.0	55323.0	61323.0
BALANCE OF PRIMARY INCOMES	813589.0	882845.0	924610.0	976415.0	1067291.0	1049568.0	1153102.0	1245640.0	1299098.0	1358491.0	1435087.0	1519375.0
II.2 Secondary distribution of income account - Resources												
BALANCE OF PRIMARY INCOMES	813589.0	882845.0	924610.0	976415.0	1067291.0	1049568.0	1153102.0	1245640.0	1299098.0	1358491.0	1435087.0	1519375.0
Social contributions	97.0	90.0	84.0	85.0	84.0	85.0	88.0	384.0	355.0	376.0	399.0	419.0
Social benefits other than social transfers in kind	235134.0	247140.0	272511.0	281112.0	287143.0	296311.0	309694.0	340719.0	367953.0	386430.0	411175.0	432508.0
Other current transfers	17365.0	17423.0	16322.0	17543.0	19143.0	17709.0	22014.0	24292.0	25378.0	25946.0	27362.0	27161.0
II.2 Secondary distribution of income account - Uses												
Current taxes on income, wealth, etc.	172553.0	176591.0	181257.0	192870.0	202738.0	211691.0	237301.0	249471.0	260418.0	276208.0	292378.0	309421.0
Social contributions	180195.0	192647.0	196692.0	207172.0	217649.0	240375.0	266088.0	306721.0	310295.0	317008.0	339311.0	366154.0
Social benefits other than social transfers in kind	97.0	90.0	84.0	85.0	84.0	85.0	88.0	384.0	355.0	376.0	399.0	419.0
Other current transfers	30992.0	31813.0	31879.0	33802.0	34207.0	32656.0	33358.0	39527.0	41033.0	42011.0	44375.0	47087.0
GROSS DISPOSABLE INCOME	682348.0	746357.0	803615.0	841226.0	918983.0	878866.0	948063.0	1014932.0	1080683.0	1135640.0	1197560.0	1256382.0
II.4.1 Use of disposable income account - Resources												
GROSS DISPOSABLE INCOME	682348.0	746357.0	803615.0	841226.0	918983.0	878866.0	948063.0	1014932.0	1080683.0	1135640.0	1197560.0	1256382.0
Adjustment for the change in net equity of households on pension funds	12269.0	19426.0	15276.0	16336.0	15399.0	21713.0	27685.0	37342.0	33979.0	31450.0	33858.0	41568.0
II.4.1 Use of disposable income account - Uses												
Final consumption expenditure	640826.0	669722.0	709860.0	757368.0	798211.0	853328.0	911319.0	958086.0	979235.0	1040627.0	1079392.0	1120013.0
Individual consumption expenditure	640826.0	669722.0	709860.0	757368.0	798211.0	853328.0	911319.0	958086.0	979235.0	1040627.0	1079392.0	1120013.0
SAVING, GROSS	53791.0	96061.0	109031.0	100194.0	136171.0	47251.0	64429.0	94188.0	135427.0	126463.0	152026.0	177937.0
III.1 Capital account - Changes in liabilities and net worth												
SAVING, GROSS	53791.0	96061.0	109031.0	100194.0	136171.0	47251.0	64429.0	94188.0	135427.0	126463.0	152026.0	177937.0
Capital transfers, receivable less payable	-294.0	-940.0	-1048.0	-1863.0	-1765.0	-2063.0	-2576.0	-1973.0	-2431.0	-2377.0	-2377.0	-1887.0

	2001	2002	2003	2004	2005	2006	2007	2008	2009	2010	2011	2012
Series	**300**											
Capital transfers, receivable	1638.0	839.0	954.0	271.0	2.0	0.0	0.0	0.0	0.0	0.0	0.0	0.0
Less: Capital transfers, payable	1932.0	1779.0	2002.0	2134.0	1767.0	2063.0	2576.0	1973.0	2431.0	2377.0	2377.0	1887.0
Equals: CHANGES IN NET WORTH DUE TO SAVINGS AND CAPITAL TRANSFERS	17130.0	57476.0	68270.0	54914.0	86354.0	-6269.0	5168.0	32488.0	71422.0	60079.0	81356.0	103692.0
	III.1 Capital account - Changes in assets											
Gross capital formation	67483.0	66205.0	66972.0	83826.0	97096.0	108363.0	121628.0	116483.0	107165.0	110540.0	139295.0	153431.0
Gross fixed capital formation	67483.0	66205.0	66972.0	83826.0	97096.0	108363.0	121628.0	116483.0	107165.0	110540.0	139295.0	153431.0
Changes in inventories	...	...	...	...	...	...	...	...	...	...	...	...
Acquisitions less disposals of valuables	0.0	0.0	0.0	0.0	0.0	0.0	0.0	0.0	0.0	0.0	0.0	0.0
Acquisitions less disposals of non-produced non-financial assets	0.0	0.0	0.0	0.0	0.0	0.0	0.0	0.0	0.0	0.0	0.0	0.0
NET LENDING (+) / NET BORROWING (-)	-13986.0	28916.0	41011.0	14505.0	37310.0	-63175.0	-59775.0	-24268.0	25831.0	13546.0	10354.0	22619.0
	III.2 Financial account - Changes in liabilities and net worth											
Net incurrence of liabilities	101320.1	102881.2	110718.9	139215.0	167569.2	181454.6	209409.6	123940.7	112048.4	144736.6	165767.5	...
Currency and deposits	...	...	...	...	...	...	...	...	...	...	...	...
Securities other than shares	-3.0	23.0	100.0	-111.0	193.0	-9.0	334.0	1.0	-34.0	0.0	0.0	...
Loans	93539.8	98955.4	110659.4	131245.0	163161.3	173235.9	190484.1	129507.7	126902.8	133565.5	154557.8	...
Shares and other equity	...	...	...	...	...	...	...	...	...	...	...	...
Insurance technical reserves	...	...	...	...	...	...	...	...	...	...	...	...
Financial derivatives	...	...	...	...	...	...	...	...	...	...	...	...
Other accounts payable	7783.3	3902.8	-40.5	8081.0	4215.0	8227.7	18591.5	-5568.0	-14820.4	11171.1	11209.7	...
NET LENDING (+) / NET BORROWING (-) [a]	-8455.6	5930.8	31396.7	2168.6	49361.5	-70774.7	-81850.3	-41664.6	3173.6	-27190.4	-30213.9	...
	III.2 Financial account - Changes in assets											
Net acquisition of financial assets	92864.5	108812.0	142115.6	141383.6	216930.8	110679.9	127559.3	82276.1	115222.0	117546.2	135553.6	...
Currency and deposits	31270.2	42648.7	26606.5	26798.6	34997.8	52997.9	61406.3	57698.7	21346.9	40499.3	62870.6	...
Securities other than shares	5027.0	1952.0	1649.0	2661.0	3314.0	-2612.0	-6484.0	-5130.0	-2545.0	-1942.0	-1532.0	...
Loans	-961.6	7745.6	11825.4	14075.6	25192.1	-6384.9	-2120.5	-6402.8	-3083.0	-4964.6	-1675.7	...
Shares and other equity	10629.1	12981.6	31486.4	34165.0	75077.0	-15665.0	-3195.0	-16629.0	11786.0	-1458.0	-6566.0	...
Insurance technical reserves	41010.7	31804.6	54040.1	52612.7	59424.8	55930.3	43655.9	46599.5	64950.4	63231.3	60301.3	...
Financial derivatives	...	...	...	...	...	...	...	...	...	...	...	...
Other accounts receivable	5889.0	11679.5	16508.1	11070.6	18925.0	26413.6	34296.5	6139.7	22766.6	22180.2	22155.4	...

[a] Net lending in the financial account has not been reconciled with Net lending in the capital account.

Table 4.7 Non-profit institutions serving households (S.15)

Series 300: 1993 SNA, Norwegian krone, Western calendar year | **Data in millions**

	2001	2002	2003	2004	2005	2006	2007	2008	2009	2010	2011	2012
Series	**300**											
	I. Production account - Resources											
Output, at basic prices (otherwise, please specify)	31131.0	33227.0	35865.0	38366.0	41692.0	44452.0	48711.0	53093.0	57541.0	58955.0	62597.0	65687.0
	I. Production account - Uses											
Intermediate consumption, at purchaser's prices	14656.0	15606.0	17482.0	17757.0	19612.0	20793.0	22386.0	24332.0	26335.0	26885.0	28657.0	29793.0
VALUE ADDED GROSS, at basic prices	16475.0	17621.0	18383.0	20609.0	22080.0	23659.0	26325.0	28761.0	31206.0	32070.0	33940.0	35894.0
Less: Consumption of fixed capital	1952.0	1988.0	2009.0	2156.0	2290.0	2512.0	2713.0	2942.0	3102.0	3339.0	3696.0	3942.0
VALUE ADDED NET, at basic prices	14523.0	15633.0	16374.0	18453.0	19790.0	21147.0	23612.0	25819.0	28104.0	28731.0	30244.0	31952.0
	II.1.1 Generation of income account - Resources											
VALUE ADDED GROSS, at basic prices	16475.0	17621.0	18383.0	20609.0	22080.0	23659.0	26325.0	28761.0	31206.0	32070.0	33940.0	35894.0
	II.1.1 Generation of income account - Uses											
Compensation of employees	14523.0	15628.0	16369.0	18448.0	19790.0	21147.0	23602.0	25808.0	28089.0	28716.0	30237.0	31945.0
Other taxes less Other subsidies on production	0.0	5.0	5.0	5.0	0.0	0.0	10.0	13.0	14.0	15.0	7.0	7.0
Other taxes on production	0.0	5.0	5.0	5.0	0.0	0.0	10.0	13.0	14.0	15.0	7.0	7.0
Less: Other subsidies on production	...	...	...	...	...	...	...	...	...	...	...	...
OPERATING SURPLUS, GROSS	1952.0	1988.0	2009.0	2156.0	2290.0	2512.0	2713.0	2940.0	3103.0	3339.0	3696.0	3942.0
	II.1.2 Allocation of primary income account - Resources											
OPERATING SURPLUS, GROSS	1952.0	1988.0	2009.0	2156.0	2290.0	2512.0	2713.0	2940.0	3103.0	3339.0	3696.0	3942.0
Property income	2775.0	2988.0	2238.0	1594.0	1856.0	1536.0	3219.0	4263.0	2492.0	2751.0	3024.0	3234.0
	II.1.2 Allocation of primary income account - Uses											
Property income	464.0	483.0	347.0	154.0	167.0	279.0	1123.0	824.0	307.0	389.0	536.0	530.0
BALANCE OF PRIMARY INCOMES	4263.0	4493.0	3900.0	3596.0	3979.0	3769.0	4809.0	6379.0	5288.0	5701.0	6184.0	6646.0
	II.2 Secondary distribution of income account - Resources											
BALANCE OF PRIMARY INCOMES	4263.0	4493.0	3900.0	3596.0	3979.0	3769.0	4809.0	6379.0	5288.0	5701.0	6184.0	6646.0
Social contributions	156.0	39.0	72.0	82.0	113.0	114.0	151.0	50.0	12.0	113.0	129.0	137.0
Other current transfers	28335.0	29927.0	31222.0	33438.0	35498.0	37117.0	39127.0	45012.0	48970.0	49825.0	52870.0	55447.0
	II.2 Secondary distribution of income account - Uses											
Current taxes on income, wealth, etc.	38.0	124.0	40.0	38.0	23.0	30.0	26.0	31.0	27.0	39.0	26.0	39.0
Social benefits other than social transfers in kind	156.0	39.0	72.0	82.0	113.0	114.0	151.0	50.0	12.0	113.0	129.0	137.0
Other current transfers	0.0	0.0	0.0	0.0	0.0	0.0	244.0	244.0	252.0	256.0	0.0	248.0
GROSS DISPOSABLE INCOME	32560.0	34296.0	35082.0	36996.0	39454.0	40856.0	43666.0	51116.0	53979.0	55231.0	59028.0	61806.0
	II.4.1 Use of disposable income account - Resources											
GROSS DISPOSABLE INCOME	32560.0	34296.0	35082.0	36996.0	39454.0	40856.0	43666.0	51116.0	53979.0	55231.0	59028.0	61806.0
	II.4.1 Use of disposable income account - Uses											
Final consumption expenditure	26738.0	28304.0	30909.0	33025.0	36413.0	38686.0	40737.0	44561.0	48479.0	49326.0	52340.0	54891.0
Individual consumption expenditure	26738.0	28304.0	30909.0	33025.0	36413.0	38686.0	40737.0	44561.0	48479.0	49326.0	52340.0	54891.0
Adjustment for the change in net equity of households on pension funds	...	...	...	...	...	...	...	...	...	...	...	...

	2001	2002	2003	2004	2005	2006	2007	2008	2009	2010	2011	2012
Series	**300**											
SAVING, GROSS	5822.0	5992.0	4173.0	3971.0	3041.0	2170.0	2929.0	6555.0	5500.0	5905.0	6688.0	6915.0
	III.1 Capital account - Changes in liabilities and net worth											
SAVING, GROSS	5822.0	5992.0	4173.0	3971.0	3041.0	2170.0	2929.0	6555.0	5500.0	5905.0	6688.0	6915.0
Capital transfers, receivable less payable	...	...	...	...	...	...	...	...	...	...	...	...
Capital transfers, receivable	...	...	...	...	...	...	...	...	...	...	...	...
Less: Capital transfers, payable	...	...	...	...	...	...	...	...	...	...	...	...
Equals: CHANGES IN NET WORTH DUE TO SAVING AND CAPITAL TRANSFERS	3870.0	4004.0	2164.0	1815.0	751.0	-342.0	216.0	3613.0	2398.0	2566.0	2992.0	2973.0
	III.1 Capital account - Changes in assets											
Gross capital formation	3085.0	3202.0	3404.0	3535.0	3915.0	4115.0	5284.0	5663.0	5881.0	6131.0	6459.0	6568.0
Gross fixed capital formation	3085.0	3202.0	3404.0	3535.0	3915.0	4115.0	5284.0	5663.0	5881.0	6131.0	6459.0	6568.0
Changes in inventories	...	...	...	...	...	...	...	...	...	...	...	...
Acquisitions less disposals of valuables	...	...	...	...	...	...	...	...	...	...	...	...
Acquisitions less disposals of non-produced non-financial assets	...	...	...	...	...	...	...	...	...	...	...	...
NET LENDING (+) / NET BORROWING (-)	2737.0	2790.0	769.0	436.0	-874.0	-1945.0	-2355.0	892.0	-381.0	-226.0	229.0	347.0
	III.2 Financial account - Changes in liabilities and net worth											
Net incurrence of liabilities	884.8	1156.4	42.4	687.4	959.6	3496.5	663.0	840.4	-1077.5	427.6	51.5	...
Currency and deposits	...	...	...	...	...	...	...	...	...	...	...	...
Securities other than shares	0.0	0.0	0.0	0.0	0.0	12.0	174.0	180.0	-17.0	0.0	0.0	...
Loans	951.7	1032.8	53.8	743.1	887.8	3295.7	303.6	789.2	-1112.9	312.7	40.7	...
Shares and other equity	...	...	...	...	...	...	...	...	...	...	...	...
Insurance technical reserves	...	...	...	...	...	...	...	...	...	...	...	...
Financial derivatives	...	...	...	...	...	...	...	...	...	...	...	...
Other accounts payable	-66.9	123.6	-11.3	-55.7	71.8	188.8	185.4	-128.8	52.4	114.9	10.8	...
NET LENDING (+) / NET BORROWING (-) [a]	1926.4	5593.5	2152.1	4665.6	5185.3	3571.3	4742.9	2566.7	4216.9	6108.6	5244.1	...
	III.2 Financial account - Changes in assets											
Net acquisition of financial assets	2811.2	6749.9	2194.5	5353.1	6144.9	7067.7	5405.9	3407.1	3139.4	6536.2	5295.5	...
Currency and deposits	224.1	5262.9	-291.6	1784.0	1686.3	3618.4	3313.5	3360.1	856.0	2991.7	3561.9	...
Securities other than shares	1653.0	-127.0	1860.0	513.0	297.0	502.0	520.0	-1063.0	705.0	93.0	478.0	...
Loans	-1.3	-162.5	0.3	-64.5	9.7	-5.2	-18.0	-0.1	0.1	-0.8	0.7	...
Shares and other equity	918.8	1617.1	729.7	3335.8	4189.0	2382.0	1391.0	989.0	1379.0	3853.0	1902.0	...
Insurance technical reserves	...	...	...	...	...	...	...	...	...	...	...	...
Financial derivatives	...	...	...	...	...	...	...	...	...	...	...	...
Other accounts receivable	16.7	159.3	-103.8	-215.2	-37.1	570.5	199.3	121.0	199.4	-400.7	-647.1	...

[a] Net lending in the financial account has not been reconciled with Net lending in the capital account.

Table 4.8 Combined Sectors: Non-Financial and Financial Corporations (S.11 + S.12)

Series 300: 1993 SNA, Norwegian krone, Western calendar year **Data in millions**

	2001	2002	2003	2004	2005	2006	2007	2008	2009	2010	2011	2012
Series	**300**											
	I. Production account - Resources											
Output, at basic prices (otherwise, please specify)	1933080.0	1906211.0	1973763.0	2181642.0	2442293.0	2802693.0	3075498.0	3444671.0	3111037.0	3255889.0	3536095.0	3753436.0
	I. Production account - Uses											
Intermediate consumption, at purchaser's prices	969361.0	968668.0	993828.0	1068941.0	1159958.0	1351590.0	1564570.0	1710130.0	1579712.0	1618935.0	1746088.0	1848841.0
VALUE ADDED GROSS, at basic prices	963719.0	937543.0	979935.0	1112701.0	1282335.0	1451103.0	1510928.0	1734541.0	1531325.0	1636954.0	1790007.0	1904595.0
Less: Consumption of fixed capital	146161.0	148160.0	149326.0	152757.0	160321.0	173828.0	192345.0	216406.0	235972.0	243026.0	251701.0	263402.0
VALUE ADDED NET, at basic prices	817558.0	789383.0	830609.0	959944.0	1122014.0	1277275.0	1318583.0	1518135.0	1295353.0	1393928.0	1538306.0	1641193.0
	II.1.1 Generation of income account - Resources											
VALUE ADDED GROSS, at basic prices	963719.0	937543.0	979935.0	1112701.0	1282335.0	1451103.0	1510928.0	1734541.0	1531325.0	1636954.0	1790007.0	1904595.0
	II.1.1 Generation of income account - Uses											
Compensation of employees	443729.0	462244.0	471514.0	493320.0	528728.0	586776.0	659575.0	731115.0	741486.0	753901.0	800867.0	857005.0
Other taxes less Other subsidies on production	-2496.0	-4565.0	-6790.0	-6553.0	-6067.0	-4268.0	-6880.0	-6124.0	-10670.0	-14131.0	-13986.0	-15561.0
Other taxes on production	14702.0	13815.0	13764.0	14043.0	14215.0	16544.0	16982.0	17351.0	16219.0	15025.0	15913.0	16521.0
Less: Other subsidies on production	17198.0	18380.0	20554.0	20596.0	20282.0	20812.0	23862.0	23475.0	26889.0	29156.0	29899.0	32082.0
OPERATING SURPLUS, GROSS	522486.0	479864.0	515211.0	625934.0	759674.0	868595.0	858233.0	1009550.0	800509.0	897184.0	1003126.0	1063151.0
	II.1.2 Allocation of primary income account - Resources											
OPERATING SURPLUS, GROSS	522486.0	479864.0	515211.0	625934.0	759674.0	868595.0	858233.0	1009550.0	800509.0	897184.0	1003126.0	1063151.0
Property income	326995.0	307442.0	301611.0	254314.0	357366.0	422612.0	516365.0	622756.0	400066.0	419151.0	440964.0	471236.0
	II.1.2 Allocation of primary income account - Uses											
Property income	462304.0	458665.0	471064.0	470977.0	623493.0	652576.0	765803.0	938249.0	641672.0	652383.0	738548.0	750131.0
BALANCE OF PRIMARY INCOMES	387177.0	328641.0	345758.0	409271.0	493547.0	638631.0	608795.0	694057.0	558903.0	663952.0	705542.0	784256.0
	II.2 Secondary distribution of income account - Resources											
BALANCE OF PRIMARY INCOMES	387177.0	328641.0	345758.0	409271.0	493547.0	638631.0	608795.0	694057.0	558903.0	663952.0	705542.0	784256.0
Social contributions	36587.0	40630.0	38304.0	40537.0	41950.0	49532.0	57676.0	80865.0	76518.0	73261.0	78895.0	88492.0
Other current transfers	87977.0	96688.0	83707.0	87681.0	93737.0	96021.0	143944.0	133873.0	134203.0	122823.0	139146.0	125252.0
	II.2 Secondary distribution of income account - Uses											
Current taxes on income, wealth, etc.	136460.0	125216.0	127965.0	173159.0	228712.0	279342.0	254250.0	312063.0	216693.0	254521.0	293659.0	302393.0
Social benefits other than social transfers in kind	24317.0	21204.0	23028.0	24201.0	25968.0	27038.0	28940.0	42074.0	41083.0	40739.0	43848.0	45521.0
Other current transfers	106008.0	105656.0	97929.0	96320.0	103159.0	106585.0	153709.0	143629.0	144975.0	133819.0	152269.0	137571.0
GROSS DISPOSABLE INCOME	244956.0	213883.0	218847.0	243809.0	271395.0	371219.0	373516.0	411029.0	366873.0	430957.0	433807.0	512515.0
	II.4.1 Use of disposable income account - Resources											
GROSS DISPOSABLE INCOME	244956.0	213883.0	218847.0	243809.0	271395.0	371219.0	373516.0	411029.0	366873.0	430957.0	433807.0	512515.0
	II.4.1 Use of disposable income account - Uses											
Adjustment for the change in net equity of households on pension funds	12269.0	19426.0	15276.0	16336.0	15399.0	21713.0	27685.0	37342.0	33979.0	31450.0	33858.0	41568.0
SAVING, GROSS	232687.0	194457.0	203571.0	227473.0	255996.0	349506.0	345831.0	373687.0	332894.0	399507.0	399949.0	470947.0

	2001	2002	2003	2004	2005	2006	2007	2008	2009	2010	2011	2012
Series	**300**											
III.1 Capital account - Changes in liabilities and net worth												
SAVING, GROSS	232687.0	194457.0	203571.0	227473.0	255996.0	349506.0	345831.0	373687.0	332894.0	399507.0	399949.0	470947.0
Capital transfers, receivable less payable	2414.0	2062.0	8089.0	2178.0	1743.0	2684.0	2140.0	2973.0	2529.0	2583.0	3694.0	3126.0
Capital transfers, receivable	3779.0	2579.0	8914.0	2671.0	1743.0	2684.0	2140.0	2973.0	2529.0	2583.0	3694.0	3126.0
Less: Capital transfers, payable	1365.0	517.0	825.0	493.0	0.0	0.0	0.0	0.0	0.0	0.0	0.0	0.0
Equals: CHANGES IN NET WORTH DUE TO SAVING AND CAPITAL TRANSFERS	88940.0	48359.0	62334.0	76894.0	97418.0	178362.0	155626.0	160254.0	99451.0	159064.0	151942.0	210671.0
III.1 Capital account - Changes in assets												
Gross capital formation	180108.0	177939.0	169386.0	216569.0	264514.0	326361.0	396295.0	426004.0	331667.0	393992.0	430074.0	478507.0
Gross fixed capital formation	166987.0	162031.0	158130.0	180121.0	220262.0	257754.0	315203.0	341202.0	316775.0	283785.0	296184.0	338699.0
Changes in inventories	13121.0	15908.0	11256.0	36448.0	44252.0	68607.0	81092.0	84802.0	14892.0	110207.0	133890.0	139808.0
Acquisitions less disposals of valuables	0.0	0.0	0.0	0.0	0.0	0.0	0.0	0.0	0.0	0.0	0.0	...
Acquisitions less disposals of non-produced non-financial assets	1770.0	582.0	1641.0	3084.0	3370.0	3037.0	2226.0	1381.0	2586.0	2298.0	2577.0	2893.0
NET LENDING (+) / NET BORROWING (-)	53223.0	17998.0	40633.0	9998.0	-10145.0	22792.0	-50550.0	-50725.0	1170.0	5800.0	-29008.0	-7327.0
III.2 Financial account - Changes in liabilities and net worth												
Net incurrence of liabilities	147029.6	361156.5	331243.6	369058.0	784577.6	936319.3	1110863.1	801088.3	234508.1	606570.0	394585.1	...
Currency and deposits	61669.6	115631.1	81909.2	74603.4	209376.0	334501.5	281866.3	277106.7	75768.4	12505.2	226830.7	...
Securities other than shares	27802.8	45050.9	68139.8	54007.3	132553.5	177291.2	191845.9	129340.9	59853.5	142114.3	90417.4	...
Loans	79807.6	104603.3	14090.0	101882.9	152199.9	208266.1	305115.2	398416.9	-42318.2	217898.4	-57406.5	...
Shares and other equity	-3565.2	24417.7	57555.0	31834.9	193904.7	74875.3	71184.9	-15563.0	69592.6	122972.4	13697.4	...
Insurance technical reserves	38539.0	30635.6	55837.7	62654.5	58357.6	59344.5	53128.8	50438.7	64029.8	62611.0	63601.3	...
Financial derivatives	...	...	...	...	...	...	...	...	...	...	...	...
Other accounts payable	-57224.2	40817.9	53712.0	44075.0	38185.8	82040.7	207722.1	-38651.9	7582.1	48468.7	57444.8	...
NET LENDING (+) / NET BORROWING (-) [a]	58033.5	38487.4	60264.0	22212.9	-20165.3	33676.4	-28443.1	-42461.2	-7741.3	57625.0	56642.1	...
III.2 Financial account - Changes in assets												
Net acquisition of financial assets	205063.1	399643.9	391507.6	391270.9	764412.3	969995.7	1082420.0	758627.1	226766.9	664194.9	451227.2	...
Monetary gold and SDRs	558.0	-590.0	-109.0	-3254.0	-106.0	752.0	-827.0	1060.0	-1214.0	-31.0	-470.0	...
Currency and deposits	-1691.0	-2813.2	34073.1	46044.2	80169.2	183244.6	149402.6	153172.0	-74085.9	11458.8	214188.2	...
Securities other than shares	-6298.5	63151.5	61967.2	61048.3	90680.1	101441.3	11466.2	99452.2	182918.3	6035.4	9909.6	...
Loans	151605.1	190669.9	116408.8	180983.8	361056.8	352082.4	445990.8	368988.8	67015.7	222840.1	230875.0	...
Shares and other equity	55055.6	13360.7	48412.9	62925.8	168744.7	178751.3	161096.9	57966.0	98666.6	195893.4	57481.0	...
Insurance technical reserves	2813.7	-515.6	1298.9	1067.9	1721.8	2051.2	7874.0	4909.2	-350.7	1527.7	207.0	...
Financial derivatives	...	...	...	...	...	...	...	...	...	...	...	...
Other accounts receivable	3020.2	136380.7	129455.6	42455.0	62145.7	151672.9	307416.6	73078.8	-46183.2	226470.7	-60963.6	...

[a] Net lending in the financial account has not been reconciled with Net lending in the capital account.

Table 4.9 Combined Sectors: Households and NPISH (S.14 + S.15)

Series 300: 1993 SNA, Norwegian krone, Western calendar year **Data in millions**

	2001	2002	2003	2004	2005	2006	2007	2008	2009	2010	2011	2012
Series	**300**											
I. Production account - Resources												
Output, at basic prices (otherwise, please specify)	266323.0	277689.0	287282.0	304967.0	342366.0	353047.0	367915.0	391744.0	395875.0	415339.0	438017.0	458485.0
I. Production account - Uses												
Intermediate consumption, at purchaser's prices	108215.0	111183.0	116192.0	131860.0	160388.0	160567.0	161952.0	182404.0	186267.0	192100.0	202718.0	215401.0
VALUE ADDED GROSS, at basic prices	158108.0	166506.0	171090.0	173107.0	181978.0	192480.0	205963.0	209340.0	209608.0	223239.0	235299.0	243084.0
Less: Consumption of fixed capital	38319.0	39633.0	41722.0	45573.0	50342.0	53969.0	59398.0	62669.0	64676.0	67346.0	71989.0	76300.0
VALUE ADDED NET, at basic prices	119789.0	126873.0	129368.0	127534.0	131636.0	138511.0	146565.0	146671.0	144932.0	155893.0	163310.0	166784.0
II.1.1 Generation of income account - Resources												
VALUE ADDED GROSS, at basic prices	158108.0	166506.0	171090.0	173107.0	181978.0	192480.0	205963.0	209340.0	209608.0	223239.0	235299.0	243084.0
II.1.1 Generation of income account - Uses												
Compensation of employees	34723.0	36662.0	35388.0	39120.0	40193.0	41638.0	44697.0	45443.0	45610.0	47277.0	49938.0	52657.0
Other taxes less Other subsidies on production	-8513.0	-9022.0	-8880.0	-8976.0	-9355.0	-9508.0	-9628.0	-13216.0	-12798.0	-13497.0	-13908.0	-14485.0
Other taxes on production	1209.0	1252.0	1381.0	1638.0	1988.0	2284.0	2571.0	3095.0	3231.0	3551.0	3538.0	3674.0
Less: Other subsidies on production	9722.0	10274.0	10261.0	10614.0	11343.0	11792.0	12199.0	16311.0	16029.0	17048.0	17446.0	18159.0
OPERATING SURPLUS, GROSS	69183.0	73387.0	73523.0	74634.0	80000.0	88229.0	93449.0	96556.0	95540.0	102317.0	106851.0	109478.0
MIXED INCOME, GROSS	62715.0	65479.0	71059.0	68329.0	71140.0	72121.0	77445.0	80557.0	81256.0	87142.0	92418.0	95434.0
II.1.2 Allocation of primary income account - Resources												
OPERATING SURPLUS, GROSS	69183.0	73387.0	73523.0	74634.0	80000.0	88229.0	93449.0	96556.0	95540.0	102317.0	106851.0	109478.0
MIXED INCOME, GROSS	62715.0	65479.0	71059.0	68329.0	71140.0	72121.0	77445.0	80557.0	81256.0	87142.0	92418.0	95434.0
Compensation of employees	671506.0	705489.0	722700.0	757260.0	802678.0	875374.0	969408.0	1062960.0	1095188.0	1127614.0	1202963.0	1284277.0
Property income	71418.0	104123.0	108144.0	104689.0	143420.0	55656.0	91237.0	115810.0	84731.0	93941.0	94898.0	98685.0
II.1.2 Allocation of primary income account - Uses												
Property income	56970.0	61140.0	46916.0	24901.0	25968.0	38044.0	73628.0	103864.0	52329.0	46822.0	55859.0	61853.0
BALANCE OF PRIMARY INCOMES	817852.0	887338.0	928510.0	980011.0	1071270.0	1053337.0	1157911.0	1252019.0	1304386.0	1364192.0	1441271.0	1526021.0
II.2 Secondary distribution of income account - Resources												
BALANCE OF PRIMARY INCOMES	817852.0	887338.0	928510.0	980011.0	1071270.0	1053337.0	1157911.0	1252019.0	1304386.0	1364192.0	1441271.0	1526021.0
Social contributions	253.0	129.0	156.0	167.0	197.0	199.0	239.0	434.0	367.0	489.0	528.0	556.0
Social benefits other than social transfers in kind	235134.0	247140.0	272511.0	281112.0	287143.0	296311.0	309694.0	340719.0	367953.0	386430.0	411175.0	432508.0
Other current transfers	45700.0	47350.0	47544.0	50981.0	54641.0	54826.0	61141.0	69304.0	74348.0	75771.0	80232.0	82608.0
II.2 Secondary distribution of income account - Uses												
Current taxes on income, wealth, etc.	172591.0	176715.0	181297.0	192908.0	202761.0	211721.0	237327.0	249502.0	260445.0	276247.0	292404.0	309460.0
Social contributions	180195.0	192647.0	196692.0	207172.0	217649.0	240375.0	266088.0	306721.0	310295.0	317008.0	339311.0	366154.0
Social benefits other than social transfers in kind	253.0	129.0	156.0	167.0	197.0	199.0	239.0	434.0	367.0	489.0	528.0	556.0
Other current transfers	30992.0	31813.0	31879.0	33802.0	34207.0	32656.0	33602.0	39771.0	41285.0	42267.0	44375.0	47335.0
GROSS DISPOSABLE INCOME	714908.0	780653.0	838697.0	878222.0	958437.0	919722.0	991729.0	1066048.0	1134662.0	1190871.0	1256588.0	1318188.0

	2001	2002	2003	2004	2005	2006	2007	2008	2009	2010	2011	2012
Series	**300**											
II.4.1 Use of disposable income account - Resources												
GROSS DISPOSABLE INCOME	714908.0	780653.0	838697.0	878222.0	958437.0	919722.0	991729.0	1066048.0	1134662.0	1190871.0	1256588.0	1318188.0
Adjustment for the change in net equity of households on pension funds	12269.0	19426.0	15276.0	16336.0	15399.0	21713.0	27685.0	37342.0	33979.0	31450.0	33858.0	41568.0
II.4.1 Use of disposable income account - Uses												
Final consumption expenditure	667564.0	698026.0	740769.0	790393.0	834624.0	892014.0	952056.0	1002647.0	1027714.0	1089953.0	1131732.0	1174904.0
Individual consumption expenditure	667564.0	698026.0	740769.0	790393.0	834624.0	892014.0	952056.0	1002647.0	1027714.0	1089953.0	1131732.0	1174904.0
SAVING, GROSS	59613.0	102053.0	113204.0	104165.0	139212.0	49421.0	67358.0	100743.0	140927.0	132368.0	158714.0	184852.0
III.1 Capital account - Changes in liabilities and net worth												
SAVING, GROSS	59613.0	102053.0	113204.0	104165.0	139212.0	49421.0	67358.0	100743.0	140927.0	132368.0	158714.0	184852.0
Capital transfers, receivable less payable	-294.0	-940.0	-1048.0	-1863.0	-1765.0	-2063.0	-2576.0	-1973.0	-2431.0	-2377.0	-2377.0	-1887.0
Capital transfers, receivable	1638.0	839.0	954.0	271.0	2.0	0.0	0.0	0.0	0.0	0.0	0.0	0.0
Less: Capital transfers, payable	1932.0	1779.0	2002.0	2134.0	1767.0	2063.0	2576.0	1973.0	2431.0	2377.0	2377.0	1887.0
Equals: CHANGES IN NET WORTH DUE TO SAVINGS AND CAPITAL TRANSFERS	21000.0	61480.0	70434.0	56729.0	87105.0	-6611.0	5384.0	36101.0	73820.0	62645.0	84348.0	106665.0
III.1 Capital account - Changes in assets												
Gross capital formation	70568.0	69407.0	70376.0	87361.0	101011.0	112478.0	126912.0	122146.0	113046.0	116671.0	145754.0	159999.0
Gross fixed capital formation	70568.0	69407.0	70376.0	87361.0	101011.0	112478.0	126912.0	122146.0	113046.0	116671.0	145754.0	159999.0
Changes in inventories	...	...	...	...	...	...	...	...	...	...	...	...
Acquisitions less disposals of valuables	0.0	0.0	0.0	0.0	0.0	0.0	0.0	0.0	0.0	0.0	0.0	0.0
Acquisitions less disposals of non-produced non-financial assets	0.0	0.0	0.0	0.0	0.0	0.0	0.0	0.0	0.0	0.0	0.0	0.0
NET LENDING (+) / NET BORROWING (-)	-11249.0	31706.0	41780.0	14941.0	36436.0	-65120.0	-62130.0	-23376.0	25450.0	13320.0	10583.0	22966.0
III.2 Financial account - Changes in liabilities and net worth												
Net incurrence of liabilities	102204.8	104037.6	110761.3	139902.4	168528.9	184951.1	210072.6	124781.1	110970.9	145164.2	165819.0	...
Currency and deposits	...	...	...	...	...	...	...	...	...	...	...	...
Securities other than shares	-3.0	23.0	100.0	-111.0	193.0	3.0	508.0	181.0	-51.0	0.0	0.0	...
Loans	94491.5	99988.2	110713.1	131988.1	164049.1	176531.5	190787.7	130296.9	125789.9	133878.3	154598.5	...
Shares and other equity	...	...	...	...	...	...	...	...	...	...	...	...
Insurance technical reserves	...	...	...	...	...	...	...	...	...	...	...	...
Financial derivatives	...	...	...	...	...	...	...	...	...	...	...	...
Other accounts payable	7716.3	4026.4	-51.8	8025.3	4286.8	8416.5	18776.9	-5696.8	-14768.0	11286.0	11220.5	...
NET LENDING (+) / NET BORROWING (-) [a]	-6529.1	11524.2	33548.8	6834.3	54546.8	-67203.5	-77107.4	-39097.9	7390.5	-21081.8	-24969.8	...
III.2 Financial account - Changes in assets												
Net acquisition of financial assets	95675.7	115561.9	144310.1	146736.6	223075.7	117747.6	132965.2	85683.2	118361.4	124082.4	140849.1	...
Currency and deposits	31494.3	47911.6	26314.9	28582.6	36684.2	56616.3	64719.9	61058.8	22202.9	43491.0	66432.6	...
Securities other than shares	6680.0	1825.0	3509.0	3174.0	3611.0	-2110.0	-5964.0	-6193.0	-1840.0	-1849.0	-1054.0	...
Loans	-962.9	7583.1	11825.7	14011.2	25201.8	-6390.1	-2138.4	-6402.8	-3082.9	-4965.4	-1675.0	...
Shares and other equity	11547.9	14598.7	32216.1	37500.7	79266.0	-13283.0	-1804.0	-15640.0	13165.0	2395.0	-4664.0	...
Insurance technical reserves	41010.7	31804.6	54040.1	52612.7	59424.8	55930.3	43655.9	46599.5	64950.4	63231.3	60301.3	...

	2001	2002	2003	2004	2005	2006	2007	2008	2009	2010	2011	2012
Series	**300**											
Financial derivatives	...	...	...	...	...	...	...	...	...	...	...	...
Other accounts receivable	5905.7	11838.8	16404.3	10855.4	18887.9	26984.1	34495.9	6260.7	22966.0	21779.5	21508.3	...

[a] Net lending in the financial account has not been reconciled with Net lending in the capital account.

Oman

Source

National accounts data are prepared by the Directorate General of Economic Statistics of the Ministry of National Economy of the Sultanate of Oman located in Muscat, Oman. The official national accounts estimates are published in the "Statistical Yearbook" publications. Each statistical yearbook contains national accounts estimates for the three prior years. The thirty-fifth (2007) and thirty-fourth (2006) edition of the "Statistical Yearbook" are available from the Ministry of National Economy website at http://www.moneoman.gov.om.

General

The Directorate General of Economic Statistics conducted a comprehensive review to update the preparation system of national accounts and others that were not previously prepared for their importance as an index used to measure economical and social development of the Sultanate. The Sultanate applies the new System of National Accounts (SNA) approved by the Economic and Social Council of UN in 1993 after presented by the Bureau of Statistics of the UN. Application of the system was in two stages; the first included the preparation of the national accounts series for the period 1980-1997 for production and income generation accounts according to the international recommendations. The results were published in the 1997 -Statistical Year Book.

The second stage started directly after the release of the updating results of the first stage. The expansion of surveys carried out has a significant impact in the preparation and construction of accounts. Together with this, direct data and methodologies were relied upon instead of the indirect methods previously used in some activities; whereas updating of methodologies for preparation of accounts of production and income generation for some economic activities was achieved. During this stage, data were classified and coded according to the classifications stated in the SNA. The work included the transference of some data collected based on commercial accounting concepts and available in database to SNA concepts. The Ministry resorted to IMF and UN and other experts for the revision and updating processes.

The current account and capital account were constructed in accordance to institutional sectors for 1998-2006, and then the preparation and construction of supply and use tables and the Integrated Economic Accounts (IEA). The updating of the national accounts system required that the MONE expands the periodic economical and social surveys to develop and improve the quality of the basic data needed for the preparation of these accounts, the result of which were used in preparation of national accounts at current and constant prices according to the new methodology for 1998-2007.

The difference in the GDP by the new methodology at current prices compared with the previous methodology was due to a number of reasons which include:

- The economic and social surveys conducted by the Ministry allowed collection of a more detailed data.
- Additional economic activities were covered in the new methodology.
- Updating the method of calculating the intermediate consumption in the new methodology according to the detailed data for some economic activities.
- Amending the methodology for preparing the value added at constant prices for most of the economic activities according to new detailed deflators and change of base year to be 2000 instead of 1988.
- Breaking up the economic activities into institutional sectors.

Constructed Accounts and Tables:
Accounts at the Sector Level:

- Production account; the balancing item is value added balance.
- Generation of income account; the balancing item is operating surplus balance.
- Allocation of primary income accounts; and ends with the balance of primary income.
- Secondary distribution of income account; the balancing item is disposable income balance.

• Redistribution of income in kind account; the balancing item is adjusted disposable income.
• Use of Income account and ends with the saving.
• Capital account; the balancing item is net lending/borrowing.

Accounts at the Overall Level:

• Zero account (Good and Service account) which displays the economy balance at the overall level.
• Integrated economic accounts which reflect the integrated accounts for all sectors including abroad sector.
• Supply and use table; which displays the disposable resources (domestic production + imports) and the disposal of these resources in detail at the economic activity level.

Methodology:

Expenditure Approach

Household Final Consumption: This is measured by the value of all the individual consumption goods and services acquired by resident households.

Government Final Consumption: It is based on the government accounts and it's calculated by taking total production minus sales of the government.

Gross Fixed Capital Formation: The Gross fixed Capital Formation represents the value of imports of machinery equipment, building and construction in addition to the intangible capital formation, which is an estimate of oil and gas survey and exploration services.

Export and Import of Goods and Services: These estimates were based on the foreign trade statistics of commodities and the estimates of the balance of payments prepared by the Central Bank of Oman.

Production Approach

Agriculture: Sources of data used in estimating output include the annual survey of agricultural production for the main crops, some studies carried out by Ministry of Agriculture and Fisheries, and the periodic survey of agricultural products and livestock prices conducted by the Directorate General of Economic Statistics. The studies and researches carried by the Ministry of Agriculture and Fisheries are utilized for calculating intermediate consumption.

Fisheries: Estimates of the output were based on the periodic surveys of traditional fishermen conducted by the Ministry of Agriculture and Fisheries and also data of commercial fishing companies. As for intermediate consumption, some studies prepared by the Ministry of Agriculture and Fisheries were used in the estimation process.

Mining and Quarrying: Crude Petroleum Output estimates are obtained by multiplying production quantities by average monthly price of oil plus the value of crude petroleum sales to Oman Refineries and Petrochemicals Company (ORPC). The production includes estimated income of services generated by oil companies. The value added of this activity is estimated by subtracting the value of intermediate consumption (estimated on the basis of detailed data analysis of current expenditure of ORPC and other oil companies) from the value of output.

Services Incidental to Oil and Gas: Output represents the cost of drilling and exploration by the oil companies. The intermediate consumption is estimated on the basis of field surveys.

Mining of Non Ferrous Metal Ores: Estimates of value added are based on the analysis of balance sheets of the companies working in this field

Quarrying of Stone Sand & Clay: Quarrying of stone, sand and clay production estimates for this activity are based on the periodic survey of quantities conducted by Ministry of Commerce and Industry.

Natural Gas: The output of the natural gas activity represents the value of the government gas consumed. The intermediate consumption is computed based on the cost of operation of the Government Gas System. It also constitutes the production of the upstream project of the government owned OLNG, which is the sales of gas to Oman Liquefied Natural Gas Company. The intermediate consumption was calculated according to the costs of production operations.

Manufacturing of Refined Petroleum Products: The value added of this industry was estimated based on the analysis of the Oman Refineries and Petrochemicals Company (ORPC) budget.

Other Manufacturing: Results of economic surveys carried out by the Directorate General of Economic Statistics and the Industrial Survey conducted by Ministry of Commerce and Industry were used in the estimates of this activity.

Manufacturing of basic chemicals: Value added based on the analysis of the budget of the companies working in this field.

Electricity: the value added of this activity is represented by the analysis of the budget of the companies operating in the area of production, transport and distribution of electricity.

Water: this activity is divided into public (government) production and private production. Government production represents total government revenues from selling water. Private production equals to the value of the water consumed by households that do not use government water.

Construction: The construction activity includes all the residential and non-residential buildings construction operations, construction of roads, electricity and water projects and land preparation etc. Estimates of this activity were based on the annual economic survey of the construction carried out by the Directorate-General for economic statistics.

Maintenance of Vehicles: Output represents the maintenance requirements of the vehicles for the different economic activities, in addition to the individual's expenditure in this field.

Wholesale and Retail Trade: The output of this activity was estimated based on the trade margins for the locally produced commodities, by type of commodity, and the total trade margin for imports, by type of commodity. Intermediate consumption is obtained from the results of economic surveys of this activity.

Repair of Personal and Household Goods: Output represents the households' expenditure on repairing personal and household goods.

Hotels and Restaurants: Estimates were based on the annual survey of hotels and restaurants carried out by the Directorate General of Economic Statistics.

Transport: Output estimates are based on the transport margin for the total supply of goods (i.e., domestic production plus imports) in addition to the analysis of financial statements of some companies working in the transport field as well as the results of the annual economic survey.

Posts, Telegraphs and Telephones: Estimates were based on the accounts of the Ministry of Transport and Telecommunication and on the final accounts of the Oman Telecommunications Company (Omantel) and Omani Qatari Telecommunications Company (Nawras).

Financial Intermediation: Estimates were based on the annual surveys of Banks, Insurance companies, other intermediaries and the analysis of final accounts of Muscat Securities Market (MSM) and the Central Bank of

Oman (CBO).

Real Estate and Business Activities: Several secondary activities come under this activity. In general, government, oil companies' employment data, the average wage, number of house by type and average rent were used to calculate the details of this activity, in addition to the analysis of economic surveys data.

Producers of Government Services: The value added of this activity represents salaries, wages and depreciation. Estimates were based on the State's final accounts. The financial accounts were re-classified into economic accounts according to the New System of National Accounts (SNA 93) in addition to the distribution of government expenditure to (14) sectors and the re-valuation of depreciation by using the Perpetual Inventory Method.

Education: Education is divided into public education and private education. Private education output represents the revenue of private schools & language schools, Private Colleges, institutes and driving schools. These estimates were based on the results of the annual economic survey conducted by the Directorate General of Economic Statistics and other quantitative statistics such as, number of students, schools and institutes. Output of public education represents salaries and wages of the government education sector, plus depreciation, and intermediate consumption.

Health: This activity is also divided into public and private Health. Private health output represents the income of all private clinics and hospitals. Estimates were based on the results of the annual economic survey. Output of public health represents salaries and wages of the health sector in the government budget, plus depreciation, and the intermediate consumption.

Other Community, Social & Personal Services: This activity is divided into public and private. The public aspect represents salaries and wages of the housing sector and the entertainment, cultural and sport sector, plus depreciation, and the intermediate consumption. The private aspect however, was estimated by using economic indicators from studies conducted by the Ministry of National Economy.

Private Households with Employed Persons: Numbers of housemaids, servants, cooks and chauffeurs, in addition to the average annual salary were used to estimate the value of output.

Table 1.1 Gross domestic product by expenditures at current prices

Series 200: 1993 SNA, Rial Omani, Western calendar year — **Data in millions**

	2001	2002	2003	2004	2005	2006	2007	2008	2009	2010	2011	2012
Series	**200**											
	Expenditures of the gross domestic product											
Final consumption expenditure	4499.6	4609.6	4957.3	5654.1	6118.4	6935.0	8329.3	10507.8	10876.4	11625.0	12703.1	
Household final consumption expenditure	2758.4	2768.5	3096.3	3508.4	3621.8	4257.6	5272.3	7179.2	7254.7	7520.1	8054.1	
NPISHs final consumption expenditure	9.2	9.2	10.5	10.9	11.9	11.6	13.1	12.2	20.6	12.9	22.1	
General government final consumption expenditure	1732.0	1831.9	1850.5	2134.8	2484.6	2665.7	3043.9	3316.4	3601.1	4092.0	4627.0	
Gross capital formation	1286.5	1458.0	1915.3	2642.0	2511.8	3709.3	5113.6	7866.6	4697.1	5477.4	6250.1	
Gross fixed capital formation	1297.5	1449.5	1850.2	2426.3	2750.6	3426.7	4927.5	7028.0	6421.3	6302.7	7082.2	
Changes in inventories	-10.9	8.6	65.1	215.7	-238.8	282.6	186.1	838.6	-1723.2	-825.3	-832.1	
Acquisitions less disposals of valuables	...	...	...	...	...	...	...	...	...	...	...	
Exports of goods and services	3867.2	3803.0	4138.9	4891.7	6965.0	8038.0	9139.0	13688.9	9420.9	12881.5	16686.0	

	2001	2002	2003	2004	2005	2006	2007	2008	2009	2010	2011	2012
Series	**200**											
Less: Imports of goods and services	2194.4	2162.3	2728.2	3700.8	3712.2	4531.0	6471.0	8707.2	6446.0	7370.3	8735.0	
Equals: GROSS DOMESTIC PRODUCT	7459.0	7708.4	8283.2	9487.0	11882.9	14151.2	16110.9	23356.0	18548.4	22613.6	26904.2	

Table 1.2 Gross domestic product by expenditures at constant prices

Series 200: 1993 SNA, Rial Omani, Western calendar year **Data in millions**

	2001	2002	2003	2004	2005	2006	2007	2008	2009	2010	2011	2012
Series	**200**											
Base year	**2000**											
Expenditures of the gross domestic product												
Final consumption expenditure	4489.3	4674.1	5070.1	5520.3	5762.9	6209.1	7227.6	8478.6	8733.9	9184.0	9597.1	
Household final consumption expenditure	2746.3	2850.0	3250.2	3447.5	3386.4	3713.4	4587.5	5749.7	5796.0	6102.8	6282.4	
NPISHs final consumption expenditure	9.2	9.4	10.7	10.9	11.7	11.7	11.7	9.7	15.9	10.0	15.9	
General government final consumption expenditure	1733.8	1814.7	1809.3	2061.9	2364.8	2484.0	2628.4	2719.2	2921.8	3071.5	3298.8	
Gross capital formation	1329.8	1478.3	1853.5	2495.4	2039.6	2522.4	3169.1	4057.3	3094.9	3740.4	3931.8	
Gross fixed capital formation	1337.2	1449.8	1791.8	2197.4	2387.2	2722.5	3725.9	4836.3	4642.6	4579.2	4941.2	
Changes in inventories	-7.5	28.5	61.7	297.9	-347.6	-200.1	-556.7	-777.3	-1547.2	-838.9	-1009.4	
Acquisitions less disposals of valuables	...	...	...	...	...	...	...	...	...	...	...	
Exports of goods and services	4258.3	4077.2	3911.5	3884.1	4167.9	4127.0	4384.4	4613.8	4188.2	4452.3	4418.2	
Less: Imports of goods and services	2182.1	2171.3	2748.5	3537.3	3274.3	3681.5	4987.0	6066.2	4571.0	5291.2	5826.4	
Equals: GROSS DOMESTIC PRODUCT	7895.3	8058.3	8086.7	8362.4	8696.1	9177.0	9794.2	11083.5	11445.9	12085.5	12120.7	

Table 1.3 Relations among product, income, savings, and net lending aggregates

Series 200: 1993 SNA, Rial Omani, Western calendar year **Data in millions**

	2001	2002	2003	2004	2005	2006	2007	2008	2009	2010	2011	2012
Series	**200**											
GROSS DOMESTIC PRODUCT	7459.0	7708.4	8283.2	9487.0	11882.9	14151.2	16110.9	23356.0	18548.4	22613.6	26904.2	
Plus: Compensation of employees - from and to the rest of the world, net	...	...	15.0	15.0	15.0	15.0	15.0	15.0	15.0	15.0	15.0	
Plus: Compensation of employees - from the rest of the world	...	...	15.0	15.0	15.0	15.0	15.0	15.0	15.0	15.0	15.0	
Less: Compensation of employees - to the rest of the world	...	...	...	...	...	...	...	...	...	...	...	
Plus: Property income - from and to the rest of the world, net	...	...	-223.0	-165.0	-408.0	-271.0	-324.0	-1076.0	-1176.0	-1076.0	-1245.0	
Plus: Property income - from the rest of the world	...	...	107.0	278.0	279.0	655.0	816.0	407.0	236.0	319.0	253.0	
Less: Property income - to the rest of the world	...	...	330.0	443.0	687.0	926.0	1140.0	1483.0	1412.0	1395.0	1498.0	
Sum of Compensation of employees and property income - from and to the rest of the world, net	-360.0	-371.0	-208.0	-150.0	-393.0	-256.0	-309.0	-1061.0	-1161.0	-1061.0	-1230.0	

	2001	2002	2003	2004	2005	2006	2007	2008	2009	2010	2011	2012
Series	**200**											
Plus: Sum of Compensation of employees and property income - from the rest of the world	...	...	122.0	293.0	294.0	670.0	831.0	422.0	251.0	334.0	268.0	
Less: Sum of Compensation of employees and property income - to the rest of the world	...	...	330.0	443.0	687.0	926.0	1140.0	1483.0	1412.0	1395.0	1498.0	
Plus: Taxes less subsidies on production and imports - from and to the rest of the world, net	...	...	...	...	...	...	...	...	...	...	...	
Equals: GROSS NATIONAL INCOME	7099.0	7337.4	8075.2	9337.0	11489.9	13895.2	15801.9	22295.0	17388.4	21552.6	25674.2	
Plus: Current transfers - from and to the rest of the world, net	-618.3	-646.3	-675.4	-739.7	-915.0	-1117.9	-1458.0	-2039.0	-2091.0	-2240.0	-2821.0	
Equals: GROSS NATIONAL DISPOSABLE INCOME	6480.7	6691.0	7399.8	8597.3	10574.9	12777.3	14343.9	20256.0	15296.4	19312.6	22853.2	
Less: Final consumption expenditure / Actual final consumption	4499.6	4609.6	4957.3	5654.1	6118.4	6935.0	8329.3	10507.8	10876.4	11625.0	12703.1	
Equals: SAVING, GROSS	1981.1	2081.4	2442.6	2943.3	4456.6	5842.3	6014.6	9748.2	4420.0	7687.6	10150.1	
Plus: Capital transfers - from and to the rest of the world, net	...	...	...	...	...	...	...	...	...	...	...	
Less: Gross capital formation	1286.5	1458.0	1915.3	2642.0	2511.8	3709.3	5113.6	7866.6	4698.1	5477.4	6250.1	
Less: Acquisitions less disposals of non-produced non-financial assets	...	...	...	...	...	...	...	...	...	...	...	
Equals: NET LENDING (+) / NET BORROWING (-) OF THE NATION	...	...	...	...	...	...	...	...	...	...	...	
	Net values: Gross National Income / Gross National Disposable Income / Saving Gross less Consumption of fixed capital											
Less: Consumption of fixed capital	...	...	...	...	...	...	...	...	...	...	...	
Equals: NET NATIONAL INCOME	5801.5	5887.9	6225.0	6910.7	8739.3	10468.5	10874.4	15267.1	10967.1	15140.9	19822.0	
Equals: NET NATIONAL DISPOSABLE INCOME	...	...	...	...	...	...	...	...	...	...	...	
Equals: SAVING, NET	...	...	...	...	...	...	...	...	...	...	...	

Table 2.1 Value added by industries at current prices (ISIC Rev. 3)

Series 200: 1993 SNA, Rial Omani, Western calendar year — **Data in millions**

	2001	2002	2003	2004	2005	2006	2007	2008	2009	2010	2011	2012
Series	**200**											
	Industries											
Agriculture, hunting, forestry; fishing	163.3	164.5	171.4	174.4	183.1	191.4	210.1	243.4	261.5	297.6	316.0	
Agriculture, hunting, forestry	112.3	111.4	114.8	108.0	107.7	117.4	133.7	153.2	162.8	187.7	199.9	
Agriculture, hunting and related service activities	112.3	111.4	114.8	108.0	107.7	117.4	133.7	153.2	162.8	187.7	199.9	
Forestry, logging and related service activities	...	...	...	...	...	...	...	...	...	...	...	
Fishing	51.0	53.1	56.6	66.5	75.4	74.0	76.5	90.3	98.8	110.0	116.2	
Mining and quarrying	3299.5	3320.3	3500.2	4102.5	5903.7	6766.6	7181.9	11914.4	7466.1	10480.1	14239.9	
Manufacturing	656.9	668.7	738.0	820.7	1006.9	1526.8	1748.6	2467.0	2189.6	2418.7	2965.2	
Electricity, gas and water supply	79.5	78.9	107.5	122.8	202.7	169.2	176.2	188.9	231.6	271.0	322.2	
Construction	182.5	228.5	275.6	311.4	456.8	566.3	791.8	1116.5	1237.6	1313.7	1390.1	
Wholesale, retail trade, repair of motor vehicles, motorcycles and personal and households goods; hotels and restaurants	655.8	661.9	737.6	889.0	947.9	1203.6	1632.8	2237.4	1795.2	1907.7	2120.3	

	2001	2002	2003	2004	2005	2006	2007	2008	2009	2010	2011	2012
Series	**200**											
Wholesale, retail trade, repair of motor vehicles, motorcycles and personal and household goods	597.5	601.4	675.0	818.1	859.2	1088.6	1489.4	2061.5	1635.5	1735.2	1945.3	
Hotels and restaurants	58.3	60.5	62.5	70.8	88.7	115.0	143.4	175.9	159.7	172.5	175.0	
Transport, storage and communications	391.7	464.2	525.9	620.3	635.6	802.9	909.0	1176.9	1138.3	1161.1	1346.1	
Land transport; transport via pipelines, water transport; air transport; Supporting and auxiliary transport activities; activities of travel agencies	255.4	300.7	345.9	415.4	425.5	545.6	587.4	799.6	741.2	754.1	905.7	
Post and telecommunications	136.3	163.5	180.0	204.9	210.0	257.3	321.6	377.2	397.1	407.0	440.4	
Financial intermediation; real estate, renting and business activities	762.6	799.7	872.4	935.9	1010.4	1141.2	1390.4	1658.8	1825.8	1958.7	2097.4	
Financial intermediation	321.1	348.7	374.0	425.2	462.4	546.5	698.0	846.3	910.7	974.5	1053.5	
Real estate, renting and business activities	441.5	451.0	498.4	510.7	548.0	594.8	692.4	812.5	915.1	984.2	1043.9	
Public administration and defence; compulsory social security	726.6	758.7	753.8	845.1	910.1	1062.6	1192.2	1282.1	1376.8	1604.5	1861.6	
Education; health and social work; other community, social and personal services	591.1	631.0	678.4	738.0	849.4	916.8	1076.6	1235.6	1378.4	1566.1	1634.3	
Education	346.0	372.0	406.8	449.3	523.3	571.7	671.9	767.2	870.5	981.2	1022.6	
Health and social work	131.8	142.7	152.5	163.8	188.0	202.1	237.6	272.5	297.6	346.9	366.9	
Other community, social and personal services	113.3	116.3	119.1	124.8	138.1	143.0	167.1	195.9	210.4	237.9	244.8	
Private households with employed persons	36.1	38.5	41.1	44.3	46.4	48.4	46.8	55.8	53.8	63.0	74.4	
Equals: VALUE ADDED, GROSS, in basic prices [a]	7382.6	7627.4	8215.0	9416.0	11939.4	14155.7	16062.9	23217.2	18529.8	22573.8	27853.8	
Less: Financial intermediation services indirectly measured (FISIM)	163.1	187.5	187.0	188.4	213.6	240.1	293.5	359.5	424.9	468.3	513.8	
Plus: Taxes less Subsidies on products	76.4	80.9	68.2	71.0	-56.4	-4.5	48.0	138.8[b]	18.5	39.8	-949.6	
Plus: Taxes on products	76.4	81.0	68.2	71.0	92.3	123.4	171.9	243.8	...	...	...	
Less: Subsidies on products	...	...	...	...	148.7	127.9	123.9	126.4	...	...	...	
Equals: GROSS DOMESTIC PRODUCT	7459.0	7708.4	8283.2	9487.0	11882.9	14151.2	16110.9	23356.0	18548.4	22613.6	26904.2	

[a] Excludes financial intermediation services indirectly measured (FISIM), but FISIM is included in industry data.
[b] Discrepancy between components and total as one or more components have not been revised.

Table 2.2 Value added by industries at constant prices (ISIC Rev. 3)

Series 200: 1993 SNA, Rial Omani, Western calendar year **Data in millions**

	2001	2002	2003	2004	2005	2006	2007	2008	2009	2010	2011	2012
Series	**200**											
Base year	**2000**											
	Industries											
Agriculture, hunting, forestry; fishing	164.1	164.8	160.7	166.6	161.8	154.3	161.4	173.1	181.4	200.8	205.2	
Agriculture, hunting, forestry	111.6	107.1	104.8	100.0	98.2	94.6	100.8	111.7	117.2	134.5	141.1	
Agriculture, hunting and related service activities	111.6	107.1	104.8	100.0	98.2	94.6	100.8	111.7	117.2	134.5	141.1	
Forestry, logging and related service activities	...	...	...	...	...	...	...	...	...	...	...	
Fishing	52.5	57.7	56.0	66.7	63.6	59.7	60.6	61.4	64.1	66.3	64.1	
Mining and quarrying	3797.4	3587.4	3298.0	3186.6	3217.7	3076.6	2932.1	3191.6	3427.9	3572.3	3653.6	

	2001	2002	2003	2004	2005	2006	2007	2008	2009	2010	2011	2012
Series	**200**											
Base year	**2000**											
Manufacturing	605.5	691.7	715.5	728.6	787.8	868.0	979.5	1081.9	1216.5	1340.3	1299.3	
Electricity, gas and water supply	87.2	107.6	211.1	256.7	277.9	173.8	188.0	198.2	215.2	246.3	285.5	
Construction	184.6	269.6	277.9	302.9	440.4	523.2	708.0	921.1	1072.8	1125.7	1144.1	
Wholesale, retail trade, repair of motor vehicles, motorcycles and personal and household goods; hotels and restaurants	666.5	692.4	772.0	851.9	854.9	1006.2	1218.7	1472.9	1146.4	1251.2	1348.5	
Wholesale, retail trade, repair of motor vehicles, motorcycles and personal and household goods	609.6	637.2	711.7	784.5	775.8	919.8	1126.4	1364.2	1056.7	1156.4	1250.9	
Hotels and restaurants	56.9	55.2	60.3	67.3	79.0	86.4	92.3	108.7	89.6	94.9	97.6	
Transport, storage and communications	389.8	452.4	499.5	552.2	637.2	767.8	797.5	1006.1	1064.1	1093.7	1239.5	
Land transport; transport via piplines, water transport; air transport; Supporting and auxiliary transport activities; activities of travel agencies	253.5	288.9	310.2	337.2	391.7	453.9	393.4	503.6	467.8	484.7	565.8	
Post and telecommunications	136.3	163.5	189.3	215.0	245.5	313.9	404.0	502.4	596.3	609.0	673.7	
Financial intermediation, real estate, renting and business activities	739.6	774.7	836.2	871.7	916.2	995.9	1104.1	1239.0	1276.1	1340.0	1384.3	
Financial intermediation	299.1	319.9	333.9	355.8	365.4	412.6	482.0	591.1	600.6	648.2	678.4	
Real estate, renting and business activities	440.5	454.8	502.2	515.9	550.8	583.3	622.1	647.9	675.5	691.8	705.9	
Public administration and defence; compulsory social security	720.2	744.6	725.0	801.2	839.7	954.7	959.9	983.9	1050.9	1103.7	1249.2	
Education; health and social work; other community, social and personal services	586.8	619.4	649.0	696.4	778.9	796.8	870.6	947.9	1039.7	1085.7	1104.6	
Education	343.8	366.2	388.9	423.9	481.3	490.6	546.2	594.0	657.9	684.5	695.7	
Health and social work	130.6	139.5	145.3	153.7	169.6	176.9	187.3	204.9	222.2	234.6	241.9	
Other community, social and personal services	112.4	113.7	114.8	118.9	128.0	129.3	137.1	149.0	159.7	166.6	167.0	
Private households with employed persons	36.0	37.9	40.7	43.9	45.9	47.9	45.3	53.2	51.3	50.7	58.4	
Equals: VALUE ADDED, GROSS, in basic prices [a]	7819.1	7976.5	8017.9	8294.6	8773.8	9169.0	9736.6	10992.3	11430.8	12064.2	12607.2	
Less: Financial intermediation services indirectly measured (FISIM)	158.6	166.0	167.7	164.0	184.5	196.2	228.4	276.4	311.4	346.1	365.0	
Plus: Taxes less Subsidies on products	76.2	81.7	68.7	67.9	-77.7	8.0	57.6	91.2	15.1	21.2	-486.6	
Equals: GROSS DOMESTIC PRODUCT	7895.3	8058.3	8086.7	8362.4	8696.1	9177.0	9794.2	11083.5	11445.8	12085.5	12120.7	

[a] Excludes financial intermediation services indirectly measured (FISIM), but FISIM is included in industry data.

Table 2.3 Output, gross value added, and fixed assets by industries at current prices (ISIC Rev. 3) Total Economy

Series 200: 1993 SNA, Rial Omani, Western calendar year **Data in millions**

	2001	2002	2003	2004	2005	2006	2007	2008	2009	2010	2011	2012
Series	**200**											
Output, at basic prices	10393.5	10898.5	11680.9	13600.9	17187.8	20358.0	24074.4	34618.1	28855.4	34452.0	41920.1	
Less: Intermediate consumption, at purchaser's prices	3010.9	3271.1	3466.0	4184.9	5248.5	6202.3	8011.5	11400.9	10325.6	11878.2	14066.3	
Equals: VALUE ADDED, GROSS, at basic prices [a]	7382.6	7627.4	8215.0	9416.0	11939.4	14155.7	16062.9	23217.2	18529.8	22573.8	27853.8	

	2001	2002	2003	2004	2005	2006	2007	2008	2009	2010	2011	2012
Series	**200**											
Compensation of employees	2165.4	2247.1	2481.2	2740.0	3151.7	3529.3	4190.3	5011.9	5283.6	6062.5	6975.6	
Taxes on production and imports, less Subsidies	37.0	82.9	84.9	102.6	72.4	97.8	154.6	161.2	160.4	162.2	-949.6	
Taxes on production and imports	62.3	88.3	88.1	106.9	79.1	111.1	173.0	181.8	175.2	177.0	...	
Taxes on products	...	...	...	...	...	...	...	...	...	...	...	
Other taxes on production	62.4	90.2	88.8	108.2	79.3	111.3	173.2	182.0	175.2	177.1	...	
Less: Subsidies	25.6	7.3	3.4	5.6	6.8	13.3	18.6	20.9	14.7	14.9	...	
Subsidies on products	...	...	...	...	...	...	...	...	...	...	...	
Other subsidies on production	25.6	7.3	3.4	5.7	6.9	13.5	18.6	20.9	14.7	14.9	...	
OPERATING SURPLUS, GROSS	4717.4	4802.0	5142.8	6033.2	8120.4	9803.4	10783.9	16843.3	11952.6	15266.5	...	
MIXED INCOME, GROSS	461.3	492.5	505.1	585.4	594.8	725.2	934.1	1197.2	1112.8	1063.9	...	
Total Economy only: Adjustment for FISIM (if FISIM is not distributed to uses)	163.1	187.5	187.0	188.4	213.6	240.1	293.5	359.5	424.9	468.3	513.8	
Less: Consumption of fixed capital	689.2	520.3	795.1	1146.7	1561.1	1907.6	1757.3	1824.3	2528.6	2585.2	...	
OPERATING SURPLUS, NET	4007.1	4273.4	4323.6	4908.0	6610.4	7951.6	9090.3	15100.8	9498.6	12764.0	...	
MIXED INCOME, NET	485.8	505.4	531.5	563.9	543.8	669.4	870.5	1125.0	1038.0	981.4	...	
Gross capital formation	1286.5	1458.0	1915.3	2642.0	2511.8	3709.3	5113.6	7856.0	4698.1	5477.4	...	
Gross fixed capital formation	1297.5	1449.5	1850.2	2426.3	2750.6	3426.7	4927.5	7028.0	6421.3	6302.7	...	
Changes in inventories	-10.9	8.6	65.1	215.7	-238.8	282.6	186.1	828.0	-1723.2	-825.3	-832.1	
Acquisitions less disposals of valuables	...	...	...	...	...	...	...	...	...	...	...	

[a] Excludes financial intermediation services indirectly measured (FISIM), but FISIM is included in industry data.

Table 2.3 Output, gross value added, and fixed assets by industries at current prices (ISIC Rev. 3) Agriculture, hunting, forestry; fishing (A+B)

Series 200: 1993 SNA, Rial Omani, Western calendar year **Data in millions**

	2001	2002	2003	2004	2005	2006	2007	2008	2009	2010	2011	2012
Series	**200**											
Output, at basic prices	234.1	238.4	245.7	250.6	262.8	274.7	302.1	338.2	362.2	407.3	432.7	
Less: Intermediate consumption, at purchaser's prices	70.8	73.9	74.3	76.2	79.7	83.4	92.0	94.8	100.8	109.6	116.6	
Equals: VALUE ADDED, GROSS, at basic prices	163.3	164.5	171.4	174.4	183.1	191.4	210.1	243.4	261.5	297.6	316.0	
Compensation of employees	25.6	26.8	27.1	25.0	30.2	24.3	27.7	31.5	31.3	34.1	36.8	
Taxes on production and imports, less Subsidies	0.1	1.9	0.7	1.3	0.2	0.2	0.2	0.2	0.2[a]	0.2[a]	0.0	
Taxes on production and imports	0.0	0.0	0.0	0.0	0.0	0.0	0.0	0.0	0.2	0.2	0.0	
Taxes on products	...	...	...	...	...	...	...	...	...	...	...	
Other taxes on production	0.1	1.9	0.7	1.3	0.2	0.2	0.2	0.2	0.2	0.2	...	
Less: Subsidies	0.1	0.1	0.1	0.1	0.0	0.0	0.0	0.0	0.0	0.0	0.0	
Subsidies on products	...	...	...	...	...	...	...	...	...	...	...	
Other subsidies on production	0.1	0.1	0.1	0.1	0.0	0.0	0.0	0.0	0.0	...	...	
OPERATING SURPLUS, GROSS	3.4	7.3	6.2	6.3	8.9	11.0	15.1	12.9	14.8	18.1	...	
MIXED INCOME, GROSS	134.3	128.6	137.6	142.0	143.7	155.9	167.1	198.8	215.2	245.2	...	

	2001	2002	2003	2004	2005	2006	2007	2008	2009	2010	2011	2012
Series	**200**											
Less: Consumption of fixed capital	7.3	8.9	8.5	9.1	9.6	8.8	10.2	11.8	12.5	13.6	...	
OPERATING SURPLUS, NET	1.9	5.0	4.0	3.9	6.0	8.1	11.2	8.6	10.2	13.2	...	
MIXED INCOME, NET	128.5	122.0	131.2	135.3	137.0	150.0	160.8	191.3	207.2	236.6	...	
Gross capital formation	...	...	...	...	...	...	...	...	...	...	...	
Gross fixed capital formation	19.7	15.5	15.7	13.6	9.1	21.2	12.3	10.2	9.5	10.1	...	
Changes in inventories	...	...	...	...	...	...	...	...	...	...	...	
Acquisitions less disposals of valuables	...	...	...	...	...	...	...	...	...	...	...	

[a] Discrepancy between components and total.

Table 2.3 Output, gross value added, and fixed assets by industries at current prices (ISIC Rev. 3) Agriculture, hunting and related service activities (01)

Series 200: 1993 SNA, Rial Omani, Western calendar year **Data in millions**

	2001	2002	2003	2004	2005	2006	2007	2008	2009	2010	2011	2012
Series	**200**											
Output, at basic prices	176.5	173.5	178.9	171.1	173.8	189.9	214.4	236.1	252.0	282.0	300.6	
Less: Intermediate consumption, at purchaser's prices	64.2	62.1	64.0	63.2	66.1	72.5	80.7	82.9	88.7	94.6	100.8	
Equals: VALUE ADDED, GROSS, at basic prices	112.3	111.4	114.8	108.0	107.7	117.4	133.7	153.2	162.8	187.7	199.9	
Compensation of employees	24.9	24.6	24.7	20.7	25.4	21.2	24.4	26.9	26.0	27.5	28.5	
Taxes on production and imports, less Subsidies	0.0	0.0	0.0	0.0	0.2	0.2	0.2	0.2	0.0	0.0	0.0	
Taxes on production and imports	0.1	0.1	0.1	0.1	0.2	0.2	0.2	0.2	0.2	...	...	
Taxes on products	...	...	...	...	...	...	...	...	...	...	...	
Other taxes on production	0.1	0.1	0.1	0.1	0.2	0.2	0.2	0.2	0.2	...	...	
Less: Subsidies	0.1	0.1	0.1	0.1	0.0	0.0	0.0	0.0	...	...	...	
Subsidies on products	...	...	...	...	...	...	...	...	...	...	...	
Other subsidies on production	0.1	0.1	0.1	0.1	0.0	0.0	0.2	0.2	0.2	0.0	0.0	
OPERATING SURPLUS, GROSS	2.5	2.4	2.5	2.4	3.4	7.3	11.2	9.5	11.7	13.3	...	
MIXED INCOME, GROSS	84.9	84.4	87.6	84.8	78.7	88.7	97.8	116.6	124.9	146.7	...	
Less: Consumption of fixed capital	6.9	6.7	6.9	6.8	7.1	7.2	8.5	9.9	10.5	10.8	...	
OPERATING SURPLUS, NET	1.2	1.2	1.2	1.2	1.7	5.2	8.2	6.2	8.2	9.7	...	
MIXED INCOME, NET	79.3	79.0	82.1	79.2	73.3	83.6	92.4	110.0	117.9	139.5	...	
Gross capital formation	...	...	...	...	...	...	...	...	...	...	...	

Table 2.3 Output, gross value added, and fixed assets by industries at current prices (ISIC Rev. 3) Fishing (B)

Series 200: 1993 SNA, Rial Omani, Western calendar year — **Data in millions**

	2001	2002	2003	2004	2005	2006	2007	2008	2009	2010	2011	2012
Series	**200**											
Output, at basic prices	57.7	64.9	66.8	79.5	88.9	84.9	87.7	102.7	111.0	125.0	132.0	
Less: Intermediate consumption, at purchaser's prices	6.7	11.8	10.2	13.0	13.5	10.8	11.2	11.9	12.2	15.0	15.9	
Equals: VALUE ADDED, GROSS, at basic prices	51.0	53.1	56.6	66.5	75.4	74.0	76.5	90.8	98.8	110.0	116.2	
Compensation of employees	0.7	2.3	2.4	4.2	4.8	3.1	3.3	4.6	5.3	6.6	8.3	
Taxes on production and imports, less Subsidies	0.0	1.8	0.6	1.2	0.1	0.0	0.0	0.0	0.0	0.0	0.0	
Taxes on production and imports	0.0	1.8	0.6	1.2	0.1	0.0	0.0	0.0	0.0	0.0	0.0	
Taxes on products	...	...	...	...	...	...	...	...	...	...	...	
Other taxes on production	0.0	1.8	0.6	1.2	0.1	0.0	0.0	0.0	0.0	...	...	
Less: Subsidies	...	...	...	...	...	...	...	...	...	...	...	
OPERATING SURPLUS, GROSS	0.9	4.9	3.7	3.9	5.5	3.7	3.9	3.4	3.1	4.8	...	
MIXED INCOME, GROSS	49.4	44.1	50.0	57.2	65.0	67.2	69.2	82.2	90.3	98.5	...	
Less: Consumption of fixed capital	0.4	2.2	1.6	2.3	2.5	1.7	1.7	1.9	2.0	2.8	...	
OPERATING SURPLUS, NET	0.7	3.8	2.9	2.7	4.3	2.8	3.0	2.4	2.0	3.4	...	
MIXED INCOME, NET	49.2	43.1	49.2	56.1	63.8	66.4	68.4	81.3	89.3	97.1	...	
Gross capital formation	...	...	...	...	...	...	...	...	...	...	...	

Table 2.3 Output, gross value added, and fixed assets by industries at current prices (ISIC Rev. 3) Mining and quarrying (C)

Series 200: 1993 SNA, Rial Omani, Western calendar year — **Data in millions**

	2001	2002	2003	2004	2005	2006	2007	2008	2009	2010	2011	2012
Series	**200**											
Output, at basic prices	3577.8	3616.3	3830.2	4443.6	6264.4	7219.4	7757.0	12572.0	8165.8	11259.9	15083.7	
Less: Intermediate consumption, at purchaser's prices	278.2	295.9	330.1	341.1	360.7	452.8	575.1	657.6	699.7	779.8	843.8	
Equals: VALUE ADDED, GROSS, at basic prices	3299.5	3320.3	3500.2	4102.5	5903.7	6766.6	7181.9	11914.4	7466.1	10480.1	14239.9	
Compensation of employees	136.6	155.8	177.3	199.5	226.8	230.3	267.6	375.6	397.4	448.2	515.3	
Taxes on production and imports, less Subsidies	1.6	1.1	1.6	3.1	2.3	4.2	0.3	0.3	0.3	1.2	...	
Taxes on production and imports	1.6	1.1	1.6	3.1	2.4	4.5	4.0	12.0	5.8	6.9	0.0	
Taxes on products	...	...	...	...	...	...	...	...	...	...	...	
Other taxes on production	1.6	1.1	1.6	3.1	2.4	4.5	4.0	12.0	5.8	6.9	...	
Less: Subsidies	0.0	0.0	0.0	0.0	0.0	0.0	3.7	11.6	5.5	5.7	0.0	
Subsidies on products	...	...	...	...	...	...	...	...	...	...	...	
Other subsidies on production	0.0	0.0	0.0	0.0	0.1	0.2	3.7	11.6	5.5	5.7	...	
OPERATING SURPLUS, GROSS	3161.3	3163.4	3321.3	3899.9	5674.5	6532.0	6914.0	11538.4	7068.3	10030.7	...	
MIXED INCOME, GROSS	...	...	...	...	...	...	...	...	...	...	...	

	2001	2002	2003	2004	2005	2006	2007	2008	2009	2010	2011	2012
Series	**200**											
Less: Consumption of fixed capital	249.4	58.1	283.5	483.6	451.8	603.6	811.6	674.1	1126.3	989.5	...	
OPERATING SURPLUS, NET	2911.8	3105.3	3037.7	3416.3	5222.7	5928.4	6102.4	10864.3	5942.0	9041.2	...	
MIXED INCOME, NET	...	...	...	...	...	...	...	...	...	...	...	
Gross capital formation	...	...	...	...	...	...	...	...	...	...	...	
Gross fixed capital formation	408.5	445.7	598.1	773.8	780.1	1021.3	1602.5	2234.2	1983.0	1873.4	...	
Changes in inventories	...	...	...	...	...	...	...	...	...	...	...	
Acquisitions less disposals of valuables	...	...	...	...	...	...	...	...	...	...	...	

Table 2.3 Output, gross value added, and fixed assets by industries at current prices (ISIC Rev. 3) Manufacturing (D)

Series 200: 1993 SNA, Rial Omani, Western calendar year **Data in millions**

	2001	2002	2003	2004	2005	2006	2007	2008	2009	2010	2011	2012
Series	**200**											
Output, at basic prices	1478.0	1598.7	1780.5	2013.3	2626.8	3647.7	4714.0	7508.5	5755.7	6873.2	8777.9	
Less: Intermediate consumption, at purchaser's prices	821.1	930.0	1042.5	1192.6	1619.8	2120.8	2965.3	5041.4	3566.0	4454.5	5812.7	
Equals: VALUE ADDED, GROSS, at basic prices	656.9	668.7	738.0	820.7	1006.9	1526.8	1748.6	2467.0	2189.6	2418.7	2965.2	
Compensation of employees	112.6	125.8	122.7	125.1	151.2	162.2	205.4	242.3	268.6	299.0	345.4	
Taxes on production and imports, less Subsidies	3.0	8.8	6.9	24.0	-1.4	3.1	32.3	32.3	32.3	32.3	...	
Taxes on production and imports	4.6	10.3	9.2	28.6	4.7	10.2	40.9	40.9	40.9	40.9	...	
Taxes on products	...	...	...	...	...	...	...	...	...	...	...	
Other taxes on production	4.6	10.3	9.2	28.6	4.7	10.2	40.9	40.9	40.9	40.9	...	
Less: Subsidies	1.6	1.5	2.3	4.6	6.1	7.2	8.6	8.6	8.6	8.6	...	
Subsidies on products	...	...	...	...	...	...	...	...	...	...	...	
Other subsidies on production	1.6	1.5	2.3	4.6	6.1	7.2	8.6	8.6	8.6	8.6	...	
OPERATING SURPLUS, GROSS	527.9	508.3	593.2	652.7	843.1	1343.8	1486.6	2158.8	1840.9	2038.5	...	
MIXED INCOME, GROSS	13.5	25.7	15.1	18.9	14.0	17.7	24.4	29.9	29.6	29.7	...	
Less: Consumption of fixed capital	79.6	88.9	83.2	86.1	94.7	128.1	139.5	222.1	296.4	435.3	...	
OPERATING SURPLUS, NET	449.6	421.8	511.4	567.6	750.0	1217.5	1349.7	1939.4	1546.2	1612.4	...	
MIXED INCOME, NET	13.9	25.7	15.5	18.0	12.4	15.9	21.7	27.2	27.3	20.5	...	
Gross capital formation	...	...	...	...	...	...	...	...	...	...	...	
Gross fixed capital formation	87.1	85.6	119.0	581.8	676.8	797.0	1337.4	1939.3	1296.2	1209.7	...	
Changes in inventories	...	...	...	...	...	...	...	...	...	...	...	
Acquisitions less disposals of valuables	...	...	...	...	...	...	...	...	...	...	...	

Table 2.3 Output, gross value added, and fixed assets by industries at current prices (ISIC Rev. 3) Electricity, gas and water supply (E)

Series 200: 1993 SNA, Rial Omani, Western calendar year **Data in millions**

	2001	2002	2003	2004	2005	2006	2007	2008	2009	2010	2011	2012
Series	**200**											
Output, at basic prices	239.1	238.6	260.7	282.4	456.2	504.0	547.4	582.1	682.0	815.1	969.1	
Less: Intermediate consumption, at purchaser's prices	159.6	159.7	153.2	159.6	253.5	334.9	371.2	393.3	450.3	544.1	646.9	
Equals: VALUE ADDED, GROSS, at basic prices	79.5	78.9	107.5	122.8	202.7	169.2	176.2	188.9	231.6	271.0	322.2	
Compensation of employees	16.3	17.5	18.6	19.5	23.4	23.1	26.6	36.5	42.2	51.0	61.7	
Taxes on production and imports, less Subsidies	0.8	0.8	0.0	0.0	0.0	0.0	0.0	0.0	0.0	0.0	0.0	
Taxes on production and imports	0.8	0.8	0.0	0.0	0.0	0.0	0.0	0.0	0.0	0.0	0.0	
Taxes on products	...	...	...	...	...	...	...	...	...	...	...	
Other taxes on production	0.8	0.8	0.0	0.0	0.0	0.0	0.0	0.0	0.0	0.0	...	
Less: Subsidies	...	...	...	...	...	...	...	...	...	...	...	
OPERATING SURPLUS, GROSS	60.8	59.0	82.5	93.1	168.8	135.6	148.1	150.7	187.7	218.1	...	
MIXED INCOME, GROSS	1.6	1.7	6.4	10.1	10.5	10.5	1.6	1.7	1.8	1.9	...	
Less: Consumption of fixed capital	43.3	44.2	51.4	55.4	85.0	74.3	70.9	81.2	91.4	98.5	...	
OPERATING SURPLUS, NET	18.6	15.9	34.2	42.6	88.3	66.1	77.8	70.2	96.9	120.2	...	
MIXED INCOME, NET	0.6	0.6	3.3	5.2	6.0	5.6	1.0	1.0	1.1	1.3	...	
Gross capital formation	...	...	...	...	...	...	...	...	...	...	...	
Gross fixed capital formation	93.7	183.5	279.8	86.6	121.9	142.2	165.2	228.5	301.5	351.0	...	
Changes in inventories	...	...	...	...	...	...	...	...	...	...	...	
Acquisitions less disposals of valuables	...	...	...	...	...	...	...	...	...	...	...	

Table 2.3 Output, gross value added, and fixed assets by industries at current prices (ISIC Rev. 3) Construction (F)

Series 200: 1993 SNA, Rial Omani, Western calendar year **Data in millions**

	2001	2002	2003	2004	2005	2006	2007	2008	2009	2010	2011	2012
Series	**200**											
Output, at basic prices	484.4	566.3	677.2	955.6	1286.5	1548.3	2153.5	3135.5	3313.8	3517.6	3722.3	
Less: Intermediate consumption, at purchaser's prices	301.9	337.8	401.6	644.2	829.7	982.0	1361.8	2019.0	2076.2	2203.9	2332.2	
Equals: VALUE ADDED, GROSS, at basic prices	182.5	228.5	275.6	311.4	456.8	566.3	791.8	1116.5	1237.6	1313.7	1390.1	
Compensation of employees	110.6	119.4	146.7	166.8	255.9	297.8	401.6	547.0	553.7	723.5	945.3	
Taxes on production and imports, less Subsidies	7.1	24.6	12.5	14.5	34.7	18.3	37.7	37.7	37.6	37.6	0.0	
Taxes on production and imports	7.7	25.6	13.1	14.6	34.9	18.3	37.7	37.7	37.7	37.7	0.0	
Taxes on products	...	...	...	...	...	...	...	...	...	...	...	
Other taxes on production	7.7	25.6	13.1	14.6	34.9	18.3	37.7	37.7	37.7	37.7	...	
Less: Subsidies	0.6	1.0	0.6	0.1	0.1	0.0	0.1	0.1	0.1	0.1	0.0	
Subsidies on products	...	...	...	...	...	...	...	...	...	...	...	

	2001	2002	2003	2004	2005	2006	2007	2008	2009	2010	2011	2012
Series	**200**											
Other subsidies on production	0.6	1.0	0.6	0.1	0.1	0.0	0.1	0.1	0.1	0.1	...	
OPERATING SURPLUS, GROSS	57.9	73.0	114.7	131.2	167.2	251.4	354.1	528.6	641.0	682.6	...	
MIXED INCOME, GROSS	5.7	9.5	0.5	-1.1	-1.0	-1.2	-1.7	3.2	5.1	-130.1	...	
Less: Consumption of fixed capital	22.2	19.7	35.8	49.4	443.6	550.3	116.1	92.8	168.0	178.4	...	
OPERATING SURPLUS, NET	35.9	53.7	79.3	83.1	-274.9	-297.3	240.4	437.0	476.0	507.4	...	
MIXED INCOME, NET	6.7	11.1	1.2	-2.5	-2.4	-2.9	-4.1	2.0	2.1	-133.3	...	
Gross capital formation	...	...	...	...	...	...	...	...	...	...	...	
Gross fixed capital formation	33.8	23.9	36.0	32.6	69.2	85.1	174.4	206.0	109.3	116.0	...	
Changes in inventories	...	...	...	...	...	...	...	...	...	...	...	
Acquisitions less disposals of valuables	...	...	...	...	...	...	...	...	...	...	...	

Table 2.3 Output, gross value added, and fixed assets by industries at current prices (ISIC Rev. 3) Wholesale retail trade, repair of motor vehicles, motorcycles, etc.; hotels and restaurants (G+H)

Series 200: 1993 SNA, Rial Omani, Western calendar year **Data in millions**

	2001	2002	2003	2004	2005	2006	2007	2008	2009	2010	2011	2012
Series	**200**											
Output, at basic prices	1003.6	1010.3	1120.9	1341.8	1442.1	1718.5	2301.1	3111.6	2722.3	2864.8	3177.8	
Less: Intermediate consumption, at purchaser's prices	347.7	348.4	383.4	452.8	494.2	514.8	668.4	874.2	927.1	957.1	1057.6	
Equals: VALUE ADDED, GROSS, at basic prices	655.8	661.9	737.6	889.0[a]	947.9	1203.6	1632.8	2237.4	1795.2	1907.7	2120.3	
Compensation of employees	303.7	255.7	358.2	412.1	447.4	508.5	640.3	872.3	837.3	915.5	1006.9	
Taxes on production and imports, less Subsidies	22.6	20.6	28.4	27.8	6.3	43.9	30.1	30.1	28.8	28.9	0.0	
Taxes on production and imports	22.6	20.6	28.4	27.9	6.7	45.5	30.7	30.7	29.4	29.4	0.0	
Taxes on products	...	...	...	...	...	...	...	...	...	...	...	
Other taxes on production	22.6	20.6	28.4	27.9	6.7	45.5	30.7	30.7	29.4	29.4	...	
Less: Subsidies	...	...	...	0.1	0.4	1.6	0.6	0.6	0.6	0.5	0.0	
Subsidies on products	...	...	...	...	...	...	...	...	...	...	...	
Other subsidies on production	...	...	...	0.1	0.4	1.6	0.6	0.6	0.6	0.5	...	
OPERATING SURPLUS, GROSS	135.4	182.7	138.6	245.1	245.1	367.7	579.2	882.0	488.2	505.6	...	
MIXED INCOME, GROSS	194.1	202.8	212.4	249.0	249.0	283.5	383.1	453.0	438.9	457.8	...	
Less: Consumption of fixed capital	18.7	13.8	19.1	111.8	82.5	109.5	122.9	161.4	166.3	184.6	...	
OPERATING SURPLUS, NET	91.7	153.6	90.5	132.9	191.3	290.8	498.4	771.1	373.1	371.7	...	
MIXED INCOME, NET	219.1	218.1	241.4	249.4	220.4	250.8	341.0	402.6	388.2	407.0	...	
Gross capital formation	...	...	...	...	...	...	...	...	...	...	...	
Gross fixed capital formation	52.1	37.8	54.9	83.5	65.0	163.3	145.8	270.0	203.2	144.4	...	
Changes in inventories	...	...	...	...	...	...	...	...	...	...	...	
Acquisitions less disposals of valuables	...	...	...	...	...	...	...	...	...	...	...	

[a] Discrepancy between components and total.

Table 2.3 Output, gross value added, and fixed assets by industries at current prices (ISIC Rev. 3) Transport, storage and communications (I)

Series 200: 1993 SNA, Rial Omani, Western calendar year **Data in millions**

	2001	2002	2003	2004	2005	2006	2007	2008	2009	2010	2011	2012
Series	**200**											
Output, at basic prices	561.0	631.8	703.7	832.9	904.8	1108.8	1298.0	1720.3	1680.6	1846.9	2152.5	
Less: Intermediate consumption, at purchaser's prices	169.3	167.7	177.8	212.6	269.3	306.0	389.0	543.4	542.3	685.8	806.4	
Equals: VALUE ADDED, GROSS, at basic prices	391.7	464.2	525.9	620.3	635.6	802.9	909.0	1176.9	1138.3	1161.1	1346.1	
Compensation of employees	83.9	90.5	112.3	119.7	141.3	177.9	199.2	227.0	251.7	281.0	323.0	
Taxes on production and imports, less Subsidies	8.0	6.2	6.6	9.2	8.1	1.5	4.7	4.7	4.7	4.7	0.0	
Taxes on production and imports	8.0	6.2	6.6	9.5	8.1	1.5	4.7	4.7	4.7	4.7	0.0	
Taxes on products	...	...	...	...	...	...	...	...	...	...	...	
Other taxes on production	7.9	6.2	6.7	9.5	8.1	1.5	4.7	4.7	4.7	4.7	...	
Less: Subsidies	...	...	...	0.4	0.0	0.0	0.0	0.0	0.0	0.0	0.0	
Subsidies on products	...	...	...	...	...	...	...	...	...	...	...	
Other subsidies on production	...	...	...	0.4	0.0	0.0	0.0	0.0	0.0	...	...	
OPERATING SURPLUS, GROSS	193.3	249.3	280.2	326.6	309.5	369.8	358.7	450.6	478.5	436.4	...	
MIXED INCOME, GROSS	106.5	118.2	126.8	164.8	176.7	253.6	346.5	494.6	403.5	439.0	...	
Less: Consumption of fixed capital	31.0	40.0	44.9	67.6	83.3	102.5	119.7	156.6	200.2	165.4	...	
OPERATING SURPLUS, NET	156.0	204.4	227.7	265.4	232.6	273.7	245.8	300.5	285.1	277.7	...	
MIXED INCOME, NET	112.8	123.1	134.4	158.4	170.3	247.2	339.7	488.2	396.7	432.2	...	
Gross capital formation	...	...	...	...	...	...	...	...	...	...	...	
Gross fixed capital formation	82.8	85.6	123.7	138.3	148.0	235.0	257.3	460.1	383.6	441.0	...	
Changes in inventories	...	...	...	...	...	...	...	...	...	...	...	
Acquisitions less disposals of valuables	...	...	...	...	...	...	...	...	...	...	...	

Table 2.3 Output, gross value added, and fixed assets by industries at current prices (ISIC Rev. 3) Financial intermediation; real estate, renting and business activities (J+K)

Series 200: 1993 SNA, Rial Omani, Western calendar year **Data in millions**

	2001	2002	2003	2004	2005	2006	2007	2008	2009	2010	2011	2012
Series	**200**											
Output, at basic prices	945.9	1017.5	1053.2	1172.4	1264.8	1448.0	1713.5	2042.1	2247.6	2430.0	2601.5	
Less: Intermediate consumption, at purchaser's prices	183.2	217.7	180.8	236.5	254.5	306.8	323.1	383.3	421.7	471.4	504.1	
Equals: VALUE ADDED, GROSS, at basic prices	762.6	799.7	872.4	935.9	1010.4	1141.2	1390.4	1658.8	1825.8	1958.7	2097.4	
Compensation of employees	189.1	205.5	234.1	249.3	289.0	314.8	367.5	451.5	497.6	526.4	564.4	
Taxes on production and imports, less Subsidies	-6.9	18.2	27.3	21.2	20.7	25.0	47.8	54.3	55.0	55.7	0.0	
Taxes on production and imports	16.3	22.8	28.0	21.5	20.8	29.5	53.4	54.3	55.0	55.7	0.0	
Taxes on products	...	...	...	...	...	...	...	...	...	...	...	
Other taxes on production	16.3	22.8	28.0	21.5	20.8	29.5	53.4	54.3	55.0	55.7	...	

	2001	2002	2003	2004	2005	2006	2007	2008	2009	2010	2011	2012
Series	**200**											
Less: Subsidies	23.2	4.5	0.1	0.3	0.1	4.5	5.7	0.0	0.0	0.0	0.0	
Subsidies on products	...	...	...	...	...	...	...	...	...	...	...	
Other subsidies on production	23.2	4.5	0.1	0.3	0.1	4.5	5.7	0.0	0.0	0.0	...	
OPERATING SURPLUS, GROSS	581.1	576.5	611.2	668.5	704.1	805.0	971.7	1148.9	1267.6	1369.4	...	
MIXED INCOME, GROSS	-0.7	-0.5	-0.1	-3.2	-3.5	-3.5	3.4	4.1	5.7	7.3	...	
Less: Consumption of fixed capital	77.6	78.1	88.6	91.2	103.8	110.3	123.8	138.2	151.2	157.6	...	
OPERATING SURPLUS, NET	503.9	498.6	522.9	577.4	600.5	694.9	848.0	1020.5	1116.7	1212.2	...	
MIXED INCOME, NET	-0.7	-0.5	-0.9	-3.3	-3.6	-3.7	3.2	3.9	5.4	6.9	...	
Gross capital formation	...	...	...	...	...	...	...	...	...	...	...	
Gross fixed capital formation	203.1	267.5	233.1	250.6	331.6	363.0	428.0	468.7	523.3	520.3	...	
Changes in inventories	...	...	...	...	...	...	...	...	...	...	...	
Acquisitions less disposals of valuables	...	...	...	...	...	...	...	...	...	...	...	

Table 2.3 Output, gross value added, and fixed assets by industries at current prices (ISIC Rev. 3) Public administration and defense; compulsory social security (L)

Series 200: 1993 SNA, Rial Omani, Western calendar year **Data in millions**

	2001	2002	2003	2004	2005	2006	2007	2008	2009	2010	2011	2012
Series	**200**											
Output, at basic prices	1072.1	1128.2	1111.1	1328.0	1546.7	1654.8	1883.1	1981.5	2129.2	2375.2	2843.1	
Less: Intermediate consumption, at purchaser's prices	345.4	369.5	357.3	482.9	636.6	592.2	690.9	699.3	752.4	771.4	981.5	
Equals: VALUE ADDED, GROSS, at basic prices	726.6	758.7	753.8	845.1	910.1	1062.6	1192.2	1282.1	1376.8	1604.5	1861.6	
Compensation of employees	629.2	656.0	645.2	728.0	783.5	926.1	1039.7	1099.7	1175.1	1370.9	1628.0	
Taxes on production and imports, less Subsidies	...	...	...	...	...	...	...	...	...	...	...	
OPERATING SURPLUS, GROSS	97.4	102.7	108.6	117.1	126.5	136.5	152.5	182.4	201.7	233.6	...	
MIXED INCOME, GROSS	...	...	...	...	...	...	...	...	...	...	...	
Less: Consumption of fixed capital	97.4	102.7	108.6	117.1	126.5	136.5	152.5	181.3	201.7	233.6	...	
OPERATING SURPLUS, NET	0.0	0.0	0.0	0.0	-0.0	0.0	0.0	1.1	0.0	0.0	...	
MIXED INCOME, NET	...	...	...	...	...	...	...	...	...	...	...	
Gross capital formation	...	...	...	...	...	...	...	...	...	...	...	
Gross fixed capital formation	208.6	193.8	248.4	312.6	346.1	364.2	519.4	789.0	1138.6	1090.7	...	
Changes in inventories	...	...	...	...	...	...	...	...	...	...	...	
Acquisitions less disposals of valuables	...	...	...	...	...	...	...	...	...	...	...	

Table 2.3 Output, gross value added, and fixed assets by industries at current prices (ISIC Rev. 3) Education; health and social work; other community, social and personal services (M+N+O)

Series 200: 1993 SNA, Rial Omani, Western calendar year **Data in millions**

	2001	2002	2003	2004	2005	2006	2007	2008	2009	2010	2011	2012
Series	**200**											
Output, at basic prices	761.6	814.1	856.6	936.0	1086.4	1185.5	1357.9	1570.7	1742.6	1999.0	2085.0	
Less: Intermediate consumption, at purchaser's prices	170.5	183.0	178.2	198.0	236.9	268.7	281.2	335.9	364.2	433.0	450.6	
Equals: VALUE ADDED, GROSS, at basic prices	591.1	631.0	678.4	738.0	849.4	916.8	1076.6	1235.6	1378.4	1566.1	1634.3	
Compensation of employees	521.8	555.6	597.9	650.5	756.5	815.7	967.9	1072.7	1174.9	1349.4	1474.3	
Taxes on production and imports, less Subsidies	0.6	0.6	0.9	1.5	1.4	1.6	1.6	1.6	1.6	1.6	0.0	
Taxes on production and imports	0.7	0.8	1.2	1.7	1.6	1.6	1.6	1.6	1.6	1.6	0.0	
Taxes on products	...	...	...	...	...	...	...	...	...	...	...	
Other taxes on production	0.7	0.8	1.2	1.7	1.6	1.6	1.6	1.6	1.6	1.6	...	
Less: Subsidies	0.1	0.2	0.3	0.1	0.2	0.0	0.0	0.0	0.0	0.0	0.0	
Subsidies on products	...	...	...	...	...	...	...	...	...	...	...	
Other subsidies on production	0.1	0.2	0.3	0.1	0.2	0.0	0.0	0.0	0.0	0.0	...	
OPERATING SURPLUS, GROSS	62.1	67.3	73.4	81.1	86.2	90.7	97.4	149.5	188.8	201.9	...	
MIXED INCOME, GROSS	6.3	6.5	6.4	4.9	5.4	8.8	9.7	11.8	13.1	13.2	...	
Less: Consumption of fixed capital	62.7	65.9	71.5	75.4	80.3	83.6	90.0	104.8	114.6	128.8	...	
OPERATING SURPLUS, NET	0.8	2.6	2.9	7.1	7.5	9.5	10.1	47.5	77.3	76.2	...	
MIXED INCOME, NET	4.9	5.3	5.4	3.5	3.8	6.4	7.1	8.9	10.0	10.1	...	
Gross capital formation	...	...	...	...	...	...	...	...	...	...	...	
Gross fixed capital formation	108.1	110.7	141.5	152.8	202.9	234.5	285.7	422.1	473.3	546.0	...	
Changes in inventories	...	...	...	...	...	...	...	...	...	...	...	
Acquisitions less disposals of valuables	...	...	...	...	...	...	...	...	...	...	...	

Table 2.3 Output, gross value added, and fixed assets by industries at current prices (ISIC Rev. 3) Private households with employed persons (P)

Series 200: 1993 SNA, Rial Omani, Western calendar year **Data in millions**

	2001	2002	2003	2004	2005	2006	2007	2008	2009	2010	2011	2012
Series	**200**											
Output, at basic prices	36.1	38.5	41.1	44.3	46.4	48.4	46.8	55.8	53.8	63.0	74.4	
Less: Intermediate consumption, at purchaser's prices	...	...	...	...	...	...	...	...	...	...	...	
Equals: VALUE ADDED, GROSS, at basic prices	36.1	38.5	41.1	44.3	46.4	48.4	46.8	55.8	53.8	63.0	74.4	
Compensation of employees	36.1	38.5	41.1	44.3	46.4	48.4	46.8	55.8	53.8	63.0	74.4	
Taxes on production and imports, less Subsidies	...	...	...	...	...	...	...	...	...	...	...	
OPERATING SURPLUS, GROSS	...	...	...	...	...	...	...	...	...	...	...	

	2001	2002	2003	2004	2005	2006	2007	2008	2009	2010	2011	2012
Series	**200**											
MIXED INCOME, GROSS	...	...	...	...	...	...	...	...	...	...	...	
Gross capital formation	...	...	...	...	...	...	...	...	...	...	...	

Table 5.1 Cross classification of Gross value added by industries and institutional sectors (ISIC Rev. 3) Non-financial corporations

Series 200: 1993 SNA, Rial Omani, Western calendar year **Data in millions**

	2001	2002	2003	2004	2005	2006	2007	2008	2009	2010	2011	2012
Series	**200**											
	Industries											
Agriculture, hunting, forestry; fishing	6.5	11.9	10.4	11.8	15.2	16.1	22.0	22.3	24.0	27.5		
Mining and quarrying	3299.5	3320.3	3500.2	4102.5	5903.7	6766.6	7181.9	11914.4	7500.7	10480.1		
Manufacturing	631.1	623.2	709.3	784.1	971.8	1485.6	1698.7	2409.1	2131.6	2365.6		
Electricity, gas and water supply	19.8	17.8	41.0	50.9	136.3	132.9	145.0	156.1	195.7	230.7		
Construction	171.7	210.7	270.6	299.5	445.0	552.0	771.9	1076.1	1196.8	1270.5		
Wholesale and retail trade; repair of motor vehicles, motorcycles and personal and household goods; hotels and restaurants	318.4	309.2	358.9	444.2	473.4	663.5	920.3	1389.6	960.5	1046.9		
Transport, storage and communications	235.3	299.2	351.0	404.2	422.9	517.0	521.4	635.9	684.3	671.3		
Financial intermediation; real estate renting and business activities	170.2	180.6	225.2	237.8	272.2	310.9	378.7	447.7	492.2	529.3		
Public administration and defence; compulsory social security	...	...	...	...	...	...	...	...	...	...		
Education; health and social work; other community, social and personal services	34.2	40.3	44.5	49.1	53.5	59.2	67.8	83.0	113.5	117.5		
Private households with employed persons	...	...	...	...	...	...	...	...	...	...		
VALUE ADDED GROSS, at basic prices	4886.8	5013.3	5510.9	6384.2	8694.1	10503.9	11707.6	18137.9	13299.2	16739.4		

Table 5.1 Cross classification of Gross value added by industries and institutional sectors (ISIC Rev. 3) Financial corporations

Series 200: 1993 SNA, Rial Omani, Western calendar year **Data in millions**

	2001	2002	2003	2004	2005	2006	2007	2008	2009	2010	2011	2012
Series	**200**											
	Industries											
Agriculture, hunting, forestry; fishing	...	...	...	...	...	...	...	...	...	...		
Mining and quarrying	...	...	...	...	...	...	...	...	...	...		
Manufacturing	...	...	...	...	...	...	...	...	...	...		
Electricity, gas and water supply	...	...	...	...	...	...	...	...	...	...		
Construction	...	...	...	...	...	...	...	...	...	...		

	2001	2002	2003	2004	2005	2006	2007	2008	2009	2010	2011	2012
Series	**200**											
Wholesale and retail trade; repair of motor vehicles, motorcycles and personal and household goods; hotels and restaurants	...	...	...	...	...	...	...	...	...	...		
Transport, storage and communications	...	...	...	...	...	...	...	...	...	...		
Financial intermediation; real estate renting and business activities	321.1	348.7	374.0	425.2	462.4	546.5	698.0	846.3	910.7	974.5		
Public administration and defence; compulsory social security	...	...	...	...	...	...	...	...	...	...		
Education; health and social work; other community, social and personal services	...	...	...	...	...	...	...	...	...	...		
Private households with employed persons	...	...	...	...	...	...	...	...	...	...		
VALUE ADDED GROSS, at basic prices	321.1	348.7	374.0	425.2	462.4	546.5	698.0	846.3	910.7	974.5		

Table 5.1 Cross classification of Gross value added by industries and institutional sectors (ISIC Rev. 3) General government

Series 200: 1993 SNA, Rial Omani, Western calendar year **Data in millions**

	2001	2002	2003	2004	2005	2006	2007	2008	2009	2010	2011	2012
Series	**200**											
Industries												
Agriculture, hunting, forestry; fishing	...	...	...	...	...	...	...	...	...	...		
Mining and quarrying	...	...	...	...	...	...	...	...	...	...		
Manufacturing	...	...	...	...	...	...	...	...	...	...		
Electricity, gas and water supply	55.9	57.3	58.2	59.6	53.5	23.6	28.1	29.4	32.5	36.7		
Construction	...	...	...	...	...	...	...	...	...	...		
Wholesale and retail trade; repair of motor vehicles, motorcycles and personal and household goods; hotels and restaurants	...	...	...	...	...	...	...	...	...	...		
Transport, storage and communications	20.0	17.7	17.7	19.8	3.9	8.7	17.6	22.9	27.0	27.3		
Financial intermediation; real estate renting and business activities	...	...	...	...	...	...	...	...	...	...		
Public administration and defence; compulsory social security	726.6	758.7	753.8	845.1	910.1	1062.6	1192.2	1282.1	1376.8	1604.5		
Education; health and social work; other community, social and personal services	525.4	558.3	599.9	651.0	752.3	808.0	954.9	1088.4	1192.6	1371.9		
Private households with employed persons	...	...	...	...	...	...	...	...	...	...		
VALUE ADDED GROSS, at basic prices	1328.0	1391.9	1429.5	1575.5	1719.8	1902.9	2192.8	2422.9	2628.8	3040.3		

Table 5.1 Cross classification of Gross value added by industries and institutional sectors (ISIC Rev. 3) Households

Series 200: 1993 SNA, Rial Omani, Western calendar year

Data in millions

	2001	2002	2003	2004	2005	2006	2007	2008	2009	2010	2011	2012
Series	**200**											
	Industries											
Agriculture, hunting, forestry; fishing	156.8	152.6	161.1	162.6	167.9	175.3	188.2	221.2	237.4	270.1		
Mining and quarrying	...	...	...	...	...	...	...	...	...	...		
Manufacturing	25.8	45.4	28.7	36.6	35.1	41.2	49.9	54.2	46.8	53.1		
Electricity, gas and water supply	3.7	3.8	8.3	12.3	12.9	12.6	3.2	3.3	3.5	3.7		
Construction	10.8	17.8	5.0	11.8	11.9	14.3	19.9	40.4	40.7	43.2		
Wholesale and retail trade; repair of motor vehicles, motorcycles and personal and household goods; hotels and restaurants	337.4	352.7	378.7	444.8	474.4	540.1	712.5	847.9	826.0	860.9		
Transport, storage and communications	136.4	147.4	157.3	196.3	208.8	277.1	370.0	518.0	427.0	462.5		
Financial intermediation; real estate renting and business activities	271.3	270.4	273.2	272.8	275.8	283.9	313.7	364.8	423.0	454.9		
Public administration and defence; compulsory social security	...	...	...	...	...	...	...	...	...	...		
Education; health and social work; other community, social and personal services	25.5	26.4	27.6	31.2	36.5	42.7	46.4	56.9	67.8	69.0		
Private households with employed persons	36.1	38.5	41.1	44.3	46.4	48.4	46.8	55.8	62.7	63.0		
VALUE ADDED GROSS, at basic prices	1003.8	1054.9	1080.9	1212.8	1269.6	1435.6	1750.6	2162.5	2135.0	2280.3		

Table 5.1 Cross classification of Gross value added by industries and institutional sectors (ISIC Rev. 3) Non-profit institutions serving households

Series 200: 1993 SNA, Rial Omani, Western calendar year

Data in millions

	2001	2002	2003	2004	2005	2006	2007	2008	2009	2010	2011	2012
Series	**200**											
	Industries											
Agriculture, hunting, forestry; fishing	...	...	...	...	...	...	...	...	...	...		
Mining and quarrying	...	...	...	...	...	...	...	...	...	...		
Manufacturing	...	...	...	...	...	...	...	...	...	...		
Electricity, gas and water supply	...	...	...	...	...	...	...	...	...	...		
Construction	...	...	...	...	...	...	...	...	...	...		
Wholesale and retail trade; repair of motor vehicles, motorcycles and personal and household goods; hotels and restaurants	...	...	...	...	...	...	...	...	...	...		
Transport, storage and communications	...	...	...	...	...	...	...	...	...	...		
Financial intermediation; real estate renting and business activities	...	...	...	...	...	...	...	...	...	...		
Public administration and defence; compulsory social security	...	...	...	...	...	...	...	...	...	...		

	2001	2002	2003	2004	2005	2006	2007	2008	2009	2010	2011	2012
Series	**200**											
Education; health and social work; other community, social and personal services	6.0	6.0	6.5	6.7	7.1	7.0	7.5	7.2	10.0	7.6		
Private households with employed persons	...	...	...	...	...	...	...	...	...	...		
VALUE ADDED GROSS, at basic prices	6.0	6.0	6.5	6.7	7.1	7.0	7.5	7.2	10.0	7.6		

Table 5.1 Cross classification of Gross value added by industries and institutional sectors (ISIC Rev. 3) Total economy

Series 200: 1993 SNA, Rial Omani, Western calendar year

Data in millions

	2001	2002	2003	2004	2005	2006	2007	2008	2009	2010	2011	2012
Series	**200**											
Industries												
Agriculture, hunting, forestry; fishing	163.3	164.5	171.4	174.4	183.1	191.4	210.1	243.4	261.5	297.6		
Mining and quarrying	3299.5	3320.3	3500.2	4102.5	5903.7	6766.6	7181.9	11914.4	7500.7	10480.1		
Manufacturing	656.9	668.7	738.0	820.7	1006.9	1526.8	1748.6	2463.4	2178.4[a]	2418.7		
Electricity, gas and water supply	79.5	78.9	107.5	122.8	202.7	169.2	176.2	188.9	231.6	271.0		
Construction	182.5	228.5	275.6	311.4	456.8	566.3	791.8	1116.5	1237.6	1313.7		
Wholesale and retail trade; repair of motor vehicles, motorcycles and personal and household goods; hotels and restaurants	655.8	661.9	737.6	889.0	947.9	1203.6	1632.8	2237.4	1786.5	1907.7		
Transport, storage and communications	391.7	464.2	525.9	620.3	635.6	802.9	909.0	1176.9	1138.3	1161.1		
Financial intermediation; real estate renting and business activities	762.6	799.7	872.4	935.9	1010.4	1141.2	1390.4	1658.8	1825.8	1958.7		
Public administration and defence; compulsory social security	726.6	758.7	753.8	845.1	910.1	1062.6	1192.2	1282.1	1376.8	1604.5		
Education; health and social work; other community, social and personal services	591.1	631.0	678.4	738.0	849.4	916.8	1076.6	1235.6	1383.9	1566.1		
Private households with employed persons	36.1	38.5	41.1	44.3	46.4	48.4	46.8	55.8	62.7[a]	63.0		
VALUE ADDED GROSS, at basic prices	7545.6	7814.9	8401.9	9604.4	12152.9	14395.8	16356.5	23576.7	18983.7	23042.1		

[a] Discrepancy with equivalent item in Table 2.1 (Value added by industries at current prices).

Pakistan

Source

Reply to the United Nations national accounts questionnaire from the Federal Bureau of Statistics, Statistics Division of the Ministry of Finance, Economic Affairs & Statistics, Islamabad. National accounts estimates are also published in the "Monthly Bulletin of Statistics" and "Statistical Pocket Book of Pakistan", "Pakistan Statistical Yearbook", "Economic Survey", and "Annual Report of the State Bank of Pakistan", and also released on FBS website, www.statpak.gov.pk.

General

The estimates shown in the following tables have been prepared in accordance with the concepts and definitions of the System of National Accounts 1993 (1993 SNA). The official estimates and methodological notes on sources and methods are published in a series of reports entitled "National Accounts of Pakistan". Estimates relate to fiscal year beginning 1 July. When the scope and coverage of the estimates differ for conceptual or statistical reasons from the definitions and classifications recommended in SNA, a footnote is indicated to the relevant tables.

Rebasing of the National Accounts estimates from 1980-81 to 1999-2000 gained prime importance as Pakistan delayed the re-basing of the national accounts for two decades. As such, many structural changes which took place since 1980-81 until 1999-2000 on the production and consumption structure of the economy were not captured in the country's national accounts. A number of economic areas remained either uncovered or under-reported and accordingly under-estimated the size of the national income. Taking cognizance of facts narrative above, the Annual Plan Coordination Committee (APCC) in its meeting in 1997 recommended to re-base the national accounts of Pakistan to make the GDP and investment figures more realistic. The journey of the re-basing exercises that began in 1997 culminated in July 2003. During the period, various technical committees were set up, a number of studies were undertaken and reviewed by experts inside and outside the country. Accordingly, the size of the overall GDP in 1999-2000 increased by 19.5 percent, agriculture by 18.5 percent, industries by 18.0 percent, and services by 20.8 percent over the old base. Per capita income in US dollar term was estimated at $526 for the year 1999-2000 compared to $441 according to the old base. Similarly, fixed investment showed an improvement of 34.3 percent in 1999-2000 mainly due to improved coverage.

Methodology:

Overview of GDP Compilation

Gross domestic product is estimated mainly through the production approach.

Expenditure Approach

The expenditure approach is used to estimate government final consumption expenditure and exports and imports of goods and services. This approach, in combination with the commodity-flow approach is used to estimate gross capital formation. Government consumption expenditure is estimated by analysing the budgets of the government bodies with an element of estimation made for the local government bodies for which all the budgets are difficult to obtain. The basic information used in estimating increase in stocks is received from the Planning Commission. The estimates of gross fixed capital formation are classified by economic sectors. Benchmark estimates of agriculture are derived from 1980 Agriculture Census adjusted for 1980-81 and non-monetized investment are based on survey results conducted by FBS. Investment in the mining and quarrying sector is estimated on the basis of data obtained from annual censuses of mining industries and from concerned source agencies. For large-scale manufacturing, investment estimates are based on annual sample surveys while the small industries surveys in 1976-77, 1983-84, 1987-88, and now 1996-97 provided data for investment in small industries. Investment in machinery and equipment of the agricultural sectors is estimated by the commodity-flow method. For the service sector, estimates are prepared from trade and domestic production data, annual budgets and annual questionnaires. Estimates of private residential construction are based on the rural construction survey, census reports, population growth and number of persons per household. Capital expenditure for the government bodies are based on the classification of their budgets. The estimates of exports of goods and services are obtained from the trade statistics of the FBS and the balance of payments statistics. For constant price estimates, all items of GDP by expenditure type are deflated by appropriate price indexes while gross fixed capital formation is deflated by sectoral deflators.

Income Approach

Domestic factor incomes consisting of compensation of employees and operating surplus, is obtained as a residual, i.e., after subtracting depreciation and net indirect taxes from gross domestic product. For depreciation, a flat rate is applied for the different sectors, 5 per cent for agriculture, mining and quarrying, small-scale manufacturing, public administration and defence and other private services, 10 per cent for large-scale manufacturing, 2.5 per cent for construction, 2 per cent for trade and 20 per cent for ownership of dwellings in the rural areas and 25 per cent in the urban areas. Data of indirect taxes and subsidies are derived from budgets of the government bodies, together with those collected by the Central Board of Revenue.

Production Approach

The table of gross domestic product by kind of economic activity is prepared in factor values. The production approach is used to estimate value added in agriculture, mining and quarrying, manufacturing and electricity. The income approach is used for most of the remaining sectors. Production data of major agricultural crops are obtained from the Ministry of Agriculture. Corresponding harvest prices are obtained from the Provincial Directorates of Land Records. Minor crops harvest prices are taken at 80 per cent of the wholesale prices. Data on livestock products are obtained from the Department of Agricultural Marketing and Grading. The current price estimates are derived indirectly by applying the wholesale price index to the constant price estimates. Production and price data of forestry/fishing are obtained from concerned departments.

The Natural Resources Division and the Provincial Mineral Development Department provide production and price data for the mining sector. Gross value of output is obtained by multiplying the output of each mineral by pit-head or well-head prices in the benchmark year while annual output and index of wholesale prices are used for the current estimates. Value added at constant factor cost thus obtained are adjusted by wholesale price index for manufacturing to arrive at current estimates. For small-scale manufacturing, benchmark 1980-81 was computed on the basis of survey reports on SHMI for 1976-77 and 1983-84 and employment data from 1981 Population Census and Labour Force Surveys 1982-83 and 1984-85. The estimates for electricity and gas are based on data furnished by concerned companies while the estimates of water are included in public administration and defence sector. For construction estimates are based on gross fixed capital formation data in construction activity collected on annual basis by FBS, and its value added coefficients obtained from concerned construction agencies/companies.

The value added of the trade sector is measured by net trade margins earned by traders on various types of products entering into wholesale and retail trade. Trade margins are derived from distributive Trade Survey 1983-84. For the transport sector, estimates are based on data supplied by concerned enterprises and FBS surveys on mechanized and non-mechanized road transport. For the financial sector, value added is based on data provided by the State Bank of Pakistan and various financial institutions. Estimates of ownership of dwellings are based on Housing Census 1980, HED Survey 1973 and Construction Survey 1986. For government services, the budgets of the government bodies are used. For private services, the number of persons engaged in the different occupations is obtained from the 1981 Population Census and extrapolated by the intercensal growth rate in the working force of this sector. Price deflation is used for forestry and fishing, electricity and gas, transport, financial and community services. For mining, the annual output of each mineral is multiplied by the base year pit-head and well-head prices. Value added of the trade sector is obtained from the distribution of agricultural produce, manufactured and imported goods. Value added of manufacturing, construction and ownership of dwellings is extrapolated by quantum indexes.

Table 1.1 Gross domestic product by expenditures at current prices

Series 100: 1993 SNA, Pakistan Rupee, Fiscal year ending 30 June — **Data in billions**

	2001	2002	2003	2004	2005	2006	2007	2008	2009	2010	2011	2012
Series	**100**											
	Expenditures of the gross domestic product											
Final consumption expenditure	3538.7	3718.3	4029.7	4647.2	5511.4	6544.5	7340.0	9113.7	11367.3	13367.6	16590.1	19752.5
Household final consumption expenditure	3211.1	3329.9	3601.0	4184.7	5001.5	5720.2	6543.8	7835.3	10338.1	12188.9	15160.0	18031.7
NPISHs final consumption expenditure	...	...	...	...	...	...	...	...	...	...	...	...
General government final consumption expenditure	327.6	388.4	428.7	462.5	509.9	824.3	796.2	1278.4	1029.2	1178.7	1430.1	1720.8
Gross capital formation	715.5	738.4	817.1	935.1	1240.2	1687.8	1953.4	2258.6	2317.7	2303.8	2357.8	2586.3
Gross fixed capital formation	659.3	680.4	736.4	844.8	1134.9	1565.8	1814.6	2094.7	2114.1	2066.9	2069.2	2255.9
Changes in inventories	56.2	58.0	80.6	90.2	105.3	122.0	138.8	163.9	203.6	236.9	288.5	330.5
Acquisitions less disposals of valuables	...	...	...	...	...	...	...	...	...	...	...	...
Exports of goods and services	617.1	677.9	815.2	883.7	1019.8	1161.3	1230.7	1316.4	1636.2	2009.5	2552.6	2575.4
Less: Imports of goods and services	661.5	681.9	786.2	825.4	1271.6	1770.4	1851.1	2446.0	2597.2	2877.2	3467.6	4260.3
Equals: GROSS DOMESTIC PRODUCT	4209.9	4452.7	4875.6	5640.6	6499.8	7623.2	8673.0	10242.8	12724.0	14803.7	18032.9	20653.9

Table 1.2 Gross domestic product by expenditures at constant prices

Series 100: 1993 SNA, Pakistan Rupee, Fiscal year ending 30 June — **Data in billions**

	2001	2002	2003	2004	2005	2006	2007	2008	2009	2010	2011	2012
Series	**100**											
Base year	**2000**											
	Expenditures of the gross domestic product											
Final consumption expenditure	3211.8	3299.4	3337.4	3642.3	4067.6	4296.6	4415.0	4518.4	4746.4	4901.1	5094.0	5657.5
Household final consumption expenditure	2899.7	2940.4	2952.6	3251.9	3670.7	3708.1	3882.9	3779.3	4240.4	4168.8	4323.7	4824.0
NPISHs final consumption expenditure	...	...	...	...	...	...	...	...	...	...	...	...
General government final consumption expenditure	312.1	359.0	384.8	390.3	396.8	588.6	532.1	739.1	506.0	732.3	770.3	833.5
Gross capital formation	687.3	685.6	729.1	691.4	780.5	923.9	1042.8	1113.7	965.4	910.2	867.7	793.4
Gross fixed capital formation	634.4	632.1	658.1	617.7	701.4	841.0	955.1	1024.7	873.1	814.6	769.4	690.9
Changes in inventories	52.9	53.5	71.1	73.7	79.1	82.9	87.6	89.0	92.2	95.5	98.3	102.5
Acquisitions less disposals of valuables	...	...	...	...	...	...	...	...	...	...	...	...
Exports of goods and services	576.9	634.4	814.4	802.0	878.9	965.9	988.2	935.3	904.4	1046.4	1071.3	927.9
Less: Imports of goods and services	574.1	591.6	658.0	601.6	845.1	1003.1	968.0	1002.1	850.7	887.7	886.6	975.0
Equals: GROSS DOMESTIC PRODUCT	3902.0	4027.8	4223.0	4534.1	4881.8	5183.4	5477.9	5565.4	5765.5	5970.0	6146.4	6403.7

Table 1.3 Relations among product, income, savings, and net lending aggregates

Series 100: 1993 SNA, Pakistan Rupee, Fiscal year ending 30 June — **Data in billions**

	2001	2002	2003	2004	2005	2006	2007	2008	2009	2010	2011	2012
Series	**100**											
GROSS DOMESTIC PRODUCT	4209.9	4452.7	4875.6	5640.6	6499.8	7623.2	8673.0	10242.8	12724.0	14803.7	18032.9	20653.9
Plus: Compensation of employees - from and to the rest of the world, net	...	...	...	...	...	...	...	...	...	...	...	...
Plus: Property income - from and to the rest of the world, net	...	...	...	...	...	...	...	...	...	...	...	...
Plus: Taxes less subsidies on production and imports - from and to the rest of the world, net	...	...	...	...	...	...	...	...	...	...	...	...
Equals: GROSS NATIONAL INCOME	4155.4	4476.3	5027.5	5765.1	6634.2	7773.1	8830.6	10451.7	13070.3	15369.9	18853.1	21679.0
Plus: Current transfers - from and to the rest of the world, net	...	...	...	...	...	...	...	...	...	...	...	...
Equals: GROSS NATIONAL DISPOSABLE INCOME	...	...	...	...	...	...	...	...	...	...	...	...
Less: Final consumption expenditure / Actual final consumption	3536.7	3718.3	4029.7	4647.2	5511.4	6544.5	7340.0	9113.7	11367.3	13367.6	16590.1	19752.5
Equals: SAVING, GROSS	...	...	...	...	...	...	...	...	...	...	...	...
Plus: Capital transfers - from and to the rest of the world, net	...	...	...	...	...	...	...	...	...	...	...	...
Less: Gross capital formation	715.5	738.4	817.1	935.1	1240.2	1687.8	1953.4	2258.6	2317.7	2303.8	2357.8	2586.3
Less: Acquisitions less disposals of non-produced non-financial assets	...	...	...	...	...	...	...	...	...	...	...	...
Equals: NET LENDING (+) / NET BORROWING (-) OF THE NATION	...	...	...	...	...	...	...	...	...	...	...	...
	Net values: Gross National Income / Gross National Disposable Income / Saving Gross less Consumption of fixed capital											
Less: Consumption of fixed capital	342.9	366.8	391.0	428.3	487.4	560.9	625.3	712.2	825.1	880.5	957.2	1100.9
Equals: NET NATIONAL INCOME	3812.5	4109.6	4636.4	5336.8	6146.8	7212.2	8205.3	9739.5	12245.2	14489.4	17895.9	20578.1
Equals: NET NATIONAL DISPOSABLE INCOME	...	...	...	...	...	...	...	...	...	...	...	...
Equals: SAVING, NET	...	...	...	...	...	...	...	...	...	...	...	...

Table 2.1 Value added by industries at current prices (ISIC Rev. 3)

Series 100: 1993 SNA, Pakistan Rupee, Fiscal year ending 30 June — **Data in billions**

	2001	2002	2003	2004	2005	2006	2007	2008	2009	2010	2011	2012
Series	**100**											
	Industries											
Agriculture, hunting, forestry; fishing	945.3	968.3	1059.3	1164.8	1314.2	1457.2	1685.2	2017.2	2611.5	2972.7	3697.1	3899.3
Mining and quarrying	106.4	117.0	137.0	208.3	182.1	219.7	252.5	301.5	346.4	437.9	391.3	446.5
Manufacturing	608.1	642.9	725.4	902.5	1136.6	1370.8	1567.3	1950.5	2069.5	2484.7	3182.0	3694.5
Electricity, gas and water supply	133.1	134.3	120.6	190.7	187.3	153.3	169.5	145.9	284.1	327.3	354.1	413.9
Construction	94.7	95.2	100.9	115.5	153.3	179.9	225.2	260.3	295.0	319.3	337.0	410.9
Wholesale, retail trade, repair of motor vehicles, motorcycles and personal and households goods; hotels and restaurants	691.9	720.8	785.8	896.4	1093.1	1262.0	1441.8	1829.9	2104.3	2463.6	3112.1	3574.1
Transport, storage and communications	513.0	542.8	609.9	675.6	759.7	908.4	1012.2	1155.9	1587.9	1832.8	2143.4	2476.8

	2001	2002	2003	2004	2005	2006	2007	2008	2009	2010	2011	2012
Series	**100**											
Financial intermediation; real estate, renting and business activities	241.4	268.9	280.1	311.5	401.7	549.1	653.4	795.7	920.3	955.7	1086.5	1267.6
Public administration and defence; compulsory social security	235.0	260.0	285.9	312.1	343.3	404.6	467.7	530.1	662.7	757.1	983.9	1119.3
Education; health and social work; other community, social and personal services	354.4	396.0	429.3	473.2	551.2	653.4	760.1	934.6	1228.7	1482.6	1805.6	2133.9
Private households with employed persons	...	...	...	...	...	...	...	...	...	...	...	...
Equals: VALUE ADDED, GROSS, in basic prices [a]	3923.2	4146.2	4534.2	5250.5	6122.6	7158.5	8235.1	9921.6	12110.5	14033.6	17092.9	19436.8
Less: Financial intermediation services indirectly measured (FISIM)	...	...	...	...	...	...	...	...	...	...	...	...
Plus: Taxes less Subsidies on products [b]	286.6	306.5	341.4	390.1	377.2	464.7	437.9	321.2	613.5	770.0	940.0	1217.0
Plus: Taxes on products	320.7	339.3	403.2	455.5	468.6	569.1	556.9	667.6	763.5	842.9	1014.9	1274.5
Less: Subsidies on products	34.0	32.8	61.8	65.5	91.4	104.4	119.0	346.4	150.0	72.9	74.9	57.4
Equals: GROSS DOMESTIC PRODUCT	4209.9	4452.7	4875.6	5640.6	6499.8	7623.2	8673.0	10242.8	12724.0	14803.7	18032.9	20653.9

[a] At factor cost.
[b] Refers to all taxes on production and imports less subsidies for the total economy.

Table 2.2 Value added by industries at constant prices (ISIC Rev. 3)

Series 100: 1993 SNA, Pakistan Rupee, Fiscal year ending 30 June

Data in billions

	2001	2002	2003	2004	2005	2006	2007	2008	2009	2010	2011	2012
Series	**100**											
Base year	**2000**											
Industries												
Agriculture, hunting, forestry; fishing	903.5	904.4	941.9	964.8	1027.4	1092.1	1137.0	1148.9	1195.0	1202.4	1231.0	1269.5
Mining and quarrying	85.5	90.4	96.4	111.5	122.6	128.3	132.3	138.0	137.3	140.4	138.6	144.7
Manufacturing	571.4	596.8	638.0	727.4	840.2	913.0	988.3	1036.1	998.8	1053.4	1085.6	1124.3
Electricity, gas and water supply	120.5	112.0	98.9	155.1	146.2	107.4	112.4	85.9	136.6	145.0	134.5	132.3
Construction	87.8	89.2	92.8	82.8	98.2	108.2	134.5	127.1	112.9	131.3	122.0	129.9
Wholesale, retail trade, repair of motor vehicles, motorcycles and personal and household goods; hotels and restaurants	649.6	667.6	707.7	766.7	858.7	838.4	887.3	934.2	921.4	962.7	996.7	1032.4
Transport, storage and communications	422.2	427.3	445.6	461.3	477.2	496.1	519.5	539.3	558.7	569.3	574.2	581.4
Financial intermediation, real estate, renting and business activities	227.0	250.4	252.5	268.5	316.7	400.9	445.1	483.9	463.4	430.7	429.6	452.9
Public administration and defence; compulsory social security	225.2	240.6	259.1	267.3	268.8	296.0	316.9	320.6	332.1	340.5	388.7	398.9
Education; health and social work; other community, social and personal services	339.4	366.3	389.1	410.1	437.2	480.2	518.3	569.0	619.4	667.9	714.0	762.4
Private households with employed persons	...	...	...	...	...	...	...	...	...	...	...	...
Equals: VALUE ADDED, GROSS, in basic prices [a]	3632.1	3745.1	3922.1	4215.6	4593.2	4860.5	5191.7	5383.0	5475.7	5643.6	5815.0	6028.6
Less: Financial intermediation services indirectly measured (FISIM)	...	...	...	...	...	...	...	...	...	...	...	...
Plus: Taxes less Subsidies on products [b]	269.9	282.7	300.9	318.5	288.6	322.9	286.2	182.4	289.8	326.4	331.4	375.1
Plus: Taxes on products	301.9	312.9	355.3	372.0	358.5	395.4	361.8	372.7	360.6	353.4	345.0	393.8

	2001	2002	2003	2004	2005	2006	2007	2008	2009	2010	2011	2012
Series	**100**											
Base year	**2000**											
Less: Subsidies on products	32.0	30.2	54.5	53.5	69.9	72.5	75.6	190.3	70.8	27.1	13.6	18.7
Equals: GROSS DOMESTIC PRODUCT	3902.0	4027.8	4223.0	4534.1	4881.8	5183.4	5477.9	5565.4	5765.5	5970.0	6146.4	6403.7

[a] At factor cost.
[b] Refers to all taxes on production and imports less subsidies for the total economy.

Table 2.3 Output, gross value added, and fixed assets by industries at current prices (ISIC Rev. 3) Total Economy

Series 100: 1993 SNA, Pakistan Rupee, Fiscal year ending 30 June **Data in billions**

	2001	2002	2003	2004	2005	2006	2007	2008	2009	2010	2011	2012
Series	**100**											
Output, at basic prices	...	...	...	...	...	...	...	...	...	...	...	...
Less: Intermediate consumption, at purchaser's prices	...	...	...	...	...	...	...	...	...	...	...	...
Equals: VALUE ADDED, GROSS, at basic prices	...	...	...	...	...	...	...	...	...	...	...	...
Compensation of employees	...	...	...	...	...	...	...	...	...	...	...	...
Taxes on production and imports, less Subsidies	...	...	...	...	...	...	...	...	...	...	...	...
OPERATING SURPLUS, GROSS	...	...	...	...	...	...	...	...	...	...	...	...
MIXED INCOME, GROSS	...	...	...	...	...	...	...	...	...	...	...	...
Gross capital formation	715.5	738.4	817.1	935.1	1240.2	1687.8	1953.4	2258.6	2317.7	2303.8	2357.8	2586.3
Gross fixed capital formation	659.3	680.4	736.4	844.8	1134.9	1565.8	1814.6	2094.7	2114.1	2066.9	2069.2	2255.9
Changes in inventories	56.2	58.0	80.6	90.2	105.3	122.0	138.8	163.9	203.6	236.9	288.5	330.5
Acquisitions less disposals of valuables	...	...	...	...	...	...	...	...	...	...	...	...

Table 2.3 Output, gross value added, and fixed assets by industries at current prices (ISIC Rev. 3) Agriculture, hunting, forestry; fishing (A+B)

Series 100: 1993 SNA, Pakistan Rupee, Fiscal year ending 30 June **Data in billions**

	2001	2002	2003	2004	2005	2006	2007	2008	2009	2010	2011	2012
Series	**100**											
Gross fixed capital formation	67.1	69.6	75.7	81.2	135.3	145.6	151.6	147.5	169.9	190.0	200.8	188.6
Changes in inventories	...	...	...	...	...	...	...	...	...	...	...	...
Acquisitions less disposals of valuables	...	...	...	...	...	...	...	...	...	...	...	...

Table 2.3 Output, gross value added, and fixed assets by industries at current prices (ISIC Rev. 3) Mining and quarrying (C)

Series 100: 1993 SNA, Pakistan Rupee, Fiscal year ending 30 June — **Data in billions**

	2001	2002	2003	2004	2005	2006	2007	2008	2009	2010	2011	2012
Series	**100**											
Gross fixed capital formation	33.7	49.0	77.4	18.7	33.4	49.6	75.6	94.8	138.4	169.5	85.9	70.1
Changes in inventories	...	...	...	...	...	...	...	...	...	...	...	...
Acquisitions less disposals of valuables	...	...	...	...	...	...	...	...	...	...	...	...

Table 2.3 Output, gross value added, and fixed assets by industries at current prices (ISIC Rev. 3) Manufacturing (D)

Series 100: 1993 SNA, Pakistan Rupee, Fiscal year ending 30 June — **Data in billions**

	2001	2002	2003	2004	2005	2006	2007	2008	2009	2010	2011	2012
Series	**100**											
Gross fixed capital formation	151.0	168.1	164.9	203.9	247.1	326.8	350.2	364.1	375.5	355.1	349.4	403.1
Changes in inventories	...	...	...	...	...	...	...	...	...	...	...	...
Acquisitions less disposals of valuables	...	...	...	...	...	...	...	...	...	...	...	...

Table 2.3 Output, gross value added, and fixed assets by industries at current prices (ISIC Rev. 3) Electricity, gas and water supply (E)

Series 100: 1993 SNA, Pakistan Rupee, Fiscal year ending 30 June — **Data in billions**

	2001	2002	2003	2004	2005	2006	2007	2008	2009	2010	2011	2012
Series	**100**											
Gross fixed capital formation	67.6	56.9	57.6	25.3	40.0	69.8	73.5	88.4	89.6	74.2	131.8	79.9
Changes in inventories	...	...	...	...	...	...	...	...	...	...	...	...
Acquisitions less disposals of valuables	...	...	...	...	...	...	...	...	...	...	...	...

Table 2.3 Output, gross value added, and fixed assets by industries at current prices (ISIC Rev. 3) Construction (F)

Series 100: 1993 SNA, Pakistan Rupee, Fiscal year ending 30 June — **Data in billions**

	2001	2002	2003	2004	2005	2006	2007	2008	2009	2010	2011	2012
Series	**100**											
Gross fixed capital formation	13.6	15.2	7.1	10.1	17.8	26.1	38.3	33.5	42.9	31.9	22.4	29.1
Changes in inventories	...	...	...	...	...	...	...	...	...	...	...	...
Acquisitions less disposals of valuables	...	...	...	...	...	...	...	...	...	...	...	...

Table 2.3 Output, gross value added, and fixed assets by industries at current prices (ISIC Rev. 3) Wholesale retail trade, repair of motor vehicles, motorcycles, etc.; hotels and restaurants (G+H)

Series 100: 1993 SNA, Pakistan Rupee, Fiscal year ending 30 June — **Data in billions**

	2001	2002	2003	2004	2005	2006	2007	2008	2009	2010	2011	2012
Series	**100**											
Gross fixed capital formation	8.6	10.4	12.5	17.2	21.4	29.2	37.2	43.1	52.0	56.9	63.0	71.1
Changes in inventories	...	...	...	...	...	...	...	...	...	...	...	...
Acquisitions less disposals of valuables	...	...	...	...	...	...	...	...	...	...	...	...

Table 2.3 Output, gross value added, and fixed assets by industries at current prices (ISIC Rev. 3) Transport, storage and communications (I)

Series 100: 1993 SNA, Pakistan Rupee, Fiscal year ending 30 June — **Data in billions**

	2001	2002	2003	2004	2005	2006	2007	2008	2009	2010	2011	2012
Series	**100**											
Gross fixed capital formation	104.7	86.4	82.9	148.6	225.0	392.7	395.2	457.2	327.8	314.5	224.6	204.2
Changes in inventories	...	...	...	...	...	...	...	...	...	...	...	...
Acquisitions less disposals of valuables	...	...	...	...	...	...	...	...	...	...	...	...

Table 2.3 Output, gross value added, and fixed assets by industries at current prices (ISIC Rev. 3) Financial intermediation; real estate, renting and business activities (J+K)

Series 100: 1993 SNA, Pakistan Rupee, Fiscal year ending 30 June — **Data in billions**

	2001	2002	2003	2004	2005	2006	2007	2008	2009	2010	2011	2012
Series	**100**											
Gross fixed capital formation	92.6	98.0	114.7	138.3	160.8	190.2	240.4	333.8	309.3	278.8	322.1	368.3
Changes in inventories	...	...	...	...	...	...	...	...	...	...	...	...
Acquisitions less disposals of valuables	...	...	...	...	...	...	...	...	...	...	...	...

Table 2.3 Output, gross value added, and fixed assets by industries at current prices (ISIC Rev. 3) Public administration and defense; compulsory social security (L)

Series 100: 1993 SNA, Pakistan Rupee, Fiscal year ending 30 June — **Data in billions**

	2001	2002	2003	2004	2005	2006	2007	2008	2009	2010	2011	2012
Series	**100**											
Gross fixed capital formation	67.0	70.4	87.3	124.8	153.0	206.1	306.1	350.2	377.1	339.6	371.0	439.7
Changes in inventories	...	...	...	...	...	...	...	...	...	...	...	...
Acquisitions less disposals of valuables	...	...	...	...	...	...	...	...	...	...	...	...

Table 2.3 Output, gross value added, and fixed assets by industries at current prices (ISIC Rev. 3) Education; health and social work; other community, social and personal services (M+N+O)

Series 100: 1993 SNA, Pakistan Rupee, Fiscal year ending 30 June — **Data in billions**

	2001	2002	2003	2004	2005	2006	2007	2008	2009	2010	2011	2012
Series	**100**											
Gross fixed capital formation	53.4	56.6	56.3	76.8	101.1	129.9	146.5	182.1	231.7	256.6	298.2	401.8
Changes in inventories	...	...	...	...	...	...	...	...	...	...	...	...
Acquisitions less disposals of valuables	...	...	...	...	...	...	...	...	...	...	...	...

Table 3.1 Government final consumption expenditure by function at current prices

Series 100: 1993 SNA, Pakistan Rupee, Fiscal year ending 30 June — **Data in billions**

	2001	2002	2003	2004	2005	2006	2007	2008	2009	2010	2011	2012
Series	**100**											
General public services	142.4	174.2	161.8	221.9	226.5	296.6	338.8	455.7	370.8	446.1	525.6	704.1
Defence	...	...	...	...	...	...	...	...	...	...	...	...
Public order and safety	14.1	26.3	34.6	48.2	50.5	45.6	76.9	98.0	103.1	143.2	174.5	180.3
Economic affairs	57.7	83.7	99.2	33.4	65.1	216.7	99.3	195.4	167.1	150.0	160.6	204.5
Environment protection	0.5	0.5	0.1	2.6	3.1	4.7	5.5	8.9	11.9	12.4	17.4	21.0
Housing and community amenities	2.6	2.6	10.2	4.9	6.2	6.9	10.0	22.2	16.4	13.9	14.0	20.6
Health	11.4	12.1	19.3	20.1	24.7	32.5	37.7	67.9	73.8	85.8	99.4	104.9
Recreation, culture and religion	0.4	1.1	1.7	1.4	2.5	2.5	3.2	15.5	7.2	8.9	10.8	12.9
Education	55.6	33.0	71.2	54.8	52.8	120.5	83.4	154.8	180.3	191.0	270.0	309.4
Social protection	65.9	73.0	61.8	78.1	82.9	100.8	89.1	228.0	117.5	144.4	182.7	186.4
Plus: (Other functions)	0.0	6.9	6.0	3.4	3.2	7.8	67.7	49.7	...	...	...	...
Equals: General government final consumption expenditure [a]	350.5	413.5	466.0	468.7	517.5	834.6	811.5	1295.9	1048.0	1195.8	1455.1	1744.3

[a] Statistical discrepancy with the equivalent item in Table 1.1 (Gross domestic product by expenditures at current prices). Includes depreciation.

Panama

Source
The preparation of national accounts statistics in Panama is undertaken by the Direccion de Estadistica y Censos Panama. Official estimates are published annually, from 1960 in "Estadistica Panamena, Serie C, Ingreso Nacional" and from 1976 in the bulletin "Situacion Economica". The latter publication also contains the most detailed description of the sources and methods used for the national accounts estimation. The following tables have been prepared from successive replies to the United Nations national accounts questionnaire.

General
The latest estimates shown in the following tables are considered to be prepared in accordance with the concepts and definitions of the System of National Accounts 1993 (1993 SNA). Previous estimates were prepared in accordance with the concepts and definitions of the United Nations System of National Accounts 1968 (1968 SNA). When the scope and coverage of the estimates differ for conceptual or statistical reasons from the definitions and classifications recommended in the SNA, a footnote provides explanation.

Methodology:

Overview of GDP Compilation
Gross domestic product is estimated mainly through the production approach.

Expenditure Approach
The expenditure approach is used to estimate government final consumption expenditure as well as imports and exports of goods and services. The commodity-flow approach is used to estimate private final consumption expenditure and, to a large extent, gross capital formation. Data on government consumption expenditure are obtained from official documents and directly from the concerned agencies. Estimates of private consumption expenditure are based on data on locally produced and imported consumer goods. The gross value of construction is obtained by adding the cost of inputs of building materials to the estimated value added of the industry. Factor and non-factor services rendered by residents of Panama to the Former Canal Zone and to the Colon Free Zone are treated uniformly as non-factor services to the rest of the world. These services are, therefore, included in exports of goods and services.

Constant prices are estimated by a combined use of extrapolation and price indexes. For government consumption expenditure, compensation of employees is extrapolated by the number of persons employed, whereas purchases of goods and services are deflated by a combination of price indexes. For private consumption expenditure, base-year estimates are extrapolated by means of indexes which refer to consumption at both current and constant prices. The final estimates are adjusted for the discrepancy between total demand and total supply. Current values of gross fixed capital formation are deflated by a price index for inputs in the case of buildings and other construction. The current value of transport equipment and machinery and equipment are extrapolated by a volume index obtained by deflating current values by an index based on the unit export value of machinery in supplier countries. Various price indexes are used for price deflation of exports and imports of goods and services.

Income Approach
Estimates of compensation of employees are based on data on average wages, and the percentage distribution of employees obtained from household surveys. Yearly estimates of salaries earned in the public and private sectors, employers' contribution to social security schemes and an estimate of the incomes of self-employed workers is added to this information. Operating surplus is compiled from various items, such as property income, saving and direct taxes. The estimates on consumption of fixed capital, which exclude depreciation of government fixed capital, are based on accounting data of the private enterprises, obtained through direct surveys, and financial information of all autonomous and semi-autonomous entities included in the public sector. Estimates of indirect

taxes are based on data from public finance, and on revenue figures from central government, municipalities and the Panamanian Institute of Tourism.

Production Approach

For the agriculture, forestry and fishing sector, value added is obtained by deducting inputs from gross value of production. Sources used to estimate agricultural production include the census of agriculture, agricultural surveys and, in the case of export products, external trade statistics. Price data are obtained from the current statistics on prices received by the agricultural producers. Value added in forestry is derived from a benchmark estimate of sawn wood produced, the number of persons occupied and the ratio of output to employment, which is obtained from periodical industrial inquiries. In the case of fishing, estimates are based on fish landings in the Gulf of Panama, as published in "Estadistica Panamena" and on the number of persons engaged in fishing, which is obtained from the latest population census.

Value added of manufacturing is estimated by extrapolating the benchmark estimate by an indicator based on the gross value of production by type of industrial activity. A similar approach is used for the electricity, gas and water sector, as well as the construction and the trade sectors. For the trade sector the indicator used is based on the current prices of products which are marketed through wholesale and retail trade. For transport, value added is estimated on the basis of the payments to factor of production. Value added for ownership of dwellings is obtained by aggregating estimates for different geographical areas of the country. For business services value added is estimated by utilizing an indicator of patent registrations in force for operating business at the end of each year. Financial reports relating to factor payments from central government, other government authorities and municipalities, form the data basis for estimates of public administration.

A similar approach is applied for other public services, whereas for other private services value added is first estimated at constant prices and then inflated by price indices to arrive at value added at current prices. For the estimation of constant prices in the agricultural sector, the current quantities are valued at base year prices. Base year estimates for the manufacturing sector, are extrapolated by various indexes such as indexes of input quantities and quantum indexes of output. For construction, value added is extrapolated by a quantity index of inputs. For electricity, trade and transport value added is extrapolated by quantity indicators of output.

For restaurants and hotels the indicators are based on tourist expenditure in Panama and on food and beverage quantities. For banks, value added is extrapolated using the balance of loans and deposits at the end of each year. For ownership of dwellings in urban areas, the construction of new dwellings is used as indicator, and for the rural areas the base year estimate is extrapolated by an index of rural population growth. The value added of government services is extrapolated by an index of number of government employees. For other private services as well value added is extrapolated using various quantity indicators.

Table 1.1 Gross domestic product by expenditures at current prices

Series 100: 1993 SNA, balboa, Western calendar year — **Data in millions**

	2001	2002	2003	2004	2005	2006	2007	2008	2009	2010	2011	2012
Series	**100**											
	Expenditures of the gross domestic product											
Final consumption expenditure	8922.4	9704.5	9822.7	11002.6	11631.0	12561.9	13581.7	14531.8	14780.8	19721.9	22721.0	...
Household final consumption expenditure	7276.3	7885.2	8015.7	9072.9	9597.2	10445.6	11345.4	12142.8	11702.7	16176.0	18860.0	...
NPISHs final consumption expenditure	...	...	...	...	...	...	...	...	...	...	...	...
General government final consumption expenditure	1646.1	1819.3	1807.0	1929.7	2033.8	2116.3	2236.3	2389.0	3078.1	3545.9	3860.0	...
Gross capital formation	2082.5	1932.9	2456.7	2651.9	2839.0	3335.0	4775.7	6355.2	6185.6	6906.8	8519.0	...
Gross fixed capital formation	1794.2	1664.8	2207.3	2351.0	2601.3	3134.9	4554.7	6100.5	5932.0	6639.3	8180.0	...

	2001	2002	2003	2004	2005	2006	2007	2008	2009	2010	2011	2012
Series	**100**											
Changes in inventories	288.3	268.1	249.4	300.9	237.7	200.0	221.0	254.7	253.6	267.5	340.0	...
Acquisitions less disposals of valuables	...	...	...	...	...	...	...	...	...	...	...	...
Exports of goods and services	8586.5	8278.9	8225.2	9586.5	11674.2	13146.6	16071.9	19595.5	19581.7	20337.0	26380.0	...
Less: Imports of goods and services	7783.9	7643.9	7571.4	9061.7	10679.5	11906.4	14635.6	17480.9	16385.2	19912.7	26303.0	...
Equals: GROSS DOMESTIC PRODUCT	11807.5	12272.4	12933.2	14179.3	15464.7	17137.0	19793.7	23001.6	24162.9	27053.0	31315.8	36252.5

Table 1.2 Gross domestic product by expenditures at constant prices

Series 100: 1993 SNA, balboa, Western calendar year — **Data in millions**

	2001	2002	2003	2004	2005	2006	2007	2008	2009	2010	2011	2012
Series	**100**											
Base year	**1996**											
Expenditures of the gross domestic product												
Final consumption expenditure	8719.5	9355.6	10040.4	10436.3	11278.0	11748.7	11907.9	11745.7	11543.1	14471.0	15443.0	...
Household final consumption expenditure	7259.8	7763.0	8441.0	8806.2	9580.0	9998.5	10085.9	9876.7	9598.4	12230.0	13100.6	...
NPISHs final consumption expenditure	...	...	...	...	...	...	...	...	...	...	...	...
General government final consumption expenditure	1459.7	1592.6	1599.4	1630.1	1698.0	1750.2	1822.0	1869.0	1944.7	2243.0	2342.4	...
Gross capital formation	2053.7	1942.2	2312.0	2540.1	2612.4	2966.1	4120.1	5115.9	4822.2	5360.7	6412.5	...
Gross fixed capital formation	1769.7	1670.0	2058.9	2252.1	2397.1	2795.3	3940.9	4937.4	4631.9	5167.4	6193.2	...
Changes in inventories	284.0	272.2	253.1	288.0	215.3	170.8	179.2	178.5	190.3	193.3	219.3	...
Acquisitions less disposals of valuables	...	...	...	...	...	...	...	...	...	...	...	...
Exports of goods and services	8617.2	8402.3	7557.2	8959.0	9973.0	11075.1	13512.5	15922.3	15763.7	16018.0	19411.2	...
Less: Imports of goods and services	7954.2	8009.0	7726.8	8836.2	9822.0	10551.3	12456.1	13971.0	12590.6	14855.0	17994.6	...
Equals: GROSS DOMESTIC PRODUCT	11436.2	11691.1	12182.8	13099.2	14041.0	15238.6	17084.4	18812.9	19538.4	20994.0	23272.1	25755.5

Table 1.3 Relations among product, income, savings, and net lending aggregates

Series 100: 1993 SNA, balboa, Western calendar year — **Data in millions**

	2001	2002	2003	2004	2005	2006	2007	2008	2009	2010	2011	2012
Series	**100**											
GROSS DOMESTIC PRODUCT	11807.5	12272.4	12933.2	14179.3	15465.0	17137.0	19793.7	23001.6	24162.9	27053.0	31315.8	
Plus: Compensation of employees - from and to the rest of the world, net	0.0	0.0	0.0	0.0	0.0	7.8	7.1	9.4	8.6	10.0	15.3	
Plus: Compensation of employees - from the rest of the world	0.0	0.0	0.0	0.0	0.0	7.8	7.1	9.4	8.6	10.0	15.3	
Less: Compensation of employees - to the rest of the world	...	...	...	...	...	...	...	...	...	...	...	
Plus: Property income - from and to the rest of the world, net	-910.0	-566.0	-969.7	-1268.9	-1436.5	-1553.8	-1748.3	-2045.0	-1830.2	-2236.6	-2358.9	
Plus: Property income - from the rest of the world	1198.6	780.2	636.1	620.7	855.8	1237.2	1588.2	1596.3	1222.9	1288.5	1606.5	
Less: Property income - to the rest of the world	2108.7	1345.9	1605.8	1889.6	2292.3	2791.0	3336.5	3641.3	3053.1	3525.1	3965.4	

	2001	2002	2003	2004	2005	2006	2007	2008	2009	2010	2011	2012
Series	**100**											
Sum of Compensation of employees and property income - from and to the rest of the world, net	-910.1	-565.7	-969.7	-1268.9	-1436.5	-1546.0	-1741.2	-2035.6	-1821.6	-2226.6	-2343.6	
Plus: Sum of Compensation of employees and property income - from the rest of the world	1198.6	780.2	636.1	620.7	855.8	1245.0	1606.8	1605.7	1231.5	1298.5	1621.8	
Less: Sum of Compensation of employees and property income - to the rest of the world	2108.7	1345.9	1605.8	1889.6	2292.3	2791.0	3352.7	3641.3	3053.1	3525.1	3965.4	
Plus: Taxes less subsidies on production and imports - from and to the rest of the world, net	...	...	...	...	...	...	...	...	...	...	...	
Equals: GROSS NATIONAL INCOME	10897.4	11706.7	11963.5	12910.4	14028.2	15591.0	18052.5	20966.0	22341.3	24826.4	28972.2	
Plus: Current transfers - from and to the rest of the world, net	159.5	170.9	180.3	151.0	165.6	153.7	150.3	122.8	-1.9	33.3	81.3	
Plus: Current transfers - from the rest of the world	211.3	225.9	244.5	231.5	262.1	289.6	313.5	334.4	620.8	686.8	688.2	
Less: Current transfers - to the rest of the world	51.8	55.0	64.2	80.5	97.0	136.0	163.2	211.6	622.7	653.5	606.9	
Equals: GROSS NATIONAL DISPOSABLE INCOME	11056.9	11877.6	12143.8	13061.4	14193.8	15744.7	18202.8	21088.8	22339.4	24859.7	29053.5	
Less: Final consumption expenditure / Actual final consumption	8922.4	9704.5	9822.7	11002.6	11631.0	12561.9	13581.7	14531.8	14780.8	19721.9	22721.0	
Equals: SAVING, GROSS	2134.5	2173.1	2321.1	2058.8	2563.0	3183.0	4621.1	6557.0	7558.6	5137.8	6333.7	
Plus: Capital transfers - from and to the rest of the world, net	1.6	0.0	10.0	9.1	0.0	15.2	43.7	56.9	30.0	42.5	8.9	
Less: Gross capital formation	2082.5	1932.9	2456.7	2651.9	2839.0	3334.9	4775.7	6355.2	6185.6	6906.8	8519.0	
Less: Acquisitions less disposals of non-produced non-financial assets	...	...	...	...	...	...	...	...	...	...	...	
Equals: NET LENDING (+) / NET BORROWING (-) OF THE NATION	53.6	240.2	-125.6	-584.0	-276.1	-136.7	-110.9	258.7	1403.0	-1726.5	-2176.4	
	Net values: Gross National Income / Gross National Disposable Income / Saving Gross less Consumption of fixed capital											
Less: Consumption of fixed capital	958.2	981.7	992.6	1039.6	1060.4	1254.0	1369.7	1362.8	1350.3	1518.0	1766.4	
Equals: NET NATIONAL INCOME	9939.2	10725.0	10970.9	11870.8	12967.9	14337.0	16682.7	19603.2	20991.0	23308.4	27205.8	
Equals: NET NATIONAL DISPOSABLE INCOME	10098.7	10895.9	11151.2	12021.8	13133.4	14490.7	16833.1	19726.0	20989.1	23341.7	27287.1	
Equals: SAVING, NET	1176.3	1191.4	1328.5	1019.2	1502.4	1928.8	3251.4	5194.2	6208.3	3619.8	4567.3	

Table 2.1 Value added by industries at current prices (ISIC Rev. 3)

Series 100: 1993 SNA, balboa, Western calendar year — **Data in millions**

	2001	2002	2003	2004	2005	2006	2007	2008	2009	2010	2011	2012
Series	**100**											
	Industries											
Agriculture, hunting, forestry; fishing	860.1	887.4	961.1	987.8	1006.6	1049.8	1098.2	1166.6	1112.2	1043.8	1088.6	...
Agriculture, hunting, forestry	601.1	581.7	610.9	631.0	688.7	746.9	829.0	880.6	859.3	873.4	940.8	...
Agriculture, hunting and related service activities	573.7	552.3	583.0	599.0	654.2	711.8	790.3	839.6	817.2	826.5	887.9	...
Forestry, logging and related service activities	27.4	29.4	27.7	32.4	34.5	35.1	38.7	41.0	42.1	46.9	52.9	...
Fishing	259.0	305.7	350.2	356.8	317.9	302.9	269.2	286.0	252.9	170.4	147.7	...
Mining and quarrying	76.8	90.1	127.8	142.7	151.1	188.9	235.0	327.4	352.6	384.9	469.3	...
Manufacturing	1033.8	973.6	969.4	1023.4	1072.4	1137.5	1225.8	1417.1	1414.8	1430.1	1529.3	...

	2001	2002	2003	2004	2005	2006	2007	2008	2009	2010	2011	2012
Series	**100**											
Electricity, gas and water supply	325.5	350.1	362.9	422.6	504.5	495.6	518.8	600.0	605.8	624.5	710.7	...
Construction	459.4	426.4	593.5	677.1	692.2	845.8	1072.8	1483.5	1607.3	1765.3	2183.5	...
Wholesale, retail trade, repair of motor vehicles, motorcycles and personal and households goods; hotels and restaurants	1927.9	1899.9	1930.1	2235.2	2566.2	2929.9	3430.2	4066.2	4173.2	4755.4	5913.6	...
Wholesale, retail trade, repair of motor vehicles, motorcycles and personal and household goods	1681.4	1645.9	1647.1	1911.1	2201.7	2507.3	2906.4	3419.6	3507.1	3980.8	5016.1	...
Hotels and restaurants	246.5	254.0	283.0	324.1	364.5	422.6	523.8	646.6	666.1	774.6	897.5	...
Transport, storage and communications	1612.5	1706.0	1855.4	2165.5	2409.9	2940.0	3386.1	3996.9	4093.9	4742.1	5638.3	...
Land transport; transport via pipelines, water transport; air transport; Supporting and auxiliary transport activities; activities of travel agencies	1227.4	1330.5	1508.6	1800.5	2013.0	2506.0	2901.9	3431.5	3518.7	4035.4	4832.7	...
Post and telecommunications	385.1	375.5	346.8	365.0	396.6	434.0	484.2	565.4	575.1	706.7	805.6	...
Financial intermediation; real estate, renting and business activities	3225.6	3415.8	3536.9	3701.3	4053.4	4437.0	5074.3	5734.9	6208.6	7369.6	8181.0	...
Financial intermediation	1155.6	1184.3	1155.1	1193.4	1343.5	1423.4	1663.3	1962.0	2037.6	2115.2	2423.4	...
Real estate, renting and business activities	2070.0	2231.5	2381.8	2507.9	2709.9	3013.6	3411.0	3772.9	4171.0	5254.4	5757.6	...
Public administration and defence; compulsory social security	589.0	609.2	542.7	645.4	637.9	698.5	826.4	899.7	1131.7	1168.2	1244.4	...
Education; health and social work; other community, social and personal services	1325.3	1405.1	1499.3	1555.8	1622.0	1692.2	1893.4	2134.0	2260.1	2415.3	2675.3	...
Education	512.0	535.9	568.0	588.4	603.5	635.3	721.1	840.7	885.2	907.2	1000.2	...
Health and social work	416.3	461.4	492.2	511.2	539.2	548.0	576.9	640.4	683.7	759.3	845.9	...
Other community, social and personal services	397.0	407.8	439.1	456.2	479.3	508.9	595.4	652.9	691.2	748.8	829.2	...
Private households with employed persons	94.4	106.0	113.0	123.1	128.9	138.3	145.7	154.8	160.7	174.1	182.4	...
Equals: VALUE ADDED, GROSS, in basic prices [a]	11530.3	11869.6	12492.2	13679.9	14845.3	16553.5	18906.7	21981.1	23120.9	25873.7	29816.6	...
Less: Financial intermediation services indirectly measured (FISIM)	402.9	370.3	404.0	404.0	422.2	467.7	452.2	527.7	602.8	657.5	796.0	...
Plus: Taxes less Subsidies on products	680.2	773.1	845.1	903.4	1041.6	1051.2	1339.2	1548.2	1644.8	1836.8	2295.2	...
Plus: Taxes on products	743.2	828.1	893.9	987.9	1128.3	1213.2	1513.3	1768.2	1827.2	2148.0	2599.5	...
Less: Subsidies on products	63.0	55.0	48.8	84.5	86.7	162.0	174.1	220.0	182.4	311.2	304.3	...
Equals: GROSS DOMESTIC PRODUCT	11807.6	12272.4	12933.2	14179.3	15464.7	17137.0	19793.7	23001.6	24162.9	27053.0	31315.8	36252.5

[a] Includes financial intermediation services indirectly measured (FISIM) of the Total Economy.

Table 2.2 Value added by industries at constant prices (ISIC Rev. 3)

Series 100: 1993 SNA, balboa, Western calendar year

Data in millions

	2001	2002	2003	2004	2005	2006	2007	2008	2009	2010	2011	2012
Series	**100**											
Base year	**1996**											
Industries												
Agriculture, hunting, forestry; fishing	849.3	877.5	958.9	971.9	997.0	1039.1	1045.0	1131.6	1043.5	895.6	889.9	929.1
Agriculture, hunting, forestry	588.3	565.2	581.1	592.9	622.0	670.6	688.8	719.5	646.5	663.3	708.4	743.1
Agriculture, hunting and related service activities	555.3	531.2	547.8	558.2	585.0	632.0	649.6	677.4	603.4	614.7	654.5	684.1
Forestry, logging and related service activities	33.0	34.0	33.3	34.7	37.0	38.6	39.2	42.1	43.1	48.6	53.9	59.0
Fishing	261.0	312.3	377.7	379.0	375.0	368.5	356.2	412.1	397.0	232.3	181.5	186.0
Mining and quarrying	75.6	89.3	120.9	136.0	136.1	159.5	197.8	259.0	270.8	290.7	353.5	459.7
Manufacturing	1026.3	999.4	965.4	985.5	1027.0	1066.7	1126.7	1170.9	1163.9	1176.7	1214.7	1259.0
Electricity, gas and water supply	357.0	381.5	387.0	410.6	433.0	447.6	484.3	502.9	540.5	575.4	610.7	682.1
Construction	419.9	390.0	516.7	588.6	594.6	704.0	857.2	1120.3	1170.4	1252.3	1489.1	1922.1
Wholesale, retail trade, repair of motor vehicles, motorcycles and personal and household goods; hotels and restaurants	1962.7	1945.5	1993.0	2229.5	2433.0	2707.2	3012.6	3231.1	3287.2	3616.5	4107.7	4466.0
Wholesale, retail trade, repair of motor vehicles, motorcycles and personal and household goods	1703.5	1668.1	1686.8	1881.9	2047.0	2274.0	2517.7	2695.2	2737.5	3009.5	3443.7	3731.9
Hotels and restaurants	259.2	277.4	306.2	347.6	386.1	433.2	494.9	535.9	549.7	607.0	664.0	734.1
Transport, storage and communications	1767.5	1803.2	1999.0	2296.3	2568.0	2920.9	3417.5	3945.8	4269.0	4890.1	5578.8	6201.2
Land transport; transport via piplines, water transport; air transport; Supporting and auxiliary transport activities; activities of travel agencies	1275.0	1289.5	1414.9	1630.5	1811.0	2044.1	2374.6	2702.1	2581.0	2929.5	3362.1	3701.3
Post and telecommunications	492.5	513.7	584.1	666.0	757.0	876.8	1042.9	1243.7	1688.0	1960.6	2216.7	2499.9
Financial intermediation, real estate, renting and business activities	2884.8	2879.4	2895.0	2990.1	3290.0	3588.4	4022.5	4410.2	4609.1	4905.5	5281.7	5716.2
Financial intermediation	1090.4	1011.9	939.4	887.0	1032.0	1187.1	1414.7	1614.6	1661.4	1754.6	1886.5	2079.7
Real estate, renting and business activities	1794.4	1867.5	1955.6	2103.1	2257.9	2401.3	2607.8	2795.6	2947.7	3150.9	3395.2	3636.5
Public administration and defence; compulsory social security	514.5	520.2	473.2	527.7	511.0	541.7	586.6	597.1	664.8	681.9	700.7	...
Education; health and social work; other community, social and personal services	1177.6	1243.0	1321.2	1321.9	1356.0	1382.2	1468.2	1557.9	1571.7	1652.7[a]	1777.4[a]	2646.7[b]
Education	438.8	449.2	484.0	474.3	475.0	483.8	507.7	537.8	531.5	531.7	566.8	156.8
Health and social work	368.0	403.2	440.0	435.2	452.0	447.8	444.2	468.9	462.0	487.1	523.8	208.1
Other community, social and personal services	370.8	390.6	397.2	412.4	429.0	450.6	516.3	551.2	578.2	614.8	644.1	733.4
Private households with employed persons	84.3	93.1	95.1	102.7	104.5	111.3	112.6	114.7	113.8	115.5	119.5	126.1
Equals: VALUE ADDED, GROSS, in basic prices [c]	11119.5	11222.1	11725.4	12560.8	13450.0	14668.6	16331.0	18041.5	18704.7	20052.7	22123.7	24408.2
Less: Financial intermediation services indirectly measured (FISIM)	369.0	288.2	300.2	262.5	289.1	374.3	379.8	403.9	430.5	446.7	470.3	502.7
Plus: Taxes less Subsidies on products	685.7	757.2	757.6	800.9	880.2	944.3	1133.2	1175.3	1264.2	1388.4	1618.7	1850.0
Plus: Taxes on products	745.7	809.0	803.0	878.6	960.0	1101.8	1291.3	1345.3	1375.0	1571.1	1787.4	2011.9

	2001	2002	2003	2004	2005	2006	2007	2008	2009	2010	2011	2012
Series	**100**											
Base year	**1996**											
Less: Subsidies on products	60.0	51.8	45.4	77.7	79.8	157.5	158.1	170.0	110.8	182.7	168.7	161.9
Equals: GROSS DOMESTIC PRODUCT	11436.2	11691.1	12182.8	13099.2	14041.2	15238.6	17084.4	18812.9	19538.4	20994.4	23272.1	23272.1

[a] Discrepancy between components and total as one or more components have not been revised.
[b] Includes Public administration and defence; compulsory social security.
[c] Includes financial intermediation services indirectly measured (FISIM) of the Total Economy.

Table 2.3 Output, gross value added, and fixed assets by industries at current prices (ISIC Rev. 3) Total Economy

Series 100: 1993 SNA, balboa, Western calendar year — **Data in millions**

	2001	2002	2003	2004	2005	2006	2007	2008	2009	2010	2011	2012
Series	**100**											
Output, at basic prices	...	...	...	...	...	...	...	...	...	...	...	
Less: Intermediate consumption, at purchaser's prices	...	...	...	...	...	...	...	...	...	...	...	
Equals: VALUE ADDED, GROSS, at basic prices [a]	11530.3	11869.6	12492.2	13679.9	14845.0	16553.5	18906.7	21981.1	23120.9	25873.7	29020.6	
Compensation of employees	4361.6	4378.8	4523.6	4919.0	5123.0	5675.5	6405.5	7276.7	7829.6	8412.0	9442.5	
Taxes on production and imports, less Subsidies	771.6	914.4	1062.4	1102.3	1279.6	1344.3	1626.9	1864.7	1929.3	2281.2	2774.1	
Taxes on production and imports	834.6	969.4	1111.2	1186.8	1366.3	1506.3	1801.0	2084.7	2111.7	2592.4	3078.4	
Taxes on products	743.2	828.1	893.9	987.9	1128.5	1213.2	1513.3	1768.2	1827.2	2148.0	2599.5	
Other taxes on production	91.4	141.3	217.3	198.9	238.0	293.1	287.7	316.5	284.5	444.4	478.9	
Less: Subsidies	63.0	55.0	48.8	84.5	86.7	162.0	174.1	220.0	182.4	311.2	304.3	
Subsidies on products	63.0	55.0	48.8	84.5	86.7	162.0	174.1	220.0	182.4	311.2	304.3	
Other subsidies on production	...	...	...	...	...	...	...	...	...	...	...	
OPERATING SURPLUS, GROSS	5234.6	5460.5	5728.0	6333.3	7066.4	7909.4	9158.4	10766.0	11203.0	12799.2	14906.0	
MIXED INCOME, GROSS	1439.7	1518.7	1619.2	1824.7	1996.0	2207.8	2602.8	3094.3	3200.9	3560.6	4193.2	
Total Economy only: Adjustment for FISIM (if FISIM is not distributed to uses)	402.9	370.3	404.0	404.0	422.2	467.7	452.2	527.7	602.8	657.5	796.0	
Less: Consumption of fixed capital	958.2	981.7	992.6	1039.6	1060.4	1254.0	1369.7	1362.8	1350.3	1518.0	1766.4	
OPERATING SURPLUS, NET	4276.4	4478.8	4735.4	5293.7	6006.0	6655.4	7788.7	9403.2	9852.7	11281.2	13139.6	
MIXED INCOME, NET	1439.7	1518.7	1619.2	1824.7	1996.0	2207.8	2602.8	3094.3	3200.9	3560.1	4193.2	
Gross capital formation	2082.5	1932.9	2456.7	2651.9	2839.0	3334.9	4775.7	6355.2	6185.6	6906.8	8519.0	
Gross fixed capital formation	1794.2	1664.8	2207.3	2351.0	2601.3	3134.9	4554.7	6100.5	5932.0	6639.3	8179.5	
Changes in inventories	288.3	268.1	249.4	300.9	237.7	200.0	221.0	254.7	253.6	267.5	339.5	
Acquisitions less disposals of valuables	...	...	...	...	...	...	...	...	...	...	...	

[a] Includes financial intermediation services indirectly measured (FISIM) of the Total Economy.

Table 3.1 Government final consumption expenditure by function at current prices

Series 100: 1993 SNA, balboa, Western calendar year — **Data in millions**

	2001	2002	2003	2004	2005	2006	2007	2008	2009	2010	2011	2012
Series	**100**											
General public services	326.5	445.6	320.4	427.0	434.5	534.7	488.2	525.8	1073.6	1353.1	1408.3	
Defence	...	...	...	...	...	...	...	...	...	...	...	
Public order and safety	262.4	262.0	335.0	282.3	245.0	248.0	290.4	303.4	309.8	408.4	410.9	
Economic affairs	106.3	112.7	110.1	154.9	268.4	202.8	220.9	222.6	162.8	154.6	214.1	
Environment protection	5.3	5.2	4.5	4.6	4.8	9.7	6.7	10.4	15.2	7.4	10.3	
Housing and community amenities	9.0	8.6	7.3	8.3	10.4	8.3	8.7	9.4	13.2	15.1	16.3	
Health	128.8	116.0	132.0	124.3	141.1	145.9	142.8	156.7	157.3	814.6	934.9	
Recreation, culture and religion	15.5	16.9	16.4	17.0	14.5	16.5	20.6	23.1	25.1	27.7	31.7	
Education	426.2	430.3	454.3	466.3	473.2	486.5	564.4	621.7	706.7	698.3	756.5	
Social protection	366.1	422.0	427.0	445.0	441.9	463.9	493.6	515.1	614.4	66.7	77.0	
Equals: General government final consumption expenditure	1646.1	1819.3	1807.0	1929.7	2033.8	2116.3	2236.3	2389.0	3078.1	3545.9	3860.0	

Table 4.1 Total Economy (S.1)

Series 100: 1993 SNA, balboa, Western calendar year — **Data in millions**

	2001	2002	2003	2004	2005	2006	2007	2008	2009	2010	2011	2012
Series	**100**											
I. Production account - Resources												
Output, at basic prices (otherwise, please specify)	...	...	...	...	...	...	...	...	...	...	...	
Less: Financial intermediation services indirectly measured (only to be deducted if FISIM is not distributed to uses)	402.9	370.3	404.0	404.0	422.2	467.7	452.2	527.7	602.8	657.5	796.0	
Plus: Taxes less Subsidies on products	680.2	773.1	845.1	903.4	1041.6	1051.2	1339.2	1548.2	1644.8	1835.9	2295.2	
Plus: Taxes on products	743.2	828.1	893.9	987.9	1128.3	1213.2	1513.3	1768.2	1827.2	2147.1	2599.5	
Less: Subsidies on products	63.0	55.0	48.9	84.5	86.7	162.0	174.1	220.0	182.4	311.2	304.3	
I. Production account - Uses												
Intermediate consumption, at purchaser's prices	...	...	...	...	...	...	...	...	...	...	...	
GROSS DOMESTIC PRODUCT	11807.5	12272.4	12933.2	14179.3	15464.7	17137.0	19793.7	23001.6	24162.9	27053.0	31315.8	
Less: Consumption of fixed capital	958.2	981.7	992.6	1039.6	1060.4	1254.0	1369.7	1362.8	1350.3	1518.0	1766.4	
NET DOMESTIC PRODUCT	10849.3	11290.7	11940.6	13164.6	14404.3	15883.0	18424.0	21627.6	22812.6	25535.0	29549.4	
II.1.1 Generation of income account - Resources												
GROSS DOMESTIC PRODUCT	11807.5	12272.4	12933.0	14179.3	15464.7	17137.0	19793.7	23001.6	24162.9	27053.0	31315.8	
II.1.1 Generation of income account - Uses												
Compensation of employees	4361.6	4378.8	4523.6	4919.0	5122.5	5675.5	6405.5	7276.7	7829.6	8412.0	9442.5	
Taxes on production and imports, less Subsidies	771.6	914.4	1062.4	1102.3	1279.6	1344.3	1626.9	1864.7	1929.3	2281.2	2774.1	
Taxes on production and imports	834.6	969.4	1111.2	1186.8	1366.3	1506.3	1801.0	2084.7	2111.7	2592.4	3078.4	
Taxes on products	743.2	828.1	893.9	987.9	1128.3	1213.2	1513.3	1768.2	1827.2	2148.0	2599.5	
Other taxes on production	91.4	141.3	217.3	198.9	238.0	293.1	287.7	316.5	284.5	444.4	478.9	

	2001	2002	2003	2004	2005	2006	2007	2008	2009	2010	2011	2012
Series	**100**											
Less: Subsidies	63.0	55.0	48.8	84.5	86.7	162.0	174.1	220.0	182.4	311.2	304.3	
Subsidies on products	...	...	...	...	...	...	...	...	...	...	...	
Other subsidies on production	...	...	...	...	...	...	...	...	...	...	...	
OPERATING SURPLUS, GROSS	5234.6	5460.5	5728.0	6333.3	7066.4	7909.4	9158.4	10766.0	11203.0	12799.2	14906.0	
MIXED INCOME, GROSS	1439.7	1518.7	1619.2	1824.7	1996.0	2207.8	2602.8	3094.3	3200.9	3560.6	4193.2	
II.1.2 Allocation of primary income account - Resources												
OPERATING SURPLUS, GROSS	5234.6	5460.5	5728.0	6333.3	7066.4	7909.4	9158.4	10766.0	11203.0	12799.0	14906.0	
MIXED INCOME, GROSS	1439.7	1518.7	1619.2	1824.7	1996.0	2207.8	2602.8	3094.3	3200.9	3560.6	4193.2	
Compensation of employees	4361.6	4378.8	4523.6	4919.0	5122.5	5675.5	6405.5	7276.7	7829.6	8412.0	9442.5	
Taxes on production and imports, less Subsidies	771.6	914.4	1062.4	1102.3	1279.6	1344.3	1626.9	1864.7	1929.3	2281.0	2774.0	
Taxes on production and imports	834.6	969.4	1111.2	1186.8	1366.3	1506.3[a]	1801.0	2084.7	2111.7	2592.0	3078.4	
Taxes on products	417.8	480.6	610.7	643.3	738.0	1132.5	1513.3	1768.2	1827.2	2147.1	2599.5	
Other taxes on production	416.8	488.8	500.5	543.5	628.3	638.0	287.7	316.5	284.5	444.4	478.9	
Less: Subsidies	63.0	55.0	48.8	84.5	86.7	162.0	174.1	220.0	182.4	311.2	304.3	
Subsidies on products	...	...	...	...	...	...	...	...	...	...	...	
Other subsidies on production	...	...	...	...	...	...	...	...	...	...	...	
Property income	-910.1[b]	-565.7[b]	-969.7[b]	-1268.9[b]	-1436.5[b]	-1546.0[b]	-1748.3[b]	-2035.6[b]	-1821.6[b]	-2226.6	-2343.6	
II.1.2 Allocation of primary income account - Uses												
Property income	...	...	...	...	...	...	...	...	...	...	...	
GROSS NATIONAL INCOME	10897.4	11706.7	11963.5	12910.4	14028.2	15591.0	18052.5	20966.0	22341.3	24826.4	28972.2	
II.2 Secondary distribution of income account - Resources												
GROSS NATIONAL INCOME	10897.4	11706.7	11963.5	12910.4	14028.2	15591.0	18052.5	20966.0	22341.3	24826.0	28972.2	
Current taxes on income, wealth, etc.	...	...	...	...	...	...	...	...	...	...	...	
Social contributions	...	...	...	...	...	...	...	...	...	...	...	
Social benefits other than social transfers in kind	...	...	...	...	...	...	...	...	...	...	...	
Other current transfers	159.5[b]	170.9[b]	180.3[b]	151.0[b]	165.6[b]	153.7[b]	150.3[b]	122.8[b]	-1.9[b]	33.3	81.3	
II.2 Secondary distribution of income account - Uses												
Current taxes on income, wealth, etc.	...	...	...	...	...	...	...	...	...	...	...	
Social contributions	...	...	...	...	...	...	...	...	...	...	...	
Social benefits other than social transfers in kind	...	...	...	...	...	...	...	...	...	...	...	
Other current transfers	...	...	...	...	...	...	...	...	...	...	...	
GROSS DISPOSABLE INCOME	11056.9	11877.6	12143.8	13061.4	14193.8	15744.7	18202.8	21088.8	22339.4	24859.7	29053.5	
II.4.1 Use of disposable income account - Resources												
GROSS DISPOSABLE INCOME	11056.9	11877.6	12143.8	13061.4	14193.8	15744.7	18202.8	21088.8	22339.4	24859.7	29053.5	
Adjustment for the change in net equity of households on pension funds	...	...	...	...	...	...	...	...	...	...	...	
II.4.1 Use of disposable income account - Uses												
Final consumption expenditure	8922.4	9704.5	9822.7	11002.6	11631.0	12561.9	13581.7	14531.8	14780.8	19721.9	22719.8	
Individual consumption expenditure	...	...	...	...	...	...	...	...	...	...	...	
Collective consumption expenditure	...	...	...	...	...	...	...	...	...	...	...	

	2001	2002	2003	2004	2005	2006	2007	2008	2009	2010	2011	2012
Series	**100**											
Adjustment for the change in net equity of households on pension funds	...	...	...	...	...	...	...	...	...	...	...	
SAVING, GROSS	2134.5	2173.1	2321.1	2058.8	2562.8	3182.8	4621.1	6557.0	7558.6	5137.8	6333.7	
III.1 Capital account - Changes in liabilities and net worth												
SAVING, GROSS	2134.5	2173.1	2321.1	2058.8	2562.8	3182.8	4621.1	6557.0	7558.6	5137.8	6333.7	
Capital transfers, receivable less payable	1.6	0.0	10.0	9.1	0.0	15.0	43.7	56.9	30.0	42.5	8.9	
Capital transfers, receivable	...	...	...	...	...	...	...	...	...	...	...	
Less: Capital transfers, payable	...	...	...	...	...	...	...	...	...	...	...	
Equals: CHANGES IN NET WORTH DUE TO SAVING AND CAPITAL TRANSFERS	...	...	...	...	...	...	...	...	...	...	...	
III.1 Capital account - Changes in assets												
Gross capital formation	2082.5	1932.9	2456.7	2651.9	2839.0	3334.9	4775.7	6355.2	6185.6	6906.8	8519.0	
Gross fixed capital formation	1794.2	1664.8	2207.3	2351.0	2601.3	3134.9	4554.7	6100.5	5932.0	6639.3	8179.5	
Changes in inventories	288.3	268.1	249.4	300.9	237.7	200.0	221.0	254.7	253.6	267.5	339.5	
Acquisitions less disposals of valuables	...	...	...	...	...	...	...	...	...	...	...	
Acquisitions less disposals of non-produced non-financial assets	...	...	...	...	...	...	...	...	...	...	...	
NET LENDING (+) / NET BORROWING (-)	53.6	240.2	-125.6	-584.0	-276.2	-137.1	-110.9	258.7	1403.0	-1726.5	-2176.4	
III.2 Financial account - Changes in liabilities and net worth												
Net incurrence of liabilities	...	...	...	...	...	...	...	...	...	...	...	
Currency and deposits	...	...	...	...	...	...	...	...	...	...	...	
Securities other than shares	...	...	...	...	...	...	...	...	...	...	...	
Loans	...	...	...	...	...	...	...	...	...	...	...	
Shares and other equity	...	...	...	...	...	...	...	...	...	...	...	
Insurance technical reserves	...	...	...	...	...	...	...	...	...	...	...	
Financial derivatives	...	...	...	...	...	...	...	...	...	...	...	
Other accounts payable	...	...	...	...	...	...	...	...	...	...	...	
NET LENDING (+) / NET BORROWING (-)	53.6	240.2	-125.6	-584.0	-276.2	-152.1[c]	-110.9	258.7	1403.0	-1726.5	-2176.4	
III.2 Financial account - Changes in assets												
Net acquisition of financial assets	...	...	...	...	...	...	...	...	...	...	...	
Monetary gold and SDRs	...	...	...	...	...	...	...	...	...	...	...	
Currency and deposits	...	...	...	...	...	...	...	...	...	...	...	
Securities other than shares	...	...	...	...	...	...	...	...	...	...	...	
Loans	...	...	...	...	...	...	...	...	...	...	...	
Shares and other equity	...	...	...	...	...	...	...	...	...	...	...	
Insurance technical reserves	...	...	...	...	...	...	...	...	...	...	...	
Financial derivatives	...	...	...	...	...	...	...	...	...	...	...	
Other accounts receivable	...	...	...	...	...	...	...	...	...	...	...	

[a] Discrepancy between components and total.
[b] Refers to net values (to/from the Rest of the World).
[c] Statistical discrepancy between net lending (+)/net borrowing (-) in the financial account and net lending (+)/net borrowing (-) in the capital account.

Papua New Guinea

Source

Reply to the United Nations national accounts questionnaire from the National Statistical Office (formerly Bureau of Statistics), Port Moresby. The official estimates are published in "Gross Domestic Product and Expenditure".

General

The latest estimates shown in the following tables have been prepared in accordance with the concepts and definitions of the System of National Accounts 1993 (1993 SNA). Previously, the estimates were prepared in accordance with the United Nations System of National Accounts 1968 (1968 SNA). A detailed description of the sources and methods used for the national accounts estimation is found in "National Accounts Statistics". When the scope and coverage of the estimates differ for conceptual or statistical reasons from the definitions and classifications recommended in SNA, a footnote is indicated to the relevant tables.

Methodology:

Overview of GDP Compilation

Gross domestic product is estimated mainly through the production approach.

Expenditure Approach

All components of gross domestic product by expenditure type are estimated through the expenditure approach. However, the commodity-flow approach is used for checking purposes in the case of a few items included under private consumption expenditure. The estimates of government consumption expenditure are based on budget papers, annual reports of the commissioner for local government, financial statements of provincial government and Australian budget papers. The market component of household consumption expenditure is estimated mainly from the results of the retail sales and selected services survey. Estimates for items not covered by this survey are obtained from sources such as budget papers, the population census, various surveys of urban markets and village industry and taxation data. For some selected items, the estimates are checked and supplemented by data from international trade statistics using the commodity-flow approach. The non-market component of household consumption consists of food and firewood for own consumption and services of owner-occupied dwellings. Estimates of food produced for own consumption are calculated by using data from the Rural Industrial Bulletin and the estimated consumption per head of population. The annual quantity of firewood used per family is multiplied by average price and the number of families gathering firewood for own use.

Construction and maintenance of housing is estimated by multiplying population data by the time spent and the minimum wage rate. Estimates of increase in stocks are based mainly on the Taxation Statistics Bulletin. For gross fixed capital formation by private industries, the principal source of information is the capital expenditure survey and for the public industries, the annual reports of the public enterprises. Exports and imports of goods and services are estimated mainly from the international trade statistics. For the constant price estimates of parts of government expenditure, private expenditure, gross fixed capital formation, increase in stocks and exports of merchandise, the current quantities are revalued at base-year prices. Regarding the market component of private consumption expenditure, building and construction, government expenditure on goods and services and imports of merchandise, the current values are deflated by appropriate price indexes.

Income Approach

Estimates of compensation of employees are based on taxation statistics, statistics of religious organizations and the Labour Information Bulletin. Adjustments are made for wages and salaries not covered by the above sources.

Imputed wages referring to work provided to government and mission authorities are shown separately. Estimates of operating surplus for the market component are based mainly on taxation returns with some adjustments made to cover imputed bank service charge and to include producers not required to submit returns. For owner-occupied dwellings, operating surplus is calculated from information contained in the Building Statistics Bulletin. Consumption of fixed capital is estimated based on taxation data supplemented by annual reports for producers not covered. The Papua New Guinea Budget papers and the annual reports of the Commissioner for Local Government provide all the information needed to estimate indirect taxes and subsidies.

Production Approach

The table of gross domestic product by kind of economic activity is prepared at market prices, i.e., producers' values. The income approach is used to estimate value added of most industries. Value added is defined as the sum of compensation of employees, operating surplus, consumption of fixed capital and net indirect taxes. The principal source is the income tax statistics, supplemented by annual reports of public and private enterprises. The reporting unit in these statistics is the enterprise (legal entity) rather than the establishment. For the major activities such as mining and quarrying, electricity, gas and water, and communication, in which cases almost the whole production is concentrated in a few enterprise units, the establishment type data are used. In cases where surveys data are used, adjustments and supplementary data are taken into account to cover activities not included. For the non-marketed production and contributions of free and partially paid labour, estimates are available separately as subdivisions of the relevant items as the amounts involved are quite substantial. As mentioned above, estimates of GDP by kind of economic activity are arrived at by subdividing the cost-structure components of total GDP into the various kinds of activity.

Compensation of employees is classified in accordance with the industry information on individuals' tax returns. If an individual has more than one source of income, he is allocated to the industry category corresponding to his major source of income and all of his income is classed to that category. Data on operating surplus of private enterprises are classified on the basis of information given in the company tax statistics and in the statistics of individuals' income other than wages and salaries, while the industry categories of the operating surplus of public enterprises are determined by the nature of their productive activities. For industry allocation of consumption of fixed capital, the taxation data supplemented by other information in respect of producers not covered by the taxation statistics provide the basis. In the case of indirect taxes and subsidies, the industry allocation is made on the basis of the nature of indirect taxes and subsidies. GDP by kind of economic activity at constant prices is not estimated.

Table 1.1 Gross domestic product by expenditures at current prices

Series 100: 1993 SNA, kina, Western calendar year — **Data in millions**

	2001	2002	2003	2004	2005	2006	2007	2008	2009	2010	2011	2012
Series	**100**											
Expenditures of the gross domestic product												
Final consumption expenditure	6650.3	8562.5	8514.5	9285.1	9676.8	10796.6						
Household final consumption expenditure	4962.3	6574.9	6676.9	7047.5	7239.2	7959.0						
NPISHs final consumption expenditure	...	...	...	...	...	...						
General government final consumption expenditure	1688.0	1987.6	1837.6	2237.6	2437.6	2837.6						
Gross capital formation	2386.1	2970.0	2827.0	2874.0	2639.0	2653.0						
Gross fixed capital formation	2199.8	2463.9	2281.0	2294.0	2489.0	2303.0						
Changes in inventories	186.3	506.1	546.0	580.2	150.0	350.0						
Acquisitions less disposals of valuables	...	...	...	...	...	...						

	2001	2002	2003	2004	2005	2006	2007	2008	2009	2010	2011	2012
Series	**100**											
Exports of goods and services	6791.9	7100.0	8724.0	9143.4	11245.7	13986.2						
Less: Imports of goods and services	5432.1	6760.6	6824.3	7843.7	8467.1	10538.9						
Equals: GROSS DOMESTIC PRODUCT	10396.3	11872.2	13241.5	13459.4	15094.7	16896.6						

Table 1.2 Gross domestic product by expenditures at constant prices

Series 100: 1993 SNA, kina, Western calendar year **Data in millions**

	2001	2002	2003	2004	2005	2006	2007	2008	2009	2010	2011	2012
Series	**100**											
Base year	**1998**											
Expenditures of the gross domestic product												
Final consumption expenditure	4406.5	5060.7	4552.6	5079.6	5423.2	5842.3						
Household final consumption expenditure	2854.8	3334.9	3068.6	3306.4	3630.2	3858.0						
NPISHs final consumption expenditure	...	...	...	...	...	...						
General government final consumption expenditure	1551.7	1725.8	1483.8	1773.2	1793.0	1984.3						
Gross capital formation	2047.0	2406.0	2132.8	2145.8	1934.6	1898.1						
Gross fixed capital formation	1887.1	1995.9	1720.8	1712.5	1824.5	1647.3						
Changes in inventories	159.9	410.1	412.1	433.3	110.0	250.8						
Acquisitions less disposals of valuables	...	...	...	...	...	...						
Exports of goods and services	5775.4	5702.8	6516.3	6703.0	7159.0	7187.0						
Less: Imports of goods and services	4479.2	5264.1	4949.0	5629.0	5892.0	6104.0						
Equals: GROSS DOMESTIC PRODUCT	7750.0	7905.5	8252.3	8299.1	8625.2	8823.0						

Table 1.3 Relations among product, income, savings, and net lending aggregates

Series 100: 1993 SNA, kina, Western calendar year **Data in millions**

	2001	2002	2003	2004	2005	2006	2007	2008	2009	2010	2011	2012
Series	**100**											
GROSS DOMESTIC PRODUCT	10396.3	11871.9	13242.0	13459.0	15094.7	16896.6						
Plus: Compensation of employees - from and to the rest of the world, net	0.0	-0.1	-0.1	0.1	0.0	0.0						
Plus: Compensation of employees - from the rest of the world	2.5	2.5	2.5	3.0	3.0	3.0						
Less: Compensation of employees - to the rest of the world	2.5	2.5	2.6	3.0	3.0	3.0						
Plus: Property income - from and to the rest of the world, net	-408.1	-414.9	-424.4	-1408.9	-1670.0	-2462.0						
Plus: Property income - from the rest of the world	55.2	54.6	56.0	61.0	81.0	215.0						
Less: Property income - to the rest of the world	463.2	469.5	480.4	1470.0	1751.0	2677.0						
Sum of Compensation of employees and property income - from and to the rest of the world, net	-408.1	-415.0	-424.5	-1408.9	-1670.0	-2462.0						

	2001	2002	2003	2004	2005	2006	2007	2008	2009	2010	2011	2012
Series	**100**											
Plus: Sum of Compensation of employees and property income - from the rest of the world	58.0	57.0	58.5	63.8	84.0	218.0						
Less: Sum of Compensation of employees and property income - to the rest of the world	466.0	472.0	483.0	1472.7	1754.0	2680.0						
Plus: Taxes less subsidies on production and imports - from and to the rest of the world, net	...	...	...	...	...	...						
Equals: GROSS NATIONAL INCOME	9988.2	11456.9	12817.5	12050.1	13424.7	14434.6						
Plus: Current transfers - from and to the rest of the world, net	44.5	87.8	116.1	799.2	808.0	726.0						
Plus: Current transfers - from the rest of the world	111.0	148.6	183.0	871.9	883.0	804.0						
Less: Current transfers - to the rest of the world	66.7	60.8	66.8	73.0	75.0	78.0						
Equals: GROSS NATIONAL DISPOSABLE INCOME	10033.0	11545.2	12932.8	12849.9	14232.7	15161.0						
Less: Final consumption expenditure / Actual final consumption	6650.3	8562.5	8514.5	9285.1	9676.8	10796.6						
Equals: SAVING, GROSS	3382.0	2982.2	4418.8	3564.9	4555.7	4364.0						
Plus: Capital transfers - from and to the rest of the world, net	241.2	183.2	212.2	254.0	260.0	243.0						
Less: Gross capital formation	2386.1	2970.0	2827.2	2874.5	2639.0	2653.0						
Less: Acquisitions less disposals of non-produced non-financial assets	...	...	...	...	...	...						
Equals: NET LENDING (+) / NET BORROWING (-) OF THE NATION	1237.5	195.5	1803.6	944.1	2177.0	1954.0						
Net values: Gross National Income / Gross National Disposable Income / Saving Gross less Consumption of fixed capital												
Less: Consumption of fixed capital	638.0	747.2	820.8	828.9	876.7	985.0						
Equals: NET NATIONAL INCOME	9350.3	10709.7	11995.8	11221.6	12548.0	13449.6						
Equals: NET NATIONAL DISPOSABLE INCOME	9394.7	10797.6	12112.4	12020.9	13356.1	14175.8						
Equals: SAVING, NET	2744.4	2235.0	3597.8	2735.7	3679.2	3379.2						

Table 2.1 Value added by industries at current prices (ISIC Rev. 3)

Series 100: 1993 SNA, kina, Western calendar year **Data in millions**

	2001	2002	2003	2004	2005	2006	2007	2008	2009	2010	2011	2012
Series	**100**											
Industries												
Agriculture, hunting, forestry; fishing	3577.5	4428.0	4820.0	4550.0	5019.9	5327.3						
Agriculture, hunting, forestry	3305.5	4167.8	4532.1	4242.0	4661.7	4870.5						
Agriculture, hunting and related service activities	3182.7	4062.1	4435.5	4163.0	4574.0	4767.0						
Forestry, logging and related service activities	122.8	105.7	96.6	78.0	87.0	104.0						
Fishing	272.0	260.2	287.2	308.0	358.0	457.0						
Mining and quarrying	2401.1	2365.0	2925.5	3199.5	4061.7	5042.8						
Manufacturing	731.1	729.3	820.8	848.0	928.0	974.7						
Electricity, gas and water supply	167.2	194.8	228.7	264.0	301.0	338.0						
Construction	702.3	995.7	1128.9	1177.0	1245.8	1437.2						

	2001	2002	2003	2004	2005	2006	2007	2008	2009	2010	2011	2012
Series	**100**											
Wholesale, retail trade, repair of motor vehicles, motorcycles and personal and households goods; hotels and restaurants	558.0	745.5	849.9	891.0	943.0	1039.0						
Transport, storage and communications	258.4	268.0	293.9	305.0	317.0	326.0						
Financial intermediation; real estate, renting and business activities	406.7	407.0	422.9	415.0	489.0	579.0						
Public administration and defence; compulsory social security	...	...	...	...	...	...						
Education; health and social work; other community, social and personal services [a]	1240.6	1351.8	1403.1	1395.0	1447.9	1526.8						
Education	...	...	...	...	...	...						
Health and social work	...	...	...	...	...	...						
Other community, social and personal services	1240.6	1351.8	1403.1	1395.0	1447.9	1526.8						
Private households with employed persons	...	...	...	...	...	...						
Equals: VALUE ADDED, GROSS, in basic prices [b]	9864.4	11299.8	12659.0	12806.4	14437.4	16200.4						
Less: Financial intermediation services indirectly measured (FISIM)	178.5	185.4	234.5	237.0	316.0	391.0						
Plus: Taxes less Subsidies on products [c]	531.9	572.3	582.4	653.0	657.0	696.0						
Plus: Taxes on products	534.5	575.0	585.3	656.0	661.0	700.0						
Less: Subsidies on products	2.6	2.8	2.9	3.0	4.0	4.0						
Equals: GROSS DOMESTIC PRODUCT	10396.3	11872.0	13241.5	13459.4	15094.7	16896.6						

[a] Includes Public administration and defence; compulsory social security.
[b] Excludes financial intermediation services indirectly measured (FISIM), but FISIM is included in industry data.
[c] Refers to import duties less subsidies.

Table 2.2 Value added by industries at constant prices (ISIC Rev. 3)

Series 100: 1993 SNA, kina, Western calendar year — **Data in millions**

	2001	2002	2003	2004	2005	2006	2007	2008	2009	2010	2011	2012
Series	**100**											
Base year	**1998**											
Industries												
Agriculture, hunting, forestry; fishing	2909.0	2891.9	3115.8	3109.0	3284.0	3318.2						
Agriculture, hunting, forestry	2702.7	2727.1	2923.8	2916.1	3086.4	3118.1						
Agriculture, hunting and related service activities	2615.8	2650.1	2850.4	2857.3	3020.7	3042.2						
Forestry, logging and related service activities	86.9	77.0	73.4	59.0	66.0	76.0						
Fishing	206.2	164.8	192.0	193.0	198.0	200.0						
Mining and quarrying	1120.9	1002.3	1133.1	1112.3	1125.8	1030.4						
Manufacturing	594.5	560.0	587.1	600.0	650.4	676.4						
Electricity, gas and water supply	116.1	120.7	124.9	127.0	133.5	135.2						
Construction	600.9	805.0	848.7	876.0	917.7	1027.9						
Wholesale, retail trade, repair of motor vehicles, motorcycles and personal and household goods; hotels and restaurants	428.2	525.5	539.4	556.0	576.0	624.0						
Transport, storage and communications	209.7	205.5	209.8	215.0	221.8	232.8						

	2001	2002	2003	2004	2005	2006	2007	2008	2009	2010	2011	2012
Series	**100**											
Base year	**1998**											
Financial intermediation, real estate, renting and business activities	343.2	324.2	313.3	303.0	333.0	366.0						
Public administration and defence; compulsory social security	...	...	...	...	...	...						
Education; health and social work; other community, social and personal services	1140.4	1173.7	1132.9	1106.0	1127.1	1160.7						
Education	...	...	...	...	...	...						
Health and social work	...	...	...	...	...	...						
Other community, social and personal services	1140.4	1173.7	1132.9	1106.0	1127.1	1160.7						
Private households with employed persons	...	...	...	...	...	...						
Equals: VALUE ADDED, GROSS, in basic prices [a]	7311.1	7459.9	7830.0	7831.0	8157.7	8333.7						
Less: Financial intermediation services indirectly measured (FISIM)	151.8	148.9	175.2	174.0	212.0	238.0						
Plus: Taxes less Subsidies on products [b]	438.6	445.6	422.4	469.0	468.0	489.0						
Plus: Taxes on products	440.8	447.7	424.5	471.0	470.0	492.0						
Less: Subsidies on products	2.2	2.2	2.1	2.0	2.0	3.0						
Equals: GROSS DOMESTIC PRODUCT	7749.7	7905.5	8252.0	8299.1	8625.0	8823.0						

[a] Excludes financial intermediation services indirectly measured (FISIM), but FISIM is included in industry data.
[b] Refers to import duties less subsidies.

Table 2.3 Output, gross value added, and fixed assets by industries at current prices (ISIC Rev. 3) Total Economy

Series 100: 1993 SNA, kina, Western calendar year — **Data in millions**

	2001	2002	2003	2004	2005	2006	2007	2008	2009	2010	2011	2012
Series	**100**											
Output, at basic prices	...	...	...	...	...	...						
Less: Intermediate consumption, at purchaser's prices	...	...	...	...	...	...						
Equals: VALUE ADDED, GROSS, at basic prices [a]	9864.4	11299.8	12659.2	12806.4	14437.4	16200.4						
Compensation of employees	2050.3	2245.4	2436.2	2450.5	2491.1	2550.9						
Taxes on production and imports, less Subsidies	390.8	299.6	338.6	363.4	564.5	670.0						
Taxes on production and imports	390.8	299.6	338.6	363.4	564.5	670.0						
Taxes on products	...	...	...	...	...	...						
Other taxes on production	390.8	299.6	338.6	363.4	564.5	670.0						
Less: Subsidies	...	...	...	...	...	...						
OPERATING SURPLUS, GROSS [b]	7423.1	8754.7	9884.5	9992.7	11381.8	12979.5						
MIXED INCOME, GROSS	...	...	...	...	...	...						
Less: Consumption of fixed capital	638.0	747.2	820.8	828.9	876.7	985.0						
OPERATING SURPLUS, NET [c]	6785.1	8007.5	9063.7	9163.8	10505.1	11994.5						
MIXED INCOME, NET	...	...	...	...	...	...						
Gross capital formation	2386.1	2970.0	2827.0	2874.5	2639.0	2653.0						

	2001	2002	2003	2004	2005	2006	2007	2008	2009	2010	2011	2012
Series	**100**											
Gross fixed capital formation	2199.8	2464.0	2281.0	2294.0	2489.0	2303.0						
Changes in inventories	186.3	506.1	546.0	580.2	150.0	350.0						
Acquisitions less disposals of valuables	...	...	...	...	...	...						

[a] Excludes financial intermediation services indirectly measured (FISIM), but FISIM is included in industry data.
[b] Includes Mixed Income, Gross.
[c] Includes Mixed Income, Net.

Table 2.3 Output, gross value added, and fixed assets by industries at current prices (ISIC Rev. 3) Agriculture, hunting, forestry; fishing (A+B)

Series 100: 1993 SNA, kina, Western calendar year **Data in millions**

	2001	2002	2003	2004	2005	2006	2007	2008	2009	2010	2011	2012
Series	**100**											
Output, at basic prices	...	...	...	...	...	...						
Less: Intermediate consumption, at purchaser's prices	...	...	...	...	...	...						
Equals: VALUE ADDED, GROSS, at basic prices	3577.5	4428.0	4820.0	4549.6	5019.9	5327.3						
Compensation of employees	142.0	175.7	197.5	204.3	206.1	218.1						
Taxes on production and imports, less Subsidies	174.2	83.3	104.1	124.0	137.1	150.0						
Taxes on production and imports	174.2	83.3	104.1	124.0	137.1	150.0						
Taxes on products	...	...	...	...	...	...						
Other taxes on production	174.2	83.3	104.1	124.0	137.1	150.0						
Less: Subsidies	...	...	...	...	...	...						
OPERATING SURPLUS, GROSS [a]	3261.3	4169.1	4518.5	4221.3	4676.7	4959.2						
MIXED INCOME, GROSS	...	...	...	...	...	...						
Less: Consumption of fixed capital	36.7	49.6	55.7	57.6	61.0	68.5						
OPERATING SURPLUS, NET [b]	3224.6	4119.5	4462.8	4163.7	4615.7	4890.7						
MIXED INCOME, NET	...	...	...	...	...	...						
Gross capital formation	...	...	...	...	...	...						

[a] Includes Mixed Income, Gross.
[b] Includes Mixed Income, Net.

Table 2.3 Output, gross value added, and fixed assets by industries at current prices (ISIC Rev. 3) Agriculture, hunting and related service activities (01)

Series 100: 1993 SNA, kina, Western calendar year **Data in millions**

	2001	2002	2003	2004	2005	2006	2007	2008	2009	2010	2011	2012
Series	**100**											
Output, at basic prices	...	...	...	...	...	...						
Less: Intermediate consumption, at purchaser's prices	...	...	...	...	...	...						
Equals: VALUE ADDED, GROSS, at basic prices	3183.0	4062.0	4436.0	4163.0	4574.0	4767.0						
Compensation of employees	126.0	161.0	181.0	187.0	189.0	200.0						

	2001	2002	2003	2004	2005	2006	2007	2008	2009	2010	2011	2012
Series	**100**											
Taxes on production and imports, less Subsidies	155.0	65.0	82.0	97.0	108.0	118.0						
Taxes on production and imports	155.0	65.0	82.0	97.0	108.0	118.0						
Taxes on products	...	...	...	...	...	...						
Other taxes on production	155.0	65.0	82.0	97.0	108.0	118.0						
Less: Subsidies	...	...	...	...	...	...						
OPERATING SURPLUS, GROSS [a]	2902.0	3835.0	4173.0	3879.0	4278.0	4449.0						
MIXED INCOME, GROSS	...	...	...	...	...	...						
Less: Consumption of fixed capital	33.0	45.0	51.0	53.0	56.0	63.0						
OPERATING SURPLUS, NET [b]	2869.0	3790.0	4122.0	3826.0	4222.0	4386.0						
MIXED INCOME, NET	...	...	...	...	...	...						
Gross capital formation	...	...	...	...	...	...						

[a] Includes Mixed Income, Gross.
[b] Includes Mixed Income, Net.

Table 2.3 Output, gross value added, and fixed assets by industries at current prices (ISIC Rev. 3) Forestry, logging and related service activities (02)

Series 100: 1993 SNA, kina, Western calendar year **Data in millions**

	2001	2002	2003	2004	2005	2006	2007	2008	2009	2010	2011	2012
Series	**100**											
Output, at basic prices	...	...	...	...	...	...						
Less: Intermediate consumption, at purchaser's prices	...	...	...	...	...	...						
Equals: VALUE ADDED, GROSS, at basic prices	122.8	105.7	96.6	77.9	87.4	103.6						
Compensation of employees	4.9	4.2	4.7	4.9	4.9	5.2						
Taxes on production and imports, less Subsidies	6.0	5.1	6.4	7.7	8.5	9.3						
Taxes on production and imports	6.0	5.1	6.4	7.7	8.5	9.3						
Taxes on products	...	...	...	...	...	...						
Other taxes on production	6.0	5.1	6.4	7.7	8.5	9.3						
Less: Subsidies	...	...	...	...	...	...						
OPERATING SURPLUS, GROSS [a]	112.0	96.3	85.4	65.4	74.1	89.1						
MIXED INCOME, GROSS	...	...	...	...	...	...						
Less: Consumption of fixed capital	1.3	1.2	1.3	1.4	1.5	1.7						
OPERATING SURPLUS, NET [b]	110.7	95.1	84.1	64.0	72.6	87.4						
MIXED INCOME, NET	...	...	...	...	...	...						
Gross capital formation	...	...	...	...	...	...						

[a] Includes Mixed Income, Gross.
[b] Includes Mixed Income, Net.

Table 2.3 Output, gross value added, and fixed assets by industries at current prices (ISIC Rev. 3) Fishing (B)

Series 100: 1993 SNA, kina, Western calendar year

Data in millions

	2001	2002	2003	2004	2005	2006	2007	2008	2009	2010	2011	2012
Series	**100**											
Output, at basic prices	...	...	...	...	...	...						
Less: Intermediate consumption, at purchaser's prices	...	...	...	...	...	...						
Equals: VALUE ADDED, GROSS, at basic prices	272.0	260.2	287.2	308.4	358.1	456.8						
Compensation of employees	10.8	10.3	11.6	12.0	12.1	12.8						
Taxes on production and imports, less Subsidies	13.2	12.7	15.8	18.9	20.9	22.8						
Taxes on production and imports	13.2	12.7	15.8	18.9	20.9	22.8						
Taxes on products	...	...	...	...	...	...						
Other taxes on production	13.2	12.7	15.8	18.9	20.9	22.8						
Less: Subsidies	...	...	...	...	...	...						
OPERATING SURPLUS, GROSS [a]	247.9	237.2	259.8	277.5	325.1	421.2						
MIXED INCOME, GROSS	...	...	...	...	...	...						
Less: Consumption of fixed capital	2.8	2.9	3.3	3.4	3.6	4.1						
OPERATING SURPLUS, NET [b]	245.1	234.3	256.5	274.1	321.5	417.1						
MIXED INCOME, NET	...	...	...	...	...	...						
Gross capital formation	...	...	...	...	...	...						

[a] Includes Mixed Income, Gross.
[b] Includes Mixed Income, Net.

Table 2.3 Output, gross value added, and fixed assets by industries at current prices (ISIC Rev. 3) Mining and quarrying (C)

Series 100: 1993 SNA, kina, Western calendar year

Data in millions

	2001	2002	2003	2004	2005	2006	2007	2008	2009	2010	2011	2012
Series	**100**											
Output, at basic prices	...	...	...	...	...	...						
Less: Intermediate consumption, at purchaser's prices	...	...	...	...	...	...						
Equals: VALUE ADDED, GROSS, at basic prices	2401.1	2365.0	2925.5	3199.5	4061.7	5042.8						
Compensation of employees	255.4	230.1	224.6	201.1	209.1	221.5						
Taxes on production and imports, less Subsidies	...	...	...	...	...	...						
OPERATING SURPLUS, GROSS [a]	2145.7	2134.9	2701.0	2998.5	3852.7	4821.3						
MIXED INCOME, GROSS	...	...	...	...	...	...						
Less: Consumption of fixed capital	185.8	182.0	177.1	157.8	166.9	187.5						
OPERATING SURPLUS, NET [b]	1959.9	1952.9	2523.9	2840.7	3685.8	4633.8						

	2001	2002	2003	2004	2005	2006	2007	2008	2009	2010	2011	2012
Series	**100**											
MIXED INCOME, NET	...	...	...	...	...	...						
Gross capital formation	...	...	...	...	...	...						

[a] Includes Mixed Income, Gross.
[b] Includes Mixed Income, Net.

Table 2.3 Output, gross value added, and fixed assets by industries at current prices (ISIC Rev. 3) Manufacturing (D)

Series 100: 1993 SNA, kina, Western calendar year **Data in millions**

	2001	2002	2003	2004	2005	2006	2007	2008	2009	2010	2011	2012
Series	**100**											
Output, at basic prices	...	...	...	...	...	...						
Less: Intermediate consumption, at purchaser's prices	...	...	...	...	...	...						
Equals: VALUE ADDED, GROSS, at basic prices	731.1	729.3	820.8	848.3	928.1	974.4						
Compensation of employees	127.0	126.7	138.5	143.1	150.3	155.1						
Taxes on production and imports, less Subsidies	166.4	166.0	181.4	187.4	255.9	310.0						
Taxes on production and imports	166.4	166.0	181.4	187.4	255.9	310.0						
Taxes on products	...	...	...	...	...	...						
Other taxes on production	166.4	166.0	181.4	187.4	255.9	310.0						
Less: Subsidies	...	...	...	...	...	...						
OPERATING SURPLUS, GROSS [a]	437.6	436.5	500.9	517.7	522.0	509.5						
MIXED INCOME, GROSS	...	...	...	...	...	...						
Less: Consumption of fixed capital	28.4	30.9	33.8	34.9	37.0	41.5						
OPERATING SURPLUS, NET [b]	409.2	405.6	467.1	482.8	485.0	468.0						
MIXED INCOME, NET	...	...	...	...	...	...						
Gross capital formation	...	...	...	...	...	...						

[a] Includes Mixed Income, Gross.
[b] Includes Mixed Income, Net.

Table 2.3 Output, gross value added, and fixed assets by industries at current prices (ISIC Rev. 3) Electricity, gas and water supply (E)

Series 100: 1993 SNA, kina, Western calendar year **Data in millions**

	2001	2002	2003	2004	2005	2006	2007	2008	2009	2010	2011	2012
Series	**100**											
Output, at basic prices	...	...	...	...	...	...						
Less: Intermediate consumption, at purchaser's prices	...	...	...	...	...	...						
Equals: VALUE ADDED, GROSS, at basic prices	167.2	194.8	228.7	263.7	301.3	337.7						
Compensation of employees	39.7	46.3	54.3	62.6	63.5	66.3						
Taxes on production and imports, less Subsidies	...	...	...	...	...	...						

	2001	2002	2003	2004	2005	2006	2007	2008	2009	2010	2011	2012
Series	**100**											
OPERATING SURPLUS, GROSS [a]	127.5	148.6	174.3	201.1	237.8	271.4						
MIXED INCOME, GROSS	...	...	...	...	...	...						
Less: Consumption of fixed capital	52.5	66.6	78.1	90.1	95.3	107.1						
OPERATING SURPLUS, NET [b]	75.0	82.0	96.2	111.0	142.5	164.3						
MIXED INCOME, NET	...	...	...	...	...	...						
Gross capital formation	...	...	...	...	...	...						

[a] Includes Mixed Income, Gross.
[b] Includes Mixed Income, Net.

Table 2.3 Output, gross value added, and fixed assets by industries at current prices (ISIC Rev. 3) Construction (F)

Series 100: 1993 SNA, kina, Western calendar year — **Data in millions**

	2001	2002	2003	2004	2005	2006	2007	2008	2009	2010	2011	2012
Series	**100**											
Output, at basic prices	...	...	...	...	...	...						
Less: Intermediate consumption, at purchaser's prices	...	...	...	...	...	...						
Equals: VALUE ADDED, GROSS, at basic prices	702.3	995.7	1128.9	1177.0	1245.8	1437.0						
Compensation of employees	162.2	234.3	281.2	293.3	283.0	315.9						
Taxes on production and imports, less Subsidies	...	...	...	...	...	...						
OPERATING SURPLUS, GROSS [a]	540.1	761.3	847.7	883.7	962.8	1121.2						
MIXED INCOME, GROSS	...	...	...	...	...	...						
Less: Consumption of fixed capital	51.2	80.6	96.8	100.9	106.8	119.9						
OPERATING SURPLUS, NET [b]	488.9	680.7	750.9	782.8	856.0	1001.3						
MIXED INCOME, NET	...	...	...	...	...	...						
Gross capital formation	...	...	...	...	...	...						

[a] Includes Mixed Income, Gross.
[b] Includes Mixed Income, Net.

Table 2.3 Output, gross value added, and fixed assets by industries at current prices (ISIC Rev. 3) Wholesale retail trade, repair of motor vehicles, motorcycles, etc.; hotels and restaurants (G+H)

Series 100: 1993 SNA, kina, Western calendar year — **Data in millions**

	2001	2002	2003	2004	2005	2006	2007	2008	2009	2010	2011	2012
Series	**100**											
Output, at basic prices	...	...	...	...	...	...						
Less: Intermediate consumption, at purchaser's prices	...	...	...	...	...	...						
Equals: VALUE ADDED, GROSS, at basic prices	558.0	745.5	849.9	890.5	942.6	1039.0						
Compensation of employees	212.3	283.6	354.8	371.8	381.6	402.2						
Taxes on production and imports, less Subsidies	6.1	8.2	10.3	10.8	131.1	165.0						

	2001	2002	2003	2004	2005	2006	2007	2008	2009	2010	2011	2012
Series	**100**											
Taxes on production and imports	6.1	8.2	10.3	10.8	131.1	165.0						
Taxes on products	...	...	...	...	...	...						
Other taxes on production	6.1	8.2	10.3	10.8	131.1	165.0						
Less: Subsidies	...	...	...	...	...	...						
OPERATING SURPLUS, GROSS [a]	339.6	453.8	484.8	508.0	430.0	471.8						
MIXED INCOME, GROSS	...	...	...	...	...	...						
Less: Consumption of fixed capital	94.9	138.2	172.9	181.1	192.0	215.2						
OPERATING SURPLUS, NET [b]	244.7	315.6	311.9	326.9	238.0	256.6						
MIXED INCOME, NET	...	...	...	...	...	...						
Gross capital formation	...	...	...	...	...	...						

[a] Includes Mixed Income, Gross.
[b] Includes Mixed Income, Net.

Table 2.3 Output, gross value added, and fixed assets by industries at current prices (ISIC Rev. 3) Transport, storage and communications (I)

Series 100: 1993 SNA, kina, Western calendar year — **Data in millions**

	2001	2002	2003	2004	2005	2006	2007	2008	2009	2010	2011	2012
Series	**100**											
Output, at basic prices	...	...	...	...	...	...						
Less: Intermediate consumption, at purchaser's prices	...	...	...	...	...	...						
Equals: VALUE ADDED, GROSS, at basic prices	258.4	268.0	293.9	304.7	317.0	326.2						
Compensation of employees	98.3	68.4	68.5	71.1	71.5	73.0						
Taxes on production and imports, less Subsidies	2.8	2.0	2.0	2.1	2.5	3.0						
Taxes on production and imports	2.8	2.0	2.0	2.1	2.5	3.0						
Taxes on products	...	...	...	...	...	...						
Other taxes on production	2.8	2.0	2.0	2.1	2.5	3.0						
Less: Subsidies	...	...	...	...	...	...						
OPERATING SURPLUS, GROSS [a]	157.2	197.6	223.4	231.6	243.0	250.1						
MIXED INCOME, GROSS	...	...	...	...	...	...						
Less: Consumption of fixed capital	43.9	33.3	33.4	34.6	36.6	41.1						
OPERATING SURPLUS, NET [b]	113.3	164.3	190.0	197.0	206.4	209.0						
MIXED INCOME, NET	...	...	...	...	...	...						
Gross capital formation	...	...	...	...	...	...						

[a] Includes Mixed Income, Gross.
[b] Includes Mixed Income, Net.

Table 2.3 Output, gross value added, and fixed assets by industries at current prices (ISIC Rev. 3) Financial intermediation; real estate, renting and business activities (J+K)

Series 100: 1993 SNA, kina, Western calendar year — **Data in millions**

	2001	2002	2003	2004	2005	2006	2007	2008	2009	2010	2011	2012
Series	**100**											
Output, at basic prices	...	...	...	...	...	...						
Less: Intermediate consumption, at purchaser's prices	...	...	...	...	...	...						
Equals: VALUE ADDED, GROSS, at basic prices	406.7	407.0	422.9	415.2	488.7	579.4						
Compensation of employees	203.5	197.6	200.6	192.3	195.0	203.5						
Taxes on production and imports, less Subsidies	41.3	40.1	40.8	39.1	37.9	42.0						
Taxes on production and imports	41.3	40.1	40.8	39.1	37.9	42.0						
Taxes on products	...	...	...	...	...	...						
Other taxes on production	41.3	40.1	40.8	39.1	37.9	42.0						
Less: Subsidies	...	...	...	...	...	...						
OPERATING SURPLUS, GROSS [a]	161.9	169.3	181.6	183.9	255.8	334.0						
MIXED INCOME, GROSS	...	...	...	...	...	...						
Less: Consumption of fixed capital	64.2	70.7	74.1	73.4	77.6	87.2						
OPERATING SURPLUS, NET [b]	97.7	98.6	107.5	110.5	178.2	246.8						
MIXED INCOME, NET	...	...	...	...	...	...						
Gross capital formation	...	...	...	...	...	...						

[a] Includes Mixed Income, Gross.
[b] Includes Mixed Income, Net.

Table 2.3 Output, gross value added, and fixed assets by industries at current prices (ISIC Rev. 3) Public administration and defense; compulsory social security (L)

Series 100: 1993 SNA, kina, Western calendar year — **Data in millions**

	2001	2002	2003	2004	2005	2006	2007	2008	2009	2010	2011	2012
Series	**100**											
Output, at basic prices	...	...	...	...	...	...						
Less: Intermediate consumption, at purchaser's prices	...	...	...	...	...	...						
Equals: VALUE ADDED, GROSS, at basic prices [a]	1241.0	1352.0	1403.0	1395.0	1448.0	1527.0						
Compensation of employees	810.0	883.0	916.0	911.0	931.0	895.0						
Taxes on production and imports, less Subsidies	...	...	...	...	...	...						
OPERATING SURPLUS, GROSS	430.0	469.0	487.0	484.0	517.0	632.0						
MIXED INCOME, GROSS	...	...	...	...	...	...						
Less: Consumption of fixed capital	80.0	95.0	99.0	98.0	104.0	117.0						
OPERATING SURPLUS, NET	350.0	374.0	388.0	386.0	413.0	515.0						
MIXED INCOME, NET	...	...	...	...	...	...						
Gross capital formation	...	...	...	...	...	...						

[a] Includes Education; health and social work; other community, social and personal services.

Table 3.1 Government final consumption expenditure by function at current prices

Series 100: 1993 SNA, kina, Western calendar year — **Data in millions**

		2001	2002	2003	2004	2005	2006	2007	2008	2009	2010	2011	2012
Series		**100**											
General public services		994.3	961.5	1294.2	1167.8	1178.9	1402.9	1788.2					
Defence		85.5	76.6	77.3	88.3	94.5	95.7	114.9					
Public order and safety		313.8	225.4	260.2	301.2	306.3	341.8	436.3					
Economic affairs		488.6	436.4	405.3	589.2	590.3	829.8	595.2					
Environment protection		...	...	...	...	...	...	...					
Housing and community amenities		246.0	116.0	116.9	226.1	153.1	213.0	247.7					
Health		364.9	195.1	332.1	390.4	358.2	489.3	505.9					
Recreation, culture and religion		26.3	17.4	21.6	69.9	54.5	38.6	42.2					
Education		645.9	619.9	605.6	767.9	704.4	846.1	494.0					
Social protection		42.3	43.4	65.6	106.8	97.1	74.7	390.5					
Plus: (Other functions)	a	385.8	300.9	256.3	687.8	1001.6	1285.5	1917.8					
Equals: General government final consumption expenditure	b	3593.6	2992.6	3434.9	4394.9	4539.0	5617.3	6533.4					

[a] Refers to the sum of Other Economic Affairs, Unallocable & other purposes
[b] Discrepancy with equivalent item in Table 1.1 (Gross domestic product by expenditures at current prices).

Table 3.2 Individual consumption expenditure of households, NPISHs, and general government at current prices

Series 100: 1993 SNA, kina, Western calendar year — **Data in millions**

		2001	2002	2003	2004	2005	2006	2007	2008	2009	2010	2011	2012
Series		**100**											
		Individual consumption expenditure of households											
Food and non-alcoholic beverages		562.0	665.0	753.0									
Alcoholic beverages, tobacco and narcotics		737.0	806.0	921.0									
Clothing and footwear		420.0	457.0	478.0									
Housing, water, electricity, gas and other fuels		257.0	265.0	281.0									
Furnishings, household equipment and routine maintenance of the house		498.0	531.0	607.0									
Health		...	...	...									
Transport	a	899.0	996.0	1216.0									
Communication		...	...	...									
Recreation and culture		...	...	...									
Education		...	...	...									
Restaurants and hotels		...	...	...									
Miscellaneous goods and services		...	...	...									

[a] Includes Communication.

Table 4.1 Total Economy (S.1)

Series 100: 1993 SNA, kina, Western calendar year — **Data in millions**

	2001	2002	2003	2004	2005	2006	2007	2008	2009	2010	2011	2012
Series	**100**											
I. Production account - Resources												
Output, at basic prices (otherwise, please specify)	...	...	...	...	...	...						
Less: Financial intermediation services indirectly measured (only to be deducted if FISIM is not distributed to uses)	...	...	...	...	...	...						
Plus: Taxes less Subsidies on products	...	...	...	...	...	...						
Plus: Taxes on products	...	...	...	...	...	...						
Less: Subsidies on products	...	...	...	...	...	...						
I. Production account - Uses												
Intermediate consumption, at purchaser's prices	...	...	...	...	...	...						
GROSS DOMESTIC PRODUCT	10396.3	11872.0	13241.5	13459.4	15094.7	16896.6						
Less: Consumption of fixed capital	638.0	747.2	820.8	828.9	876.7	985.0						
NET DOMESTIC PRODUCT	9758.3	11124.8	12420.7	12630.5	14218.0	15911.6						
II.1.1 Generation of income account - Resources												
GROSS DOMESTIC PRODUCT	10396.3	11872.0	13241.5	13459.4	15094.7	16896.6						
II.1.1 Generation of income account - Uses												
Compensation of employees	2050.3	2245.4	2436.2	2450.5	2491.1	2550.9						
Taxes on production and imports, less Subsidies	923.0	872.0	921.0	1016.0	1222.0	1366.0						
Taxes on production and imports	926.0	875.0	924.0	1019.0	1225.0	1370.0						
Taxes on products	...	...	...	...	...	...						
Other taxes on production	...	...	...	...	...	...						
Less: Subsidies	2.6	2.8	2.9	3.0	4.0	4.0						
Subsidies on products	...	...	...	...	...	...						
Other subsidies on production	...	...	...	...	...	...						
OPERATING SURPLUS, GROSS	7423.1	8754.7	9884.5	9992.7	11381.8	12979.5						
MIXED INCOME, GROSS	...	...	...	...	...	...						
II.1.2 Allocation of primary income account - Resources												
OPERATING SURPLUS, GROSS	7423.1	8754.7	9884.5	9992.7	11381.8	12979.5						
MIXED INCOME, GROSS	...	...	...	...	...	...						
Compensation of employees	2050.3	2245.4	2436.2	2450.5	2491.1	2550.9						
Taxes on production and imports, less Subsidies	922.8	871.9	920.8	1016.4	1221.9	1366.2						
Taxes on production and imports	...	...	...	...	...	...						
Taxes on products	...	...	...	...	...	...						
Other taxes on production	...	...	...	...	...	...						
Less: Subsidies	...	...	...	...	...	...						
Subsidies on products	...	...	...	...	...	...						
Other subsidies on production	...	...	...	...	...	...						
Property income [a]	-408.1	-414.9	-424.4	-1409.0	-1670.0	-2467.0						

	2001	2002	2003	2004	2005	2006	2007	2008	2009	2010	2011	2012
Series	**100**											
II.1.2 Allocation of primary income account - Uses												
Property income	...	...	...	...	...	...						
GROSS NATIONAL INCOME	9988.0	11457.2	12816.8	12050.9	13424.7	14435.0						
II.2 Secondary distribution of income account - Resources												
GROSS NATIONAL INCOME	9988.0	11457.2	12816.8	12050.9	13424.7	14435.0						
Current taxes on income, wealth, etc.	...	...	...	...	...	...						
Social contributions	...	...	...	...	...	...						
Social benefits other than social transfers in kind	...	...	...	...	...	...						
Other current transfers [b]	44.5	87.8	116.1	799.0	808.0	726.0						
II.2 Secondary distribution of income account - Uses												
Current taxes on income, wealth, etc.	...	...	...	...	...	...						
Social contributions	...	...	...	...	...	...						
Social benefits other than social transfers in kind	...	...	...	...	...	...						
Other current transfers	...	...	...	...	...	...						
GROSS DISPOSABLE INCOME	10033.0	11545.2	12932.8	12849.9	14232.7	15161.0						
II.4.1 Use of disposable income account - Resources												
GROSS DISPOSABLE INCOME	10033.0	11545.2	12932.8	12849.9	14232.7	15161.0						
Adjustment for the change in net equity of households on pension funds	...	...	...	...	...	...						
II.4.1 Use of disposable income account - Uses												
Final consumption expenditure	6650.3	8562.0	8514.0	9285.0	9677.0	10797.0						
Individual consumption expenditure	...	...	...	...	...	...						
Collective consumption expenditure	...	...	...	...	...	...						
Adjustment for the change in net equity of households on pension funds	...	...	...	...	...	...						
SAVING, GROSS	3382.0	2982.2	4418.8	3564.9	4555.7	4364.0						
III.1 Capital account - Changes in liabilities and net worth												
SAVING, GROSS	3382.0	2982.2	4418.8	3564.9	4555.7	4364.0						
Capital transfers, receivable less payable	241.2	183.2	212.2	254.0	261.0	243.0						
Capital transfers, receivable	...	...	...	...	...	...						
Less: Capital transfers, payable	...	...	...	...	...	...						
Equals: CHANGES IN NET WORTH DUE TO SAVING AND CAPITAL TRANSFERS	...	...	...	...	...	...						
III.1 Capital account - Changes in assets												
Gross capital formation	2386.1	2970.0	2827.0	2874.0	2639.0	2653.0						
Gross fixed capital formation	2199.8	2464.0	2281.0	2294.0	2489.0	2303.0						
Changes in inventories	186.3	506.0	546.0	580.0	150.0	350.0						
Acquisitions less disposals of valuables	...	...	...	...	...	...						

	2001	2002	2003	2004	2005	2006	2007	2008	2009	2010	2011	2012
Series	**100**											
Acquisitions less disposals of non-produced non-financial assets	...	...	...	...	...	...						
NET LENDING (+) / NET BORROWING (-)	1238.0	196.0	1804.0	944.0	2177.0	1954.0						

[a] Refers to net property income from the Rest of the world
[b] Refers to net current transfers from the Rest of the World.

Table 4.2 Rest of the world (S.2)

Series 100: 1993 SNA, kina, Western calendar year

Data in millions

	2001	2002	2003	2004	2005	2006	2007	2008	2009	2010	2011	2012
Series	**100**											
V.I External account of goods and services - Resources												
Imports of goods and services	5432.1	6760.6	6824.3	7844.0	8467.0	10539.0						
Imports of goods	...	...	...	...	...	...						
Imports of services	...	...	...	...	...	...						
V.I External account of goods and services - Uses												
Exports of goods and services	6791.9	7100.0	8724.0	9143.0	11246.0	13986.0						
Exports of goods	...	...	...	...	...	...						
Exports of services	...	...	...	...	...	...						
EXTERNAL BALANCE OF GOODS AND SERVICES	-1359.8	-339.5	-1899.7	-1300.0	-2779.0	-3447.0						
V.II External account of primary income and current transfers - Resources												
EXTERNAL BALANCE OF GOODS AND SERVICES	-1360.0	-339.0	-1900.0	-1300.0	-2779.0	-3447.0						
Compensation of employees	2.5	2.5	2.6	3.0	3.0	3.0						
Taxes on production and imports, less Subsidies	...	...	...	...	...	...						
Taxes on production and imports	...	...	...	...	...	...						
Taxes on products	...	...	...	...	...	...						
Other taxes on production	...	...	...	...	...	...						
Less: Subsidies	...	...	...	...	...	...						
Subsidies on products	...	...	...	...	...	...						
Other subsidies on production	...	...	...	...	...	...						
Property income	463.2	469.5	480.4	1470.0	1751.0	2677.0						
Current taxes on income, wealth, etc.	...	...	...	...	...	...						
Social contributions	...	...	...	...	...	...						
Social benefits other than social transfers in kind	...	...	...	...	...	...						
Other current transfers	66.7	60.8	66.8	73.0	75.0	78.0						
Adjustment for the change in net equity of households on pension funds	...	...	...	...	...	...						
V.II External account of primary income and current transfers - Uses												
Compensation of employees	3.0	3.0	3.0	3.0	3.0	3.0						
Taxes on production and imports, less Subsidies	...	...	...	...	...	...						
Taxes on production and imports	...	...	...	...	...	...						

	2001	2002	2003	2004	2005	2006	2007	2008	2009	2010	2011	2012
Series	**100**											
Taxes on products	...	...	...	...	...	...						
Other taxes on production	...	...	...	...	...	...						
Less: Subsidies	...	...	...	...	...	...						
Subsidies on products	...	...	...	...	...	...						
Other subsidies on production	...	...	...	...	...	...						
Property income	55.2	54.6	56.0	61.0	81.0	215.0						
Current taxes on income and wealth, etc.	...	...	...	...	...	...						
Social contributions	...	...	...	...	...	...						
Social benefits other than social transfers in kind	...	...	...	...	...	...						
Other current transfers	111.3	148.6	183.0	872.0	883.0	804.0						
Adjustment for the change in net equity of households on pension funds	...	...	...	...	...	...						
CURRENT EXTERNAL BALANCE	-996.2	-12.3	-1591.4	-690.0	-1917.0	-1712.0						
	V.III.1 Capital account - Changes in liabilities and net worth											
CURRENT EXTERNAL BALANCE	-996.2	-12.3	-1591.4	-690.0	-1917.0	-1712.0						
Capital transfers, receivable less payable	-241.2	-183.2	-212.2	-254.0	-261.0	-243.0						
Capital transfers, receivable	...	...	...	...	...	...						
Less: Capital transfers, payable	...	...	...	...	...	...						
Equals: CHANGES IN NET WORTH DUE TO SAVING AND CAPITAL TRANSFERS	...	...	...	...	...	...						
	V.III.1 Capital account - Changes in assets											
Acquisitions less disposals of non-produced non-financial assets	...	...	...	...	...	...						
NET LENDING (+) / NET BORROWING (-)	-1238.0	-196.0	-1804.0	-944.0	-2177.0	-1954.0						

Paraguay

Source
The preparation of national accounts statistics in Paraguay is undertaken by the Departamento de Estudios Economicos of the Banco Central del Paraguay, Asuncion. The official estimates are published by the Department in "Cuentas Nacionales".

General
The estimates are generally in accordance with the classifications and definitions recommended in the United Nations System of National Accounts 1993 (1993 SNA). When the scope and coverage of the estimates differ for conceptual or statistical reasons from the definitions and classifications recommended in the SNA, a footnote provides explanation.

Methodology:

Overview of GDP Compilation
Gross domestic product is estimated mainly through the production approach.

Expenditure Approach
The expenditure approach is used to estimate government final consumption expenditure and exports and imports of goods and services. The commodity-flow approach is used for the estimation of gross fixed capital formation. Private final consumption expenditure is arrived at as a residual. The information needed to estimate government consumption expenditure is obtained from the Ministerio de Hacienda, which controls the budget of the public sector institutions. Increase in stock is estimated for livestock only. It is assumed to be the annual increase of the cattle production minus the number of cattle slaughtered. Gross fixed capital formation is estimated on the basis of import statistics for machinery, equipment, transport and communication. Estimates of the domestic production of these items as well as the gross value of production in the construction sector are also included. Exports and imports of goods and services are estimated on the basis of information furnished by the Division de Balanza de Pagos of the Banco Central. For the constant price estimates, the only information available is that the wholesale price index is used as a deflator.

Income Approach
Compensation of employees is estimated by combining the information on the number of persons employed, by economic sectors and the average wages paid in each productive sector. Depreciation is estimated on the basis of the average lifetime of each type of capital good established in the respective depreciation tables. Information on indirect taxes and subsidies are supplied by the Ministerio de Hacienda. Operating surplus is obtained as a residual.

Production Approach
The table of gross domestic product by kind of economic activity is prepared at market prices, i.e., producers' values. The production approach is used to estimate the value added of most industries. The income approach is used to estimate the value added of public administration and defence, part of transport and communication, and part of other private services. The gross output of the trade sector is based on the commodity-flow approach, applying a fixed percentage for value added. The value of agricultural production is obtained by multiplying quantities by prices. Information on prices and on most quantities are obtained from Ministerio de Agricultura y Ganaderia. Remaining quantities are estimated through the use of indirect indicators such as the rate of population growth. The value of livestock production is estimated by type of livestock. Slaughtering is estimated on the basis of information provided by the Direccion de Impuestos and the meat-processing industries while stocks of cattle are based on the 1956 agricultural census. Inputs for the agricultural section are assumed to be a certain

percentage of the gross value of production.

The production of mining and quarrying is estimated on the basis of the industrial production coefficients of lime and cement. Information on the manufacturing sector is obtained from the surveys of the Banco Central, and the 1955 and 1963 industrial censuses. The value added of each industrial group is determined on the basis of coefficients from the 1963 industrial census applied to the gross production values. The value added of electricity and water is mainly based on information from the concerned enterprises. For construction, the source used is the production index for construction materials. This index is compared with permits granted by the municipalities expressed in quantitative measures, multiplied by the base year value and inflated by the implicit price index of construction materials.

Value added of the trade sector is assumed to be 30 per cent of the values of locally manufactured goods, imported goods and agricultural products net of farm consumption. For motor transport, the number of vehicles by category is multiplied by the number of days worked and the gross income earned in the base year. The resulting amounts are then multiplied by value added coefficients for each category of vehicle. Non-mechanical transport is calculated on the basis of the index of agricultural production transported in rural areas by carts. For ownership of dwellings, the estimates are prepared on the basis of the number of dwellings by type of construction materials used. Value added is estimated by multiplying the paid and imputed rents by the number of dwellings. The value added of public administration and defence is estimated as the total compensation paid to government employees based on information furnished by the Presupuesto General de la Nacion. The value of public education is determined directly from the Presupuesto General de Gastos de la Nacion while that of private education is estimated at constant prices by multiplying the number of students enrolled by the annual education costs plus registration fees minus 20 per cent for intermediate consumption.

For health, information is obtained directly from the public health services and social security services and from the Ministerio de Salud Publica y Bienestar Social for the private sector. Estimates for domestic services are obtained by multiplying actual annual wages by employment figures which are assumed to increase at a rate of 3.3 per cent in the urban area and 2.6 per cent in the rural area. For other services, benchmark estimates, based on the 1963 economic census, are projected by a specially constructed growth rate. For the constant price estimates, double deflation is used for the agricultural sector. The current quantities of mining and manufacturing are revalued at base year prices. Value added of construction, transport and financial sectors is extrapolated by using quantity indicators. For electricity, gas and water, trade and services sectors, value added is deflated by using appropriate price indexes.

Table 1.1 Gross domestic product by expenditures at current prices

Series 100: 1993 SNA, guarani, Western calendar year **Data in billions**

	2001	2002	2003	2004	2005	2006	2007	2008	2009	2010	2011	2012
Series	**100**											
	Expenditures of the gross domestic product											
Final consumption expenditure	24070.0	24724.0	29097.4	33967.5	38710.2	44284.0	51981.3	64042.5	63234.6	76578.5	90870.5	
Household final consumption expenditure	20865.9	21425.0	25368.5	29877.1	33700.2	38422.9	45582.2	56864.1	54592.8	66661.8	79714.3	
NPISHs final consumption expenditure	...	...	...	...	...	...	...	...	...	...	...	
General government final consumption expenditure	3204.1	3299.0	3728.9	4090.3	5010.0	5861.1	6399.2	7178.3	8641.8	9916.6	11156.2	
Gross capital formation	4954.2	5443.6	7185.9	7983.9	9182.7	10283.2	10951.4	13243.9	10911.5	15404.4	17632.7	
Gross fixed capital formation	4597.5	5023.8	6778.2	7749.3	8963.9	9971.1	10562.8	12936.1	10684.8	15049.5	17231.6	
Changes in inventories	356.8	419.8	407.8	234.6	218.9	312.1	388.6	307.8	226.7	355.0	401.1	
Acquisitions less disposals of valuables	...	...	...	...	...	...	...	...	...	...	...	
Exports of goods and services	9202.6[a]	19134.1[b]	22998.4[b]	25802.9[b]	30931.1[b]	34976.3[b]	39087.0[b]	43802.2[b]	40479.9[b]	51863.0[b]	53148.4[b]	

	2001	2002	2003	2004	2005	2006	2007	2008	2009	2010	2011	2012
Series	**100**											
Exports of goods	7757.0	10620.2	13964.9	17097.6	20706.9	24801.0	28445.4	34026.2	29137.2	39544.6	...	
Exports of services	1445.7	2019.3	2335.3	2373.1	2487.1	2755.3	3096.6	3491.3	5190.5	5247.6	...	
Less: Imports of goods and services	11761.2	13145.5[b]	16957.5[b]	19755.2[b]	24861.7[b]	29547.0[b]	32593.5[b]	40353.9[b]	35508.9[b]	48911.6[b]	52857.0[b]	
Imports of goods	10277.0	12220.1	15741.6	18556.1	23564.2	28300.3	31127.6	38668.2	34317.8	47047.5	...	
Imports of services	1484.3	1854.8	2032.0	1723.2	2042.0	2064.4	2246.5	2475.0	2568.4	3399.4	...	
Equals: GROSS DOMESTIC PRODUCT	26465.7[a]	36156.2	42324.2	47999.0	53962.3	59996.5	69426.3	80734.8	79117.2	94934.3	108794.6	

[a] Does not incorporate export of binacional hydroelectric power at market prices.
[b] Discrepancy between components and total as one or more components have not been revised.

Table 1.2 Gross domestic product by expenditures at constant prices

Series 100: 1993 SNA, guarani, Western calendar year

Data in billions

	2001	2002	2003	2004	2005	2006	2007	2008	2009	2010	2011	2012
Series	**100**											
Base year	**1994**											
	Expenditures of the gross domestic product											
Final consumption expenditure	11825.0	11335.4	12202.3	12841.7	13240.3	13622.7	14339.0	15358.8	15285.6	17352.0	18774.2	
Household final consumption expenditure	10620.6	10169.1	11059.3	11629.9	11889.7	12218.1	12892.4	13861.5	13583.6	15445.7	16766.9	
NPISHs final consumption expenditure	...	...	...	...	...	...	...	...	...	...	...	
General government final consumption expenditure	1204.4	1166.3	1143.0	1211.9	1350.7	1404.5	1446.7	1497.3	1702.0	1906.3	2007.3	
Gross capital formation	2945.1	3118.4	3439.6	3504.9	3078.9	3332.1	3492.2	4210.4	3682.1	4518.9	5006.8	
Gross fixed capital formation	2294.6	2256.0	2537.2	2652.2	2724.6	2835.3	3187.9	3755.8	3496.2	4255.0	4723.1	
Changes in inventories	650.5	862.3	902.5	852.7	354.3	496.8	304.2	454.7	185.9	263.9	283.7	
Acquisitions less disposals of valuables	...	...	...	...	...	...	...	...	...	...	...	
Exports of goods and services	4863.5[a]	8018.5[b]	8969.3[b]	9709.8[b]	10795.8[b]	11202.7[b]	12249.9[b]	12495.0[c]	11333.2[c]	13570.3[c]	13953.4[c]	
Exports of goods	4099.5	4466.5	5228.5	5991.8	6756.8	7398.5	8367.1	8549.1	7107.6	9450.4	...	
Exports of services	764.0	849.2	874.3	831.6	1194.1	821.9	910.9	877.2	1266.1	1254.1	...	
Less: Imports of goods and services	5541.5	6262.3[b]	7700.8[b]	8459.9[b]	9143.1[b]	9321.5[b]	10224.1[b]	10944.4[b]	10018.6[b]	12503.4[b]	13800.9[b]	
Imports of goods	4842.2	4935.1	6304.8	7264.5	7917.6	8228.6	9007.5	9893.8	8916.2	11327.1	...	
Imports of services	699.3	749.1	813.9	674.6	686.1	600.2	650.1	633.3	667.3	818.4	...	
Equals: GROSS DOMESTIC PRODUCT	14092.1[a]	16210.0	16910.4	17596.5	17971.9	18835.9	19857.1	21119.8	20282.3	22937.8	23933.5	

[a] Does not incorporate export of binacional hydroelectric power at market prices.
[b] Discrepancy between components and total as one or more components have not been revised.
[c] Discrepancy between components and total as one or more components have not been revised. Does not incorporate export of binacional hydroelectric power at market prices.

Table 2.1 Value added by industries at current prices (ISIC Rev. 3)

Series 100: 1993 SNA, guarani, Western calendar year — **Data in billions**

	2001	2002	2003	2004	2005	2006	2007	2008	2009	2010	2011	2012
Series	**100**											
Industries												
Agriculture, hunting, forestry; fishing	4308.1	5056.5	7199.8	9010.1	9756.2	10560.0	13533.4	17379.3	13657.7	19339.4	21143.9	
Agriculture, hunting, forestry	4285.2	5032.3	7174.0	8982.5	9721.3	10519.9	13492.9	17335.2	13615.4	19296.6	21095.0	
Agriculture, hunting and related service activities	3913.0	4639.6	6661.7	8361.5	8919.7	9599.3	12466.6	16188.7	12447.4	18110.8	19682.1	
Forestry, logging and related service activities	372.2	392.7	512.4	621.0	801.6	920.5	1026.3	1146.4	1168.0	1185.7	1412.9	
Fishing	22.8	24.2	25.7	27.6	35.0	40.2	40.6	44.2	42.2	42.8	48.9	
Mining and quarrying	29.2	30.5	36.5	45.9	55.5	65.7	68.9	88.7	105.7	114.7	136.0	
Manufacturing	4201.1	4580.3	5349.6	5898.7	6414.8	7141.2	7901.7	9241.4	9186.7	10614.5	11535.7	
Electricity, gas and water supply	654.9[a]	7786.3	7532.9	7392.3	8733.9	8751.1	8962.6	8113.2	9221.3	9272.3	8430.6	
Construction	1214.5	1327.2	1779.1	1941.5	2132.6	2457.5	3269.5	4498.0	4625.1	5844.9	7096.0	
Wholesale, retail trade, repair of motor vehicles, motorcycles and personal and households goods; hotels and restaurants	4857.3	5449.5	6956.1	8699.9	9586.0	11423.3	12641.5	14597.7	13524.1	15887.7	22114.9	
Wholesale, retail trade, repair of motor vehicles, motorcycles and personal and household goods	4515.4	5058.7	6509.8	8230.6	9093.4	10859.9	11982.5	13820.5	12734.6	14963.2	21064.4	
Hotels and restaurants	341.8	390.8	446.3	469.3	492.7	563.5	659.0	777.2	789.4	924.5	1050.5	
Transport, storage and communications	1970.3	2265.2	2536.0	2829.1	3547.6	3959.2	4863.5	5167.6	5164.4	5470.4	5737.0	
Land transport; transport via pipelines, water transport; air transport; Supporting and auxiliary transport activities; activities of travel agencies	1012.8	1132.9	1454.6	1664.5	2076.5	2355.5	2687.4	3014.1	2925.4	2994.0	3075.2	
Post and telecommunications	957.5	1132.3	1081.4	1164.7	1471.1	1603.7	2176.0	2153.5	2239.0	2476.3	2661.7	
Financial intermediation; real estate, renting and business activities	2175.9	2284.4	2309.4	2406.9	2742.6	3221.2	3613.3	4709.5	5113.3	6283.6	7602.9	
Financial intermediation	856.8	890.5	880.9	895.5	1095.5	1352.7	1540.0	2365.2	2505.7	3393.4	4345.9	
Real estate, renting and business activities	1319.1	1393.9	1428.6	1511.4	1647.1	1868.6	2073.3	2344.3	2607.6	2890.2	3257.0	
Public administration and defence; compulsory social security	2734.5	2808.9	3210.0	3446.0	4186.8	4827.2	5640.0	6297.2	7480.8	8523.9	9703.1	
Education; health and social work; other community, social and personal services	...	...	...	...	...	...	...	...	...	...	...	
Private households with employed persons [b]	2064.3	2296.6	2475.7	2534.7	2721.5	2903.9	3263.4	3719.2	4118.9	4497.6	5230.7	
Equals: VALUE ADDED, GROSS, in basic prices	24210.0[a]	33885.4	39385.0	44205.2	49877.5	55310.5	63757.9	73811.8	72197.9	85848.8	98730.7	
Less: Financial intermediation services indirectly measured (FISIM)	...	...	...	...	...	...	...	...	...	...	...	
Plus: Taxes less Subsidies on products	2255.7	2270.9	2939.2	3793.8	4084.9	4686.1	5668.4	6923.0	6919.2	9085.4	10063.9	
Equals: GROSS DOMESTIC PRODUCT	26465.7[a]	36156.2	42324.2	47999.0	53962.3	59996.5	69426.3	80734.8	79117.2	94934.3	108794.6	

[a] Does not incorporate value added generated by binacional hydroelectric plants.
[b] Includes Education; health and social work; other community, social and personal services as well as Private households with employed persons.

Table 2.2 Value added by industries at constant prices (ISIC Rev. 3)

Series 100: 1993 SNA, guarani, Western calendar year

Data in billions

	2001	2002	2003	2004	2005	2006	2007	2008	2009	2010	2011	2012
Series	**100**											
Base year	**1994**											
	Industries											
Agriculture, hunting, forestry; fishing	3417.5	3559.6	3845.3	3995.3	3990.5	4134.6	4727.5	5161.4	4268.0	5729.2	5943.4	
Agriculture, hunting, forestry	3403.6	3546.2	3832.0	3981.9	3976.8	4120.8	4713.5	5147.3	4253.6	5715.5	5929.4	
Agriculture, hunting and related service activities	3130.9	3274.9	3555.3	3696.6	3672.2	3810.0	4395.0	4815.8	3936.4	5426.8	5632.0	
Forestry, logging and related service activities	272.7	271.3	276.7	285.3	304.7	310.8	318.5	331.5	317.2	288.7	297.4	
Fishing	13.9	13.4	13.3	13.4	13.6	13.8	14.0	14.1	14.3	13.8	14.0	
Mining and quarrying	15.2	13.8	16.0	16.4	17.7	17.3	17.9	18.8	19.4	20.0	21.1	
Manufacturing	2142.6	2112.5	2128.1	2198.2	2256.9	2314.0	2285.4	2330.0	2311.7	2456.9	2418.7	
Electricity, gas and water supply	241.5[a]	2368.8	2539.5	2630.1	2577.5	2784.6	2718.0	2974.8	2863.2	2864.2	3072.6	
Construction	554.0	504.7	577.1	589.5	616.0	594.5	637.3	707.4	721.5	815.3	827.5	
Wholesale, retail trade, repair of motor vehicles, motorcycles and personal and household goods; hotels and restaurants	2755.8	2711.1	2860.7	3005.6	3076.4	3247.0	3412.7	3554.5	3441.6	3810.9	3931.8	
Wholesale, retail trade, repair of motor vehicles, motorcycles and personal and household goods	2581.5	2536.0	2683.1	2826.1	2893.3	3061.1	3220.3	3352.3	3238.3	3590.4	3698.1	
Hotels and restaurants	174.2	175.1	177.6	179.5	183.2	185.9	192.4	202.3	203.3	220.5	233.8	
Transport, storage and communications	982.0	1001.5	1008.7	1105.9	1185.8	1312.3	1452.9	1527.8	1478.8	1576.1	1719.1	
Land transport; transport via piplines, water transport; air transport; Supporting and auxiliary transport activities; activities of travel agencies	509.0	519.4	554.2	613.2	626.8	675.0	739.2	779.8	697.9	746.8	765.5	
Post and telecommunications	473.0	482.2	454.5	492.6	559.0	637.2	713.7	748.0	780.9	829.3	953.7	
Financial intermediation, real estate, renting and business activities	1003.9	1012.4	962.5	983.1	1022.5	1063.3	1104.1	1191.3	1280.6	1372.3	1490.1	
Financial intermediation	335.5	334.9	312.5	314.7	327.7	344.6	362.8	431.4	459.9	515.1	604.2	
Real estate, renting and business activities	668.4	677.5	650.0	668.3	694.8	718.7	741.3	759.9	820.8	857.3	885.9	
Public administration and defence; compulsory social security	1015.5	997.7	991.3	1025.5	1105.1	1154.5	1189.1	1230.7	1417.8	1602.1	1698.2	
Education; health and social work; other community, social and personal services	...	...	...	...	...	...	...	...	...	...	...	
Private households with employed persons [b]	840.0	837.0	852.9	868.3	901.2	939.0	967.4	1010.9	1081.7	1124.9	1198.1	
Equals: VALUE ADDED, GROSS, in basic prices	12968.1[a]	15119.2	15782.1	16417.8	16749.6	17561.0	18512.1	19707.6	18884.2	21372.0	22320.6	
Less: Financial intermediation services indirectly measured (FISIM)	...	...	...	...	...	...	...	...	...	...	...	
Plus: Taxes less Subsidies on products	1124.1	1090.8	1128.3	1178.7	1222.3	1274.8	1345.0	1412.2	1398.1	1565.8	1612.8	
Equals: GROSS DOMESTIC PRODUCT	14092.1[a]	16210.0	16910.4	17596.5	17971.9	18835.9	19857.1	21119.8	20282.3	22937.8	23933.5	

[a] Does not incorporate value added generated by binacional hydroelectric plants.
[b] Includes Education; health and social work; other community, social and personal services as well as Private households with employed persons.

Table 2.3 Output, gross value added, and fixed assets by industries at current prices (ISIC Rev. 3) Total Economy

Series 100: 1993 SNA, guarani, Western calendar year — **Data in billions**

	2001	2002	2003	2004	2005	2006	2007	2008	2009	2010	2011	2012
Series	**100**											
Output, at basic prices	53196.0[a]	65402.4	77082.0	85707.2	96800.4	108454.1	124051.8	146435.9	143534.6	168425.0	188986.6	
Less: Intermediate consumption, at purchaser's prices	26730.3	31517.0	37697.0	41502.0	46922.9	53143.6	60293.9	72624.2	71336.7	82576.2	90256.0	
Equals: VALUE ADDED, GROSS, at basic prices	26465.7[b]	33885.4	39385.0	44205.2	49877.5	55310.5	63757.9	73811.8	72197.9	85848.8	98730.7	
Compensation of employees	10198.2	11621.6	12882.8	14262.4	16115.5	18764.7	21359.2	23525.7	25105.4	27777.1	31341.7	
Taxes on production and imports, less Subsidies	185.3	207.4	256.5	314.3	821.9	788.6	488.7	689.5	654.6	956.3	870.5	
OPERATING SURPLUS, GROSS [c]	13826.5	22056.3	26245.7	29628.6	32940.0	35757.1	41910.0	49596.6	46437.9	57115.4	66518.5	
MIXED INCOME, GROSS	...	...	...	...	...	...	...	...	...	...	...	
Less: Consumption of fixed capital	1150.1	1650.0	1882.1	2051.8	2341.0	2576.8	2947.0	3333.8	3324.1	3840.1	4271.6	
OPERATING SURPLUS, NET	6084.8	13394.3	16762.6	19178.8	21317.0	22789.9	26800.8	33195.3	29900.6	39438.9	45647.3	
MIXED INCOME, NET	6591.6	7012.0	7601.1	8398.0	9282.0	10390.5	12162.3	13067.5	13213.2	13836.4	16599.7	
Gross capital formation	4954.2	5443.6	7185.9	7983.9	9182.7	10283.2	10951.4	13243.9	10911.5	15404.4	17632.7	
Gross fixed capital formation	4597.5	5023.8	6778.2	7749.3	8963.9	9971.1	10562.8	12936.1	10684.8	15049.5	17231.6	
Changes in inventories	356.8	419.8	407.8	234.6	218.9	312.1	388.6	307.8	226.7	355.0	401.1	
Acquisitions less disposals of valuables	...	...	...	...	...	...	...	...	...	...	...	

[a] At producers' prices.
[b] Refers to Gross Domestic Product. Does not incorporate value added generated by binacional hydroelectric plants.
[c] Includes Mixed Income, Gross.

Table 2.3 Output, gross value added, and fixed assets by industries at current prices (ISIC Rev. 3) Agriculture, hunting, forestry; fishing (A+B)

Series 100: 1993 SNA, guarani, Western calendar year — **Data in billions**

	2001	2002	2003	2004	2005	2006	2007	2008	2009	2010	2011	2012
Series	**100**											
Output, at basic prices	6641.2	7882.5	10701.5	12932.4	14198.1	15585.5	19300.6	24673.8	20037.3	28056.9	30654.5	
Less: Intermediate consumption, at purchaser's prices	2334.1	2826.0	3501.7	3922.2	4441.8	5025.4	5767.2	7294.5	6379.7	8717.5	9510.7	
Equals: VALUE ADDED, GROSS, at basic prices	4307.1	5056.5	7199.8	9010.1	9756.2	10560.0	13533.4	17379.3	13657.7	19339.4	21143.9	
Compensation of employees	1047.7	1188.8	1360.2	1537.0	1745.2	2035.9	2356.6	2670.2	2699.5	3170.6	4027.8	
Taxes on production and imports, less Subsidies	20.2	24.5	30.3	37.1	97.0	93.1	57.7	81.4	77.3	112.9	102.7	
OPERATING SURPLUS, GROSS [a]	3240.1	3843.3	5809.3	7436.0	7914.0	8431.0	11119.2	14627.8	10880.9	16055.9	17013.3	
MIXED INCOME, GROSS	...	...	...	...	...	...	...	...	...	...	...	
Less: Consumption of fixed capital	139.2	157.6	221.0	275.6	302.8	332.2	419.3	538.8	432.9	607.1	662.9	
OPERATING SURPLUS, NET	971.6	1438.6	3079.7	4311.3	4408.7	4703.7	6471.0	9297.5	5601.8	10234.5	10303.0	
MIXED INCOME, NET	2129.3	2247.0	2508.6	2849.1	3202.6	3395.1	4228.9	4791.5	4846.2	5214.4	6047.4	
Gross capital formation	...	...	...	...	...	...	...	...	...	...	...	

[a] Includes Mixed Income, Gross.

Table 2.3 Output, gross value added, and fixed assets by industries at current prices (ISIC Rev. 3) Fishing (B)

Series 100: 1993 SNA, guarani, Western calendar year

Data in billions

	2001	2002	2003	2004	2005	2006	2007	2008	2009	2010	2011	2012
Series	**100**											
Output, at basic prices	37.0	39.3	47.0	50.6	60.7	68.2	68.9	76.6	75.9	76.6	85.9	
Less: Intermediate consumption, at purchaser's prices	14.0	15.1	21.3	23.0	25.8	28.0	28.3	32.5	33.7	33.8	37.0	
Equals: VALUE ADDED, GROSS, at basic prices	23.0	24.2	25.7	27.6	35.0	40.2	40.6	44.2	42.2	42.8	48.9	
Compensation of employees	...	...	...	...	...	...	...	...	...	...	...	
Taxes on production and imports, less Subsidies	0.0	0.0	0.0	0.0	0.0	0.0	0.0	0.0	0.0	0.0	0.0	
OPERATING SURPLUS, GROSS	...	...	...	...	...	...	...	...	...	...	...	
MIXED INCOME, GROSS	23.0	24.2	25.7	27.6	34.9	40.2	40.6	44.1	42.2	42.8	48.8	
Gross capital formation	...	...	...	...	...	...	...	...	...	...	...	

Table 2.3 Output, gross value added, and fixed assets by industries at current prices (ISIC Rev. 3) Mining and quarrying (C)

Series 100: 1993 SNA, guarani, Western calendar year

Data in billions

	2001	2002	2003	2004	2005	2006	2007	2008	2009	2010	2011	2012
Series	**100**											
Output, at basic prices	81.0[a]	78.6	99.3	113.8	134.9	148.0	154.5	190.9	216.6	234.2	271.3	
Less: Intermediate consumption, at purchaser's prices	51.0	48.1	62.8	67.9	79.4	82.3	85.5	102.3	110.9	119.6	135.3	
Equals: VALUE ADDED, GROSS, at basic prices	29.0	30.5	36.5	45.9	55.5	65.7	68.9	88.7	105.7	114.7	136.0	
Compensation of employees	22.0	23.3	26.0	29.7	32.8	38.0	40.7	43.8	44.2	44.9	48.3	
Taxes on production and imports, less Subsidies	...	0.1	0.1	0.1	0.2	0.2	0.1	0.2	0.2	0.3	0.3	
OPERATING SURPLUS, GROSS [b]	6.7	7.1	10.4	16.1	22.4	27.5	28.1	44.7	61.3	69.5	87.4	
MIXED INCOME, GROSS	...	...	...	...	...	...	...	...	...	...	...	
Less: Consumption of fixed capital	3.9	4.1	4.9	6.1	7.4	8.8	9.2	11.8	14.1	15.3	18.1	
OPERATING SURPLUS, NET	0.3	0.5	2.7	6.6	11.2	14.4	14.3	27.8	42.1	49.0	62.9	
MIXED INCOME, NET	2.4	2.5	2.8	3.4	3.8	4.4	4.7	5.0	5.1	5.2	6.3	
Gross capital formation	...	...	...	...	...	...	...	...	...	...	...	

[a] Discrepancy between components and total.
[b] Includes Mixed Income, Gross.

Table 2.3 Output, gross value added, and fixed assets by industries at current prices (ISIC Rev. 3) Manufacturing (D)

Series 100: 1993 SNA, guarani, Western calendar year

Data in billions

	2001	2002	2003	2004	2005	2006	2007	2008	2009	2010	2011	2012
Series	**100**											
Output, at basic prices	17372.0	19264.4	22656.3	25010.5	27583.4	31204.0	34788.1	41723.4	41222.0	47604.7	52014.7	
Less: Intermediate consumption, at purchaser's prices	13170.0	14684.1	17306.7	19111.8	21168.6	24062.8	26886.4	32482.0	32035.3	36990.2	40479.0	
Equals: VALUE ADDED, GROSS, at basic prices	4202.0	4580.3	5349.6	5898.7	6414.8	7141.2	7901.7	9241.4	9186.7	10614.5	11535.7	
Compensation of employees	1719.0	1861.4	2070.2	2326.0	2556.0	2930.2	3098.7	3119.7	3143.0	3305.9	3691.0	
Taxes on production and imports, less Subsidies	1.7	2.0	2.5	3.0	7.5	7.2	4.6	6.2	5.9	8.6	7.9	
OPERATING SURPLUS, GROSS [a]	2480.0	2716.9	3276.9	3569.7	3851.3	4203.8	4798.5	6115.5	6037.9	7299.9	7836.9	
MIXED INCOME, GROSS	...	...	...	...	...	...	...	...	...	...	...	
Less: Consumption of fixed capital	335.0	371.0	434.8	473.7	513.6	577.6	637.8	731.9	751.3	871.8	983.9	
OPERATING SURPLUS, NET	1710.0	1874.4	2318.2	2487.1	2605.4	2832.5	3350.1	4596.1	4491.1	5622.3	5834.4	
MIXED INCOME, NET	435.0	471.5	523.9	608.9	732.3	793.8	810.6	787.5	795.4	805.8	1018.5	
Gross capital formation	...	...	...	...	...	...	...	...	...	...	...	

[a] Includes Mixed Income, Gross.

Table 2.3 Output, gross value added, and fixed assets by industries at current prices (ISIC Rev. 3) Electricity, gas and water supply (E)

Series 100: 1993 SNA, guarani, Western calendar year

Data in billions

	2001	2002	2003	2004	2005	2006	2007	2008	2009	2010	2011	2012
Series	**100**											
Output, at basic prices	1133.0	9895.8	9974.8	9808.7	11351.2	11527.0	12138.6	11206.5	12676.6	12636.6	11654.8	
Less: Intermediate consumption, at purchaser's prices	478.0	2109.6	2442.0	2416.4	2617.3	2775.9	3176.0	3093.3	3455.2	3364.3	3224.2	
Equals: VALUE ADDED, GROSS, at basic prices	655.0[a]	7786.3	7532.9	7392.3	8733.9	8751.1	8962.6	8113.2	9221.3	9272.3	8430.6	
Compensation of employees	162.0	810.4	861.8	912.3	994.8	1144.5	1249.9	1352.4	1438.6	1713.3	1757.5	
Taxes on production and imports, less Subsidies	0.1	0.1	0.1	0.1	0.4	0.3	0.2	0.3	0.3	0.4	0.4	
OPERATING SURPLUS, GROSS	493.0	6975.7[b]	6671.0[b]	6479.8[b]	7738.8[b]	7606.3[b]	7712.5[b]	6760.4[b]	7782.4[b]	7558.5[b]	6672.7[b]	
MIXED INCOME, GROSS	...	...	...	...	...	...	...	...	...	...	...	
Less: Consumption of fixed capital	154.0	528.8	542.7	543.3	615.3	632.1	647.1	606.6	666.9	681.1	688.1	
OPERATING SURPLUS, NET	339.0	6447.0[c]	6128.3[c]	5936.5[c]	7123.5[c]	6974.3[c]	7065.5[c]	6153.8[c]	7115.5[c]	6877.5[c]	5984.6[c]	
MIXED INCOME, NET	...	...	...	...	...	...	...	...	...	...	...	
Gross capital formation	...	...	...	...	...	...	...	...	...	...	...	

[a] Does not incorporate value added generated by binacional hydroelectric plants.
[b] Includes Mixed Income, Gross.
[c] Includes Mixed Income, Net.

Table 2.3 Output, gross value added, and fixed assets by industries at current prices (ISIC Rev. 3) Construction (F)

Series 100: 1993 SNA, guarani, Western calendar year — **Data in billions**

	2001	2002	2003	2004	2005	2006	2007	2008	2009	2010	2011	2012
Series	**100**											
Output, at basic prices	2827.0	3089.9	4127.3	4627.0	5077.5	5666.4	7162.4	9642.9	10151.6	12319.4	14049.0	
Less: Intermediate consumption, at purchaser's prices	1612.0	1762.7	2348.2	2685.5	2944.9	3208.9	3892.9	5144.9	5526.4	6474.5	6953.0	
Equals: VALUE ADDED, GROSS, at basic prices	1215.0	1327.2	1779.1	1941.5	2132.6	2457.5	3269.5	4498.0	4625.1	5844.9	7096.0	
Compensation of employees	885.0	943.4	1064.9	1162.9	1301.7	1498.9	1749.1	2241.4	2275.0	2499.1	2751.2	
Taxes on production and imports, less Subsidies	5.0	5.5	6.8	8.3	21.6	20.8	12.9	18.2	17.2	25.2	22.9	
Taxes on production and imports	5.0	5.5	6.8	8.3	21.6	20.8	12.9	18.2	17.2	25.2	22.9	
Less: Subsidies	...	...	...	...	...	...	...	...	...	...	...	
OPERATING SURPLUS, GROSS [a]	325.0	378.4	707.4	770.3	809.2	937.9	1507.5	2238.5	2332.9	3320.7	4321.9	
MIXED INCOME, GROSS	...	...	...	...	...	...	...	...	...	...	...	
Less: Consumption of fixed capital	53.0	68.3	91.5	99.9	109.7	126.4	168.2	231.4	238.0	300.7	365.1	
OPERATING SURPLUS, NET	-40.0	-21.4	246.7	269.3	250.5	294.4	736.0	1234.0	1312.4	2227.6	3021.8	
MIXED INCOME, NET	312.0	331.5	369.2	401.1	449.0	517.0	603.3	773.1	782.6	792.4	935.1	
Gross capital formation	...	...	...	...	...	...	...	...	...	...	...	

[a] Includes Mixed Income, Gross.

Table 2.3 Output, gross value added, and fixed assets by industries at current prices (ISIC Rev. 3) Wholesale retail trade, repair of motor vehicles, motorcycles, etc.; hotels and restaurants (G+H)

Series 100: 1993 SNA, guarani, Western calendar year — **Data in billions**

	2001	2002	2003	2004	2005	2006	2007	2008	2009	2010	2011	2012
Series	**100**											
Output, at basic prices	8796.0	9845.9	12418.8	14675.2	16151.3	19088.1	21166.8	25414.0	23004.3	26856.1	33829.8	
Less: Intermediate consumption, at purchaser's prices	3938.0	4396.4	5462.7	5975.3	6565.2	7664.8	8525.3	10816.3	9480.2	10968.4	11714.9	
Equals: VALUE ADDED, GROSS, at basic prices	4858.0	5449.5	6956.1	8699.9	9586.0	11423.3	12641.5	14597.7	13524.1	15887.7	22114.9	
Compensation of employees	1414.0	1565.9	1764.8	2044.9	2263.8	2619.6	2931.2	3303.8	3408.0	3674.0	4132.3	
Taxes on production and imports, less Subsidies	19.0	23.9	29.5	36.2	95.0	91.2	56.4	79.8	75.7	110.6	100.7	
OPERATING SURPLUS, GROSS [a]	3423.0	3859.7	5161.8	6618.8	7227.1	8712.5	9653.9	11214.1	10040.3	12103.0	17881.9	
MIXED INCOME, GROSS	...	...	...	...	...	...	...	...	...	...	...	
Less: Consumption of fixed capital	48.0	50.5	64.6	80.9	89.1	106.2	117.5	135.7	125.7	147.6	205.7	
OPERATING SURPLUS, NET	1228.0	1571.4	2608.6	3903.9	4194.2	5226.6	5740.1	6850.2	5639.1	7497.0	12356.4	
MIXED INCOME, NET	2147.0	2237.7	2488.6	2634.1	2943.8	3379.7	3796.3	4228.2	4275.5	4458.4	5319.8	
Gross capital formation	...	...	...	...	...	...	...	...	...	...	...	

[a] Includes Mixed Income, Gross.

Table 2.3 Output, gross value added, and fixed assets by industries at current prices (ISIC Rev. 3) Transport, storage and communications (I)

Series 100: 1993 SNA, guarani, Western calendar year **Data in billions**

	2001	2002	2003	2004	2005	2006	2007	2008	2009	2010	2011	2012
Series	**100**											
Output, at basic prices	4347.0	4959.6	5925.4	6623.0	8513.7	9787.5	11364.1	12690.5	12129.3	13080.6	14447.3	
Less: Intermediate consumption, at purchaser's prices	2377.0	2694.3	3389.4	3793.8	4966.2	5828.3	6500.6	7522.8	6964.9	7610.2	8710.3	
Equals: VALUE ADDED, GROSS, at basic prices	1970.0	2265.2	2536.0	2829.1	3547.6	3959.2	4863.5	5167.6	5164.4	5470.4	5737.0	
Compensation of employees	825.0	896.3	1010.3	1132.5	1232.0	1619.2	1931.6	2301.4	2343.5	2467.3	2623.5	
Taxes on production and imports, less Subsidies	40.0	48.0	59.4	72.8	190.3	182.6	113.1	159.6	151.5	221.4	201.5	
OPERATING SURPLUS, GROSS [a]	1106.1	1320.9	1466.3	1623.9	2125.3	2157.4	2818.7	2706.6	2669.4	2781.7	2912.0	
MIXED INCOME, GROSS	...	...	...	...	...	...	...	...	...	...	...	
Less: Consumption of fixed capital	297.6	339.0	388.0	434.7	544.6	609.5	739.4	792.8	788.4	830.4	867.9	
OPERATING SURPLUS, NET	659.7	819.8	897.2	985.8	1352.3	1261.4	1730.9	1486.8	1448.8	1506.3	1554.5	
MIXED INCOME, NET	148.8	162.1	181.1	203.3	228.4	286.5	348.4	426.9	432.1	445.1	489.6	
Gross capital formation	...	...	...	...	...	...	...	...	...	...	...	

[a] Includes Mixed Income, Gross.

Table 2.3 Output, gross value added, and fixed assets by industries at current prices (ISIC Rev. 3) Financial intermediation; real estate, renting and business activities (J+K)

Series 100: 1993 SNA, guarani, Western calendar year **Data in billions**

	2001	2002	2003	2004	2005	2006	2007	2008	2009	2010	2011	2012
Series	**100**											
Output, at basic prices	3075.0	3241.4	3243.3	3439.4	3884.7	4496.2	5026.4	6422.2	7044.6	8493.6	10115.2	
Less: Intermediate consumption, at purchaser's prices	900.0	957.1	933.8	1032.5	1142.2	1274.9	1413.1	1712.7	1931.3	2210.0	2512.3	
Equals: VALUE ADDED, GROSS, at basic prices	2175.0	2284.4	2309.4	2406.9	2742.6	3221.2	3613.3	4709.5	5113.3	6283.6	7602.9	
Compensation of employees	587.5	620.3	534.5	569.7	617.5	681.3	745.2	842.9	873.7	933.2	1076.6	
Taxes on production and imports, less Subsidies	88.2	90.1	111.4	136.5	357.0	342.6	212.3	299.5	284.4	415.4	378.1	
OPERATING SURPLUS, GROSS [a]	1500.1	1574.0	1663.6	1700.7	1768.0	2197.4	2655.8	3567.1	3955.2	4935.0	6148.2	
MIXED INCOME, GROSS	...	...	...	...	...	...	...	...	...	...	...	
Less: Consumption of fixed capital	65.3	73.6	73.0	74.6	90.8	111.8	127.3	192.3	204.5	274.4	349.8	
OPERATING SURPLUS, NET	1110.8	1139.2	1347.3	1362.4	1498.8	1856.4	2263.3	3082.1	3454.7	4361.3	5432.1	
MIXED INCOME, NET	324.1	361.2	243.3	263.7	178.5	229.2	265.2	292.7	296.0	299.3	366.3	
Gross capital formation	...	...	...	...	...	...	...	...	...	...	...	

[a] Includes Mixed Income, Gross.

Table 2.3 Output, gross value added, and fixed assets by industries at current prices (ISIC Rev. 3) Public administration and defense; compulsory social security (L)

Series 100: 1993 SNA, guarani, Western calendar year | **Data in billions**

	2001	2002	2003	2004	2005	2006	2007	2008	2009	2010	2011	2012
Series	**100**											
Output, at basic prices	3504.0	3595.3	4109.7	4498.1	5570.2	6280.4	7747.7	8487.5	10478.4	11987.9	13701.1	
Less: Intermediate consumption, at purchaser's prices	770.0	786.4	899.7	1052.1	1383.3	1453.1	2107.7	2190.4	2997.6	3464.0	3998.0	
Equals: VALUE ADDED, GROSS, at basic prices	2734.0	2808.9	3210.0	3446.0	4186.8	4827.2	5640.0	6297.2	7480.8	8523.9	9703.1	
Compensation of employees	2734.3	2808.6	3209.7	3445.6	4185.8	4826.2	5639.4	6296.3	7480.0	8522.7	9702.0	
Taxes on production and imports, less Subsidies	0.3	0.3	0.3	0.4	1.0	1.0	0.6	0.9	0.8	1.2	1.1	
OPERATING SURPLUS, GROSS	...	...	...	...	...	...	...	...	...	...	...	
MIXED INCOME, GROSS	...	...	...	...	...	...	...	...	...	...	...	
Gross capital formation	...	...	...	...	...	...	...	...	...	...	...	

Table 2.3 Output, gross value added, and fixed assets by industries at current prices (ISIC Rev. 3) Private households with employed persons (P)

Series 100: 1993 SNA, guarani, Western calendar year | **Data in billions**

	2001	2002	2003	2004	2005	2006	2007	2008	2009	2010	2011	2012
Series	**100**											
Output, at basic prices	3164.0	3548.9	3825.7	3979.3	4335.5	4671.1	5202.5	5984.3	6574.0	7155.0	8249.0	
Less: Intermediate consumption, at purchaser's prices	1100.0	1252.3	1350.0	1444.6	1614.0	1767.2	1939.2	2265.1	2455.1	2657.4	3018.3	
Equals: VALUE ADDED, GROSS, at basic prices	2064.0	2296.6	2475.7	2534.7	2721.5	2903.9	3263.4	3719.2	4118.9	4497.6	5230.7	
Compensation of employees	819.0	903.3	980.4	1101.8	1185.8	1371.0	1616.9	1353.9	1399.9	1446.1	1481.5	
Taxes on production and imports, less Subsidies	10.8	13.1	16.2	19.8	51.8	49.7	30.8	43.5	41.3	60.3	54.9	
OPERATING SURPLUS, GROSS [a]	1234.0	1380.2	1479.1	1413.1	1483.8	1483.2	1615.6	2321.9	2677.7	2991.1	3694.3	
MIXED INCOME, GROSS	...	...	...	...	...	...	...	...	...	...	...	
Less: Consumption of fixed capital	53.8	57.1	61.5	63.0	67.7	72.2	81.1	92.5	102.4	111.8	130.0	
OPERATING SURPLUS, NET	87.2	124.6	134.1	-84.2	-127.6	-373.7	-570.4	466.9	795.0	1063.4	1181.8	
MIXED INCOME, NET	1092.9	1198.5	1283.5	1434.3	1543.7	1784.8	2104.9	1762.5	1780.3	1815.9	2382.5	
Gross capital formation	...	...	...	...	...	...	...	...	...	...	...	

[a] Includes Mixed Income, Gross.

Peru

Source

The National Directorate of National Accounts in Lima, which is part of the National Statistics and Information Institute of Peru ('Instituto Nacional de Estadísticas e Informática'), is responsible for preparing the annual statistics presented in the country's national accounts. Official estimates are published quarterly and annually and included in the National Statistics Compendium ('Compendio Estadístico Nacional). They are also posted on the Internet (www.inei.gob.pe). The concepts, definitions, sources of basic statistics and methods of estimation used are described in detail in the publications corresponding to each benchmark year: those for 1979 were published in March 1985; and for 1994, a methodological collection was published in July 2000. The quarterly and annual publications also include a chapter on the methodology and sources of information used to calculate the national accounts.

General

The most recent estimates include the following tables that have been prepared in accordance with the concepts and definitions of the System of National Accounts, 1993 (1993 SNA). In the past, estimates were made in accordance with the United Nations System of National Accounts, 1968 (1968 SNA). Input-output tables were published for the years 1979, 1981, 1982, 1983, 1984, 1985, 1986, 1987, 1988, 1989, 1990 and 1991. The input-output table for 1994 was published in July 2000 using the United Nations System of National Accounts, 1993 (1993 SNA). Any estimates that, for conceptual or statistical reasons, diverge from the definitions and classifications recommended in the System of National Accounts are explained in a footnote at the end of each table.

On 1 February 1985, a new monetary unit, the inti, which was equivalent to 1,000 soles, was introduced. The inti in turn was replaced on 1 July 1991 with the nuevo sol, which was equivalent to one million intis.

Methodology:

Overview of GDP Compilation

GDP is estimated primarily on the basis of production and expenditure calculations. The input-output tables are not prepared annually: separate estimates are calculated for each variable or economic activity, and then an aggregate balance is calculated for the economy.

Expenditure Approach

Estimates of the Government's final consumption expenditures are made on the basis of the production accounts, which are in turn calculated on the basis of the administrative records of the institutions that make up the Government (official budget expenditures less income obtained from the sale of goods and services). Estimates of constant prices for the Government's final consumption expenditures are based on the deflation of intermediate consumption, wages and consumption of fixed capital.

Values of private consumption expenditures on goods and services are mainly obtained by the product flow method and from the national household surveys. Data sources include production statistics for agriculture, manufacturing, electric power, water supply and foreign trade, by product, as well as statistical records on vehicle registrations and the communications sector. The national household surveys also provide information on products at current purchaser prices. The consumer price index is used to obtain current value data.

Own-account consumption (imputed rents for housing) is valued at producer prices in the case of owner-occupied housing. In the case of private expenditures on services, estimates are principally based on the statistics obtained from the national household surveys and the pertinent economic activities. In the case of private consumption expenditure, the current values provided by the national household surveys are deflated using appropriate price indices (consumer price indices), and the internal demand method is used to calculate the estimates for non-food products.

Data on inventory changes are based on regular annual surveys, from which the trends for this variable are determined. The data are reconciled with the values obtained by inflating constant values. Constant values are determined by the difference between supply and demand and by deflating current values of any other reference data obtained from the surveys.
Gross fixed capital formation (GFCF) is determined on the basis of the value of domestic production plus imports (the relevant percentage on the basis of customs information is applied) less exports and is adjusted to include transportation costs, trade margins, etc.

In the case of the construction sector, the gross value of production for the individual branch is calculated on the basis of cement sales, the physical progress of public works undertaken by the Ministry of Transport, and rural population growth figures. Own-account construction of dwellings and buildings is included.

GFCF at constant prices is calculated by using a production and foreign trade index to extrapolate constant values.
The estimates of imports and exports of goods and services are based on foreign trade and balance-of-payments statistics. The constant values of imports and exports are obtained by using a foreign trade index to deflate current values.

Income Approach

Estimates of wages are calculated using data from the annual economic surveys and information provided directly by enterprises. Information on the following sectors is also directly available: Government, banking, insurance, pension funds, electricity and water supply. The gross operating surplus is calculated in the same way as a residual balance. No differentiation is made between the business surplus and the household surplus (mixed income). Estimates of stock depreciation are obtained from accounting information in the annual economic surveys and administrative records. Figures for taxes on products and other taxes on production and imports are obtained directly from Government records.

Production Approach

GDP by type of economic activity is calculated on the basis of producer values. Using production estimates, it is possible to make reasonably accurate estimates of the value added in all industries. In the case of public administration, national defence and non-market production activities, output is calculated on the basis of costs incurred.

The value added of agriculture is obtained by deducting intermediate consumption, including a figure imputed for the sector's own consumption, from the gross value of production. The calculations are based on the results of the agricultural censuses and in non-census years on the statistics for production volumes and prices obtained from the regular monthly and annual surveys conducted by the Ministry of Agriculture. Constant values are determined by applying the prices of the benchmark year.

In the case of fisheries (extractive and processed), mining (extractive and processed), manufacturing, construction, electricity, gas and water and other service sectors, value added is calculated by deducting intermediate consumption from the gross value of production. The estimates are based on the information obtained from the economic censuses and from the monthly and annual accounts reported in the years between censuses. Constant values are determined by extrapolating the values for the benchmark year.

In the case of financial institutions, the value added is derived from the financial statements of banking and other financial institutions, insurance companies and private pension funds. Estimates at constant prices for financial and insurance entities are obtained through a double deflation process, whereby the price index is applied to production and intermediate consumption, the value added being the difference. In the case of private pension funds, value added is extrapolated using a quantum indicator for production; intermediate consumption is determined by deflation using a price index, and value added is calculated as the difference between the gross value of production and intermediate consumption.

The value added of the public sector as a whole is obtained by aggregating the value added of the various institutions that make up the Government as a whole, in other words, by aggregating the production costs obtained from their executed budgets. The estimates of constant prices used in the calculation of the Government's value added are based on the deflation of wages and consumption of fixed capital.

Table 1.1 Gross domestic product by expenditures at current prices

Series 100: 1993 SNA, new sol, Western calendar year — **Data in millions**

	2001	2002	2003	2004	2005	2006	2007	2008	2009	2010	2011	2012
Series	**100**											
	Expenditures of the gross domestic product											
Final consumption expenditure	157053.1	164235.9	173278.4	186540.2	199347.8	215454.5	236335.0	270652.2	288422.0	311316.4	341845.9	378007.9
Household final consumption expenditure	136821.9	144044.7	151363.0	162840.4	173050.2	186644.5	206187.0	237340.0	248969.9	269045.1	296004.0	326381.1
NPISHs final consumption expenditure	...	...	...	...	...	...	...	...	...	...	...	...
General government final consumption expenditure	20231.2	20191.3	21915.3	23699.8	26297.6	28810.1	30148.1	33312.2	39452.1	42271.3	45841.9	51626.8
Gross capital formation	35505.9	36741.3	39340.2	42704.4	46809.1	60580.0	77185.0	102856.0	87401.5	118266.2	134582.0	153818.1
Gross fixed capital formation	35132.5	35134.9	38052.2	42551.2	47966.4	58391.4	72762.5	98487.3	94266.7	117172.1	129321.3	150471.2
Changes in inventories	374.0	1606.0	1288.0	153.2	-1157.3	2188.6	4422.5	4368.7	-6865.1	1094.1	5260.8	3347.0
Acquisitions less disposals of valuables	...	...	...	...	...	...	...	...	...	...	...	...
Exports of goods and services	29819.8	32682.1	38060.6	51041.0	65647.0	86233.7	97814.8	102830.9	93707.5	114094.9	141468.5	136169.0
Less: Imports of goods and services	33166.1	34009.4	37254.3	42383.9	50150.7	60013.1	74996.4	98776.4	77601.8	98896.6	120065.6	128132.4
Equals: GROSS DOMESTIC PRODUCT	189212.7	199649.9	213424.9	237901.7	261653.2	302255.1	336339.0	377562.0	391929.2	444780.9	497830.9	539862.7[a]

[a] Data for this year refers to preliminary data.

Table 1.2 Gross domestic product by expenditures at constant prices

Series 100: 1993 SNA, new sol, Western calendar year — **Data in millions**

	2001	2002	2003	2004	2005	2006	2007	2008	2009	2010	2011	2012
Series	**100**											
Base year	**1994**											
	Expenditures of the gross domestic product											
Final consumption expenditure	98920.9	103229.2	106769.9	110713.8	116385.5	124041.8	133808.0	144461.0	150154.8	159958.6	169942.7	180740.8
Household final consumption expenditure	87456.3	91769.4	94860.4	98312.5	102856.7	109482.7	118618.0	128954.0	132095.7	140475.8	149255.5	158157.8
NPISHs final consumption expenditure	...	...	...	...	...	...	...	...	...	...	...	...
General government final consumption expenditure	11464.5	11459.8	11909.5	12401.3	13528.8	14559.1	15190.9	15507.4	18059.1	19482.9	20687.2	22583.0
Gross capital formation	22017.4	22669.7	23744.3	24813.6	27024.9	34177.8	43168.5	55884.1	45493.4	62497.4	69910.6	79145.2
Gross fixed capital formation	21784.6	21672.8	22952.5	24722.7	27699.6	32905.2	40624.5	53417.6	49145.6	61953.8	67512.8	77690.2
Changes in inventories	233.0	997.0	792.0	90.9	-674.7	1272.6	2544.0	2466.0	-3652.2	543.6	2397.8	1455.0
Acquisitions less disposals of valuables	...	...	...	...	...	...	...	...	...	...	...	...
Exports of goods and services	21451.2	23070.0	24491.2	28221.2	32511.7	32771.7	34787.1	38236.2	37134.6	38914.2	43558.4	45266.5

	2001	2002	2003	2004	2005	2006	2007	2008	2009	2010	2011	2012
Series	**100**											
Base year	**1994**											
Less: Imports of goods and services	21072.4	21561.4	22460.6	24607.4	27282.1	30845.8	37416.0	47214.7	39675.1	51307.7	58787.4	66356.6
Equals: GROSS DOMESTIC PRODUCT	121317.1	127407.4	132544.9	139141.3	148640.0	160145.5	174348.0	191367.0	193107.8	210062.6	224624.3	238795.8[a]

[a] Data for this year refers to preliminary data.

Table 2.1 Value added by industries at current prices (ISIC Rev. 3)

Series 100: 1993 SNA, new sol, Western calendar year — **Data in millions**

	2001	2002	2003	2004	2005	2006	2007	2008	2009	2010	2011	2012
Series	**100**											
	Industries											
Agriculture, hunting, forestry; fishing	14297.0	14401.0	14896.0	15784.0	17176.0	19206.0	21525.0	24921.0	26389.0	27555.0	31589.0	
Agriculture, hunting, forestry	12867.0	12668.0	13470.0	14213.0	15135.0	17107.0	19342.0	22352.0	23834.0	24996.0	28077.0	
Fishing	1430.0	1733.0	1426.0	1571.0	2041.0	2099.0	2183.0	2569.0	2555.0	2559.0	3512.0	
Mining and quarrying	9312.0	10961.0	12929.0	18264.0	23139.0	35248.0	38413.0	39267.0	37377.0	46535.0	56220.0	
Manufacturing	27737.0	28954.0	30352.0	35373.0	39077.0	44234.0	49035.0	54921.0	51667.0	59808.0	67149.0	
Electricity, gas and water supply	4334.0	4442.0	4651.0	4895.0	5379.0	5656.0	6011.0	6539.0	7440.0	7758.0	8619.0	
Construction	9882.0	10737.0	11561.0	12885.0	14214.0	17122.0	20395.0	24112.0	27082.0	32690.0	34802.0	
Wholesale, retail trade, repair of motor vehicles, motorcycles and personal and households goods; hotels and restaurants	33688.0	35130.0	36661.0	39898.0	42537.0	48365.0	53798.0	62113.0	66656.0	76023.0	85772.0	
Wholesale, retail trade, repair of motor vehicles, motorcycles and personal and household goods	25818.0	26945.0	28000.0	30734.0	32726.0	37845.0	42104.0	48602.0	52025.0	59545.0	66790.0	
Hotels and restaurants	7870.0	8185.0	8661.0	9164.0	9811.0	10520.0	11694.0	13511.0	14631.0	16478.0	18982.0	
Transport, storage and communications	14991.0	15406.0	16747.0	18226.0	20075.0	22772.0	28622.0	32210.0	34115.0	37701.0	42718.0	
Land transport; transport via pipelines, water transport; air transport; Supporting and auxiliary transport activities; activities of travel agencies	11078.0	11460.0	12578.0	13645.0	15302.0	16887.0	22154.0	25151.0	26850.0	30535.0	34429.0	
Post and telecommunications	3913.0	3946.0	4169.0	4581.0	4773.0	5885.0	6468.0	7059.0	7265.0	7166.0	8289.0	
Financial intermediation; real estate, renting and business activities	26601.0	28536.0	30047.0	31810.0	34442.0	37806.0	41844.0	47277.0	51618.0	56568.0	62562.0	
Financial intermediation	4698.0	5724.0	6299.0	6644.0	7762.0	8821.0	10102.0	12049.0	14083.0	15800.0	18260.0	
Real estate, renting and business activities	21903.0	22812.0	23748.0	25166.0	26680.0	28985.0	31742.0	35228.0	37535.0	40768.0	44302.0	
Public administration and defence; compulsory social security	14211.0	15044.0	16274.0	17474.0	19249.0	20970.0	21630.0	23922.0	27108.0	28051.0	30294.0	
Education; health and social work; other community, social and personal services	17053.0	17899.0	19353.0	20562.0	21614.0	23356.0	25153.0	27615.0	30095.0	32650.0	35406.0	
Education	7152.0	7464.0	8125.0	8738.0	9204.0	9926.0	10667.0	11413.0	12271.0	13157.0	14057.0	
Health and social work	3537.0	3776.0	4179.0	4449.0	4715.0	5123.0	5341.0	5861.0	6378.0	6890.0	7459.0	
Other community, social and personal services	6364.0	6659.0	7049.0	7375.0	7695.0	8307.0	9145.0	10341.0	11446.0	12603.0	13890.0	
Private households with employed persons	1219.0	1252.0	1321.0	1382.0	1436.0	1517.0	1586.0	1741.0	1881.0	2033.0	2198.0	
Equals: VALUE ADDED, GROSS, in basic prices	173326.0	182762.0	194791.0	216554.0	238338.0	276251.0	308012.0	344641.0	361425.0	407372.0	457329.0	

	2001	2002	2003	2004	2005	2006	2007	2008	2009	2010	2011	2012
Series	**100**											
Less: Financial intermediation services indirectly measured (FISIM)	...	...	...	...	...	...	...	...	...	...	...	
Plus: Taxes less Subsidies on products	15887.0	16888.0	18634.0	21348.0	23315.0	26004.0	28326.0	32922.0	30504.0	37408.0	40502.0	
Equals: GROSS DOMESTIC PRODUCT	189213.0	199650.0	213425.0	237902.0	261653.0	302255.0	336339.0	377562.0	391929.0	444781.0	497831.0	
Memorandum Item: FISIM, if distributed to uses	4085.0	4578.0	4681.0	4815.0	5742.0	6923.0	8281.0	9922.0	11775.0	13208.0	...	

Table 2.2 Value added by industries at constant prices (ISIC Rev. 3)

Series 100: 1993 SNA, new sol, Western calendar year **Data in millions**

	2001	2002	2003	2004	2005	2006	2007	2008	2009	2010	2011	2012
Series	**100**											
Base year	**1994**											
Industries												
Agriculture, hunting, forestry; fishing	11422.0	12119.0	12391.0	12408.1	13063.0	14109.0	14597.0	15640.0	15994.0	16595.0	17545.0	18266.0
Agriculture, hunting, forestry	10796.3	11454.7	11795.4	11629.5	12259.4	13286.4	13717.6	14705.9	15100.0	15820.0	16526.0	17365.0
Fishing	625.6	663.5	595.5	778.6	803.6	822.5	879.0	934.4	894.0	775.0	1019.0	901.0
Mining and quarrying	7262.8	8132.9	8578.6	9031.4	9789.9	9926.0	10195.3	10972.9	11055.0	11088.0	11105.0	11350.0
Manufacturing	18118.1	19146.6	19830.2	21300.1	22887.4	24606.6	27337.1	29824.6	27722.0	31492.0	33382.0	33821.0
Electricity, gas and water supply	2566.4	2706.3	2805.2	2930.6	3094.4	3307.5	3587.7	3866.5	3912.0	4218.0	4528.0	4765.0
Construction	5699.8	6136.4	6412.5	6712.1	7275.7	8349.5	9737.2	11339.4	12036.0	14135.0	14566.0	16774.0
Wholesale, retail trade, repair of motor vehicles, motorcycles and personal and household goods; hotels and restaurants	22230.0	22945.0	23615.0	24998.2	26505.3	29231.7	32015.0	35993.0	35954.0	39520.0	43046.0	46133.0
Wholesale, retail trade, repair of motor vehicles, motorcycles and personal and household goods	17443.5	18013.1	18452.6	19604.2	20821.3	23247.7	25497.8	28752.6	28543.0	31500.0	34251.0	36557.0
Hotels and restaurants	4786.0	4932.0	5162.0	5394.0	5684.0	5984.0	6517.0	7240.0	7411.0	8020.0	8795.0	9576.0
Transport, storage and communications	9511.0	9859.0	10346.0	11010.0	11949.0	13047.0	15513.0	17070.0	17131.0	18295.0	20256.0	21906.0
Land transport; transport via piplines, water transport; air transport; Supporting and auxiliary transport activities; activities of travel agencies	7196.0	7438.0	7721.0	8168.0	8845.0	9079.0	10005.0	10899.0	10826.0	11982.0	12808.0	13681.0
Post and telecommunications	2315.0	2421.0	2625.0	2842.0	3104.0	3968.0	5508.0	6171.0	6305.0	6313.0	7448.0	8225.0
Financial intermediation, real estate, renting and business activities	14602.0	15322.0	15953.0	16573.0	17653.0	18972.0	20746.0	22860.0	23925.0	25830.0	28041.0	30064.0
Financial intermediation	2879.0	3198.0	3420.0	3462.0	3836.0	4349.0	4915.0	5539.0	6331.0	7027.0	7804.0	8484.0
Real estate, renting and business activities	11723.0	12124.0	12533.0	13111.0	13817.0	14623.0	15831.0	17321.0	17594.0	18803.0	20237.0	21580.0
Public administration and defence; compulsory social security	7410.0	7752.0	8246.0	8598.0	9321.0	10029.0	10339.0	10742.0	11874.0	12297.0	12950.0	13542.0
Education; health and social work; other community, social and personal services	10168.0	10479.0	10900.0	11269.0	11617.0	12139.0	12828.0	13579.0	14257.0	15095.0	16009.0	17214.0
Education	3990.0	4070.0	4243.0	4394.0	4526.0	4696.0	4889.0	5056.0	5212.0	5393.0	5567.0	5978.0
Health and social work	1985.0	2065.0	2144.0	2199.0	2251.0	2355.0	2416.0	2526.0	2622.0	2740.0	2871.0	3083.0
Other community, social and personal services	4193.0	4344.0	4513.0	4676.0	4840.0	5088.0	5523.0	5997.0	6423.0	6962.0	7571.0	8153.0
Private households with employed persons	703.0	724.0	751.0	777.0	807.0	829.0	856.0	932.0	995.0	1063.0	1134.0	1218.0

	2001	2002	2003	2004	2005	2006	2007	2008	2009	2010	2011	2012
Series	**100**											
Base year	**1994**											
Equals: VALUE ADDED, GROSS, in basic prices	109692.6	115323.2	119828.0	125607.5	133961.0	144546.9	157752.0	172819.0	174856.0	189627.0	202562.0	215049.0
Less: Financial intermediation services indirectly measured (FISIM)	...	...	...	...	...	...	...	...	...	...	...	...
Plus: Taxes less Subsidies on products	11624.5	12084.3	12716.8	13533.7	14679.0	15598.6	16596.5	18547.3	18252.0	20435.0	22062.0	23747.0
Equals: GROSS DOMESTIC PRODUCT	121317.1	127407.4	132544.9	139141.3	148640.0	160145.5	174348.0	191367.0	193108.0	210063.0	224624.0	238796.0[a]
Memorandum Item: FISIM, if distributed to uses	0.0	0.0	0.0	0.0	2931.0	3473.0	4080.0	4663.0	5453.0	6015.0	...	...

[a] Data for this year refers to preliminary data.

Table 2.3 Output, gross value added, and fixed assets by industries at current prices (ISIC Rev. 3) Total Economy

Series 100: 1993 SNA, new sol, Western calendar year — **Data in millions**

		2001	2002	2003	2004	2005	2006	2007	2008	2009	2010	2011	2012
Series		**100**											
Output, at basic prices		...	...	...	...	...	...	...	...	...	...	...	
Less: Intermediate consumption, at purchaser's prices		...	...	...	...	...	...	...	...	...	...	...	
Equals: VALUE ADDED, GROSS, at basic prices		173326.0	182762.0	194791.0	216554.0	238338.0	276251.0	308012.0	344640.0	361425.0	407372.0	457329.0	
Compensation of employees		47551.0	49918.0	53312.0	56977.0	60324.0	66320.0	72840.0	78966.0	85634.0	93340.0	104374.0	
Taxes on production and imports, less Subsidies		1217.0	766.0	822.0	839.0	1557.0	1864.0	2119.0	2455.0[a]	2870.0	3015.0	3619.0	
Taxes on production and imports		1217.0	766.0	822.0	839.0	1557.0	1864.0	2119.0	2455.0[a]	2870.0	3015.0	3619.0	
Taxes on products		...	...	...	...	...	...	...	...	...	...	...	
Other taxes on production		1217.0	766.0	822.0	839.0	1557.0	1864.0	2119.0	2455.0[a]	2870.0	3015.0	3619.0	
Less: Subsidies		...	...	...	...	...	...	...	...	...	...	...	
OPERATING SURPLUS, GROSS	b	124557.0	132078.0	140657.0	158738.0	176458.0	208067.0	233053.0	263219.0	272921.0	311017.0	349337.0	
MIXED INCOME, GROSS		...	...	...	...	...	...	...	...	...	...	...	
Less: Consumption of fixed capital		14209.0	14789.0	15355.0	16910.0	18512.0	20900.0	23201.0	25349.0	26677.0	29259.0	31873.0	
OPERATING SURPLUS, NET	c	110348.0	117289.0	125302.0	141828.0	157946.0	187167.0	209852.0	237870.0	246244.0	281758.0	317464.0	
MIXED INCOME, NET		...	...	...	...	...	...	...	...	...	...	...	
Gross capital formation		35506.0	36741.0	39340.0	42704.4	46809.1	60580.0	77185.0	102856.0	87402.0	118266.0	134582.0	
Gross fixed capital formation		35132.0	35135.0	38052.0	42551.2	47966.4	58391.4	72762.5	98487.3	94267.0	117172.0	129321.0	
Changes in inventories		374.0	1606.0	1288.0	153.2	-1157.3	2188.6	4422.5	4368.7	-6865.0	1094.0	5261.0	
Acquisitions less disposals of valuables		...	...	...	...	...	...	...	...	...	...	...	

[a] Discrepancy between the data for the total economy and the data by industries.
[b] Includes Mixed Income, Gross.
[c] Includes Mixed Income, Net.

Table 2.3 Output, gross value added, and fixed assets by industries at current prices (ISIC Rev. 3) Agriculture, hunting, forestry; fishing (A+B)

Series 100: 1993 SNA, new sol, Western calendar year — **Data in millions**

	2001	2002	2003	2004	2005	2006	2007	2008	2009	2010	2011	2012
Series	**100**											
Output, at basic prices	...	...	...	...	...	...	...	...	...	...	...	
Less: Intermediate consumption, at purchaser's prices	...	...	...	...	...	...	...	...	...	...	...	
Equals: VALUE ADDED, GROSS, at basic prices	14298.0	14401.0	14896.0	15784.0	17177.0	19206.0	21525.0	24922.0	26389.0	27555.0	31589.0	
Compensation of employees	2653.0	2633.0	2746.0	3159.0	3232.0	3638.0	3825.0	4049.0	4223.0	4435.0	5148.0	
Taxes on production and imports, less Subsidies	11.0	10.0	9.0[a]	11.0	13.0	14.0	16.0	19.0	21.0	21.0	24.0	
Taxes on production and imports	11.0	10.0	9.0[a]	11.0	13.0	14.0	16.0	19.0	21.0	21.0	24.0	
Taxes on products	...	...	...	...	...	...	...	...	...	...	...	
Other taxes on production	11.0	10.0	9.0[a]	11.0	13.0	14.0	16.0	19.0	21.0	21.0	24.0	
Less: Subsidies	...	...	...	...	...	...	...	...	...	...	...	
OPERATING SURPLUS, GROSS [b]	11634.0	11758.0	12141.0	12614.0	13932.0	15554.0	17684.0	20853.0	22145.0	23099.0	26417.0	
MIXED INCOME, GROSS	...	...	...	...	...	...	...	...	...	...	...	
Less: Consumption of fixed capital	513.0	540.0	514.0	597.0	647.0	665.0	699.0	781.0	771.0	791.0	1000.0	
OPERATING SURPLUS, NET [c]	11121.0	11218.0	11627.0	12017.0	13285.0	14889.0	16985.0	20072.0	21374.0	22308.0	25417.0	
MIXED INCOME, NET	...	...	...	...	...	...	...	...	...	...	...	
Gross capital formation	...	...	...	...	...	...	...	...	...	...	...	

[a] Discrepancy between agricultural sub-industries and total.
[b] Includes Mixed Income, Gross.
[c] Includes Mixed Income, Net.

Table 2.3 Output, gross value added, and fixed assets by industries at current prices (ISIC Rev. 3) Agriculture, hunting and related service activities (01)

Series 100: 1993 SNA, new sol, Western calendar year — **Data in millions**

	2001	2002	2003	2004	2005	2006	2007	2008	2009	2010	2011	2012
Series	**100**											
Output, at basic prices	...	...	...	...	...	...	...	...	...	...	...	
Less: Intermediate consumption, at purchaser's prices	...	...	...	...	...	...	...	...	...	...	...	
Equals: VALUE ADDED, GROSS, at basic prices	12867.0	12668.0	13470.0	14213.0	15135.0	17107.0	19342.0	22352.0	23835.0	24996.0	28077.0	
Compensation of employees	2383.0	2324.0	2491.0	2718.0	2869.0	3269.0	3441.0	3596.0	3807.0	4010.0	4556.0	
Taxes on production and imports, less Subsidies	5.0	4.0	5.0	4.0	7.0	7.0	8.0	9.0	10.0	10.0	12.0	
Taxes on production and imports	5.0	4.0	5.0	4.0	7.0	7.0	8.0	9.0	10.0	10.0	12.0	
Taxes on products	...	...	...	...	...	...	...	...	...	...	...	
Other taxes on production	5.0	4.0	5.0	4.0	7.0	7.0	8.0	9.0	10.0	10.0	12.0	
Less: Subsidies	...	...	...	...	...	...	...	...	...	...	...	
OPERATING SURPLUS, GROSS [a]	10479.0	10340.0	10975.0	11491.0	12260.0	13831.0	15893.0	18748.0	20018.0	20976.0	23509.0	
MIXED INCOME, GROSS	...	...	...	...	...	...	...	...	...	...	...	

	2001	2002	2003	2004	2005	2006	2007	2008	2009	2010	2011	2012
Series	**100**											
Less: Consumption of fixed capital	307.0	304.0	318.0	332.0	339.0	342.0	363.0	384.0	407.0	426.0	491.0	
OPERATING SURPLUS, NET [b]	10172.0	10036.0	10656.0	11159.0	11921.0	13489.0	15530.0	18364.0	19611.0	20550.0	23018.0	
MIXED INCOME, NET	...	...	...	...	...	...	...	...	...	...	...	
Gross capital formation	...	...	...	...	...	...	...	...	...	...	...	

[a] Includes Mixed Income, Gross.
[b] Includes Mixed Income, Net.

Table 2.3 Output, gross value added, and fixed assets by industries at current prices (ISIC Rev. 3) Fishing (B)

Series 100: 1993 SNA, new sol, Western calendar year — **Data in millions**

	2001	2002	2003	2004	2005	2006	2007	2008	2009	2010	2011	2012
Series	**100**											
Output, at basic prices	...	...	...	...	...	...	...	...	...	...	...	
Less: Intermediate consumption, at purchaser's prices	...	...	...	...	...	...	...	...	...	...	...	
Equals: VALUE ADDED, GROSS, at basic prices	1430.0	1733.0	1426.0	1571.0	2041.0	2099.0	2183.0	2569.0	2554.0	2560.0	3512.0	
Compensation of employees	269.0	310.0	255.0	441.0	363.0	369.0	384.0	454.0	416.0	426.0	592.0	
Taxes on production and imports, less Subsidies	6.0	6.0	5.0	7.0	6.0	7.0	8.0	10.0	11.0	11.0	13.0	
Taxes on production and imports	6.0	6.0	5.0	7.0	6.0	7.0	8.0	10.0	11.0	11.0	13.0	
Taxes on products	...	...	...	...	...	...	...	...	...	...	...	
Other taxes on production	6.0	6.0	5.0	7.0	6.0	7.0	8.0	10.0	11.0	11.0	13.0	
Less: Subsidies	...	...	...	...	...	...	...	...	...	...	...	
OPERATING SURPLUS, GROSS [a]	1155.0	1418.0	1166.0	1123.0	1672.0	1723.0	1791.0	2106.0	2127.0	2123.0	2907.0	
MIXED INCOME, GROSS	...	...	...	...	...	...	...	...	...	...	...	
Less: Consumption of fixed capital	206.0	237.0	195.0	265.0	308.0	323.0	336.0	397.0	364.0	365.0	508.0	
OPERATING SURPLUS, NET [b]	949.0	1181.0	971.0	858.0	1364.0	1400.0	1455.0	1709.0	1763.0	1758.0	2399.0	
MIXED INCOME, NET	...	...	...	...	...	...	...	...	...	...	...	
Gross capital formation	...	...	...	...	...	...	...	...	...	...	...	

[a] Includes Mixed Income, Gross.
[b] Includes Mixed Income, Net.

Table 2.3 Output, gross value added, and fixed assets by industries at current prices (ISIC Rev. 3) Mining and quarrying (C)

Series 100: 1993 SNA, new sol, Western calendar year — **Data in millions**

	2001	2002	2003	2004	2005	2006	2007	2008	2009	2010	2011	2012
Series	**100**											
Output, at basic prices	...	...	...	...	...	...	...	...	...	...	...	
Less: Intermediate consumption, at purchaser's prices	...	...	...	...	...	...	...	...	...	...	...	
Equals: VALUE ADDED, GROSS, at basic prices	9312.0	10961.0	12929.0	18264.0	23139.0	35248.0	38413.0	39267.0	37376.0	46535.0	56220.0	

	2001	2002	2003	2004	2005	2006	2007	2008	2009	2010	2011	2012
Series	**100**											
Compensation of employees	2810.0	2775.0	2957.0	3223.0	3304.0	3745.0	4091.0	4319.0	4211.0	5094.0	6123.0	
Taxes on production and imports, less Subsidies	36.0	21.0	22.0	20.0	64.0	81.0	87.0	86.0	98.0	101.0	123.0	
Taxes on production and imports	36.0	21.0	22.0	20.0	64.0	81.0	87.0	86.0	98.0	101.0	123.0	
Taxes on products	...	...	...	...	...	...	...	...	...	...	...	
Other taxes on production	36.0	21.0	22.0	20.0	64.0	81.0	87.0	86.0	98.0	101.0	123.0	
Less: Subsidies	...	...	...	...	...	...	...	...	...	...	...	
OPERATING SURPLUS, GROSS [a]	6466.0	8165.0	9950.0	15021.0	19770.0	31421.0	34231.0	34854.0	33067.0	41340.0	49974.0	
MIXED INCOME, GROSS	...	...	...	...	...	...	...	...	...	...	...	
Less: Consumption of fixed capital	667.0	700.0	711.0	995.0	1321.0	1885.0	2042.0	2222.0	2056.0	2597.0	3204.0	
OPERATING SURPLUS, NET [b]	5799.0	7465.0	9239.0	14026.0	18449.0	29536.0	32193.0	32641.0	31011.0	38743.0	46770.0	
MIXED INCOME, NET	...	...	...	...	...	...	...	...	...	...	...	
Gross capital formation	...	...	...	...	...	...	...	...	...	...	...	

[a] Includes Mixed Income, Gross.
[b] Includes Mixed Income, Net.

Table 2.3 Output, gross value added, and fixed assets by industries at current prices (ISIC Rev. 3) Manufacturing (D)

Series 100: 1993 SNA, new sol, Western calendar year

Data in millions

	2001	2002	2003	2004	2005	2006	2007	2008	2009	2010	2011	2012
Series	**100**											
Output, at basic prices	...	...	...	...	...	...	...	...	...	...	...	
Less: Intermediate consumption, at purchaser's prices	...	...	...	...	...	...	...	...	...	...	...	
Equals: VALUE ADDED, GROSS, at basic prices	27737.0	28954.0	30352.0	35373.0	39077.0	44234.0	49035.0	54921.0	51667.0	59809.0	67140.0	
Compensation of employees	7289.0	7531.0	7794.0	8293.0	8511.0	8969.0	9648.0	10063.0	10522.0	11420.0	12765.0	
Taxes on production and imports, less Subsidies	180.0	138.0	148.0	134.0	364.0	443.0	488.0	520.0	581.0	593.0	715.0	
Taxes on production and imports	180.0	138.0	148.0	134.0	364.0	443.0	488.0	520.0	581.0	593.0	715.0	
Taxes on products	...	...	...	...	...	...	...	...	...	...	...	
Other taxes on production	180.0	138.0	148.0	134.0	364.0	443.0	488.0	520.0	581.0	593.0	715.0	
Less: Subsidies	...	...	...	...	...	...	...	...	...	...	...	
OPERATING SURPLUS, GROSS [a]	20268.0	21285.0	22409.0	26946.0	30202.0	34823.0	38898.0	44337.0	40564.0	47796.0	53668.0	
MIXED INCOME, GROSS	...	...	...	...	...	...	...	...	...	...	...	
Less: Consumption of fixed capital	2756.0	2904.0	2997.0	3543.0	3844.0	4464.0	4845.0	5161.0	5296.0	5655.0	6453.0	
OPERATING SURPLUS, NET [b]	17512.0	18381.0	19412.0	23403.0	26358.0	30359.0	34053.0	39176.0	35268.0	42141.0	47215.0	
MIXED INCOME, NET	...	...	...	...	...	...	...	...	...	...	...	
Gross capital formation	...	...	...	...	...	...	...	...	...	...	...	

[a] Includes Mixed Income, Gross.
[b] Includes Mixed Income, Net.

Table 2.3 Output, gross value added, and fixed assets by industries at current prices (ISIC Rev. 3) Electricity, gas and water supply (E)

Series 100: 1993 SNA, new sol, Western calendar year — **Data in millions**

	2001	2002	2003	2004	2005	2006	2007	2008	2009	2010	2011	2012
Series	**100**											
Output, at basic prices	...	...	...	...	...	...	...	...	...	...	...	
Less: Intermediate consumption, at purchaser's prices	...	...	...	...	...	...	...	...	...	...	...	
Equals: VALUE ADDED, GROSS, at basic prices	4334.0	4442.0	4651.0	4895.0	5379.0	5656.0	6011.0	6539.0	7440.0	7758.0	8619.0	
Compensation of employees	624.0	628.0	666.0	713.0	725.0	775.0	803.0	832.0	921.0	1008.0	1119.0	
Taxes on production and imports, less Subsidies	29.0	17.0	19.0	17.0	121.0	165.0	182.0	210.0	239.0	248.0	299.0	
Taxes on production and imports	29.0	17.0	19.0	17.0	121.0	165.0	182.0	210.0	239.0	248.0	299.0	
Taxes on products	...	...	...	...	...	...	...	...	...	...	...	
Other taxes on production	29.0	17.0	19.0	17.0	121.0	165.0	182.0	210.0	239.0	248.0	299.0	
Less: Subsidies	...	...	...	...	...	...	...	...	...	...	...	
OPERATING SURPLUS, GROSS [a]	3681.0	3796.0	3965.0	4164.0	4533.0	4715.0	5025.0	5497.0	6280.0	6502.0	7201.0	
MIXED INCOME, GROSS	...	...	...	...	...	...	...	...	...	...	...	
Less: Consumption of fixed capital	1110.0	1138.0	1200.0	1255.0	1458.0	1466.0	1558.0	1696.0	1705.0	1821.0	2019.0	
OPERATING SURPLUS, NET [b]	2571.0	2658.0	2765.0	2909.0	3075.0	3249.0	3467.0	3801.0	4575.0	4681.0	5182.0	
MIXED INCOME, NET	...	...	...	...	...	...	...	...	...	...	...	
Gross capital formation	...	...	...	...	...	...	...	...	...	...	...	

[a] Includes Mixed Income, Gross.
[b] Includes Mixed Income, Net.

Table 2.3 Output, gross value added, and fixed assets by industries at current prices (ISIC Rev. 3) Construction (F)

Series 100: 1993 SNA, new sol, Western calendar year — **Data in millions**

	2001	2002	2003	2004	2005	2006	2007	2008	2009	2010	2011	2012
Series	**100**											
Output, at basic prices	...	...	...	...	...	...	...	...	...	...	...	
Less: Intermediate consumption, at purchaser's prices	...	...	...	...	...	...	...	...	...	...	...	
Equals: VALUE ADDED, GROSS, at basic prices	9882.0	10737.0	11561.0	12885.0	14214.0	17122.0	20395.0	24112.0	27082.0	32690.0	34802.0	
Compensation of employees	2943.0	3197.0	3711.0	4137.0	4563.0	5471.0	7045.0	8329.0	9200.0	10669.0	11761.0	
Taxes on production and imports, less Subsidies	132.0	54.0	57.0	52.0	152.0	198.0	253.0	305.0	345.0	373.0	453.0	
Taxes on production and imports	132.0	54.0	57.0	52.0	152.0	198.0	253.0	305.0	345.0	373.0	453.0	
Taxes on products	...	...	...	...	...	...	...	...	...	...	...	
Other taxes on production	132.0	54.0	57.0	52.0	152.0	198.0	253.0	305.0	345.0	373.0	453.0	
Less: Subsidies	...	...	...	...	...	...	...	...	...	...	...	
OPERATING SURPLUS, GROSS [a]	6807.0	7486.0	7792.0	8697.0	9498.0	11452.0	13097.0	15478.0	17537.0	21648.0	22588.0	
MIXED INCOME, GROSS	...	...	...	...	...	...	...	...	...	...	...	
Less: Consumption of fixed capital	660.0	717.0	782.0	871.0	975.0	1184.0	1439.0	1701.0	1880.0	2096.0	2091.0	

	2001	2002	2003	2004	2005	2006	2007	2008	2009	2010	2011	2012
Series	**100**											
OPERATING SURPLUS, NET [b]	6147.0	6769.0	7010.0	7826.0	8524.0	10268.0	11658.0	13777.0	15657.0	19552.0	20497.0	
MIXED INCOME, NET	...	...	...	...	...	...	...	...	...	...	...	
Gross capital formation	...	...	...	...	...	...	...	...	...	...	...	

[a] Includes Mixed Income, Gross.
[b] Includes Mixed Income, Net.

Table 2.3 Output, gross value added, and fixed assets by industries at current prices (ISIC Rev. 3) Wholesale retail trade, repair of motor vehicles, motorcycles, etc.; hotels and restaurants (G+H)

Series 100: 1993 SNA, new sol, Western calendar year **Data in millions**

	2001	2002	2003	2004	2005	2006	2007	2008	2009	2010	2011	2012
Series	**100**											
Output, at basic prices	...	...	...	...	...	...	...	...	...	...	...	
Less: Intermediate consumption, at purchaser's prices	...	...	...	...	...	...	...	...	...	...	...	
Equals: VALUE ADDED, GROSS, at basic prices	33688.0	35130.0	36661.0	39898.0	42538.0	48365.0	53798.0	62113.0	66655.0	76022.0	85773.0	
Compensation of employees	4936.0	5401.0	5661.0	6087.0	6223.0	6847.0	7290.0	7862.0	8454.0	9266.0	10716.0	
Taxes on production and imports, less Subsidies	286.0	113.0	124.0	110.0	145.0	183.0	213.0	260.0	309.0	335.0	442.0	
Taxes on production and imports	286.0	113.0	124.0	110.0	145.0	183.0	213.0	260.0	309.0	335.0	442.0	
Taxes on products	...	...	...	...	...	...	...	...	...	...	...	
Other taxes on production	286.0	113.0	124.0	110.0	145.0	183.0	213.0	260.0	309.0	335.0	442.0	
Less: Subsidies	...	...	...	...	...	...	...	...	...	...	...	
OPERATING SURPLUS, GROSS [a]	28466.0	29616.0	30876.0	33700.0	36169.0	41335.0	46295.0	53991.0	57892.0	66421.0	74615.0	
MIXED INCOME, GROSS	...	...	...	...	...	...	...	...	...	...	...	
Less: Consumption of fixed capital	651.0	689.0	748.0	781.0	866.0	981.0	1090.0	1259.0	1411.0	1582.0	1768.0	
OPERATING SURPLUS, NET [b]	27815.0	28927.0	30128.0	32919.0	35303.0	40354.0	45205.0	52732.0	56481.0	64839.0	72847.0	
MIXED INCOME, NET	...	...	...	...	...	...	...	...	...	...	...	
Gross capital formation	...	...	...	...	...	...	...	...	...	...	...	

[a] Includes Mixed Income, Gross.
[b] Includes Mixed Income, Net.

Table 2.3 Output, gross value added, and fixed assets by industries at current prices (ISIC Rev. 3) Transport, storage and communications (I)

Series 100: 1993 SNA, new sol, Western calendar year **Data in millions**

	2001	2002	2003	2004	2005	2006	2007	2008	2009	2010	2011	2012
Series	**100**											
Output, at basic prices	...	...	...	...	...	...	...	...	...	...	...	
Less: Intermediate consumption, at purchaser's prices	...	...	...	...	...	...	...	...	...	...	...	
Equals: VALUE ADDED, GROSS, at basic prices	14991.0	15406.0	16747.0	18226.0	20075.0	22772.0	28622.0	32210.0	34114.0	37701.0	42717.0	
Compensation of employees	3640.0	3678.0	3912.0	3953.0	3980.0	4013.0	5020.0	5173.0	5490.0	6429.0	7314.0	

	2001	2002	2003	2004	2005	2006	2007	2008	2009	2010	2011	2012
Series	**100**											
Taxes on production and imports, less Subsidies	51.0	19.0	20.0	21.0	132.0	155.0	201.0	239.0	273.0	286.0	343.0	
Taxes on production and imports	51.0	19.0	20.0	21.0	132.0	155.0	201.0	239.0	273.0	286.0	343.0	
Taxes on products	...	...	...	...	...	...	...	...	...	...	...	
Other taxes on production	51.0	19.0	20.0	21.0	132.0	155.0	201.0	239.0	273.0	286.0	343.0	
Less: Subsidies	...	...	...	...	...	...	...	...	...	...	...	
OPERATING SURPLUS, GROSS [a]	11300.0	11708.0	12815.0	14252.0	15963.0	18605.0	23401.0	26798.0	28351.0	30986.0	35060.0	
MIXED INCOME, GROSS	...	...	...	...	...	...	...	...	...	...	...	
Less: Consumption of fixed capital	2626.0	2709.0	2960.0	3246.0	3591.0	4143.0	5214.0	5868.0	6539.0	7380.0	8083.0	
OPERATING SURPLUS, NET [b]	8674.0	8999.0	9855.0	11006.0	12372.0	14462.0	18187.0	20930.0	21812.0	23606.0	26977.0	
MIXED INCOME, NET	...	...	...	...	...	...	...	...	...	...	...	
Gross capital formation	...	...	...	...	...	...	...	...	...	...	...	

[a] Includes Mixed Income, Gross.
[b] Includes Mixed Income, Net.

Table 2.3 Output, gross value added, and fixed assets by industries at current prices (ISIC Rev. 3) Financial intermediation; real estate, renting and business activities (J+K)

Series 100: 1993 SNA, new sol, Western calendar year — **Data in millions**

	2001	2002	2003	2004	2005	2006	2007	2008	2009	2010	2011	2012
Series	**100**											
Output, at basic prices	...	...	...	...	...	...	...	...	...	...	...	
Less: Intermediate consumption, at purchaser's prices	...	...	...	...	...	...	...	...	...	...	...	
Equals: VALUE ADDED, GROSS, at basic prices	26600.0	28536.0	30046.0	31810.0	34442.0	37806.0	41844.0	47277.0	51617.0	56568.0	62561.0	
Compensation of employees	5812.0	6120.0	6299.0	6477.0	6963.0	7981.0	8851.0	9397.0	9947.0	10679.0	12196.0	
Taxes on production and imports, less Subsidies	255.0	195.0	208.0	209.0	227.0	257.0	294.0	350.0	400.0	409.0	450.0	
Taxes on production and imports	255.0	195.0	208.0	209.0	227.0	257.0	294.0	350.0	400.0	409.0	450.0	
Taxes on products	...	...	...	...	...	...	...	...	...	...	...	
Other taxes on production	255.0	195.0	208.0	209.0	227.0	257.0	294.0	350.0	400.0	409.0	450.0	
Less: Subsidies	...	...	...	...	...	...	...	...	...	...	...	
OPERATING SURPLUS, GROSS [a]	20533.0	22221.0	23539.0	25124.0	27252.0	29568.0	32699.0	37530.0	41270.0	45480.0	49915.0	
MIXED INCOME, GROSS	...	...	...	...	...	...	...	...	...	...	...	
Less: Consumption of fixed capital	1894.0	2023.0	2031.0	2037.0	2060.0	2164.0	2528.0	2741.0	2965.0	3187.0	2906.0	
OPERATING SURPLUS, NET [b]	18639.0	20198.0	21508.0	23087.0	25192.0	27404.0	30171.0	34789.0	38305.0	42293.0	47009.0	
MIXED INCOME, NET	...	...	...	...	...	...	...	...	...	...	...	
Gross capital formation	...	...	...	...	...	...	...	...	...	...	...	

[a] Includes Mixed Income, Gross.
[b] Includes Mixed Income, Net.

Table 2.3 Output, gross value added, and fixed assets by industries at current prices (ISIC Rev. 3) Public administration and defense; compulsory social security (L)

Series 100: 1993 SNA, new sol, Western calendar year **Data in millions**

	2001	2002	2003	2004	2005	2006	2007	2008	2009	2010	2011	2012
Series	**100**											
Output, at basic prices	...	...	...	...	...	...	...	...	...	...	...	
Less: Intermediate consumption, at purchaser's prices	...	...	...	...	...	...	...	...	...	...	...	
Equals: VALUE ADDED, GROSS, at basic prices	14211.0	15044.0	16274.0	17474.0	19249.0	20970.0	21630.0	23922.0	27108.0	28051.0	30294.0	
Compensation of employees	12026.0	12844.0	14125.0	15156.0	16806.0	18426.0	19382.0	21666.0	24777.0	25781.0	27930.0	
Taxes on production and imports, less Subsidies	165.0	160.0	172.0	226.0	258.0	276.0	281.0	346.0	472.0	503.0	605.0	
Taxes on production and imports	165.0	160.0	172.0	226.0	258.0	276.0	281.0	346.0	472.0	503.0	605.0	
Taxes on products	...	...	...	...	...	...	...	...	...	...	...	
Other taxes on production	165.0	160.0	172.0	226.0	258.0	276.0	281.0	346.0	472.0	503.0	605.0	
Less: Subsidies	...	...	...	...	...	...	...	...	...	...	...	
OPERATING SURPLUS, GROSS	2020.0	2041.0	1978.0	2093.0	2185.0	2267.0	1966.0	1910.0	1859.0[a]	1767.0[a]	1759.0[a]	
MIXED INCOME, GROSS	...	...	...	...	...	...	...	...	...	...	...	
Less: Consumption of fixed capital	2020.0	2041.0	1978.0	2093.0	2185.0	2267.0	1966.0	1910.0	1859.0	1767.0	1759.0	
OPERATING SURPLUS, NET	...	...	...	...	...	...	...	...	...	...	...	
MIXED INCOME, NET	...	...	...	...	...	...	...	...	...	...	...	
Gross capital formation	...	...	...	...	...	...	...	...	...	...	...	

[a] Includes Mixed Income, Gross.

Table 2.3 Output, gross value added, and fixed assets by industries at current prices (ISIC Rev. 3) Education; health and social work; other community, social and personal services (M+N+O)

Series 100: 1993 SNA, new sol, Western calendar year **Data in millions**

	2001	2002	2003	2004	2005	2006	2007	2008	2009	2010	2011	2012
Series	**100**											
Output, at basic prices	...	...	...	...	...	...	...	...	...	...	...	
Less: Intermediate consumption, at purchaser's prices	...	...	...	...	...	...	...	...	...	...	...	
Equals: VALUE ADDED, GROSS, at basic prices	17053.0	17899.0	19352.0	20562.0	21614.0	23356.0	25153.0	27615.0	30093.0	32651.0	35406.0	
Compensation of employees	3679.0	3935.0	4206.0	4479.0	4667.0	5028.0	5393.0	5643.0	6124.0	6652.0	7238.0	
Taxes on production and imports, less Subsidies	64.0	31.0	35.0	31.0	72.0	82.0	92.0	107.0	118.0	131.0	147.0	
Taxes on production and imports	64.0	31.0	35.0	31.0	72.0	82.0	92.0	107.0	118.0	131.0	147.0	
Taxes on products	...	...	...	...	...	...	...	...	...	...	...	
Other taxes on production	64.0	31.0	35.0	31.0	72.0	82.0	92.0	107.0	118.0	131.0	147.0	
Less: Subsidies	...	...	...	...	...	...	...	...	...	...	...	
OPERATING SURPLUS, GROSS [a]	13309.0	13933.0	15112.0	16052.0	16876.0	18246.0	19668.0	21865.0	23851.0	25868.0	28021.0	
MIXED INCOME, GROSS	...	...	...	...	...	...	...	...	...	...	...	
Less: Consumption of fixed capital	1239.0	1259.0	1356.0	1418.0	1487.0	1600.0	1735.0	1914.0	2091.0	2273.0	2471.0	

	2001	2002	2003	2004	2005	2006	2007	2008	2009	2010	2011	2012
Series	**100**											
OPERATING SURPLUS, NET [b]	12070.0	12674.0	13756.0	14635.0	15389.0	16646.0	17933.0	19951.0	21760.0	23595.0	25550.0	
MIXED INCOME, NET	...	...	...	...	...	...	...	...	...	...	...	
Gross capital formation	...	...	...	...	...	...	...	...	...	...	...	

[a] Includes Mixed Income, Gross.
[b] Includes Mixed Income, Net.

Table 2.3 Output, gross value added, and fixed assets by industries at current prices (ISIC Rev. 3) Private households with employed persons (P)

Series 100: 1993 SNA, new sol, Western calendar year **Data in millions**

	2001	2002	2003	2004	2005	2006	2007	2008	2009	2010	2011	2012
Series	**100**											
Output, at basic prices	...	...	...	...	...	...	...	...	...	...	...	
Less: Intermediate consumption, at purchaser's prices	...	...	...	...	...	...	...	...	...	...	...	
Equals: VALUE ADDED, GROSS, at basic prices	1219.0	1252.0	1321.0	1382.0	1436.0	1517.0	1586.0	1741.0	1881.0	2032.0	2197.0	
Compensation of employees	1139.0	1174.0	1235.0	1300.0	1349.0	1427.0	1491.0	1633.0	1764.0	1907.0	2063.0	
Taxes on production and imports, less Subsidies	8.0	8.0	8.0	7.0	9.0	10.0	11.0	13.0	14.0	15.0	16.0	
Taxes on production and imports	8.0	8.0	8.0	7.0	9.0	10.0	11.0	13.0	14.0	15.0	16.0	
Taxes on products	...	...	...	...	...	...	...	...	...	...	...	
Other taxes on production	8.0	8.0	8.0	7.0	9.0	10.0	11.0	13.0	14.0	15.0	16.0	
Less: Subsidies	...	...	...	...	...	...	...	...	...	...	...	
OPERATING SURPLUS, GROSS [a]	73.0	70.0	78.0	75.0	78.0	81.0	84.0	95.0	103.0	110.0	118.0	
MIXED INCOME, GROSS	...	...	...	...	...	...	...	...	...	...	...	
Less: Consumption of fixed capital	73.0	70.0	78.0	75.0	78.0	81.0	84.0	95.0	103.0	110.0	118.0	
OPERATING SURPLUS, NET	...	...	...	...	...	...	...	...	...	...	...	
MIXED INCOME, NET	...	...	...	...	...	...	...	...	...	...	...	
Gross capital formation	...	...	...	...	...	...	...	...	...	...	...	

[a] Includes Mixed Income, Gross.

Philippines

Source

Reply to the United Nations national accounts questionnaire from the National Statistical Coordination Board (NSCB), Manila.

General

The National Statistical Coordination Board (NSCB) is tasked, among others, with the development, compilation and maintenance of the Philippine System of National Accounts (PSNA). The NSCB was created in 1987 as the highest policy-making and coordinating body on statistical matters by virtue of Executive Order (EO) 121, "Reorganizing and Strengthening the Philippine Statistical System (PSS) and for Other Purposes."

The current PSNA follows the prescribed statistical standards and concepts of the 1993 United Nations System of National Accounts (UNSNA) and to a limited extent, the 2008 SNA. It also applies the following standard classification systems: the Philippine Standard Industrial Classification (PSIC), based on the International Standard Industry Classification (ISIC) Rev.3.1 for all economic activities in the country; the Philippine Standard Commodity Classification (PSCC), based on the Standard International Trade Commodity (SITC) Rev.3; and the Philippine Central Product Classification (PCPC), based on the United Nations' Central Product Classification (UN-CPC) Version 1.1 for the detailed classification of products and external and domestic commodities that enter the Philippine trade as well as Philippine Classification of Individual Consumption by Purpose (PCOICOP) for the classification of household final consumption expenditures.

The official estimates of the national accounts are published on a quarterly and annual basis in "the National Accounts of the Philippines" with a time lag of two months after the reference quarter for the 1st to 3rd quarter estimates and one month after the reference quarter for the 4th quarter estimates. The public is duly informed of the schedule of releases of the national accounts and its related accounts for the current year through the Advance Release Calendar (ARC) which is uploaded on the NSCB website (http://www.nscb.gov.ph/sna/schedule.asp) at the beginning of the year.

The quarterly PSNA compiles the GDP using two approaches, the production approach or by industrial origin, and the expenditure approach. The third approach, the income approach is used to compile the Income and Outlay Accounts on an annual basis.

Regional dimensions are available both for the production and expenditure accounts through the Gross Regional Domestic Product (GRDP) and the Gross Regional Domestic Expenditure (GRDE), which are likewise compiled on an annual basis.

However, both the GDP income approach and the regional accounts following the present revised series and at base year 2000 is still on-going activities. These are scheduled for release in June 2012 for the GDP by income approach, July 2012 for the GRDP and August 2012 for the GRDE.

But recognizing the need for sub-regional accounts in regional planning and development, the NSCB has embarked on the pilot compilation of the Provincial Product Accounts (PPA) in the provinces of Palawan for benchmark years 1988 and 1994 and Guimaras, covering the period 2000-2004. The NSCB has strategized the development of the PPA as a demand-driven activity in partnership with Local Government Units (LGUs). Given the limited financial and manpower resources of the NSCB, priority is being given to interested LGUs who are willing to invest their own resources for the PPA and are committed to support its institutionalization in their respective localities.

The production and expenditure accounts are expressed at current and constant prices. The growth rate of GDP is determined from the production side of the accounts as data support on production is stronger and more reliable.

Hence, a Statistical Discrepancy is reported as a residual item of the expenditure accounts.

The Statistical Discrepancy (SD) is the difference between the GDP level from the production and the expenditure accounts. Statistical Discrepancy occurs as a result of the independent process of compiling the production and expenditure accounts, the use of different data sources and variations in the quality of data. The combination of survey and other measurement errors likewise contribute to the difference between the estimates. The practice of showing the SD in the PSNA is a way of reflecting transparency in the estimates.

The NSCB maintains a link series of the national accounts: the annual series starts from 1946 onwards; the quarterly series from 1981; the GRDP from 1975; and GRDE from 1988. Work on the linking of the series for the annual, quarterly as well as for the annual regional accounts is still on-going activities with scheduled releases mentioned earlier.

Methodology:

Expenditure Approach

GDP by expenditure is the sum of the final uses of goods and services in the economy, valued at purchaser's prices. Final uses refer to the final consumption of households and non-profit institutions serving households Household Final Consumption Expenditure (HFCE); Government Final Consumption Expenditure (GFCE); gross fixed capital formation (GFCF) and for exports (net of exports) to the rest of the world. Gross Fixed Capital Formation consists of fixed capital formation and Changes in Inventories. Fixed capital formation is composed of expenditures on Construction; Durable Equipment; Breeding Stocks and Orchard Development; and Intellectual Property Products. Benchmark estimates of Household Final Consumption Expenditure (HFCE) consider the structure of the latest Family Income and Expenditure Survey (FIES) of the National Statistics Office (NSO), which is conducted every three years.

For quarterly estimates, HFCE adopts extrapolation using the trend (or 1+G) of the gross output-classified-according-to-HFCE-sub-component each sub-component of HFCE to be able to derive its corresponding estimates. The chosen estimate of each sub-component was either deflated (if estimate started at current prices) or inflated (if the estimate started at constant prices) using the appropriate CPI to derive the constant or current prices.

GFCE is the sum of the estimate for public administration and defence including compulsory social security schemes on the production side and the government's total expenditures. Estimates of quarterly expenditures for the national and local governments and social security are extrapolated using the trend of the Department of Budget and Management (DBM) report of the quarterly cash disbursement for MOOE of the national government. Annual and quarterly benchmarks were estimated once the Commission on Audit (COA)'s annual financial reports for national and local governments are available. Investments on Durable Equipment originating from domestic and foreign sources utilize the commodity flow approach for the quarterly estimates. The Foreign Trade Statistics (FTS) and the QSPBI in Manufacturing from the National Statistics Office (NSO), provide the basic data for imported and local durable equipment, respectively. Investments in Construction are estimated as the sum of the gross value of private and public construction and transfer costs. Public construction includes construction in progress and land improvements of the national and local governments and government corporations. Estimates on Public Construction are extrapolated using the trend of the value of actual cash disbursements from DBM. For private construction, gross value is estimated as the sum of the value of physical accomplishments of residential and non-residential construction based on the data on building permits from the NSO.

Annual estimates of Exports and Imports are built up from quarterly estimates. Exports and Imports of Goods adopt the direct estimation method based on the reported data of the NSO's Foreign Trade Statistics. The value of gold demonetized by the Bangko Sentral ng Pilipinas (BSP) is excluded in the Exports of Goods. Both Exports and Imports of Goods are valued at Free on Board (FOB). Meanwhile Exports and Imports of Services use the Balance of Payment (BOP) data except for Travel wherein data are sourced from the Department of Tourism (DOT). The compilation of the Philippine BOP has adopted the Balance of Payment Manual 5 (BPM5) starting CY 2000.

However, there are still some items in the BOP that cannot be readily used for national accounting due to the limitations of its source of data. Travel under Import of Services is one item wherein there is a divergence between the BOP and national accounts. Estimate of Travel is based on the trend of tourist receipts/travel tax.

Changes in Inventories are estimated for agriculture, crude and petroleum, general government, government-owned and controlled corporations and all establishments. The first four sub-sectors are estimated using direct estimation while Changes in Inventories for establishments use the fixed ratio of inventory to production based on the Census of Establishments for Business and Industry. Lastly, expenditures on Breeding Stocks and Orchard Development are based on extrapolation using the trend of the composite growths of the value of production of selected crops, livestock, poultry and forestry. The constant price estimates of GFCE, Construction, Changes in Inventories, Export and Import of Goods and Services are derived by deflating the current price estimates by their respective appropriate indices. On the other hand, Durable Equipment adopt the quantity revaluation method where the volume of goods (reported in Gross Kilos) are valued at base year's prices.

Income Approach

The third approach of compiling the GDP is the income approach, where the income generated by factor shares, i.e., the Gross Value Added (GVA) from the production accounts is distributed to the institutional sector to which it accrues. This is shown in the Income and Outlay accounts, through the current receipts and disbursements of the four institutional sectors-financial corporation, non-financial, government corporations, general government and households, unincorporated enterprises including NPISH. The latest Census of Philippine Business and Industry (CPBI), the annual Surveys of Philippine Business and Industry (ASPBI), government reports on financial institutions and public utilities, administrative data sources, financial statements of private corporations and studies on production costs are some of the primary sources of data for the estimation of the factors of production by institutional sector. The estimates of indirect taxes and subsidies are based on the reports of the Commission On Audit (COA), and the Bureau of Internal Revenue (BIR). However, the compilation of GDP by income approach is still an on-going activity which is scheduled for released in June 2012.

Production Approach

GDP by industrial origin (production) is the aggregate of the Gross Value Added (GVA) of all resident producing units in the domestic economy valued at producers' prices. The production side of the accounts consists of three major industries: (1) Agriculture, Hunting, Forestry and Fishing (AFF); (2) Industry; and (3) Services.

Gross Value Added (GVA) by Industrial Origin or by Economic Activity, is estimated for each of the production sectors of the economy, namely: (i) Agriculture, Hunting, Forestry and Fishing; (ii) Mining and Quarrying; (iii) Manufacturing; (iv) Construction; (v) Electricity and Water; (vi) Transportation, Communication and Storage (TCS); (vii) Trade; (viii) Financial Intermediation; (ix) Real Estate, Renting and Business Activities (RERBA); (x) Other Services; and (xi) Public Administration and Defence.

The production side of the accounts uses three major approaches in the estimation of the GVA, namely: a) Direct approach – GVA is derived by deducting the cost of goods and services used up in the process of production (intermediate consumption) from the total value of goods and services (gross output) during the period. This approach is generally used to generate the annual benchmark estimates of the production sectors using data from the latest Censuses and annual Surveys. b) Indirect approach or the use of ICR (intermediate consumption ratio) – When the required data is not sufficient to estimate the GVA using the direct approach, as in the case of the quarterly national accounts, the use of ICR. The GVA for Agriculture, Hunting, Forestry and Fishing; Mining and Quarrying; and Construction are derived using ICR appropriate to the sector. Since the quarterly data differs from the annual benchmark data due to limitations in detail and coverage, the quarterly data for AHFF, Mining and Construction are adjusted for under coverage by applying an under coverage ratio (UCR) relevant to the sector.

The respective ICRs and UCRs are computed from the latest Census of Philippine Business and Industry (CPBI), Census of Agriculture and Fishery (CAF) or the Annual Survey of Philippine Business and Industry (ASPBI); and administrative reports from source agencies. c) Volume/Value Extrapolation – This approach utilizes the use of output indicators to extrapolate the GVA for the quarterly estimates. Public Administration and Defence use the trend of the quarterly cash disbursement of personal services of the national government workers from the Department of Budget and Management (DBM). Estimates on Public Administration and Defence are benchmarked annually and quarterly based on the Commission on Audit (COA) annual financial reports for the national and local governments with lag time of one year from the reference year.

Manufacturing, Electricity and Water, TCS, Trade, Financial Intermediation, Real Estate, Renting and Business Activities and Other Services sectors rely on the trend of revenues from the Monthly Integrated Survey of Selected Industries (MISSI) for Manufacturing and the Quarterly Survey of Philippine Business and Industry (QSPBI) of the National Statistics Office (NSO) supplemented by other indicators to extrapolate the GVA. However, for Ownership of Dwellings (OD) in the ODRE sector, the GVA is based on the trend of stock of residential structures. The current PSNA still uses the fixed base-year method for constant price estimates with 2000 as the base year. AHFF uses the quantity revaluation method while Mining and Quarrying adopts the volume extrapolation method to derive the constant price estimates. Manufacturing and the Services sectors apply the single deflation method using the appropriate price indices. For Electricity and Water and Other Services, specific composite price indices were developed as deflators to estimate the constant prices.

Table 1.1 Gross domestic product by expenditures at current prices

Series 100: 1993 SNA, Philippine peso, Western calendar year — **Data in billions**

	2001	2002	2003	2004	2005	2006	2007	2008	2009	2010	2011	2012
Series	**100**											
	Expenditures of the gross domestic product											
Final consumption expenditure	3294.4	3546.4	3845.6	4295.3	4772.4	5253.7	5704.4	6421.5	6784.8	7317.3	8074.4	8950.5
Household final consumption expenditure [a]	2863.5	3102.4	3381.6	3814.9	4259.1	4678.0	5064.5	5739.6	5993.4	6442.0	7132.6	7837.9
NPISHs final consumption expenditure	...	...	...	...	...	...	...	...	...	...	...	...
General government final consumption expenditure	430.9	443.9	464.0	480.4	513.3	575.7	640.0	681.9	791.4	875.3	941.8	1112.6
Gross capital formation	861.0	1027.3	1045.2	1106.6	1223.6	1129.4	1195.0	1489.2	1331.7	1849.4	1985.9	1950.5
Gross fixed capital formation[b]	810.6	863.5	941.0	1041.6	1129.9	1261.9	1371.6	1518.2	1526.1	1847.8	1817.2	2048.0
Changes in inventories	50.4	163.9	104.2	65.0	93.6	-132.6	-176.6	-29.0	-194.4	1.6	168.7	-97.4
Acquisitions less disposals of valuables	...	...	...	...	...	...	...	...	...	...	...	...
Exports of goods and services	1789.9	1962.6	2144.8	2487.1	2619.5	2921.0	2981.8	2849.9	2587.0	3133.5	3103.0	3254.5
Exports of goods	1599.7	1751.1	1918.4	2167.8	2232.9	2404.1	2298.3	2152.1	1799.7	2259.9	2034.5	2120.2
Exports of services	190.2	211.5	226.3	319.3	386.6	516.9	683.5	697.8	787.3	873.6	1068.5	1134.3
Less: Imports of goods and services	2056.5	2338.0	2487.5	2768.6	2937.8	3032.9	2988.6	3039.7	2677.4	3296.7	3457.1	3590.6
Imports of goods	1703.7	1992.2	2134.8	2395.0	2531.8	2599.7	2504.4	2512.0	2104.8	2635.8	2826.1	2875.9
Imports of services	352.7	345.8	352.6	373.6	406.0	433.2	484.2	527.8	572.6	661.0	630.9	714.7
Plus: Statistical discrepancy	0.0	0.0	0.0	0.0	-0.0	-0.0	-0.0	0.0	0.0	0.0	0.0	0.0
Equals: GROSS DOMESTIC PRODUCT	3888.8	4198.4	4548.1	5120.4	5677.8	6271.2	6892.7	7720.9	8026.1	9003.5	9706.3	10564.9

[a] Includes NPISH final consumption expenditure.
[b] Includes intellectual property products.

Table 1.2 Gross domestic product by expenditures at constant prices

Series 100: 1993 SNA, Philippine peso, Western calendar year **Data in billions**

	2001	2002	2003	2004	2005	2006	2007	2008	2009	2010	2011	2012
Series	**100**											
Base year	**2000**											
	Expenditures of the gross domestic product											
Final consumption expenditure	3093.4	3214.8	3384.2	3570.4	3718.7	3901.0	4091.4	4225.2	4366.2	4516.0	4751.0	5095.6
Household final consumption expenditure [a]	2690.9	2828.3	2983.7	3161.9	3301.8	3439.9	3598.4	3730.9	3817.9	3945.8	4168.9	4442.5
NPISHs final consumption expenditure	...	...	...	...	...	...	...	...	...	...	...	...
General government final consumption expenditure	402.5	386.5	400.4	408.5	416.9	461.1	492.9	494.4	548.3	570.2	582.1	653.1
Gross capital formation	815.4	943.1	938.9	917.9	945.0	802.1	798.3	984.8	899.3	1183.7	1206.8	1168.4
Gross fixed capital formation[b]	769.4	792.1	844.8	863.0	883.3	931.0	979.7	1010.6	992.9	1182.2	1159.0	1280.0
Changes in inventories	46.0	151.0	94.1	54.9	61.7	-128.9	-181.4	-25.8	-93.6	1.4	47.8	-111.7
Acquisitions less disposals of valuables	...	...	...	...	...	...	...	...	...	...	...	...
Exports of goods and services	1709.4	1789.1	1869.8	2108.4	2212.8	2491.6	2659.7	2588.6	2385.8	2886.1	2805.4	3054.1
Exports of goods	1534.5	1600.9	1677.9	1848.9	1919.2	2121.3	2186.9	2139.3	1898.8	2367.5	2199.4	2426.5
Exports of services	174.9	188.3	191.9	259.5	293.6	370.3	472.8	449.2	487.1	518.6	606.1	627.6
Less: Imports of goods and services	1933.8	2128.4	2184.4	2319.7	2395.2	2478.4	2521.1	2561.5	2354.1	2884.3	2854.2	3006.4
Imports of goods	1612.8	1815.5	1885.7	2023.8	2074.1	2117.5	2095.3	2093.1	1887.9	2330.1	2344.0	2415.2
Imports of services	321.1	312.8	298.7	295.9	321.2	360.9	425.8	468.4	466.2	554.2	510.2	591.2
Plus: Statistical discrepancy	-0.0	0.0	0.0	-0.0	-0.0	0.0	0.0	0.0	0.0	0.0	0.0	0.0
Equals: GROSS DOMESTIC PRODUCT	3684.3	3818.7	4008.5	4276.9	4481.3	4716.2	5028.3	5237.1	5297.2	5701.5	5909.0	6311.7

[a] Includes NPISH final consumption expenditure.
[b] Includes intellectual property products.

Table 1.3 Relations among product, income, savings, and net lending aggregates

Series 100: 1993 SNA, Philippine peso, Western calendar year **Data in billions**

	2001	2002	2003	2004	2005	2006	2007	2008	2009	2010	2011	2012
Series	**100**											
GROSS DOMESTIC PRODUCT	3888.8	4198.3	4548.1	5120.4	5677.7	6271.2	6892.7	7720.9	8026.1	9003.5	9706.3	10564.9
Plus: Compensation of employees - from and to the rest of the world, net	...	...	...	...	...	...	...	...	1934.4	2058.3	2129.0	2346.9
Plus: Compensation of employees - from the rest of the world	...	...	...	...	...	...	...	...	1934.4	2058.3	2129.0	2346.9
Less: Compensation of employees - to the rest of the world	...	...	...	...	...	...	...	...	...	...	...	...
Plus: Property income - from and to the rest of the world, net	...	...	...	...	...	...	...	...	-222.3	-209.3	-237.1	-303.0
Plus: Property income - from the rest of the world	...	...	...	...	...	...	...	...	53.7	43.6	58.3	52.5
Less: Property income - to the rest of the world	...	...	...	...	...	...	...	...	276.0	252.9	295.3	355.6
Sum of Compensation of employees and property income - from and to the rest of the world, net	705.2	780.8	1022.8	1184.7	1472.6	1611.9	1741.4	2055.3	1712.1	1849.0	1891.9	2043.8

	2001	2002	2003	2004	2005	2006	2007	2008	2009	2010	2011	2012
Series	**100**											
Plus: Sum of Compensation of employees and property income - from the rest of the world	...	...	...	...	...	...	...	...	1988.1	2101.9	2187.3	2399.4
Less: Sum of Compensation of employees and property income - to the rest of the world	...	...	...	...	...	...	...	...	276.0	252.9	295.3	355.6
Plus: Taxes less subsidies on production and imports - from and to the rest of the world, net	...	...	...	...	...	...	...	...	...	...	...	...
Equals: GROSS NATIONAL INCOME	4594.0	4979.2	5570.9	6305.1	7150.3	7883.1	8634.1	9776.2	10652.5[a]	10852.4	11598.2	12608.7
Plus: Current transfers - from and to the rest of the world, net	...	...	...	...	...	...	...	...	54.2	18.3	53.8	50.4
Plus: Current transfers - from the rest of the world	...	...	...	...	...	...	...	...	84.3	55.8	74.2	73.4
Less: Current transfers - to the rest of the world	...	...	...	...	...	...	...	...	30.1	37.4	20.4	23.1
Equals: GROSS NATIONAL DISPOSABLE INCOME	...	...	...	...	...	...	...	...	10706.7[a]	10870.7	11652.0	12659.1
Less: Final consumption expenditure / Actual final consumption	...	...	...	...	...	...	...	...	6784.8	7317.3	8074.4	8950.5
Equals: SAVING, GROSS	889.5	1055.7	1211.0	1448.1	1637.1	1752.8	2006.0	2282.9	3921.9[a]	3553.4	3577.6	3708.6
Plus: Capital transfers - from and to the rest of the world, net	...	...	...	...	...	...	...	...	7.9	7.7	11.0	10.8
Less: Gross capital formation	...	...	...	...	...	...	...	...	1331.7	1849.4	1985.9	1950.5
Less: Acquisitions less disposals of non-produced non-financial assets	...	...	...	...	...	...	...	...	...	...	...	...
Equals: NET LENDING (+) / NET BORROWING (-) OF THE NATION	...	...	...	...	...	...	...	...	1683.8	1711.7	1602.7	1768.9
	Net values: Gross National Income / Gross National Disposable Income / Saving Gross less Consumption of fixed capital											
Less: Consumption of fixed capital	...	...	...	...	...	...	...	...	882.9	990.4	1009.3	1127.8
Equals: NET NATIONAL INCOME	...	...	...	...	...	...	...	...	9544.6	9862.0	10588.9	11480.9
Equals: NET NATIONAL DISPOSABLE INCOME	...	...	...	...	...	...	...	...	9598.8	9880.4	10642.7	11531.3
Equals: SAVING, NET	...	...	...	...	...	...	...	...	3039.0	2563.0	2568.3	2580.8

[a] Discrepancy between components and total as one or more components have not been revised.

Table 2.1 Value added by industries at current prices (ISIC Rev. 3)

Series 100: 1993 SNA, Philippine peso, Western calendar year

Data in billions

	2001	2002	2003	2004	2005	2006	2007	2008	2009	2010	2011	2012
Series	**100**											
	Industries											
Agriculture, hunting, forestry; fishing	513.4	551.9	577.8	681.3	719.1	775.7	861.4	1022.5	1049.9	1108.7	1235.0	1250.6
Agriculture, hunting, forestry	...	...	...	...	...	...	...	...	871.0	928.6	1052.2	1057.0
Agriculture, hunting and related service activities	...	...	...	...	...	...	...	...	867.3	926.2	1048.3	1053.7
Forestry, logging and related service activities	2.7	1.8	2.1	4.3	4.5	5.1	4.2	3.6	3.8	2.4	3.9	3.2
Fishing	...	...	...	...	...	...	...	...	178.9	180.1	182.8	193.7
Mining and quarrying	22.1	40.0	51.1	54.2	69.6	76.5	93.9	95.4	106.4	128.7	143.0	121.4
Manufacturing	959.2	1036.7	1120.8	1226.3	1365.7	1481.3	1567.7	1760.9	1706.4	1930.8	2047.7	2170.9
Electricity, gas and water supply	156.7	161.9	171.4	191.9	216.6	234.3	251.1	262.8	271.9	321.5	330.3	374.1

	2001	2002	2003	2004	2005	2006	2007	2008	2009	2010	2011	2012
Series	**100**											
Construction	203.6	213.3	228.6	255.9	269.1	308.2	365.5	419.4	460.4	551.2	521.0	618.1
Wholesale, retail trade, repair of motor vehicles, motorcycles and personal and households goods; hotels and restaurants	620.3[a]	663.7[a]	718.2[a]	817.2[a]	931.1[a]	1053.2[a]	1178.8[a]	1316.1[a]	1489.0	1709.0	1857.3	2047.2
Wholesale, retail trade, repair of motor vehicles, motorcycles and personal and household goods	620.3	663.7	718.2	817.2	931.1	1053.2	1178.8	1316.1	1359.5	1563.8	1695.9	1868.4
Hotels and restaurants	...	...	...	...	...	...	...	...	129.5	145.2	161.3	178.8
Transport, storage and communications	263.5	296.8	336.0	395.0	443.5	476.9	514.5	548.9	561.1	586.2	627.3	685.3
Land transport; transport via pipelines, water transport; air transport; Supporting and auxiliary transport activities; activities of travel agencies	...	...	...	...	...	...	...	...	282.9	304.4	337.8	372.3
Post and telecommunications	...	...	...	...	...	...	...	...	278.2	281.8	289.5	312.9
Financial intermediation; real estate, renting and business activities	565.6	611.7	678.5	772.1	894.1	1027.9	1150.4	1316.5	1428.7	1601.5	1789.2	2000.2
Financial intermediation	208.6	225.3	247.5	280.7	334.0	396.9	449.7	499.9	544.5	622.4	684.1	763.7
Real estate, renting and business activities	357.0	386.4	431.0	491.5	560.1	631.0	700.8	816.5	884.1	979.1	1105.1	1236.5
Public administration and defence; compulsory social security	196.6	200.4	207.8	225.7	233.8	260.2	269.3	285.9	323.6	372.3	404.3	455.5
Education; health and social work; other community, social and personal services	387.8[b]	421.9[b]	457.9[b]	500.9[b]	535.1[b]	576.9[b]	640.1[b]	692.7[b]	628.8	693.4	751.2	841.7
Education	...	...	...	...	...	...	...	...	342.1	355.2	385.6	411.6
Health and social work	...	...	...	...	...	...	...	...	114.9	125.5	139.7	158.6
Other community, social and personal services	...	...	...	...	...	...	...	...	171.8	212.7	225.9	271.5
Private households with employed persons	...	...	...	...	...	...	...	...	...	...	...	...
Equals: VALUE ADDED, GROSS, in basic prices [c]	3888.8	4198.3	4548.1	5120.4	5677.7	6271.2	6892.7	7720.9	8026.1	9003.5	9706.3	10564.9
Less: Financial intermediation services indirectly measured (FISIM)	...	...	...	...	...	...	...	...	...	...	...	...
Plus: Taxes less Subsidies on products	...	...	...	...	...	...	...	...	539.5	588.7	635.9	710.4
Plus: Taxes on products	...	...	...	...	...	...	...	...	596.3	645.7	708.6	823.1
Less: Subsidies on products	...	...	...	...	...	...	...	...	56.8	57.0	72.6	112.7
Equals: GROSS DOMESTIC PRODUCT	3888.8	4198.3	4548.1	5120.4	5677.7	6271.2	6892.7	7720.9	8026.1	9003.5	9706.3	10564.9

[a] Excludes Hotels and restaurants.
[b] Includes Hotels and restaurants.
[c] Value Added refers to GDP.

Table 2.2 Value added by industries at constant prices (ISIC Rev. 3)

Series 100: 1993 SNA, Philippine peso, Western calendar year

Data in billions

	2001	2002	2003	2004	2005	2006	2007	2008	2009	2010	2011	2012
Series	**100**											
Base year	**2000**											
Industries												
Agriculture, hunting, forestry; fishing	517.3	534.5	559.5	583.6	596.7	618.5	647.7	668.5	663.7	662.7	679.8	698.9
Agriculture, hunting, forestry	...	...	...	...	...	...	...	...	526.6	526.2	549.3	568.9
Agriculture, hunting and related service activities	...	...	...	...	...	...	...	...	522.7	523.6	545.5	565.1
Forestry, logging and related service activities	3.0	2.2	2.8	4.3	4.4	5.2	3.9	4.0	3.9	2.7	3.8	3.8
Fishing	...	...	...	...	...	...	...	...	137.1	136.4	130.5	130.0
Mining and quarrying	21.3	35.0	39.5	37.6	43.6	43.5	51.6	50.9	59.1	65.9	70.5	72.0
Manufacturing	899.8	927.1	961.3	1011.6	1062.6	1106.1	1145.5	1194.9	1137.5	1264.5	1324.3	1395.7
Electricity, gas and water supply	135.4	138.1	148.3	158.7	160.9	165.6	174.7	186.6	184.9	203.3	204.5	214.9
Construction	189.1	181.5	187.3	198.4	198.2	217.6	249.4	266.8	285.0	325.8	293.9	339.9
Wholesale, retail trade, repair of motor vehicles, motorcycles and personal and household goods; hotels and restaurants	595.6	618.8	650.5	698.8	740.3	784.4	851.9	863.7	966.3	1047.6	1087.7	1169.3
Wholesale, retail trade, repair of motor vehicles, motorcycles and personal and household goods	595.6	618.8	650.5	698.8	740.3	784.4	851.9	863.7	875.6	948.7	980.5	1054.4
Hotels and restaurants	...	...	...	...	...	...	...	...	90.6	98.9	107.2	114.9
Transport, storage and communications	242.9	267.9	300.7	337.0	360.9	376.4	408.1	424.0	423.4	427.8	446.0	482.1
Land transport; transport via piplines, water transport; air transport; Supporting and auxiliary transport activities; activities of travel agencies	...	...	...	...	...	...	...	...	152.0	154.1	165.1	178.8
Post and telecommunications	...	...	...	...	...	...	...	...	271.4	273.7	280.9	303.3
Financial intermediation, real estate, renting and business activities	528.1	545.4	576.1	625.7	676.8	734.8	799.6	848.8	888.2	963.7	1032.6	1113.2
Financial intermediation	194.8	204.8	217.5	232.7	257.3	287.8	317.1	322.7	340.3	374.7	394.4	426.8
Real estate, renting and business activities	333.3	340.6	358.7	393.0	419.5	447.0	482.5	526.1	547.9	588.9	638.2	686.4
Public administration and defence; compulsory social security	187.9	189.5	196.0	210.7	212.1	219.6	222.7	227.2	241.0	255.1	260.0	275.8
Education; health and social work; other community, social and personal services	366.9	380.9	389.2	414.7	429.2	449.8	477.1	505.7	448.0	485.2	509.6	549.7
Education	...	...	...	...	...	...	...	...	256.5	261.8	272.7	277.3
Health and social work	...	...	...	...	...	...	...	...	71.0	75.6	81.8	91.1
Other community, social and personal services	...	...	...	...	...	...	...	...	120.6	147.9	155.1	181.3
Private households with employed persons	...	...	...	...	...	...	...	...	...	...	...	...
Equals: VALUE ADDED, GROSS, in basic prices [a]	3684.3	3818.7	4008.5	4276.9	4481.3	4716.2	5028.3	5237.1	5297.2	5701.5	5909.0	6311.7
Less: Financial intermediation services indirectly measured (FISIM)	...	...	...	...	...	...	...	...	...	...	...	...
Plus: Taxes less Subsidies on products	...	...	...	...	...	...	...	...	...	...	...	...
Equals: GROSS DOMESTIC PRODUCT	3684.3	3818.7	4008.5	4276.9	4481.3	4716.2	5028.3	5237.1	5297.2	5701.5	5909.0	6311.7

[a] Value Added refers to GDP.

Table 2.4 Value added by industries at current prices (ISIC Rev. 4)

Series 100: 1993 SNA, Philippine peso, Western calendar year

Data in billions

	2001	2002	2003	2004	2005	2006	2007	2008	2009	2010	2011	2012
Series	**100**											
Industries												
Agriculture, forestry and fishing	513.4	551.9	577.8	681.3	719.1	775.7	861.4	1022.5	1049.9	1108.7	1235.0	1250.6
Crop and animal production, hunting and related service activities	...	...	...	...	...	...	...	...	867.3	926.2	1048.3	1053.7
Forestry and logging	2.7	1.8	2.1	4.3	4.5	5.1	4.2	3.6	3.8	2.4	3.9	3.2
Fishing and aquaculture	...	...	...	...	...	...	...	...	178.9	180.1	182.8	193.7
Manufacturing, mining and quarrying and other industrial activities	1138.0	1238.7	1343.3	1472.4	1651.9	1792.2	1912.7	2119.1	2084.7	2381.1	2521.1	2666.4
Mining and quarrying	22.1	40.0	51.1	54.2	69.6	76.5	93.9	95.4	106.4	128.7	143.0	121.4
Manufacturing	959.2	1036.7	1120.8	1226.3	1365.7	1481.3	1567.7	1760.9	1706.4	1930.8	2047.7	2170.9
Electricity, gas, steam and air conditioning supply	156.7[a]	161.9[a]	171.4[a]	191.9[a]	216.6[a]	234.3[a]	251.1[a]	262.8[a]	229.9	275.3	279.7	317.0
Water supply; sewerage, waste management and remediation activities	...	...	...	...	...	...	...	...	42.0	46.2	50.6	57.1
Construction	203.6	213.3	228.6	255.9	269.1	308.2	365.5	419.4	460.4	551.2	521.0	618.1
Wholesale and retail trade, transportation and storage, accommodation and food service activities	883.8	960.5	1054.2	1212.1	1374.6	1530.1	1693.3	1864.9	1920.6	2150.0	2323.2	2553.7
Wholesale and retail trade; repair of motor vehicles and motorcycles	620.3	663.7	718.2	817.2	931.1	1053.2	1178.8	1316.1	1359.5	1563.8	1695.9	1868.4
Transportation and storage	263.5	296.8	336.0	395.0	443.5	476.9	514.5	548.9	561.1	586.2	627.3	685.3
Accommodation and food service activities	...	...	...	...	...	...	...	...	...	...	...	...
Information and communication	...	...	...	...	...	...	...	...	...	...	...	...
Financial and insurance activities	208.6	225.3	247.5	280.7	334.0	396.9	449.7	499.9	544.5	622.4	684.1	763.7
Real estate activities	357.0	386.4	431.0	491.5	560.1	631.0	700.8	816.5	884.1	979.1	1105.1	1236.5
Professional, scientific, technical, administrative and support service activities	...	...	...	...	...	...	...	...	...	...	...	...
Public administration and defence, education, human health and social work activities	196.6	200.4	207.8	225.7	233.8	260.2	269.3	285.9	323.6	372.3	404.3	455.5
Public administration and defence; compulsory social security	196.6	200.4	207.8	225.7	233.8	260.2	269.3	285.9	323.6	372.3	404.3	455.5
Education	...	...	...	...	...	...	...	...	...	...	...	...
Human health and social work activities	...	...	...	...	...	...	...	...	...	...	...	...
Other service activities	387.8	421.9	457.9	500.9	535.1	576.9	640.1	692.7	758.3	838.7	912.5	1020.5
Arts, entertainment and recreation	...	...	...	...	...	...	...	...	...	...	...	...
Other service activities [b]	387.8	421.9	457.9	500.9	535.1	576.9	640.1	692.7	758.3	838.7	912.5	1020.5
Private households with employed persons	...	...	...	...	...	...	...	...	...	...	...	...
Equals: VALUE ADDED, GROSS, at basic prices [c]	3888.8	4198.4	4548.1	5120.4	5677.8	6271.2	6892.7	7720.9	8026.1	9003.5	9706.3	10564.9
Less: Financial intermediation services indirectly measured (FISIM)	...	...	...	...	...	...	...	...	...	...	...	...
Plus: Taxes less Subsidies on products	...	...	...	...	...	...	...	...	539.5	588.7	635.9	710.4
Plus: Taxes on products	...	...	...	...	...	...	...	...	596.3	645.7	708.6	823.1

	2001	2002	2003	2004	2005	2006	2007	2008	2009	2010	2011	2012
Series	**100**											
Less: Subsidies on products	...	...	...	...	...	...	...	...	56.8	57.0	72.6	112.7
Equals: GROSS DOMESTIC PRODUCT	3888.8	4198.4	4548.1	5120.4	5677.8	6271.2	6892.7	7720.9	8026.1[d]	9003.5[d]	9706.3[d]	10564.9[d]

[a] Includes industry E (ISIC 4): water supply; sewerage, waste management and remediation services.
[b] Includes Arts, entertainment and recreation (R), and Private households with employed persons (T) of ISIC Revision IV industry classification.
[c] Value Added refers to GDP.
[d] Discrepancy between Value Added, FISIM, Taxes less Subsidies on products, Gross Domestic Product in the amount of Taxes less Subsidies on products.

Table 2.5 Value added by industries at constant prices (ISIC Rev. 4)

Series 100: 1993 SNA, Philippine peso, Western calendar year

Data in billions

	2001	2002	2003	2004	2005	2006	2007	2008	2009	2010	2011	2012
Series	**100**											
Base year	**2000**											
Industries												
Agriculture, forestry and fishing	517.3	534.5	559.5	583.6	596.7	618.5	647.7	668.5	663.7	662.7	679.8	698.9
Crop and animal production, hunting and related service activities	...	...	...	...	...	...	...	...	522.7	523.6	545.5	565.1
Forestry and logging	3.0	2.2	2.8	4.3	4.4	5.2	3.9	4.0	3.9	2.7	3.8	3.8
Fishing and aquaculture	...	...	...	...	...	...	...	...	137.1	136.4	130.5	130.0
Manufacturing, mining and quarrying and other industrial activities	1056.5	1100.1	1149.1	1207.9	1267.1	1315.2	1371.8	1432.4	1381.6	1533.7	1599.4	1682.7
Mining and quarrying	21.3	35.0	39.5	37.6	43.6	43.5	51.6	50.9	59.1	65.9	70.5	72.0
Manufacturing	899.8	927.1	961.3	1011.6	1062.6	1106.1	1145.5	1194.9	1137.5	1264.5	1324.3	1395.7
Electricity, gas, steam and air conditioning supply	135.4[a]	138.1[a]	148.3[a]	158.7[a]	160.9[a]	165.6[a]	174.7[a]	186.6[a]	167.1	184.8	186.0	195.1
Water supply; sewerage, waste management and remediation activities	...	...	...	...	...	...	...	...	17.9	18.5	18.5	19.8
Construction	189.1	181.5	187.3	198.4	198.2	217.6	249.4	266.8	285.0	325.8	293.9	339.9
Wholesale and retail trade, transportation and storage, accommodation and food service activities	838.5	886.7	951.2	1035.9	1101.2	1160.8	1260.0	1287.7	1299.0	1376.5	1426.5	1536.5
Wholesale and retail trade; repair of motor vehicles and motorcycles	595.6	618.8	650.5	698.8	740.3	784.4	851.9	863.7	875.6	948.7	980.5	1054.4
Transportation and storage	242.9	267.9	300.7	337.0	360.9	376.4	408.1	424.0	423.4	427.8	446.0	482.1
Accommodation and food service activities	...	...	...	...	...	...	...	...	...	...	...	...
Information and communication	...	...	...	...	...	...	...	...	...	...	...	...
Financial and insurance activities	194.8	204.8	217.5	232.7	257.3	287.8	317.1	322.7	340.3	374.7	394.4	426.8
Real estate activities	333.3	340.6	358.7	393.0	419.5	447.0	482.5	526.1	547.9	588.9	638.2	686.4
Professional, scientific, technical, administrative and support service activities	...	...	...	...	...	...	...	...	...	...	...	...
Public administration and defence, education, human health and social work activities	187.9	189.5	196.0	210.7	212.1	219.6	222.7	227.2	241.0	255.1	260.0	275.8
Public administration and defence; compulsory social security	187.9	189.5	196.0	210.7	212.1	219.6	222.7	227.2	241.0	255.1	260.0	275.8
Education	...	...	...	...	...	...	...	...	...	...	...	...

	2001	2002	2003	2004	2005	2006	2007	2008	2009	2010	2011	2012
Series	**100**											
Base year	**2000**											
Human health and social work activities	...	...	...	...	...	...	...	...	...	...	...	...
Other service activities	366.9	380.9	389.2	414.7	429.2	449.8	477.1	505.7	538.7	584.1	616.8	664.6
Arts, entertainment and recreation	...	...	...	...	...	...	...	...	...	...	...	...
Other service activities [b]	366.9	380.9	389.2	414.7	429.2	449.8	477.1	505.7	538.7	584.1	616.8	664.6
Private households with employed persons	...	...	...	...	...	...	...	...	...	...	...	...
Equals: VALUE ADDED, GROSS, at basic prices [c]	3684.3	3818.7	4008.5	4276.9	4481.3	4716.2	5028.3	5237.1	5297.2	5701.5	5909.0	6311.7
Less: Financial intermediation services indirectly measured (FISIM)	...	...	...	...	...	...	...	...	...	...	...	...
Plus: Taxes less Subsidies on products	...	...	...	...	...	...	...	...	539.5	588.7	635.9	710.4
Plus: Taxes on products	...	...	...	...	...	...	...	...	596.3	645.7	708.6	823.1
Less: Subsidies on products	...	...	...	...	...	...	...	...	56.8	57.0	72.6	112.7
Equals: GROSS DOMESTIC PRODUCT	3684.3	3818.7	4008.5	4276.9	4481.3	4716.2	5028.3	5237.1	5297.2[d]	5701.5[d]	5909.0[d]	6311.7[d]

[a] Includes industry E (ISIC 4): water supply; sewerage, waste management and remediation services.
[b] Includes Arts, entertainment and recreation (R), and Private households with employed persons (T) of ISIC Revision IV industry classification.
[c] Value Added refers to GDP.
[d] Discrepancy between Value Added, FISIM, Taxes less Subsidies on products, Gross Domestic Product in the amount of Taxes less Subsidies on products.

Table 2.6 Output, gross value added and fixed assets by industries at current prices (ISIC Rev. 4) Total economy

Series 100: 1993 SNA, Philippine peso, Western calendar year — **Data in billions**

	2001	2002	2003	2004	2005	2006	2007	2008	2009	2010	2011	2012
Series	**100**											
Output, at basic prices	7875.8	8493.3	9122.0	10247.2	11367.0	12561.9	13580.4	14976.3	15328.2	17407.1	18615.6	20202.2
Less: Intermediate consumption, at purchaser's prices	3987.0	4295.0	4573.9	5126.7	5689.3	6290.8	6687.7	7255.4	7302.0	8403.6	8909.4	9637.3
Equals: VALUE ADDED, GROSS, at basic prices [a]	3888.8	4198.4	4548.1	5120.4	5677.8	6271.2	6892.7	7720.9	8026.1	9003.5	9706.3	10564.9
Compensation of employees	...	...	...	...	...	...	...	...	1934.4	2058.3	2129.0	2346.9
Taxes on production and imports, less Subsidies	...	...	...	...	...	...	...	...	539.5	588.7	635.9	710.4
Taxes on production and imports	...	...	...	...	...	...	...	...	596.3	645.7	708.6	823.1
Less: Subsidies	...	...	...	...	...	...	...	...	56.8	57.0	72.6	112.7
OPERATING SURPLUS, GROSS	...	...	...	...	...	...	...	...	...	...	...	...
MIXED INCOME, GROSS	...	...	...	...	...	...	...	...	...	...	...	...
Less: Consumption of fixed capital	...	...	...	...	...	...	...	...	882.9	990.4	1009.3	1127.8
OPERATING SURPLUS, NET	...	...	...	...	...	...	...	...	3970.9	4523.3	4613.2	4954.7
MIXED INCOME, NET	...	...	...	...	...	...	...	...	...	...	...	...
Gross capital formation	861.0	1027.3	1045.2	1106.6	1223.6	1129.4	1195.0	1489.2	1331.7	1849.4	1985.9	1950.5
Gross fixed capital formation	810.6	863.5	941.0	1041.6	1129.9	1261.9	1371.6	1518.2	1526.1	1847.8	1817.2	2048.0
Changes in inventories	50.4	163.9	104.2	65.0	93.6	-132.6	-176.6	-29.0	-194.4	1.6	168.7	-97.4
Acquisitions less disposals of valuables	...	...	...	...	...	...	...	...	...	...	...	...

[a] Value Added refers to GDP.

Table 2.6 Output, gross value added and fixed assets by industries at current prices (ISIC Rev. 4) Agriculture, forestry and fishing (A)

Series 100: 1993 SNA, Philippine peso, Western calendar year — **Data in billions**

	2001	2002	2003	2004	2005	2006	2007	2008	2009	2010	2011	2012
Series	**100**											
Output, at basic prices	706.5	753.8	795.6	937.5	994.1	1077.4	1184.0	1409.3	1450.2	1536.5	1702.5	1735.4
Less: Intermediate consumption, at purchaser's prices	193.1	201.9	217.8	256.2	275.0	301.7	322.6	386.8	400.3	427.8	467.5	484.7
Equals: VALUE ADDED, GROSS, at basic prices	513.4	551.9	577.8	681.3	719.1	775.7	861.4	1022.5	1049.9	1108.7	1235.0	1250.6
Compensation of employees	...	...	...	...	...	...	...	...	...	...	...	...
Taxes on production and imports, less Subsidies	...	...	...	...	...	...	...	...	...	...	...	...
OPERATING SURPLUS, GROSS	...	...	...	...	...	...	...	...	...	...	...	...
MIXED INCOME, GROSS	...	...	...	...	...	...	...	...	...	...	...	...
Gross capital formation	...	...	...	...	...	...	...	...	...	...	...	...

Table 2.6 Output, gross value added and fixed assets by industries at current prices (ISIC Rev. 4) Forestry and logging (02)

Series 100: 1993 SNA, Philippine peso, Western calendar year — **Data in billions**

	2001	2002	2003	2004	2005	2006	2007	2008	2009	2010	2011	2012
Series	**100**											
Equals: VALUE ADDED, GROSS, at basic prices	2.7	1.8	2.1	4.3	4.5	5.1	4.2	3.6	3.8	2.4	3.9	3.2
Compensation of employees	...	...	...	...	...	...	...	...	...	...	...	...

Table 2.6 Output, gross value added and fixed assets by industries at current prices (ISIC Rev. 4) Fishing and aquaculture (03)

Series 100: 1993 SNA, Philippine peso, Western calendar year — **Data in billions**

	2001	2002	2003	2004	2005	2006	2007	2008	2009	2010	2011	2012
Series									**100**			
Equals: VALUE ADDED, GROSS, at basic prices									178.9	180.1	182.8	193.7
Compensation of employees									...	...	...	...

Table 2.6 Output, gross value added and fixed assets by industries at current prices (ISIC Rev. 4) Manufacturing, mining and quarrying and other industrial activities (B+C+D+E)

Series 100: 1993 SNA, Philippine peso, Western calendar year | **Data in billions**

	2001	2002	2003	2004	2005	2006	2007	2008	2009	2010	2011	2012
Series	**100**											
Output, at basic prices	3396.5	3700.4	3928.7	4366.8	4877.0	5314.5	5498.7	5936.5	5693.8	6614.4	6945.8	7045.6
Less: Intermediate consumption, at purchaser's prices	2415.1	2623.7	2756.9	3086.3	3441.7	3756.7	3837.1	4080.2	3881.0	4554.9	4755.1	4753.3
Equals: VALUE ADDED, GROSS, at basic prices	1138.0	1238.7	1343.3	1472.4	1651.9	1792.2	1912.7	2119.1	2084.7	2381.1	2521.1	2666.4
Compensation of employees	...	...	...	...	...	...	...	...	...	...	...	...
Taxes on production and imports, less Subsidies	...	...	...	...	...	...	...	...	...	...	...	...
OPERATING SURPLUS, GROSS	...	...	...	...	...	...	...	...	...	...	...	...
MIXED INCOME, GROSS	...	...	...	...	...	...	...	...	...	...	...	...
Gross capital formation	...	...	...	...	...	...	...	...	...	...	...	...

Table 2.6 Output, gross value added and fixed assets by industries at current prices (ISIC Rev. 4) Mining and quarrying (B)

Series 100: 1993 SNA, Philippine peso, Western calendar year | **Data in billions**

	2001	2002	2003	2004	2005	2006	2007	2008	2009	2010	2011	2012
Series	**100**											
Output, at basic prices	34.8	61.1	77.6	81.8	103.2	115.1	143.5	143.3	162.6	200.6	224.7	228.2
Less: Intermediate consumption, at purchaser's prices	12.7	21.1	26.6	27.6	33.6	38.5	49.6	47.9	56.2	71.9	81.6	106.8
Equals: VALUE ADDED, GROSS, at basic prices	22.1	40.0	51.1	54.2	69.6	76.5	93.9	95.4	106.4	128.7	143.0	121.4
Compensation of employees	...	...	...	...	...	...	...	...	...	...	...	...
Taxes on production and imports, less Subsidies	...	...	...	...	...	...	...	...	...	...	...	...
OPERATING SURPLUS, GROSS	...	...	...	...	...	...	...	...	...	...	...	...
MIXED INCOME, GROSS	...	...	...	...	...	...	...	...	...	...	...	...
Gross capital formation	...	...	...	...	...	...	...	...	...	...	...	...

Table 2.6 Output, gross value added and fixed assets by industries at current prices (ISIC Rev. 4) Manufacturing (C)

Series 100: 1993 SNA, Philippine peso, Western calendar year | **Data in billions**

	2001	2002	2003	2004	2005	2006	2007	2008	2009	2010	2011	2012
Series	**100**											
Output, at basic prices	3361.7	3639.3	3851.1	4285.0	4773.8	5199.4	5355.2	5793.2	5531.2	6413.8	6721.1	6817.4
Less: Intermediate consumption, at purchaser's prices	2402.4	2602.6	2730.3	3058.7	3408.1	3718.1	3787.5	4032.3	3824.9	4483.1	4673.4	4646.5
Equals: VALUE ADDED, GROSS, at basic prices	959.2	1036.7	1120.8	1226.3	1365.7	1481.3	1567.7	1760.9	1706.4	1930.8	2047.7	2170.9
Compensation of employees	...	...	...	...	...	...	...	...	...	...	...	...

	2001	2002	2003	2004	2005	2006	2007	2008	2009	2010	2011	2012
Series	**100**											
Taxes on production and imports, less Subsidies	...	...	...	...	...	...	...	...	...	...	...	...
OPERATING SURPLUS, GROSS	...	...	...	...	...	...	...	...	...	...	...	...
MIXED INCOME, GROSS	...	...	...	...	...	...	...	...	...	...	...	...
Gross capital formation	...	...	...	...	...	...	...	...	...	...	...	...

Table 2.6 Output, gross value added and fixed assets by industries at current prices (ISIC Rev. 4) Electricity, gas, steam and air conditioning supply (D)

Series 100: 1993 SNA, Philippine peso, Western calendar year — **Data in billions**

	2001	2002	2003	2004	2005	2006	2007	2008	2009	2010	2011	2012
Series								**100**				
Equals: VALUE ADDED, GROSS, at basic prices								0.0	229.9	275.3	279.7	317.0
Compensation of employees								...	...	...	...	...

Table 2.6 Output, gross value added and fixed assets by industries at current prices (ISIC Rev. 4) Water supply; sewerage, waste management and remediation activities (E)

Series 100: 1993 SNA, Philippine peso, Western calendar year — **Data in billions**

	2001	2002	2003	2004	2005	2006	2007	2008	2009	2010	2011	2012
Series								**100**				
Equals: VALUE ADDED, GROSS, at basic prices								0.0	42.0	46.2	50.6	57.1
Compensation of employees								...	...	...	...	...

Table 2.6 Output, gross value added and fixed assets by industries at current prices (ISIC Rev. 4) Construction (F)

Series 100: 1993 SNA, Philippine peso, Western calendar year — **Data in billions**

	2001	2002	2003	2004	2005	2006	2007	2008	2009	2010	2011	2012
Series	**100**											
Output, at basic prices	366.9	379.4	409.3	459.3	479.9	552.7	639.1	734.4	793.4	951.4	896.5	1064.5
Less: Intermediate consumption, at purchaser's prices	163.3	166.2	180.7	203.4	210.8	244.5	273.6	315.0	333.0	400.2	375.5	446.5
Equals: VALUE ADDED, GROSS, at basic prices	203.6	213.3	228.6	255.9	269.1	308.2	365.5	419.4	460.4	551.2	521.0	618.1
Compensation of employees	...	...	...	...	...	...	...	...	...	...	...	...
Taxes on production and imports, less Subsidies	...	...	...	...	...	...	...	...	...	...	...	...
OPERATING SURPLUS, GROSS	...	...	...	...	...	...	...	...	...	...	...	...
MIXED INCOME, GROSS	...	...	...	...	...	...	...	...	...	...	...	...
Gross capital formation	...	...	...	...	...	...	...	...	...	...	...	...

Table 2.6 Output, gross value added and fixed assets by industries at current prices (ISIC Rev. 4) Wholesale and retail trade, transportation and storage, accommodation and food service activities (G+H+I)

Series 100: 1993 SNA, Philippine peso, Western calendar year **Data in billions**

	2001	2002	2003	2004	2005	2006	2007	2008	2009	2010	2011	2012
Series	**100**											
Output, at basic prices	1432.8	1541.0	1687.2	1958.7	2212.8	2450.9	2711.8	2973.9	3070.9	3438.6	3721.5	4089.6
Less: Intermediate consumption, at purchaser's prices	549.0	580.6	633.0	746.6	838.2	920.8	1018.5	1109.0	1150.3	1288.6	1398.4	1535.9
Equals: VALUE ADDED, GROSS, at basic prices	883.8	960.5	1054.2	1212.1	1374.6	1530.1	1693.3	1864.9	1920.6	2150.0	2323.2	2553.7
Compensation of employees	...	...	...	...	...	...	...	...	...	...	...	...
Taxes on production and imports, less Subsidies	...	...	...	...	...	...	...	...	...	...	...	...
OPERATING SURPLUS, GROSS	...	...	...	...	...	...	...	...	...	...	...	...
MIXED INCOME, GROSS	...	...	...	...	...	...	...	...	...	...	...	...
Gross capital formation	...	...	...	...	...	...	...	...	...	...	...	...

Table 2.6 Output, gross value added and fixed assets by industries at current prices (ISIC Rev. 4) Wholesale and retail trade; repair of motor vehicles and motorcycles (G)

Series 100: 1993 SNA, Philippine peso, Western calendar year **Data in billions**

	2001	2002	2003	2004	2005	2006	2007	2008	2009	2010	2011	2012
Series	**100**											
Output, at basic prices	913.8	964.9	1048.4	1205.4	1370.8	1553.3	1738.0	1935.9	2003.8	2302.5	2496.5	2754.6
Less: Intermediate consumption, at purchaser's prices	293.5	301.2	330.2	388.2	439.6	500.1	559.2	619.8	644.3	738.7	800.6	886.1
Equals: VALUE ADDED, GROSS, at basic prices	620.3	663.7	718.2	817.2	931.1	1053.2	1178.8	1316.1	1359.5	1563.8	1695.9	1868.4
Compensation of employees	...	...	...	...	...	...	...	...	...	...	...	...
Taxes on production and imports, less Subsidies	...	...	...	...	...	...	...	...	...	...	...	...
OPERATING SURPLUS, GROSS	...	...	...	...	...	...	...	...	...	...	...	...
MIXED INCOME, GROSS	...	...	...	...	...	...	...	...	...	...	...	...
Gross capital formation	...	...	...	...	...	...	...	...	...	...	...	...

Table 2.6 Output, gross value added and fixed assets by industries at current prices (ISIC Rev. 4) Transportation and storage (H)

Series 100: 1993 SNA, Philippine peso, Western calendar year **Data in billions**

	2001	2002	2003	2004	2005	2006	2007	2008	2009	2010	2011	2012
Series	**100**											
Output, at basic prices	519.0	576.1	638.9	753.3	842.1	897.6	973.8	1038.0	1067.2	1136.1	1225.0	1335.0
Less: Intermediate consumption, at purchaser's prices	255.6	279.3	302.8	358.4	398.6	420.7	459.3	489.2	506.1	549.9	597.7	649.8
Equals: VALUE ADDED, GROSS, at basic prices	263.5	296.8	336.0	395.0	443.5	476.9	514.5	548.9	561.1	586.2	627.3	685.3
Compensation of employees	...	...	...	...	...	...	...	...	...	...	...	...

	2001	2002	2003	2004	2005	2006	2007	2008	2009	2010	2011	2012
Series	**100**											
Taxes on production and imports, less Subsidies	...	...	...	...	...	...	...	...	...	...	...	...
OPERATING SURPLUS, GROSS	...	...	...	...	...	...	...	...	...	...	...	...
MIXED INCOME, GROSS	...	...	...	...	...	...	...	...	...	...	...	...
Gross capital formation	...	...	...	...	...	...	...	...	...	...	...	...

Table 2.6 Output, gross value added and fixed assets by industries at current prices (ISIC Rev. 4) Financial and insurance activities (K)

Series 100: 1993 SNA, Philippine peso, Western calendar year **Data in billions**

	2001	2002	2003	2004	2005	2006	2007	2008	2009	2010	2011	2012
Series	**100**											
Output, at basic prices	330.0	354.7	379.6	396.6	448.4	576.3	654.4	711.2	768.1	883.2	974.7	1086.4
Less: Intermediate consumption, at purchaser's prices	121.4	129.4	132.1	116.0	114.4	179.4	204.8	211.3	223.6	260.8	290.6	322.7
Equals: VALUE ADDED, GROSS, at basic prices	208.6	225.3	247.5	280.7	334.0	396.9	449.7	499.9	544.5	622.4	684.1	763.7
Compensation of employees	...	...	...	...	...	...	...	...	...	...	...	...
Taxes on production and imports, less Subsidies	...	...	...	...	...	...	...	...	...	...	...	...
OPERATING SURPLUS, GROSS	...	...	...	...	...	...	...	...	...	...	...	...
MIXED INCOME, GROSS	...	...	...	...	...	...	...	...	...	...	...	...
Gross capital formation	...	...	...	...	...	...	...	...	...	...	...	...

Table 2.6 Output, gross value added and fixed assets by industries at current prices (ISIC Rev. 4) Real estate activities (L)

Series 100: 1993 SNA, Philippine peso, Western calendar year **Data in billions**

	2001	2002	2003	2004	2005	2006	2007	2008	2009	2010	2011	2012
Series	**100**											
Output, at basic prices	471.5	508.3	569.0	665.5	757.2	858.7	970.1	1143.4	1238.9	1386.1	1583.7	1783.5
Less: Intermediate consumption, at purchaser's prices	114.5	121.9	138.1	174.1	197.1	227.6	269.3	326.8	354.8	407.0	478.5	547.0
Equals: VALUE ADDED, GROSS, at basic prices	357.0	386.4	431.0	491.5	560.1	631.0	700.8	816.5	884.1	979.1	1105.1	1236.5
Compensation of employees	...	...	...	...	...	...	...	...	...	...	...	...
Taxes on production and imports, less Subsidies	...	...	...	...	...	...	...	...	...	...	...	...
OPERATING SURPLUS, GROSS	...	...	...	...	...	...	...	...	...	...	...	...
MIXED INCOME, GROSS	...	...	...	...	...	...	...	...	...	...	...	...
Gross capital formation	...	...	...	...	...	...	...	...	...	...	...	...

Table 2.6 Output, gross value added and fixed assets by industries at current prices (ISIC Rev. 4) Public administration and defence, education, human health and social work activities (O+P+Q)

Series 100: 1993 SNA, Philippine peso, Western calendar year **Data in billions**

	2001	2002	2003	2004	2005	2006	2007	2008	2009	2010	2011	2012
Series	**100**											
Output, at basic prices	305.3	316.6	332.7	348.5	377.2	415.4	484.9	510.5	599.4	672.2	725.3	1112.6
Less: Intermediate consumption, at purchaser's prices	108.8	116.2	124.9	122.9	143.4	155.2	215.6	224.7	275.7	299.9	321.0	657.1
Equals: VALUE ADDED, GROSS, at basic prices	196.6	200.4	207.8	225.7	233.8	260.2	269.3	285.9	323.6	372.3	404.3	455.5
Compensation of employees	...	...	...	...	...	...	...	...	...	...	...	...
Taxes on production and imports, less Subsidies	...	...	...	...	...	...	...	...	...	...	...	...
OPERATING SURPLUS, GROSS	...	...	...	...	...	...	...	...	...	...	...	...
MIXED INCOME, GROSS	...	...	...	...	...	...	...	...	...	...	...	...
Gross capital formation	...	...	...	...	...	...	...	...	...	...	...	...

Table 2.6 Output, gross value added and fixed assets by industries at current prices (ISIC Rev. 4) Public administration and defence; compulsory social security (O)

Series 100: 1993 SNA, Philippine peso, Western calendar year **Data in billions**

	2001	2002	2003	2004	2005	2006	2007	2008	2009	2010	2011	2012
Series	**100**											
Output, at basic prices	305.3	316.6	332.7	348.5	377.2	415.4	484.9	510.5	599.4	672.2	725.3	1112.6
Less: Intermediate consumption, at purchaser's prices	108.8	116.2	124.9	122.9	143.4	155.2	215.6	224.7	275.7	299.9	321.0	657.1
Equals: VALUE ADDED, GROSS, at basic prices	196.6	200.4	207.8	225.7	233.8	260.2	269.3	285.9	323.6	372.3	404.3	455.5
Compensation of employees	...	...	...	...	...	...	...	...	...	...	...	...
Taxes on production and imports, less Subsidies	...	...	...	...	...	...	...	...	...	...	...	...
OPERATING SURPLUS, GROSS	...	...	...	...	...	...	...	...	...	...	...	...
MIXED INCOME, GROSS	...	...	...	...	...	...	...	...	...	...	...	...
Gross capital formation	...	...	...	...	...	...	...	...	...	...	...	...

Table 3.2 Individual consumption expenditure of households, NPISHs, and general government at current prices

Series 100: 1993 SNA, Philippine peso, Western calendar year **Data in billions**

	2001	2002	2003	2004	2005	2006	2007	2008	2009	2010	2011	2012
Series	**100**											
	Individual consumption expenditure of households											
Food and non-alcoholic beverages	...	...	...	...	...	...	...	...	2544.0	2709.8	3053.3	3343.4
Alcoholic beverages, tobacco and narcotics	...	...	...	...	...	...	...	...	83.8	87.8	91.8	100.9
Clothing and footwear	...	...	...	...	...	...	...	...	89.5	94.9	100.9	108.5
Housing, water, electricity, gas and other fuels	...	...	...	...	...	...	...	...	712.3	805.5	879.3	965.8

	2001	2002	2003	2004	2005	2006	2007	2008	2009	2010	2011	2012
Series	**100**											
Furnishings, household equipment and routine maintenance of the house	...	...	...	...	...	...	...	...	257.8	269.9	291.9	310.2
Health	...	...	...	...	...	...	...	...	141.1	157.1	173.4	199.8
Transport	...	...	...	...	...	...	...	...	663.6	715.7	770.4	837.6
Communication	...	...	...	...	...	...	...	...	216.7	220.2	225.4	247.9
Recreation and culture	...	...	...	...	...	...	...	...	113.0	123.0	129.6	142.9
Education	...	...	...	...	...	...	...	...	239.1	256.8	282.8	302.8
Restaurants and hotels	...	...	...	...	...	...	...	...	219.3	238.0	263.7	291.5
Miscellaneous goods and services	...	...	...	...	...	...	...	...	713.3	763.4	870.0	986.6
Equals: Household final consumption expenditure in domestic market	2863.5	3102.4	3381.6	3814.9	4259.1	4678.0	5064.5	5739.6	5993.4	6442.0	7132.6	7837.9
Plus: Direct purchases abroad by residents	...	...	...	...	...	...	...	...	...	...	...	...
Less: Direct purchases in domestic market by non-residents	...	...	...	...	...	...	...	...	...	...	...	...
Equals: Household final consumption expenditure	2863.5	3102.4	3381.6	3814.9	4259.1	4678.0	5064.5	5739.6	5993.4	6442.0	7132.6	7837.9
	Individual consumption expenditure of non-profit institutions serving households (NPISHs)											
Equals: NPISHs final consumption expenditure	...	...	...	...	...	...	...	...	...	...	...	...
	Individual consumption expenditure of general government											
Equals: Individual consumption expenditure of general government	...	...	...	...	...	...	...	...	...	...	...	...
Equals: Total actual individual consumption	...	...	...	...	...	...	...	...	...	...	...	...

Table 4.1 Total Economy (S.1)

Series 100: 1993 SNA, Philippine peso, Western calendar year — **Data in billions**

	2001	2002	2003	2004	2005	2006	2007	2008	2009	2010	2011	2012
Series	**100**											
	I. Production account - Resources											
Output, at basic prices (otherwise, please specify)	7875.8	8493.3	9122.0	10247.2	11367.0	12561.9	13580.4	14976.3	15328.2[a]	17407.1[a]	18615.6[a]	20202.2[a]
Less: Financial intermediation services indirectly measured (only to be deducted if FISIM is not distributed to uses)	...	...	...	...	...	...	...	...	...	...	...	...
Plus: Taxes less Subsidies on products	...	...	...	...	...	...	...	...	539.5	588.7	645.9[b]	710.4
Plus: Taxes on products	...	...	...	...	...	...	...	...	596.3	645.7	718.6	823.1
Less: Subsidies on products	...	...	...	...	...	...	...	...	56.8	57.0	72.6	112.7
	I. Production account - Uses											
Intermediate consumption, at purchaser's prices	3987.0	4295.0	4573.9	5126.7	5689.3	6290.8	6687.7	7255.4	7302.0	8403.6	8909.4	9637.3
GROSS DOMESTIC PRODUCT	3888.8	4198.3	4548.1	5120.4	5677.7	6271.2	6892.7	7720.9	8026.1	9003.5	9706.3	10564.9
Less: Consumption of fixed capital	...	...	...	...	...	...	...	...	882.9	990.4	1009.3	1127.8
NET DOMESTIC PRODUCT	...	...	...	...	...	...	...	...	7143.3	8013.1	8697.0	9437.1
	II.1.1 Generation of income account - Resources											
GROSS DOMESTIC PRODUCT	3888.8	4198.3	4548.1	5120.4	5677.7	6271.2	6892.7	7720.9	8026.1	9003.5	9706.3	10564.9

	2001	2002	2003	2004	2005	2006	2007	2008	2009	2010	2011	2012
Series	**100**											
	II.1.1 Generation of income account - Uses											
Compensation of employees	...	...	...	...	...	...	...	...	1934.4	2058.3	2129.0	2346.9
Taxes on production and imports, less Subsidies	...	...	...	...	...	...	...	...	539.5	588.7	645.9	710.4
Taxes on production and imports	...	...	...	...	...	...	...	...	596.3	645.7	718.6	823.1
Taxes on products	...	...	...	...	...	...	...	...	...	...	...	...
Other taxes on production	...	...	...	...	...	...	...	...	...	...	...	...
Less: Subsidies	...	...	...	...	...	...	...	...	56.8	57.0	72.6	112.7
Subsidies on products	...	...	...	...	...	...	...	...	...	...	...	...
Other subsidies on production	...	...	...	...	...	...	...	...	...	...	...	...
OPERATING SURPLUS, GROSS	...	...	...	...	...	...	...	...	...	...	...	...
MIXED INCOME, GROSS	...	...	...	...	...	...	...	...	...	...	...	...
	II.1.2 Allocation of primary income account - Resources											
OPERATING SURPLUS, GROSS	...	...	...	...	...	...	...	...	...	...	...	...
MIXED INCOME, GROSS	...	...	...	...	...	...	...	...	...	...	...	...
Compensation of employees	...	...	...	...	...	...	...	...	1934.4	2058.3	2129.0	2346.9
Taxes on production and imports, less Subsidies	...	...	...	...	...	...	...	...	539.5	588.7	645.9	710.4
Taxes on production and imports	...	...	...	...	...	...	...	...	596.3	645.7	718.6	823.1
Taxes on products	...	...	...	...	...	...	...	...	...	...	...	...
Other taxes on production	...	...	...	...	...	...	...	...	...	...	...	...
Less: Subsidies	...	...	...	...	...	...	...	...	56.8	57.0	72.6	112.7
Subsidies on products	...	...	...	...	...	...	...	...	...	...	...	...
Other subsidies on production	...	...	...	...	...	...	...	...	...	...	...	...
Property income	...	...	...	...	...	...	...	...	1063.9	1324.5	1043.9	1087.5
	II.1.2 Allocation of primary income account - Uses											
Property income	...	...	...	...	...	...	...	...	1452.9	1313.1	1467.5	1562.0
GROSS NATIONAL INCOME	4594.0	4979.2	5570.9	6305.1	7150.3	7883.1	8634.1	9776.2	10652.5	10852.4	11598.2	12608.7
	II.2 Secondary distribution of income account - Resources											
GROSS NATIONAL INCOME	4594.0	4979.2	5570.9	6305.1	7150.3	7883.1	8634.1	9776.2	10652.5	10852.4	11598.2	12608.7
Current taxes on income, wealth, etc.	...	...	...	...	...	...	...	...	...	...	...	...
Social contributions	...	...	...	...	...	...	...	...	...	...	...	...
Social benefits other than social transfers in kind	...	...	...	...	...	...	...	...	...	...	...	...
Other current transfers	...	...	...	...	...	...	...	...	384.0	391.9	441.4	389.9
	II.2 Secondary distribution of income account - Uses											
Current taxes on income, wealth, etc.	...	...	...	...	...	...	...	...	...	...	...	...
Social contributions	...	...	...	...	...	...	...	...	...	...	...	...
Social benefits other than social transfers in kind	...	...	...	...	...	...	...	...	...	...	...	...
Other current transfers	...	...	...	...	...	...	...	...	...	...	...	...
GROSS DISPOSABLE INCOME	...	...	...	...	...	...	...	...	...	...	...	...

[a] At producers' prices.
[b] Statistical discrepancy with equivalent items in other tables.

Table 4.4 Financial Corporations (S.12)

Series 10: 1968 SNA, Philippine peso, Western calendar year

Data in billions

	2001	2002	2003	2004	2005	2006	2007	2008	2009	2010	2011	2012
Series	**10**											
I. Production account - Resources												
Output, at basic prices (otherwise, please specify)	...	...	...	...	...	...	...	...				
I. Production account - Uses												
Intermediate consumption, at purchaser's prices	...	...	...	...	...	...	...	...				
VALUE ADDED GROSS, at basic prices	1387.0	1764.5	1864.6	2606.0[a]	2974.3[a]	3245.0[a]	3534.5[a]	3918.1[a]				
Less: Consumption of fixed capital	253.9	260.5	257.4	445.3	497.6	547.6	601.9	661.0				
VALUE ADDED NET, at basic prices	1133.0	1504.0	1607.2	2160.7[b]	2476.7[b]	2697.4[b]	2932.6[b]	3257.1[b]				
II.1.1 Generation of income account - Resources												
VALUE ADDED GROSS, at basic prices	1387.0	1764.5	1864.6	2606.0[a]	2974.3[a]	3245.0[a]	3534.5[a]	3918.1[a]				
II.1.1 Generation of income account - Uses												
Compensation of employees	201.0	570.7	633.8	912.7	1045.3	1171.5	1318.0	1486.3				
Other taxes less Other subsidies on production	144.9	155.9	210.0	281.0[c]	336.1[c]	376.5[c]	351.5[c]	325.8[c]				
Other taxes on production	152.4[d]	165.1[d]	233.8[d]	299.0[d]	361.6[e]	401.2[e]	399.4[e]	420.0[e]				
Less: Other subsidies on production	7.6	9.2	23.8	18.0	25.5	24.7	48.0	94.2				
OPERATING SURPLUS, GROSS	1041.2	1037.9	1020.7	1412.3	1593.0	1696.9	1865.1	2106.0				
II.1.2 Allocation of primary income account - Resources												
OPERATING SURPLUS, GROSS	1041.2	1037.9	1020.7	1412.3	1593.0	1696.9	1865.1	2106.0				
Property income [f]	175.0	81.3	118.5	115.5	129.1	170.3	177.8	194.6				
II.1.2 Allocation of primary income account - Uses												
Property income	327.9[g]	235.7[g]	273.7[g]	268.5[g]	308.8[g]	379.1	381.2	370.3				
BALANCE OF PRIMARY INCOMES	888.3	883.5	865.5	1259.4	1413.2	1488.2	1661.7	1930.3				
II.2 Secondary distribution of income account - Resources												
BALANCE OF PRIMARY INCOMES	888.3	883.5	865.5	1259.4	1413.2	1488.2	1661.7	1930.3				
Social contributions	...	...	...	...	...	...	...	...				
Other current transfers	13.0	12.2	12.7	21.5	15.0	15.6	16.5	17.5				
II.2 Secondary distribution of income account - Uses												
Current taxes on income, wealth, etc.	147.3	110.8	115.3	127.1	146.5	181.5	228.4	259.9				
Social benefits other than social transfers in kind	...	...	...	...	...	...	...	...				
Other current transfers	22.2	15.2	14.8	34.0	17.3	21.3	24.1	26.0				
GROSS DISPOSABLE INCOME	731.7	769.8	748.1	1119.8	1264.4	1300.9	1425.7	1661.9				
II.4.1 Use of disposable income account - Resources												
GROSS DISPOSABLE INCOME	731.7	769.8	748.1	1119.8	1264.4	1300.9	1425.7	1661.9				
II.4.1 Use of disposable income account - Uses												
Adjustment for the change in net equity of households on pension funds	...	...	...	...	...	...	...	...				
SAVING, GROSS	731.7	769.8	748.1	1119.8	1264.4	1300.9	1425.7	1661.9				

	2001	2002	2003	2004	2005	2006	2007	2008	2009	2010	2011	2012
Series	**10**											
	III.1 Capital account - Changes in liabilities and net worth											
SAVING, GROSS	731.7	769.8	748.1	1119.8	1264.4	1300.9	1425.7	1661.9				
Capital transfers, receivable less payable	...	...	...	...	...	...	...	...				
Capital transfers, receivable	...	...	...	...	...	...	...	...				
Less: Capital transfers, payable	...	...	...	...	...	...	...	...				
Equals: CHANGES IN NET WORTH DUE TO SAVING AND CAPITAL TRANSFERS	...	...	...	...	...	...	...	...				
	III.1 Capital account - Changes in assets											
Gross capital formation	...	...	...	...	...	...	...	...				
Gross fixed capital formation	...	...	...	...	...	...	...	...				
Changes in inventories	...	...	...	...	...	...	...	...				
Acquisitions less disposals of valuables	...	...	...	...	...	...	...	...				
Acquisitions less disposals of non-produced non-financial assets	...	...	...	...	...	...	...	...				
NET LENDING (+) / NET BORROWING (-)	...	...	...	...	...	...	...	...				

[a] Value Added refers to GDP.
[b] Value Added net refers to Net Domestic Product
[c] Includes Taxes less subsidies on products.
[d] Excludes import duties and taxes
[e] Includes taxes on products
[f] Refers to property income for private corporations, interest income for public corporations
[g] Refers to interest payments

Table 4.5 General Government (S.13)

Series 10: 1968 SNA, Philippine peso, Western calendar year — **Data in billions**

	2001	2002	2003	2004	2005	2006	2007	2008	2009	2010	2011	2012
Series	**10**											
	I. Production account - Resources											
Output, at basic prices (otherwise, please specify)	...	...	...	...	...	...	...	...				
	I. Production account - Uses											
Intermediate consumption, at purchaser's prices	...	...	...	...	...	...	...	...				
VALUE ADDED GROSS, at basic prices	338.7	362.8	378.6	384.1[a]	416.5[a]	453.8[a]	475.5[a]	522.0[a]				
Less: Consumption of fixed capital	15.5	16.5	18.0	19.4	20.2	22.9	24.3	26.4				
VALUE ADDED NET, at basic prices	323.3	346.3	360.7	364.7[b]	396.3[b]	430.9[b]	451.1[b]	495.6[b]				
	II.1.1 Generation of income account - Resources											
VALUE ADDED GROSS, at basic prices	338.7	362.8	378.6	384.1[a]	416.5[a]	453.8[a]	475.5[a]	522.0[a]				
	II.1.1 Generation of income account - Uses											
Compensation of employees	321.2	342.1	357.8	360.6	384.0	416.4	436.8	479.6				
Other taxes less Other subsidies on production	1.5	3.4	1.6	2.7[c]	10.0[c]	12.3[c]	12.2[c]	13.7[c]				
Other taxes on production	1.5[d]	3.4[d]	1.6[d]	2.7[e]	10.0[f]	12.3[f]	12.1[f]	13.7[f]				
Less: Other subsidies on production	...	...	...	...	...	...	...	...				
OPERATING SURPLUS, GROSS	16.0	17.2	19.2	20.8	22.5	25.1	26.4	28.7				

		2001	2002	2003	2004	2005	2006	2007	2008	2009	2010	2011	2012
Series		**10**											
		II.1.2 Allocation of primary income account - Resources											
OPERATING SURPLUS, GROSS		16.0	17.2	19.2	20.8	22.5	25.1	26.4	28.7				
Taxes on production and imports, less Subsidies		278.5	291.4	318.8	340.8	389.0	497.7	495.4	521.8				
Taxes on production and imports		286.1	300.6	342.5	358.8	414.5	522.4	543.3	616.0				
Taxes on products		...	...	...	...	...	...	...	...				
Other taxes on production		...	...	...	...	...	...	...	...				
Less: Subsidies		7.6	9.2	23.8	18.0	25.5	24.7	48.0	94.2				
Subsidies on products		...	...	...	...	...	...	...	...				
Other subsidies on production		...	...	...	...	...	...	...	...				
Property income	g	105.3	121.2	127.4	173.7	172.2	197.1	257.2	241.7				
		II.1.2 Allocation of primary income account - Uses											
Property income	h	202.8	196.0	234.8	280.1	314.4	326.4	275.3	298.3				
BALANCE OF PRIMARY INCOMES		197.1	233.8	230.5	255.2	269.2	393.5	503.6	494.0				
		II.2 Secondary distribution of income account - Resources											
BALANCE OF PRIMARY INCOMES		197.1	233.8	230.5	255.2	269.2	393.5	503.6	494.0				
Current taxes on income, wealth, etc.		241.4	239.7	251.5	288.9	337.7	388.0	442.6	502.1				
Social contributions		80.1	85.5	92.3	105.8	104.3	113.8	126.4	139.5				
Other current transfers		4.0	2.8	4.2	3.2	3.7	4.2	6.0	6.4				
		II.2 Secondary distribution of income account - Uses											
Current taxes on income, wealth, etc.		...	...	...	...	...	...	...	...				
Social benefits other than social transfers in kind	i	69.2	74.4	80.8	88.4	94.6	99.9	112.1	126.8				
Other current transfers		10.2	6.7	9.8	9.4	6.1	9.3	9.7	11.0				
GROSS DISPOSABLE INCOME		443.2	480.7	487.9	555.2	614.2	790.3	956.9	1004.2				
		II.4.1 Use of disposable income account - Resources											
GROSS DISPOSABLE INCOME		443.2	480.7	487.9	555.2	614.2	790.3	956.9	1004.2				
		II.4.1 Use of disposable income account - Uses											
Final consumption expenditure		444.8	456.9	477.4	492.1	527.0	589.9	653.8	716.5				
Individual consumption expenditure		...	...	...	...	...	...	...	...				
Collective consumption expenditure		...	...	...	...	...	...	...	...				
Adjustment for the change in net equity of households on pension funds		...	...	...	...	...	...	...	...				
SAVING, GROSS		-1.6	23.8	10.5	63.1	87.1	200.3	303.1	287.6				

[a] Value Added refers to GDP.
[b] Value Added net refers to Net Domestic Product
[c] Includes Taxes less subsidies on products.
[d] Excludes import duties and taxes
[e] Excludes import duties and taxes Includes taxes on products
[f] Includes taxes on products
[g] Refers to property income, compulsory fines and fees
[h] Refers to interest on public debt.
[i] Includes social benefits and net casualty insurance premiums

Table 4.6 Households (S.14)

Series 10: 1968 SNA, Philippine peso, Western calendar year

Data in billions

	2001	2002	2003	2004	2005	2006	2007	2008	2009	2010	2011	2012
Series	**10**											
I. Production account - Resources												
Output, at basic prices (otherwise, please specify)	...	...	...	...	...	...	...	...				
I. Production account - Uses												
Intermediate consumption, at purchaser's prices	...	...	...	...	...	...	...	...				
VALUE ADDED GROSS, at basic prices	1804.2	1729.0	2010.2	1881.4[a]	2053.2[a]	2332.4[a]	2637.4[a]	2983.1[a]				
Less: Consumption of fixed capital	46.3	69.9	108.6	93.2	114.1	125.8	137.3	153.5				
VALUE ADDED NET, at basic prices	1757.9	1659.1	1901.5	1788.3[b]	1939.1[b]	2207.2[b]	2500.0[b]	2829.6[b]				
II.1.1 Generation of income account - Resources												
VALUE ADDED GROSS, at basic prices	1804.2	1729.0	2010.2	1881.4[a]	2053.2[a]	2332.4[a]	2637.4[a]	2983.1[a]				
II.1.1 Generation of income account - Uses												
Compensation of employees	391.4	72.0	63.7	72.2	78.5	87.2	95.8	103.7				
Other taxes less Other subsidies on production	30.4	24.5	44.1	57.1[c]	42.8[c]	108.9[c]	131.7[c]	182.3[c]				
Other taxes on production	30.4[d]	24.5[d]	44.1[d]	57.1[e]	42.8[f]	108.9[f]	131.7[f]	182.3[f]				
Less: Other subsidies on production	...	...	...	...	...	...	...	...				
OPERATING SURPLUS, GROSS [g]	1382.4	1632.5	1902.4	1752.1	1931.9	2136.4	2409.9	2697.1				
MIXED INCOME, GROSS	...	...	...	...	...	...	...	...				
II.1.2 Allocation of primary income account - Resources												
OPERATING SURPLUS, GROSS [g]	1382.2	1632.5	1902.4	1752.1	1931.9	2136.4	2409.9	2697.1				
MIXED INCOME, GROSS	...	...	...	...	...	...	...	...				
Compensation of employees	1278.9	1387.6	1525.0	1885.9	2130.7	2382.0	2613.1	3071.7				
Property income [h]	211.7	161.8	225.5	218.8	288.7	278.2	211.0	233.4				
II.1.2 Allocation of primary income account - Uses												
Property income	81.5	80.4	117.4	123.2	142.6	146.1	172.0	176.2				
BALANCE OF PRIMARY INCOMES	2791.2	3101.6	3535.5	3733.5	4208.7	4650.5	5061.9	5826.0				
II.2 Secondary distribution of income account - Resources												
BALANCE OF PRIMARY INCOMES	2791.2	3101.6	3535.5	3733.5	4208.7	4650.5	5061.9	5826.0				
Social contributions	...	...	...	...	...	...	...	...				
Social benefits other than social transfers in kind	70.5	75.6	82.1	90.0	94.6	99.9	112.1	126.8				
Other current transfers	54.3	80.2	84.3	79.6	77.6	77.9	86.1	81.6				
II.2 Secondary distribution of income account - Uses												
Current taxes on income, wealth, etc.	94.1	128.9	136.2	161.8	191.2	206.5	214.3	242.2				
Social contributions	81.4	86.8	93.6	107.1	104.3	113.8	126.4	139.5				
Social benefits other than social transfers in kind	...	...	...	...	...	...	...	...				
Other current transfers	3.2	16.4	18.7	22.0	27.8	27.0	30.5	38.2				
GROSS DISPOSABLE INCOME	2737.3	3025.3	3453.3	3612.2	4057.7	4481.0	4888.9	5614.5				

	2001	2002	2003	2004	2005	2006	2007	2008	2009	2010	2011	2012
Series	**10**											
	II.4.1 Use of disposable income account - Resources											
GROSS DISPOSABLE INCOME	2737.3	3025.3	3453.3	3612.2	4057.7	4481.0	4888.9	5614.5				
Adjustment for the change in net equity of households on pension funds	...	...	...	...	...	...	...	...				
	II.4.1 Use of disposable income account - Uses											
Final consumption expenditure	2565.0	2751.0	2988.2	3346.7	3772.2	4229.5	4611.9	5281.1				
Individual consumption expenditure	...	...	...	...	...	...	...	...				
SAVING, GROSS	172.3	274.3	465.1	265.4	285.5	251.5	277.0	333.4				

[a] Value Added refers to GDP.
[b] Value Added net refers to Net Domestic Product
[c] Includes Taxes less subsidies on products.
[d] Excludes import duties and taxes
[e] Excludes import duties and taxes Includes taxes on products
[f] Includes taxes on products
[g] Includes Mixed Income, Gross.
[h] Refers to interest on public debt and other interest income

Poland

Source
The preparation of annual national accounts statistics in Poland is undertaken by the National Accounts and Finance Division, the Central Statistical Office located in Warsaw. The official estimates are published annually on the internet (www.stat.gov.pl), in "National accounts by institutional sectors and sub-sectors" (CSO), as well as in the annual statistical yearbooks: Concise Statistical Yearbook of Poland and Statistical Yearbook of the Republic of Poland. The concepts, definitions, sources and methods of estimation were described in above-mentioned publications.

In December 2006 a complete methodological inventory on GDP compilation was submitted by central Statistical Office to EUROSTAT. This inventory describes in detail all methods applied in compiling the accounts and presents numerical examples.

General
The estimates shown in tables have been prepared in accordance with the concepts and definitions of System of National Accounts 1993 and European System of Accounts 1995.

Two kinds of revisions of national accounts are conducted: the routine and the cyclic revisions. The routine revisions concern the successive versions of estimation from provisional to final version of national accounts. The routine revisions are regular conducted and are made four times. The cyclic revisions caused by methodological changes, changes in law and other reasons takes place every few years and always comprises full time series- in the case of PNA starting from the data for the year 1995.

In Polish national accounts the constant price calculation is carrying out at previous year prices. For calculation at constant prices the broad range of price data is used.

Methodology:

Overview of GDP Compilation
Gross domestic product is estimated from both the production and expenditure sides. The income approach is calculated independently.

Expenditure Approach
Expenditure approach is the one from the main approaches for GDP estimation. Expenditure components of GDP are calculated separately for final consumption expenditure, for gross capital formation, and for exports less imports.

Household final consumption expenditure is estimated according to COICOP classification scheme. HFCE estimates are independent, complete and consistent with the output approach. It is calculated as a bottom up estimate .Household consumption expenditure is recorded at purchasers' prices. The main data sources for compiling HFCE are: retail statistics based on statistical reports, households budget survey, balance of agricultural products, surveys on travel abroad and on border traffic, balance of payments, administrative sources.

For the government final consumption expenditure estimation the data are obtained from budgetary statistics and supplementary sources for units that are not obliged to provide the budgetary reports. For the social security funds the data are derived from budgetary reporting, accounting data of social insurance institutions, Insurance and Pension Funds Yearbook. GFCE is distributed into individual consumption expenditure and collective consumption expenditure.

Gross fixed capital formation data are elaborated by kind of fixed assets, by kind of activity according to NACE, by institutional sectors as well. All estimates are based on the statistical and budgetary reports. Gross fixed capital formation is valued at purchasers' prices.

The annual data for changes in inventories are based on quarterly estimations. Changes in inventories are estimated at average constant prices of previous year. In order to estimate them at current prices the obtained value of changes in inventories at constant prices in quarterly periods is converted into current prices using quarterly price indices for sale in enterprises' sector (previous year=100). The main data sources are statistical reports.

The main data source for value of exports and imports of goods is the foreign trade statistics compiled by CSO on the basis of custom statistics (data from INTRASTAT and SAD). The value of exports of goods is shown on the FOB basis, while imports of goods – on CIF basis. Data for exports of transport services come from the banking statistics that registers settlements with non-residents and it is increased by the cost of transport rendered by Polish carriers and included in the invoices of trade in goods. For foreign travel data are obtained from Institute of Tourism. Information on other services comes mainly from the statistics provided by banks and from reports received from non-financial corporations involved in trade of services with non-residents. Data sources and methods to calculate the imports of services are the same as in the case of exports.

Every aggregate of expenditure approach is calculated at constant prices using the broad range of price indices. In addition, the data for retail trade and information on quantitative dynamics of purchased goods (food and non-food) and services from Households Budget Survey are used.

Income Approach

For income approach the same data sources are used as in the output approach. Compensation of employees is expressed in gross term: income tax and social contributions payable by employees and employers are included. In general, data sources for calculation are the same as for compilation of gross output and intermediate consumption (statistical reports, budgetary reports supplemented by other sources for units that are not obliged to provide the budgetary reporting, annual report of central bank and reports of commercial banks). Additional adjustments are made for compensation of employees in individual farms, for tips and for hidden economy.

Taxes and subsidies are calculated on accrual basis. Data are derived from administrative sources mainly from budgetary statistics. Gross operating surplus and mixed income do not exist in the bookkeeping system of units in Poland thus gross operating surplus is calculated as a residual item. Mixed income is calculated only for households sector as the difference between gross value added and compensation of employees and other taxes on production.

Production Approach

Production approach is the main approach for estimating GDP. The basic data for compilation of estimates from output approach come from structural business statistics and from other supplementary data sources.

For general government sector data are obtained from budgetary statistics and supplementary sources for units that are not obliged to provide the budgetary reporting. Basic data for compiling the output approach of financial institutions come from the reports on financial results of banks, insurance units and other financial institutions.

Gross output is valued at basic prices. Valuation of gross output is made on the basis of the statistical sources mentioned above. The value of output of the private farms is estimated using the method of direct calculation, i.e. quantity of produced crop and animal products multiplied by their appropriate prices.

Data regarding dwelling stocks is compiled on the basis of the results of general censuses as well as the Population and Housing Census as of 2002 and the balance of dwelling stocks as of 31 December, in each administrative division. Imputed rents are estimated with the User Cost Method according to Commission Decision of 18 July 1995.

Output for private households with employed persons is estimated at the level of compensation of employees. Intermediate consumption is valued at purchasers' prices. These prices include basic prices, transport costs, trade margin and non-deductible taxes on products.

Gross value added is valued at the same prices as gross output – at basic prices. It is calculated as a residual item.

Double deflation is used in output approach. Each element of output approach aggregates is deflated separately using the broad range of price indices.

Table 1.1 Gross domestic product by expenditures at current prices

Series 300: 1993 SNA, Zloty, Western calendar year — **Data in millions**

	2001	2002	2003	2004	2005	2006	2007	2008	2009	2010	2011	2012
Series	**300**											
	Expenditures of the gross domestic product											
Final consumption expenditure	646210.0	685992.0	707815.0	760730.0	801145.0	856020.0	922899.0	1021294.0	1069928.0	1136237.0	1208639.0	1260681.0
Household final consumption expenditure	498981.0	532925.0	546241.0	589390.0	614294.0	652827.0	701556.0	773822.0	809737.0	856184.0	921561.0	962722.0
NPISHs final consumption expenditure	7772.0	8416.0	8748.0	8684.0	9066.0	9486.0	10316.0	11293.0	11299.0	11626.0	12320.0	12982.0
General government final consumption expenditure	139457.0	144651.0	152826.0	162656.0	177785.0	193707.0	211027.0	236179.0	248892.0	268427.0	274758.0	284977.0
Individual consumption expenditure	81472.0	82733.0	87237.0	91265.0	99337.0	108129.0	118024.0	133443.0	143266.0	153523.0	158222.0	164427.0
Collective consumption expenditure	57985.0	61918.0	65589.0	71391.0	78448.0	85578.0	93003.0	102736.0	105626.0	114904.0	116536.0	120550.0
Gross capital formation	161923.0	150588.0	158028.0	185542.0	189445.0	223162.0	287657.0	304848.0	273568.0	297449.0	337076.0	329610.0
Gross fixed capital formation	161277.0	151472.0	153758.0	167158.0	179180.0	208308.0	253729.0	283906.0	284649.0	281320.0	308692.0	309258.0
Changes in inventories	512.0	-1070.0	4021.0	18127.0	9979.0	14670.0	33729.0	20728.0	-11273.0	15924.0	28199.0	20149.0
Acquisitions less disposals of valuables	134.0	186.0	249.0	257.0	286.0	184.0	199.0	214.0	192.0	205.0	185.0	203.0
Exports of goods and services	210919.0	231535.0	280888.0	346631.0	364658.0	427776.0	479606.0	508887.0	530278.0	598369.0	688738.0	736306.0
Exports of goods	170600.0	190540.0	237257.0	297657.0	311959.0	363893.0	400193.0	423712.0	439835.0	499337.0	577332.0	613312.0
Exports of services	40319.0	40995.0	43631.0	48974.0	52699.0	63883.0	79413.0	85175.0	90443.0	99032.0	111406.0	122994.0
Less: Imports of goods and services	239488.0	259537.0	303575.0	368365.0	371946.0	446927.0	513425.0	559521.0	529269.0	615470.0	706326.0	731333.0
Imports of goods	201889.0	220063.0	259533.0	318433.0	320972.0	385361.0	446794.0	486094.0	453188.0	524425.0	609659.0	626511.0
Imports of services	37599.0	39474.0	44042.0	49932.0	50974.0	61566.0	66631.0	73427.0	76081.0	91045.0	96667.0	104822.0
Equals: GROSS DOMESTIC PRODUCT	779564.0	808578.0	843156.0	924538.0	983302.0	1060031.0	1176737.0	1275508.0	1344505.0	1416585.0	1528127.0	1595264.0

Table 1.2 Gross domestic product by expenditures at constant prices

Series 300: 1993 SNA, Zloty, Western calendar year — **Data in millions**

	2001	2002	2003	2004	2005	2006	2007	2008	2009	2010	2011	2012
Series	**300**											
Base year	**2005**											
	Expenditures of the gross domestic product											
Final consumption expenditure	706886.0	728068.2	747635.0	779960.7	801145.0	842984.0	882137.5	936048.4	955218.6	987331.3	1003166.1	1009474.9
Household final consumption expenditure	544107.2	562827.8	574710.1	601948.4	614294.0	644992.0	676690.9	715589.6	730398.5	753457.7	773274.0	779362.4
NPISHs final consumption expenditure	8474.8	8773.5	8928.9	8880.9	9066.0	9450.0	10042.7	10544.1	10384.4	10458.9	10634.3	10819.0

	2001	2002	2003	2004	2005	2006	2007	2008	2009	2010	2011	2012
Series	**300**											
Base year	**2005**											
General government final consumption expenditure	154222.3	156347.8	163952.8	169061.5	177785.0	188542.0	195433.2	209842.5	214349.8	223241.0	219506.8	219611.5
Individual consumption expenditure	90091.4	89416.8	93580.0	94867.3	99337.0	105245.0	109301.8	118561.9	123381.9	127678.5	126404.4	...
Collective consumption expenditure	64130.4	66930.7	70372.5	74194.3	78448.0	83297.0	86131.4	91280.6	90967.8	95562.5	93102.4	...
Gross capital formation	169852.6	157636.3	162823.2	186795.2	189445.0	219994.0	273418.7	284227.8	251522.5	274950.1	305781.2	295651.9
Gross fixed capital formation	168932.2	158323.5	158199.1	168294.5	179180.0	205912.0	242052.5	265278.1	262025.5	260931.9	283092.4	280805.2
Changes in inventories	552.4	-1138.2	4194.1	18227.5	9979.0	13900.0	30598.0	18822.0	-9844.1	13436.7	21443.5	14841.4
Acquisitions less disposals of valuables	144.7	197.7	262.5	262.5	286.0	182.0	191.9	198.6	172.7	180.7	156.9	165.4
Exports of goods and services	247537.8	259479.4	296337.8	337766.7	364658.0	418036.0	456151.9	488314.2	455078.5	510088.3	549391.2	564684.3
Exports of goods	200323.8	213547.9	250992.2	287885.2	311959.0	355036.0	379838.3	409496.9	374514.3	423564.3	456121.1	465575.6
Exports of services	47226.8	45953.5	45369.5	49939.6	52699.0	63000.0	76395.3	78865.7	80311.0	86078.4	92792.1	98793.3
Less: Imports of goods and services	272083.5	279627.3	306574.3	355123.3	371946.0	436477.0	496081.0	535951.0	469314.6	534447.9	563660.3	553372.2
Imports of goods	232873.6	241269.7	260854.1	305075.1	320972.0	375011.0	431498.0	468202.9	401464.1	456386.1	484655.6	470933.8
Imports of services	39506.9	38835.5	45867.9	50113.9	50974.0	61466.0	64446.2	67597.3	67341.4	77481.4	78466.0	82012.4
Equals: GROSS DOMESTIC PRODUCT [a]	854948.8	867290.0	900829.5	948977.0	983302.0	1044537.0	1115411.7	1172593.8	1191687.1	1237861.8	1293823.1	1317952.4

[a] Chain-linked volume measures are presented in this table, thus discrepancies between components and total may exist.

Table 1.3 Relations among product, income, savings, and net lending aggregates

Series 300: 1993 SNA, Zloty, Western calendar year **Data in millions**

	2001	2002	2003	2004	2005	2006	2007	2008	2009	2010	2011	2012
Series	**300**											
GROSS DOMESTIC PRODUCT	779564.0	808578.0	843156.0	924538.0	983302.0	1060031.0	1176737.0	1275508.0	1344505.0	1416585.0	1523245.0	
Plus: Compensation of employees - from and to the rest of the world, net	2950.0	3363.0	4862.0	10804.0	12797.0	14665.0	13883.0	9554.0	9588.0	7443.0	...	
Plus: Compensation of employees - from the rest of the world	3971.0	4451.0	5998.0	13110.0	15127.0	17130.0	17126.0	13539.0	13658.0	12019.0	...	
Less: Compensation of employees - to the rest of the world	1021.0	1088.0	1136.0	2306.0	2330.0	2465.0	3243.0	3985.0	4070.0	4576.0	...	
Plus: Property income - from and to the rest of the world, net	-4867.0	-6098.0	-13046.0	-40508.0	-34381.0	-44879.0	-58924.0	-39300.0	-60256.0	-63659.0	...	
Plus: Property income - from the rest of the world	9745.0	7051.0	7036.0	6691.0	7761.0	10741.0	10558.0	12773.0	6110.0	12052.0	...	
Less: Property income - to the rest of the world	14612.0	13149.0	20082.0	47199.0	42142.0	55620.0	69482.0	52073.0	66366.0	75711.0	...	
Sum of Compensation of employees and property income - from and to the rest of the world, net	-1917.0	-2735.0	-8184.0	-26230.0[a]	-19246.0[a]	-26958.0[a]	-42037.0[a]	-25730.0[a]	-46593.0[a]	-54142.0[a]	-63391.0[a]	
Plus: Sum of Compensation of employees and property income - from the rest of the world	13716.0	11502.0	13034.0	25167.0[b]	27796.0[b]	33803.0[b]	33904.0[b]	33885.0[b]	27021.0[b]	29503.0[b]	30885.0[b]	
Less: Sum of Compensation of employees and property income - to the rest of the world	15633.0	14237.0	21218.0	51397.0[c]	47042.0[c]	60761.0[c]	75941.0[c]	59615.0[c]	73614.0[c]	83645.0[c]	94276.0[c]	
Plus: Taxes less subsidies on production and imports - from and to the rest of the world, net	...	...	...	3474.0	2338.0	3256.0	3004.0	4016.0	4075.0	2073.0	...	
Plus: Taxes less subsidies on production and imports - from the rest of the world	...	...	...	...	...	...	...	...	...	...	...	

	2001	2002	2003	2004	2005	2006	2007	2008	2009	2010	2011	2012
Series	**300**											
Less: Taxes less subsidies on production and imports - to the rest of the world [d]	...	...	...	-3474.0	-2338.0	-3256.0	-3004.0	-4016.0	-4075.0	-2073.0	...	
Equals: GROSS NATIONAL INCOME	777647.0	805843.0	834972.0	898308.0	964056.0	1033073.0	1134700.0	1249778.0	1297912.0	1362443.0	1459854.0	
Plus: Current transfers - from and to the rest of the world, net	11827.0	13381.0	16466.0	-370.0	4515.0	3593.0	4426.0	4508.0	3969.0	10403.0	12349.0	
Plus: Current transfers - from the rest of the world	15299.0	17061.0	20667.0	8270.0	16274.0	17392.0	18493.0	19740.0	25781.0	26228.0	27917.0	
Less: Current transfers - to the rest of the world	3472.0	3680.0	4201.0	8640.0	11759.0	13799.0	14067.0	15232.0	21812.0	15825.0	15568.0	
Equals: GROSS NATIONAL DISPOSABLE INCOME	789474.0	819224.0	851438.0	897938.0	968571.0	1036666.0	1139126.0	1254286.0	1301881.0	1372846.0	1472203.0	
Less: Final consumption expenditure / Actual final consumption	646210.0	685992.0	707815.0	760730.0	801145.0	856020.0	922899.0	1021294.0	1069928.0	1136237.0	1207585.0	
Equals: SAVING, GROSS	143264.0	133232.0	143623.0	137208.0	167426.0	180646.0	216227.0	232992.0	231953.0	236609.0	264618.0	
Plus: Capital transfers - from and to the rest of the world, net	310.0	-25.0	-178.0	1855.0	3202.0	9783.0	11316.0	8764.0	16363.0	22196.0	27472.0	
Plus: Capital transfers - from the rest of the world	458.0	190.0	233.0	2382.0	3818.0	11222.0	13058.0	11070.0	17604.0	23969.0	32658.0	
Less: Capital transfers - to the rest of the world	148.0	215.0	411.0	527.0	616.0	1439.0	1742.0	2306.0	1241.0	1773.0	5186.0	
Less: Gross capital formation	161923.0	150588.0	158028.0	185542.0	189445.0	223162.0	287657.0	304848.0	273568.0	297449.0	333187.0	
Less: Acquisitions less disposals of non-produced non-financial assets	...	...	...	...	...	...	...	...	...	0.0	0.0	
Equals: NET LENDING (+) / NET BORROWING (-) OF THE NATION	-18349.0	-17381.0	-14583.0	-46479.0	-18817.0	-32733.0	-60114.0	-63092.0	-25252.0	-38644.0	-41097.0	
	Net values: Gross National Income / Gross National Disposable Income / Saving Gross less Consumption of fixed capital											
Less: Consumption of fixed capital	106103.0	109819.0	115537.0	121469.0	126936.0	134952.0	142219.0	145746.0	148493.0	151142.0	156742.0	
Equals: NET NATIONAL INCOME	671544.0	696024.0	719435.0	776839.0	837120.0	898121.0	992481.0	1104032.0	1149419.0	1211301.0	1303112.0	
Equals: NET NATIONAL DISPOSABLE INCOME	683371.0	709405.0	735901.0	776469.0	841635.0	901714.0	996907.0	1108540.0	1153388.0	1221704.0	1315461.0	
Equals: SAVING, NET	37161.0	23413.0	28086.0	15739.0	40490.0	45694.0	74008.0	87246.0	83460.0	85467.0	107876.0	

[a] Refers to net primary income (i.e. net compensation of employee, net property income and net taxes less subsidies on production from/to the rest of the world).
[b] Refers to primary income receivable from the rest of the world.
[c] Refers to primary income payable to the rest of the world.
[d] Refers to net taxes less subsidies on production and imports (to/from the rest of the world).

Table 2.4 Value added by industries at current prices (ISIC Rev. 4)

Series 300: 1993 SNA, Zloty, Western calendar year — **Data in millions**

	2001	2002	2003	2004	2005	2006	2007	2008	2009	2010	2011	2012
Series	**300**											
	Industries											
Agriculture, forestry and fishing	35428.0	32438.0	32745.0	41819.0	39795.0	39640.0	44112.0	41290.0	43060.0	46637.0	54089.0	56654.0
Manufacturing, mining and quarrying and other industrial activities	153893.0	157355.0	175123.0	206269.0	212752.0	229422.0	251117.0	268378.0	293422.0	300296.0	332498.0	350317.0
Manufacturing	109629.0	110834.0	125461.0	150652.0	153824.0	167920.0	185493.0	197199.0	215039.0	209714.0	233641.0	248678.0
Construction	51175.0	48363.0	46174.0	47853.0	54470.0	62775.0	76253.0	85582.0	96624.0	101026.0	110539.0	104978.0
Wholesale and retail trade, transportation and storage, accommodation and food service activities	181391.0	187934.0	189123.0	204953.0	221300.0	238903.0	258506.0	278593.0	306889.0	325587.0	343651.0	367645.0
Information and communication	26717.0	31146.0	32515.0	38040.0	37333.0	38306.0	41188.0	46150.0	48602.0	47448.0	49538.0	51748.0

	2001	2002	2003	2004	2005	2006	2007	2008	2009	2010	2011	2012
Series	**300**											
Financial and insurance activities	31980.0	30193.0	31529.0	34863.0	38160.0	42566.0	54787.0	59236.0	46926.0	55110.0	59314.0	65028.0
Real estate activities	44919.0	49623.0	52110.0	53239.0	55707.0	59207.0	62433.0	67704.0	67362.0	70094.0	75322.0	81435.0
Professional, scientific, technical, administrative and support service activities	45804.0	45364.0	46837.0	50002.0	54463.0	59307.0	67203.0	76582.0	84253.0	85944.0	93059.0	100722.0
Public administration and defence, education, human health and social work activities	99409.0	106791.0	111586.0	117354.0	121887.0	129460.0	140140.0	155497.0	168387.0	175928.0	183712.0	193081.0
Other service activities	24539.0	25865.0	26615.0	27273.0	30462.0	31593.0	33703.0	37540.0	39305.0	39581.0	40664.0	41806.0
Equals: VALUE ADDED, GROSS, at basic prices	695255.0	715072.0	744357.0	821665.0	866329.0	931179.0	1029442.0	1116552.0	1194830.0	1247651.0	1342386.0	1413414.0
Less: Financial intermediation services indirectly measured (FISIM)	...	...	...	...	...	...	...	...	...	...	...	...
Plus: Taxes less Subsidies on products	84309.0	93506.0	98799.0	102873.0	116973.0	128852.0	147295.0	158956.0	149675.0	168934.0	185741.0	181850.0
Plus: Taxes on products	86450.0	95000.0	99812.0	108252.0	119921.0	131808.0	151582.0	164244.0	154744.0	173578.0	190276.0	185325.0
Less: Subsidies on products	2141.0	1494.0	1013.0	5379.0	2948.0	2956.0	4287.0	5288.0	5069.0	4644.0	4535.0	3475.0
Equals: GROSS DOMESTIC PRODUCT	779564.0	808578.0	843156.0	924538.0	983302.0	1060031.0	1176737.0	1275508.0	1344505.0	1416585.0	1528127.0	1595264.0

Table 2.5 Value added by industries at constant prices (ISIC Rev. 4)

Series 300: 1993 SNA, Zloty, Western calendar year **Data in millions**

	2001	2002	2003	2004	2005	2006	2007	2008	2009	2010	2011	2012
Series	**300**											
Base year	**2005**											
Industries												
Agriculture, forestry and fishing	35592.1	36049.2	37078.3	39673.6	39795.0	38073.0	36515.1	35890.1	39166.2	37468.1	38011.2	38103.9
Manufacturing, mining and quarrying and other industrial activities	170902.1	170630.0	185450.0	205581.0	212752.0	233731.0	257057.0	272447.7	275799.7	296023.5	320257.8	323682.9
Manufacturing	114276.6	116137.2	130236.0	148171.6	153824.0	178668.0	201777.2	217753.5	225879.6	242448.8	264718.6	269622.2
Construction	56199.5	51957.3	50522.0	51089.8	54470.0	61262.0	67027.6	70909.3	79106.2	84145.3	94048.6	93348.4
Wholesale and retail trade, transportation and storage, accommodation and food service activities	196754.6	201871.2	202796.0	210357.9	221300.0	233899.0	244515.9	255448.4	261635.8	272756.3	276257.2	284262.3
Information and communication	27947.1	31970.2	33190.6	38613.0	37333.0	39025.0	41553.6	45480.1	46996.8	46944.6	49936.5	51767.1
Financial and insurance activities	31186.6	30630.7	32840.3	35446.3	38160.0	40138.0	52297.5	60328.2	43748.0	46175.7	47996.4	50665.9
Real estate activities	52124.1	55304.8	56959.8	56012.1	55707.0	57738.0	56333.7	55774.3	57552.1	60415.9	62352.6	63824.5
Professional, scientific, technical, administrative and support service activities	49372.6	47840.9	49461.8	51997.4	54463.0	57739.0	64317.4	70038.7	74414.8	74957.1	79451.4	80398.2
Public administration and defence, education, human health and social work activities	111094.3	114141.9	119626.1	120538.4	121887.0	124314.0	127718.1	130023.8	134096.0	134803.2	136047.6	137907.8
Other service activities	28792.5	29882.5	30134.4	29433.5	30462.0	32005.0	32131.6	34324.4	33981.5	32722.7	32820.3	32975.2
Equals: VALUE ADDED, GROSS, at basic prices	759640.3	769819.0	797654.6	838860.9	866329.0	917924.0	979425.9	1029610.2	1048430.0	1087737.2	1136270.1	1156186.4
Less: Financial intermediation services indirectly measured (FISIM)	...	...	...	...	...	...	...	...	...	...	...	...
Plus: Taxes less Subsidies on products	95256.7	97445.2	103086.2	109985.1	116973.0	126613.0	135983.3	142980.3	143304.1	150293.4	157742.5	161963.3
Plus: Taxes on products	100627.9	102102.7	107398.0	115599.3	119921.0	129528.0	140056.7	147832.8	147742.8	154274.2	161501.0	164721.2

	2001	2002	2003	2004	2005	2006	2007	2008	2009	2010	2011	2012
Series	**300**											
Base year	**2005**											
Less: Subsidies on products	5927.1	4072.3	2747.5	5487.0	2948.0	2915.0	4076.7	4872.6	4448.7	4045.9	3835.1	2840.6
Equals: GROSS DOMESTIC PRODUCT [a]	854948.8	867290.0	900829.5	948977.0	983302.0	1044537.0	1115411.7	1172593.8	1191687.1	1237861.8	1293823.1	1317952.4

[a] Chain-linked volume measures are presented in this table, thus discrepancies between components and total may exist.

Table 2.6 Output, gross value added and fixed assets by industries at current prices (ISIC Rev. 4) Total economy

Series 300: 1993 SNA, Zloty, Western calendar year — **Data in millions**

	2001	2002	2003	2004	2005	2006	2007	2008	2009	2010	2011	2012
Series	**300**											
Output, at basic prices	1533367.0	1567168.0	1649864.0	1854941.0	1952502.0	2156192.0	2438084.0	2643647.0	...	...	...	...
Less: Intermediate consumption, at purchaser's prices	838112.0	852096.0	905507.0	1033276.0	1086173.0	1225013.0	1408642.0	1527095.0	...	...	...	...
Equals: VALUE ADDED, GROSS, at basic prices	695255.0	715072.0	744357.0	821665.0	866329.0	931179.0	1029442.0	1116552.0	1194830.0	1247651.0	1342386.0	1413414.0
Compensation of employees	319824.0	316553.0	322046.0	334464.0	352169.0	376527.0	418206.0	476010.0	495789.0	521499.0	548926.0	...
Taxes on production and imports, less Subsidies	9803.0	10199.0	9395.0	6915.0	8799.0	12263.0	8769.0	9671.0	11751.0	14616.0	15153.0	...
OPERATING SURPLUS, GROSS [a]	365628.0	388320.0	412916.0	480286.0	505361.0	542389.0	602467.0	630871.0	687290.0	711536.0	773425.0	...
MIXED INCOME, GROSS	...	...	...	...	...	...	...	...	...	...	...	...
Less: Consumption of fixed capital	106103.0	109819.0	115537.0	121469.0	126936.0	134952.0	142219.0	145746.0	148493.0	151142.0	156742.0	...
OPERATING SURPLUS, NET [b]	259525.0	278501.0	297379.0	358817.0	378425.0	407437.0	460248.0	485125.0	538797.0	560394.0	616683.0	...
MIXED INCOME, NET	...	...	...	...	...	...	...	...	...	...	...	...
Gross capital formation	161923.0	150588.0	158028.0	185542.0	189445.0	223162.0	287657.0	304848.0	273568.0	297449.0	337076.0	329610.0
Gross fixed capital formation	161277.0	151472.0	153758.0	167158.0	179180.0	208308.0	253729.0	283906.0	284649.0	281320.0	308692.0	309258.0
Changes in inventories	512.0	-1070.0	4021.0	18127.0	9979.0	14670.0	33729.0	20728.0	-11273.0	15924.0	28199.0	20149.0
Acquisitions less disposals of valuables	134.0	186.0	249.0	257.0	286.0	184.0	199.0	214.0	192.0	205.0	185.0	203.0
Employment (average, in 1000 persons)	14194.8	13766.3	13606.1	13760.2	14057.0	14503.9	15155.9	15739.8	15803.4	15876.3	16034.5	15777.3

[a] Includes Mixed Income, Gross.
[b] Includes Mixed Income, Net.

Table 2.6 Output, gross value added and fixed assets by industries at current prices (ISIC Rev. 4) Agriculture, forestry and fishing (A)

Series 300: 1993 SNA, Zloty, Western calendar year — **Data in millions**

	2001	2002	2003	2004	2005	2006	2007	2008	2009	2010	2011	2012
Series	**300**											
Equals: VALUE ADDED, GROSS, at basic prices	35428.0	32438.0	32745.0	41819.0	39795.0	39640.0	44112.0	41290.0	43060.0	46637.0	54089.0	56654.0
Compensation of employees	7864.0	7395.0	7242.0	7521.0	7705.0	7016.0	7452.0	7755.0	8239.0	7929.0	9034.0	...
Employment (average, in 1000 persons)	...	...	...	2469.3	2426.6	2276.3	2218.6	2198.6	2098.8	2039.6	2032.6	1965.8

Table 2.6 Output, gross value added and fixed assets by industries at current prices (ISIC Rev. 4) Manufacturing, mining and quarrying and other industrial activities (B+C+D+E)

Series 300: 1993 SNA, Zloty, Western calendar year — **Data in millions**

	2001	2002	2003	2004	2005	2006	2007	2008	2009	2010	2011	2012
Series	**300**											
Equals: VALUE ADDED, GROSS, at basic prices	153893.0	157355.0	175123.0	206269.0	212752.0	229422.0	251117.0	268378.0	293422.0	300296.0	332498.0	350317.0
Compensation of employees	92560.0	89032.0	90877.0	95898.0	99304.0	105971.0	117445.0	134349.0	132344.0	138166.0	142545.0	...
Employment (average, in 1000 persons)	...	...	...	3205.3	3313.8	3466.2	3634.2	3785.4	3608.8	3508.0	3585.5	3522.0

Table 2.6 Output, gross value added and fixed assets by industries at current prices (ISIC Rev. 4) Manufacturing (C)

Series 300: 1993 SNA, Zloty, Western calendar year — **Data in millions**

	2001	2002	2003	2004	2005	2006	2007	2008	2009	2010	2011	2012
Series	**300**											
Equals: VALUE ADDED, GROSS, at basic prices	109629.0	110834.0	125461.0	150652.0	153824.0	167920.0	185493.0	197199.0	215039.0	209714.0	233641.0	248678.0
Compensation of employees	68269.0	64313.0	65844.0	70822.0	73228.0	78949.0	88576.0	102172.0	97622.0	101770.0	104784.0	...
Employment (average, in 1000 persons)	...	...	...	2672.7	2762.5	2901.1	3068.9	3213.0	3046.0	2944.9	3000.8	2935.6

Table 2.6 Output, gross value added and fixed assets by industries at current prices (ISIC Rev. 4) Construction (F)

Series 300: 1993 SNA, Zloty, Western calendar year — **Data in millions**

	2001	2002	2003	2004	2005	2006	2007	2008	2009	2010	2011	2012
Series	**300**											
Equals: VALUE ADDED, GROSS, at basic prices	51175.0	48363.0	46174.0	47853.0	54470.0	62775.0	76253.0	85582.0	96624.0	101026.0	110539.0	104978.0
Compensation of employees	22263.0	19014.0	17920.0	18628.0	20281.0	22074.0	26184.0	31880.0	34900.0	37563.0	41900.0	...
Employment (average, in 1000 persons)	...	...	...	797.4	839.9	914.8	1047.0	1214.7	1281.5	1250.2	1286.1	1231.8

Table 2.6 Output, gross value added and fixed assets by industries at current prices (ISIC Rev. 4) Wholesale and retail trade, transportation and storage, accommodation and food service activities (G+H+I)

Series 300: 1993 SNA, Zloty, Western calendar year — **Data in millions**

	2001	2002	2003	2004	2005	2006	2007	2008	2009	2010	2011	2012
Series	**300**											
Equals: VALUE ADDED, GROSS, at basic prices	181391.0	187934.0	189123.0	204953.0	221300.0	238903.0	258506.0	278593.0	306889.0	325587.0	343651.0	367645.0
Compensation of employees	61822.0	61349.0	62548.0	63707.0	67966.0	73647.0	81880.0	91556.0	95182.0	100660.0	105898.0	...
Employment (average, in 1000 persons)	...	...	...	2925.9	2996.4	3123.1	3372.0	3517.1	3538.4	3597.7	3616.9	3567.9

Table 2.6 Output, gross value added and fixed assets by industries at current prices (ISIC Rev. 4) Information and communication (J)

Series 300: 1993 SNA, Zloty, Western calendar year — **Data in millions**

	2001	2002	2003	2004	2005	2006	2007	2008	2009	2010	2011	2012
Series	**300**											
Equals: VALUE ADDED, GROSS, at basic prices	26717.0	31146.0	32515.0	38040.0	37333.0	38306.0	41188.0	46150.0	48602.0	47448.0	49538.0	51748.0
Compensation of employees	10713.0	10539.0	10430.0	10819.0	11011.0	11661.0	12764.0	15699.0	16152.0	16642.0	17694.0	...
Employment (average, in 1000 persons)	...	...	...	217.9	215.9	252.7	285.5	294.1	318.7	315.2	316.3	325.3

Table 2.6 Output, gross value added and fixed assets by industries at current prices (ISIC Rev. 4) Financial and insurance activities (K)

Series 300: 1993 SNA, Zloty, Western calendar year — **Data in millions**

	2001	2002	2003	2004	2005	2006	2007	2008	2009	2010	2011	2012
Series	**300**											
Equals: VALUE ADDED, GROSS, at basic prices	31980.0	30193.0	31529.0	34863.0	38160.0	42566.0	54787.0	59236.0	46926.0	55110.0	59314.0	65028.0
Compensation of employees	13122.0	12489.0	12456.0	13094.0	13944.0	15510.0	16956.0	19220.0	19757.0	20464.0	21428.0	...
Employment (average, in 1000 persons)	...	...	...	272.4	294.7	328.7	363.2	340.5	372.2	370.5	388.6	403.6

Table 2.6 Output, gross value added and fixed assets by industries at current prices (ISIC Rev. 4) Real estate activities (L)

Series 300: 1993 SNA, Zloty, Western calendar year — **Data in millions**

	2001	2002	2003	2004	2005	2006	2007	2008	2009	2010	2011	2012
Series	**300**											
Equals: VALUE ADDED, GROSS, at basic prices	44919.0	49623.0	52110.0	53239.0	55707.0	59207.0	62433.0	67704.0	67362.0	70094.0	75322.0	81435.0
Compensation of employees	4974.0	5193.0	5117.0	4900.0	4883.0	5113.0	5950.0	6242.0	6124.0	6242.0	7524.0	...
Employment (average, in 1000 persons)	...	...	...	146.3	136.0	123.1	128.8	143.1	156.3	174.1	169.8	149.6

Table 2.6 Output, gross value added and fixed assets by industries at current prices (ISIC Rev. 4) Professional, scientific, technical, administrative and support service activities (M+N)

Series 300: 1993 SNA, Zloty, Western calendar year — **Data in millions**

	2001	2002	2003	2004	2005	2006	2007	2008	2009	2010	2011	2012
Series	**300**											
Equals: VALUE ADDED, GROSS, at basic prices	45804.0	45364.0	46837.0	50002.0	54463.0	59307.0	67203.0	76582.0	84253.0	85944.0	93059.0	100722.0
Compensation of employees	16081.0	16436.0	16776.0	17521.0	18409.0	21181.0	25224.0	29243.0	31320.0	34807.0	37645.0	...
Employment (average, in 1000 persons)	...	...	...	608.6	640.9	669.7	753.8	776.4	845.5	904.8	956.4	958.5

Table 2.6 Output, gross value added and fixed assets by industries at current prices (ISIC Rev. 4) Public administration and defence, education, human health and social work activities (O+P+Q)

Series 300: 1993 SNA, Zloty, Western calendar year

Data in millions

	2001	2002	2003	2004	2005	2006	2007	2008	2009	2010	2011	2012
Series	**300**											
Equals: VALUE ADDED, GROSS, at basic prices	99409.0	106791.0	111586.0	117354.0	121887.0	129460.0	140140.0	155497.0	168387.0	175928.0	183712.0	193081.0
Compensation of employees	80112.0	84141.0	86810.0	90540.0	94772.0	101175.0	110003.0	124392.0	135082.0	141561.0	146279.0	...
Employment (average, in 1000 persons)	...	...	...	2742.9	2813.4	2920.7	2927.6	3025.1	3128.0	3238.6	3216.7	3187.4

Table 2.6 Output, gross value added and fixed assets by industries at current prices (ISIC Rev. 4) Other service activities (R+S+T)

Series 300: 1993 SNA, Zloty, Western calendar year

Data in millions

	2001	2002	2003	2004	2005	2006	2007	2008	2009	2010	2011	2012
Series	**300**											
Equals: VALUE ADDED, GROSS, at basic prices	24539.0	25865.0	26615.0	27273.0	30462.0	31593.0	33703.0	37540.0	39305.0	39581.0	40664.0	41806.0
Compensation of employees	10313.0	10965.0	11870.0	11836.0	13894.0	13179.0	14348.0	15674.0	16689.0	17465.0	18979.0	...
Employment (average, in 1000 persons)	...	...	...	374.2	379.4	428.7	425.2	445.0	455.1	477.6	465.6	465.4

Table 3.1 Government final consumption expenditure by function at current prices

Series 300: 1993 SNA, Zloty, Western calendar year

Data in millions

	2001	2002	2003	2004	2005	2006	2007	2008	2009	2010	2011	2012
Series	**300**											
General public services	...	19727.0	22062.0	23623.5	22501.0	23924.0	24529.0	26576.0	26254.0	29842.0	29861.0	...
Defence	...	7593.0	7670.2	7320.4	8200.2	9812.0	13892.0	16374.0	13405.0	17745.0	16695.0	...
Public order and safety	...	11031.0	12721.0	13947.1	16114.1	18172.0	19281.0	22055.0	23885.0	24594.0	24936.0	...
Economic affairs	...	10821.6	10137.9	9412.9	11494.0	14505.0	16188.0	19606.0	22978.0	23336.0	24460.0	...
Environment protection	...	1805.0	1890.9	1811.6	2131.0	2407.1	2441.0	3460.0	3880.0	4456.0	4644.0	...
Housing and community amenities	...	7004.0	7283.6	7755.1	9295.4	8194.0	8725.0	10592.0	11287.0	10842.0	11340.0	...
Health	...	30124.0	31537.7	35082.3	37878.3	40428.0	43442.0	50375.0	55632.0	61164.0	63881.0	...
Recreation, culture and religion	...	4765.3	4858.6	4459.5	4914.6	6138.0	7541.0	7472.0	8157.0	8432.0	8670.0	...
Education	...	40621.0	41963.0	45149.8	49103.0	51863.0	55352.0	58923.0	62317.0	66401.0	69835.0	...
Social protection	...	11159.0	12701.2	14094.1	16153.5	18264.0	20227.0	20746.0	21097.0	21615.0	20436.0	...
Equals: General government final consumption expenditure	139457.0	144650.9	152826.0	162656.0	177784.9	193707.0	211618.0	236179.0	248892.0	268427.0	274758.0	284977.0

Table 3.2 Individual consumption expenditure of households, NPISHs, and general government at current prices

Series 300: 1993 SNA, Zloty, Western calendar year | **Data in millions**

	2001	2002	2003	2004	2005	2006	2007	2008	2009	2010	2011	2012
Series	**300**											
	Individual consumption expenditure of households											
Food and non-alcoholic beverages	114457.0	116010.0	115260.0	125247.0	129513.0	136441.0	144636.0	156078.0	162454.0	167862.0	174261.0	...
Alcoholic beverages, tobacco and narcotics	33593.0	35160.0	35816.0	38598.0	40661.0	43047.0	46507.0	50991.0	56313.0	57934.0	59508.0	...
Clothing and footwear	24675.0	25703.0	26069.0	28106.0	28350.0	29976.0	29098.0	31442.0	31767.0	35528.0	38788.0	...
Housing, water, electricity, gas and other fuels	109675.0	122843.0	126727.0	134471.0	145871.0	154287.0	162663.0	181464.0	197831.0	206060.0	223472.0	...
Furnishings, household equipment and routine maintenance of the house	21412.0	23518.0	23596.0	25298.0	26802.0	28446.0	30522.0	33793.0	35889.0	38630.0	41112.0	...
Health	18602.0	20627.0	21344.0	24753.0	24648.0	26137.0	27973.0	30557.0	33521.0	35515.0	40944.0	...
Transport	45519.0	48419.0	49771.0	53301.0	53527.0	55968.0	62385.0	72264.0	74653.0	79673.0	91826.0	...
Communication	14704.0	15867.0	16823.0	18333.0	20711.0	21649.0	22723.0	24415.0	24542.0	26153.0	26979.0	...
Recreation and culture	38187.0	38833.0	41855.0	46301.0	46587.0	47850.0	52004.0	58822.0	62211.0	66716.0	71107.0	...
Education	6428.0	7159.0	7466.0	8003.0	7664.0	8420.0	9039.0	9247.0	9759.0	10778.0	10968.0	...
Restaurants and hotels	14972.0	15417.0	15861.0	16994.0	17465.0	19057.0	20119.0	21663.0	23486.0	24392.0	25961.0	...
Miscellaneous goods and services	56757.0	63369.0	65653.0	69985.0	72495.0	81549.0	93887.0	103086.0	97311.0	106943.0	115581.0	...
Equals: Household final consumption expenditure in domestic market	498981.0	532925.0	546241.0	589390.0	614294.0	652827.0	701556.0	773822.0	809737.0	856184.0	920507.0	...
Plus: Direct purchases abroad by residents	...	...	...	...	...	...	...	...	...	...	...	...
Less: Direct purchases in domestic market by non-residents	...	...	...	...	...	...	...	...	...	...	...	...
Equals: Household final consumption expenditure	498981.0	532925.0	546241.0	589390.0	614294.0	652827.0	701556.0	773822.0	809737.0	856184.0	921561.0	962722.0
	Individual consumption expenditure of non-profit institutions serving households (NPISHs)											
Equals: NPISHs final consumption expenditure	7772.0	8416.0	8748.0	8684.0	9066.0	9486.0	10316.0	11293.0	11299.0	11626.0	12320.0	12982.0
	Individual consumption expenditure of general government											
Equals: Individual consumption expenditure of general government	81472.0	82733.0	87237.0	91265.0	99337.0	108129.0	118024.0	133443.0	143266.0	153523.0	158222.0	164427.0
Equals: Total actual individual consumption	588225.0	624074.0	642226.0	689339.0	722697.0	770442.0	829896.0	918558.0	964302.0	1021333.0	1092103.0	1140131.0

Table 4.1 Total Economy (S.1)

Series 300: 1993 SNA, Zloty, Western calendar year | **Data in millions**

	2001	2002	2003	2004	2005	2006	2007	2008	2009	2010	2011	2012
Series	**300**											
	I. Production account - Resources											
Output, at basic prices (otherwise, please specify)	1533367.0	1567168.0	1649864.0	1854941.0	1952502.0	2156192.0	2438084.0	2643647.0	2685117.0	2864769.0	3136279.0	...
Less: Financial intermediation services indirectly measured (only to be deducted if FISIM is not distributed to uses)	...	...	...	...	...	...	...	...	...	...	...	...
Plus: Taxes less Subsidies on products	84309.0	93506.0	98799.0	102873.0	116982.0	128852.0	147295.0	158956.0	149675.0	168934.0	185741.0	181850.0

	2001	2002	2003	2004	2005	2006	2007	2008	2009	2010	2011	2012
Series	**300**											
Plus: Taxes on products	86449.0	95000.0	99812.0	108252.0	119921.0	131808.0	151582.0	164244.0	154744.0	173578.0	190276.0	185325.0
Less: Subsidies on products	2140.0	1494.0	1013.0	5379.0	2948.0	2956.0	4287.0	5288.0	5069.0	4644.0	4535.0	3475.0
	I. Production account - Uses											
Intermediate consumption, at purchaser's prices	838112.0	852096.0	905507.0	1033276.0	1086173.0	1225013.0	1408642.0	1527095.0	1490287.0	1617118.0	1798775.0	...
GROSS DOMESTIC PRODUCT	779564.0	808578.0	843156.0	924538.0	983302.0	1060031.0	1176737.0	1275508.0	1344505.0	1416585.0	1523245.0	...
Less: Consumption of fixed capital	106103.0	109819.0	115537.0	121469.0	126936.0	134952.0	142219.0	145746.0	148493.0	151142.0	156742.0	...
NET DOMESTIC PRODUCT	673461.0	698759.0	727619.0	803069.0	856366.0	925079.0	1034518.0	1129762.0	1196012.0	1265443.0	1366503.0	...
	II.1.1 Generation of income account - Resources											
GROSS DOMESTIC PRODUCT	779564.0	808578.0	843156.0	924538.0	983302.0	1060031.0	1176737.0	1275508.0	1344505.0	1416585.0	1523245.0	...
	II.1.1 Generation of income account - Uses											
Compensation of employees	319824.0	316553.0	322046.0	334464.0	352169.0	376527.0	418206.0	476010.0	495789.0	521499.0	548926.0	...
Taxes on production and imports, less Subsidies	94112.0	103705.0	108194.0	109788.0	125772.0	141115.0	156064.0	168627.0	161426.0	183550.0	200894.0	...
Taxes on production and imports	97407.0	106642.0	111015.0	120843.0	136241.0	153195.0	169518.0	184133.0	175837.0	195705.0	213749.0	...
Taxes on products	86449.0	95000.0	99812.0	108252.0	119921.0	131808.0	151582.0	164244.0	154744.0	173578.0	190276.0	...
Other taxes on production	10958.0	11642.0	11203.0	12591.0	16320.0	21387.0	17936.0	19889.0	21093.0	22127.0	23473.0	...
Less: Subsidies	3295.0	2937.0	2821.0	11055.0	10469.0	12080.0	13454.0	15506.0	14411.0	12155.0	12855.0	...
Subsidies on products	2140.0	1494.0	1013.0	5379.0	2948.0	2956.0	4287.0	5288.0	5069.0	4644.0	4535.0	...
Other subsidies on production	1155.0	1443.0	1808.0	5676.0	7521.0	9124.0	9167.0	10218.0	9342.0	7511.0	8320.0	...
OPERATING SURPLUS, GROSS	178228.0	195559.0	217670.0	264117.0	278780.0	300048.0	338303.0	357104.0	395218.0	411650.0	473539.0	...
MIXED INCOME, GROSS	187400.0	192761.0	195246.0	216169.0	226581.0	242341.0	264164.0	273767.0	292072.0	299886.0	299886.0	...
	II.1.2 Allocation of primary income account - Resources											
OPERATING SURPLUS, GROSS	178228.0	195559.0	217670.0	264117.0	278780.0	300048.0	338303.0	357104.0	395218.0	411650.0	473539.0	...
MIXED INCOME, GROSS	187400.0	192761.0	195246.0	216169.0	226581.0	242341.0	264164.0	273767.0	292072.0	299886.0	299886.0	...
Compensation of employees	322774.0	319916.0	326908.0	345268.0	364966.0	391192.0	432089.0	485564.0	505377.0	528942.0	554623.0	...
Taxes on production and imports, less Subsidies	94112.0	103705.0	108194.0	113262.0	128110.0	144371.0	159068.0	172643.0	165501.0	185624.0	203195.0	...
Taxes on production and imports	97407.0	106642.0	111015.0	118951.0	133671.0	150519.0	166302.0	180576.0	172659.0	192347.0	210153.0	...
Taxes on products	86449.0	95000.0	99812.0	106360.0	117351.0	129132.0	148366.0	160687.0	151566.0	170220.0	186680.0	...
Other taxes on production	10958.0	11642.0	11203.0	12591.0	16320.0	21387.0	17936.0	19889.0	21093.0	22127.0	23473.0	...
Less: Subsidies	3295.0	2937.0	2821.0	5689.0	5561.0	6148.0	7234.0	7933.0	7158.0	6723.0	6958.0	...
Subsidies on products	2140.0	1494.0	1013.0	3780.0	2207.0	1938.0	3473.0	4334.0	4384.0	4089.0	4047.0	...
Other subsidies on production	1155.0	1443.0	1808.0	1909.0	3354.0	4210.0	3761.0	3599.0	2774.0	2634.0	2911.0	...
Property income	118985.0	112594.0	92946.0	103351.0	116878.0	109195.0	129857.0	165735.0	145157.0	154313.0	175841.0	...
	II.1.2 Allocation of primary income account - Uses											
Property income	123852.0	118692.0	105992.0	143859.0	151259.0	154074.0	188781.0	205035.0	205413.0	217972.0	247230.0	...
GROSS NATIONAL INCOME	777647.0	805843.0	834972.0	898308.0	964056.0	1033073.0	1134700.0	1249778.0	1297912.0	1362443.0	1459854.0	...
	II.2 Secondary distribution of income account - Resources											
GROSS NATIONAL INCOME	777647.0	805843.0	834972.0	898308.0	964056.0	1033073.0	1134700.0	1249778.0	1297912.0	1362443.0	1459854.0	...
Current taxes on income, wealth, etc.	49145.0	54560.0	54526.0	59881.0	68684.0	79920.0	100615.0	109747.0	100013.0	98293.0	107196.0	...
Social contributions	115019.0	116972.0	117795.0	124505.0	134401.0	142634.0	158022.0	165676.0	175456.0	180582.0	189697.0	...
Social benefits other than social transfers in kind	132040.0	137322.0	142779.0	148289.0	153946.0	161336.0	166880.0	179112.0	197755.0	210072.0	215523.0	...

	2001	2002	2003	2004	2005	2006	2007	2008	2009	2010	2011	2012
Series	**300**											
Other current transfers	50997.0	58493.0	65747.0	58531.0	70654.0	85697.0	93124.0	116856.0	143806.0	141178.0	151139.0	...
	II.2 Secondary distribution of income account - Uses											
Current taxes on income, wealth, etc.	49145.0	54560.0	54526.0	59881.0	68684.0	79920.0	100615.0	109747.0	100013.0	98293.0	107196.0	...
Social contributions	115019.0	116972.0	117795.0	124505.0	134401.0	142634.0	158022.0	165676.0	175456.0	180582.0	189697.0	...
Social benefits other than social transfers in kind	132040.0	137322.0	142779.0	148289.0	153946.0	161336.0	166880.0	179112.0	197755.0	210072.0	215523.0	...
Other current transfers	39170.0	45112.0	49281.0	58901.0	66139.0	82104.0	88698.0	112348.0	139837.0	130775.0	138790.0	...
GROSS DISPOSABLE INCOME	789474.0	819224.0	851438.0	897938.0	968571.0	1036666.0	1139126.0	1254286.0	1301881.0	1372846.0	1472203.0	...
	II.4.1 Use of disposable income account - Resources											
GROSS DISPOSABLE INCOME	789474.0	819224.0	851438.0	897938.0	968571.0	1036666.0	1139126.0	1254286.0	1301881.0	1372846.0	1472203.0	...
Adjustment for the change in net equity of households on pension funds	9409.0	11528.0	13421.0	17368.0	23656.0	30379.0	23231.0	-1875.0	38775.0	41180.0	3354.0	...
	II.4.1 Use of disposable income account - Uses											
Final consumption expenditure	646210.0	685992.0	707815.0	760730.0	801145.0	856020.0	922899.0	1021294.0	1069928.0	1136237.0	1207585.0	...
Individual consumption expenditure	588225.0	624074.0	642226.0	689339.0	722697.0	770442.0	829896.0	918558.0	964302.0	1021333.0	1091049.0	...
Collective consumption expenditure	57985.0	61918.0	65589.0	71391.0	78448.0	85578.0	93003.0	102736.0	105626.0	114904.0	116536.0	...
Adjustment for the change in net equity of households on pension funds	9409.0	11528.0	13421.0	17368.0	23656.0	30379.0	23231.0	-1875.0	38775.0	41180.0	3354.0	...
SAVING, GROSS	143264.0	133232.0	143623.0	137208.0	167426.0	180646.0	216227.0	232992.0	231953.0	236609.0	264618.0	...
	III.1 Capital account - Changes in liabilities and net worth											
SAVING, GROSS	143264.0	133232.0	143623.0	137208.0	167426.0	180646.0	216227.0	232992.0	231953.0	236609.0	264618.0	...
Capital transfers, receivable less payable	310.0	-25.0	-178.0	1855.0	3202.0	9783.0	11316.0	8764.0	16363.0	22196.0	27472.0	...
Capital transfers, receivable	6200.0	5275.0	10564.0	7088.0	17356.0	21565.0	21225.0	23073.0	30317.0	34306.0	44695.0	...
Less: Capital transfers, payable	5890.0	5300.0	10742.0	5233.0	14154.0	11782.0	9909.0	14309.0	13954.0	12110.0	17223.0	...
Equals: CHANGES IN NET WORTH DUE TO SAVING AND CAPITAL TRANSFERS	37471.0	23388.0	27908.0	17594.0	43692.0	55477.0	85324.0	96010.0	99823.0	107663.0	135348.0	...
	III.1 Capital account - Changes in assets											
Gross capital formation	161923.0	150588.0	158028.0	185542.0	189445.0	223162.0	287657.0	304848.0	273568.0	297449.0	333187.0	...
Gross fixed capital formation	161277.0	151472.0	153758.0	167158.0	179180.0	208308.0	253729.0	283906.0	284649.0	281320.0	309744.0	...
Changes in inventories	512.0	-1070.0	4021.0	18127.0	9979.0	14670.0	33729.0	20728.0	-11273.0	15924.0	23259.0	...
Acquisitions less disposals of valuables	134.0	186.0	249.0	257.0	286.0	184.0	199.0	214.0	192.0	205.0	184.0	...
Acquisitions less disposals of non-produced non-financial assets	0.0	0.0	0.0	0.0	0.0	...	...	...	...	0.0	...	...
NET LENDING (+) / NET BORROWING (-)	-18349.0	-17381.0	-14583.0	-46479.0	-18817.0	-32733.0	-60114.0	-63092.0	-25252.0	-38644.0	-41097.0	...
	III.2 Financial account - Changes in liabilities and net worth											
Net incurrence of liabilities	143962.5	70380.5	127135.4	170037.0	206709.0	372678.0	464278.0	403432.0	248511.0	318981.0	313302.0	...
Currency and deposits	37824.1	-14011.4	27903.3	34541.0	45033.0	66116.0	116742.0	112819.0	72074.0	64150.0	81309.0	...
Securities other than shares	35116.1	41556.4	49977.1	59956.0	67188.0	53781.0	42443.0	63358.0	39232.0	82904.0	46226.0	...
Loans	15530.8	13308.9	17873.3	16579.0	20517.0	97299.0	150239.0	188096.0	88234.0	81537.0	128604.0	...
Shares and other equity	14873.1	27107.0	37180.0	33803.0	36105.0	66831.0	91319.0	-16247.0	37615.0	34737.0	-5333.0	...
Insurance technical reserves	6345.2	7027.5	5802.8	20669.0	20056.0	25765.0	28198.0	32613.0	18753.0	28321.0	16324.0	...
Financial derivatives	...	...	...	...	...	...	...	...	...	...	...	...

	2001	2002	2003	2004	2005	2006	2007	2008	2009	2010	2011	2012
Series	**300**											
Other accounts payable	34273.2	-4607.9	-11601.1	4490.0	17810.0	62887.0	35339.0	22793.0	-7398.0	27332.0	46171.0	...
Adjustment to reconcile Net Lending of Financial Account and Capital Account	-391.2	-300.0	264.1	-14311.0	-26425.0	2774.0	-11532.0	104554.0	25754.0	-4694.0	13201.0	...
NET LENDING (+) / NET BORROWING (-)	-21137.8[a]	-20149.0[a]	-18313.1[a]	-32168.0	7608.0	-35507.0	-48582.0	-167647.0	-51008.0	-27419.0[a]	-49450.0[a]	...
	III.2 Financial account - Changes in assets											
Net acquisition of financial assets	122824.7	50231.5	108822.3	137869.0	214317.0	337172.0	415696.0	235785.0	197503.0	291562.0	263851.0	...
Monetary gold and SDRs	2.0	1.3	0.0	-829.0	1.0	0.0	0.0	-603.0	-182.0	-101.0	-127.0	...
Currency and deposits	50544.3	-22311.8	18321.5	58133.0	55459.0	60903.0	85688.0	40159.0	51277.0	65254.0	85219.0	...
Securities other than shares	26013.2	33482.0	52996.7	28019.0	45423.0	53499.0	53753.0	80147.0	36521.0	63447.0	26014.0	...
Loans	11915.5	16744.5	18992.4	24782.0	37383.0	78134.0	122314.0	149496.0	70393.0	78807.0	115256.0	...
Shares and other equity	-5341.4	16108.8	20231.0	-492.0	39814.0	56332.0	90340.0	-79423.0	33157.0	15802.0	-19558.0	...
Insurance technical reserves	6559.1	6921.7	5841.3	20686.0	20071.0	25668.0	27934.0	33495.0	18925.0	29179.0	16463.0	...
Financial derivatives	...	...	...	...	...	...	...	...	...	...	...	...
Other accounts receivable	33132.0	-715.0	-7560.6	7571.0	16167.0	62636.0	35668.0	12514.0	-12587.0	39173.0	40586.0	...

[a] Statistical discrepancy between Net lending in the financial account and Net lending in the capital account.

Table 4.2 Rest of the world (S.2)

Series 300: 1993 SNA, Zloty, Western calendar year **Data in millions**

	2001	2002	2003	2004	2005	2006	2007	2008	2009	2010	2011	2012
Series	**300**											
	V.I External account of goods and services - Resources											
Imports of goods and services	239488.0	259537.0	303575.0	368365.0	371946.0	446927.0	513425.0	559521.0	529269.0	615470.0	706266.0	
Imports of goods	201889.0	220063.0	259533.0	318433.0	320972.0	385361.0	446794.0	486094.0	453188.0	524425.0	609658.0	
Imports of services	37599.0	39474.0	44042.0	49932.0	50974.0	61566.0	66631.0	73427.0	76081.0	91045.0	96608.0	
	V.I External account of goods and services - Uses											
Exports of goods and services	210919.0	231535.0	280888.0	346631.0	364658.0	427776.0	479606.0	508887.0	530278.0	598369.0	688739.0	
Exports of goods	170600.0	190540.0	237257.0	297657.0	311959.0	363893.0	400193.0	423712.0	439835.0	499337.0	577332.0	
Exports of services	40319.0	40995.0	43631.0	48974.0	52699.0	63883.0	79413.0	85175.0	90443.0	99032.0	111407.0	
EXTERNAL BALANCE OF GOODS AND SERVICES	28569.0	28002.0	22687.0	21734.0	7288.0	19151.0	33819.0	50634.0	-1009.0	17101.0	17527.0	
	V.II External account of primary income and current transfers - Resources											
EXTERNAL BALANCE OF GOODS AND SERVICES	28569.0	28002.0	22687.0	21734.0	7288.0	19151.0	33819.0	50634.0	-1009.0	17101.0	17527.0	
Compensation of employees	1021.0	1088.0	1136.0	2306.0	2330.0	2465.0	3243.0	3985.0	4070.0	4576.0	5610.0	
Taxes on production and imports, less Subsidies	...	...	...	-3474.0	-2338.0	-3256.0	-3004.0	-4016.0	-4075.0	-2074.0	-2301.0	
Taxes on production and imports	...	...	...	1892.0	2570.0	2676.0	3216.0	3557.0	3178.0	3358.0	3596.0	
Taxes on products	...	...	...	1892.0	2570.0	2676.0	3216.0	3557.0	3178.0	3358.0	3596.0	
Other taxes on production	...	...	...	...	...	...	...	...	...	...	...	
Less: Subsidies	...	...	...	5366.0	4908.0	5932.0	6220.0	7573.0	7253.0	5432.0	5897.0	
Subsidies on products	...	...	...	1599.0	741.0	1018.0	814.0	954.0	685.0	555.0	488.0	
Other subsidies on production	...	...	...	3767.0	4167.0	4914.0	5406.0	6619.0	6568.0	4877.0	5409.0	
Property income	14612.0	13149.0	20082.0	47199.0	42142.0	55620.0	69482.0	52073.0	66366.0	75711.0	85070.0	

	2001	2002	2003	2004	2005	2006	2007	2008	2009	2010	2011	2012
Series	**300**											
Current taxes on income, wealth, etc.	...	...	...	...	...	...	...	...	...	...	...	
Social contributions	...	...	...	...	...	...	...	...	...	...	...	
Social benefits other than social transfers in kind	...	...	...	...	...	...	...	...	...	...	...	
Other current transfers	3472.0	3680.0	4201.0	8640.0	11759.0	13799.0	14067.0	15232.0	21812.0	15825.0	15568.0	
Adjustment for the change in net equity of households on pension funds	...	...	...	...	...	...	...	...	...	...	...	
V.II External account of primary income and current transfers - Uses												
Compensation of employees	3971.0	4451.0	5998.0	13110.0	15127.0	17130.0	17126.0	13539.0	13658.0	12019.0	11307.0	
Taxes on production and imports, less Subsidies	...	...	...	...	...	...	...	...	...	...	...	
Taxes on production and imports	...	...	...	...	...	...	...	...	...	...	...	
Taxes on products	...	...	...	...	...	...	...	...	...	...	...	
Other taxes on production	...	...	...	...	...	...	...	...	...	...	...	
Less: Subsidies	...	...	...	...	...	...	...	...	...	...	...	
Subsidies on products	...	...	...	...	...	...	...	...	...	...	...	
Other subsidies on production	...	...	...	...	...	...	...	...	...	...	...	
Property income	9745.0	7051.0	7036.0	6691.0	7761.0	10741.0	10558.0	12773.0	6110.0	12052.0	13681.0	
Current taxes on income and wealth, etc.	...	...	...	...	...	...	...	...	...	...	...	
Social contributions	...	...	...	...	...	...	...	...	...	...	...	
Social benefits other than social transfers in kind	...	...	...	...	...	...	...	...	...	...	...	
Other current transfers	15299.0	17061.0	20667.0	8270.0	16274.0	17392.0	18493.0	19740.0	25781.0	26228.0	27917.0	
Adjustment for the change in net equity of households on pension funds	...	...	...	...	...	...	...	...	...	...	...	
CURRENT EXTERNAL BALANCE	18659.0	17356.0	14405.0	48334.0	22019.0	42516.0	71430.0	71856.0	41615.0	60840.0	68569.0	
V.III.1 Capital account - Changes in liabilities and net worth												
CURRENT EXTERNAL BALANCE	18659.0	17356.0	14405.0	48334.0	22019.0	42516.0	71430.0	71856.0	41615.0	60840.0	68569.0	
Capital transfers, receivable less payable	-310.0	25.0	178.0	-1855.0	-3202.0	-9783.0	-11316.0	-8764.0	-16363.0	-22196.0	-27472.0	
Capital transfers, receivable	148.0	215.0	411.0	527.0	616.0	1439.0	1742.0	2306.0	1241.0	1773.0	5186.0	
Less: Capital transfers, payable	458.0	190.0	233.0	2382.0	3818.0	11222.0	13058.0	11070.0	17604.0	23969.0	32658.0	
Equals: CHANGES IN NET WORTH DUE TO SAVING AND CAPITAL TRANSFERS	18349.0	17381.0	14583.0	46479.0	18817.0	32733.0	60114.0	63092.0	25252.0	38644.0	41097.0	
V.III.1 Capital account - Changes in assets												
Acquisitions less disposals of non-produced non-financial assets	...	...	...	...	...	...	...	...	...	...	...	
NET LENDING (+) / NET BORROWING (-)	18349.0	17381.0	14583.0	46479.0	18817.0	32733.0	60114.0	63092.0	25252.0	38644.0	41097.0	
V.III.2 Financial account - Changes in liabilities and net worth												
Net incurrence of liabilities	13112.1	-95.4	30487.1	31301.0	61128.0	55876.0	65111.0	1779.0	25904.0	113834.0	74667.0	
Currency and deposits	13299.7	-12172.3	-3052.5	21819.0	14540.0	-2064.0	5074.0	-46511.0	-12047.0	14089.0	10979.0	
Securities other than shares	-5523.4	7693.5	19841.4	2854.0	23569.0	10834.0	16742.0	27732.0	18829.0	40134.0	22820.0	
Loans	-476.7	-917.4	1576.8	594.0	3526.0	2629.0	5595.0	10814.0	697.0	18776.0	10354.0	
Shares and other equity	592.5	1911.6	-339.0	2094.0	11851.0	34869.0	28012.0	4150.0	17381.0	6111.0	14010.0	
Insurance technical reserves	0.0	0.0	0.0	17.0	15.0	-97.0	-264.0	882.0	171.0	858.0	139.0	

	2001	2002	2003	2004	2005	2006	2007	2008	2009	2010	2011	2012
Series	**300**											
Financial derivatives	...	...	...	...	...	...	...	...	...	...	...	
Other accounts payable	5220.0	3389.2	12460.4	3923.0	7628.0	9705.0	9952.0	4713.0	872.0	33866.0	16365.0	
Adjustment to reconcile Net Lending of Financial Account and Capital Account	391.2	299.7	-264.1	14311.0	26425.0	-2774.0	11532.0	-104554.0	-25754.0	4694.0	-13201.0	
NET LENDING (+) / NET BORROWING (-)	21137.8[a]	20149.3[a]	18313.1[a]	32168.0	-7608.0	35507.0	48582.0	167647.0	51008.0	27419.0[a]	49450.0[a]	
	V.III.2 Financial account - Changes in assets											
Net acquisition of financial assets	34249.9	20053.9	48800.2	63469.0	53519.0	91383.0	113693.0	169426.0	76912.0	141253.0	124117.0	
Monetary gold and SDRs	-2.0	-1.0	0.0	829.0	-1.0	0.0	0.0	603.0	182.0	101.0	127.0	
Currency and deposits	579.5	-3871.9	6529.3	-1774.0	4114.0	3148.0	36128.0	26149.0	8750.0	12985.0	7069.0	
Securities other than shares	3579.5	15767.9	16821.8	34792.0	45334.0	11115.0	5432.0	10943.0	21541.0	59590.0	43032.0	
Loans	3138.6	-4353.0	457.7	-7609.0	-13340.0	21794.0	33520.0	49414.0	18538.0	21506.0	23703.0	
Shares and other equity	20807.0	12909.8	16610.0	36390.0	8142.0	45369.0	28990.0	67327.0	21840.0	25046.0	28235.0	
Insurance technical reserves	-213.9	105.8	-38.5	0.0	0.0	0.0	0.0	0.0	0.0	0.0	0.0	
Financial derivatives	...	...	...	...	...	...	...	...	...	...	...	
Other accounts receivable	6361.2	-503.7	8419.9	842.0	9271.0	9956.0	9623.0	14992.0	6061.0	22025.0	21950.0	

[a] Statistical discrepancy between Net lending in the financial account and Net lending in the capital account.

Table 4.3 Non-financial Corporations (S.11)

Series 300: 1993 SNA, Zloty, Western calendar year **Data in millions**

	2001	2002	2003	2004	2005	2006	2007	2008	2009	2010	2011	2012
Series	**300**											
	I. Production account - Resources											
Output, at basic prices (otherwise, please specify)	912691.0	932111.0	996203.0	1159523.0	1230139.0	1380173.0	1571704.0	1714995.0	1728805.0	1864990.0	2076753.0	
	I. Production account - Uses											
Intermediate consumption, at purchaser's prices	608983.0	619801.0	664286.0	777482.0	828042.0	939354.0	1081781.0	1179678.0	1138266.0	1245241.0	1406591.0	
VALUE ADDED GROSS, in basic prices	303708.0	312310.0	331917.0	382041.0	402097.0	440819.0	489923.0	535317.0	590539.0	619749.0	670162.0	
Less: Consumption of fixed capital	69587.0	73383.0	77156.0	81051.0	84737.0	90699.0	94677.0	96469.0	97760.0	99187.0	103170.0	
VALUE ADDED NET, at basic prices	234121.0	238927.0	254761.0	300990.0	317360.0	350120.0	395246.0	438848.0	492779.0	520562.0	566992.0	
	II.1.1 Generation of income account - Resources											
VALUE ADDED GROSS, at basic prices	303708.0	312310.0	331917.0	382041.0	402097.0	440819.0	489923.0	535317.0	590539.0	619749.0	670162.0	
	II.1.1 Generation of income account - Uses											
Compensation of employees	194445.0	186496.0	186016.0	193846.0	204245.0	220556.0	250005.0	283454.0	288627.0	307485.0	328541.0	
Other taxes less Other subsidies on production	6640.0	7022.0	6116.0	7181.0	8064.0	12799.0	9697.0	11625.0	11144.0	12995.0	13041.0	
Other taxes on production	7766.0	8461.0	7918.0	9080.0	11557.0	16212.0	13036.0	14629.0	14831.0	15530.0	15969.0	
Less: Other subsidies on production	1126.0	1439.0	1802.0	1899.0	3493.0	3413.0	3339.0	3004.0	3687.0	2535.0	2928.0	
OPERATING SURPLUS, GROSS	102623.0	118792.0	139785.0	181014.0	189788.0	207464.0	230221.0	240238.0	290768.0	299269.0	328580.0	
	II.1.2 Allocation of primary income account - Resources											
OPERATING SURPLUS, GROSS	102623.0	118792.0	139785.0	181014.0	189788.0	207464.0	230221.0	240238.0	290768.0	299269.0	328580.0	
Property income	13680.0	8194.0	12242.0	9268.0	9709.0	10053.0	9599.0	16404.0	6674.0	16156.0	21202.0	

	2001	2002	2003	2004	2005	2006	2007	2008	2009	2010	2011	2012
Series	**300**											
	II.1.2 Allocation of primary income account - Uses											
Property income	44621.0	47619.0	48357.0	71516.0	72992.0	79653.0	98672.0	84810.0	97679.0	99094.0	104918.0	
BALANCE OF PRIMARY INCOMES	71682.0	79367.0	103670.0	118766.0	126505.0	137864.0	141148.0	171832.0	199763.0	216331.0	244864.0	
	II.2 Secondary distribution of income account - Resources											
BALANCE OF PRIMARY INCOMES	71682.0	79367.0	103670.0	118766.0	126505.0	137864.0	141148.0	171832.0	199763.0	216331.0	244864.0	
Social contributions	0.0	0.0	0.0	0.0	0.0	0.0	0.0	0.0	0.0	0.0	0.0	
Other current transfers	2817.0	2105.0	2447.0	2647.0	3862.0	6957.0	7234.0	8678.0	15062.0	19387.0	21486.0	
	II.2 Secondary distribution of income account - Uses											
Current taxes on income, wealth, etc.	11038.0	12369.0	14402.0	19519.0	18184.0	24421.0	31026.0	32245.0	28686.0	27292.0	29650.0	
Social benefits other than social transfers in kind	...	...	...	...	...	...	...	...	...	...	...	
Other current transfers	6617.0	5852.0	3639.0	8471.0	6553.0	11776.0	10409.0	11616.0	15890.0	16795.0	16215.0	
GROSS DISPOSABLE INCOME	56844.0	63251.0	88076.0	93423.0	105630.0	108624.0	106947.0	136649.0	170249.0	191631.0	220485.0	
	II.4.1 Use of disposable income account - Resources											
GROSS DISPOSABLE INCOME	56844.0	63251.0	88076.0	93423.0	105630.0	108624.0	106947.0	136649.0	170249.0	191631.0	220485.0	
	II.4.1 Use of disposable income account - Uses											
Adjustment for the change in net equity of households on pension funds	...	...	...	...	...	...	...	...	...	...	...	
SAVING, GROSS	56844.0	63251.0	88076.0	93423.0	105630.0	108624.0	106947.0	136649.0	170249.0	191631.0	220485.0	
	III.1 Capital account - Changes in liabilities and net worth											
SAVING, GROSS	56844.0	63251.0	88076.0	93423.0	105630.0	108624.0	106947.0	136649.0	170249.0	191631.0	220485.0	
Capital transfers, receivable less payable	2832.0	1772.0	5639.0	5297.0	5667.0	9355.0	8196.0	10961.0	15552.0	9262.0	6789.0	
Capital transfers, receivable	3665.0	2616.0	7141.0	5768.0	10090.0	11578.0	10676.0	12825.0	16778.0	11138.0	12639.0	
Less: Capital transfers, payable	833.0	844.0	1502.0	471.0	4423.0	2223.0	2480.0	1864.0	1226.0	1876.0	5850.0	
Equals: CHANGES IN NET WORTH DUE TO SAVING AND CAPITAL TRANSFERS	-9911.0	-8360.0	16559.0	17669.0	26560.0	27280.0	20466.0	51141.0	88041.0	101706.0	124104.0	
	III.1 Capital account - Changes in assets											
Gross capital formation	90029.0	77368.0	82622.0	99618.0	101363.0	126190.0	167539.0	168712.0	134863.0	138658.0	168361.0	
Gross fixed capital formation	89246.0	78856.0	79132.0	85472.0	92078.0	110422.0	136611.0	149922.0	140057.0	129769.0	146106.0	
Changes in inventories	732.0	-1537.0	3444.0	14110.0	9225.0	15730.0	30887.0	18746.0	-5234.0	8846.0	22215.0	
Acquisitions less disposals of valuables	51.0	49.0	46.0	36.0	60.0	38.0	41.0	44.0	40.0	43.0	40.0	
Acquisitions less disposals of non-produced non-financial assets	...	...	...	...	...	...	...	...	...	2304.0	4639.0	
NET LENDING (+) / NET BORROWING (-)	-30353.0	-12345.0	11093.0	-898.0	9934.0	-8211.0	-52396.0	-21102.0	50938.0	59931.0	54274.0	
	III.2 Financial account - Changes in liabilities and net worth											
Net incurrence of liabilities	43574.9	19162.6	18541.8	39607.0	40786.0	133212.0	147550.0	86095.0	21983.0	31781.0	100775.0	
Currency and deposits	0.0	0.0	0.0	0.0	0.0	0.0	0.0	0.0	0.0	0.0	0.0	
Securities other than shares	1504.7	-1714.8	-2589.9	-1651.0	2720.0	3984.0	4261.0	812.0	-1164.0	6935.0	8072.0	
Loans	17237.4	4370.4	5561.2	93.0	12943.0	44286.0	55404.0	66175.0	821.0	-2744.0	60134.0	
Shares and other equity	-1792.0	11469.6	26266.2	35773.0	13737.0	41969.0	57320.0	8559.0	25055.0	3369.0	-6008.0	
Insurance technical reserves	0.0	0.0	0.0	0.0	0.0	0.0	0.0	0.0	0.0	0.0	0.0	
Financial derivatives	...	...	...	...	...	...	...	...	...	...	...	

	2001	2002	2003	2004	2005	2006	2007	2008	2009	2010	2011	2012
Series	**300**											
Other accounts payable	26624.8	5037.4	-10695.7	5392.0	11385.0	42973.0	30566.0	10549.0	-2729.0	24221.0	38576.0	
Adjustment to reconcile Net Lending of Financial Account and Capital Account	237.3	-683.1	-78.1	7642.0	19291.0	28832.0	57383.0	23664.0	58449.0	26252.0	115000.0	
NET LENDING (+) / NET BORROWING (-)	-30979.3[a]	-11739.9[a]	11167.1	-8540.0	-9357.0	-37043.0	-109779.0	-44826.0[a]	-8008.0[a]	40463.0[a]	-50428.0[a]	
	III.2 Financial account - Changes in assets											
Net acquisition of financial assets	12595.6	7422.7	29708.9	31067.0	31429.0	96169.0	37771.0	41268.0	13975.0	72244.0	50347.0	
Monetary gold and SDRs	...	...	...	...	...	...	...	...	...	...	...	
Currency and deposits	9377.3	-5998.2	13046.2	23925.0	16259.0	25972.0	21177.0	1544.0	15042.0	16488.0	19638.0	
Securities other than shares	-616.8	-2963.9	11784.5	6736.0	-882.0	3.0	1848.0	1032.0	2528.0	12953.0	364.0	
Loans	0.2	770.6	254.4	1065.0	2849.0	2178.0	2695.0	6566.0	3316.0	20180.0	5984.0	
Shares and other equity	754.6	2641.1	1484.7	-753.0	1092.0	8610.0	6758.0	24856.0	-2041.0	958.0	9636.0	
Insurance technical reserves	1135.2	285.3	870.4	1052.0	235.0	1199.0	785.0	1249.0	1101.0	1872.0	2268.0	
Financial derivatives	...	...	...	...	...	...	...	...	...	...	...	
Other accounts receivable	1945.1	12687.8	2268.7	-958.0	11876.0	58207.0	4509.0	6021.0	-5971.0	19792.0	12457.0	

[a] Statistical discrepancy between Net lending in the financial account and Net lending in the capital account.

Table 4.4 Financial Corporations (S.12)

Series 300: 1993 SNA, Zloty, Western calendar year — **Data in millions**

	2001	2002	2003	2004	2005	2006	2007	2008	2009	2010	2011	2012
Series	**300**											
	I. Production account - Resources											
Output, at basic prices (otherwise, please specify)	54491.0	51414.0	54992.0	60167.0	64853.0	76008.0	93090.0	101468.0	91331.0	100785.0	107395.0	
	I. Production account - Uses											
Intermediate consumption, at purchaser's prices	22982.0	21711.0	23961.0	26003.0	27243.0	34350.0	39047.0	43098.0	44523.0	45800.0	48395.0	
VALUE ADDED GROSS, at basic prices	31509.0	29703.0	31031.0	34164.0	37610.0	41658.0	54043.0	58370.0	46808.0	54985.0	59000.0	
Less: Consumption of fixed capital	5089.0	4298.0	4475.0	4658.0	4860.0	4995.0	5217.0	5297.0	5392.0	5423.0	5413.0	
VALUE ADDED NET, at basic prices	26420.0	25405.0	26556.0	29506.0	32750.0	36663.0	48826.0	53073.0	41416.0	49562.0	53587.0	
	II.1.1 Generation of income account - Resources											
VALUE ADDED GROSS, at basic prices	31509.0	29703.0	31031.0	34164.0	37610.0	41658.0	54043.0	58370.0	46808.0	54985.0	59000.0	
	II.1.1 Generation of income account - Uses											
Compensation of employees	13054.0	12418.0	12383.0	13021.0	13856.0	15415.0	16862.0	19111.0	19662.0	20369.0	21332.0	
Other taxes less Other subsidies on production	577.0	552.0	515.0	472.0	858.0	1035.0	982.0	1202.0	1346.0	1351.0	1906.0	
Other taxes on production	606.0	556.0	521.0	502.0	922.0	1092.0	1054.0	1235.0	1366.0	1456.0	1942.0	
Less: Other subsidies on production	29.0	4.0	6.0	30.0	64.0	57.0	72.0	33.0	20.0	105.0	36.0	
OPERATING SURPLUS, GROSS	17878.0	16733.0	18133.0	20671.0	22896.0	25208.0	36199.0	38057.0	25800.0	33265.0	35762.0	
	II.1.2 Allocation of primary income account - Resources											
OPERATING SURPLUS, GROSS	17878.0	16733.0	18133.0	20671.0	22896.0	25208.0	36199.0	38057.0	25800.0	33265.0	35762.0	
Property income	40638.0	36975.0	23419.0	37382.0	43627.0	38643.0	49578.0	77275.0	64670.0	63948.0	74950.0	

	2001	2002	2003	2004	2005	2006	2007	2008	2009	2010	2011	2012
Series	**300**											
	II.1.2 Allocation of primary income account - Uses											
Property income	44128.0	37954.0	26753.0	42092.0	45511.0	42380.0	49639.0	72884.0	61164.0	66715.0	83641.0	
BALANCE OF PRIMARY INCOMES	14388.0	15754.0	14799.0	15961.0	21012.0	21471.0	36138.0	42448.0	29306.0	30498.0	27071.0	
	II.2 Secondary distribution of income account - Resources											
BALANCE OF PRIMARY INCOMES	14388.0	15754.0	14799.0	15961.0	21012.0	21471.0	36138.0	42448.0	29306.0	30498.0	27071.0	
Social contributions	10593.0	12368.0	9891.0	10462.0	13311.0	13550.0	17377.0	21098.0	23013.0	23601.0	15110.0	
Other current transfers	10903.0	12054.0	15331.0	16585.0	15749.0	16812.0	19479.0	29626.0	40244.0	36958.0	40099.0	
	II.2 Secondary distribution of income account - Uses											
Current taxes on income, wealth, etc.	2715.0	2570.0	3052.0	2821.0	2961.0	3547.0	5078.0	4874.0	4715.0	4777.0	5968.0	
Social benefits other than social transfers in kind	...	...	...	...	...	...	...	...	...	...	...	
Other current transfers	11148.0	12272.0	15608.0	16777.0	15918.0	17042.0	19854.0	30067.0	44657.0	37579.0	40791.0	
GROSS DISPOSABLE INCOME	22021.0	25334.0	21361.0	23410.0	31193.0	31244.0	48062.0	58231.0	43191.0	48701.0	35521.0	
	II.4.1 Use of disposable income account - Resources											
GROSS DISPOSABLE INCOME	22021.0	25334.0	21361.0	23410.0	31193.0	31244.0	48062.0	58231.0	43191.0	48701.0	35521.0	
	II.4.1 Use of disposable income account - Uses											
Adjustment for the change in net equity of households on pension funds	9409.0	11528.0	13421.0	17368.0	23656.0	30379.0	23231.0	-1875.0	38775.0	41180.0	3354.0	
SAVING, GROSS	12612.0	13806.0	7940.0	6042.0	7537.0	865.0	24831.0	60106.0	4416.0	7521.0	32167.0	
	III.1 Capital account - Changes in liabilities and net worth											
SAVING, GROSS	12612.0	13806.0	7940.0	6042.0	7537.0	865.0	24831.0	60106.0	4416.0	7521.0	32167.0	
Capital transfers, receivable less payable	66.0	55.0	76.0	53.0	229.0	59.0	62.0	58.0	345.0	444.0	481.0	
Capital transfers, receivable	66.0	55.0	76.0	53.0	229.0	59.0	62.0	58.0	345.0	444.0	481.0	
Less: Capital transfers, payable	0.0	0.0	0.0	0.0	0.0	0.0	0.0	0.0	0.0	0.0	0.0	
Equals: CHANGES IN NET WORTH DUE TO SAVING AND CAPITAL TRANSFERS	7589.0	9563.0	3541.0	1437.0	2906.0	-4071.0	19676.0	54867.0	-631.0	2542.0	27235.0	
	III.1 Capital account - Changes in assets											
Gross capital formation	8911.0	5950.0	4535.0	4941.0	5078.0	5833.0	7331.0	7194.0	6681.0	5458.0	5235.0	
Gross fixed capital formation	8879.0	5905.0	4495.0	4897.0	5032.0	5790.0	7278.0	7137.0	6633.0	5405.0	5189.0	
Changes in inventories	0.0	0.0	0.0	0.0	0.0	0.0	0.0	0.0	0.0	0.0	0.0	
Acquisitions less disposals of valuables	32.0	45.0	40.0	44.0	46.0	43.0	53.0	57.0	48.0	53.0	46.0	
Acquisitions less disposals of non-produced non-financial assets	...	...	...	...	...	...	...	...	...	53.0	84.0	
NET LENDING (+) / NET BORROWING (-)	3767.0	7911.0	3481.0	1154.0	2688.0	-4909.0	17562.0	52970.0	-1920.0	2454.0	27329.0	
	III.2 Financial account - Changes in liabilities and net worth											
Net incurrence of liabilities	60970.0	5158.1	47745.4	64614.0	94381.0	144402.0	199773.0	182721.0	80154.0	142954.0	105139.0	
Currency and deposits	37824.1	-13975.7	27887.5	34549.0	45070.0	66118.0	116745.0	112818.0	72074.0	64150.0	81309.0	
Securities other than shares	483.4	1921.7	1884.6	4102.0	2493.0	1508.0	-1922.0	22704.0	-22998.0	2784.0	4770.0	
Loans	-1254.3	-1093.2	836.3	7857.0	1314.0	12989.0	23014.0	35014.0	2889.0	17451.0	-3386.0	
Shares and other equity	16665.1	15637.4	10913.8	-1969.0	22368.0	24862.0	33999.0	-24806.0	12560.0	31369.0	675.0	
Insurance technical reserves	6345.2	7027.5	5802.8	20669.0	20056.0	25765.0	28198.0	32613.0	18753.0	28321.0	16324.0	
Financial derivatives	...	...	...	...	...	...	...	...	...	...	...	

	2001	2002	2003	2004	2005	2006	2007	2008	2009	2010	2011	2012
Series	**300**											
Other accounts payable	906.5	-4359.6	420.4	-593.0	3081.0	13160.0	-261.0	4379.0	-3125.0	-1121.0	5446.0	
Adjustment to reconcile Net Lending of Financial Account and Capital Account	-437.8	-386.6	179.3	-295.0	-386.0	-12696.0	-21254.0	47610.0	-36344.0	1069.0	-23630.0	
NET LENDING (+) / NET BORROWING (-)	12479.8[a]	18538.6[a]	15135.7[a]	1449.0	3074.0	7787.0	38816.0	5359.0	34423.0	2087.0[a]	47680.0[a]	
	III.2 Financial account - Changes in assets											
Net acquisition of financial assets	73449.8	23696.7	62881.1	66064.0	97455.0	152189.0	238589.0	188080.0	114578.0	145041.0	152819.0	
Monetary gold and SDRs	2.0	1.3	0.0	-829.0	1.0	0.0	0.0	-603.0	-182.0	-101.0	-127.0	
Currency and deposits	13299.7	-14261.3	-2525.5	20851.0	14377.0	-2106.0	3419.0	-44645.0	-12146.0	14356.0	11529.0	
Securities other than shares	29078.7	32381.9	39246.6	20893.0	48158.0	54435.0	53228.0	77829.0	36776.0	50748.0	25396.0	
Loans	11162.7	15534.1	18591.4	21575.0	33448.0	76089.0	119783.0	141015.0	64410.0	59470.0	108021.0	
Shares and other equity	-4051.6	493.0	5086.2	-1794.0	2349.0	24175.0	40817.0	11797.0	22507.0	15311.0	-1648.0	
Insurance technical reserves	0.0	0.0	0.0	17.0	15.0	-97.0	-264.0	882.0	171.0	858.0	139.0	
Financial derivatives	...	...	...	...	...	...	...	...	...	...	...	
Other accounts receivable	23958.3	-10452.3	2482.4	5351.0	-893.0	-306.0	21606.0	1804.0	3041.0	4399.0	9509.0	

[a] Statistical discrepancy between Net lending in the financial account and Net lending in the capital account.

Table 4.5 General Government (S.13)

Series 300: 1993 SNA, Zloty, Western calendar year

Data in millions

	2001	2002	2003	2004	2005	2006	2007	2008	2009	2010	2011	2012
Series	**300**											
	I. Production account - Resources											
Output, at basic prices (otherwise, please specify)	158157.0	164241.0	169185.0	176103.0	187950.0	200128.0	216933.0	241610.0	251371.0	270066.0	274226.0	283634.0
	I. Production account - Uses											
Intermediate consumption, at purchaser's prices	47249.0	49106.0	50850.0	53531.0	57348.0	63556.0	69991.0	78882.0	76469.0	88311.0	87090.0	89159.0
VALUE ADDED GROSS, at basic prices	110908.0	115135.0	118335.0	122572.0	130602.0	136572.0	146942.0	162728.0	174902.0	181755.0	187136.0	194475.0
Less: Consumption of fixed capital	16959.0	17092.0	17817.0	18834.0	19706.0	20758.0	22191.0	22542.0	24339.0	25329.0	26404.0	27621.0
VALUE ADDED NET, at basic prices	93949.0	98043.0	100518.0	103738.0	110896.0	115814.0	124751.0	140186.0	150563.0	156426.0	160732.0	...
	II.1.1 Generation of income account - Resources											
VALUE ADDED GROSS, at basic prices	110908.0	115135.0	118335.0	122572.0	130602.0	136572.0	146942.0	162728.0	174902.0	181755.0	187136.0	194475.0
	II.1.1 Generation of income account - Uses											
Compensation of employees	83286.0	86957.0	90021.0	93014.0	98815.0	104067.0	113165.0	127570.0	138604.0	144340.0	148626.0	154061.0
Other taxes less Other subsidies on production	871.0	865.0	834.0	964.0	1117.0	1120.0	1245.0	1233.0	1785.0	1486.0	1528.0	1641.0
Other taxes on production	871.0	865.0	834.0	964.0	1117.0	1120.0	1245.0	1233.0	1785.0	1486.0	1528.0	...
Less: Other subsidies on production	0.0	0.0	0.0	0.0	0.0	0.0	0.0	0.0	0.0	0.0	0.0	...
OPERATING SURPLUS, GROSS	26751.0	27313.0	27480.0	28594.0	30670.0	31385.0	32532.0	33925.0	34513.0	35929.0	36982.0	38773.0
	II.1.2 Allocation of primary income account - Resources											
OPERATING SURPLUS, GROSS	26751.0	27313.0	27480.0	28594.0	30670.0	31385.0	32532.0	33925.0	34513.0	35929.0	36982.0	38773.0
Taxes on production and imports, less Subsidies	94112.0	103705.0	108194.0	113262.0	128110.0	144371.0	159068.0	172643.0	165501.0	185624.0	203195.0	199679.0
Taxes on production and imports	97407.0	106642.0	111015.0	118951.0	133671.0	150519.0	166302.0	180576.0	172659.0	192347.0	210153.0	205603.0

	2001	2002	2003	2004	2005	2006	2007	2008	2009	2010	2011	2012
Series	**300**											
Taxes on products	86449.0	95000.0	99812.0	106360.0	117351.0	129132.0	148366.0	160687.0	151566.0	170220.0	186680.0	...
Other taxes on production	10958.0	11642.0	11203.0	12591.0	16320.0	21387.0	17936.0	19889.0	21093.0	22127.0	23473.0	...
Less: Subsidies	3295.0	2937.0	2821.0	5689.0	5561.0	6148.0	7234.0	7933.0	7158.0	6723.0	6958.0	5924.0
Subsidies on products	2140.0	1494.0	1013.0	3780.0	2207.0	1938.0	3473.0	4334.0	4384.0	4089.0	4047.0	...
Other subsidies on production	1155.0	1443.0	1808.0	1909.0	3354.0	4210.0	3761.0	3599.0	2774.0	2634.0	2911.0	...
Property income	8436.0	10308.0	10709.0	8546.0	15362.0	16147.0	18306.0	17546.0	18780.0	15004.0	16957.0	21617.0
II.1.2 Allocation of primary income account - Uses												
Property income	24335.0	23354.0	25056.0	25485.0	27746.0	28132.0	27211.0	28363.0	35524.0	38112.0	41030.0	45324.0
BALANCE OF PRIMARY INCOMES	104964.0	117972.0	121327.0	124917.0	146396.0	163771.0	182695.0	195751.0	183270.0	198445.0	216104.0	214745.0
II.2 Secondary distribution of income account - Resources												
BALANCE OF PRIMARY INCOMES	104964.0	117972.0	121327.0	124917.0	146396.0	163771.0	182695.0	195751.0	183270.0	198445.0	216104.0	214745.0
Current taxes on income, wealth, etc.	49145.0	54560.0	54526.0	59881.0	68684.0	79920.0	100615.0	109747.0	100013.0	98293.0	107196.0	115171.0
Social contributions	104426.0	104604.0	107904.0	114043.0	121090.0	129084.0	140645.0	144578.0	152443.0	156981.0	174587.0	196123.0
Other current transfers	7523.0	6593.0	6810.0	9430.0	13795.0	16130.0	12919.0	14153.0	16724.0	18348.0	18979.0	18639.0
II.2 Secondary distribution of income account - Uses												
Current taxes on income, wealth, etc.	0.0	14.0	8.0	4.0	13.0	35.0	23.0	28.0	35.0	55.0	93.0	137.0
Social benefits other than social transfers in kind	132040.0	137322.0	142779.0	148289.0	153946.0	161336.0	166880.0	179112.0	197755.0	210072.0	215523.0	226334.0
Other current transfers	3989.0	9437.0	9869.0	11628.0	20526.0	26886.0	29313.0	31781.0	29750.0	33149.0	34639.0	37369.0
GROSS DISPOSABLE INCOME	130029.0	136956.0	137911.0	148350.0	175480.0	200648.0	240658.0	253308.0	224910.0	228791.0	266611.0	280838.0
II.4.1 Use of disposable income account - Resources												
GROSS DISPOSABLE INCOME	130029.0	136956.0	137911.0	148350.0	175480.0	200648.0	240658.0	253308.0	224910.0	228791.0	266611.0	280838.0
II.4.1 Use of disposable income account - Uses												
Final consumption expenditure	139457.0	144651.0	152826.0	162656.0	177785.0	193707.0	211027.0	236179.0	248892.0	268427.0	274758.0	284977.0
Individual consumption expenditure	81472.0	82733.0	87237.0	91265.0	99337.0	108129.0	118024.0	133443.0	143266.0	153523.0	158222.0	164427.0
Collective consumption expenditure	57985.0	61918.0	65589.0	71391.0	78448.0	85578.0	93003.0	102736.0	105626.0	114904.0	116536.0	120550.0
Adjustment for the change in net equity of households on pension funds	...	...	...	...	...	...	...	...	...	...	...	...
SAVING, GROSS	-9428.0	-7695.0	-14915.0	-14306.0	-2305.0	6941.0	29631.0	17129.0	-23982.0	-39636.0	-8147.0	-4139.0
III.1 Capital account - Changes in liabilities and net worth												
SAVING, GROSS	-9428.0	-7695.0	-14915.0	-14306.0	-2305.0	6941.0	29631.0	17129.0	-23982.0	-39636.0	-8147.0	-4139.0
Capital transfers, receivable less payable	-4940.0	-4370.0	-8693.0	-3610.0	-3365.0	-3550.0	-1009.0	-5930.0	-4376.0	8660.0	16052.0	11020.0
Capital transfers, receivable	-102.0	-111.0	353.0	678.0	5730.0	5714.0	5857.0	5916.0	7885.0	18472.0	27051.0	21786.0
Less: Capital transfers, payable	4838.0	4259.0	9046.0	4288.0	9095.0	9264.0	6866.0	11846.0	12261.0	9812.0	10999.0	10766.0
Equals: CHANGES IN NET WORTH DUE TO SAVING AND CAPITAL TRANSFERS	-31327.0	-29157.0	-41425.0	-36750.0	-25376.0	-17367.0	6431.0	-11343.0	-52697.0	-56305.0	-18499.0	...
III.1 Capital account - Changes in assets												
Gross capital formation	26727.0	28252.0	28604.0	31862.0	34378.0	41862.0	50168.0	58184.0	71237.0	80925.0	88714.0	74275.0
Gross fixed capital formation	26455.0	27845.0	28079.0	31019.0	33494.0	41429.0	49018.0	58587.0	70142.0	79681.0	87333.0	73845.0
Changes in inventories	0.0	4.0	-12.0	268.0	271.0	-101.0	564.0	-1034.0	542.0	646.0	840.0	430.0
Acquisitions less disposals of valuables	272.0	403.0	537.0	575.0	613.0	534.0	586.0	631.0	553.0	598.0	541.0	...

	2001	2002	2003	2004	2005	2006	2007	2008	2009	2010	2011	2012
Series	**300**											
Acquisitions of non-produced non-financial assets	...	...	...	...	...	...	...	...	...	-598.0	-4078.0	-4678.0
NET LENDING (+) / NET BORROWING (-)	-41095.0	-40317.0	-52212.0	-49778.0	-40048.0	-38471.0	-21546.0	-46985.0	-99595.0	-111303.0	-76731.0	-62716.0
	III.2 Financial account - Changes in liabilities and net worth											
Net incurrence of liabilities	26767.7	42918.7	48789.1	45599.0	43732.0	41694.0	36562.0	47029.0	96300.0	103854.0	65524.0	...
Currency and deposits	0.0	-35.7	15.8	-8.0	-37.0	-2.0	-3.0	1.0	0.0	0.0	0.0	...
Securities other than shares	33125.5	41343.4	50686.4	57505.0	61974.0	48289.0	40104.0	39842.0	63394.0	73185.0	33384.0	...
Loans	-7925.8	743.2	-2517.1	-10536.0	-20751.0	-10716.0	-8542.0	-60.0	33647.0	26996.0	31039.0	...
Shares and other equity	0.0	0.0	0.0	0.0	0.0	0.0	0.0	0.0	0.0	0.0	0.0	...
Insurance technical reserves	0.0	0.0	0.0	0.0	0.0	0.0	0.0	0.0	0.0	0.0	0.0	...
Financial derivatives	...	...	...	...	...	...	...	...	...	...	...	...
Other accounts payable	1568.0	867.8	604.0	-1363.0	2546.0	4123.0	5003.0	7246.0	-741.0	3674.0	1101.0	...
Adjustment to reconcile Net Lending of Financial Account and Capital Account	-336.6	-23.5	-57.5	-6306.0	-9018.0	-7145.0	-14138.0	-4948.0	12328.0	12925.0	-6580.0	...
NET LENDING (+) / NET BORROWING (-)	-39614.4[a]	-40463.5[a]	-52774.5[a]	-43472.0	-31030.0	-31326.0	-7408.0	-41977.0[a]	-111427.0[a]	-124118.0[a]	-71430.0[a]	...
	III.2 Financial account - Changes in assets											
Net acquisition of financial assets	-12846.7	2455.2	-3985.4	2127.0	12702.0	10368.0	29154.0	5052.0	-15127.0	-20264.0	-5906.0	...
Monetary gold and SDRs	...	...	...	0.0	0.0	0.0	0.0	0.0	0.0	0.0	0.0	...
Currency and deposits	-2270.5	93.2	3123.7	9080.0	8541.0	3459.0	25206.0	4458.0	-1079.0	-5159.0	-5576.0	...
Securities other than shares	-995.8	-155.8	0.7	62.0	122.0	185.0	-59.0	-83.0	27.0	-28.0	134.0	...
Loans	738.0	431.7	130.2	183.0	773.0	-520.0	1642.0	869.0	971.0	151.0	1645.0	...
Shares and other equity	-8913.5	-3615.4	-4183.1	-11021.0	-2478.0	850.0	-1305.0	-2151.0	-5700.0	-28931.0	-19821.0	...
Insurance technical reserves	66.8	69.3	57.7	-85.0	507.0	-88.0	100.0	16.0	110.0	281.0	0.0	...
Financial derivatives	...	...	...	...	...	...	...	...	...	...	...	...
Other accounts receivable	-1471.7	5632.2	-3114.6	3909.0	5237.0	6482.0	3570.0	1943.0	-9456.0	13423.0	17713.0	...

[a] Statistical discrepancy between Net lending in the financial account and Net lending in the capital account.

Table 4.6 Households (S.14)

Series 300: 1993 SNA, Zloty, Western calendar year — **Data in millions**

	2001	2002	2003	2004	2005	2006	2007	2008	2009	2010	2011	2012
Series	**300**											
	I. Production account - Resources											
Output, at basic prices (otherwise, please specify)	391856.0	402244.0	410966.0	439721.0	449092.0	478108.0	533454.0	561691.0	589364.0	604174.0	653335.0	
	I. Production account - Uses											
Intermediate consumption, at purchaser's prices	151776.0	153948.0	158133.0	167796.0	164613.0	178278.0	207800.0	214867.0	220434.0	226932.0	245928.0	
VALUE ADDED GROSS, at basic prices	240080.0	248296.0	252833.0	271925.0	284479.0	299830.0	325654.0	346824.0	368930.0	377242.0	407407.0	
Less: Consumption of fixed capital	14287.0	14859.0	15884.0	16711.0	17409.0	18273.0	19896.0	21190.0	20743.0	20937.0	21481.0	
VALUE ADDED NET, at basic prices	225793.0	233437.0	236949.0	255214.0	267070.0	281557.0	305758.0	325634.0	348187.0	356305.0	385926.0	
	II.1.1 Generation of income account - Resources											
VALUE ADDED GROSS, at basic prices	240080.0	248296.0	252833.0	271925.0	284479.0	299830.0	325654.0	346824.0	368930.0	377242.0	407407.0	

	2001	2002	2003	2004	2005	2006	2007	2008	2009	2010	2011	2012
Series	**300**											
II.1.1 Generation of income account - Uses												
Compensation of employees	24277.0	25538.0	27994.0	28506.0	28807.0	29666.0	30932.0	38569.0	41100.0	41137.0	42012.0	
Other taxes less Other subsidies on production	1410.0	1473.0	1669.0	-1969.0	-1692.0	-3140.0	-3716.0	-4964.0	-3147.0	-1873.0	-2011.0	
Other taxes on production	1410.0	1473.0	1669.0	1755.0	2175.0	2375.0	2000.0	2175.0	2457.0	2973.0	3334.0	
Less: Other subsidies on production	...	...	...	3724.0	3867.0	5515.0	5716.0	7139.0	5604.0	4846.0	5345.0	
OPERATING SURPLUS, GROSS	26993.0	28524.0	27924.0	29219.0	30783.0	30963.0	34274.0	39452.0	38905.0	38092.0	67520.0	
MIXED INCOME, GROSS	187400.0	192761.0	195246.0	216169.0	226581.0	242341.0	264164.0	273767.0	292072.0	299886.0	299886.0	
II.1.2 Allocation of primary income account - Resources												
OPERATING SURPLUS, GROSS	26993.0	28524.0	27924.0	29219.0	30783.0	30963.0	34274.0	39452.0	38905.0	38092.0	67520.0	
MIXED INCOME, GROSS	187400.0	192761.0	195246.0	216169.0	226581.0	242341.0	264164.0	273767.0	292072.0	299886.0	299886.0	
Compensation of employees	322774.0	319916.0	326908.0	345268.0	364966.0	391192.0	432089.0	485564.0	505377.0	528942.0	554623.0	
Property income	54653.0	55798.0	46028.0	47844.0	46451.0	43902.0	51802.0	53575.0	54355.0	58602.0	62091.0	
II.1.2 Allocation of primary income account - Uses												
Property income	10564.0	9707.0	5825.0	4501.0	4037.0	3880.0	13186.0	18853.0	10941.0	13933.0	17485.0	
BALANCE OF PRIMARY INCOMES	581256.0	587292.0	590281.0	633999.0	664744.0	704518.0	769143.0	833505.0	879768.0	911589.0	966635.0	
II.2 Secondary distribution of income account - Resources												
BALANCE OF PRIMARY INCOMES	581256.0	587292.0	590281.0	633999.0	664744.0	704518.0	769143.0	833505.0	879768.0	911589.0	966635.0	
Social contributions	...	...	...	...	...	...	...	...	...	...	...	
Social benefits other than social transfers in kind	132040.0	137322.0	142779.0	148289.0	153946.0	161336.0	166880.0	179112.0	197755.0	210072.0	215523.0	
Other current transfers	23705.0	31020.0	34788.0	22886.0	29985.0	37951.0	45091.0	55229.0	59078.0	54590.0	60610.0	
II.2 Secondary distribution of income account - Uses												
Current taxes on income, wealth, etc.	35392.0	39607.0	37064.0	37537.0	47526.0	51917.0	64488.0	72600.0	66577.0	66169.0	71485.0	
Social contributions	115019.0	116972.0	117795.0	124505.0	134401.0	142634.0	158022.0	165676.0	175456.0	180582.0	189697.0	
Social benefits other than social transfers in kind	...	...	...	...	...	...	...	...	...	...	...	
Other current transfers	16802.0	16821.0	18963.0	20616.0	21963.0	24941.0	27546.0	37254.0	47111.0	43252.0	47145.0	
GROSS DISPOSABLE INCOME	569788.0	582234.0	594026.0	622516.0	644785.0	684313.0	731058.0	792316.0	847457.0	886248.0	934441.0	
II.4.1 Use of disposable income account - Resources												
GROSS DISPOSABLE INCOME	569788.0	582234.0	594026.0	622516.0	644785.0	684313.0	731058.0	792316.0	847457.0	886248.0	934441.0	
Adjustment for the change in net equity of households on pension funds	9409.0	11528.0	13421.0	17368.0	23656.0	30379.0	23231.0	-1875.0	38775.0	41180.0	3354.0	
II.4.1 Use of disposable income account - Uses												
Final consumption expenditure	498981.0	532925.0	546241.0	589390.0	614294.0	652827.0	701556.0	773822.0	809737.0	856184.0	920507.0	
Individual consumption expenditure	498981.0	532925.0	546241.0	589390.0	614294.0	652827.0	701556.0	773822.0	809737.0	856184.0	920507.0	
SAVING, GROSS	80216.0	60837.0	61206.0	50494.0	54147.0	61865.0	52733.0	16619.0	76495.0	71244.0	17288.0	
III.1 Capital account - Changes in liabilities and net worth												
SAVING, GROSS	80216.0	60837.0	61206.0	50494.0	54147.0	61865.0	52733.0	16619.0	76495.0	71244.0	17288.0	
Capital transfers, receivable less payable	2326.0	2488.0	2767.0	81.0	1009.0	3874.0	3915.0	3593.0	4647.0	3546.0	3771.0	
Capital transfers, receivable	2545.0	2685.0	2961.0	555.0	1261.0	4169.0	4478.0	4192.0	5033.0	3880.0	4082.0	
Less: Capital transfers, payable	219.0	197.0	194.0	474.0	252.0	295.0	563.0	599.0	386.0	334.0	311.0	

	2001	2002	2003	2004	2005	2006	2007	2008	2009	2010	2011	2012
Series	**300**											
Equals: CHANGES IN NET WORTH DUE TO SAVINGS AND CAPITAL TRANSFERS	68255.0	48466.0	48089.0	33864.0	37747.0	47466.0	36752.0	-978.0	60399.0	53853.0	-422.0	
III.1 Capital account - Changes in assets												
Gross capital formation	35910.0	38685.0	41941.0	48754.0	48259.0	48877.0	62139.0	70266.0	60288.0	71925.0	70379.0	
Gross fixed capital formation	36351.0	38533.0	41726.0	45403.0	48209.0	50267.0	60342.0	67768.0	67318.0	65982.0	70618.0	
Changes in inventories	-220.0	463.0	589.0	3749.0	483.0	-959.0	2278.0	3016.0	-6581.0	6432.0	204.0	
Acquisitions less disposals of valuables	-221.0	-311.0	-374.0	-398.0	-433.0	-431.0	-481.0	-518.0	-449.0	-489.0	-443.0	
Acquisitions less disposals of non-produced non-financial assets	...	...	...	...	...	...	...	...	...	-1759.0	-645.0	
NET LENDING (+) / NET BORROWING (-)	46632.0	24640.0	22032.0	1821.0	6897.0	16862.0	-5491.0	-50054.0	20854.0	4624.0	-48675.0	
III.2 Financial account - Changes in liabilities and net worth												
Net incurrence of liabilities	12935.2	3195.0	12247.7	10019.9[a]	32181.9[a]	56086.5[a]	73218.2[a]	108276.7[a]	...	...	...	
Currency and deposits	...	...	...	...	...	...	...	...	...	...	...	
Securities other than shares	2.5	6.1	-4.0	76.7[a]	0.0	0.0	0.0	0.0	...	...	...	
Loans	7920.3	9062.4	14180.2	14468.7[a]	28745.7[a]	53148.5[a]	71046.2[a]	108225.9[a]	...	...	...	
Shares and other equity	...	...	...	...	...	...	...	...	...	...	...	
Insurance technical reserves	...	...	...	...	...	...	...	...	...	...	...	
Financial derivatives	...	...	...	...	...	...	...	...	...	...	...	
Other accounts payable	5012.4	-5873.5	-1928.5	-4525.5[a]	3436.2[a]	2938.0[a]	2172.0[a]	50.8[a]	...	...	...	
Adjustment to reconcile Net Lending of Financial Account and Capital Account	-249.1	-351.5	-234.4	-166.0[a]	-239.5[a]	-647.0[a]	-242.0[a]	690.2[a]	...	...	...	
NET LENDING (+) / NET BORROWING (-) [b]	34204.7	10813.9	7190.9	-3232.1	14669.5	18183.0	13533.0	-16031.2	...	...	...	
III.2 Financial account - Changes in assets												
Net acquisition of financial assets	47139.9	14008.9	19438.6	6787.8[a]	46851.4[a]	74269.5[a]	86751.2[a]	92245.5[a]	...	...	...	
Currency and deposits	27741.1	-1117.1	3473.9	-562.6[a]	12385.1[a]	24057.5[a]	32028.4[a]	82739.7[a]	...	...	...	
Securities other than shares	-1444.2	4044.7	1657.4	-466.7[a]	323.1[a]	-7162.7[a]	-10781.5[a]	6683.3[a]	...	...	...	
Loans	14.6	8.1	16.4	25.4[a]	-606.1[a]	-1461.7[a]	-930.4[a]	1502.0[a]	...	...	...	
Shares and other equity	6736.8	16322.0	17570.9	680.8[a]	5376.6[a]	23148.8[a]	29235.0[a]	-18718.9[a]	...	...	...	
Insurance technical reserves	5357.1	6567.1	4913.2	4771.7[a]	28951.1[a]	35804.1[a]	30949.7[a]	13759.2[a]	...	...	...	
Financial derivatives	...	...	...	...	...	...	...	...	...	...	...	
Other accounts receivable	8734.5	-11815.9	-8193.2	2339.2[a]	421.6[a]	-116.5[a]	6250.0[a]	6280.2[a]	...	...	...	

[a] Data for this item has not been revised.

[b] Excludes Adjustment to reconcile Net Lending of the Financial Account and the Capital Account. Statistical discrepancy between Net lending in the financial account and Net lending in the capital account.

Table 4.7 Non-profit institutions serving households (S.15)

Series 300: 1993 SNA, Zloty, Western calendar year **Data in millions**

	2001	2002	2003	2004	2005	2006	2007	2008	2009	2010	2011	2012
Series	**300**											
I. Production account - Resources												
Output, at basic prices (otherwise, please specify)	16172.0	17158.0	18518.0	19427.0	20468.0	21775.0	22903.0	23883.0	24246.0	24754.0	24570.0	
I. Production account - Uses												
Intermediate consumption, at purchaser's prices	7122.0	7530.0	8277.0	8464.0	8927.0	9475.0	10023.0	10570.0	10595.0	10834.0	10771.0	
VALUE ADDED GROSS, at basic prices	9050.0	9628.0	10241.0	10963.0	11541.0	12300.0	12880.0	13313.0	13651.0	13920.0	13799.0	
Less: Consumption of fixed capital	181.0	187.0	205.0	215.0	224.0	227.0	238.0	248.0	259.0	266.0	274.0	
VALUE ADDED NET, at basic prices	8869.0	9441.0	10036.0	10748.0	11317.0	12073.0	12642.0	13065.0	13392.0	13654.0	13525.0	
II.1.1 Generation of income account - Resources												
VALUE ADDED GROSS, at basic prices	9050.0	9628.0	10241.0	10963.0	11541.0	12300.0	12880.0	13313.0	13651.0	13920.0	13799.0	
II.1.1 Generation of income account - Uses												
Compensation of employees	4762.0	5144.0	5632.0	6077.0	6446.0	6823.0	7242.0	7306.0	7796.0	8168.0	8415.0	
Other taxes less Other subsidies on production	305.0	287.0	261.0	267.0	452.0	449.0	561.0	575.0	623.0	657.0	689.0	
Other taxes on production	305.0	287.0	261.0	290.0	549.0	588.0	601.0	617.0	654.0	682.0	700.0	
Less: Other subsidies on production	...	...	...	23.0	97.0	139.0	40.0	42.0	31.0	25.0	11.0	
OPERATING SURPLUS, GROSS	3983.0	4197.0	4348.0	4619.0	4643.0	5028.0	5077.0	5432.0	5232.0	5095.0	4695.0	
II.1.2 Allocation of primary income account - Resources												
OPERATING SURPLUS, GROSS	3983.0	4197.0	4348.0	4619.0	4643.0	5028.0	5077.0	5432.0	5232.0	5095.0	4695.0	
Property income	1578.0	1319.0	548.0	311.0	1729.0	450.0	572.0	935.0	678.0	603.0	641.0	
II.1.2 Allocation of primary income account - Uses												
Property income	204.0	58.0	1.0	265.0	973.0	29.0	73.0	125.0	105.0	118.0	156.0	
BALANCE OF PRIMARY INCOMES	5357.0	5458.0	4895.0	4665.0	5399.0	5449.0	5576.0	6242.0	5805.0	5580.0	5180.0	
II.2 Secondary distribution of income account - Resources												
BALANCE OF PRIMARY INCOMES	5357.0	5458.0	4895.0	4665.0	5399.0	5449.0	5576.0	6242.0	5805.0	5580.0	5180.0	
Social contributions	...	...	...	...	...	...	...	...	...	...	...	
Other current transfers	6049.0	6721.0	6371.0	6983.0	7263.0	7847.0	8401.0	9170.0	12698.0	11895.0	9965.0	
II.2 Secondary distribution of income account - Uses												
Current taxes on income, wealth, etc.	...	...	...	...	...	...	...	...	...	...	...	
Social benefits other than social transfers in kind	...	...	...	...	...	...	...	...	...	...	...	
Other current transfers	614.0	730.0	1202.0	1409.0	1179.0	1459.0	1576.0	1630.0	2429.0	0.0	0.0	
GROSS DISPOSABLE INCOME	10792.0	11449.0	10064.0	10239.0	11483.0	11837.0	12401.0	13782.0	16074.0	17475.0	15145.0	
II.4.1 Use of disposable income account - Resources												
GROSS DISPOSABLE INCOME	10792.0	11449.0	10064.0	10239.0	11483.0	11837.0	12401.0	13782.0	16074.0	17475.0	15145.0	
II.4.1 Use of disposable income account - Uses												
Final consumption expenditure	7772.0	8416.0	8748.0	8684.0	9066.0	9486.0	10316.0	11293.0	11299.0	11626.0	12320.0	
Individual consumption expenditure	7772.0	8416.0	8748.0	8684.0	9066.0	9486.0	10316.0	11293.0	11299.0	11626.0	12320.0	
Adjustment for the change in net equity of households on pension funds	...	...	...	...	...	...	...	...	...	...	...	

	2001	2002	2003	2004	2005	2006	2007	2008	2009	2010	2011	2012
Series	**300**											
SAVING, GROSS	3020.0	3033.0	1316.0	1555.0	2417.0	2351.0	2085.0	2489.0	4775.0	5849.0	2825.0	
III.1 Capital account - Changes in liabilities and net worth												
SAVING, GROSS	3020.0	3033.0	1316.0	1555.0	2417.0	2351.0	2085.0	2489.0	4775.0	5849.0	2825.0	
Capital transfers, receivable less payable	26.0	30.0	33.0	34.0	-338.0	45.0	152.0	82.0	195.0	284.0	379.0	
Capital transfers, receivable	26.0	30.0	33.0	34.0	46.0	45.0	152.0	82.0	276.0	372.0	442.0	
Less: Capital transfers, payable	...	...	...	...	384.0	...	...	...	81.0	88.0	63.0	
Equals: CHANGES IN NET WORTH DUE TO SAVING AND CAPITAL TRANSFERS	2865.0	2876.0	1144.0	1374.0	1855.0	2169.0	1999.0	2323.0	4711.0	5867.0	2930.0	
III.1 Capital account - Changes in assets												
Gross capital formation	346.0	333.0	326.0	367.0	367.0	400.0	480.0	492.0	499.0	483.0	498.0	
Gross fixed capital formation	346.0	333.0	326.0	367.0	367.0	400.0	480.0	492.0	499.0	483.0	498.0	
Changes in inventories	...	...	...	...	...	...	...	...	...	...	...	
Acquisitions less disposals of valuables	...	...	...	...	...	...	...	...	...	...	...	
Acquisitions less disposals of non-produced non-financial assets	...	...	...	...	...	...	...	...	...	...	...	
NET LENDING (+) / NET BORROWING (-)	2700.0	2730.0	1023.0	1222.0	1712.0	1996.0	1757.0	2079.0	4471.0	5650.0	2706.0	
III.2 Financial account - Changes in liabilities and net worth												
Net incurrence of liabilities	-285.3	-53.9	-188.6	-52.7[a]	49.2[a]	190.9[a]	647.4[a]	620.9[a]	...	...	...	
Currency and deposits	...	...	...	...	...	...	...	...	...	...	...	
Securities other than shares	...	...	...	...	...	...	...	...	...	...	...	
Loans	-446.8	226.1	-187.3	-52.7[a]	49.2[a]	190.9[a]	647.4[a]	620.9[a]	...	...	...	
Shares and other equity	...	...	...	...	...	...	...	...	...	...	...	
Insurance technical reserves	...	...	...	...	...	...	...	...	...	...	...	
Financial derivatives	...	...	...	...	...	...	...	...	...	...	...	
Other accounts payable	161.5	-280.0	-1.3	...	...	...	...	...	...	...	...	
Adjustment to reconcile Net Lending of Financial Account and Capital Account	...	...	...	...	-175.6	378.1	175.0	-283.6	...	...	...	
NET LENDING (+) / NET BORROWING (-)	2771.4[b]	2701.9[b]	967.7[b]	1467.9[c]	1887.6[d]	1617.9[d]	1603.0[d]	2343.6[d]	...	...	...	
III.2 Financial account - Changes in assets												
Net acquisition of financial assets	2486.1	2648.0	779.1	1415.2[a]	1936.8[a]	1808.8[a]	2250.4[a]	2964.5[a]	...	...	...	
Currency and deposits	2396.7	-1028.4	1203.2	52.5[a]	1932.2[a]	2286.9[a]	1832.8[a]	3216.7[a]	...	...	...	
Securities other than shares	-8.7	175.1	307.5	342.4[a]	-1.8[a]	-732.8[a]	0.0[a]	0.0[a]	...	...	...	
Loans	0.0	0.0	0.0	0.0[a]	0.0[a]	0.2[a]	0.8[a]	-0.7[a]	...	...	...	
Shares and other equity	132.3	268.1	272.3	-7.3[a]	6.4[a]	254.5[a]	400.5[a]	-237.3[a]	...	...	...	
Insurance technical reserves	...	...	...	...	...	...	...	...	...	...	...	
Financial derivatives	...	...	...	...	...	...	...	...	...	...	...	
Other accounts receivable	-34.2	3233.2	-1003.9	1027.6[a]	0.0[a]	0.0[a]	16.3[a]	-14.2[a]	...	...	...	

[a] Data for this item has not been revised.
[b] Statistical discrepancy between Net lending in the financial account and Net lending in the capital account.
[c] Data for this item has not been revised. Statistical discrepancy between Net lending in the financial account and Net lending in the capital account.
[d] Data for this item has not been revised. Excludes Adjustment to reconcile Net Lending of the Financial Account and the Capital Account.

Table 4.8 Combined Sectors: Non-Financial and Financial Corporations (S.11 + S.12)

Series 300: 1993 SNA, Zloty, Western calendar year

Data in millions

	2001	2002	2003	2004	2005	2006	2007	2008	2009	2010	2011	2012
Series	**300**											
	I. Production account - Resources											
Output, at basic prices (otherwise, please specify)	967182.0	983525.0	1051195.0	1219690.0	1294992.0	1456181.0	1664794.0	1816463.0	1820136.0	1965775.0	2184148.0	
	I. Production account - Uses											
Intermediate consumption, at purchaser's prices	631965.0	641512.0	688247.0	803485.0	855285.0	973704.0	1120828.0	1222776.0	1182789.0	1291041.0	1454986.0	
VALUE ADDED GROSS, at basic prices	335217.0	342013.0	362948.0	416205.0	439707.0	482477.0	543966.0	593687.0	637347.0	674734.0	729162.0	
Less: Consumption of fixed capital	74676.0	77681.0	81631.0	85709.0	89597.0	95694.0	99894.0	101766.0	103152.0	104610.0	108583.0	
VALUE ADDED NET, at basic prices	260541.0	264332.0	281317.0	330496.0	350110.0	386783.0	444072.0	491921.0	534195.0	570124.0	620579.0	
	II.1.1 Generation of income account - Resources											
VALUE ADDED GROSS, at basic prices	335217.0	342013.0	362948.0	416205.0	439707.0	482477.0	543966.0	593687.0	637347.0	674734.0	729162.0	
	II.1.1 Generation of income account - Uses											
Compensation of employees	207499.0	198914.0	198399.0	206867.0	218101.0	235971.0	266867.0	302565.0	308289.0	327854.0	349873.0	
Other taxes less Other subsidies on production	7217.0	7574.0	6631.0	7653.0	8922.0	13834.0	10679.0	12827.0	12490.0	14346.0	14947.0	
Other taxes on production	8372.0	9017.0	8439.0	9582.0	12479.0	17304.0	14090.0	15864.0	16197.0	16986.0	17911.0	
Less: Other subsidies on production	1155.0	1443.0	1808.0	1929.0	3557.0	3470.0	3411.0	3037.0	3707.0	2640.0	2964.0	
OPERATING SURPLUS, GROSS	120501.0	135525.0	157918.0	201685.0	212684.0	232672.0	266420.0	278295.0	316568.0	332534.0	364342.0	
	II.1.2 Allocation of primary income account - Resources											
OPERATING SURPLUS, GROSS	120501.0	135525.0	157918.0	201685.0	212684.0	232672.0	266420.0	278295.0	316568.0	332534.0	364342.0	
Property income	54318.0	45169.0	35661.0	46650.0	53336.0	48696.0	59177.0	93679.0	71344.0	80104.0	96152.0	
	II.1.2 Allocation of primary income account - Uses											
Property income	88749.0	85573.0	75110.0	113608.0	118503.0	122033.0	148311.0	157694.0	158843.0	165809.0	188559.0	
BALANCE OF PRIMARY INCOMES	86070.0	95121.0	118469.0	134727.0	147517.0	159335.0	177286.0	214280.0	229069.0	246829.0	271935.0	
	II.2 Secondary distribution of income account - Resources											
BALANCE OF PRIMARY INCOMES	86070.0	95121.0	118469.0	134727.0	147517.0	159335.0	177286.0	214280.0	229069.0	246829.0	271935.0	
Social contributions	10593.0	12368.0	9891.0	10462.0	13311.0	13550.0	17377.0	21098.0	23013.0	23601.0	15110.0	
Other current transfers	13720.0	14159.0	17778.0	19232.0	19611.0	23769.0	26713.0	38304.0	55306.0	56345.0	61585.0	
	II.2 Secondary distribution of income account - Uses											
Current taxes on income, wealth, etc.	13753.0	14939.0	17454.0	22340.0	21145.0	27968.0	36104.0	37119.0	33401.0	32069.0	35618.0	
Social benefits other than social transfers in kind	...	...	...	...	...	...	...	...	...	...	...	
Other current transfers	17765.0	18124.0	19247.0	25248.0	22471.0	28818.0	30263.0	41683.0	60547.0	54374.0	57006.0	
GROSS DISPOSABLE INCOME	78865.0	88585.0	109437.0	116833.0	136823.0	139868.0	155009.0	194880.0	213440.0	240332.0	256006.0	
	II.4.1 Use of disposable income account - Resources											
GROSS DISPOSABLE INCOME	78865.0	88585.0	109437.0	116833.0	136823.0	139868.0	155009.0	194880.0	213440.0	240332.0	256006.0	
	II.4.1 Use of disposable income account - Uses											
Adjustment for the change in net equity of households on pension funds	9409.0	11528.0	13421.0	17368.0	23656.0	30379.0	23231.0	-1875.0	38775.0	41180.0	...	
SAVING, GROSS	69456.0	77057.0	96016.0	99465.0	113167.0	109489.0	131778.0	196755.0	174665.0	199152.0	252652.0	

	2001	2002	2003	2004	2005	2006	2007	2008	2009	2010	2011	2012
Series	**300**											
	III.1 Capital account - Changes in liabilities and net worth											
SAVING, GROSS	69456.0	77057.0	96016.0	99465.0	113167.0	109489.0	131778.0	196755.0	174665.0	199152.0	252652.0	
Capital transfers, receivable less payable	2898.0	1827.0	5715.0	5350.0	5896.0	9414.0	8258.0	11019.0	15897.0	9706.0	7270.0	
Capital transfers, receivable	3731.0	2671.0	7217.0	5821.0	10319.0	11637.0	10738.0	12883.0	17123.0	11582.0	13120.0	
Less: Capital transfers, payable	833.0	844.0	1502.0	471.0	4423.0	2223.0	2480.0	1864.0	1226.0	1876.0	5850.0	
Equals: CHANGES IN NET WORTH DUE TO SAVING AND CAPITAL TRANSFERS	-2322.0	1203.0	20100.0	19106.0	29466.0	23209.0	40142.0	106008.0	87410.0	104248.0	151339.0	
	III.1 Capital account - Changes in assets											
Gross capital formation	98940.0	83318.0	87157.0	104559.0	106441.0	132023.0	174870.0	175906.0	141544.0	144116.0	173596.0	
Gross fixed capital formation	98125.0	84761.0	83627.0	90369.0	97110.0	116212.0	143889.0	157059.0	146690.0	135174.0	151295.0	
Changes in inventories	732.0	-1537.0	3444.0	14110.0	9225.0	15730.0	30887.0	18746.0	-5234.0	8846.0	22215.0	
Acquisitions less disposals of valuables	83.0	94.0	86.0	80.0	106.0	81.0	94.0	101.0	88.0	96.0	86.0	
Acquisitions less disposals of non-produced non-financial assets	...	...	...	...	...	...	...	...	...	2357.0	4723.0	
NET LENDING (+) / NET BORROWING (-)	-26586.0	-4434.0	14574.0	256.0	12622.0	-13120.0	-34834.0	31868.0	49018.0	62385.0	81603.0	
	III.2 Financial account - Changes in liabilities and net worth											
Net incurrence of liabilities	104544.9	24320.7	66287.2	104221.0	135167.0	277614.0	347323.0	268816.0	102137.0	174735.0	205914.0	
Currency and deposits	37824.1	-13975.7	27887.5	34549.0	45070.0	66118.0	116745.0	112818.0	72074.0	64150.0	81309.0	
Securities other than shares	1988.1	206.9	-705.3	2451.0	5213.0	5492.0	2339.0	23516.0	-24162.0	9719.0	12842.0	
Loans	15983.1	3277.2	6397.5	7950.0	14257.0	57275.0	78418.0	101189.0	3710.0	14707.0	56748.0	
Shares and other equity	14873.1	27107.0	37180.0	33804.0	36105.0	66831.0	91319.0	-16247.0	37615.0	34738.0	-5333.0	
Insurance technical reserves	6345.2	7027.5	5802.8	20669.0	20056.0	25765.0	28198.0	32613.0	18753.0	28321.0	16324.0	
Financial derivatives	...	...	...	...	...	...	...	...	...	...	...	
Other accounts payable	27531.3	677.8	-10275.3	4799.0	14466.0	56133.0	30305.0	14928.0	-5854.0	23100.0	44022.0	
NET LENDING (+) / NET BORROWING (-) [a]	-18499.5	6798.7	26302.8	-7091.0	-6283.0	-29256.0	-70963.0	-39467.0	26415.0	42550.0	-2748.0	
	III.2 Financial account - Changes in assets											
Net acquisition of financial assets	86045.4	31119.4	92590.0	97131.0	128884.0	248358.0	276360.0	229348.0	128553.0	217285.0	203166.0	
Monetary gold and SDRs	2.0	1.3	0.0	-829.0	1.0	-1.0	-1.0	-603.0	-182.0	-101.0	...	
Currency and deposits	22677.0	-20259.5	10520.7	44776.0	30636.0	23866.0	24596.0	-43101.0	2896.0	30844.0	31167.0	
Securities other than shares	28461.9	29418.0	51031.1	27629.0	47276.0	54438.0	55076.0	78861.0	39304.0	63701.0	25760.0	
Loans	11162.9	16304.7	18845.8	22640.0	36297.0	78267.0	122478.0	147581.0	67726.0	79650.0	114005.0	
Shares and other equity	-3297.0	3134.1	6570.9	-2547.0	3441.0	32785.0	47575.0	36653.0	20466.0	16269.0	7988.0	
Insurance technical reserves	1135.2	285.3	870.4	1069.0	250.0	1102.0	521.0	2131.0	1272.0	2730.0	2407.0	
Financial derivatives	...	...	...	...	...	...	...	...	...	...	...	
Other accounts receivable	25903.4	2235.5	4751.1	4393.0	10983.0	57901.0	26115.0	7825.0	-2930.0	24191.0	21966.0	

[a] Net lending in the financial account and Net lending in the capital account have not been reconciled.

Table 4.9 Combined Sectors: Households and NPISH (S.14 + S.15)

Series 300: 1993 SNA, Zloty, Western calendar year — **Data in millions**

	2001	2002	2003	2004	2005	2006	2007	2008	2009	2010	2011	2012
Series	**300**											
	I. Production account - Resources											
Output, at basic prices (otherwise, please specify)	408028.0	419402.0	429484.0	459148.0	469560.0	499883.0	556357.0	585574.0	613610.0	628928.0	677905.0	
	I. Production account - Uses											
Intermediate consumption, at purchaser's prices	158898.0	161478.0	166410.0	176260.0	173540.0	187753.0	217823.0	225437.0	231029.0	237766.0	256699.0	
VALUE ADDED GROSS, at basic prices	249130.0	257924.0	263074.0	282888.0	296020.0	312130.0	338534.0	360137.0	382581.0	391162.0	421206.0	
Less: Consumption of fixed capital	14468.0	15046.0	16089.0	16926.0	17633.0	18500.0	20134.0	21438.0	21002.0	21203.0	21755.0	
VALUE ADDED NET, at basic prices	234662.0	242878.0	246985.0	265962.0	278387.0	293630.0	318400.0	338699.0	361579.0	369959.0	399451.0	
	II.1.1 Generation of income account - Resources											
VALUE ADDED GROSS, at basic prices	249130.0	257924.0	263074.0	282888.0	296020.0	312130.0	338534.0	360137.0	382581.0	391162.0	421206.0	
	II.1.1 Generation of income account - Uses											
Compensation of employees	29039.0	30682.0	33626.0	34583.0	35253.0	36489.0	38174.0	45875.0	48896.0	49305.0	50427.0	
Other taxes less Other subsidies on production	1715.0	1760.0	1930.0	-1702.0	-1240.0	-2691.0	-3155.0	-4389.0	-2524.0	-1216.0	-1322.0	
Other taxes on production	1715.0	1760.0	1930.0	2045.0	2724.0	2963.0	2601.0	2792.0	3111.0	3655.0	4034.0	
Less: Other subsidies on production	...	...	...	3747.0	3964.0	5654.0	5756.0	7181.0	5635.0	4871.0	5356.0	
OPERATING SURPLUS, GROSS	30976.0	32721.0	32272.0	33838.0	35426.0	35991.0	39351.0	44884.0	44137.0	43187.0	72215.0	
MIXED INCOME, GROSS	187400.0	192761.0	195246.0	216169.0	226581.0	242341.0	264164.0	273767.0	292072.0	299886.0	299886.0	
	II.1.2 Allocation of primary income account - Resources											
OPERATING SURPLUS, GROSS	30976.0	32721.0	32272.0	33838.0	35426.0	35991.0	39351.0	44884.0	44137.0	43187.0	72215.0	
MIXED INCOME, GROSS	187400.0	192761.0	195246.0	216169.0	226581.0	242341.0	264164.0	273767.0	292072.0	299886.0	299886.0	
Compensation of employees	322774.0	319916.0	326908.0	345268.0	364966.0	391192.0	432089.0	485564.0	505377.0	528942.0	554623.0	
Property income	56231.0	57117.0	46576.0	48155.0	48180.0	44352.0	52374.0	54510.0	55033.0	59205.0	62732.0	
	II.1.2 Allocation of primary income account - Uses											
Property income	10768.0	9765.0	5826.0	4766.0	5010.0	3909.0	13259.0	18978.0	11046.0	14051.0	17641.0	
BALANCE OF PRIMARY INCOMES	586613.0	592750.0	595176.0	638664.0	670143.0	709967.0	774719.0	839747.0	885573.0	917169.0	971815.0	
	II.2 Secondary distribution of income account - Resources											
BALANCE OF PRIMARY INCOMES	586613.0	592750.0	595176.0	638664.0	670143.0	709967.0	774719.0	839747.0	885573.0	917169.0	971815.0	
Social contributions	0.0	0.0	0.0	0.0	0.0	0.0	0.0	0.0	0.0	0.0	0.0	
Social benefits other than social transfers in kind	132040.0	137322.0	142779.0	148289.0	153946.0	161336.0	166880.0	179112.0	197755.0	210072.0	215523.0	
Other current transfers	29754.0	37741.0	41159.0	29869.0	37248.0	45798.0	53492.0	64399.0	71776.0	66485.0	70575.0	
	II.2 Secondary distribution of income account - Uses											
Current taxes on income, wealth, etc.	35392.0	39607.0	37064.0	37537.0	47526.0	51917.0	64488.0	72600.0	66577.0	66169.0	71485.0	
Social contributions	115019.0	116972.0	117795.0	124505.0	134401.0	142634.0	158022.0	165676.0	175456.0	180582.0	189697.0	
Social benefits other than social transfers in kind	0.0	0.0	0.0	0.0	0.0	0.0	0.0	0.0	0.0	0.0	0.0	
Other current transfers	17416.0	17551.0	20165.0	22025.0	23142.0	26400.0	29122.0	38884.0	49540.0	43252.0	47145.0	
GROSS DISPOSABLE INCOME	580580.0	593683.0	604090.0	632755.0	656268.0	696150.0	743459.0	806098.0	863531.0	903723.0	949586.0	

	2001	2002	2003	2004	2005	2006	2007	2008	2009	2010	2011	2012
Series	**300**											
II.4.1 Use of disposable income account - Resources												
GROSS DISPOSABLE INCOME	580580.0	593683.0	604090.0	632755.0	656268.0	696150.0	743459.0	806098.0	863531.0	903723.0	949586.0	
Adjustment for the change in net equity of households on pension funds	9409.0	11528.0	13421.0	17368.0	23656.0	30379.0	23231.0	-1875.0	38775.0	41180.0	3354.0	
II.4.1 Use of disposable income account - Uses												
Final consumption expenditure	506753.0	541341.0	554989.0	598074.0	623360.0	662313.0	711872.0	785115.0	821036.0	867810.0	932827.0	
Individual consumption expenditure	506753.0	541341.0	554989.0	598074.0	623360.0	662313.0	711872.0	785115.0	821036.0	867810.0	932827.0	
SAVING, GROSS	83236.0	63870.0	62522.0	52049.0	56564.0	64216.0	54818.0	19108.0	81270.0	77093.0	20113.0	
III.1 Capital account - Changes in liabilities and net worth												
SAVING, GROSS	83236.0	63870.0	62522.0	52049.0	56564.0	64216.0	54818.0	19108.0	81270.0	77093.0	20113.0	
Capital transfers, receivable less payable	2352.0	2518.0	2800.0	115.0	671.0	3919.0	4067.0	3675.0	4842.0	3830.0	4150.0	
Capital transfers, receivable	2571.0	2715.0	2994.0	589.0	1307.0	4214.0	4630.0	4274.0	5309.0	4252.0	4524.0	
Less: Capital transfers, payable	219.0	197.0	194.0	474.0	636.0	295.0	563.0	599.0	467.0	422.0	374.0	
Equals: CHANGES IN NET WORTH DUE TO SAVINGS AND CAPITAL TRANSFERS	71120.0	51342.0	49233.0	35238.0	39602.0	49635.0	38751.0	1345.0	65110.0	59720.0	2508.0	
III.1 Capital account - Changes in assets												
Gross capital formation	36256.0	39018.0	42267.0	49121.0	48626.0	49277.0	62619.0	70758.0	60787.0	72408.0	70877.0	
Gross fixed capital formation	36697.0	38866.0	42052.0	45770.0	48576.0	50667.0	60822.0	68260.0	67817.0	66465.0	71116.0	
Changes in inventories	-220.0	463.0	589.0	3749.0	483.0	-959.0	2278.0	3016.0	-6581.0	6432.0	204.0	
Acquisitions less disposals of valuables	-221.0	-311.0	-374.0	-398.0	-433.0	-431.0	-481.0	-518.0	-449.0	-489.0	-443.0	
Acquisitions less disposals of non-produced non-financial assets	...	...	...	...	...	...	...	...	...	-1759.0	-645.0	
NET LENDING (+) / NET BORROWING (-)	49332.0	27370.0	23055.0	3043.0	8609.0	18858.0	-3734.0	-47975.0	25325.0	10274.0	-45969.0	
III.2 Financial account - Changes in liabilities and net worth												
Net incurrence of liabilities	12649.9	3141.1	12059.1	20217.0	27809.0	53370.0	80393.0	87588.0	50073.0	40392.0	41864.0	
Currency and deposits	...	...	...	...	...	...	...	...	...	...	...	
Securities other than shares	2.5	6.1	-4.0	0.0	0.0	0.0	0.0	0.0	0.0	0.0	...	
Loans	7473.5	9288.5	13992.9	19164.0	27011.0	50739.0	80362.0	86967.0	50877.0	39834.0	40817.0	
Shares and other equity	...	...	...	...	...	...	...	...	...	...	...	
Insurance technical reserves	...	...	...	...	...	...	...	...	...	...	...	
Financial derivatives	...	...	...	...	...	...	...	...	...	...	...	
Other accounts payable	5173.9	-6153.5	-1929.8	1053.0	798.0	2631.0	31.0	620.0	-804.0	559.0	1047.0	
NET LENDING (+) / NET BORROWING (-)	36976.1[a]	13515.8[a]	8158.6[a]	18489.0	44917.0	25076.0[a]	29789.0[a]	-86203.0[a]	34005.0[a]	54148.0[a]	24727.0[a]	
III.2 Financial account - Changes in assets												
Net acquisition of financial assets	49626.0	16656.9	20217.7	38707.0	72727.0	78446.0	110182.0	1385.0	84078.0	94541.0	66591.0	
Currency and deposits	30137.8	-2145.5	4677.1	4277.0	16282.0	33579.0	35886.0	78802.0	49460.0	39569.0	59627.0	
Securities other than shares	-1452.9	4219.8	1964.9	328.0	-1976.0	-1124.0	-1265.0	1369.0	-2811.0	-226.0	120.0	
Loans	14.6	8.1	16.4	2051.0	311.0	387.0	-1806.0	1045.0	1696.0	-995.0	-394.0	
Shares and other equity	6869.1	16590.1	17843.2	13079.0	38848.0	22697.0	44071.0	-113925.0	18391.0	28464.0	-7725.0	
Insurance technical reserves	5357.1	6567.1	4913.2	19703.0	19314.0	24654.0	27313.0	31347.0	17543.0	26168.0	14056.0	

	2001	2002	2003	2004	2005	2006	2007	2008	2009	2010	2011	2012
Series	**300**											
Financial derivatives	...	...	...	...	...	...	...	...	...	...	...	
Other accounts receivable	8700.3	-8582.7	-9197.1	-731.0	-53.0	-1747.0	5982.0	2747.0	-201.0	1560.0	907.0	

[a] Statistical discrepancy between Net lending in the financial account and Net lending in the capital account.

Portugal

Source

The preparation of national accounts statistics in Portugal is undertaken by the Statistics Portugal (INE), Lisbon. The official estimates are disseminated in the official website, quarterly and annually, under the theme "National Accounts", INE. The present inventory of sources and methods describes the methodology used by the Portuguese System of National Accounts (SNCP) base 2000. The description seeks essentially to explain the processes applied in the base year. The following tables have been prepared from successive replies to the United Nations national accounts questionnaire. The data was received through the Organisation for Economic Co-operation and Development (OECD), Paris.

General

The latest estimates shown in the following tables have been prepared in accordance with the concepts and definitions of System of National Accounts 1993 (1993 SNA). Previously the estimates were prepared in accordance with the United Nations System of National Accounts 1968 (1968 SNA). The National Accounts in Portugal are according to the European System of National Accounts, ESA95, which is an EU regulation meaning that it is mandatory for the EU countries. Some ESA95 transmission tables are regularly transmitted to Eurostat. Presently Statistics Portugal compiles annual full fledged Supply and Uses Tables and Integrated Economic Accounts. Estimates of annual GDP are normally available on a provisional basis 9 months after the reference year, on an A6 level and for the main components of GDP. Also this level of detail is available for quarterly National Accounts and these are disclosed 70 days after the reference quarter. All data since 1995 are available in Euro, the present national currency. When the scope and coverage of the estimates differ for conceptual or statistical reasons from the definitions and classifications recommended in SNA, a footnote is indicated to the relevant tables.

On 1 January 1999 the conversion rate of the national currencies to the new currency euro was irrevocably fixed and the euro became the single currency of the 11 member countries of the European Monetary Union (EMU). For these 11 countries all data starting 1999 is in euro. The data before 1999 is still in national currency but it was converted to 'euro' using the fixed exchange rates to allow for easy comparison of national time series data. In this publication the currency name of this data consists of the year of accession plus the ISO currency code of the national currency and the word 'euro'. In the case of Portugal the currency name for the data before 1999 is "1999 PTE euro". For international comparisons, like for example when converting national data into US dollar the data before the euro introduction has first to be converted back into national currency using the fixed 6-digit Euro conversion rate of 1 Euro = 200.482 Portuguese escudo. The name of the currency of the newly submitted data is "1999 PTE euro" for the data before 1999 and "euro" for the data from 1999 on. In the database this newly submitted data is stored as a new series of data and will be shown in this yearbook as a new row of data if in the same table there is also previously submitted data. Previously submitted data for Portugal, like for example all old data following the 1968 SNA is still in "Portuguese escudo", although this is not specifically indicated in the tables.

Methodology:

Overview of GDP Compilation

Gross Domestic Product is estimated mainly through the production approach. One of the principal aims of the Portuguese System of National Accounts is to ensure the highest level of exhaustiveness in the determining GDP given the statistical sources. The final phase of compiling national accounts is bringing everything together, and this relies in particular on comparison of all the data obtained automatically with a view to ensuring their coherence. The theory behind establishing this balance means that the estimation of aggregates is only deemed to be final after compilation and comparison of the Supply/Use Table (SUT) and the Integrated Economic Accounts Table.

Special note should be taken of the balancing of the SUT, since it is in the context of the balance between sources and uses (supply and demand) for products that the principal decisions are taken influencing the computation of GDP.

Expenditure Approach

The methodology used to compute the variables governing GDP from the expenditure approach was as follows:

Final consumption expenditure of households – the basis for this variable is the Household Budget Survey where the values are extrapolated, encoded by NPCN and adjusted in order to bring them into line with the concepts of national accounts.

Final consumption expenditure of NPISH – this variable results from the transfer of goods and individual non-market services, their value being equal to the value of non-market production.

Final consumption expenditure of general government – this is computed from other non-market production, it is estimated from costs, less payments made by households.

GFCF – GFCF from the expenditure approach is determined from data obtained via institutional sectors (S12, S13 and S15) and in data obtained from the Structural Business Survey (for units of Sector S11 and unincorporated enterprises of S14). For Sectors S12 and S13 the data are exhaustive; for others they are incomplete. This situation results in adjustments based on GFCF obtained from the production approach, through compilation of sources and uses balances. For reasons of exhaustiveness and economic consistency, the prevailing approach is that of supply.

Acquisitions less cessions of valuables (ACOV) – comprises the acquisition of non-financial assets which are neither used in the production process nor consumed, do not under normal conditions deteriorate over time, and are generally acquired and held as a store of value. The value for ACOV is the result of compilation of sources and uses balances, based on identification of codes in the PRODCOM and the foreign trade classification giving rise to ACOV.

Variations in stocks – a preliminary approximation to the value of variations in stocks is made taking data from the Structural Business Survey, and this is then filled out with data from the Annual Industrial Output Survey. Available data allows this flow to be disaggregated into variations in stocks at the producer, in commerce and with the user. A transition is subsequently made from data by activity to data by products.

Exports / Imports – these variables are obtained from statistics of international trade for their goods components, and the balance of payments for services. Since external trade statistics are not exhaustive an estimate is made from foreign trade (Intrastat) data.

Income Approach

The income approach has not played a major role in determining GDP, for lack of suitable statistical sources. These results in the computation of gross operating surplus as a balance from the operating account, with compensation of employees, taxes and subsidies computed independently. For the components of GDP from the income approach computed independently, the following estimation methods were applied:

a) Compensations – direct estimation from data of the Structural Business survey, Income tax data and exhaustive sector data (S13 and S12);

b) Other taxes and other subsidies on production – direct method, from accounting data provided by the units making up general government.

Production Approach

Production transactions can be estimated by all three types of producer: market producers, non-market producers and producers for own final consumption. Taking the various statistical sources together allows the variables necessary for computation of GVA to be obtained for virtually all products and branches.

The transition from business bookkeeping and administrative data to ESA95, National Accounts concepts through the use of bridge tables, where an exhaustive importance is given of the takeover of data from the Structural Business Survey, the Annual Industrial Output Survey, the Survey of Credit Institutions and Financial Corporations and data from General Government.

One of the important factors affecting exhaustiveness is the estimation of two components which may be ignored in business accounting: benefits in kind and tips and gratuities. The production of each branch includes the adjustments made for each of these components.

The methodology for determining GDP from the production approach varies according to branch:

a) In agriculture, forestry and fisheries, production is computed from the application of prices to quantities produced. The principal sources are Estatísticas Agrícolas, published by the Department of Statistics of Agriculture and Fisheries which compiles, inter alia, the Statistics of Crop Production; Statistics of Animal Production and Forestry Statistics.

b) In the non-market and market branches of general government and NPISH, production is obtained from accounting data of general government bodies, or, for NPISH, fiscal sources. Non-market production is valued by reference to production costs;

c) For the production of market goods and services, data are obtained in particular from the Structural Business Survey, the Annual Industrial Output Survey and data specific to certain products. This survey is the main source for these branches, other than NACE J – Financial intermediation – which because of its nature is the subject of specific surveys which enable the estimation of the transactions necessary to determine GVA.

Values for taxes and subsidies on products are obtained from accounting data provided by the units making up general government.

Table 1.1 Gross domestic product by expenditures at current prices

Series 400: 1993 SNA, 1999 PTE euro / euro, Western calendar year — **Data in millions**

	2001	2002	2003	2004	2005	2006	2007	2008	2009	2010	2011	2012
Series	**400**											
	Expenditures of the gross domestic product											
Final consumption expenditure	110979.7	116056.1	119528.5	125921.5	132465.0	137749.9	144214.0	149488.9	146960.0	151314.4	148073.4	139821.9
Household final consumption expenditure	82386.9	85744.5	88072.6	92739.2	96881.3	101660.6	107220.1	111363.3	106206.8	110395.2	110243.5	106209.9
NPISHs final consumption expenditure	2488.5	2648.8	2727.3	2858.1	2965.6	3087.0	3414.8	3593.4	3567.9	3584.4	3535.0	3369.1
General government final consumption expenditure	26104.3	27662.8	28728.6	30324.2	32618.1	33002.3	33579.1	34532.2	37185.3	37334.8	34294.9	30242.9
Individual consumption expenditure	15267.4	16250.3	16927.1	17759.6	18875.3	18814.9	18727.8	19116.0	20395.4	20431.6	18925.0	16705.9
Collective consumption expenditure	10836.9	11412.5	11801.5	12564.6	13742.8	14187.4	14851.3	15416.2	16789.9	16903.2	15369.9	13537.0
Gross capital formation	37270.4	36182.9	33700.3	35810.5	36325.5	37078.1	38651.9	39817.2	34050.8	34874.8	30461.2	26408.5
Gross fixed capital formation	36268.2	35978.1	33846.6	34699.7	35412.8	35890.2	37629.2	38634.7	34629.4	33829.7	30552.3	26160.0

	2001	2002	2003	2004	2005	2006	2007	2008	2009	2010	2011	2012
Series	**400**											
Changes in inventories	876.9	81.3	-248.4	1007.9	768.7	1039.8	903.3	1040.5	-702.6	915.6	-218.4	104.1
Acquisitions less disposals of valuables	125.3	123.5	102.1	102.9	144.0	148.1	119.4	142.0	124.0	129.5	127.3	144.4
Exports of goods and services	37753.0	38797.5	39630.9	41874.7	42668.7	49712.6	54498.0	55801.8	47235.7	54109.4	61126.1	64038.2
Exports of goods	29554.1	30202.0	31020.5	32413.8	32750.4	37670.2	40342.5	40999.7	33717.0	39421.3	45098.2	47739.7
Exports of services	8198.9	8595.5	8610.4	9460.9	9918.3	12042.4	14155.5	14802.1	13518.7	14688.1	16027.9	16298.5
Less: Imports of goods and services	51532.0	50469.7	49388.0	54294.2	57190.5	63685.2	68044.7	73124.8	59717.3	67439.1	68607.6	65021.8
Imports of goods	45184.1	44104.9	43233.2	47601.8	49878.1	55154.7	58746.5	63270.5	50573.8	57666.0	58391.6	55465.4
Imports of services	6347.9	6364.8	6154.8	6692.4	7312.4	8530.5	9298.2	9854.3	9143.5	9773.1	10216.0	9556.4
Plus: Statistical discrepancy	0.0	0.0	0.0	0.0	0.0	0.0	0.0	0.0	0.0	0.0	0.0	0.0
Equals: GROSS DOMESTIC PRODUCT	134471.1	140566.8	143471.7	149312.5	154268.7	160855.4	169319.2	171983.1	168529.2	172859.5	171053.1	165246.8

Table 1.2 Gross domestic product by expenditures at constant prices

Series 400: 1993 SNA, 1999 PTE euro / euro, Western calendar year **Data in millions**

	2001	2002	2003	2004	2005	2006	2007	2008	2009	2010	2011	2012
Series	**400**											
Base year	**2006**											
Expenditures of the gross domestic product												
Final consumption expenditure	128133.1	130006.0	129914.9	133306.3	136079.2	137749.8	140550.6	142080.1	141127.6	143824.2	138152.6	130771.9
Household final consumption expenditure	94787.8	95934.1	95725.0	98262.9	99867.7	101660.7	104089.9	105424.0	102890.1	105586.4	101525.7	95773.1
NPISHs final consumption expenditure	2713.9	2859.6	2842.3	2933.5	3015.7	3087.0	3297.5	3377.5	3380.6	3335.7	3231.9	3077.5
General government final consumption expenditure	30631.4	31212.3	31347.6	32109.9	33195.8	33002.1	33163.2	33278.6	34856.9	34902.1	33395.0	31921.3
Individual consumption expenditure	17962.6	18078.0	18345.3	18462.6	19170.0	18814.9	18852.0	18946.7	19855.5	19920.7	19383.3	18484.9
Collective consumption expenditure	12668.8	13134.3	13002.3	13647.3	14025.8	14187.2	14311.2	14331.9	15001.4	14981.4	14011.7	13436.4
Gross capital formation	41539.6	39411.4	36301.3	37648.0	37304.5	37078.2	37843.6	37801.8	32785.6	33232.4	28686.6	24821.1
Gross fixed capital formation	40611.5	39327.5	36541.1	36535.7	36369.2	35890.2	36830.7	36716.3	33553.9	32504.9	29047.3	24831.3
Changes in inventories	698.5	96.9	-239.8	973.8	781.9	1039.8	895.5	955.1	-819.4	646.8	-434.5	-91.9
Acquisitions less disposals of valuables	162.2	152.6	123.4	121.0	156.4	148.1	117.1	131.6	110.6	106.9	96.0	101.0
Exports of goods and services	40092.4	41203.2	42698.6	44446.3	44549.4	49712.6	53463.4	53413.7	47581.6	52444.7	56181.1	57999.0
Exports of goods	30858.0	31757.0	33473.8	34552.9	34321.6	37670.2	39789.0	39548.4	34631.4	38520.5	41328.6	43101.1
Exports of services	9234.4	9446.2	9224.8	9893.4	10227.8	12042.4	13674.4	13865.3	12950.2	13924.2	14852.5	14897.9
Less: Imports of goods and services	54505.1	54251.7	54007.2	58104.3	59422.8	63685.2	67197.4	68769.3	61880.5	66839.9	62888.2	58660.5
Imports of goods	47225.2	47108.9	47194.2	50899.1	51850.9	55154.7	58165.0	59390.4	53094.1	57638.4	53624.6	50119.0
Imports of services	7279.9	7142.8	6813.0	7205.2	7571.9	8530.5	9032.4	9378.9	8786.4	9201.5	9263.6	8541.5
Plus: Statistical discrepancy	-99.4	-22.2	14.6	43.2	48.7	0.0	0.0	119.9	243.4	291.8	287.4	276.2
Equals: GROSS DOMESTIC PRODUCT	155160.6	156346.7	154922.2	157339.5	158559.0	160855.4	164660.2	164646.2	159857.7	162953.2	160419.5	155207.7

Table 1.3 Relations among product, income, savings, and net lending aggregates

Series 400: 1993 SNA, 1999 PTE euro / euro, Western calendar year **Data in millions**

	2001	2002	2003	2004	2005	2006	2007	2008	2009	2010	2011	2012
Series	**400**											
GROSS DOMESTIC PRODUCT	134471.1	140566.8	143471.7	149312.5	154268.7	160855.4	169319.2	171983.1	168529.2	172859.5	171053.1	165246.8
Plus: Compensation of employees - from and to the rest of the world, net	...	...	...	...	...	...	...	...	...	...	...	...
Plus: Property income - from and to the rest of the world, net	...	...	...	...	...	...	...	...	...	...	...	...
Sum of Compensation of employees and property income - from and to the rest of the world, net	-3434.5	-2246.2	-1382.8	-1589.3	-2288.2	-4856.2	-5373.7	-6147.4	-6864.3	-5924.9	-6445.0	-4176.2
Plus: Sum of Compensation of employees and property income - from the rest of the world	7513.1	6708.0	7301.1	8314.6	9478.5	12730.3	14444.4	14458.5	10541.2	14034.1	12543.7	10126.2
Less: Sum of Compensation of employees and property income - to the rest of the world	10947.6	8954.2	8683.9	9903.9	11766.7	17586.5	19818.1	20605.9	17405.5	19959.0	18988.7	14302.4
Plus: Taxes less subsidies on production and imports - from and to the rest of the world, net	...	...	...	...	...	...	...	...	...	...	...	...
Equals: GROSS NATIONAL INCOME	131036.6	138320.6	142088.9	147723.2	151980.5	155999.2	163945.5	165835.7	161664.9	166934.6	164608.1	161070.6
Plus: Current transfers - from and to the rest of the world, net	2961.3	1952.0	1544.4	1666.1	898.3	1572.3	1712.7	1800.6	1160.3	1362.7	1535.5	1938.8
Plus: Current transfers - from the rest of the world	4995.8	4298.0	3854.0	4248.5	4018.9	4665.2	4841.0	4894.5	4580.9	4876.6	5065.5	5337.5
Less: Current transfers - to the rest of the world	2034.5	2346.0	2309.6	2582.4	3120.6	3092.9	3128.3	3093.9	3420.6	3513.9	3530.0	3398.7
Equals: GROSS NATIONAL DISPOSABLE INCOME	133997.9	140272.6	143633.3	149389.3	152878.8	157571.5	165658.2	167636.3	162825.2	168297.3	166143.6	163009.4
Less: Final consumption expenditure / Actual final consumption	110979.7	116056.1	119528.5	125921.5	132465.0	137749.9	144214.0	149488.9	146960.0	151314.4	148073.4	139821.9
Equals: SAVING, GROSS	23018.2	24216.5	24104.8	23467.8	20413.8	19821.6	21444.2	18147.4	15865.2	16982.9	18070.2	23187.5
Plus: Capital transfers - from and to the rest of the world, net	2206.2	2516.6	3246.8	2529.2	2217.0	2014.2	1940.6	1670.0	1968.2	2415.9	2713.1	3695.6
Plus: Capital transfers - from the rest of the world	2393.7	2717.8	3417.8	2718.1	2381.3	2187.4	2181.4	2033.7	2232.4	2688.3	2958.3	3897.4
Less: Capital transfers - to the rest of the world	187.5	201.2	171.0	188.9	164.3	173.2	240.8	363.7	264.2	272.4	245.2	201.8
Less: Gross capital formation	37270.4	36182.9	33700.3	35810.5	36325.5	37078.1	38651.9	39817.2	34050.8	34874.8	30461.2	26408.5
Less: Acquisitions less disposals of non-produced non-financial assets	16.6	-1.9	-13.2	-38.3	-48.5	-7.3	-159.7	-442.2	4.0	13.7	-136.3	-77.9
Equals: NET LENDING (+) / NET BORROWING (-) OF THE NATION	-12062.6	-9447.9	-6335.5	-9775.2	-13646.2	-15235.0	-15107.4	-19557.6	-16221.4	-15489.7	-9541.6	552.5
	Net values: Gross National Income / Gross National Disposable Income / Saving Gross less Consumption of fixed capital											
Less: Consumption of fixed capital	21655.0	23083.6	23991.2	25043.6	26259.2	27299.9	28350.7	29745.5	29795.2	30444.1	30987.6	31102.9
Equals: NET NATIONAL INCOME	109381.6	115237.0	118097.7	122679.6	125721.3	128699.3	135594.8	136090.2	131869.7	136490.5	133620.5	129967.7
Equals: NET NATIONAL DISPOSABLE INCOME	112342.9	117189.0	119642.1	124345.7	126619.6	130271.6	137307.5	137890.8	133030.0	137853.2	135156.0	131906.5
Equals: SAVING, NET	1363.2	1132.9	113.6	-1575.8	-5845.4	-7478.3	-6906.5	-11598.1	-13930.0	-13461.2	-12917.4	-7915.4

Table 2.4 Value added by industries at current prices (ISIC Rev. 4)

Series 400: 1993 SNA, 1999 PTE euro / euro, Western calendar year — **Data in millions**

	2001	2002	2003	2004	2005	2006	2007	2008	2009	2010	2011	2012
Series	**400**											
Industries												
Agriculture, forestry and fishing	4032.8	3910.0	3896.4	3974.7	3659.1	3760.8	3515.0	3517.8	3410.8	3467.3	3239.9	3221.2
Manufacturing, mining and quarrying and other industrial activities	23315.3	23800.3	23765.7	24196.7	23999.9	25033.4	26333.7	25897.7	24700.7	26748.7	27136.5	26594.8
Manufacturing	19584.1	19887.7	19412.6	19534.0	19432.5	19747.8	20561.5	20456.1	18742.7	20221.1	20960.0	20572.9
Construction	9843.9	10075.2	9633.3	10026.6	9968.0	10033.7	10699.9	10887.7	9964.2	9465.2	8516.9	7066.3
Wholesale and retail trade, transportation and storage, accommodation and food service activities	27301.6	28483.3	28788.7	30447.5	30890.9	32057.0	33953.7	34317.2	35366.5	35708.8	35871.1	35762.4
Information and communication	4308.9	4635.2	4706.4	4933.1	5083.2	5304.4	5504.5	5675.1	5719.4	5515.2	5350.8	5046.9
Financial and insurance activities	7248.3	7349.8	7738.6	8117.6	8366.4	9988.1	11013.9	11503.5	10399.1	10375.1	10188.6	9456.6
Real estate activities	8823.8	9362.4	10027.6	10128.6	10669.8	10774.3	11835.6	12325.5	12115.5	12861.3	13561.1	14212.3
Professional, scientific, technical, administrative and support service activities	6710.2	6950.1	7164.5	7607.6	7992.4	8152.1	9120.1	9829.3	10013.1	10114.8	9968.1	10003.6
Public administration and defence, education, human health and social work activities	23778.8	25448.8	26537.5	27744.3	29461.5	29816.6	30505.4	31288.2	32788.5	32823.4	30998.2	28243.0
Other service activities	2567.2	2837.3	2988.6	3168.7	3274.5	3429.9	3726.9	4069.1	4239.2	4346.7	4441.0	4510.9
Equals: VALUE ADDED, GROSS, at basic prices	117930.8	122852.4	125247.3	130345.4	133365.7	138350.3	146208.7	149311.1	148717.0	151426.5	149272.2	144118.0
Less: Financial intermediation services indirectly measured (FISIM)	...	...	...	...	...	...	...	...	...	...	...	...
Plus: Taxes less Subsidies on products	16540.3	17714.4	18224.4	18967.1	20903.0	22505.1	23110.5	22672.0	19812.2	21433.0	21637.0	20795.3
Plus: Taxes on products	17237.7	18423.8	18988.1	19784.6	21675.8	23130.8	23660.6	23206.0	20334.8	21996.4	22299.1	21247.2
Less: Subsidies on products	697.4	709.4	763.7	817.5	772.8	625.7	550.1	534.0	522.6	563.4	662.1	451.9
Plus: Statistical discrepancy	0.0	0.0	0.0	0.0	0.0	0.0	0.0	0.0	0.0	0.0	143.9	333.5
Equals: GROSS DOMESTIC PRODUCT	134471.1	140566.8	143471.7	149312.5	154268.7	160855.4	169319.2	171983.1	168529.2	172859.5	171053.1	165246.8

Table 2.5 Value added by industries at constant prices (ISIC Rev. 4)

Series 400: 1993 SNA, 1999 PTE euro / euro, Western calendar year — **Data in millions**

	2001	2002	2003	2004	2005	2006	2007	2008	2009	2010	2011	2012
Series	**400**											
Base year	**2006**											
Industries												
Agriculture, forestry and fishing	3660.1	3769.5	3678.9	3887.7	3673.2	3760.8	3588.6	3698.6	3559.7	3615.2	3637.6	3602.7
Manufacturing, mining and quarrying and other industrial activities	24416.9	24431.3	24503.2	24709.0	24396.6	25033.3	25697.7	25564.3	23265.3	24984.5	25196.6	24631.4
Manufacturing	19881.7	19920.8	19704.1	19765.0	19539.1	19747.7	20290.3	20031.8	18087.5	19411.3	19751.9	19292.7
Construction	12100.0	11656.0	10657.9	10610.7	10304.6	10033.7	10231.5	9728.2	8688.4	8215.2	7407.9	6237.0
Wholesale and retail trade, transportation and storage, accommodation and food service activities	30383.5	30435.8	30011.0	31084.1	31286.9	32056.8	32948.1	32751.9	32537.3	33399.2	33095.2	32590.4

	2001	2002	2003	2004	2005	2006	2007	2008	2009	2010	2011	2012
Series	**400**											
Base year	**2006**											
Information and communication	4311.5	4624.6	4675.3	4882.1	5073.7	5304.3	5544.9	5745.3	5820.0	5659.2	5444.5	5154.5
Financial and insurance activities	7090.9	7651.0	8297.8	8695.9	8862.6	9988.1	10877.8	11398.8	11586.6	11808.3	11560.7	11142.3
Real estate activities	10992.7	10893.0	10872.4	10724.1	10894.8	10774.3	10887.8	10968.5	11055.8	11081.2	11268.2	11480.5
Professional, scientific, technical, administrative and support service activities	7472.2	7531.9	7532.2	7735.8	8074.3	8152.2	8644.4	8994.5	9036.6	9279.8	9058.3	8931.1
Public administration and defence, education, human health and social work activities	28873.6	29365.3	29268.7	29463.7	30079.5	29816.7	30071.1	30024.3	30131.3	30206.3	29722.3	29336.7
Other service activities	3193.9	3274.5	3310.8	3321.6	3366.0	3429.8	3617.6	3835.1	3830.6	3868.2	3870.0	3843.2
Equals: VALUE ADDED, GROSS, at basic prices	132495.3	133632.9	132808.2	135114.7	136012.2	138350.0	142109.5	142709.5	139511.6	142117.1	140261.3	136949.8
Less: Financial intermediation services indirectly measured (FISIM)	...	...	...	...	...	...	...	...	...	...	...	...
Plus: Taxes less Subsidies on products	22796.4	22832.0	22165.8	22242.3	22584.1	22505.4	22550.7	21934.0	20332.2	20830.9	19927.5	18317.8
Plus: Taxes on products	23603.2	23584.6	22915.9	23065.2	23325.3	23131.0	23077.7	22438.4	20827.5	21346.8	20438.6	18797.3
Less: Subsidies on products	806.8	752.6	750.1	822.9	741.2	625.6	527.0	504.4	495.3	515.9	511.1	479.5
Plus: Statistical discrepancy	-131.1	-118.2	-51.8	-17.5	-37.3	0.0	0.0	2.7	13.9	5.2	230.7	-59.9
Equals: GROSS DOMESTIC PRODUCT	155160.6	156346.7	154922.2	157339.5	158559.0	160855.4	164660.2	164646.2	159857.7	162953.2	160419.5	155207.7

Table 2.6 Output, gross value added and fixed assets by industries at current prices (ISIC Rev. 4) Total economy

Series 400: 1993 SNA, 1999 PTE euro / euro, Western calendar year — **Data in millions**

	2001	2002	2003	2004	2005	2006	2007	2008	2009	2010	2011	2012
Series	**400**											
Output, at basic prices	...	...	...	...	...	...	...	...	...	...	...	...
Less: Intermediate consumption, at purchaser's prices	...	...	...	...	...	...	...	...	...	...	...	...
Equals: VALUE ADDED, GROSS, at basic prices	117930.8	122852.4	125247.3	130345.4	133365.7	138350.3	146208.7	149311.1	148717.0	151426.5	149272.2	144118.0
Compensation of employees	66109.7	69374.4	71223.1	73648.2	77358.8	79663.4	82861.1	85692.6	85888.4	86813.8	85454.7	79243.5
Taxes on production and imports, less Subsidies	-1117.9	-858.5	-333.3	-1008.6	-1136.8	-941.1	-865.8	-578.1	-700.1	-968.6	-820.5	-809.5
OPERATING SURPLUS, GROSS [a]	52939.0	54336.5	54357.5	57705.8	57143.7	59628.0	64213.5	64196.6	63528.6	65581.2	64763.1	66001.2
MIXED INCOME, GROSS	...	...	...	...	...	...	...	...	...	...	...	...
Less: Consumption of fixed capital	21655.0	23083.6	23991.2	25043.6	26259.2	27299.9	28350.7	29745.5	29795.2	30444.1	30987.6	31102.9
OPERATING SURPLUS, NET [b]	31284.0	31252.9	30366.3	32662.2	30884.5	32328.1	35862.8	34451.1	33733.4	35137.1	33775.5	34898.3
MIXED INCOME, NET	...	...	...	...	...	...	...	...	...	...	...	...
Gross capital formation	37270.4	36182.9	33700.3	35810.5	36325.5	37078.1	38651.9	39817.2	34050.8	34874.8	30461.2	26408.5
Gross fixed capital formation	36268.2	35978.1	33846.6	34699.7	35412.8	35890.2	37629.2	38634.7	34629.4	33829.7	30552.3	26160.0
Changes in inventories	876.9	81.3	-248.4	1007.9	768.7	1039.8	903.3	1040.5	-702.6	915.6	-218.4	104.1
Acquisitions less disposals of valuables	125.3	123.5	102.1	102.9	144.0	148.1	119.4	142.0	124.0	129.5	127.3	144.4
Employment (average, in 1000 persons)	5121.3	5151.2	5120.7	5116.7	5099.9	5126.1	5123.8	5147.1	5014.2	4937.0	4861.2	4655.6

[a] Includes Mixed Income, Gross.
[b] Includes Mixed Income, Net.

Table 2.6 Output, gross value added and fixed assets by industries at current prices (ISIC Rev. 4) Agriculture, forestry and fishing (A)

Series 400: 1993 SNA, 1999 PTE euro / euro, Western calendar year **Data in millions**

	2001	2002	2003	2004	2005	2006	2007	2008	2009	2010	2011	2012
Series	**400**											
Equals: VALUE ADDED, GROSS, at basic prices	4032.8	3910.0	3896.4	3974.7	3659.1	3760.8	3515.0	3517.8	3410.8	3467.3	3239.9	3221.2
Compensation of employees	891.7	865.0	903.1	931.3	980.1	990.1	1032.0	1045.3	1036.7	1047.1	1066.4	1086.3
Employment (average, in 1000 persons)	631.2	612.4	617.8	593.4	583.9	583.7	572.3	568.6	558.8	533.4	517.1	514.1

Table 2.6 Output, gross value added and fixed assets by industries at current prices (ISIC Rev. 4) Manufacturing, mining and quarrying and other industrial activities (B+C+D+E)

Series 400: 1993 SNA, 1999 PTE euro / euro, Western calendar year **Data in millions**

	2001	2002	2003	2004	2005	2006	2007	2008	2009	2010	2011	2012
Series	**400**											
Equals: VALUE ADDED, GROSS, at basic prices	23315.3	23800.3	23765.7	24196.7	23999.9	25033.4	26333.7	25897.7	24700.7	26748.7	27136.5	26594.8
Compensation of employees	12616.3	12950.1	12879.3	13034.4	13222.6	13670.2	13942.6	14182.5	13453.0	13587.5	13704.7	12967.8
Employment (average, in 1000 persons)	1032.2	1018.9	991.8	966.9	939.2	928.0	912.1	896.7	836.1	810.7	800.9	756.5

Table 2.6 Output, gross value added and fixed assets by industries at current prices (ISIC Rev. 4) Manufacturing (C)

Series 400: 1993 SNA, 1999 PTE euro / euro, Western calendar year **Data in millions**

	2001	2002	2003	2004	2005	2006	2007	2008	2009	2010	2011	2012
Series	**400**											
Equals: VALUE ADDED, GROSS, at basic prices	19584.1	19887.7	19412.6	19534.0	19432.5	19747.8	20561.5	20456.1	18742.7	20221.1	20960.0	20572.9
Compensation of employees	11311.7	11594.7	11452.1	11555.1	11702.5	12055.3	12281.5	12499.6	11694.7	11797.4	11878.0	11257.0
Employment (average, in 1000 persons)	965.6	954.0	924.4	900.6	874.6	863.2	848.1	831.8	770.6	744.5	734.3	694.5

Table 2.6 Output, gross value added and fixed assets by industries at current prices (ISIC Rev. 4) Construction (F)

Series 400: 1993 SNA, 1999 PTE euro / euro, Western calendar year **Data in millions**

	2001	2002	2003	2004	2005	2006	2007	2008	2009	2010	2011	2012
Series	**400**											
Equals: VALUE ADDED, GROSS, at basic prices	9843.9	10075.2	9633.3	10026.6	9968.0	10033.7	10699.9	10887.7	9964.2	9465.2	8516.9	7066.3
Compensation of employees	5571.1	6042.8	5992.9	6137.0	6389.5	6639.6	7194.2	7221.4	6627.0	6495.4	6074.3	4906.5
Employment (average, in 1000 persons)	592.5	611.0	585.7	576.5	554.3	543.1	547.7	533.7	491.1	468.2	440.8	369.4

Table 2.6 Output, gross value added and fixed assets by industries at current prices (ISIC Rev. 4) Wholesale and retail trade, transportation and storage, accommodation and food service activities (G+H+I)

Series 400: 1993 SNA, 1999 PTE euro / euro, Western calendar year — **Data in millions**

	2001	2002	2003	2004	2005	2006	2007	2008	2009	2010	2011	2012
Series	**400**											
Equals: VALUE ADDED, GROSS, at basic prices	27301.6	28483.3	28788.7	30447.5	30890.9	32057.0	33953.7	34317.2	35366.5	35708.8	35871.1	35762.4
Compensation of employees	15051.9	15491.3	16048.3	16820.3	17647.6	18692.9	19674.2	20395.0	20084.8	20582.3	20767.6	19990.2
Employment (average, in 1000 persons)	1181.8	1180.5	1197.7	1230.3	1243.5	1274.5	1270.8	1285.9	1246.8	1236.3	1219.3	1174.2

Table 2.6 Output, gross value added and fixed assets by industries at current prices (ISIC Rev. 4) Information and communication (J)

Series 400: 1993 SNA, 1999 PTE euro / euro, Western calendar year — **Data in millions**

	2001	2002	2003	2004	2005	2006	2007	2008	2009	2010	2011	2012
Series	**400**											
Equals: VALUE ADDED, GROSS, at basic prices	4308.9	4635.2	4706.4	4933.1	5083.2	5304.4	5504.5	5675.1	5719.4	5515.2	5350.8	5046.9
Compensation of employees	1695.0	1857.8	1901.5	1930.4	1992.1	2118.2	2279.5	2478.1	2635.5	2616.3	2586.6	2529.4
Employment (average, in 1000 persons)	60.1	62.1	61.7	63.1	65.4	67.3	69.5	73.6	75.9	77.8	78.1	77.2

Table 2.6 Output, gross value added and fixed assets by industries at current prices (ISIC Rev. 4) Financial and insurance activities (K)

Series 400: 1993 SNA, 1999 PTE euro / euro, Western calendar year — **Data in millions**

	2001	2002	2003	2004	2005	2006	2007	2008	2009	2010	2011	2012
Series	**400**											
Equals: VALUE ADDED, GROSS, at basic prices	7248.3	7349.8	7738.6	8117.6	8366.4	9988.1	11013.9	11503.5	10399.1	10375.1	10188.6	9456.6
Compensation of employees	3271.0	3318.0	3439.1	3513.6	4030.1	4361.3	4518.3	4587.3	4674.9	4785.7	4766.3	4468.5
Employment (average, in 1000 persons)	106.4	104.7	102.0	99.3	100.2	102.2	104.1	103.2	105.1	105.7	107.7	104.7

Table 2.6 Output, gross value added and fixed assets by industries at current prices (ISIC Rev. 4) Real estate activities (L)

Series 400: 1993 SNA, 1999 PTE euro / euro, Western calendar year — **Data in millions**

	2001	2002	2003	2004	2005	2006	2007	2008	2009	2010	2011	2012
Series	**400**											
Equals: VALUE ADDED, GROSS, at basic prices	8823.8	9362.4	10027.6	10128.6	10669.8	10774.3	11835.6	12325.5	12115.5	12861.3	13561.1	14212.3
Compensation of employees	392.8	406.3	419.4	394.6	429.4	452.2	531.4	538.3	499.2	523.4	582.5	555.0
Employment (average, in 1000 persons)	37.2	36.7	36.6	34.7	35.5	35.6	38.8	39.6	38.8	39.0	40.6	40.4

Table 2.6 Output, gross value added and fixed assets by industries at current prices (ISIC Rev. 4) Professional, scientific, technical, administrative and support service activities (M+N)

Series 400: 1993 SNA, 1999 PTE euro / euro, Western calendar year — **Data in millions**

	2001	2002	2003	2004	2005	2006	2007	2008	2009	2010	2011	2012
Series	**400**											
Equals: VALUE ADDED, GROSS, at basic prices	6710.2	6950.1	7164.5	7607.6	7992.4	8152.1	9120.1	9829.3	10013.1	10114.8	9968.1	10003.6
Compensation of employees	3856.9	3981.4	4093.8	4341.0	4641.2	4658.6	5207.2	5692.4	5834.7	5988.0	6007.9	5889.5
Employment (average, in 1000 persons)	298.0	302.9	309.5	322.7	334.5	342.5	354.2	373.1	377.6	380.2	381.1	370.3

Table 2.6 Output, gross value added and fixed assets by industries at current prices (ISIC Rev. 4) Public administration and defence, education, human health and social work activities (O+P+Q)

Series 400: 1993 SNA, 1999 PTE euro / euro, Western calendar year — **Data in millions**

	2001	2002	2003	2004	2005	2006	2007	2008	2009	2010	2011	2012
Series	**400**											
Equals: VALUE ADDED, GROSS, at basic prices	23778.8	25448.8	26537.5	27744.3	29461.5	29816.6	30505.4	31288.2	32788.5	32823.4	30998.2	28243.0
Compensation of employees	20666.6	22198.7	23160.1	24065.2	25399.4	25284.3	25468.5	26309.9	27703.3	27734.3	26292.0	23220.2
Employment (average, in 1000 persons)	929.4	964.2	957.1	967.9	976.9	979.9	975.8	984.2	999.4	1004.0	996.3	975.8

Table 2.6 Output, gross value added and fixed assets by industries at current prices (ISIC Rev. 4) Other service activities (R+S+T)

Series 400: 1993 SNA, 1999 PTE euro / euro, Western calendar year — **Data in millions**

	2001	2002	2003	2004	2005	2006	2007	2008	2009	2010	2011	2012
Series	**400**											
Equals: VALUE ADDED, GROSS, at basic prices	2567.2	2837.3	2988.6	3168.7	3274.5	3429.9	3726.9	4069.1	4239.2	4346.7	4441.0	4510.9
Compensation of employees	2096.4	2263.0	2385.6	2480.4	2626.8	2796.0	3013.2	3242.4	3339.3	3453.8	3606.4	3630.1
Employment (average, in 1000 persons)	252.4	257.8	260.8	261.9	266.6	269.3	278.3	288.4	284.7	281.6	279.3	273.0

Table 3.1 Government final consumption expenditure by function at current prices

Series 400: 1993 SNA, 1999 PTE euro / euro, Western calendar year — **Data in millions**

	2001	2002	2003	2004	2005	2006	2007	2008	2009	2010	2011	2012
Series	**400**											
General public services	2318.1	2298.6	2581.5	3052.5	3499.9	3447.2	3755.1	3966.0	4225.2	4250.8	3886.4	...
Defence	1873.4	1842.7	1839.1	1890.3	2008.5	2017.9	1933.3	2125.7	2485.2	3338.3	2250.7	...
Public order and safety	2119.3	2382.5	2627.5	2636.2	2781.0	2899.7	2919.9	3070.6	3258.6	3256.3	3166.9	...
Economic affairs	2249.3	2539.8	2468.5	2646.5	2968.8	3155.2	3598.9	3456.5	3621.6	3057.0	2975.1	...
Environment protection	632.3	673.6	665.8	563.3	601.5	738.7	722.9	760.8	767.1	740.7	744.3	...
Housing and community amenities	373.6	403.0	328.2	403.6	441.0	472.6	490.7	559.6	595.3	551.8	545.8	...
Health	7067.0	7548.6	7900.4	8577.2	9079.8	9007.7	9189.9	9206.0	10232.4	10151.5	9810.5	...

	2001	2002	2003	2004	2005	2006	2007	2008	2009	2010	2011	2012
Series	**400**											
Recreation, culture and religion	820.0	773.1	737.6	706.4	864.7	931.6	966.6	988.6	1003.7	967.8	990.4	...
Education	7575.0	8197.8	8531.6	8850.4	9381.9	9280.8	9029.6	9366.3	9648.3	9841.1	8945.9	...
Social protection	1076.3	1003.4	1048.6	997.6	991.1	1050.6	972.2	1031.8	1323.0	1155.5	955.2	...
Equals: General government final consumption expenditure	26104.4	27663.0	28728.9	30324.0	32618.2	33002.1	33579.0	34532.0	37160.4	37310.8	34271.0	30242.9

Table 3.2 Individual consumption expenditure of households, NPISHs, and general government at current prices

Series 400: 1993 SNA, 1999 PTE euro / euro, Western calendar year **Data in millions**

	2001	2002	2003	2004	2005	2006	2007	2008	2009	2010	2011	2012
Series	**400**											
Individual consumption expenditure of households												
Food and non-alcoholic beverages	14781.1	15311.3	15925.1	16340.6	16529.9	17338.5	18139.6	19226.7	18728.1	18898.3	19401.0	...
Alcoholic beverages, tobacco and narcotics	3113.0	3203.1	3370.9	3482.9	3506.3	3741.1	3423.9	3356.2	3355.7	3766.4	3544.2	...
Clothing and footwear	5365.1	5817.7	5811.5	6043.0	6115.7	6329.9	6501.0	6581.4	6481.5	6717.6	6948.1	...
Housing, water, electricity, gas and other fuels	11330.6	12115.6	12960.4	13796.2	14531.9	15083.7	15991.3	16866.6	17230.1	18013.7	17671.3	...
Furnishings, household equipment and routine maintenance of the house	5885.1	6207.9	6218.4	6285.1	6498.7	6779.5	7124.4	7223.7	6737.7	6866.7	6693.8	...
Health	3953.5	4267.1	4554.2	4880.6	5075.1	5329.1	5896.6	6322.1	6441.0	6568.4	6791.5	...
Transport	13399.3	13222.6	12809.8	13817.7	14789.2	15235.3	16070.8	16205.5	13993.4	15783.0	14600.8	...
Communication	2648.4	2905.5	2982.5	3187.6	3264.8	3373.4	3426.9	3515.6	3351.6	3453.5	3588.5	...
Recreation and culture	6962.0	7052.1	6980.4	7303.9	7724.3	7980.9	8166.3	8321.3	8000.9	8088.2	8328.5	...
Education	913.5	964.4	1003.9	1080.0	1149.5	1217.6	1277.2	1393.6	1434.3	1539.1	1537.6	...
Restaurants and hotels	9473.0	9917.7	9965.2	10606.5	11039.5	11603.1	12324.8	12326.6	12109.0	12821.6	12980.7	...
Miscellaneous goods and services	8284.6	8567.2	9187.6	9881.3	10483.2	11788.9	13593.7	14686.4	12684.2	12677.8	13435.1	...
Equals: Household final consumption expenditure in domestic market	86109.1	89552.3	91770.1	96705.1	100708.2	105800.9	111936.1	116025.7	110547.5	115193.7	115521.1	111955.2
Plus: Direct purchases abroad by residents	1836.3	1722.6	1610.6	1656.7	1798.6	1914.9	2019.3	2086.7	1925.8	2096.6	2111.4	2091.8
Less: Direct purchases in domestic market by non-residents	5558.5	5530.5	5308.2	5622.7	5625.6	6055.1	6735.5	6749.2	6266.6	6895.3	7389.1	7806.3
Equals: Household final consumption expenditure	82386.9	85744.5	88072.6	92739.2	96881.3	101660.6	107220.1	111363.3	106206.8	110395.2	110243.5	106209.9
Individual consumption expenditure of non-profit institutions serving households (NPISHs)												
Equals: NPISHs final consumption expenditure	2488.5	2648.8	2727.3	2858.1	2965.6	3087.0	3414.8	3593.4	3567.9	3584.4	3535.0	3369.1
Individual consumption expenditure of general government												
Equals: Individual consumption expenditure of general government	15267.4	16250.3	16927.1	17759.6	18875.3	18814.9	18727.8	19116.0	20395.4	20431.6	18925.0	16705.9
Equals: Total actual individual consumption	100142.8	104643.6	107727.0	113356.9	118722.2	123562.5	129362.7	134072.7	130170.1	134411.2	132703.5	126284.9

Table 4.1 Total Economy (S.1)

Series 400: 1993 SNA, 1999 PTE euro / euro, Western calendar year **Data in millions**

	2001	2002	2003	2004	2005	2006	2007	2008	2009	2010	2011	2012
Series	**400**											
I. Production account - Resources												
Output, at basic prices (otherwise, please specify)	255077.1	260681.5	263894.6	276474.7	287332.0	298573.4	317575.6	330273.3	311378.5	323625.1	...	...
Less: Financial intermediation services indirectly measured (only to be deducted if FISIM is not distributed to uses)	...	...	...	...	...	...	...	...	...	...	...	...
Plus: Taxes less Subsidies on products	16540.3	17714.4	18224.4	18967.1	20903.0	22505.1	23110.5	22672.0	19812.2	21433.0	21637.0	20795.3
Plus: Taxes on products	17237.5	18423.8	18987.9	19784.6	21675.9	23130.7	23660.6	23206.0	20334.8	21996.5	22299.0	21247.2
Less: Subsidies on products	697.3	709.4	763.7	817.5	772.9	625.6	550.1	534.0	522.6	563.4	662.0	451.9
I. Production account - Uses												
Intermediate consumption, at purchaser's prices	137146.3	137829.0	138647.2	146129.3	153966.3	160223.2	171366.8	180962.2	162661.5	172198.6	...	...
GROSS DOMESTIC PRODUCT	134471.1	140566.8	143471.7	149312.5	154268.7	160855.4	169319.2	171983.1	168529.2	172859.5	171064.7	165409.3
Less: Consumption of fixed capital	21655.0	23083.6	23991.2	25043.6	26259.1	27299.9	28350.7	29745.5	29795.2	30444.2	30987.6	31112.1
NET DOMESTIC PRODUCT	112816.0	117483.2	119480.5	124268.9	128009.6	133555.5	140968.5	142237.5	138734.1	142415.3	140077.1	134297.2
II.1.1 Generation of income account - Resources												
GROSS DOMESTIC PRODUCT	134471.1	140566.8	143471.7	149312.5	154268.7	160855.4	169319.2	171983.1	168529.2	172859.5	171064.7	165409.3
II.1.1 Generation of income account - Uses												
Compensation of employees	66109.7	69374.2	71223.1	73648.4	77359.1	79663.1	82861.3	85692.4	85888.4	86813.9	85454.8	79243.7
Taxes on production and imports, less Subsidies	15422.4	16855.8	17891.2	17958.7	19766.4	21563.9	22244.7	22093.9	19112.0	20464.4	20816.5	19985.7
Taxes on production and imports	18091.0	19680.2	20896.0	20787.6	22746.3	24310.6	24981.7	24645.6	21872.7	23493.1	23857.3	22913.1
Taxes on products	17237.5	18423.8	18987.9	19784.6	21675.9	23130.7	23660.6	23206.0	20334.8	21996.5	22299.0	21247.2
Other taxes on production	853.5	1256.4	1908.1	1003.1	1070.4	1179.9	1321.1	1439.6	1537.9	1496.7	1558.3	1665.9
Less: Subsidies	2668.6	2824.3	3004.8	2829.0	2979.9	2746.7	2737.0	2551.7	2760.7	3028.7	3040.8	2927.5
Subsidies on products	697.3	709.4	763.7	817.5	772.9	625.6	550.1	534.0	522.6	563.4	662.0	451.9
Other subsidies on production	1971.3	2114.9	2241.2	2011.5	2207.0	2121.0	2186.9	2017.7	2238.1	2465.3	2378.8	2475.6
OPERATING SURPLUS, GROSS	31859.0	32523.0	31798.0	34530.0	33902.0	42631.0	47136.4	46745.0	45784.2	47945.4	...	...
MIXED INCOME, GROSS	21079.8	21814.1	22558.1	23176.6	23241.2	16997.3	17076.8	17451.7	17744.6	17635.7	...	...
II.1.2 Allocation of primary income account - Resources												
OPERATING SURPLUS, GROSS	31859.0	32523.0	31798.0	34530.0	33902.0	42631.0	47136.4	46745.0	45784.2	47945.4	...	...
MIXED INCOME, GROSS	21079.8	21814.1	22558.1	23176.6	23241.2	16997.3	17076.8	17451.7	17744.6	17635.7	...	...
Compensation of employees	66076.8	69314.8	71204.3	73530.2	77198.4	79519.9	82856.6	85661.0	85757.0	86694.4	85311.0	79146.6
Taxes on production and imports, less Subsidies	15812.7	17640.2	18708.2	19032.8	20936.9	22453.9	23178.2	23045.8	20227.9	21757.0	22202.2	21483.7
Taxes on production and imports	17471.7	19204.2	20455.1	20402.0	22383.5	23902.0	24527.3	24213.5	21486.7	23039.5	23389.8	22522.4
Taxes on products	16618.2	17947.8	18547.1	19398.9	21313.1	22722.1	23206.2	22777.7	19949.5	21542.8	21831.4	20856.5
Other taxes on production	853.5	1256.4	1908.1	1003.1	1070.4	1179.9	1321.1	1435.8	1537.2	1496.7	1558.3	1665.9
Less: Subsidies	1659.0	1564.0	1746.9	1369.2	1446.6	1448.0	1349.2	1167.7	1258.8	1282.6	1187.6	1038.8
Subsidies on products	197.6	192.6	213.6	197.9	239.1	257.6	258.5	261.0	243.4	277.7	349.5	198.0
Other subsidies on production	1461.4	1371.4	1533.3	1171.3	1207.5	1190.4	1090.7	906.7	1015.5	1004.9	838.1	840.7
Property income	30840.5	27593.9	26994.0	31058.0	34319.9	45354.8	56929.3	65854.1	40537.6	39694.4	47882.0	46971.1

	2001	2002	2003	2004	2005	2006	2007	2008	2009	2010	2011	2012
Series	**400**											
II.1.2 Allocation of primary income account - Uses												
Property income	34632.3	30565.0	29174.9	33603.2	37617.9	50957.8	63231.9	72922.0	48386.5	46792.4	55569.0	52548.1
GROSS NATIONAL INCOME	131036.6	138320.6	142089.0	147723.3	151980.5	155999.2	163945.5	165835.7	161664.8	166934.5	164619.6	161233.2
II.2 Secondary distribution of income account - Resources												
GROSS NATIONAL INCOME	131036.6	138320.6	142089.0	147723.3	151980.5	155999.2	163945.5	165835.7	161664.8	166934.5	164619.6	161233.2
Current taxes on income, wealth, etc.	12202.0	12651.4	12035.5	12401.1	12662.3	13851.8	16084.4	16644.2	15146.3	15222.3	16962.6	15291.3
Social contributions	18910.1	19960.8	20970.1	21337.6	23220.1	24553.4	25191.9	26673.5	26727.7	26874.6	26672.4	24610.1
Social benefits other than social transfers in kind	19458.7	20983.5	23045.5	24313.8	25728.9	27808.0	29586.3	31961.6	34080.5	34812.8	34732.0	34294.8
Other current transfers	12164.7	12117.4	11194.9	12770.2	12435.2	13541.0	14324.6	14133.7	14147.9	13754.7	14301.7	14245.4
II.2 Secondary distribution of income account - Uses												
Current taxes on income, wealth, etc.	12208.5	12653.9	12039.2	12395.0	12654.2	13846.1	16091.8	16649.1	15144.9	15218.0	16962.0	15296.1
Social contributions	18890.0	19938.4	20959.7	21297.4	23167.0	24503.0	25181.0	26654.0	26682.5	26810.9	26617.7	24569.5
Social benefits other than social transfers in kind	19493.0	21028.7	23103.1	24377.7	25823.5	27900.9	29680.2	32063.5	34210.5	34946.4	34882.0	34426.3
Other current transfers	9182.7	10140.1	9599.6	11086.7	11503.3	11931.8	12521.3	12245.6	12904.2	12326.5	12671.5	12239.9
GROSS DISPOSABLE INCOME	133997.8	140272.5	143633.3	149389.3	152878.9	157571.6	165658.3	167636.5	162825.2	168297.1	166155.1	163142.9
II.4.1 Use of disposable income account - Resources												
GROSS DISPOSABLE INCOME	133997.8	140272.5	143633.3	149389.3	152878.9	157571.6	165658.3	167636.5	162825.2	168297.1	166155.1	163142.9
Adjustment for the change in net equity of households on pension funds	573.7	410.4	308.8	367.4	1306.7	1101.6	568.7	193.4	189.2	212.5	201.7	186.4
II.4.1 Use of disposable income account - Uses												
Final consumption expenditure	110979.8	116056.0	119528.6	125921.5	132465.1	137749.8	144214.0	149488.6	146959.9	151314.4	148073.3	139853.3
Individual consumption expenditure	100142.7	104643.3	107726.7	113357.3	118722.2	123562.5	129362.8	134072.6	130170.1	134411.5	132703.5	126316.0
Collective consumption expenditure	10837.0	11412.7	11801.8	12564.2	13742.9	14187.2	14851.2	15416.0	16789.8	16902.9	15369.8	13537.3
Adjustment for the change in net equity of households on pension funds	573.7	410.4	308.8	367.4	1306.7	1101.6	568.7	193.4	189.2	212.5	201.7	186.4
SAVING, GROSS	23018.0	24216.5	24104.7	23467.8	20413.9	19821.8	21444.3	18147.8	15865.3	16982.7	18081.8	23289.7
III.1 Capital account - Changes in liabilities and net worth												
SAVING, GROSS	23018.0	24216.5	24104.7	23467.8	20413.9	19821.8	21444.3	18147.8	15865.3	16982.7	18081.8	23289.7
Capital transfers, receivable less payable	2206.2	2516.6	3246.8	2529.1	2216.9	2014.3	1940.7	1669.9	1968.1	2416.0	2713.1	3695.5
Capital transfers, receivable	6535.7	7870.8	8113.9	9799.8	8489.8	3830.6	3282.5	6687.6	3763.6	9060.9	12174.1	8389.8
Less: Capital transfers, payable	4329.5	5354.2	4867.1	7270.7	6272.8	1816.3	1341.7	5017.7	1795.5	6644.9	9461.0	4694.3
Equals: CHANGES IN NET WORTH DUE TO SAVING AND CAPITAL TRANSFERS	3569.2	3649.5	3360.4	953.4	-3628.3	-5463.9	-4965.7	-9927.8	-11961.7	-11045.5	-10192.7	-4126.9
III.1 Capital account - Changes in assets												
Gross capital formation	37270.3	36182.9	33700.3	35810.5	36325.3	37078.1	38651.9	39817.3	34050.9	34874.8	30442.5	26389.2
Gross fixed capital formation	36268.3	35977.9	33846.6	34699.7	35412.8	35890.1	37629.2	38634.7	34629.5	33829.9	30533.6	26146.5
Changes in inventories	876.9	81.5	-248.4	1007.9	768.5	1039.9	903.4	1040.7	-702.6	915.4	-218.4	98.5
Acquisitions less disposals of valuables	125.2	123.5	102.1	102.9	144.0	148.1	119.3	141.9	124.1	129.5	127.2	144.2
Acquisitions less disposals of non-produced non-financial assets	16.6	-1.9	-13.1	-38.3	-48.5	-7.2	-159.8	-442.3	4.1	13.7	-136.4	-77.9
NET LENDING (+) / NET BORROWING (-)	-12062.7	-9447.9	-6335.6	-9775.2	-13646.0	-15234.8	-15107.1	-19557.3	-16221.5	-15489.8	-9511.2	673.9[a]

	2001	2002	2003	2004	2005	2006	2007	2008	2009	2010	2011	2012
Series	**400**											
	III.2 Financial account - Changes in liabilities and net worth											
Net incurrence of liabilities	70559.8	50578.7	68572.9	58122.9	64030.7	66385.4	84351.6	57867.6	72161.4	64589.6	-6049.7	...
Currency and deposits	17330.8	7735.3	6415.7	13537.3	16930.8	24022.7	20697.7	7326.2	5531.7	38956.1	-19069.0	...
Securities other than shares	12775.9	9051.7	3474.4	6548.6	11332.0	10528.1	24165.9	27233.5	34749.1	12604.6	-18836.6	...
Loans	26667.9	20943.0	24095.1	12291.1	20306.2	24375.2	30973.9	21800.8	5845.9	2177.7	37589.7	...
Shares and other equity	6030.2	10654.7	22436.4	14685.9	14200.1	6399.4	-3476.0	-501.2	15874.4	3108.5	-5931.3	...
Insurance technical reserves	5271.4	4178.4	3399.4	4809.6	8057.4	6011.9	5780.8	-243.5	4721.5	6237.8	-5950.5	...
Financial derivatives	...	...	...	...	...	...	...	...	...	...	...	...
Other accounts payable	2483.6	-1984.3	8751.8	6250.3	-6795.9	-4951.9	6209.3	2251.9	5438.7	1504.9	6148.0	...
Adjustment to reconcile Net Lending of Financial Account and Capital Account	517.1	-251.1	312.5	625.5	394.0	812.4	-221.1	-361.0	1060.6	704.4	...	...
NET LENDING (+) / NET BORROWING (-)	-12579.8[b]	-9196.8[b]	-6648.2[b]	-10400.7[b]	-14040.0[b]	-16047.3[b]	-14886.0[b]	-19196.3[b]	-17282.2[b]	-16194.2[b]	-9737.0[c]	...
	III.2 Financial account - Changes in assets											
Net acquisition of financial assets	57980.1	41381.9	61924.7	47722.1	49990.6	50338.2	69465.6	38671.3	54879.2	48395.3	-15786.7	...
Monetary gold and SDRs	12.6	-144.6	-768.8	-584.3	-507.0	-561.0	-1.4	6.3	-11.5	12.2	-45.7	...
Currency and deposits	5571.7	6251.8	9417.5	5046.2	11129.8	20849.9	15834.6	-3854.2	2187.8	14103.2	7040.6	...
Securities other than shares	10087.0	8289.8	12089.1	9248.3	14584.3	5400.7	11736.0	19219.9	21167.9	21604.7	-20168.2	...
Loans	26026.8	19623.7	15265.5	12633.1	13880.6	18675.3	31582.5	28372.2	9037.5	12164.8	411.9	...
Shares and other equity	8751.9	4620.0	13958.4	11109.3	8721.8	3983.8	-1197.6	-7850.4	12390.9	-5479.8	-5095.1	...
Insurance technical reserves	5342.7	4167.4	3559.0	4589.5	8128.7	5750.8	5770.5	-245.6	4773.6	6273.8	-5932.0	...
Financial derivatives	...	...	...	...	...	...	...	...	...	...	...	...
Other accounts receivable	2187.3	-1426.1	8404.0	5680.0	-5947.5	-3761.4	5740.9	3023.0	5332.9	-283.6	8001.9	...

[a] Integrated accounts data updated with one year delay resulting in discrepancy with equivalent items in other tables.
[b] Excludes Adjustment to reconcile Net Lending of the Financial Account and the Capital Account.
[c] Statistical discrepancy between net lending (+)/net borrowing (-) in the financial account and net lending (+)/net borrowing (-) in the capital account.

Table 4.2 Rest of the world (S.2)

Series 400: 1993 SNA, 1999 PTE euro / euro, Western calendar year **Data in millions**

	2001	2002	2003	2004	2005	2006	2007	2008	2009	2010	2011	2012
Series	**400**											
	V.I External account of goods and services - Resources											
Imports of goods and services	51532.1	50469.7	49388.0	54294.2	57190.5	63685.2	68044.8	73124.7	59717.2	67439.1	68619.2	64906.6
Imports of goods	45184.1	44104.9	43233.2	47601.8	49878.1	55154.6	58746.7	63270.5	50573.7	57666.0	58403.2	55350.1
Imports of services	6347.9	6364.8	6154.8	6692.4	7312.4	8530.6	9298.1	9854.2	9143.5	9773.1	10216.0	9556.5
	V.I External account of goods and services - Uses											
Exports of goods and services	37753.0	38797.6	39630.8	41874.7	42668.8	49712.7	54498.2	55801.8	47235.7	54109.4	61168.1	64073.4
Exports of goods	29554.1	30202.0	31020.5	32413.8	32750.4	37670.2	40342.7	40999.7	33716.9	39421.3	45140.3	47774.9
Exports of services	8198.9	8595.6	8610.3	9460.9	9918.4	12042.4	14155.4	14802.1	13518.8	14688.1	16027.8	16298.5
EXTERNAL BALANCE OF GOODS AND SERVICES	13779.0	11672.1	9757.2	12419.5	14521.7	13972.5	13546.7	17322.9	12481.5	13329.7	7451.1	833.2

	2001	2002	2003	2004	2005	2006	2007	2008	2009	2010	2011	2012
Series	**400**											
	V.II External account of primary income and current transfers - Resources											
EXTERNAL BALANCE OF GOODS AND SERVICES	13779.0	11672.1	9757.2	12419.5	14521.7	13972.5	13546.7	17322.9	12481.5	13329.7	7451.1	833.2
Compensation of employees	279.5	271.8	229.0	302.9	349.8	354.2	251.7	265.7	370.1	370.4	428.3	388.2
Taxes on production and imports, less Subsidies	-390.3	-784.3	-817.0	-1074.1	-1170.5	-890.0	-933.5	-951.9	-1115.8	-1292.5	-1385.7	-1498.0
Taxes on production and imports	619.4	476.0	440.9	385.7	362.8	408.6	454.4	432.1	386.0	453.6	467.5	390.7
Taxes on products	619.4	476.0	440.9	385.7	362.8	408.6	454.4	428.3	385.3	453.6	467.5	390.7
Other taxes on production	0.0	0.0	0.0	0.0	0.0	0.0	0.0	3.8	0.7	0.0	0.0	0.0
Less: Subsidies	1009.6	1260.3	1257.9	1459.8	1533.3	1298.6	1387.9	1384.0	1501.8	1746.2	1853.2	1888.7
Subsidies on products	499.7	516.8	550.0	619.6	533.8	368.0	291.6	273.0	279.2	285.7	312.6	253.9
Other subsidies on production	509.9	743.5	707.9	840.2	999.5	930.6	1096.2	1111.0	1222.6	1460.4	1540.6	1634.9
Property income	10048.7	8206.4	8014.0	9215.3	11054.0	16823.6	19112.0	19908.1	16649.4	19135.0	18092.9	13523.4
Current taxes on income, wealth, etc.	29.8	25.7	23.5	20.3	20.4	23.2	28.0	26.5	30.1	32.1	36.2	37.4
Social contributions	58.5	54.1	54.0	45.0	45.3	49.2	59.9	55.2	63.6	61.6	72.3	71.6
Social benefits other than social transfers in kind	66.9	74.9	83.5	93.8	129.0	136.9	141.6	157.5	176.2	182.7	206.4	189.7
Other current transfers	1879.4	2191.4	2148.6	2423.3	2925.8	2883.5	2898.8	2854.5	3150.7	3237.5	3215.1	3129.1
Adjustment for the change in net equity of households on pension funds	...	...	...	...	...	...	...	...	...	...	...	...
	V.II External account of primary income and current transfers - Uses											
Compensation of employees	246.6	212.4	210.2	184.7	189.1	211.0	247.1	234.3	238.8	250.9	284.6	291.1
Taxes on production and imports, less Subsidies	...	...	...	...	...	...	...	...	...	...	...	...
Taxes on production and imports	...	...	...	...	...	...	...	...	...	...	...	...
Taxes on products	...	...	...	...	...	...	...	...	...	...	...	...
Other taxes on production	...	...	...	...	...	...	...	...	...	...	...	...
Less: Subsidies	...	...	...	...	...	...	...	...	...	...	...	...
Subsidies on products	...	...	...	...	...	...	...	...	...	...	...	...
Other subsidies on production	...	...	...	...	...	...	...	...	...	...	...	...
Property income	6256.9	5235.3	5833.0	6670.2	7756.0	11220.7	12809.4	12840.2	8800.4	12037.0	10405.9	7946.4
Current taxes on income and wealth, etc.	23.3	23.3	19.8	26.4	28.5	28.9	20.5	21.7	31.6	36.4	36.8	32.6
Social contributions	78.6	76.4	64.4	85.2	98.3	99.6	70.8	74.7	108.8	125.3	127.0	112.2
Social benefits other than social transfers in kind	32.6	29.7	25.9	30.0	34.4	44.0	47.7	55.6	46.2	49.2	56.4	58.2
Other current transfers	4861.4	4168.6	3744.0	4106.9	3857.7	4492.8	4702.0	4742.6	4394.3	4665.7	4845.3	5134.6
Adjustment for the change in net equity of households on pension funds	...	...	...	...	...	...	...	...	...	...	...	...
CURRENT EXTERNAL BALANCE	14252.3	11966.4	9595.6	12342.7	15911.5	17256.3	17207.6	21669.5	18185.6	17892.1	12360.7	3099.5
	V.III.1 Capital account - Changes in liabilities and net worth											
CURRENT EXTERNAL BALANCE	14252.3	11966.4	9595.6	12342.7	15911.5	17256.3	17207.6	21669.5	18185.6	17892.1	12360.7	3099.5
Capital transfers, receivable less payable	-2206.2	-2516.6	-3246.8	-2529.1	-2216.9	-2014.3	-1940.7	-1669.9	-1968.1	-2416.0	-2713.1	-3695.5
Capital transfers, receivable	187.6	201.2	171.0	188.9	164.3	173.2	240.7	363.7	264.2	272.4	245.2	201.9
Less: Capital transfers, payable	2393.8	2717.7	3417.9	2718.1	2381.2	2187.4	2181.5	2033.7	2232.3	2688.3	2958.3	3897.4
Equals: CHANGES IN NET WORTH DUE TO SAVING AND CAPITAL TRANSFERS	12046.1	9449.8	6348.7	9813.6	13694.5	15242.1	15266.9	19999.6	16217.5	15476.1	9647.6	-596.0

	2001	2002	2003	2004	2005	2006	2007	2008	2009	2010	2011	2012
Series	**400**											
	V.III.1 Capital account - Changes in assets											
Acquisitions less disposals of non-produced non-financial assets	-16.6	1.9	13.1	38.3	48.5	7.2	159.8	442.3	-4.1	-13.7	136.4	77.9
NET LENDING (+) / NET BORROWING (-)	12062.7	9447.9	6335.6	9775.2	13646.1	15234.8	15107.1	19557.3	16221.5	15489.8	9511.2	-673.9
	V.III.2 Financial account - Changes in liabilities and net worth											
Net incurrence of liabilities	24176.6	15290.7	29443.0	16178.5	17832.2	25608.6	24689.0	4019.6	19926.4	6680.2	-15377.7	...
Currency and deposits	3239.3	3821.4	8455.4	1562.4	3370.7	13650.9	9119.6	-15241.0	898.3	6401.6	-6731.8	...
Securities other than shares	7948.5	7355.8	13663.1	8778.1	14343.8	2405.2	5361.9	12700.5	14948.0	3135.7	-21703.8	...
Loans	5920.3	3862.5	77.6	-1572.0	-2350.7	144.8	5067.9	5094.6	2428.8	4137.0	9333.4	...
Shares and other equity	7709.9	-1183.6	6929.1	6940.2	1949.1	8283.2	4955.8	1729.9	1045.7	-6480.5	-71.5	...
Insurance technical reserves	78.7	-7.2	167.7	-213.0	82.5	-252.6	-0.5	-5.1	56.7	18.5	22.3	...
Financial derivatives	...	...	...	...	...	...	...	...	...	...	...	...
Other accounts payable	-720.1	1441.8	150.1	682.7	437.0	1377.2	184.4	-259.3	548.9	-531.9	3773.7	...
Adjustment to reconcile Net Lending of Financial Account and Capital Account	-517.1	251.2	-312.6	-625.2	-393.9	-812.3	221.2	361.0	-1060.7	-704.4	...	...
NET LENDING (+) / NET BORROWING (-)	12579.8[a]	9196.8[a]	6648.2[a]	10400.5[a]	14040.0[a]	16047.1[a]	14886.0[a]	19196.3[a]	17282.2[a]	16194.2[a]	9737.0[b]	...
	V.III.2 Financial account - Changes in assets											
Net acquisition of financial assets	36756.3	24487.5	36091.2	26578.9	31872.2	41655.8	39575.0	23215.9	37208.6	22874.5	-5640.6	...
Monetary gold and SDRs	-12.6	144.6	768.8	584.3	507.0	561.0	1.4	-6.3	11.5	-12.2	45.7	...
Currency and deposits	14998.4	5304.9	5453.6	10053.6	9171.7	16823.7	13982.7	-4060.6	4242.1	31254.5	-32841.3	...
Securities other than shares	10637.4	8117.6	5048.5	6078.2	11091.4	7532.6	17791.8	20714.1	28529.2	-5864.4	-20372.2	...
Loans	6561.3	5181.7	8907.3	-1914.0	4074.9	5844.6	4459.3	-1476.9	-762.8	-5850.1	46511.2	...
Shares and other equity	4988.2	4851.1	15407.0	10516.9	7427.3	10698.7	2677.3	9079.1	4529.2	2107.8	-907.7	...
Insurance technical reserves	7.4	3.8	8.2	7.1	11.2	8.5	9.8	-3.0	4.6	-17.6	3.8	...
Financial derivatives	...	...	...	...	...	...	...	...	...	...	...	...
Other accounts receivable	-423.7	883.7	497.9	1253.0	-411.4	186.6	652.7	-1030.4	654.8	1256.5	1919.8	...

[a] Excludes Adjustment to reconcile Net Lending of the Financial Account and the Capital Account.
[b] Statistical discrepancy between net lending (+)/net borrowing (-) in the financial account and net lending (+)/net borrowing (-) in the capital account.

Table 4.3 Non-financial Corporations (S.11)

Series 400: 1993 SNA, 1999 PTE euro / euro, Western calendar year — **Data in millions**

	2001	2002	2003	2004	2005	2006	2007	2008	2009	2010	2011	2012
Series	**400**											
	I. Production account - Resources											
Output, at basic prices (otherwise, please specify)	174630.0	178060.9	180669.3	190044.4	198270.3	207420.5	223467.4	233665.1	215143.1	227074.6	...	...
	I. Production account - Uses											
Intermediate consumption, at purchaser's prices	112649.9	113471.4	114924.1	121067.7	128103.3	133801.7	143874.7	152644.2	134148.7	143677.4	...	...
VALUE ADDED GROSS, in basic prices	61980.0	64589.5	65745.2	68976.7	70167.0	73618.8	79592.7	81020.9	80994.4	83397.1	82910.6	81575.9
Less: Consumption of fixed capital	11707.9	12590.3	13133.3	13644.6	14216.7	14553.3	15048.9	15773.2	15754.2	15960.2	16081.3	16057.3
VALUE ADDED NET, at basic prices	50272.1	51999.2	52611.9	55332.1	55950.3	59065.5	64543.8	65247.7	65240.2	67436.9	66829.3	65518.6

	2001	2002	2003	2004	2005	2006	2007	2008	2009	2010	2011	2012
Series	**400**											
II.1.1 Generation of income account - Resources												
VALUE ADDED GROSS, at basic prices	61980.0	64589.5	65745.2	68976.7	70167.0	73618.8	79592.7	81020.9	80994.4	83397.1	82910.6	81575.9
II.1.1 Generation of income account - Uses												
Compensation of employees	38013.7	39753.6	41683.6	43155.6	44983.8	47162.7	50339.6	52786.6	52311.3	53493.6	53846.0	51366.7
Other taxes less Other subsidies on production	-565.6	-188.0	187.1	-349.5	-332.9	-279.8	-256.6	-85.7	-103.2	-257.3	-827.8	-847.4
Other taxes on production	494.0	806.4	1298.9	499.8	542.7	583.4	651.9	709.8	814.6	764.9	802.1	848.9
Less: Other subsidies on production	1059.6	994.4	1111.8	849.3	875.6	863.2	908.6	795.5	917.8	1022.3	1629.9	1696.3
OPERATING SURPLUS, GROSS	24532.0	25023.9	23874.4	26170.6	25516.2	26736.0	29509.8	28320.0	28786.3	30160.9	29892.4	31056.6
II.1.2 Allocation of primary income account - Resources												
OPERATING SURPLUS, GROSS	24532.0	25023.9	23874.4	26170.6	25516.2	26736.0	29509.8	28320.0	28786.3	30160.9	29892.4	31056.6
Property income	3715.9	2989.6	4001.9	5011.8	5882.5	8843.9	10056.0	10532.3	7513.9	8986.3	10302.7	8936.4
II.1.2 Allocation of primary income account - Uses												
Property income	11115.8	9605.6	10609.5	13598.3	16312.6	20454.2	23226.3	26008.0	21674.0	22081.2	25146.9	23967.6
BALANCE OF PRIMARY INCOMES	17132.1	18407.9	17266.8	17584.1	15086.1	15125.7	16339.5	12844.3	14626.2	17065.9	15048.3	16025.4
II.2 Secondary distribution of income account - Resources												
BALANCE OF PRIMARY INCOMES	17132.1	18407.9	17266.8	17584.1	15086.1	15125.7	16339.5	12844.3	14626.2	17065.9	15048.3	16025.4
Social contributions	2091.6	2116.5	1977.2	1609.1	1287.9	1771.3	1671.7	1808.5	1828.5	1868.3	1880.6	1794.0
Other current transfers	604.2	688.5	753.2	866.1	801.0	885.3	917.8	755.4	884.7	935.0	910.1	833.7
II.2 Secondary distribution of income account - Uses												
Current taxes on income, wealth, etc.	4002.5	4352.4	3707.8	4089.4	3951.1	4040.6	4949.1	5525.0	4357.9	4556.9	5411.6	4160.0
Social benefits other than social transfers in kind	2091.6	2116.5	1977.2	1609.1	1287.9	1771.3	1671.7	1808.5	1828.5	1868.3	1880.6	1794.0
Other current transfers	2049.7	2321.7	1694.9	1984.1	1760.0	1961.9	2455.3	2234.8	2238.2	1867.2	1976.8	2292.3
GROSS DISPOSABLE INCOME	11684.1	12422.3	12617.3	12376.7	10176.1	10008.5	9852.9	5839.9	8914.8	11576.8	8569.9	10406.8
II.4.1 Use of disposable income account - Resources												
GROSS DISPOSABLE INCOME	11684.1	12422.3	12617.3	12376.7	10176.1	10008.5	9852.9	5839.9	8914.8	11576.8	8569.9	10406.8
II.4.1 Use of disposable income account - Uses												
Adjustment for the change in net equity of households on pension funds	...	...	...	...	...	...	...	...	...	...	...	...
SAVING, GROSS	11684.1	12422.3	12617.3	12376.7	10176.1	10008.5	9852.9	5839.9	8914.8	11576.8	8569.9	10406.8
III.1 Capital account - Changes in liabilities and net worth												
SAVING, GROSS	11684.1	12422.3	12617.3	12376.7	10176.1	10008.5	9852.9	5839.9	8914.8	11576.8	8569.9	10406.8
Capital transfers, receivable less payable	-183.4	-135.3	679.2	728.7	1697.9	1263.4	1336.7	1877.1	1610.9	-1784.5	2277.4	2827.9
Capital transfers, receivable	129.1	350.4	2421.5	1910.3	1821.1	1284.9	1458.3	1996.4	1712.6	1221.0	2673.6	3213.9
Less: Capital transfers, payable	312.5	485.7	1742.3	1181.6	123.2	21.5	121.7	119.4	101.7	3005.5	396.2	386.0
Equals: CHANGES IN NET WORTH DUE TO SAVING AND CAPITAL TRANSFERS	-207.2	-303.3	163.2	-539.1	-2342.8	-3281.4	-3859.4	-8056.3	-5228.5	-6167.9	-5233.9	-2822.6
III.1 Capital account - Changes in assets												
Gross capital formation	19023.5	17797.7	17097.4	18197.9	19186.2	19973.6	22544.1	23928.7	19805.5	19617.4	17766.6	15820.1
Gross fixed capital formation	18118.8	17694.6	17286.4	17262.9	18526.9	19023.5	21716.6	22953.4	20521.5	18789.6	17963.2	15730.3
Changes in inventories	901.5	100.5	-191.0	932.9	657.0	948.0	826.0	974.0	-716.7	827.2	-197.3	89.0

	2001	2002	2003	2004	2005	2006	2007	2008	2009	2010	2011	2012
Series	**400**											
Acquisitions less disposals of valuables	3.3	2.6	2.0	2.0	2.3	2.1	1.4	1.3	0.7	0.7	0.7	0.8
Acquisitions less disposals of non-produced non-financial assets	1285.9	1745.0	1354.0	1266.3	1268.1	1942.6	2771.3	3429.3	2115.7	2099.4	1922.9	2350.7
NET LENDING (+) / NET BORROWING (-)	-8808.8	-7255.8	-5154.9	-6358.7	-8580.4	-10644.3	-14125.8	-19641.1	-11395.4	-11924.5	-8842.2	-4936.1
	III.2 Financial account - Changes in liabilities and net worth											
Net incurrence of liabilities	22658.2	10677.2	23307.4	12367.2	7603.6	13540.5	19645.8	22905.2	16975.1	14731.3	9843.1	...
Currency and deposits	...	...	...	...	...	...	...	...	...	...	...	...
Securities other than shares	1968.4	2429.4	-752.6	1496.8	4460.9	2159.0	5476.2	5206.6	2101.8	832.5	2661.2	...
Loans	14328.3	3279.6	6595.4	746.3	5010.1	9426.0	17336.4	17717.9	4044.6	3425.2	-2969.3	...
Shares and other equity	2341.7	5712.4	10587.9	6288.8	4528.1	6951.4	-2450.4	185.8	5353.2	6912.2	4335.8	...
Insurance technical reserves	498.1	-750.6	1251.3	540.3	-93.3	-103.0	350.9	29.7	-123.5	381.1	-102.9	...
Financial derivatives	...	...	...	...	...	...	...	...	...	...	...	...
Other accounts payable	3521.7	6.3	5625.5	3295.1	-6302.3	-4892.9	-1067.3	-234.9	5598.9	3180.4	5918.2	...
Adjustment to reconcile Net Lending of Financial Account and Capital Account	490.1	-253.7	501.3	529.3	166.6	598.7	-288.0	-655.8	839.0	709.8	...	...
NET LENDING (+) / NET BORROWING (-)	-9298.9[a]	-7002.1[a]	-5656.2[a]	-6887.9[a]	-8746.9[a]	-11243.0[a]	-13837.8[a]	-18985.3[a]	-12246.0[a]	-12646.3[a]	-6904.1[b]	...
	III.2 Financial account - Changes in assets											
Net acquisition of financial assets	13359.3	3675.1	17651.2	5479.3	-1143.4	2297.5	5808.0	3919.9	4729.1	2085.0	2939.1	...
Monetary gold and SDRs	...	...	...	...	...	...	...	...	...	...	...	...
Currency and deposits	1574.3	396.3	2806.4	1140.0	4219.7	3015.3	-289.5	-916.3	-172.8	5994.5	-4941.7	...
Securities other than shares	4474.8	2330.8	503.2	767.2	-1503.8	-696.9	183.8	-218.8	109.5	-1485.2	-331.9	...
Loans	1204.7	4353.9	473.5	-1926.4	1843.4	2503.5	5178.1	3908.6	1785.2	6587.9	4877.1	...
Shares and other equity	-148.6	-2443.8	4053.8	3117.7	4.8	527.7	229.4	3349.2	1205.0	-7432.7	3671.5	...
Insurance technical reserves	137.3	66.2	142.6	123.4	194.9	165.6	131.9	-40.9	62.5	-236.5	51.1	...
Financial derivatives	...	...	...	...	...	...	...	...	...	...	...	...
Other accounts receivable	6116.8	-1028.3	9671.8	2257.3	-5902.4	-3217.7	374.3	-2161.8	1739.7	-1342.9	-387.1	...

[a] Excludes Adjustment to reconcile Net Lending of the Financial Account and the Capital Account.
[b] Statistical discrepancy between net lending (+)/net borrowing (-) in the financial account and net lending (+)/net borrowing (-) in the capital account.

Table 4.4 Financial Corporations (S.12)

Series 400: 1993 SNA, 1999 PTE euro / euro, Western calendar year **Data in millions**

	2001	2002	2003	2004	2005	2006	2007	2008	2009	2010	2011	2012
Series	**400**											
	I. Production account - Resources											
Output, at basic prices (otherwise, please specify)	10656.7	10916.7	11272.9	11803.5	12451.8	14577.3	16185.3	16884.4	15725.2	15992.4	...	...
	I. Production account - Uses											
Intermediate consumption, at purchaser's prices	3426.7	3598.9	3571.4	3720.3	4108.2	4623.3	5207.0	5327.8	5238.1	5516.7	...	...
VALUE ADDED GROSS, at basic prices	7230.0	7317.8	7701.5	8083.2	8343.5	9954.0	10978.3	11556.6	10487.1	10475.7	10292.2	9474.3
Less: Consumption of fixed capital	592.1	580.3	558.6	559.9	576.7	622.6	673.0	730.8	739.3	767.6	808.6	848.1
VALUE ADDED NET, at basic prices	6637.9	6737.4	7142.9	7523.3	7766.8	9331.5	10305.3	10825.8	9747.8	9708.1	9483.5	8626.2

	2001	2002	2003	2004	2005	2006	2007	2008	2009	2010	2011	2012
Series	**400**											
II.1.1 Generation of income account - Resources												
VALUE ADDED GROSS, at basic prices	7230.0	7317.8	7701.5	8083.2	8343.5	9954.0	10978.3	11556.6	10487.1	10475.7	10292.2	9474.3
II.1.1 Generation of income account - Uses												
Compensation of employees	2947.4	2979.7	3081.9	3137.8	3633.1	3991.2	4136.7	4201.2	4260.0	4308.0	4280.4	3991.4
Other taxes less Other subsidies on production	18.4	15.0	20.3	23.8	18.5	21.7	26.8	29.3	28.2	29.1	31.8	34.9
Other taxes on production	22.7	18.1	26.1	28.2	22.6	25.6	30.2	31.8	32.9	32.3	33.4	35.8
Less: Other subsidies on production	4.3	3.1	5.8	4.4	4.1	3.9	3.4	2.5	4.6	3.2	1.5	0.9
OPERATING SURPLUS, GROSS	4264.2	4323.0	4599.3	4921.6	4692.0	5941.1	6814.8	7326.2	6198.9	6138.7	5979.9	5448.0
II.1.2 Allocation of primary income account - Resources												
OPERATING SURPLUS, GROSS	4264.2	4323.0	4599.3	4921.6	4692.0	5941.1	6814.8	7326.2	6198.9	6138.7	5979.9	5448.0
Property income	15437.1	12991.3	11053.5	11975.9	13362.7	19261.3	25748.7	31323.0	17787.2	16198.0	20141.9	18797.3
II.1.2 Allocation of primary income account - Uses												
Property income	16636.9	14177.0	12405.0	12288.6	13483.0	20382.7	26645.3	31629.6	17996.2	17269.0	19665.1	17873.3
BALANCE OF PRIMARY INCOMES	3064.4	3137.3	3247.8	4608.9	4571.7	4819.7	5918.2	7019.5	5989.9	5067.6	6456.7	6372.0
II.2 Secondary distribution of income account - Resources												
BALANCE OF PRIMARY INCOMES	3064.4	3137.3	3247.8	4608.9	4571.7	4819.7	5918.2	7019.5	5989.9	5067.6	6456.7	6372.0
Social contributions	2236.6	2129.1	2219.2	2408.0	3495.5	3679.7	3772.6	4261.3	3772.6	3645.8	3772.1	3498.1
Other current transfers	1764.9	1903.6	2024.3	2070.9	2045.8	2208.2	2256.9	2200.3	2319.9	2110.5	2141.4	2080.5
II.2 Secondary distribution of income account - Uses												
Current taxes on income, wealth, etc.	579.0	530.1	466.5	392.6	393.4	914.0	1398.8	1014.7	636.8	572.3	444.6	777.0
Social benefits other than social transfers in kind	1783.1	1827.5	1949.5	2111.3	2245.7	2636.5	3270.7	4162.6	3627.1	3434.4	3264.9	2756.0
Other current transfers	1774.0	1903.9	1995.4	2080.9	2054.0	2221.9	2278.8	2229.5	2346.7	2006.3	2066.0	2052.2
GROSS DISPOSABLE INCOME	2929.8	2908.5	3079.8	4502.9	5419.9	4935.2	4999.5	6074.3	5471.9	4811.0	6594.7	6365.4
II.4.1 Use of disposable income account - Resources												
GROSS DISPOSABLE INCOME	2929.8	2908.5	3079.8	4502.9	5419.9	4935.2	4999.5	6074.3	5471.9	4811.0	6594.7	6365.4
II.4.1 Use of disposable income account - Uses												
Adjustment for the change in net equity of households on pension funds	573.7	410.4	308.8	367.4	1306.7	1101.6	568.7	193.4	189.2	212.5	201.7	186.4
SAVING, GROSS	2356.1	2498.1	2771.0	4135.6	4113.2	3833.6	4430.8	5880.9	5282.7	4598.4	6393.0	6178.9
III.1 Capital account - Changes in liabilities and net worth												
SAVING, GROSS	2356.1	2498.1	2771.0	4135.6	4113.2	3833.6	4430.8	5880.9	5282.7	4598.4	6393.0	6178.9
Capital transfers, receivable less payable	-1204.6	-1637.2	-1092.5	-3502.6	-2260.0	-320.6	2.8	-1416.2	-58.0	2229.3	-5394.8	522.8
Capital transfers, receivable	1263.2	1838.7	664.6	966.2	2013.4	368.7	7.1	1447.1	77.0	2330.8	1122.6	2113.5
Less: Capital transfers, payable	2467.8	3475.8	1757.0	4468.8	4273.4	689.3	4.4	2863.3	135.0	101.5	6517.3	1590.7
Equals: CHANGES IN NET WORTH DUE TO SAVING AND CAPITAL TRANSFERS	559.4	280.6	1120.0	73.1	1276.5	2890.5	3760.5	3733.8	4485.4	6060.1	189.6	5853.6
III.1 Capital account - Changes in assets												
Gross capital formation	998.3	1248.7	1063.8	1563.8	999.7	2324.1	1683.4	1435.2	1064.4	1018.4	1056.5	984.9
Gross fixed capital formation	997.1	1245.6	1062.3	1561.3	964.6	2323.8	1683.3	1434.9	1065.3	1019.0	1056.5	984.9
Changes in inventories	0.0	0.0	0.0	0.0	0.0	0.0	0.0	0.0	0.0	0.0	0.0	0.0

	2001	2002	2003	2004	2005	2006	2007	2008	2009	2010	2011	2012
Series	**400**											
Acquisitions less disposals of valuables	1.2	3.1	1.4	2.5	35.1	0.3	0.1	0.3	-0.9	-0.7	0.0	0.0
Acquisitions less disposals of non-produced non-financial assets	70.8	330.3	161.3	261.3	363.7	770.9	58.7	102.6	2.9	93.3	41.6	30.6
NET LENDING (+) / NET BORROWING (-)	82.5	-718.0	453.5	-1192.2	489.8	418.1	2691.5	2926.8	4157.3	5716.0	-99.8	5686.2
	III.2 Financial account - Changes in liabilities and net worth											
Net incurrence of liabilities	32445.4	22748.4	30711.6	28365.5	34805.0	33484.6	43459.1	21775.2	33909.5	24402.8	-32262.2	...
Currency and deposits	16241.7	6550.3	5744.5	13680.1	16393.2	21971.3	19769.6	7853.2	6063.3	39791.2	-15958.9	...
Securities other than shares	5415.0	879.5	1894.4	585.0	-4489.5	3208.6	16694.6	12573.8	16411.7	-6025.6	-10372.9	...
Loans	1567.0	6325.8	6431.7	-1307.2	3284.6	2973.3	477.3	-2018.4	-2867.3	-7868.2	9640.1	...
Shares and other equity	3688.6	4942.3	11848.5	8397.1	9672.0	-552.0	-1025.6	-687.0	10521.2	-3803.7	-10267.1	...
Insurance technical reserves	4773.2	4929.0	2148.2	4269.3	8150.7	6114.9	5429.9	-273.3	4845.0	5856.7	-5847.6	...
Financial derivatives	...	...	...	...	...	...	...	...	...	...	...	...
Other accounts payable	759.9	-878.5	2644.3	2741.1	1794.0	-231.3	2113.2	4326.9	-1064.4	-3547.7	544.2	...
Adjustment to reconcile Net Lending of Financial Account and Capital Account	26.9	2.6	-188.8	96.2	227.4	213.8	66.9	294.7	221.6	-5.4	...	...
NET LENDING (+) / NET BORROWING (-)	55.5[a]	-720.5[a]	642.3[a]	-1288.4[a]	262.4[a]	204.3[a]	2624.6[a]	2632.2[a]	3935.7[a]	5721.4[a]	-2362.3[b]	...
	III.2 Financial account - Changes in assets											
Net acquisition of financial assets	32501.0	22027.8	31353.9	27077.1	35067.4	33688.9	46083.7	24407.4	37845.2	30124.3	-34624.4	...
Monetary gold and SDRs	12.6	-144.6	-768.8	-584.3	-507.0	-561.0	-1.4	6.3	-11.5	12.2	-45.7	...
Currency and deposits	-1113.9	1872.4	7794.3	1243.8	5039.0	10927.8	6407.8	-15505.2	1782.9	4615.9	-6911.8	...
Securities other than shares	3451.8	3531.8	8516.5	6786.6	15751.3	6163.5	9166.6	18266.9	20617.3	21401.5	-19082.2	...
Loans	25176.8	15356.0	15019.0	14966.4	12533.8	15460.5	26864.0	21690.1	8071.1	4414.1	-4896.1	...
Shares and other equity	3758.2	976.5	2070.5	3878.2	2444.4	1672.4	2904.4	-3321.3	3695.8	886.5	-5267.1	...
Insurance technical reserves	78.7	-7.2	167.7	-213.0	82.5	-252.6	-0.5	-5.1	56.7	18.5	22.3	...
Financial derivatives	...	...	...	...	...	...	...	...	...	...	...	...
Other accounts receivable	1136.8	442.9	-1445.3	999.4	-276.4	278.5	742.8	3275.7	3632.8	-1224.5	1556.1	...

[a] Excludes Adjustment to reconcile Net Lending of the Financial Account and the Capital Account.
[b] Statistical discrepancy between net lending (+)/net borrowing (-) in the financial account and net lending (+)/net borrowing (-) in the capital account.

Table 4.5 General Government (S.13)

Series 400: 1993 SNA, 1999 PTE euro / euro, Western calendar year **Data in millions**

	2001	2002	2003	2004	2005	2006	2007	2008	2009	2010	2011	2012
Series	**400**											
	I. Production account - Resources											
Output, at basic prices (otherwise, please specify)	27020.7	28539.9	27906.1	29255.2	31304.9	30967.0	30957.8	31509.7	32923.1	33293.7	30747.0	27238.2
	I. Production account - Uses											
Intermediate consumption, at purchaser's prices	6107.8	6246.9	5864.1	6311.4	6973.5	6987.0	7380.2	7637.1	8411.0	8942.3	8039.2	7535.7
VALUE ADDED GROSS, at basic prices	20912.9	22292.9	22042.0	22943.8	24331.4	23980.0	23577.6	23872.7	24512.1	24351.4	22707.8	19702.5
Less: Consumption of fixed capital	2589.2	2757.3	2852.9	3006.3	3209.9	3383.3	3501.6	3572.7	3591.6	3733.6	3867.0	3884.2
VALUE ADDED NET, at basic prices	18323.7	19535.6	19189.1	19937.4	21121.5	20596.7	20076.0	20299.9	20920.5	20617.8	18840.8	15818.3

	2001	2002	2003	2004	2005	2006	2007	2008	2009	2010	2011	2012
Series	**400**											
	II.1.1 Generation of income account - Resources											
VALUE ADDED GROSS, at basic prices	20912.9	22292.9	22042.0	22943.8	24331.4	23980.0	23577.6	23872.7	24512.1	24351.4	22707.8	19702.5
	II.1.1 Generation of income account - Uses											
Compensation of employees	18645.4	19935.4	19579.2	20328.4	21523.2	21009.4	20473.2	20676.9	21399.5	21157.3	19438.4	16308.9
Other taxes less Other subsidies on production	-281.4	-376.3	-353.5	-340.4	-361.7	-351.4	-341.3	-280.2	-389.8	-485.8	-503.3	-399.1
Other taxes on production	...	...	...	...	...	...	...	...	...	...	...	...
Less: Other subsidies on production	281.4	376.3	353.5	340.4	361.7	351.4	341.3	280.2	389.8	485.8	503.3	399.1
OPERATING SURPLUS, GROSS	2548.9	2733.8	2816.4	2955.7	3169.8	3322.1	3445.8	3476.0	3502.4	3679.8	3772.7	3792.7
	II.1.2 Allocation of primary income account - Resources											
OPERATING SURPLUS, GROSS	2548.9	2733.8	2816.4	2955.7	3169.8	3322.1	3445.8	3476.0	3502.4	3679.8	3772.7	3792.7
Taxes on production and imports, less Subsidies	15812.7	17640.2	18708.2	19032.8	20936.9	22453.9	23178.2	23045.8	20227.9	21757.0	22202.2	21483.7
Taxes on production and imports	17471.7	19204.2	20455.1	20402.0	22383.5	23902.0	24527.3	24213.5	21486.7	23039.5	23389.8	22522.4
Taxes on products	16618.2	17947.8	18547.1	19398.9	21313.1	22722.1	23206.2	22777.7	19949.5	21542.8	21831.4	20856.5
Other taxes on production	853.5	1256.4	1908.1	1003.1	1070.4	1179.9	1321.1	1435.8	1537.2	1496.7	1558.3	1665.9
Less: Subsidies	1659.0	1564.0	1746.9	1369.2	1446.6	1448.0	1349.2	1167.7	1258.8	1282.6	1187.6	1038.8
Subsidies on products	197.6	192.6	213.6	197.9	239.1	257.6	258.5	261.0	243.4	277.7	349.5	198.0
Other subsidies on production	1461.4	1371.4	1533.3	1171.3	1207.5	1190.4	1090.7	906.7	1015.5	1004.9	838.1	840.7
Property income	1049.9	1124.4	1114.1	1212.9	778.6	1207.6	1545.4	1660.8	1291.0	1117.5	1080.9	1209.1
	II.1.2 Allocation of primary income account - Uses											
Property income	3988.5	3982.2	3898.2	3920.6	3877.5	4505.2	5094.2	5322.6	4824.8	4906.5	6932.8	7306.7
BALANCE OF PRIMARY INCOMES	15423.1	17516.1	18740.5	19280.7	21007.8	22478.5	23075.1	22860.1	20196.5	21647.7	20122.9	19178.8
	II.2 Secondary distribution of income account - Resources											
BALANCE OF PRIMARY INCOMES	15423.1	17516.1	18740.5	19280.7	21007.8	22478.5	23075.1	22860.1	20196.5	21647.7	20122.9	19178.8
Current taxes on income, wealth, etc.	12202.0	12651.4	12035.5	12401.1	12662.3	13851.8	16084.4	16644.2	15146.3	15222.3	16962.6	15291.3
Social contributions	14489.6	15620.1	16679.1	17234.4	18356.2	19007.8	19648.1	20502.8	21032.5	21269.8	20928.6	19230.4
Other current transfers	706.7	925.1	1054.6	1649.3	1334.9	1741.9	2157.8	1974.4	2048.8	1588.8	1996.3	2410.4
	II.2 Secondary distribution of income account - Uses											
Current taxes on income, wealth, etc.	0.0	0.0	0.0	0.0	0.0	15.2	20.9	32.7	7.9	7.8	18.0	4.2
Social benefits other than social transfers in kind	15526.1	16989.7	19081.7	20571.0	22209.4	23398.6	24638.3	25991.5	28660.8	29552.9	29645.4	29788.7
Other current transfers	2298.3	2891.8	2860.4	3291.4	3483.0	3832.9	3883.8	3733.9	4275.7	4870.4	4380.6	3823.4
GROSS DISPOSABLE INCOME	24997.0	26831.2	26567.5	26703.0	27668.7	29833.4	32422.3	32223.4	25479.7	25297.4	25966.3	22494.6
	II.4.1 Use of disposable income account - Resources											
GROSS DISPOSABLE INCOME	24997.0	26831.2	26567.5	26703.0	27668.7	29833.4	32422.3	32223.4	25479.7	25297.4	25966.3	22494.6
	II.4.1 Use of disposable income account - Uses											
Final consumption expenditure	26104.4	27663.0	28728.9	30324.0	32618.2	33002.1	33579.0	34532.0	37185.3	37334.5	34294.9	30243.1
Individual consumption expenditure	15267.4	16250.3	16927.1	17759.7	18875.3	18814.9	18727.8	19116.0	20395.5	20431.6	18925.1	16705.9
Collective consumption expenditure	10837.0	11412.7	11801.8	12564.2	13742.9	14187.2	14851.2	15416.0	16789.8	16902.9	15369.8	13537.3
Adjustment for the change in net equity of households on pension funds	...	...	...	...	...	...	...	...	...	...	...	...
SAVING, GROSS	-1107.4	-831.7	-2161.3	-3621.0	-4949.4	-3168.8	-1156.6	-2308.6	-11705.6	-12037.1	-8328.6	-7748.6

	2001	2002	2003	2004	2005	2006	2007	2008	2009	2010	2011	2012
Series	**400**											
III.1 Capital account - Changes in liabilities and net worth												
SAVING, GROSS	-1107.4	-831.7	-2161.3	-3621.0	-4949.4	-3168.8	-1156.6	-2308.6	-11705.6	-12037.1	-8328.6	-7748.6
Capital transfers, receivable less payable	553.5	1082.7	2400.0	3418.0	397.0	411.8	226.7	-622.4	-190.1	1586.5	5210.6	-194.3
Capital transfers, receivable	1895.1	2202.2	3482.3	4852.7	2050.9	1357.5	1317.7	1250.4	1247.2	4911.9	7641.0	2170.0
Less: Capital transfers, payable	1341.7	1119.5	1082.4	1434.6	1653.9	945.7	1091.0	1872.7	1437.4	3325.4	2430.5	2364.3
Equals: CHANGES IN NET WORTH DUE TO SAVING AND CAPITAL TRANSFERS	-3143.2	-2506.3	-2614.3	-3209.3	-7762.3	-6140.3	-4431.6	-6503.7	-15487.3	-14184.2	-6985.1	-11827.1
III.1 Capital account - Changes in assets												
Gross capital formation	5910.9	5717.9	5565.0	5703.2	5510.5	4565.4	4588.3	5068.1	5077.6	6500.2	4440.1	3060.3
Gross fixed capital formation	5910.7	5717.7	5559.4	5696.1	5504.4	4560.1	4578.5	5059.4	5066.6	6496.5	4435.5	3056.7
Changes in inventories	...	...	...	...	...	...	...	...	...	...	...	...
Acquisitions less disposals of valuables	0.2	0.2	5.6	7.1	6.1	5.4	9.9	8.7	11.0	3.7	4.6	3.7
Acquisitions of non-produced non-financial assets	4.5	-642.0	46.5	127.0	-52.7	120.6	-79.3	-1640.7	173.0	76.7	-34.1	-378.9
NET LENDING (+) / NET BORROWING (-)	-6469.4	-4824.9	-5372.9	-6033.2	-10010.2	-7443.0	-5439.1	-6358.3	-17146.3	-17027.6	-7524.0	-10624.3
III.2 Financial account - Changes in liabilities and net worth												
Net incurrence of liabilities	5740.6	8989.0	5228.7	6998.7	10813.4	7200.2	5276.5	7607.6	18194.8	21892.8	22033.0	...
Currency and deposits	1089.1	1185.0	671.2	-142.8	537.6	2051.4	928.1	-527.0	-531.7	-835.1	-3110.1	...
Securities other than shares	5392.4	5742.8	2333.5	4464.9	11425.7	5191.4	1975.4	9455.4	16235.3	17787.4	-11144.8	...
Loans	1644.7	1661.4	1355.8	2502.7	224.2	66.5	1222.5	-970.1	1718.5	3704.8	35483.2	...
Shares and other equity	...	...	...	...	...	...	...	...	...	...	...	...
Insurance technical reserves	...	...	...	...	...	...	...	...	...	...	...	...
Financial derivatives	...	...	...	...	...	...	...	...	...	...	...	...
Other accounts payable	-2385.6	399.8	868.0	173.9	-1374.1	-109.1	1150.5	-350.7	772.7	1235.7	804.8	...
Adjustment to reconcile Net Lending of Financial Account and Capital Account	0.0	0.0	0.1	-0.3	0.0	0.0	0.0	0.0	0.0	0.0	...	...
NET LENDING (+) / NET BORROWING (-)	-6469.4	-4824.9	-5373.0	-6032.9	-10010.2	-7443.0	-5439.1	-6358.3	-17135.4	-17016.7	-7506.2	...
III.2 Financial account - Changes in assets												
Net acquisition of financial assets	-728.8	4164.1	-144.3	965.8	803.1	-242.8	-162.5	1249.3	1059.4	4876.0	14526.9	...
Monetary gold and SDRs	...	...	...	...	...	...	...	...	...	...	...	...
Currency and deposits	-1825.9	1575.3	-1290.0	-196.0	880.4	918.9	-400.5	-588.7	-506.3	712.7	10247.3	...
Securities other than shares	460.8	90.1	217.2	-126.1	520.2	406.9	-76.2	-943.5	324.8	-509.9	142.1	...
Loans	331.8	340.8	497.3	103.3	303.9	61.4	-2047.3	671.9	-191.8	1282.9	446.0	...
Shares and other equity	-377.3	1198.6	408.7	-163.7	-525.4	-1678.4	1504.3	1992.1	1001.4	1591.7	-336.4	...
Insurance technical reserves	0.9	0.8	1.7	1.5	2.4	1.9	0.9	-0.3	0.4	-1.6	0.3	...
Financial derivatives	...	...	...	...	...	...	...	...	...	...	...	...
Other accounts receivable	680.9	958.5	20.8	1346.9	-378.2	46.6	856.2	117.8	430.9	1800.2	4027.6	...

Table 4.6 Households (S.14)

Series 400: 1993 SNA, 1999 PTE euro / euro, Western calendar year

Data in millions

	2001	2002	2003	2004	2005	2006	2007	2008	2009	2010	2011	2012
Series	400											
I. Production account - Resources												
Output, at basic prices (otherwise, please specify)	39156.6	39371.5	40106.4	41205.0	40967.0	41069.4	42050.4	42936.7	42297.2	41873.3		
I. Production account - Uses												
Intermediate consumption, at purchaser's prices	13383.2	12865.9	12566.2	13166.0	12825.8	12761.4	12667.1	12930.7	12470.1	11724.5		
VALUE ADDED GROSS, at basic prices	25773.4	26505.6	27540.2	28038.9	28141.2	28308.0	29383.3	30006.0	29827.2	30148.8		
Less: Consumption of fixed capital	6302.9	6672.1	6955.1	7328.5	7738.8	8208.4	8575.8	9108.5	9144.8	9392.0		
VALUE ADDED NET, at basic prices	19470.5	19833.5	20585.1	20710.4	20402.3	20099.7	20807.6	20897.5	20682.4	20756.8		
II.1.1 Generation of income account - Resources												
VALUE ADDED GROSS, at basic prices	25773.4	26505.6	27540.2	28038.9	28141.2	28308.0	29383.3	30006.0	29827.2	30148.8		
II.1.1 Generation of income account - Uses												
Compensation of employees	4726.3	4797.8	4911.9	4995.2	5117.9	5306.3	5599.1	5555.2	5284.2	5116.0		
Other taxes less Other subsidies on production	-32.7	-106.3	70.2	-132.9	-217.8	-102.9	-114.9	-76.0	64.8	16.6		
Other taxes on production	334.4	429.0	579.8	472.0	501.8	567.1	634.8	694.2	687.0	695.8		
Less: Other subsidies on production	367.1	535.3	509.6	604.9	719.6	670.0	749.7	770.2	622.2	679.2		
OPERATING SURPLUS, GROSS	...	...	...	...	...	6107.3	6822.3	7075.1	6733.5	7380.5		
MIXED INCOME, GROSS	21079.8	21814.1	22558.1	23176.6	23241.2	16997.3	17076.8	17451.7	17744.6	17635.7		
II.1.2 Allocation of primary income account - Resources												
OPERATING SURPLUS, GROSS	...	...	...	...	...	6107.3	6822.3	7075.1	6733.5	7380.5		
MIXED INCOME, GROSS	21079.8	21814.1	22558.1	23176.6	23241.2	16997.3	17076.8	17451.7	17744.6	17635.7		
Compensation of employees	66076.8	69314.8	71204.3	73530.2	77198.4	79519.9	82856.6	85661.0	85757.0	86694.4		
Property income	10382.8	10235.4	10591.6	12581.8	13972.7	15615.1	19011.3	21658.0	13626.4	13112.5		
II.1.2 Allocation of primary income account - Uses												
Property income	2751.9	2676.6	2163.2	3696.4	3843.4	5485.7	8100.9	9759.7	3846.7	2477.6		
BALANCE OF PRIMARY INCOMES	94787.4	98687.8	102190.8	105592.1	110568.9	112753.9	117666.2	122086.1	120014.9	122345.5		
II.2 Secondary distribution of income account - Resources												
BALANCE OF PRIMARY INCOMES	94787.4	98687.8	102190.8	105592.1	110568.9	112753.9	117666.2	122086.1	120014.9	122345.5		
Social contributions	55.8	56.5	53.5	43.4	35.1	47.6	50.4	48.8	41.9	38.0		
Social benefits other than social transfers in kind	19458.7	20983.5	23045.5	24313.8	25728.9	27808.0	29586.3	31961.6	34080.5	34812.8		
Other current transfers	6271.2	5863.4	5196.0	5577.3	5772.3	6438.4	6667.1	6725.9	6420.5	6651.4		
II.2 Secondary distribution of income account - Uses												
Current taxes on income, wealth, etc.	7623.2	7766.9	7861.4	7909.3	8305.8	8871.5	9717.5	10071.8	10136.8	10076.9		
Social contributions	18890.0	19938.4	20959.7	21297.4	23167.0	24503.0	25181.0	26654.0	26682.5	26810.9		
Social benefits other than social transfers in kind	55.8	56.5	53.5	43.4	35.1	47.6	50.4	48.8	41.9	38.0		
Other current transfers	3033.8	2993.6	3010.6	3684.1	4159.2	3855.1	3836.8	3972.0	3951.7	3491.3		
GROSS DISPOSABLE INCOME	90970.2	94835.7	98600.5	102592.4	106438.1	109770.7	115184.3	120075.7	119744.9	123430.4		

	2001	2002	2003	2004	2005	2006	2007	2008	2009	2010	2011	2012
Series	**400**											
	II.4.1 Use of disposable income account - Resources											
GROSS DISPOSABLE INCOME	90970.2	94835.7	98600.5	102592.4	106438.1	109770.7	115184.3	120075.7	119744.9	123430.4		
Adjustment for the change in net equity of households on pension funds	573.7	410.4	308.8	367.4	1306.7	1101.6	568.7	193.4	189.2	212.5		
	II.4.1 Use of disposable income account - Uses											
Final consumption expenditure	82387.0	85744.3	88072.4	92739.4	96881.3	101660.6	107220.2	111363.1	106206.7	110395.5		
Individual consumption expenditure	82387.0	85744.3	88072.4	92739.4	96881.3	101660.6	107220.2	111363.1	106206.7	110395.5		
SAVING, GROSS	9157.0	9501.9	10836.8	10220.4	10863.6	9211.7	8532.8	8905.9	13727.4	13247.5		
	III.1 Capital account - Changes in liabilities and net worth											
SAVING, GROSS	9157.0	9501.9	10836.8	10220.4	10863.6	9211.7	8532.8	8905.9	13727.4	13247.5		
Capital transfers, receivable less payable	2872.1	3071.7	1105.7	1742.2	2207.2	436.2	85.9	1556.1	250.1	79.2		
Capital transfers, receivable	3072.8	3339.3	1365.9	1924.5	2422.7	593.8	209.4	1689.5	369.1	291.3		
Less: Capital transfers, payable	200.6	267.6	260.2	182.3	215.5	157.6	123.6	133.4	119.0	212.0		
Equals: CHANGES IN NET WORTH DUE TO SAVINGS AND CAPITAL TRANSFERS	5726.2	5901.5	4987.5	4634.0	5332.0	1439.5	42.9	1353.5	4832.7	3934.8		
	III.1 Capital account - Changes in assets											
Gross capital formation	10368.3	10475.5	9109.6	9627.9	10078.2	9499.0	9288.7	8693.2	7269.2	6858.5		
Gross fixed capital formation	10274.8	10380.2	9076.2	9464.3	9869.0	9269.8	9106.0	8642.9	7144.7	6647.2		
Changes in inventories	-24.7	-18.9	-57.4	75.0	111.5	91.8	77.4	66.7	14.1	88.3		
Acquisitions less disposals of valuables	118.1	114.3	90.8	88.7	97.6	137.4	105.3	-16.4	110.5	123.1		
Acquisitions less disposals of non-produced non-financial assets	-1344.6	-1435.2	-1575.0	-1692.9	-1627.6	-2844.5	-2915.2	-2350.0	-2295.0	-2259.0		
NET LENDING (+) / NET BORROWING (-)	3005.4	3533.2	4407.9	4027.5	4620.2	2993.3	2245.2	4118.8	9003.2	8727.3		

Table 4.7 Non-profit institutions serving households (S.15)

Series 400: 1993 SNA, 1999 PTE euro / euro, Western calendar year

Data in millions

	2001	2002	2003	2004	2005	2006	2007	2008	2009	2010	2011	2012
Series	**400**											
	I. Production account - Resources											
Output, at basic prices (otherwise, please specify)	3613.1	3792.6	3939.9	4166.7	4338.0	4539.2	4914.6	5277.3	5289.8	5391.0		
	I. Production account - Uses											
Intermediate consumption, at purchaser's prices	1578.7	1645.9	1721.4	1863.8	1955.5	2049.8	2237.8	2422.4	2393.5	2337.7		
VALUE ADDED GROSS, at basic prices	2034.5	2146.7	2218.6	2302.9	2382.6	2489.4	2676.8	2854.9	2896.3	3053.3		
Less: Consumption of fixed capital	462.9	483.5	491.3	504.3	517.0	532.4	551.4	560.2	565.3	590.7		
VALUE ADDED NET, at basic prices	1571.6	1663.1	1727.2	1798.6	1865.6	1957.0	2125.3	2294.7	2331.0	2462.6		
	II.1.1 Generation of income account - Resources											
VALUE ADDED GROSS, at basic prices	2034.5	2146.7	2218.6	2302.9	2382.6	2489.4	2676.8	2854.9	2896.3	3053.3		
	II.1.1 Generation of income account - Uses											
Compensation of employees	1776.8	1907.7	1966.5	2031.3	2101.2	2193.5	2312.8	2472.5	2633.5	2739.1		

	2001	2002	2003	2004	2005	2006	2007	2008	2009	2010	2011	2012
Series	**400**											
Other taxes less Other subsidies on production	-256.4	-202.9	-257.2	-209.5	-242.7	-228.7	-179.7	-165.4	-300.3	-271.2		
Other taxes on production	2.4	2.9	3.2	3.1	3.4	3.8	4.2	3.9	3.4	3.6		
Less: Other subsidies on production	258.8	205.9	260.4	212.6	246.1	232.5	183.9	169.2	303.7	274.9		
OPERATING SURPLUS, GROSS	514.1	441.8	509.3	481.0	524.1	524.6	543.7	547.8	563.1	585.5		
	II.1.2 Allocation of primary income account - Resources											
OPERATING SURPLUS, GROSS	514.1	441.8	509.3	481.0	524.1	524.6	543.7	547.8	563.1	585.5		
Property income	254.8	253.3	232.8	275.7	323.4	427.0	567.9	680.0	319.1	280.2		
	II.1.2 Allocation of primary income account - Uses											
Property income	139.2	123.7	99.1	99.2	101.5	130.1	165.2	202.1	44.8	58.0		
BALANCE OF PRIMARY INCOMES	629.6	571.5	643.0	657.5	746.0	821.5	946.5	1025.7	837.4	807.8		
	II.2 Secondary distribution of income account - Resources											
BALANCE OF PRIMARY INCOMES	629.6	571.5	643.0	657.5	746.0	821.5	946.5	1025.7	837.4	807.8		
Social contributions	36.5	38.6	41.2	42.8	45.4	46.9	49.1	52.1	52.2	52.7		
Other current transfers	2817.7	2736.8	2166.9	2606.7	2481.1	2267.3	2324.9	2477.7	2473.9	2469.1		
	II.2 Secondary distribution of income account - Uses											
Current taxes on income, wealth, etc.	3.7	4.5	3.4	3.7	3.9	4.8	5.5	4.8	5.5	4.1		
Social benefits other than social transfers in kind	36.5	38.6	41.2	42.8	45.4	46.9	49.1	52.1	52.2	52.7		
Other current transfers	26.9	29.1	38.4	46.2	47.1	60.1	66.6	75.4	92.0	91.3		
GROSS DISPOSABLE INCOME	3416.7	3274.7	2768.2	3214.3	3176.1	3023.8	3199.3	3423.2	3213.8	3181.5		
	II.4.1 Use of disposable income account - Resources											
GROSS DISPOSABLE INCOME	3416.7	3274.7	2768.2	3214.3	3176.1	3023.8	3199.3	3423.2	3213.8	3181.5		
	II.4.1 Use of disposable income account - Uses											
Final consumption expenditure	2488.4	2648.8	2727.3	2858.2	2965.6	3087.0	3414.8	3593.5	3567.8	3584.5		
Individual consumption expenditure	2488.4	2648.8	2727.3	2858.2	2965.6	3087.0	3414.8	3593.5	3567.8	3584.5		
Adjustment for the change in net equity of households on pension funds	...	...	...	...	...	...	...	...	...	...		
SAVING, GROSS	928.3	626.0	40.9	356.1	210.4	-63.2	-215.5	-170.3	-354.1	-403.0		
	III.1 Capital account - Changes in liabilities and net worth											
SAVING, GROSS	928.3	626.0	40.9	356.1	210.4	-63.2	-215.5	-170.3	-354.1	-403.0		
Capital transfers, receivable less payable	168.7	134.6	154.4	142.8	174.9	223.4	288.8	275.4	355.3	305.5		
Capital transfers, receivable	175.5	140.1	179.6	146.2	181.7	225.7	289.9	304.3	357.6	305.9		
Less: Capital transfers, payable	6.9	5.5	25.2	3.4	6.8	2.2	1.1	28.9	2.3	0.5		
Equals: CHANGES IN NET WORTH DUE TO SAVING AND CAPITAL TRANSFERS	634.1	277.1	-296.0	-5.3	-131.7	-372.1	-478.2	-455.1	-564.0	-688.2		
	III.1 Capital account - Changes in assets											
Gross capital formation	969.3	943.1	864.5	717.7	550.8	716.0	547.5	692.1	834.1	880.3		
Gross fixed capital formation	966.9	939.8	862.2	715.1	547.9	713.0	544.9	544.1	831.4	877.6		
Changes in inventories	...	...	...	...	...	...	...	...	...	...		
Acquisitions less disposals of valuables	2.4	3.3	2.3	2.6	2.9	3.0	2.6	148.0	2.8	2.7		

	2001	2002	2003	2004	2005	2006	2007	2008	2009	2010	2011	2012
Series	**400**											
Acquisitions less disposals of non-produced non-financial assets	0.0	0.0	0.0	0.0	0.0	3.2	4.7	16.6	7.5	3.3		
NET LENDING (+) / NET BORROWING (-)	127.6	-182.5	-669.2	-218.8	-165.5	-558.9	-478.9	-603.6	-840.4	-981.0		

Table 4.8 Combined Sectors: Non-Financial and Financial Corporations (S.11 + S.12)

Series 400: 1993 SNA, 1999 PTE euro / euro, Western calendar year **Data in millions**

	2001	2002	2003	2004	2005	2006	2007	2008	2009	2010	2011	2012
Series	**400**											
	I. Production account - Resources											
Output, at basic prices (otherwise, please specify)	185286.7	188977.5	191942.2	201847.9	210722.1	221997.8	239652.8	250549.5	230868.4	243067.0	...	...
	I. Production account - Uses											
Intermediate consumption, at purchaser's prices	116076.6	117070.2	118495.5	124788.0	132211.5	138425.0	149081.7	157971.9	139386.9	149194.1	...	...
VALUE ADDED GROSS, at basic prices	69210.0	71907.3	73446.7	77059.9	78510.6	83572.8	90571.0	92577.5	91481.5	93872.9	93202.8	91050.2
Less: Consumption of fixed capital	12300.0	13170.7	13691.9	14204.5	14793.4	15175.8	15721.9	16504.0	16493.5	16727.8	16889.9	16905.4
VALUE ADDED NET, at basic prices	56910.0	58736.6	59754.8	62855.4	63717.1	68397.0	74849.1	76073.5	74988.0	77145.0	76312.9	74144.8
	II.1.1 Generation of income account - Resources											
VALUE ADDED GROSS, at basic prices	69210.0	71907.3	73446.7	77059.9	78510.6	83572.8	90571.0	92577.5	91481.5	93872.9	93202.8	91050.2
	II.1.1 Generation of income account - Uses											
Compensation of employees	40961.1	42733.3	44765.6	46293.4	48616.8	51153.9	54476.2	56987.8	56571.2	57801.6	58126.4	55358.2
Other taxes less Other subsidies on production	-547.3	-173.0	207.4	-325.7	-314.4	-258.1	-229.9	-56.4	-74.9	-228.2	-796.0	-812.5
Other taxes on production	516.7	824.5	1325.0	528.0	565.2	609.0	682.1	741.6	847.5	797.3	835.5	884.7
Less: Other subsidies on production	1064.0	997.5	1117.6	853.7	879.6	867.1	912.0	798.0	922.4	1025.5	1631.5	1697.1
OPERATING SURPLUS, GROSS	28796.2	29346.9	28473.7	31092.2	30208.2	32677.0	36324.7	35646.2	34985.2	36299.6	35872.3	36504.5
	II.1.2 Allocation of primary income account - Resources											
OPERATING SURPLUS, GROSS	28796.2	29346.9	28473.7	31092.2	30208.2	32677.0	36324.7	35646.2	34985.2	36299.6	35872.3	36504.5
Property income	19153.0	15980.8	15055.4	16987.7	19245.2	28105.2	35804.7	41855.3	25301.1	25184.2	30444.6	27733.8
	II.1.2 Allocation of primary income account - Uses											
Property income	27752.7	23782.6	23014.5	25886.9	29795.5	40836.8	49871.6	57637.6	39670.2	39350.2	44812.0	41840.9
BALANCE OF PRIMARY INCOMES	20196.5	21545.2	20514.6	22193.0	19657.8	19945.4	22257.8	19863.8	20616.1	22133.5	21505.0	22397.4
	II.2 Secondary distribution of income account - Resources											
BALANCE OF PRIMARY INCOMES	20196.5	21545.2	20514.6	22193.0	19657.8	19945.4	22257.8	19863.8	20616.1	22133.5	21505.0	22397.4
Social contributions	4328.2	4245.6	4196.4	4017.1	4783.4	5451.0	5444.4	6069.8	5601.1	5514.1	5652.7	5292.1
Other current transfers	2369.1	2592.0	2777.5	2937.0	2846.8	3093.4	3174.7	2955.7	3204.6	3045.5	3051.4	2914.2
	II.2 Secondary distribution of income account - Uses											
Current taxes on income, wealth, etc.	4581.5	4882.5	4174.4	4482.0	4344.5	4954.6	6347.9	6539.7	4994.7	5129.2	5856.1	4937.0
Social benefits other than social transfers in kind	3874.6	3943.9	3926.7	3720.5	3533.6	4407.8	4942.5	5971.1	5455.6	5302.7	5145.5	4550.0
Other current transfers	3823.7	4225.6	3690.3	4065.0	3813.9	4183.7	4734.1	4464.4	4584.8	3873.5	4042.9	4344.6
GROSS DISPOSABLE INCOME	14613.9	15330.8	15697.1	16879.6	15596.0	14943.7	14852.4	11914.1	14386.7	16387.8	15164.7	16772.2

	2001	2002	2003	2004	2005	2006	2007	2008	2009	2010	2011	2012
Series	**400**											
II.4.1 Use of disposable income account - Resources												
GROSS DISPOSABLE INCOME	14613.9	15330.8	15697.1	16879.6	15596.0	14943.7	14852.4	11914.1	14386.7	16387.8	15164.7	16772.2
II.4.1 Use of disposable income account - Uses												
Adjustment for the change in net equity of households on pension funds	573.7	410.4	308.8	367.4	1306.7	1101.6	568.7	193.4	189.2	212.5	201.7	186.4
SAVING, GROSS	14040.2	14920.4	15388.4	16512.3	14289.3	13842.1	14283.7	11720.8	14197.5	16175.2	14962.9	16585.7
III.1 Capital account - Changes in liabilities and net worth												
SAVING, GROSS	14040.2	14920.4	15388.4	16512.3	14289.3	13842.1	14283.7	11720.8	14197.5	16175.2	14962.9	16585.7
Capital transfers, receivable less payable	-1388.0	-1772.5	-413.2	-2773.9	-562.1	942.8	1339.4	460.8	1552.8	444.8	-3117.3	3350.7
Capital transfers, receivable	1392.3	2189.1	3086.1	2876.5	3834.4	1653.6	1465.5	3443.5	1789.6	3551.8	3796.2	5327.4
Less: Capital transfers, payable	2780.3	3961.6	3499.3	5650.4	4396.6	710.8	126.0	2982.7	236.8	3107.0	6913.5	1976.6
Equals: CHANGES IN NET WORTH DUE TO SAVING AND CAPITAL TRANSFERS	352.2	-22.7	1283.2	-466.1	-1066.3	-390.9	-98.8	-4322.4	-743.1	-107.8	-5044.3	3031.0
III.1 Capital account - Changes in assets												
Gross capital formation	20021.8	19046.4	18161.2	19761.6	20185.9	22297.7	24227.5	25363.9	20869.9	20635.8	18823.1	16805.1
Gross fixed capital formation	19115.8	18940.3	18348.7	18824.2	19491.4	21347.3	23399.9	24388.4	21586.8	19808.6	19019.7	16715.2
Changes in inventories	901.5	100.5	-191.0	932.9	657.0	948.0	826.0	974.0	-716.7	827.2	-197.3	89.0
Acquisitions less disposals of valuables	4.5	5.7	3.4	4.5	37.4	2.4	1.5	1.6	-0.2	0.0	0.7	0.8
Acquisitions less disposals of non-produced non-financial assets	1356.6	2075.3	1515.3	1527.6	1631.8	2713.5	2830.0	3531.9	2118.6	2192.7	1964.5	2381.3
NET LENDING (+) / NET BORROWING (-)	-8726.3	-7973.8	-4701.4	-7550.8	-8090.6	-10226.3	-11434.3	-16714.2	-7238.1	-6208.5	-8942.0	750.1
III.2 Financial account - Changes in liabilities and net worth												
Net incurrence of liabilities	55103.6	33425.5	54019.0	40732.7	42408.6	47025.1	63104.9	44680.4	50884.6	39134.1	-22419.0	...
Currency and deposits	16241.7	6550.3	5744.5	13680.1	16393.2	21971.3	19769.6	7853.2	6063.3	39791.2	-15958.9	...
Securities other than shares	7383.4	3308.9	1141.7	2081.8	-28.6	5367.6	22170.8	17780.4	18513.5	-5193.1	-7711.6	...
Loans	15895.3	9605.4	13027.1	-560.9	8294.7	12399.3	17813.8	15699.5	1177.3	-4443.0	6670.9	...
Shares and other equity	6030.2	10654.7	22436.4	14685.9	14200.1	6399.4	-3476.0	-501.2	15874.4	3108.5	-5931.3	...
Insurance technical reserves	5271.4	4178.4	3399.4	4809.6	8057.4	6011.9	5780.8	-243.5	4721.5	6237.8	-5950.5	...
Financial derivatives	...	...	...	...	...	...	...	...	...	...	...	...
Other accounts payable	4281.5	-872.1	8269.8	6036.2	-4508.3	-5124.3	1045.9	4092.1	4534.6	-367.3	6462.4	...
NET LENDING (+) / NET BORROWING (-) [a]	-9243.3	-7722.6	-5013.9	-8176.3	-8484.5	-11038.7	-11213.2	-16353.1	-8310.3	-6924.9	-9266.3	...
III.2 Financial account - Changes in assets												
Net acquisition of financial assets	45860.2	25702.9	49005.1	32556.4	33924.0	35986.4	51891.7	28327.3	42574.3	32209.3	-31685.4	...
Monetary gold and SDRs	12.6	-144.6	-768.8	-584.3	-507.0	-561.0	-1.4	6.3	-11.5	12.2	-45.7	...
Currency and deposits	460.4	2268.7	10600.7	2383.9	9258.6	13943.1	6118.3	-16421.6	1610.1	10610.4	-11853.5	...
Securities other than shares	7926.6	5862.6	9019.7	7553.9	14247.5	5466.6	9350.4	18048.1	20726.8	19916.3	-19414.1	...
Loans	26381.5	19709.9	15492.5	13040.0	14377.2	17963.9	32042.0	25598.7	9856.3	11002.0	-19.0	...
Shares and other equity	3609.6	-1467.3	6124.3	6995.8	2449.2	2200.1	3133.9	27.8	4900.8	-6546.3	-1595.5	...
Insurance technical reserves	216.0	59.0	310.3	-89.6	277.4	-87.0	131.4	-46.0	119.2	-218.0	73.4	...

	2001	2002	2003	2004	2005	2006	2007	2008	2009	2010	2011	2012
Series	**400**											
Financial derivatives	...	...	...	...	...	...	...	...	...	...	...	...
Other accounts receivable	7253.6	-585.4	8226.5	3256.7	-6178.9	-2939.2	1117.1	1113.8	5372.6	-2567.3	1169.1	...

[a] Statistical discrepancy between net lending (+)/net borrowing (-) in the financial account and net lending (+)/net borrowing (-) in the capital account.

Table 4.9 Combined Sectors: Households and NPISH (S.14 + S.15)

Series 400: 1993 SNA, 1999 PTE euro / euro, Western calendar year **Data in millions**

	2001	2002	2003	2004	2005	2006	2007	2008	2009	2010	2011	2012
Series	**400**											
	I. Production account - Resources											
Output, at basic prices (otherwise, please specify)	42769.7	43164.1	44046.3	45371.6	45305.0	45608.6	46965.0	48214.1	47587.0	47264.3	...	...
	I. Production account - Uses											
Intermediate consumption, at purchaser's prices	14961.9	14511.9	14287.6	15029.8	14781.3	14811.2	14904.9	15353.2	14863.6	14062.1	...	...
VALUE ADDED GROSS, at basic prices	27807.8	28652.3	29758.8	30341.8	30523.8	30797.4	32060.1	32860.9	32723.4	33202.2	33517.2	33861.2
Less: Consumption of fixed capital	6765.8	7155.6	7446.4	7832.8	8255.8	8740.8	9127.2	9668.8	9710.1	9982.8	10230.7	10322.5
VALUE ADDED NET, at basic prices	21042.1	21496.7	22312.3	22509.0	22267.9	22056.6	22932.9	23192.2	23013.4	23219.4	23286.5	23538.7
	II.1.1 Generation of income account - Resources											
VALUE ADDED GROSS, at basic prices	27807.8	28652.3	29758.8	30341.8	30523.8	30797.4	32060.1	32860.9	32723.4	33202.2	33517.2	33861.2
	II.1.1 Generation of income account - Uses											
Compensation of employees	6503.2	6705.5	6878.4	7026.5	7219.1	7499.9	7911.9	8027.7	7917.6	7855.1	7889.9	7576.7
Other taxes less Other subsidies on production	-289.1	-309.2	-187.0	-342.4	-460.5	-331.6	-294.6	-241.4	-235.4	-254.6	478.8	401.9
Other taxes on production	336.8	431.9	583.0	475.1	505.2	570.9	639.0	698.1	690.4	699.4	722.8	781.3
Less: Other subsidies on production	625.9	741.1	770.0	817.4	965.7	902.5	933.6	939.4	925.8	954.0	244.0	379.4
OPERATING SURPLUS, GROSS	514.1	441.8	509.3	481.0	524.1	6631.8	7366.0	7622.9	7296.6	7966.0	...	...
MIXED INCOME, GROSS	21079.8	21814.1	22558.1	23176.6	23241.2	16997.3	17076.8	17451.7	17744.6	17635.7	...	...
	II.1.2 Allocation of primary income account - Resources											
OPERATING SURPLUS, GROSS	514.1	441.8	509.3	481.0	524.1	6631.8	7366.0	7622.9	7296.6	7966.0	...	...
MIXED INCOME, GROSS	21079.8	21814.1	22558.1	23176.6	23241.2	16997.3	17076.8	17451.7	17744.6	17635.7	...	...
Compensation of employees	66076.8	69314.8	71204.3	73530.2	77198.4	79519.9	82856.6	85661.0	85757.0	86694.4	85311.0	79146.6
Property income	10637.6	10488.7	10824.5	12857.5	14296.1	16042.0	19579.2	22338.1	13945.5	13392.7	16356.5	18028.2
	II.1.2 Allocation of primary income account - Uses											
Property income	2891.2	2800.2	2262.2	3795.6	3944.9	5615.7	8266.1	9961.9	3891.5	2535.6	3824.2	3400.5
BALANCE OF PRIMARY INCOMES	95417.0	99259.3	102833.9	106249.7	111314.9	113575.4	118612.7	123111.8	120852.3	123153.3	122991.8	119657.0
	II.2 Secondary distribution of income account - Resources											
BALANCE OF PRIMARY INCOMES	95417.0	99259.3	102833.9	106249.7	111314.9	113575.4	118612.7	123111.8	120852.3	123153.3	122991.8	119657.0
Social contributions	92.3	95.1	94.7	86.2	80.5	94.6	99.4	100.9	94.1	90.7	91.1	87.5
Social benefits other than social transfers in kind	19458.7	20983.5	23045.5	24313.8	25728.9	27808.0	29586.3	31961.6	34080.5	34812.8	34732.0	34294.8
Other current transfers	9088.9	8600.2	7362.9	8183.9	8253.4	8705.7	8992.0	9203.6	8894.5	9120.4	9254.0	8920.7

	2001	2002	2003	2004	2005	2006	2007	2008	2009	2010	2011	2012
Series	**400**											
	II.2 Secondary distribution of income account - Uses											
Current taxes on income, wealth, etc.	7626.9	7771.4	7864.8	7913.0	8309.7	8876.3	9723.0	10076.6	10142.3	10081.0	11087.8	10355.0
Social contributions	18890.0	19938.4	20959.7	21297.4	23167.0	24503.0	25181.0	26654.0	26682.5	26810.9	26617.7	24569.5
Social benefits other than social transfers in kind	92.3	95.1	94.7	86.2	80.5	94.6	99.4	100.9	94.1	90.7	91.1	87.5
Other current transfers	3060.7	3022.7	3049.0	3730.3	4206.3	3915.2	3903.4	4047.4	4043.8	3582.6	4248.0	4071.9
GROSS DISPOSABLE INCOME	94386.9	98110.5	101368.6	105806.7	109614.2	112794.5	118383.6	123498.9	122958.7	126612.0	125024.2	123876.2
	II.4.1 Use of disposable income account - Resources											
GROSS DISPOSABLE INCOME	94386.9	98110.5	101368.6	105806.7	109614.2	112794.5	118383.6	123498.9	122958.7	126612.0	125024.2	123876.2
Adjustment for the change in net equity of households on pension funds	573.7	410.4	308.8	367.4	1306.7	1101.6	568.7	193.4	189.2	212.5	201.7	186.4
	II.4.1 Use of disposable income account - Uses											
Final consumption expenditure	84875.4	88393.0	90799.7	95597.5	99846.9	104747.6	110635.0	114956.6	109774.6	113979.9	113778.4	109610.1
Individual consumption expenditure	84875.4	88393.0	90799.7	95597.5	99846.9	104747.6	110635.0	114956.6	109774.6	113979.9	113778.4	109610.1
SAVING, GROSS	10085.3	10127.9	10877.7	10576.5	11074.1	9148.5	8317.3	8735.7	13373.3	12844.6	11447.5	14452.5
	III.1 Capital account - Changes in liabilities and net worth											
SAVING, GROSS	10085.3	10127.9	10877.7	10576.5	11074.1	9148.5	8317.3	8735.7	13373.3	12844.6	11447.5	14452.5
Capital transfers, receivable less payable	3040.8	3206.3	1260.1	1885.0	2382.1	659.6	374.7	1831.4	605.4	384.7	619.9	539.1
Capital transfers, receivable	3248.3	3479.4	1545.6	2070.7	2604.4	819.5	499.3	1993.7	726.8	597.2	736.8	892.4
Less: Capital transfers, payable	207.5	273.2	285.4	185.6	222.4	159.8	124.7	162.3	121.4	212.5	116.9	353.3
Equals: CHANGES IN NET WORTH DUE TO SAVINGS AND CAPITAL TRANSFERS	6360.2	6178.5	4691.4	4628.7	5200.3	1067.3	-435.3	898.3	4268.7	3246.5	1836.7	4669.1
	III.1 Capital account - Changes in assets											
Gross capital formation	11337.6	11418.6	9974.1	10345.7	10629.0	10215.0	9836.1	9385.3	8103.4	7738.8	7179.2	6523.8
Gross fixed capital formation	11241.7	11319.9	9938.4	10179.4	10416.9	9982.8	9650.8	9187.0	7976.0	7524.7	7078.4	6374.6
Changes in inventories	-24.7	-18.9	-57.4	75.0	111.5	91.8	77.4	66.7	14.1	88.3	-21.1	9.5
Acquisitions less disposals of valuables	120.5	117.6	93.1	91.3	100.5	140.4	107.9	131.6	113.2	125.8	121.9	139.7
Acquisitions less disposals of non-produced non-financial assets	-1344.6	-1435.2	-1575.0	-1692.9	-1627.6	-2841.3	-2910.5	-2333.5	-2287.5	-2255.8	-2066.8	-2080.3
NET LENDING (+) / NET BORROWING (-)	3133.0	3350.7	3738.7	3808.8	4454.7	2434.4	1766.3	3515.2	8162.8	7746.3	6954.9	10548.1

Puerto Rico

Source

Reply to the United Nations national accounts questionnaire from the Planning Board, San Juan. Official estimates are published periodically by the Board in "Ingreso y Producto-Puerto Rico Income and Product". The following presentation of sources and methods is mainly based on information received from the Planning Board.

General

The estimates provided in the following tables have been prepared in accordance with the United Nations System of National Accounts 1968 (1968 SNA). When the scope and coverage of the estimates differ for conceptual or statistical reasons from the definitions and classifications recommended in the SNA, a footnote provides explanation.

Methodology:

Overview of GDP Compilation

Gross domestic product is estimated mainly through the expenditure approach.

Expenditure Approach

All components of gross domestic product by expenditure type are estimated through the expenditure approach except private final consumption expenditure of goods and private investment in machinery and equipment which are estimated through the commodity-flow approach. Estimates of government consumption expenditure are based on special tabulations prepared by the accounting division of the Department of the Treasury. For personal consumption expenditure on goods, import data in f.o.b. values are obtained from the trade statistics whereas transport costs by commodity are computed by the Division of Economic Accounts. Estimates of locally produced goods are prepared by using the Puerto Rican censuses of manufactures as benchmarks and extrapolating these data for other years. Estimates of local sales of agricultural products are furnished by the Division of Agricultural Statistics. Adjustments for changes in trade inventories and mark-ups are made on the basis of data obtained from income tax returns and from the firms concerned. For some goods, the estimated quantity consumed is multiplied by the average price believed to have been paid by the consumer.

Estimates of services are based on the gross receipts of the firms or organizations providing the services. Estimates of changes in stocks for the manufacturing sector are obtained through the use of census data which are extrapolated for the non-census years. For sugar and tobacco, quantity data from official sources are multiplied by the average export prices. For trade, inventories are calculated as percentages of sales from a sample of income tax returns. These percentages are then applied to the estimated total sales. Farm inventories of livestock are computed from data supplied by the Department of Agriculture. Estimates of gross fixed domestic investment in construction are obtained directly through surveys among the contractors. For those not covered by the surveys, data from building permits are used. Private investment in machinery and equipment is estimated on the basis of import statistics.

For the government sector, capital expenditure estimates are based on direct surveys within the agencies and on special tabulations prepared by the accounting division of the Department of the Treasury. Sales to the rest of the world, i.e., to the federal government and other non-residents of Puerto Rico, include wages and salaries paid to federal employees and all purchases of goods and services by the federal government. These data are obtained from the records of the agencies themselves. Data on imports are obtained from the trade statistics issued by the United States Department of Commerce. For the constant price estimates, private final consumption expenditure is obtained by multiplying quantities by base year prices where quantity data are available. Otherwise, the current estimates are deflated by appropriate price indexes. For all other components of GDP by expenditure type, price deflation is used.

Income Approach

Basic data on wages and salaries are derived from records of the Bureau of Unemployment Insurance, from censuses of business and manufacturers and from income tax returns and other financial reports of private businesses and public corporations. The method used for estimating operating surplus in manufacturing, construction and some services consists in calculating, from a sample of income tax returns, ratios of profits and other property income to wages and salaries. These ratios are then applied to total wages and salaries. For some industries, the method is based on ratios of profits to gross receipts as reported on the income tax returns. Rental income of persons is estimated by deducting from the total rent paid the rent received by businesses, government and the rest of the world. Depreciation is estimated by applying to the total wages and salaries the ratio of depreciation charges to wages and salaries or to gross receipts, in the case of trade, derived from income tax returns. Data on indirect taxes and subsidies are obtained in detail from government reports.

Production Approach

The table of gross domestic product by kind of economic activity is prepared at market prices, i.e., producers' values. The income approach by distributive shares is used to estimate the value added of each industrial sector. The net income by distributive shares is available by industrial sector. Business transfer payments, depreciation and subsidies are distributed using direct information. Indirect business taxes are obtained from government reports and are broken down by industrial sector, using economic indicators such as data on local production and imports. For the constant price estimates, price deflation is used for the different economic activities of GDP.

Table 1.1 Gross domestic product by expenditures at current prices

Series 10: 1968 SNA, US dollar, Fiscal year beginning 1 July
Series 20: 1968 SNA, US dollar, Fiscal year beginning 1 July

Data in millions

	2001	2002	2003	2004	2005	2006	2007	2008	2009	2010	2011	2012
Series	**10**					**20**						
	Expenditures of the gross domestic product											
Final consumption expenditure	47201.0	49706.0	52497.0	56600.0	59990.0	62521.0[a]						
						62461.0	65079.0	66697.0				
Household final consumption expenditure	37167.0	39224.0	41629.0	44676.0	47704.0	48997.0						
						49977.0	52444.0	53306.0				
NPISHs final consumption expenditure	1678.0	1749.0	1767.0	1859.0	1956.0	2012.0						
						1972.0	2117.0	2258.0				
General government final consumption expenditure	8356.0	8733.0	9101.0	10065.0	10330.0	10512.0						
						10512.0	10321.0	11133.0				
Gross capital formation	11599.0	11619.0	12303.0	12249.0	12211.0	11981.0						
						11987.0	11373.0	10205.0				
Gross fixed capital formation	11356.0	11362.0	11961.0	11902.0	11833.0	11670.0						
						11674.0	10974.0	9842.0				
Changes in inventories	243.0	257.0	342.0	347.0	378.0	311.0						
						313.0	399.0	363.0				
Acquisitions less disposals of valuables	...	...	...	...	...	...						
						...	...	...				
Exports of goods and services	54095.0	60958.0	64538.0	65460.0	69125.0	70700.0						
						70287.0	74836.0	71895.0				
Exports of goods	49610.0	56335.0	59447.0	59901.0	63588.0	64603.0						
						64203.0	68551.0	66078.0				
Exports of services	4487.0	4623.0	5091.0	5559.0	5537.0	6097.0						
						6084.0	6285.0	5817.0				
Less: Imports of goods and services	41271.0	47455.0	50128.0	51500.0	55168.0	56300.0						
						56332.0	58362.0	53089.0				
Imports of goods	38192.0	44137.0	46573.0	47841.0	51732.0	52795.0						
						53029.0	54918.0	49734.0				
Imports of services	3312.0	3318.0	3355.0	3659.0	3436.0	3505.0						
						3302.0	3444.0	3355.0				
Equals: GROSS DOMESTIC PRODUCT	71624.0	74827.0	79209.0	82809.0	86157.0	88902.0						
						88405.0	92926.0	95708.0				

[a] Discrepancy between components and total.

Table 1.2 Gross domestic product by expenditures at constant prices

Series 10: 1968 SNA, US dollar, Fiscal year beginning 1 July
Series 20: 1968 SNA, US dollar, Fiscal year beginning 1 July

Data in millions

	2001	2002	2003	2004	2005	2006	2007	2008	2009	2010	2011	2012
Series	**10**					**20**						
Base year	**1954**											
	Expenditures of the gross domestic product											
Final consumption expenditure	9983.0	10330.0	10705.0	11096.0	11269.0	11418.0 11423.0	11288.0	11093.0[a]				
Household final consumption expenditure	8179.0	8483.0	8847.0	9161.0	9333.0	9508.0 9513.0	9468.0	9240.0				
NPISHs final consumption expenditure	...	...	...	...	...	... ...	...	...				
General government final consumption expenditure	1804.0	1847.0	1858.0	1935.0	1936.0	1910.0 1852.0	1709.0	1519.0				
Gross capital formation	1872.0	1871.0	2015.0	1936.0	1929.0	1850.0 1852.0	1709.0	1520.0				
Gross fixed capital formation	1827.0	1824.0	1941.0	1859.0	1844.0	1796.0 1798.0	1635.0	1442.0				
Changes in inventories	45.0	47.0	75.0	78.0	84.0	54.0 ...	...	78.0				
Acquisitions less disposals of valuables	...	...	...	...	...	... ...	...	...				
Exports of goods and services	5874.0	6550.0	6785.0	6781.0	6880.0	6792.0 6627.0	6708.0	6394.0				
Less: Imports of goods and services	7058.0	8078.0	8507.0	8723.0	9004.0	9140.0 9098.0	9035.0	8594.0				
Equals: GROSS DOMESTIC PRODUCT	10670.0	10675.0	10999.0	11090.0	11073.0	10920.0 10804.0	10669.0	10411.0				

[a] Discrepancy between components and total.

Table 1.3 Relations among product, income, savings, and net lending aggregates

Series 10: 1968 SNA, US dollar, Fiscal year beginning 1 July

Data in millions

	2001	2002	2003	2004	2005	2006	2007	2008	2009	2010	2011	2012
Series	**10**											
GROSS DOMESTIC PRODUCT	71624.0	74827.0	79209.0	82809.0	86157.0	88902.0	93263.0					
Plus: Compensation of employees - from and to the rest of the world, net	975.0	985.0	961.0	1084.0	1037.0	949.0	987.0					
Plus: Compensation of employees - from the rest of the world	982.0	994.0	968.0	1093.0	1044.0	953.0	991.0					
Less: Compensation of employees - to the rest of the world	7.0	9.0	7.0	9.0	7.0	4.0	4.0					
Plus: Property income - from and to the rest of the world, net	-27944.0	-28753.0	-29838.0	-30495.0	-30798.0	-31696.0	-33961.0					
Plus: Property income - from the rest of the world	1114.0	1125.0	1315.0	2121.0	2586.0	1835.0	2012.0					
Less: Property income - to the rest of the world	29058.0	29878.0	31153.0	32626.0	33384.0	33531.0	35973.0					
Sum of Compensation of employees and property income - from and to the rest of the world, net	-26969.0	-27768.0	-28879.0	-29411.0	-29761.0	-30747.0	-32974.0					
Plus: Sum of Compensation of employees and property income - from the rest of the world	2096.0	2119.0	2281.0	3214.0	3630.0	2788.0	3003.0					
Less: Sum of Compensation of employees and property income - to the rest of the world	29065.0	29887.0	31160.0	32635.0	33391.0	33535.0	35977.0					
Plus: Taxes less subsidies on production and imports - from and to the rest of the world, net	...	...	...	...	...	...	...					

	2001	2002	2003	2004	2005	2006	2007	2008	2009	2010	2011	2012
Series	**10**											
Equals: GROSS NATIONAL INCOME	44655.0	47059.0	50332.0	53398.0	56396.0	58155.0	60289.0					
Plus: Current transfers - from and to the rest of the world, net	9436.0	10191.0	9228.0	9342.0	10126.0	10719.0	12494.0					
Plus: Current transfers - from the rest of the world	12587.0	13537.0	12813.0	13037.0	13987.0	14496.0	16243.0					
Less: Current transfers - to the rest of the world	3151.0	3346.0	3585.0	3695.0	3861.0	3777.0	3749.0					
Equals: GROSS NATIONAL DISPOSABLE INCOME	54091.0	57250.0	59560.0	62740.0	66522.0	68874.0	72783.0					
Less: Final consumption expenditure / Actual final consumption	47201.0	49706.0	52497.0	56600.0	59990.0	62521.0	64675.0					
Equals: SAVING, GROSS [a]	2664.0	2767.0	3638.0	5138.0	6059.0	6264.0	6582.0					
Plus: Capital transfers - from and to the rest of the world, net	...	...	...	...	...	...	...					
Less: Gross capital formation	11599.0	11619.0	12303.0	12249.0	12211.0	11981.0	11381.0					
Less: Acquisitions less disposals of non-produced non-financial assets	...	...	...	...	...	...	...					
Equals: NET LENDING (+) / NET BORROWING (-) OF THE NATION	...	...	...	...	...	...	...					
	Net values: Gross National Income / Gross National Disposable Income / Saving Gross less Consumption of fixed capital											
Less: Consumption of fixed capital	4977.0	5005.0	5350.0	5741.0	6533.0	6354.0	8108.0					
Equals: NET NATIONAL INCOME	39678.0	42054.0	44982.0	47657.0	50337.0	51891.0	53707.0[b]					
Equals: NET NATIONAL DISPOSABLE INCOME [b]	44888.0	47468.0	50785.0	55997.0	59516.0	62431.0	63149.0					
Equals: SAVING, NET	-2313.0	-2238.0	-1712.0	-603.0	-474.0	-70.0	-1526.0					

[a] Discrepancy between Gross Saving, Final Consumption and Gross National Disposable Income.
[b] Discrepancy between net value, consumption of fixed capital and gross value.

Table 2.1 Value added by industries at current prices (ISIC Rev. 3)

Series 10: 1968 SNA, US dollar, Fiscal year beginning 1 July
Series 20: 1968 SNA, US dollar, Fiscal year beginning 1 July

Data in millions

	2001	2002	2003	2004	2005	2006	2007	2008	2009	2010	2011	2012
Series	**10**					**20**						
	Industries											
Agriculture, hunting, forestry; fishing	276.0	333.0	414.0	375.0	394.0	418.0						
						435.0	620.0	640.0				
Mining and quarrying	53.0	54.0	58.0	66.0	62.0	63.0						
						53.0	54.0	46.0				
Manufacturing	31243.0	31532.0	33267.0	34534.0	35638.0	36309.0						
						36863.0	39781.0	42757.0				
Electricity, gas and water supply	1618.0	1750.0	1722.0	1753.0	1963.0	2187.0						
						2229.0	2129.0	2132.0				
Construction [a]	1595.0	1718.0	1847.0	1782.0	1726.0	1866.0						
						1900.0	1862.0	1653.0				
Wholesale, retail trade, repair of motor vehicles, motorcycles and personal and households goods; hotels and restaurants	9303.0	9848.0	10476.0	10955.0	11377.0	11766.0						
						8419.0	8590.0	8684.0				
Transport, storage and communications	3330.0	3429.0	3621.0	3555.0	3943.0	3923.0						
						2854.0	2877.0	2898.0				
Financial intermediation; real estate, renting and business activities	12810.0	14103.0	14781.0	16134.0	16760.0	17968.0						
						16918.0	17394.0	16757.0				
Public administration and defence; compulsory social security	6303.0	6948.0	7389.0	8151.0	8424.0	8585.0						
						8585.0	8762.0	9254.0				
Education; health and social work; other community, social and personal services	4164.0	4311.0	4514.0	4655.0	4910.0	5125.0						
						6770.0	7206.0	7468.0				

	2001	2002	2003	2004	2005	2006	2007	2008	2009	2010	2011	2012
Series	**10**					**20**						
Private households with employed persons	635.0	657.0	706.0	738.0	738.0	756.0 0.0	0.0	0.0				
Equals: VALUE ADDED, GROSS, in basic prices [b]	71330.0	74683.0	78795.0	82665.0	85935.0	88966.0 85026.0	89275.0	92289.0				
Less: Financial intermediation services indirectly measured (FISIM)	...	...	...	...	...	... ...	...	...				
Plus: Taxes less Subsidies on products	2854.0	3195.0	3309.0	3196.0	3654.0	3842.0 3843.0	3866.0	3956.0				
Plus: Taxes on products	3669.0	3998.0	4152.0	4039.0	4350.0	4615.0 4616.0	4714.0	4753.0				
Less: Subsidies on products	815.0	803.0	843.0	843.0	696.0	773.0 773.0	848.0	797.0				
Plus: Statistical discrepancy	294.0	144.0	414.0	144.0	131.0	-58.0 -464.0	-215.0	-538.0				
Equals: GROSS DOMESTIC PRODUCT	71624.0	74827.0	79209.0	82809.0	86158.0	88902.0 88405.0	92926.0	95708.0				

[a] Refers to contract construction only.
[b] At producers' prices.

Table 2.2 Value added by industries at constant prices (ISIC Rev. 3)

Series 10: 1968 SNA, US dollar, Fiscal year beginning 1 July
Series 20: 1968 SNA, US dollar, Fiscal year beginning 1 July

Data in millions

	2001	2002	2003	2004	2005	2006	2007	2008	2009	2010	2011	2012
Series	**10**					**20**						
Base year	**1954**											
	Industries											
Agriculture, hunting, forestry; fishing	119.0	136.0	169.0	156.0	157.0	168.0 172.0	219.0	212.0				
Mining and quarrying	10.0	10.0	11.0	13.0	9.0	10.0 11.0	11.0	11.0				
Manufacturing	4689.0	4556.0	4767.0	4820.0	4754.0	4680.0 4645.0	5005.0	4374.0				
Electricity, gas and water supply	314.0	293.0	284.0	256.0	224.0	234.0 502.0	458.0	441.0				
Construction [a]	232.0	246.0	256.0	233.0	219.0	230.0 240.0	229.0	200.0				
Wholesale, retail trade, repair of motor vehicles, motorcycles and personal and household goods; hotels and restaurants	1913.0	1995.0	2167.0	2210.0	2256.0	2304.0 1619.0	1567.0	1537.0				
Transport, storage and communications	931.0	945.0	988.0	941.0	1033.0	995.0 1123.0	1037.0	944.0				
Financial intermediation, real estate, renting and business activities	2603.0	3069.0	3161.0	3120.0	2767.0	2665.0 2643.0	2607.0	2439.0				
Public administration and defence; compulsory social security	1342.0	1435.0	1471.0	1512.0	1529.0	1497.0 1560.0	1516.0	1542.0				
Education; health and social work; other community, social and personal services	607.0	617.0	632.0	632.0	628.0	633.0 849.0	884.0	888.0				
Private households with employed persons	85.0	82.0	81.0	73.0	67.0	60.0 0.0	0.0	0.0				
Equals: VALUE ADDED, GROSS, in basic prices	12845.0	13384.0	13987.0	13967.0	13643.0	13476.0 13364.0	13533.0	13588.0[b]				
Less: Financial intermediation services indirectly measured (FISIM)	...	...	...	...	...	... ...	...	...				
Plus: Taxes less Subsidies on products	...	...	...	...	...	... ...	...	...				
Equals: GROSS DOMESTIC PRODUCT	10670.0	10676.0	10999.0	11090.0	11073.0	10920.0 10803.0	10669.0	10411.0				

[a] Refers to contract construction only.
[b] Discrepancy between components and total.

Table 3.2 Individual consumption expenditure of households, NPISHs, and general government at current prices

Series 10: 1968 SNA, US dollar, Fiscal year beginning 1 July | **Data in millions**

	2001	2002	2003	2004	2005	2006	2007	2008	2009	2010	2011	2012
Series	**10**											
	Individual consumption expenditure of households											
Food and non-alcoholic beverages	5569.0	5984.0	6061.0	6535.0	6982.0	7315.0	7954.0					
Alcoholic beverages, tobacco and narcotics	1435.0	1513.0	1541.0	1739.0	1765.0	1783.0	1721.0					
Clothing and footwear	2654.0	2694.0	2852.0	2957.0	3085.0	3544.0	3646.0					
Housing, water, electricity, gas and other fuels	6704.0	7307.0	7823.0	8498.0	9312.0	10017.0	10821.0					
Furnishings, household equipment and routine maintenance of the house	2227.0	2272.0	2156.0	2390.0	2674.0	2912.0	2810.0					
Health	5184.0	5352.0	5546.0	5820.0	6214.0	6434.0	6665.0					
Transport	2146.0	2148.0	2228.0	2687.0	2520.0	2149.0	2155.0					
Communication	3638.0	3763.0	4204.0	4644.0	5043.0	5466.0	5995.0					
Recreation and culture	1497.0	1613.0	1662.0	1667.0	1840.0	1923.0	1895.0					
Education	1311.0	1345.0	1589.0	1628.0	1820.0	1845.0	1856.0					
Restaurants and hotels	1816.0	2187.0	2740.0	2879.0	2970.0	3032.0	3120.0					
Miscellaneous goods and services	4467.0	4651.0	4863.0	5004.0	5310.0	5447.0	5587.0					
Equals: Household final consumption expenditure in domestic market	...	...	...	...	...	...	...					
Plus: Direct purchases abroad by residents	...	...	...	...	...	...	...					
Less: Direct purchases in domestic market by non-residents	...	...	...	...	...	...	...					
Equals: Household final consumption expenditure	37167.0	39224.0	41629.0	44676.0	47704.0	48997.0	52238.0					
	Individual consumption expenditure of non-profit institutions serving households (NPISHs)											
Housing	...	...	...	...	...	...	...					
Health	1504.0	1525.0	1532.0	1627.0	1706.0	1764.0	1851.0					
Recreation and culture	...	...	...	...	...	...	...					
Education	...	...	...	...	...	...	...					
Social protection	...	...	...	...	...	...	...					
Other services	...	...	...	...	...	...	...					
Equals: NPISHs final consumption expenditure	1678.0	1749.0	1767.0	1859.0	1956.0	2012.0	2116.0					
	Individual consumption expenditure of general government											
Equals: Individual consumption expenditure of general government	...	...	...	...	...	...	...					
Equals: Total actual individual consumption	...	...	...	...	...	...	...					

Qatar

Source

Reply to the United Nations national accounts questionnaire from the Central Statistical Organization, Doha.

General

The latest estimates shown in the following tables have been prepared in accordance with the concepts and definitions of the System of National Accounts 1993 (1993 SNA). The previous estimates are generally in accordance with the classifications and definitions recommended in the United Nations System of National Accounts 1968 (1968 SNA) as far as the existing data would permit.

Table 1.1 Gross domestic product by expenditures at current prices

Series 100: 1993 SNA, Qatar riyal, Western calendar year — **Data in millions**

	2001	2002	2003	2004	2005	2006	2007	2008	2009	2010	2011	2012
Series	**100**											
	Expenditures of the gross domestic product											
Final consumption expenditure	21746.0	24766.0	27328.0	35260.0	49061.9	68802.5	85718.5	107371.7	124275.3	137334.8	156745.6	
Household final consumption expenditure	9855.0	12983.0	14131.0	20166.0	25889.9	36186.3	49728.6	64675.8	68622.9	73645.7	79905.7	
NPISHs final consumption expenditure	...	...	...	...	...	...	...	...	...	...	...	
General government final consumption expenditure	11891.0	11783.0	13197.0	15094.0	23172.0[a]	32616.2	35989.9	42695.9	55652.3	63689.1	76839.9	
Individual consumption expenditure	1453.0	1210.0	1277.0	5382.0	6181.0	...	...	...	...	...	...	
Collective consumption expenditure	10438.0	10573.0	11920.0	9712.0	11588.0	...	...	...	...	...	...	
Gross capital formation	18590.0	23010.0	29871.0	36399.0[a]	55609.5[a]	92830.1[a]	133518.1	172524.2	152946.2	143011.1	183872.5	
Gross fixed capital formation	14917.0	20453.0	25894.0	34810.0	51887.0	70745.0	...	...	...	...	...	
Changes in inventories	3673.0	2557.0	3977.0	3756.0	2953.0	4012.0	...	...	...	...	...	
Acquisitions less disposals of valuables	...	...	...	...	...	...	...	...	...	...	...	
Exports of goods and services	42066.0	42532.0	52852.0	74122.3	105496.6	139210.7	174896.0	257466.0	182034.0	283270.5	442959.8	
Exports of goods	39571.0	39960.0	48711.0	68012.3	93773.6	123947.7	161821.0	244998.0	174746.0	272309.5	415905.5	
Exports of services	2495.0	2572.0	4141.0	6110.0	11723.0	15263.0	13075.0	12468.0	7288.0	10961.0	27054.3	
Less: Imports of goods and services	18562.0	19825.0	24386.0	30269.0	48077.0	79233.0	103981.0	117779.0	103269.0	108171.0	159405.2	
Imports of goods	12324.0	13287.0	15865.0	19691.0	32992.0	53911.0	76832.0	91492.0	81726.0	76210.0	98010.1	
Imports of services	6238.0	6538.0	8521.0	10578.0	15085.0	25322.0	27149.0	26287.0	21543.0	31961.0	61395.1	
Equals: GROSS DOMESTIC PRODUCT	63840.0	70484.0	85663.0	115512.4	162091.0	221610.3	290151.6	419582.8	355986.5	455445.4	624172.7	

[a] Discrepancy between components and total as one or more components have not been revised.

Table 1.2 Gross domestic product by expenditures at constant prices

Series 100: 1993 SNA, Qatar riyal, Western calendar year — **Data in millions**

	2001	2002	2003	2004	2005	2006	2007	2008	2009	2010	2011	2012
Series	**100**											
Base year	**2001**			**2004**								
Expenditures of the gross domestic product												
Final consumption expenditure	21746.0	23675.0	24395.0	28637.0								
				35260.0	45675.0	58608.8	65385.9	71866.1	87578.5	98174.3	106152.8	
Household final consumption expenditure	9855.0	12952.0	13785.0	18420.0								
				20166.0	23585.3	29094.0	34932.2	39393.1	44428.5	49718.9	52818.9	
NPISHs final consumption expenditure	...	...	...	...								
				...	...	...	...	...	...	...	...	
General government final consumption expenditure	11891.0	10723.0	10610.0	10217.0								
				15094.0	22089.7	29514.8	30453.8	32473.0	43150.0	48455.3	53334.0	
Individual consumption expenditure	1453.0	1101.0	1026.0	3643.0								
				...	...	...	...	...	...	...	...	
Collective consumption expenditure	10438.0	9622.0	9584.0	6574.0								
				...	...	...	...	...	...	...	...	
Gross capital formation	18590.0	18608.0	32338.0	32881.0								
				36399.0	42660.5	75494.0	102100.4	116955.6	114166.8	110912.6	126416.2	
Gross fixed capital formation	14917.0	16125.0	29197.0	30240.0								
				...	...	...	...	...	...	...	...	
Changes in inventories	3673.0	2483.0	3141.0	2641.0								
				...	...	...	...	...	...	...	...	
Acquisitions less disposals of valuables	...	...	...	...								
				...	...	...	...	...	...	...	...	
Exports of goods and services	42066.0	44083.0	40418.0	55041.0								
				74122.3	81811.6	95208.2	108386.7	125087.5	127692.8	162551.0	201519.8	
Less: Imports of goods and services	18562.0	17827.0	26629.0	31158.0								
				30269.0	45980.8	72648.9	91033.6	96421.5	85946.3	87405.5	113015.4[a]	
Imports of goods	12324.0	11948.0	17324.0	20996.0								
				19691.0	31335.6	48826.9	66053.8	74244.9	67584.1	60929.2	98010.1	
Imports of services	6238.0	5879.0	9305.0	10162.0								
				10578.0	14645.2	23822.0	24979.9	22176.6	18362.3	26476.3	61395.1	
Plus: Statistical discrepancy	...	-145.0	259.0	123.0								
				...	...	...	...	...	...	...	...	
Equals: GROSS DOMESTIC PRODUCT	63840.0	68394.0	70781.0	85524.0								
				115512.4	124166.3	156662.0	184839.4	217487.6	243491.8	284232.3	321073.5	

[a] Discrepancy between components and total.

Table 1.3 Relations among product, income, savings, and net lending aggregates

Series 100: 1993 SNA, Qatar riyal, Western calendar year — **Data in millions**

	2001	2002	2003	2004	2005	2006	2007	2008	2009	2010	2011	2012
Series	**100**											
GROSS DOMESTIC PRODUCT	63840.0	70484.0	85663.0	115512.4	162091.0	221610.3	290151.6	419582.8	355986.5	455445.4	624172.7	
Plus: Compensation of employees - from and to the rest of the world, net	...	...	...	...	...	...	...	...	...	...	...	
Plus: Property income - from and to the rest of the world, net	-2562.0	-3266.0	-1516.0	-8160.0	-20805.0[a]	-11941.0	-15430.0	-24614.0	-34262.0	-47115.0	-48306.0	
Plus: Property income - from the rest of the world	3231.0	2582.0	4927.0	4633.0	5139.0	7207.0	...	...	...	...	...	
Less: Property income - to the rest of the world	5793.0	5848.0	6443.0	12793.0	10264.0	19148.0	...	...	...	...	...	
Sum of Compensation of employees and property income - from and to the rest of the world, net	-2562.0	-3266.0	-1516.0	-8160.0	-20805.0	-11941.0	-15430.0	-24614.0	-34262.0	-47115.0	-48306.0	
Plus: Taxes less subsidies on production and imports - from and to the rest of the world, net	...	...	...	...	...	...	...	...	...	...	...	
Equals: GROSS NATIONAL INCOME	61278.0	67218.0	84147.0	107352.4	141286.0	209669.3	274721.6	394968.8	321724.5	408330.4	575866.7	
Plus: Current transfers - from and to the rest of the world, net[b]	-5829.0	-5522.0	-6007.0	-8205.0	-9380.0	-13604.0	-13779.0	-18270.0	-21247.0	-41362.0	-46048.0	

	2001	2002	2003	2004	2005	2006	2007	2008	2009	2010	2011	2012
Series	**100**											
Plus: Current transfers - from the rest of the world	...	...	...	...	...	...	...	...	...	...	...	
Less: Current transfers - to the rest of the world	5829.0	5522.0	6007.0	8205.0	9380.0	...	...	...	...	...	...	
Equals: GROSS NATIONAL DISPOSABLE INCOME	55449.0	61696.0	78140.0	99147.4	131906.0	196065.3	260942.6	376698.8	300477.5	366968.4	529818.7	
Less: Final consumption expenditure / Actual final consumption	21746.0	24766.0	27328.0	35260.0	49061.9	68802.5	85718.5	107371.7	124275.3	137334.8	156745.6	
Equals: SAVING, GROSS	33703.0	36930.0	50812.0	63887.4	82844.2	127262.8	175224.1	269327.2	176202.2	229633.6	373073.1	
Plus: Capital transfers - from and to the rest of the world, net	...	...	...	...	...	...	...	...	...	...	...	
Less: Gross capital formation	18590.0	23010.0	29871.0	36399.0	55609.5	92830.1	133518.1	172524.2	152946.2	143011.1	183872.5	
Less: Acquisitions less disposals of non-produced non-financial assets	...	...	...	...	...	...	...	...	...	...	...	
Equals: NET LENDING (+) / NET BORROWING (-) OF THE NATION	15113.0	13920.0	20941.0	27488.3	27234.6	34432.7	41706.0	96803.0	23256.0	86622.5	189200.6	
	Net values: Gross National Income / Gross National Disposable Income / Saving Gross less Consumption of fixed capital											
Less: Consumption of fixed capital	7459.0	7174.0	7734.0	10735.0	5906.0	28700.3	...	...	...	...	...	
Equals: NET NATIONAL INCOME	53819.0	60044.0	76413.0	96617.0	135380.0	180969.0	...	...	...	...	...	
Equals: NET NATIONAL DISPOSABLE INCOME	47990.0	54522.0	70406.0	88412.0	126000.0	167365.0	...	...	...	...	...	
Equals: SAVING, NET	...	...	...	...	...	109188.0	...	...	...	...	...	

[a] Discrepancy between components and total as one or more components have not been revised.
[b] Includes Compensation of Employees

Table 2.1 Value added by industries at current prices (ISIC Rev. 3)

Series 100: 1993 SNA, Qatar riyal, Western calendar year — **Data in millions**

	2001	2002	2003	2004	2005	2006	2007	2008	2009	2010	2011	2012
Series	**100**											
	Industries											
Agriculture, hunting, forestry; fishing	240.0	181.0	201.0	210.0	216.0	270.0	319.0	523.0	439.0	537.0	590.0	
Mining and quarrying	36812.0	40717.0	50551.0	61675.6	94488.9	117469.2	150014.4	230312.1	159467.3	239744.8	370160.6	
Manufacturing	3909.0	5076.0	6553.0	13241.4	15994.0	20616.6	26810.4	44853.5	33569.7	40831.9	56742.1	
Electricity, gas and water supply	433.0	409.0	1205.0	1482.9	1525.7	1568.5	1819.9	2063.0	1794.0	2113.0	2350.9	
Construction	2938.0	3593.0	4654.0	6425.0	8744.0	10846.0	15925.0	27199.0	25522.0	27500.0	28340.0	
Wholesale, retail trade, repair of motor vehicles, motorcycles and personal and households goods; hotels and restaurants	3918.0	3969.0	4345.0	6521.1	7289.4	14789.3	20847.8	23429.4	29838.6	31500.7	35603.3	
Wholesale, retail trade, repair of motor vehicles, motorcycles and personal and household goods	3478.0	3491.0	3787.0	5615.0	5971.7	12972.3	18800.3	20565.5	26646.6	28218.0	31847.0	
Hotels and restaurants	441.0	478.0	558.0	906.0	1317.7	1817.0	2047.4	2863.9	3192.0	3282.7	3756.3	
Transport, storage and communications	2223.0	2489.0	2911.0	4019.8	5431.0[a]	6885.0[a]	8697.0	14775.0	16212.0	18068.9	20992.9	
Land transport; transport via pipelines, water transport; air transport; Supporting and auxiliary transport activities; activities of travel agencies	939.0	994.0	1438.0	1897.0	2219.0	3881.0	...	...	...	...	...	
Post and telecommunications	1284.0	1495.0	1473.0	2123.0	2895.0	3278.0	...	...	...	...	...	

	2001	2002	2003	2004	2005	2006	2007	2008	2009	2010	2011	2012
Series	**100**											
Financial intermediation; real estate, renting and business activities	5196.0	5802.0	6446.0	9924.1	14727.3	29370.8	41982.2	51580.1	58099.3	60291.6	65592.7	
Financial intermediation	2221.0	2694.0	3222.0	3747.9	7060.8	11800.4	15676.6	19397.4	25084.1	27217.2	31760.8	
Real estate, renting and business activities	2975.0	3108.0	3224.0	6176.2	7666.5	17570.4	26305.6	32182.6	33015.2	33074.5	33831.9	
Public administration and defence; compulsory social security	8468.0[b]	8804.0[b]	9495.0[b]	7512.8	7547.2	12727.1	14389.7	16423.9	20029.5	23028.5	29147.0	
Education; health and social work; other community, social and personal services	608.0[c]	615.0[c]	644.0[c]	5066.6	6504.8	8480.2	10569.7	13371.8	16225.6	18881.3	22085.4	
Education	204.0	219.0	222.0	2203.4	2767.4	3386.9	4487.0	5969.5	7199.8	8486.2	10103.5	
Health and social work	43.0	51.0	51.0	1780.1	2102.1	2838.2	3176.9	4153.8	5014.8	5675.8	6377.5	
Other community, social and personal services	361.0	345.0	371.0	1083.1	1635.3	2255.0	2905.9	3248.5	4011.0	4719.2	5604.4	
Private households with employed persons	548.0	571.0	617.0	987.0	1057.0	1236.9	1565.1	1660.9	1827.0	1881.0	2012.5	
Equals: VALUE ADDED, GROSS, in basic prices [d]	65295.0	72227.0	87623.0	117066.4	163525.2	224259.5	292940.1	426191.6	363024.1	464378.7	633617.3	
Less: Financial intermediation services indirectly measured (FISIM)	1821.0	2208.0	2491.0	2761.0	3173.1	5352.5	6734.3	10148.8	10151.5	12726.0	13365.0	
Plus: Taxes less Subsidies on products	367.0	466.0	532.0	1207.0	1738.9	2703.2	3945.7	3540.0	3113.9	3792.7	3920.4	
Plus: Taxes on products	367.0	466.0	532.0	1207.0	1738.9	2703.2	3945.7	3540.0	3113.9	3792.7	3920.4	
Less: Subsidies on products	...	...	...	...	...	...	...	...	...	...	...	
Equals: GROSS DOMESTIC PRODUCT	63840.0	70484.0	85663.0	115512.4	162091.0	221610.3	290151.6	419582.8	355986.5	455445.4	624172.7	

[a] Discrepancy between components and total as one or more components have not been revised.
[b] Includes the provision of public health, education and other miscellaneous services.
[c] Refers to social services.
[d] At producers' prices. Includes financial intermediation services indirectly measured (FISIM) of the Total Economy.

Table 2.2 Value added by industries at constant prices (ISIC Rev. 3)

Series 100: 1993 SNA, Qatar riyal, Western calendar year **Data in millions**

	2001	2002	2003	2004	2005	2006	2007	2008	2009	2010	2011	2012
Series	**100**											
Base year	**2001**			**2004**								
	Industries											
Agriculture, hunting, forestry; fishing	240.0	179.0	199.0	201.0 210.0	248.9	289.9	319.0	436.0	361.5	433.2	456.5	
Mining and quarrying	36812.0	40144.0	40468.0	47765.0 61675.6	65047.6	72653.0	82669.9	93591.3	97816.5	126099.7	145936.9	
Manufacturing	3909.0	4316.0	4628.0	4929.0 13241.4	14360.0	15039.9	16058.4	19087.8	21709.0	25522.0	28171.6	
Electricity, gas and water supply	433.0	414.0	974.0	1143.0 1482.9	1595.5	1757.3	1816.7	2040.4	2031.0	2305.2	2486.6	
Construction	2938.0	3287.0	4245.0	4601.0 6425.0	6386.2	10518.7	14804.0	26531.8	28352.0	31047.9	34343.2	
Wholesale, retail trade, repair of motor vehicles, motorcycles and personal and household goods; hotels and restaurants	3919.0	3957.0	4239.0	5616.0 6521.1	6878.8	13226.1	17207.5	18313.5	21185.6	21716.5	24508.3	
Wholesale, retail trade, repair of motor vehicles, motorcycles and personal and household goods	...	...	...	... 5615.0	5854.2	12057.1	15881.3	16607.4	19214.8	19671.2	22039.0	
Hotels and restaurants	...	...	...	... 906.0	1024.6	1169.0	1326.1	1706.0	1970.8	2045.3	2469.3	
Transport, storage and communications	2223.0	2757.0	2933.0	4010.0 4019.8	5326.3	6832.3	8825.3	13327.3	16347.0	18013.4	20241.9	

	2001	2002	2003	2004	2005	2006	2007	2008	2009	2010	2011	2012
Series	**100**											
Base year	**2001**			**2004**								
Financial intermediation, real estate, renting and business activities	5196.0	5677.0	5437.0	7484.0 9924.1	11028.4	17688.3	21953.0	23896.7	30051.3	32278.9	34329.5	
Financial intermediation	...	...	...	... 3747.9	4688.9	5636.3	7514.6	8644.3	12164.0	12038.8	13902.4	
Real estate, renting and business activities	...	...	...	... 6176.2	6339.5	12052.0	14438.4	15252.4	17887.3	20240.1	20427.0	
Public administration and defence; compulsory social security	8468.0	8130.0	7920.0	8619.0 7512.8	7349.5	12024.8	12976.8	13441.7	16617.0	17826.5	20600.2	
Education; health and social work; other community, social and personal services	608.0	614.0	628.0	1008.0 5066.6	6334.4	8012.2	9531.9	10943.9	13460.8	14624.0	15669.8	
Education	...	...	...	... 2203.4	2693.0	3207.9	4081.2	4914.2	5822.3	6578.5	7148.6	
Health and social work	...	...	...	... 1780.1	2043.1	2665.4	2854.1	3383.9	4095.1	4380.8	4495.3	
Other community, social and personal services	...	...	...	... 1083.1	1598.3	2138.9	2596.6	2645.8	3543.5	3664.7	4026.0	
Private households with employed persons	548.0	611.0	636.0	985.0 987.0	999.7	1126.6	1328.6	1379.5	1438.0	1469.4	1481.8	
Equals: VALUE ADDED, GROSS, in basic prices [a] [b]	65294.0	70086.0	72307.0	86361.0 117066.4	125555.4	159169.1	187491.2	222989.9	249370.2	291336.7	328226.2	
Less: Financial intermediation services indirectly measured (FISIM)	1821.0	2158.0	2058.0	2044.0 2761.0	3088.5	4982.0	5997.2	8131.2	8209.4	9850.2	9865.2	
Plus: Taxes less Subsidies on products	367.0	466.0	532.0	1207.0 1207.0	1699.3	2474.9	3345.4	2629.0	2331.0	2745.7	2712.4	
Plus: Taxes on products	...	...	...	... 1207.0	1699.3	2474.9	3345.4	2629.0	2331.0	2745.7	2712.4	
Less: Subsidies on products	...	...	...	... ...	...	...	...	...	...	...	...	
Equals: GROSS DOMESTIC PRODUCT	63840.0	68394.0	70781.0	85524.0 115512.4	124166.3	156662.0	184839.4	217487.6	243491.8	284232.3	321073.5	

[a] Includes financial intermediation services indirectly measured (FISIM) of the Total Economy.
[b] At producers' prices. Includes financial intermediation services indirectly measured (FISIM) of the Total Economy.

Table 2.3 Output, gross value added, and fixed assets by industries at current prices (ISIC Rev. 3) Total Economy

Series 100: 1993 SNA, Qatar riyal, Western calendar year — **Data in millions**

	2001	2002	2003	2004	2005	2006	2007	2008	2009	2010	2011	2012
Series	**100**											
Output, at basic prices	86913.0	94383.0	114248.0	153842.6	213750.0	290300.2	379836.5	553888.7	496352.1	653051.2	...	
Less: Intermediate consumption, at purchaser's prices	21618.0	22156.0	26625.0	36776.2	50224.8	66040.6	86896.4	127697.1	133328.0	188672.5	...	
Equals: VALUE ADDED, GROSS, at basic prices	65295.0	72227.0	87623.0	117066.4	163525.2	224259.5	292940.1	426191.6	363024.1	464378.7	633617.3	
Compensation of employees	14617.0	15980.0	17422.0	22702.5	27477.2	40074.0	51256.0	64553.2	79232.0	86660.0	...	
Taxes on production and imports, less Subsidies	-506.0[a]	-546.0	-593.0	-2225.2	-3196.0	-3323.7	-4847.9	-4913.9	-6337.5	-5879.7	...	
Taxes on production and imports	99.0[a]	80.0	88.0[a]	114.6	175.9	183.1	217.8	381.1	349.2	377.6	...	
Taxes on products	...	...	...	...	...	...	...	...	...	...	...	
Other taxes on production	99.0[a]	80.0	88.0	114.6	175.9	183.1	...	...	...	...	...	
Less: Subsidies	605.0	626.0	681.0	2339.8	3371.9	3506.7	5065.7	5294.9	6686.7	6257.2	...	
Subsidies on products	...	...	...	...	...	...	...	...	...	...	...	
Other subsidies on production	605.0	626.0	681.0	2339.8	3371.9	3506.7	...	...	...	...	...	
OPERATING SURPLUS, GROSS	46758.0	51971.0	65582.0	93828.1[b]	136071.1[b]	182156.7[b]	239797.8[c]	356403.5[c]	279978.0[c]	370872.4[c]	...	
MIXED INCOME, GROSS	2603.0	2612.0	2722.0	...	...	...	...	...	...	...	...	

	2001	2002	2003	2004	2005	2006	2007	2008	2009	2010	2011	2012
Series	**100**											
Total Economy only: Adjustment for FISIM (if FISIM is not distributed to uses)	1821.0	2208.0	2491.0	2761.0	3173.0	5352.5	6734.3	10148.8	10151.5	12726.0	13365.0	
Less: Consumption of fixed capital	7459.0	7174.0	7734.0	10735.0	5906.0[a]	28700.3[a]	...	...	...	...	...	
OPERATING SURPLUS, NET	39663.0	45190.0	58253.0	79179.0	111073.0[a]	...	...	...	...	...	...	
MIXED INCOME, NET	2240.0	2219.0	2318.0	...	...	...	...	...	...	...	...	
Gross capital formation	18590.0	23010.0	29871.0	38566.0	54840.0	74757.0	133518.1	172494.8	157414.9	158685.7	...	
Gross fixed capital formation	14917.0	20453.0	25894.0	34810.0	51887.0	70745.0	...	...	...	...	...	
Changes in inventories	3673.0	2557.0	3977.0	3756.0	2953.0	4012.0	...	...	...	...	...	
Acquisitions less disposals of valuables	...	...	...	...	...	...	...	...	...	...	...	

[a] Discrepancy between the data for the total economy and the data by industries.
[b] Includes Mixed Income, Gross. Discrepancy between components and total as one or more components have not been revised.
[c] Includes Mixed Income, Gross.

Table 2.3 Output, gross value added, and fixed assets by industries at current prices (ISIC Rev. 3) Agriculture, hunting, forestry; fishing (A+B)

Series 100: 1993 SNA, Qatar riyal, Western calendar year **Data in millions**

	2001	2002	2003	2004	2005	2006	2007	2008	2009	2010	2011	2012
Series	**100**											
Output, at basic prices	327.0	342.0	361.0	343.0	348.0	435.0	514.0	844.0	676.0	826.9		
Less: Intermediate consumption, at purchaser's prices	87.0	161.0	160.0	133.0	132.0	165.0	195.0	321.0	237.0	289.9		
Equals: VALUE ADDED, GROSS, at basic prices	240.0	181.0	201.0	210.0	216.0	270.0	319.0	523.0	439.0	537.0		
Compensation of employees	105.0	106.0	107.0	63.0	64.8	81.0	95.7	156.9	131.7	145.1		
Taxes on production and imports, less Subsidies	-21.0	-12.0	-12.0	...	...	...	...	...	...	...		
Taxes on production and imports	...	...	...	...	...	...	...	...	...	...		
Less: Subsidies	21.0	12.0	12.0	...	...	...	...	...	...	...		
Subsidies on products	...	...	...	...	...	...	...	...	...	...		
Other subsidies on production	21.0	12.0	12.0	...	...	...	...	...	...	...		
OPERATING SURPLUS, GROSS [a]	156.0	87.0	106.0	147.0	151.2	189.0	223.3	366.1	307.3	391.9		
MIXED INCOME, GROSS	...	...	...	...	...	...	...	...	...	...		
Less: Consumption of fixed capital	97.0	95.0	91.0	86.0	78.0	93.0	...	...	...	...		
OPERATING SURPLUS, NET	...	...	...	...	...	...	...	...	...	...		
MIXED INCOME, NET	...	...	...	...	...	...	...	...	...	...		
Gross capital formation	9.0	14.0	39.0	25.0[b]	70.0[b]	...	...	...	...	...		
Gross fixed capital formation	9.0	14.0	39.0	25.0	70.0	...	...	...	...	...		
Changes in inventories	...	...	...	...	...	...	...	...	...	...		
Acquisitions less disposals of valuables	...	...	...	...	...	...	...	...	...	...		

[a] Includes Mixed Income, Gross.
[b] Data for this year(s) have not been revised.

Table 2.3 Output, gross value added, and fixed assets by industries at current prices (ISIC Rev. 3) Mining and quarrying (C)

Series 100: 1993 SNA, Qatar riyal, Western calendar year **Data in millions**

	2001	2002	2003	2004	2005	2006	2007	2008	2009	2010	2011	2012
Series	**100**											
Output, at basic prices	40400.0	44042.0	54045.0	66445.1	103752.1	128578.6	166612.4	251943.4	181527.0	276335.2	...	
Less: Intermediate consumption, at purchaser's prices	3588.0	3325.0	3494.0	4769.5	9263.3	11109.5	16598.0	21631.3	22059.6	36590.4	...	
Equals: VALUE ADDED, GROSS, at basic prices	36812.0	40717.0	50551.0	61675.6	94488.9	117469.2	150014.4	230312.1	159467.3	239744.8	370160.6	
Compensation of employees	1021.0	1403.0	1473.0	1693.7	2312.2	3874.9	5277.3	9545.0	11993.3	11971.4	...	
Taxes on production and imports, less Subsidies	6.0	5.0	3.0	3.4	5.4	22.7	17.1	14.7	19.2	12.1	...	
Taxes on production and imports	6.0	5.0	3.0	3.4	5.4	22.7	17.1	14.7	19.2	12.1	...	
Taxes on products	...	...	...	...	...	...	...	...	...	...	...	
Other taxes on production	6.0	5.0	3.0	3.4	5.4	22.7	...	...	...	...	...	
Less: Subsidies	...	...	...	...	...	...	...	...	...	...	...	
OPERATING SURPLUS, GROSS [a]	35785.0	39309.0	49075.0	59978.5[b]	92171.2[b]	113571.5[b]	144720.0	220752.3	147454.8	227761.3	...	
MIXED INCOME, GROSS	...	...	...	...	...	...	...	...	...	...	...	
Less: Consumption of fixed capital	3701.0	2958.0	3034.0	4700.0	6773.0	3779.0	...	...	...	...	...	
OPERATING SURPLUS, NET [c]	32084.0	36351.0	46041.0	56521.0	82978.0	...	...	...	...	...	...	
MIXED INCOME, NET	...	...	...	...	...	...	...	...	...	...	...	
Gross capital formation	8017.0	7898.0	10367.0	15087.0[d]	18846.0[d]	...	...	...	...	...	...	
Gross fixed capital formation	6444.0	6860.0	8540.0	13829.0	18517.0	...	...	...	...	...	...	
Changes in inventories	1573.0	1038.0	1827.0	1258.0	329.0	...	...	...	...	...	...	
Acquisitions less disposals of valuables	...	...	...	...	...	...	...	...	...	...	...	

[a] Includes Mixed Income, Gross.
[b] Discrepancy between components and total as one or more components have not been revised.
[c] Includes Mixed Income, Net.
[d] Data for this year(s) have not been revised.

Table 2.3 Output, gross value added, and fixed assets by industries at current prices (ISIC Rev. 3) Manufacturing (D)

Series 100: 1993 SNA, Qatar riyal, Western calendar year **Data in millions**

	2001	2002	2003	2004	2005	2006	2007	2008	2009	2010	2011	2012
Series	**100**											
Output, at basic prices	7711.0	7832.0	11052.0	20926.3	24620.2	34342.0	46341.1	78769.1	58702.1	84816.1		
Less: Intermediate consumption, at purchaser's prices	3802.0	2757.0	4499.0	7684.8	8626.2	13725.4	19530.7	33915.7	25132.3	43984.2		
Equals: VALUE ADDED, GROSS, at basic prices	3909.0	5075.0	6553.0	13241.4	15994.0	20616.6	26810.4	44853.5	33569.7	40831.9		
Compensation of employees	812.0	833.0	939.0	1316.0	1505.5	2142.4	3122.2	3999.2	4702.0	5202.5		
Taxes on production and imports, less Subsidies	-24.0	-37.0	-42.0	11.8	19.6	19.5	14.9	111.4	29.1	59.8		
Taxes on production and imports	11.0	9.0	8.0	11.8	19.6	19.5	14.9	111.4	29.1	31.5		
Taxes on products	...	...	...	...	...	...	...	...	...	...		
Other taxes on production	11.0	9.0	8.0	11.8	19.6	19.5	...	...	...	...		

	2001	2002	2003	2004	2005	2006	2007	2008	2009	2010	2011	2012
Series	**100**											
Less: Subsidies	35.0	46.0	50.0	0.0	0.0	0.0	0.0	0.0	0.0	-28.2		
Subsidies on products	...	...	...	...	...	...	...	...	...	...		
Other subsidies on production	35.0	46.0	50.0	0.0	0.0	0.0	...	...	...	...		
OPERATING SURPLUS, GROSS [a]	3122.0	4280.0	5657.0	11913.7[b]	14468.9[b]	18454.8[b]	23673.3	40742.9	28838.7	35569.6		
MIXED INCOME, GROSS	...	...	...	...	...	...	...	...	...	...		
Less: Consumption of fixed capital	695.0	859.0	789.0	1311.0	1505.0	1521.0	...	...	...	...		
OPERATING SURPLUS, NET [c]	2426.0	3420.0	4867.0	9427.0	10081.0	...	...	...	...	...		
MIXED INCOME, NET	...	...	...	...	...	...	...	...	...	...		
Gross capital formation	1408.0	3035.0	3979.0	2301.0[d]	3118.0[d]	...	...	...	...	...		
Gross fixed capital formation	811.0	2941.0	3217.0	2178.0	2834.0	...	...	...	...	...		
Changes in inventories	597.0	94.0	762.0	123.0	284.0	...	...	...	...	...		
Acquisitions less disposals of valuables	...	...	...	...	...	...	...	...	...	...		

[a] Includes Mixed Income, Gross.
[b] Discrepancy between components and total as one or more components have not been revised.
[c] Includes Mixed Income, Net.
[d] Data for this year(s) have not been revised.

Table 2.3 Output, gross value added, and fixed assets by industries at current prices (ISIC Rev. 3) Electricity, gas and water supply (E)

Series 100: 1993 SNA, Qatar riyal, Western calendar year — **Data in millions**

	2001	2002	2003	2004	2005	2006	2007	2008	2009	2010	2011	2012
Series	**100**											
Output, at basic prices	1499.0	1499.0	2291.0	3128.5	2769.9	2411.3	3045.0	2976.2	5737.4	8791.3		
Less: Intermediate consumption, at purchaser's prices	1066.0	1090.0	1087.0	1645.6	1244.2	842.8	1225.1	913.3	3943.4	6678.3		
Equals: VALUE ADDED, GROSS, at basic prices	432.0	409.0	1204.0	1482.9	1525.7	1568.5	1819.9	2063.0	1794.0	2113.0		
Compensation of employees	244.0	249.0	255.0	415.2	618.9	540.3	522.6	785.1	840.3	906.6		
Taxes on production and imports, less Subsidies	-542.0	-557.0	-592.0	-1796.0	-1941.5	-1505.6	-1864.5	-2186.0	-2280.6	-2391.4		
Taxes on production and imports	0.0	0.0	1.0	4.0	8.5	5.9	0.5	0.5	0.4	0.5		
Taxes on products	...	...	...	...	...	...	...	...	...	...		
Other taxes on production	...	0.0	1.0	4.0	8.5	5.9	...	...	...	...		
Less: Subsidies	542.0	557.0	593.0	1800.0	1950.0	1511.5	1865.0	2186.5	2281.0	2391.8		
Subsidies on products	...	...	...	...	...	...	...	...	...	...		
Other subsidies on production	542.0	557.0	593.0	1800.0	1950.0	1511.5	...	...	...	...		
OPERATING SURPLUS, GROSS [a]	730.0	717.0	1541.0	2863.7[b]	2848.3[b]	2533.9[b]	3161.8	3463.8	3234.4	3597.8		
MIXED INCOME, GROSS	...	...	...	...	...	...	...	...	...	...		
Less: Consumption of fixed capital	193.0	211.0	353.0	109.0	163.0	997.0	...	...	...	...		
OPERATING SURPLUS, NET [c]	537.0	506.0	1188.0	2864.0	3366.0	...	...	...	...	...		
MIXED INCOME, NET	...	...	...	...	...	...	...	...	...	...		
Gross capital formation	589.0	838.0	838.0	2836.0[d]	4229.0[d]	...	...	...	...	...		
Gross fixed capital formation	318.0	577.0	600.0	2520.0	3757.0	...	...	...	...	...		

	2001	2002	2003	2004	2005	2006	2007	2008	2009	2010	2011	2012
Series	**100**											
Changes in inventories	271.0	261.0	238.0	316.0	472.0	...	...	...	...	...		
Acquisitions less disposals of valuables	...	...	...	...	...	...	...	...	...	...		

[a] Includes Mixed Income, Gross.
[b] Discrepancy between components and total as one or more components have not been revised.
[c] Includes Mixed Income, Net.
[d] Data for this year(s) have not been revised.

Table 2.3 Output, gross value added, and fixed assets by industries at current prices (ISIC Rev. 3) Construction (F)

Series 100: 1993 SNA, Qatar riyal, Western calendar year — **Data in millions**

	2001	2002	2003	2004	2005	2006	2007	2008	2009	2010	2011	2012
Series	**100**											
Output, at basic prices	7321.0	9051.0	11029.0	14296.0	19134.0	23831.0	34103.0	56664.0	56802.0	68629.0		
Less: Intermediate consumption, at purchaser's prices	4383.0	5457.0	6375.0	7871.0	10390.0	12985.0	18178.0	29465.0	31280.0	41129.0		
Equals: VALUE ADDED, GROSS, at basic prices	2938.0	3594.0	4654.0	6425.0	8744.0	10846.0	15925.0	27199.0	25522.0	27500.0		
Compensation of employees	1750.0	2121.0	2579.0	3146.1	4061.4	4896.6	7351.5	9103.0	11329.2	13682.6		
Taxes on production and imports, less Subsidies	21.0	15.0	18.0	21.8	37.7	45.4	97.4	150.0	-1292.4	-273.2		
Taxes on production and imports	21.0	15.0	18.0	21.8	37.7	45.4	97.4	150.0	114.8	131.4		
Taxes on products	...	...	...	...	...	...	...	...	...	...		
Other taxes on production	21.0	15.0	18.0	21.8	37.7	45.4	...	...	...	...		
Less: Subsidies	0.0	0.0	0.0	0.0	0.0	0.0	0.0	0.0	1407.2	404.6		
OPERATING SURPLUS, GROSS [a]	1167.0	1458.0	2057.0	3257.1[b]	4644.9[b]	5904.0[b]	8476.1	17945.9	15485.2	14090.6		
MIXED INCOME, GROSS	...	...	...	...	...	...	...	...	...	...		
Less: Consumption of fixed capital	351.0	448.0	518.0	615.0	804.0	1168.0	...	...	...	...		
OPERATING SURPLUS, NET [c]	817.0	1010.0	1539.0	2544.0	4794.0	...	...	...	...	...		
MIXED INCOME, NET	...	...	...	...	...	...	...	...	...	...		
Gross capital formation	858.0	392.0	444.0	739.0[d]	1065.0[d]	...	...	...	...	...		
Gross fixed capital formation	862.0	352.0	399.0	550.0	824.0	...	...	...	...	...		
Changes in inventories	-4.0	40.0	45.0	189.0	241.0	...	...	...	...	...		
Acquisitions less disposals of valuables	...	...	...	...	...	...	...	...	...	...		

[a] Includes Mixed Income, Gross.
[b] Discrepancy between components and total as one or more components have not been revised.
[c] Includes Mixed Income, Net.
[d] Data for this year(s) have not been revised.

Table 2.3 Output, gross value added, and fixed assets by industries at current prices (ISIC Rev. 3) Wholesale retail trade, repair of motor vehicles, motorcycles, etc.; hotels and restaurants (G+H)

Series 100: 1993 SNA, Qatar riyal, Western calendar year — **Data in millions**

	2001	2002	2003	2004	2005	2006	2007	2008	2009	2010	2011	2012
Series	**100**											
Output, at basic prices	4976.0	4998.0	5489.0	8873.1	10074.8	19110.0	26413.7	29623.0	37140.5	38004.1		
Less: Intermediate consumption, at purchaser's prices	1058.0	1029.0	1144.0	2352.1	2785.4	4320.8	5566.0	6193.6	7301.9	6503.4		
Equals: VALUE ADDED, GROSS, at basic prices	3918.0	3969.0	4345.0	6521.1	7289.4	14789.3	20847.8	23429.4	29838.6	31500.7		
Compensation of employees	1030.0	1084.0	1197.0	1918.4	2179.0	3571.5	5205.1	5827.2	6747.9	7232.4		
Taxes on production and imports, less Subsidies	25.0	21.0	5.0	33.4	35.5	15.5	-147.5	-166.4	-29.7	-137.6		
Taxes on production and imports	29.0	30.0	28.0	53.8	76.9	56.3	51.8	49.5	101.8	118.5		
Taxes on products	...	...	...	...	...	...	...	...	...	...		
Other taxes on production	29.0	30.0	28.0	53.8	76.9	56.3	...	...	...	...		
Less: Subsidies	4.0	9.0	23.0	20.3	41.3	40.8	199.3	215.9	131.6	256.1		
Subsidies on products	...	...	...	...	...	...	...	...	...	...		
Other subsidies on production	4.0	9.0	23.0	20.3	41.3	40.8	...	...	...	...		
OPERATING SURPLUS, GROSS [a]	2862.0	2864.0	3143.0	4569.3[b]	5074.9[b]	11202.2[b]	15790.2	17768.7	23120.4	24405.9		
MIXED INCOME, GROSS	...	...	...	...	...	...	...	...	...	...		
Less: Consumption of fixed capital	266.0	272.0	267.0	417.0	475.0	720.0	...	...	...	...		
OPERATING SURPLUS, NET [c]	2596.0	2592.0	2876.0	3967.0	4374.0	...	...	...	...	...		
MIXED INCOME, NET	...	...	...	...	...	...	...	...	...	...		
Gross capital formation	465.0	757.0	1139.0	1482.0[d]	1629.0[d]	...	...	...	...	...		
Gross fixed capital formation	199.0	206.0	231.0	362.0	503.0	...	...	...	...	...		
Changes in inventories	266.0	551.0	908.0	1120.0	1126.0	...	...	...	...	...		
Acquisitions less disposals of valuables	...	...	...	...	...	...	...	...	...	...		

[a] Includes Mixed Income, Gross.
[b] Discrepancy between components and total as one or more components have not been revised.
[c] Includes Mixed Income, Net.
[d] Data for this year(s) have not been revised.

Table 2.3 Output, gross value added, and fixed assets by industries at current prices (ISIC Rev. 3) Transport, storage and communications (I)

Series 100: 1993 SNA, Qatar riyal, Western calendar year — **Data in millions**

	2001	2002	2003	2004	2005	2006	2007	2008	2009	2010	2011	2012
Series	**100**											
Output, at basic prices	3831.0	4673.0	5665.0	7989.0	10317.5	13033.8	15507.0	26711.0	28483.4	32826.1		
Less: Intermediate consumption, at purchaser's prices	1608.0	2184.0	2753.0	3969.2	4886.5	6148.8	6810.0	11936.0	12271.4	14757.2		
Equals: VALUE ADDED, GROSS, at basic prices	2223.0	2489.0	2912.0	4019.8	5431.0	6885.0	8697.0	14775.0	16212.0	18068.9		
Compensation of employees	694.0	808.0	901.0	1292.0	1537.8	2431.5	3474.9	3903.5	5566.9	5421.6		
Taxes on production and imports, less Subsidies	5.0	4.0	6.0	-0.8	-19.0	-42.2	-62.4	-72.9	-52.3	-85.3		
Taxes on production and imports	5.0	4.0	6.0	6.2	9.2	7.8	10.6	14.0	19.0	14.1		

	2001	2002	2003	2004	2005	2006	2007	2008	2009	2010	2011	2012
Series	**100**											
Taxes on products	...	...	...	...	...	...	...	...	...	...		
Other taxes on production	5.0	4.0	6.0	6.2	9.2	7.8	...	...	...	...		
Less: Subsidies	0.0	0.0	0.0	7.0	28.2	50.0	72.9	86.9	71.3	99.4		
Subsidies on products	...	...	...	...	...	...	...	...	...	...		
Other subsidies on production	...	...	...	7.0	28.2	50.0	72.9	86.9	71.3	99.4		
OPERATING SURPLUS, GROSS	1342.0	1468.0	1810.0	2728.6[a]	3912.3[a]	4495.8[a]	5284.5[b]	10944.4[b]	10697.4[b]	12732.7[b]		
MIXED INCOME, GROSS	183.0	208.0	195.0	...	...	...	...	...	...	...		
Less: Consumption of fixed capital	321.0	419.0	608.0	758.0	934.0	954.0	...	...	...	...		
OPERATING SURPLUS, NET	1041.0	1069.0	1229.0	1860.0	2526.0	...	...	...	...	...		
MIXED INCOME, NET	163.0	189.0	168.0	206.0	211.0	...	...	...	...	...		
Gross capital formation	1769.0	2647.0	3118.0	3176.0[c]	3703.0[c]	...	...	...	...	...		
Gross fixed capital formation	901.0	2038.0	3068.0	2868.0	3378.0	...	...	...	...	...		
Changes in inventories	868.0	609.0	50.0	308.0	325.0	...	...	...	...	...		
Acquisitions less disposals of valuables	...	...	...	...	...	...	...	...	...	...		

[a] Includes Mixed Income, Gross. Discrepancy between components and total as one or more components have not been revised.
[b] Includes Mixed Income, Gross.
[c] Data for this year(s) have not been revised.

Table 2.3 Output, gross value added, and fixed assets by industries at current prices (ISIC Rev. 3) Financial intermediation; real estate, renting and business activities (J+K)

Series 100: 1993 SNA, Qatar riyal, Western calendar year **Data in millions**

	2001	2002	2003	2004	2005	2006	2007	2008	2009	2010	2011	2012
Series	**100**											
Output, at basic prices	6536.0	7207.0	7992.0	11224.0	16257.7	32020.3	45352.8	56807.3	63910.5	70397.9		
Less: Intermediate consumption, at purchaser's prices	1340.0	1405.0	1544.0	1299.9	1530.4	2649.4	3370.7	5227.2	5811.2	10106.3		
Equals: VALUE ADDED, GROSS, at basic prices	5196.0	5802.0	6448.0	9924.1	14727.3	29370.8	41982.2	51580.1	58099.3	60291.6		
Compensation of employees	826.0	966.0	988.0	1358.8	1606.9	2955.4	3608.9	5106.1	7163.9	7666.6		
Taxes on production and imports, less Subsidies	15.0	14.0	18.0	-28.5	-79.5	-193.4	-137.1	-212.1	-203.6	-154.8		
Taxes on production and imports	15.0	14.0	18.0	10.1	13.1	19.7	20.5	32.2	45.3	58.2		
Taxes on products	...	...	...	...	...	...	...	...	...	...		
Other taxes on production	15.0	14.0	18.0	10.1	13.1	19.7	...	...	...	...		
Less: Subsidies	0.0	0.0	0.0	38.6	92.6	213.1	157.6	244.3	248.9	213.1		
Subsidies on products	...	...	...	...	...	...	...	...	...	...		
Other subsidies on production	...	...	...	38.6	92.6	213.1	157.6	244.3	248.9	213.1		
OPERATING SURPLUS, GROSS	2069.0	2478.0	3054.0	8593.8[a]	13199.9[a]	26608.7[a]	38510.3[b]	46686.1[b]	51138.9[b]	52779.9[b]		
MIXED INCOME, GROSS	2286.0	2343.0	2387.0	...	...	...	...	...	...	...		
Less: Consumption of fixed capital	488.0	532.0	533.0	758.0	1042.0	1150.0	...	...	...	...		
OPERATING SURPLUS, NET	1828.0	2224.0	2807.0	4489.0	7726.0	...	...	...	...	...		
MIXED INCOME, NET	2039.0	2064.0	2101.0	3286.0	4330.0	...	...	...	...	...		
Gross capital formation	1887.0	1836.0	3137.0	4027.0[c]	5875.0[c]	...	...	...	...	...		

	2001	2002	2003	2004	2005	2006	2007	2008	2009	2010	2011	2012
Series	**100**											
Gross fixed capital formation	1807.0	1915.0	3020.0	3649.0	5765.0	...	...	...	...	...		
Changes in inventories	80.0	-79.0	117.0	378.0	110.0	...	...	...	...	...		
Acquisitions less disposals of valuables	...	...	...	...	...	...	...	...	...	...		

[a] Includes Mixed Income, Gross. Discrepancy between components and total as one or more components have not been revised.
[b] Includes Mixed Income, Gross.
[c] Data for this year(s) have not been revised.

Table 2.3 Output, gross value added, and fixed assets by industries at current prices (ISIC Rev. 3) Public administration and defense; compulsory social security (L)

Series 100: 1993 SNA, Qatar riyal, Western calendar year — **Data in millions**

	2001	2002	2003	2004	2005	2006	2007	2008	2009	2010	2011	2012
Series	**100**											
Output, at basic prices	12886.0	13134.0	14604.0	12347.6	14319.7	21278.0	24976.3	28889.2	39113.0	44085.6		
Less: Intermediate consumption, at purchaser's prices	4418.0	4330.0	5109.0	4834.7	6772.6	8550.9	10586.6	12465.3	19083.5	21057.2		
Equals: VALUE ADDED, GROSS, at basic prices	8468.0[a]	8804.0[a]	9495.0[a]	7512.8	7547.2	12727.1	14389.7	16423.9	20029.5	23028.5		
Compensation of employees	7179.0	7491.0	8035.0	5758.4	5964.7	10917.3	12074.3	12916.2	14687.2	16124.5		
Taxes on production and imports, less Subsidies	...	...	...	...	...	...	...	...	...	...		
OPERATING SURPLUS, GROSS	1289.0	1313.0	1460.0	1754.4[b]	1582.4[b]	1809.8[b]	2315.4[b]	3507.7[b]	5342.3[b]	6903.9[b]		
MIXED INCOME, GROSS	...	...	...	...	...	...	...	...	...	...		
Less: Consumption of fixed capital	1289.0	1313.0	1460.0	1754.4	1582.4	1809.8	...	...	...	...		
OPERATING SURPLUS, NET	...	...	...	...	...	...	...	...	...	...		
MIXED INCOME, NET	...	...	...	...	...	...	...	...	...	...		
Gross capital formation	3538.0	5524.0	6755.0	8689.0[c]	16088.0[c]	...	...	...	...	...		
Gross fixed capital formation	3538.0	5524.0	6755.0	8689.0	16088.0	...	...	...	...	...		
Changes in inventories	...	...	...	...	...	...	...	...	...	...		
Acquisitions less disposals of valuables	...	...	...	...	...	...	...	...	...	...		

[a] Includes the provision of public health, education and other miscellaneous services.
[b] Includes Mixed Income, Gross.
[c] Data for this year(s) have not been revised.

Table 2.3 Output, gross value added, and fixed assets by industries at current prices (ISIC Rev. 3) Education; health and social work; other community, social and personal services (M+N+O)

Series 100: 1993 SNA, Qatar riyal, Western calendar year — **Data in millions**

	2001	2002	2003	2004	2005	2006	2007	2008	2009	2010	2011	2012
Series	**100**											
Output, at basic prices	879.0	1034.0	1102.0	7283.0	11099.1	14023.3	15406.1	19000.6	22433.3	26457.9	...	
Less: Intermediate consumption, at purchaser's prices	271.0	419.0	458.0	2216.4	4594.3	5543.1	4836.4	5628.8	6207.7	7576.6	...	
Equals: VALUE ADDED, GROSS, at basic prices	608.0[a]	615.0[a]	644.0[a]	5066.6	6504.8	8480.2	10569.7	13371.8	16225.6	18881.3	22085.4	
Compensation of employees	408.0	348.0	365.0	4753.9	6569.0	7426.1	8958.4	11550.1	14242.7	16425.6	...	

	2001	2002	2003	2004	2005	2006	2007	2008	2009	2010	2011	2012
Series	**100**											
Taxes on production and imports, less Subsidies	-1.0	0.0	4.0	-470.3	-1254.2	-1685.5	-2765.9	-2552.7	-2527.2	-2909.2	...	
Taxes on production and imports	2.0	3.0	7.0	3.6	5.5	5.9	5.0	8.6	19.6	11.2	...	
Taxes on products	...	...	...	...	...	...	...	...	...	...	...	
Other taxes on production	2.0	3.0	7.0	3.6	5.5	5.9	...	...	...	...	...	
Less: Subsidies	3.0	3.0	3.0	473.9	1259.7	1691.3	2770.9	2561.3	2546.8	2920.4	...	
Subsidies on products	...	...	...	...	...	...	...	...	...	...	...	
Other subsidies on production	3.0	3.0	3.0	473.9	1259.7	1691.3	...	...	...	...	...	
OPERATING SURPLUS, GROSS [b]	201.0	267.0	275.0	783.0[c]	1190.0[c]	2739.5[c]	4377.2	4374.4	4510.1	5364.9	...	
MIXED INCOME, GROSS	...	...	...	...	...	...	...	...	...	...	...	
Less: Consumption of fixed capital	58.0	68.0	80.0	127.0	160.0	694.0	...	...	...	...	...	
OPERATING SURPLUS, NET [d]	143.0	199.0	195.0	266.0	211.0	...	...	...	...	...	...	
MIXED INCOME, NET	...	...	...	...	...	...	...	...	...	...	...	
Gross capital formation	51.0	69.0	56.0	205.0[e]	216.0[e]	...	...	...	...	...	...	
Gross fixed capital formation	29.0	26.0	25.0	139.0	150.0	...	...	...	...	...	...	
Changes in inventories	22.0	43.0	31.0	66.0	66.0	...	...	...	...	...	...	
Acquisitions less disposals of valuables	...	...	...	...	...	...	...	...	...	...	...	

[a] Refers to social services.
[b] Includes Mixed Income, Gross.
[c] Discrepancy between components and total as one or more components have not been revised.
[d] Includes Mixed Income, Net.
[e] Data for this year(s) have not been revised.

Table 2.3 Output, gross value added, and fixed assets by industries at current prices (ISIC Rev. 3) Private households with employed persons (P)

Series 100: 1993 SNA, Qatar riyal, Western calendar year

Data in millions

	2001	2002	2003	2004	2005	2006	2007	2008	2009	2010	2011	2012
Series	**100**											
Output, at basic prices	548.0	571.0	617.0	987.0	1057.0	1236.9	1565.1	1660.9	1827.0	1881.0		
Less: Intermediate consumption, at purchaser's prices	...	...	...	...	...	...	...	...	...	...		
Equals: VALUE ADDED, GROSS, at basic prices	548.0	571.0	617.0	987.0	1057.0	1236.9	1565.1	1660.9	1827.0	1881.0		
Compensation of employees	548.0	571.0	617.0	987.0	1057.0	1236.9	1565.1	1660.9	1827.0	1881.0		
Taxes on production and imports, less Subsidies	...	...	...	...	...	...	...	...	...	...		
OPERATING SURPLUS, GROSS	...	...	...	...	...	...	...	...	...	...		
MIXED INCOME, GROSS	...	...	...	...	...	...	...	...	...	...		
Gross capital formation	...	...	...	...	...	...	...	...	...	...		

Table 4.1 Total Economy (S.1)

Series 100: 1993 SNA, Qatar riyal, Western calendar year

Data in millions

	2001	2002	2003	2004	2005	2006	2007	2008	2009	2010	2011	2012
Series	**100**											
I. Production account - Resources												
Output, at basic prices (otherwise, please specify)	86913.0	94383.0	114248.0	155082.0[a]	204669.0[a]							
Less: Financial intermediation services indirectly measured (only to be deducted if FISIM is not distributed to uses)	1821.0	2208.0	2491.0	2761.0	4985.0[a]							
Plus: Taxes less Subsidies on products	367.0	466.0	532.0	1207.0	1739.0							
Plus: Taxes on products	367.0	466.0	532.0	1207.0	1739.0							
Less: Subsidies on products	...	...	...	...	...							
I. Production account - Uses												
Intermediate consumption, at purchaser's prices [b]	21619.0	22157.0	26624.0	38014.0[a]	46858.0[a]							
GROSS DOMESTIC PRODUCT	63840.0	70484.0	85665.0	115514.0	154565.0[a]							
Less: Consumption of fixed capital	7459.0	7174.0	7734.0	10735.0	14059.0							
NET DOMESTIC PRODUCT	56381.0	63310.0	77931.0	104779.0	140506.0							
II.1.1 Generation of income account - Resources												
GROSS DOMESTIC PRODUCT	63840.0	70484.0	85665.0	115514.0	154565.0							
II.1.1 Generation of income account - Uses												
Compensation of employees	14617.0	15980.0	17422.0	22703.0	24966.0[a]							
Taxes on production and imports, less Subsidies	-139.0	-80.0	-61.0	-640.0	-111.0							
Taxes on production and imports	466.0	546.0	620.0	1398.0	1953.0							
Taxes on products	367.0	466.0	532.0	1207.0	1739.0							
Other taxes on production	99.0	80.0	88.0	191.0	214.0							
Less: Subsidies	605.0	626.0	681.0	2038.0	2064.0							
Subsidies on products	...	...	...	...	...							
Other subsidies on production	605.0	626.0	681.0	2038.0	2064.0							
OPERATING SURPLUS, GROSS [c]	49362.0	54584.0	68304.0	93451.0	129710.0							
MIXED INCOME, GROSS	...	...	...	...	...							
II.1.2 Allocation of primary income account - Resources												
OPERATING SURPLUS, GROSS	49362.0	54584.0	68304.0	93451.0	129710.0							
MIXED INCOME, GROSS	...	...	...	...	...							
Compensation of employees	14617.0	15980.0	17422.0	22703.0	24828.0							
Taxes on production and imports, less Subsidies	-139.0	-80.0	-61.0	-640.0	-111.0							
Taxes on production and imports	466.0	546.0	620.0	1398.0	1953.0							
Taxes on products	367.0	466.0	532.0	1207.0	1739.0							
Other taxes on production	99.0	80.0	88.0	191.0	214.0							
Less: Subsidies	605.0	626.0	681.0	2038.0	2064.0							
Subsidies on products	...	...	...	...	...							
Other subsidies on production	605.0	626.0	681.0	2038.0	2064.0							
Property income	17710.0	22821.0	26006.0	40126.0	48579.0							

		2001	2002	2003	2004	2005	2006	2007	2008	2009	2010	2011	2012
Series		**100**											
		II.1.2 Allocation of primary income account - Uses											
Property income		20271.0	26088.0	27522.0	48286.0	53566.0							
GROSS NATIONAL INCOME	d	61278.0	67218.0	84149.0	107354.0	149440.0[a]							
		II.2 Secondary distribution of income account - Resources											
GROSS NATIONAL INCOME		61278.0	67218.0	84149.0	107354.0	149440.0[a]							
Current taxes on income, wealth, etc.		12939.0	13757.0	13943.0	34453.0	36518.0							
Social contributions		...	...	...	...	...							
Social benefits other than social transfers in kind		96.0	107.0	110.0	129.0	129.0							
Other current transfers		2313.0	3169.0	3251.0	4785.0	5516.0							
		II.2 Secondary distribution of income account - Uses											
Current taxes on income, wealth, etc.		12939.0	13757.0	13943.0	34452.0	36517.0							
Social contributions		...	...	...	...	...							
Social benefits other than social transfers in kind		96.0	107.0	110.0	129.0	129.0							
Other current transfers		8142.0	8691.0	9257.0	12990.0	14895.0							
GROSS DISPOSABLE INCOME	d	55449.0	61696.0	78142.0	99149.0	140060.0[a]							
		II.4.1 Use of disposable income account - Resources											
GROSS DISPOSABLE INCOME		55449.0	61696.0	78142.0	99149.0	140060.0[a]							
Adjustment for the change in net equity of households on pension funds		...	...	...	...	...							
		II.4.1 Use of disposable income account - Uses											
Final consumption expenditure		21746.0	24766.0	27328.0	35260.0	45934.0[a]							
Individual consumption expenditure		11308.0	14193.0	15408.0	25548.0	34346.0[a]							
Collective consumption expenditure		10438.0	10573.0	11920.0	9712.0	11588.0							
Adjustment for the change in net equity of households on pension funds		...	...	...	...	...							
SAVING, GROSS	d	33703.0	36930.0	50814.0	63889.0	94126.0[a]							
		III.1 Capital account - Changes in liabilities and net worth											
SAVING, GROSS		33703.0	36930.0	50814.0	63889.0	94126.0							
Capital transfers, receivable less payable		...	...	...	...	...							
Capital transfers, receivable		...	...	...	...	...							
Less: Capital transfers, payable		...	...	...	...	...							
Equals: CHANGES IN NET WORTH DUE TO SAVING AND CAPITAL TRANSFERS	e	33703.0	36930.0	50814.0	63889.0	94126.0							
		III.1 Capital account - Changes in assets											
Gross capital formation		18590.0	23010.0	29871.0	38566.0[a]	54840.0[a]							
Gross fixed capital formation		14917.0	20453.0	25894.0	34810.0	51887.0							
Changes in inventories		3673.0	2557.0	3977.0	3756.0	2953.0							
Acquisitions less disposals of valuables		...	...	...	...	...							

	2001	2002	2003	2004	2005	2006	2007	2008	2009	2010	2011	2012
Series	**100**											
Acquisitions less disposals of non-produced non-financial assets	...	...	...	...	...							
NET LENDING (+) / NET BORROWING (-) [d]	15113.0	13920.0	20943.0	25323.0	39286.0[a]							

[a] Data in this table have not been updated, resulting in discrepancies with equivalent items in other tables.
[b] Excludes financial intermediation services indirectly measured (FISIM).
[c] Includes Mixed Income, Gross. Discrepancy between Total Economy and the sum of the domestic sectors as Total Economy excludes FISIM, but FISIM is included in the domestic sectors.
[d] Discrepancy between Total Economy and the sum of the domestic sectors as Total Economy excludes FISIM, but FISIM is included in the domestic sectors.
[e] Item does not consider consumption of fixed capital. Discrepancy between Total Economy and the sum of the domestic sectors as Total Economy excludes FISIM, but FISIM is included in the domestic sectors.

Table 4.2 Rest of the world (S.2)

Series 100: 1993 SNA, Qatar riyal, Western calendar year

Data in millions

	2001	2002	2003	2004	2005	2006	2007	2008	2009	2010	2011	2012
Series	**100**											
V.I External account of goods and services - Resources												
Imports of goods and services	18562.0	19825.0	24386.0	32434.0[a]	51706.0[a]							
Imports of goods	12324.0	13287.0	15865.0	21856.0[a]	36621.0[a]							
Imports of services	6238.0	6538.0	8521.0	10578.0	15085.0							
V.I External account of goods and services - Uses												
Exports of goods and services	42066.0	42532.0	52852.0	74123.0	105497.0							
Exports of goods	39571.0	39960.0	48711.0	68013.0	93774.0							
Exports of services	2495.0	2572.0	4141.0	6110.0	11723.0							
EXTERNAL BALANCE OF GOODS AND SERVICES	-23504.0	-22707.0	-28466.0	-41689.0	-53791.0							
V.II External account of primary income and current transfers - Resources												
EXTERNAL BALANCE OF GOODS AND SERVICES	-23504.0	-22707.0	-28466.0	-41689.0	-53791.0							
Compensation of employees	...	...	...	...	...							
Taxes on production and imports, less Subsidies	...	...	...	...	...							
Taxes on production and imports	...	...	...	...	...							
Taxes on products	...	...	...	...	...							
Other taxes on production	...	...	...	...	...							
Less: Subsidies	...	...	...	...	...							
Subsidies on products	...	...	...	...	...							
Other subsidies on production	...	...	...	...	...							
Property income	5793.0	5848.0	6443.0	12793.0	10264.0							
Current taxes on income, wealth, etc.	...	...	...	...	...							
Social contributions	...	...	...	...	...							
Social benefits other than social transfers in kind	...	...	...	...	...							
Other current transfers	5829.0	5522.0	6007.0	8205.0	9380.0							
Adjustment for the change in net equity of households on pension funds	...	...	...	...	...							

	2001	2002	2003	2004	2005	2006	2007	2008	2009	2010	2011	2012
Series	**100**											
	V.II External account of primary income and current transfers - Uses											
Compensation of employees	...	...	...	...	...							
Taxes on production and imports, less Subsidies	...	...	...	...	...							
Taxes on production and imports	...	...	...	...	...							
Taxes on products	...	...	...	...	...							
Other taxes on production	...	...	...	...	...							
Less: Subsidies	...	...	...	...	...							
Subsidies on products	...	...	...	...	...							
Other subsidies on production	...	...	...	...	...							
Property income	3231.0	2582.0	4927.0	4633.0	5139.0							
Current taxes on income and wealth, etc.	...	...	...	...	...							
Social contributions	...	...	...	...	...							
Social benefits other than social transfers in kind	...	...	...	...	...							
Other current transfers	...	...	...	...	...							
Adjustment for the change in net equity of households on pension funds	...	...	...	...	...							
CURRENT EXTERNAL BALANCE	-15113.0	-13919.0	-20943.0	-25324.0	-39286.0							
	V.III.1 Capital account - Changes in liabilities and net worth											
CURRENT EXTERNAL BALANCE	-15113.0	-13919.0	-20943.0	-25324.0	-39286.0							
Capital transfers, receivable less payable	...	...	...	...	...							
Capital transfers, receivable	...	...	...	...	...							
Less: Capital transfers, payable	...	...	...	...	...							
Equals: CHANGES IN NET WORTH DUE TO SAVING AND CAPITAL TRANSFERS	-15113.0	-13919.0	-20943.0	-25324.0	-39286.0							
	V.III.1 Capital account - Changes in assets											
Acquisitions less disposals of non-produced non-financial assets	...	...	...	...	...							
NET LENDING (+) / NET BORROWING (-)	-15113.0	-13919.0	-20943.0	-25324.0	-39286.0							

[a] Data in this table have not been updated, resulting in discrepancies with equivalent items in other tables.

Table 4.3 Non-financial Corporations (S.11)

Series 100: 1993 SNA, Qatar riyal, Western calendar year **Data in millions**

	2001	2002	2003	2004	2005	2006	2007	2008	2009	2010	2011	2012
Series	**100**											
	I. Production account - Resources											
Output, at basic prices (otherwise, please specify)	67035.0	73749.0	91307.0	125792.0	167623.0							
	I. Production account - Uses											
Intermediate consumption, at purchaser's prices	15928.0	16513.0	20039.0	29527.0	35845.0							
VALUE ADDED GROSS, in basic prices	51107.0	57236.0	71268.0	96265.0	131778.0							
Less: Consumption of fixed capital	5701.0	5367.0	5754.0	8380.0	11158.0							

	2001	2002	2003	2004	2005	2006	2007	2008	2009	2010	2011	2012
Series	**100**											
VALUE ADDED NET, at basic prices	45406.0	51869.0	65514.0	87885.0	120620.0							
	II.1.1 Generation of income account - Resources											
VALUE ADDED GROSS, at basic prices	51107.0	57236.0	71268.0	96265.0	131778.0							
	II.1.1 Generation of income account - Uses											
Compensation of employees	6027.0	7033.0	7880.0	10722.0	12399.0							
Other taxes less Other subsidies on production	-505.0	-544.0	-593.0	-1841.0	-1849.0							
Other taxes on production	79.0	71.0	76.0	180.0	203.0							
Less: Other subsidies on production	584.0	615.0	669.0	2021.0	2052.0							
OPERATING SURPLUS, GROSS	45585.0	50747.0	63981.0	87384.0	121228.0							
	II.1.2 Allocation of primary income account - Resources											
OPERATING SURPLUS, GROSS	45585.0	50747.0	63981.0	87384.0	121228.0							
Property income	972.0	1032.0	640.0	1050.0	1384.0							
	II.1.2 Allocation of primary income account - Uses											
Property income	13663.0	20568.0	21888.0	37445.0	44777.0							
BALANCE OF PRIMARY INCOMES	32894.0	31211.0	42733.0	50989.0	77835.0							
	II.2 Secondary distribution of income account - Resources											
BALANCE OF PRIMARY INCOMES	32894.0	31211.0	42733.0	50989.0	77835.0							
Social contributions	...	...	...	...	...							
Other current transfers	185.0	806.0	477.0	1739.0	2311.0							
	II.2 Secondary distribution of income account - Uses											
Current taxes on income, wealth, etc.	12876.0	13681.0	13865.0	34393.0	36383.0							
Social benefits other than social transfers in kind	...	...	...	...	...							
Other current transfers	613.0	950.0	1069.0	1526.0	2243.0							
GROSS DISPOSABLE INCOME	19590.0	17386.0	28276.0	16809.0	41520.0							
	II.4.1 Use of disposable income account - Resources											
GROSS DISPOSABLE INCOME	19590.0	17386.0	28276.0	16809.0	41520.0							
	II.4.1 Use of disposable income account - Uses											
Adjustment for the change in net equity of households on pension funds	...	...	...	...	...							
SAVING, GROSS	19590.0	17386.0	28276.0	16809.0	41520.0							
	III.1 Capital account - Changes in liabilities and net worth											
SAVING, GROSS	19590.0	17386.0	28276.0	16809.0	41520.0							
Capital transfers, receivable less payable	...	...	...	...	...							
Capital transfers, receivable	...	...	...	...	...							
Less: Capital transfers, payable	...	...	...	...	...							
Equals: CHANGES IN NET WORTH DUE TO SAVING AND CAPITAL TRANSFERS	13889.0	12019.0	22522.0	8429.0	30362.0							
	III.1 Capital account - Changes in assets											
Gross capital formation	13366.0	15743.0	20290.0	26429.0	33252.0							
Gross fixed capital formation	9740.0	13162.0	16315.0	22757.0	30313.0							

	2001	2002	2003	2004	2005	2006	2007	2008	2009	2010	2011	2012
Series	**100**											
Changes in inventories	3626.0	2581.0	3975.0	3672.0	2939.0							
Acquisitions less disposals of valuables	...	...	...	...	...							
Acquisitions less disposals of non-produced non-financial assets	...	...	...	...	...							
NET LENDING (+) / NET BORROWING (-)	6224.0	1643.0	7986.0	-9620.0	8268.0							

Table 4.4 Financial Corporations (S.12)

Series 100: 1993 SNA, Qatar riyal, Western calendar year **Data in millions**

	2001	2002	2003	2004	2005	2006	2007	2008	2009	2010	2011	2012
Series	**100**											
	I. Production account - Resources											
Output, at basic prices (otherwise, please specify)	2679.0	3096.0	3700.0	4432.0	7937.0							
	I. Production account - Uses											
Intermediate consumption, at purchaser's prices	458.0	402.0	477.0	682.0	824.0							
VALUE ADDED GROSS, at basic prices	2221.0	2694.0	3223.0	3750.0	7113.0							
Less: Consumption of fixed capital	105.0	102.0	116.0	125.0	222.0							
VALUE ADDED NET, at basic prices	2116.0	2592.0	3107.0	3625.0	6891.0							
	II.1.1 Generation of income account - Resources											
VALUE ADDED GROSS, at basic prices	2221.0	2694.0	3223.0	3750.0	7113.0							
	II.1.1 Generation of income account - Uses											
Compensation of employees	512.0	570.0	584.0	684.0	899.0							
Other taxes less Other subsidies on production	4.0	4.0	7.0	7.0	4.0							
Other taxes on production	4.0	4.0	7.0	7.0	4.0							
Less: Other subsidies on production	...	...	...	...	...							
OPERATING SURPLUS, GROSS	1705.0	2120.0	2632.0	3059.0	6210.0							
	II.1.2 Allocation of primary income account - Resources											
OPERATING SURPLUS, GROSS	1705.0	2120.0	2632.0	3059.0	6210.0							
Property income	2010.0	1099.0	1028.0	1365.0	2740.0							
	II.1.2 Allocation of primary income account - Uses											
Property income	2140.0	1269.0	1190.0	1492.0	2996.0							
BALANCE OF PRIMARY INCOMES	1575.0	1950.0	2470.0	2932.0	5954.0							
	II.2 Secondary distribution of income account - Resources											
BALANCE OF PRIMARY INCOMES	1575.0	1950.0	2470.0	2932.0	5954.0							
Social contributions	...	...	...	...	...							
Other current transfers	343.0	508.0	790.0	85.0	190.0							
	II.2 Secondary distribution of income account - Uses											
Current taxes on income, wealth, etc.	63.0	76.0	78.0	59.0	134.0							
Social benefits other than social transfers in kind	...	...	...	...	...							

	2001	2002	2003	2004	2005	2006	2007	2008	2009	2010	2011	2012
Series	**100**											
Other current transfers	434.0	607.0	979.0	247.0	386.0							
GROSS DISPOSABLE INCOME	1421.0	1775.0	2203.0	2711.0	5624.0							
	II.4.1 Use of disposable income account - Resources											
GROSS DISPOSABLE INCOME	1421.0	1775.0	2203.0	2711.0	5624.0							
	II.4.1 Use of disposable income account - Uses											
Adjustment for the change in net equity of households on pension funds	18.0	28.0	11.0	32.0	283.0							
SAVING, GROSS	1403.0	1747.0	2192.0	2679.0	5341.0							
	III.1 Capital account - Changes in liabilities and net worth											
SAVING, GROSS	1403.0	1747.0	2192.0	2679.0	5341.0							
Capital transfers, receivable less payable	...	...	...	...	...							
Capital transfers, receivable	...	...	...	...	...							
Less: Capital transfers, payable	...	...	...	...	...							
Equals: CHANGES IN NET WORTH DUE TO SAVING AND CAPITAL TRANSFERS	1298.0	1645.0	2076.0	2554.0	5119.0							
	III.1 Capital account - Changes in assets											
Gross capital formation	191.0	138.0	158.0	302.0	308.0							
Gross fixed capital formation	143.0	162.0	156.0	218.0	294.0							
Changes in inventories	48.0	-24.0	2.0	84.0	14.0							
Acquisitions less disposals of valuables	...	...	...	...	...							
Acquisitions less disposals of non-produced non-financial assets	...	...	...	...	...							
NET LENDING (+) / NET BORROWING (-)	1212.0	1609.0	2034.0	2377.0	5033.0							

Table 4.5 General Government (S.13)

Series 100: 1993 SNA, Qatar riyal, Western calendar year

Data in millions

	2001	2002	2003	2004	2005	2006	2007	2008	2009	2010	2011	2012
Series	**100**											
	I. Production account - Resources											
Output, at basic prices (otherwise, please specify)	12886.0	13134.0	14604.0	18536.0	21263.0							
	I. Production account - Uses											
Intermediate consumption, at purchaser's prices	4418.0	4330.0	5109.0	6688.0	8874.0							
VALUE ADDED GROSS, at basic prices	8468.0	8804.0	9495.0	11848.0	12389.0							
Less: Consumption of fixed capital	1289.0	1313.0	1460.0	1854.0	2126.0							
VALUE ADDED NET, at basic prices	7179.0	7491.0	8035.0	9994.0	10263.0							
	II.1.1 Generation of income account - Resources											
VALUE ADDED GROSS, at basic prices	8468.0	8804.0	9495.0	11848.0	12389.0							
	II.1.1 Generation of income account - Uses											
Compensation of employees	7179.0	7491.0	8035.0	9994.0	10263.0							

	2001	2002	2003	2004	2005	2006	2007	2008	2009	2010	2011	2012
Series	**100**											
Other taxes less Other subsidies on production	...	...	...	...	...							
Other taxes on production	...	...	...	...	...							
Less: Other subsidies on production	...	...	...	...	...							
OPERATING SURPLUS, GROSS	1289.0	1313.0	1460.0	1854.0	2126.0							
II.1.2 Allocation of primary income account - Resources												
OPERATING SURPLUS, GROSS	1289.0	1313.0	1460.0	1854.0	2126.0							
Taxes on production and imports, less Subsidies	-139.0	-80.0	-61.0	-640.0	-110.0							
Taxes on production and imports	466.0	546.0	620.0	1398.0	1954.0							
Taxes on products	367.0	466.0	532.0	1207.0	1739.0							
Other taxes on production	99.0	80.0	88.0	191.0	215.0							
Less: Subsidies	605.0	626.0	681.0	2038.0	2064.0							
Subsidies on products	...	...	...	...	...							
Other subsidies on production	605.0	626.0	681.0	2038.0	2064.0							
Property income	7841.0	11133.0	12555.0	24830.0	26392.0							
II.1.2 Allocation of primary income account - Uses												
Property income	2819.0	2437.0	2328.0	1694.0	1632.0							
BALANCE OF PRIMARY INCOMES	6172.0	9929.0	11626.0	24350.0	26776.0							
II.2 Secondary distribution of income account - Resources												
BALANCE OF PRIMARY INCOMES	6172.0	9929.0	11626.0	24350.0	26776.0							
Current taxes on income, wealth, etc.	12939.0	13757.0	13943.0	34453.0	36518.0							
Social contributions	...	...	...	...	...							
Other current transfers	311.0	225.0	181.0	1325.0	1325.0							
II.2 Secondary distribution of income account - Uses												
Current taxes on income, wealth, etc.	...	...	...	...	...							
Social benefits other than social transfers in kind	96.0	107.0	110.0	129.0	129.0							
Other current transfers	1408.0	1186.0	1188.0	1585.0	1632.0							
GROSS DISPOSABLE INCOME	17918.0	22618.0	24452.0	58414.0	62858.0							
II.4.1 Use of disposable income account - Resources												
GROSS DISPOSABLE INCOME	17918.0	22618.0	24452.0	58414.0	62858.0							
II.4.1 Use of disposable income account - Uses												
Final consumption expenditure	11891.0	11783.0	13197.0	15094.0	17769.0							
Individual consumption expenditure	1453.0	1210.0	1277.0	5382.0	6181.0							
Collective consumption expenditure	10438.0	10573.0	11920.0	9712.0	11588.0							
Adjustment for the change in net equity of households on pension funds	...	...	...	...	...							
SAVING, GROSS	6027.0	10835.0	11255.0	43320.0	45089.0							
III.1 Capital account - Changes in liabilities and net worth												
SAVING, GROSS	6027.0	10835.0	11255.0	43320.0	45089.0							
Capital transfers, receivable less payable	...	...	...	...	...							
Capital transfers, receivable	...	...	...	...	...							

	2001	2002	2003	2004	2005	2006	2007	2008	2009	2010	2011	2012
Series	**100**											
Less: Capital transfers, payable	...	...	...	...	...							
Equals: CHANGES IN NET WORTH DUE TO SAVING AND CAPITAL TRANSFERS	4738.0	9522.0	9795.0	41466.0	42963.0							
	III.1 Capital account - Changes in assets											
Gross capital formation	3538.0	5524.0	6755.0	8689.0	16088.0							
Gross fixed capital formation	3538.0	5524.0	6755.0	8689.0	16088.0							
Changes in inventories	...	...	...	...	...							
Acquisitions less disposals of valuables	...	...	...	...	...							
Acquisitions of non-produced non-financial assets	337.0	130.0	123.0	761.0	776.0							
NET LENDING (+) / NET BORROWING (-)	2152.0	5181.0	4377.0	33870.0	28225.0							

Table 4.6 Households (S.14)

Series 100: 1993 SNA, Qatar riyal, Western calendar year

Data in millions

	2001	2002	2003	2004	2005	2006	2007	2008	2009	2010	2011	2012
Series	**100**											
	I. Production account - Resources											
Output, at basic prices (otherwise, please specify)	4313.0	4404.0	4637.0	6322.0	7846.0							
	I. Production account - Uses											
Intermediate consumption, at purchaser's prices	815.0	913.0	999.0	1117.0	1315.0							
VALUE ADDED GROSS, at basic prices	3498.0	3491.0	3638.0	5205.0	6531.0							
Less: Consumption of fixed capital	364.0	393.0	405.0	377.0	552.0							
VALUE ADDED NET, at basic prices	3134.0	3098.0	3233.0	4828.0	5979.0							
	II.1.1 Generation of income account - Resources											
VALUE ADDED GROSS, at basic prices	3498.0	3491.0	3638.0	5205.0	6531.0							
	II.1.1 Generation of income account - Uses											
Compensation of employees	899.0	886.0	923.0	1303.0	1405.0							
Other taxes less Other subsidies on production	-5.0	-8.0	-7.0	-11.0	-4.0							
Other taxes on production	16.0	4.0	5.0	6.0	8.0							
Less: Other subsidies on production	21.0	12.0	12.0	17.0	12.0							
OPERATING SURPLUS, GROSS	...	...	...	...	...							
MIXED INCOME, GROSS	2604.0	2613.0	2722.0	3913.0	5130.0							
	II.1.2 Allocation of primary income account - Resources											
OPERATING SURPLUS, GROSS	...	...	...	...	...							
MIXED INCOME, GROSS	2604.0	2613.0	2722.0	3913.0	5130.0							
Compensation of employees	14617.0	15980.0	17422.0	22703.0	24828.0							
Property income	6887.0	9557.0	11783.0	12881.0	18063.0							
	II.1.2 Allocation of primary income account - Uses											
Property income	1649.0	1814.0	2116.0	7655.0	4161.0							

	2001	2002	2003	2004	2005	2006	2007	2008	2009	2010	2011	2012
Series	**100**											
BALANCE OF PRIMARY INCOMES	22459.0	26336.0	29811.0	31842.0	43860.0							
	II.2 Secondary distribution of income account - Resources											
BALANCE OF PRIMARY INCOMES	22459.0	26336.0	29811.0	31842.0	43860.0							
Social contributions	...	...	...	...	...							
Social benefits other than social transfers in kind	96.0	107.0	110.0	129.0	129.0							
Other current transfers	1474.0	1630.0	1803.0	1636.0	1690.0							
	II.2 Secondary distribution of income account - Uses											
Current taxes on income, wealth, etc.	...	...	...	...	...							
Social contributions	...	...	...	...	...							
Social benefits other than social transfers in kind	...	...	...	...	...							
Other current transfers	5687.0	5948.0	6021.0	9632.0	10634.0							
GROSS DISPOSABLE INCOME	18342.0	22125.0	25703.0	23975.0	35045.0							
	II.4.1 Use of disposable income account - Resources											
GROSS DISPOSABLE INCOME	18342.0	22125.0	25703.0	23975.0	35045.0							
Adjustment for the change in net equity of households on pension funds	18.0	28.0	11.0	32.0	283.0							
	II.4.1 Use of disposable income account - Uses											
Final consumption expenditure	9855.0	12984.0	14131.0	20166.0	28165.0							
Individual consumption expenditure	9855.0	12984.0	14131.0	20166.0	28165.0							
SAVING, GROSS	8505.0	9169.0	11583.0	3841.0	7163.0							
	III.1 Capital account - Changes in liabilities and net worth											
SAVING, GROSS	8505.0	9169.0	11583.0	3841.0	7163.0							
Capital transfers, receivable less payable	...	...	...	...	...							
Capital transfers, receivable	...	...	...	...	...							
Less: Capital transfers, payable	...	...	...	...	...							
Equals: CHANGES IN NET WORTH DUE TO SAVINGS AND CAPITAL TRANSFERS	8141.0	8776.0	11178.0	3464.0	6611.0							
	III.1 Capital account - Changes in assets											
Gross capital formation	1496.0	1605.0	2668.0	3146.0	5192.0							
Gross fixed capital formation	1496.0	1605.0	2668.0	3146.0	5192.0							
Changes in inventories	...	...	...	...	...							
Acquisitions less disposals of valuables	...	...	...	...	...							
Acquisitions less disposals of non-produced non-financial assets	-337.0	-130.0	-123.0	-761.0	-776.0							
NET LENDING (+) / NET BORROWING (-)	7346.0	7694.0	9038.0	1456.0	2747.0							

Republic of Moldova

Source

The National Bureau of Statistics of the Republic of Moldova (NBS), Division of Macroeconomic Statistics and National Accounts is responsible for the production and dissemination of official statistics on the National Accounts of the Republic of Moldova. The latest data was received through the United Nations Economic Commission for Europe (UN/ECE).

Statistical data are disseminated to users via quarterly reports on National Accounts and other publications issued by the NBS:
• "Social-economic development of the Republic of Moldova";
• various quarterly newsletters, statistical yearbooks and publications on national accounts, as presented on the official website of the NBS: www.statistica.md

The latest statistical publications on National Accounts are:
• National Accounts, 2011;
• Balancing of quarterly GDP with annuals, 1995 -2010.

General

National Accounts of the Republic of Moldova are developed based on methodological principles of the System of National Accounts (SNA) approved in 1993 by the Commission of European Community, International Monetary Fund, Organisation for Economic Cooperation and Development, the United Nations and the World Bank.

According to this standard, the main principle of recording of economic operations is the "accrual method", used for the compilation of the National Accounts of Moldova.

Since 1990, the calculations are performed based on this standard. Data from quarterly and annual statistical surveys, financial, banking and administrative records, a sample survey of agriculture, the Household Budget Survey, the Labour Force Survey and the Structural Business Survey, as well as the statistics of the Balance of Payments are used in the compilation of the accounts.

The methodology of National Accounts (information on concepts, definitions and classifications) is posted on the official website of the NBS: www.statistica.md. Besides, methodological notes are presented in specialised issues, such as “Statistical Yearbook”.

At the beginning of each calendar year, NBS publishes the programme of preliminary and revised data on National Accounts, as part of the Programme of Statistical Works. The calculations of annual indicators are revised over a two year period: the first preliminary version comes eleven months after the end of the reporting period; the second revision is published one year after the end of reporting period. The cycle of revisions is determined and communicated to users. Revised data are published accompanied by explanatory notes. The information on the significant changes in methodologies, primary data and statistical methods is presented well in advance in the annual Programme of Statistical Works.

The main changes in the compilation of National Accounts in Moldova:

• In 2001, the adoption of NACE Classification; since 2004 – revision NACE 1.1;
• In 1993, the currency change from Rubbles to Moldovan Lei;
• The prices of the previous year are taken as a basis for the calculation of the indices of physical volume;
• 2000 was taken as a basic year for the calculations in constant prices.
• Financial year = calendar year.

Methodology:

Overview of GDP Compilation

Three methods are used for the calculation of Gross Domestic Product in the Republic of Moldova:
1) Production approach;
2) Income approach;
3) Expenditure approach.

The production approach is used at the stage of production of goods and services in the GDP calculation. Gross Domestic Product equals the sum of Gross Value Added of all economic activities, by institutional sectors of the economy, plus taxes, excluding subsidies on products.

In the income approach, the Gross Value Added is determined as the sum of primary incomes, distributed by economic units-residents, between the producers of goods and services. This calculation method is auxiliary, due to the fact that gross revenue and mixed income are determined by the difference between the Gross Domestic Product, calculated using the production approach, and the compensation of employees and taxes, excluding subsidies, on production and import.

The expenditure approach calculates GDP as the sum of final consumption, gross capital formation and the balance of exports and imports of goods and services.

GDP is calculated at current market prices and at the prices of the previous year. The integrated table on national accounts and the annual Supply and Use Table for 53 economic activities are compiled on an annual basis.

It should be mentioned that the quarterly GDP calculations are performed on a discrete basis, which are later balanced with the annual data in constant prices and seasonally adjusted. Currently, 2000 is taken as a base year. At the moment, the NBS disseminates time series of quarterly national accounts for 1995-2010. Both the quarterly and annual GDP are adjusted to include estimations of the Non-Observed Economy (formal sector, informal sector and the household production for own consumption, except illegal activity).

Annual National Accounts are internally coordinated. The estimation of GDP by economic activities and components of expenditures are coordinated during a process of detailed balancing based on Supply and Use Tables. The estimations in current prices are harmonised with corresponding data in constant prices and deflators. The estimations in current prices, volume indicators and hidden deflators are harmonised in the framework of the "value=volume x price" relationship. Quarterly GDP estimations are summed up to get the annual estimations.

The concepts, definitions and classifications for quarterly GDP are analogical to those used for annual estimations.

The harmonised times series are available for the 1989–2010 period. Harmonised quarterly data for 1995-2010 are available and published. Time series are revised according to changes in methodologies.

In general, national accounts statistics are aligned with the Balance of Payments (BP) statistics and the statistics of government finance. Currently, the BP is the main source of statistical data on the transactions with the rest of the world, while the account of current operations of BP is used as a "mirror account" in National Accounts. National accounts statistics and data on the sector of general government are also harmonised.

Expenditure Approach

GDP by expenditure includes the expenditures of the institutional sectors in the final consumption of goods and services, gross capital formation and exports, excluding imports, of goods and services.

Final consumption expenditure represents the expenditures of institutional economic units in the purchase of goods and services, used directly to satisfy current individual and collective needs.

Final consumption expenditure of households includes the expenditures on goods and services from own sources; reception of goods and services in kind, and production for own consumption.

The data on population purchases of goods and services represent the primary information for the calculation of household expenditures on final consumption. The following adjustments are made to make these data correspond to expenditure indicators on household final consumption in the SNA:

The following are excluded from the total volume of goods and services purchased by households (statistical data on goods and services)
• Expenditures related to other SNA categories (payment for goods by social protection agencies, goods for intermediate consumption, jewellery and other valuable goods, payment of work related travel and hotel expenses within the country, services for intermediate consumption, capital services)

The following are added
• Services provided to households, and paid by enterprises (housing and communal services, education, tourist and excursion services, etc.)
• Household expenditure for the purchase of services not considered in the accounts of paid services (lottery services, etc.)
• Changes in debts on housing rent and payment of communal services
• Household consumption of goods and services in kind
• Balance of purchases of goods and services by residents abroad and by non-residents.

Final consumption expenditure of the general government is financed by the National Public Budget, the National Social Insurance House, and resources from the National Company of Medical Insurance.

The expenditure on final consumption of the general government comprises expenditures of institutional units of this sector on goods and services provided by units of other sectors, free of charge or at prices that are not economically significant.

They include:
- the cost of non-market goods and services, provided by institutional units of other sectors free of charge or at prices that are not economically significant;
- the cost of consumption of goods and services purchased by units of the general government from market producers and to be transferred to households without any transformation;
- compensation to households for expenditures on goods and services from budget funds and public extra-budget social funds.
Individual final consumption expenditure of the general government represents the expenditure of the general government institutions for the consumption of goods and services by individual households.

Collective final consumption expenditure of the general government includes the expenditures on services provided from the National Public Budget by enterprises and organisations, which satisfy the needs of society in general and of separate groups of the population.

The calculations are based on the report of implementation of National Public Budget, the report of the National Social Insurance House, and on the report of the National Company of Medical Insurance.

The final consumption expenditure of not-for-profit organisations serving households includes expenditures of social organisations for the consumption of goods and services provided to households free of charge as social transfers in kind. The calculation is based on statistical and administrative information according to the international classification of expenditures of non-for-profit organisations serving households.

Gross fixed capital formation represents the capital investments of resident units in fixed assets to generate revenue by using them in production. The calculation of gross fixed capital formation is performed by the following scheme:

The following are excluded from the capital investments:
• Expenditures that do not increase the value of fixed assets (expenditures on training, building conservation, compensation provided to citizens when buildings belonging to them are demolished on land allotted for construction, etc.);
• The cost of low value, quickly expendable tools and equipment included in the construction estimates.

The following are added:
• Changes in inventories of equipment requiring installation;
• Increases in fixed assets in livestock;
• Expenditures on capital repair of fixed assets;
• Acquisition of equipment and inventory by state financed organisations;
• Acquisition of books for libraries;
• Expenditures on the development and acquisition of software and databases;
• Acquisition of originals literary works of art;

The sources of information used to asses the gross fixed capital formation are investment data and the implementation report of the National Public Budget.

Changes in inventories represent the difference in stocks at the beginning and at the end of the period. Stocks represent the goods not included in the gross fixed capital formation, and available in the enterprise. Based on the data of bookkeeping balance, the changes in inventories are broken down in three groups: producer inventories, consumer inventories and trade inventories. In order to exclude the influence of price changes on the calculation of changes in inventories, a special computation method is used, which consists in assessing stocks at the beginning and end of reporting period in average prices of the reporting period. It should be mentioned that all indices are calculated on the same basis.

Households (as consumers) do not have inventories. Central government and non-commercial organisations serving households, providing non-market services, do not have inventories except the strategic ones.

The volume of export and import of goods and services is determined on the basis of Balance of Payments of the Republic of Moldova, and the current account of the Balance of Payments is used as a “mirror” account for the national accounts.

Income Approach

Compensation of employees covers all types of work remuneration including various premiums, copayments accrued in cash or in kind. It is calculated before the payment of contributions to social insurance funds, income taxes and other deductions according to legislation. The goods and services paid to employees are estimated in market prices in case of remuneration in kind.

The calculation of compensation of employees is performed based on the statistical and administrative data taking into account the non-observed economic activity.

Actual payments for social insurance include the payments by employers to the Pension Fund and the social insurance funds, and are determined as the amount of payments to the funds by all types of social insurance. The calculation is based on structural business survey, the implementation of National Public Budget and the reports of corresponding funds of social insurance.

Imputed contributions of employers to social insurance funds are paid by employers, at their own expense without involving a third party, directly to their employees, ex-employees or the family members that are entitled to.

Other production related taxes include the payments of enterprises and organisations to budgetary and non-budgetary funds, related to production factors, as well as payments for licences and permits to perform a production activity and other compulsory payments, necessary for the production activity of resident units.

Other production related subsidies are received by enterprises from the bodies of central administration in connection to their production activity.

The calculation of production related taxes and subsidies is based on the data on the implementation of National Public Budget.

The Gross Operating Surplus and Mixed Income are the balancing items.

Production Approach

GDP using the production approach is calculated as the sum of Gross Value Added of all institutional sectors of economy and all economic activities in basic prices, including the taxes on products excluding the subsidies on products.

The output of goods and services includes the value of goods and services, which are the result of production activity of resident-units during the reporting period. The Non-Observed Economic activity is included as well.

Market production is estimated based on the direct data on production output (works, services) or revenues from sales. The non-market production for own final consumption is estimated in market prices on similar goods and services, or by current expenditures for their production.

A specially developed and implemented statistical survey 5-C “Enterprise expenditures”, where every reporting unit presents the volume of executed works and expenditures (detailed description) for the production of that volume is used to determine the production and intermediate consumption by economic activities. The volume for agricultural and industrial production and constructions is verified with the data from other sources received from branch statistics.

Non-market production and intermediate consumption is calculated from the implementation of National Public Budget.
Intermediate consumption includes the expenditures on goods, material and non-material services, used by institutional units in the production process.

Gross Value Added is calculated by balancing method, as the difference between the production and the intermediate consumption. The calculations are presented in basic prices. Gross Value Added is corrected with the payment of financial intermediation services, which is not distributed between the users of these services.

Other taxes on products are calculated proportionally to the cost of goods or services, produced, sold or imported by residents.

Other subsidies on products are paid proportionally to the quantity or cost of goods and services produced, sold or imported by residents. Taxes and subsidies on products are calculated based on the data on implementation of the National Public Budget.

The calculation of indicators on production, intermediate consumption and Gross Value Added is performed by economic activities according to NACE Rev. 1.1. The calculations are performed by institutional sectors of the economy.

Overview of the Compilation of the Integrated Economic Accounts

Currently, the System of National Accounts of Moldova includes the following accounts:

- account of goods and services;
- production account;
- income account;
- primary distribution of income account;
- secondary distribution of income account;
- use of gross disposable income account;
- redistribution of in kind account;
- adjusted gross disposable income;
- capital account;
- Rest of the world account.

The accounts are balanced with balancing items.

The accounts are produced for the economy as a whole, by economic activities and institutional sectors:

- Non-financial corporations;
- Financial corporations;
- General government;
- Households;
- Non-commercial institutions serving households.

The Rest of the world account is produced to reflect the operations with non-resident units, gathering all institutional non-resident units that are involved in economic relations with resident units. The “Rest of the world account” includes institutional non-resident units located on the geographic territory of Moldova. The “Rest of the world account” is based on Balance of payments data, produced by the Central Bank of Moldova.

Linking of indicators of institutional sectors accounts is performed in an integrated table, which reflects main Intersectoral economic flows.

Table 1.1 Gross domestic product by expenditures at current prices

Series 200: 1993 SNA, Moldovan leu, Western calendar year — **Data in millions**

	2001	2002	2003	2004	2005	2006	2007	2008	2009	2010	2011	2012
Series	**200**											
Expenditures of the gross domestic product												
Final consumption expenditure	19262.7	23289.3	30450.6	33297.7	41368.4	50972.5	60618.1	71451.4	68574.0	83240.3	96090.5	102953.9
Household final consumption expenditure	16384.7	18492.9	24711.3	28125.2	34694.1	41360.3	49178.3	57804.4	53352.6	66051.8	78104.1	83372.9
NPISHs final consumption expenditure	141.7	234.0	304.0	398.4	485.2	667.5	781.7	802.4	861.0	1257.8	1402.8	1509.3
General government final consumption expenditure	2736.3	4562.4	5435.3	4774.1	6189.1	8944.8	10658.1	12844.5	14360.5	15930.7	16583.6	18071.7
Individual consumption expenditure	1784.6	2718.6	3450.0	2609.6	3337.6	5704.3	6730.9	8581.7	10177.5	11667.2	13044.0	12877.6
Collective consumption expenditure	951.7	1843.8	1985.3	2164.5	2851.5	3240.5	3927.2	4262.8	4183.0	4263.4	3539.6	5194.1
Gross capital formation	4435.6	4885.6	6401.4	8443.4	11606.4	14656.1	20359.8	24683.0	13984.6	16910.7	19904.0	20537.3
Gross fixed capital formation	3190.0	3681.8	5127.3	6786.8	9257.9	12691.5	18221.7	21391.4	13655.0	16262.6	19178.8	20540.6
Changes in inventories	1245.7	1203.9	1274.1	1656.5	2348.5	1964.6	2138.1	3291.6	329.7	648.1	725.2	-3.2
Acquisitions less disposals of valuables	...	...	...	...	...	...	...	...	...	...	...	...
Exports of goods and services	9536.3	11833.7	14724.6	16398.4	19264.1	20254.0	24353.6	25684.0	22281.8	28197.2	37033.6	38457.5

	2001	2002	2003	2004	2005	2006	2007	2008	2009	2010	2011	2012
Series	**200**											
Exports of goods	7507.5	8973.7	11717.4	12817.4	14728.4	14490.6	16505.4	17019.5	14835.1	19549.7	26708.5	27004.7
Exports of services	2028.8	2860.0	3007.2	3581.1	4535.7	5763.4	7848.3	8664.5	7446.6	8647.6	10325.1	11452.8
Less: Imports of goods and services	14183.0	17452.7	23957.6	26107.7	34587.1	41128.2	51901.9	58896.8	44410.6	56462.7	70679.4	74101.4
Imports of goods	12423.8	14117.6	21288.6	23298.9	31079.7	36997.8	44311.2	50364.6	36476.9	46952.6	60317.6	62452.7
Imports of services	1759.3	3335.1	2669.0	2808.8	3507.4	4130.4	7590.7	8532.2	7933.7	9510.1	10361.8	11648.6
Equals: GROSS DOMESTIC PRODUCT	19051.5	22555.9	27618.9	32031.8	37651.9	44754.4	53429.6	62921.5	60429.8	71885.5	82348.7	87847.3[a]

[a] Data for this year refers to preliminary data.

Table 1.2 Gross domestic product by expenditures at constant prices

Series 200: 1993 SNA, Moldovan leu, Western calendar year **Data in millions**

	2001	2002	2003	2004	2005	2006	2007	2008	2009	2010	2011	2012
Series	**200**											
Base year	**2000**	**2001**	**2002**	**2003**	**2004**	**2005**	**2006**	**2007**	**2008**	**2009**	**2010**	**2011**
Expenditures of the gross domestic product												
Final consumption expenditure	17220.8	21125.5	26864.9	31057.1	37883.4	44687.6	52955.3	64069.8	66494.7	73600.9	89338.7	96932.5
Household final consumption expenditure	14893.5	17344.5	21916.7	26248.5	31970.3	37408.7	42832.6	52053.3	53117.4	58242.8	72271.9	78857.8
NPISHs final consumption expenditure	125.9	216.0	286.4	329.6	444.6	521.4	703.2	821.4	794.4	1155.6	1292.8	1403.2
General government final consumption expenditure	2201.5	3565.1	4661.7	4479.0	5468.5	6757.4	9419.5	11195.0	12583.0	14202.5	15774.1	16671.5
Individual consumption expenditure	1434.0	2198.8	2691.5	2364.1	2884.9	3954.9	5964.8	6971.4	8787.6	10479.1	11792.6	12294.8
Collective consumption expenditure	767.5	1366.3	1970.3	2114.9	2583.6	2802.5	3454.7	4223.6	3795.4	3723.4	3981.5	4376.7
Gross capital formation	4035.7	4482.3	5547.0	7071.0	9972.6	13023.1	17881.8	21749.1	15102.6	16517.6	19121.2	19346.9
Gross fixed capital formation	2900.8	3372.4	4365.4	5545.8	7766.9	11230.5	15929.7	18623.2	14790.0	15997.0	18370.6	19258.4
Changes in inventories	1135.0	1109.9	1181.6	1525.3	2205.7	1792.6	1952.1	3125.9	312.6	520.6	750.7	88.4
Acquisitions less disposals of valuables	...	...	...	...	...	...	...	...	...	...	...	...
Exports of goods and services	9312.9	11345.0	14107.7	16344.9	18803.0	19475.0	22382.8	25182.7	22577.5	25340.4	35925.9	37867.6
Exports of goods	7367.2	9147.5	11179.5	12953.7	14477.3	14490.6	15164.6	15061.5	15615.9	17569.0	25930.5	27154.8
Exports of services	1945.7	2197.5	2928.3	3391.2	4325.7	4984.4	7218.2	10121.2	6961.6	7771.4	9995.3	10712.9
Less: Imports of goods and services	13566.1	16413.5	22469.8	24820.4	32224.4	37732.3	47123.6	53384.4	45022.0	50742.1	67600.9	72470.7
Imports of goods	11866.5	14563.8	19871.0	21913.1	28884.4	33905.4	40232.9	43417.8	37605.1	42195.6	57445.3	61339.1
Imports of services	1699.6	1849.6	2598.9	2907.4	3340.0	3826.9	6890.7	9966.6	7416.9	8546.6	10155.6	11131.6
Equals: GROSS DOMESTIC PRODUCT	17003.4	20539.4	24049.8	29652.6	34434.6	39453.4	46096.3	57617.2	59152.8	64716.7	76784.9	81676.3[a]

[a] Data for this year refers to preliminary data.

Table 1.3 Relations among product, income, savings, and net lending aggregates

Series 200: 1993 SNA, Moldovan leu, Western calendar year **Data in millions**

	2001	2002	2003	2004	2005	2006	2007	2008	2009	2010	2011	2012
Series	**200**											
GROSS DOMESTIC PRODUCT	19051.5	22555.9	27618.9	32031.8	37651.9	44754.4	53429.6	62921.5	60429.8	71885.5	82348.7	87847.3[a]
Plus: Compensation of employees - from and to the rest of the world, net	2401.1	3252.7	4090.0	5469.2	6013.7	6879.5	7134.5	7892.1	5557.8	8282.3	10105.4	...
Plus: Compensation of employees - from the rest of the world	2871.2	3644.3	4619.5	5900.1	6557.7	7541.3	7813.9	8713.5	6295.5	9012.0	10525.8	...
Less: Compensation of employees - to the rest of the world	470.1	391.6	529.5	430.9	544.0	661.7	679.4	821.4	737.6	729.7	420.4	...
Plus: Property income - from and to the rest of the world, net	-968.9	-1003.8	-871.4	-1087.1	-925.3	-1608.0	-2154.4	-1716.1	-2154.0	-2283.4	-3475.1	...
Plus: Property income - from the rest of the world	156.5	114.7	122.5	123.8	243.0	431.7	734.1	653.8	293.2	227.9	333.4	...
Less: Property income - to the rest of the world	1125.4	1118.5	993.8	1210.9	1168.3	2039.7	2888.5	2369.8	2447.2	2511.3	3808.5	...
Sum of Compensation of employees and property income - from and to the rest of the world, net	1432.2	2248.9	3218.6	4382.1	5088.4	5271.5	4980.1	6176.0	3403.8	5998.9	6630.3	...
Plus: Sum of Compensation of employees and property income - from the rest of the world	3027.7	3759.0	4741.9	6023.9	6800.7	7973.0	8548.0	9367.3	6588.7	9239.9	10859.2	...
Less: Sum of Compensation of employees and property income - to the rest of the world	1595.5	1510.1	1523.4	1641.9	1712.3	2701.4	3567.9	3191.3	3184.9	3241.0	4228.9	...
Plus: Taxes less subsidies on production and imports - from and to the rest of the world, net	...	...	...	...	...	...	...	...	...	...	...	...
Equals: GROSS NATIONAL INCOME	20483.7	24804.7	30837.5	36413.8	42740.3	50025.9	58409.7	69097.5	63833.6	77884.3	88979.0	...
Plus: Current transfers - from and to the rest of the world, net	2002.6	2101.4	4237.2	4495.9	7191.9	10279.2	13819.0	16381.5	13040.7	15671.7	17124.6	...
Plus: Current transfers - from the rest of the world	2236.4	2302.0	4620.4	4928.7	7735.2	11067.5	14787.1	17540.0	14187.5	16730.7	18291.7	...
Less: Current transfers - to the rest of the world	233.8	200.6	383.2	432.8	543.3	788.3	968.1	1158.5	1146.8	1059.0	1167.1	...
Equals: GROSS NATIONAL DISPOSABLE INCOME	22486.4	26906.1	35074.7	40909.8	49932.1	60305.1	72228.6	85479.1	76874.3	93556.0	106103.7	...
Less: Final consumption expenditure / Actual final consumption	19262.7	23289.3	30450.6	33297.7	41368.4	50972.5	60618.1	71451.4	68574.0	83240.3	96090.5	...
Equals: SAVING, GROSS	3223.7	3616.9	4624.1	7612.1	8563.7	9332.6	11610.6	14027.7	8300.3	10315.7	10013.2	...
Plus: Capital transfers - from and to the rest of the world, net	-25.8	-207.9	-178.1	-68.1	-48.4	-46.7	275.0	238.9	399.5	233.4	221.6	...
Plus: Capital transfers - from the rest of the world	14.3	11.0	48.5	130.8	230.2	332.8	456.4	486.8	731.5	749.2	794.7	...
Less: Capital transfers - to the rest of the world	40.1	218.9	226.7	198.8	278.6	379.4	181.4	248.0	332.1	515.9	573.1	...
Less: Gross capital formation	4435.6	4885.6	6401.4	8443.4	11606.4	14656.1	20359.8	24683.0	13984.6	16910.7	19904.0	...
Less: Acquisitions less disposals of non-produced non-financial assets	...	...	...	...	...	...	...	...	...	...	-93.0	...
Equals: NET LENDING (+) / NET BORROWING (-) OF THE NATION	-1237.8	-1476.7	-1955.4	-899.4	-3091.1	-5370.2	-8474.2	-10416.4	-5284.9	-6361.6	-9576.3	...
	Net values: Gross National Income / Gross National Disposable Income / Saving Gross less Consumption of fixed capital											
Less: Consumption of fixed capital	...	...	...	...	...	...	...	...	...	...	...	...
Equals: NET NATIONAL INCOME	...	...	...	...	...	...	...	...	...	...	...	...

	2001	2002	2003	2004	2005	2006	2007	2008	2009	2010	2011	2012
Series	**200**											
Equals: NET NATIONAL DISPOSABLE INCOME	...	...	...	...	...	...	...	...	...	...	...	...
Equals: SAVING, NET	...	...	...	...	...	...	...	...	...	...	...	...

[a] Data for this year refers to preliminary data.

Table 2.1 Value added by industries at current prices (ISIC Rev. 3)

Series 200: 1993 SNA, Moldovan leu, Western calendar year

Data in millions

	2001	2002	2003	2004	2005	2006	2007	2008	2009	2010	2011	2012
Series	**200**											
Industries												
Agriculture, hunting, forestry; fishing	4271.4	4741.7	5062.1	5633.4	6174.9	6488.8	5333.9	5544.0	5134.5	8657.4	10095.2	9585.8
Agriculture, hunting, forestry	4260.8	4729.9	5048.2	5619.0	6158.1	6475.0	5316.6	5524.9	5110.9	8633.4	10068.6	9553.6
Fishing	10.5	11.8	13.9	14.4	16.8	13.9	17.3	19.1	23.6	24.0	26.6	32.2
Mining and quarrying	35.6	49.6	70.4	106.0	143.7	224.4	262.6	315.1	241.2	270.0	348.8	380.6
Manufacturing	3005.3	3352.4	4265.3	4650.8	5022.0	5599.2	6300.2	7093.9	6390.8	7618.9	9354.7	9968.6
Electricity, gas and water supply	523.3	498.6	524.4	711.7	770.1	757.2	1053.1	1328.1	1398.8	1645.8	1814.8	1958.5
Construction	583.5	665.3	811.6	1101.2	1257.0	1776.5	2585.9	3115.0	2108.7	2437.5	2719.9	3070.7
Wholesale, retail trade, repair of motor vehicles, motorcycles and personal and households goods; hotels and restaurants	2453.9	2680.6	3227.6	3693.9	4327.1	5613.7	7325.8	8993.7	8763.8	10124.2	12125.7	13361.9
Wholesale, retail trade, repair of motor vehicles, motorcycles and personal and household goods	2287.2	2488.1	2966.8	3383.9	3928.6	5144.8	6713.8	8148.6	7954.1	9212.9	11119.2	12250.5
Hotels and restaurants	166.7	192.5	260.8	310.0	398.6	468.9	612.0	845.1	809.7	911.3	1006.5	1111.4
Transport, storage and communications	1974.3	2254.5	2977.0	3780.2	4603.9	5288.7	6582.0	7601.1	7226.0	8099.2	9001.6	9481.2
Land transport; transport via pipelines, water transport; air transport; Supporting and auxiliary transport activities; activities of travel agencies	1191.6	1250.4	1631.0	2006.1	2158.1	2391.6	2999.2	3684.5	3073.2	3472.1	4076.1	4357.1
Post and telecommunications	782.8	1004.1	1346.0	1774.1	2445.8	2897.0	3582.8	3916.5	4152.8	4627.0	4925.6	5124.2
Financial intermediation; real estate, renting and business activities	1819.1	2165.7	2680.6	3508.7	4156.3	5228.2	6935.6	8971.1	9034.8	9932.2	10977.6	11812.1
Financial intermediation	862.5	979.1	1251.9	1516.9	1726.8	2224.8	3223.3	3781.2	3850.9	4105.6	4135.6	4186.5
Real estate, renting and business activities	956.6	1186.6	1428.7	1991.8	2429.5	3003.5	3712.3	5189.9	5183.9	5826.7	6841.9	7625.6
Public administration and defence; compulsory social security	671.1	1269.7	1379.3	1337.7	1607.4	2101.1	2453.1	2642.0	2857.0	2740.4	3038.4	3406.2
Education; health and social work; other community, social and personal services	1845.8	2438.9	3091.0	3679.6	4257.3	5282.0	6665.3	7342.0	8487.0	9727.1	10565.5	11919.7
Education	964.8	1231.1	1575.9	1734.9	2109.7	2632.0	3058.0	3523.3	4250.4	4837.1	5184.0	5724.1
Health and social work	484.0	824.6	1022.1	1305.9	1374.4	1582.1	2033.3	2379.5	2685.4	3007.5	3310.7	3671.6
Other community, social and personal services	397.0	383.2	493.0	638.7	773.2	1067.9	1574.0	1439.2	1551.2	1882.5	2070.8	2524.1
Private households with employed persons	22.7	34.8	80.7	44.3	53.0	95.4	131.1	136.6	151.5	166.6	121.7	121.1
Equals: VALUE ADDED, GROSS, in basic prices	17206.0	20152.0	24170.1	28247.4	32372.8	38455.2	45628.7	53082.7	51794.0	61419.5	70164.0	75066.4
Less: Financial intermediation services indirectly measured (FISIM)	432.9	462.7	647.0	729.8	756.9	1116.5	1215.8	1309.1	984.8	1498.8	1774.5	1746.6

	2001	2002	2003	2004	2005	2006	2007	2008	2009	2010	2011	2012
Series	**200**											
Plus: Taxes less Subsidies on products	2278.5	2866.6	4095.9	4514.2	6035.9	7415.6	9016.7	11148.0	9620.6	11964.8	13959.1	14527.5
Plus: Taxes on products	2372.2	2974.8	4220.2	4775.3	6401.6	7929.7	9816.4	11823.4	10076.4	12349.2	14376.2	14911.9
Less: Subsidies on products	93.8	108.3	124.3	261.1	365.6	514.1	799.7	675.4	455.8	384.4	417.0	384.4
Equals: GROSS DOMESTIC PRODUCT	19051.5	22555.9	27618.9	32031.8	37651.9	44754.4	53429.6	62921.5	60429.8	71885.5	82348.7	87847.3[a]

[a] Data for this year refers to preliminary data.

Table 2.2 Value added by industries at constant prices (ISIC Rev. 3)

Series 200: 1993 SNA, Moldovan leu, Western calendar year **Data in millions**

	2001	2002	2003	2004	2005	2006	2007	2008	2009	2010	2011	2012
Series	**200**											
Base year	**2000**	**2001**	**2002**	**2003**	**2004**	**2005**	**2006**	**2007**	**2008**	**2009**	**2010**	**2011**
	Industries											
Agriculture, hunting, forestry; fishing	4371.0	4487.9	4224.0	6093.5	5717.1	6000.5	4220.7	7528.5	4992.5	5514.1	9104.1	7738.0
Agriculture, hunting, forestry	4359.8	4476.1	4208.7	6078.3	5703.2	5983.8	4204.7	7510.4	4971.3	5495.9	9078.4	7707.6
Fishing	11.3	11.8	15.4	15.2	14.0	16.7	16.0	18.1	21.2	18.1	25.7	30.4
Mining and quarrying	28.5	44.8	60.1	89.7	113.0	177.7	234.0	274.7	221.9	258.8	345.9	355.8
Manufacturing	2407.1	3092.1	3950.0	4599.1	4769.4	4806.3	5528.4	6372.0	5539.0	7077.1	8580.8	9447.4
Electricity, gas and water supply	360.0	421.0	513.8	528.9	783.5	816.3	764.9	1024.0	1240.2	1413.0	1584.7	1768.3
Construction	538.6	616.6	776.7	1033.8	1124.3	1488.0	2152.8	2594.1	2281.2	2376.8	2484.9	2766.5
Wholesale, retail trade, repair of motor vehicles, motorcycles and personal and household goods; hotels and restaurants	2147.6	2532.4	2884.9	3093.2	3872.0	4572.0	6499.1	7991.3	8896.5	9463.5	11249.0	12648.0
Wholesale, retail trade, repair of motor vehicles, motorcycles and personal and household goods	2020.0	2364.1	2647.8	2846.0	3523.8	4205.4	5993.5	7312.2	8143.6	8626.5	10336.3	11586.2
Hotels and restaurants	127.6	168.3	237.1	247.2	348.2	366.6	505.6	679.1	752.8	836.9	912.7	1061.9
Transport, storage and communications	1666.0	2160.6	2456.5	3131.1	4356.1	5289.9	6283.3	6907.2	6944.6	7955.7	8673.2	9258.0
Land transport; transport via piplines, water transport; air transport; Supporting and auxiliary transport activities; activities of travel agencies	956.0	1197.6	1404.4	1752.4	1910.1	2406.4	2700.3	3010.3	2879.4	3335.4	3805.1	4163.0
Post and telecommunications	710.0	963.0	1052.1	1378.7	2446.0	2883.5	3583.1	3896.9	4065.1	4620.3	4868.0	5095.0
Financial intermediation, real estate, renting and business activities	1674.8	2051.3	2390.5	3220.8	3879.2	4380.6	5784.1	7055.3	8723.3	9394.9	10491.0	11371.4
Financial intermediation	850.4	928.0	1089.3	1377.2	1685.2	1825.5	2627.2	3476.7	3827.6	3963.1	4419.4	4275.9
Real estate, renting and business activities	824.3	1123.3	1301.2	1843.6	2194.0	2555.1	3156.9	3578.5	4895.7	5431.8	6071.6	7095.5
Public administration and defence; compulsory social security	545.1	802.0	1318.2	1392.2	1423.8	1615.5	2071.4	2570.0	2730.7	2615.6	2738.4	3045.1
Education; health and social work; other community, social and personal services	1493.5	2053.1	2432.1	2913.4	3743.6	4405.0	6038.6	6525.2	7682.4	9099.0	9826.9	10785.6
Education	829.2	1040.2	1203.5	1535.2	1766.0	2047.8	2770.8	3109.3	3677.2	4431.2	4723.1	5236.2
Health and social work	391.3	640.6	795.4	862.3	1259.2	1462.4	1912.7	2086.7	2518.3	2910.0	3139.7	3412.4
Other community, social and personal services	273.0	372.3	433.2	515.9	718.4	894.8	1355.2	1329.2	1486.9	1757.9	1964.2	2137.0
Private households with employed persons	20.7	33.2	73.1	39.4	49.2	83.2	114.7	117.2	140.0	152.7	111.8	114.3

	2001	2002	2003	2004	2005	2006	2007	2008	2009	2010	2011	2012
Series	**200**											
Base year	**2000**	**2001**	**2002**	**2003**	**2004**	**2005**	**2006**	**2007**	**2008**	**2009**	**2010**	**2011**
Equals: VALUE ADDED, GROSS, in basic prices	15252.9	18295.1	21080.0	26135.0	29831.2	33635.1	39692.2	48959.5	49392.2	55321.1	65190.7	69298.4
Less: Financial intermediation services indirectly measured (FISIM)	418.3	437.9	567.6	665.6	889.4	883.1	1509.6	1542.2	920.3	1346.6	1517.3	1760.7
Plus: Taxes less Subsidies on products	2168.8	2682.2	3537.4	4183.2	5492.8	6701.3	7913.8	10199.8	10680.9	10742.2	13111.5	14138.7
Plus: Taxes on products	2232.7	2770.7	3642.1	4434.2	5809.3	7163.3	8599.4	10829.3	11166.5	11074.1	13505.0	14468.6
Less: Subsidies on products	63.9	88.6	104.7	251.0	316.5	461.9	685.7	629.5	485.6	331.8	393.5	329.9
Equals: GROSS DOMESTIC PRODUCT	17003.4	20539.4	24049.8	29652.6	34434.6	39453.4	46096.3	57617.2	59152.8	64716.7	76784.9	81676.3[a]

[a] Data for this year refers to preliminary data.

Table 2.3 Output, gross value added, and fixed assets by industries at current prices (ISIC Rev. 3) Total Economy

Series 200: 1993 SNA, Moldovan leu, Western calendar year

Data in millions

	2001	2002	2003	2004	2005	2006	2007	2008	2009	2010	2011	2012
Series	**200**											
Output, at basic prices	40304.3	49107.4	60226.6	70811.8	82670.7	97395.3	119502.1	143002.5	127666.4	149858.7	168167.3	175015.0[a]
Less: Intermediate consumption, at purchaser's prices [b]	23531.2	29418.2	36703.6	43294.2	51054.8	60056.6	75089.3	91228.9	76857.2	89938.0	99777.8	101695.2
Equals: VALUE ADDED, GROSS, at basic prices [c]	16773.1	19689.2	23523.0	27517.6	31615.9	37338.7	44412.8	51773.6	50809.2	59920.7	68389.6	73319.8
Compensation of employees	6793.2	8630.3	11569.4	13383.9	15767.6	18985.9	22231.4	27786.8	29196.5	31445.8	34914.4	...
Taxes on production and imports, less Subsidies	290.1	299.9	309.0	377.5	247.4	493.0	108.3	388.1	49.8	317.6	331.0	...
Taxes on production and imports	292.6	317.3	346.7	419.1	525.7	632.5	634.5	926.6	562.4	694.8	694.9	...
Taxes on products	...	...	...	...	...	...	...	...	...	...	...	...
Other taxes on production	292.6	317.3	346.7	419.1	525.7	632.5	634.5	926.6	562.4	694.8	694.9	...
Less: Subsidies	2.6	17.3	37.7	41.5	278.3	139.5	526.3	538.6	512.6	377.1	363.9	...
Subsidies on products	...	...	...	...	...	...	...	...	...	...	...	...
Other subsidies on production	2.6	17.3	37.7	41.5	278.3	139.5	526.3	538.6	512.6	377.1	363.9	...
OPERATING SURPLUS, GROSS	5243.8	5326.2	5807.6	7827.4	9161.5	10748.8	14638.5	15075.4	14121.2	18351.6	22887.5	...
MIXED INCOME, GROSS	4446.0	5432.8	5837.0	5928.7	6439.4	7111.0	7434.5	8523.2	7441.7	9805.6	10256.6	...
Total Economy only: Adjustment for FISIM (if FISIM is not distributed to uses)	432.9	462.7	647.0	729.8	756.9	1116.5	1215.8	1309.1	984.8	1498.8	1774.5	...
Gross capital formation	4435.6	4885.6	6401.4	8443.4	11606.4	14656.1	20359.8	24683.0	13984.6	16910.7	19904.0	...
Gross fixed capital formation	3190.0	3681.8	5127.3	6786.9	9257.9	12691.5	18221.7	21391.4	13655.0	16262.6	19178.8	...
Changes in inventories	1245.7	1203.9	1274.2	1656.5	2348.5	1964.6	2138.1	3291.6	329.7	648.1	725.2	...
Acquisitions less disposals of valuables	...	...	...	...	...	...	...	...	...	...	...	...
Closing stocks of fixed assets (produced assets)	95009.4	100914.5	101890.2	106760.8	112502.0	125225.4	137252.0	155533.6	167613.7	180364.0	199397.8	...
Employment (average, in 1000 persons)	1499.0	1505.0	1356.0	1316.0	1319.0	1257.0	1247.0	1251.0	1184.0	1143.0	1173.0	...

[a] Data for this year refers to preliminary data.
[b] FISIM is added to Intermediate Consumption.
[c] FISIM is deducted from Value added gross.

Table 2.3 Output, gross value added, and fixed assets by industries at current prices (ISIC Rev. 3) Agriculture, hunting, forestry; fishing (A+B)

Series 200: 1993 SNA, Moldovan leu, Western calendar year **Data in millions**

	2001	2002	2003	2004	2005	2006	2007	2008	2009	2010	2011	2012
Series	**200**											
Output, at basic prices	8773.7	9620.3	10493.0	11965.7	12866.4	13956.5	13068.9	16739.8	13594.1	20137.0	22938.7	20019.9
Less: Intermediate consumption, at purchaser's prices	4502.3	4878.7	5430.9	6332.3	6691.6	7467.7	7735.0	11195.8	8459.6	11479.6	12843.5	10434.1
Equals: VALUE ADDED, GROSS, at basic prices	4271.4	4741.7	5062.1	5633.4	6174.9	6488.8	5333.9	5544.0	5134.5	8657.4	10095.2	9585.8
Compensation of employees	639.2	796.1	919.4	997.1	1104.4	976.6	1025.6	1277.7	1149.4	1154.9	1327.5	...
Taxes on production and imports, less Subsidies	144.7	130.8	124.9	126.7	-105.2	-18.1	-289.7	-151.8	-219.4	-47.1	-26.1	...
Taxes on production and imports	147.3	148.2	162.6	168.2	173.2	121.4	120.5	254.0	154.1	190.4	160.6	...
Taxes on products	...	...	...	...	...	...	...	...	...	...	...	...
Other taxes on production	147.3	148.2	162.6	168.2	173.2	121.4	120.5	254.0	154.1	190.4	160.6	...
Less: Subsidies	2.6	17.3	37.7	41.5	278.3	139.5	410.3	405.8	373.5	237.6	186.7	...
Subsidies on products	...	...	...	...	...	...	...	...	...	...	...	...
Other subsidies on production	2.6	17.3	37.7	41.5	278.3	139.5	410.3	405.8	373.5	237.6	186.7	...
OPERATING SURPLUS, GROSS	493.1	458.9	245.7	917.1	858.2	536.4	681.8	-119.3	650.2	2180.2	2716.0	...
MIXED INCOME, GROSS	2994.3	3355.9	3772.0	3592.6	4317.5	4993.9	3916.2	4537.5	3554.3	5369.5	6077.8	...
Gross capital formation	267.6	314.4	-35.0	233.9	382.6	484.8	-22.5	2157.0	638.7	828.8	1037.1	...
Gross fixed capital formation	226.1	115.0	109.4	115.6	141.8	395.3	738.6	933.2	585.2	723.5	853.3	...
Changes in inventories	41.5	199.4	-144.4	118.3	240.8	89.5	-761.1	1223.8	53.5	105.2	183.8	...
Acquisitions less disposals of valuables	...	...	...	...	...	...	...	...	...	...	...	...
Closing stocks of fixed assets (produced assets)	8189.3	7998.0	5477.9	5661.6	5738.9	5865.4	6444.9	7129.5	8619.8	9104.0	10667.5	...
Employment (average, in 1000 persons)	764.0	747.0	583.0	533.0	537.0	422.0	409.0	389.0	334.0	315.0	323.0	...

Table 2.3 Output, gross value added, and fixed assets by industries at current prices (ISIC Rev. 3) Agriculture, hunting and related service activities (01)

Series 200: 1993 SNA, Moldovan leu, Western calendar year **Data in millions**

	2001	2002	2003	2004	2005	2006	2007	2008	2009	2010	2011	2012
Series	**200**											
Output, at basic prices	8742.1	9585.1	10453.3	11937.6	12832.4	13926.3	13031.1	16697.6	13546.5	20090.1	22885.8	19964.9
Less: Intermediate consumption, at purchaser's prices	4481.2	4855.2	5405.1	6318.7	6674.4	7451.3	7714.5	11172.7	8435.7	11456.7	12817.2	10411.3
Equals: VALUE ADDED, GROSS, at basic prices	4260.8	4729.9	5048.2	5619.0	6158.1	6475.0	5316.6	5524.9	5110.9	8633.4	10068.6	9553.6
Compensation of employees	635.1	790.7	907.8	986.8	1091.9	965.9	1016.3	1263.6	1126.7	1135.7	1308.0	...
Taxes on production and imports, less Subsidies	144.5	130.8	124.9	126.4	-105.7	-18.3	-290.1	-153.8	-220.2	-48.1	-28.1	...
Taxes on production and imports	147.0	148.1	162.6	167.9	172.6	121.2	120.2	252.0	153.4	189.4	158.7	...
Taxes on products	...	...	...	...	...	...	...	...	...	...	...	...
Other taxes on production	147.0	148.1	162.6	167.9	172.6	121.2	120.2	252.0	153.4	189.4	158.7	...
Less: Subsidies	2.6	17.3	37.7	41.5	278.3	139.5	410.3	405.8	373.5	237.6	186.7	...

	2001	2002	2003	2004	2005	2006	2007	2008	2009	2010	2011	2012
Series	**200**											
Subsidies on products	...	...	...	...	...	...	...	...	...	...	...	...
Other subsidies on production	2.6	17.3	37.7	41.5	278.3	139.5	410.3	405.8	373.5	237.6	186.7	...
OPERATING SURPLUS, GROSS	492.6	457.7	244.9	915.8	857.9	536.1	681.7	-119.6	650.1	2179.4	2715.9	...
MIXED INCOME, GROSS	2988.7	3350.7	3770.6	3590.0	4314.0	4991.3	3908.6	4534.7	3554.3	5366.5	6072.8	...
Gross capital formation	267.6	314.4	-37.6	233.0	379.0	482.0	-26.3	2151.9	638.2	827.8	1037.9	...
Gross fixed capital formation	226.1	115.0	109.4	115.6	141.8	395.3	738.6	933.2	585.2	723.5	853.3	...
Changes in inventories	41.5	199.4	-146.9	117.4	237.0	86.7	-764.9	1218.7	53.0	104.2	184.6	...
Acquisitions less disposals of valuables	...	...	...	...	...	...	...	...	...	...	...	...
Closing stocks of fixed assets (produced assets)	8021.4	7830.5	5362.7	5497.4	5583.0	5708.1	1161.3	6853.1	8330.9	8928.3	10495.3	...
Employment (average, in 1000 persons)	763.0	745.0	582.0	532.0	536.0	421.0	408.0	388.0	333.0	314.0	322.0	...

Table 2.3 Output, gross value added, and fixed assets by industries at current prices (ISIC Rev. 3) Fishing (B)

Series 200: 1993 SNA, Moldovan leu, Western calendar year — **Data in millions**

	2001	2002	2003	2004	2005	2006	2007	2008	2009	2010	2011	2012
Series	**200**											
Output, at basic prices	31.6	35.2	39.7	28.0	34.0	30.2	37.9	42.1	47.5	46.9	52.9	55.0
Less: Intermediate consumption, at purchaser's prices	21.1	23.4	25.8	13.6	17.2	16.4	20.5	23.0	23.9	22.9	26.3	22.8
Equals: VALUE ADDED, GROSS, at basic prices	10.5	11.8	13.9	14.4	16.8	13.9	17.3	19.1	23.6	24.0	26.6	32.2
Compensation of employees	4.1	5.4	11.6	10.3	12.5	10.7	9.3	14.1	22.7	19.2	19.5	...
Taxes on production and imports, less Subsidies	0.2	0.1	0.0	0.2	0.5	0.2	0.8	2.0	0.8	1.0	1.9	...
Taxes on production and imports	0.2	0.1	0.0	0.2	0.5	0.2	0.4	2.0	0.8	1.0	1.9	...
Taxes on products	...	...	...	...	...	...	...	...	...	...	...	...
Other taxes on production	0.2	0.1	0.0	0.2	0.5	0.2	0.4	2.0	0.8	1.0	1.9	...
Less: Subsidies	...	...	...	...	...	...	...	...	...	...	...	...
OPERATING SURPLUS, GROSS	0.5	1.2	0.8	1.3	0.3	0.3	-0.3	0.3	0.1	0.8	0.1	...
MIXED INCOME, GROSS	5.6	5.1	1.4	2.6	3.5	2.7	7.6	2.8	0.0	3.0	5.1	...
Gross capital formation	...	...	2.6	0.9	3.8	2.8	3.8	5.1	0.5	1.0	-0.8	...
Gross fixed capital formation	...	...	...	...	...	...	...	...	...	...	...	...
Changes in inventories	...	...	2.6	0.9	3.8	2.8	3.8	5.1	0.5	1.0	-0.8	...
Acquisitions less disposals of valuables	...	...	...	...	...	...	...	...	...	...	...	...
Closing stocks of fixed assets (produced assets)	167.8	167.5	115.2	164.2	155.9	157.3	283.6	276.3	288.9	175.7	172.1	...
Employment (average, in 1000 persons)	1.0	2.0	1.0	1.0	1.0	1.0	1.0	1.0	1.0	1.0	1.0	...

Table 2.3 Output, gross value added, and fixed assets by industries at current prices (ISIC Rev. 3) Mining and quarrying (C)

Series 200: 1993 SNA, Moldovan leu, Western calendar year — **Data in millions**

	2001	2002	2003	2004	2005	2006	2007	2008	2009	2010	2011	2012
Series	**200**											
Output, at basic prices	79.2	106.6	153.4	218.4	299.7	472.4	555.4	670.2	515.9	575.6	737.8	789.4
Less: Intermediate consumption, at purchaser's prices	43.7	56.9	83.0	112.5	156.1	248.0	292.8	355.0	274.6	305.5	389.0	408.8
Equals: VALUE ADDED, GROSS, at basic prices	35.6	49.6	70.4	106.0	143.7	224.4	262.6	315.1	241.2	270.0	348.8	380.6
Compensation of employees	24.2	32.8	47.7	60.0	80.5	113.6	147.0	184.6	189.3	197.1	257.1	...
Taxes on production and imports, less Subsidies	1.2	0.7	1.6	3.4	3.8	6.5	6.5	13.8	8.4	10.3	2.2	...
Taxes on production and imports	1.2	0.7	1.6	3.4	3.8	6.5	6.5	13.8	8.4	10.3	2.2	...
Taxes on products	...	...	...	...	...	...	...	...	...	...	...	...
Other taxes on production	1.2	0.7	1.6	3.4	3.8	6.5	6.5	13.8	8.4	10.3	2.2	...
Less: Subsidies	...	...	...	...	...	...	...	...	...	...	...	...
OPERATING SURPLUS, GROSS	9.6	16.1	20.4	42.4	59.2	102.9	109.2	116.8	43.6	62.6	89.4	...
MIXED INCOME, GROSS	0.7	...	0.7	0.2	0.1	1.4	...	...	...	...	...	...
Gross capital formation	...	...	20.9	1.6	5.1	17.8	33.6	31.9	28.7	106.5	100.7	...
Gross fixed capital formation	...	...	...	...	...	...	...	...	...	...	...	...
Changes in inventories	...	...	20.9	1.6	5.1	17.8	33.6	31.9	28.7	106.5	100.7	...
Acquisitions less disposals of valuables	...	...	...	...	...	...	...	...	...	...	...	...
Closing stocks of fixed assets (produced assets)	192.0	200.8	199.2	213.3	264.0	345.0	392.7	446.8	459.9	527.7	640.0	...
Employment (average, in 1000 persons)	2.0	3.0	1.0	1.0	2.0	4.0	4.0	4.0	5.0	5.0	5.0	...

Table 2.3 Output, gross value added, and fixed assets by industries at current prices (ISIC Rev. 3) Manufacturing (D)

Series 200: 1993 SNA, Moldovan leu, Western calendar year — **Data in millions**

	2001	2002	2003	2004	2005	2006	2007	2008	2009	2010	2011	2012
Series	**200**											
Output, at basic prices	11229.5	13743.1	17916.1	19859.2	22730.7	24524.0	27790.2	31411.3	26963.8	32001.0	39016.7	39953.4
Less: Intermediate consumption, at purchaser's prices	8224.2	10390.8	13650.8	15208.4	17708.7	18924.8	21490.0	24317.3	20573.0	24382.1	29662.0	29984.8
Equals: VALUE ADDED, GROSS, at basic prices	3005.3	3352.4	4265.3	4650.8	5022.0	5599.2	6300.2	7093.9	6390.8	7618.9	9354.7	9968.6
Compensation of employees	1518.5	1767.3	2659.2	2854.4	3038.7	3393.6	3816.2	4657.5	4385.9	4482.0	4953.1	...
Taxes on production and imports, less Subsidies	42.3	30.1	32.0	38.9	80.2	94.0	109.2	126.9	77.0	95.1	54.1	...
Taxes on production and imports	42.3	30.1	32.0	38.9	80.2	94.0	109.2	126.9	77.0	95.1	54.1	...
Taxes on products	...	...	...	...	...	...	...	...	...	...	...	...
Other taxes on production	42.3	30.1	32.0	38.9	80.2	94.0	109.2	126.9	77.0	95.1	54.1	...
Less: Subsidies	...	...	...	...	...	...	...	...	...	...	...	...
OPERATING SURPLUS, GROSS	1148.5	910.1	885.0	1184.8	1373.4	1698.0	1786.9	1473.2	1279.9	2274.0	3547.4	...
MIXED INCOME, GROSS	296.1	644.9	689.1	572.7	529.7	413.7	587.8	836.4	648.0	767.8	800.1	...

	2001	2002	2003	2004	2005	2006	2007	2008	2009	2010	2011	2012
Series	**200**											
Gross capital formation	2656.6	2581.5	3716.8	3749.8	5661.2	6633.0	9328.1	8870.7	4559.1	6113.2	7433.2	...
Gross fixed capital formation	1452.4	1577.1	2319.2	2213.1	3558.6	4775.7	6462.6	6843.2	4311.7	5676.8	6992.4	...
Changes in inventories	1204.2	1004.5	1397.6	1536.6	2102.6	1857.3	2865.5	2027.5	247.4	436.3	440.8	...
Acquisitions less disposals of valuables	...	...	...	...	...	...	...	...	...	...	...	...
Closing stocks of fixed assets (produced assets)	15526.8	16466.3	17200.3	18459.9	19333.3	25261.8	26755.8	28416.3	29148.0	30119.5	31088.0	...
Employment (average, in 1000 persons)	137.0	142.0	137.0	135.0	132.0	134.0	128.0	136.0	128.0	121.0	128.0	...

Table 2.3 Output, gross value added, and fixed assets by industries at current prices (ISIC Rev. 3) Electricity, gas and water supply (E)

Series 200: 1993 SNA, Moldovan leu, Western calendar year **Data in millions**

	2001	2002	2003	2004	2005	2006	2007	2008	2009	2010	2011	2012
Series	**200**											
Output, at basic prices	1982.0	2102.8	2157.9	2266.5	2489.5	2400.1	3240.4	4204.5	4416.8	5153.0	5646.8	6026.1
Less: Intermediate consumption, at purchaser's prices	1458.8	1604.1	1633.5	1554.9	1719.3	1642.9	2187.3	2876.4	3018.1	3507.2	3832.0	4067.6
Equals: VALUE ADDED, GROSS, at basic prices	523.3	498.6	524.4	711.7	770.1	757.2	1053.1	1328.1	1398.8	1645.8	1814.8	1958.5
Compensation of employees	354.1	453.8	506.5	588.1	722.1	756.3	937.4	1112.3	1225.8	1336.8	1427.0	...
Taxes on production and imports, less Subsidies	25.2	21.0	11.6	14.7	13.2	0.6	8.5	103.7	62.9	77.7	12.4	...
Taxes on production and imports	25.2	21.0	11.6	14.7	13.2	0.6	8.5	103.7	62.9	77.7	12.4	...
Taxes on products	...	...	...	...	...	...	...	...	...	...	...	...
Other taxes on production	25.2	21.0	11.6	14.7	13.2	0.6	8.5	103.7	62.9	77.7	12.4	...
Less: Subsidies	...	...	...	...	...	...	...	...	...	...	...	...
OPERATING SURPLUS, GROSS	140.8	23.2	6.3	108.9	34.8	0.3	107.2	112.2	110.1	231.2	375.4	...
MIXED INCOME, GROSS	3.3	0.6	...	...	...	...	...	...	...	...	...	...
Gross capital formation	...	...	...	...	...	...	...	8.4	0.0	0.0	0.0	...
Gross fixed capital formation	...	...	...	...	...	...	...	...	...	...	...	...
Changes in inventories	...	...	...	...	...	...	...	8.4	...	...	...	...
Acquisitions less disposals of valuables	...	...	...	...	...	...	...	...	...	...	...	...
Closing stocks of fixed assets (produced assets)	9718.6	13492.2	14277.0	14364.8	14731.6	15210.9	15912.5	19516.2	20417.2	21412.4	22227.4	...
Employment (average, in 1000 persons)	26.0	26.0	26.0	26.0	25.0	23.0	26.0	23.0	22.0	20.0	20.0	...

Table 2.3 Output, gross value added, and fixed assets by industries at current prices (ISIC Rev. 3) Construction (F)

Series 200: 1993 SNA, Moldovan leu, Western calendar year | **Data in millions**

	2001	2002	2003	2004	2005	2006	2007	2008	2009	2010	2011	2012
Series	**200**											
Output, at basic prices	1583.5	2146.2	2951.6	5248.8	6778.8	9712.6	14202.8	17057.0	10645.4	12206.6	13542.7	14936.3
Less: Intermediate consumption, at purchaser's prices	1000.0	1480.9	2139.9	4147.6	5521.8	7936.2	11616.9	13941.9	8536.7	9769.0	10822.8	11865.6
Equals: VALUE ADDED, GROSS, at basic prices	583.5	665.3	811.6	1101.2	1257.0	1776.5	2585.9	3115.0	2108.7	2437.5	2719.9	3070.7
Compensation of employees	335.2	295.6	397.6	562.8	694.5	1049.3	1332.4	1583.4	1187.3	1204.2	1256.9	...
Taxes on production and imports, less Subsidies	5.1	3.3	5.9	7.9	11.7	19.7	14.0	24.1	14.6	18.1	17.3	...
Taxes on production and imports	5.1	3.3	5.9	7.9	11.7	19.7	14.0	24.1	14.6	18.1	17.3	...
Taxes on products	...	...	...	...	...	...	...	...	...	...	...	...
Other taxes on production	5.1	3.3	5.9	7.9	11.7	19.7	14.0	24.1	14.6	18.1	17.3	...
Less: Subsidies	...	...	...	...	...	...	...	...	...	...	...	...
OPERATING SURPLUS, GROSS	189.8	143.5	94.4	144.5	150.8	360.3	469.3	482.4	207.9	357.8	464.2	...
MIXED INCOME, GROSS	53.4	222.9	313.8	386.1	400.0	347.2	770.1	1025.1	698.9	857.5	981.5	...
Gross capital formation	1362.8	1796.2	2503.4	4177.9	5242.0	7087.7	10416.6	12678.4	7950.1	9078.8	10399.8	...
Gross fixed capital formation	1362.8	1796.2	2503.4	4177.9	5242.0	7087.7	10416.6	12678.4	7950.1	9078.8	10399.8	...
Changes in inventories	...	...	...	...	...	...	...	...	...	...	...	...
Acquisitions less disposals of valuables	...	...	...	...	...	...	...	...	...	...	...	...
Closing stocks of fixed assets (produced assets)	2005.3	1884.5	1777.8	1778.2	1922.7	2153.9	2531.8	5555.5	5636.0	4009.6	4767.7	...
Employment (average, in 1000 persons)	43.0	46.0	53.0	52.0	52.0	67.0	76.0	83.0	73.0	67.0	67.0	...

Table 2.3 Output, gross value added, and fixed assets by industries at current prices (ISIC Rev. 3) Wholesale retail trade, repair of motor vehicles, motorcycles, etc.; hotels and restaurants (G+H)

Series 200: 1993 SNA, Moldovan leu, Western calendar year | **Data in millions**

	2001	2002	2003	2004	2005	2006	2007	2008	2009	2010	2011	2012
Series	**200**											
Output, at basic prices	4341.7	5022.9	6284.5	6906.3	8301.4	10793.3	14124.5	17513.2	16974.3	19510.9	23195.3	25304.3
Less: Intermediate consumption, at purchaser's prices	1887.8	2342.3	3056.9	3212.4	3974.3	5179.6	6798.7	8519.6	8210.6	9386.7	11069.6	11942.4
Equals: VALUE ADDED, GROSS, at basic prices	2453.9	2680.6	3227.6	3693.9	4327.1	5613.7	7325.8	8993.7	8763.8	10124.2	12125.7	13361.9
Compensation of employees	650.0	842.8	1249.8	1600.3	2060.7	2414.6	3055.1	4317.0	4499.1	4966.6	5523.6	...
Taxes on production and imports, less Subsidies	31.3	47.4	42.9	74.1	98.0	192.3	191.7	260.9	158.4	195.6	312.5	...
Taxes on production and imports	31.3	47.4	42.9	74.1	98.0	192.3	191.7	260.9	158.4	195.6	312.5	...
Taxes on products	...	...	...	...	...	...	...	...	...	...	...	...
Other taxes on production	31.3	47.4	42.9	74.1	98.0	192.3	191.7	260.9	158.4	195.6	312.5	...
Less: Subsidies	...	...	...	...	...	...	...	...	...	...	...	...
OPERATING SURPLUS, GROSS	863.0	816.5	1108.7	1021.0	1384.4	1978.0	2519.8	3132.3	2303.6	2940.1	4686.5	...
MIXED INCOME, GROSS	909.5	974.0	826.2	998.5	784.1	1028.8	1559.2	1283.5	1802.7	2021.8	1603.2	...

	2001	2002	2003	2004	2005	2006	2007	2008	2009	2010	2011	2012
Series	**200**											
Gross capital formation	...	...	...	...	...	...	...	0.0	0.0	0.0	0.0	...
Closing stocks of fixed assets (produced assets)	4817.9	5386.3	5836.1	6449.6	7412.7	9007.5	11326.3	16470.9	15105.1	16649.3	18949.9	...
Employment (average, in 1000 persons)	164.0	175.0	176.0	179.0	183.0	196.0	198.0	209.0	217.0	213.0	223.0	...

Table 2.3 Output, gross value added, and fixed assets by industries at current prices (ISIC Rev. 3) Transport, storage and communications (I)

Series 200: 1993 SNA, Moldovan leu, Western calendar year **Data in millions**

	2001	2002	2003	2004	2005	2006	2007	2008	2009	2010	2011	2012
Series	**200**											
Output, at basic prices	4955.9	6023.8	8135.8	9622.0	11862.5	13676.8	17180.8	20100.1	17498.3	19580.9	21962.1	23083.8
Less: Intermediate consumption, at purchaser's prices	2981.6	3769.3	5158.8	5841.7	7258.6	8388.1	10598.9	12499.0	10272.3	11481.8	12960.4	13602.6
Equals: VALUE ADDED, GROSS, at basic prices	1974.3	2254.5	2977.0	3780.2	4603.9	5288.7	6582.0	7601.1	7226.0	8099.2	9001.6	9481.2
Compensation of employees	779.1	779.1	1363.7	1576.1	1961.8	2213.2	2458.8	3286.0	3007.3	3164.4	3620.1	...
Taxes on production and imports, less Subsidies	23.7	57.2	74.3	93.0	122.1	137.6	109.4	60.0	36.4	43.1	59.6	...
Taxes on production and imports	23.7	57.2	74.3	93.0	122.1	137.6	109.4	60.0	36.4	45.0	63.7	...
Taxes on products	...	...	...	...	...	...	...	...	...	...	...	...
Other taxes on production	23.7	57.2	74.3	93.0	122.1	137.6	109.4	60.0	36.4	45.0	63.7	...
Less: Subsidies	...	...	...	...	...	...	...	...	...	1.8	4.1	...
Subsidies on products	...	...	...	...	...	...	...	...	...	...	...	...
Other subsidies on production	...	...	...	...	...	...	...	...	...	1.8	4.1	...
OPERATING SURPLUS, GROSS	1076.8	1292.6	1472.5	1908.6	2307.7	2816.2	3833.9	3948.1	3850.1	4555.3	5054.4	...
MIXED INCOME, GROSS	94.8	125.6	66.6	202.6	212.4	121.6	179.8	307.0	332.1	336.3	267.5	...
Gross capital formation	...	...	...	...	...	...	...	0.0	0.0	0.0	0.0	...
Closing stocks of fixed assets (produced assets)	21157.6	14819.6	15652.3	16716.7	18125.4	20359.0	22865.5	21001.1	25324.7	39505.9	33756.3	...
Employment (average, in 1000 persons)	64.0	62.0	68.0	73.0	71.0	65.0	69.0	71.0	68.0	64.0	67.0	...

Table 2.3 Output, gross value added, and fixed assets by industries at current prices (ISIC Rev. 3) Financial intermediation; real estate, renting and business activities (J+K)

Series 200: 1993 SNA, Moldovan leu, Western calendar year **Data in millions**

	2001	2002	2003	2004	2005	2006	2007	2008	2009	2010	2011	2012
Series	**200**											
Output, at basic prices	2916.4	3631.7	4501.2	6127.6	7414.9	9520.1	14016.1	18154.9	18202.5	19983.2	19051.8	20267.8
Less: Intermediate consumption, at purchaser's prices	1097.3	1465.9	1820.6	2618.9	3258.6	4291.9	7080.4	9183.8	9167.7	10051.0	8074.3	8455.7
Equals: VALUE ADDED, GROSS, at basic prices	1819.1	2165.7	2680.6	3508.7	4156.3	5228.2	6935.6	8971.1	9034.8	9932.2	10977.6	11812.1
Compensation of employees	692.3	846.4	1066.7	1330.6	1574.4	1901.7	2553.3	3373.7	3574.9	4030.6	4607.6	...
Taxes on production and imports, less Subsidies	10.5	5.7	12.9	15.7	19.2	21.4	21.8	48.4	20.3	25.1	34.1	...

	2001	2002	2003	2004	2005	2006	2007	2008	2009	2010	2011	2012
Series	**200**											
Taxes on production and imports	10.5	5.7	12.9	15.7	19.2	21.4	21.8	48.4	20.3	25.1	34.1	...
Taxes on products	...	...	...	...	...	...	...	...	...	...	...	...
Other taxes on production	10.5	5.7	12.9	15.7	19.2	21.4	21.8	48.4	20.3	25.1	34.1	...
Less: Subsidies	...	...	...	...	...	...	...	...	...	...	...	...
OPERATING SURPLUS, GROSS	1099.7	1278.1	1569.1	2092.9	2513.7	3264.2	4266.9	5447.5	5381.0	5794.9	6242.4	...
MIXED INCOME, GROSS	16.6	35.6	31.9	69.5	48.9	40.9	93.7	101.5	58.6	81.6	93.5	...
Gross capital formation	148.7	193.4	195.3	280.2	315.5	432.8	603.9	936.6	808.0	783.5	933.3	...
Gross fixed capital formation	148.7	193.4	195.3	280.2	315.5	432.8	603.9	936.6	808.0	783.5	933.3	...
Changes in inventories	...	...	...	...	...	...	...	...	...	...	...	...
Acquisitions less disposals of valuables	...	...	...	...	...	...	...	...	...	...	...	...
Closing stocks of fixed assets (produced assets)	11379.1	18302.0	18606.5	19244.6	14795.2	15605.7	17831.5	21367.8	24754.1	19358.0	30529.3	...
Employment (average, in 1000 persons)	45.0	38.0	36.0	39.0	42.0	46.0	44.0	53.0	55.0	58.0	60.0	...

Table 2.3 Output, gross value added, and fixed assets by industries at current prices (ISIC Rev. 3) Public administration and defense; compulsory social security (L)

Series 200: 1993 SNA, Moldovan leu, Western calendar year **Data in millions**

	2001	2002	2003	2004	2005	2006	2007	2008	2009	2010	2011	2012
Series	**200**											
Output, at basic prices	1109.9	2174.2	2350.1	2374.7	2761.1	3422.0	3950.3	4482.0	4800.6	4590.4	4629.2	5139.5
Less: Intermediate consumption, at purchaser's prices	438.7	904.5	970.8	1037.0	1153.7	1320.9	1497.2	1840.0	1943.6	1849.9	1590.8	1733.3
Equals: VALUE ADDED, GROSS, at basic prices	671.1	1269.7	1379.3	1337.7	1607.4	2101.1	2453.1	2642.0	2857.0	2740.4	3038.4	3406.2
Compensation of employees	571.8	853.0	977.9	979.9	1200.6	1779.0	1926.9	1927.7	2282.9	2260.3	2515.2	...
Taxes on production and imports, less Subsidies	...	...	...	...	...	...	...	...	...	...	...	...
OPERATING SURPLUS, GROSS	99.4	416.7	401.3	357.8	406.8	322.1	526.2	714.3	574.1	480.2	523.2	...
MIXED INCOME, GROSS	...	...	...	...	...	...	...	...	...	...	...	...
Gross capital formation	...	...	...	...	...	...	...	0.0	0.0	0.0	0.0	...
Closing stocks of fixed assets (produced assets)	4238.0	5934.0	5116.4	6270.9	12256.7	12860.1	13467.6	14314.3	15179.1	15658.1	16453.4	...
Employment (average, in 1000 persons)	50.0	53.0	58.0	58.0	58.0	58.0	58.0	57.0	58.0	58.0	58.0	...

Table 2.3 Output, gross value added, and fixed assets by industries at current prices (ISIC Rev. 3) Education; health and social work; other community, social and personal services (M+N+O)

Series 200: 1993 SNA, Moldovan leu, Western calendar year — **Data in millions**

	2001	2002	2003	2004	2005	2006	2007	2008	2009	2010	2011	2012
Series	**200**											
Output, at basic prices	3309.6	4501.0	5202.4	6178.3	7112.7	8822.1	11241.6	12533.1	13903.2	15953.5	17324.5	19373.4
Less: Intermediate consumption, at purchaser's prices	1463.9	2062.1	2111.4	2498.8	2855.4	3540.1	4576.3	5191.1	5416.2	6226.3	6759.0	7453.7
Equals: VALUE ADDED, GROSS, at basic prices	1845.8	2438.9	3091.0	3679.6	4257.3	5282.0	6665.3	7342.0	8487.0	9727.1	10565.5	11919.7
Compensation of employees	1228.9	1873.5	2381.0	2834.8	3329.9	4387.9	4978.6	6067.1	7694.6	8648.8	9426.3	...
Taxes on production and imports, less Subsidies	6.2	3.7	3.0	3.1	4.2	39.0	-63.1	-97.8	-108.9	-100.4	-135.1	...
Taxes on production and imports	6.2	3.7	3.0	3.1	4.2	39.0	52.9	34.9	30.2	37.3	38.0	...
Taxes on products	...	...	...	...	...	...	...	...	...	...	...	...
Other taxes on production	6.2	3.7	3.0	3.1	4.2	39.0	52.9	34.9	30.2	37.3	38.0	...
Less: Subsidies	...	...	...	...	...	...	116.0	132.7	139.1	137.7	173.1	...
Subsidies on products	...	...	...	...	...	...	...	...	...	...	...	...
Other subsidies on production	...	...	...	...	...	...	116.0	132.7	139.1	137.7	173.1	...
OPERATING SURPLUS, GROSS	556.0	523.2	651.2	779.3	829.4	787.0	1553.3	1076.9	705.5	974.2	963.0	...
MIXED INCOME, GROSS	54.6	38.5	55.9	62.3	93.7	68.1	196.6	295.7	195.7	204.6	311.3	...
Gross capital formation	...	...	...	...	...	...	...	...	...	...	...	...
Closing stocks of fixed assets (produced assets)	17784.8	16430.8	17746.8	17601.2	17921.5	18556.1	19723.4	21315.0	22969.9	24019.5	30318.4	...
Employment (average, in 1000 persons)	204.0	209.0	214.0	217.0	214.0	236.0	229.0	221.0	219.0	217.0	219.0	...

Table 2.3 Output, gross value added, and fixed assets by industries at current prices (ISIC Rev. 3) Private households with employed persons (P)

Series 200: 1993 SNA, Moldovan leu, Western calendar year — **Data in millions**

	2001	2002	2003	2004	2005	2006	2007	2008	2009	2010	2011	2012
Series	**200**											
Output, at basic prices	22.7	34.8	80.7	44.3	53.0	95.4	131.1	136.6	151.5	166.6	121.7	121.1
Less: Intermediate consumption, at purchaser's prices	...	...	...	...	...	...	...	...	...	...	...	...
Equals: VALUE ADDED, GROSS, at basic prices	22.7	34.8	80.7	44.3	53.0	95.4	131.1	136.6	151.5	166.6	121.7	121.1
Compensation of employees	...	...	...	...	...	...	...	...	...	...	...	...
Taxes on production and imports, less Subsidies	...	...	...	...	...	...	...	...	...	...	...	...
OPERATING SURPLUS, GROSS	...	...	...	...	...	...	...	...	...	...	...	...
MIXED INCOME, GROSS	22.7	34.8	80.7	44.3	53.0	95.4	131.1	136.6	151.5	166.6	121.7	...
Gross capital formation	...	...	...	...	...	...	...	...	...	...	...	...
Employment (average, in 1000 persons)	...	4.0	4.0	3.0	3.0	5.0	5.0	5.0	5.0	5.0	3.0	...

Table 3.1 Government final consumption expenditure by function at current prices

Series 200: 1993 SNA, Moldovan leu, Western calendar year — **Data in millions**

		2001	2002	2003	2004	2005	2006	2007	2008	2009	2010	2011	2012
Series		**200**											
General public services	a	728.5	1608.2	1658.6	1713.7	2141.6	2595.0	3041.3	3257.7	3300.8	3234.1	2710.0	
Defence		...	...	...	...	...	...	...	...	...	...	...	
Public order and safety		...	...	...	...	...	...	...	...	...	...	...	
Economic affairs	b	332.1	350.2	444.2	569.9	811.8	771.3	997.6	901.2	706.8	956.8	899.4	
Environment protection		...	...	...	...	...	...	...	...	...	...	...	
Housing and community amenities	c	37.4	44.3	59.9	74.5	121.2	152.1	203.2	270.4	333.0	336.2	338.4	
Health		507.4	1027.9	1251.9	183.1	296.3	1820.1	2205.7	3159.0	3543.2	3809.3	4038.8	
Recreation, culture and religion	d	75.0	94.0	148.0	192.0	146.0	250.0	263.8	315.7	356.6	397.3	...	
Education		946.4	1299.5	1696.3	1805.4	2343.2	3061.5	3412.1	4147.1	5249.7	6031.9	6956.2	
Social protection		40.6	66.1	78.1	93.4	126.6	98.7	215.8	501.4	609.1	766.0	831.9	
Plus: (Other functions)		69.0[e]	72.0[e]	98.0[e]	142.0[e]	201.0[e]	197.0[e]	318.6[e]	292.0[e]	261.3[e]	399.0[e]	808.9[f]	
Equals: General government final consumption expenditure		2736.3	4562.4	5435.3	4774.1	6189.1	8944.8	10658.1	12844.6	14360.5	15930.7	16583.6	

[a] Includes Defence.
[b] Includes Agriculture, Transport, and other branches of the economy.
[c] Refers to real estate transactions
[d] Refers to Culture from "Other Services".
[e] Refers to Other Services, excluding Culture.
[f] Refers to Other services.

Table 3.2 Individual consumption expenditure of households, NPISHs, and general government at current prices

Series 200: 1993 SNA, Moldovan leu, Western calendar year — **Data in millions**

	2001	2002	2003	2004	2005	2006	2007	2008	2009	2010	2011	2012
Series	**200**											
Individual consumption expenditure of households												
Food and non-alcoholic beverages	...	...	...	...	9215.0	...	...	...	...	...	...	
Alcoholic beverages, tobacco and narcotics	...	...	...	...	2954.0	...	...	...	...	...	...	
Clothing and footwear	...	...	...	...	1709.0	...	...	...	...	...	...	
Housing, water, electricity, gas and other fuels	...	...	...	...	5410.0	...	...	...	...	...	...	
Furnishings, household equipment and routine maintenance of the house	...	...	...	...	2659.0	...	...	...	...	...	...	
Health	...	...	...	...	1539.0	...	...	...	...	...	...	
Transport	...	...	...	...	3777.0	...	...	...	...	...	...	
Communication	...	...	...	...	1771.0	...	...	...	...	...	...	
Recreation and culture	...	...	...	...	2207.0	...	...	...	...	...	...	
Education	...	...	...	...	522.0	...	...	...	...	...	...	
Restaurants and hotels	...	...	...	...	627.0	...	...	...	...	...	...	
Miscellaneous goods and services	...	...	...	...	1858.0	...	...	...	...	...	...	
Equals: Household final consumption expenditure in domestic market	15901.0	18020.0	24072.0	27582.0	34248.0	40395.0	48569.4	57045.5	52501.4	64834.1	76818.9	

	2001	2002	2003	2004	2005	2006	2007	2008	2009	2010	2011	2012
Series	**200**											
Plus: Direct purchases abroad by residents	978.0	950.0	1241.0	1372.0	1719.0	2139.0	2177.5	2406.3	2183.1	2881.4	3103.5	
Less: Direct purchases in domestic market by non-residents	494.0	477.0	602.0	829.0	1273.0	1174.0	1568.6	1647.4	1331.9	1663.7	1818.2	
Equals: Household final consumption expenditure	16384.7	18492.9	24711.3	28125.2	34694.1	41360.0	49178.3	57804.4	53352.6	66051.8	78104.1	
	Individual consumption expenditure of non-profit institutions serving households (NPISHs)											
Housing	...	...	...	...	...	...	...	...	...	...	...	
Health	18.3	27.3	43.2	54.6	17.4	16.4	20.2	20.9	28.6	26.0	28.5	
Recreation and culture	0.5	0.6	0.9	1.5	3.0	3.0	3.6	6.9	4.4	3.2	3.9	
Education	9.7	10.2	11.7	16.0	21.0	16.9	22.8	29.0	29.8	34.1	36.0	
Social protection	...	...	...	...	...	...	...	...	...	...	...	
Other services	113.2	195.9	248.2	326.3	443.8	631.2	735.1	745.6	798.2	1194.5	1334.4	
Equals: NPISHs final consumption expenditure	141.7	234.0	304.0	398.4	485.2	667.5	781.7	802.4	861.0	1257.8	1402.8	
	Individual consumption expenditure of general government											
Housing	...	...	...	...	...	...	...	...	...	...	...	
Health	507.4	1027.9	1251.9	183.1	296.3	1820.1	2205.7	3159.0	3543.2	3809.3	4038.8	
Recreation and culture	74.7	94.4	147.7	191.8	146.3	250.3	263.8	315.7	356.6	428.5	515.5	
Education	946.4	1299.5	1696.3	1805.4	2343.2	3061.5	3412.1	4147.1	5249.7	6031.9	6956.2	
Social protection	40.6	66.1	78.1	93.4	126.6	98.7	215.8	501.4	609.1	766.0	831.9	
Plus:	215.5	230.7	276.1	335.8	425.2	473.7	633.5	458.5	419.0	631.6	701.7	
Equals: Individual consumption expenditure of general government	1784.6	2718.6	3450.0	2609.6	3337.6	5704.3	6730.9	8581.7	10177.5	11667.2	13044.0	
Equals: Total actual individual consumption	18311.0	21445.5	28465.3	31133.2	38516.9	47731.7	56690.9	67188.6	64391.1	78976.9	92550.9	

Table 4.1 Total Economy (S.1)

Series 200: 1993 SNA, Moldovan leu, Western calendar year

Data in millions

	2001	2002	2003	2004	2005	2006	2007	2008	2009	2010	2011	2012
Series	**200**											
	I. Production account - Resources											
Output, at basic prices (otherwise, please specify)	40304.2	49107.4	60226.6	70811.8	82670.7	97395.3	119502.2	143002.5	127666.4	149858.7	168167.3	
Less: Financial intermediation services indirectly measured (only to be deducted if FISIM is not distributed to uses)	432.9	462.7	647.0	729.8	756.9	1116.5	1215.8	1309.1	984.8	1498.8	1774.5	
Plus: Taxes less Subsidies on products	2278.5	2866.6	4095.9	4514.2	6035.9	7415.6	9016.7	11148.0	9620.6	11964.8	13959.1	
Plus: Taxes on products	2372.2	2974.8	4220.2	4775.3	6401.6	7929.7	9816.4	11823.4	10076.4	12349.2	14376.2	
Less: Subsidies on products	93.8	108.3	124.3	261.1	365.6	514.1	799.7	675.4	455.8	384.4	417.0	
	I. Production account - Uses											
Intermediate consumption, at purchaser's prices [a]	23531.2	29418.1	36703.6	43294.2	51054.8	60056.5	75089.3	91228.9	76857.2	89938.0	99777.8	
GROSS DOMESTIC PRODUCT	19051.5	22555.9	27618.9	32031.8	37651.9	44754.4	53429.6	62921.5	60429.8	71885.5	82348.7	
Less: Consumption of fixed capital	...	...	...	...	...	...	...	...	...	...	...	
NET DOMESTIC PRODUCT	...	...	...	...	...	...	...	...	...	...	...	

	2001	2002	2003	2004	2005	2006	2007	2008	2009	2010	2011	2012
Series	**200**											
	II.1.1 Generation of income account - Resources											
GROSS DOMESTIC PRODUCT	19051.5	22555.9	27618.9	32031.8	37651.9	44754.4	53429.6	62921.5	60429.8	71885.5	82348.7	
	II.1.1 Generation of income account - Uses											
Compensation of employees	6793.2	8630.3	11569.4	13383.9	15767.6	18985.9	22231.4	27786.8	29196.5	31445.8	34914.4	
Taxes on production and imports, less Subsidies	2568.6	3166.5	4404.9	4891.7	6283.3	7908.6	9124.9	11536.1	9670.4	12282.4	14290.1	
Taxes on production and imports	2664.9	3292.1	4566.9	5194.3	6927.3	8562.2	10450.9	12750.1	10638.8	13043.9	15071.0	
Taxes on products	2372.2	2974.8	4220.2	4775.3	6401.6	7929.7	9816.4	11823.4	10076.4	12349.2	14376.2	
Other taxes on production	292.6	317.3	346.7	419.1	525.7	632.5	634.5	926.6	562.4	694.8	694.9	
Less: Subsidies	96.3	125.6	162.0	302.6	644.0	653.6	1326.0	1214.0	968.4	761.5	780.9	
Subsidies on products	93.8	108.3	124.3	261.1	365.6	514.1	799.7	675.4	455.8	384.4	417.0	
Other subsidies on production	2.6	17.3	37.7	41.5	278.3	139.5	526.3	538.6	512.6	377.1	363.9	
OPERATING SURPLUS, GROSS	5243.8	5326.3	5807.6	7827.4	9161.6	10748.8	14638.7	15075.4	14121.2	18351.6	22887.5	
MIXED INCOME, GROSS	4446.0	5432.8	5837.0	5928.7	6439.4	7111.0	7434.5	8523.2	7441.7	9805.6	10256.6	
	II.1.2 Allocation of primary income account - Resources											
OPERATING SURPLUS, GROSS	5243.8	5326.3	5807.6	7827.4	9161.6	10748.8	14638.7	15075.4	14121.2	18351.6	22887.5	
MIXED INCOME, GROSS	4446.0	5432.8	5837.0	5928.7	6439.4	7111.0	7434.5	8523.2	7441.7	9805.6	10256.6	
Compensation of employees	9194.3	11883.0	15659.3	18853.1	21781.3	25865.4	29366.0	35678.9	34754.4	39728.1	45019.8	
Taxes on production and imports, less Subsidies	2568.6	3166.5	4404.9	4891.7	6283.3	7908.6	9124.9	11536.1	9670.4	12282.4	14290.1	
Taxes on production and imports	2664.9	3292.1	4566.9	5194.3	6927.3	8562.2	10450.9	12750.1	10638.8	13043.9	15071.0	
Taxes on products	2372.2	2974.8	4220.2	4775.3	6401.6	7929.7	9816.4	11823.4	10076.4	12349.2	14376.2	
Other taxes on production	292.6	317.3	346.7	419.1	525.7	632.5	634.5	926.6	562.4	694.8	694.9	
Less: Subsidies	96.3	125.6	162.0	302.6	644.0	653.6	1326.0	1214.0	968.4	761.5	780.9	
Subsidies on products	93.8	108.3	124.3	261.1	365.6	514.1	799.7	675.4	455.8	384.4	417.0	
Other subsidies on production	2.6	17.3	37.7	41.5	278.3	139.5	526.3	538.6	512.6	377.1	363.9	
Property income	1396.1	1372.5	1799.0	2467.2	3022.8	4658.5	7380.9	10004.1	8757.6	7629.3	9026.2	
	II.1.2 Allocation of primary income account - Uses											
Property income	2365.0	2376.3	2670.3	3554.4	3948.1	6266.5	9535.3	11720.2	10911.6	9912.7	12501.3	
GROSS NATIONAL INCOME	20483.7	24804.7	30837.5	36413.8	42740.3	50025.9	58409.8	69097.5	63833.6	77884.3	88979.0	
	II.2 Secondary distribution of income account - Resources											
GROSS NATIONAL INCOME	20483.7	24804.7	30837.5	36413.8	42740.3	50025.9	58409.8	69097.5	63833.6	77884.3	88979.0	
Current taxes on income, wealth, etc.	...	...	...	...	...	...	...	...	...	...	...	
Social contributions	...	...	...	...	...	...	...	...	...	...	...	
Social benefits other than social transfers in kind	...	...	...	...	...	...	...	...	...	...	...	
Other current transfers	7409.9	8622.4	12500.9	15348.0	22109.1	28629.3	34535.6	41303.4	41233.7	48769.8	52130.8	
	II.2 Secondary distribution of income account - Uses											
Current taxes on income, wealth, etc.	...	...	...	...	...	...	...	...	...	...	...	
Social contributions	...	...	...	...	...	...	...	...	...	...	...	
Social benefits other than social transfers in kind	...	...	...	...	...	...	...	...	...	...	...	
Other current transfers	5407.2	6521.0	8263.7	10852.1	14917.2	18350.1	20716.7	24921.9	28193.0	33098.1	35006.2	
GROSS DISPOSABLE INCOME	22486.4	26906.1	35074.7	40909.8	49932.1	60305.1	72228.7	85479.1	76874.3	93556.0	106103.7	

	2001	2002	2003	2004	2005	2006	2007	2008	2009	2010	2011	2012
Series	**200**											
	II.4.1 Use of disposable income account - Resources											
GROSS DISPOSABLE INCOME	22486.4	26906.1	35074.7	40909.8	49932.1	60305.1	72228.7	85479.1	76874.3	93556.0	106103.7	
Adjustment for the change in net equity of households on pension funds	-4.8	-4.6	-4.4	-5.2	-4.7	-7.4	-7.5	-5.6	0.4	0.6	0.5	
	II.4.1 Use of disposable income account - Uses											
Final consumption expenditure	19262.7	23289.3	30450.6	33297.7	41368.4	50972.5	60618.1	71451.4	68574.0	83240.3	96090.5	
Individual consumption expenditure	18310.9	21445.5	28465.3	31133.2	38516.9	47732.0	56690.9	67188.6	64391.1	78976.9	92550.9	
Collective consumption expenditure	951.7	1843.8	1985.3	2164.5	2851.5	3240.5	3927.2	4262.8	4183.0	4263.4	3539.6	
Adjustment for the change in net equity of households on pension funds	-4.8	-4.6	-4.4	-5.2	-4.7	-7.4	-7.5	-5.6	0.4	0.6	0.5	
SAVING, GROSS	3223.7	3616.9	4624.1	7612.1	8563.7	9332.6	11610.7	14027.7	8300.3	10315.7	10013.2	
	III.1 Capital account - Changes in liabilities and net worth											
SAVING, GROSS	3223.7	3616.9	4624.1	7612.1	8563.7	9332.6	11610.7	14027.7	8300.3	10315.7	10013.2	
Capital transfers, receivable less payable	-25.8	-207.9	-178.1	-68.1	-48.4	-46.7	275.0	238.9	399.5	233.4	221.6	
Capital transfers, receivable [b]	14.3	11.0	48.5	130.8	230.2	332.8	3353.4	486.8	731.5	749.2	794.7	
Less: Capital transfers, payable [c]	40.1	218.9	226.7	198.8	278.6	379.4	3078.4	248.0	332.1	515.9	573.1	
Equals: CHANGES IN NET WORTH DUE TO SAVING AND CAPITAL TRANSFERS [d]	3197.9	3408.9	4446.0	7544.0	8515.3	9285.9	11885.7	14266.6	8699.7	10549.1	10234.7	
	III.1 Capital account - Changes in assets											
Gross capital formation	4435.6	4885.6	6401.4	8443.4	11606.4	14656.1	20359.8	24683.0	13984.6	16910.7	19904.0	
Gross fixed capital formation	3190.0	3681.8	5127.3	6786.8	9257.9	12691.5	18221.7	21391.4	13655.0	16262.6	19178.8	
Changes in inventories	1245.7	1203.9	1274.1	1656.5	2348.5	1964.6	2138.1	3291.6	329.7	648.1	725.2	
Acquisitions less disposals of valuables	...	...	...	...	...	...	...	...	...	...	...	
Acquisitions less disposals of non-produced non-financial assets	...	...	...	...	...	...	...	...	...	...	-93.0	
NET LENDING (+) / NET BORROWING (-)	-1237.8	-1476.7	-1955.4	-899.4	-3091.1	-5370.2	-8474.1	-10416.4	-5284.9	-6361.6	-9576.3	

[a] FISIM is added to Intermediate Consumption.
[b] Refers to net capital transfers, receivable, from the Rest of the World.
[c] Refers to net capital transfers, payable, to the Rest of the World.
[d] Item does not consider consumption of fixed capital.

Table 4.2 Rest of the world (S.2)

Series 200: 1993 SNA, Moldovan leu, Western calendar year — **Data in millions**

	2001	2002	2003	2004	2005	2006	2007	2008	2009	2010	2011	2012
Series	**200**											
	V.I External account of goods and services - Resources											
Imports of goods and services	14183.0	17452.7	23957.6	26107.7	34587.1	41128.2	51901.9	58896.8	44410.6	56462.7	70679.4	
Imports of goods	12423.8	14117.6	21288.6	23298.9	31079.7	36997.8	44311.2	50364.6	36476.9	46952.6	60317.6	
Imports of services	1759.3	3335.1	2669.0	2808.8	3507.4	4130.4	7590.7	8532.2	7933.7	9510.1	10361.8	
	V.I External account of goods and services - Uses											
Exports of goods and services	9536.3	11833.7	14724.6	16398.4	19264.1	20254.0	24353.6	25684.0	22281.8	28197.2	37033.6	
Exports of goods	7507.5	8973.7	11717.4	12817.4	14728.4	14490.6	16505.4	17019.5	14835.1	19549.7	26708.5	

	2001	2002	2003	2004	2005	2006	2007	2008	2009	2010	2011	2012
Series	**200**											
Exports of services	2028.8	2860.0	3007.2	3581.1	4535.7	5763.4	7848.3	8664.5	7446.6	8647.6	10325.1	
EXTERNAL BALANCE OF GOODS AND SERVICES	4646.8	5619.1	9233.1	9709.3	15323.0	20874.2	27548.3	33212.8	22128.8	28265.5	33645.8	
	V.II External account of primary income and current transfers - Resources											
EXTERNAL BALANCE OF GOODS AND SERVICES	4646.8	5619.1	9233.1	9709.3	15323.0	20874.2	27548.3	33212.8	22128.8	28265.5	33645.8	
Compensation of employees	470.1	391.6	529.5	430.9	544.0	661.7	679.4	821.4	737.6	729.7	420.4	
Taxes on production and imports, less Subsidies	...	...	...	...	...	...	...	...	...	...	...	
Taxes on production and imports	...	...	...	...	...	...	...	...	...	...	...	
Taxes on products	...	...	...	...	...	...	...	...	...	...	...	
Other taxes on production	...	...	...	...	...	...	...	...	...	...	...	
Less: Subsidies	...	...	...	...	...	...	...	...	...	...	...	
Subsidies on products	...	...	...	...	...	...	...	...	...	...	...	
Other subsidies on production	...	...	...	...	...	...	...	...	...	...	...	
Property income	1125.4	1118.5	993.8	1210.9	1168.3	2039.7	2888.5	2369.8	2447.2	2511.3	3808.5	
Current taxes on income, wealth, etc.	...	...	...	...	...	...	...	...	...	...	...	
Social contributions	...	...	...	...	...	...	...	...	...	...	...	
Social benefits other than social transfers in kind	...	...	...	...	...	...	...	...	...	...	...	
Other current transfers	233.8	200.6	383.2	432.8	543.3	788.3	968.1	1158.5	1146.8	1059.0	1167.1	
Adjustment for the change in net equity of households on pension funds	...	...	...	...	...	...	...	...	...	...	...	
	V.II External account of primary income and current transfers - Uses											
Compensation of employees	2871.2	3644.3	4619.5	5900.1	6557.7	7541.3	7813.9	8713.5	6295.5	9012.0	10525.8	
Taxes on production and imports, less Subsidies	...	...	...	...	...	...	...	...	...	...	...	
Taxes on production and imports	...	...	...	...	...	...	...	...	...	...	...	
Taxes on products	...	...	...	...	...	...	...	...	...	...	...	
Other taxes on production	...	...	...	...	...	...	...	...	...	...	...	
Less: Subsidies	...	...	...	...	...	...	...	...	...	...	...	
Subsidies on products	...	...	...	...	...	...	...	...	...	...	...	
Other subsidies on production	...	...	...	...	...	...	...	...	...	...	...	
Property income	156.5	114.7	122.5	123.8	243.0	431.7	734.1	653.8	293.2	227.9	333.4	
Current taxes on income and wealth, etc.	...	...	...	...	...	...	...	...	...	...	...	
Social contributions	...	...	...	...	...	...	...	...	...	...	...	
Social benefits other than social transfers in kind	...	...	...	...	...	...	...	...	...	...	...	
Other current transfers	2236.4	2302.0	4620.4	4928.7	7735.2	11067.5	14787.1	17540.0	14187.5	16730.7	18291.7	
Adjustment for the change in net equity of households on pension funds	...	...	...	...	...	...	...	...	...	...	...	
CURRENT EXTERNAL BALANCE	1212.0	1268.8	1777.3	831.3	3042.8	5323.5	8749.2	10655.3	5684.3	6594.9	9890.9	
	V.III.1 Capital account - Changes in liabilities and net worth											
CURRENT EXTERNAL BALANCE	1212.0	1268.8	1777.3	831.3	3042.8	5323.5	8749.2	10655.3	5684.3	6594.9	9890.9	
Capital transfers, receivable less payable	25.8	207.9	178.1	68.1	48.4	46.7	-275.0	-238.9	-399.5	-233.4	-221.6	
Capital transfers, receivable	40.1	218.9	226.7	198.8	278.6	379.4	181.4	248.0	332.1	515.9	573.1	

	2001	2002	2003	2004	2005	2006	2007	2008	2009	2010	2011	2012
Series	**200**											
Less: Capital transfers, payable	14.3	11.0	48.5	130.8	230.2	332.8	456.4	486.8	731.5	749.2	794.7	
Equals: CHANGES IN NET WORTH DUE TO SAVING AND CAPITAL TRANSFERS	1237.8	1476.7	1955.4	899.4	3091.1	5370.2	8474.2	10416.4	5284.9	6361.6	9669.3	
	V.III.1 Capital account - Changes in assets											
Acquisitions less disposals of non-produced non-financial assets	...	...	...	...	...	...	...	...	...	...	93.0	
NET LENDING (+) / NET BORROWING (-)	1237.8	1476.7	1955.4	899.4	3091.1	5370.2	8474.2	10416.4	5284.9	6361.6	9576.3	

Table 4.3 Non-financial Corporations (S.11)

Series 200: 1993 SNA, Moldovan leu, Western calendar year

Data in millions

	2001	2002	2003	2004	2005	2006	2007	2008	2009	2010	2011	2012
Series	**200**											
	I. Production account - Resources											
Output, at basic prices (otherwise, please specify)	26904.3	31215.9	39522.3	48397.4	56940.7	68912.8	82032.7	96069.7	83538.7	98089.7	116925.8	
	I. Production account - Uses											
Intermediate consumption, at purchaser's prices	17257.2	21025.9	27088.5	31913.1	37952.6	46381.4	55090.7	64597.5	53349.4	61887.9	73477.5	
VALUE ADDED GROSS, in basic prices	9647.1	10190.0	12433.8	16484.3	18988.1	22531.4	26942.0	31472.3	30189.3	36201.8	43448.3	
Less: Consumption of fixed capital	...	...	...	...	...	...	...	...	...	...	...	
VALUE ADDED NET, at basic prices	...	...	...	...	...	...	...	...	...	...	...	
	II.1.1 Generation of income account - Resources											
VALUE ADDED GROSS, at basic prices	9647.1	10190.0	12433.8	16484.3	18988.1	22531.4	26942.0	31472.3	30189.3	36201.8	43448.3	
	II.1.1 Generation of income account - Uses											
Compensation of employees	4836.7	5729.5	7921.7	9968.5	11553.5	13405.9	15899.5	20308.3	20359.2	21907.1	24580.6	
Other taxes less Other subsidies on production	235.6	195.1	159.5	217.3	47.3	337.7	-130.3	106.3	-121.2	106.4	91.3	
Other taxes on production	238.2	212.5	197.2	258.9	325.7	477.2	395.9	644.9	391.4	483.5	455.1	
Less: Other subsidies on production	2.6	17.3	37.7	41.5	278.3	139.5	526.3	538.6	512.6	377.1	363.9	
OPERATING SURPLUS, GROSS	4574.8	4265.4	4352.6	6298.5	7387.2	8787.9	11172.8	11057.7	9951.4	14188.3	18776.5	
	II.1.2 Allocation of primary income account - Resources											
OPERATING SURPLUS, GROSS	4574.8	4265.4	4352.6	6298.5	7387.2	8787.9	11172.8	11057.7	9951.4	14188.3	18776.5	
Property income	95.8	115.5	162.0	193.8	206.4	383.6	433.9	522.8	754.3	709.4	916.2	
	II.1.2 Allocation of primary income account - Uses											
Property income	1037.1	1357.1	1558.9	1866.3	1973.5	3821.7	5385.9	5750.3	5926.8	6432.7	7867.2	
BALANCE OF PRIMARY INCOMES	3633.4	3023.8	2955.7	4626.0	5620.1	5349.8	6220.8	5830.1	4778.8	8465.0	11825.5	
	II.2 Secondary distribution of income account - Resources											
BALANCE OF PRIMARY INCOMES	3633.4	3023.8	2955.7	4626.0	5620.1	5349.8	6220.8	5830.1	4778.8	8465.0	11825.5	
Social contributions	...	...	...	...	...	...	...	...	...	...	...	
Other current transfers	375.1	286.0	242.2	716.6	1010.2	2427.5	4041.6	5572.6	5925.9	6088.9	2547.4	
	II.2 Secondary distribution of income account - Uses											
Current taxes on income, wealth, etc.	...	...	...	...	...	...	...	...	...	...	...	

	2001	2002	2003	2004	2005	2006	2007	2008	2009	2010	2011	2012
Series	**200**											
Social benefits other than social transfers in kind	...	...	...	...	...	...	...	...	...	...	...	
Other current transfers	933.2	729.9	932.3	1441.9	1815.4	2295.9	2718.7	2258.8	1717.5	1679.3	1403.3	
GROSS DISPOSABLE INCOME	3075.3	2579.9	2265.6	3900.7	4814.9	5481.4	7543.7	9143.9	8987.2	12874.5	12969.7	
	II.4.1 Use of disposable income account - Resources											
GROSS DISPOSABLE INCOME	3075.3	2579.9	2265.6	3900.7	4814.9	5481.4	7543.7	9143.9	8987.2	12874.5	12969.7	
	II.4.1 Use of disposable income account - Uses											
Adjustment for the change in net equity of households on pension funds	...	...	...	...	...	...	...	...	...	...	...	
SAVING, GROSS	3075.3	2579.9	2265.6	3900.7	4814.9	5481.4	7543.7	9143.9	8987.2	12874.5	12969.7	
	III.1 Capital account - Changes in liabilities and net worth											
SAVING, GROSS	3075.3	2579.9	2265.6	3900.7	4814.9	5481.4	7543.7	9143.9	8987.2	12874.5	12969.7	
Capital transfers, receivable less payable	155.3	192.4	206.2	550.3	1094.5	1754.1	2391.9	2220.7	1769.6	2038.4	2884.9	
Capital transfers, receivable	155.3	192.4	206.2	550.3	1094.5	1754.3	2393.3	2228.7	1789.1	2171.8	2971.1	
Less: Capital transfers, payable	...	...	...	...	...	...	1.4	8.0	19.5	133.4	86.2	
Equals: CHANGES IN NET WORTH DUE TO SAVING AND CAPITAL TRANSFERS [a]	3230.6	2772.3	2471.8	4451.0	5909.4	7235.5	9935.6	11364.6	10756.8	14912.9	15854.6	
	III.1 Capital account - Changes in assets											
Gross capital formation	3598.4	3791.6	5603.1	6926.4	9299.0	11936.7	18573.3	20450.1	11303.0	13925.6	16385.1	
Gross fixed capital formation	2352.8	2588.0	4026.6	5415.8	7160.8	9972.0	15419.5	17803.6	10828.7	13505.3	15717.9	
Changes in inventories	1245.5	1203.7	1576.6	1510.6	2138.2	1964.7	3153.8	2646.5	474.2	420.3	667.2	
Acquisitions less disposals of valuables	...	...	...	...	...	...	...	...	...	...	...	
Acquisitions less disposals of non-produced non-financial assets	...	14.3	60.2	69.0	96.0	268.1	230.6	322.8	283.1	450.1	243.5	
NET LENDING (+) / NET BORROWING (-)	-367.8	-1033.6	-3191.5	-2544.3	-3485.6	-4969.3	-8868.2	-9408.3	-829.2	537.2	-774.0	

[a] Item does not consider consumption of fixed capital.

Table 4.4 Financial Corporations (S.12)

Series 200: 1993 SNA, Moldovan leu, Western calendar year — **Data in millions**

	2001	2002	2003	2004	2005	2006	2007	2008	2009	2010	2011	2012
Series	**200**											
	I. Production account - Resources											
Output, at basic prices (otherwise, please specify)	1101.9	1340.5	1699.3	2076.7	2409.9	3174.6	6470.4	7703.3	7855.4	8341.6	5579.2	
	I. Production account - Uses											
Intermediate consumption, at purchaser's prices	239.3	361.3	447.4	559.7	683.1	949.8	3247.1	3922.1	4004.5	4236.0	1443.5	
VALUE ADDED GROSS, at basic prices	862.5	979.1	1251.9	1516.9	1726.8	2224.8	3223.3	3781.2	3850.9	4105.6	4135.6	
Less: Consumption of fixed capital	...	...	...	...	...	...	...	...	...	...	...	
VALUE ADDED NET, at basic prices	...	...	...	...	...	...	...	...	...	...	...	
	II.1.1 Generation of income account - Resources											
VALUE ADDED GROSS, at basic prices	862.5	979.1	1251.9	1516.9	1726.8	2224.8	3223.3	3781.2	3850.9	4105.6	4135.6	

	2001	2002	2003	2004	2005	2006	2007	2008	2009	2010	2011	2012
Series	**200**											
II.1.1 Generation of income account - Uses												
Compensation of employees	319.3	378.2	439.1	590.9	655.9	669.9	1055.1	1321.1	1436.1	1520.1	1868.4	
Other taxes less Other subsidies on production	0.4	0.3	0.6	1.0	1.2	2.0	1.0	2.9	1.7	2.2	0.7	
Other taxes on production	0.4	0.3	0.6	1.0	1.2	2.0	1.0	2.9	1.7	2.2	0.7	
Less: Other subsidies on production	...	...	...	...	...	...	...	...	...	...	...	
OPERATING SURPLUS, GROSS	542.8	600.6	812.2	924.9	1069.7	1552.9	2167.2	2457.2	2413.1	2583.3	2266.5	
II.1.2 Allocation of primary income account - Resources												
OPERATING SURPLUS, GROSS	542.8	600.6	812.2	924.9	1069.7	1552.9	2167.2	2457.2	2413.1	2583.3	2266.5	
Property income	1052.5	934.1	1331.8	1687.6	1961.4	2748.4	4274.7	5706.1	4808.4	4113.2	4720.4	
Adjustment entry for FISIM (balanced by Nominal Sector)	-432.9	-462.7	-647.0	-729.8	-756.9	-1116.5	-1215.8	-1309.1	-984.8	-1498.8	-1774.5	
II.1.2 Allocation of primary income account - Uses												
Property income	492.3	501.7	523.4	813.7	1195.0	1349.8	2554.8	3737.8	2892.4	2084.2	3154.7	
BALANCE OF PRIMARY INCOMES	670.1	570.2	973.6	1069.1	1079.1	1835.0	2671.3	3116.4	3344.4	3113.6	2057.8	
II.2 Secondary distribution of income account - Resources												
BALANCE OF PRIMARY INCOMES	670.1	570.2	973.6	1069.1	1079.1	1835.0	2671.3	3116.4	3344.4	3113.6	2057.8	
Social contributions	...	...	...	...	...	...	...	...	...	...	...	
Other current transfers	132.2	182.5	222.1	293.7	342.1	442.4	576.8	670.2	1021.3	935.6	962.8	
II.2 Secondary distribution of income account - Uses												
Current taxes on income, wealth, etc.	...	...	...	...	...	...	...	...	...	...	...	
Social benefits other than social transfers in kind	...	...	...	...	...	...	...	...	...	...	...	
Other current transfers	387.3	371.5	518.4	382.2	620.2	703.7	1028.7	656.2	966.5	1231.2	957.0	
GROSS DISPOSABLE INCOME	414.9	381.2	677.2	980.5	801.1	1573.7	2219.4	3130.4	3399.1	2817.9	2063.7	
II.4.1 Use of disposable income account - Resources												
GROSS DISPOSABLE INCOME	414.9	381.2	677.2	980.5	801.1	1573.7	2219.4	3130.4	3399.1	2817.9	2063.7	
II.4.1 Use of disposable income account - Uses												
Adjustment for the change in net equity of households on pension funds	-4.8	-4.6	-4.4	-5.2	-4.7	-7.4	-7.5	-5.6	0.4	0.6	0.5	
SAVING, GROSS	419.7	385.8	681.6	985.8	805.7	1581.1	2227.0	3136.0	3398.7	2817.3	2063.2	
III.1 Capital account - Changes in liabilities and net worth												
SAVING, GROSS	419.7	385.8	681.6	985.8	805.7	1581.1	2227.0	3136.0	3398.7	2817.3	2063.2	
Capital transfers, receivable less payable	...	...	...	...	...	...	...	...	...	...	...	
Capital transfers, receivable	...	...	...	...	...	...	...	...	...	...	...	
Less: Capital transfers, payable	...	...	...	...	...	...	...	...	...	...	...	
Equals: CHANGES IN NET WORTH DUE TO SAVING AND CAPITAL TRANSFERS [a]	419.7	385.8	681.6	985.8	805.7	1581.1	2227.0	3136.0	3398.7	2817.3	2063.2	
III.1 Capital account - Changes in assets												
Gross capital formation	151.4	155.3	122.1	165.4	274.3	261.0	202.7	519.9	329.2	358.5	345.2	
Gross fixed capital formation	151.4	155.3	122.1	165.4	274.3	261.0	202.7	519.9	329.2	358.5	345.2	
Changes in inventories	...	...	...	...	...	...	...	...	...	...	...	
Acquisitions less disposals of valuables	...	...	...	...	...	...	...	...	...	...	...	

	2001	2002	2003	2004	2005	2006	2007	2008	2009	2010	2011	2012
Series	**200**											
Acquisitions less disposals of non-produced non-financial assets	...	...	...	...	...	...	...	...	...	...	...	
NET LENDING (+) / NET BORROWING (-)	268.3	230.5	559.5	820.4	531.5	1320.1	2024.3	2616.1	3069.6	2458.8	1718.0	

[a] Item does not consider consumption of fixed capital.

Table 4.5 General Government (S.13)

Series 200: 1993 SNA, Moldovan leu, Western calendar year **Data in millions**

	2001	2002	2003	2004	2005	2006	2007	2008	2009	2010	2011	2012
Series	**200**											
I. Production account - Resources												
Output, at basic prices (otherwise, please specify)	3112.9	5244.7	6323.3	5690.6	6945.7	8456.6	9924.6	11746.3	12630.4	13454.0	13818.1	
I. Production account - Uses												
Intermediate consumption, at purchaser's prices	1297.9	2294.0	2400.4	2178.1	2640.1	2915.5	3620.4	4649.2	4569.0	4800.2	4708.8	
VALUE ADDED GROSS, at basic prices	1815.0	2950.7	3923.0	3512.6	4305.6	5541.1	6304.2	7097.0	8061.4	8653.8	9109.3	
Less: Consumption of fixed capital	...	...	...	...	...	...	...	...	...	...	...	
VALUE ADDED NET, at basic prices	...	...	...	...	...	...	...	...	...	...	...	
II.1.1 Generation of income account - Resources												
VALUE ADDED GROSS, at basic prices	1815.0	2950.7	3923.0	3512.6	4305.6	5541.1	6304.2	7097.0	8061.4	8653.8	9109.3	
II.1.1 Generation of income account - Uses												
Compensation of employees	1586.8	2475.6	3111.2	2681.2	3397.4	4685.2	5052.3	5879.8	7048.4	7528.1	7993.1	
Other taxes less Other subsidies on production	...	...	...	...	...	...	...	...	...	...	...	
Other taxes on production	...	...	...	...	...	...	...	...	...	...	...	
Less: Other subsidies on production	...	...	...	...	...	...	...	...	...	...	...	
OPERATING SURPLUS, GROSS	228.2	475.1	811.8	831.4	908.2	855.9	1251.9	1217.3	1012.9	1125.7	1116.1	
II.1.2 Allocation of primary income account - Resources												
OPERATING SURPLUS, GROSS	228.2	475.1	811.8	831.4	908.2	855.9	1251.9	1217.3	1012.9	1125.7	1116.1	
Taxes on production and imports, less Subsidies	2568.6	3166.5	4404.9	4891.7	6283.3	7908.6	9124.9	11536.1	9670.4	12282.4	14290.1	
Taxes on production and imports	2664.9	3292.1	4566.9	5194.3	6927.3	8562.2	10450.9	12750.1	10638.8	13043.9	15071.0	
Taxes on products	2372.2	2974.8	4220.2	4775.3	6401.6	7929.7	9816.4	11823.4	10076.4	12349.2	14376.2	
Other taxes on production	292.6	317.3	346.7	419.1	525.7	632.5	634.5	926.6	562.4	694.8	694.9	
Less: Subsidies	96.3	125.6	162.0	302.6	644.0	653.6	1326.0	1214.0	968.4	761.5	780.9	
Subsidies on products	93.8	108.3	124.3	261.1	365.6	514.1	799.7	675.4	455.8	384.4	417.0	
Other subsidies on production	2.6	17.3	37.7	41.5	278.3	139.5	526.3	538.6	512.6	377.1	363.9	
Property income	80.7	88.9	98.8	106.3	184.1	333.5	517.2	255.6	217.1	341.5	419.7	
II.1.2 Allocation of primary income account - Uses												
Property income	813.4	496.0	588.1	777.4	487.5	454.6	634.6	732.7	843.1	557.6	673.3	
BALANCE OF PRIMARY INCOMES	2064.1	3234.5	4727.4	5052.0	6888.1	8643.5	10259.5	12276.2	10057.4	13192.0	15152.7	
II.2 Secondary distribution of income account - Resources												
BALANCE OF PRIMARY INCOMES	2064.1	3234.5	4727.4	5052.0	6888.1	8643.5	10259.5	12276.2	10057.4	13192.0	15152.7	

	2001	2002	2003	2004	2005	2006	2007	2008	2009	2010	2011	2012
Series	**200**											
Current taxes on income, wealth, etc.	...	...	...	...	...	...	...	...	...	...	...	
Social contributions	...	...	...	...	...	...	...	...	...	...	...	
Other current transfers	4182.4	4807.2	5565.8	5969.7	9240.2	11029.4	13893.1	16112.9	17619.4	21514.2	21731.4	
	II.2 Secondary distribution of income account - Uses											
Current taxes on income, wealth, etc.	...	...	...	...	...	...	...	...	...	...	...	
Social benefits other than social transfers in kind	...	...	...	...	...	...	...	...	...	...	...	
Other current transfers	2055.6	2838.1	3364.1	4705.0	7499.7	9491.4	9763.8	12186.9	15129.8	17848.9	18765.8	
GROSS DISPOSABLE INCOME	4190.8	5203.6	6929.1	6316.6	8628.6	10181.5	14388.8	16202.3	12547.0	16857.3	18118.3	
	II.4.1 Use of disposable income account - Resources											
GROSS DISPOSABLE INCOME	4190.8	5203.6	6929.1	6316.6	8628.6	10181.5	14388.8	16202.3	12547.0	16857.3	18118.3	
	II.4.1 Use of disposable income account - Uses											
Final consumption expenditure	2736.3	4562.4	5435.3	4774.1	6189.1	8944.8	10658.1	12844.5	14360.5	15930.7	16583.6	
Individual consumption expenditure	1784.6	2718.6	3450.0	2609.6	3337.6	5704.3	6730.9	8581.7	10177.5	11667.2	13044.0	
Collective consumption expenditure	951.7	1843.8	1985.3	2164.5	2851.5	3240.5	3927.2	4262.8	4183.0	4263.4	3539.6	
Adjustment for the change in net equity of households on pension funds	...	...	...	...	...	...	...	...	...	...	...	
SAVING, GROSS	1454.5	641.2	1493.8	1542.5	2439.5	1236.7	3730.7	3357.8	-1813.4	926.7	1534.7	
	III.1 Capital account - Changes in liabilities and net worth											
SAVING, GROSS	1454.5	641.2	1493.8	1542.5	2439.5	1236.7	3730.7	3357.8	-1813.4	926.7	1534.7	
Capital transfers, receivable less payable	-155.3	-192.3	-206.3	-479.1	-998.0	-1589.5	-2105.7	-2028.4	-1190.5	-1620.1	-2366.6	
Capital transfers, receivable	35.6	50.0	68.9	112.8	572.1	793.1	791.4	751.5	943.1	1082.0	978.7	
Less: Capital transfers, payable	190.8	242.2	275.3	591.9	1570.0	2382.6	2897.1	2779.9	2133.6	2702.1	3345.3	
Equals: CHANGES IN NET WORTH DUE TO SAVING AND CAPITAL TRANSFERS [a]	1299.2	449.0	1287.5	1063.4	1441.6	-352.8	1625.0	1329.3	-3003.9	-693.5	-831.9	
	III.1 Capital account - Changes in assets											
Gross capital formation	272.9	497.0	596.7	685.9	1039.8	1595.5	1608.8	1901.0	1154.5	1081.3	1165.2	
Gross fixed capital formation	272.9	497.0	596.7	685.9	1039.8	1595.5	1608.8	1901.0	1154.5	1081.3	1141.1	
Changes in inventories	...	...	...	...	...	...	...	...	...	...	...	
Acquisitions less disposals of valuables	...	...	...	...	...	...	...	...	...	...	24.2	
Acquisitions of non-produced non-financial assets	-34.0	-23.0	-60.2	-69.0	-96.0	-268.1	-230.6	-328.1	-185.8	-189.3	-195.7	
NET LENDING (+) / NET BORROWING (-)	1060.3	-25.0	751.0	446.5	497.7	-1680.3	246.9	-243.6	-3972.6	-1585.5	-1801.5	

[a] Item does not consider consumption of fixed capital.

Table 4.6 Households (S.14)

Series 200: 1993 SNA, Moldovan leu, Western calendar year **Data in millions**

	2001	2002	2003	2004	2005	2006	2007	2008	2009	2010	2011	2012
Series	**200**											
	I. Production account - Resources											
Output, at basic prices (otherwise, please specify)	9032.8	11072.0	12374.9	14242.9	15884.2	16137.4	20233.3	26558.8	22669.1	28715.5	30441.5	
	I. Production account - Uses											
Intermediate consumption, at purchaser's prices	4213.9	5135.3	5940.9	7682.8	8727.9	8259.6	11419.3	16203.6	13384.7	16785.6	17591.8	
VALUE ADDED GROSS, at basic prices	4818.9	5936.7	6434.0	6560.1	7156.3	7877.8	8814.0	10355.2	9284.4	11930.0	12849.8	
Less: Consumption of fixed capital	...	...	...	...	...	...	...	...	...	...	...	
VALUE ADDED NET, at basic prices	...	...	...	...	...	...	...	...	...	...	...	
	II.1.1 Generation of income account - Resources											
VALUE ADDED GROSS, at basic prices	4818.9	5936.7	6434.0	6560.1	7156.3	7877.8	8814.0	10355.2	9284.4	11930.0	12849.8	
	II.1.1 Generation of income account - Uses											
Compensation of employees	...	...	...	...	...	...	...	...	...	...	...	
Other taxes less Other subsidies on production	53.8	104.2	148.5	158.7	198.3	152.9	236.9	278.2	168.8	208.6	238.5	
Other taxes on production	53.8	104.2	148.5	158.7	198.3	152.9	236.9	278.2	168.8	208.6	238.5	
Less: Other subsidies on production	...	...	...	...	...	...	...	...	...	...	...	
OPERATING SURPLUS, GROSS	319.1	399.7	448.5	472.7	518.6	613.9	1142.6	1553.8	1674.0	1915.8	2354.6	
MIXED INCOME, GROSS	4446.0	5432.8	5837.0	5928.7	6439.4	7111.0	7434.5	8523.2	7441.7	9805.6	10256.6	
	II.1.2 Allocation of primary income account - Resources											
OPERATING SURPLUS, GROSS	319.1	399.7	448.5	472.7	518.6	613.9	1142.6	1553.8	1674.0	1915.8	2354.6	
MIXED INCOME, GROSS	4446.0	5432.8	5837.0	5928.7	6439.4	7111.0	7434.5	8523.2	7441.7	9805.6	10256.6	
Compensation of employees	9194.3	11883.0	15659.3	18853.1	21781.3	25865.4	29366.0	35678.9	34754.4	39728.1	45019.8	
Property income	167.2	234.0	206.4	479.5	670.8	1192.8	2153.9	3515.9	2975.2	2462.5	2968.1	
	II.1.2 Allocation of primary income account - Uses											
Property income	22.3	21.5	...	96.9	292.0	640.3	959.9	1499.2	1249.2	836.7	805.6	
BALANCE OF PRIMARY INCOMES	14104.3	17928.0	22151.3	25637.1	29118.1	34142.8	39137.1	47772.6	45596.0	53075.3	59793.6	
	II.2 Secondary distribution of income account - Resources											
BALANCE OF PRIMARY INCOMES	14104.3	17928.0	22151.3	25637.1	29118.1	34142.8	39137.1	47772.6	45596.0	53075.3	59793.6	
Social contributions	...	...	...	...	...	...	...	...	...	...	...	
Social benefits other than social transfers in kind	...	...	...	...	...	...	...	...	...	...	...	
Other current transfers	2507.5	3239.5	6145.8	7939.6	10990.4	14059.6	15239.7	18119.1	15752.8	18965.7	25616.0	
	II.2 Secondary distribution of income account - Uses											
Current taxes on income, wealth, etc.	...	...	...	...	...	...	...	...	...	...	...	
Social contributions	...	...	...	...	...	...	...	...	...	...	...	
Social benefits other than social transfers in kind	...	...	...	...	...	...	...	...	...	...	...	
Other current transfers	1922.3	2439.9	3305.0	4171.1	4853.1	5739.8	7067.1	9662.3	10191.9	12105.8	13636.3	
GROSS DISPOSABLE INCOME	14689.5	18727.6	24992.1	29405.6	35255.4	42462.6	47309.7	56229.5	51156.9	59935.2	71773.3	

	2001	2002	2003	2004	2005	2006	2007	2008	2009	2010	2011	2012
Series	**200**											
	II.4.1 Use of disposable income account - Resources											
GROSS DISPOSABLE INCOME	14689.5	18727.6	24992.1	29405.6	35255.4	42462.6	47309.7	56229.5	51156.9	59935.2	71773.3	
Adjustment for the change in net equity of households on pension funds	-4.8	-4.6	-4.4	-5.2	-4.7	-7.4	-7.5	-5.6	0.4	0.6	0.5	
	II.4.1 Use of disposable income account - Uses											
Final consumption expenditure	16384.7	18492.9	24711.3	28125.2	34694.1	41360.3	49178.3	57804.4	53352.6	66051.8	78104.1	
Individual consumption expenditure	16384.7	18492.9	24711.3	28125.2	34694.1	41360.3	49178.3	57804.4	53352.6	66051.8	78104.1	
SAVING, GROSS	-1700.0	230.1	276.4	1275.2	556.6	1094.9	-1876.2	-1580.6	-2195.3	-6116.0	-6330.4	
	III.1 Capital account - Changes in liabilities and net worth											
SAVING, GROSS	-1700.0	230.1	276.4	1275.2	556.6	1094.9	-1876.2	-1580.6	-2195.3	-6116.0	-6330.4	
Capital transfers, receivable less payable	-25.8	-208.1	-178.0	-139.3	-144.9	-211.2	-11.2	46.6	-179.6	-184.9	-296.7	
Capital transfers, receivable	14.3	11.0	48.5	59.5	133.7	168.0	168.7	286.6	152.5	323.4	275.7	
Less: Capital transfers, payable	40.1	219.1	226.5	198.8	278.6	379.2	180.0	239.9	332.1	508.3	572.4	
Equals: CHANGES IN NET WORTH DUE TO SAVINGS AND CAPITAL TRANSFERS [a]	-1725.8	22.1	98.4	1135.9	411.7	883.7	-1887.4	-1534.0	-2375.0	-6300.9	-6627.1	
	III.1 Capital account - Changes in assets											
Gross capital formation	406.4	435.8	73.1	660.9	971.1	822.2	-106.5	1703.8	1121.4	1528.5	1966.3	
Gross fixed capital formation	406.3	435.6	375.5	515.0	760.8	822.3	909.2	1058.6	1266.0	1300.8	1932.4	
Changes in inventories	0.1	0.2	-302.4	146.0	210.3	-0.1	-1015.7	645.2	-144.6	227.7	33.9	
Acquisitions less disposals of valuables	...	...	...	...	...	...	...	...	...	...	...	
Acquisitions less disposals of non-produced non-financial assets	34.0	8.7	...	...	...	...	...	5.3	-97.3	-260.8	-140.8	
NET LENDING (+) / NET BORROWING (-)	-2166.2	-422.5	25.3	474.9	-559.4	61.6	-1780.8	-3243.0	-3399.1	-7568.6	-8452.6	

[a] Item does not consider consumption of fixed capital.

Table 4.7 Non-profit institutions serving households (S.15)

Series 200: 1993 SNA, Moldovan leu, Western calendar year — **Data in millions**

	2001	2002	2003	2004	2005	2006	2007	2008	2009	2010	2011	2012
Series	**200**											
	I. Production account - Resources											
Output, at basic prices (otherwise, please specify)	152.4	234.3	306.7	404.2	490.2	713.9	841.2	924.3	972.7	1257.8	1402.8	
	I. Production account - Uses											
Intermediate consumption, at purchaser's prices	89.9	138.9	179.3	230.7	294.2	433.7	496.1	547.4	564.8	729.5	781.7	
VALUE ADDED GROSS, at basic prices	62.5	95.4	127.4	173.5	196.0	280.2	345.1	376.9	407.9	528.3	621.1	
Less: Consumption of fixed capital	...	...	...	...	...	...	...	...	...	...	...	
VALUE ADDED NET, at basic prices	...	...	...	...	...	...	...	...	...	...	...	
	II.1.1 Generation of income account - Resources											
VALUE ADDED GROSS, at basic prices	62.5	95.4	127.4	173.5	196.0	280.2	345.1	376.9	407.9	528.3	621.1	
	II.1.1 Generation of income account - Uses											
Compensation of employees	50.4	47.0	97.4	143.3	160.8	224.9	224.5	277.7	352.9	490.4	472.3	

	2001	2002	2003	2004	2005	2006	2007	2008	2009	2010	2011	2012
Series	**200**											
Other taxes less Other subsidies on production	0.3	0.3	0.4	0.4	0.5	0.5	0.7	0.7	0.4	0.5	0.5	
Other taxes on production	0.3	0.3	0.4	0.4	0.5	0.5	0.7	0.7	0.4	0.5	0.5	
Less: Other subsidies on production	...	...	...	...	...	...	...	...	...	...	...	
OPERATING SURPLUS, GROSS	11.9	48.1	29.6	29.7	34.8	54.8	119.8	98.5	54.6	37.3	148.2	
	II.1.2 Allocation of primary income account - Resources											
OPERATING SURPLUS, GROSS	11.9	48.1	29.6	29.7	34.8	54.8	119.8	98.5	54.6	37.3	148.2	
Property income	0.0	0.0	...	...	...	0.2	1.3	3.7	2.6	2.7	1.7	
	II.1.2 Allocation of primary income account - Uses											
Property income	...	...	...	...	...	0.1	...	0.1	0.2	1.5	0.5	
BALANCE OF PRIMARY INCOMES	11.9	48.1	29.6	29.7	34.8	54.8	121.2	102.1	57.0	38.5	149.4	
	II.2 Secondary distribution of income account - Resources											
BALANCE OF PRIMARY INCOMES	11.9	48.1	29.6	29.7	34.8	54.8	121.2	102.1	57.0	38.5	149.4	
Social contributions	...	...	...	...	...	...	...	...	...	...	...	
Other current transfers	212.7	107.2	324.9	428.5	526.1	670.4	784.4	828.7	914.2	1265.4	1273.2	
	II.2 Secondary distribution of income account - Uses											
Current taxes on income, wealth, etc.	...	...	...	...	...	...	...	...	...	...	...	
Social benefits other than social transfers in kind	...	...	...	...	...	...	...	...	...	...	...	
Other current transfers	108.8	141.6	143.8	151.9	128.8	119.4	138.5	157.8	187.3	232.9	243.9	
GROSS DISPOSABLE INCOME	115.8	13.8	210.7	306.3	432.2	605.8	767.1	773.0	784.0	1071.0	1178.7	
	II.4.1 Use of disposable income account - Resources											
GROSS DISPOSABLE INCOME	115.8	13.8	210.7	306.3	432.2	605.8	767.1	773.0	784.0	1071.0	1178.7	
	II.4.1 Use of disposable income account - Uses											
Final consumption expenditure	141.7	234.0	304.0	398.4	485.2	667.5	781.7	802.4	861.0	1257.8	1402.8	
Individual consumption expenditure	141.7	234.0	304.0	398.4	485.2	667.5	781.7	802.4	861.0	1257.8	1402.8	
Adjustment for the change in net equity of households on pension funds	...	...	...	...	...	...	...	...	...	...	...	
SAVING, GROSS	-25.9	-220.2	-93.3	-92.1	-53.1	-61.6	-14.6	-29.4	-76.9	-186.8	-224.1	
	III.1 Capital account - Changes in liabilities and net worth											
SAVING, GROSS	-25.9	-220.2	-93.3	-92.1	-53.1	-61.6	-14.6	-29.4	-76.9	-186.8	-224.1	
Capital transfers, receivable less payable	...	...	...	...	...	...	...	...	...	...	...	
Capital transfers, receivable	...	...	...	...	...	...	...	...	...	...	...	
Less: Capital transfers, payable	...	...	...	...	...	...	...	...	...	...	...	
Equals: CHANGES IN NET WORTH DUE TO SAVING AND CAPITAL TRANSFERS [a]	-25.9	-220.2	-93.3	-92.1	-53.1	-61.6	-14.6	-29.4	-76.9	-186.8	-224.1	
	III.1 Capital account - Changes in assets											
Gross capital formation	6.6	5.9	6.5	4.8	22.3	40.6	81.6	108.3	76.6	16.7	42.1	
Gross fixed capital formation	6.6	5.9	6.5	4.8	22.3	40.6	81.6	108.3	76.6	16.7	42.1	
Changes in inventories	...	...	...	...	...	...	...	...	...	...	...	
Acquisitions less disposals of valuables	...	...	...	...	...	...	...	...	...	...	...	

	2001	2002	2003	2004	2005	2006	2007	2008	2009	2010	2011	2012
Series	**200**											
Acquisitions less disposals of non-produced non-financial assets	...	...	...	...	...	...	...	...	...	...	...	
NET LENDING (+) / NET BORROWING (-)	-32.4	-226.1	-99.7	-96.9	-75.4	-102.2	-96.2	-137.6	-153.5	-203.5	-266.2	

[a] Item does not consider consumption of fixed capital.

Table 5.1 Cross classification of Gross value added by industries and institutional sectors (ISIC Rev. 3) Non-financial corporations

Series 200: 1993 SNA, Moldovan leu, Western calendar year **Data in millions**

	2001	2002	2003	2004	2005	2006	2007	2008	2009	2010	2011	2012
Series	**200**											
	Industries											
Agriculture, hunting, forestry; fishing	1213.4	1309.4	1175.5	1921.2	1664.4	1379.1	1290.2	808.3	1382.9	3090.4	3839.2	
Mining and quarrying	34.9	49.6	69.7	105.8	143.2	222.5	262.6	315.1	241.2	270.0	348.8	
Manufacturing	2706.8	2705.1	3568.4	4067.1	4479.9	5170.8	5687.2	6227.2	5724.3	6828.3	8544.1	
Electricity, gas and water supply	520.0	498.0	524.4	711.7	770.1	757.2	1053.1	1328.1	1398.8	1645.8	1814.8	
Construction	529.8	442.1	497.7	652.3	793.1	1360.1	1776.9	2015.1	1373.8	1534.7	1736.9	
Wholesale and retail trade; repair of motor vehicles, motorcycles and personal and household goods; hotels and restaurants	1542.3	1680.7	2390.7	2679.2	3511.3	4521.8	5703.8	7626.8	6910.4	8039.8	10421.1	
Transport, storage and communications	1856.2	2098.7	2831.8	3525.5	4319.7	5146.9	6314.6	7246.0	6864.7	7726.8	8683.1	
Financial intermediation; real estate renting and business activities	591.6	718.2	900.0	1392.7	1774.0	2237.6	2336.7	3356.6	3248.9	3600.7	4159.2	
Public administration and defence; compulsory social security	...	...	...	...	...	...	...	...	...	...	...	
Education; health and social work; other community, social and personal services	652.1	688.0	475.6	1428.8	1532.3	1735.4	2516.8	2549.0	3044.3	3465.3	3901.3	
Private households with employed persons	...	...	...	...	...	...	...	...	...	...	...	
VALUE ADDED GROSS, at basic prices	9647.1	10190.0	12433.8	16484.3	18988.1	22531.4	26942.0	31472.3	30189.3	36201.8	43448.3	

Table 5.1 Cross classification of Gross value added by industries and institutional sectors (ISIC Rev. 3) Financial corporations

Series 200: 1993 SNA, Moldovan leu, Western calendar year **Data in millions**

	2001	2002	2003	2004	2005	2006	2007	2008	2009	2010	2011	2012
Series	**200**											
	Industries											
Agriculture, hunting, forestry; fishing	...	...	...	...	...	...	...	...	...	...	...	
Mining and quarrying	...	...	...	...	...	...	...	...	...	...	...	
Manufacturing	...	...	...	...	...	...	...	...	...	...	...	
Electricity, gas and water supply	...	...	...	...	...	...	...	...	...	...	...	
Construction	...	...	...	...	...	...	...	...	...	...	...	

	2001	2002	2003	2004	2005	2006	2007	2008	2009	2010	2011	2012
Series	**200**											
Wholesale and retail trade; repair of motor vehicles, motorcycles and personal and household goods; hotels and restaurants	...	...	...	...	...	...	...	...	...	...	...	
Transport, storage and communications	...	...	...	...	...	...	...	...	...	...	...	
Financial intermediation; real estate renting and business activities	862.5	979.1	1251.9	1516.9	1726.8	2224.8	3223.3	3781.2	3850.9	4105.6	4135.6	
Public administration and defence; compulsory social security	...	...	...	...	...	...	...	...	...	...	...	
Education; health and social work; other community, social and personal services	...	...	...	...	...	...	...	...	...	...	...	
Private households with employed persons	...	...	...	...	...	...	...	...	...	...	...	
VALUE ADDED GROSS, at basic prices	862.5	979.1	1251.9	1516.9	1726.8	2224.8	3223.3	3781.2	3850.9	4105.6	4135.6	

Table 5.1 Cross classification of Gross value added by industries and institutional sectors (ISIC Rev. 3) General government

Series 200: 1993 SNA, Moldovan leu, Western calendar year **Data in millions**

	2001	2002	2003	2004	2005	2006	2007	2008	2009	2010	2011	2012
Series	**200**											
Industries												
Agriculture, hunting, forestry; fishing	17.0	12.1	29.6	41.2	111.4	62.8	74.7	88.8	131.0	115.6	108.2	
Mining and quarrying	...	...	...	...	...	...	...	...	...	...	...	
Manufacturing	...	...	...	...	...	...	...	...	...	...	...	
Electricity, gas and water supply	...	...	...	...	...	...	...	...	...	...	...	
Construction	...	...	...	62.1	63.0	68.4	37.7	72.6	34.6	43.7	...	
Wholesale and retail trade; repair of motor vehicles, motorcycles and personal and household goods; hotels and restaurants	...	...	...	...	...	...	...	...	...	...	...	
Transport, storage and communications	21.9	19.1	33.8	...	0.9	...	...	...	...	...	...	
Financial intermediation; real estate renting and business activities	28.7	33.0	48.4	56.9	87.9	111.0	139.3	177.9	202.5	228.6	234.7	
Public administration and defence; compulsory social security	671.1	1269.7	1379.3	1337.7	1607.4	2101.1	2453.1	2642.0	2857.0	2740.4	3038.4	
Education; health and social work; other community, social and personal services	1076.2	1616.7	2431.9	2014.6	2434.8	3197.8	3599.4	4115.7	4836.2	5525.5	5727.9	
Private households with employed persons	...	...	...	...	...	...	...	...	...	...	...	
VALUE ADDED GROSS, at basic prices	1815.0	2950.7	3923.0	3512.6	4305.6	5541.1	6304.2	7097.0	8061.4	8653.8	9109.3	

Table 5.1 Cross classification of Gross value added by industries and institutional sectors (ISIC Rev. 3) Households

Series 200: 1993 SNA, Moldovan leu, Western calendar year — **Data in millions**

	2001	2002	2003	2004	2005	2006	2007	2008	2009	2010	2011	2012
Series	**200**											
Industries												
Agriculture, hunting, forestry; fishing	3041.0	3420.1	3856.9	3670.9	4399.0	5046.9	3969.0	4646.9	3620.7	5451.5	6147.8	
Mining and quarrying	0.7	...	0.7	0.2	0.5	1.9	...	...	...	...	...	
Manufacturing	298.4	647.2	696.9	583.7	542.1	428.4	613.0	866.8	666.4	790.6	810.7	
Electricity, gas and water supply	3.3	0.6	...	...	...	...	...	...	...	...	...	
Construction	53.7	223.2	313.9	386.8	400.9	348.0	771.2	1027.3	700.2	859.1	983.1	
Wholesale and retail trade; repair of motor vehicles, motorcycles and personal and household goods; hotels and restaurants	911.6	999.9	837.0	1014.6	815.8	1091.9	1622.0	1366.9	1853.3	2084.4	1704.7	
Transport, storage and communications	96.2	136.7	111.4	254.7	283.4	141.8	267.3	355.1	361.3	372.4	318.6	
Financial intermediation; real estate renting and business activities	336.3	435.3	480.3	542.2	567.5	654.9	1236.3	1655.3	1732.5	1997.4	2448.1	
Public administration and defence; compulsory social security	...	...	...	...	...	...	...	...	...	...	...	
Education; health and social work; other community, social and personal services	55.0	38.8	56.1	62.7	94.1	68.7	204.1	300.4	198.5	208.1	315.2	
Private households with employed persons	22.7	34.8	80.7	44.3	53.0	95.4	131.1	136.6	151.5	166.6	121.7	
VALUE ADDED GROSS, at basic prices	4818.9	5936.7	6434.0	6560.1	7156.3	7877.8	8814.0	10355.2	9284.4	11930.0	12849.8	

Table 5.1 Cross classification of Gross value added by industries and institutional sectors (ISIC Rev. 3) Non-profit institutions serving households

Series 200: 1993 SNA, Moldovan leu, Western calendar year — **Data in millions**

	2001	2002	2003	2004	2005	2006	2007	2008	2009	2010	2011	2012
Series	**200**											
Industries												
Agriculture, hunting, forestry; fishing	...	...	...	...	...	...	...	...	...	...	...	
Mining and quarrying	...	...	...	...	...	...	...	...	...	...	...	
Manufacturing	...	...	...	...	...	...	...	...	...	...	...	
Electricity, gas and water supply	...	...	...	...	...	...	...	...	...	...	...	
Construction	...	...	...	...	...	...	...	...	...	...	...	
Wholesale and retail trade; repair of motor vehicles, motorcycles and personal and household goods; hotels and restaurants	...	...	...	...	...	...	...	...	...	...	...	
Transport, storage and communications	...	...	...	...	...	...	...	...	...	...	...	
Financial intermediation; real estate renting and business activities	...	...	...	...	...	...	...	...	...	...	...	
Public administration and defence; compulsory social security	...	...	...	...	...	...	...	...	...	...	...	

	2001	2002	2003	2004	2005	2006	2007	2008	2009	2010	2011	2012
Series	**200**											
Education; health and social work; other community, social and personal services	62.5	95.4	127.4	173.5	196.0	280.2	345.1	376.9	407.9	528.3	621.1	
Private households with employed persons	...	...	...	...	...	...	...	...	...	...	...	
VALUE ADDED GROSS, at basic prices	62.5	95.4	127.4	173.5	196.0	280.2	345.1	376.9	407.9	528.3	621.1	

Table 5.1 Cross classification of Gross value added by industries and institutional sectors (ISIC Rev. 3) Total economy

Series 200: 1993 SNA, Moldovan leu, Western calendar year **Data in millions**

		2001	2002	2003	2004	2005	2006	2007	2008	2009	2010	2011	2012
Series		**200**											
	Industries												
Agriculture, hunting, forestry; fishing		4271.4	4741.7	5062.1	5633.4	6174.9	6488.8	5333.9	5544.0	5134.5	8657.4	10095.2	
Mining and quarrying		35.6	49.6	70.4	106.0	143.7	224.4	262.6	315.1	241.2	270.0	348.8	
Manufacturing		3005.3	3352.4	4265.3	4650.8	5022.0	5599.2	6300.2	7093.9	6390.8	7618.9	9354.7	
Electricity, gas and water supply		523.3	498.6	524.4	711.7	770.1	757.2	1053.1	1328.1	1398.8	1645.8	1814.8	
Construction		583.5	665.3	811.6	1101.2	1257.0	1776.5	2585.9	3115.0	2108.7	2437.5	2719.9	
Wholesale and retail trade; repair of motor vehicles, motorcycles and personal and household goods; hotels and restaurants		2453.9	2680.6	3227.6	3693.9	4327.1	5613.7	7325.8	8993.7	8763.8	10124.2	12125.7	
Transport, storage and communications		1974.3	2254.5	2977.0	3780.2	4603.9	5288.7	6582.0	7601.1	7226.0	8099.2	9001.6	
Financial intermediation; real estate renting and business activities		1819.1	2165.7	2680.6	3508.7	4156.3	5228.2	6935.6	8971.1	9034.8	9932.2	10977.6	
Public administration and defence; compulsory social security		671.1	1269.7	1379.3	1337.7	1607.4	2101.1	2453.1	2642.0	2857.0	2740.4	3038.4	
Education; health and social work; other community, social and personal services		1845.8	2438.9	3091.0	3679.6	4257.3	5282.0	6665.3	7342.0	8487.0	9727.1	10565.5	
Private households with employed persons		22.7	34.8	80.7	44.3	53.0	95.4	131.1	136.6	151.5	166.6	121.7	
Plus: Statistical discrepancy (otherwise, please specify)	a	-432.9	-462.7	-647.0	-729.8	-756.9	-1116.5	-1215.8	-1309.1	-984.8	-1498.8	-1774.5	
VALUE ADDED GROSS, at basic prices	b	16773.0	19689.3	23523.0	27517.6	31615.9	37338.7	44412.9	51773.6	50809.2	59920.7	68389.6	

[a] Refers to financial intermediation services indirectly measured (FISIM).
[b] Excludes financial intermediation services indirectly measured (FISIM).

Romania

Source

In Romania, annual non-financial national accounts are elaborated by Department of National Accounts and Macroeconomic Synthesis from General Department of National Accounts and Macroeconomic Synthesis, National Institute of Statistics (NIS) located in Bucharest.

The financial national accounts and Balance of payments statistics are separately elaborated by National Bank of Romania, Statistics Division, Monetary and Financial Statistics Department.

The official estimates together with the main concepts of non-financial national accounts are annually published in Romanian Statistical Yearbook, within Chapter dedicated to National Accounts. This publication can be found on the internet NIS web-site (www.insse.ro) under the label "Anuarul statistic", "Conturi naționale" chapter.

All data series are available in the database called TEMPO which is accessible via the NIS web-site. The final version of annual national accounts in current and constant prices is published within "National Accounts" brochure yearly issued both in Romanian and English versions. The brochure contains information on evolution of the Romanian macroeconomic figures, the explanations of the ESA95 concepts.

Starting in 2007, since Romania is European Union Member State, the Romanian national accounts are subject to European Commission direct monitoring and control. In the framework of the European legislation regarding "EU own resources", Romania has produced GNI Inventory report containing Romanian national accounts methodology. This report is still under revision, is not available to the public as yet.

General

The latest estimates of Romanian national accounts are compiled according to European System of Accounts 1995 (ESA95), compatible with System of National Accounts 1993 (1993 SNA). 1993 SNA/ESA95 has been applied since the 1998 compilation year; the annual series 1995-1997 were revised according ESA95/SNA93, while the annual data for 1990-1994 are available according to ESA79/1968 SNA.

The main synthesis tables published also in the National Accounts brochure each year are the Supply-Use/Input-Output Tables and the Table of Integrated Economic Accounts (the sequence of accounts). The symmetric Input-Output table in current and constant prices according to the required classification by Eurostat is performed once at 5 years.

The fiscal year is the calendar year.

The constant prices estimation is based on the previous year prices. The main indicators used for the deflation and extrapolation are:
- Consumer price indices (CPI)
- Industrial producer price indices (IPPI)
- Turnover indices
- Turnover volume indices
- Price index of agricultural production, calculated by products
- Volume index of industrial production
- Cost index of construction
- Unit value indices for imports and exports of goods
- Volume index of investments.

Some of these series are compiled and provided by other departments of the NIS while others are estimated within the national accounts department.

The classification NACE Rev.2 was introduced in 2008. A revision process is performed in order to bring the series by industry for years 1995-2007 to NACE Rev.2. The preferred working level of detail by industry is 99 divisions.

Romania receives the National Accounts Questionnaire annually from UNSD which is filled with data on GDP (in current and constant prices) and aggregates from institutional sectors accounts.

Methodology:

Overview of GDP Compilation

Gross Domestic Product is estimated based on the three methods: production approach, expenditure approach and income approach. They are available in the provisional (T+75 days), semi-final (T+12 months) and final (T+21 months) versions of GDP/National accounts. The sequence of accounts of institutional sectors is compiled also in provisional (T+90 days), semi-final (T+12 months) and final (T+21 months) versions. The GDP aggregates are compiled both by industries and by institutional sectors. For constant prices estimates of GDP, only the output and expenditure approaches are applied. The GDP approaches are reconciled within the Supply and Uses Tables, both in current and constant prices.

Expenditure Approach

The expenditure approach represents, for Romanian NA, a base approach, together with the production approach for GDP. It represents the uses side of the economy, shown in the supply and use tables, in current and constant prices.

The main data sources used to compile GDP by expenditure approach are:
- Statistical data sources: Structural Business Survey (SBS), Households Budget Survey (HBS), balance of agricultural products, retail trade data/ commodity flow, Census on population and dwellings, other statistical sources;
- Administrative data sources: accounting statements of enterprises submitted to the Ministry of Public Finance (MoPF); Budgetary execution (covering central government, social security, local and special funds), plus autonomous public institutions' budgets (financed by extra budgetary funds); Balance of payments (BoP) from the National Bank of Romania; Declarations on global income from the MoPF submitted by the self-employed and family associations (referred to also unincorporated enterprises).

The majority of the expenditure is accounted for by households spending on goods and services. The calculation of expenditure is essentially linked to the HBS and SBS.

HBS offers information regarding:
- The food products and alcoholic drinks;
- Purchases of non-food goods;
- Expenditures for rendering services: rents, health services, transport services, postal services;
- Expenditures on investments;
- Endowment of goods;

Structural business survey comprises detailed information about retail trade and services. Imputed rent, non-observed economy part and products obtained for own use is separately compiled and added.

The consumption expenditure of NPISHs is valued as the sum of costs involved by rendering these services. It is computed as the difference between the total output of NPISHs and the value of the market output of this sector. Consumption expenditures incurred by government units is made by:
- expenditures for individual consumption, and
- expenditures for collective consumption.

The consumption expenditure of general government is valued as the sum of costs incurred to produce these services.

Gross fixed capital formation for a unit includes all the expenses for acquiring new fixed assets to the unit, less sales, or for improving existing assets, including major renovations. Gross fixed capital formation for tangible fixed assets is estimated both by product and by institutional sectors. GFCF by product and for the economy in total therefore refers to acquisition of new assets only. GFCF by institutional sectors covers acquisitions less disposals of existing assets. These two different totals, in the input-output table and in the Integrated Economic Accounts Table for sectors, are reconciled.

Changes in inventories are measured by the value of entries into inventories less the value of withdrawals. In Romanian business accounts, enterprises record the values of inventories at the beginning and the end of the accounting periods, based on 'historic cost' (accounting value of inventories). National Accounts has to apply the valuation based on actual period prices, so inventories had to be re-valued. In this sense, it was applied the method of "middle of the year" prices for re-valuation and obtaining the economic value of inventories.

The estimates of exports and imports of goods and services are presented by 99 product divisions NACE Rev.2, as integrated in SUTs. Data on exports and imports of goods are available from INTRA and EXTRASTAT statistics by product level-Combined Nomenclature, being further re-classified by CPA2008. Data for exports and imports of services are obtained from Balance of payments.

Regarding data on constant prices, the above enumerated indices are used. The final consumption expenditure is estimated by each component, as follows:
- For households final consumption consumer price indices, price indices of agricultural products, price indices of market rent;
- The government final consumption estimates are tightly linked to the output data, price indices of non-market output and consumer price indices for market output are used.
- For the Gross Fixed Capital Formation, aggregated indices of output and import of goods entering within this category are used, specifically basic price IPPI are adjusted to the purchase price valuation basis of GFCF.
- The constant prices estimate of changes in inventories is undertaken by deflating values of the changes in inventories adjusted for holding gains and losses in current prices with the same type of synthetic indices which are calculated and used to deflate intermediate consumption and to estimate holding gains and losses.
- The deflation of import-export components is made in special using unit value indices, producer price indices and exchange rate changes.

Income Approach

The generation of income account, which is the base for income approach of GDP, is compiled both by homogenous branches (formed by Local Kind of Activity Units (LKAU)) and by institutional sectors in parallel with the production account. It is an integral part of supply and use tables and Integrated Economic Accounts Table, constituting the table of primary inputs.

In Romania, the GDP by income approach is estimated using independent sources by institutional sectors. By homogenous branches the gross operating surplus is not allocated using directly the data sources, thus is compiled as residual.

The main data sources used to compile the generation of income accounts are:
- by homogenous branches: SBS, Labour Force Survey (LFS), HBS, Labour cost survey (S3), balance of agricultural products; Budgetary execution
- by institutional sectors: Accounting statements submitted by financial enterprises, non-financial enterprises and non profit institutions serving households to the Ministry of Public Finance, Declarations on global income of self-employed and family associations submitted to Ministry of Public Finance, Budgetary execution.

Compensation of employees is directly compiled using the statistics on wages (SBS, S3), accounting statements, budgetary execution and Declarations on global income of self-employed and family associations. The employees' social contributions are compiled based on information regarding the quantum legally established to be paid to: state funds for social security, for unemployment, for health, a.s.o.

Other taxes and subsidies on production are valuated on accrual basis, being identified/classified and adjusted from the budgetary execution.

Aggregates of the income approach are not estimated in constant prices.

During the latest years, there were developed the estimates on employment according to ESA95. Employment is compiled in number of persons and hours-worked by employees and self-employed persons. They are correlated to the estimates on Compensation of employees (D.1). The main data source for Employment based on ESA95 is Labour Force Survey, completed by administrative data and plausibility adjustments.

Production Approach

This approach is for Romania the base one, due to various data sources available and enhanced by the compilation process.

The output approach to GDP is compiled both by institutional sector and by kind of activity, covering the goods and services and production accounts. Final estimates by kind of activity and by institutional sectors are simultaneously elaborated in the framework of the resources-uses tables.

All exhaustiveness adjustments are specified by institutional sector and also at the level of LKAU/homogenous branches.

The data sources used for the estimations for the final version of GDP are: Structural business survey, Households budget survey, Economic Agricultural Accounts, accounting statements of financial, insurance and non-financial corporations and non-profit institutions, General government budgetary execution, Balance of Payment, income declaration for self employed and family associations etc.

Output is valued at basic prices, this valuation being directly identified or assuming the basic prices of the similar products from the market. The products/services used for intermediate consumption are valued at the purchasers' prices. Taxes and subsidies on products and production are evaluated on accrual basis in national accounts. Gross value added is mostly compiled as difference between output and intermediate consumption.

Measurement of output for General government and NPISHs is based on costs available by economic classification, by adding up the items of both intermediate consumption and gross value added (GVA is obtained directly, not as a balancing item).

The output and intermediate consumption for agriculture are supplied by the specialised department of the NIS, based on balance of agricultural products and Economic Accounts of Agriculture, including also the estimations for output produced for own-consumption.

Data for most manufacturing industries are based on direct methods, that is, sample surveys and financial statements for producers and administrative records of government. The SBS covers all businesses and collects detailed data on production and intermediate consumption (e.g. distribution of expenditures from intermediate consumption over consuming activities of enterprise (NACE classes) and by products and services according to their provenience.

Separate special surveys, administrated by special departments of NIS, give more information on industries as: trade (for turnover), transport (also volume indicators), construction, hotels and restaurants, telecommunications etc. The statistical surveys held by NIS are mostly adapted to the SNA93/ ESA95 concepts in order to supply direct information for national accounts estimations.

For the estimation of imputed rent, the "Stratification method" is applied, together with consumer price indices. The real estate (physical) data are based on the benchmark data from Census of population and dwellings and other statistical reports.

For the financial institutions, value added is derived from accounting statements of these institutions and also from the financial records of the supervisory boards in the field.

The value added of government services is estimated by adding the cost items obtained from budgetary reports. The method is also applied for public health services. The estimation of other services is based on annual turnover statistics.

Regarding the non-observed economy in Romania, the exhaustiveness adjustments are made for:
- under-reported value added by registered institutional units in the non-financial corporations because of the underground utilisation of labour;
- value added taxes evasion/fraud for non-financial corporations sector;
- for activities performed by family associations and self-employed not elsewhere registered.

For the constant prices estimations, double deflation is mostly applied, using the price and volume indices as for expenditure approach. Some indices are resultant indices from the balancing process between resources and uses within the synthesis table. Also, the intermediate consumption matrix is obtained in current and constant prices, by applying the appropriate price indices (CPI mostly) and technical coefficients.

Overview of the Compilation of the Integrated Economic Accounts

According to ESA95, units are classified into institutional sectors, as follows:
- Non-financial corporations (S11)
- Financial corporations (S.12)
- General government (S.13),
- Households (S.14)
- Non-profit institutions serving households (S.15)
- Rest of the world (S.2)

The main non-financial accounts that are elaborated in the framework of national accounting according to the ESA95 methodology are the following:
- production account
- primary distribution of income account:
- generation of income account
- allocation of primary income account
- entrepreneurial income account
- allocation of other primary income account
- secondary distribution of income account
- redistribution of income in kind account
- use of income account
- use of disposable income account
- use of adjusted disposable income account
- capital account:
- change in net worth due to saving and capital transfers account
- acquisitions of non-financial assets account
- external account of goods and services

Data sources

The main data sources used for the compilation of the annual sector accounts are:

a. Financial-accounting data sources:
- Financial statements of financial corporations;

- Financial statements of non-financial corporations and NPISHs.

b. Administrative data sources:
- state budget execution, local budget execution, execution account of external loans, state social security budget execution, budget execution of National Fund of Health Insurance, unemployment budget execution, expenditures and incomes of public institutions financed wholly and partly from own revenues, expenditures and incomes of public institutions financed from own revenues
- Balance of Payments.

c. Statistical data sources:
- Households budget survey;
- Labour force survey
- Labour cost survey
- Economic Accounts of Agriculture;
- Balance of agricultural products;
- Structural Business Survey;
- Census of population and dwellings;
- External trade statistics (Intrastat system, Extrastat system)
- Statistical survey on changes in dwellings stock
- Statistical survey on prices and tariffs of goods and services

Table 1.1 Gross domestic product by expenditures at current prices

Series 200: 1993 SNA, New Romanian Leu, Western calendar year — **Data in millions**

	2001	2002	2003	2004	2005	2006	2007	2008	2009	2010	2011	2012
Series	**200**											
	Expenditures of the gross domestic product											
Final consumption expenditure	100731.7	127118.8	168818.7	211054.6	251038.1	294867.6	344937.0	420917.5	404275.5	419801.2	436485.0	459012.1
Household final consumption expenditure	80170.3	102412.2	128437.9	167644.3	197069.2	233134.9	273418.1	327927.7	304667.1	327241.5	345046.6	358514.1
NPISHs final consumption expenditure	1444.0	1814.7	2302.4	3129.1	3803.2	4319.8	4940.4	5865.9	6704.8	7115.7	7672.5	8240.2
General government final consumption expenditure	19117.2	22891.9	38078.4	40281.2	50165.7	57412.9	66578.5	87123.9	92903.6	85444.0	83765.9	92257.8
Individual consumption expenditure	10562.8	12668.8	18655.5	20725.6	26056.3	30986.6	34864.8	47314.5	49030.2	48089.0	48617.7	53546.4
Collective consumption expenditure	8554.4	10223.1	19422.9	19555.6	24109.4	26426.3	31713.7	39809.4	43873.4	37355.0	35148.2	38711.4
Gross capital formation	26186.2	33446.1	43370.2	58551.4	67286.6	91188.3	128858.7	160896.9	127137.4	133898.6	149909.4	158780.5
Gross fixed capital formation	24171.4	32366.5	42496.6	53850.3	68526.6	88272.0	125645.3	164279.4	122441.9	129421.8	144558.2	156927.6
Changes in inventories [a]	2014.8	1079.6	873.6	4701.1	-1240.0	2916.3	3213.4	-3382.5	4695.5	4476.8	5351.2	1852.9
Acquisitions less disposals of valuables	...	...	...	...	...	...	...	...	...	...	...	...
Exports of goods and services	38997.4	53763.0	68657.9	88646.4	95595.6	111250.3	121895.7	156629.3	153355.5	185499.7	222873.0	234974.9
Exports of goods	32984.8	45905.1	58525.3	76794.0	80662.7	91471.7	98578.5	123812.4	123344.5	157435.8	191913.9	200730.8
Exports of services	6012.6	7857.9	10132.6	11852.4	14932.9	19778.6	23317.2	32816.9	30011.0	28063.9	30959.1	34244.1
Less: Imports of goods and services	47969.5	62310.9	83419.2	110884.4	124965.7	152655.6	179684.6	223743.7	183629.0	215506.2	252559.0	265268.1
Imports of goods	41699.8	54563.4	73596.7	98262.3	108866.8	132995.4	158130.6	193957.1	152456.0	189317.2	223253.0	233648.1
Imports of services	6269.7	7747.5	9822.5	12622.1	16098.9	19660.2	21554.0	29786.6	31173.0	26189.0	29306.0	31620.0
Equals: GROSS DOMESTIC PRODUCT	117945.8	152017.0	197427.6	247368.0	288954.6	344650.6	416006.8	514700.0	501139.4	523693.3	556708.4[b]	587499.4[c]

[a] Includes Acquisitions less disposals of valuables.
[b] Data for this year refers to semi-final data.
[c] Data for this year refers to provisional data.

Table 1.2 Gross domestic product by expenditures at constant prices

Series 200: 1993 SNA, New Romanian Leu, Western calendar year **Data in millions**

	2001	2002	2003	2004	2005	2006	2007	2008	2009	2010	2011	2012
Series	**200**											
Base year	**2000**	**2001**	**2002**	**2003**	**2004**	**2005**	**2006**	**2007**	**2008**	**2009**	**2010**	**2011**
Expenditures of the gross domestic product												
Final consumption expenditure	74175.9	104961.5	138007.4	186255.2	229794.3	274563.5	323036.3	374798.7	389944.7	398978.4	423780.4	441595.9
Household final consumption expenditure	59595.1	85192.9	110977.8	148703.6	184539.9	222471.6	261032.4	298007.1	293784.9	303945.3	331078.0	348442.5
NPISHs final consumption expenditure	1066.2	1444.8	1902.8	2759.2	3441.8	3994.4	4633.5	5402.8	6366.1	6525.2	7085.5	8000.8
General government final consumption expenditure	13514.6	18323.8	25126.8	34792.4	41812.6	48097.5	57370.4	71388.8	89793.7	88507.9	85616.9	85152.6
Individual consumption expenditure	7019.0	10336.3	13825.9	17292.5	21813.1	26754.0	30296.4	37699.5	46187.5	50646.9	48377.5	49167.8
Collective consumption expenditure	6495.6	7987.5	11300.9	17499.9	19999.5	21343.5	27074.0	33689.3	43606.2	37861.0	37239.4	35984.8
Gross capital formation	18297.7	27175.8	35814.1	51446.7	61130.1	84829.8	117804.9	133666.0	122155.0	126756.3	143703.6	153072.6
Gross fixed capital formation	16753.9	26329.7	35201.5	47179.7	62107.8	82143.4	115027.4	145188.4	118140.1	120209.6	138858.9	151701.2
Changes in inventories [a]	1543.8	846.1	612.6	4267.0	-977.7	2686.4	2777.5	-11522.4	4014.9	6546.7	4844.7	1371.4
Acquisitions less disposals of valuables	...	...	...	...	...	...	...	...	...	...	...	...
Exports of goods and services	29755.6	45662.8	58752.2	78304.7	95368.9	105575.6	119971.1	131999.4	146534.0	173614.9	204656.3	216150.6
Exports of goods	25127.3	39026.6	49447.3	68093.7	80870.5	87951.1	98113.8	102363.0[b]	119335.9	146851.7	175011.1	183591.1
Exports of services	4628.3	6636.2	9304.9	10211.0	14498.4	17624.5	21857.3	29636.4	27198.1	26763.2	29645.2	32559.5
Less: Imports of goods and services	36645.6	53866.2	72596.0	101816.9	128650.5	153259.7	194389.5	193885.8	177780.3	203968.3	237146.3	250274.4
Imports of goods	32080.1	47131.7	69020.6	98079.8	122409.4	144068.6	174102.8	165504.7	149199.5	178421.0	208830.1	220579.4
Imports of services	4565.5	6734.5	3575.4	3737.1	6241.1	9191.1	20286.7	28381.1	28580.8	25547.3	28316.2	29695.0
Equals: GROSS DOMESTIC PRODUCT	85583.6	123933.9	159977.7	214189.7	257642.8	311709.2	366422.8	446578.3	480853.4	495381.3	534994.0[b]	560544.7[c]

[a] Includes Acquisitions less disposals of valuables.
[b] Data for this year refers to semi-final data.
[c] Data for this year refers to provisional data.

Table 1.3 Relations among product, income, savings, and net lending aggregates

Series 200: 1993 SNA, New Romanian Leu, Western calendar year **Data in millions**

	2001	2002	2003	2004	2005	2006	2007	2008	2009	2010	2011	2012
Series	**200**											
GROSS DOMESTIC PRODUCT	117946.0	152017.0	197428.0	247368.0	288955.0	344651.0	416007.0	514700.0	501139.0	523693.3	556708.4[a]	587499.4[b]
Plus: Compensation of employees - from and to the rest of the world, net	319.0	433.8	344.2	348.5	2723.0	3124.5	3823.9	3832.7	1892.0	1758.0	1727.0	2147.0
Plus: Compensation of employees - from the rest of the world	329.4	452.7	367.2	368.8	2788.1	3243.9	3954.1	4260.1	2086.0	2040.0	2118.0	2547.0
Less: Compensation of employees - to the rest of the world	10.4	18.9	23.0	20.3	65.1	119.4	130.2	427.4	194.0	282.0	391.0	400.0
Plus: Property income - from and to the rest of the world, net	-1210.9	-2036.6	-4915.5	-10714.7	-11213.8	-14660.6	-17702.9	-17853.9	-10015.0	-9966.9	-11232.0	-10286.1
Plus: Property income - from the rest of the world	1011.1	903.7	858.8	958.8	1600.8	2736.3	4141.8	4079.0	2925.0	1801.3	3312.8	3412.4
Less: Property income - to the rest of the world	2222.0	2940.3	5774.3	11673.5	12814.6	17396.9	21844.7	21932.9	12940.0	11768.2	14544.8	13698.5
Sum of Compensation of employees and property income - from and to the rest of the world, net	-891.9	-1602.8	-4571.3	-10366.2	-8490.8	-11536.1	-13878.8	-14021.2	-8123.0	-8208.9	-9505.0	-8139.1

	2001	2002	2003	2004	2005	2006	2007	2008	2009	2010	2011	2012
Series	**200**											
Plus: Sum of Compensation of employees and property income - from the rest of the world	1340.5	1356.4	1226.0	1327.6	4388.9	5980.2	8095.9	8339.1	5011.0	3841.3	5430.8	5959.4
Less: Sum of Compensation of employees and property income - to the rest of the world	2232.4	2959.2	5797.3	11693.8	12879.7	17516.3	21974.7	22360.3	13134.0	12050.2	14935.8	14098.5
Plus: Taxes less subsidies on production and imports - from and to the rest of the world, net	...	...	...	...	...	...	-1046.6	-895.7	1312.3	1794.3	2215.3	3126.9
Plus: Taxes less subsidies on production and imports - from the rest of the world	...	...	...	...	...	...	...	...	...	...	...	...
Less: Taxes less subsidies on production and imports - to the rest of the world	...	...	...	...	...	...	1046.6	895.7	-1312.3	-1794.3	-2215.3	-3126.9
Equals: GROSS NATIONAL INCOME	117054.0	150414.0	192856.0	237002.0	280464.0	333115.0	401081.0	499783.0	494329.0	517278.7	549418.7	582487.2
Plus: Current transfers - from and to the rest of the world, net	3248.2	8477.3	9658.9	18242.0	12200.9	16442.8	16055.9	23279.3	16185.7	13456.3	11963.1	11764.8
Plus: Current transfers - from the rest of the world	4013.4	9357.1	10759.4	19801.7	13835.5	18676.1	23979.4	32481.0	25946.5	22557.4	21037.1	20948.2
Less: Current transfers - to the rest of the world	765.1	879.8	1100.5	1559.7	1634.6	2233.3	7923.5	9201.7	9760.8	9101.1	9074.0	9183.4
Equals: GROSS NATIONAL DISPOSABLE INCOME	120302.0	158892.0	202515.0	255244.0	292665.0	349557.0	417137.0	523062.0	510514.0	530735.0	561381.8	594252.0
Less: Final consumption expenditure / Actual final consumption	100732.0	127119.0	168819.0	211055.0	251038.0	294868.0	344937.0	420918.0	404276.0	419801.2	436485.0	459012.1
Equals: SAVING, GROSS	19570.4	31772.7	33696.5	44189.2	41626.6	54689.7	72200.3	102145.0	106239.0	110933.8	124896.8	135239.9
Plus: Capital transfers - from and to the rest of the world, net	391.1	505.1	911.7	2302.8	2961.3	507.6	2383.3	2290.8	2174.7	969.5	2367.1	7219.3
Plus: Capital transfers - from the rest of the world	455.6	553.6	972.0	2420.2	3330.5	3196.9	3316.4	3258.6	3353.4	2001.5	3580.7	8057.1
Less: Capital transfers - to the rest of the world	64.5	48.5	60.3	117.4	369.2	2689.3	933.1	967.8	1178.7	1032.0	1213.6	837.8
Less: Gross capital formation	26186.2	33446.1	43370.2	58551.4	67286.6	91188.3	128859.0	160897.0	127137.0	133898.6	149909.4	158780.5
Less: Acquisitions less disposals of non-produced non-financial assets	...	...	...	...	...	...	-359.6	-18.8	-563.8	-73.8	-684.3	-1272.6
Equals: NET LENDING (+) / NET BORROWING (-) OF THE NATION	-6224.7	-1168.3	-8762.0	-12059.4	-22698.7	-35991.0	-53915.5	-56442.4	-18160.0	-21921.5	-21961.2	-15048.7
	Net values: Gross National Income / Gross National Disposable Income / Saving Gross less Consumption of fixed capital											
Less: Consumption of fixed capital	23508.2	34041.3	46110.2	49195.9	54117.9	59843.1	66579.9	79002.4	90297.0	93309.2	...	...
Equals: NET NATIONAL INCOME	93545.8	116372.7	146745.8	187806.1	226346.1	273271.9	334501.1	420780.6	404032.0	423969.5	...	...
Equals: NET NATIONAL DISPOSABLE INCOME	96793.8	124850.7	156404.8	206048.1	238547.1	289713.9	350557.1	444059.6	420217.0	437425.8	...	...
Equals: SAVING, NET	-3937.8	-2268.6	-12413.7	-5006.7	-12491.3	-5153.4	5620.4	23142.6	15942.0	17624.6	...	...

[a] Data for this year refers to semi-final data.
[b] Data for this year refers to provisional data.

Table 2.1 Value added by industries at current prices (ISIC Rev. 3)

Series 200: 1993 SNA, New Romanian Leu, Western calendar year | **Data in millions**

	2001	2002	2003	2004	2005	2006	2007	2008	2009	2010	2011	2012
Series	**200**											
	Industries											
Agriculture, hunting, forestry; fishing	15641.6	17289.3	22847.5	31055.0	24291.8	26861.9	23992.2	34126.3	31734.9	30728.6		
Agriculture, hunting, forestry	15634.8	17280.6	22833.5	31041.2	24278.0	26845.8	23966.3	34081.9	31689.0	...		
Agriculture, hunting and related service activities	15121.9	16592.2	21810.4	29931.3	23139.6	25571.9	22491.9	32412.4	...	...		
Forestry, logging and related service activities	512.9	688.4	1023.1	1109.9	1138.4	1273.9	1474.4	1669.5	...	...		
Fishing	6.8	8.7	14.0	13.8	13.8	16.1	25.9	44.4	45.9	...		
Mining and quarrying	2142.1	2733.2	2741.0	3271.2	3788.5	4744.6	5657.5	5175.4	121842.5[a]	135472.0[a]		
Manufacturing	26134.9	33424.8	40412.6	52061.7	61250.3	72416.3	86951.9	102836.3	...	...		
Electricity, gas and water supply	2970.4	4937.5	5624.5	6294.3	6692.4	7395.1	8538.6	10474.3	...	...		
Construction	6237.3	8648.8	11318.4	14649.0	18865.2	25547.8	37923.8	54628.2	49350.0	45481.9		
Wholesale, retail trade, repair of motor vehicles, motorcycles and personal and households goods; hotels and restaurants	12658.5	15649.1	20626.2	26153.5	33221.0	41629.3	50843.3	63277.1	60618.6	62435.7		
Wholesale, retail trade, repair of motor vehicles, motorcycles and personal and household goods	10620.6	12919.1	17512.0	22349.9	28131.1	35007.8	43026.0	54549.8	52083.8	53075.0		
Hotels and restaurants	2037.9	2730.0	3114.2	3803.6	5089.9	6621.5	7817.3	8727.3	8534.8	9360.7		
Transport, storage and communications	11302.3	14479.4	19470.1	24827.0	29345.8	34803.3	43532.5	51485.4	46937.6	46066.6		
Land transport; transport via pipelines, water transport; air transport; Supporting and auxiliary transport activities; activities of travel agencies	7277.6	9621.3	13285.8	16909.5	20963.3	25007.1	31752.0	37782.7	32598.2	32982.3		
Post and telecommunications	4024.7	4858.1	6184.3	7917.5	8382.5	9796.2	11780.5	13702.7	14339.4	13084.3		
Financial intermediation; real estate, renting and business activities	16023.4	21572.8	24299.4	30426.1	38189.9	45694.1	57006.0	68622.0	68265.8	71473.4[b]		
Financial intermediation	4067.6	3857.2	3685.5	5592.9	5826.4	6181.6	7923.1	11425.0	10555.9	10970.6		
Real estate, renting and business activities	11955.8	17715.6	20613.9	24833.2	32363.5	39512.5	49082.9	57197.0	57709.9	60502.8[b]		
Public administration and defence; compulsory social security	4542.7	6059.5	12329.3	11604.8	14613.0	16015.5	19567.1	22169.9	22057.2	64265.9[c]		
Education; health and social work; other community, social and personal services	8466.8	12127.9	15971.9	20588.7	24974.8	29161.9	34343.4	45740.6	47040.6	...		
Education	3489.2	4431.4	6104.6	8345.7	9744.5	10924.5	12079.1	17340.0	16840.2	...		
Health and social work	2351.6	3853.8	4949.4	6137.6	7692.1	8372.4	10304.0	13945.3	14586.6	...		
Other community, social and personal services	2626.0	3842.7	4917.9	6105.4	7538.2	9865.0	11960.3	14455.3	15613.8	...		
Private households with employed persons	...	...	...	...	...	...	...	...	...	...		
Equals: VALUE ADDED, GROSS, in basic prices	106120.0	136922.3	175640.9	220931.3	255232.7	304269.8	368356.3	458535.5	447847.2	455924.1		
Less: Financial intermediation services indirectly measured (FISIM)	...	...	...	...	...	...	...	...	...	...		
Plus: Taxes less Subsidies on products	11825.8	15094.7	21786.7	26436.7	33721.9	40380.8	47650.5	56164.5	50160.3	57716.7		
Plus: Taxes on products	12591.4	16688.4	23025.4	27854.5	35811.8	41950.3	49238.3	57607.9	51366.1	58807.7		
Less: Subsidies on products	765.6	1593.7	1238.7	1417.8	2089.9	1569.5	1587.8	1443.4	1205.8	1091.0		

	2001	2002	2003	2004	2005	2006	2007	2008	2009	2010	2011	2012
Series	**200**											
Equals: GROSS DOMESTIC PRODUCT	117945.8	152017.0	197427.6	247368.0	288954.6	344650.6	416006.8	514700.0	498007.5[d]	513640.8[d]		
Memorandum Item: FISIM, if distributed to uses	1798.5	1681.0	2802.6	3494.4	4723.2	4832.1	6404.7	7978.2	7858.8	7841.2		

[a] Includes Manufacturing, and Electricity, gas and water supply.
[b] Includes other community, social and personal services
[c] Includes Education, Health and Social work.
[d] Data for this year(s) have not been revised. Discrepancy with corresponding item in Table 1.1 - Gross domestic product by expenditures at current prices.

Table 2.2 Value added by industries at constant prices (ISIC Rev. 3)

Series 200: 1993 SNA, New Romanian Leu, Western calendar year **Data in millions**

	2001	2002	2003	2004	2005	2006	2007	2008	2009	2010	2011	2012
Series	**200**											
Base year	**2000**	**2001**	**2002**	**2003**	**2004**	**2005**	**2006**	**2007**	**2008**	**2009**		
	Industries											
Agriculture, hunting, forestry; fishing	11250.0	14558.7	18159.4	27105.3	25721.3	25126.8	22743.9	28957.3	29249.8	31479.6		
Agriculture, hunting, forestry	11247.0	14551.4	18149.6	27092.7	25707.3	25112.5	22727.5	28920.5	29206.0	...		
Agriculture, hunting and related service activities	10865.5	13994.8	17422.0	26103.4	24603.3	23927.3	21367.2	27397.8	...	...		
Forestry, logging and related service activities	381.5	556.5	727.6	989.3	1104.0	1185.2	1360.3	1522.7	...	...		
Fishing	3.2	7.3	9.8	12.6	14.0	14.3	16.4	36.8	43.8	...		
Mining and quarrying	1707.4	1985.1	2725.6	2858.0	3252.1	3848.4	4760.6	4728.7	116783.0[a]	128017.0[a]		
Manufacturing	18253.1	27573.9	35139.6	44184.7	53929.4	66055.3	76989.2	89013.7	...	...		
Electricity, gas and water supply	2154.9	3420.5	5033.0	5436.9	6044.9	6964.6	7374.8	9298.7	...	...		
Construction	4331.8	6788.7	9258.1	12381.5	16282.8	23271.0	34204.4	47854.9	47364.3	44074.8		
Wholesale, retail trade, repair of motor vehicles, motorcycles and personal and household goods; hotels and restaurants	10048.0	13173.8	17605.8	22977.2	30263.2	38940.6	47586.9	56371.4	57325.3	59071.5		
Wholesale, retail trade, repair of motor vehicles, motorcycles and personal and household goods	8325.1	11020.3	14828.8	19726.5	26021.6	33073.0	40503.7	48161.3	49164.4	50094.2		
Hotels and restaurants	1722.9	2153.5	2777.0	3250.7	4241.6	5867.6	7083.2	8210.1	8160.9	8977.3		
Transport, storage and communications	7906.3	12073.4	15596.9	21539.4	26608.0	31869.5	36686.7	45775.0	45505.9	44198.9		
Land transport; transport via piplines, water transport; air transport; Supporting and auxiliary transport activities; activities of travel agencies	4831.2	7745.5	10468.7	14676.1	18549.3	22631.1	26184.7	33071.7	31544.1	31318.9		
Post and telecommunications	3075.1	4327.9	5128.2	6863.3	8058.7	9238.4	10502.0	12703.3	13961.8	12880.0		
Financial intermediation, real estate, renting and business activities	12064.2	17756.2	21637.4	26620.7	33524.4	42724.1	48967.1	59492.1	79813.2[b]	68824.1[b]		
Financial intermediation	3105.7	3708.7	3522.6	4688.0	5723.3	5908.0	7230.6	8948.8	10349.2	10342.4		
Real estate, renting and business activities	8958.5	14047.5	18114.8	21932.7	27801.1	36816.1	41736.5	50543.3	69464.0[b]	58481.7[b]		
Public administration and defence; compulsory social security	3488.4	4761.1	6502.5	10339.6	11860.4	11970.5	15659.1	18610.7	22298.7[c]	67150.5[c]		
Education; health and social work; other community, social and personal services	5794.6	9320.4	12255.3	17121.3	21316.3	24433.8	30188.5	36034.8	30837.8	...		
Education	2149.0	3634.8	4625.5	6649.9	8489.8	9330.1	11010.3	13370.3	16924.5	...		
Health and social work	1329.2	2773.3	3906.8	5117.9	6374.7	6786.7	8584.7	10677.0	13913.3	...		

	2001	2002	2003	2004	2005	2006	2007	2008	2009	2010	2011	2012
Series	**200**											
Base year	**2000**	**2001**	**2002**	**2003**	**2004**	**2005**	**2006**	**2007**	**2008**	**2009**		
Other community, social and personal services	2316.4	2912.3	3723.0	5353.5	6451.8	8317.0	10593.5	11987.5	...	...		
Private households with employed persons	...	...	...	...	...	...	...	...	...	...		
Equals: VALUE ADDED, GROSS, in basic prices	76998.7	111411.8	143913.6	190564.6	228802.8	275204.6	325161.2	396137.3	429178.0	442816.4		
Less: Financial intermediation services indirectly measured (FISIM)	...	...	...	...	...	...	...	...	...	...		
Plus: Taxes less Subsidies on products	8584.9	12522.1	16064.1	23625.1	28840.0	36504.6	41261.6	50441.0	49089.6	48883.5		
Plus: Taxes on products	9480.4	13407.8	17728.0	24842.0	30261.1	37593.5	42350.5	51620.4	50294.0	50073.7		
Less: Subsidies on products	895.5	885.7	1663.9	1216.9	1421.1	1088.9	1088.9	1179.4	1204.4	1190.2		
Equals: GROSS DOMESTIC PRODUCT	85583.6	123933.9	159977.7	214189.7	257642.8	311709.2	366422.8	446578.3	478267.6[d]	491699.9[d]		
Memorandum Item: FISIM, if distributed to uses	1337.1	1238.5	...	...	...	...	...	...	...	...		

[a] Includes Manufacturing, and Electricity, gas and water supply.
[b] Includes other community, social and personal services
[c] Includes Education, Health and Social work.
[d] Data for this year(s) have not been revised. Discrepancy with equivalent item in Table 1.2 (Base year).

Table 2.4 Value added by industries at current prices (ISIC Rev. 4)

Series 200: 1993 SNA, New Romanian Leu, Western calendar year **Data in millions**

	2001	2002	2003	2004	2005	2006	2007	2008	2009	2010	2011	2012
Series					**200**							
	Industries											
Agriculture, forestry and fishing					24306.9	26761.4	23912.3	34126.4	32297.8	29874.2	36438.6	30897.7
Crop and animal production, hunting and related service activities					23154.7	25471.4	22411.8	32412.6	30540.2	27841.0	33669.2	...
Forestry and logging					1138.4	1274.0	1474.3	1669.4	1657.3	1879.5	2516.7	...
Fishing and aquaculture					13.8	16.0	26.2	44.4	100.3	153.7	252.7	...
Manufacturing, mining and quarrying and other industrial activities					71699.4	84633.7	101254.8	118240.1	120637.4	148553.1	160927.9	167081.0
Mining and quarrying					3788.0	4744.7	5657.2	5174.4	5914.7	8672.0	9222.4	...
Manufacturing					60407.9	71436.5	85773.3	100991.0	99186.8	113158.2	120399.0	...
Electricity, gas, steam and air conditioning supply					6110.6	6807.3	7821.3	9712.2	12261.6	19406.8	22811.7	...
Water supply; sewerage, waste management and remediation activities					1392.9	1645.2	2003.0	2362.5	3274.3	7316.1	8494.8	...
Construction					19917.3	26957.3	39334.8	56130.6	52809.4	47762.3	47563.4	50448.9
Wholesale and retail trade, transportation and storage, accommodation and food service activities					53684.7	65787.3	81393.2	99593.8	94359.5	69740.4	62764.2	67319.7
Wholesale and retail trade; repair of motor vehicles and motorcycles					27780.5	34571.8	42214.6	53994.8	46968.9	26173.2	25164.7	...
Transportation and storage					20814.3	24593.9	31361.8	37071.0	38933.0	38415.4	32914.5	...
Accommodation and food service activities					5089.9	6621.6	7816.8	8528.0	8457.6	5151.8	4685.0	...
Information and communication					11399.3	13978.6	17501.3	20047.9	19520.6	17811.8	17917.4	23391.2
Financial and insurance activities					5826.1	6181.9	7923.9	11407.3	11250.1	11681.0	14170.3	14766.8
Real estate activities					21611.1	24192.7	28971.2	31671.5	32699.0	46250.9	47449.7	49081.0

	2001	2002	2003	2004	2005	2006	2007	2008	2009	2010	2011	2012
Series					**200**							
Professional, scientific, technical, administrative and support service activities					8537.5	12356.3	15971.7	19739.5	20044.0	24716.8	30599.8	34420.3
Professional, scientific and technical activities					5519.8	8211.0	10413.0	13294.9	13901.1	14823.2	20274.8	...
Administrative and support service activities					3017.7	4145.3	5558.7	6444.6	6142.9	9893.6	10325.0	...
Public administration and defence, education, human health and social work activities					32050.3	35311.7	41978.0	55789.9	55668.2	56607.7	55110.2	61067.0
Public administration and defence; compulsory social security					14613.0	16015.0	19567.8	24343.8	24566.3	22343.0	21775.6	...
Education					9744.8	10924.4	12078.2	17510.0	17199.9	18439.6	17695.6	...
Human health and social work activities					7692.5	8372.3	10332.0	13936.1	13902.0	15825.1	15639.0	...
Other service activities					6200.1	8108.9	10115.1	11788.8	11693.1	13398.8	14385.3	15329.2
Arts, entertainment and recreation					2381.7	3117.8	3779.4	3673.1	4954.3	7434.4	7604.8	...
Other service activities					3818.4	4991.1	6335.7	8115.7	6738.8	5964.4	6780.5	...
Private households with employed persons					...	...	...	...	...	...	...	...
Equals: VALUE ADDED, GROSS, at basic prices					255232.7	304269.8	368356.3	458536.0	450979.0	466397.0	487326.8[a]	513802.8[b]
Less: Financial intermediation services indirectly measured (FISIM)					...	...	...	...	...	...	...	...
Plus: Taxes less Subsidies on products					33721.9	40380.8	47650.5	56164.5	50160.3	57296.3	69381.6	73696.6
Plus: Taxes on products					35811.8	41950.3	49238.3	57607.9	51366.1	59475.3	70208.9	74790.7
Less: Subsidies on products					2089.9	1569.5	1587.8	1443.4	1205.8	2179.0	827.3	1094.1
Equals: GROSS DOMESTIC PRODUCT					288954.6	344650.6	416006.8	514700.0	501139.0	523693.3	556708.4[a]	587499.4[b]
Memorandum Item: FISIM, if distributed to uses					4723.2	4907.5	6404.8	7978.2	7852.8	8193.1	9297.4	...

[a] Data for this year refers to semi-final data.
[b] Data for this year refers to provisional data.

Table 2.5 Value added by industries at constant prices (ISIC Rev. 4)

Series 200: 1993 SNA, New Romanian Leu, Western calendar year — **Data in millions**

	2001	2002	2003	2004	2005	2006	2007	2008	2009	2010	2011	2012
Series						**200**						
Base year						**2005**	**2006**	**2007**	**2008**	**2009**	**2010**	**2011**
Industries												
Agriculture, forestry and fishing						25115.4	22752.1	28882.7	33009.7	30522.5	33566.2	28577.0
Crop and animal production, hunting and related service activities						23915.9	21374.9	27323.1	31388.7	28357.0	30985.3	...
Forestry and logging						1185.2	1360.5	1522.7	1573.8	2113.6	2349.4	...
Fishing and aquaculture						14.3	16.7	36.9	47.2	51.9	231.5	...
Manufacturing, mining and quarrying and other industrial activities						76891.1	89630.2	102598.6	116599.1	125513.8	148665.4	159369.7
Mining and quarrying						3848.1	4758.1	4728.6	5469.0	6956.8	8414.7	...
Manufacturing						65186.1	76406.8	87661.6	97298.7	102098.0	113843.6	...
Electricity, gas, steam and air conditioning supply						6414.4	6733.5	8245.5	11272.0	10734.6	19803.5	...

	2001	2002	2003	2004	2005	2006	2007	2008	2009	2010	2011	2012
Series						**200**						
Base year						**2005**	**2006**	**2007**	**2008**	**2009**	**2010**	**2011**
Water supply; sewerage, waste management and remediation activities						1442.5	1731.8	1962.9	2559.4	5724.4	6603.6	...
Construction						24413.0	35425.8	49374.1	50578.5	50416.4	44721.5	47401.0
Wholesale and retail trade, transportation and storage, accommodation and food service activities						60769.6	72718.7	88496.9	88804.7	92140.3	68294.4	63710.8
Wholesale and retail trade; repair of motor vehicles and motorcycles						32660.8	39998.1	47560.9	46852.4	52357.0	25862.0	...
Transportation and storage						22241.3	25669.8	32726.3	34113.6	34751.1	37480.7	...
Accommodation and food service activities						5867.5	7050.8	8209.7	7838.7	5032.2	4951.7	...
Information and communication						12877.5	15552.0	18425.9	19542.7	19501.0	17981.8	23138.0
Financial and insurance activities						5908.0	7072.1	8948.9	10478.8	10387.2	13611.1	14141.3
Real estate activities						23444.2	25499.3	29679.1	29094.0	31508.5	47622.4	48226.4
Professional, scientific, technical, administrative and support service activities						10688.4	12432.7	16959.5	18664.8	19641.7	29328.9	33626.4
Professional, scientific and technical activities						7053.4	8149.2	11094.0	12496.9	13729.4	19365.7	...
Administrative and support service activities						3635.0	4283.5	5865.5	6167.9	5912.3	9963.2	...
Public administration and defence, education, human health and social work activities						28087.7	35176.7	42884.5	55098.8	54200.7	56610.0	56340.8
Public administration and defence; compulsory social security						11970.3	15659.5	18610.7	23993.5	25346.3	20801.3	...
Education						9330.6	11003.8	13597.6	17250.5	16877.3	18720.1	...
Human health and social work activities						6786.8	8513.4	10676.2	13854.8	11977.1	17088.6	...
Other service activities						7009.7	8901.6	9887.1	9892.6	9103.8	13809.3	14831.3
Arts, entertainment and recreation						2627.9	3343.4	3790.7	3700.3	3623.7	7434.8	...
Other service activities						4381.8	5558.2	6096.4	6192.3	5480.1	6374.5	...
Private households with employed persons						...	...	...	...	...	...	...
Equals: VALUE ADDED, GROSS, at basic prices						275204.6	325161.2	396137.3	431764.0	442935.9	474211.0[a]	489362.7[b]
Less: Financial intermediation services indirectly measured (FISIM)						...	...	...	...	...	...	...
Plus: Taxes less Subsidies on products						36504.6	41261.6	50441.0	49089.7	52445.4	60783.0	71182.0
Plus: Taxes on products						37593.5	42350.5	51620.4	50294.1	54504.7	63477.6	71964.2
Less: Subsidies on products						1088.9	1088.9	1179.4	1204.4	2059.3	2694.6	782.2
Equals: GROSS DOMESTIC PRODUCT						311709.2	366422.8	446578.3	480853.0	495381.3	534994.0[a]	560544.7[b]

[a] Data for this year refers to semi-final data.
[b] Data for this year refers to provisional data.

Table 2.6 Output, gross value added and fixed assets by industries at current prices (ISIC Rev. 4) Total economy

Series 200: 1993 SNA, New Romanian Leu, Western calendar year **Data in millions**

	2001	2002	2003	2004	2005	2006	2007	2008	2009	2010	2011	2012
Series					**200**							
Output, at basic prices					547894.3	656511.9	784007.5	985670.9	976996.6	1030336.7	1132017.7	1191865.2
Less: Intermediate consumption, at purchaser's prices					292661.6	352242.1	415651.2	527135.4	526017.2	563939.7	644690.9	678062.4
Equals: VALUE ADDED, GROSS, at basic prices					255232.7	304269.8	368356.3	458535.5	450979.4	466397.0	487326.8[a]	513802.8[b]
Compensation of employees					112996.9	132194.9	161938.1	216151.5	203244.5	189790.9	200528.4	...
Taxes on production and imports, less Subsidies					-756.5	-2582.9	-980.9	-741.7	-1914.5	229.7	-1398.0	...
Taxes on production and imports					1436.2	1961.0	3203.4	4029.8	3476.1	3765.0	3475.9	...
Taxes on products					...	...	...	...	...	...	...	...
Other taxes on production					1436.2	1961.0	3203.4	4029.8	3476.1	3765.0	3475.9	...
Less: Subsidies					2192.7	4543.9	4184.3	4771.5	5390.6	3535.3	4873.9	...
Subsidies on products					...	...	...	...	...	...	...	...
Other subsidies on production					2192.7	4543.9	4184.3	4771.5	5390.6	3535.3	4873.9	...
OPERATING SURPLUS, GROSS					142992.3[c]	174657.8[c]	207399.1[c]	243125.7[c]	249649.4[c]	194676.0	195881.5	...
MIXED INCOME, GROSS					...	...	...	...	...	81700.4	92314.9	...
Less: Consumption of fixed capital					...	...	...	79002.4	90297.0	93309.2	...	...
OPERATING SURPLUS, NET [d]					...	...	...	164123.0	159352.0	183067.0	...	...
MIXED INCOME, NET					...	...	...	...	...	...	...	...
Gross capital formation					67286.6	91188.3	128858.7	160897.0	127137.0	133898.6	149909.4	158780.5
Gross fixed capital formation					68526.6	88272.0	125645.3	164279.0	122442.0	129421.8	144558.2	156927.6
Changes in inventories					-1240.0	2916.3	3213.4	-3382.5	4695.5	4476.8	5351.2	1852.9
Acquisitions less disposals of valuables					...	...	...	...	...	...	...	...
Employment (average, in 1000 persons)					...	...	...	9365.9	9181.0	9156.3	9058.0	9229.0

[a] Data for this year refers to semi-final data.
[b] Data for this year refers to provisional data.
[c] Includes Mixed Income, Gross.
[d] Includes Mixed Income, Net.

Table 2.6 Output, gross value added and fixed assets by industries at current prices (ISIC Rev. 4) Agriculture, forestry and fishing (A)

Series 200: 1993 SNA, New Romanian Leu, Western calendar year **Data in millions**

	2001	2002	2003	2004	2005	2006	2007	2008	2009	2010	2011	2012
Series					**200**							
Output, at basic prices					49705.1	54172.7	52951.0	73276.6	67468.3	64441.0	77914.9	67395.9
Less: Intermediate consumption, at purchaser's prices					25398.2	27411.3	29038.7	39150.2	35170.5	34566.8	41476.3	36498.2
Equals: VALUE ADDED, GROSS, at basic prices					24306.9	26761.4	23912.3	34126.4	32297.8	29874.2	36438.6[a]	30897.7[b]
Compensation of employees					5802.5	6641.1	8083.5	10581.6	10841.2	13539.1	...	...
Taxes on production and imports, less Subsidies					-1459.5	-2109.2	-2252.4	-2834.7	-4651.0	-2671.6	...	...

	2001	2002	2003	2004	2005	2006	2007	2008	2009	2010	2011	2012
Series					**200**							
Taxes on production and imports					95.5	123.8	202.3	175.8	108.1	112.5	...	...
Taxes on products					...	...	...	...	...	...	...	...
Other taxes on production					95.5	123.8	202.3	175.8	108.1	112.5	...	...
Less: Subsidies					1555.0	2233.0	2454.7	3010.5	4759.1	2784.1	...	...
Subsidies on products					...	...	...	...	...	...	...	...
Other subsidies on production					1555.0	2233.0	2454.7	3010.5	4759.1	2784.1	...	...
OPERATING SURPLUS, GROSS					19963.9[c]	22229.5[c]	18081.2[c]	26379.5[c]	26107.6[c]	-4018.2	...	...
MIXED INCOME, GROSS					...	...	...	...	...	23024.9	...	...
Gross capital formation					...	...	...	...	...	...	...	...
Employment (average, in 1000 persons)					...	...	...	2767.8	2764.2	2905.2	2731.3	2809.4

[a] Data for this year refers to semi-final data.
[b] Data for this year refers to provisional data.
[c] Includes Mixed Income, Gross.

Table 2.6 Output, gross value added and fixed assets by industries at current prices (ISIC Rev. 4) Crop and animal production, hunting and related service activities (01)

Series 200: 1993 SNA, New Romanian Leu, Western calendar year

Data in millions

	2001	2002	2003	2004	2005	2006	2007	2008	2009	2010	2011	2012
Series					**200**							
Output, at basic prices					47717.2	51929.1	50384.6	70314.1	64320.4	60478.1	72266.9	
Less: Intermediate consumption, at purchaser's prices					24562.5	26457.7	27972.8	37901.5	33780.2	32637.1	38597.7	
Equals: VALUE ADDED, GROSS, at basic prices					23154.7	25471.4	22411.8	32412.6	30540.2	27841.0	33669.2[a]	
Compensation of employees					4971.2	5690.1	6870.1	8963.4	10067.9	12387.2	...	
Taxes on production and imports, less Subsidies					-1463.3	-2115.8	-2263.3	-2844.1	-4666.2	-2686.3	...	
Taxes on production and imports					91.7	117.2	191.4	166.4	92.9	97.7	...	
Taxes on products					...	...	...	...	...	...	...	
Other taxes on production					91.7	117.2	191.4	166.4	92.9	97.7	...	
Less: Subsidies					1555.0	2233.0	2454.7	3010.5	4759.1	2784.0	...	
Subsidies on products					...	...	...	...	...	...	...	
Other subsidies on production					1555.0	2233.0	2454.7	3010.5	4759.1	2784.0	...	
OPERATING SURPLUS, GROSS					19646.8[b]	21897.1[b]	17805.0[b]	26293.3[b]	25138.5[b]	-4683.5	...	
MIXED INCOME, GROSS					...	...	...	...	...	22823.6	...	
Gross capital formation					...	...	...	...	...	...	...	
Employment (average, in 1000 persons)					...	...	...	2712.6	2726.0	2874.9	...	

[a] Data for this year refers to semi-final data.
[b] Includes Mixed Income, Gross.

Table 2.6 Output, gross value added and fixed assets by industries at current prices (ISIC Rev. 4) Forestry and logging (02)

Series 200: 1993 SNA, New Romanian Leu, Western calendar year **Data in millions**

	2001	2002	2003	2004	2005	2006	2007	2008	2009	2010	2011	2012
Series					**200**							
Output, at basic prices					1920.9	2164.0	2470.2	2797.8	2780.5	3782.3	5354.7	
Less: Intermediate consumption, at purchaser's prices					782.5	890.0	995.9	1128.4	1123.2	1902.8	2838.0	
Equals: VALUE ADDED, GROSS, at basic prices					1138.4	1274.0	1474.3	1669.4	1657.3	1879.5	2516.7	
Compensation of employees					818.6	936.5	1194.8	1593.5	742.3	1115.0	...	
Taxes on production and imports, less Subsidies					3.7	6.4	10.5	9.1	13.4	13.8	...	
Taxes on production and imports					3.7	6.4	10.5	9.1	13.4	13.8	...	
Taxes on products					...	...	...	...	...	...	...	
Other taxes on production					3.7	6.4	10.5	9.1	13.4	13.8	...	
Less: Subsidies					...	...	...	...	...	...	...	
OPERATING SURPLUS, GROSS					316.1[a]	331.1[a]	269.0[a]	66.8[a]	901.6[a]	570.2	...	
MIXED INCOME, GROSS					...	...	...	...	...	...	...	
Total Economy only: Adjustment for FISIM (if FISIM is not distributed to uses)					...	...	...	...	...	180.5	...	
Gross capital formation					...	...	...	...	...	...	...	
Employment (average, in 1000 persons)					...	...	...	53.0	36.1	19.8	...	

[a] Includes Mixed Income, Gross.

Table 2.6 Output, gross value added and fixed assets by industries at current prices (ISIC Rev. 4) Fishing and aquaculture (03)

Series 200: 1993 SNA, New Romanian Leu, Western calendar year **Data in millions**

	2001	2002	2003	2004	2005	2006	2007	2008	2009	2010	2011	2012
Series					**200**							
Output, at basic prices					67.0	79.6	96.2	164.7	367.4	180.6	293.3	
Less: Intermediate consumption, at purchaser's prices					53.2	63.6	70.0	120.3	267.1	26.9	40.6	
Equals: VALUE ADDED, GROSS, at basic prices					13.8	16.0	26.2	44.4	100.3	153.7	252.7[a]	
Compensation of employees					12.7	14.5	18.6	24.7	31.0	36.9	...	
Taxes on production and imports, less Subsidies					0.1	0.2	0.4	0.3	1.8	0.9	...	
Taxes on production and imports					0.1	0.2	0.4	0.3	1.8	1.0	...	
Taxes on products					...	...	...	...	...	...	...	
Other taxes on production					0.1	0.2	0.4	0.3	1.8	1.0	...	
Less: Subsidies					0.0	0.0	0.0	0.0	0.0	0.1	...	
Subsidies on products					...	...	...	...	...	...	...	
Other subsidies on production					0.0	0.0	0.0	0.0	0.0	0.1	...	
OPERATING SURPLUS, GROSS					1.0[b]	1.3[b]	7.2[b]	19.4[b]	67.5[b]	95.1	...	
MIXED INCOME, GROSS					...	...	...	...	...	...	...	

	2001	2002	2003	2004	2005	2006	2007	2008	2009	2010	2011	2012
Series					**200**							
Total Economy only: Adjustment for FISIM (if FISIM is not distributed to uses)					...	...	...	...	...	20.8	...	
Gross capital formation					...	...	...	...	...	...	...	
Employment (average, in 1000 persons)					...	...	...	2.2	2.1	1.5	...	

[a] Data for this year refers to semi-final data.
[b] Includes Mixed Income, Gross.

Table 2.6 Output, gross value added and fixed assets by industries at current prices (ISIC Rev. 4) Manufacturing, mining and quarrying and other industrial activities (B+C+D+E)

Series 200: 1993 SNA, New Romanian Leu, Western calendar year

Data in millions

	2001	2002	2003	2004	2005	2006	2007	2008	2009	2010	2011	2012
Series					**200**							
Output, at basic prices					214910.1	253047.3	293525.1	348902.6	352806.8	370126.3	423678.9	443069.7
Less: Intermediate consumption, at purchaser's prices					143210.7	168413.6	192270.3	230662.5	232169.2	221573.2	262751.0	275988.7
Equals: VALUE ADDED, GROSS, at basic prices					71699.4	84633.7	101254.8	118240.1	120637.6	148553.1	160927.9[a]	167081.0[b]
Compensation of employees					38663.5	43343.0	53193.3	70717.8	51332.1	51039.7	...	...
Taxes on production and imports, less Subsidies					363.5	594.5	1000.0	901.6	1225.3	1758.4	...	...
Taxes on production and imports					399.3	639.1	1043.4	933.7	1265.3	2204.8	...	...
Taxes on products					...	...	...	...	...	...	...	...
Other taxes on production					399.3	639.1	1043.4	933.7	1265.3	2204.8	...	...
Less: Subsidies					35.8	44.6	43.4	32.1	40.0	446.4	...	...
Subsidies on products					...	...	...	...	...	...	...	...
Other subsidies on production					35.8	44.6	43.4	32.1	40.0	446.4	...	...
OPERATING SURPLUS, GROSS					32672.4[c]	40696.2[c]	47061.5[c]	46620.7[c]	68080.2[c]	75842.9	...	...
MIXED INCOME, GROSS					...	...	...	...	...	19912.1	...	...
Gross capital formation					...	...	...	...	...	...	...	...
Employment (average, in 1000 persons)					...	...	...	2217.9	2008.0	1931.6	1938.6	1962.4

[a] Data for this year refers to semi-final data.
[b] Data for this year refers to provisional data.
[c] Includes Mixed Income, Gross.

Table 2.6 Output, gross value added and fixed assets by industries at current prices (ISIC Rev. 4) Mining and quarrying (B)

Series 200: 1993 SNA, New Romanian Leu, Western calendar year

Data in millions

	2001	2002	2003	2004	2005	2006	2007	2008	2009	2010	2011	2012
Series					**200**							
Output, at basic prices					10621.5	13596.8	15729.4	13728.9	15711.3	17719.0	21545.0	
Less: Intermediate consumption, at purchaser's prices					6833.5	8852.1	10072.2	8554.5	9796.6	9047.0	12322.6	
Equals: VALUE ADDED, GROSS, at basic prices					3788.0	4744.7	5657.2	5174.4	5914.7	8672.0	9222.4[a]	

	2001	2002	2003	2004	2005	2006	2007	2008	2009	2010	2011	2012
Series					**200**							
Compensation of employees					3224.0	3419.1	3964.9	5202.8	5060.5	5012.4	...	
Taxes on production and imports, less Subsidies					21.3	35.5	57.7	50.0	50.3	276.4	...	
Taxes on production and imports					21.3	35.5	57.7	50.0	50.3	417.0	...	
Taxes on products					...	...	...	...	...	...	...	
Other taxes on production					21.3	35.5	57.7	50.0	50.3	417.0	...	
Less: Subsidies					0.0	0.0	0.0	0.0	0.0	140.6	...	
Subsidies on products					...	...	...	...	...	...	...	
Other subsidies on production					0.0	0.0	0.0	0.0	0.0	140.6	...	
OPERATING SURPLUS, GROSS					542.7[b]	1290.1[b]	1634.6[b]	-78.4[b]	803.9[b]	3345.9	...	
MIXED INCOME, GROSS					...	...	...	...	...	37.3	...	
Gross capital formation					...	...	...	...	...	...	...	
Employment (average, in 1000 persons)					...	...	...	107.0	95.3	95.0	...	

[a] Data for this year refers to semi-final data.
[b] Includes Mixed Income, Gross.

Table 2.6 Output, gross value added and fixed assets by industries at current prices (ISIC Rev. 4) Manufacturing (C)

Series 200: 1993 SNA, New Romanian Leu, Western calendar year

Data in millions

	2001	2002	2003	2004	2005	2006	2007	2008	2009	2010	2011	2012
Series					**200**							
Output, at basic prices					170142.1	201240.2	234292.8	280184.0	267269.0	283309.2	320273.2	...
Less: Intermediate consumption, at purchaser's prices					109734.2	129803.7	148519.5	179193.0	168082.0	170151.0	199874.2	...
Equals: VALUE ADDED, GROSS, at basic prices					60407.9	71436.5	85773.3	100991.0	99186.8	113158.2	120399.0[a]	...
Compensation of employees					31352.7	35179.4	43563.1	57963.5	37075.4	37374.8	...	...
Taxes on production and imports, less Subsidies					263.3	473.7	802.9	710.4	887.2	421.7	...	...
Taxes on production and imports					299.1	518.3	846.3	742.5	927.2	492.3	...	...
Taxes on products					...	...	...	...	...	...	...	...
Other taxes on production					299.1	518.3	846.3	742.5	927.2	492.3	...	...
Less: Subsidies					35.8	44.6	43.4	32.1	40.0	70.6	...	...
Subsidies on products					...	...	...	...	...	...	...	...
Other subsidies on production					35.8	44.6	43.4	32.1	40.0	70.6	...	...
OPERATING SURPLUS, GROSS					28791.9[b]	35783.4[b]	41407.3[b]	42316.8[b]	61224.2[b]	55627.2	...	...
MIXED INCOME, GROSS					...	...	...	...	...	19734.5	...	...
Gross capital formation					...	...	...	...	...	...	...	...
Employment (average, in 1000 persons)					...	...	...	1900.3	1715.4	1601.9	1626.1	1651.2

[a] Data for this year refers to semi-final data.
[b] Includes Mixed Income, Gross.

Table 2.6 Output, gross value added and fixed assets by industries at current prices (ISIC Rev. 4) Electricity, gas, steam and air conditioning supply (D)

Series 200: 1993 SNA, New Romanian Leu, Western calendar year **Data in millions**

	2001	2002	2003	2004	2005	2006	2007	2008	2009	2010	2011	2012
Series					**200**							
Output, at basic prices					30978.4	34472.4	39049.3	49845.8	62219.1	54178.6	64643.9	
Less: Intermediate consumption, at purchaser's prices					24867.8	27665.1	31228.0	40133.6	49957.5	34771.8	41832.2	
Equals: VALUE ADDED, GROSS, at basic prices					6110.6	6807.3	7821.3	9712.2	12261.6	19406.8	22811.7[a]	
Compensation of employees					3149.1	3672.9	4294.6	5902.3	6861.3	5964.4	...	
Taxes on production and imports, less Subsidies					57.5	74.4	121.7	105.6	246.7	997.6	...	
Taxes on production and imports					57.5	74.4	121.7	105.6	246.7	1232.8	...	
Taxes on products					...	...	...	...	...	...	...	
Other taxes on production					57.5	74.4	121.7	105.6	246.7	1232.8	...	
Less: Subsidies					0.0	0.0	0.0	0.0	0.0	235.2	...	
Subsidies on products					...	...	...	...	...	...	...	
Other subsidies on production					0.0	0.0	0.0	0.0	0.0	235.2	...	
OPERATING SURPLUS, GROSS					2904.0[b]	3060.0[b]	3405.0[b]	3704.3[b]	5153.6[b]	12441.6	...	
MIXED INCOME, GROSS					...	...	...	...	...	3.2	...	
Gross capital formation					...	...	...	...	...	...	...	
Employment (average, in 1000 persons)					...	...	...	141.7	133.6	124.4	...	

[a] Data for this year refers to semi-final data.
[b] Includes Mixed Income, Gross.

Table 2.6 Output, gross value added and fixed assets by industries at current prices (ISIC Rev. 4) Water supply; sewerage, waste management and remediation activities (E)

Series 200: 1993 SNA, New Romanian Leu, Western calendar year **Data in millions**

	2001	2002	2003	2004	2005	2006	2007	2008	2009	2010	2011	2012
Series					**200**							
Output, at basic prices					3168.1	3737.9	4453.6	5143.9	7607.4	14919.5	17216.8	
Less: Intermediate consumption, at purchaser's prices					1775.2	2092.7	2450.6	2781.4	4333.1	7603.4	8722.0	
Equals: VALUE ADDED, GROSS, at basic prices					1392.9	1645.2	2003.0	2362.5	3274.3	7316.1	8494.8[a]	
Compensation of employees					937.7	1071.6	1370.7	1649.2	2334.9	2688.1	...	
Taxes on production and imports, less Subsidies					21.4	10.9	17.7	35.6	41.1	62.7	...	
Taxes on production and imports					21.4	10.9	17.7	35.6	41.1	62.7	...	
Taxes on products					...	...	...	...	...	...	...	
Other taxes on production					21.4	10.9	17.7	35.6	41.1	62.7	...	
Less: Subsidies					...	...	...	...	...	...	...	
OPERATING SURPLUS, GROSS					433.8[b]	562.7[b]	614.6[b]	677.7[b]	898.3[b]	4428.2	...	
MIXED INCOME, GROSS					...	...	...	...	...	137.1	...	

	2001	2002	2003	2004	2005	2006	2007	2008	2009	2010	2011	2012
Series					**200**							
Gross capital formation					...	...	...	...	...	...	...	
Employment (average, in 1000 persons)					...	...	...	68.9	63.7	110.3	...	

[a] Data for this year refers to semi-final data.
[b] Includes Mixed Income, Gross.

Table 2.6 Output, gross value added and fixed assets by industries at current prices (ISIC Rev. 4) Construction (F)

Series 200: 1993 SNA, New Romanian Leu, Western calendar year **Data in millions**

	2001	2002	2003	2004	2005	2006	2007	2008	2009	2010	2011	2012
Series					**200**							
Output, at basic prices					43011.5	57828.1	83189.9	119820.0	115140.0	132595.7	136027.2	140080.1
Less: Intermediate consumption, at purchaser's prices					23094.2	30870.8	43855.1	63689.7	62330.5	84833.4	88463.8	89631.2
Equals: VALUE ADDED, GROSS, at basic prices					19917.3	26957.3	39334.8	56130.6	52809.4	47762.3	47563.4[a]	50448.9[b]
Compensation of employees					7847.2	8923.7	11490.8	16119.0	18166.2	11829.3	...	...
Taxes on production and imports, less Subsidies					80.0	-612.3	221.7	289.6	389.2	128.9	...	...
Taxes on production and imports					80.0	136.3	221.7	289.6	389.2	155.5	...	...
Taxes on products					...	...	...	...	...	...	...	...
Other taxes on production					80.0	136.3	221.7	289.6	389.2	155.5	...	...
Less: Subsidies					0.0	748.6	0.0	0.0	0.0	26.6	...	...
Subsidies on products					...	...	...	...	...	...	...	...
Other subsidies on production					0.0	748.6	0.0	0.0	0.0	26.6	...	...
OPERATING SURPLUS, GROSS					11990.1[c]	18645.9[c]	27622.3[c]	39722.0[c]	34254.0[c]	18747.9	...	...
MIXED INCOME, GROSS					...	...	...	...	...	17056.2	...	...
Gross capital formation					...	...	...	...	...	...	...	...
Employment (average, in 1000 persons)					...	...	...	733.1	724.4	701.6	677.6	697.5

[a] Data for this year refers to semi-final data.
[b] Data for this year refers to provisional data.
[c] Includes Mixed Income, Gross.

Table 2.6 Output, gross value added and fixed assets by industries at current prices (ISIC Rev. 4) Wholesale and retail trade, transportation and storage, accommodation and food service activities (G+H+I)

Series 200: 1993 SNA, New Romanian Leu, Western calendar year **Data in millions**

	2001	2002	2003	2004	2005	2006	2007	2008	2009	2010	2011	2012
Series					**200**							
Output, at basic prices					95531.7	118212.7	144005.7	178107.1	171478.1	195589.5	200808.6	213938.6
Less: Intermediate consumption, at purchaser's prices					41847.0	52425.4	62612.5	78513.3	77118.6	125849.1	138044.4	146618.9
Equals: VALUE ADDED, GROSS, at basic prices					53684.7	65787.3	81393.2	99593.8	94359.5	69740.4	62764.2[a]	67319.7[b]
Compensation of employees					21689.9	24897.9	29673.5	40205.3	43686.9	38403.7	...	...
Taxes on production and imports, less Subsidies					-395.0	-1039.3	-282.2	-484.1	-41.7	340.5	...	...

	2001	2002	2003	2004	2005	2006	2007	2008	2009	2010	2011	2012
Series					**200**							
Taxes on production and imports					206.9	478.4	781.6	733.4	496.5	589.5	...	...
Taxes on products					...	...	...	...	...	...	...	...
Other taxes on production					206.9	478.4	781.6	733.4	496.5	589.5	...	...
Less: Subsidies					601.9	1517.7	1063.8	1217.5	538.2	249.0	...	...
Subsidies on products					...	...	...	...	...	...	...	...
Other subsidies on production					601.9	1517.7	1063.8	1217.5	538.2	249.0	...	...
OPERATING SURPLUS, GROSS					32389.8[c]	41928.7[c]	52001.9[c]	59872.6[c]	50714.3[c]	20733.9	...	...
MIXED INCOME, GROSS					...	...	...	...	...	10262.3	...	...
Gross capital formation					...	...	...	...	...	...	...	...
Employment (average, in 1000 persons)					...	...	...	1756.4	1746.8	1715.1	1741.4	1778.1

[a] Data for this year refers to semi-final data.
[b] Data for this year refers to provisional data.
[c] Includes Mixed Income, Gross.

Table 2.6 Output, gross value added and fixed assets by industries at current prices (ISIC Rev. 4) Wholesale and retail trade; repair of motor vehicles and motorcycles (G)

Series 200: 1993 SNA, New Romanian Leu, Western calendar year **Data in millions**

	2001	2002	2003	2004	2005	2006	2007	2008	2009	2010	2011	2012
Series					**200**							
Output, at basic prices					46046.6	57405.3	69717.0	90475.9	78746.3	98765.2	103988.7	
Less: Intermediate consumption, at purchaser's prices					18266.1	22833.5	27502.4	36481.1	31777.4	72592.0	78824.0	
Equals: VALUE ADDED, GROSS, at basic prices					27780.5	34571.8	42214.6	53994.8	46968.9	26173.2	25164.7[a]	
Compensation of employees					11239.4	12985.2	15725.4	21536.9	25795.8	22494.3	...	
Taxes on production and imports, less Subsidies					81.9	296.0	483.4	424.9	235.7	255.7	...	
Taxes on production and imports					81.9	296.0	483.4	424.9	235.7	277.8	...	
Taxes on products					...	...	...	...	...	...	...	
Other taxes on production					81.9	296.0	483.4	424.9	235.7	277.8	...	
Less: Subsidies					0.0	0.0	0.0	0.0	0.0	22.1	...	
Subsidies on products					...	...	...	...	...	...	...	
Other subsidies on production					0.0	0.0	0.0	0.0	0.0	22.1	...	
OPERATING SURPLUS, GROSS					16459.2[b]	21290.6[b]	26005.8[b]	32033.0[b]	20937.4[b]	-1083.3	...	
MIXED INCOME, GROSS					...	...	...	...	...	4506.5	...	
Gross capital formation					...	...	...	...	...	...	...	
Employment (average, in 1000 persons)					...	...	...	1163.3	1138.7	1105.0	...	

[a] Data for this year refers to semi-final data.
[b] Includes Mixed Income, Gross.

Table 2.6 Output, gross value added and fixed assets by industries at current prices (ISIC Rev. 4) Transportation and storage (H)

Series 200: 1993 SNA, New Romanian Leu, Western calendar year — **Data in millions**

	2001	2002	2003	2004	2005	2006	2007	2008	2009	2010	2011	2012
Series					**200**							
Output, at basic prices					38178.5	45531.9	56416.6	67310.4	72404.0	82697.5	82346.3	
Less: Intermediate consumption, at purchaser's prices					17364.2	20938.0	25054.8	30239.4	33471.0	44282.1	49431.8	
Equals: VALUE ADDED, GROSS, at basic prices					20814.3	24593.9	31361.8	37071.0	38933.0	38415.4	32914.5[a]	
Compensation of employees					8458.1	9719.8	11319.7	15239.3	14826.2	13272.5	...	
Taxes on production and imports, less Subsidies					-495.9	-1369.0	-820.8	-956.8	-329.7	38.9	...	
Taxes on production and imports					106.0	148.7	243.0	260.7	208.5	265.8	...	
Taxes on products					...	...	...	...	...	...	...	
Other taxes on production					106.0	148.7	243.0	260.7	208.5	265.8	...	
Less: Subsidies					601.9	1517.7	1063.8	1217.5	538.2	226.9	...	
Subsidies on products					...	...	...	...	...	...	...	
Other subsidies on production					601.9	1517.7	1063.8	1217.5	538.2	226.9	...	
OPERATING SURPLUS, GROSS					12852.1[b]	16243.1[b]	20862.9[b]	22788.5[b]	24436.5[b]	20232.6	...	
MIXED INCOME, GROSS					...	...	...	...	...	4871.4	...	
Gross capital formation					...	...	...	...	...	...	...	
Employment (average, in 1000 persons)					...	...	...	456.9	450.4	440.2	...	

[a] Data for this year refers to semi-final data.
[b] Includes Mixed Income, Gross.

Table 2.6 Output, gross value added and fixed assets by industries at current prices (ISIC Rev. 4) Accommodation and food service activities (I)

Series 200: 1993 SNA, New Romanian Leu, Western calendar year — **Data in millions**

	2001	2002	2003	2004	2005	2006	2007	2008	2009	2010	2011	2012
Series					**200**							
Output, at basic prices					11306.6	15275.5	17872.1	20320.8	20327.8	14126.8	14473.6	
Less: Intermediate consumption, at purchaser's prices					6216.7	8653.9	10055.3	11792.8	11870.2	8975.0	9788.6	
Equals: VALUE ADDED, GROSS, at basic prices					5089.9	6621.6	7816.8	8528.0	8457.6	5151.8	4685.0[a]	
Compensation of employees					1992.4	2192.9	2628.4	3429.1	3064.9	2636.9	...	
Taxes on production and imports, less Subsidies					19.0	33.7	55.2	47.8	52.3	45.9	...	
Taxes on production and imports					19.0	33.7	55.2	47.8	52.3	45.9	...	
Taxes on products					...	...	...	...	...	...	...	
Other taxes on production					19.0	33.7	55.2	47.8	52.3	45.9	...	
Less: Subsidies					...	...	...	...	...	...	...	
OPERATING SURPLUS, GROSS					3078.5[b]	4395.0[b]	5133.2[b]	5051.1[b]	5340.4[b]	1584.6	...	
MIXED INCOME, GROSS					...	...	...	...	...	884.4	...	

	2001	2002	2003	2004	2005	2006	2007	2008	2009	2010	2011	2012
Series					**200**							
Gross capital formation					...	...	...	...	...	...	...	
Employment (average, in 1000 persons)					...	...	...	136.2	157.7	169.9	...	

[a] Data for this year refers to semi-final data.
[b] Includes Mixed Income, Gross.

Table 2.6 Output, gross value added and fixed assets by industries at current prices (ISIC Rev. 4) Information and communication (J)

Series 200: 1993 SNA, New Romanian Leu, Western calendar year **Data in millions**

	2001	2002	2003	2004	2005	2006	2007	2008	2009	2010	2011	2012
Series					**200**							
Output, at basic prices					18871.3	23273.9	28380.9	33300.4	32926.1	38159.3	40097.8	50695.8
Less: Intermediate consumption, at purchaser's prices					7472.0	9295.3	10879.6	13252.5	13405.5	20347.5	22180.4	27304.6
Equals: VALUE ADDED, GROSS, at basic prices					11399.3	13978.6	17501.3	20047.9	19520.6	17811.8	17917.4[a]	23391.2[b]
Compensation of employees					4186.1	4811.6	5554.2	7628.5	6181.0	6506.4	...	...
Taxes on production and imports, less Subsidies					51.5	62.6	102.3	122.3	123.2	336.2	...	...
Taxes on production and imports					51.5	62.6	102.3	122.3	158.3	360.7	...	...
Taxes on products					...	...	...	...	...	...	...	...
Other taxes on production					51.5	62.6	102.3	122.3	158.3	360.7	...	...
Less: Subsidies					0.0	0.0	0.0	0.0	35.1	24.5	...	...
Subsidies on products					...	...	...	...	...	...	...	...
Other subsidies on production					0.0	0.0	0.0	0.0	35.1	24.5	...	...
OPERATING SURPLUS, GROSS					7161.7[c]	9104.4[c]	11844.8[c]	12297.1[c]	13216.4[c]	8887.4	...	...
MIXED INCOME, GROSS					...	...	...	...	...	2081.8	...	...
Gross capital formation					...	...	...	...	...	...	...	...
Employment (average, in 1000 persons)					...	...	...	123.5	122.1	124.5	127.5	150.9

[a] Data for this year refers to semi-final data.
[b] Data for this year refers to provisional data.
[c] Includes Mixed Income, Gross.

Table 2.6 Output, gross value added and fixed assets by industries at current prices (ISIC Rev. 4) Financial and insurance activities (K)

Series 200: 1993 SNA, New Romanian Leu, Western calendar year **Data in millions**

	2001	2002	2003	2004	2005	2006	2007	2008	2009	2010	2011	2012
Series					**200**							
Output, at basic prices					8790.7	9648.3	14659.0	20664.3	19032.0	18722.6	22753.3	23682.1
Less: Intermediate consumption, at purchaser's prices					2964.6	3466.4	6735.1	9257.0	7781.9	7041.6	8583.0	8915.3
Equals: VALUE ADDED, GROSS, at basic prices					5826.1	6181.9	7923.9	11407.3	11250.1	11681.0	14170.3[a]	14766.8[b]
Compensation of employees					3066.4	4312.7	5011.7	6082.2	5700.0	6083.0	...	...
Taxes on production and imports, less Subsidies					239.0	146.0	238.6	1032.6	562.4	28.8	...	...

	2001	2002	2003	2004	2005	2006	2007	2008	2009	2010	2011	2012
Series					**200**							
Taxes on production and imports					239.0	146.0	238.6	1032.6	562.4	28.8	...	...
Taxes on products					...	...	...	...	...	...	...	...
Other taxes on production					239.0	146.0	238.6	1032.6	562.4	28.8	...	...
Less: Subsidies					...	...	...	...	...	...	...	...
OPERATING SURPLUS, GROSS [c]					2520.7	1723.2	2673.6	4292.5	4987.7	5569.2	...	...
MIXED INCOME, GROSS					...	...	...	...	...	...	...	...
Gross capital formation					...	...	...	...	...	...	...	...
Employment (average, in 1000 persons)					...	...	...	98.0	91.5	91.7	101.8	98.1

[a] Data for this year refers to semi-final data.
[b] Data for this year refers to provisional data.
[c] Includes Mixed Income, Gross.

Table 2.6 Output, gross value added and fixed assets by industries at current prices (ISIC Rev. 4) Real estate activities (L)

Series 200: 1993 SNA, New Romanian Leu, Western calendar year — **Data in millions**

	2001	2002	2003	2004	2005	2006	2007	2008	2009	2010	2011	2012
Series					**200**							
Output, at basic prices					33457.1	37598.6	44582.9	54536.0	56484.3	55671.7	57103.0	59711.9
Less: Intermediate consumption, at purchaser's prices					11846.0	13405.9	15611.7	22864.5	23785.3	9420.8	9653.3	10630.9
Equals: VALUE ADDED, GROSS, at basic prices					21611.1	24192.7	28971.2	31671.5	32699.0	46250.9	47449.7[a]	49081.0[b]
Compensation of employees					654.5	756.6	1106.7	1721.6	887.1	1171.9	...	...
Taxes on production and imports, less Subsidies					115.8	122.5	200.2	182.2	52.9	141.0	...	...
Taxes on production and imports					115.8	122.5	200.2	182.2	52.9	141.0	...	...
Taxes on products					...	...	...	...	...	...	...	...
Other taxes on production					115.8	122.5	200.2	182.2	52.9	141.0	...	...
Less: Subsidies					...	...	...	...	...	...	...	...
OPERATING SURPLUS, GROSS					20840.8[c]	23313.6[c]	27664.3[c]	29767.7[c]	31759.0[c]	44644.5	...	...
MIXED INCOME, GROSS					...	...	...	...	...	293.5	...	...
Gross capital formation					...	...	...	...	...	...	...	...
Employment (average, in 1000 persons)					...	...	...	59.7	46.9	39.4	38.1	33.5

[a] Data for this year refers to semi-final data.
[b] Data for this year refers to provisional data.
[c] Includes Mixed Income, Gross.

Table 2.6 Output, gross value added and fixed assets by industries at current prices (ISIC Rev. 4) Professional, scientific, technical, administrative and support service activities (M+N)

Series 200: 1993 SNA, New Romanian Leu, Western calendar year — **Data in millions**

	2001	2002	2003	2004	2005	2006	2007	2008	2009	2010	2011	2012
Series					**200**							
Output, at basic prices					20832.3	30436.4	36762.4	45662.0	46188.5	51978.4	66614.2	76731.6
Less: Intermediate consumption, at purchaser's prices					12294.8	18080.1	20790.7	25922.5	26144.5	27261.6	36014.4	42311.3
Equals: VALUE ADDED, GROSS, at basic prices					8537.5	12356.3	15971.7	19739.5	20044.0	24716.8	30599.8[a]	34420.3[b]
Compensation of employees					4223.3	4901.9	6276.9	8332.5	10153.0	10194.5	...	...
Taxes on production and imports, less Subsidies					59.2	79.4	-493.0	-375.0	204.4	93.0	...	...
Taxes on production and imports					59.2	79.4	129.4	112.5	204.4	97.7	...	...
Taxes on products					...	...	...	...	...	...	...	...
Other taxes on production					59.2	79.4	129.4	112.5	204.4	97.7	...	...
Less: Subsidies					0.0	0.0	622.4	487.5	0.0	4.7	...	...
Subsidies on products					...	...	...	...	...	...	...	...
Other subsidies on production					0.0	0.0	622.4	487.5	0.0	4.7	...	...
OPERATING SURPLUS, GROSS					4255.0[c]	7375.0[c]	10187.8[c]	11782.0[c]	9686.6[c]	11407.1	...	...
MIXED INCOME, GROSS					...	...	...	...	...	3022.2	...	...
Gross capital formation					...	...	...	...	...	...	...	...
Employment (average, in 1000 persons)					...	...	...	274.8	314.8	304.2	317.6	333.5

[a] Data for this year refers to semi-final data.
[b] Data for this year refers to provisional data.
[c] Includes Mixed Income, Gross.

Table 2.6 Output, gross value added and fixed assets by industries at current prices (ISIC Rev. 4) Professional, scientific and technical activities (M)

Series 200: 1993 SNA, New Romanian Leu, Western calendar year — **Data in millions**

	2001	2002	2003	2004	2005	2006	2007	2008	2009	2010	2011	2012
Series					**200**							
Output, at basic prices					13765.6	20506.7	24443.9	30576.7	31286.0	35814.3	49198.5	
Less: Intermediate consumption, at purchaser's prices					8245.8	12295.7	14030.9	17281.8	17384.9	20991.1	28923.7	
Equals: VALUE ADDED, GROSS, at basic prices					5519.8	8211.0	10413.0	13294.9	13901.1	14823.2	20274.8[a]	
Compensation of employees					3101.1	3597.8	4601.3	6136.4	6219.2	6041.6	...	
Taxes on production and imports, less Subsidies					38.3	52.0	-537.7	-412.9	134.3	79.2	...	
Taxes on production and imports					38.3	52.0	84.7	74.6	134.3	83.9	...	
Taxes on products					...	...	...	...	...	...	...	
Other taxes on production					38.3	52.0	84.7	74.6	134.3	83.9	...	
Less: Subsidies					0.0	0.0	622.4	487.5	0.0	4.7	...	
Subsidies on products					...	...	...	...	...	...	...	
Other subsidies on production					0.0	0.0	622.4	487.5	0.0	4.7	...	

	2001	2002	2003	2004	2005	2006	2007	2008	2009	2010	2011	2012
Series					**200**							
OPERATING SURPLUS, GROSS					2380.4[b]	4561.2[b]	6349.4[b]	7571.4[b]	7547.6[b]	5865.1	...	
MIXED INCOME, GROSS					...	...	...	...	...	2837.3	...	
Gross capital formation					...	...	...	...	...	...	...	
Employment (average, in 1000 persons)					...	...	...	208.1	202.1	141.9	...	

[a] Data for this year refers to semi-final data.
[b] Includes Mixed Income, Gross.

Table 2.6 Output, gross value added and fixed assets by industries at current prices (ISIC Rev. 4) Administrative and support service activities (N)

Series 200: 1993 SNA, New Romanian Leu, Western calendar year **Data in millions**

	2001	2002	2003	2004	2005	2006	2007	2008	2009	2010	2011	2012
Series					**200**							
Output, at basic prices					7066.7	9929.7	12318.5	15085.3	14902.5	16164.1	17415.7	
Less: Intermediate consumption, at purchaser's prices					4049.0	5784.4	6759.8	8640.7	8759.6	6270.5	7090.7	
Equals: VALUE ADDED, GROSS, at basic prices					3017.7	4145.3	5558.7	6444.6	6142.9	9893.6	10325.0[a]	
Compensation of employees					1122.2	1304.1	1675.6	2196.1	3933.8	4152.9	...	
Taxes on production and imports, less Subsidies					20.9	27.4	44.7	37.9	70.1	13.8	...	
Taxes on production and imports					20.9	27.4	44.7	37.9	70.1	13.8	...	
Taxes on products					...	...	...	...	...	...	...	
Other taxes on production					20.9	27.4	44.7	37.9	70.1	13.8	...	
Less: Subsidies					...	...	...	...	...	...	...	
OPERATING SURPLUS, GROSS					1874.6[b]	2813.8[b]	3838.4[b]	4210.6[b]	2139.0[b]	5542.0	...	
MIXED INCOME, GROSS					...	...	...	...	...	184.9	...	
Gross capital formation					...	...	...	...	...	...	...	
Employment (average, in 1000 persons)					...	...	...	66.7	112.7	162.3	...	

[a] Data for this year refers to semi-final data.
[b] Includes Mixed Income, Gross.

Table 2.6 Output, gross value added and fixed assets by industries at current prices (ISIC Rev. 4) Public administration and defence, education, human health and social work activities (O+P+Q)

Series 200: 1993 SNA, New Romanian Leu, Western calendar year **Data in millions**

	2001	2002	2003	2004	2005	2006	2007	2008	2009	2010	2011	2012
Series					**200**							
Output, at basic prices					48980.1	54223.7	63977.5	85148.2	86307.6	78944.9	81057.4	88906.3
Less: Intermediate consumption, at purchaser's prices					16929.8	18912.0	21999.5	29358.3	30639.4	22337.2	25947.2	27839.3
Equals: VALUE ADDED, GROSS, at basic prices					32050.3	35311.7	41978.0	55789.9	55668.2	56607.7	55110.2[a]	61067.0[b]
Compensation of employees					23694.8	29831.0	36302.6	48314.4	50543.8	45369.9	...	...
Taxes on production and imports, less Subsidies					49.7	125.1	204.4	177.3	17.6	6.9	...	...

	2001	2002	2003	2004	2005	2006	2007	2008	2009	2010	2011	2012
Series					**200**							
Taxes on production and imports					49.7	125.1	204.4	177.3	17.6	6.9	...	...
Taxes on products					...	...	...	...	...	...	...	...
Other taxes on production					49.7	125.1	204.4	177.3	17.6	6.9	...	...
Less: Subsidies					...	...	...	...	...	...	...	...
OPERATING SURPLUS, GROSS					8305.8[c]	5355.6[c]	5471.0[c]	7298.2[c]	5106.8[c]	6261.1	...	...
MIXED INCOME, GROSS					...	...	...	...	...	4969.8	...	...
Gross capital formation					...	...	...	...	...	...	...	...
Employment (average, in 1000 persons)					...	...	...	1083.1	1114.6	1117.3	1118.1	1096.2

[a] Data for this year refers to semi-final data.
[b] Data for this year refers to provisional data.
[c] Includes Mixed Income, Gross.

Table 2.6 Output, gross value added and fixed assets by industries at current prices (ISIC Rev. 4) Public administration and defence; compulsory social security (O)

Series 200: 1993 SNA, New Romanian Leu, Western calendar year **Data in millions**

	2001	2002	2003	2004	2005	2006	2007	2008	2009	2010	2011	2012
Series					**200**							
Output, at basic prices					19228.4	21190.3	25209.3	31359.8	30440.9	29458.1	30074.2	
Less: Intermediate consumption, at purchaser's prices					4615.4	5175.3	5641.5	7016.0	5874.6	7115.1	8298.6	
Equals: VALUE ADDED, GROSS, at basic prices					14613.0	16015.0	19567.8	24343.8	24566.3	22343.0	21775.6[a]	
Compensation of employees					10379.0	13928.4	18209.1	22931.8	22717.7	20882.7	...	
Taxes on production and imports, less Subsidies					...	...	...	...	...	...	...	
OPERATING SURPLUS, GROSS					4234.0	2086.6	1358.7	1412.0	1848.6	1460.3	...	
MIXED INCOME, GROSS					...	...	...	...	...	...	...	
Gross capital formation					...	...	...	...	...	...	...	
Employment (average, in 1000 persons)					...	...	...	307.0	379.9	359.0	...	

[a] Data for this year refers to semi-final data.

Table 2.6 Output, gross value added and fixed assets by industries at current prices (ISIC Rev. 4) Education (P)

Series 200: 1993 SNA, New Romanian Leu, Western calendar year **Data in millions**

	2001	2002	2003	2004	2005	2006	2007	2008	2009	2010	2011	2012
Series					**200**							
Output, at basic prices					13649.1	15391.9	17027.8	24590.5	24193.3	22260.3	22061.2	
Less: Intermediate consumption, at purchaser's prices					3904.3	4467.5	4949.6	7080.5	6993.4	3820.7	4365.6	
Equals: VALUE ADDED, GROSS, at basic prices					9744.8	10924.4	12078.2	17510.0	17199.9	18439.6	17695.6[a]	
Compensation of employees					7567.2	8659.9	9669.9	14015.3	15023.0	12463.0	...	
Taxes on production and imports, less Subsidies					22.8	39.2	64.1	55.6	2.3	1.0	...	

	2001	2002	2003	2004	2005	2006	2007	2008	2009	2010	2011	2012
Series					**200**							
Taxes on production and imports					22.8	39.2	64.1	55.6	2.3	1.0	...	
Taxes on products					...	...	...	...	...	...	...	
Other taxes on production					22.8	39.2	64.1	55.6	2.3	1.0	...	
Less: Subsidies					...	...	...	...	...	...	...	
OPERATING SURPLUS, GROSS					2154.8[b]	2225.3[b]	2344.2[b]	3439.1[b]	2174.6[b]	2073.6	...	
MIXED INCOME, GROSS					...	...	...	...	...	3902.0	...	
Gross capital formation					...	...	...	...	...	...	...	
Employment (average, in 1000 persons)					...	...	...	389.0	363.1	371.2	...	

[a] Data for this year refers to semi-final data.
[b] Includes Mixed Income, Gross.

Table 2.6 Output, gross value added and fixed assets by industries at current prices (ISIC Rev. 4) Human health and social work activities (Q)

Series 200: 1993 SNA, New Romanian Leu, Western calendar year — **Data in millions**

	2001	2002	2003	2004	2005	2006	2007	2008	2009	2010	2011	2012
Series					**200**							
Output, at basic prices					16102.6	17641.5	21740.4	29197.9	31673.4	27226.5	28922.0	
Less: Intermediate consumption, at purchaser's prices					8410.1	9269.2	11408.4	15261.8	17771.4	11401.4	13283.0	
Equals: VALUE ADDED, GROSS, at basic prices					7692.5	8372.3	10332.0	13936.1	13902.0	15825.1	15639.0[a]	
Compensation of employees					5748.6	7242.7	8423.6	11367.3	12803.1	12024.2	...	
Taxes on production and imports, less Subsidies					26.9	85.9	140.3	121.7	15.3	5.9	...	
Taxes on production and imports					26.9	85.9	140.3	121.7	15.3	5.9	...	
Taxes on products					...	...	...	...	...	...	...	
Other taxes on production					26.9	85.9	140.3	121.7	15.3	5.9	...	
Less: Subsidies					...	...	...	...	...	...	...	
OPERATING SURPLUS, GROSS					1917.0[b]	1043.7[b]	1768.1[b]	2447.1[b]	1083.6[b]	2727.2	...	
MIXED INCOME, GROSS					...	...	...	...	...	1067.8	...	
Gross capital formation					...	...	...	...	...	...	...	
Employment (average, in 1000 persons)					...	...	...	387.1	371.6	387.1	...	

[a] Data for this year refers to semi-final data.
[b] Includes Mixed Income, Gross.

Table 2.6 Output, gross value added and fixed assets by industries at current prices (ISIC Rev. 4) Other service activities (R+S+T)

Series 200: 1993 SNA, New Romanian Leu, Western calendar year — **Data in millions**

	2001	2002	2003	2004	2005	2006	2007	2008	2009	2010	2011	2012
Series					**200**							
Output, at basic prices					13804.4	18070.2	21973.1	26253.7	29164.9	24107.3	25962.4	27653.2
Less: Intermediate consumption, at purchaser's prices					7604.3	9961.3	11858.0	14464.9	17471.8	10708.5	11577.1	12324.0
Equals: VALUE ADDED, GROSS, at basic prices					6200.1	8108.9	10115.1	11788.8	11693.1	13398.8	14385.3[a]	15329.2[b]
Compensation of employees					3168.7	3775.4	5244.9	6448.6	5753.2	5653.4	...	...
Taxes on production and imports, less Subsidies					139.3	47.8	79.5	246.5	203.2	67.6	...	...
Taxes on production and imports					139.3	47.8	79.5	270.4	221.4	67.6	...	...
Taxes on products					...	...	...	...	...	...	...	...
Other taxes on production					139.3	47.8	79.5	270.4	221.4	67.6	...	...
Less: Subsidies					0.0	0.0	0.0	23.9	18.2	0.0	...	...
Subsidies on products					...	...	...	...	...	...	...	...
Other subsidies on production					0.0	0.0	0.0	23.9	18.2	0.0	...	...
OPERATING SURPLUS, GROSS					2892.1[c]	4285.7[c]	4790.7[c]	5093.7[c]	5736.7[c]	6600.2	...	...
MIXED INCOME, GROSS					...	...	...	...	...	1077.6	...	...
Gross capital formation					...	...	...	...	...	...	...	...
Employment (average, in 1000 persons)					...	...	...	251.6	247.7	234.7	266.1	269.3

[a] Data for this year refers to semi-final data.
[b] Data for this year refers to provisional data.
[c] Includes Mixed Income, Gross.

Table 2.6 Output, gross value added and fixed assets by industries at current prices (ISIC Rev. 4) Arts, entertainment and recreation (R)

Series 200: 1993 SNA, New Romanian Leu, Western calendar year — **Data in millions**

	2001	2002	2003	2004	2005	2006	2007	2008	2009	2010	2011	2012
Series					**200**							
Output, at basic prices					5277.9	6901.4	8382.6	10022.7	14132.7	11126.4	11964.2	
Less: Intermediate consumption, at purchaser's prices					2896.2	3783.6	4603.2	6349.6	9178.4	3692.0	4359.4	
Equals: VALUE ADDED, GROSS, at basic prices					2381.7	3117.8	3779.4	3673.1	4954.3	7434.4	7604.8[a]	
Compensation of employees					1205.9	1441.1	2013.0	2071.1	1910.1	1740.6	...	
Taxes on production and imports, less Subsidies					55.6	18.4	30.1	148.7	32.1	19.1	...	
Taxes on production and imports					55.6	18.4	30.1	172.6	32.1	19.1	...	
Taxes on products					...	...	...	...	...	...	...	
Other taxes on production					55.6	18.4	30.1	172.6	32.1	19.1	...	
Less: Subsidies					0.0	0.0	0.0	23.9	0.0	0.0	...	
Subsidies on products					...	...	...	...	...	...	...	
Other subsidies on production					0.0	0.0	0.0	23.9	0.0	0.0	...	

	2001	2002	2003	2004	2005	2006	2007	2008	2009	2010	2011	2012
Series					**200**							
OPERATING SURPLUS, GROSS					1120.2[b]	1658.3[b]	1736.3[b]	1453.3[b]	3012.1[b]	5555.1	...	
MIXED INCOME, GROSS					...	...	...	...	...	119.6	...	
Gross capital formation					...	...	...	...	...	...	...	
Employment (average, in 1000 persons)					...	...	...	71.4	74.2	65.6	...	

[a] Data for this year refers to semi-final data.
[b] Includes Mixed Income, Gross.

Table 2.6 Output, gross value added and fixed assets by industries at current prices (ISIC Rev. 4) Other service activities (S)

Series 200: 1993 SNA, New Romanian Leu, Western calendar year **Data in millions**

	2001	2002	2003	2004	2005	2006	2007	2008	2009	2010	2011	2012
Series					**200**							
Output, at basic prices					8526.5	11168.8	13590.5	16231.0	15032.2	12980.9	13998.2	
Less: Intermediate consumption, at purchaser's prices					4708.1	6177.7	7254.8	8115.3	8293.4	7016.5	7217.7	
Equals: VALUE ADDED, GROSS, at basic prices					3818.4	4991.1	6335.7	8115.7	6738.8	5964.4	6780.5[a]	
Compensation of employees					1962.8	2334.3	3231.9	4377.5	3843.1	3912.8	...	
Taxes on production and imports, less Subsidies					83.7	29.4	49.4	97.8	171.1	48.5	...	
Taxes on production and imports					83.7	29.4	49.4	97.8	189.3	48.5	...	
Taxes on products					...	...	...	...	...	...	...	
Other taxes on production					83.7	29.4	49.4	97.8	189.3	48.5	...	
Less: Subsidies					0.0	0.0	0.0	0.0	18.2	0.0	...	
Subsidies on products					...	...	...	...	...	...	...	
Other subsidies on production					0.0	0.0	0.0	0.0	18.2	0.0	...	
OPERATING SURPLUS, GROSS					1771.9[b]	2627.4[b]	3054.4[b]	3640.4[b]	2724.6[b]	1045.1	...	
MIXED INCOME, GROSS					...	...	...	...	...	958.0	...	
Gross capital formation					...	...	...	...	...	...	...	
Employment (average, in 1000 persons)					...	...	...	180.2	173.5	169.1	...	

[a] Data for this year refers to semi-final data.
[b] Includes Mixed Income, Gross.

Table 3.1 Government final consumption expenditure by function at current prices

Series 200: 1993 SNA, New Romanian Leu, Western calendar year **Data in millions**

	2001	2002	2003	2004	2005	2006	2007	2008	2009	2010	2011	2012
Series	**200**											
General public services	2909.2	3331.2	3591.4	3664.9	4141.4	4936.8	7364.0	9733.1	8313.6	6462.4	8180.8	
Defence	1969.9	2919.7	4643.2	5170.8	7696.9	7326.6	6945.7	7233.0	7310.5	7266.6	4667.1	
Public order and safety	1566.8	2216.5	3245.3	4011.0	5647.8	7441.4	9697.2	10168.2	9793.6	10608.9	11507.6	
Economic affairs	1645.3	1394.3	3071.9	3361.2	5434.2	5221.9	8644.9	12325.4	12555.0	12566.1	11007.8	
Environment protection	133.3	95.9	94.0	108.3	673.7	943.6	1195.3	1819.3	1779.7	1731.4	2276.4	

	2001	2002	2003	2004	2005	2006	2007	2008	2009	2010	2011	2012
Series	**200**											
Housing and community amenities	1001.6	1135.9	2999.2	2978.9	2838.8	3037.2	3032.7	3835.5	4646.3	3027.3	3368.9	
Health	4354.0	5638.5	6214.9	5960.2	7288.5	8684.9	11336.4	15165.2	17287.1	17413.2	16208.8	
Recreation, culture and religion	451.2	474.1	962.9	1042.1	1362.5	2254.7	2637.7	3572.5	3577.1	3336.3	3443.5	
Education	3499.5	4333.7	5130.8	7057.4	8315.3	10350.4	10975.2	16666.7	15857.6	13175.2	11633.6	
Social protection	1586.4	1351.9	3633.8	5535.0	6118.0	7480.2	8312.6	10689.5	9800.2	9856.6	11471.4	
Equals: General government final consumption expenditure	19117.2	22891.7	33587.4[a]	38889.8[a]	49517.1[a]	57677.7[a]	70141.7[a]	91208.4[a]	90920.7[a]	85444.0	83765.9	

[a] Discrepancy between item and corresponding item in Table 1.1 (Gross domestic product by expenditures at current prices).

Table 4.1 Total Economy (S.1)

Series 200: 1993 SNA, New Romanian Leu, Western calendar year **Data in millions**

	2001	2002	2003	2004	2005	2006	2007	2008	2009	2010	2011	2012
Series	**200**											
I. Production account - Resources												
Output, at basic prices (otherwise, please specify)	228796.5	295622.9	381863.6	483917.4	547894.3	656511.9	784007.5	985671.0	976996.0	1030336.7	1132017.7	1191865.3
Less: Financial intermediation services indirectly measured (only to be deducted if FISIM is not distributed to uses)	...	...	...	...	...	...	...	...	...	...	...	...
Plus: Taxes less Subsidies on products	11825.8	15094.7	21786.7	26436.7	33721.9	40380.8	47650.5	56164.6	50160.3	57296.3	69381.6	73696.6
Plus: Taxes on products	12591.4	16688.4	23025.4	27854.5	35811.8	41950.3	49238.3	57607.9	51366.1	59475.3	70208.9	74790.7
Less: Subsidies on products	765.6	1593.7	1238.7	1417.8	2089.9	1569.5	1587.8	1443.3	1205.8	2179.0	827.3	1094.1
I. Production account - Uses												
Intermediate consumption, at purchaser's prices	122676.5	158700.6	206222.7	262986.1	292661.6	352242.1	415651.2	527135.0	526017.0	563939.7	644690.9	678062.5
GROSS DOMESTIC PRODUCT	117945.8	152017.0	197427.6	247368.0	288954.6	344650.6	416006.8	514700.0	501139.0	523693.3	556708.4[a]	587499.4[b]
Less: Consumption of fixed capital	23508.2	34041.3	46110.2	49195.9	54117.9	59843.1	66579.9	79002.4	90297.0	93309.2	...	...
NET DOMESTIC PRODUCT	94437.6	117975.7	151317.4	198172.1	234836.7	284807.5	349426.9	435698.0	410842.0	430384.1	...	...
II.1.1 Generation of income account - Resources												
GROSS DOMESTIC PRODUCT	117945.8	152017.0	197427.6	247368.0	288954.6	344650.6	416006.8	514700.0	501139.0	523693.3	556708.4	...
II.1.1 Generation of income account - Uses												
Compensation of employees	48604.9	60172.8	73674.2	91039.3	112996.9	132194.9	161938.1	216152.0	203245.0	189790.9	200528.4	...
Taxes on production and imports, less Subsidies	11833.2	15219.2	21450.8	25305.2	32965.4	37797.8	46669.6	55422.8	48245.8	57526.0	67983.6	...
Taxes on production and imports	13328.0	17664.2	24213.8	29029.6	37248.0	43911.3	52441.7	61637.7	54842.2	63240.3	73684.8	...
Taxes on products	12591.4	16688.4	23025.4	27854.5	35811.8	41950.3	49238.3	57607.9	51366.1	59475.3	70208.9	...
Other taxes on production	736.6	975.8	1188.4	1175.1	1436.2	1961.0	3203.4	4029.8	3476.1	3765.0	3475.9	...
Less: Subsidies	1494.8	2445.0	2763.0	3724.4	4282.6	6113.5	5772.1	6214.9	6596.4	5714.3	5701.2	...
Subsidies on products	765.6	1593.7	1238.7	1417.8	2089.9	1569.5	1587.8	1443.4	1205.8	2179.0	827.3	...
Other subsidies on production	729.2	851.3	1524.3	2306.6	2192.7	4544.0	4184.3	4771.5	5390.6	3535.3	4873.9	...
OPERATING SURPLUS, GROSS	57507.7[c]	76625.0[c]	102302.6[c]	131023.5[c]	142992.3[c]	174657.9[c]	207399.1[c]	243126.0[c]	249649.0[c]	194676.0	195881.5	...
MIXED INCOME, GROSS	...	...	...	...	...	...	...	...	...	81700.4	92314.9	...
II.1.2 Allocation of primary income account - Resources												
OPERATING SURPLUS, GROSS	57507.7[c]	76625.0[c]	102302.6[c]	131023.5[c]	142992.3[c]	174657.9[c]	207399.1[c]	243126.0[c]	249649.0[c]	194676.0	195881.5	...

	2001	2002	2003	2004	2005	2006	2007	2008	2009	2010	2011	2012
Series	**200**											
MIXED INCOME, GROSS	...	...	...	...	...	...	...	...	...	81700.4	92314.9	...
Compensation of employees	48923.9	60606.6	74018.4	91387.8	115719.9	135319.4	165762.2	219984.0	205137.0	191548.9	202255.4	...
Taxes on production and imports, less Subsidies	11833.2	15219.2	21450.8	25305.2	32965.4	37797.8	45623.0	54527.1	49558.1	59320.3	70198.9	...
Taxes on production and imports	13328.0	17664.2	24213.8	29029.6	37248.0	43911.3	51370.5	60291.9	53721.9	62250.5	72661.6	...
Taxes on products	12591.4	16688.4	23025.4	27854.5	35811.8	41950.3	48167.1	56265.6	50249.6	58485.5	69185.7	...
Other taxes on production	736.6	975.8	1188.4	1175.1	1436.2	1961.0	3203.4	4026.3	3472.3	3765.0	3475.9	...
Less: Subsidies	1494.8	2445.0	2763.0	3724.4	4282.6	6113.5	5747.5	5764.8	4163.8	2930.2	2462.7	...
Subsidies on products	765.6	1593.7	1238.7	1417.8	2089.9	1569.5	1587.8	1443.4	1205.8	2179.0	827.3	...
Other subsidies on production	729.2	851.3	1524.3	2306.6	2192.7	4544.0	4159.7	4321.4	2958.0	751.2	1635.4	...
Property income	15033.3	11620.6	13409.9	16222.6	19665.8	26049.2	35545.7	30896.0	59099.0	52956.9	37135.5	...
II.1.2 Allocation of primary income account - Uses												
Property income	16244.2	13657.2	18325.4	26937.3	30879.6	40709.8	53248.6	48749.9	69114.0	62923.8	48367.5	...
GROSS NATIONAL INCOME	117053.9	150414.2	192856.3	237001.8	280463.8	333114.5	401081.4	499783.0	494329.0	517278.7	549418.7	...
II.2 Secondary distribution of income account - Resources												
GROSS NATIONAL INCOME	117053.9	150414.2	192856.3	237001.8	280463.8	333114.5	401081.4	499783.0	494329.0	517278.7	549418.7	...
Current taxes on income, wealth, etc.	7491.8	8765.9	11811.5	15711.7	15376.9	20965.4	27887.2	34573.5	32790.0	31632.4	33297.8	...
Social contributions	13242.3	16899.5	19528.4	23887.8	29649.6	35604.2	43639.1	51988.2	51267.0	51144.6	52827.1	...
Social benefits other than social transfers in kind	11453.9	14116.6	16667.5	21609.5	25641.8	30358.4	38345.9	53323.0	63537.7	67692.9	66892.2	...
Other current transfers	11780.4	16365.5	20025.6	32573.5	27558.2	33550.8	32738.7	42598.8	38862.9	42459.3	50664.4	...
II.2 Secondary distribution of income account - Uses												
Current taxes on income, wealth, etc.	7216.2	8605.8	11744.6	15654.9	15330.0	20853.4	28056.5	34649.9	32928.0	31978.2	33665.4	...
Social contributions	13242.3	16899.5	19528.4	23887.8	29649.6	35604.2	43639.1	51988.2	51260.6	51144.6	52827.1	...
Social benefits other than social transfers in kind	11453.9	14116.6	16667.5	21609.5	25641.8	30358.4	38345.9	53323.0	63537.7	67690.7	66802.6	...
Other current transfers	8807.8	8048.3	10433.6	14388.3	15404.2	17220.0	16513.5	19243.1	22545.6	28659.4	38423.3	...
GROSS DISPOSABLE INCOME	120302.1	158891.5	202515.2	255243.8	292664.7	349557.3	417137.3	523062.0	510514.0	530735.0	561381.8	...
II.4.1 Use of disposable income account - Resources												
GROSS DISPOSABLE INCOME	120302.1	158891.5	202515.2	255243.8	292664.7	349557.3	417137.3	523062.0	510514.0	530735.0	561381.8	...
Adjustment for the change in net equity of households on pension funds	...	...	...	...	...	...	...	...	...	...	...	...
II.4.1 Use of disposable income account - Uses												
Final consumption expenditure	100731.7	127118.8	168818.7	211054.6	251038.1	294867.6	344937.0	420918.0	404276.0	419801.2	436485.0	...
Individual consumption expenditure	92177.3	116895.7	149395.8	191499.0	226928.7	268441.3	313223.3	381108.0	360402.0	382446.2	401336.8	...
Collective consumption expenditure	8554.4	10223.1	19422.9	19555.6	24109.4	26426.3	31713.7	39809.4	43873.4	37355.0	35148.2	...
Adjustment for the change in net equity of households on pension funds	...	...	...	...	...	...	...	...	...	...	...	...
SAVING, GROSS	19570.4	31772.7	33696.5	44189.2	41626.6	54689.7	72200.3	102145.0	106239.0	110933.8	124896.8	...
III.1 Capital account - Changes in liabilities and net worth												
SAVING, GROSS	19570.4	31772.7	33696.5	44189.2	41626.6	54689.7	72200.3	102145.0	106239.0	110933.8	124896.8	...
Capital transfers, receivable less payable	391.1	505.1	911.7	2302.8	2961.3	507.6	2383.3	2290.8	2174.7	969.5	2367.1	...
Capital transfers, receivable	1530.4	2117.1	3377.9	7333.0	5765.7	5797.4	7261.9	9006.3	5726.1	5366.8	16027.7	...
Less: Capital transfers, payable	1139.3	1612.0	2466.2	5030.2	2804.4	5289.8	4878.6	6715.5	3551.4	4397.3	13660.6	...

	2001	2002	2003	2004	2005	2006	2007	2008	2009	2010	2011	2012
Series	**200**											
Equals: CHANGES IN NET WORTH DUE TO SAVING AND CAPITAL TRANSFERS	-3546.7	-1763.5	-11502.0	-2703.9	-9530.0	-4645.8	8003.7	25433.3	18116.6	18594.1	127263.9[d]	...
	III.1 Capital account - Changes in assets											
Gross capital formation	26186.2	33446.1	43370.2	58551.4	67286.6	91188.3	128858.7	160897.0	127137.0	133898.6	149909.4	...
Gross fixed capital formation	24171.4	32366.5	42496.6	53850.3	68526.6	88272.0	125645.3	164279.0	122442.0	129421.8	144558.2	...
Changes in inventories [e]	2014.8	1079.6	873.6	4701.1	-1240.0	2916.3	3213.4	-3382.5	4695.5	4476.8	5351.2	...
Acquisitions less disposals of valuables	...	...	...	...	...	...	...	...	...	...	...	...
Acquisitions less disposals of non-produced non-financial assets	...	...	...	...	...	...	-359.6	-18.8	-563.8	-73.8	-684.3	...
NET LENDING (+) / NET BORROWING (-)	-6224.7	-1168.3	-8762.0	-12059.4	-22698.7	-35991.0	-53915.5	-56442.4	-18160.0	-21921.5	-21961.2	...

[a] Data for this year refers to semi-final data.
[b] Data for this year refers to provisional data.
[c] Includes Mixed Income, Gross.
[d] Item does not consider consumption of fixed capital.
[e] Includes Acquisitions less disposals of valuables.

Table 4.2 Rest of the world (S.2)

Series 200: 1993 SNA, New Romanian Leu, Western calendar year **Data in millions**

	2001	2002	2003	2004	2005	2006	2007	2008	2009	2010	2011	2012
Series	**200**											
	V.I External account of goods and services - Resources											
Imports of goods and services	47969.5	62310.9	83419.2	110884.4	124965.7	152655.6	179685.0	223744.0	183629.0	215506.2	252559.0	265268.1
Imports of goods	41699.8	54563.4	73596.7	98262.3	108866.8	132995.4	158131.0	193957.0	152456.0	189317.2	223253.0	233648.1
Imports of services	6269.7	7747.5	9822.5	12622.1	16098.9	19660.2	21554.0	29786.6	31173.0	26189.0	29306.0	31620.0
	V.I External account of goods and services - Uses											
Exports of goods and services	38997.4	53763.0	68657.9	88646.4	95595.6	111250.3	121896.0	156629.0	153356.0	185499.7	222873.0	234974.9
Exports of goods	32984.8	45905.1	58525.3	76794.0	80662.7	91471.7	98578.5	123812.0	123345.0	157435.8	191913.9	200730.8
Exports of services	6012.6	7857.9	10132.6	11852.4	14932.9	19778.6	23317.2	32816.9	30011.0	28063.9	30959.1	34244.1
EXTERNAL BALANCE OF GOODS AND SERVICES	8972.1	8547.9	14761.3	22238.0	29370.1	41405.3	57788.9	67114.4	30273.5	30006.5	29686.0[a]	30293.2[b]
	V.II External account of primary income and current transfers - Resources											
EXTERNAL BALANCE OF GOODS AND SERVICES	8972.1	8547.9	14761.3	22238.0	29370.1	41405.3	57788.9	67114.4	30273.5	30006.5	29686.0	30293.2
Compensation of employees	10.4	18.9	23.0	20.3	65.1	119.4	130.0	427.5	194.0	282.0	391.0	400.0
Taxes on production and imports, less Subsidies	...	...	...	...	...	...	1046.6	895.7	-1312.3	-1794.3	-2215.3	-3126.9
Taxes on production and imports	...	...	...	...	...	...	1071.2	1345.8	1120.3	989.8	1023.2	1204.5
Taxes on products	...	...	...	...	...	...	1071.2	1342.3	1116.5	989.8	1023.2	1204.5
Other taxes on production	...	...	...	...	...	...	0.0	3.5	3.8	0.0	0.0	0.0
Less: Subsidies	...	...	...	...	...	...	24.6	450.1	2432.6	2784.1	3238.5	4331.4
Subsidies on products	...	...	...	...	...	...	...	...	...	...	...	...
Other subsidies on production	...	...	...	...	...	...	24.6	450.1	2432.6	2784.1	3238.5	4331.4
Property income	2222.0	2940.3	5774.3	11673.5	12814.6	17396.9	21844.7	21932.9	12940.0	11768.2	14544.8	13698.5
Current taxes on income, wealth, etc.	...	...	...	...	40.1	3.5	359.1	286.5	350.7	613.0	790.2	628.6
Social contributions	...	...	...	...	...	...	...	...	...	...	...	...

	2001	2002	2003	2004	2005	2006	2007	2008	2009	2010	2011	2012
Series	**200**											
Social benefits other than social transfers in kind	...	...	...	...	...	...	...	...	0.1	0.0	0.0	2.3
Other current transfers	765.1	879.8	1100.5	1559.7	1594.5	2229.8	7564.4	8915.2	9410.0	8488.1	8283.8	8552.5
Adjustment for the change in net equity of households on pension funds	...	...	...	...	...	...	...	...	...	...	...	...
	V.II External account of primary income and current transfers - Uses											
Compensation of employees	329.4	452.7	367.2	368.8	2788.1	3243.9	3954.1	4260.1	2086.0	2040.0	2118.0	2547.0
Taxes on production and imports, less Subsidies	...	...	...	...	...	...	...	...	...	...	...	...
Taxes on production and imports	...	...	...	...	...	...	...	...	...	...	...	...
Taxes on products	...	...	...	...	...	...	...	...	...	...	...	...
Other taxes on production	...	...	...	...	...	...	...	...	...	...	...	...
Less: Subsidies	...	...	...	...	...	...	...	...	...	...	...	...
Subsidies on products	...	...	...	...	...	...	...	...	...	...	...	...
Other subsidies on production	...	...	...	...	...	...	...	...	...	...	...	...
Property income	1011.1	903.7	858.8	958.8	1600.8	2736.3	4141.8	4079.0	2925.0	1801.3	3312.8	3412.4
Current taxes on income and wealth, etc.	275.9	160.1	66.9	56.8	87.0	115.5	189.8	210.1	212.7	267.2	422.6	556.3
Social contributions	...	...	...	...	...	...	...	...	6.5	0.0	0.0	0.0
Social benefits other than social transfers in kind	...	...	...	...	...	...	...	...	...	2.2	89.6	10.4
Other current transfers	3737.5	9197.0	10692.5	19744.9	13748.5	18560.6	23789.6	32270.9	25727.3	22288.0	20524.9	20381.5
Adjustment for the change in net equity of households on pension funds	...	...	...	...	...	...	...	...	...	...	...	...
CURRENT EXTERNAL BALANCE	6615.8	1673.4	9673.7	14362.2	25660.0	36498.6	56658.4	58752.0	20898.5	22964.8	25012.6	23540.6
	V.III.1 Capital account - Changes in liabilities and net worth											
CURRENT EXTERNAL BALANCE	6615.8	1673.4	9673.7	14362.2	25660.0	36498.6	56658.4	58752.0	20898.5	22964.8	25012.6	23540.6
Capital transfers, receivable less payable	-391.1	-505.1	-911.7	-2302.8	-2961.3	-507.6	-2383.3	-2290.8	-2174.7	-969.5	-2367.1	-7219.3
Capital transfers, receivable	64.5	48.5	60.3	117.4	369.2	2689.3	933.1	967.8	1178.7	1032.0	1213.6	837.8
Less: Capital transfers, payable	455.6	553.6	972.0	2420.2	3330.5	3196.9	3316.4	3258.6	3353.4	2001.5	3580.7	8057.1
Equals: CHANGES IN NET WORTH DUE TO SAVING AND CAPITAL TRANSFERS	6224.7	1168.3	8762.0	12059.4	22698.7	35991.0	54275.1	56461.2	18723.8	21995.3	22645.5	16321.3
	V.III.1 Capital account - Changes in assets											
Acquisitions less disposals of non-produced non-financial assets	...	...	...	...	...	...	359.6	18.8	563.8	73.8	684.3	1272.6
NET LENDING (+) / NET BORROWING (-)	6224.7	1168.3	8762.0	12059.4	22698.7	35991.0	53915.5	56442.4	18160.0	21921.5	21961.2	15048.7

[a] Data for this year refers to semi-final data.
[b] Data for this year refers to provisional data.

Table 4.3 Non-financial Corporations (S.11)

Series 200: 1993 SNA, New Romanian Leu, Western calendar year **Data in millions**

	2001	2002	2003	2004	2005	2006	2007	2008	2009	2010	2011	2012
Series	**200**											
	I. Production account - Resources											
Output, at basic prices (otherwise, please specify)	145423.8	194046.5	250338.5	317260.0	363785.3	443149.0	539359.4	681309.0	677752.0	705047.9	783268.8	830692.6
	I. Production account - Uses											
Intermediate consumption, at purchaser's prices	89446.3	117487.4	152468.9	194941.7	218434.4	267405.4	322320.8	405874.0	409653.0	438829.3	505936.6	536879.4
VALUE ADDED GROSS, in basic prices	55977.5	76559.1	97869.6	122318.3	145350.9	175743.6	217038.6	275435.0	268100.0	266218.6	277332.2[a]	293813.2[b]
Less: Consumption of fixed capital	13086.2	19486.4	21594.3	24668.9	26958.7	30172.3	34707.9	43351.0	49290.3	52488.1	...	...
VALUE ADDED NET, at basic prices	42891.3	57072.7	76275.3	97649.4	118392.2	145571.3	182330.7	232084.0	218809.0	213730.5	...	...
	II.1.1 Generation of income account - Resources											
VALUE ADDED GROSS, at basic prices	55977.5	76559.1	97869.6	122318.3	145350.9	175743.6	217038.6	275435.0	268100.0	266218.6	277332.2	...
	II.1.1 Generation of income account - Uses											
Compensation of employees	35928.8	42842.6	51834.7	63268.9	77048.5	87101.9	105548.0	143308.0	129390.0	128715.3	144671.5	...
Other taxes less Other subsidies on production	-107.3	-62.5	-596.1	-1379.0	-1087.2	-3007.9	-1678.3	-1991.2	-2708.2	61.3	-2209.8	...
Other taxes on production	621.8	788.8	928.2	927.6	1105.5	1536.1	2506.0	2780.3	2682.4	3596.6	2664.1	...
Less: Other subsidies on production	729.1	851.3	1524.3	2306.6	2192.7	4544.0	4184.3	4771.5	5390.6	3535.3	4873.9	...
OPERATING SURPLUS, GROSS	20156.0	33779.0	46631.0	60428.4	69389.6	91649.6	113168.9	134118.0	141418.0	137442.0	134870.5	...
	II.1.2 Allocation of primary income account - Resources											
OPERATING SURPLUS, GROSS	20156.0	33779.0	46631.0	60428.4	69389.6	91649.6	113168.9	134118.0	141418.0	137442.0	134870.5	...
Property income	3050.6	2780.9	945.5	909.3	3441.9	3547.5	3185.0	8010.5	8507.3	7087.9	2389.1	...
	II.1.2 Allocation of primary income account - Uses											
Property income	6631.8	3798.8	9457.5	15060.9	15953.5	23329.9	26962.4	32358.5	25464.2	26310.3	16135.5	...
BALANCE OF PRIMARY INCOMES	16574.8	32761.1	38119.0	46276.8	56878.0	71867.2	89391.5	109770.0	124461.0	118219.6	121124.1	...
	II.2 Secondary distribution of income account - Resources											
BALANCE OF PRIMARY INCOMES	16574.8	32761.1	38119.0	46276.8	56878.0	71867.2	89391.5	109770.0	124461.0	118219.6	121124.1	...
Social contributions	...	...	...	...	...	...	...	...	...	...	...	...
Other current transfers	4070.6	1183.2	1138.3	1341.1	1492.5	1791.0	2686.0	2462.0	3458.5	5456.0	9200.6	...
	II.2 Secondary distribution of income account - Uses											
Current taxes on income, wealth, etc.	2086.3	3389.2	4733.6	7122.8	7205.1	9879.5	13153.1	15408.9	12275.7	10955.7	12290.2	...
Social benefits other than social transfers in kind	...	...	...	...	...	...	...	...	...	...	...	...
Other current transfers	3.4	253.2	62.8	93.8	165.9	199.0	509.0	768.4	1221.9	1728.4	2052.8	...
GROSS DISPOSABLE INCOME	18555.7	30301.9	34460.9	40401.3	50999.5	63579.7	78415.4	96054.8	114422.0	110991.5	115981.7	...
	II.4.1 Use of disposable income account - Resources											
GROSS DISPOSABLE INCOME	18555.7	30301.9	34460.9	40401.3	50999.5	63579.7	78415.4	96054.8	114422.0	110991.5	115981.7	...
	II.4.1 Use of disposable income account - Uses											
Adjustment for the change in net equity of households on pension funds	...	...	...	...	...	...	...	...	...	...	...	...
SAVING, GROSS	18555.7	30301.9	34460.9	40401.3	50999.5	63579.7	78415.4	96054.8	114422.0	110991.5	115981.7	...

	2001	2002	2003	2004	2005	2006	2007	2008	2009	2010	2011	2012
Series	**200**											
	III.1 Capital account - Changes in liabilities and net worth											
SAVING, GROSS	18555.7	30301.9	34460.9	40401.3	50999.5	63579.7	78415.4	96054.8	114422.0	110991.5	115981.7	...
Capital transfers, receivable less payable	1173.6	1804.0	2751.3	4737.6	3002.5	3418.8	3790.7	3112.5	2428.5	1206.2	7506.7	...
Capital transfers, receivable	1173.6	1804.0	2751.3	4737.6	3002.5	3418.8	3790.7	3112.5	2428.5	1206.2	7506.7	...
Less: Capital transfers, payable	0.0	...	...	...	...	...	...	...	...	...	...	...
Equals: CHANGES IN NET WORTH DUE TO SAVING AND CAPITAL TRANSFERS	6643.1	12619.5	15617.9	20470.0	27043.3	36826.2	47498.2	55816.3	67560.0	59709.6	123488.4[c]	...
	III.1 Capital account - Changes in assets											
Gross capital formation	19146.2	25841.9	32946.5	46714.3	52422.9	67993.1	93502.9	121094.0	87738.8	69070.8	76074.0	...
Gross fixed capital formation	17763.1	25035.1	32328.5	42588.2	53268.6	66104.8	91364.1	123507.0	84726.9	68301.2	74506.6	...
Changes in inventories	1383.1	806.8	618.0	4126.1	-845.7	1888.3	2138.8	-2412.9[d]	3011.9[d]	769.6[d]	1567.4[d]	...
Acquisitions less disposals of valuables	...	...	...	...	...	...	...	...	...	...	...	...
Acquisitions less disposals of non-produced non-financial assets	23744.3	2477.7	14721.6	9965.6	7420.2	8904.2	32181.3	20348.8	13294.1	14998.5	10895.6	...
NET LENDING (+) / NET BORROWING (-)	-23161.2	3786.3	-10455.9	-11541.0	-5841.1	-9898.8	-43478.1	-42275.6	15817.4	28128.4	36518.8	...

[a] Data for this year refers to semi-final data.
[b] Data for this year refers to provisional data.
[c] Item does not consider consumption of fixed capital.
[d] Includes Acquisitions less disposals of valuables.

Table 4.4 Financial Corporations (S.12)

Series 200: 1993 SNA, New Romanian Leu, Western calendar year — **Data in millions**

	2001	2002	2003	2004	2005	2006	2007	2008	2009	2010	2011	2012
Series	**200**											
	I. Production account - Resources											
Output, at basic prices (otherwise, please specify)	5199.7	5215.8	5711.3	8052.7	8790.8	9648.2	14632.9	20664.3	19031.9	18722.6	22753.3	23682.1
	I. Production account - Uses											
Intermediate consumption, at purchaser's prices	1143.2	1456.1	2038.6	2501.2	2964.3	3466.6	6735.9	9257.5	7781.8	7041.6	8583.0	8915.3
VALUE ADDED GROSS, at basic prices	4056.5	3759.7	3672.7	5551.5	5826.5	6181.6	7897.0	11406.8	11250.1	11681.0	14170.3[a]	14766.8[b]
Less: Consumption of fixed capital	872.9	1281.8	1430.7	1689.0	1786.2	1968.6	1872.6	1365.6	1356.1	1392.9	...	...
VALUE ADDED NET, at basic prices	3183.6	2477.9	2242.0	3862.5	4040.3	4213.0	6024.4	10041.2	9894.0	10288.1	...	...
	II.1.1 Generation of income account - Resources											
VALUE ADDED GROSS, at basic prices	4056.5	3759.7	3672.7	5551.5	5826.5	6181.6	7897.0	11406.8	11250.1	11681.0	14170.3	...
	II.1.1 Generation of income account - Uses											
Compensation of employees	1379.6	1372.3	1835.0	2527.3	3066.3	3855.3	5011.7	6082.2	5700.0	6083.0	6965.9	...
Other taxes less Other subsidies on production	85.9	132.7	194.7	187.1	239.9	315.2	519.9	1032.7	562.4	28.8	528.5	...
Other taxes on production	86.0	132.7	194.7	187.1	239.9	315.2	519.9	1032.7	562.4	28.8	528.5	...
Less: Other subsidies on production	0.1	0.0	0.0	0.0	0.0	0.0	...	...	...	0.0	0.0	...
OPERATING SURPLUS, GROSS	2590.9	2254.7	1643.0	2837.1	2520.3	2011.1	2365.4	4291.9	4987.7	5569.2	6675.9	...
	II.1.2 Allocation of primary income account - Resources											
OPERATING SURPLUS, GROSS	2590.9	2254.7	1643.0	2837.1	2520.3	2011.1	2365.4	4291.9	4987.7	5569.2	6675.9	...

	2001	2002	2003	2004	2005	2006	2007	2008	2009	2010	2011	2012
Series	**200**											
Property income	2290.5	3038.1[c]	7707.6	10070.3	8737.7	12487.2	19145.5	7379.2	37222.1	32711.7	26194.2	...
II.1.2 Allocation of primary income account - Uses												
Property income	5293.2	5498.0	4557.2	6128.2	9361.6	10023.8	17687.7	8330.7	30543.6	22460.4	13301.2	...
BALANCE OF PRIMARY INCOMES	-411.8	-205.2	4793.4	6779.2	1896.4	4474.5	3823.2	3340.4	11666.2	15820.5	19568.9	...
II.2 Secondary distribution of income account - Resources												
BALANCE OF PRIMARY INCOMES	-411.8	-205.2	4793.4	6779.2	1896.4	4474.5	3823.2	3340.4	11666.2	15820.5	19568.9	...
Social contributions	0.7	0.0	0.5	0.0	0.0	0.0	...	...	...	1593.0	2019.0	...
Other current transfers	2039.1	1801.9	3016.1	3930.1	5372.3	8653.3	4785.9	4935.8	8666.7	9812.2	13089.2	...
II.2 Secondary distribution of income account - Uses												
Current taxes on income, wealth, etc.	294.7	121.3	326.1	483.5	328.5	452.4	335.9	690.9	1616.9	1291.2	347.4	...
Social benefits other than social transfers in kind	0.0	0.0	0.5	0.0	0.0	0.0	...	...	...	...	...	...
Other current transfers	2012.9	2319.9	3166.3	4314.6	4458.5	7296.6	3142.2	4614.7	9012.9	8697.5	11120.4	...
GROSS DISPOSABLE INCOME	-680.4	-844.5	4317.1	5911.2	2481.7	5378.8	5131.0	2970.6	9703.1	17237.0	23209.3	...
II.4.1 Use of disposable income account - Resources												
GROSS DISPOSABLE INCOME	-680.4	-844.5	4317.1	5911.2	2481.7	5378.8	5131.0	2970.6	9703.1	17237.0	23209.3	...
II.4.1 Use of disposable income account - Uses												
Adjustment for the change in net equity of households on pension funds	...	...	...	...	...	...	...	...	...	...	...	...
SAVING, GROSS	-680.4	-844.5	4317.1	5911.2	2481.7	5378.8	5131.0	2970.6	9703.1	17237.0	23209.3	...
III.1 Capital account - Changes in liabilities and net worth												
SAVING, GROSS	-680.4	-844.5	4317.1	5911.2	2481.7	5378.8	5131.0	2970.6	9703.1	17237.0	23209.3	...
Capital transfers, receivable less payable	...	...	...	...	...	...	...	...	...	...	...	...
Capital transfers, receivable	...	...	...	...	...	...	...	...	...	...	...	...
Less: Capital transfers, payable	...	...	...	...	...	...	...	...	...	...	...	...
Equals: CHANGES IN NET WORTH DUE TO SAVING AND CAPITAL TRANSFERS	-1552.6	-2126.3	2886.9	4222.2	695.5	3410.2	3258.4	1605.0	8347.0	15844.1	23209.3[d]	...
III.1 Capital account - Changes in assets												
Gross capital formation	978.2	1120.1	1348.3	1710.4	907.0	1905.9	2704.8	1742.5	1034.4	1159.4	6054.9	...
Gross fixed capital formation	910.4	1090.7	1318.9	1550.8	1247.6	1497.2	2206.0	2241.3	1014.1	1140.7	6054.9	...
Changes in inventories	67.8	29.4	29.4	159.6	-340.6	408.7	498.8	-498.8[e]	20.3[e]	18.7[e]	0.0[e]	...
Acquisitions less disposals of valuables	...	...	...	...	...	...	...	...	...	...	...	...
Acquisitions less disposals of non-produced non-financial assets	69.4	65.1	33.1	57.1	63.1	32.3	45.1	38.7	33.5	30.3	152.3	...
NET LENDING (+) / NET BORROWING (-)	-1728.0	-2029.7	2935.7	4143.7	1511.6	3440.6	2381.1	1189.4	8635.2	16047.3	17002.1	...

[a] Data for this year refers to semi-final data.
[b] Data for this year refers to provisional data.
[c] Excludes financial intermediation services indirectly measured (FISIM).
[d] Item does not consider consumption of fixed capital.
[e] Includes Acquisitions less disposals of valuables.

Table 4.5 General Government (S.13)

Series 200: 1993 SNA, New Romanian Leu, Western calendar year **Data in millions**

	2001	2002	2003	2004	2005	2006	2007	2008	2009	2010	2011	2012
Series	**200**											
I. Production account - Resources												
Output, at basic prices (otherwise, please specify)	20196.4	25422.4	39687.2	42753.5	53072.1	61336.8	72801.4	93860.6	101083.0	92738.0	91061.5	96574.9
I. Production account - Uses												
Intermediate consumption, at purchaser's prices	8991.0	10738.9	13312.8	15457.1	20271.0	21973.9	25863.5	33698.6	34673.6	30325.2	33724.5	34628.2
VALUE ADDED GROSS, at basic prices	11205.4	14683.5	26374.4	27296.4	32801.1	39362.9	46937.9	60162.0	66409.5	62412.8	57337.0[a]	61946.7[b]
Less: Consumption of fixed capital	1418.4	1742.2	10238.7	7167.1	7525.5	7901.7	8296.8	8711.7	12960.5	11733.1	...	...
VALUE ADDED NET, at basic prices	9787.0	12941.3	16135.7	20129.3	25275.6	31461.2	38641.1	51450.3	53449.0	50679.7	...	...
II.1.1 Generation of income account - Resources												
VALUE ADDED GROSS, at basic prices	11205.4	14683.5	26374.4	27296.4	32801.1	39362.9	46937.9	60162.0	66409.5	62412.8	57337.0	...
II.1.1 Generation of income account - Uses												
Compensation of employees	9787.0	12941.3	16135.7	20126.7	25265.0	31458.0	38637.5	51446.6	53407.2	50587.8	43978.9	...
Other taxes less Other subsidies on production	0.2	0.0	0.0	2.6	10.6	3.2	3.6	3.7	41.7	92.0	98.0	...
Other taxes on production	0.2	0.0	0.0	2.6	10.6	3.2	3.6	3.7	41.7	92.0	98.0	...
Less: Other subsidies on production	...	...	...	...	...	...	...	...	...	...	...	...
OPERATING SURPLUS, GROSS	1418.4	1742.2	10238.7	7167.1	7525.5	7901.7	8296.8	8711.7	12960.6	11733.0	13260.1	...
II.1.2 Allocation of primary income account - Resources												
OPERATING SURPLUS, GROSS	1418.4	1742.2	10238.7	7167.1	7525.5	7901.7	8296.8	8711.7	12960.6	11733.0	13260.1	...
Taxes on production and imports, less Subsidies	11833.2	15219.2	21450.8	25305.2	32965.4	37797.8	45623.0	54527.1	49558.1	59320.3	70198.9	...
Taxes on production and imports	13328.0	17664.2	24213.8	29029.6	37248.0	43911.3	51370.5	60291.9	53721.9	62250.5	72661.6	...
Taxes on products	12591.4	16688.4	23025.4	27854.5	35811.8	41950.3	48167.1	56265.6	50249.6	58485.5	69185.7	...
Other taxes on production	736.6	975.8	1188.4	1175.1	1436.2	1961.0	3203.4	4026.3	3472.3	3765.0	3475.9	...
Less: Subsidies	1494.8	2445.0	2763.0	3724.4	4282.6	6113.5	5747.5	5764.8	4163.8	2930.2	2462.7	...
Subsidies on products	765.6	1593.7	1238.7	1417.8	2089.9	1569.5	1587.8	1443.4	1205.8	2179.0	827.3	...
Other subsidies on production	729.2	851.3	1524.3	2306.6	2192.7	4544.0	4159.7	4321.4	2958.0	751.2	1635.4	...
Property income	1987.6	2042.4	2092.5	2004.4	1744.0	3338.2	3916.3	4399.9	4199.1	4146.4	4649.7	...
II.1.2 Allocation of primary income account - Uses												
Property income	4042.0	3742.4	3158.4	3537.1	3167.1	2982.3	3342.8	4072.1	7636.4	8265.6	9388.1	...
BALANCE OF PRIMARY INCOMES	11197.2	15261.4	30623.6	30939.6	39067.8	46055.4	54493.3	63566.6	59081.4	66934.1	78720.6	...
II.2 Secondary distribution of income account - Resources												
BALANCE OF PRIMARY INCOMES	11197.2	15261.4	30623.6	30939.6	39067.8	46055.4	54493.3	63566.6	59081.4	66934.1	78720.6	...
Current taxes on income, wealth, etc.	7491.8	8765.9	11811.5	15711.7	15376.9	20965.4	27887.2	34573.5	32790.0	31632.4	33297.8	...
Social contributions	13242.3	16899.5	19528.4	23887.8	29649.6	35604.2	43639.1	51988.2	51267.0	49551.6	50808.1	...
Other current transfers	364.7	1666.9	1726.7	3848.4	3336.6	3187.1	3479.0	3763.1	5094.9	9862.9	7346.6	...
II.2 Secondary distribution of income account - Uses												
Current taxes on income, wealth, etc.	0.0	0.0	0.0	0.0	0.0	0.0	...	...	...	...	...	...
Social benefits other than social transfers in kind	11453.9	14116.6	16667.5	21609.5	25641.8	30358.4	38345.9	53323.0	63537.7	67690.7	66802.6	...

	2001	2002	2003	2004	2005	2006	2007	2008	2009	2010	2011	2012
Series	**200**											
Other current transfers	1137.2	1863.4	2417.1	4085.7	1880.2	3181.5	7117.9	6678.3	5690.5	9764.1	10892.6	...
GROSS DISPOSABLE INCOME	19704.9	26613.7	44605.6	48692.3	59908.9	72272.2	84034.8	93890.1	79005.1	80526.2	92477.9	...
	II.4.1 Use of disposable income account - Resources											
GROSS DISPOSABLE INCOME	19704.9	26613.7	44605.6	48692.3	59908.9	72272.2	84034.8	93890.1	79005.1	80526.2	92477.9	...
	II.4.1 Use of disposable income account - Uses											
Final consumption expenditure	19117.2	22891.9	38078.4	40281.2	50165.7	57412.9	66578.5	87123.9	92903.6	85444.0	83765.9	...
Individual consumption expenditure	10562.8	12668.8	18655.5	20725.6	26056.3	30986.6	34864.8	47314.5	49030.2	48089.0	48617.7	...
Collective consumption expenditure	8554.4	10223.1	19422.9	19555.6	24109.4	26426.3	31713.7	39809.4	43873.4	37355.0	35148.2	...
Adjustment for the change in net equity of households on pension funds	...	...	...	...	...	...	...	...	...	...	...	...
SAVING, GROSS	587.7	3721.8	6527.2	8411.1	9743.2	14859.3	17456.3	6766.2	-13898.5	-4917.8	8712.0	...
	III.1 Capital account - Changes in liabilities and net worth											
SAVING, GROSS	587.7	3721.8	6527.2	8411.1	9743.2	14859.3	17456.3	6766.2	-13898.5	-4917.8	8712.0	...
Capital transfers, receivable less payable	-1025.2	-1515.2	-2369.6	-4009.8	-2064.0	-4863.5	-4335.7	-6104.8	-2018.9	-741.9	-10488.7	...
Capital transfers, receivable	114.1	96.8	96.6	1020.4	740.4	426.3	542.9	610.7	1532.5	3655.4	3171.9	...
Less: Capital transfers, payable	1139.3	1612.0	2466.2	5030.2	2804.4	5289.8	4878.6	6715.5	3551.4	4397.3	13660.6	...
Equals: CHANGES IN NET WORTH DUE TO SAVING AND CAPITAL TRANSFERS	-1855.9	464.4	-6081.1	-2765.8	153.7	2094.1	4823.8	-8050.3	-28877.9	-17392.8	-1776.7[c]	...
	III.1 Capital account - Changes in assets											
Gross capital formation	3678.1	5249.1	7110.0	7619.9	11223.3	17821.8	23586.3	28592.3	26515.6	29957.5	30256.8	...
Gross fixed capital formation	3226.2	5111.0	6942.3	7474.6	11168.0	17673.7	23581.8	28452.5	26490.4	29860.6	30200.4	...
Changes in inventories	451.9	138.1	167.7	145.3	55.3	148.1	4.5	139.8[d]	25.2[d]	96.9[d]	56.4[d]	...
Acquisitions less disposals of valuables	...	...	...	...	...	...	...	...	...	...	...	...
Acquisitions of non-produced non-financial assets	...	...	...	-203.5	...	-179.7	...	...	...	129.7	-29.6	...
NET LENDING (+) / NET BORROWING (-)	-4115.6	-3042.5	-2952.4	-3015.1	-3544.1	-7646.3	-10465.7	-27930.9	-42433.0	-35746.9	-32003.9	...

[a] Data for this year refers to semi-final data.
[b] Data for this year refers to provisional data.
[c] Item does not consider consumption of fixed capital.
[d] Includes Acquisitions less disposals of valuables.

Table 4.6 Households (S.14)

Series 200: 1993 SNA, New Romanian Leu, Western calendar year — **Data in millions**

	2001	2002	2003	2004	2005	2006	2007	2008	2009	2010	2011	2012
Series	**200**											
	I. Production account - Resources											
Output, at basic prices (otherwise, please specify)	56325.6	68764.1	83334.9	111713.3	117726.9	135519.1	148665.8	180651.0	170025.0	205040.2	225827.3	230866.8
	I. Production account - Uses											
Intermediate consumption, at purchaser's prices	22103.3	27748.5	36832.1	47903.0	49109.6	55154.4	55225.6	72989.0	68812.3	82236.8	90998.6	91624.2
VALUE ADDED GROSS, at basic prices	34222.3	41015.6	46502.8	63810.3	68617.3	80364.7	93440.2	107662.0	101213.0	122803.4	134828.7[a]	139242.6[b]
Less: Consumption of fixed capital	8053.8	11448.5	12767.9	15623.9	17799.4	19759.7	21662.5	25486.9	26570.0	27562.6	...	...
VALUE ADDED NET, at basic prices	26168.5	29567.1	33734.9	48186.4	50817.9	60605.0	71777.7	82175.5	74642.8	95240.8	...	...

	2001	2002	2003	2004	2005	2006	2007	2008	2009	2010	2011	2012
Series	**200**											
	II.1.1 Generation of income account - Resources											
VALUE ADDED GROSS, at basic prices	34222.3	41015.6	46502.8	63810.3	68617.3	80364.7	93440.2	107662.0	101213.0	122803.4	134828.7	...
	II.1.1 Generation of income account - Uses											
Compensation of employees	1044.1	2220.3	2997.4	4353.3	5245.1	7632.8	10020.1	11610.5	11572.8	1281.5	1425.6	...
Other taxes less Other subsidies on production	0.0	0.0	0.0	0.0	0.0	0.0	...	...	...	0.0	0.0	...
Other taxes on production	0.0	0.0	0.0	0.0	0.0	0.0	...	...	...	0.0	0.0	...
Less: Other subsidies on production	...	...	...	...	...	...	...	...	...	0.0	0.0	...
OPERATING SURPLUS, GROSS	33178.2	38795.3	43505.4	59457.0	63372.2	72731.9	83420.1	96051.9	89640.0	39821.5	41088.2	...
MIXED INCOME, GROSS	...	...	...	...	...	...	...	...	...	81700.4	92314.9	...
	II.1.2 Allocation of primary income account - Resources											
OPERATING SURPLUS, GROSS	33178.2	38795.3	43505.4	59457.0	63372.2	72731.9	83420.1	96051.9	89640.0	39821.5	41088.2	...
MIXED INCOME, GROSS	...	...	...	...	...	...	...	...	...	81700.4	92314.9	...
Compensation of employees	48923.9	60606.6	74018.4	91387.8	115719.9	135319.4	165762.2	219984.0	205137.0	191548.9	202255.4	...
Property income	7540.4	3619.7	2614.7	3163.9	5594.1	6421.3	9209.9	10141.0	8290.1	8601.5	3616.2	...
	II.1.2 Allocation of primary income account - Uses											
Property income	266.1	605.8	1145.7	2136.4	2384.7	4345.0	5219.9	3883.0	5398.8	5862.8	9244.9	...
BALANCE OF PRIMARY INCOMES	89376.4	102415.8	118992.8	151872.3	182301.5	210127.6	253172.3	322294.0	297668.0	315809.5	330029.8	...
	II.2 Secondary distribution of income account - Resources											
BALANCE OF PRIMARY INCOMES	89376.4	102415.8	118992.8	151872.3	182301.5	210127.6	253172.3	322294.0	297668.0	315809.5	330029.8	...
Social contributions	...	...	...	...	...	...	...	...	...	...	...	...
Social benefits other than social transfers in kind	11453.9	14116.6	16667.5	21609.5	25641.8	30358.4	38345.9	53323.0	63537.7	67692.9	66892.2	...
Other current transfers	5302.4	10577.1	11361.2	20172.9	14969.6	12218.2	13355.4	20017.5	14166.0	15020.7	17415.3	...
	II.2 Secondary distribution of income account - Uses											
Current taxes on income, wealth, etc.	4833.6	5092.0	6678.6	8031.0	7792.0	10519.8	14539.2	18397.3	19006.3	19117.0	21027.8	...
Social contributions	13242.3	16899.5	19528.4	23887.8	29649.6	35604.2	43639.1	51988.2	51260.6	51144.6	52827.1	...
Social benefits other than social transfers in kind	...	...	...	...	...	...	...	...	...	...	...	...
Other current transfers	3180.2	3407.4	4686.8	5764.2	8687.4	6091.9	5070.1	6162.3	6207.5	8333.0	13249.3	...
GROSS DISPOSABLE INCOME	84876.6	101710.6	116127.7	155971.7	176783.9	200488.3	241625.2	319087.0	298897.0	319928.5	327233.1	...
	II.4.1 Use of disposable income account - Resources											
GROSS DISPOSABLE INCOME	84876.6	101710.6	116127.7	155971.7	176783.9	200488.3	241625.2	319087.0	298897.0	319928.5	327233.1	...
Adjustment for the change in net equity of households on pension funds	...	...	...	...	...	...	...	...	...	...	...	...
	II.4.1 Use of disposable income account - Uses											
Final consumption expenditure	80170.3	102412.2	128437.9	167644.3	197069.2	233134.9	273418.1	327928.0	304667.0	327241.5	345046.6	...
Individual consumption expenditure	80170.3	102412.2	128437.9	167644.3	197069.2	233134.9	273418.1	327928.0	304667.0	327241.5	345046.6	...
SAVING, GROSS	4706.3	-701.6	-12310.2	-11672.6	-20285.3	-32646.6	-31792.9	-8840.9	-5770.0	-7313.0	-17813.5	...
	III.1 Capital account - Changes in liabilities and net worth											
SAVING, GROSS	4706.3	-701.6	-12310.2	-11672.6	-20285.3	-32646.6	-31792.9	-8840.9	-5770.0	-7313.0	-17813.5	...
Capital transfers, receivable less payable	192.9	157.5	431.7	1251.9	1550.2	1782.5	2673.5	2775.0	775.0	196.1	4948.0	...
Capital transfers, receivable	192.9	157.5	431.7	1251.9	1550.2	1782.5	2673.5	2775.0	775.0	196.1	4948.0	...

	2001	2002	2003	2004	2005	2006	2007	2008	2009	2010	2011	2012
Series	**200**											
Less: Capital transfers, payable	...	...	...	...	...	...	...	...	...	...	...	...
Equals: CHANGES IN NET WORTH DUE TO SAVINGS AND CAPITAL TRANSFERS	-3154.6	-11992.6	-24646.4	-26044.6	-36534.5	-50623.8	-50781.9	-31552.8	-31565.0	-34679.5	-12865.5[c]	...
	III.1 Capital account - Changes in assets											
Gross capital formation	2001.8	1048.2	1692.3	2227.0	2602.7	3149.1	8749.8	8818.2	11090.4	33474.2	36153.8	...
Gross fixed capital formation	1894.7	945.0	1635.9	1963.1	2740.8	2783.4	8284.0	9284.0	9624.6	29886.0	32735.7	...
Changes in inventories	107.0[d]	103.2[d]	56.4[d]	263.9[d]	-138.1	365.7[d]	465.8[d]	-465.8[d]	1465.8[d]	3588.2[d]	3418.1[d]	...
Acquisitions less disposals of valuables	...	...	...	...	...	...	...	...	...	...	...	...
Acquisitions less disposals of non-produced non-financial assets	-23813.6	-2542.8	-14754.7	-9819.2	-7483.3	-8756.8	-32586.0	-20406.3	-13891.4	-15232.3	-11702.6	...
NET LENDING (+) / NET BORROWING (-)	26711.1	950.5	1183.9	-2828.5	-13854.5	-25256.4	-5283.2	5522.2	-2194.0	-25358.8	-37316.7	...

[a] Data for this year refers to semi-final data.
[b] Data for this year refers to provisional data.
[c] Item does not consider consumption of fixed capital.
[d] Includes Acquisitions less disposals of valuables.

Table 4.7 Non-profit institutions serving households (S.15)

Series 200: 1993 SNA, New Romanian Leu, Western calendar year **Data in millions**

	2001	2002	2003	2004	2005	2006	2007	2008	2009	2010	2011	2012
Series	**200**											
	I. Production account - Resources											
Output, at basic prices (otherwise, please specify)	1651.0	2174.1	2791.7	4137.9	4519.2	6858.8	8548.0	9185.2	9104.0	8788.0	9106.8	10048.9
	I. Production account - Uses											
Intermediate consumption, at purchaser's prices	992.7	1269.7	1570.3	2183.1	1882.3	4241.8	5505.4	5316.2	5096.9	5506.8	5448.2	6015.4
VALUE ADDED GROSS, at basic prices	658.3	904.4	1221.4	1954.8	2636.9	2617.0	3042.6	3869.0	4007.1	3281.2	3658.6[a]	4033.5[b]
Less: Consumption of fixed capital	76.9	82.4	78.6	47.0	48.1	40.8	40.1	87.2	120.1	132.5	...	...
VALUE ADDED NET, at basic prices	581.4	822.0	1142.8	1907.8	2588.8	2576.2	3002.5	3781.8	3887.0	3148.7	3658.6	...
	II.1.1 Generation of income account - Resources											
VALUE ADDED GROSS, at basic prices	658.3	904.4	1221.4	1954.8	2636.9	2617.0	3042.6	3869.0	4007.1	3281.2	3658.6	...
	II.1.1 Generation of income account - Uses											
Compensation of employees	465.9	796.3	871.9	763.1	2372.0	2146.9	2720.8	3703.8	3174.5	3123.3	3486.5	...
Other taxes less Other subsidies on production	28.8	54.3	65.5	57.8	80.2	106.5	173.9	213.1	189.6	47.6	185.3	...
Other taxes on production	28.8	54.3	65.5	57.8	80.2	106.5	173.9	213.1	189.6	47.6	185.3	...
Less: Other subsidies on production	0.0	0.0	0.0	0.0	0.0	0.0	...	...	...	...	...	...
OPERATING SURPLUS, GROSS	163.6	53.8	284.0	1133.9	184.7	363.6	147.9	-47.9	643.0	110.3	-13.2	...
	II.1.2 Allocation of primary income account - Resources											
OPERATING SURPLUS, GROSS	163.6	53.8	284.0	1133.9	184.7	363.6	147.9	-47.9	643.0	110.3	-13.2	...
Property income	164.2	139.5	49.6	74.7	148.1	255.0	86.8	965.4	880.4	409.4	286.3	...
	II.1.2 Allocation of primary income account - Uses											
Property income	11.9	12.2	6.6	74.7	12.7	28.8	33.6	105.6	71.0	24.7	297.8	...
BALANCE OF PRIMARY INCOMES	316.6	181.1	327.0	1133.9	320.1	589.8	201.1	811.9	1452.4	495.0	-24.7	...

	2001	2002	2003	2004	2005	2006	2007	2008	2009	2010	2011	2012
Series	**200**											
	II.2 Secondary distribution of income account - Resources											
BALANCE OF PRIMARY INCOMES	316.6	181.1	327.0	1133.9	320.1	589.8	201.1	811.9	1452.4	495.0	-24.7	...
Social contributions	0.0	0.0	0.0	0.0	0.0	0.0	...	...	...	...	...	...
Other current transfers	3.6	1136.4	2783.3	3281.0	2387.2	7701.2	8434.6	11420.4	7476.8	2307.5	3612.7	...
	II.2 Secondary distribution of income account - Uses											
Current taxes on income, wealth, etc.	1.6	3.3	6.3	17.6	4.4	1.7	28.3	152.8	29.1	614.3	0.0	...
Social benefits other than social transfers in kind	0.0	0.0	0.0	0.0	0.0	0.0	...	...	...	...	...	...
Other current transfers	2474.0	204.4	100.6	130.0	212.2	451.0	676.5	1019.4	412.8	136.4	1108.2	...
GROSS DISPOSABLE INCOME	-2155.4	1109.8	3003.4	4267.3	2490.7	7838.3	7930.9	11060.1	8487.3	2051.8	2479.8	...
	II.4.1 Use of disposable income account - Resources											
GROSS DISPOSABLE INCOME	-2155.4	1109.8	3003.4	4267.3	2490.7	7838.3	7930.9	11060.1	8487.3	2051.8	2479.8	...
	II.4.1 Use of disposable income account - Uses											
Final consumption expenditure	1444.0	1814.7	2302.4	3129.1	3803.2	4319.8	4940.4	5865.9	6704.8	7115.7	7672.5	...
Individual consumption expenditure	1444.0	1814.7	2302.4	3129.1	3803.2	4319.8	4940.4	5865.9	6704.8	7115.7	7672.5	...
Adjustment for the change in net equity of households on pension funds	...	...	...	...	...	...	...	...	...	...	...	...
SAVING, GROSS	-3599.6	-704.9	701.0	1138.2	-1312.5	3518.5	2990.5	5194.2	1782.5	-5063.9	-5192.7	...
	III.1 Capital account - Changes in liabilities and net worth											
SAVING, GROSS	-3599.6	-704.9	701.0	1138.2	-1312.5	3518.5	2990.5	5194.2	1782.5	-5063.9	-5192.7	...
Capital transfers, receivable less payable	49.8	58.8	98.3	323.1	472.6	169.8	254.8	2508.1	990.1	309.1	401.1	...
Capital transfers, receivable	49.8	58.8	98.3	323.1	472.6	169.8	254.8	2508.1	990.1	309.1	401.1	...
Less: Capital transfers, payable	...	...	...	...	...	...	...	...	...	...	...	...
Equals: CHANGES IN NET WORTH DUE TO SAVING AND CAPITAL TRANSFERS	-3626.7	-728.5	720.7	1414.3	-888.0	3647.5	3205.2	7615.1	2652.5	-4887.3	-4791.6[c]	...
	III.1 Capital account - Changes in assets											
Gross capital formation	381.9	186.8	273.1	279.8	130.7	318.4	314.9	649.8	758.2	236.7	1369.9	...
Gross fixed capital formation	377.0	184.7	271.0	273.6	101.6	212.9	209.4	794.6	585.9	233.3	1060.6	...
Changes in inventories	4.9[d]	2.1	2.1	6.2	29.1	105.5	105.5	-144.8	172.3[d]	3.4	309.3	...
Acquisitions less disposals of valuables	...	...	...	...	...	...	...	...	...	...	...	...
Acquisitions less disposals of non-produced non-financial assets	...	...	...	...	...	...	...	...	...	...	...	...
NET LENDING (+) / NET BORROWING (-)	-3931.7	-832.9	526.2	1181.5	-970.6	3369.9	2930.4	7052.5	2014.4	-4991.5	-6161.5	...

[a] Data for this year refers to semi-final data.
[b] Data for this year refers to provisional data.
[c] Item does not consider consumption of fixed capital.
[d] Includes Acquisitions less disposals of valuables.

Table 5.2 Cross classification of Gross value added by industries and institutional sectors (ISIC Rev. 4) Non-financial corporations

Series 200: 1993 SNA, New Romanian Leu, Western calendar year **Data in millions**

	2001	2002	2003	2004	2005	2006	2007	2008	2009	2010	2011	2012
Series								**200**				
Industries												
Agriculture, forestry and fishing								2568.8	6677.6	4866.7	6463.9	5578.9
Manufacturing, mining and quarrying and other industrial activities								100196.0	102063.0	126393.9	135204.8	144454.6
Of which: manufacturing								...	...	...	...	...
Construction								44210.4	37946.8	30327.9	31994.0	35359.2
Wholesale and retail trade, transportation and storage, accommodation and food service activities								77045.9	73155.1	49729.5	47197.7	49842.7
Information and communication								19964.6	19434.1	15558.3	15215.8	15433.7
Financial and insurance activities								...	...	...	...	...
Real estate activities								6994.2	6158.6	5932.8	5865.7	6566.0
Professional, scientific, technical, administrative and support service activities								19179.8	17472.5	20749.5	21892.3	23198.0
Public administration and defence, education, human health and social work activities								2063.7	2464.3	5141.8	5491.9	5083.0
Other service activities								3212.4	2727.9	7518.2	8006.3	8297.1
VALUE ADDED GROSS, at basic prices								275435.0	268100.0	266218.6	277332.3[a]	293813.2[b]

[a] Data for this year refers to semi-final data.
[b] Data for this year refers to provisional data.

Table 5.2 Cross classification of Gross value added by industries and institutional sectors (ISIC Rev. 4) Financial corporations

Series 200: 1993 SNA, New Romanian Leu, Western calendar year **Data in millions**

	2001	2002	2003	2004	2005	2006	2007	2008	2009	2010	2011	2012
Series								**200**				
Industries												
Agriculture, forestry and fishing								...	...	...	...	...
Manufacturing, mining and quarrying and other industrial activities								...	...	...	...	...
Of which: manufacturing								...	...	...	...	...
Construction								...	...	...	...	...
Wholesale and retail trade, transportation and storage, accommodation and food service activities								...	...	...	...	...
Information and communication								...	...	...	...	...
Financial and insurance activities								11406.8	11250.1	11681.0	14170.2	14766.8
Real estate activities								...	...	...	...	...
Professional, scientific, technical, administrative and support service activities								...	...	...	...	...

	2001	2002	2003	2004	2005	2006	2007	2008	2009	2010	2011	2012
Series								**200**				
Public administration and defence, education, human health and social work activities								...	...	...	...	...
Other service activities								...	...	...	...	...
VALUE ADDED GROSS, at basic prices								11406.8	11250.1	11681.0	14170.2[a]	14766.8[b]

[a] Data for this year refers to semi-final data.
[b] Data for this year refers to provisional data.

Table 5.2 Cross classification of Gross value added by industries and institutional sectors (ISIC Rev. 4) General government

Series 200: 1993 SNA, New Romanian Leu, Western calendar year **Data in millions**

	2001	2002	2003	2004	2005	2006	2007	2008	2009	2010	2011	2012
Series								**200**				
Industries												
Agriculture, forestry and fishing								2386.1	3265.7	1972.3	1837.6	2119.4
Manufacturing, mining and quarrying and other industrial activities								22.4	28.8	2062.0	3255.0	3640.7
Of which: manufacturing								...	...	...	...	...
Construction								1568.9	1634.9	2.6	2043.1	2184.6
Wholesale and retail trade, transportation and storage, accommodation and food service activities								1961.1	5211.0	9254.2	5478.1	6013.7
Information and communication								65.3	71.5	103.6	101.4	121.9
Financial and insurance activities								...	...	...	...	...
Real estate activities								...	...	192.6	18.5	19.2
Professional, scientific, technical, administrative and support service activities								318.2	911.0	813.5	293.0	350.5
Public administration and defence, education, human health and social work activities								50765.6	51325.9	46470.4	42923.4	45875.9
Other service activities								3074.4	3960.7	1541.6	1387.0	1620.7
VALUE ADDED GROSS, at basic prices								60162.0	66409.5	62412.8	57337.0[a]	61946.7[b]

[a] Data for this year refers to semi-final data.
[b] Data for this year refers to provisional data.

Table 5.2 Cross classification of Gross value added by industries and institutional sectors (ISIC Rev. 4) Households

Series 200: 1993 SNA, New Romanian Leu, Western calendar year — **Data in millions**

	2001	2002	2003	2004	2005	2006	2007	2008	2009	2010	2011	2012
Series								**200**				
Industries												
Agriculture, forestry and fishing								29171.5	22354.5	23035.2	28137.1	23199.6
Manufacturing, mining and quarrying and other industrial activities								17829.4	18402.6	19972.3	22361.8	18871.7
Of which: manufacturing								...	...	...	...	...
Construction								10351.3	13227.7	17431.8	13526.3	12905.2
Wholesale and retail trade, transportation and storage, accommodation and food service activities								20399.3	15853.8	10756.7	10088.4	11463.3
Information and communication								18.1	15.0	2149.9	2600.3	7835.5
Financial and insurance activities								0.0	0.0	0.0	0.0	0.0
Real estate activities								24677.3	26540.4	40125.5	41565.5	42495.6
Professional, scientific, technical, administrative and support service activities								241.6	1660.5	3153.8	8414.6	10871.8
Public administration and defence, education, human health and social work activities								2960.7	1878.0	4995.5	6694.9	10108.1
Other service activities								2013.2	1280.3	1182.7	1439.7	1491.8
VALUE ADDED GROSS, at basic prices								107662.4	101212.8	122803.4	134828.6[a]	139242.6[b]

[a] Data for this year refers to semi-final data.
[b] Data for this year refers to provisional data.

Table 5.2 Cross classification of Gross value added by industries and institutional sectors (ISIC Rev. 4) Non-profit institutions serving households

Series 200: 1993 SNA, New Romanian Leu, Western calendar year — **Data in millions**

	2001	2002	2003	2004	2005	2006	2007	2008	2009	2010	2011	2012
Series								**200**				
Industries												
Agriculture, forestry and fishing								...	...	...	...	...
Manufacturing, mining and quarrying and other industrial activities								192.5	143.3	124.9	106.2	113.7
Of which: manufacturing								...	...	...	...	...
Construction								...	...	...	...	...
Wholesale and retail trade, transportation and storage, accommodation and food service activities								187.5	139.6	0.0	0.0	0.0
Information and communication								...	...	...	...	...
Financial and insurance activities								...	...	...	...	...
Real estate activities								...	...	...	...	...
Professional, scientific, technical, administrative and support service activities								...	...	...	...	...

	2001	2002	2003	2004	2005	2006	2007	2008	2009	2010	2011	2012
Series								**200**				
Public administration and defence, education, human health and social work activities								...	...	...	...	...
Other service activities								3489.0	3724.2	3156.3	3552.4	3919.8
VALUE ADDED GROSS, at basic prices								3869.0	4007.1	3281.2	3658.6[a]	4033.5[b]

[a] Data for this year refers to semi-final data.
[b] Data for this year refers to provisional data.

Table 5.2 Cross classification of Gross value added by industries and institutional sectors (ISIC Rev. 4) Total economy

Series 200: 1993 SNA, New Romanian Leu, Western calendar year **Data in millions**

	2001	2002	2003	2004	2005	2006	2007	2008	2009	2010	2011	2012
Series								**200**				
Industries												
Agriculture, forestry and fishing								34126.4	32297.8	29874.2	36438.6	30897.9
Manufacturing, mining and quarrying and other industrial activities								118239.8	120637.4	148553.1	160927.8	167080.7
Of which: manufacturing								...	...	...	...	...
Construction								56130.6	52809.4	47762.3	47563.4	50449.0
Wholesale and retail trade, transportation and storage, accommodation and food service activities								99593.8	94359.5	69740.4	62764.2	67319.7
Information and communication								20048.0	19520.6	17811.8	17917.4	23391.1
Financial and insurance activities								11406.8	11250.1	11681.0	14170.2	14766.8
Real estate activities								31671.5	32699.0	46250.9	47449.7	49080.8
Professional, scientific, technical, administrative and support service activities								19739.6	20044.0	24716.8	30599.9	34420.3
Public administration and defence, education, human health and social work activities								55790.0	55668.2	56607.7	55110.2	61067.0
Other service activities								11789.0	11693.1	13398.8	14385.4	15329.4
VALUE ADDED GROSS, at basic prices								458535.5	450979.1	466397.0	487326.8[a]	513802.8[b]

[a] Data for this year refers to semi-final data.
[b] Data for this year refers to provisional data.

Russian Federation

Source
Data on national accounts are compiled by the Federal State Statistics Service (Rosstat) and published in the annual "National Accounts of Russia" (an electronic version is posted on the Rosstat website). Furthermore, quarterly and annual gross domestic product (GDP) estimates are regularly posted on the Rosstat website.

General
The Russian System of National Accounts includes the following accounts and tables:

(a) Value added by type of economic activity and GDP in current and constant prices;
(b) GDP components by expenditure in current and constant prices;
(c) Production account;
(d) Generation of income account;
(e) Allocation of primary income account;
(f) Secondary distribution of income account;
(g) Use of income account;
(h) Capital account;
(i) Rest of the world account.

Accounts are classified according to institutional sector. However, separate tables contain units in financial and non-financial sectors.

The following additional accounts and tables are regularly compiled:

(a) Quarterly value added and GDP in current and constant prices by type of activity;
(b) Quarterly GDP components by expenditure in current and constant prices;
(c) Quarterly generation of income account;

No financial account is compiled.

Rosstat also compiles regional indicators on an annual basis: gross regional product by type of activity, actual final consumption of households, and gross fixed capital formation for 83 constituent entities of the Russian Federation. Furthermore, components of the generation of income account are compiled for constituent entities of the Russian Federation.

Classification systems:

• Operations, flows and institutional sectors: in accordance with the 1993 SNA;
• Final consumption of households: according to the COICOP;
• Final consumption of government: following the Classification of Individual Consumption According to Purpose (COICOP) and the Classification of the Functions of Government (COFOG);
• Foreign trade: according to the commodity nomenclature of foreign economic activity, developed on the basis of the international Harmonized Commodity Description and Coding System;
• Types of activity by industry: until 2003, following the Russian Classification of Branches of the National Economy; data after 2003, in accordance with the Russian Classification of Types of Economic Activity, which is fully compatible with the first version of the Statistical Classification of Economic Activities in the European Community (NACE Rev.1.1);
• Goods and services: based on the national classification.

Relationship with international methodological instruments:

• Classification of products: All-Russia classification of products by kinds of economic activities OK 034-2007 (OKPD), harmonized with statistical classification of products by activity in the European economic community (CPA 2002)
• Final consumption of households: consumption of households is based on COICOP.

Methodology:

Overview of GDP Compilation

The conceptual framework for Russian national accounts is the System of National Accounts 1993 (1993 SNA), developed under the auspices of the Inter-Secretariat Working Group on National Accounts, which was established by the Statistical Office of the European Communities (EUROSTAT), the International Monetary Fund, the Organization for Economic Cooperation and Development, the United Nations and the World Bank.

GDP is calculated by three methods: the output method, the income use method and the sources of income method. GDP obtained using the sources of income method is not independent since, with the methodology used, not all income indicators are obtained by direct calculation and some of them are calculated by the balance method.

Because the main method for calculating GDP is the output method, a breakdown of GDP by category of expenditure includes a statistical discrepancy: the difference between GDP calculated by the output method and by the income use method. The statistical discrepancy between closing estimates of GDP by type of activity and component of income use is, on average, less than two per cent of GDP.

Expenditure Approach

The information database for calculating GDP aggregates uses the following data:

• Final consumption expenditure of households: data on the volume of retail turnover, data on the volume of paid services to the public, household budget surveys, and balance of payments data;
• Final consumption expenditure of government: data on the execution of the State budget, and data from the statistical observation of activity of State extrabudgetary funds;
• Final consumption expenditure of non-profit institutions serving households: a sample statistical survey of non-profit institutions serving households;
• Gross fixed capital formation: a statistical survey of investments in fixed capital, and data on livestock population and on prices for the sale of animals from the main herd;
• Changes in inventories: data from the balance sheet and from a statistical survey of inventory availability by type;
• Export and import of goods and services: balance of payments data.

Estimation procedure: All components of GDP calculated by the income use method are obtained independently.
• Final consumption expenditure of households is estimated for aggregated groups of goods and services. Final consumption expenditure of households is estimated using data on the volume of retail turnover. Expenditure by residents abroad is included in final consumption expenditure of households, but expenditure by non-residents in the domestic economy is excluded;
• Agricultural production for own final consumption is included in the estimate. It is obtained by the balance method based on data on household economic output and trends for its use;
• Data on in kind goods and services received by households are obtained from company surveys, and Federal Customs Service data on humanitarian assistance;
• Final consumption expenditure of government is compiled in the context of COICOP and COFOG;
• Gross fixed capital formation is calculated on the basis of company survey data on investments (in the construction of buildings and installations, acquisition of machinery and equipment, etc.);
• Data on changes in inventories are obtained from surveys of inventories by type. Estimates are adjusted for holding gains.

Each of the three methods for calculating GDP contains adjustments for the unobserved economy, i.e. hidden and informal economic activity.

Annual GDP growth series estimates have been available since 1990, and quarterly ones since 1995. However, estimates prior to 1995 have not been reviewed and the individual components of GDP are not compatible with the data for later periods. Furthermore, following the transition to the Russian Classification of Types of Economic Activity, starting with data for 2003, estimates of components of GDP produced are not compatible with similar data for earlier periods.

Growth series / Base year

1995-2000 / 1995
2000-2002 / 2000
2002-2010 / 2003
2002-2011 / 2008

GDP growth series and components of GDP in constant prices are obtained by multiplying data on GDP and its components in the base period (for annual calculations: the year 2008; for quarterly calculations: the notional average for one quarter of 2008 (the value for 2008 divided by four)) for the corresponding chain volume indices. Volume indices of GDP and its components for the corresponding period of the preceding year are calculated as the quotient from the division of the reporting period indicator (in annual average prices for the previous year) by a similar indicator for the corresponding period of the preceding year (in annual average prices).

This approach results in discrepancies between GDP as a whole and the sum of its components, calculated in constant prices, as a result of the change in the weighting pattern.

Rosstat conducts regular reviews of GDP:

• A preliminary set of annual estimates is disseminated on the last working day of the month following the end of the period, and a definitive set of data is disseminated 24 months following the end of the period;
• A first set of preliminary quarterly estimates is disseminated 50 working days following the end of the period. A second set is disseminated 90 working days following the end of the period. A set of quarterly calendar year estimates is finalized 27 months following the end of a given calendar year.

Production Approach

Basic data are compiled from a combination of annual and quarterly company surveys, data from administrative sources, and annual household budget surveys. Administrative data include budget execution data, tax data and so forth.

Estimates of output, intermediate consumption and value added are published at the one-digit and two-digit level of the Russian Classification of Types of Economic Activity.

• Private homes: the output of private homes is estimated as the cost of repairs and maintenance, net insurance premiums, taxes paid by owners and consumption of fixed capital. The market value of rental housing actually rented is also estimated;

• Adjustment for changes in inventories: changes in inventories are estimated using data from the balance sheet and from a statistical survey of inventory availability by type. Estimates of changes in inventories are adjusted for income arising from appreciation in the value of assets as a result of price increases;

• Consumption of fixed capital: the perpetual inventory method is used to assess consumption of fixed capital.

Table 1.1 Gross domestic product by expenditures at current prices

Series 300: 1993 SNA, Russian ruble (re-denom. 1:1000), Western calendar year
Series 400: 1993 SNA, Russian ruble (re-denom. 1:1000), Western calendar year

Data in billions

	2001	2002	2003	2004	2005	2006	2007	2008	2009	2010	2011	2012
Series	**300**		**400**									
Expenditures of the gross domestic product												
Final consumption expenditure	5886.9	7443.2	9024.8									
			9058.7	11477.8	14438.1	17809.7	21968.6	27543.5	29269.6	32514.7	37439.3	42471.5
Household final consumption expenditure	4318.1	5400.3	6540.1									
			6537.4	8438.5	10652.9	12974.7	16031.7	19967.0	20985.9	23617.6	27164.5	30543.5
NPISHs final consumption expenditure	98.8	131.5	154.0									
			154.9	149.6	139.4	154.6	185.9	216.7	217.0	225.7	234.1	263.3
General government final consumption expenditure	1470.0	1911.3	2330.6									
			2366.4	2889.8	3645.9	4680.4	5751.0	7359.8	8066.7	8671.3	10040.8	11664.8
Individual consumption expenditure	596.9	858.2	1015.5									
			1015.5	1260.4	1662.9	2154.3	2710.0	3500.2	3836.0	4118.6	4788.3	5487.1
Collective consumption expenditure	873.0	1053.2	1315.1									
			1350.9	1629.4	1983.0	2526.1	3041.0	3859.7	4230.7	4552.7	5252.5	6177.7
Gross capital formation	1963.1	2169.3	2755.0									
			2755.0	3559.0	4338.7	5698.7	8034.1	10526.1	7344.8	10472.6	14207.8	16264.5
Gross fixed capital formation	1671.0	1924.5	2412.9									
			2432.3	3130.5	3836.9	4980.6	6853.4	8943.0	8222.4	9647.5	11595.2	13164.2
Changes in inventories	273.8	230.0	322.8									
			322.8	428.4	501.8	718.2	1053.7	1325.3	-1190.9	458.3	2132.0	2496.5
Acquisitions less disposals of valuables	18.3	14.9	19.4									
			...	...	...	...	127.0	257.8	313.3	366.8	480.6	603.8
Exports of goods and services	3299.6	3813.7	4655.9									
			4655.9	5860.4	7607.3	9079.3	10028.8	12923.6	10842.0	13529.3	16940.9	18428.0
Exports of goods	2965.3	3386.3	4159.1									
			...	...	...	...	...	11652.0	9529.1	12162.6	15353.3	16571.6
Exports of services	334.3	427.4	496.7									
			...	...	...	...	...	1271.6	1312.9	1366.7	1587.6	1856.4
Less: Imports of goods and services	2165.9	2646.2	3153.9									
			3153.9	3773.9	4648.3	5653.4	7162.2	9111.0	7954.3	9789.6	12164.4	13860.1
Imports of goods	1565.1	1908.5	2324.2									
			...	...	...	...	...	7238.2	6016.9	7549.6	9519.0	10499.7
Imports of services	600.8	737.7	829.7									
			...	...	...	...	...	1872.8	1937.4	2240.0	2645.4	3360.4
Plus: Statistical discrepancy	-40.0	50.5	-38.5									
			-107.5	-96.1	-126.1	-17.2	378.3	-605.3	-694.9	-418.5	-624.0	-704.8
Equals: GROSS DOMESTIC PRODUCT	8943.6	10830.5	13243.2									
			13208.2	17027.2	21609.8	26917.2	33247.5	41276.8	38807.2	46308.5	55799.6	62599.1

Table 1.2 Gross domestic product by expenditures at constant prices

Series 300: 1993 SNA, Russian ruble (re-denom. 1:1000), Western calendar year
Series 400: 1993 SNA, Russian ruble (re-denom. 1:1000), Western calendar year

Data in billions

	2001	2002	2003	2004	2005	2006	2007	2008	2009	2010	2011	2012
Series	**300**	**400**										
Base year	**2000**	**2008**										
Expenditures of the gross domestic product												
Final consumption expenditure	4782.6	5118.2										
		16458.0	17458.5	19092.6	20835.0	22821.5	25369.6	27543.5	26460.5	27399.7	28717.4	30110.1
Household final consumption expenditure	3608.2	3914.8										
		10366.6	11159.8	12550.7	14087.4	15799.7	18060.7	19967.0	18946.6	19993.8	21271.7	22710.2
NPISHs final consumption expenditure	80.6	81.3										
		299.6	300.0	266.7	217.8	214.0	219.9	216.7	199.4	198.4	188.8	186.9
General government final consumption expenditure	1093.8	1122.2										
		6390.0	6540.2	6679.0	6775.3	6931.9	7120.7	7359.8	7314.5	7205.7	7259.9	7246.2
Individual consumption expenditure	438.0	448.7										
		3028.6	3090.5	3123.7	3278.9	3320.8	3388.7	3500.2	3470.0	3387.3	3367.5	3398.3
Collective consumption expenditure	655.8	673.5										
		3360.0	3446.8	3547.1	3501.5	3612.8	3732.1	3859.7	3844.5	3818.6	3893.4	3846.9
Gross capital formation	1594.3	1552.4										
		4723.1	5396.9	6056.2	6631.1	7806.4	9526.5	10526.1	6209.8	7982.2	9782.4	10428.7
Gross fixed capital formation	1341.4	1382.9										
		4065.8	4629.4	5183.4	5710.1	6733.4	8152.4	8943.0	7631.1	8119.9	8967.1	9529.3

	2001	2002	2003	2004	2005	2006	2007	2008	2009	2010	2011	2012
Series	**300**	**400**										
Base year	**2000**	**2008**										
Changes in inventories	236.0	156.5 625.3	729.9	798.9	810.6	935.9	1210.2	1325.3	-1667.5	521.9	...	...
Acquisitions less disposals of valuables	16.9	13.0 32.2	40.4	76.5	110.6	137.3	159.6	257.8	246.2	226.1	236.2	235.1
Exports of goods and services	3354.6	3698.9 8401.8	9463.8	10581.3	11264.7	12089.8	12847.6	12923.6	12311.5	13179.1	13220.4	13399.0
Exports of goods	3033.3	3315.6 8362.5	9340.1	10317.7	10817.2	11445.4	11954.1	11652.0	11266.7	12052.8	11840.7	11888.7
Exports of services	321.3	383.3 361.1	437.9	538.8	651.9	796.1	987.9	1271.6	1044.8	1123.7	1334.5	1474.6
Less: Imports of goods and services	2084.4	2388.3 3076.3	3607.9	4447.1	5186.7	6290.1	7938.4	9111.0	6339.5	7975.9	9593.9	10504.1
Imports of goods	1532.5	1783.0 2477.4	2937.0	3608.1	4223.5	5211.5	6523.1	7238.2	4795.1	6112.1	7318.6	7800.1
Imports of services	551.9	605.3 595.2	677.6	843.0	972.9	1113.5	1447.6	1872.8	1544.3	1863.8	2276.2	2730.4
Plus: Statistical discrepancy	30.5	60.6 -247.6	-302.7	-424.6	-534.1	-486.5	-573.0	-605.3	-593.7	-685.9	-695.4	-634.8
Equals: GROSS DOMESTIC PRODUCT [a]	7677.6	8041.8 27312.3	29304.9	31407.8	33410.5	36134.6	39218.7	41276.8	38048.6	39762.2	41468.4	42895.9

[a] Chain-linked volume measures are presented in this table, thus discrepancies between components and total may exist.

Table 1.3 Relations among product, income, savings, and net lending aggregates

Series 300: 1993 SNA, Russian ruble (re-denom. 1:1000), Western calendar year
Series 400: 1993 SNA, Russian ruble (re-denom. 1:1000), Western calendar year

Data in billions

	2001	2002	2003	2004	2005	2006	2007	2008	2009	2010	2011	2012
Series	**300**							**400**				
GROSS DOMESTIC PRODUCT	8943.6	10830.5	13243.2	17048.1	21625.4	26903.5	33258.1	41444.7 41276.8	38807.2	46308.5	55799.6	62599.1
Plus: Compensation of employees - from and to the rest of the world, net	3.8	6.2	-4.3	-7.5	-34.4	-112.7	-185.9	-350.6 -355.1	-280.1	-258.8	-277.8	-366.3
Plus: Compensation of employees - from the rest of the world	18.2	22.1	25.0	34.7	48.5	51.5	66.7	93.9 93.9	105.3	109.9	115.4	123.1
Less: Compensation of employees - to the rest of the world	14.4	15.9	29.2	42.2	82.9	164.2	252.6	444.6 449.0	385.4	368.7	393.2	489.3
Plus: Property income - from and to the rest of the world, net	-127.4	-212.9	-397.2	-360.8	-504.6	-683.8	-597.6	-853.8 -855.3	-981.0	-1219.1	-1484.4	-1693.9
Plus: Property income - from the rest of the world	179.3	154.5	316.8	310.1	442.5	755.7	1143.3	1444.7 1432.4	948.7	1024.0	1128.1	1378.3
Less: Property income - to the rest of the world	306.7	367.3	714.0	670.9	947.1	1439.4	1741.0	2298.6 2287.7	1929.7	2243.1	2612.5	3072.2
Sum of Compensation of employees and property income - from and to the rest of the world, net	-123.6	-206.7	-401.4	-368.2	-539.0	-796.5	-783.6	-1204.5 -1210.4	-1261.1	-1477.8	-1762.2	-2060.2
Plus: Sum of Compensation of employees and property income - from the rest of the world	197.5	176.5	341.8	344.9	491.0	807.2	1210.0	1538.7 1526.3	1054.1	1133.9	1243.4	1501.3
Less: Sum of Compensation of employees and property income - to the rest of the world	321.1	383.2	743.2	713.1	1030.0	1603.7	1993.6	2743.1 2736.7	2315.2	2611.7	3005.6	3561.5
Plus: Taxes less subsidies on production and imports - from and to the rest of the world, net	...	...	...	...	...	...	...	... ...	...	...	...	...
Equals: GROSS NATIONAL INCOME	8819.9	10623.8	12841.8	16679.9	21086.4	26107.0	32474.6	40240.2 40066.4	37546.1	44830.7	54037.4	60538.9
Plus: Current transfers - from and to the rest of the world, net	-23.9	-11.2	-12.0	-19.7	-29.6	-41.0	-88.4	-70.8 -70.7	-89.0	-109.9	-94.8	-189.8
Plus: Current transfers - from the rest of the world	21.7	52.8	77.3	104.7	127.1	173.6	215.0	270.5 270.5	282.0	302.4	480.3	512.9
Less: Current transfers - to the rest of the world	45.7	64.0	89.3	124.4	156.7	214.6	303.3	341.3 341.3	370.9	412.4	575.1	702.7
Equals: GROSS NATIONAL DISPOSABLE INCOME	8796.0	10612.7	12829.8	16660.2	21056.8	26066.0	32386.2	40169.5 39995.7	37457.2	44720.8	53942.5	60349.1

	2001	2002	2003	2004	2005	2006	2007	2008	2009	2010	2011	2012
Series	**300**							**400**				
Less: Final consumption expenditure / Actual final consumption	5886.9	7443.2	9024.8	11401.4	14319.0	17629.7	21937.9	27417.3 27543.5	29269.6	32514.7	37439.3	42471.5
Equals: SAVING, GROSS	2909.2	3169.5	3805.1	5258.8	6737.8	8436.3	10448.3	12752.2 12452.2	8187.5	12206.1	16503.2	17877.6
Plus: Capital transfers - from and to the rest of the world, net	-273.7	-391.9	-30.0	-45.7	-365.0	2.4	-261.7	7.4 7.4	-376.8	-4.5	-7.6	-147.6
Plus: Capital transfers - from the rest of the world	58.2	230.4	14.8	20.4	12.3	20.0	22.3	25.4 25.4	35.0	20.0	16.9	8.7
Less: Capital transfers - to the rest of the world	331.9	622.3	44.8	66.1	377.3	17.6	283.9	18.1 18.1	411.8	24.4	24.4	156.4
Less: Gross capital formation	1963.1	2169.3	2755.0	3559.0	4338.7	5748.7	8037.8	10523.1 10526.1	7344.8	10472.6	14207.8	16264.5
Less: Acquisitions less disposals of non-produced non-financial assets	...	...	...	...	...	...	...	... 5.8	7.2	0.0	0.0	12.5
Plus: Statistical discrepancy	40.0	-50.5	38.5	-1.2	-8.7	-102.5	-391.2	307.7 605.3	694.9	-418.5	-624.0	-704.8
Equals: NET LENDING (+) / NET BORROWING (-) OF THE NATION	712.3	557.7	1058.5	1653.0	2025.4	2587.5	1757.7	2538.4 2533.0	458.7[a]	1729.0[a]	2287.9[a]	1452.9[a]
Net values: Gross National Income / Gross National Disposable Income / Saving Gross less Consumption of fixed capital												
Less: Consumption of fixed capital	724.9	845.9	959.1	1099.1	1289.5	1369.8	1619.3	1994.9 1994.9	2230.5	2365.9	2614.9	0.0
Equals: NET NATIONAL INCOME	8095.1	9778.0	11882.7	15580.8	19796.8	24737.2	30855.3	38245.3 38071.5	35315.7	42464.8	51422.4	60538.9
Equals: NET NATIONAL DISPOSABLE INCOME	8071.1	9766.8	11870.7	15561.1	19767.2	24696.2	30766.9	38174.5 38000.8	35226.7	42354.9	51327.6	60349.1
Equals: SAVING, NET	2184.3	2323.6	2846.0	4159.6	5448.3	7066.5	8829.0	10757.3 10457.3	5957.1	9840.2	13888.3	17877.6

[a] Excludes the statistical discrepancy between expenditure-based and production-based GDP amounts.

Table 2.1 Value added by industries at current prices (ISIC Rev. 3)

Series 400: 1993 SNA, Russian ruble (re-denom. 1:1000), Western calendar year **Data in billions**

	2001	2002	2003	2004	2005	2006	2007	2008	2009	2010	2011	2012
Series	**400**											
Industries												
Agriculture, hunting, forestry; fishing	544.8	602.8	726.8	835.1	919.7	1039.4	1256.4	1549.3	1585.1	1548.5	2072.4	2060.9
Agriculture, hunting, forestry	544.8	573.8	667.4	773.4	864.2	981.3	1194.8	1486.6	1504.4	1451.5	1973.5	1952.0
Agriculture, hunting and related service activities	536.2	573.8	622.0	718.7	804.7	915.2	1114.6	1421.8	1444.3	1376.8	1892.2	1862.2
Forestry, logging and related service activities	8.5	...	45.5	54.6	59.5	66.1	80.2	64.8	60.2	74.7	81.3	89.8
Fishing	...	29.0	59.4	61.7	55.5	58.1	61.6	62.7	80.6	97.0	98.9	108.9
Mining and quarrying	...	638.4	769.8	1411.6	2064.3	2509.4	2865.5	3284.6	2885.4	3842.8	5157.3	5801.4
Manufacturing	...	1634.3	1897.7	2590.9	3388.5	4116.0	5025.2	6163.9	5005.3	5934.7	7385.5	8091.7
Electricity, gas and water supply	...	349.4	414.1	548.3	608.4	727.0	855.9	1034.0	1388.7	1527.1	1814.5	1845.8
Construction	...	513.5	703.0	847.1	989.9	1202.0	1633.9	2225.3	2101.5	2587.8	3101.8	3445.0
Wholesale, retail trade, repair of motor vehicles, motorcycles and personal and households goods; hotels and restaurants	...	2280.6	2666.1	3152.1	3778.3	4880.3	6031.3	7495.7	6404.2	8424.2	9791.8	11028.4
Wholesale, retail trade, repair of motor vehicles, motorcycles and personal and household goods	...	2192.6	2572.2	3012.2	3610.5	4673.6	5745.0	7137.7	6060.5	8021.0	9329.7	10514.1
Hotels and restaurants	...	88.0	93.9	139.9	167.8	206.7	286.3	358.0	343.7	403.3	462.0	514.3
Transport, storage and communications	...	978.7	1244.2	1642.4	1897.0	2247.6	2750.9	3258.3	3249.6	3662.5	3971.5	4350.6

	2001	2002	2003	2004	2005	2006	2007	2008	2009	2010	2011	2012
Series	**400**											
Land transport; transport via pipelines, water transport; air transport; Supporting and auxiliary transport activities; activities of travel agencies	...	...	987.0	1231.8	1421.1	1700.5	2050.9	2444.7	2358.0	2800.7	3055.8	3356.2
Post and telecommunications	...	...	257.2	410.6	475.9	547.1	700.0	813.6	891.7	861.7	915.7	994.4
Financial intermediation; real estate, renting and business activities	...	1300.1	1634.8	1882.2	2529.9	3264.7	4356.6	5497.2	5927.8	6675.0	7601.8	8614.0
Financial intermediation	...	280.3	388.0	474.1	701.2	977.2	1253.8	1537.8	1707.2	1773.5	1956.0	2328.5
Real estate, renting and business activities	...	1019.7	1246.7	1408.0	1828.8	2287.6	3102.8	3959.4	4220.6	4901.5	5645.8	6285.6
Public administration and defence; compulsory social security	...	488.7	651.3	802.5	959.1	1189.2	1466.4	1884.4	2203.2	2423.5	2672.6	3520.8
Education; health and social work; other community, social and personal services	...	783.4	912.0	1146.5	1382.6	1801.8	2242.4	2790.0	3080.5	3413.9	3936.2	4525.9
Education	...	280.0	317.9	400.1	493.2	619.3	769.9	970.7	1134.2	1226.0	1386.3	1584.0
Health and social work	...	321.5	375.9	472.6	564.7	765.5	950.5	1197.8	1360.3	1487.3	1773.0	2081.9
Other community, social and personal services	...	182.0	218.2	273.8	324.7	417.1	522.1	621.5	586.0	700.6	776.9	860.0
Private households with employed persons	...	...	...	...	...	...	...	...	...	0.0	0.0	0.0
Equals: VALUE ADDED, GROSS, in basic prices	...	9570.0	11619.8	14858.8	18517.7	22977.3	28484.5	35182.7	33831.3	40040.1	47505.5	53284.5
Less: Financial intermediation services indirectly measured (FISIM)	...	...	...	...	...	...	...	...	...	...	...	...
Plus: Taxes less Subsidies on products	...	1249.2	1588.5	2168.4	3092.1	3939.9	4763.0	6094.2	4975.9	6268.5	8294.1	9314.5
Plus: Taxes on products	...	1415.2	1775.1	2352.1	3248.2	4090.1	4977.6	6323.8	5202.1	6462.6	8463.3	9492.3
Less: Subsidies on products	...	165.9	186.6	183.7	156.1	150.2	214.5	229.7	226.2	194.1	169.3	177.8
Equals: GROSS DOMESTIC PRODUCT	...	10819.2	13208.2	17027.2	21609.8	26917.2	33247.5	41276.8	38807.2	46308.5	55799.6	62599.1

Table 2.2 Value added by industries at constant prices (ISIC Rev. 3)

Series 300: 1993 SNA, Russian ruble (re-denom. 1:1000), Western calendar year
Series 400: 1993 SNA, Russian ruble (re-denom. 1:1000), Western calendar year

Data in billions

	2001	2002	2003	2004	2005	2006	2007	2008	2009	2010	2011	2012
Series	**300**	**400**										
Base year	**2000**	**2008**										
Industries												
Agriculture, hunting, forestry; fishing	484.7	498.8										
		1420.0	1398.5	1414.7	1407.8	1447.1	1464.4	1549.3	1574.8	1386.1	1582.2	1526.9
Agriculture, hunting, forestry [a]	484.7	498.8										
		1348.5	1324.3	1338.1	1342.6	1379.1	1397.3	1486.6	1508.6	1325.6	1522.0	1464.9
Agriculture, hunting and related service activities	468.1	481.7										
		...	1245.9	1257.2	1260.8	1293.8	1314.2	1421.8	1446.6	1255.8	1454.4	1392.3
Forestry, logging and related service activities	7.0	7.5										
		...	75.3	77.4	78.2	81.4	79.6	64.8	62.0	70.3	67.7	73.3
Fishing	...	...										
		69.5	70.7	72.4	64.6	67.2	66.6	62.7	66.2	60.1	62.6	63.6
Mining and quarrying	...	...										
		2687.7	2976.7	3374.1	3425.5	3325.6	3253.5	3284.6	3207.1	3419.8	3518.4	3552.1
Manufacturing	2211.9	2296.3										
		4476.2	4870.1	5262.3	5495.8	5857.0	6297.6	6163.9	5263.0	5716.1	6019.0	6217.6
Electricity, gas and water supply	...	...										
		926.0	934.5	1008.1	1016.9	1063.0	1026.5	1034.0	985.6	1025.4	1030.4	1031.0
Construction	471.3	484.5										
		1152.2	1298.0	1426.4	1572.1	1772.9	2003.5	2225.3	1898.2	1982.3	2071.6	2114.0

	2001	2002	2003	2004	2005	2006	2007	2008	2009	2010	2011	2012
Series	**300**	**400**										
Base year	**2000**	**2008**										
Wholesale, retail trade, repair of motor vehicles, motorcycles and personal and household goods; hotels and restaurants	1602.3	1733.7 3955.9	4463.9	4911.3	5360.6	6102.4	6822.2	7495.7	7025.0	7435.0	7682.6	8178.2
Wholesale, retail trade, repair of motor vehicles, motorcycles and personal and household goods	...	... 3740.5	4237.9	4669.4	5096.4	5815.7	6496.9	7137.7	6720.6	7110.2	7346.0	7826.0
Hotels and restaurants	...	... 226.1	229.8	242.8	265.3	286.2	325.3	358.0	304.5	324.2	335.9	352.0
Transport, storage and communications	626.0	661.7 2237.0	2399.2	2540.9	2691.3	2953.0	3096.0	3258.3	2978.9	3142.1	3348.0	3433.9
Land transport; transport via piplines, water transport; air transport; Supporting and auxiliary transport activities; activities of travel agencies	...	... ...	2082.8	2081.9	2155.3	2328.4	2364.1	2444.7	2145.7	2284.3	2454.9	2518.5
Post and telecommunications	...	... ...	382.3	492.1	556.6	638.9	735.5	813.6	833.2	857.2	888.0	909.9
Financial intermediation, real estate, renting and business activities	657.7	682.8 2762.8	2983.3	3005.3	3496.2	3995.9	4924.7	5497.2	5343.8	5576.2	5854.0	6275.5
Financial intermediation	...	... 437.6	564.7	647.8	837.1	1049.4	1354.5	1537.8	1561.5	1566.1	1622.7	1855.1
Real estate, renting and business activities	...	... 2422.9	2490.0	2399.9	2687.7	2957.8	3571.7	3959.4	3782.3	4008.8	4228.4	4428.5
Public administration and defence; compulsory social security	313.2	322.6 1715.6	1738.3	1817.4	1719.4	1761.9	1830.1	1884.4	1883.4	1878.5	1816.1	1802.7
Education; health and social work; other community, social and personal services	483.7	491.1 2556.4	2537.0	2589.2	2627.6	2694.1	2770.6	2790.0	2649.9	2647.2	2655.5	2691.4
Education	...	... 938.8	950.0	953.4	956.4	961.0	971.5	970.7	957.1	940.2	932.2	932.9
Health and social work	...	... 1163.5	1126.0	1137.7	1156.6	1173.3	1186.7	1197.8	1195.6	1199.4	1216.0	1251.8
Other community, social and personal services	...	... 476.1	480.1	510.3	524.9	564.5	612.8	621.5	497.2	507.9	508.3	508.3
Private households with employed persons	...	... ...	...	...	...	...	...	...	...	...	...	...
Equals: VALUE ADDED, GROSS, in basic prices [b]	6850.9	7171.5 23521.3	25283.1	26952.7	28567.8	30835.4	33438.3	35182.7	32809.6	34150.3	35473.8	36668.1
Less: Financial intermediation services indirectly measured (FISIM)	58.1	62.1 ...	...	...	...	...	...	...	...	...	...	...
Plus: Taxes less Subsidies on products	884.8	932.3 3819.6	3988.3	4441.4	4841.5	5298.8	5780.1	6094.2	5239.0	5623.7	6014.2	6247.2
Plus: Taxes on products	1033.4	1080.6 4100.3	4313.9	4740.8	5071.6	5515.4	6016.2	6323.8	5454.9	5789.7	6153.5	6387.2
Less: Subsidies on products	148.6	148.3 280.7	279.8	272.7	226.3	215.0	234.4	229.7	215.9	171.9	146.1	146.1
Equals: GROSS DOMESTIC PRODUCT [c]	7677.6	8041.8 27312.3	29304.9	31407.8	33410.5	36134.6	39218.7	41276.8	38048.6	39762.2	41468.4	42895.9

[a] Discrepancy between components and total.
[b] Includes financial intermediation services indirectly measured (FISIM).
[c] Chain-linked volume measures are presented in this table, thus discrepancies between components and total may exist.

Table 2.3 Output, gross value added, and fixed assets by industries at current prices (ISIC Rev. 3) Total Economy

Series 300: 1993 SNA, Russian ruble (re-denom. 1:1000), Western calendar year
Series 400: 1993 SNA, Russian ruble (re-denom. 1:1000), Western calendar year

Data in billions

	2001	2002	2003	2004	2005	2006	2007	2008	2009	2010	2011	2012
Series	**300**					**400**						
Output, at basic prices	15922.8	18990.5	23298.4	29543.4	37091.3	46330.0						
						...	...	70741.8[a]	68116.4	82054.6	97365.4	107956.1
Less: Intermediate consumption, at purchaser's prices	7947.0	9229.9	11432.1	14356.5	18115.2	22787.8						
						...	...	35559.1[a]	34285.1	42014.5	49859.9	54671.6
Equals: VALUE ADDED, GROSS, at basic prices [b]	7975.8	9760.6	11866.3	15186.8	18976.1	23542.2						
						...	...	35182.7	33831.3	40040.1	47505.5	53284.5
Compensation of employees [c]	3848.4	5065.1[d]	6231.4[d]	7845.0[d]	9474.3[d]	11985.9[d]						
						...	...	19559.8	20411.6	22995.6	27646.5	31577.9
Taxes on production and imports, less Subsidies	305.1	1845.8[e]	2110.2[e]	2872.7[e]	4244.5[e]	5381.7[e]						
						...	...	2124.3	1498.6	1950.7	2585.9	3095.0
Taxes on production and imports	316.9	2027.0[f]	2315.9[f]	3076.3[f]	4406.9[f]	5537.3[f]						
						...	...	2174.7	1606.3	2032.1	2731.0	3252.8
Taxes on products	...	1415.2	1775.1	2352.1	3248.2	4090.1						
						...	...	...	...	...	...	...
Other taxes on production	316.9	611.8	540.8	724.1	1158.6	1447.2						
						...	...	2174.7	1606.3	2032.1	2731.0	3252.8
Less: Subsidies	11.8	181.2[g]	205.7[g]	203.6[g]	162.4[g]	155.6[g]						
						...	...	50.4	107.6	81.4	145.1	157.8
Subsidies on products	...	165.9	186.6	183.7	156.1	150.2						
						...	...	...	...	...	...	...
Other subsidies on production	11.8	15.3	19.1	19.9	6.3	5.3						
						...	...	50.4	107.6	81.4	145.1	157.8
OPERATING SURPLUS, GROSS [h] [i]	3692.6	3919.7[d]	4901.6[d]	6330.4[d]	7906.6[d]	9535.9[d]						
						...	...	13498.7	11921.1	15093.7	17273.1	18611.6
MIXED INCOME, GROSS	...	...	...	...	...	...						
						...	...	...	...	...	...	...
Total Economy only: Adjustment for FISIM (if FISIM is not distributed to uses)	129.7	179.3	211.6	307.1	442.9	578.6						
						...	...	...	...	...	...	...
Gross capital formation	1963.1	2169.3	2755.0	3559.0	4338.7	5748.7						
						5698.7	8034.1	10526.1	7344.8	10472.6	14207.8	16264.5
Gross fixed capital formation	1671.0	1924.5	2412.9	3091.5	3775.3	4890.2						
						4890.2	6853.4	8943.0	8222.4	9647.5	11595.2	13164.2
Changes in inventories	273.8	230.0	322.8	428.4	501.8	768.2						
						718.2	1053.7	1325.3	-1190.9	458.3	2132.0	2496.5
Acquisitions less disposals of valuables	18.3	14.9	19.4	39.1	61.6	90.3						
						...	127.0	257.8	313.3	366.8	480.6	603.8
Closing stocks of fixed assets (produced assets)	...	...	...	34873.7	41493.6	47489.5						
						...	60391.5	74441.1	82303.0	93185.6	108001.2	117196.8
Employment (average, in 1000 persons)	64980.0	65574.0	65979.0	66407.0	66792.0	67174.0						
						...	68019.0	68474.0	67343.0	67577.0	67727.0	67969.0

[a] Discrepancy with equivalent item in Table 4.1 (Total Economy).
[b] Includes financial intermediation services indirectly measured (FISIM).
[c] Discrepancy between total economy and sum of data by industry due to different allocation of value added to compensation of employees and gross operating surplus.
[d] Discrepancy between the data for the total economy and the data by industries.
[e] Refers to all taxes on production and imports less subsidies for the total economy.
[f] Includes taxes on products
[g] Includes subsidies on products.
[h] Includes Mixed Income, Gross.
[i] Includes Mixed Income, Gross. Discrepancy between total economy and sum of data by industry due to different allocation of value added to compensation of employees and gross operating surplus.

Table 2.3 Output, gross value added, and fixed assets by industries at current prices (ISIC Rev. 3) Agriculture, hunting, forestry; fishing (A+B)

Series 300: 1993 SNA, Russian ruble (re-denom. 1:1000), Western calendar year
Series 400: 1993 SNA, Russian ruble (re-denom. 1:1000), Western calendar year

Data in billions

	2001	2002	2003	2004	2005	2006	2007	2008	2009	2010	2011	2012
Series			**300**				**400**					
Output, at basic prices			1469.4				...	2819.6	3072.1	3211.7	3982.7	3981.6
Less: Intermediate consumption, at purchaser's prices			678.3				...	1270.3	1487.0	1663.1	1910.3	1920.7
Equals: VALUE ADDED, GROSS, at basic prices			791.1				...	1549.3	1585.1	1548.5	2072.4	2060.9
Compensation of employees			208.2				...	375.5	390.5	368.9	463.8	497.2
Taxes on production and imports, less Subsidies			-10.6				...	-17.8	-53.1	-17.1	-63.9	-57.1
Taxes on production and imports			2.8				...	20.4	23.8	29.4	20.7	30.3
Taxes on products			...				...	...	...	...	...	...
Other taxes on production			2.8				...	20.4	23.8	29.4	20.7	30.3
Less: Subsidies			13.4				...	38.2	76.9	46.5	84.6	87.4
Subsidies on products			...				...	...	...	...	...	...
Other subsidies on production			13.4				...	38.2	76.9	46.5	84.6	87.4
OPERATING SURPLUS, GROSS [a]			593.5				...	1191.5	1247.6	1196.8	1672.6	1620.8
MIXED INCOME, GROSS			...				...	...	...	...	...	...
Gross capital formation			...				...	...	...	...	...	...
Closing stocks of fixed assets (produced assets)			...				2042.6	2350.8	2664.3	2973.0	3260.0	3583.7
Employment (average, in 1000 persons)			7912.0				7070.0	6817.0	6879.0	6799.0	6730.0	6570.0

[a] Includes Mixed Income, Gross.

Table 2.3 Output, gross value added, and fixed assets by industries at current prices (ISIC Rev. 3) Agriculture, hunting and related service activities (01)

Series 300: 1993 SNA, Russian ruble (re-denom. 1:1000), Western calendar year
Series 400: 1993 SNA, Russian ruble (re-denom. 1:1000), Western calendar year

Data in billions

	2001	2002	2003	2004	2005	2006	2007	2008	2009	2010	2011	2012
Series			**300**	**400**								
Output, at basic prices			1361.9	...	...	...	...	2684.0	2760.8	2855.5	3604.0	3561.5
Less: Intermediate consumption, at purchaser's prices			631.8	...	...	...	...	1262.2	1316.5	1478.7	1711.8	1699.3
Equals: VALUE ADDED, GROSS, at basic prices			730.1	...	...	...	...	1421.8	1444.3	1376.8	1892.2	1862.2
Compensation of employees			198.1	...	...	...	...	307.1	316.9	294.8	382.1	411.8
Taxes on production and imports, less Subsidies			-10.6	...	...	...	...	-18.7	-54.2	-19.5	-65.7	-59.9
Taxes on production and imports			2.5	...	...	...	...	19.4	22.6	26.3	18.1	26.7
Taxes on products			...	...	...	...	...	...	...	...	...	...
Other taxes on production			2.5	...	...	...	...	19.4	22.6	26.3	18.1	26.7
Less: Subsidies			13.1	...	...	...	...	38.1	76.8	45.8	83.8	86.6
Subsidies on products			...	...	...	...	...	...	...	...	...	...

	2001	2002	2003	2004	2005	2006	2007	2008	2009	2010	2011	2012
Series			**300**	**400**								
Other subsidies on production			13.1	...	...	...	...	38.1	76.8	45.8	83.8	86.6
OPERATING SURPLUS, GROSS [a]			542.6	...	...	...	...	1133.4	1181.6	1101.5	1575.8	1510.3
MIXED INCOME, GROSS			...	...	...	...	...	...	...	...	...	...
Gross capital formation			...	...	...	...	...	...	...	...	...	...
Closing stocks of fixed assets (produced assets)			...	1395.8	1440.1	1574.7	1963.3	2259.6	2566.9	2859.9	3127.2	3444.8
Employment (average, in 1000 persons)			7796.0	...	...	...	6239.0	6028.0	6103.0	6045.0	5996.0	5861.0

[a] Includes Mixed Income, Gross.

Table 2.3 Output, gross value added, and fixed assets by industries at current prices (ISIC Rev. 3) Forestry, logging and related service activities (02)

Series 400: 1993 SNA, Russian ruble (re-denom. 1:1000), Western calendar year **Data in billions**

	2001	2002	2003	2004	2005	2006	2007	2008	2009	2010	2011	2012
Series			**400**									
Output, at basic prices			96.1	104.6	110.8	130.2	146.3	135.6	131.7	167.7	171.5	190.4
Less: Intermediate consumption, at purchaser's prices			50.6	50.0	51.3	64.1	66.1	70.8	71.6	93.0	90.2	100.6
Equals: VALUE ADDED, GROSS, at basic prices			45.5	54.6	59.5	66.1	80.2	64.8	60.2	74.7	81.3	89.8
Compensation of employees			30.3	32.1	32.6	35.5	41.5	38.2	39.4	41.4	44.6	46.6
Taxes on production and imports, less Subsidies			0.3	0.4	0.3	0.3	0.4	0.5	0.5	0.2	0.8	0.9
Taxes on production and imports			0.3	0.4	0.3	0.3	0.4	0.5	0.5	0.7	1.3	1.4
Taxes on products			...	...	...	...	...	...	...	...	...	...
Other taxes on production			0.3	0.4	0.3	0.3	0.4	0.5	0.5	0.7	1.3	1.4
Less: Subsidies			...	...	...	...	...	...	0.0	0.5	0.5	0.6
Subsidies on products			...	...	...	...	...	...	...	...	...	...
Other subsidies on production			...	...	...	...	...	...	0.0	0.5	0.5	0.6
OPERATING SURPLUS, GROSS [a]			14.9	22.1	26.5	30.2	38.3	26.1	20.3	33.2	35.9	42.3
MIXED INCOME, GROSS			...	...	...	...	...	...	...	...	...	...
Gross capital formation			...	...	...	...	...	...	...	...	...	...
Employment (average, in 1000 persons)			...	...	...	...	687.0	647.0	630.0	611.0	587.0	567.0

[a] Includes Mixed Income, Gross.

Table 2.3 Output, gross value added, and fixed assets by industries at current prices (ISIC Rev. 3) Fishing (B)

Series 300: 1993 SNA, Russian ruble (re-denom. 1:1000), Western calendar year
Series 400: 1993 SNA, Russian ruble (re-denom. 1:1000), Western calendar year

Data in billions

	2001	2002	2003	2004	2005	2006	2007	2008	2009	2010	2011	2012
Series	**400**		**300**									
Output, at basic prices	...		107.5				...	151.5	179.5	188.5	207.2	229.7
Less: Intermediate consumption, at purchaser's prices	...		46.5				...	88.8	98.9	91.5	108.3	120.7
Equals: VALUE ADDED, GROSS, at basic prices	...		61.0				...	62.7	80.6	97.0	98.9	108.9
Compensation of employees	...		10.1				...	30.2	34.2	32.7	37.1	38.8
Taxes on production and imports, less Subsidies	...		0.1				...	0.5	0.6	2.2	1.0	1.9
Taxes on production and imports	...		0.3				...	0.5	0.8	2.3	1.3	2.2
Taxes on products	...		...				...	...	...	...	...	...
Other taxes on production	...		0.3				...	0.5	0.8	2.3	1.3	2.2
Less: Subsidies	...		0.2				...	0.1	0.1	0.2	0.3	0.2
Subsidies on products	...		...				...	...	...	...	...	...
Other subsidies on production	...		0.2				...	0.1	0.1	0.2	0.3	0.2
OPERATING SURPLUS, GROSS [a]	...		50.8				...	32.0	45.8	62.2	60.8	68.2
MIXED INCOME, GROSS	...		...				...	...	...	...	...	...
Gross capital formation	...		...				...	...	...	...	...	...
Closing stocks of fixed assets (produced assets)	...		...				79.3	91.2	97.4	113.1	132.7	138.9
Employment (average, in 1000 persons)	134000.0		116.0				145.0	142.0	146.0	143.0	147.0	142.0

[a] Includes Mixed Income, Gross.

Table 2.3 Output, gross value added, and fixed assets by industries at current prices (ISIC Rev. 3) Mining and quarrying (C)

Series 300: 1993 SNA, Russian ruble (re-denom. 1:1000), Western calendar year
Series 400: 1993 SNA, Russian ruble (re-denom. 1:1000), Western calendar year

Data in billions

	2001	2002	2003	2004	2005	2006	2007	2008	2009	2010	2011	2012
Series			**300**				**400**					
Output, at basic prices			1609.7				...	4972.9	4748.1	5982.2	7774.2	8811.7
Less: Intermediate consumption, at purchaser's prices			824.7				...	1688.3	1862.7	2139.4	2616.9	3010.4
Equals: VALUE ADDED, GROSS, at basic prices			785.0				...	3284.6	2885.4	3842.8	5157.3	5801.4
Compensation of employees			264.6				...	568.4	550.8	604.9	742.9	832.5
Taxes on production and imports, less Subsidies			350.5				...	1437.1	910.6	1206.6	2072.6	2498.2
Taxes on production and imports			350.6				...	1437.6	911.1	1206.8	2072.6	2498.2
Taxes on products			...				...	...	...	...	...	...
Other taxes on production			350.6				...	1437.6	911.1	1206.8	2072.6	2498.2
Less: Subsidies			0.0				...	0.5	0.5	0.3	0.0	0.0
Subsidies on products			...				...	...	...	...	...	...

	2001	2002	2003	2004	2005	2006	2007	2008	2009	2010	2011	2012
Series			**300**				**400**					
Other subsidies on production			...				...	0.5	0.5	0.3	0.0	0.0
OPERATING SURPLUS, GROSS [a]			169.8				...	1279.1	1423.9	2031.3	2341.8	2470.7
MIXED INCOME, GROSS			...				...	...	...	...	...	...
Gross capital formation			...				...	...	...	...	...	...
Closing stocks of fixed assets (produced assets)			...				4976.9	6365.5	7861.1	9084.6	10574.3	11681.7
Employment (average, in 1000 persons)			1112.0				1040.0	1044.0	1067.0	1057.0	1063.0	1068.0

[a] Includes Mixed Income, Gross.

Table 2.3 Output, gross value added, and fixed assets by industries at current prices (ISIC Rev. 3) Manufacturing (D)

Series 300: 1993 SNA, Russian ruble (re-denom. 1:1000), Western calendar year
Series 400: 1993 SNA, Russian ruble (re-denom. 1:1000), Western calendar year

Data in billions

	2001	2002	2003	2004	2005	2006	2007	2008	2009	2010	2011	2012
Series			**300**				**400**					
Output, at basic prices			6300.0				...	20190.4	16869.2	21067.7	25631.4	28032.1
Less: Intermediate consumption, at purchaser's prices			4323.7				...	14026.4	11863.9	15133.1	18246.0	19940.4
Equals: VALUE ADDED, GROSS, at basic prices			1976.3				...	6163.9	5005.3	5934.7	7385.5	8091.7
Compensation of employees			1006.2				...	2308.7	2138.2	2375.5	2806.0	3071.3
Taxes on production and imports, less Subsidies			36.7				...	381.1	258.0	332.1	106.8	118.7
Taxes on production and imports			37.5				...	382.6	262.7	342.1	124.4	139.6
Taxes on products			...				...	...	...	...	...	...
Other taxes on production			37.5				...	382.6	262.7	342.1	124.4	139.6
Less: Subsidies			0.8				...	1.5	4.7	10.1	17.5	20.9
Subsidies on products			...				...	...	...	...	...	...
Other subsidies on production			0.8				...	1.5	4.7	10.1	17.5	20.9
OPERATING SURPLUS, GROSS [a]			933.4				...	3474.1	2609.2	3227.0	4472.7	4901.7
MIXED INCOME, GROSS			...				...	...	...	...	...	...
Gross capital formation			...				...	...	...	...	...	...
Closing stocks of fixed assets (produced assets)			...				5122.5	6001.5	6951.7	7989.0	8876.6	9868.5
Employment (average, in 1000 persons)			11932.0				11368.0	11191.0	10401.0	10292.0	10281.0	10230.0

[a] Includes Mixed Income, Gross.

Table 2.3 Output, gross value added, and fixed assets by industries at current prices (ISIC Rev. 3) Electricity, gas and water supply (E)

Series 300: 1993 SNA, Russian ruble (re-denom. 1:1000), Western calendar year
Series 400: 1993 SNA, Russian ruble (re-denom. 1:1000), Western calendar year

Data in billions

	2001	2002	2003	2004	2005	2006	2007	2008	2009	2010	2011	2012
Series			**300**				**400**					
Output, at basic prices			1186.5				...	3109.9	3727.4	4536.9	5201.9	5291.1
Less: Intermediate consumption, at purchaser's prices			758.5				...	2076.0	2338.7	3009.8	3387.5	3445.3
Equals: VALUE ADDED, GROSS, at basic prices			428.0				...	1034.0	1388.7	1527.1	1814.5	1845.8
Compensation of employees			215.0				...	548.9	631.9	688.1	821.7	892.2
Taxes on production and imports, less Subsidies			23.5				...	44.4	45.7	55.4	34.0	38.3
Taxes on production and imports			23.5				...	44.8	46.4	55.8	34.4	38.7
Taxes on products			...				...	...	...	...	...	...
Other taxes on production			23.5				...	44.8	46.4	55.8	34.4	38.7
Less: Subsidies			...				...	0.4	0.7	0.4	0.4	0.4
Subsidies on products			...				...	...	...	...	...	...
Other subsidies on production			...				...	0.4	0.7	0.4	0.4	0.4
OPERATING SURPLUS, GROSS [a]			189.5				...	440.7	711.1	783.6	958.8	915.2
MIXED INCOME, GROSS			...				...	...	...	...	...	...
Gross capital formation			...				...	...	...	...	...	...
Closing stocks of fixed assets (produced assets)			...				4087.4	4925.3	5741.0	6769.1	8528.5	9257.5
Employment (average, in 1000 persons)			1890.0				1909.0	1884.0	1929.0	1945.0	1950.0	1960.0

[a] Includes Mixed Income, Gross.

Table 2.3 Output, gross value added, and fixed assets by industries at current prices (ISIC Rev. 3) Construction (F)

Series 300: 1993 SNA, Russian ruble (re-denom. 1:1000), Western calendar year
Series 400: 1993 SNA, Russian ruble (re-denom. 1:1000), Western calendar year

Data in billions

	2001	2002	2003	2004	2005	2006	2007	2008	2009	2010	2011	2012
Series			**300**				**400**					
Output, at basic prices			1461.1				...	5317.8	4906.3	5791.3	6921.6	7695.7
Less: Intermediate consumption, at purchaser's prices			744.9				...	3092.4	2804.9	3203.5	3819.8	4250.7
Equals: VALUE ADDED, GROSS, at basic prices			716.2				...	2225.3	2101.5	2587.8	3101.8	3445.0
Compensation of employees			285.9				...	1056.7	975.2	1082.5	1255.6	1386.6
Taxes on production and imports, less Subsidies			4.1				...	9.4	6.4	8.0	35.4	41.1
Taxes on production and imports			4.1				...	10.2	10.9	12.0	40.4	47.0
Taxes on products			...				...	...	...	...	...	...
Other taxes on production			4.1				...	10.2	10.9	12.0	40.4	47.0
Less: Subsidies			0.0				...	0.8	4.5	4.0	5.0	5.9
Subsidies on products			...				...	...	...	...	...	...

	2001	2002	2003	2004	2005	2006	2007	2008	2009	2010	2011	2012
Series			**300**				**400**					
Other subsidies on production			...				...	0.8	4.5	4.0	5.0	5.9
OPERATING SURPLUS, GROSS [a]			426.2				...	1159.3	1119.8	1497.3	1810.8	2017.3
MIXED INCOME, GROSS			...				...	...	...	...	...	...
Gross capital formation			...				...	...	...	...	...	...
Closing stocks of fixed assets (produced assets)			...				992.9	1220.9	1391.1	1499.9	1553.0	1732.4
Employment (average, in 1000 persons)			4555.0				5273.0	5474.0	5315.0	5380.0	5474.0	5581.0

[a] Includes Mixed Income, Gross.

Table 2.3 Output, gross value added, and fixed assets by industries at current prices (ISIC Rev. 3) Wholesale retail trade, repair of motor vehicles, motorcycles, etc.; hotels and restaurants (G+H)

Series 300: 1993 SNA, Russian ruble (re-denom. 1:1000), Western calendar year
Series 400: 1993 SNA, Russian ruble (re-denom. 1:1000), Western calendar year

Data in billions

	2001	2002	2003	2004	2005	2006	2007	2008	2009	2010	2011	2012
Series			**300**				**400**					
Output, at basic prices			3776.6				...	11196.8	10519.7	13830.7	16152.9	18222.8
Less: Intermediate consumption, at purchaser's prices			1092.0				...	3701.1	4115.6	5406.4	6361.1	7194.4
Equals: VALUE ADDED, GROSS, at basic prices			2684.6				...	7495.7	6404.2	8424.2	9791.8	11028.4
Compensation of employees			325.4				...	1864.4	1541.2	2243.6	3085.0	3421.5
Taxes on production and imports, less Subsidies			32.3				...	79.0	61.4	70.6	32.4	34.8
Taxes on production and imports			32.3				...	86.2	77.0	86.1	58.4	64.6
Taxes on products			...				...	...	...	...	...	...
Other taxes on production			32.3				...	86.2	77.0	86.1	58.4	64.6
Less: Subsidies			...				...	7.2	15.6	15.5	26.0	29.8
Subsidies on products			...				...	...	...	...	...	...
Other subsidies on production			...				...	7.2	15.6	15.5	26.0	29.8
OPERATING SURPLUS, GROSS [a]			2327.0				...	5552.3	4801.6	6110.1	6674.3	7572.0
MIXED INCOME, GROSS			...				...	...	...	...	...	...
Gross capital formation			...				...	...	...	...	...	...
Closing stocks of fixed assets (produced assets)			...				2044.7	2600.3	3040.8	3645.0	4343.2	5055.6
Employment (average, in 1000 persons)			11612.0				12973.0	13294.0	13085.0	13240.0	13392.0	13650.0

[a] Includes Mixed Income, Gross.

Table 2.3 Output, gross value added, and fixed assets by industries at current prices (ISIC Rev. 3) Transport, storage and communications (I)

Series 300: 1993 SNA, Russian ruble (re-denom. 1:1000), Western calendar year
Series 400: 1993 SNA, Russian ruble (re-denom. 1:1000), Western calendar year

Data in billions

	2001	2002	2003	2004	2005	2006	2007	2008	2009	2010	2011	2012
Series			**300**				**400**					
Output, at basic prices			2221.8				...	6425.5	6410.4	7286.1	8408.8	9243.9
Less: Intermediate consumption, at purchaser's prices			960.2				...	3167.2	3160.8	3623.6	4437.3	4893.3
Equals: VALUE ADDED, GROSS, at basic prices			1261.6				...	3258.3	3249.6	3662.5	3971.5	4350.6
Compensation of employees			521.4				...	1311.1	1384.6	1355.6	1799.7	1949.7
Taxes on production and imports, less Subsidies			41.0				...	73.3	75.5	89.8	69.5	77.4
Taxes on production and imports			41.0				...	74.7	77.6	91.3	75.7	84.4
Taxes on products			...				...	...	...	...	...	...
Other taxes on production			41.0				...	74.7	77.6	91.3	75.7	84.4
Less: Subsidies			...				...	1.4	2.2	1.5	6.2	7.0
Subsidies on products			...				...	...	...	...	...	...
Other subsidies on production			...				...	1.4	2.2	1.5	6.2	7.0
OPERATING SURPLUS, GROSS [a]			699.3				...	1873.9	1789.6	2217.0	2102.3	2323.6
MIXED INCOME, GROSS			...				...	...	...	...	...	...
Gross capital formation			...				...	...	...	...	...	...
Closing stocks of fixed assets (produced assets)			...				17942.2	21525.5	23283.5	25950.3	30737.0	32165.1
Employment (average, in 1000 persons)			5205.0				5450.0	5451.0	5306.0	5347.0	5361.0	5381.0

[a] Includes Mixed Income, Gross.

Table 2.3 Output, gross value added, and fixed assets by industries at current prices (ISIC Rev. 3) Financial intermediation; real estate, renting and business activities (J+K)

Series 300: 1993 SNA, Russian ruble (re-denom. 1:1000), Western calendar year
Series 400: 1993 SNA, Russian ruble (re-denom. 1:1000), Western calendar year

Data in billions

	2001	2002	2003	2004	2005	2006	2007	2008	2009	2010	2011	2012
Series			**300**				**400**					
Output, at basic prices			2439.8				...	8312.2	8884.3	10285.5	11727.0	13260.2
Less: Intermediate consumption, at purchaser's prices			782.8				...	2815.0	2956.5	3610.5	4125.1	4646.1
Equals: VALUE ADDED, GROSS, at basic prices			1656.9				...	5497.2	5927.8	6675.0	7601.8	8614.0
Compensation of employees			546.5				...	2200.1	2286.0	2409.9	2838.2	3217.8
Taxes on production and imports, less Subsidies			43.3				...	107.1	121.1	132.3	202.7	234.7
Taxes on production and imports			43.3				...	107.5	123.7	135.4	208.0	241.1
Taxes on products			...				...	...	...	...	...	...
Other taxes on production			43.3				...	107.5	123.7	135.4	208.0	241.1
Less: Subsidies			...				...	0.4	2.6	3.1	5.4	6.4
Subsidies on products			...				...	...	...	...	...	...

	2001	2002	2003	2004	2005	2006	2007	2008	2009	2010	2011	2012
Series			**300**				**400**					
Other subsidies on production			...				...	0.4	2.6	3.1	5.4	6.4
OPERATING SURPLUS, GROSS [a]			1067.2				...	3190.0	3520.7	4132.9	4561.0	5161.5
MIXED INCOME, GROSS			...				...	...	...	...	...	...
Gross capital formation			...				...	...	...	...	...	...
Closing stocks of fixed assets (produced assets)			...				14703.5	20088.7	21474.7	24050.2	27078.8	29537.2
Employment (average, in 1000 persons)			5630.0				6050.0	6277.0	6406.0	6502.0	6696.0	6872.0

[a] Includes Mixed Income, Gross.

Table 2.3 Output, gross value added, and fixed assets by industries at current prices (ISIC Rev. 3) Public administration and defense; compulsory social security (L)

Series 300: 1993 SNA, Russian ruble (re-denom. 1:1000), Western calendar year
Series 400: 1993 SNA, Russian ruble (re-denom. 1:1000), Western calendar year

Data in billions

	2001	2002	2003	2004	2005	2006	2007	2008	2009	2010	2011	2012
Series			**300**				**400**					
Output, at basic prices			1340.2				...	3897.2	4242.8	4716.0	5394.9	6328.1
Less: Intermediate consumption, at purchaser's prices			688.8				...	2012.8	2039.6	2292.5	2722.3	2807.2
Equals: VALUE ADDED, GROSS, at basic prices			651.3				...	1884.4	2203.2	2423.5	2672.6	3520.8
Compensation of employees			618.8				...	1818.3	2108.1	2333.6	2577.5	3418.6
Taxes on production and imports, less Subsidies			0.6				...	0.7	24.6	19.7	19.7	21.4
Taxes on production and imports			0.6				...	0.7	24.6	19.7	19.7	21.4
Taxes on products			...				...	...	...	...	...	...
Other taxes on production			0.6				...	0.7	24.6	19.7	19.7	21.4
Less: Subsidies			...				...	...	...	...	...	...
OPERATING SURPLUS, GROSS			31.9				...	65.4	70.4	70.2	75.4	80.9
MIXED INCOME, GROSS			...				...	...	...	...	...	...
Gross capital formation			...				...	...	...	...	...	...
Closing stocks of fixed assets (produced assets)			...				2854.0	3261.0	3538.6	4253.0	5365.0	6036.0
Employment (average, in 1000 persons)			3266.0				3618.0	3727.0	3876.0	3905.0	3801.0	3760.0

Table 2.3 Output, gross value added, and fixed assets by industries at current prices (ISIC Rev. 3) Education; health and social work; other community, social and personal services (M+N+O)

Series 300: 1993 SNA, Russian ruble (re-denom. 1:1000), Western calendar year
Series 400: 1993 SNA, Russian ruble (re-denom. 1:1000), Western calendar year

Data in billions

	2001	2002	2003	2004	2005	2006	2007	2008	2009	2010	2011	2012
Series			**300**				**400**					
Output, at basic prices			1493.3				...	4499.6	4736.1	5346.4	6169.9	7089.0
Less: Intermediate consumption, at purchaser's prices			578.1				...	1709.7	1655.6	1932.5	2233.7	2563.1
Equals: VALUE ADDED, GROSS, at basic prices			915.2				...	2790.0	3080.5	3413.9	3936.2	4525.9
Compensation of employees			743.1				...	2307.6	2615.0	2900.9	3388.0	3872.5
Taxes on production and imports, less Subsidies			0.3				...	9.9	48.3	53.4	76.7	87.5
Taxes on production and imports			5.2				...	9.9	48.3	53.4	76.7	87.5
Taxes on products			...				...	...	...	...	...	...
Other taxes on production			5.2				...	9.9	48.3	53.4	76.7	87.5
Less: Subsidies			4.9				...	...	...	...	...	...
Subsidies on products			...				...	...	...	...	...	...
Other subsidies on production			4.9				...	...	...	...	...	...
OPERATING SURPLUS, GROSS [a]			171.8				...	472.4	417.1	459.6	471.4	565.9
MIXED INCOME, GROSS			...				...	...	...	...	...	...
Gross capital formation			...				...	...	...	...	...	...
Closing stocks of fixed assets (produced assets)			...				5624.6	6101.5	6356.2	6971.5	7684.8	8279.0
Employment (average, in 1000 persons)			12856.0				13233.0	13268.0	13143.0	13054.0	12923.0	12840.0

[a] Includes Mixed Income, Gross.

Table 2.3 Output, gross value added, and fixed assets by industries at current prices (ISIC Rev. 3) Private households with employed persons (P)

Series 400: 1993 SNA, Russian ruble (re-denom. 1:1000), Western calendar year

Data in billions

	2001	2002	2003	2004	2005	2006	2007	2008	2009	2010	2011	2012
Series					**400**							
Output, at basic prices					...	...	...	...	...	0.1	0.1	0.1
Less: Intermediate consumption, at purchaser's prices					...	...	...	...	...	0.0	0.0	0.0
Equals: VALUE ADDED, GROSS, at basic prices					...	...	...	...	...	0.0	0.0	0.0
Compensation of employees					...	...	...	...	...	0.0	0.0	0.0
Taxes on production and imports, less Subsidies					...	...	...	...	...	0.0	0.0	0.0
Taxes on production and imports					...	...	...	...	...	0.0	0.0	0.0
Taxes on products					...	...	...	...	...	...	...	...
Other taxes on production					...	...	...	...	...	0.0	0.0	0.0
Less: Subsidies					...	...	...	...	...	...	...	...
OPERATING SURPLUS, GROSS [a]					...	...	...	...	...	0.0	0.0	0.0

	2001	2002	2003	2004	2005	2006	2007	2008	2009	2010	2011	2012
Series					**400**							
MIXED INCOME, GROSS					...	...	...	...	...	...	...	...
Gross capital formation					...	...	...	...	...	...	...	...
Employment (average, in 1000 persons)					24.0	25.0	33.0	46.0	55.0	55.0	56.0	56.0

[a] Includes Mixed Income, Gross.

Table 3.1 Government final consumption expenditure by function at current prices

Series 300: 1993 SNA, Russian ruble (re-denom. 1:1000), Western calendar year
Series 400: 1993 SNA, Russian ruble (re-denom. 1:1000), Western calendar year

Data in billions

	2001	2002	2003	2004	2005	2006	2007	2008	2009	2010	2011	2012
Series	**300**							**400**				
General public services	841.6[a]	994.0[a]	1240.9[a]	1500.3[a]	292.6	431.4	661.9	748.8				
								681.5	730.1	789.4	826.6	
Defence	...	...	...	...	...	...	...	...				
								...	...	1188.0	1338.7	
Public order and safety [a]	...	...	...	...	1062.6	1321.3	1481.7	1700.5				
								1900.3[a]	2199.3	1173.3	1362.3	
Economic affairs	11.8[b]	32.7[b]	38.8[b]	45.2[b]	270.8	318.1	428.8	620.4				
								620.4	683.2	698.2	845.5	
Environment protection	...	...	...	...	8.7	9.8	12.3	16.3				
								16.3	16.8	17.1	22.6	
Housing and community amenities	20.9	38.2	66.8	84.9	92.0	148.4	188.0	267.4				
								267.4	206.3	247.1	347.7	
Health	299.5	460.5	529.0	656.0	621.1	806.1	1035.3	1300.9				
								1333.9	1437.4	1468.2	1757.2	
Recreation, culture and religion	29.9	54.8	68.3	82.0	97.6	119.9	160.9	209.7				
								209.7	213.6	222.9	239.5	
Education	246.6	304.6	351.5	437.5	707.4	901.3	1131.9	1445.3				
								1445.3	1580.4	1634.9	1741.7	
Social protection	...	...	...	...	438.0	532.9	644.4	881.7				
								885.1	999.5	1024.1	1107.3	
Plus: (Other functions) [c]	19.7	26.5	35.3	41.6	...	...	...	...				
								...	...	...	...	
Equals: General government final consumption expenditure	1470.0	1911.3	2330.6	2847.5	3590.7	4589.2	5745.2	7191.0				
								7359.8	8066.7	8671.3[d]	10040.8[d]	

[a] Includes Defence.
[b] Refers to Agriculture, geology, exploration, hydrometeorology, transport, and communication.
[c] Refers to Science.
[d] Discrepancy between components and total due to budgetary and extra-budgetary activities of autonomous institutions.

Table 3.2 Individual consumption expenditure of households, NPISHs, and general government at current prices

Series 300: 1993 SNA, Russian ruble (re-denom. 1:1000), Western calendar year
Series 400: 1993 SNA, Russian ruble (re-denom. 1:1000), Western calendar year

Data in billions

	2001	2002	2003	2004	2005	2006	2007	2008	2009	2010	2011	2012
Series	**300**							**400**				
Individual consumption expenditure of households												
Food and non-alcoholic beverages	...	...	...	...	...	...	...	...				
								5630.0	6292.8	7139.3	8155.0	...
Alcoholic beverages, tobacco and narcotics	...	...	...	...	...	...	...	...				
								1523.5	1722.1	1926.2	2211.3	...
Clothing and footwear	...	...	...	...	...	...	...	...				
								1855.4	1983.4	2193.1	2437.8	...
Housing, water, electricity, gas and other fuels	...	...	...	...	...	...	...	...				
								1851.5	2059.1	2448.7	2738.5	...
Furnishings, household equipment and routine maintenance of the house	...	...	...	...	...	...	...	...				
								1027.6	1059.1	1202.6	1322.0	...
Health	...	...	...	...	...	...	...	...				
								656.5	768.6	861.6	970.9	...

	2001	2002	2003	2004	2005	2006	2007	2008	2009	2010	2011	2012
Series	**300**							**400**				
Transport	...	...	...	...	...	...	...	...				
								2820.9	2430.7	2714.3	3322.8	...
Communication	...	...	...	...	...	...	...	...				
								1039.6	1069.9	1144.3	1238.2	...
Recreation and culture	...	...	...	...	...	...	...	...				
								1095.2	1059.3	1141.2	1373.2	...
Education	...	...	...	...	...	...	...	...				
								244.1	266.6	280.8	283.9	...
Restaurants and hotels	...	...	...	...	...	...	...	...				
								768.6	750.6	782.1	898.9	...
Miscellaneous goods and services	...	...	...	...	...	...	...	...				
								1158.4	1160.3	1243.5	1594.2	...
Equals: Household final consumption expenditure in domestic market	4182.4	5216.4	6334.8	8104.3	10262.3	12600.3	15730.9	19713.3				
								19671.2	20622.4	23077.5	26546.7	30194.8
Plus: Direct purchases abroad by residents	240.1	314.8	343.1	454.2	494.0	494.2	517.0	588.0				
								588.0	659.5	808.5	952.1	1345.1
Less: Direct purchases in domestic market by non-residents	104.4	130.9	137.8	152.9	166.3	206.6	241.1	291.7				
								292.2	295.9	268.4	334.3	348.7
Equals: Household final consumption expenditure	4318.1	5400.3	6540.1	8405.6	10590.0	12887.9	16006.8	20009.6				
								19967.0	20985.9	23617.6	27164.5	30543.5
Individual consumption expenditure of non-profit institutions serving households (NPISHs)												
Housing	...	...	...	...	...	...	...	...				
								...	...	...	...	...
Health	31.7	21.0	24.7	22.6	13.3	14.1	15.2	14.6				
								14.6	13.7	13.6	15.0	16.9
Recreation and culture	4.9	24.5	29.7	28.7	36.9	40.9	53.1	62.9				
								62.9	34.6	33.1	35.2	39.6
Education	5.8	10.1	12.0	8.1	7.6	6.1	5.4	6.1				
								6.1	9.1	9.7	9.4	10.5
Social protection	...	...	...	9.8	8.5	11.0	13.4	14.5				
								14.5	9.5	9.7	11.4	12.9
Other services	56.4	75.9	87.6	79.2	71.9	80.4	98.8	118.5				
								118.5	150.1	159.6	163.1	183.4
Equals: NPISHs final consumption expenditure	98.8	131.5	154.0	148.4	138.2	152.6	185.9	216.7				
								216.7	217.0	225.7	234.1	263.3
Individual consumption expenditure of general government												
Housing	20.9	38.2	66.8	84.9	105.2	150.1	216.3	295.4				
								299.1	350.7	369.6	365.3	399.4
Health	299.5	460.5	529.0	440.9	585.9	753.9	982.0	1220.2				
								1253.2	1346.1	1416.8	1698.6	1977.9
Recreation and culture	29.9	54.8	68.3	82.0	111.7	139.7	179.3	226.5				
								226.5	231.2	298.5	348.4	389.1
Education	246.6	304.6	351.5	437.5	551.6	694.8	884.3	1118.1				
								1118.1	1228.2	1295.3	1497.1	1722.8
Social protection	...	...	...	215.1	308.5	381.7	442.3	603.3				
								603.3	679.9	738.4	879.0	998.0
Equals: Individual consumption expenditure of general government	596.9	858.2	1015.5	1260.4	1662.9	2120.2	2704.3	3463.4				
								3500.2	3836.0	4118.6	4788.3	5487.1
Equals: Total actual individual consumption	5013.8	6390.0	7709.7	9814.3	12391.1	15160.8	18897.0	23689.7				
								23683.8	25038.9	27962.0	32186.9	36293.9

Table 4.1 Total Economy (S.1)

Series 300: 1993 SNA, Russian ruble (re-denom. 1:1000), Western calendar year
Series 400: 1993 SNA, Russian ruble (re-denom. 1:1000), Western calendar year

Data in billions

	2001	2002	2003	2004	2005	2006	2007	2008	2009	2010	2011	2012
Series	**300**							**400**				
I. Production account - Resources												
Output, at basic prices (otherwise, please specify)	15922.8	18990.5	23298.4	29543.4	37091.3	46330.0		71601.7	68116.4	82054.6	97365.4	107956.1
Less: Financial intermediation services indirectly measured (only to be deducted if FISIM is not distributed to uses)	129.7	179.3	211.6	307.1	442.9	578.6		...	...	...	...	...
Plus: Taxes less Subsidies on products	1097.5	1249.2	1588.5	2168.4	3092.1	3939.9		6094.2	4975.9	6268.5	8294.1	9314.5
Plus: Taxes on products	1268.9	1415.2	1775.1	2352.1	3248.2	4090.1		6323.8	5202.1	6462.6	8463.3	9492.3
Less: Subsidies on products	171.4	165.9	186.6	183.7	156.1	150.2		229.7	226.2	194.1	169.3	177.8
I. Production account - Uses												
Intermediate consumption, at purchaser's prices	7947.0	9229.9	11432.1	14356.5	18115.2	22787.8		36419.0	34285.1	42014.5	49859.9	54671.6
GROSS DOMESTIC PRODUCT	8943.6	10830.5	13243.2	17048.1	21625.4	26903.5		41276.8	38807.2	46308.5	55799.6	62599.1
Less: Consumption of fixed capital	724.9	845.9	959.1	1099.1	1289.5	...		1994.9	2230.5	2365.9	2614.9	...
NET DOMESTIC PRODUCT	8218.7	9984.7	12284.1	15949.0	20330.6	...		39281.9	36576.8	43942.6	53184.7	...
II.1.1 Generation of income account - Resources												
GROSS DOMESTIC PRODUCT	8943.6	10830.5	13243.2	17048.1	21625.4	26903.5		41276.8	38807.2	46308.5	55799.6	62599.1
II.1.1 Generation of income account - Uses												
Compensation of employees	3848.4	5065.1	6231.4	7845.0	9474.3	11985.9[a]		19559.8	20411.6	22995.6	27646.5	31577.9
Taxes on production and imports, less Subsidies	1402.6	1845.8	2110.2	2872.7	4244.5	5381.7		8218.4	6474.5	8219.2	10880.0	12409.5
Taxes on production and imports	1585.8	2027.0	2315.9	3076.3	4406.9	5537.3		8498.5	6808.4	8494.6	11194.3	12745.1
Taxes on products	1268.9	1415.2	1775.1	2352.1	3248.2	4090.1		6323.8	5202.1	6462.6	8463.3	9492.3
Other taxes on production	316.9	611.8	540.8	724.1	1158.6	1447.2		2174.7	1606.3	2032.1	2731.0	3252.8
Less: Subsidies	183.3	181.2	205.7	203.6	162.4	155.6		280.1	333.9	275.5	314.3	335.7
Subsidies on products	171.4	165.9	186.6	183.7	156.1	150.2		229.7	226.2	194.1	169.3	177.8
Other subsidies on production	11.8	15.3	19.1	19.9	6.3	5.3		50.4	107.6	81.4	145.1	157.8
OPERATING SURPLUS, GROSS [b]	3692.6	3919.7	4901.6	6330.4	7906.6	9535.9		10204.5	8302.9	11529.9	13106.8	14176.2
MIXED INCOME, GROSS	...	...	...	...	...	...		3294.2	3618.2	3563.8	4166.2	4435.5
II.1.2 Allocation of primary income account - Resources												
OPERATING SURPLUS, GROSS [b]	3692.6	3919.7	4901.6	6330.4	7906.6	9535.9		10204.5	8302.9	11529.9	13106.8	14176.2
MIXED INCOME, GROSS	...	...	...	...	...	...		3294.2	3618.2	3563.8	4166.2	4435.5
Compensation of employees	3852.2	5071.3	6227.1	7837.6	9433.1	11697.4		19204.7	20131.5	22736.9	27368.7	31211.7
Taxes on production and imports, less Subsidies	1402.6	1845.8	2110.2	2872.7	4244.5	5381.7		8218.4	6474.5	8219.2	10880.0	12409.5
Taxes on production and imports	1585.8	2027.0	2315.9	3076.3	4406.9	5537.3		8498.5	6808.4	8494.6	11194.3	12745.1
Taxes on products	1268.9	1415.2	1775.1	2352.1	3248.2	4090.1		6323.8	5202.1	6462.6	8463.3	9492.3
Other taxes on production	316.9	611.8	540.8	724.1	1158.6	1447.2		2174.7	1606.3	2032.1	2731.0	3252.8
Less: Subsidies	183.3	181.2	205.7	203.6	162.4	155.6		280.1	333.9	275.5	314.3	335.7
Subsidies on products	171.4	165.9	186.6	183.7	156.1	150.2		229.7	226.2	194.1	169.3	177.8

	2001	2002	2003	2004	2005	2006	2007	2008	2009	2010	2011	2012
Series	**300**							**400**				
Other subsidies on production	11.8	15.3	19.1	19.9	6.3	5.3		50.4	107.6	81.4	145.1	157.8
Property income [c]	179.3	154.5	316.8	352.3	525.3	836.9		1432.4	948.7	1024.0	1128.1	1378.3
II.1.2 Allocation of primary income account - Uses												
Property income [d]	306.7	367.3	714.0	713.1	1031.4	1489.6		2287.7	1929.7	2243.1	2612.5	3072.2
GROSS NATIONAL INCOME	8819.9	10623.8	12841.8	16679.9	21079.5	26009.7		40066.4	37546.1	44830.7	54037.4	60538.9
II.2 Secondary distribution of income account - Resources												
GROSS NATIONAL INCOME	8819.9	10623.8	12841.8	16679.9	21079.5	26009.7		40066.4	37546.1	44830.7	54037.4	60538.9
Current taxes on income, wealth, etc.	...	...	...	...	...	...		4411.1	3220.3	4044.2	4610.5	...
Social contributions	...	...	...	...	...	...		2740.7	2897.2	3067.4	4418.0	...
Social benefits other than social transfers in kind	...	...	...	...	...	...		3199.7	3887.7	5261.7	5419.3	...
Other current transfers [e] [e]	21.7	52.8	77.3	104.7	132.8	179.4		270.5	282.0	302.4	480.3	512.9
II.2 Secondary distribution of income account - Uses												
Current taxes on income, wealth, etc.	...	...	...	...	...	...		4411.1	3220.3	4044.2	4610.5	...
Social contributions	...	...	...	...	...	...		2740.7	2897.2	3067.4	4418.0	...
Social benefits other than social transfers in kind	...	...	...	...	...	...		3199.7	3887.7	5261.7	5419.3	...
Other current transfers [f] [g]	45.7	64.0	89.3	124.4	164.8	214.5		341.3	370.9	412.4	575.1	702.7
GROSS DISPOSABLE INCOME	8796.0	10612.7	12829.8	16660.2	21047.5	25974.7		39995.7	37457.2	44720.8	53942.5	60349.1
II.4.1 Use of disposable income account - Resources												
GROSS DISPOSABLE INCOME	8796.0	10612.7	12829.8	16660.2	21047.5	25974.7		39995.7	37457.2	44720.8	53942.5	60349.1
Adjustment for the change in net equity of households on pension funds	...	...	...	...	...	...		47.5	102.8	83.0	57.1	...
II.4.1 Use of disposable income account - Uses												
Final consumption expenditure	5886.9	7443.2	9024.8	11401.4	14363.5	17742.6		27543.5	29269.6	32514.7	37439.3	42471.5
Individual consumption expenditure	5013.8	6390.0	7709.7	9814.3	12419.3	15212.9		23683.8	25038.9	27962.0	32186.9	36293.9
Collective consumption expenditure	873.0	1053.2	1315.1	1587.1	1944.2	2529.7[h]		3859.7	4230.7	4552.7	5252.5	6177.7
Adjustment for the change in net equity of households on pension funds	...	...	...	...	...	...		47.5	102.8	83.0	57.1	...
SAVING, GROSS	2909.2	3169.5	3805.1	5258.8	6684.0	8232.1		12452.2	8187.5	12206.1	16503.2	17877.6
III.1 Capital account - Changes in liabilities and net worth												
SAVING, GROSS	2909.2	3169.5	3805.1	5258.8	6684.0	8232.1		12452.2	8187.5	12206.1	16503.2	17877.6
Capital transfers, receivable less payable	-273.7	-391.9	-30.0	-45.7	-365.0	2.3		7.4	-376.8	-4.5	-7.6	-147.6
Capital transfers, receivable [i]	58.2	230.4	14.8	20.4	12.3	19.9		25.4	35.0	20.0	16.9	8.7
Less: Capital transfers, payable [j]	331.9	622.3	44.8	66.1	377.3	17.6		18.1	411.8	24.4	24.4	156.4
Equals: CHANGES IN NET WORTH DUE TO SAVING AND CAPITAL TRANSFERS [k] [k]	2635.4	2777.6	3775.1	5213.1	6319.0	8234.4		12459.5	7810.7	12201.6	16495.6	17729.9
III.1 Capital account - Changes in assets												
Gross capital formation	1963.1	2169.3	2755.0	3559.0	4349.9[h]	5415.8[h]		10526.1	7344.8	10472.6	14207.8	16264.5
Gross fixed capital formation	1671.0	1924.5	2412.9	3091.5	3785.6	4719.7[h]		8943.0	8222.4	9647.5	11595.2	13164.2
Changes in inventories	273.8	230.0	322.8	428.4	501.5	620.2[h]		1325.3	-1190.9	458.3	2132.0	2496.5
Acquisitions less disposals of valuables	18.3	14.9	19.4	39.1	62.8	75.9[h]		257.8	313.3	366.8	480.6	603.8

	2001	2002	2003	2004	2005	2006	2007	2008	2009	2010	2011	2012
Series	**300**							**400**				
Acquisitions less disposals of non-produced non-financial assets	...	...	...	...	...	...		5.8	7.2	0.0	0.0	12.5
NET LENDING (+) / NET BORROWING (-) [l]	672.3	608.3	1020.0	1654.2	1969.1	2818.6		1927.7[l]	458.7	1729.0	2287.9	1452.9
	III.2 Financial account - Changes in liabilities and net worth											
Net incurrence of liabilities	...	...	...	...	...	...		...	...	...	...	...
Currency and deposits	...	...	...	...	...	...		...	...	...	...	...
Securities other than shares	...	...	...	...	...	...		...	...	...	...	...
Loans	...	...	...	...	...	...		...	...	...	...	...
Shares and other equity	...	...	...	...	...	...		...	...	...	...	...
Insurance technical reserves	...	...	...	...	...	...		...	...	...	...	...
Financial derivatives	...	...	...	...	...	...		...	...	...	...	...
Other accounts payable	...	...	...	...	...	...		...	...	...	...	...
NET LENDING (+) / NET BORROWING (-)	672.3	608.3	1020.0	1654.2	1969.1	2818.6		1927.7	458.7	1729.0	2287.9	1452.9
	III.2 Financial account - Changes in assets											
Net acquisition of financial assets	...	...	...	...	...	...		...	...	...	...	...
Monetary gold and SDRs	...	...	...	...	...	...		...	...	...	...	...
Currency and deposits	...	...	...	...	...	...		...	...	...	...	...
Securities other than shares	...	...	...	...	...	...		...	...	...	...	...
Loans	...	...	...	...	...	...		...	...	...	...	...
Shares and other equity	...	...	...	...	...	...		...	...	...	...	...
Insurance technical reserves	...	...	...	...	...	...		...	...	...	...	...
Financial derivatives	...	...	...	...	...	...		...	...	...	...	...
Other accounts receivable	...	...	...	...	...	...		...	...	...	...	...

[a] Discrepancy between the Total Economy and the Rest of the World account.
[b] Includes Mixed Income, Gross.
[c] Refers to Property income from the rest of the world.
[d] Refers to Property income to the rest of the world.
[e] Refers to current transfer from the rest of the world.
[f] Refers to current transfer to the rest of the world. Includes Social benefits other than social transfers in kind to the rest of the world.
[g] Refers to current transfer to the rest of the world.
[h] Discrepancy with equivalent item in Table 1.1 (Gross domestic product by expenditures at current prices). Data needs to be revised/updated.
[i] Refers to capital transfers from the rest of the world
[j] Refers to capital transfers to the rest of the world
[k] Item does not consider consumption of fixed capital.
[l] Excludes the statistical discrepancy between expenditure-based and production-based GDP amounts.

Table 4.2 Rest of the world (S.2)

Series 300: 1993 SNA, Russian ruble (re-denom. 1:1000), Western calendar year
Series 400: 1993 SNA, Russian ruble (re-denom. 1:1000), Western calendar year

Data in billions

	2001	2002	2003	2004	2005	2006	2007	2008	2009	2010	2011	2012
Series	**300**							**400**				
	V.I External account of goods and services - Resources											
Imports of goods and services	2165.9	2646.2	3153.9	3773.9	4660.1	5679.1		9111.0	7954.3	9789.6	12164.4	13860.1
Imports of goods	1565.1	1908.5	2324.2	2801.0	3543.2	4452.7		7238.2	6016.9	7549.6	9519.0	10499.7
Imports of services	600.8	737.7	829.7	972.8	1117.0[a]	1226.4[a]		1872.8	1937.4	2240.0	2645.4	3360.4
	V.I External account of goods and services - Uses											
Exports of goods and services	3299.6	3813.7	4655.9	5860.4	7592.1	9069.1		12923.6	10842.0	13529.3	16940.9	18428.0
Exports of goods	2965.3	3386.3	4159.1	5273.5	6893.3	8246.3		11652.0	9529.1	12162.6	15353.3	16571.6
Exports of services	334.3	427.4	496.7	586.9	698.7[a]	822.8[a]		1271.6	1312.9	1366.7	1587.6	1856.4
EXTERNAL BALANCE OF GOODS AND SERVICES	-1133.6	-1167.5	-1502.0	-2086.5	-2931.9	-3390.0		-3812.6	-2887.7	-3739.7	-4776.5	-4567.8
	V.II External account of primary income and current transfers - Resources											
EXTERNAL BALANCE OF GOODS AND SERVICES	-1133.6	-1167.5	-1502.0	-2086.5	-2931.9	-3390.0		-3812.6	-2887.7	-3739.7	-4776.5	-4567.8
Compensation of employees	14.4	15.9	29.2	42.2	82.9	163.4		449.0	385.4	368.7	393.2	489.3
Taxes on production and imports, less Subsidies	...	...	...	...	...	...		...	...	...	...	...
Taxes on production and imports	...	...	...	...	...	...		...	...	...	...	...
Taxes on products	...	...	...	...	...	...		...	...	...	...	...
Other taxes on production	...	...	...	...	...	...		...	...	...	...	...
Less: Subsidies	...	...	...	...	...	...		...	...	...	...	...
Subsidies on products	...	...	...	...	...	...		...	...	...	...	...
Other subsidies on production	...	...	...	...	...	...		...	...	...	...	...
Property income	306.7	367.3	714.0	670.9	948.5	1326.1		2287.7	1929.7	2243.1	2612.5	3072.2
Current taxes on income, wealth, etc.	...	...	...	...	...	...		...	...	...	...	...
Social contributions	...	...	...	...	...	...		...	...	...	...	...
Social benefits other than social transfers in kind	0.1	0.3	0.5	0.5	0.6	1.1		...	...	...	...	...
Other current transfers	45.6	63.7	88.8	123.9	164.2	213.3		341.3	370.9	412.4	575.1	702.7
Adjustment for the change in net equity of households on pension funds	...	...	...	...	...	...		...	...	...	...	...
	V.II External account of primary income and current transfers - Uses											
Compensation of employees	18.2	22.1	25.0	34.7	48.5	44.7		93.9	105.3	109.9	115.4	123.1
Taxes on production and imports, less Subsidies	...	...	...	...	...	...		...	...	...	...	...
Taxes on production and imports	...	...	...	...	...	...		...	...	...	...	...
Taxes on products	...	...	...	...	...	...		...	...	...	...	...
Other taxes on production	...	...	...	...	...	...		...	...	...	...	...
Less: Subsidies	...	...	...	...	...	...		...	...	...	...	...
Subsidies on products	...	...	...	...	...	...		...	...	...	...	...
Other subsidies on production	...	...	...	...	...	...		...	...	...	...	...
Property income	179.3	154.5	316.8	310.1	442.3	673.4		1432.4	948.7	1024.0	1128.1	1378.3

	2001	2002	2003	2004	2005	2006	2007	2008	2009	2010	2011	2012
Series	**300**							**400**				
Current taxes on income and wealth, etc.	...	...	...	...	...	...		...	...	...	...	...
Social contributions	...	...	...	...	...	...		...	...	...	...	...
Social benefits other than social transfers in kind	...	...	...	...	...	...		...	...	...	...	...
Other current transfers	21.7	52.8	77.3	104.7	132.8	179.4		270.5	282.0	302.4	480.3	512.9
Adjustment for the change in net equity of households on pension funds	...	...	...	...	...	...		...	...	...	...	...
CURRENT EXTERNAL BALANCE	-986.1	-949.6	-1088.5	-1698.6	-2359.3	-2583.6		-2531.4	-1537.6	-2151.9	-2919.5	-2317.9
	V.III.1 Capital account - Changes in liabilities and net worth											
CURRENT EXTERNAL BALANCE	-986.1	-949.6	-1088.5	-1698.6	-2359.3	-2583.6		-2531.4	-1537.6	-2151.9	-2919.5	-2317.9
Capital transfers, receivable less payable	273.7	391.9	30.0	45.7	365.0	-2.3		-7.4	376.8	4.5	7.6	147.6
Capital transfers, receivable	331.9	622.3	44.8	66.1	377.3	17.6		18.1	411.8	24.4	24.4	156.4
Less: Capital transfers, payable	58.2	230.4	14.8	20.4	12.3	19.9		25.4	35.0	20.0	16.9	8.7
Equals: CHANGES IN NET WORTH DUE TO SAVING AND CAPITAL TRANSFERS	-712.3	-557.7	-1058.5	-1653.0	-1994.3	-2585.9		-2538.8	-1160.8	-2147.5	-2911.9	-2170.2
	V.III.1 Capital account - Changes in assets											
Acquisitions less disposals of non-produced non-financial assets	...	...	...	...	...	...		-5.8	-7.2	0.0	0.0	-12.5
NET LENDING (+) / NET BORROWING (-) [b]	-712.3	-557.7	-1058.5	-1653.0	-1994.3	-2585.9		-2533.0	-1153.6	-2147.5	-2911.9	-2157.7

[a] Data for this year(s) have not been revised. Discrepancy with equivalent item in Table 1.1 (Gross domestic product by expenditures at current prices).
[b] Discrepancy with equivalent item in other tables by the same amount as the statistical discrepancy to adjust GDP by expenditure approach and GDP by production approach.

Table 4.3 Non-financial Corporations (S.11)

Series 400: 1993 SNA, Russian ruble (re-denom. 1:1000), Western calendar year **Data in billions**

	2001	2002	2003	2004	2005	2006	2007	2008	2009	2010	2011	2012
Series								**400**				
	I. Production account - Resources											
Output, at basic prices (otherwise, please specify)								56953.3	52424.1	63922.0	76536.6	
	I. Production account - Uses											
Intermediate consumption, at purchaser's prices								30642.1	28624.9	34951.1	41690.2	
VALUE ADDED GROSS, in basic prices								26311.2	23799.2	28970.9	34846.4	
Less: Consumption of fixed capital								1663.5	1849.0	1971.3	2192.6	
VALUE ADDED NET, at basic prices								24647.7	21950.1	26999.6	32653.8	
	II.1.1 Generation of income account - Resources											
VALUE ADDED GROSS, at basic prices								26311.2	23799.2	28970.9	34846.4	
	II.1.1 Generation of income account - Uses											
Compensation of employees								15068.1	15395.3	16843.4	20583.7	
Other taxes less Other subsidies on production								2028.0	1327.9	1759.7	2363.4	
Other taxes on production								2078.4	1435.6	1841.0	2508.5	
Less: Other subsidies on production								50.4	107.6	81.4	145.1	

	2001	2002	2003	2004	2005	2006	2007	2008	2009	2010	2011	2012
Series								**400**				
OPERATING SURPLUS, GROSS								9215.1	7075.9	10367.8	11899.3	
II.1.2 Allocation of primary income account - Resources												
OPERATING SURPLUS, GROSS								9215.1	7075.9	10367.8	11899.3	
Property income								1486.9	1394.8	1573.4	1703.4	
II.1.2 Allocation of primary income account - Uses												
Property income								4395.7	4746.5	4922.6	5326.6	
BALANCE OF PRIMARY INCOMES								6306.4	3724.3	7018.6	8276.1	
II.2 Secondary distribution of income account - Resources												
BALANCE OF PRIMARY INCOMES								6306.4	3724.3	7018.6	8276.1	
Social contributions								139.4	155.6	169.8	189.4	
Other current transfers								503.9	603.6	647.7	586.5	
II.2 Secondary distribution of income account - Uses												
Current taxes on income, wealth, etc.								2446.0	1277.9	1750.2	2049.5	
Social benefits other than social transfers in kind								88.5	101.4	104.9	114.5	
Other current transfers								701.7	576.2	940.4	857.2	
GROSS DISPOSABLE INCOME								3713.5	2528.1	5040.6	6030.7	
II.4.1 Use of disposable income account - Resources												
GROSS DISPOSABLE INCOME								3713.5	2528.1	5040.6	6030.7	
II.4.1 Use of disposable income account - Uses												
Adjustment for the change in net equity of households on pension funds								...	...	...	...	
SAVING, GROSS								3713.5	2528.1	5040.6	6030.7	
III.1 Capital account - Changes in liabilities and net worth												
SAVING, GROSS								3713.5	2528.1	5040.6	6030.7	
Capital transfers, receivable less payable								482.8	522.1	588.6	509.5	
Capital transfers, receivable								492.4	529.5	597.3	519.2	
Less: Capital transfers, payable								9.6	7.4	8.7	9.7	
Equals: CHANGES IN NET WORTH DUE TO SAVING AND CAPITAL TRANSFERS								4196.3[a]	3050.2[a]	3657.9	4347.6	
III.1 Capital account - Changes in assets												
Gross capital formation								7292.7	4321.5	7249.4	10072.9	
Gross fixed capital formation								5775.4	5326.4	6438.9	7672.8	
Changes in inventories								1352.5	-1216.4	556.2	2057.5	
Acquisitions less disposals of valuables								164.7	211.5	254.3	342.7	
Acquisitions less disposals of non-produced non-financial assets								44.3	45.5	36.6	43.3	
NET LENDING (+) / NET BORROWING (-)								-3140.7	-1316.9	-1656.9	-3576.0	

[a] Item does not consider consumption of fixed capital.

Table 4.4 Financial Corporations (S.12)

Series 400: 1993 SNA, Russian ruble (re-denom. 1:1000), Western calendar year **Data in billions**

	2001	2002	2003	2004	2005	2006	2007	2008	2009	2010	2011	2012
Series								**400**				
I. Production account - Resources												
Output, at basic prices (otherwise, please specify)								2203.8	2373.1	2465.1	2796.8	
I. Production account - Uses												
Intermediate consumption, at purchaser's prices								665.9	666.0	710.6	860.3	
VALUE ADDED GROSS, at basic prices								1537.8	1707.2	1754.5	1936.5	
Less: Consumption of fixed capital								40.6	38.4	41.0	43.1	
VALUE ADDED NET, at basic prices								1497.2	1668.8	1713.5	1893.4	
II.1.1 Generation of income account - Resources												
VALUE ADDED GROSS, at basic prices								1537.8	1707.2	1754.5	1936.5	
II.1.1 Generation of income account - Uses												
Compensation of employees								697.5	646.3	762.9	890.9	
Other taxes less Other subsidies on production								71.6	71.0	80.5	99.0	
Other taxes on production								71.6	71.0	80.5	99.0	
Less: Other subsidies on production								...	...	...	...	
OPERATING SURPLUS, GROSS								768.7	989.8	911.1	946.6	
II.1.2 Allocation of primary income account - Resources												
OPERATING SURPLUS, GROSS								768.7	989.8	911.1	946.6	
Property income								1812.2	1959.1	1615.0	1747.4	
II.1.2 Allocation of primary income account - Uses												
Property income								1538.2	1729.2	1583.8	1614.3	
BALANCE OF PRIMARY INCOMES								1042.7	1219.8	942.3	1079.8	
II.2 Secondary distribution of income account - Resources												
BALANCE OF PRIMARY INCOMES								1042.7	1219.8	942.3	1079.8	
Social contributions								71.9	134.0	117.7	96.3	
Other current transfers								660.6	802.7	888.3	994.2	
II.2 Secondary distribution of income account - Uses												
Current taxes on income, wealth, etc.								193.1	162.3	367.5	392.5	
Social benefits other than social transfers in kind								25.7	31.2	34.7	39.2	
Other current transfers								633.5	750.9	787.2	927.1	
GROSS DISPOSABLE INCOME								922.8	1212.1	758.9	811.5	
II.4.1 Use of disposable income account - Resources												
GROSS DISPOSABLE INCOME								922.8	1212.1	758.9	811.5	
II.4.1 Use of disposable income account - Uses												
Adjustment for the change in net equity of households on pension funds								47.5	102.8	83.0	57.1	
SAVING, GROSS								875.3	1109.3	675.9	754.4	

	2001	2002	2003	2004	2005	2006	2007	2008	2009	2010	2011	2012
Series								**400**				
	III.1 Capital account - Changes in liabilities and net worth											
SAVING, GROSS								875.3	1109.3	675.9	754.4	
Capital transfers, receivable less payable								-0.0	-0.1	-0.1	-0.1	
Capital transfers, receivable								0.0	0.0	0.0	0.0	
Less: Capital transfers, payable								0.0	0.1	0.1	0.1	
Equals: CHANGES IN NET WORTH DUE TO SAVING AND CAPITAL TRANSFERS								875.2[a]	1109.2[a]	634.8	711.2	
	III.1 Capital account - Changes in assets											
Gross capital formation								151.6	145.3	148.0	194.3	
Gross fixed capital formation								151.3	145.1	147.1	193.8	
Changes in inventories								0.3	0.2	0.9	0.5	
Acquisitions less disposals of valuables								...	...	...	...	
Acquisitions less disposals of non-produced non-financial assets								...	...	...	...	
NET LENDING (+) / NET BORROWING (-)								723.6	963.9	527.8	560.0	

[a] Item does not consider consumption of fixed capital.

Table 4.5 General Government (S.13)

Series 400: 1993 SNA, Russian ruble (re-denom. 1:1000), Western calendar year — **Data in billions**

	2001	2002	2003	2004	2005	2006	2007	2008	2009	2010	2011	2012
Series								**400**				
	I. Production account - Resources											
Output, at basic prices (otherwise, please specify)								7137.8	7764.6	8901.4	10322.3	
	I. Production account - Uses											
Intermediate consumption, at purchaser's prices								3222.4	3201.6	3710.1	4397.0	
VALUE ADDED GROSS, at basic prices								3915.5	4563.0	5191.3	5925.3	
Less: Consumption of fixed capital								139.6	158.8	158.1	171.6	
VALUE ADDED NET, at basic prices								3775.9	4404.2	5033.2	5753.8	
	II.1.1 Generation of income account - Resources											
VALUE ADDED GROSS, at basic prices								3915.5	4563.0	5191.3	5925.3	
	II.1.1 Generation of income account - Uses											
Compensation of employees								3700.4	4268.7	4879.4	5597.4	
Other taxes less Other subsidies on production								1.0	68.4	71.7	80.5	
Other taxes on production								1.0	68.4	71.7	80.5	
Less: Other subsidies on production								...	...	...	...	
OPERATING SURPLUS, GROSS								214.0	226.0	240.2	247.4	
	II.1.2 Allocation of primary income account - Resources											
OPERATING SURPLUS, GROSS								214.0	226.0	240.2	247.4	
Taxes on production and imports, less Subsidies								8218.4	6474.5	8219.2	10880.0	

	2001	2002	2003	2004	2005	2006	2007	2008	2009	2010	2011	2012
Series								**400**				
Taxes on production and imports								8498.5	6808.4	8494.6	11194.3	
Taxes on products								6323.8	5202.1	6462.6	8463.3	
Other taxes on production								2174.7	1606.3	2032.1	2731.0	
Less: Subsidies								280.1	333.9	275.5	314.3	
Subsidies on products								229.7	226.2	194.1	169.3	
Other subsidies on production								50.4	107.6	81.4	145.1	
Property income								606.6	705.9	578.5	668.7	
II.1.2 Allocation of primary income account - Uses												
Property income								164.5	195.3	243.2	319.7	
BALANCE OF PRIMARY INCOMES								8874.5	7211.1	8794.7	11476.4	
II.2 Secondary distribution of income account - Resources												
BALANCE OF PRIMARY INCOMES								8874.5	7211.1	8794.7	11476.4	
Current taxes on income, wealth, etc.								4411.1	3220.3	4044.2	4610.5	
Social contributions								2529.1	2607.2	2779.5	4131.9	
Other current transfers								808.4	881.4	1057.0	1323.0	
II.2 Secondary distribution of income account - Uses												
Current taxes on income, wealth, etc.								...	...	...	...	
Social benefits other than social transfers in kind								3034.7	3735.3	5100.8	5224.0	
Other current transfers								785.3	956.5	984.2	1181.9	
GROSS DISPOSABLE INCOME								12803.2	9228.2	10590.5	15135.9	
II.4.1 Use of disposable income account - Resources												
GROSS DISPOSABLE INCOME								12803.2	9228.2	10590.5	15135.9	
II.4.1 Use of disposable income account - Uses												
Final consumption expenditure								7359.8	8066.7	8671.3	10040.8	
Individual consumption expenditure								3500.2	3836.0	4118.6	4788.3	
Collective consumption expenditure								3859.7	4230.7	4552.7	5252.5	
Adjustment for the change in net equity of households on pension funds								...	...	...	...	
SAVING, GROSS								5443.4	1161.5	1919.2	5095.1	
III.1 Capital account - Changes in liabilities and net worth												
SAVING, GROSS								5443.4	1161.5	1919.2	5095.1	
Capital transfers, receivable less payable								-1619.2	-2674.0	-1706.0	-1599.6	
Capital transfers, receivable								5.2	4.1	1.8	2.2	
Less: Capital transfers, payable								1624.3	2678.1	1707.9	1601.9	
Equals: CHANGES IN NET WORTH DUE TO SAVING AND CAPITAL TRANSFERS								3824.2[a]	-1512.5[a]	55.1	3323.9	
III.1 Capital account - Changes in assets												
Gross capital formation								868.6	79.2	816.8	1211.7	
Gross fixed capital formation								870.7	84.8	827.3	1215.9	
Changes in inventories								...	...	...	...	

	2001	2002	2003	2004	2005	2006	2007	2008	2009	2010	2011	2012
Series								**400**				
Acquisitions less disposals of valuables								-2.1	-5.6	-10.5	-4.3	
Acquisitions of non-produced non-financial assets								-38.5	-38.3	-36.6	-43.3	
NET LENDING (+) / NET BORROWING (-)								2994.1	-1553.3	-567.0	2327.1	

[a] Item does not consider consumption of fixed capital.

Table 4.6 Households (S.14)

Series 400: 1993 SNA, Russian ruble (re-denom. 1:1000), Western calendar year **Data in billions**

	2001	2002	2003	2004	2005	2006	2007	2008	2009	2010	2011	2012
Series								**400**				
I. Production account - Resources												
Output, at basic prices (otherwise, please specify)								5086.3	5337.3	6540.3	7464.4	
I. Production account - Uses												
Intermediate consumption, at purchaser's prices								1769.4	1689.0	2534.6	2796.8	
VALUE ADDED GROSS, at basic prices								3316.9	3648.3	4005.6	4667.6	
Less: Consumption of fixed capital								145.7	174.8	186.3	196.7	
VALUE ADDED NET, at basic prices								3171.2	3473.5	3819.3	4470.9	
II.1.1 Generation of income account - Resources												
VALUE ADDED GROSS, at basic prices								3316.9	3648.3	4005.6	4667.6	
II.1.1 Generation of income account - Uses												
Compensation of employees								...	...	404.4	459.2	
Other taxes less Other subsidies on production								22.7	30.1	37.4	42.2	
Other taxes on production								22.7	30.1	37.4	42.2	
Less: Other subsidies on production								...	...	...	...	
OPERATING SURPLUS, GROSS								...	...	...	...	
MIXED INCOME, GROSS								3294.2	3618.2	3563.8	4166.2	
II.1.2 Allocation of primary income account - Resources												
OPERATING SURPLUS, GROSS								...	...	...	...	
MIXED INCOME, GROSS								3294.2	3618.2	3563.8	4166.2	
Compensation of employees								19204.7	20131.5	22736.9	27368.7	
Property income								1615.9	1937.1	1986.4	1897.1	
II.1.2 Allocation of primary income account - Uses												
Property income								279.5	309.7	227.4	265.9	
BALANCE OF PRIMARY INCOMES								23835.2	25377.1	28059.7	33166.1	
II.2 Secondary distribution of income account - Resources												
BALANCE OF PRIMARY INCOMES								23835.2	25377.1	28059.7	33166.1	
Social contributions								...	...	...	...	
Social benefits other than social transfers in kind								3197.5	3884.9	5257.3	5413.5	
Other current transfers								203.1	243.9	235.0	252.5	

	2001	2002	2003	2004	2005	2006	2007	2008	2009	2010	2011	2012
Series								**400**				
	II.2 Secondary distribution of income account - Uses											
Current taxes on income, wealth, etc.								1771.9	1780.2	1926.6	2167.8	
Social contributions								2740.7	2897.2	3067.4	4418.0	
Social benefits other than social transfers in kind								...	...	...	...	
Other current transfers								438.8	576.4	503.4	594.7	
GROSS DISPOSABLE INCOME								22284.4	24252.1	28054.6	31651.6	
	II.4.1 Use of disposable income account - Resources											
GROSS DISPOSABLE INCOME								22284.4	24252.1	28054.6	31651.6	
Adjustment for the change in net equity of households on pension funds								47.5	102.8	83.0	57.1	
	II.4.1 Use of disposable income account - Uses											
Final consumption expenditure								19967.0	20985.9	23617.6	27164.5	
Individual consumption expenditure								19967.0	20985.9	23617.6	27164.5	
SAVING, GROSS								2364.9	3369.0	4520.0	4544.3	
	III.1 Capital account - Changes in liabilities and net worth											
SAVING, GROSS								2364.9	3369.0	4520.0	4544.3	
Capital transfers, receivable less payable								1143.7	1775.2	1113.1	1082.7	
Capital transfers, receivable								1161.7	1791.8	1131.2	1104.9	
Less: Capital transfers, payable								18.0	16.7	18.1	22.2	
Equals: CHANGES IN NET WORTH DUE TO SAVINGS AND CAPITAL TRANSFERS								3508.7[a]	5144.2[a]	5446.8	5430.3	
	III.1 Capital account - Changes in assets											
Gross capital formation								2196.6	2792.8	2252.0	2714.7	
Gross fixed capital formation								2128.9	2660.0	2227.9	2498.5	
Changes in inventories								-27.5	25.3	-98.9	74.0	
Acquisitions less disposals of valuables								95.2	107.4	123.0	142.2	
Acquisitions less disposals of non-produced non-financial assets								...	...	...	...	
NET LENDING (+) / NET BORROWING (-)								1312.1	2351.4	3381.0	2912.2	

[a] Item does not consider consumption of fixed capital.

Table 4.7 Non-profit institutions serving households (S.15)

Series 400: 1993 SNA, Russian ruble (re-denom. 1:1000), Western calendar year **Data in billions**

	2001	2002	2003	2004	2005	2006	2007	2008	2009	2010	2011	2012
Series								**400**				
	I. Production account - Resources											
Output, at basic prices (otherwise, please specify)								220.4	217.4	225.9	245.3	
	I. Production account - Uses											
Intermediate consumption, at purchaser's prices								119.2	103.7	108.1	115.6	
VALUE ADDED GROSS, at basic prices								101.2	113.7	117.7	129.7	

	2001	2002	2003	2004	2005	2006	2007	2008	2009	2010	2011	2012
Series								**400**				
Less: Consumption of fixed capital								5.5	9.5	9.3	11.0	
VALUE ADDED NET, at basic prices								95.8	104.2	108.5	118.7	
II.1.1 Generation of income account - Resources												
VALUE ADDED GROSS, at basic prices								101.2	113.7	117.7	129.7	
II.1.1 Generation of income account - Uses												
Compensation of employees								93.7	101.3	105.4	115.3	
Other taxes less Other subsidies on production								0.9	1.2	1.5	0.9	
Other taxes on production								0.9	1.2	1.5	0.9	
Less: Other subsidies on production								...	...	...	...	
OPERATING SURPLUS, GROSS								6.7	11.1	10.9	13.5	
II.1.2 Allocation of primary income account - Resources												
OPERATING SURPLUS, GROSS								6.7	11.1	10.9	13.5	
Property income								1.1	2.9	4.6	25.6	
II.1.2 Allocation of primary income account - Uses												
Property income								0.0	0.3	0.1	0.1	
BALANCE OF PRIMARY INCOMES								7.7	13.8	15.4	38.9	
II.2 Secondary distribution of income account - Resources												
BALANCE OF PRIMARY INCOMES								7.7	13.8	15.4	38.9	
Social contributions								0.3	0.4	0.4	0.4	
Other current transfers								352.6	277.3	319.9	339.2	
II.2 Secondary distribution of income account - Uses												
Current taxes on income, wealth, etc.								...	...	...	0.7	
Social benefits other than social transfers in kind								50.7	19.9	21.2	41.6	
Other current transfers								38.0	35.0	38.3	23.6	
GROSS DISPOSABLE INCOME								271.8	236.6	276.2	312.7	
II.4.1 Use of disposable income account - Resources												
GROSS DISPOSABLE INCOME								271.8	236.6	276.2	312.7	
II.4.1 Use of disposable income account - Uses												
Final consumption expenditure								216.7	217.0	225.7	234.1	
Individual consumption expenditure								...	...	...	...	
Adjustment for the change in net equity of households on pension funds								...	...	...	...	
SAVING, GROSS								55.1	19.6	50.5	78.6	
III.1 Capital account - Changes in liabilities and net worth												
SAVING, GROSS								55.1	19.6	50.5	78.6	
Capital transfers, receivable less payable								...	...	...	...	
Capital transfers, receivable								...	...	...	...	
Less: Capital transfers, payable								...	...	...	...	
Equals: CHANGES IN NET WORTH DUE TO SAVING AND CAPITAL TRANSFERS								55.1[a]	19.6[a]	41.2	67.6	

	2001	2002	2003	2004	2005	2006	2007	2008	2009	2010	2011	2012
Series								**400**				
	III.1 Capital account - Changes in assets											
Gross capital formation								16.6	6.0	6.4	14.1	
Gross fixed capital formation								16.6	6.0	6.4	14.1	
Changes in inventories								...	...	...	...	
Acquisitions less disposals of valuables								...	...	...	...	
Acquisitions less disposals of non-produced non-financial assets								...	...	...	...	
NET LENDING (+) / NET BORROWING (-)								38.5	13.6	44.1	64.5	

[a] Item does not consider consumption of fixed capital.

Table 5.1 Cross classification of Gross value added by industries and institutional sectors (ISIC Rev. 3) Non-financial corporations

Series 300: 1993 SNA, Russian ruble (re-denom. 1:1000), Western calendar year
Series 400: 1993 SNA, Russian ruble (re-denom. 1:1000), Western calendar year

Data in billions

	2001	2002	2003	2004	2005	2006	2007	2008	2009	2010	2011	2012
Series		**300**						**400**				
	Industries											
Agriculture, hunting, forestry; fishing		218.2	317.4	393.6	420.1	485.6	616.4	759.8				
								755.5	686.2	588.5	854.2	864.2
Mining and quarrying		649.6	783.8	1426.8	2084.4	2527.9	2864.4	3299.3				
								3284.4	2885.3	3842.6	5157.1	5801.1
Manufacturing		1607.7	1933.1	2648.6	3451.8	4190.8	4925.7	6063.2				
								6055.8	4921.5	5836.4	7300.9	8002.9
Electricity, gas and water supply		359.6	428.0	565.0	632.0	754.8	862.8	1034.4				
								1033.7	1388.4	1526.6	1813.9	1845.3
Construction		473.6	657.2	782.9	914.2	1122.4	1485.5	2028.6				
								2040.6	1905.4	2388.2	2866.8	3188.0
Wholesale and retail trade; repair of motor vehicles, motorcycles and personal and household goods; hotels and restaurants		1755.9	2093.1	2453.8	2911.0	3769.2	4701.3	6179.5				
								6152.0	4910.3	7024.5	8135.4	9254.4
Transport, storage and communications		944.6	1205.6	1605.5	1850.1	2180.4	2612.8	3024.5				
								3073.4	3040.8	3407.3	3681.2	4048.1
Financial intermediation; real estate renting and business activities		841.5	1055.4	1044.5	1361.7	1701.8	2409.0	3161.7				
								3157.4	3325.1	3662.8	4290.2	4787.4
Public administration and defence; compulsory social security		10.7	18.6	...	...	...	...	...				
								...	...	...	...	...
Education; health and social work; other community, social and personal services		198.2	248.1	322.0	395.0	503.4	626.1	743.2				
								758.4	736.1	694.0	746.7	835.2
Private households with employed persons		...	...	...	...	...	...	...				
								...	...	0.0	0.0	...
VALUE ADDED GROSS, at basic prices		7059.7	8740.3	11242.7	14020.3	17236.3	21104.0	26294.2				
								26311.2	23799.2	28970.9	34846.4	38626.6

Table 5.1 Cross classification of Gross value added by industries and institutional sectors (ISIC Rev. 3) Financial corporations

Series 300: 1993 SNA, Russian ruble (re-denom. 1:1000), Western calendar year
Series 400: 1993 SNA, Russian ruble (re-denom. 1:1000), Western calendar year

Data in billions

	2001	2002	2003	2004	2005	2006	2007	2008	2009	2010	2011	2012
Series		300						400				
Industries												
Agriculture, hunting, forestry; fishing		...	...	...	...	...	...	...				
								...	...	...	...	...
Mining and quarrying		...	...	...	...	...	...	...				
								...	...	...	...	...
Manufacturing		...	...	...	...	...	...	...				
								...	...	...	...	...
Electricity, gas and water supply		...	...	...	...	...	...	...				
								...	...	...	...	...
Construction		...	...	...	...	...	...	...				
								...	...	...	...	...
Wholesale and retail trade; repair of motor vehicles, motorcycles and personal and household goods; hotels and restaurants		...	...	...	...	...	...	...				
								...	...	...	...	...
Transport, storage and communications		...	...	...	...	...	...	...				
								...	...	...	...	...
Financial intermediation; real estate renting and business activities		297.4	399.0	511.4	759.0	1050.1	1253.8	1539.8				
								1537.8	1707.2	1754.5	1936.5	2308.1
Public administration and defence; compulsory social security		...	...	...	...	...	...	...				
								...	...	...	...	...
Education; health and social work; other community, social and personal services		...	...	...	...	...	...	...				
								...	...	...	...	...
Private households with employed persons		...	...	...	...	...	...	...				
								...	...	...	...	...
VALUE ADDED GROSS, at basic prices		297.4	399.0	511.4	759.0	1050.1	1253.8	1539.8				
								1537.8	1707.2	1754.5	1936.5	2308.1

Table 5.1 Cross classification of Gross value added by industries and institutional sectors (ISIC Rev. 3) General government

Series 300: 1993 SNA, Russian ruble (re-denom. 1:1000), Western calendar year
Series 400: 1993 SNA, Russian ruble (re-denom. 1:1000), Western calendar year

Data in billions

	2001	2002	2003	2004	2005	2006	2007	2008	2009	2010	2011	2012
Series		300						400				
Industries												
Agriculture, hunting, forestry; fishing		9.4	11.0	14.8	12.8	14.5	17.6	19.5				
								19.5	26.5	25.2	27.7	28.1
Mining and quarrying		...	...	...	...	...	...	...				
								...	...	...	...	...
Manufacturing		...	...	...	0.5	1.0	1.5	2.3				
								2.3	2.5	2.6	2.4	2.7
Electricity, gas and water supply		...	...	...	...	...	...	...				
								...	...	...	...	...
Construction		2.7	3.3	2.9	3.1	3.5	5.3	5.0				
								5.0	4.9	6.2	5.1	5.7
Wholesale and retail trade; repair of motor vehicles, motorcycles and personal and household goods; hotels and restaurants		...	...	...	...	...	...	...				
								...	...	2.3	2.7	2.9
Transport, storage and communications		...	...	...	4.7	5.2	5.3	8.3				
								8.3	18.7	23.6	24.9	28.9
Financial intermediation; real estate renting and business activities		54.6	68.7	82.0	86.1	114.4	123.3	140.2				
								140.2	147.7	182.8	199.6	185.7

	2001	2002	2003	2004	2005	2006	2007	2008	2009	2010	2011	2012
Series		**300**						**400**				
Public administration and defence; compulsory social security		478.1	632.7	802.5	959.1	1189.2	1466.4	1884.4				
								1884.4	2203.2	2423.5	2672.6	3520.8
Education; health and social work; other community, social and personal services		488.1	553.2	711.5	867.3	1159.0	1460.1	1855.8				
								1855.8	2159.6	2525.2	2990.3	3456.0
Private households with employed persons		...	...	...	...	...	...	...				
								...	...	...	...	...
VALUE ADDED GROSS, at basic prices		1033.0	1269.0	1613.7	1933.6	2486.9	3079.4	3915.5				
								3915.5	4563.0	5191.3	5925.3	7230.8

Table 5.1 Cross classification of Gross value added by industries and institutional sectors (ISIC Rev. 3) Households

Series 300: 1993 SNA, Russian ruble (re-denom. 1:1000), Western calendar year
Series 400: 1993 SNA, Russian ruble (re-denom. 1:1000), Western calendar year

Data in billions

	2001	2002	2003	2004	2005	2006	2007	2008	2009	2010	2011	2012
Series		**300**						**400**				
	Industries											
Agriculture, hunting, forestry; fishing		417.4	462.7	504.6	595.0	671.8	622.4	775.4				
								774.2	872.4	934.8	1190.6	1168.6
Mining and quarrying		1.0	1.2	0.2	0.5	0.7	1.1	0.2				
								0.2	0.1	0.2	0.3	0.3
Manufacturing		83.1	43.2	38.9	68.7	81.0	100.4	106.8				
								105.9	81.3	95.7	82.2	86.1
Electricity, gas and water supply		...	...	1.5	0.4	0.4	0.3	0.2				
								0.3	0.3	0.5	0.5	0.5
Construction		46.3	55.8	77.3	94.8	105.8	143.1	180.2				
								179.7	191.2	193.5	229.9	251.3
Wholesale and retail trade; repair of motor vehicles, motorcycles and personal and household goods; hotels and restaurants		536.4	586.7	724.2	902.8	1161.4	1322.7	1537.4				
								1335.6	1487.6	1392.0	1647.7	1764.4
Transport, storage and communications		49.1	56.0	56.5	70.3	98.2	134.0	177.4				
								176.6	190.1	231.5	265.4	273.5
Financial intermediation; real estate renting and business activities		131.2	130.9	291.6	399.3	493.7	569.4	676.9				
								660.6	727.9	1053.9	1146.9	1300.7
Public administration and defence; compulsory social security		...	...	...	...	...	...	...				
								...	...	...	...	...
Education; health and social work; other community, social and personal services		29.6	34.1	40.7	55.7	72.0	76.3	84.0				
								83.8	97.4	103.5	104.1	127.3
Private households with employed persons		...	...	...	...	...	...	...				
								...	...	0.0	0.0	0.0
VALUE ADDED GROSS, at basic prices		1294.1	1370.5	1735.7	2187.5	2684.9	2969.6	3538.5				
								3316.9	3648.3	4005.6	4667.6	4972.7

Table 5.1 Cross classification of Gross value added by industries and institutional sectors (ISIC Rev. 3) Non-profit institutions serving households

Series 300: 1993 SNA, Russian ruble (re-denom. 1:1000), Western calendar year
Series 400: 1993 SNA, Russian ruble (re-denom. 1:1000), Western calendar year

Data in billions

	2001	2002	2003	2004	2005	2006	2007	2008	2009	2010	2011	2012
Series		**300**						**400**				
	Industries											
Agriculture, hunting, forestry; fishing		...	...	...	...	...	...	...				
								...	...	...	...	...
Mining and quarrying		...	...	...	...	...	...	...				
								...	...	...	...	...
Manufacturing		...	...	...	...	...	...	...				
								...	...	...	...	...
Electricity, gas and water supply		...	...	...	...	...	...	...				
								...	...	...	...	...
Construction		...	...	...	...	...	...	...				
								...	...	...	...	...
Wholesale and retail trade; repair of motor vehicles, motorcycles and personal and household goods; hotels and restaurants		4.4	4.8	3.8	6.2	6.7	7.3	8.0				
								8.0	6.3	5.5	5.9	6.7
Transport, storage and communications		...	...	...	...	...	...	...				
								...	...	...	...	...
Financial intermediation; real estate renting and business activities		2.2	2.9	3.2	1.0	1.4	1.2	1.2				
								1.2	19.9	21.1	28.6	32.3
Public administration and defence; compulsory social security		...	...	...	...	...	...	...				
								...	...	...	...	...
Education; health and social work; other community, social and personal services		69.8	79.8	76.3	68.5	75.8	79.9	92.0				
								92.0	87.4	91.2	95.1	107.3
Private households with employed persons		...	...	...	...	...	...	...				
								...	...	...	...	...
VALUE ADDED GROSS, at basic prices		76.4	87.5	83.3	75.8	83.9	88.3	101.2				
								101.2	113.7	117.7	129.7	146.3

Table 5.1 Cross classification of Gross value added by industries and institutional sectors (ISIC Rev. 3) Total economy

Series 300: 1993 SNA, Russian ruble (re-denom. 1:1000), Western calendar year
Series 400: 1993 SNA, Russian ruble (re-denom. 1:1000), Western calendar year

Data in billions

	2001	2002	2003	2004	2005	2006	2007	2008	2009	2010	2011	2012
Series		**300**						**400**				
	Industries											
Agriculture, hunting, forestry; fishing		645.1	791.1	913.0	1027.9	1172.0	1256.4	1554.7				
								1549.3	1585.1	1548.5	2072.4	2060.9
Mining and quarrying		650.6	785.0	1426.9	2084.9	2528.6	2865.5	3299.5				
								3284.6	2885.4	3842.8	5157.3	5801.4
Manufacturing		1690.9	1976.3	2687.6	3521.0	4272.8	5027.6	6172.3				
								6163.9	5005.3	5934.7	7385.5	8091.7
Electricity, gas and water supply		359.6	428.0	566.5	632.5	755.2	863.1	1034.7				
								1034.0	1388.7	1527.1	1814.5	1845.8
Construction		522.6	716.2	863.1	1012.0	1231.8	1633.9	2213.8				
								2225.3	2101.5	2587.8	3101.8	3445.0
Wholesale and retail trade; repair of motor vehicles, motorcycles and personal and household goods; hotels and restaurants		2296.7	2684.6	3181.8	3820.0	4937.3	6031.2	7724.9				
								7495.7	6404.2	8424.2	9791.8	11028.4
Transport, storage and communications		993.7	1261.6	1662.0	1925.1	2283.8	2752.1	3210.2				
								3258.3	3249.6	3662.5	3971.5	4350.6
Financial intermediation; real estate renting and business activities		1327.0	1656.9	1932.7	2607.1	3361.3	4356.6	5519.8				
								5497.2	5927.8	6675.0	7601.8	8614.0

	2001	2002	2003	2004	2005	2006	2007	2008	2009	2010	2011	2012
Series		**300**						**400**				
Public administration and defence; compulsory social security		488.8	651.3	802.5	959.1	1189.2	1466.4	1884.4 1884.4	2203.2	2423.5	2672.6	3520.8
Education; health and social work; other community, social and personal services		785.7	915.2	1150.6	1386.5	1810.3	2242.4	2774.9 2790.0	3080.5	3413.9	3936.2	4525.9
Private households with employed persons		...	...	...	...	...	...	... ...	...	0.0	0.0	0.0
VALUE ADDED GROSS, at basic prices		9760.6[a]	11866.3[a]	15186.8[a]	18976.1[a]	23542.2[a]	28495.1[b]	35389.2[b] 35182.7	33831.3	40040.1	47505.5	53284.5

[a] Includes financial intermediation services indirectly measured (FISIM).

[b] Excludes financial intermediation services indirectly measured (FISIM) but FISIM is not distributed by uses. It is also excluded from tables by industry.

Rwanda

Source
Reply to the United Nations national accounts questionnaire from the National Institute of Statistics of Rwanda (NSIR). National accounts are estimated on an annual basis by the NSIR. From time to time, the estimation methodology is revised due to reasons that include, improvement in data sources and systems and changes in the national economic structure. In this regard the first benchmark of 2001 was done in 2003 and currently, the NSIR is in the process of rebasing the benchmark to 2006. The rebasing exercise is practically possible two years after the intended base year which in this case is 2006. This allows for the use of final approved data for 2006 base year and 2007 current year.

General
The estimates shown in the following tables have been prepared in accordance with the United Nations System of National Accounts 1993 (1993 SNA) so far as the existing data would permit. When the scope and coverage of the estimates differ for conceptual or statistical reasons from the definitions and classifications recommended in the SNA, a footnote provides explanation.

Methodology:

Overview of GDP Compilation
Due to technical reasons that include huge informal and non-monetary sectors (about 65% of the economy in 2006) and data availability among others, in Rwanda National Accounts are only compiled using the Production approach. On the other hand as far as the expenditure approach is concerned, it is only the final household expenditure that cannot be measured on a yearly basis. Hence, in this case it can then be calculated by subtracting as a balancing item from the production approach.

GDP and its components are evaluated quarterly at both current prices (for the levels) and constant 2006 prices (for measuring real growth rates). Annual estimates for calendar years and for years ending June (which from July 2009 are the government□ s fiscal years) are obtained by summing the relevant quarterly estimates.

GDP estimates of both the production and expenditure approaches are computed annually in Rwanda. National Accounts are estimated by economic activities which are classified according the International Standard Industrial Classification of all economic activities (ISIC). This is used along side the United Nations Central Product Classification (CPC) that is linked to the Harmonized System (HS) used for classifying international trade. All these are adapted to Rwanda's development level keeping their framework as much as possible.

Expenditure Approach
The expenditure approach aims to measure GDP (at market prices) by aggregating final consumption expenditures (by households, NGOs and government), capital formation, and exports less imports of goods and (non-factor) services. In Rwanda, except in a benchmark year (see below), no direct information is currently available on household expenditure on a regular basis, so it is not possible to prepare direct quarterly estimates of GDP according to the expenditure approach. Final expenditures by NGOs are also not covered at present.

Direct quarterly and annual estimates are also available for most of the expenditure components. HFCE is therefore calculated by subtraction as a balancing item. It therefore includes all the error and omissions that may have occurred since the base year.

It may be noted that while up-to-date estimates of Household Final Consumption Expenditure (HFCE) are obtained as a residual, the benchmark estimates are based on direct observations from the Integrated Living Conditions Surveys (EICV) and this plays a key role in establishing the benchmark level of GDP.

Production Approach

One of the benefits of the benchmark is that estimates can be made according to mode of production. This classification allows rough estimates to be made of informal activity, albeit indirectly, as a residual. Reliable direct estimates are very difficult to obtain, so the production approach provides a cost effective alternative.
Modes of production have been split into four groups: a) Formal private sector; b) Informal activity (monetary); c) Non-monetary production; and d) Government and NGOs

For practical reasons, the formal sector has been defined as businesses registered for VAT at the Rwanda Revenue Authority (agricultural activity is excluded, although registered agro-industries such as tea and coffee processing are included). The formal sector also includes the VAT and other taxes on products, whether collected on imports or on locally produced goods and services (classified under adjustments in the table).

Informal activity covers marketed production by all other private producers not registered for VAT. By definition, there are no regular, readily available sources of information on these producers, except in the case of major crop production (for which food security forecasts have been the main source). Most informal activity is not subject to tax.

Non-monetary production covers goods (mostly crops) and housing services that are consumed by the producer (auto-consumption). The proportions of production that are consumed by the producer were available from the EICV (Integrated Living Conditions Survey) and used to distinguish between monetary and non-monetary production in the benchmark exercise. These proportions are assumed to be constant between benchmarks.

The Government and NGO mode of production is assumed to be activity carried out in three branches, namely public administration, education and health.

Since 2001, when VAT was introduced in Rwanda, the total turnover of VAT registered traders by type of activity has been used both in the benchmark and to extrapolate the benchmark to estimate formal sector (defined as registered traders) activity. In several cases, this serves merely to split the overall estimates within a given activity (such as in the case of construction and commercial trade). In other cases, separate estimates are made for the informal sector only, and thus the VAT-based data contributes directly to the GDP, as well as indirectly through the use of production data to estimate trade and transport margins.

Quarterly production data are obtained from some of the largest enterprises, for example OCIR-Thé and OCIR-Café for tea and coffee production (both crops and manufacturing output). Other major producers covered include those producing beverages, tobacco, textiles, soap, cement, electricity and water, and telecommunications.

Table 1.1 Gross domestic product by expenditures at current prices

Series 100: 1993 SNA, Rwanda franc, Western calendar year — **Data in millions**

	2001	2002	2003	2004	2005	2006	2007	2008	2009	2010	2011	2012
Series	**100**											
	Expenditures of the gross domestic product											
Final consumption expenditure	757317.0	822793.0	1004569.0	1189676.0	1410995.0	1685998.0	1970061.0	2397557.0	2919897.0	3265786.0	3659239.0	4224702.0
Household final consumption expenditure	618589.0	666733.0	813889.0	968310.0	1149286.0	1374461.0	1632174.0	2019207.0	2465654.0	2742203.0	3090375.0	3559975.0
NPISHs final consumption expenditure	...	...	...	...	...	...	...	...	...	...	...	...
General government final consumption expenditure	138728.0	156061.0	190680.0	221366.0	261708.0	311537.0	337887.0	378350.0	454243.0	523583.0	568864.0	664726.0
Gross capital formation	101846.0	107530.0	137798.0	181108.0	227432.0	274663.0	368855.0	584524.0	643964.0	687767.0	817903.0	996969.0

	2001	2002	2003	2004	2005	2006	2007	2008	2009	2010	2011	2012
Series	**100**											
Gross fixed capital formation	101846.0	107530.3	137797.6	181108.2	227432.1	274664.8	369065.0	584523.9	643963.8	687766.6	817903.6	...
Changes in inventories	...	...	...	...	...	...	...	...	...	...	...	...
Acquisitions less disposals of valuables	...	...	...	...	...	...	...	...	...	...	...	...
Exports of goods and services	62824.0	56149.6	83901.6	134177.0	164526.0	189803.0	228269.0	372488.0	302548.0	329498.0	513701.0	574568.0
Exports of goods	41453.1	31735.0	33305.0	54825.0	67128.0	78540.0	96641.0	142842.0	108745.0	148518.0	255181.0	310497.0
Exports of services	21370.9	24415.2	50597.7	79351.9	97398.2	111262.0	131628.0	229645.0	193802.0	180980.0	258519.0	264070.0
Less: Imports of goods and services	180115.0	189024.0	233652.0	298691.0	363038.0	433987.0	522587.0	777963.0	881411.0	1003228.0	1176425.0	1432901.0
Imports of goods	102026.0	100469.0	124553.0	161816.0	204952.0	249729.0	323589.0	493292.0	584404.0	678671.0	805107.0	1011518.0
Imports of services	78088.9	88555.0	109099.0	136875.0	158086.0	184258.0	198998.0	284670.0	297007.0	324557.0	371317.0	421382.0
Equals: GROSS DOMESTIC PRODUCT	741872.0	797450.0	992618.0	1206269.0	1439915.0	1716476.0	2044598.0	2576606.0	2984998.0	3279823.0	3814419.0	4363338.0

Table 1.2 Gross domestic product by expenditures at constant prices

Series 100: 1993 SNA, Rwanda franc, Western calendar year **Data in millions**

	2001	2002	2003	2004	2005	2006	2007	2008	2009	2010	2011	2012
Series	**100**											
Base year	**2006**											
	Expenditures of the gross domestic product											
Final consumption expenditure	1168552.0	1324946.0	1276779.0	1365093.0	1487588.0	1685997.0	1799773.0	1885371.0	2139088.0	2320747.0	2444099.0	2600225.0
Household final consumption expenditure	988056.0	1118900.0	1039188.0	1103571.0	1201051.0	1374460.0	1484815.0	1563252.0	1779202.0	1923668.0	2029262.0	2122142.0
NPISHs final consumption expenditure	...	...	...	...	...	...	...	...	...	...	...	...
General government final consumption expenditure	186162.0	212247.0	237323.0	260037.0	284671.0	311537.0	315046.0	322250.0	360062.0	397079.0	414837.0	478083.0
Gross capital formation	149771.0	160723.0	177180.0	202528.0	233636.0	274662.0	344270.0	454798.0	466473.0	500519.0	560916.0	651496.0
Gross fixed capital formation	149771.0	160723.0	177180.0	202528.0	233636.0	274662.0	344270.0	454798.0	466473.0	500519.0	560916.0	651496.0
Changes in inventories	...	...	...	...	...	...	...	...	...	...	...	...
Acquisitions less disposals of valuables	...	...	...	...	...	...	...	...	...	...	...	...
Exports of goods and services	99352.0	104428.0	125819.0	165781.0	184290.0	189803.0	211992.0	296335.0	222244.0	234639.0	346513.0	465481.0
Exports of goods	73618.0	73367.0	59851.0	72081.0	78638.0	78540.0	91045.0	113728.0	83115.0	107734.0	174853.0	300594.0
Exports of services	31371.0	36290.0	67318.0	94303.0	106065.0	111262.0	120695.0	183039.0	139128.0	126905.0	171659.0	164887.0
Less: Imports of goods and services	258849.0	278889.0	243885.0	296159.0	334444.0	433987.0	508888.0	585290.0	644559.0	716533.0	819402.0	982985.0
Imports of goods	146625.0	148233.0	130008.0	160444.0	188809.0	249728.0	313516.0	369647.0	426869.0	485293.0	560525.0	694431.0
Imports of services	112224.0	130655.0	113877.0	135715.0	145634.0	184258.0	195316.0	215628.0	217690.0	231240.0	258877.0	288554.0
Equals: GROSS DOMESTIC PRODUCT	1155821.0	1308298.0	1337112.0	1436695.0	1571427.0	1716476.0	1847444.0	2053641.0	2181871.0	2339373.0	2532127.0	2734218.0

Table 2.1 Value added by industries at current prices (ISIC Rev. 3)

Series 100: 1993 SNA, Rwanda franc, Western calendar year — **Data in millions**

	2001	2002	2003	2004	2005	2006	2007	2008	2009	2010	2011	2012
Series	**100**											
Industries												
Agriculture, hunting, forestry; fishing	276986.0	282190.0	379786.0	465146.0	552755.0	659735.0	728806.0	834431.0	1012337.0	1057502.0	1222563.0	1437770.0
Agriculture, hunting, forestry	274135.0	278806.0	375844.0	460640.0	547521.0	653730.0	722148.0	825833.0	1002348.0	1046255.0	1209151.0	1422959.0
Agriculture, hunting and related service activities	263727.0	266123.0	360609.0	434498.0	512357.0	601732.0	669102.0	757052.0	928994.0	969224.0	1125261.0	1321584.0
Forestry, logging and related service activities	10408.0	12683.0	15235.0	26142.0	35164.0	51998.0	53046.0	68781.0	73354.0	77031.0	83890.0	101375.0
Fishing	2850.9	3383.8	3942.5	4505.8	5233.7	6004.9	6658.4	8598.2	9988.9	11247.4	13412.0	14811.0
Mining and quarrying	5640.8	2486.2	2610.0	8157.1	10046.1	10957.3	20726.3	24610.4	15696.9	21450.2	47959.6	39078.0
Manufacturing	51252.2	59703.1	67445.2	83697.4	101219.0	116698.0	124718.0	158653.0	190439.0	217788.0	252116.0	258789.0
Electricity, gas and water supply	3337.0	3401.8	2114.1	1385.6	2900.7	3376.4	7940.8	5304.7	6153.2	7141.5	8282.2	10471.0
Construction	44794.6	45339.4	55147.1	74168.5	88301.0	105123.0	131705.0	193410.0	218284.0	244341.0	316559.0	386665.0
Wholesale, retail trade, repair of motor vehicles, motorcycles and personal and households goods; hotels and restaurants	80496.0	92309.0	115576.0	146592.0	187315.0	232807.0	288594.0	413706.0	445916.0	500121.0	561733.0	643964.0
Wholesale, retail trade, repair of motor vehicles, motorcycles and personal and household goods	73599.0	82335.0	99899.0	125506.0	155524.0	192464.0	239926.0	355546.0	384930.0	432009.0	489439.0	563500.0
Hotels and restaurants	6897.0	9974.0	15677.0	21086.0	31791.0	40343.0	48668.0	58160.0	60986.0	68112.0	72294.0	80464.0
Transport, storage and communications	43130.0	52974.0	59505.0	73590.0	90156.0	116569.0	144690.0	196240.0	223314.0	256471.0	287619.0	344057.0
Financial intermediation; real estate, renting and business activities	94313.0	96701.0	118014.0	131186.0	145557.0	162371.0	229502.0	297995.0	345978.0	373008.0	405971.0	466833.0
Financial intermediation	22030.0	21928.0	29984.0	37257.0	41217.0	49137.0	58439.0	64142.0	63604.0	80405.0	99975.0	130171.0
Real estate, renting and business activities	72283.0	74773.0	88030.0	93929.0	104340.0	113234.0	171063.0	233853.0	282374.0	292603.0	305996.0	336662.0
Public administration and defence; compulsory social security	54977.0	55710.0	63264.0	68498.0	74621.0	86566.0	97293.0	111709.0	128395.0	150901.0	181047.0	212810.0
Education; health and social work; other community, social and personal services	44471.0	54006.0	64555.0	76805.0	98116.0	121940.0	151246.0	176620.0	213777.0	251613.0	295058.0	297605.0
Education	25590.0	32104.0	35394.0	42772.0	58881.0	76059.0	94599.0	110323.0	139610.0	167362.0	207843.0	202596.0
Health and social work	12735.0	14329.0	18899.0	21197.0	20898.0	22831.0	29676.0	36291.0	43833.0	51431.0	52852.0	58988.0
Other community, social and personal services	6146.0	7573.0	10262.0	12836.0	18337.0	23050.0	26971.0	30006.0	30334.0	32820.0	34363.0	36021.0
Private households with employed persons	...	...	...	...	...	...	...	...	...	...	...	...
Equals: VALUE ADDED, GROSS, in basic prices	699396.0	744821.0	928018.0	1129227.0	1350988.0	1616141.0	1925224.0	2412678.0	2800292.0	3080336.0	3578908.0	4098039.0
Less: Financial intermediation services indirectly measured (FISIM)	12526.0	11173.0	13698.0	17126.0	19329.0	23590.0	31293.0	40007.0	40985.0	49610.0	69470.0	85942.0
Plus: Taxes less Subsidies on products	55002.0	63802.0	78298.0	94168.0	108256.0	123925.0	150667.0	203935.0	225691.0	249097.0	304981.0	351242.0
Equals: GROSS DOMESTIC PRODUCT	741872.0	797450.0	992618.0	1206269.0	1439915.0	1716476.0	2044598.0	2576606.0	2984998.0	3279823.0	3814419.0	4363339.0

Table 2.2 Value added by industries at constant prices (ISIC Rev. 3)

Series 100: 1993 SNA, Rwanda franc, Western calendar year **Data in millions**

	2001	2002	2003	2004	2005	2006	2007	2008	2009	2010	2011	2012
Series	**100**											
Base year	**2006**											
	Industries											
Agriculture, hunting, forestry; fishing	522607.0	610903.0	592163.0	602884.0	641987.0	659735.0	676905.0	720556.0	776217.0	814909.0	853078.0	878839.0
Agriculture, hunting, forestry	517326.0	605485.0	586604.0	597180.0	636135.0	653730.0	670737.0	714219.0	769707.0	808221.0	846207.0	871779.0
Agriculture, hunting and related service activities	483111.0	568018.0	545738.0	552764.0	588013.0	601732.0	617039.0	658534.0	712669.0	749381.0	785852.0	809036.0
Forestry, logging and related service activities	34215.0	37467.0	40866.0	44416.0	48122.0	51997.5	53698.0	55685.0	57038.0	58840.0	60355.0	62743.0
Fishing	5281.0	5418.0	5559.0	5704.0	5852.0	6004.9	6168.0	6337.0	6510.0	6688.0	6871.0	7060.0
Mining and quarrying	10804.0	8191.0	6514.0	9745.0	12710.0	10957.3	15648.0	13185.0	10826.0	9660.0	14462.0	13050.0
Manufacturing	70223.0	80870.0	84512.0	94914.0	102943.0	116698.0	117610.0	124154.0	127826.0	139715.0	151053.0	146597.0
Electricity, gas and water supply	7222.0	7135.0	6467.0	4368.0	3882.0	3376.4	3547.0	4189.0	4801.0	5534.0	6375.0	7452.0
Construction	63958.0	65615.0	70995.0	85201.0	92931.0	105123.0	120819.0	154844.0	156910.0	170686.0	211028.0	243443.0
Wholesale, retail trade, repair of motor vehicles, motorcycles and personal and household goods; hotels and restaurants	119041.0	138188.0	146786.0	167809.0	195632.0	232806.0	262489.0	307684.0	315722.0	341974.0	373925.0	417505.0
Wholesale, retail trade, repair of motor vehicles, motorcycles and personal and household goods	110355.0	125547.0	127740.0	143760.0	162792.0	192464.0	220850.0	263734.0	274316.0	297287.0	327493.0	367574.0
Hotels and restaurants	8686.0	12641.0	19046.0	24049.0	32840.0	40342.6	41639.0	43950.0	41406.0	44687.0	46432.0	49931.0
Transport, storage and communications	55088.0	64766.0	68826.0	81441.0	95124.0	116569.0	134069.0	166015.0	181280.0	197138.0	207508.0	247601.0
Financial intermediation, real estate, renting and business activities	123319.0	126682.0	138629.0	144671.0	153431.0	162353.0	180146.0	200529.0	210110.0	224266.0	237382.0	266028.0
Financial intermediation	34795.0	33958.0	40917.0	44277.0	44885.0	49137.0	54855.0	55822.0	53522.0	66148.0	79555.0	93461.0
Real estate, renting and business activities	88524.0	92724.0	97712.0	100394.0	108546.0	113216.0	125291.0	144707.0	156588.0	158118.0	157827.0	172567.0
Public administration and defence; compulsory social security	72218.0	72544.0	76798.0	77305.0	79259.0	86566.0	91789.0	96290.0	103330.0	118259.0	135690.0	152158.0
Education; health and social work; other community, social and personal services	61307.0	79708.0	83127.0	96538.0	111803.0	121941.0	139662.0	149396.0	166833.0	183123.0	204781.0	217781.0
Education	38172.0	53203.0	50524.0	60310.0	71375.0	76059.0	87288.0	93350.0	107812.0	117060.0	138078.0	146780.0
Health and social work	15420.0	16821.0	20208.0	21858.0	21131.0	22831.0	26094.0	29207.0	33607.0	38876.0	39700.0	43709.0
Other community, social and personal services	7715.0	9684.0	12395.0	14370.0	19297.0	23050.4	26280.0	26839.0	25414.0	27187.0	27003.0	27292.0
Private households with employed persons	...	...	...	...	...	...	...	...	...	...	...	...
Equals: VALUE ADDED, GROSS, in basic prices	1080592.0	1221122.0	1252454.0	1349842.0	1478379.0	1616092.0	1742686.0	1936840.0	2053854.0	2205266.0	2395282.0	2590454.0
Less: Financial intermediation services indirectly measured (FISIM)	18388.0	16608.0	18225.0	20353.0	21049.0	23590.0	28624.0	31468.0	29511.0	34790.0	45970.0	53641.0
Plus: Taxes less Subsidies on products	93729.0	103158.0	102612.0	107195.0	113964.0	123923.0	133382.0	148269.0	157527.0	168899.0	182815.0	197406.0
Equals: GROSS DOMESTIC PRODUCT	1155821.0	1308298.0	1337112.0	1436695.0	1571427.0	1716424.0	1847444.0	2053641.0	2181871.0	2339374.0	2532127.0	2734219.0

Saint Kitts and Nevis

Source

Reply to the United Nations national accounts questionnaire from the Ministry of Finance, St. Kitts-Nevis. Latest revisions were as published by the Statistics Division, Planning Unit, Ministry of Finance, Technology and Sustainable Development of St. Kitts and Nevis.

General

The estimates shown in the following tables have been prepared in accordance with the United Nations System of National Accounts 1993 (1993 SNA) so far as the existing data would permit. When the scope and coverage of the estimates differ for conceptual or statistical reasons from the definitions and classifications recommended in the SNA, a footnote provides explanation.

Table 1.1 Gross domestic product by expenditures at current prices

Series 100: 1993 SNA, EC dollar, Western calendar year — **Data in millions**

	2001	2002	2003	2004	2005	2006	2007	2008	2009	2010	2011	2012
Series	**100**											
Expenditures of the gross domestic product												
Final consumption expenditure	860.7	894.0	887.0	980.3	1067.0	1309.9	1415.0	1850.8	1764.7	1811.2	1820.0	1762.8
Household final consumption expenditure	726.5	769.6	771.2	836.0	912.5	1157.3	1244.7	1646.9	1556.7	1604.2	1608.1	1550.9
NPISHs final consumption expenditure	...	...	...	...	...	...	...	...	...	...	...	...
General government final consumption expenditure	134.2	124.4	115.9	144.3	154.6	152.6	170.2	204.0	207.9	207.0	211.9	211.9
Individual consumption expenditure	...	...	...	...	...	...	...	...	...	...	...	...
Collective consumption expenditure	134.2	124.4	115.9	144.3	154.6	152.6	170.2	204.0	207.9	207.0	211.9	211.9
Gross capital formation	730.2	722.8	572.3	570.7	619.4	726.4	831.0	807.0	776.3	638.7	581.8	546.3
Gross fixed capital formation	730.2	722.8	572.3	570.7	619.4	726.4	831.0	807.0	776.3	638.7	581.8	546.3
Changes in inventories	...	...	...	...	...	...	...	...	...	...	...	...
Acquisitions less disposals of valuables	...	...	...	...	...	...	...	...	...	...	...	...
Exports of goods and services	413.9	446.0	536.1	523.7	612.0	636.4	629.2	633.7	471.9	562.0	668.5	670.8
Exports of goods	170.2	154.7	153.6	158.7	171.5	157.4	155.5	186.2	101.6	156.9	183.8	179.4
Exports of services	243.7	291.3	382.5	364.9	440.5	479.0	473.6	447.4	370.3	405.1	484.7	491.4
Less: Imports of goods and services	757.3	755.3	731.7	711.7	824.5	946.7	1024.5	1294.7	1086.4	1076.0	1041.5	915.7
Imports of goods	544.9	538.9	509.3	493.4	568.3	673.7	745.4	957.0	815.2	775.3	734.3	613.9
Imports of services	212.5	216.4	222.4	218.2	256.3	273.0	279.1	337.7	271.2	300.7	307.2	301.8
Equals: GROSS DOMESTIC PRODUCT	1247.4	1307.4	1263.7	1363.0	1473.8	1726.0	1850.6	1996.7	1926.5	1935.9	2028.7	2064.2

Table 1.3 Relations among product, income, savings, and net lending aggregates

Series 100: 1993 SNA, EC dollar, Western calendar year **Data in millions**

	2001	2002	2003	2004	2005	2006	2007	2008	2009	2010	2011	2012
Series	**100**											
GROSS DOMESTIC PRODUCT	1247.4	1307.4	1263.7	1363.0	1473.8	1726.0	1850.6	1996.7	1926.5	1935.9	2028.7	2064.2
Plus: Compensation of employees - from and to the rest of the world, net	-7.3	-7.4	-8.9	-7.7	-6.3	-2.2	-1.4	-1.5	-1.5	-1.1	-0.1	-0.1
Plus: Compensation of employees - from the rest of the world	2.6	1.2	0.8	0.6	0.8	0.7	0.8	0.6	0.6	0.6	1.0	1.0
Less: Compensation of employees - to the rest of the world	9.8	8.6	9.7	8.4	7.1	2.9	2.1	2.1	2.1	1.7	1.1	1.1
Plus: Property income - from and to the rest of the world, net	-86.1	-95.4	-109.2	-97.3	-88.5	-85.2	-82.2	-90.7	-90.1	-77.7	-79.0	-70.9
Plus: Property income - from the rest of the world	10.0	13.7	14.6	19.8	28.1	35.2	39.0	26.4	27.7	20.2	16.3	15.8
Less: Property income - to the rest of the world	96.2	109.0	123.8	117.1	116.6	120.3	121.2	117.1	117.8	97.9	95.3	86.6
Sum of Compensation of employees and property income - from and to the rest of the world, net	-93.4	-102.8	-118.1	-105.0	-94.9	-87.3	-83.6	-92.2	-91.5	-78.8	-79.1	-71.0
Plus: Sum of Compensation of employees and property income - from the rest of the world	12.6	14.9	15.3	20.4	28.8	35.9	39.8	27.0	28.3	20.8	17.2	16.8
Less: Sum of Compensation of employees and property income - to the rest of the world	106.0	117.7	133.5	125.5	123.7	123.2	123.3	119.2	119.9	99.6	96.4	87.8
Plus: Taxes less subsidies on production and imports - from and to the rest of the world, net	...	...	...	...	...	...	...	...	...	...	...	...
Equals: GROSS NATIONAL INCOME	1154.1	1204.6	1145.6	1258.0	1379.0	1638.7	1767.0	1904.6	1834.9	1857.1	1949.6	1993.2
Plus: Current transfers - from and to the rest of the world, net	43.4	44.4	50.2	0.0	64.5	87.0	84.3	89.4	121.9	125.6	125.8	114.7
Plus: Current transfers - from the rest of the world	71.9	76.5	81.0	84.0	99.3	121.2	118.5	137.9	164.1	173.0	183.2	173.7
Less: Current transfers - to the rest of the world	28.5	32.1	30.8	84.0	34.8	34.2	34.2	48.5	42.2	47.4	57.4	59.0
Equals: GROSS NATIONAL DISPOSABLE INCOME	1197.4	1249.0	1195.8	1258.0	1443.5	1725.7	1851.3	1994.0	1956.9	1982.7	2075.4	2107.9
Less: Final consumption expenditure / Actual final consumption	860.7	894.0	887.0	980.3	1067.0	1309.9	1415.0	1850.8	1764.7	1811.2	1820.0	1762.8
Equals: SAVING, GROSS	336.7	355.0	308.7	277.7	376.4	415.8	436.3	143.2	192.2	171.5	255.4	345.1
Plus: Capital transfers - from and to the rest of the world, net	29.4	38.9	14.0	14.5	39.8	35.7	54.9	91.6	69.6	162.5	183.9	169.3
Plus: Capital transfers - from the rest of the world	29.9	39.4	14.5	15.0	40.4	36.3	55.5	92.3	70.3	163.2	184.7	170.1
Less: Capital transfers - to the rest of the world	0.5	0.5	0.5	0.5	0.6	0.6	0.7	0.7	0.7	0.7	0.8	0.8
Less: Gross capital formation	730.2	722.8	572.3	570.7	619.4	726.4	831.0	807.0	776.3	638.7	581.8	546.3
Less: Acquisitions less disposals of non-produced non-financial assets	0.0	-0.5	-0.5	0.0	0.0	-0.2	0.0	0.0	0.0	0.0	0.0	0.0
Equals: NET LENDING (+) / NET BORROWING (-) OF THE NATION	-364.0	-328.4	-249.0	-278.5	-203.2	-274.7	-339.8	-572.2	-514.5	-304.7	-142.5	-31.9
Net values: Gross National Income / Gross National Disposable Income / Saving Gross less Consumption of fixed capital												
Less: Consumption of fixed capital	...	...	...	...	...	...	...	...	...	...	...	...
Equals: NET NATIONAL INCOME	...	...	...	...	...	...	...	...	...	...	...	...

	2001	2002	2003	2004	2005	2006	2007	2008	2009	2010	2011	2012
Series	**100**											
Equals: NET NATIONAL DISPOSABLE INCOME	...	...	...	...	...	...	...	...	...	...	...	...
Equals: SAVING, NET	...	...	...	...	...	...	...	...	...	...	...	...

Table 2.1 Value added by industries at current prices (ISIC Rev. 3)

Series 100: 1993 SNA, EC dollar, Western calendar year — **Data in millions**

	2001	2002	2003	2004	2005	2006	2007	2008	2009	2010	2011	2012
Series	**100**											
Industries												
Agriculture, hunting, forestry; fishing	21.5	23.2	22.6	24.4	24.5	20.7	21.5	25.7	23.5	26.7	29.2	27.4
Agriculture, hunting, forestry	15.7	16.8	15.5	16.7	15.5	13.2	14.0	16.9	15.9	18.8	19.5	17.8
Agriculture, hunting and related service activities	15.2	16.3	15.0	16.2	15.0	12.7	13.5	16.3	15.3	18.2	19.0	17.2
Forestry, logging and related service activities	0.5	0.5	0.5	0.5	0.5	0.5	0.5	0.6	0.6	0.6	0.6	0.6
Fishing	5.8	6.4	7.1	7.7	9.0	7.4	7.5	8.8	7.6	7.9	9.7	9.7
Mining and quarrying	3.0	3.6	2.4	2.6	2.7	3.1	2.7	2.1	3.1	2.2	1.4	1.4
Manufacturing	82.5	74.4	84.9	89.1	94.5	102.5	111.1	120.3	150.6	173.8	167.6	182.8
Electricity, gas and water supply	21.4	24.7	22.7	21.0	21.6	22.2	26.5	23.7	25.4	26.1	26.0	24.9
Construction	271.2	268.7	198.7	198.1	209.8	275.0	320.3	319.2	277.6	235.2	223.6	210.5
Wholesale, retail trade, repair of motor vehicles, motorcycles and personal and households goods; hotels and restaurants	133.5	141.8	160.0	187.6	211.6	235.1	240.6	264.4	224.1	229.6	225.7	220.1
Wholesale, retail trade, repair of motor vehicles, motorcycles and personal and household goods	78.3	88.8	90.1	96.2	104.2	113.2	124.1	144.9	138.9	138.9	130.3	123.3
Hotels and restaurants	55.1	53.0	69.9	91.4	107.4	121.9	116.5	119.5	85.2	90.7	95.4	96.8
Transport, storage and communications	110.0	119.8	124.4	123.2	118.7	153.9	180.7	196.0	184.4	202.7	225.1	221.1
Land transport; transport via pipelines, water transport; air transport; Supporting and auxiliary transport activities; activities of travel agencies	53.7	53.8	57.2	65.0	63.4	83.6	97.3	122.8	105.3	116.9	137.9	131.1
Post and telecommunications	56.3	66.1	67.3	58.2	55.2	70.3	83.4	73.2	79.1	85.8	87.2	90.0
Financial intermediation; real estate, renting and business activities	307.7	328.0	301.2	332.0	369.5	427.3	458.1	482.2	492.0	496.5	491.7	504.8
Financial intermediation	142.2	150.9	123.0	140.5	164.9	202.6	216.6	213.5	207.8	206.2	205.4	214.0
Real estate, renting and business activities	165.5	177.1	178.2	191.5	204.6	224.7	241.5	268.7	284.2	290.3	286.2	290.8
Public administration and defence; compulsory social security	85.3	90.3	90.6	103.2	109.7	114.2	122.8	139.2	148.3	147.4	163.5	165.8
Education; health and social work; other community, social and personal services	98.0	102.9	106.6	117.5	123.4	136.6	154.6	169.5	179.3	177.7	180.6	181.1
Education	42.7	45.3	46.7	53.2	57.5	63.0	72.3	80.5	85.7	90.5	90.1	92.3
Health and social work	27.9	29.2	29.6	32.3	33.2	37.2	40.9	44.1	46.7	43.6	45.1	46.0
Other community, social and personal services	27.5	28.5	30.2	32.0	32.7	36.4	41.3	44.8	47.0	43.6	45.4	42.9
Private households with employed persons	4.9	4.9	4.4	4.6	5.3	5.3	5.4	6.0	5.9	5.3	5.6	5.1
Equals: VALUE ADDED, GROSS, in basic prices [a]	1138.9	1182.2	1118.4	1203.2	1291.4	1495.9	1644.5	1748.2	1714.3	1723.3	1739.9	1744.8

	2001	2002	2003	2004	2005	2006	2007	2008	2009	2010	2011	2012
Series	**100**											
Less: Financial intermediation services indirectly measured (FISIM)	23.2	20.3	19.1	24.0	22.9	28.1	31.1	27.8	24.5	22.8	23.9	25.0
Plus: Taxes less Subsidies on products	131.7	145.5	164.4	183.9	205.3	258.2	237.2	276.3	236.7	235.3	312.7	344.3
Plus: Taxes on products	132.5	145.6	164.5	196.5	237.5	267.2	265.4	278.9	238.8	235.3	312.7	344.3
Less: Subsidies on products	0.8	0.1	0.2	12.6	32.2	9.0	28.1	2.6	2.1	0.0	0.0	0.0
Equals: GROSS DOMESTIC PRODUCT	1247.4	1307.4	1263.7	1363.0	1473.8	1726.0	1850.6	1996.7	1926.5	1935.9	2028.7	2064.2

[a] Includes financial intermediation services indirectly measured (FISIM).

Table 2.2 Value added by industries at constant prices (ISIC Rev. 3)

Series 100: 1993 SNA, EC dollar, Western calendar year **Data in millions**

	2001	2002	2003	2004	2005	2006	2007	2008	2009	2010	2011	2012
Series	**100**											
Base year	**2006**											
Industries												
Agriculture, hunting, forestry; fishing	20.9	25.8	26.3	30.1	31.8	20.7	21.3	22.6	20.2	20.7	23.0	21.3
Agriculture, hunting, forestry	14.1	18.1	18.2	20.8	22.6	13.2	14.0	14.5	13.2	13.7	13.8	12.4
Agriculture, hunting and related service activities	13.6	17.5	17.6	20.2	22.1	12.7	13.5	14.1	12.9	13.4	13.5	12.0
Forestry, logging and related service activities	0.5	0.5	0.6	0.6	0.5	0.5	0.5	0.4	0.3	0.3	0.3	0.4
Fishing	6.8	7.8	8.1	9.3	9.2	7.4	7.3	8.1	6.9	6.9	9.2	8.9
Mining and quarrying	3.9	4.6	2.5	2.8	2.9	3.1	2.7	1.9	2.9	2.2	1.4	1.3
Manufacturing	122.0	92.2	100.6	108.5	117.1	102.5	108.8	119.9	117.4	107.3	91.0	98.3
Electricity, gas and water supply	17.7	18.5	18.9	19.9	20.4	22.2	22.3	22.9	24.4	24.0	27.0	25.3
Construction	297.4	310.4	236.5	214.4	228.7	275.0	315.5	303.1	249.0	216.4	207.0	192.9
Wholesale, retail trade, repair of motor vehicles, motorcycles and personal and household goods; hotels and restaurants	168.0	166.7	184.3	212.1	236.6	235.1	217.6	233.7	196.3	200.0	186.2	180.3
Wholesale, retail trade, repair of motor vehicles, motorcycles and personal and household goods	104.6	105.4	104.4	108.8	113.5	113.2	109.7	121.8	114.3	113.7	99.5	93.3
Hotels and restaurants	63.5	61.2	79.9	103.3	123.1	121.9	107.9	111.9	81.9	86.3	86.6	87.0
Transport, storage and communications	114.7	119.8	118.7	132.2	148.1	153.9	168.5	185.3	188.5	202.2	207.9	203.8
Land transport; transport via piplines, water transport; air transport; Supporting and auxiliary transport activities; activities of travel agencies	70.7	70.1	69.2	80.1	85.9	83.6	90.5	101.7	97.7	103.3	107.4	101.0
Post and telecommunications	44.0	49.7	49.5	52.1	62.2	70.3	77.9	83.7	90.8	99.0	100.6	102.8
Financial intermediation, real estate, renting and business activities	355.0	376.7	372.6	379.7	402.2	427.3	443.3	453.4	462.4	496.4	485.2	494.0
Financial intermediation	164.3	169.3	172.6	172.1	184.0	202.6	203.5	199.3	201.0	226.9	223.5	230.5
Real estate, renting and business activities	190.7	207.3	200.0	207.6	218.2	224.7	239.8	254.1	261.4	269.5	261.8	263.5
Public administration and defence; compulsory social security	93.9	99.4	99.7	103.2	109.7	114.2	117.0	123.9	132.0	131.2	145.6	146.1
Education; health and social work; other community, social and personal services	107.5	111.3	113.9	118.0	124.9	136.6	146.0	153.3	160.9	156.1	155.2	154.2

		2001	2002	2003	2004	2005	2006	2007	2008	2009	2010	2011	2012
Series		**100**											
Base year		**2006**											
Education		47.0	49.8	51.4	54.2	58.9	63.0	68.3	72.1	76.2	77.9	76.8	77.7
Health and social work		32.2	32.5	32.6	32.9	33.9	37.2	39.0	39.9	41.5	38.5	39.4	39.7
Other community, social and personal services		28.3	29.0	29.9	30.9	32.1	36.4	38.7	41.4	43.1	39.6	39.1	36.7
Private households with employed persons		5.5	5.5	4.6	5.3	5.6	5.3	5.3	5.2	5.1	4.8	5.2	4.7
Equals: VALUE ADDED, GROSS, in basic prices	a	1306.5	1331.0	1278.6	1326.1	1427.9	1495.9	1568.3	1625.2	1559.0	1561.3	1534.7	1522.2
Less: Financial intermediation services indirectly measured (FISIM)		22.8	23.4	27.5	31.8	25.4	28.1	29.4	26.1	27.3	28.8	30.6	31.7
Plus: Taxes less Subsidies on products	b	151.0	162.2	187.0	202.3	230.2	258.2	222.6	252.8	216.7	215.1	214.4	...
Plus: Taxes on products	b	151.9	162.3	187.2	216.2	266.3	267.2	249.0	255.2	218.6	215.1	214.4	...
Less: Subsidies on products	b	0.9	0.1	0.2	13.9	36.1	9.0	26.4	2.4	1.9	0.0	0.0	...
Equals: GROSS DOMESTIC PRODUCT	b	1410.5	1437.5	1416.4	1478.3	1624.5	1700.7	1737.0	1827.8	1703.8	1662.2	1661.4	...

[a] Includes financial intermediation services indirectly measured (FISIM).
[b] Data for this year(s) have not been revised.

Table 2.3 Output, gross value added, and fixed assets by industries at current prices (ISIC Rev. 3) Total Economy

Series 100: 1993 SNA, EC dollar, Western calendar year — **Data in millions**

		2001	2002	2003	2004	2005	2006	2007	2008	2009	2010	2011	2012
Series		**100**											
Output, at basic prices		1941.2	1975.8	1859.6	1999.6	2175.5	2509.5	2735.6	2984.8	2853.1	2879.2	2875.8	2894.9
Less: Intermediate consumption, at purchaser's prices	a	825.5	813.9	760.3	820.4	907.0	1041.7	1122.2	1264.4	1163.4	1186.4	1159.7	1150.1
Equals: VALUE ADDED, GROSS, at basic prices	a	1138.9	1182.2	1118.4	1203.2	1291.4	1495.9	1644.5	1748.2	1714.3	1723.3	1739.9	1744.8
Compensation of employees		...	...	...	...	...	...	...	...	...	...	...	...
Taxes on production and imports, less Subsidies		...	...	...	...	...	...	...	...	...	...	...	...
OPERATING SURPLUS, GROSS		...	...	...	...	...	...	...	...	...	...	...	...
MIXED INCOME, GROSS		...	...	...	...	...	...	...	...	...	...	...	...
Total Economy only: Adjustment for FISIM (if FISIM is not distributed to uses)		23.2	20.3	19.1	24.0	22.9	28.1	31.1	27.8	24.5	22.8	23.9	25.0
Gross capital formation		730.2	722.8	572.3	570.7	619.4	726.4	831.0	807.0	776.3	638.7	581.8	546.3
Gross fixed capital formation		730.2	722.8	572.3	570.7	619.4	726.4	831.0	807.0	776.3	638.7	581.8	546.3
Changes in inventories		...	...	...	...	...	...	...	...	...	...	...	...
Acquisitions less disposals of valuables		...	...	...	...	...	...	...	...	...	...	...	...
Employment (average, in 1000 persons)		22.0	26.6	27.2	27.7	30.3	29.5	29.5	31.0	30.8	30.6	29.1	19.8

[a] Includes financial intermediation services indirectly measured (FISIM).

Saint Lucia

Source

The estimates were published in "Economic Survey and Projections", by the British Development Division in the Caribbean. Reply to the United Nations national accounts questionnaire by the British Development Division.

General

The estimates shown in the following tables have been prepared in accordance with the United Nations System of National Accounts 1993 (1993 SNA) so far as the existing data would permit. When the scope and coverage of the estimates differ for conceptual or statistical reasons from the definitions and classifications recommended in the SNA, a footnote provides explanation.

Table 1.1 Gross domestic product by expenditures at current prices

Series 100: 1993 SNA, EC dollar, Western calendar year — **Data in millions**

	2001	2002	2003	2004	2005	2006	2007	2008	2009	2010	2011	2012
Series	**100**											
	Expenditures of the gross domestic product											
Final consumption expenditure	1722.8	1790.4	1995.0	1876.0	1989.0	2478.8	2974.8	2938.0	2546.2	2922.6	3188.6	3130.2
Household final consumption expenditure	1407.7	1494.2	1670.3	1562.0	1675.5	2115.4	2602.1	2524.1	2107.4	2446.6	2703.8	2617.3
NPISHs final consumption expenditure	...	...	...	...	...	...	...	...	...	...	...	...
General government final consumption expenditure	315.1	296.2	324.7	314.0	313.5	363.4	372.7	413.9	438.9	476.0	484.7	512.9
Gross capital formation	472.4	433.3	476.0	591.7	728.4	1088.1	902.2	1026.1	920.5	940.9	980.8	931.2
Gross fixed capital formation	472.4	433.3	476.0	591.7	728.4	1088.1	902.2	1026.1	920.5	940.9	980.8	931.2
Changes in inventories	...	...	...	...	...	...	...	...	...	...	...	...
Acquisitions less disposals of valuables	...	...	...	...	...	...	...	...	...	...	...	...
Exports of goods and services	885.1	861.8	1053.3	1253.4	1417.3	1188.6	1234.2	1447.4	1468.7	1644.0	1544.8	1589.6
Exports of goods	738.5	674.7	859.5	993.4	1177.6	927.6	961.0	981.7	952.1	999.0	1027.8	1076.3
Exports of services	146.5	187.2	193.9	260.1	239.7	261.0	273.3	465.7	516.6	645.0	517.0	513.3
Less: Imports of goods and services	1087.3	1082.6	1349.2	1350.8	1606.1	1908.1	2017.9	2214.8	1749.5	2126.1	2214.5	2097.8
Imports of goods	734.6	734.1	957.2	939.6	1128.9	1406.6	1462.6	1633.0	1236.5	1574.1	1662.5	1564.2
Imports of services	352.7	348.5	392.1	411.2	477.2	501.4	555.4	581.7	513.0	552.0	552.0	533.6
Equals: GROSS DOMESTIC PRODUCT	1992.9	2003.0	2175.1	2370.3	2528.6	2847.4	3093.3	3196.7	3185.9	3381.4	3499.7	3559.5

Table 1.2 Gross domestic product by expenditures at constant prices

Series 20: 1968 SNA, EC dollar, Western calendar year — **Data in millions**

	2001	2002	2003	2004	2005	2006	2007	2008	2009	2010	2011	2012
Series	**20**											
Base year	**1990**											
	Expenditures of the gross domestic product											
Final consumption expenditure	1006.4	1107.2	1360.4	1298.2	1313.7	1286.8	1522.7					
Household final consumption expenditure	758.5	834.2	1075.8	1019.4	1029.3	1021.7	1128.5					
NPISHs final consumption expenditure	...	...	...	...	...	...	...					
General government final consumption expenditure	248.0	272.9	284.6	278.8	284.4	265.1	394.2					
Gross capital formation	416.0	372.9	358.1	397.3	483.8	639.2	615.7					
Gross fixed capital formation	416.0	372.9	358.1	397.3	483.8	639.2	615.7					
Changes in inventories	...	...	...	...	...	...	...					
Acquisitions less disposals of valuables	...	...	...	...	...	...	...					
Exports of goods and services	973.8	1002.3	1033.2	1081.6	1119.5	1069.1	989.8					
Less: Imports of goods and services	1034.7	1084.1	1288.6	1246.1	1291.0	1311.7	1412.0					
Equals: GROSS DOMESTIC PRODUCT	1361.5	1398.0	1463.2	1531.0	1625.9	1683.4	1716.1					

Table 1.3 Relations among product, income, savings, and net lending aggregates

Series 100: 1993 SNA, EC dollar, Western calendar year — **Data in millions**

	2001	2002	2003	2004	2005	2006	2007	2008	2009	2010	2011	2012
Series	**100**											
GROSS DOMESTIC PRODUCT	1992.9	2003.0	2175.1	2370.3	2528.6	2847.4	3093.3	3196.7	3185.9	3381.4	3499.7	3559.5
Plus: Compensation of employees - from and to the rest of the world, net	...	...	...	...	...	...	...	...	...	...	...	...
Plus: Property income - from and to the rest of the world, net	...	...	...	...	...	...	...	...	...	...	...	...
Sum of Compensation of employees and property income - from and to the rest of the world, net [a]	-126.9	-98.1	-137.3	-186.3	-195.8	-147.1	-183.5	-194.1	-121.9	-106.8	-42.0	-37.3
Plus: Taxes less subsidies on production and imports - from and to the rest of the world, net	...	...	...	...	...	...	...	...	...	...	...	...
Equals: GROSS NATIONAL INCOME [a]	1778.7	1844.0	1966.2	2105.9	2246.4	2580.7	2854.4	2951.6	3028.7	3131.9	3227.7	3165.5
Plus: Current transfers - from and to the rest of the world, net[a]	38.6	32.6	34.8	37.5	35.0	32.4	36.6	43.8	33.5	41.5	53.8	47.8
Equals: GROSS NATIONAL DISPOSABLE INCOME [a]	1817.3	1876.7	2001.0	2143.5	2281.4	2613.0	2891.0	2995.4	3062.2	3173.4	3281.5	3213.3
Less: Final consumption expenditure / Actual final consumption	1722.8	1790.4	1995.0	1876.0	1989.0	2478.8	2974.8	2938.0	2546.2	2922.6	3188.6	3130.2
Equals: SAVING, GROSS	181.9	147.1	77.7	345.6	378.8	253.8	-28.4	108.5	551.3	393.4	322.9	433.4
Plus: Capital transfers - from and to the rest of the world, net	...	...	...	...	...	...	...	...	...	...	...	...
Less: Gross capital formation	472.4	433.3	476.0	591.7	728.4	1088.1	902.2	1026.1	920.5	940.9	980.8	931.2
Less: Acquisitions less disposals of non-produced non-financial assets	...	...	...	...	...	...	...	...	...	...	...	...
Equals: NET LENDING (+) / NET BORROWING (-) OF THE NATION	...	...	...	...	...	...	...	...	...	...	...	...

	2001	2002	2003	2004	2005	2006	2007	2008	2009	2010	2011	2012
Series	**100**											
	Net values: Gross National Income / Gross National Disposable Income / Saving Gross less Consumption of fixed capital											
Less: Consumption of fixed capital	...	...	...	...	...	...	...	...	...	...	...	...
Equals: NET NATIONAL INCOME	...	...	...	...	...	...	...	...	...	...	...	...
Equals: NET NATIONAL DISPOSABLE INCOME	...	...	...	...	...	...	...	...	...	...	...	...
Equals: SAVING, NET	...	...	...	...	...	...	...	...	...	...	...	...

[a] Data for this item has not been revised.

Table 2.1 Value added by industries at current prices (ISIC Rev. 3)

Series 100: 1993 SNA, EC dollar, Western calendar year **Data in millions**

	2001	2002	2003	2004	2005	2006	2007	2008	2009	2010	2011	2012
Series	**100**											
	Industries											
Agriculture, hunting, forestry; fishing	84.9	94.8	88.8	92.0	76.3	88.7	88.2	121.1	116.1	94.5	84.0	92.9
Agriculture, hunting, forestry	69.1	82.1	67.2	78.0	62.7	73.6	71.6	100.8	95.6	73.8	62.9	71.3
Agriculture, hunting and related service activities	67.8	80.9	66.1	76.8	61.5	72.5	70.4	99.7	94.5	72.7	61.8	70.5
Forestry, logging and related service activities	1.3	1.2	1.2	1.2	1.1	1.1	1.1	1.1	1.1	1.1	1.0	0.8
Fishing	15.8	12.7	21.6	14.0	13.6	15.1	16.7	20.3	20.5	20.7	21.1	21.6
Mining and quarrying	6.1	6.0	6.0	5.9	5.7	6.8	7.6	7.2	7.1	7.0	7.0	7.2
Manufacturing	73.3	74.3	82.1	95.8	113.7	121.3	133.0	120.5	108.3	103.5	110.9	109.6
Electricity, gas and water supply	88.3	84.0	87.4	97.8	92.6	94.9	98.0	103.0	115.8	118.1	113.4	117.0
Construction	119.7	115.0	129.4	162.2	197.8	300.8	222.7	255.5	249.8	232.0	238.3	228.7
Wholesale, retail trade, repair of motor vehicles, motorcycles and personal and households goods; hotels and restaurants	314.3	299.8	370.4	407.7	435.2	479.7	605.7	587.4	553.5	677.6	712.8	738.4
Wholesale, retail trade, repair of motor vehicles, motorcycles and personal and household goods	130.9	132.8	154.6	162.2	194.0	227.2	241.9	249.6	219.0	219.4	263.7	259.2
Hotels and restaurants	183.3	167.0	215.9	245.4	241.2	252.5	363.8	337.8	334.5	458.2	449.2	479.2
Transport, storage and communications	342.9	344.2	380.7	414.9	433.7	448.1	507.4	498.5	485.8	562.9	574.0	579.5
Land transport; transport via pipelines, water transport; air transport; Supporting and auxiliary transport activities; activities of travel agencies	216.6	207.7	236.5	263.5	268.7	290.6	328.8	314.0	295.0	367.7	391.9	399.0
Post and telecommunications	126.3	136.5	144.2	151.4	165.0	157.6	178.6	184.5	190.8	195.2	182.1	180.6
Financial intermediation; real estate, renting and business activities	425.9	429.3	439.3	471.2	509.9	564.2	650.3	685.7	691.5	681.8	701.4	716.9
Financial intermediation	122.9	118.8	115.4	133.1	148.0	170.0	218.1	231.2	218.6	186.9	177.4	178.1
Real estate, renting and business activities	303.1	310.5	323.9	338.1	361.9	394.2	432.2	454.5	473.0	494.8	524.0	538.8
Public administration and defence; compulsory social security	140.5	135.8	138.3	128.2	128.0	147.0	154.4	167.0	173.5	187.3	202.0	212.0
Education; health and social work; other community, social and personal services	179.9	178.3	180.4	185.3	193.2	221.2	243.2	263.8	295.6	318.5	339.9	345.7
Education	83.0	83.1	83.2	85.9	83.4	96.0	101.9	107.8	118.2	127.0	130.3	130.9

	2001	2002	2003	2004	2005	2006	2007	2008	2009	2010	2011	2012
Series	**100**											
Health and social work	39.9	39.8	39.6	40.2	41.3	45.7	48.0	49.8	52.1	54.0	57.9	63.6
Other community, social and personal services	57.0	55.4	57.6	59.2	68.6	79.6	93.3	106.2	125.2	137.5	151.6	151.3
Private households with employed persons	2.9	2.9	2.9	3.0	3.1	3.3	3.4	3.6	3.7	3.8	4.2	4.3
Equals: VALUE ADDED, GROSS, in basic prices	1750.1	1734.9	1876.8	2033.6	2155.3	2431.7	2649.3	2740.5	2727.0	2919.9	3024.1	3089.6
Less: Financial intermediation services indirectly measured (FISIM)	28.4	29.4	28.9	30.4	33.7	44.2	64.7	72.7	73.6	67.1	63.6	62.5
Plus: Taxes less Subsidies on products	242.8	268.1	298.3	336.7	373.3	415.8	444.0	456.1	458.9	461.5	475.6	469.9
Plus: Taxes on products	255.6	280.4	310.9	349.2	386.2	429.8	458.0	470.8	474.5	477.4	491.9	430.0
Less: Subsidies on products	12.8	12.3	12.7	12.5	13.0	14.0	14.0	14.7	15.7	16.0	16.3	16.6
Equals: GROSS DOMESTIC PRODUCT	1992.9	2003.0	2175.3	2370.3	2528.6	2847.4	3093.3	3196.7	3185.9	3381.4	3499.7	3559.5

Table 2.2 Value added by industries at constant prices (ISIC Rev. 3)

Series 100: 1993 SNA, EC dollar, Western calendar year — **Data in millions**

	2001	2002	2003	2004	2005	2006	2007	2008	2009	2010	2011	2012
Series	**100**											
Base year	**2006**											
Industries												
Agriculture, hunting, forestry; fishing	105.8	115.4	102.8	105.3	81.3	88.7	88.5	113.3	109.1	85.8	74.5	80.7
Agriculture, hunting, forestry	85.2	101.4	81.1	88.7	66.8	73.6	71.2	93.9	89.3	66.1	54.5	60.6
Agriculture, hunting and related service activities	84.0	100.2	79.9	87.5	65.7	72.5	70.1	92.9	88.3	65.2	53.5	59.8
Forestry, logging and related service activities	1.3	1.2	1.2	1.2	1.1	1.1	1.1	1.0	1.0	1.0	0.9	0.8
Fishing	20.5	14.0	21.7	16.6	14.5	15.1	17.3	19.4	19.8	19.7	20.1	20.1
Mining and quarrying	2.0	2.0	0.6	0.7	1.5	6.8	10.9	8.3	6.9	7.6	7.3	13.0
Manufacturing	104.8	99.8	100.2	113.2	117.8	121.3	137.0	129.7	137.0	132.9	138.2	138.3
Electricity, gas and water supply	84.7	81.7	85.1	89.4	92.6	94.9	99.3	101.0	105.1	107.6	108.8	109.5
Construction	192.5	189.5	213.0	266.9	198.8	300.8	215.8	273.5	272.2	246.6	251.8	239.1
Wholesale, retail trade, repair of motor vehicles, motorcycles and personal and household goods; hotels and restaurants	346.4	346.1	398.8	415.4	456.7	479.7	488.1	482.2	443.2	455.2	488.3	474.5
Wholesale, retail trade, repair of motor vehicles, motorcycles and personal and household goods	142.5	143.9	166.4	169.7	198.5	227.2	234.1	236.4	199.6	194.0	232.4	211.6
Hotels and restaurants	203.9	202.2	232.4	245.7	258.2	252.5	254.0	245.8	243.6	261.2	255.9	262.9
Transport, storage and communications	432.5	417.0	438.3	478.8	469.3	448.1	512.4	523.8	527.6	533.1	510.9	493.4
Land transport; transport via piplines, water transport; air transport; Supporting and auxiliary transport activities; activities of travel agencies	289.9	265.1	279.3	317.6	299.6	290.6	345.5	353.2	354.2	361.7	347.0	338.2
Post and telecommunications	142.7	151.9	159.0	161.2	169.6	157.6	166.8	170.7	173.5	171.4	163.9	155.2
Financial intermediation, real estate, renting and business activities	479.9	484.5	494.2	502.5	522.7	564.2	587.8	614.8	618.2	640.9	650.1	656.9
Financial intermediation	132.9	132.9	133.3	139.5	150.1	170.0	184.0	195.9	191.6	190.2	194.5	197.3
Real estate, renting and business activities	347.1	351.5	360.9	363.0	372.6	394.2	403.8	418.9	426.6	450.7	455.6	459.6

		2001	2002	2003	2004	2005	2006	2007	2008	2009	2010	2011	2012
Series		**100**											
Base year		**2006**											
Public administration and defence; compulsory social security		153.7	144.8	140.4	142.3	145.2	147.0	147.7	151.0	155.1	160.1	164.7	168.4
Education; health and social work; other community, social and personal services		213.5	201.2	199.3	200.8	210.3	221.2	237.1	250.5	270.1	277.1	292.3	291.3
Education		100.9	95.1	92.1	93.3	94.4	96.0	99.1	100.7	103.2	106.5	109.5	112.0
Health and social work		47.1	44.2	43.0	43.6	45.1	45.7	47.4	47.5	48.9	50.3	51.8	53.2
Other community, social and personal services		65.5	61.8	64.1	63.9	70.8	79.6	90.6	102.3	118.0	120.3	131.1	126.1
Private households with employed persons		3.1	3.1	3.2	3.2	3.2	3.3	3.3	3.3	3.8	3.5	3.5	3.4
Equals: VALUE ADDED, GROSS, in basic prices		2089.7	2055.0	2147.6	2289.4	2264.6	2431.6	2472.1	2590.1	2584.0	2587.6	2626.2	2604.2
Less: Financial intermediation services indirectly measured (FISIM)		29.3	29.9	28.4	29.1	35.0	44.2	55.6	61.5	64.2	62.7	64.2	64.3
Plus: Taxes less Subsidies on products	a	287.1	310.8	334.3	372.4	382.7	415.8	405.2	422.5	425.9	417.6	432.2	371.9
Equals: GROSS DOMESTIC PRODUCT	a	2253.1	2252.0	2357.8	2535.3	2503.7	2727.8	2772.1	2913.7	2924.1	2930.7	2971.5	2881.2

[a] Data for this item has not been revised.

Saint Vincent and the Grenadines

Source

The National Accounts data for Saint Vincent and the Grenadines are produced by the Statistical Office in collaboration with the Eastern Caribbean Central Bank (ECCB). The Statistical Office disseminates detailed national accounts statistics. The national accounts framework is based on the "System of National Accounts 1993" (1993 SNA).

General

The national accounts framework is based on the "System of National Accounts 1993" (1993 SNA). When the scope and coverage of the estimates differ for conceptual or statistical reasons from the definitions and classifications recommended in the SNA, a footnote provides explanation.

Methodology:

Overview of GDP Compilation

The Statistical Office produces and disseminates the following data on an annual basis:

Gross Value Added by Economic Activity at basic prices in current prices for 15 major economic activities, 25 sub-activities: Agriculture (Crops: Banana, Other Crops; Livestock, Forestry, Fishing); Mining & Quarrying; Manufacturing; Electricity & Water (Electricity, Water); Construction; Wholesale, & Retail Trade; Hotels & Restaurants; Transport, Storage & Communication (Road, Sea, Air, Auxiliary transport activities & storage and Communications); Financial Intermediation (Banks, Insurance & Auxiliary Financial intermediation); Real Estate, Renting & Business Activities (Owner Occupied Dwellings, Real Estate Activities, Renting of Machinery & Equipment, Computer & Related Services and Business Services); Public Administration, Defence & Compulsory Social Security ; Education (Public and Private); Health and Social Work (Public & Private); Other community, Social and Personal Services): Private Households with employed Persons.

Gross Value Added (GVA) by Economic Activity at basic prices in constant (2006) prices for 15 major economic activities, 25 sub-activities: Agriculture (Crops: Banana, Other Crops; Livestock, Forestry, Fishing); Mining & Quarrying; Manufacturing; Electricity & Water (Electricity, Water); Construction; Wholesale, & Retail Trade; Hotels & Restaurants; Transport, Storage & Communication (Road, Sea, Air, Auxiliary transport activities & storage, & Communications); Financial Intermediation (Banks, Insurance & Auxiliary financial intermediation); Real Estate, Renting & Business Activities (Owner Occupied Dwellings, Real Estate Activities, Renting of Machinery & Equipment, Computer & Related Services and Business Services); Public Administration, Defence & Compulsory Social Security; Education (Public and Private); Health and Social Work (Public & Private); Other community, Social and Personal Services; Private Households with employed Persons.

GVA and GDP are compiled from the production approach and GDP by the expenditure approach. GVA by the production approach is total output at basic prices less intermediate consumption at market (purchasers') prices. Producer units are grouped according to principal economic activity. GDP from the expenditure approach is the sum of final uses of goods and services in the total economy, less the value of imports of goods and services. Financial intermediation services are allocated entirely to intermediate consumption and excluded from GVA. Economic activities are classified using the International Standard Industrial Classification of All Economic Activities, revision 3.1 (ISIC Rev. 3.1). The 15 activities covered differ from the ISIC Rev. 3.1 presentation by combining some sectors. They comprise the categories shown in parentheses; Agriculture (A-B), Mining and quarrying (C), Manufacturing (D), Electricity, Gas water supply (E), Construction (F), Wholesale and retail trade (G), Hotels and Restaurants (H), Transportation, Storage & Communication (I), Financial Intermediation (J), Real estate, Renting and Business Activities (K), Public Administration (L), Education (M); Health & Social Work (N); Other Community, Social and Personal Services Activities (O) and Private Households with Employed Persons (P).

General government final consumption expenditure is classified according to classification of functions of government (COFOG). In 2005, the CSO embarked on an exercise to rebase its system of National Accounts to reference year 2006. All economic activities have been classified according to ISIC Rev. 3.1. Implementation of the rebased series took place in 2010.

Expenditure Approach

Estimation of current price data for Private Consumption is determined as the residual of GVA using the production method less government consumption, gross capital formation, and exports less imports of goods and services. It thus effectively includes increase in stocks (change in inventories). Gross fixed capital formation comprises investment in equipment and structures. Equipment investment is estimated via a commodity flow method principally using data on imports, and structures investment is the gross output of the construction industry. There are no adjustments to equipment investment to include set-up costs. As noted above, exports and imports of goods and services are derived from the Balance of Payments prepared by the Statistical Office. The estimates from the production and expenditure approaches are not independently determined as private final consumption is calculated as a residual and reconcile by definition. Exports and imports of goods and services used in the calculation of GDP and net factor incomes from abroad used in the calculation of (GNI) are taken from the Balance of Payments, and therefore reconcile with those data by definition.

Production Approach

Coverage adjustments:
Various methods are used for the treatment of missing values of output and intermediate consumption for individual establishments in the National Establishment Survey and other sources. Among these are estimating current intermediate consumption on the basis of its share in a similar establishment's output, estimating output on the basis of the ratio of output to selected cost data of a similar establishment. Commodity flow approach to output estimation is used for construction to limit potential coverage problems from incomplete survey coverage of informal and/or non-reporting establishments.

Estimation of current price data:
Value added (VA) by industry is the value of output less intermediate consumption. The value of output and intermediate consumption for banana crops, mining & Quarrying, manufacturing, electricity and water, air and sea transport, auxiliary transport services, communications, wholesale and retail trade, hotels and restaurant, financial intermediation, real estate, renting and business services excluding owner occupied. Education (private), health & social work (private) other community, social and personal services are compiled from financial statements, annual national accounts establishment survey and administrative records. The output of banking is measured in GVA by economic activity as net interest and other income. There are insufficient data to allocate this output to intermediate and final consumption. Consequently, net interest income is treated as intermediate consumption to a notional industry. For general government, education (public) and health & social work (public) value added is compiled using compensation of employee data for government employees. The output for construction is estimated using a commodity flow method, as the sum of production costs for materials and labour unique to the industry, plus trade and transport margins for those items. For non-banana crops, fishing and road transport, output is produced from estimates of quantity produced multiplied by average price and intermediate consumption is estimated as ratio to value of output. For owner-occupied dwelling, value of output was estimated using imputed rent obtained from administrative records for selected areas multiplied by the number of owned and rent free dwellings. The intermediate consumption was derived as a ratio of output.

Estimation of constant price data:
Two methods are used for compiling constant price data, depending on the industry. In the first method, a price index of commodities is computed to deflate the gross output. Gross Value Added at constant prices is derived by extrapolating the base year value by a volume index of the deflated gross output. The activities employing this method are communications; wholesale and retail trade; construction; insurance and health. For the second method, volume index of commodities are used to extrapolate the base year value added to derive the constant prices for the activities relating to agriculture excluding bananas; manufacturing; electricity & water; hotels &

restaurants; transport and storage, financial intermediation excluding insurances, real estate, renting and business services; education; other community, social and personal services. In the case of bananas a double deflation method is used. For central government services; education (public) and health and social work (public), value added is deflated by an index of wage and salary.

Table 1.1 Gross domestic product by expenditures at current prices

Series 100: 1993 SNA, EC dollar, Western calendar year — **Data in thousands**

	2001	2002	2003	2004	2005	2006	2007	2008	2009	2010	2011	2012
Series	**100**											
	Expenditures of the gross domestic product											
Final consumption expenditure	982735.0	1055760.0	1126900.0	1271480.0	1358870.0	1486960.0	1849740.0	1921240.0	1912040.0	1931910.0	1910920.0	2009150.0
Household final consumption expenditure	798095.0	853824.0	925274.0	1050360.0	1124740.0	1238600.0	1559170.0	1604020.0	1597610.0	1647130.0	1596670.0	1669540.0
NPISHs final consumption expenditure	...	...	...	...	...	...	...	...	...	...	...	...
General government final consumption expenditure	184640.0	201940.0	201630.0	221120.0	234130.0	248360.0	290570.0	317220.0	314440.0	284780.0	314250.0	339620.0
Gross capital formation	268860.0	289890.0	359040.0	374590.0	372850.0	469560.0	509910.0	552090.0	438590.0	463970.0	440340.0	443110.0
Gross fixed capital formation	268860.0	289890.0	359040.0	374590.0	372850.0	469560.0	509910.0	552090.0	438590.0	463970.0	440340.0	443110.0
Changes in inventories	...	...	...	...	...	...	...	...	...	...	...	...
Acquisitions less disposals of valuables	...	...	...	...	...	...	...	...	...	...	...	...
Exports of goods and services	475050.0	481447.0	466696.0	498196.0	541470.0	572385.0	572994.0	567454.0	519231.0	494600.0	493544.0	507900.0
Exports of goods	115444.0	111348.0	108240.0	106106.0	114947.0	111142.0	138654.0	154413.0	144069.0	121512.0	117256.0	129040.0
Exports of services	359606.0	370099.0	358456.0	392090.0	426523.0	461243.0	434341.0	413042.0	375162.0	373089.0	376288.0	378860.0
Less: Imports of goods and services	565539.0	580015.0	651763.0	734929.0	786222.0	879804.0	1085710.0	1163210.0	1047720.0	1050780.0	1016870.0	1085320.0
Imports of goods	410318.0	425976.0	477375.0	537231.0	573456.0	641741.0	777360.0	887434.0	793282.0	803835.0	789167.0	850570.0
Imports of services	155221.0	154039.0	174388.0	197698.0	212767.0	238063.0	308352.0	275773.0	254436.0	246942.0	227704.0	234750.0
Equals: GROSS DOMESTIC PRODUCT	1161110.0	1247090.0	1300880.0	1409330.0	1486970.0	1649100.0	1846930.0	1877580.0	1822150.0	1839700.0	1827930.0	1874850.0

Table 1.3 Relations among product, income, savings, and net lending aggregates

Series 100: 1993 SNA, EC dollar, Western calendar year — **Data in thousands**

	2001	2002	2003	2004	2005	2006	2007	2008	2009	2010	2011	2012
Series	**100**											
GROSS DOMESTIC PRODUCT	1161110.0	1247090.0	1300880.0	1409330.0	1486970.0	1649100.0	1846930.0	1877580.0	1822150.0	1839700.0	1827930.0	1874850.0
Plus: Compensation of employees - from and to the rest of the world, net	314.0	2009.0	1624.0	1796.0	1257.0	8476.0	15812.0	11004.0	19078.0	16596.0	16143.0	19691.0
Plus: Compensation of employees - from the rest of the world	314.0	2009.0	1624.0	1796.0	2892.0	9928.0	17266.0	11020.0	19115.0	17330.0	16840.0	21150.0
Less: Compensation of employees - to the rest of the world	0.0	0.0	0.0	0.0	1635.0	1452.0	1454.0	16.0	37.0	735.0	698.0	1460.0
Plus: Property income - from and to the rest of the world, net	-44819.0	-49537.0	-65970.0	-81675.0	-81183.0	-77860.0	-75229.0	-72679.0	-54209.0	-49749.0	-51087.0	-30003.0
Plus: Property income - from the rest of the world	6090.0	7097.0	8528.0	11527.0	19779.0	26791.0	18934.0	16294.0	17832.0	16881.0	8889.0	17030.0
Less: Property income - to the rest of the world	50909.0	56634.0	74501.0	93202.0	100962.0	104651.0	94163.0	88972.0	72042.0	66630.0	59975.0	47040.0
Sum of Compensation of employees and property income - from and to the rest of the world, net	-44505.0	-47528.0	-64349.0	-79879.0	-79926.0	-69384.0	-59417.0	-61675.0	-35131.0	-33153.0	-34944.0	-10312.0

	2001	2002	2003	2004	2005	2006	2007	2008	2009	2010	2011	2012
Series	**100**											
Plus: Sum of Compensation of employees and property income - from the rest of the world	6404.0	9106.0	10152.0	13322.0	22671.0	36719.0	36200.0	27314.0	36948.0	34212.0	25729.0	38185.0
Less: Sum of Compensation of employees and property income - to the rest of the world	50909.0	56634.0	74501.0	93202.0	102597.0	106103.0	95617.0	88988.0	72078.0	67365.0	60673.0	48497.0
Plus: Taxes less subsidies on production and imports - from and to the rest of the world, net	...	...	...	...	...	...	...	...	...	...	...	...
Equals: GROSS NATIONAL INCOME	1116600.0	1199560.0	1236530.0	1329450.0	1407040.0	1579720.0	1787520.0	1815910.0	1787020.0	1806550.0	1792990.0	1864540.0
Plus: Current transfers - from and to the rest of the world, net	34049.0	32783.0	34833.0	38098.0	48743.0	54449.0	54422.0	35537.0	30836.0	26885.0	21298.0	63740.0
Plus: Current transfers - from the rest of the world	62754.0	64089.0	65596.0	67855.0	71284.0	87015.0	95643.0	75259.0	69687.0	75438.0	71041.0	99997.0
Less: Current transfers - to the rest of the world	28705.0	31306.0	30762.0	29757.0	22540.0	32566.0	41221.0	39722.0	38850.0	48553.0	49743.0	36257.0
Equals: GROSS NATIONAL DISPOSABLE INCOME	1150650.0	1232340.0	1271360.0	1367550.0	1455790.0	1634170.0	1841940.0	1851450.0	1817860.0	1833440.0	1814290.0	1928280.0
Less: Final consumption expenditure / Actual final consumption	982735.0	1055760.0	1126900.0	1271480.0	1358870.0	1486960.0	1849740.0	1921240.0	1912040.0	1931910.0	1910920.0	2009150.0
Equals: SAVING, GROSS	167915.0	176577.0	144457.0	96076.0	96915.0	147206.0	-7803.0	-69790.0	-94190.0	-98470.0	-96630.0	-80880.0
Plus: Capital transfers - from and to the rest of the world, net	23654.0	28633.0	38775.0	51126.0	38433.0	22016.0	198763.0	131885.0	146440.0	148040.0	104311.0	91724.0
Plus: Capital transfers - from the rest of the world	27074.0	32053.0	42195.0	54815.0	42284.0	26281.0	203510.0	136813.0	151380.0	153040.0	109450.0	96991.0
Less: Capital transfers - to the rest of the world	3420.0	3420.0	3420.0	3689.0	3852.0	4265.0	4747.0	4928.0	4940.0	5010.0	5140.0	5267.0
Less: Gross capital formation	268860.0	289890.0	359040.0	374590.0	372850.0	469560.0	509910.0	552090.0	438590.0	463970.0	440340.0	443110.0
Less: Acquisitions less disposals of non-produced non-financial assets	...	...	...	...	...	...	...	...	...	...	...	...
Equals: NET LENDING (+) / NET BORROWING (-) OF THE NATION	-77291.0	-84680.0	-175808.0	-227388.0	-237502.0	-300338.0	-318950.0	-489995.0	-386340.0	-414400.0	-432659.0	-432266.0
	Net values: Gross National Income / Gross National Disposable Income / Saving Gross less Consumption of fixed capital											
Less: Consumption of fixed capital	...	...	...	...	...	...	...	...	...	...	...	...
Equals: NET NATIONAL INCOME	...	...	...	...	...	...	...	...	...	...	...	...
Equals: NET NATIONAL DISPOSABLE INCOME	...	...	...	...	...	...	...	...	...	...	...	...
Equals: SAVING, NET	...	...	...	...	...	...	...	...	...	...	...	...

Table 2.1 Value added by industries at current prices (ISIC Rev. 3)

Series 100: 1993 SNA, EC dollar, Western calendar year — **Data in thousands**

	2001	2002	2003	2004	2005	2006	2007	2008	2009	2010	2011	2012
Series	**100**											
	Industries											
Agriculture, hunting, forestry; fishing	72927.0	79316.0	71901.0	73314.0	81402.0	86918.0	99445.0	105925.0	107858.0	111808.0	116150.0	114960.0
Agriculture, hunting, forestry	67347.0	75035.0	66443.0	67303.0	75357.0	80539.0	91455.0	99436.0	99351.0	104058.0	108909.0	108030.0
Agriculture, hunting and related service activities	66515.0	74219.0	65644.0	66519.0	74461.0	79626.0	90390.0	98392.0	98338.0	103076.0	107946.0	107090.0
Forestry, logging and related service activities	832.0	816.0	800.0	784.0	896.0	914.0	1065.0	1044.0	1013.0	982.0	963.0	940.0
Fishing	5580.0	4281.0	5458.0	6011.0	6045.0	6378.0	7991.0	6489.0	8507.0	7750.0	7241.0	6930.0
Mining and quarrying	1720.0	1730.0	1831.0	2725.0	3631.0	4180.0	5020.0	5020.0	5210.0	4110.0	3070.0	2290.0

	2001	2002	2003	2004	2005	2006	2007	2008	2009	2010	2011	2012
Series	**100**											
Manufacturing	64647.0	58614.0	62169.0	71529.0	76577.0	72170.0	87429.0	76811.0	81261.0	88700.0	86670.0	79830.0
Electricity, gas and water supply	50653.0	52560.0	53351.0	56561.0	55191.0	56782.0	68125.0	62088.0	63110.0	70884.0	66390.0	72910.0
Construction	78560.0	81535.0	93487.0	105988.0	108231.0	137991.0	169306.0	156808.0	145567.0	139442.0	137184.0	134590.0
Wholesale, retail trade, repair of motor vehicles, motorcycles and personal and households goods; hotels and restaurants	176362.0	185732.0	197601.0	216486.0	232436.0	264871.0	290447.0	304944.0	262132.0	254010.0	256890.0	266170.0
Wholesale, retail trade, repair of motor vehicles, motorcycles and personal and household goods	147250.0	152990.0	165880.0	180660.0	195840.0	215420.0	234810.0	254530.0	226532.0	222280.0	219440.0	228610.0
Hotels and restaurants	29112.0	32742.0	31721.0	35826.0	36596.0	49451.0	55637.0	50414.0	35600.0	31730.0	37450.0	37560.0
Transport, storage and communications	133015.0	162391.0	171962.0	191833.0	195639.0	218001.0	235793.0	233963.0	222042.0	217440.0	216290.0	219760.0
Land transport; transport via pipelines, water transport; air transport; Supporting and auxiliary transport activities; activities of travel agencies	94249.0	107248.0	115804.0	124477.0	130495.0	145812.0	154181.0	153033.0	150101.0	150610.0	145350.0	146780.0
Post and telecommunications	38766.0	55144.0	56158.0	67356.0	65144.0	72188.0	81612.0	80931.0	71942.0	66830.0	70940.0	72980.0
Financial intermediation; real estate, renting and business activities	258376.0	268081.0	284399.0	298774.0	323569.0	337559.0	354249.0	355487.0	342381.0	350330.0	337250.0	350400.0
Financial intermediation	57605.0	62219.0	75433.0	82873.0	101685.0	110042.0	121426.0	119967.0	111315.0	114130.0	94910.0	105760.0
Real estate, renting and business activities	200771.0	205861.0	208966.0	215900.0	221884.0	227516.0	232823.0	235520.0	231067.0	236200.0	242340.0	244640.0
Public administration and defence; compulsory social security	75859.0	82415.0	82128.0	88476.0	94589.0	105647.0	117786.0	130664.0	143425.0	168593.0	178040.0	187280.0
Education; health and social work; other community, social and personal services	103351.0	112636.0	111919.0	124109.0	133490.0	140970.0	166675.0	156469.0	167869.0	167957.0	174010.0	183730.0
Education	57537.0	61462.0	62470.0	67393.0	73544.0	78181.0	90085.0	71882.0	83737.0	85813.0	92160.0	96800.0
Health and social work	26496.0	29176.0	30377.0	30889.0	34320.0	36681.0	42169.0	45197.0	43652.0	47594.0	49250.0	51780.0
Other community, social and personal services	19319.0	21999.0	19072.0	25827.0	25626.0	26108.0	34420.0	39390.0	40480.0	34550.0	32600.0	35150.0
Private households with employed persons	2360.0	2623.0	2867.0	3036.0	3155.0	3352.0	3585.0	4010.0	4292.0	4576.0	4740.0	4910.0
Equals: VALUE ADDED, GROSS, in basic prices [a]	1005720.0	1078200.0	1121100.0	1219850.0	1293780.0	1412800.0	1577920.0	1570690.0	1525920.0	1556860.0	1557630.0	1596630.0
Less: Financial intermediation services indirectly measured (FISIM)	12112.0	9433.0	12519.0	12985.0	14125.0	15640.0	19937.0	21501.0	19230.0	20900.0	19050.0	20210.0
Plus: Taxes less Subsidies on products	155389.0	168885.0	179781.0	189487.0	193184.0	236300.0	269010.0	306890.0	296230.0	282841.0	270300.0	278221.0
Plus: Taxes on products	155779.0	169395.0	180131.0	190237.0	194034.0	237100.0	270010.0	307940.0	297380.0	284361.0	271400.0	279321.0
Less: Subsidies on products	390.0	510.0	350.0	750.0	850.0	800.0	1000.0	1050.0	1150.0	1520.0	1100.0	1100.0
Equals: GROSS DOMESTIC PRODUCT	1161110.0	1247090.0	1300880.0	1409330.0	1486970.0	1649100.0	1846930.0	1877580.0	1822150.0	1839700.0	1827930.0	1874850.0
Memorandum Item: FISIM, if distributed to uses	...	...	...	...	...	...	...	...	...	21000.0	19050.0	20210.0

[a] Excludes financial intermediation services indirectly measured (FISIM), but FISIM is included in industry data.

Table 2.2 Value added by industries at constant prices (ISIC Rev. 3)

Series 100: 1993 SNA, EC dollar, Western calendar year **Data in thousands**

	2001	2002	2003	2004	2005	2006	2007	2008	2009	2010	2011	2012
Series	**100**											
Base year	**2006**											
Industries												
Agriculture, hunting, forestry; fishing	80592.0	89858.0	85321.0	82138.0	83972.0	86920.0	96459.0	93048.0	106576.0	87400.0	87240.0	88030.0
Agriculture, hunting, forestry	74668.0	84938.0	79153.0	76056.0	77599.0	80542.0	88468.0	87738.0	99106.0	81060.0	81090.0	82800.0
Agriculture, hunting and related service activities	73696.0	83986.0	78220.0	75142.0	76703.0	79628.0	87536.0	86830.0	98220.0	80200.0	80250.0	82000.0
Forestry, logging and related service activities	971.0	952.0	933.0	914.0	896.0	914.0	932.0	910.0	890.0	860.0	840.0	800.0
Fishing	5924.0	4921.0	6169.0	6082.0	6373.0	6378.0	7991.0	5310.0	7470.0	6340.0	6150.0	5230.0
Mining and quarrying	2165.0	2089.0	2367.0	3846.0	3981.0	4180.0	4755.0	5000.0	5130.0	4010.0	3020.0	2130.0
Manufacturing	66112.0	64315.0	69365.0	67484.0	72429.0	72170.0	67820.0	69597.0	63939.0	62223.0	65840.0	64340.0
Electricity, gas and water supply	45467.0	46721.0	49302.0	51916.0	55487.0	56782.0	59028.0	58095.0	59979.0	57250.0	56000.0	58720.0
Construction	88134.0	96149.0	115997.0	127546.0	127091.0	137991.0	155981.0	139885.0	128268.0	124270.0	120080.0	115840.0
Wholesale, retail trade, repair of motor vehicles, motorcycles and personal and household goods; hotels and restaurants	186886.0	191575.0	212403.0	232346.0	244790.0	264871.0	284168.0	290560.0	262330.0	254900.0	246440.0	248650.0
Wholesale, retail trade, repair of motor vehicles, motorcycles and personal and household goods	161456.0	167139.0	180136.0	195700.0	205233.0	215420.0	234842.0	243938.0	224100.0	222090.0	212500.0	215750.0
Hotels and restaurants	25429.0	24435.0	32266.0	36647.0	39558.0	49451.0	49326.0	46615.0	38230.0	32810.0	33940.0	32900.0
Transport, storage and communications	124438.0	152645.0	184557.0	194183.0	197569.0	218001.0	214184.0	217040.0	213274.0	209910.0	209240.0	210770.0
Land transport; transport via piplines, water transport; air transport; Supporting and auxiliary transport activities; activities of travel agencies	97815.0	115375.0	124922.0	133658.0	133951.0	145812.0	153047.0	154800.0	154960.0	153910.0	156000.0	157060.0
Post and telecommunications	26623.0	37270.0	59634.0	60525.0	63618.0	72188.0	61137.0	62240.0	58315.0	53686.0	53240.0	53710.0
Financial intermediation, real estate, renting and business activities	292980.0	302450.0	307615.0	318221.0	320797.0	337559.0	334918.0	338340.0	332080.0	325190.0	330050.0	339300.0
Financial intermediation	89409.0	96561.0	100082.0	105501.0	104986.0	110042.0	105755.0	104360.0	101930.0	95680.0	99200.0	107510.0
Real estate, renting and business activities	203571.0	205889.0	207532.0	212720.0	215811.0	227516.0	229163.0	233980.0	230150.0	229510.0	230850.0	231790.0
Public administration and defence; compulsory social security	86951.0	89590.0	91855.0	95584.0	98806.0	105647.0	112194.0	121480.0	132730.0	144490.0	150590.0	156010.0
Education; health and social work; other community, social and personal services	122957.0	127389.0	129086.0	131783.0	139179.0	140970.0	139424.0	130581.0	129790.0	132440.0	136751.0	143490.0
Education	69389.0	72438.0	74890.0	77991.0	80306.0	78181.0	76061.0	60584.0	62332.0	61470.0	...	66160.0
Health and social work	31703.0	33890.0	34895.0	34079.0	36259.0	36681.0	38486.0	40576.0	39540.0	40258.0	42130.0	43530.0
Other community, social and personal services	21865.0	21061.0	19302.0	19713.0	22615.0	26108.0	24877.0	29421.0	27922.0	30713.0	31720.0	33800.0
Private households with employed persons	2684.0	3083.0	3343.0	3247.0	3275.0	3352.0	3064.0	3352.0	3112.0	3160.0	3209.0	3410.0
Equals: VALUE ADDED, GROSS, in basic prices	[a] 1085520.0	1152010.0	1236620.0	1293620.0	1332750.0	1412800.0	1455380.0	1448560.0	1419200.0	1387150.0	1391020.0	1412210.0
Less: Financial intermediation services indirectly measured (FISIM)	13850.0	13850.0	14594.0	14678.0	14631.0	15640.0	16617.0	18412.0	18018.0	18100.0	17441.0	18480.0
Plus: Taxes less Subsidies on products	167718.0	180447.0	198306.0	200946.0	199001.0	236301.0	248118.0	283030.0	275510.0	252010.0	241390.0	246090.0
Plus: Taxes on products	...	...	...	...	...	...	...	284000.0	276580.0	253360.0	242370.0	247060.0
Less: Subsidies on products	...	...	...	...	...	...	...	970.0	1070.0	1350.0	980.0	970.0

	2001	2002	2003	2004	2005	2006	2007	2008	2009	2010	2011	2012
Series	**100**											
Base year	**2006**											
Equals: GROSS DOMESTIC PRODUCT	1253240.0	1332460.0	1434920.0	1494560.0	1531750.0	1649100.0	1703500.0	1731590.0	1694710.0	1639160.0	1632410.0	1658300.0
Memorandum Item: FISIM, if distributed to uses	...	...	...	...	...	...	...	18410.0	18020.0	18100.0	17440.0	18480.0

[a] Excludes financial intermediation services indirectly measured (FISIM).

Table 2.3 Output, gross value added, and fixed assets by industries at current prices (ISIC Rev. 3) Total Economy

Series 100: 1993 SNA, EC dollar, Western calendar year — **Data in thousands**

	2001	2002	2003	2004	2005	2006	2007	2008	2009	2010	2011	2012
Series	**100**											
Output, at basic prices	1821310.0	1964850.0	2106300.0	2292940.0	2452060.0	2778460.0	3054790.0	3134063.0	2804050.0	2810550.0	2898690.0	...
Less: Intermediate consumption, at purchaser's prices [a]	813640.0	884640.0	983600.0	1071470.0	1156460.0	1365270.0	1475050.0	1563376.0	1281940.0	1257510.0	1342900.0	...
Equals: VALUE ADDED, GROSS, at basic prices [b]	1005720.0	1078200.0	1121100.0	1219850.0	1293780.0	1412800.0	1577920.0	1570688.0	1525910.0	1556850.0	1555790.0	...
Compensation of employees	...	...	...	...	...	...	...	...	...	...	...	...
Taxes on production and imports, less Subsidies	...	...	...	...	...	...	...	...	...	...	...	...
OPERATING SURPLUS, GROSS	...	...	...	...	...	...	...	...	...	...	...	...
MIXED INCOME, GROSS	...	...	...	...	...	...	...	...	...	...	...	...
Gross capital formation	268860.0	289890.0	359040.0	374600.0	372850.0	469600.0	509910.0	552090.0	438590.0	463970.0	440340.0	443110.0
Gross fixed capital formation	268860.0	289890.0	359040.0	374600.0	372850.0	469600.0	509910.0	552090.0	438590.0	463970.0	440340.0	443110.0
Changes in inventories	...	...	...	...	...	...	...	...	...	...	...	...
Acquisitions less disposals of valuables	...	...	...	...	...	...	...	...	...	...	...	...

[a] Includes financial intermediation services indirectly measured (FISIM).
[b] Excludes financial intermediation services indirectly measured (FISIM).

Table 2.3 Output, gross value added, and fixed assets by industries at current prices (ISIC Rev. 3) Agriculture, hunting, forestry; fishing (A+B)

Series 100: 1993 SNA, EC dollar, Western calendar year — **Data in thousands**

	2001	2002	2003	2004	2005	2006	2007	2008	2009	2010	2011	2012
Series	**100**											
Output, at basic prices	102750.0	109940.0	102270.0	105970.0	116600.0	123580.0	140500.0	152153.0	153450.0	156100.0	159880.0	
Less: Intermediate consumption, at purchaser's prices	29820.0	30620.0	30370.0	32660.0	35190.0	36660.0	41050.0	46228.0	45590.0	44290.0	43730.0	
Equals: VALUE ADDED, GROSS, at basic prices	72930.0	79320.0	71900.0	73310.0	81400.0	86920.0	99450.0	105925.0	107860.0	111810.0	116150.0	
Compensation of employees	...	...	...	...	...	...	...	...	...	...	...	
Taxes on production and imports, less Subsidies	...	...	...	...	...	...	...	...	...	...	...	
OPERATING SURPLUS, GROSS	...	...	...	...	...	...	...	...	...	...	...	
MIXED INCOME, GROSS	...	...	...	...	...	...	...	...	...	...	...	
Gross capital formation	...	...	...	...	...	...	...	...	...	...	...	

Table 2.3 Output, gross value added, and fixed assets by industries at current prices (ISIC Rev. 3) Agriculture, hunting and related service activities (01)

Series 100: 1993 SNA, EC dollar, Western calendar year **Data in thousands**

	2001	2002	2003	2004	2005	2006	2007	2008	2009	2010	2011	2012
Series	**100**											
Output, at basic prices	94510.0	103430.0	94220.0	97350.0	107960.0	114300.0	128830.0	142486.0	141360.0	144850.0	148940.0	
Less: Intermediate consumption, at purchaser's prices	27990.0	29210.0	28570.0	30830.0	33500.0	34670.0	38440.0	44094.0	43020.0	41770.0	40990.0	
Equals: VALUE ADDED, GROSS, at basic prices	66520.0	74220.0	65650.0	66520.0	74460.0	79630.0	90390.0	98392.0	98340.0	103080.0	107940.0	
Compensation of employees	...	...	...	...	...	...	...	...	...	...	...	
Taxes on production and imports, less Subsidies	...	...	...	...	...	...	...	...	...	...	...	
OPERATING SURPLUS, GROSS	...	...	...	...	...	...	...	...	...	...	...	
MIXED INCOME, GROSS	...	...	...	...	...	...	...	...	...	...	...	
Gross capital formation	...	...	...	...	...	...	...	...	...	...	...	

Table 2.3 Output, gross value added, and fixed assets by industries at current prices (ISIC Rev. 3) Forestry, logging and related service activities (02)

Series 100: 1993 SNA, EC dollar, Western calendar year **Data in thousands**

	2001	2002	2003	2004	2005	2006	2007	2008	2009	2010	2011	2012
Series	**100**											
Output, at basic prices	860.0	840.0	820.0	800.0	920.0	940.0	1100.0	1076.0	1040.0	1010.0	990.0	
Less: Intermediate consumption, at purchaser's prices	30.0	30.0	20.0	20.0	20.0	30.0	30.0	32.0	30.0	30.0	30.0	
Equals: VALUE ADDED, GROSS, at basic prices	830.0	820.0	800.0	780.0	900.0	910.0	1070.0	1044.0	1010.0	980.0	960.0	
Compensation of employees	...	...	...	...	...	...	...	...	...	...	...	
Taxes on production and imports, less Subsidies	...	...	...	...	...	...	...	...	...	...	...	
OPERATING SURPLUS, GROSS	...	...	...	...	...	...	...	...	...	...	...	
MIXED INCOME, GROSS	...	...	...	...	...	...	...	...	...	...	...	
Gross capital formation	...	...	...	...	...	...	...	...	...	...	...	

Table 2.3 Output, gross value added, and fixed assets by industries at current prices (ISIC Rev. 3) Fishing (B)

Series 100: 1993 SNA, EC dollar, Western calendar year **Data in thousands**

	2001	2002	2003	2004	2005	2006	2007	2008	2009	2010	2011	2012
Series	**100**											
Output, at basic prices	7380.0	5660.0	7220.0	7810.0	7710.0	8340.0	10570.0	8591.0	11050.0	10240.0	9950.0	
Less: Intermediate consumption, at purchaser's prices	1800.0	1380.0	1760.0	1800.0	1660.0	1960.0	2580.0	2102.0	2540.0	2490.0	2710.0	
Equals: VALUE ADDED, GROSS, at basic prices	5580.0	4280.0	5460.0	6010.0	6050.0	6380.0	7990.0	6489.0	8510.0	7750.0	7240.0	
Compensation of employees	...	...	...	...	...	...	...	...	...	...	...	

	2001	2002	2003	2004	2005	2006	2007	2008	2009	2010	2011	2012
Series	**100**											
Taxes on production and imports, less Subsidies	...	...	...	...	...	...	...	...	...	...	...	
OPERATING SURPLUS, GROSS	...	...	...	...	...	...	...	...	...	...	...	
MIXED INCOME, GROSS	...	...	...	...	...	...	...	...	...	...	...	
Gross capital formation	...	...	...	...	...	...	...	...	...	...	...	

Table 2.3 Output, gross value added, and fixed assets by industries at current prices (ISIC Rev. 3) Mining and quarrying (C)

Series 100: 1993 SNA, EC dollar, Western calendar year **Data in thousands**

	2001	2002	2003	2004	2005	2006	2007	2008	2009	2010	2011	2012
Series	**100**											
Output, at basic prices	2520.0	2540.0	2690.0	4450.0	4890.0	6130.0	7360.0	8875.0	9140.0	7660.0	5480.0	
Less: Intermediate consumption, at purchaser's prices	800.0	810.0	860.0	1720.0	1260.0	1950.0	2340.0	3855.0	3930.0	3570.0	2420.0	
Equals: VALUE ADDED, GROSS, at basic prices	1720.0	1730.0	1830.0	2730.0	3630.0	4180.0	5020.0	5020.0	5210.0	4100.0	3070.0	
Compensation of employees	...	...	...	...	...	...	...	...	...	...	...	
Taxes on production and imports, less Subsidies	...	...	...	...	...	...	...	...	...	...	...	
OPERATING SURPLUS, GROSS	...	...	...	...	...	...	...	...	...	...	...	
MIXED INCOME, GROSS	...	...	...	...	...	...	...	...	...	...	...	
Gross capital formation	...	...	...	...	...	...	...	...	...	...	...	

Table 2.3 Output, gross value added, and fixed assets by industries at current prices (ISIC Rev. 3) Manufacturing (D)

Series 100: 1993 SNA, EC dollar, Western calendar year **Data in thousands**

	2001	2002	2003	2004	2005	2006	2007	2008	2009	2010	2011	2012
Series	**100**											
Output, at basic prices	210600.0	183220.0	181350.0	198200.0	224620.0	220840.0	225630.0	270913.0	269860.0	258690.0	261930.0	
Less: Intermediate consumption, at purchaser's prices	145950.0	124610.0	119180.0	126670.0	148040.0	149830.0	138200.0	194101.0	188600.0	169990.0	175260.0	
Equals: VALUE ADDED, GROSS, at basic prices	64650.0	58610.0	62170.0	71530.0	76580.0	72170.0	87430.0	76812.0	81260.0	88700.0	86670.0	
Compensation of employees	...	...	...	...	...	...	...	...	...	...	...	
Taxes on production and imports, less Subsidies	...	...	...	...	...	...	...	...	...	...	...	
OPERATING SURPLUS, GROSS	...	...	...	...	...	...	...	...	...	...	...	
MIXED INCOME, GROSS	...	...	...	...	...	...	...	...	...	...	...	
Gross capital formation	...	...	...	...	...	...	...	...	...	...	...	

Table 2.3 Output, gross value added, and fixed assets by industries at current prices (ISIC Rev. 3) Electricity, gas and water supply (E)

Series 100: 1993 SNA, EC dollar, Western calendar year **Data in thousands**

	2001	2002	2003	2004	2005	2006	2007	2008	2009	2010	2011	2012
Series	**100**											
Output, at basic prices	82470.0	89290.0	97190.0	108140.0	125880.0	135750.0	149730.0	164773.0	135880.0	149880.0	163430.0	
Less: Intermediate consumption, at purchaser's prices	31820.0	36730.0	43840.0	51580.0	70690.0	78970.0	81600.0	102685.0	72770.0	79000.0	97030.0	
Equals: VALUE ADDED, GROSS, at basic prices	50650.0	52560.0	53350.0	56560.0	55190.0	56780.0	68130.0	62089.0	63110.0	70880.0	66390.0	
Compensation of employees	...	...	...	...	...	...	...	...	...	...	...	
Taxes on production and imports, less Subsidies	...	...	...	...	...	...	...	...	...	...	...	
OPERATING SURPLUS, GROSS	...	...	...	...	...	...	...	...	...	...	...	
MIXED INCOME, GROSS	...	...	...	...	...	...	...	...	...	...	...	
Gross capital formation	...	...	...	...	...	...	...	...	...	...	...	

Table 2.3 Output, gross value added, and fixed assets by industries at current prices (ISIC Rev. 3) Construction (F)

Series 100: 1993 SNA, EC dollar, Western calendar year **Data in thousands**

	2001	2002	2003	2004	2005	2006	2007	2008	2009	2010	2011	2012
Series	**100**											
Output, at basic prices	102880.0	194130.0	233720.0	264970.0	270580.0	328550.0	393740.0	364671.0	338530.0	324280.0	319030.0	
Less: Intermediate consumption, at purchaser's prices	24320.0	112590.0	140230.0	158980.0	162350.0	190560.0	224430.0	207862.0	192960.0	184840.0	181850.0	
Equals: VALUE ADDED, GROSS, at basic prices	78560.0	81540.0	93490.0	105990.0	108230.0	137990.0	169310.0	156808.0	145570.0	139440.0	137180.0	
Compensation of employees	...	...	...	...	...	...	...	...	...	...	...	
Taxes on production and imports, less Subsidies	...	...	...	...	...	...	...	...	...	...	...	
OPERATING SURPLUS, GROSS	...	...	...	...	...	...	...	...	...	...	...	
MIXED INCOME, GROSS	...	...	...	...	...	...	...	...	...	...	...	
Gross capital formation	...	...	...	...	...	...	...	...	...	...	...	

Table 2.3 Output, gross value added, and fixed assets by industries at current prices (ISIC Rev. 3) Wholesale retail trade, repair of motor vehicles, motorcycles, etc.; hotels and restaurants (G+H)

Series 100: 1993 SNA, EC dollar, Western calendar year **Data in thousands**

	2001	2002	2003	2004	2005	2006	2007	2008	2009	2010	2011	2012
Series	**100**											
Output, at basic prices	355780.0	337680.0	362850.0	401910.0	444940.0	459370.0	524970.0	567706.0	439720.0	424480.0	495310.0	
Less: Intermediate consumption, at purchaser's prices	179420.0	151950.0	165250.0	185420.0	212500.0	194500.0	234520.0	262761.0	177590.0	170460.0	238410.0	
Equals: VALUE ADDED, GROSS, at basic prices	176360.0	185730.0	197600.0	216490.0	232440.0	264870.0	290450.0	304944.0	262130.0	254010.0	256890.0	
Compensation of employees	...	...	...	...	...	...	...	...	...	...	...	

	2001	2002	2003	2004	2005	2006	2007	2008	2009	2010	2011	2012
Series	**100**											
Taxes on production and imports, less Subsidies	...	...	...	...	...	...	...	...	...	...	...	
OPERATING SURPLUS, GROSS	...	...	...	...	...	...	...	...	...	...	...	
MIXED INCOME, GROSS	...	...	...	...	...	...	...	...	...	...	...	
Gross capital formation	...	...	...	...	...	...	...	...	...	...	...	

Table 2.3 Output, gross value added, and fixed assets by industries at current prices (ISIC Rev. 3) Transport, storage and communications (I)

Series 100: 1993 SNA, EC dollar, Western calendar year **Data in thousands**

	2001	2002	2003	2004	2005	2006	2007	2008	2009	2010	2011	2012
Series	**100**											
Output, at basic prices	251390.0	311020.0	372900.0	394260.0	401280.0	451480.0	442370.0	455734.0	439350.0	425860.0	434430.0	
Less: Intermediate consumption, at purchaser's prices	118380.0	148630.0	200940.0	202430.0	205640.0	233470.0	206580.0	221771.0	217310.0	208410.0	218140.0	
Equals: VALUE ADDED, GROSS, at basic prices	133010.0	162390.0	171960.0	191830.0	195640.0	218000.0	235790.0	233963.0	222040.0	217440.0	216290.0	
Compensation of employees	...	...	...	...	...	...	...	...	...	...	...	
Taxes on production and imports, less Subsidies	...	...	...	...	...	...	...	...	...	...	...	
OPERATING SURPLUS, GROSS	...	...	...	...	...	...	...	...	...	...	...	
MIXED INCOME, GROSS	...	...	...	...	...	...	...	...	...	...	...	
Gross capital formation	...	...	...	...	...	...	...	...	...	...	...	

Table 2.3 Output, gross value added, and fixed assets by industries at current prices (ISIC Rev. 3) Financial intermediation; real estate, renting and business activities (J+K)

Series 100: 1993 SNA, EC dollar, Western calendar year **Data in thousands**

	2001	2002	2003	2004	2005	2006	2007	2008	2009	2010	2011	2012
Series	**100**											
Output, at basic prices	371330.0	371110.0	392680.0	417940.0	446090.0	467600.0	484770.0	507974.0	502690.0	508330.0	508740.0	
Less: Intermediate consumption, at purchaser's prices	112960.0	103030.0	108280.0	119170.0	122520.0	130040.0	130520.0	152489.0	160310.0	157990.0	171490.0	
Equals: VALUE ADDED, GROSS, at basic prices	258370.0	268080.0	284400.0	298770.0	323570.0	337560.0	354250.0	355486.0	342380.0	350340.0	337250.0	
Compensation of employees	...	...	...	...	...	...	...	...	...	...	...	
Taxes on production and imports, less Subsidies	...	...	...	...	...	...	...	...	...	...	...	
OPERATING SURPLUS, GROSS	...	...	...	...	...	...	...	...	...	...	...	
MIXED INCOME, GROSS	...	...	...	...	...	...	...	...	...	...	...	
Gross capital formation	...	...	...	...	...	...	...	...	...	...	...	

Table 2.3 Output, gross value added, and fixed assets by industries at current prices (ISIC Rev. 3) Public administration and defense; compulsory social security (L)

Series 100: 1993 SNA, EC dollar, Western calendar year — **Data in thousands**

	2001	2002	2003	2004	2005	2006	2007	2008	2009	2010	2011	2012
Series	**100**											
Output, at basic prices	121660.0	131960.0	129040.0	142260.0	151910.0	176210.0	192060.0	185740.0	237770.0	284340.0	268660.0	
Less: Intermediate consumption, at purchaser's prices	43850.0	47530.0	45300.0	52160.0	55500.0	69010.0	72460.0	55075.0	98150.0	119560.0	90610.0	
Equals: VALUE ADDED, GROSS, at basic prices	75859.0	82415.0	82128.0	88476.0	94589.0	105647.0	117786.0	130665.0	143430.0	168590.0	178040.0	
Compensation of employees	...	...	...	...	...	...	...	...	...	...	...	
Taxes on production and imports, less Subsidies	...	...	...	...	...	...	...	...	...	...	...	
OPERATING SURPLUS, GROSS	...	...	...	...	...	...	...	...	...	...	...	
MIXED INCOME, GROSS	...	...	...	...	...	...	...	...	...	...	...	
Gross capital formation	...	...	...	...	...	...	...	...	...	...	...	

Table 2.3 Output, gross value added, and fixed assets by industries at current prices (ISIC Rev. 3) Education; health and social work; other community, social and personal services (M+N+O)

Series 100: 1993 SNA, EC dollar, Western calendar year — **Data in thousands**

	2001	2002	2003	2004	2005	2006	2007	2008	2009	2010	2011	2012
Series	**100**											
Output, at basic prices	217580.0	231340.0	228750.0	251760.0	262110.0	405570.0	490090.0	451517.0	273370.0	266350.0	277060.0	
Less: Intermediate consumption, at purchaser's prices	114220.0	118700.0	116830.0	127660.0	128630.0	264610.0	323410.0	295048.0	105500.0	98400.0	104900.0	
Equals: VALUE ADDED, GROSS, at basic prices	103360.0	112640.0	111920.0	124100.0	133480.0	140960.0	166680.0	156469.0	167870.0	167960.0	172160.0	
Compensation of employees	...	...	...	...	...	...	...	...	...	...	...	
Taxes on production and imports, less Subsidies	...	...	...	...	...	...	...	...	...	...	...	
OPERATING SURPLUS, GROSS	...	...	...	...	...	...	...	...	...	...	...	
MIXED INCOME, GROSS	...	...	...	...	...	...	...	...	...	...	...	
Gross capital formation	...	...	...	...	...	...	...	...	...	...	...	

Table 2.3 Output, gross value added, and fixed assets by industries at current prices (ISIC Rev. 3) Private households with employed persons (P)

Series 100: 1993 SNA, EC dollar, Western calendar year — **Data in thousands**

	2001	2002	2003	2004	2005	2006	2007	2008	2009	2010	2011	2012
Series	**100**											
Output, at basic prices	2360.0	2620.0	2870.0	3040.0	3150.0	3350.0	3580.0	4009.0	4290.0	4580.0	4740.0	
Less: Intermediate consumption, at purchaser's prices	...	...	...	...	...	...	...	0.0	0.0	...	...	
Equals: VALUE ADDED, GROSS, at basic prices	2360.0	2620.0	2870.0	3040.0	3150.0	3350.0	3580.0	4009.0	4290.0	4580.0	4740.0	
Compensation of employees	...	...	...	...	...	...	...	...	...	...	...	

	2001	2002	2003	2004	2005	2006	2007	2008	2009	2010	2011	2012
Series	**100**											
Taxes on production and imports, less Subsidies	...	...	...	...	...	...	...	...	...	...	...	
OPERATING SURPLUS, GROSS	...	...	...	...	...	...	...	...	...	...	...	
MIXED INCOME, GROSS	...	...	...	...	...	...	...	...	...	...	...	
Gross capital formation	...	...	...	...	...	...	...	...	...	...	...	

Table 3.1 Government final consumption expenditure by function at current prices

Series 10: 1968 SNA, EC dollar, Western calendar year
Series 100: 1993 SNA, EC dollar, Western calendar year

Data in thousands

	2001	2002	2003	2004	2005	2006	2007	2008	2009	2010	2011	2012
Series	**10**							**100**				
General public services	23000.0	20000.0	22000.0	24000.0	25000.0	23960.0	33490.0	36130.0	50207.0	20673.0	34676.0	48358.0
Defence	...	...	...	...	...	...	...	...	...	...	...	...
Public order and safety	22000.0	24000.0	24000.0	26000.0	28000.0	30000.0	34430.0	40613.0	38847.0	46473.0	47673.0	48150.0
Economic affairs	43000.0	46000.0	44000.0	54000.0	57000.0	56000.0	71050.0	65380.0	50460.0	35619.0	33785.0	35537.0
Environment protection	...	...	...	...	...	...	...	...	...	...	...	...
Housing and community amenities	2000.0	3000.0	3000.0	3000.0	3000.0	4000.0	4260.0	4193.0	5157.0	5018.0	9026.0	10584.0
Health	34000.0	38000.0	37000.0	38000.0	40000.0	45000.0	47700.0	53340.0	49996.0	52730.0	59586.0	58963.0
Recreation, culture and religion	...	...	...	...	...	...	...	...	...	...	...	...
Education	48000.0	52000.0	51000.0	55000.0	58000.0	63000.0	73510.0	77927.0	83353.0	81656.0	85232.0	89234.0
Social protection	14000.0	16000.0	16000.0	18000.0	19000.0	22000.0	22000.0	28774.0	30681.0	35456.0	36319.0	40629.0
Plus: (Other functions)	-1000.0	3000.0	5000.0	3000.0	4000.0	4000.0	4000.0	...	...	...	...	...
Equals: General government final consumption expenditure [a]	185000.0	202000.0	202000.0	221000.0	234000.0	248360.0	290510.0	317222.0	314436.0	284779.0	314252.0	339618.0

[a] Discrepancy between components and total.

Samoa

Source

Data received from the Finance Statistics Division, Samoa Bureau of Statistics.

General

The estimates shown in the following tables have been prepared in accordance with the concepts and definitions of the System of National Accounts 1993 (1993 SNA), using the production approach. The Bureau is currently undergoing a development to compile GDP by the expenditure approach, and also other aggregated accounts. This information is expected to be published in the near future.

Table 2.1 Value added by industries at current prices (ISIC Rev. 3)

Series 100: 1993 SNA, Tala, Western calendar year — **Data in thousands**

	2001	2002	2003	2004	2005	2006	2007	2008	2009	2010	2011	2012
Series	**100**											
Industries												
Agriculture, hunting, forestry; fishing	124660.6	129810.5	118817.0	143056.0	146451.6	152354.6	174040.1	167660.8	168695.0	146749.0	157346.0	154821.0
Agriculture, hunting, forestry	55951.9	62099.6	63601.4	82273.3	87543.6	78133.6	84543.4	87947.5	89081.0	69215.7	75104.0	71142.0
Fishing	68708.7	67711.0	55215.1	60783.0	58908.0	74221.0	89496.7	79713.3	79614.0	77534.0	82242.0	83678.0
Mining and quarrying	...	...	...	...	...	...	...	...	...	...	...	...
Manufacturing	139536.8	148688.1	174089.9	172759.1	184832.3	166064.0	196407.9	163505.7	123063.7	141843.5	127198.0	134008.0
Electricity, gas and water supply	38797.0	42097.0	43441.0	46906.0	52676.0	58658.0	64903.0	67864.0	72352.0	75910.0	78663.0	80383.0
Construction	58470.4	63004.2	74796.1	108943.1	126414.1	151880.5	186204.0	181048.1	177389.5	193849.8	228755.0	227144.0
Wholesale, retail trade, repair of motor vehicles, motorcycles and personal and households goods; hotels and restaurants	168097.2	186347.3	193150.9	212152.0	234929.0	257167.0	312384.1	329921.3	336816.1	354162.0	372453.0	373418.0
Wholesale, retail trade, repair of motor vehicles, motorcycles and personal and household goods	147827.2	166357.3	169460.9	186392.0	204839.0	224917.0	268544.1	281671.3	284606.1	303322.0	326253.0	331658.0
Hotels and restaurants	20270.0	19990.0	23690.0	25760.0	30090.0	32250.0	43840.0	48250.0	52210.0	50840.0	46200.0	41760.0
Transport, storage and communications	96988.9	106825.0	121520.0	135632.0	157454.0	167067.0	181490.8	185446.3	199288.1	206443.2	199023.0	205103.0
Financial intermediation; real estate, renting and business activities [a]	97023.0	105000.9	115245.2	126273.3	136888.4	150086.0	157818.5	163976.3	170837.3	177394.1	190192.0	190428.0
Public administration and defence; compulsory social security	68913.0	71011.0	73694.7	76483.9	85932.4	100970.6	113353.5	124820.5	135744.3	144198.0	147990.0	150736.0
Education; health and social work; other community, social and personal services [b]	48967.9	48978.0	53025.0	60984.0	65573.0	62949.0	63686.0	65849.4	60227.0	62411.0	66333.0	66785.0
Private households with employed persons	...	...	...	...	...	...	...	...	...	...	...	...
Equals: VALUE ADDED, GROSS, in basic prices [c]	841484.4	901762.0	967779.0	1083106.0	1191204.0	1266984.0	1450288.0	1450092.3	1444413.0	1502961.0	1567953.0	1582824.0
Less: Financial intermediation services indirectly measured (FISIM)	8979.0	10197.0	11753.0	13184.0	14215.0	14776.0	15738.0	17027.0	19102.0	19590.0	20562.0	20805.0
Plus: Taxes less Subsidies on products	...	...	...	...	...	...	...	...	...	...	...	...
Equals: GROSS DOMESTIC PRODUCT	832505.4	891565.0	956026.0	1069922.0	1176989.0	1252208.0	1434550.0	1433065.3	1425311.0	1483371.0	1547391.0	1562019.0

[a] Refers to ownership of dwellings, finance and business services.
[b] Refers to personal and other services.
[c] At producers' prices.

Table 2.2 Value added by industries at constant prices (ISIC Rev. 3)

Series 100: 1993 SNA, Tala, Western calendar year **Data in thousands**

	2001	2002	2003	2004	2005	2006	2007	2008	2009	2010	2011	2012
Series	**100**											
Base year	**2002**											
Industries												
Agriculture, hunting, forestry; fishing	138487.9	129809.5	121878.9	115288.0	121032.0	116800.1	121057.7	108559.4	108374.7	101152.0	102290.0	96599.0
Agriculture, hunting, forestry	67599.0	62098.6	67920.0	63213.0	73324.0	68475.0	67849.4	60901.0	59112.7	53873.2	55378.0	48899.0
Fishing	70888.9	67711.0	53958.9	52075.0	47798.0	48325.1	53208.3	47658.4	49262.0	47278.0	46912.0	47700.0
Mining and quarrying	...	...	...	...	...	...	...	...	...	...	...	...
Manufacturing	141668.0	148687.8	167072.0	157756.0	159903.0	134860.0	156929.7	127353.2	101803.9	111729.6	95015.0	97391.0
Electricity, gas and water supply	38082.0	42098.0	43009.0	44118.0	45548.0	47633.0	48464.0	49394.0	52534.0	54754.0	55915.0	56485.0
Construction	59279.4	63004.2	71529.7	94398.6	104881.4	118740.5	135805.2	128978.8	126551.4	133278.4	154271.0	155841.0
Wholesale, retail trade, repair of motor vehicles, motorcycles and personal and household goods; hotels and restaurants	171258.4	186347.3	188170.3	194373.2	205762.6	222154.0	230749.0	230999.2	228246.3	230654.0	239887.0	245697.0
Wholesale, retail trade, repair of motor vehicles, motorcycles and personal and household goods	150540.5	166357.3	164828.1	170440.7	179571.0	189755.9	194446.1	192750.3	192005.7	196876.0	207746.0	210011.0
Hotels and restaurants	20717.9	19990.0	23342.3	23932.6	26191.6	32398.0	36302.9	38248.9	36240.6	33777.4	32141.0	35686.0
Transport, storage and communications	107868.2	106822.0	118683.0	129804.0	140323.0	142079.0	148231.6	150124.9	160579.3	165380.9	158948.0	161881.0
Financial intermediation, real estate, renting and business activities [a]	99817.5	104997.8	113173.6	120806.0	124579.6	129250.0	131622.5	134172.9	137715.9	137982.9	140247.0	139802.0
Public administration and defence; compulsory social security	67579.4	71011.0	75009.7	78892.9	81067.7	81924.4	84194.9	87098.5	91034.0	93023.6	95224.6	97444.0
Education; health and social work; other community, social and personal services [b]	49690.0	48978.0	55089.0	59779.0	62836.0	57830.0	58440.0	58055.0	53718.0	54701.0	53871.0	53199.0
Private households with employed persons	...	...	...	...	...	...	...	...	...	...	...	...
Equals: VALUE ADDED, GROSS, in basic prices [c]	873731.0	901755.0	953615.0	995216.0	1045934.0	1051271.0	1115452.7	1074736.0	1060557.0	1082655.0	1095669.0	1104337.0
Less: Financial intermediation services indirectly measured (FISIM)	9568.0	10196.0	10944.0	11593.0	12039.0	12274.0	12667.0	13175.0	13956.0	14135.0	14478.0	14565.0
Plus: Taxes less Subsidies on products	...	...	...	...	...	...	...	...	...	...	...	...
Equals: GROSS DOMESTIC PRODUCT	864163.0	891559.0	942671.0	983623.0	1033895.0	1038997.0	1102828.0	1061561.0	1046601.0	1068520.0	1081191.0	1089772.0

[a] Refers to ownership of dwellings, finance and business services.
[b] Refers to personal and other services.
[c] At producers' prices.

San Marino

Source

The following tables have been prepared from reply to the UN National Accounts Questionnaire by the Statistical Office of San Marino.

General

Subsequent to a Technical Assistance Mission by the IMF in September 2011, methodology revisions were made regarding the compilation of national accounts.

The aim of the mission consisted in an analysis of the former method utilized, the income approach, and an analysis of the data that is presently available to the Statistics Office, with the purpose of being able to estimate GDP both by the production and the expenditure approach, on a yearly and quarterly basis, and furthermore to be in a position to produce GDP projections.

During the course of the mission, it was decided upon to compile national accounts using the expenditure and production approach following the United Nations System of National Accounts 1993 (1993 SNA) methodology.

The data entered in the grey areas of the questionnaire reflect the revised data based on the production approach.

Methodology:

Expenditure Approach

Household Final Consumption Expenditure comprises the expenses of Households made in the domestic economic territory as well as purchases made abroad. Data for estimating HH expenditure is taken from the annual Household Budget Survey. Expenses for home and car insurance, telephone services and vacations were treated as purchases made abroad even though the transactions were effected inside the national territory.

Estimates of imputed rent for home owners are also now included in Household Final Consumption Expenditure as well as in Gross Output.

Government Final Consumption Expenditure was determined as the sum of Compensation of Employees, Intermediate Consumption, Consumption of Fixed Capital minus Sales Revenues plus purchases of Goods & Services for Households.

Gross Fixed Capital Formation for machinery and equipment is calculated as the net acquisitions of such goods and the data is supplied by the Tax Office and includes both goods purchased outside the economic territory as well as purchases made in the domestic market.

With regards to construction, estimates were made based on data supplied annually from the Building Department regarding new constructions. Estimates of new constructions represent the sole value of the construction excluding land.

Changes in Inventory represent the difference between last period's ending inventory and the current period's ending inventory.

Net Exports: Data on Imports and Exports is supplied by the Tax Office. However a series of adjustments are needed in order to account for the import and export of services that are not contemplated in the Tax Office's data.

Based on the data from the HBS, the yearend Corporate Operating Statements and from Income Tax returns, we proceeded to make adjustments to Imports for the following items:

a) Purchases by residents abroad;
b) Construction services by non-residents;
c) Telephone and insurance Services;
d) Business travel.

Adjustments were also made to Exports to account for the purchases made in the domestic market by non residents.
A further adjustment was made by the IMF to account for transportation services.

Production Approach

Data availability is as follows:
1) For the Non-Financial Corporations and the Financial Corporations, the data sources are the yearend Financial and Operating Statements, that said corporations are obliged to present to the Chamber of Commerce who then subsequently transmits the data to the Statistics Office. From these records we are able to estimate Gross Output, Intermediate Consumption, Gross Value Added, Gross Operating Surplus, Compensation and Consumption of Fixed Capital. A further breakdown of GDP contribution by Economic Activity was also put in place.

2) For the Household Sector (unincorporated) the data source is the Tax Office .The data is taken from the income tax returns and permits us to estimate the aforementioned items.

3) Data regarding the NPISHs were elaborated for the first time and were included in the experimental GDP by production approach.

4) Data regarding the Government is taken from the compilation of GFS Statistics whose source is the year-end financial and operating statements. Government Output is measured as the sum of Compensation of Employees, Intermediate consumption and Consumption of Fixed Capital. (Gross Value Added is the sum of Compensation and CFC).

With regards to the Financial Sector, it was agreed upon by the Statistics Office and The IMF Statistics Division, to further explore the compilation method in that it could prove more plausible to adopt the procedure used in estimating Government and Non-Profit GDP.

Table 1.1 Gross domestic product by expenditures at current prices

Series 20: 1968 SNA, euro, Western calendar year
Series 100: 1993 SNA, euro, Western calendar year

Data in millions

	2001	2002	2003	2004	2005	2006	2007	2008	2009	2010	2011	2012
Series	**20**						**100**					
Expenditures of the gross domestic product												
Final consumption expenditure	475.0	480.0	495.0	513.0	533.0	553.0	571.0 754.2	762.7	770.0	733.0	738.9	
Household final consumption expenditure	...	...	...	...	...	...	... 544.1	538.6	539.5	500.3	507.0	
NPISHs final consumption expenditure	...	...	...	...	...	...	... ...	...	...	...	...	
General government final consumption expenditure	...	...	...	...	...	...	... 210.1	224.1	230.5	232.7	231.9	
Gross capital formation	498.0	551.0	584.0	592.0	614.0	621.0	632.0 626.3	568.6	432.0	364.4	380.7	
Gross fixed capital formation	475.0	563.0	570.0	569.0	586.0	598.0	575.0 569.2	548.3	468.6	382.9	403.2	
Changes in inventories	23.0	-12.0	14.0	23.0	28.0	23.0	57.0 57.2	20.3	-36.6	-18.5	-22.5	
Acquisitions less disposals of valuables	...	...	...	...	...	...	... ...	...	...	...	...	
Exports of goods and services	1683.0	1660.0	1763.0	1975.0	2035.0	2307.0	2491.0 3799.7	3952.5	3296.1	2907.5	2580.1	

	2001	2002	2003	2004	2005	2006	2007	2008	2009	2010	2011	2012
Series	**20**						**100**					
Less: Imports of goods and services	1744.0	1756.0	1847.0	2019.0	2076.0	2310.0	2461.0					
							3348.1	3515.5	2887.7	2520.3	2239.0	
Equals: GROSS DOMESTIC PRODUCT	911.0	935.0	995.0	1061.0	1106.0	1171.0	1233.0					
							1832.1	1768.2	1610.3	1484.6	1460.7	

Table 1.2 Gross domestic product by expenditures at constant prices

Series 20: 1968 SNA, euro, Western calendar year
Series 100: 1993 SNA, euro, Western calendar year

Data in millions

	2001	2002	2003	2004	2005	2006	2007	2008	2009	2010	2011	2012
Series	**20**						**100**					
Base year	**1995**						**2007**					
	Expenditures of the gross domestic product											
Final consumption expenditure	412.0	407.0	410.0	416.0	425.0	433.0	439.0					
							754.2	736.9	738.3	691.5	679.3	
Household final consumption expenditure	...	...	...	...	...	...	...					
							544.1	520.4	517.3	471.9	466.2	
NPISHs final consumption expenditure	...	...	...	...	...	...	...					
							...	...	...	...	...	
General government final consumption expenditure	...	...	...	...	...	...	...					
							210.1	216.5	221.0	219.5	213.2	
Gross capital formation	432.0	467.0	484.0	481.0	489.0	486.0	486.0					
							626.3	555.5	418.8	344.9	348.0	
Gross fixed capital formation	412.0	477.0	472.0	462.0	467.0	468.0	442.0					
							569.2	535.7	452.8	362.5	368.2	
Changes in inventories	20.0	-10.0	12.0	19.0	22.0	18.0	44.0					
							57.2	19.8	-35.0	-17.6	-21.1	
Acquisitions less disposals of valuables	...	...	...	...	...	...	...					
							...	...	...	...	...	
Exports of goods and services	1461.0	1408.0	1459.0	1603.0	1624.0	1805.0	1916.0					
							3799.7	3854.8	3148.8	2766.8	2423.7	
Less: Imports of goods and services	1514.0	1490.0	1529.0	1639.0	1657.0	1808.0	1893.0					
							3348.1	3408.1	2778.8	2390.8	2072.7	
Equals: GROSS DOMESTIC PRODUCT	791.0	793.0	824.0	862.0	882.0	916.0	948.0					
							1832.1	1739.1	1526.2	1412.3	1377.4	

Table 1.3 Relations among product, income, savings, and net lending aggregates

Series 20: 1968 SNA, euro, Western calendar year

Data in millions

	2001	2002	2003	2004	2005	2006	2007	2008	2009	2010	2011	2012
Series	**20**											
GROSS DOMESTIC PRODUCT	911.0	935.0	995.0	1061.0	1106.0	1171.0	1233.0	1259.0	1102.0			
Plus: Compensation of employees - from and to the rest of the world, net	...	...	...	...	...	...	...	...	...			
Plus: Property income - from and to the rest of the world, net	...	...	...	...	...	...	...	...	...			
Plus: Taxes less subsidies on production and imports - from and to the rest of the world, net	...	...	...	...	...	...	...	...	...			
Equals: GROSS NATIONAL INCOME	790.0	829.0	891.0	942.0	970.0	1034.0	1097.0	1098.0	938.0			
Plus: Current transfers - from and to the rest of the world, net	-140.0	-131.0	-128.0	-136.0	-140.0	-152.0	-156.0	-187.0	-156.0			
Equals: GROSS NATIONAL DISPOSABLE INCOME	650.0	698.0	763.0	807.0	830.0	882.0	941.0	911.0	782.0			
Less: Final consumption expenditure / Actual final consumption	...	...	...	...	...	...	...	...	...			
Equals: SAVING, GROSS	...	...	...	...	...	...	...	...	...			
Plus: Capital transfers - from and to the rest of the world, net	...	...	...	...	...	...	...	...	...			

	2001	2002	2003	2004	2005	2006	2007	2008	2009	2010	2011	2012
Series	**20**											
Less: Gross capital formation	...	...	...	...	...	...	...	...	...			
Less: Acquisitions less disposals of non-produced non-financial assets	...	...	...	...	...	...	...	...	...			
Equals: NET LENDING (+) / NET BORROWING (-) OF THE NATION	...	...	...	...	...	...	...	...	...			
Net values: Gross National Income / Gross National Disposable Income / Saving Gross less Consumption of fixed capital												
Less: Consumption of fixed capital	...	...	...	...	...	...	...	...	...			
Equals: NET NATIONAL INCOME	...	...	...	...	...	...	...	...	...			
Equals: NET NATIONAL DISPOSABLE INCOME	...	...	...	...	...	...	...	...	...			
Equals: SAVING, NET	...	...	...	...	...	...	...	...	...			

Table 2.1 Value added by industries at current prices (ISIC Rev. 3)

Series 100: 1993 SNA, euro, Western calendar year **Data in millions**

	2001	2002	2003	2004	2005	2006	2007	2008	2009	2010	2011	2012
Series									**100**			
Industries												
Agriculture, hunting, forestry; fishing									0.7	0.7		
Agriculture, hunting, forestry									...	...		
Fishing									0.1	...		
Mining and quarrying									...	...		
Manufacturing									370.3	386.5		
Electricity, gas and water supply									...	...		
Construction									61.8	59.1		
Wholesale, retail trade, repair of motor vehicles, motorcycles and personal and households goods; hotels and restaurants									204.5	171.6		
Wholesale, retail trade, repair of motor vehicles, motorcycles and personal and household goods									189.4	151.7		
Hotels and restaurants									15.1	19.8		
Transport, storage and communications									45.1	40.6		
Financial intermediation; real estate, renting and business activities									245.0	191.6		
Financial intermediation									16.9	-7.8		
Real estate, renting and business activities									228.1	199.4		
Public administration and defence; compulsory social security									197.3	202.3		
Education; health and social work; other community, social and personal services									51.9	48.0		
Education									0.5	0.6		
Health and social work									10.2	9.7		
Other community, social and personal services									41.2	37.7		

	2001	2002	2003	2004	2005	2006	2007	2008	2009	2010	2011	2012
Series									**100**			
Private households with employed persons									273.3	258.8		
Equals: VALUE ADDED, GROSS, in basic prices									1450.0	1359.1		
Less: Financial intermediation services indirectly measured (FISIM)									...	...		
Plus: Taxes less Subsidies on products									126.8	116.5		
Plus: Statistical discrepancy									-0.0	...		
Equals: GROSS DOMESTIC PRODUCT [a]									1576.8	1475.6		

[a] Discrepancy with equivalent item in Table 1.1 (Gross domestic product by expenditures at current prices).

Table 2.2 Value added by industries at constant prices (ISIC Rev. 3)

Series 100: 1993 SNA, euro, Western calendar year — **Data in millions**

	2001	2002	2003	2004	2005	2006	2007	2008	2009	2010	2011	2012
Series									**100**			
Base year									**2007**			
Industries												
Agriculture, hunting, forestry; fishing									0.7	0.7		
Mining and quarrying									...	...		
Manufacturing									352.4	365.6		
Electricity, gas and water supply									...	...		
Construction									58.8	55.9		
Wholesale, retail trade, repair of motor vehicles, motorcycles and personal and household goods; hotels and restaurants									194.6	162.3		
Wholesale, retail trade, repair of motor vehicles, motorcycles and personal and household goods									180.2	143.5		
Hotels and restaurants									14.4	18.8		
Transport, storage and communications									43.0	38.4		
Financial intermediation, real estate, renting and business activities									233.1	181.2		
Financial intermediation									16.0	-7.4		
Real estate, renting and business activities									217.1	188.6		
Public administration and defence; compulsory social security									187.7	191.4		
Education; health and social work; other community, social and personal services									49.4	45.4		
Education									0.5	0.6		
Health and social work									9.7	9.1		
Other community, social and personal services									39.2	35.7		
Private households with employed persons									260.1	244.7		
Equals: VALUE ADDED, GROSS, in basic prices									1379.8	1285.4		
Less: Financial intermediation services indirectly measured (FISIM)									...	...		

	2001	2002	2003	2004	2005	2006	2007	2008	2009	2010	2011	2012
Series									**100**			
Base year									**2007**			
Plus: Taxes less Subsidies on products									120.7	110.2		
Equals: GROSS DOMESTIC PRODUCT [a]									1500.5	1395.6		

[a] Discrepancy with equivalent item in Table 1.2 (Gross domestic product by expenditures at constant prices).

Table 2.6 Output, gross value added and fixed assets by industries at current prices (ISIC Rev. 4) Total economy

Series 100: 1993 SNA, euro, Western calendar year **Data in millions**

	2001	2002	2003	2004	2005	2006	2007	2008	2009	2010	2011	2012
Series							**100**					
Output, at basic prices							5997.2	6359.1	5514.8	4859.2	4401.3	
Less: Intermediate consumption, at purchaser's prices							4423.6	4747.4	4064.8	3494.5	3082.2	
Equals: VALUE ADDED, GROSS, at basic prices							1573.6	1611.8	1450.0	1364.7[a]	1319.0	
Compensation of employees							638.7	690.6	693.7	703.4	673.9	
Taxes on production and imports, less Subsidies							164.9	166.8	138.1	126.1	108.6	
OPERATING SURPLUS, GROSS							624.8	614.4	510.0	425.1	421.3	
MIXED INCOME, GROSS							310.1	306.7	246.3	236.2	223.8	
Less: Consumption of fixed capital							302.2	367.1	383.8	346.3	280.4	
OPERATING SURPLUS, NET							330.0	254.9	133.5	86.1	147.5	
MIXED INCOME, NET							302.6	299.1	239.0	229.0	217.2	
Gross capital formation							626.3	568.6	432.0	364.4	380.7	
Gross fixed capital formation							569.2	548.3	468.6	382.9	403.2	
Changes in inventories							57.2	20.3	-36.6	-18.5	-22.5	
Acquisitions less disposals of valuables							...	...	...	...	...	
Employment (average, in 1000 persons)							21.4	22.1	22.1	21.9	22.1	

[a] Discrepancy with equivalent item in Table 2.1 (Value added by industries at current prices).

Table 2.6 Output, gross value added and fixed assets by industries at current prices (ISIC Rev. 4) Agriculture, forestry and fishing (A)

Series 100: 1993 SNA, euro, Western calendar year **Data in millions**

	2001	2002	2003	2004	2005	2006	2007	2008	2009	2010	2011	2012
Series									**100**			
Output, at basic prices									3.6	2.5		
Less: Intermediate consumption, at purchaser's prices									2.8	1.8		
Equals: VALUE ADDED, GROSS, at basic prices									0.7	0.7		
Compensation of employees									0.4	0.3		
Taxes on production and imports, less Subsidies									...	...		
OPERATING SURPLUS, GROSS [a]									0.4	0.4		

	2001	2002	2003	2004	2005	2006	2007	2008	2009	2010	2011	2012
Series									**100**			
MIXED INCOME, GROSS									...	...		
Less: Consumption of fixed capital									0.0	0.1		
OPERATING SURPLUS, NET									...	...		
MIXED INCOME, NET [b]									0.3	0.2		
Gross capital formation									...	...		
Employment (average, in 1000 persons)									75.0	75.0		

[a] Includes Mixed Income, Gross.
[b] Net Operating Surplus.

Table 2.6 Output, gross value added and fixed assets by industries at current prices (ISIC Rev. 4) Fishing and aquaculture (03)

Series 100: 1993 SNA, euro, Western calendar year — **Data in millions**

	2001	2002	2003	2004	2005	2006	2007	2008	2009	2010	2011	2012
Series									**100**			
Output, at basic prices									0.5			
Less: Intermediate consumption, at purchaser's prices									0.4			
Equals: VALUE ADDED, GROSS, at basic prices									0.1			
Compensation of employees									...			
Taxes on production and imports, less Subsidies									...			
OPERATING SURPLUS, GROSS									0.1			
MIXED INCOME, GROSS									...			
Less: Consumption of fixed capital									0.0			
OPERATING SURPLUS, NET									0.0			
MIXED INCOME, NET									...			
Gross capital formation									...			

Table 2.6 Output, gross value added and fixed assets by industries at current prices (ISIC Rev. 4) Manufacturing (C)

Series 100: 1993 SNA, euro, Western calendar year — **Data in millions**

	2001	2002	2003	2004	2005	2006	2007	2008	2009	2010	2011	2012
Series									**100**			
Output, at basic prices									1467.3	1643.7		
Less: Intermediate consumption, at purchaser's prices									1097.0	1257.1		
Equals: VALUE ADDED, GROSS, at basic prices									370.3	386.5		
Compensation of employees									191.4	198.1		
Taxes on production and imports, less Subsidies									...	...		
OPERATING SURPLUS, GROSS [a]									179.0	188.4		

	2001	2002	2003	2004	2005	2006	2007	2008	2009	2010	2011	2012
Series									**100**			
MIXED INCOME, GROSS									...	...		
Less: Consumption of fixed capital									45.8	50.8		
OPERATING SURPLUS, NET [b]									133.2	137.6		
MIXED INCOME, NET									...	...		
Gross capital formation									...	...		
Employment (average, in 1000 persons)									6129.0	5900.0		

[a] Includes Mixed Income, Gross.
[b] Includes Mixed Income, Net.

Table 2.6 Output, gross value added and fixed assets by industries at current prices (ISIC Rev. 4) Construction (F)

Series 100: 1993 SNA, euro, Western calendar year — **Data in millions**

	2001	2002	2003	2004	2005	2006	2007	2008	2009	2010	2011	2012
Series									**100**			
Output, at basic prices									182.1	175.9		
Less: Intermediate consumption, at purchaser's prices									120.4	116.9		
Equals: VALUE ADDED, GROSS, at basic prices									61.8	59.1		
Compensation of employees									38.4	40.2		
Taxes on production and imports, less Subsidies									...	...		
OPERATING SURPLUS, GROSS [a]									23.4	18.9		
MIXED INCOME, GROSS									...	...		
Less: Consumption of fixed capital									6.7	4.5		
OPERATING SURPLUS, NET [b]									16.7	14.4		
MIXED INCOME, NET									...	...		
Gross capital formation									...	...		
Employment (average, in 1000 persons)									1674.0	1599.0		

[a] Includes Mixed Income, Gross.
[b] Includes Mixed Income, Net.

Table 2.6 Output, gross value added and fixed assets by industries at current prices (ISIC Rev. 4) Wholesale and retail trade; repair of motor vehicles and motorcycles (G)

Series 100: 1993 SNA, euro, Western calendar year — **Data in millions**

	2001	2002	2003	2004	2005	2006	2007	2008	2009	2010	2011	2012
Series									**100**			
Output, at basic prices									1640.8	1105.1		
Less: Intermediate consumption, at purchaser's prices									1451.4	953.4		
Equals: VALUE ADDED, GROSS, at basic prices									189.4	151.7		
Compensation of employees									82.9	76.1		

	2001	2002	2003	2004	2005	2006	2007	2008	2009	2010	2011	2012
Series									**100**			
Taxes on production and imports, less Subsidies									...	...		
OPERATING SURPLUS, GROSS [a]									106.4	75.7		
MIXED INCOME, GROSS									...	...		
Less: Consumption of fixed capital									20.4	19.0		
OPERATING SURPLUS, NET [b]									86.1	56.7		
MIXED INCOME, NET									...	...		
Gross capital formation									...	...		
Employment (average, in 1000 persons)									3712.0	3712.0		

[a] Includes Mixed Income, Gross.
[b] Includes Mixed Income, Net.

Table 2.6 Output, gross value added and fixed assets by industries at current prices (ISIC Rev. 4) Transportation and storage (H)

Series 100: 1993 SNA, euro, Western calendar year **Data in millions**

	2001	2002	2003	2004	2005	2006	2007	2008	2009	2010	2011	2012
Series									**100**			
Output, at basic prices									246.2	271.7		
Less: Intermediate consumption, at purchaser's prices									201.0	231.1		
Equals: VALUE ADDED, GROSS, at basic prices									45.1	40.6		
Compensation of employees									21.3	20.4		
Taxes on production and imports, less Subsidies									...	...		
OPERATING SURPLUS, GROSS [a]									23.8	20.2		
MIXED INCOME, GROSS									...	...		
Less: Consumption of fixed capital									5.6	4.8		
OPERATING SURPLUS, NET [b]									18.2	15.4		
MIXED INCOME, NET									...	...		
Gross capital formation									...	...		
Employment (average, in 1000 persons)									621.0	664.0		

[a] Includes Mixed Income, Gross.
[b] Includes Mixed Income, Net.

Table 2.6 Output, gross value added and fixed assets by industries at current prices (ISIC Rev. 4) Accommodation and food service activities (I)

Series 100: 1993 SNA, euro, Western calendar year | **Data in millions**

	2001	2002	2003	2004	2005	2006	2007	2008	2009	2010	2011	2012
Series									**100**			
Output, at basic prices									30.7	27.6		
Less: Intermediate consumption, at purchaser's prices									15.6	7.8		
Equals: VALUE ADDED, GROSS, at basic prices									15.1	19.8		
Compensation of employees									9.9	5.5		
Taxes on production and imports, less Subsidies									...	...		
OPERATING SURPLUS, GROSS [a]									5.2	14.3		
MIXED INCOME, GROSS									...	...		
Less: Consumption of fixed capital									2.8	1.4		
OPERATING SURPLUS, NET [b]									2.4	12.9		
MIXED INCOME, NET									...	...		
Gross capital formation									...	...		
Employment (average, in 1000 persons)									231.0	218.0		

[a] Includes Mixed Income, Gross.
[b] Includes Mixed Income, Net.

Table 2.6 Output, gross value added and fixed assets by industries at current prices (ISIC Rev. 4) Financial and insurance activities (K)

Series 100: 1993 SNA, euro, Western calendar year | **Data in millions**

	2001	2002	2003	2004	2005	2006	2007	2008	2009	2010	2011	2012
Series									**100**			
Output, at basic prices									88.9	61.0		
Less: Intermediate consumption, at purchaser's prices									72.1	68.8		
Equals: VALUE ADDED, GROSS, at basic prices									16.9	-7.8		
Compensation of employees									69.0	69.7		
Taxes on production and imports, less Subsidies									...	...		
OPERATING SURPLUS, GROSS [a]									-52.1	-77.5		
MIXED INCOME, GROSS									...	...		
Less: Consumption of fixed capital									86.6	57.8		
OPERATING SURPLUS, NET [b]									-138.7	-135.3		
MIXED INCOME, NET									...	...		
Gross capital formation									...	...		
Employment (average, in 1000 persons)									1048.0	1080.0		

[a] Includes Mixed Income, Gross.
[b] Includes Mixed Income, Net.

Table 2.6 Output, gross value added and fixed assets by industries at current prices (ISIC Rev. 4) Real estate activities (L)

Series 100: 1993 SNA, euro, Western calendar year — **Data in millions**

	2001	2002	2003	2004	2005	2006	2007	2008	2009	2010	2011	2012
Series									**100**			
Output, at basic prices									947.7	729.9		
Less: Intermediate consumption, at purchaser's prices									719.6	530.5		
Equals: VALUE ADDED, GROSS, at basic prices									228.1	199.4		
Compensation of employees									56.9	64.5		
Taxes on production and imports, less Subsidies									...	...		
OPERATING SURPLUS, GROSS [a]									171.2	134.9		
MIXED INCOME, GROSS									...	...		
Less: Consumption of fixed capital									47.4	49.0		
OPERATING SURPLUS, NET [b]									123.8	85.9		
MIXED INCOME, NET									...	...		
Gross capital formation									...	...		
Employment (average, in 1000 persons)									2999.0	2962.0		

[a] Includes Mixed Income, Gross.
[b] Includes Mixed Income, Net.

Table 2.6 Output, gross value added and fixed assets by industries at current prices (ISIC Rev. 4) Administrative and support service activities (N)

Series 100: 1993 SNA, euro, Western calendar year — **Data in millions**

	2001	2002	2003	2004	2005	2006	2007	2008	2009	2010	2011	2012
Series									**100**			
Employment (average, in 1000 persons)									4180.0	4196.0		

Table 2.6 Output, gross value added and fixed assets by industries at current prices (ISIC Rev. 4) Public administration and defence; compulsory social security (O)

Series 100: 1993 SNA, euro, Western calendar year — **Data in millions**

	2001	2002	2003	2004	2005	2006	2007	2008	2009	2010	2011	2012
Series									**100**			
Output, at basic prices									340.7	504.7		
Less: Intermediate consumption, at purchaser's prices									143.7	302.4		
Equals: VALUE ADDED, GROSS, at basic prices									197.0	202.3		
Compensation of employees									177.2	181.1		
Taxes on production and imports, less Subsidies									...	...		
OPERATING SURPLUS, GROSS [a]									19.9	21.2		
MIXED INCOME, GROSS									...	...		

	2001	2002	2003	2004	2005	2006	2007	2008	2009	2010	2011	2012
Series									**100**			
Less: Consumption of fixed capital									19.9	21.2		
OPERATING SURPLUS, NET									0.0	0.0		
MIXED INCOME, NET									...	...		
Gross capital formation									...	...		
Employment (average, in 1000 persons)									4180.0	4196.0		

[a] Includes Mixed Income, Gross.

Table 2.6 Output, gross value added and fixed assets by industries at current prices (ISIC Rev. 4) Education (P)

Series 100: 1993 SNA, euro, Western calendar year **Data in millions**

	2001	2002	2003	2004	2005	2006	2007	2008	2009	2010	2011	2012
Series									**100**			
Output, at basic prices									1.5	1.4		
Less: Intermediate consumption, at purchaser's prices									0.9	0.8		
Equals: VALUE ADDED, GROSS, at basic prices									0.5	0.6		
Compensation of employees									0.3	0.3		
Taxes on production and imports, less Subsidies									...	...		
OPERATING SURPLUS, GROSS [a]									0.3	0.4		
MIXED INCOME, GROSS									...	...		
Less: Consumption of fixed capital									0.1	0.1		
OPERATING SURPLUS, NET [b]									0.2	0.3		
MIXED INCOME, NET									...	...		
Gross capital formation									...	...		
Employment (average, in 1000 persons)									44.0	47.0		

[a] Includes Mixed Income, Gross.
[b] Includes Mixed Income, Net.

Table 2.6 Output, gross value added and fixed assets by industries at current prices (ISIC Rev. 4) Human health and social work activities (Q)

Series 100: 1993 SNA, euro, Western calendar year **Data in millions**

	2001	2002	2003	2004	2005	2006	2007	2008	2009	2010	2011	2012
Series									**100**			
Output, at basic prices									27.5	21.4		
Less: Intermediate consumption, at purchaser's prices									17.4	11.7		
Equals: VALUE ADDED, GROSS, at basic prices									10.2	9.7		
Compensation of employees									4.9	4.7		
Taxes on production and imports, less Subsidies									...	...		
OPERATING SURPLUS, GROSS [a]									5.2	5.0		

	2001	2002	2003	2004	2005	2006	2007	2008	2009	2010	2011	2012
Series									**100**			
MIXED INCOME, GROSS									...	...		
Less: Consumption of fixed capital									1.5	1.5		
OPERATING SURPLUS, NET [b]									3.8	3.5		
MIXED INCOME, NET									...	...		
Gross capital formation									...	...		
Employment (average, in 1000 persons)									206.0	243.0		

[a] Includes Mixed Income, Gross.
[b] Includes Mixed Income, Net.

Table 2.6 Output, gross value added and fixed assets by industries at current prices (ISIC Rev. 4) Other service activities (S)

Series 100: 1993 SNA, euro, Western calendar year — **Data in millions**

	2001	2002	2003	2004	2005	2006	2007	2008	2009	2010	2011	2012
Series									**100**			
Output, at basic prices									124.6	95.0		
Less: Intermediate consumption, at purchaser's prices									83.2	57.3		
Equals: VALUE ADDED, GROSS, at basic prices									41.5	37.7		
Compensation of employees									14.7	15.2		
Taxes on production and imports, less Subsidies									...	...		
OPERATING SURPLUS, GROSS [a]									26.8	22.6		
MIXED INCOME, GROSS									...	...		
Less: Consumption of fixed capital									5.7	6.5		
OPERATING SURPLUS, NET [b]									21.1	16.1		
MIXED INCOME, NET									...	...		
Gross capital formation									...	...		
Employment (average, in 1000 persons)									1160.0	1208.0		

[a] Includes Mixed Income, Gross.
[b] Includes Mixed Income, Net.

Table 2.6 Output, gross value added and fixed assets by industries at current prices (ISIC Rev. 4) Private households with employed persons (T)

Series 100: 1993 SNA, euro, Western calendar year — **Data in millions**

	2001	2002	2003	2004	2005	2006	2007	2008	2009	2010	2011	2012
Series									**100**			
Output, at basic prices									412.7	389.6		
Less: Intermediate consumption, at purchaser's prices									139.4	130.9		
Equals: VALUE ADDED, GROSS, at basic prices									273.3	258.8		
Compensation of employees									26.4	27.4		

	2001	2002	2003	2004	2005	2006	2007	2008	2009	2010	2011	2012
Series									**100**			
Taxes on production and imports, less Subsidies									...	...		
OPERATING SURPLUS, GROSS									...	...		
MIXED INCOME, GROSS									247.0	231.3		
Less: Consumption of fixed capital									7.9	7.9		
OPERATING SURPLUS, NET									...	...		
MIXED INCOME, NET									...	...		
Gross capital formation									239.0	223.4		

Table 3.1 Government final consumption expenditure by function at current prices

Series 20: 1968 SNA, euro, Western calendar year **Data in millions**

	2001	2002	2003	2004	2005	2006	2007	2008	2009	2010	2011	2012
Series			**20**									
General public services			71.6	66.5								
Defence			12.5	12.9								
Public order and safety			...	...								
Economic affairs			...	...								
Environment protection			5.2	8.5								
Housing and community amenities			8.9	13.7								
Health			61.3	65.9								
Recreation, culture and religion			11.2	13.0								
Education			39.9	38.8								
Social protection			31.1	63.6								
Equals: General government final consumption expenditure [a]			270.6	313.8								

[a] Discrepancy between components and total.

Table 4.1 Total Economy (S.1)

Series 20: 1968 SNA, euro, Western calendar year **Data in millions**

	2001	2002	2003	2004	2005	2006	2007	2008	2009	2010	2011	2012
Series	**20**											
II.1.1 Generation of income account - Resources												
GROSS DOMESTIC PRODUCT	911.0	935.0	995.0	1061.0	1106.0	1171.0						
II.1.1 Generation of income account - Uses												
Compensation of employees	446.0	459.0	466.0	513.0	532.0	569.0						
Taxes on production and imports, less Subsidies	148.0	145.0	161.0	170.0	174.0	174.0						
Taxes on production and imports	153.0	150.0	167.0	175.0	180.0	181.0						
Taxes on products	...	...	...	...	...	...						
Other taxes on production	...	...	...	...	...	...						
Less: Subsidies	5.0	5.0	6.0	5.0	6.0	7.0						

		2001	2002	2003	2004	2005	2006	2007	2008	2009	2010	2011	2012
Series		**20**											
Subsidies on products		...	...	...	...	...	...						
Other subsidies on production		...	...	...	...	...	...						
OPERATING SURPLUS, GROSS		317.0	331.0	369.0	379.0	399.0	428.0						
MIXED INCOME, GROSS		...	...	...	...	...	...						
		II.1.2 Allocation of primary income account - Resources											
OPERATING SURPLUS, GROSS	a	219.0	238.0	281.0	290.0	317.0	339.0						
MIXED INCOME, GROSS		...	...	...	...	...	...						
Compensation of employees		333.0	346.0	353.0	385.0	391.0	422.0						
Taxes on production and imports, less Subsidies		148.0	145.0	161.0	170.0	174.0	174.0						
Taxes on production and imports		153.0	150.0	167.0	175.0	180.0	181.0						
Taxes on products		...	...	...	...	...	...						
Other taxes on production		...	...	...	...	...	...						
Less: Subsidies		5.0	5.0	6.0	5.0	6.0	7.0						
Subsidies on products		...	...	...	...	...	...						
Other subsidies on production		...	...	...	...	...	...						
Property income		90.0	100.0	97.0	99.0	88.0	100.0						
		II.1.2 Allocation of primary income account - Uses											
Property income		...	...	...	...	...	...						
GROSS NATIONAL INCOME		790.0	829.0	891.0	942.0	970.0	1034.0						
		II.2 Secondary distribution of income account - Resources											
GROSS NATIONAL INCOME		790.0	829.0	891.0	942.0	970.0	1034.0						
Current taxes on income, wealth, etc.	b	-97.0	-100.0	-104.0	-108.0	-116.0	-128.0						
Social contributions	b	-11.0	-7.0	-3.0	-2.0	4.0	1.0						
Social benefits other than social transfers in kind		...	...	...	...	...	...						
Other current transfers	b	-32.0	-24.0	-21.0	-26.0	-28.0	-24.0						
		II.2 Secondary distribution of income account - Uses											
Current taxes on income, wealth, etc.		...	...	...	...	...	...						
Social contributions		...	...	...	...	...	...						
Social benefits other than social transfers in kind		...	...	...	...	...	...						
Other current transfers		...	...	...	...	...	...						
GROSS DISPOSABLE INCOME		650.0	698.0	763.0	807.0	830.0	882.0						
		II.4.1 Use of disposable income account - Resources											
GROSS DISPOSABLE INCOME		650.0	698.0	763.0	807.0	830.0	882.0						
Adjustment for the change in net equity of households on pension funds		...	...	...	...	...	...						
		II.4.1 Use of disposable income account - Uses											
Final consumption expenditure	c	472.0	482.0	505.0	528.0	547.0	566.0						
Individual consumption expenditure		...	...	...	...	...	...						
Collective consumption expenditure		...	...	...	...	...	...						

	2001	2002	2003	2004	2005	2006	2007	2008	2009	2010	2011	2012
Series	**20**											
Adjustment for the change in net equity of households on pension funds	...	...	...	...	...	...						
SAVING, GROSS	177.0	215.0	257.0	278.0	283.0	316.0						

[a] Discrepancy with equivalent item in the generation of income account.
[b] Refers to Net Value.
[c] Statistical discrepancy with equivalent item in Table 1.1 (Gross domestic product by expenditures at current prices).

Sao Tome and Principe

Source

Reply to the United Nations National Accounts Questionnaire from the Instituto Nacional de Estatistica (INE), Sao Tome.

General

The estimates are generally in accordance with the classifications and definitions recommended in the United Nations System of National Accounts 1993 (1993 SNA). When the scope and coverage of the estimates differ for conceptual or statistical reasons from the definitions and classifications recommended in SNA, a footnote is indicated to the relevant tables.

Table 2.1 Value added by industries at current prices (ISIC Rev. 3)

Series 100: 1993 SNA, dobra, Western calendar year **Data in millions**

	2001	2002	2003	2004	2005	2006	2007	2008	2009	2010	2011	2012
Series	**100**											
Industries												
Agriculture, hunting, forestry; fishing	131813.4	162773.0	193579.7	215281.3	245510.9	304792.5	371998.7	511201.4	716786.8	835420.1	993428.7	
Agriculture, hunting, forestry	91412.6	117391.9	137677.0	147160.8	173250.6	215744.0	262683.7	359707.7	515514.9	587435.3	705027.4	
Fishing	40400.8	45381.1	55902.8	68120.5	72260.3	89048.4	109315.0	151493.7	201272.0	247984.8	288401.3	
Mining and quarrying	2818.9	2864.0	4097.0	5139.0	6203.0	8189.0	10718.0	16478.0	18452.0	19792.0	20612.0	
Manufacturing	50052.4	61202.8	70883.4	76750.0	91024.0	115263.0	133458.8	240659.0	261356.2	314142.8	360317.6	
Electricity, gas and water supply	9595.0	13840.7	18132.5	22343.3	31221.5	42136.0	50440.8	83629.5	93741.9	102213.7	128429.8	
Construction	63813.8	49359.1	60698.9	76307.9	99237.8	123046.3	160503.5	245614.2	272494.1	285264.2	299121.5	
Wholesale, retail trade, repair of motor vehicles, motorcycles and personal and households goods; hotels and restaurants	175021.6	200159.2	246297.6	283029.7	331152.8	444774.9	527070.2	813582.9	929804.0	1080545.6	1231773.5	
Wholesale, retail trade, repair of motor vehicles, motorcycles and personal and household goods	165455.0	187913.0	232358.6	265483.0	313558.2	423144.5	497804.3	772014.8	883809.7	1021939.7	1157584.1	
Hotels and restaurants	9566.6	12246.2	13939.0	17546.7	17594.6	21630.3	29265.9	41568.2	45994.2	58605.9	74189.4	
Transport, storage and communications	77231.0	96257.7	119020.2	149928.5	203006.7	342482.5	289813.0	468616.8	505983.0	554989.3	685620.5	
Financial intermediation; real estate, renting and business activities	41721.8	48378.4	83342.5	107718.2	139086.8[a]	176891.7	218312.5	303391.0	546992.1	576867.4	595937.5	
Financial intermediation	15755.8	16679.4	44293.2	59905.6	87811.5	108120.4	128230.0	176313.7	426756.2	429134.7	429191.2	
Real estate, renting and business activities	25966.0	31699.0	39383.2	47308.3	55770.0	68771.2	90082.5	127077.3	120235.9	147732.7	166746.4	
Public administration and defence; compulsory social security	35441.1	39354.3	52739.7	73164.3	104912.5	116810.7	107004.0	111907.4	109455.7	110681.5	110068.6	
Education; health and social work; other community, social and personal services	39148.4	44753.8	51110.1	56562.7	68925.6	83743.2	103350.7	138725.1	163409.1[a]	207538.7	248262.2	
Education	6213.0	7049.8	8423.2	9496.2	9937.7	9422.9	10208.2	10960.5	14236.5	17126.2	18729.5	
Health and social work	3169.0	3929.8	5010.6	6016.2	6342.9	6580.2	7271.3	7894.7	9005.0	11099.3	11809.1	
Other community, social and personal services	29766.4	33314.1	37676.3	41050.4	52645.0	67740.1	85871.5	119869.9	149172.7	179313.2	217723.6	
Private households with employed persons	...	...	...	...	...	...	...	...	...	...	...	
Equals: VALUE ADDED, GROSS, in basic prices	626657.0	718943.0	899901.8	1066224.8	1320282.3	1758130.1	1972670.2	2933805.3	3618474.9	4087455.4	4673572.0	

	2001	2002	2003	2004	2005	2006	2007	2008	2009	2010	2011	2012
Series	**100**											
Less: Financial intermediation services indirectly measured (FISIM)	11837.7	13036.9	27339.4	42348.6	65030.3	80036.7	94882.8	141650.1	298248.3	312153.6	305200.9	
Plus: Taxes less Subsidies on products	23848.3	...	...	...	...	...	...	...	...	...	...	
Equals: GROSS DOMESTIC PRODUCT	638668.1	736639.4	914694.2	1071295.2	1317426.6	1718916.5	2043040.4	2946702.4	3517390.2	4010068.7	4592737.2	

[a] Discrepancy between components and total.

Table 2.2 Value added by industries at constant prices (ISIC Rev. 3)

Series 100: 1993 SNA, dobra, Western calendar year **Data in millions**

	2001	2002	2003	2004	2005	2006	2007	2008	2009	2010	2011	2012
Series	**100**											
Base year	**2001**											
	Industries											
Agriculture, hunting, forestry; fishing	131813.4	131831.0	135101.4	140164.0	142386.4	150806.6	155012.1	168331.9	174902.7	172690.3	174485.8	
Agriculture, hunting, forestry	91412.6	90029.5	91265.7	94846.6	96456.7	103500.9	106327.6	118268.6	123460.6	119869.4	120286.1	
Fishing	40400.8	41801.5	43835.7	45317.4	45929.7	47305.7	48684.5	50063.3	51442.1	52820.9	54199.7	
Mining and quarrying	2818.9	2278.9	2518.9	2741.8	2813.2	3002.1	3084.9	3205.5	3354.3	3521.4	3551.3	
Manufacturing	50052.4	52310.1	54091.0	55567.1	57554.4	60422.5	62384.1	67162.2	68948.2	69303.5	74851.4	
Electricity, gas and water supply	9595.0	11227.4	12350.4	13110.8	14483.5	15871.1	16468.1	17443.2	18842.5	20649.2	23263.5	
Construction	63813.8	49097.8	53929.5	58684.9	60235.9	64463.2	67728.5	70557.8	74295.5	79296.4	79805.2	
Wholesale, retail trade, repair of motor vehicles, motorcycles and personal and household goods; hotels and restaurants	175021.6	185409.7	199153.6	215488.1	217211.6	246950.5	250944.3	282365.2	285575.9	288720.6	290645.4	
Wholesale, retail trade, repair of motor vehicles, motorcycles and personal and household goods	165455.0	174114.0	187307.5	203144.2	204767.5	233442.1	237434.0	268194.2	271295.3	273985.9	275077.8	
Hotels and restaurants	9566.6	11295.7	11846.1	12343.9	12444.1	13508.4	13510.2	14171.0	14280.6	14734.7	15567.6	
Transport, storage and communications	77231.0	88767.3	98772.1	107930.9	117083.2	136354.2	140607.3	161593.0	164030.7	167393.0	175589.7	
Financial intermediation, real estate, renting and business activities	41721.8	42585.8	44659.7	46321.5	46467.6	50779.2	51264.5	54912.3	54286.1	54338.4	56478.9	
Financial intermediation	15755.8	16082.1	16865.3	17492.8	17548.0	19176.3	19359.5	20737.1	20500.6	20520.4	21328.7	
Real estate, renting and business activities	25966.0	26503.7	27794.4	28828.6	28919.6	31603.0	31905.0	34175.2	33785.5	33818.1	35150.2	
Public administration and defence; compulsory social security	35441.1	35825.8	40358.9	38092.3	36835.4	37591.0	38188.5	38552.5	38964.6	39376.7	40164.3	
Education; health and social work; other community, social and personal services	39148.4	40080.9	42078.4	41882.1	45192.6	47080.9	49795.9	52391.0	55101.6	57842.8	61165.8	
Education	6213.0	6208.1	6780.6	7142.7	7505.4	7804.0	7843.2	8236.6	8421.3	8811.4	9297.3	
Health and social work	3169.0	3587.3	4103.7	4474.3	4569.9	4660.3	4921.3	4993.1	5026.9	4854.8	4948.2	
Other community, social and personal services	29766.4	30285.6	31194.1	30265.1	33117.3	34616.7	37031.4	39161.3	41653.4	44176.6	46920.3	
Private households with employed persons	...	...	...	...	...	...	...	...	...	...	...	
Equals: VALUE ADDED, GROSS, in basic prices	626657.4	639414.9	683013.5	719983.6	740263.8	813321.2	835478.3	916514.7	938302.0	953132.3	980001.4	
Less: Financial intermediation services indirectly measured (FISIM)	11837.7	11863.7	24900.9	37382.3	55509.5	65030.3	80036.7	107318.1	138333.5	152391.9	147718.7	

	2001	2002	2003	2004	2005	2006	2007	2008	2009	2010	2011	2012
Series	**100**											
Base year	**2001**											
Plus: Taxes less Subsidies on products	23848.3	23910.2	36475.4	43358.3	52887.0	80445.0	96040.4	119728.6	165587.9	208851.3	227115.4	
Equals: GROSS DOMESTIC PRODUCT	638668.1	651461.0	694588.4	725959.3	737641.2	828735.8	851482.0	928925.2	965556.4	1009591.7	1054865.1	

Saudi Arabia

Source

The Central Department of Statistics and Information of the Ministry of Economy and Planning, in Riyadh, is the authority responsible for preparing the national accounts statistics in the Kingdom of Saudi Arabia. The Department officially publishes national accounts data in a yearly bulletin entitled “National accounts of the Kingdom of Saudi Arabia”. The accounts are compiled on the basis of the detailed results of the various statistical studies carried out periodically by the Department, primarily the annual economic studies and social studies, as well as the data of the Saudi Arabian Monetary Institute, the State’s final accounts data provided by the Ministry of Finance, and other economic indicators.

General

Generally speaking, the methods and procedures employed in the preparation and calculation of national accounts data and the compilation of the related accounts are based on statistical sources available through the country’s statistics development programmes in accordance with international specifications and definitions. The Department follows the 1968 System of National Accounts for the issuance of its yearly bulletin. In addition, the Department has begun a trial application of the 1993 System of National Accounts (1993 SNA), issuing a new bulletin in accordance with the 1993 SNA side by side with the previous bulletin. The base year for calculations of the gross domestic product (GDP) at constant prices is 1999. The development of such statistics unquestionably requires coordination and cooperation on the part of the State authorities concerned, such as the Saudi Arabian Monetary Institute, the Ministry of Finance, etc.
In 2012 (2011NAQ), the Department submitted data for Output and Gross Value Added, and the Integrated Economic Accounts partially in accordance with the 2008 SNA. The data was originally published in the 2009 Bulletin of National Accounts "National Accounts of Saudi Arabia 2002-2009, According to System of National Accounts 2008". The document is available in the Department's website:
http://www.cdsi.gov.sa/english/index.php?option=com_docman&task=cat_view&gid=120&Itemid=113.
This submission is stored under series 100 in the National Accounts Database.

Methodology:

Overview of GDP Compilation

From the accounts compiled, GDP can be calculated using the output method or the expenditure method.

Expenditure Approach

The calculation of GDP using the expenditure method is based on a number of sources. With regard to the household sector, it is calculated by means of a survey of household expenditure and income carried out by the Department of General Statistics and Information, in 1999, which up to the present time has been the principal source for calculating the final consumption expenditure of the household (family) sector, taking into account population growth rates and price change rates (the Department is currently carrying out a new survey of household expenditure and income).

Final consumption expenditure of general government comprises total government expenditure (inputs + wages and salaries + depreciation) less market and non-market sales. The final accounts of government units issued by the Ministry of Finance are the principal source of these data.

Gross fixed capital formation is calculated by means of the economic studies carried out by the Department of General Statistics and Information, which cover all economic activities; the surveys provide data on gross fixed capital formation by type of fixed asset. In addition, the final accounts of the State provide information on expenditure on government gross fixed capital formation. The surveys also provide, by means of questionnaires, the item on depreciation (depreciation of fixed capital) other than governmental, depreciation being calculated indirectly.

With regard to exports and imports, reliance is placed on the data issued by the Directorate of Foreign Trade Statistics, within the Department, covering exports and imports of goods, and on balance of payments data provided by the Saudi Arabian Monetary Institute which includes exports and imports of services and their various subcategories.

Lastly, changes in inventory are measured by means of economic studies carried out by the Department of General Statistics and Information using questionnaires to obtain data on changes in inventory in the government sector.

Production Approach

GDP tables are prepared by type of economic activity classified by economic sector, as specified below.

(a) Non-financial sector

This covers all economic activities in accordance with the registry of economic activities (ISIC Rev.3) apart from banking and insurance activities, and ancillary financial services. In general, it can be said that the production approach has been used to calculate value added (output less inputs being equal to value added) for all activities comprising this sector. These activities can be classified as follows:

1. Agriculture, hunting and fishing
This activity includes plant production, animal production, fishing, the production of honey, etc. The Ministry of Agriculture is the primary source of data on this activity and provides data on the various kinds of agricultural output based on the results of computations and agricultural studies made by the Ministry. It provides data on output and intermediate consumption from which value added is calculated. The Ministry also provides data on wages and salaries paid and on capital formation, from which the surplus in the income-generation account is calculated. To compile the other accounts, a sample of farms and agricultural enterprises is taken and, in the light of the data provided by their final accounts, indicators are prepared for use in compiling the remaining accounts for this activity.

2. Extraction of crude petroleum and natural gas

(a) Crude petroleum

The Ministry of Oil and Mineral Resources is the principal source of data, whether monthly or annual, on crude petroleum extracted by oil companies working in the Kingdom. The Ministry provides data on the quantities and value of annual output, the source of the crude petroleum, as well as on the refineries and banks involved in production in connection with the activity of extraction in the Kingdom of Saudi Arabia only; value added is calculated for the oil extraction activity and use is made of the annual reports provided by these companies to calculate capital formation by type of capital asset, together with other information pertaining to wages and salaries, taxes, royal revenue, current and capital transfers in order to compile the current and capital accounts.

(b) Exploitation of other mines and quarries

Use is made of the results of economic studies carried out annually by the Department using questionnaires specially designed for the purpose which provide full information on outputs, inputs, wages and salaries, taxes, subsidies, current and capital transfers and royal revenue. From these data a calculation is made of value added, and of current account and capital formation.

3. Manufacturing
Studies carried out annually by the Department of General Statistics and Information using questionnaires specially designed for the purpose are the principal source of data on all manufacturing industries. By means of a comprehensive listing of all establishments with 50 employees or more and a sampling of establishments with

fewer than 50 employees, by administrative district and economic activity, the questionnaire provides all necessary data for compiling the accounts, ranging from the output account to the capital account.

4. Electricity, gas and water
The annual economic surveys made by the Department of General Statistics and Information, together with the final accounts of the Consolidated Saudi Electricity Company and the National Gas and Industrialization Company are the principal source of data on electricity; the State budget provides data on water through the budget of the water authorities in various regions of the Kingdom. On the basis of these data, the value added is calculated and the remaining current accounts and the capital account are compiled.

5. Construction and building
Construction and building activity includes all operations for the construction of residential and non-residential buildings, the construction and surfacing of roads, the building of bridges and tunnels, railways, drainage, water, sewerage, electricity and telephone projects, the drilling of wells, land reclamation, etc. The results of the annual economic surveys provide data and indicators that are used to measure the necessary changes in such activities.

6. Wholesale and retail trade
The measurements and accounts for this activity are based on the data provided by the annual economic surveys of trade and distribution statistics made by the Department of General Statistics and Information using a comprehensive listing of establishments with 50 employees or more, and a sampling of establishments with fewer than 50 employees. The annual surveys provide data on sales and purchases, wages and salaries, inputs, new fixed assets purchased and all types of expenditures and other income necessary for compiling the accounts.

7. Hotels and restaurants
The activities of hotels and restaurants are separated from wholesale and resale trade and the calculations and compilation of the accounts for this activity are based on the results of the economic surveys made by the Department of General Statistics and Information. The questionnaires provide data on the income and expenditures of the units engaged in this activity.

8. Transport, storage and communications
This activity includes transport by land, sea and air, together with communications activities, whether in the public, private or mixed sector. Use is made of economic studies and of the data provided on communications activities and on companies engaged in that field. Value added is measured and accounts compiled using the output method.

9. Real estate and business services
This includes housing rentals together with business services, such as advisory services, accountants, auditors, etc. Housing rentals are measured using data from surveys of household expenditure and income after taking into account population growth rates and rental cost indices. Figures for business services are based on the results of the annual economic survey.

10. Social, recreational and personal services
This includes educational services, health services, entertainment and recreation together with laundry, cleaning services, barbershops, etc. among personal services. The economic survey is the principal source of such data.

(b) Financial sector

This sector covers financial intermediation projects and the final accounts of units engaged in banking, and insurance companies. The annual survey made by the Department is the principal source of data on this sector. As regards the actual provision of financial intermediation services, the methodology applied is that recommended in the System of National Accounts for measuring financial intermediation services, namely measuring the services indirectly and globally as they have not yet been delivered to the entities using them.

(c) General government sector

As we have indicated, the general government sector offers goods and services either free of charge or at nominal prices. It follows that the output of government services has no market value and output in the government sector is therefore measured by means of expenditures, in other words, total output is equal to production inputs plus the remuneration of employees and depreciation. By subtracting production inputs from the value of output one obtains the overall value added which is equal to the remuneration of employees plus depreciation; subtracting marketed and unmarketed sales from total expenditures, we obtain the final consumption costs of the Government. The total current and capital accounts are compiled from the data provided in the final accounts of the State.

(d) Household sector (family sector) (covers informal enterprises)

Output for this sector is measured using a survey of family expenditures and income by measuring remuneration for household services, together with units in which fewer than five persons are employed, engaged in various unregulated economic activities. That being so, such units are excluded from the scope of the annual economic surveys; the overall current accounts, and the capital account are compiled together with such enterprises.

(e) Non-profit institutions serving households

Such institutions provide services and goods without charge or at nominal prices and their output therefore has no market value. It is therefore measured, as in the case of the general government sector, by the expenditure method (inputs + remuneration of employees + depreciation = output). By subtracting production inputs we obtain the value added. The annual economic survey is the principal source of data on this sector and provides all that is needed for compiling the current accounts and the capital account, as well as for measuring the final consumption costs, after deduction of marketed and unmarketed sales.

(f) The rest of the world

The balance of payments prepared by the Saudi Arabian Monetary Institute is the principal source of data for compiling the accounts for this sector, together with a number of other financial reports.

Table 1.1 Gross domestic product by expenditures at current prices

Series 20: 1968 SNA, Saudi Arabian riyal, Fiscal year beginning 1 July — **Data in millions**

	2001	2002	2003	2004	2005	2006	2007	2008	2009	2010	2011	2012
Series	**20**											
	Expenditures of the gross domestic product											
Final consumption expenditure	448245.0	444917.0	468128.0	516652.0	586804.0	678442.0	756273.0	869045.0	948829.0	1039589.8	1163989.0	1256308.0
Household final consumption expenditure [a]	259550.0	260400.0	269980.0	294854.0	324154.0	367360.0	434187.0	523947.0	591814.0	639417.0	674143.0	718725.0
NPISHs final consumption expenditure	...	...	...	...	...	...	...	...	...	...	...	...
General government final consumption expenditure	188695.0	184517.0	198148.0	221798.0	262650.0	311082.0	322086.0	345098.0	357015.0	400172.8	489846.0	537583.0
Gross capital formation	129592.0	139109.0	159473.0	192743.0	248306.0	313565.0	412667.0	532060.0	510336.0	607347.1	678374.4	726783.9
Gross fixed capital formation	126095.0	128066.0	148098.0	185872.0	237691.0	288680.0	368687.0	444499.0	414452.0	483921.3	574660.0	609931.7
Changes in inventories	3497.0	11043.0	11375.0	6871.0	10615.0	24885.0	43980.0	87561.0	95884.0	123425.9	103714.3	116852.2
Acquisitions less disposals of valuables	...	...	...	...	...	...	...	...	...	...	...	...
Exports of goods and services	273677.0	291155.0	371088.0	494702.0	702164.0	844522.0	934321.0	1210701.0	757711.0	981867.0	1410702.0	1525587.0
Exports of goods	...	...	...	472735.0	677144.0	791338.0	874403.0	1175552.0	721152.0	941785.0	1367619.0	1485171.0

	2001	2002	2003	2004	2005	2006	2007	2008	2009	2010	2011	2012
Series	**20**											
Exports of services	...	...	...	21967.0	25020.0	53184.0	59918.0	35149.0	36559.0	40082.0	43083.0	40416.0
Less: Imports of goods and services	165219.0	168114.0	194041.0	233814.0	306503.0	425038.0	544434.0	662568.0	607759.0	653261.0	742415.0	781279.0
Imports of goods	...	...	...	166938.0	222985.0	261402.0	338089.0	431753.0	358290.0	400735.0	493449.1	533096.0
Imports of services	...	...	...	66876.0	83518.0	163636.0	206345.0	230815.0	249469.0	252526.0	248965.9	248183.0
Equals: GROSS DOMESTIC PRODUCT	686296.0	707067.0	804648.0	970283.0	1230771.0	1411491.0	1558827.0	1949238.0	1609117.0	1975542.9	2510650.4	2727399.9

[a] Includes Final consumption expenditure of NPISH.

Table 1.2 Gross domestic product by expenditures at constant prices

Series 20: 1968 SNA, Saudi Arabian riyal, Fiscal year beginning 1 July **Data in millions**

	2001	2002	2003	2004	2005	2006	2007	2008	2009	2010	2011	2012
Series	**20**											
Base year	**1999**											
	Expenditures of the gross domestic product											
Final consumption expenditure	452970.0	456149.0	473533.0	520337.0	576721.0	640960.0	698055.0	766847.0	801780.0	830354.0	882486.0	
Household final consumption expenditure [a]	266123.0	268215.0	274589.0	298761.0	326578.0	360706.0	411077.0	460599.0	492616.0	511289.0	525948.0	
NPISHs final consumption expenditure	...	...	...	...	...	...	...	...	...	...	...	
General government final consumption expenditure	186848.0	187934.0	198944.0	221576.0	250143.0	280254.0	286978.0	306248.0	309164.0	319065.0	356538.0	
Gross capital formation	128103.0	143886.0	160055.0	184059.0	224473.0	276502.0	346309.0	412249.0	385538.0	444304.0	505117.0	
Gross fixed capital formation	125783.0	129736.0	148629.0	180981.0	220692.0	263307.0	314299.0	361899.0	339606.0	389104.0	442765.0	
Changes in inventories	2320.0	14150.0	11426.0	3078.0	3781.0	13195.0	32010.0	50350.0	45932.0	55200.0	62352.0	
Acquisitions less disposals of valuables	...	...	...	...	...	...	...	...	...	...	...	
Exports of goods and services	220078.0	203734.0	242968.0	265134.0	286572.0	312465.0	320928.0	307345.0	284966.0	298349.0	324322.0	
Less: Imports of goods and services	164735.0	166540.0	190518.0	220006.0	283856.0	381185.0	465691.0	511030.0	479031.0	505912.0	554350.0	
Equals: GROSS DOMESTIC PRODUCT	636417.0	637230.0	686037.0	749524.0	803910.0	848742.0	899601.0	975412.0	993254.0	1067097.0	1157577.0	

[a] Includes Final consumption expenditure of NPISH.

Table 1.3 Relations among product, income, savings, and net lending aggregates

Series 20: 1968 SNA, Saudi Arabian riyal, Fiscal year beginning 1 July **Data in millions**

	2001	2002	2003	2004	2005	2006	2007	2008	2009	2010	2011	2012
Series	**20**											
GROSS DOMESTIC PRODUCT	686296.0	707067.0	804648.0	970283.0	1230771.0	1411491.0	1558827.0	1949238.0	1609117.0	1975542.9	2510650.4	2727399.9
Plus: Compensation of employees - from and to the rest of the world, net	-8505.0	-8918.0	-8316.0	-7625.0	-1891.0	-2095.0	-2163.0	-2004.0	-2129.0	-2449.0	-2382.0	-2278.0
Plus: Compensation of employees - from the rest of the world	...	...	...	0.0	352.0	396.0	463.0	811.0	804.0	887.0	914.0	984.0
Less: Compensation of employees - to the rest of the world	8505.0	8918.0	8316.0	7625.0	2243.0	2491.0	2626.0	2815.0	2933.0	3336.0	3296.0	3262.0
Plus: Property income - from and to the rest of the world, net	15155.0	13797.0	11093.0	15629.0	3510.0	16457.0	26134.0	36373.0	34528.0	28865.0	38698.0	42762.0
Plus: Property income - from the rest of the world	15467.0	13929.0	11163.0	16042.0	18600.0	38857.0	56267.0	79808.0	73267.0	67257.0	73208.0	86907.0
Less: Property income - to the rest of the world	312.0	132.0	70.0	413.0	15090.0	22400.0	30133.0	43435.0	38739.0	38392.0	34510.0	44145.0

	2001	2002	2003	2004	2005	2006	2007	2008	2009	2010	2011	2012
Series	**20**											
Sum of Compensation of employees and property income - from and to the rest of the world, net	6650.0	4879.0	2777.0	8004.0	1619.0	14362.0	23971.0	34369.0	32399.0	26416.0	36316.0	40484.0
Plus: Sum of Compensation of employees and property income - from the rest of the world	15467.0	13929.0	11163.0	16042.0	18952.0	39253.0	56730.0	80619.0	74071.0	68144.0	74122.0	87891.0
Less: Sum of Compensation of employees and property income - to the rest of the world	8817.0	9050.0	8386.0	8038.0	17333.0	24891.0	32759.0	46250.0	41672.0	41728.0	37806.0	47407.0
Plus: Taxes less subsidies on production and imports - from and to the rest of the world, net	...	...	...	...	...	...	...	...	...	...	...	...
Equals: GROSS NATIONAL INCOME	692946.0	711946.0	807425.0	978287.0	1232390.0	1425853.0	1582798.0	1983607.0	1641516.0	2001958.9	2546966.4	2767883.9
Plus: Current transfers - from and to the rest of the world, net	-80032.0	-83395.0	-74645.0	-74261.0	-55374.0	-62844.0	-63870.0	-86294.0	-103772.0	-104704.0	-110197.0	-115610.0
Plus: Current transfers - from the rest of the world	...	...	...	...	...	...	...	...	...	...	...	...
Less: Current transfers - to the rest of the world	80032.0	83395.0	74645.0	74261.0	55374.0	62844.0	63870.0	86294.0	103772.0	104704.0	110327.0	115876.0
Equals: GROSS NATIONAL DISPOSABLE INCOME	612914.0	628551.0	732780.0	904026.0	1177016.0	1363009.0	1518928.0	1897313.0	1537744.0	1897254.9	2436769.4	2652273.9
Less: Final consumption expenditure / Actual final consumption	448246.0	444917.0	468128.0	516652.0	586804.0	678442.0	756273.0	869045.0	948829.0	1039590.0	1163989.0	1256308.0
Equals: SAVING, GROSS	164668.0	183634.0	264652.0	387374.0	590212.0	684567.0	762655.0	1028268.0	588915.0	857664.9	1272780.4	1395965.9
Plus: Capital transfers - from and to the rest of the world, net	...	...	...	...	...	...	...	...	...	...	...	...
Less: Gross capital formation	129592.0	139109.0	159473.0	192743.0	248306.0	313565.0	412667.0	532060.0	510336.0	607347.1	678374.4	726783.9
Less: Acquisitions less disposals of non-produced non-financial assets	...	...	...	...	...	...	...	...	...	...	...	...
Equals: NET LENDING (+) / NET BORROWING (-) OF THE NATION	...	...	...	...	...	...	...	...	...	...	...	...
	Net values: Gross National Income / Gross National Disposable Income / Saving Gross less Consumption of fixed capital											
Less: Consumption of fixed capital	71691.0	65839.0	76287.0	78683.0	82356.0	90257.0	98742.0	113453.0	109457.0	111395.0	155660.0	163500.0
Equals: NET NATIONAL INCOME	621255.0	646107.0	731138.0	899604.0	1150034.0	1335596.0	1484056.0	1870154.0	1532059.0	1890563.9	2391306.4	2604383.9
Equals: NET NATIONAL DISPOSABLE INCOME	541223.0	562712.0	656492.0	825343.0	1094660.0	1272752.0	1420186.0	1783860.0	1428287.0	1785859.9	2281109.4	2488773.9
Equals: SAVING, NET	92977.0	117795.0	188364.0	308691.0	507856.0	594310.0	663913.0	914815.0	479458.0	746269.9	1117120.4	1232465.9

Table 2.1 Value added by industries at current prices (ISIC Rev. 3)

Series 20: 1968 SNA, Saudi Arabian riyal, Fiscal year beginning 1 July
Series 200: 1993 SNA, Saudi Arabian riyal, Western calendar year

Data in millions

	2001	2002	2003	2004	2005	2006	2007	2008	2009	2010	2011	2012
Series	**20**			**200**								
	Industries											
Agriculture, hunting, forestry; fishing	35708.0	36101.0	36454.0	37187.0								
				37852.0	39641.0	41619.0	43182.0	45161.0	45926.0	47063.4	48162.7	49902.5
Mining and quarrying	230250.0	236926.0	294111.0	384468.0								
				384921.0	571892.0	669827.0	734756.0	1028053.0	608783.0	821228.3	1215517.7	1286804.2
Manufacturing	69206.0	72975.0	86267.0	95827.0								
				100254.0	117466.0	135471.0	154959.0	175100.0	174600.0	218170.8	252003.2	279538.2
Electricity, gas and water supply	8928.0	9303.0	9870.0	10406.0								
				16055.0	16753.0	17571.0	18562.0	18412.0	21575.0	26280.9	28284.7	30669.7
Construction	43185.0	44739.0	47137.0	51141.0								
				53529.0	58380.0	64636.0	74325.0	79681.0	80379.0	90780.5	107021.1	124658.2

	2001	2002	2003	2004	2005	2006	2007	2008	2009	2010	2011	2012
Series	**20**			**200**								
Wholesale, retail trade, repair of motor vehicles, motorcycles and personal and households goods; hotels and restaurants	49793.0	51735.0	53856.0	58132.0								
				66652.0	77122.0	91203.0	110366.0	133338.0	147836.0	174505.8	197926.2	219072.6
Transport, storage and communications	30559.0	31934.0	33224.0	35667.0								
				38977.0	43576.0	49813.0	61041.0	77774.0	88870.0	101204.8	115272.3	129277.9
Financial intermediation; real estate, renting and business activities	78873.0	82072.0	85843.0	91218.0								
				97132.0	108339.0	122233.0	136812.0	153304.0	171300.0	182603.9	195053.6	216759.0
Public administration and defence; compulsory social security [a]	123589.0	124486.0	139929.0	155371.0								
				155371.0	176350.0	196386.0	200306.0	209278.0	241047.0	280863.0	312308.0	344723.0
Education; health and social work; other community, social and personal services	23064.0	24124.0	25114.0	26478.0								
				26666.0	27877.0	29284.0	30996.0	33021.0	35207.0	37767.6	41892.5	46509.0
Private households with employed persons	...	...	...	...								
				...	...	...	...	...	...	...	...	...
Equals: VALUE ADDED, GROSS, in basic prices [b]	693155.0	714395.0	811805.0	945896.0								
[c]				977409.0	1237396.0	1418043.0	1565305.0	1953122.0	1615523.0	1980469.0	2513442.1	2727914.4
Less: Financial intermediation services indirectly measured (FISIM)	13991.0	14714.0	15244.0	15950.0								
				15950.0	16739.0	17575.0	18280.0	18825.0	19299.4	19595.1	20076.8	20615.5
Plus: Taxes less Subsidies on products [d]	7133.0	7386.0	8087.0	8825.0								
[d]				8825.0	10115.0	11025.0	11801.0	14940.0	12895.0	14669.0	17285.0	20101.0
Equals: GROSS DOMESTIC PRODUCT	686296.0	707067.0	804648.0	938771.0								
				970283.0	1230771.0	1411491.0	1558827.0	1949238.0	1609116.6	1975542.9	2510650.4	2727399.9[e]

[a] Includes Private households with employed persons.
[b] At producers' prices. Includes financial intermediation services indirectly measured (FISIM) of the Total Economy.
[c] At producers' prices.
[d] Import duties only.
[e] Data for this year refers to preliminary data.

Table 2.2 Value added by industries at constant prices (ISIC Rev. 3)

Series 20: 1968 SNA, Saudi Arabian riyal, Fiscal year beginning 1 July
Series 200: 1993 SNA, Saudi Arabian riyal, Western calendar year

Data in millions

	2001	2002	2003	2004	2005	2006	2007	2008	2009	2010	2011	2012
Series	**20**			**200**								
Base year	**1999**											
	Industries											
Agriculture, hunting, forestry; fishing	35992.0	36454.0	36751.0	37874.0								
				38070.0	38473.0	38862.0	39619.0	40145.0	40559.3	40156.5	41026.5	42078.3
Mining and quarrying	179937.0	164901.0	195055.0	207742.0								
				208159.0	222173.0	220245.0	211982.0	221537.0	203177.0	204166.4	224077.1	236719.4
Manufacturing	68700.0	71082.0	76142.0	81314.0								
				86470.0	93069.0	102500.0	113315.0	125193.0	128462.0	141478.1	160848.5	173059.2
Electricity, gas and water supply	9515.0	9955.0	10569.0	11259.0								
				15185.0	16001.0	17031.0	17722.0	18353.0	21382.0	26216.3	27583.1	29597.9
Construction	42123.0	43181.0	45550.0	48517.0								
				49603.0	53539.0	58172.0	64930.0	67430.0	68474.0	75818.3	83300.2	91846.8
Wholesale, retail trade, repair of motor vehicles, motorcycles and personal and household goods; hotels and restaurants	50079.0	52210.0	54204.0	56893.0								
				64004.0	72220.0	83517.0	97371.0	112681.0	114347.0	133657.7	143400.7	155341.8
Transport, storage and communications	31277.0	33455.0	35046.0	37863.0								
				39733.0	44065.0	49513.0	61236.0	78238.0	87247.0	96460.3	109768.2	121459.5
Financial intermediation, real estate, renting and business activities	79114.0	82560.0	84793.0	88490.0								
				95946.0	106232.0	116819.0	127142.0	139478.0	149597.0	156667.0	159946.3	166924.6
Public administration and defence; compulsory social security [a]	123075.0	126040.0	129326.0	132148.0								
				132148.0	136565.0	139142.0	141821.0	145210.0	152509.7	162926.0	175858.5	185078.7
Education; health and social work; other community, social and personal services	23481.0	24792.0	25552.0	26754.0								
				26936.0	28128.0	29346.0	30658.0	31720.0	33265.0	35114.4	37018.7	39152.5
Education	...	...	...	...								
				...	...	...	...	...	...	...	...	...
Health and social work	...	...	...	...								
				...	...	...	...	...	...	...	...	...

	2001	2002	2003	2004	2005	2006	2007	2008	2009	2010	2011	2012
Series	**20**			**200**								
Base year	**1999**											
Other community, social and personal services	23481.0	24792.0	25552.0	26754.0								
				26936.0	28128.0	29346.0	30658.0	31720.0	33265.0	35114.4	37018.7	39152.5
Private households with employed persons	...	...	...	...								
				...	...	...	...	...	...	...	...	...
Equals: VALUE ADDED, GROSS, in basic prices [b]	643293.0	644630.0	692988.0	728853.0								
[c]				756254.0	810465.0	855147.0	905796.0	979985.0	999020.0	1072660.8	1162827.7	1241258.7
Less: Financial intermediation services indirectly measured (FISIM)	14029.0	14859.0	14804.0	14954.0								
				14954.0	15194.0	15395.0	15508.0	15529.0	15869.0	16103.6	16316.2	16653.5
Plus: Taxes less Subsidies on products [d]	7152.0	7459.0	7854.0	8274.0								
[d]				8225.0	8641.0	8992.0	9312.0	10955.0	10104.0	10539.4	11065.4	11758.5
Equals: GROSS DOMESTIC PRODUCT	636417.0	637230.0	686037.0	722173.0								
				749524.0	803910.0	848742.0	899601.0	975412.0	993254.0	1067096.7	1157577.0	1236363.7[e]

[a] Includes Private households with employed persons.
[b] At producers' prices. Includes financial intermediation services indirectly measured (FISIM) of the Total Economy.
[c] At producers' prices.
[d] Import duties only.
[e] Data for this year refers to preliminary data.

Table 2.3 Output, gross value added, and fixed assets by industries at current prices (ISIC Rev. 3) Total Economy

Series 20: 1968 SNA, Saudi Arabian riyal, Fiscal year beginning 1 July — **Data in millions**

	2001	2002	2003	2004	2005	2006	2007	2008	2009	2010	2011	2012
Series	**20**											
Output, at basic prices	...	...	...	...	...							
Less: Intermediate consumption, at purchaser's prices	...	...	...	...	...							
Equals: VALUE ADDED, GROSS, at basic prices [a]	686296.0	707067.0	804648.0	938771.0	1160742.0[b]							
Compensation of employees	217502.0	222925.0	241968.0	263412.0	...							
Taxes on production and imports, less Subsidies [c]	18404.0	19194.0	18068.0	15217.0	...							
OPERATING SURPLUS, GROSS [d]	450390.0	464949.0	544610.0	660142.0	...							
MIXED INCOME, GROSS	...	...	...	...	...							
Total Economy only: Adjustment for FISIM (if FISIM is not distributed to uses)	13991.0	14714.0	15244.0	15950.0	...							
Less: Consumption of fixed capital	71691.0	65839.0	76287.0	78683.0	...							
OPERATING SURPLUS, NET [e]	378699.0	399110.0	468323.0	581459.0	...							
MIXED INCOME, NET	...	...	...	...	...							
Gross capital formation	129592.0	139109.0	159473.0	180156.0	...							
Gross fixed capital formation	126095.0	128066.0	148098.0	156347.0	...							
Changes in inventories	3498.0	11043.0	11375.0	23809.0	...							
Acquisitions less disposals of valuables	...	...	...	...	...							

[a] Refers to Gross Domestic Product.
[b] Data for this year(s) have not been revised.
[c] Refers to all taxes less subsidies on production and imports.
[d] Includes Mixed Income, Gross.
[e] Includes Mixed Income, Net.

Table 2.3 Output, gross value added, and fixed assets by industries at current prices (ISIC Rev. 3) Agriculture, hunting, forestry; fishing (A+B)

Series 20: 1968 SNA, Saudi Arabian riyal, Fiscal year beginning 1 July
Series 200: 1993 SNA, Saudi Arabian riyal, Western calendar year

Data in millions

	2001	2002	2003	2004	2005	2006	2007	2008	2009	2010	2011	2012
Series	**20**	**200**										
Output, at basic prices	...	...										
		48873.0	49352.0	51162.0[a]	53509.0[a]	54556.0[a]	58223.0[a]	60881.0[a]	59230.0[a]	...	...	...
Less: Intermediate consumption, at purchaser's prices	...	...										
		12949.0	13055.0	14157.0	15477.0	15423.0	18335.0	20023.0	18039.0	...	...	...
Equals: VALUE ADDED, GROSS, at basic prices	35708.0	36101.0										
		35924.0	36297.0	37852.0[b]	39641.0[b]	41619.0[b]	43182.0[b]	45161.0[b]	45926.0[b]	47063.4	48162.7	49902.5
Compensation of employees	...	...										
		7040.0	7109.0	7289.0	7350.0	7796.0	7950.0	8145.0	8201.0	...	...	...
Taxes on production and imports, less Subsidies	...	...										
		-1100.0	-2448.0	-3492.0	-2440.0	-2112.0	-3335.0	-8778.0	-8898.0	...	...	...
Taxes on production and imports	...	...										
		218.0	229.0	224.0	209.0	274.0	248.0	272.0	261.0	...	...	...
Taxes on products	...	...										
		...	...	...	...	...	...	...	...	...	...	...
Other taxes on production	...	...										
		218.0	229.0	224.0	209.0	274.0	248.0	272.0	261.0	...	...	...
Less: Subsidies	...	...										
		1318.0	2677.0	3716.0	2649.0	2386.0	3583.0	9050.0	9159.0	...	...	...
Subsidies on products	...	...										
		...	...	...	...	...	...	...	...	...	...	...
Other subsidies on production	...	...										
		1318.0	2677.0	3716.0	2649.0	2386.0	3583.0	9050.0	9159.0	...	...	...
OPERATING SURPLUS, GROSS [c]	...	...										
		29984.0	31637.0	33209.0	33123.0	33449.0	35272.0	41491.0	41888.0	...	...	...
MIXED INCOME, GROSS	...	...										
		...	...	...	...	...	...	...	...	...	...	...
Less: Consumption of fixed capital	...	...										
		2594.0	2819.0	2843.0	3088.0	3388.0	3817.0	4482.0	4082.0	...	...	...
OPERATING SURPLUS, NET [d]	...	...										
		27390.0	28818.0	30366.0	30034.0	30062.0	31456.0	37009.0	37806.0	...	...	...
MIXED INCOME, NET	...	...										
		...	...	...	...	...	...	...	...	...	...	...
Gross capital formation	...	...										
		710.0	796.0	640.0	754.0	818.0	994.0	670.0	945.0	...	...	...
Gross fixed capital formation	...	...										
		839.0	952.0	962.0	992.0	1005.0	1124.0	1320.0	1291.0	...	...	...
Changes in inventories	...	...										
		-129.0	-156.0	-322.0	-238.0	-187.0	-130.0	-650.0	-346.0	...	...	...
Acquisitions less disposals of valuables	...	...										
		...	...	...	...	...	...	...	...	...	...	...

[a] Discrepancy between components and total.
[b] Discrepancy between components and total as one or more components have not been revised.
[c] Includes Mixed Income, Gross.
[d] Includes Mixed Income, Net.

Table 2.3 Output, gross value added, and fixed assets by industries at current prices (ISIC Rev. 3) Mining and quarrying (C)

Series 20: 1968 SNA, Saudi Arabian riyal, Fiscal year beginning 1 July
Series 200: 1993 SNA, Saudi Arabian riyal, Western calendar year

Data in millions

	2001	2002	2003	2004	2005	2006	2007	2008	2009	2010	2011	2012
Series	**20**	**200**										
Output, at basic prices	...	...										
		241338.0	301366.0	393662.0[a]	580924.0[a]	679363.0[a]	745423.0[a]	1038601.0[a]	618085.0[a]	...	...	...
Less: Intermediate consumption, at purchaser's prices	...	...										
		4462.0	7295.0	9254.0	10000.0	11005.0	12888.0	13540.0	13041.0	...	...	...
Equals: VALUE ADDED, GROSS, at basic prices	230250.0	236925.0										
		236876.0	294071.0	384921.0[b]	571892.0[b]	669827.0[b]	734756.0[b]	1028053.0[b]	608783.0[b]	821228.3	1215517.7	1286804.2
Compensation of employees	...	...										
		13340.0	13815.0	16002.0	20128.0	20140.0	20682.0	24464.0	23500.0	...	...	...

	2001	2002	2003	2004	2005	2006	2007	2008	2009	2010	2011	2012
Series	**20**	**200**										
Taxes on production and imports, less Subsidies	...	... 153.0	161.0	157.0	147.0	192.0	174.0	191.0	183.0	...	...	...
Taxes on production and imports	...	... 153.0	161.0	157.0	147.0	192.0	174.0	191.0	183.0	...	...	...
Taxes on products	...	... ...	...	...	...	...	...	...	...	...	...	...
Other taxes on production	...	... 153.0	161.0	157.0	147.0	192.0	174.0	191.0	183.0	...	...	...
Less: Subsidies	...	... ...	...	...	...	...	...	...	...	...	...	...
OPERATING SURPLUS, GROSS [c]	...	... 223383.0	280096.0	368250.0	550649.0	648025.0	711677.0	1000406.0	581361.0	...	...	...
MIXED INCOME, GROSS	...	... ...	...	...	...	...	...	...	...	...	...	...
Less: Consumption of fixed capital	...	... 5922.0	12077.0	11810.0	11103.0	12773.0	12862.0	15074.0	17397.0	...	...	...
OPERATING SURPLUS, NET [d]	...	... 217461.0	268019.0	356439.0	539545.0	635252.0	698815.0	985332.0	563964.0	...	...	...
MIXED INCOME, NET	...	... ...	...	...	...	...	...	...	...	...	...	...
Gross capital formation	...	... 4276.0	3008.0	4738.0	24964.0	45287.0	70564.0	72398.0	56684.0	...	...	...
Gross fixed capital formation	...	... 2567.0	2891.0	3241.0	22935.0	41740.0	66972.0	68807.0	56914.0	...	...	...
Changes in inventories	...	... 1709.0	117.0	1497.0	2029.0	3547.0	3592.0	3591.0	-230.0	...	...	...
Acquisitions less disposals of valuables	...	... ...	...	...	...	...	...	...	...	...	...	...

[a] Discrepancy between components and total.
[b] Discrepancy between components and total as one or more components have not been revised.
[c] Includes Mixed Income, Gross.
[d] Includes Mixed Income, Net.

Table 2.3 Output, gross value added, and fixed assets by industries at current prices (ISIC Rev. 3) Manufacturing (D)

Series 20: 1968 SNA, Saudi Arabian riyal, Fiscal year beginning 1 July
Series 200: 1993 SNA, Saudi Arabian riyal, Western calendar year

Data in millions

	2001	2002	2003	2004	2005	2006	2007	2008	2009	2010	2011	2012
Series	**20**	**200**										
Output, at basic prices	...	... 244892.0	258674.0	284678.0[a]	306715.0[a]	313856.0[a]	351977.0[a]	404737.0[a]	355042.0[a]	...	...	...
Less: Intermediate consumption, at purchaser's prices	...	... 174589.0	175097.0	191278.0	198566.0	192690.0	218716.0	260659.0	212084.0	...	...	...
Equals: VALUE ADDED, GROSS, at basic prices	69206.0	72976.0 70303.0	83577.0	100254.0[b]	117466.0[b]	135471.0[b]	154959.0[b]	175100.0[b]	174600.0[b]	218170.8	252003.2	279538.2
Compensation of employees	...	... 19646.0	20705.0	21700.0	22683.0	23726.0	24914.0	25942.0	28038.0	...	...	...
Taxes on production and imports, less Subsidies	...	... 7454.0	6429.0	3131.0	6548.0	8773.0	9035.0	10209.0	11828.0	...	...	...
Taxes on production and imports	...	... 10171.0	10642.0	11097.0	11519.0	11700.0	11279.0	12439.0	12828.0	...	...	...
Taxes on products	...	... ...	...	...	...	...	...	...	...	...	...	...
Other taxes on production	...	... 10171.0	10642.0	11097.0	11519.0	11700.0	11279.0	12439.0	12828.0	...	...	...
Less: Subsidies	...	... 2717.0	4213.0	7966.0	4971.0	2927.0	2244.0	2230.0	1000.0	...	...	...
Subsidies on products	...	... ...	...	...	...	...	...	...	...	...	...	...
Other subsidies on production	...	... 2717.0	4213.0	7966.0	4971.0	2927.0	2244.0	2230.0	1000.0	...	...	...
OPERATING SURPLUS, GROSS [c]	...	... 43202.0	56443.0	68568.0	78919.0	88667.0	99312.0	107926.0	103091.0	...	...	...
MIXED INCOME, GROSS	...	... ...	...	...	...	...	...	...	...	...	...	...
Less: Consumption of fixed capital	...	... 22693.0	24171.0	26361.0	28193.0	30774.0	34762.0	40472.0	37638.0	...	...	...

	2001	2002	2003	2004	2005	2006	2007	2008	2009	2010	2011	2012
Series	**20**	**200**										
OPERATING SURPLUS, NET [d]	...	...										
		20509.0	32272.0	42207.0	50725.0	57892.0	64550.0	67454.0	65453.0	...	...	...
MIXED INCOME, NET	...	...										
		...	...	...	...	...	...	...	...	...	...	...
Gross capital formation	...	...										
		36895.0	42275.0	47446.0	38469.0	49316.0	49324.0	72634.0	64209.0	...	...	...
Gross fixed capital formation	...	...										
		32044.0	36444.0	36311.0	28718.0	42323.0	43475.0	50818.0	50406.0	...	...	...
Changes in inventories	...	...										
		4851.0	5831.0	11135.0	9751.0	6993.0	5849.0	21816.0	13803.0	...	...	...
Acquisitions less disposals of valuables	...	...										
		...	...	...	...	...	...	...	...	...	...	...

[a] Discrepancy between components and total.
[b] Discrepancy between components and total as one or more components have not been revised.
[c] Includes Mixed Income, Gross.
[d] Includes Mixed Income, Net.

Table 2.3 Output, gross value added, and fixed assets by industries at current prices (ISIC Rev. 3) Electricity, gas and water supply (E)

Series 20: 1968 SNA, Saudi Arabian riyal, Fiscal year beginning 1 July
Series 200: 1993 SNA, Saudi Arabian riyal, Western calendar year

Data in millions

	2001	2002	2003	2004	2005	2006	2007	2008	2009	2010	2011	2012
Series	**20**	**200**										
Output, at basic prices	...	...										
		14817.0	15721.0	16801.0[a]	18543.0[a]	19527.0[a]	20469.0[a]	22035.0[a]	22550.0[a]	...	...	...
Less: Intermediate consumption, at purchaser's prices	...	...										
		5721.0	6102.0	6699.0	7802.0	8159.0	8409.0	9399.0	9454.0	...	...	...
Equals: VALUE ADDED, GROSS, at basic prices	8928.0	9303.0										
		9097.0	9619.0	16055.0[b]	16753.0[b]	17571.0[b]	18562.0[b]	18412.0[b]	21575.0[b]	26280.9	28284.7	30669.7
Compensation of employees	...	...										
		2278.0	2357.0	3516.0	3746.0	4020.0	4132.0	4248.0	4342.0	...	...	...
Taxes on production and imports, less Subsidies	...	...										
		128.0	401.0	393.0	366.0	480.0	361.0	476.0	457.0	...	...	...
Taxes on production and imports	...	...										
		382.0	401.0	393.0	366.0	480.0	435.0	476.0	457.0	...	...	...
Taxes on products	...	...										
		...	...	...	...	...	...	...	...	...	...	...
Other taxes on production	...	...										
		382.0	401.0	393.0	366.0	480.0	435.0	476.0	457.0	...	...	...
Less: Subsidies	...	...										
		254.0	0.0	0.0	0.0	...	74.0	0.0	0.0	...	...	...
Subsidies on products	...	...										
		...	...	...	...	...	...	...	...	...	...	...
Other subsidies on production	...	...										
		254.0	0.0	0.0	0.0	0.0	74.0	0.0	0.0	...	...	...
OPERATING SURPLUS, GROSS [c]	...	...										
		6691.0	6861.0	6193.0	6629.0	6868.0	7568.0	7913.0	8298.0	...	...	...
MIXED INCOME, GROSS	...	...										
		...	...	...	...	...	...	...	...	...	...	...
Less: Consumption of fixed capital	...	...										
		5312.0	5772.0	5821.0	6324.0	6937.0	7816.0	9178.0	8358.0	...	...	...
OPERATING SURPLUS, NET [d]	...	...										
		1379.0	1089.0	372.0	305.0	-68.0	-247.0	-1266.0	-61.0	...	...	...
MIXED INCOME, NET	...	...										
		...	...	...	...	...	...	...	...	...	...	...
Gross capital formation	...	...										
		19368.0	21978.0	22285.0	22926.0	23218.0	25926.0	30648.0	29862.0	...	...	...
Gross fixed capital formation	...	...										
		19315.0	21914.0	22154.0	22829.0	23142.0	25873.0	30383.0	29721.0	...	...	...
Changes in inventories	...	...										
		53.0	64.0	131.0	97.0	76.0	53.0	265.0	141.0	...	...	...
Acquisitions less disposals of valuables	...	...										
		...	...	...	...	...	...	...	...	...	...	...

[a] Discrepancy between components and total.
[b] Discrepancy between components and total as one or more components have not been revised.
[c] Includes Mixed Income, Gross.
[d] Includes Mixed Income, Net.

Table 2.3 Output, gross value added, and fixed assets by industries at current prices (ISIC Rev. 3) Construction (F)

Series 20: 1968 SNA, Saudi Arabian riyal, Fiscal year beginning 1 July
Series 200: 1993 SNA, Saudi Arabian riyal, Western calendar year

Data in millions

	2001	2002	2003	2004	2005	2006	2007	2008	2009	2010	2011	2012
Series	**20**	**200**										
Output, at basic prices	...	... 113649.0	119741.0	131027.0[a]	141975.0[a]	152092.0[a]	162495.0[a]	172223.0[a]	178618.0[a]	...	...	...
Less: Intermediate consumption, at purchaser's prices	...	... 71009.0	74615.0	81780.0	89098.0	95196.0	99712.0	106362.0	112776.0	...	...	...
Equals: VALUE ADDED, GROSS, at basic prices	43185.0	44739.0 42640.0	45125.0	53529.0[b]	58380.0[b]	64636.0[b]	74325.0[b]	79681.0[b]	80379.0[b]	90780.5	107021.1	124658.2
Compensation of employees	...	... 11909.0	12385.0	12732.0	13140.0	13455.0	13778.0	14109.0	14405.0	...	...	...
Taxes on production and imports, less Subsidies	...	... 458.0	481.0	471.0	439.0	576.0	522.0	571.0	548.0	...	...	...
Taxes on production and imports [c]	...	... 458.0	481.0	471.0	439.0	576.0	522.0	571.0	548.0	...	...	...
Taxes on products	...	... ...	...	...	...	...	...	...	...	...	...	...
Other taxes on production [c]	...	... 458.0	481.0	471.0	439.0	576.0	522.0	571.0	548.0	...	...	...
Less: Subsidies	...	... ...	...	...	...	...	...	...	...	...	...	...
OPERATING SURPLUS, GROSS [d]	...	... 30273.0	32259.0	36045.0	39299.0	42865.0	48483.0	51181.0	50889.0	...	...	...
MIXED INCOME, GROSS	...	... ...	...	...	...	...	...	...	...	...	...	...
Less: Consumption of fixed capital	...	... 1410.0	1532.0	1545.0	1678.0	1841.0	2074.0	2436.0	2218.0	...	...	...
OPERATING SURPLUS, NET [e]	...	... 28863.0	30727.0	34500.0	37620.0	41024.0	46408.0	48745.0	48671.0	...	...	...
MIXED INCOME, NET	...	... ...	...	...	...	...	...	...	...	...	...	...
Gross capital formation	...	... 9594.0	10908.0	11416.0	11542.0	11572.0	12751.0	16148.0	15110.0	...	...	...
Gross fixed capital formation	...	... 9288.0	10538.0	10654.0	10978.0	11129.0	12442.0	14611.0	14292.0	...	...	...
Changes in inventories	...	... 306.0	370.0	762.0	564.0	443.0	309.0	1537.0	818.0	...	...	...
Acquisitions less disposals of valuables	...	... ...	...	...	...	...	...	...	...	...	...	...

[a] Discrepancy between components and total.
[b] Discrepancy between components and total as one or more components have not been revised.
[c] Refers to net taxes on production.
[d] Includes Mixed Income, Gross.
[e] Includes Mixed Income, Net.

Table 2.3 Output, gross value added, and fixed assets by industries at current prices (ISIC Rev. 3) Wholesale retail trade, repair of motor vehicles, motorcycles, etc.; hotels and restaurants (G+H)

Series 20: 1968 SNA, Saudi Arabian riyal, Fiscal year beginning 1 July
Series 200: 1993 SNA, Saudi Arabian riyal, Western calendar year

Data in millions

	2001	2002	2003	2004	2005	2006	2007	2008	2009	2010	2011	2012
Series	**20**	**200**										
Output, at basic prices	...	... 73980.0	77014.0	84219.0[a]	92099.0[a]	98890.0[a]	105284.0[a]	112863.0[a]	123500.0[a]	...	...	...
Less: Intermediate consumption, at purchaser's prices	...	... 33022.0	34510.0	37906.0	41923.0	45246.0	46404.0	48347.0	55582.0	...	...	...
Equals: VALUE ADDED, GROSS, at basic prices	49793.0	51735.0 40958.0	42503.0	66652.0[b]	77122.0[b]	91203.0[b]	110366.0[b]	133338.0[b]	147836.0[b]	174505.8	197926.2	219072.6
Compensation of employees	...	... 21342.0	22164.0	23051.0	23835.0	24716.0	25630.0	26580.0	27377.0	...	...	...
Taxes on production and imports, less Subsidies	...	... 2791.0	2932.0	2871.0	2674.0	3508.0	3180.0	3482.0	3340.0	...	...	...

	Series	2001	2002	2003	2004	2005	2006	2007	2008	2009	2010	2011	2012
Taxes on production and imports[c]	20	...	...										
	200		2791.0	2932.0	2871.0	2674.0	3508.0	3180.0	3482.0	3340.0	...	...	...
Taxes on products	20	...	...										
	200		...	...	...	...	...	...	...	...	...	...	...
Other taxes on production[c]	20	...	...										
	200		2791.0	2932.0	2871.0	2674.0	3508.0	3180.0	3482.0	3340.0	...	...	...
Less: Subsidies	20	...	...										
	200		...	...	...	...	...	...	...	...	...	...	...
OPERATING SURPLUS, GROSS[d]	20	...	...										
	200		16825.0	17407.0	20391.0	23667.0	25420.0	30068.0	34454.0	37202.0	...	...	...
MIXED INCOME, GROSS	20	...	...										
	200		...	...	...	...	...	...	...	...	...	...	...
Less: Consumption of fixed capital	20	...	...										
	200		4822.0	5239.0	5283.0	5740.0	6296.0	7094.0	8330.0	7586.0	...	...	...
OPERATING SURPLUS, NET[e]	20	...	...										
	200		12003.0	12169.0	15109.0	17927.0	19125.0	22974.0	26124.0	29616.0	...	...	...
MIXED INCOME, NET	20	...	...										
	200		...	...	...	...	...	...	...	...	...	...	...
Gross capital formation	20	...	...										
	200		12330.0	14224.0	18316.0	16630.0	15552.0	15493.0	30106.0	22499.0	...	...	...
Gross fixed capital formation	20	...	...										
	200		9231.0	10473.0	10588.0	10910.0	11060.0	12365.0	14521.0	14204.0	...	...	...
Changes in inventories	20	...	...										
	200		3099.0	3751.0	7728.0	5720.0	4492.0	3128.0	15585.0	8295.0	...	...	...
Acquisitions less disposals of valuables	20	...	...										
	200		...	...	...	...	...	...	...	...	...	...	...

[a] Discrepancy between components and total.
[b] Discrepancy between components and total as one or more components have not been revised.
[c] Refers to net taxes on production.
[d] Includes Mixed Income, Gross.
[e] Includes Mixed Income, Net.

Table 2.3 Output, gross value added, and fixed assets by industries at current prices (ISIC Rev. 3) Transport, storage and communications (I)

Series 20: 1968 SNA, Saudi Arabian riyal, Fiscal year beginning 1 July
Series 200: 1993 SNA, Saudi Arabian riyal, Western calendar year

Data in millions

	Series	2001	2002	2003	2004	2005	2006	2007	2008	2009	2010	2011	2012
Output, at basic prices	20	...	...										
	200		60230.0	62664.0	68053.0[a]	74165.0[a]	79332.0[a]	84605.0[a]	93487.0[a]	100764.0[a]	...	...	...
Less: Intermediate consumption, at purchaser's prices	20	...	...										
	200		29354.0	30345.0	33153.0	36399.0	38350.0	39477.0	41879.0	45115.0	...	...	...
Equals: VALUE ADDED, GROSS, at basic prices	20	30559.0	31934.0										
	200		30876.0	32319.0	38977.0[b]	43576.0[b]	49813.0[b]	61041.0[b]	77774.0[b]	88870.0[b]	101204.8	115272.3	129277.9
Compensation of employees	20	...	...										
	200		11381.0	11973.0	12595.0	13238.0	13846.0	14483.0	15150.0	15740.0	...	...	...
Taxes on production and imports, less Subsidies	20	...	...										
	200		228.0	250.0	205.0	191.0	263.0	235.0	76.0	292.0	...	...	...
Taxes on production and imports	20	...	...										
	200		244.0	256.0	251.0	234.0	306.0	278.0	304.0	292.0	...	...	...
Taxes on products	20	...	...										
	200		...	...	...	...	...	...	...	...	...	...	...
Other taxes on production	20	...	...										
	200		244.0[c]	256.0[c]	251.0[c]	234.0[c]	306.0[c]	278.0[c]	304.0[c]	292.0[d]	...	...	...
Less: Subsidies	20	...	...										
	200		16.0	6.0	46.0	43.0	43.0	43.0	228.0	0.0	...	...	...
Subsidies on products	20	...	...										
	200		...	...	...	...	...	...	...	...	...	...	...
Other subsidies on production	20	...	...										
	200		16.0[e]	6.0[e]	46.0[e]	43.0[e]	43.0[e]	43.0[e]	228.0[e]	0.0	...	...	...
OPERATING SURPLUS, GROSS[f]	20	...	...										
	200		19268.0	20095.0	22101.0	24338.0	26873.0	30410.0	36382.0	39616.0	...	...	...
MIXED INCOME, GROSS	20	...	...										
	200		...	...	...	...	...	...	...	...	...	...	...
Less: Consumption of fixed capital	20	...	...										
	200		3957.0	4299.0	4336.0	4710.0	5167.0	5821.0	6836.0	6225.0	...	...	...
OPERATING SURPLUS, NET[g]	20	...	...										
	200		15311.0	15796.0	17765.0	19628.0	21706.0	24589.0	29546.0	33391.0	...	...	...

	2001	2002	2003	2004	2005	2006	2007	2008	2009	2010	2011	2012
Series	**20**	**200**										
MIXED INCOME, NET	...	... ...	...	...	...	...	...	...	...	...	...	...
Gross capital formation	...	... 24696.0	28020.0	28348.0	29199.0	29594.0	33076.0	38903.0	38020.0	...	...	...
Gross fixed capital formation	...	... 24680.0	28001.0	28308.0	29170.0	29571.0	33060.0	38823.0	37977.0	...	...	...
Changes in inventories	...	... 16.0	19.0	40.0	29.0	23.0	16.0	80.0	43.0	...	...	...
Acquisitions less disposals of valuables	...	... ...	...	...	...	...	...	...	...	...	...	...

[a] Discrepancy between components and total.
[b] Discrepancy between components and total as one or more components have not been revised.
[c] Refers to all Taxes on production and imports.
[d] Refers to net taxes on production.
[e] Refers to all subsidies on production and imports
[f] Includes Mixed Income, Gross.
[g] Includes Mixed Income, Net.

Table 2.3 Output, gross value added, and fixed assets by industries at current prices (ISIC Rev. 3) Financial intermediation; real estate, renting and business activities (J+K)

Series 20: 1968 SNA, Saudi Arabian riyal, Fiscal year beginning 1 July
Series 200: 1993 SNA, Saudi Arabian riyal, Western calendar year

Data in millions

	2001	2002	2003	2004	2005	2006	2007	2008	2009	2010	2011	2012
Series	**20**	**200**										
Output, at basic prices	...	... 54547.0	57068.0	61789.0[a]	66883.0[a]	71338.0[a]	75696.0[a]	80362.0[a]	85699.0[a]	...	...	...
Less: Intermediate consumption, at purchaser's prices	...	... 7444.0	7625.0	9221.0	10422.0	10842.0	11528.0	12117.0	12932.0	...	...	...
Equals: VALUE ADDED, GROSS, at basic prices	78873.0	82072.0 47103.0	49442.0	97132.0[b]	108339.0[b]	122233.0[b]	136812.0[b]	153304.0[b]	171300.0[b]	182603.9	195053.6	216759.0
Compensation of employees	...	... 4539.0	4719.0	4798.0	4940.0	5299.0	6033.0	6516.0	6819.0	...	...	...
Taxes on production and imports, less Subsidies	...	... 316.0	332.0	325.0	303.0	398.0	361.0	395.0	379.0	...	...	...
Taxes on production and imports [c]	...	... 316.0	332.0	325.0	303.0	398.0	361.0	395.0	379.0	...	...	...
Taxes on products	...	... ...	...	...	...	...	...	...	...	...	...	...
Other taxes on production [c]	...	... 316.0	332.0	325.0	303.0	398.0	361.0	395.0	379.0	...	...	...
Less: Subsidies	...	... ...	...	...	...	...	...	...	...	...	...	...
OPERATING SURPLUS, GROSS [d]	...	... 42248.0	44391.0	47444.0	51218.0	54800.0	57775.0	61334.0	65569.0	...	...	...
MIXED INCOME, GROSS	...	... ...	...	...	...	...	...	...	...	...	...	...
Less: Consumption of fixed capital	...	... 1667.0	1812.0	1827.0	1985.0	2177.0	2453.0	2881.0	2624.0	...	...	...
OPERATING SURPLUS, NET [e]	...	... 40580.0	42579.0	45617.0	49233.0	52622.0	55322.0	58453.0	62945.0	...	...	...
MIXED INCOME, NET	...	... ...	...	...	...	...	...	...	...	...	...	...
Gross capital formation	...	... 2372.0	2685.0	2612.0	2750.0	2822.0	3205.0	3453.0	3558.0	...	...	...
Gross fixed capital formation	...	... 2453.0	2783.0	2813.0	2899.0	2939.0	3286.0	3858.0	3774.0	...	...	...
Changes in inventories	...	... -81.0	-98.0	-201.0	-149.0	-117.0	-81.0	-405.0	-216.0	...	...	...
Acquisitions less disposals of valuables	...	... ...	...	...	...	...	...	...	...	...	...	...

[a] Discrepancy between components and total.
[b] Discrepancy between components and total as one or more components have not been revised.
[c] Refers to all taxes less subsidies on production and imports.
[d] Includes Mixed Income, Gross.
[e] Includes Mixed Income, Net.

Table 2.3 Output, gross value added, and fixed assets by industries at current prices (ISIC Rev. 3) Public administration and defense; compulsory social security (L)

Series 20: 1968 SNA, Saudi Arabian riyal, Fiscal year beginning 1 July
Series 200: 1993 SNA, Saudi Arabian riyal, Western calendar year

Data in millions

		2001	2002	2003	2004	2005	2006	2007	2008	2009	2010	2011	2012
Series		**20**			**200**								
Output, at basic prices		...	...		...	...	...	...	...	...	...	...	...
Less: Intermediate consumption, at purchaser's prices		...	...		...	...	...	...	...	...	...	...	...
Equals: VALUE ADDED, GROSS, at basic prices	[a] [a]	123589.0	124486.0		155371.0	176350.0	196386.0	200306.0	209278.0	241047.0	280863.0	312308.0	344723.0
Compensation of employees		...	...		...	...	...	...	...	...	...	...	...
Taxes on production and imports, less Subsidies		...	...		...	...	...	...	...	...	...	...	...
OPERATING SURPLUS, GROSS		...	...		...	...	...	...	...	...	...	...	...
MIXED INCOME, GROSS		...	...		...	...	...	...	...	...	...	...	...
Gross capital formation		...	...		...	...	...	...	...	...	...	...	...

[a] Includes Private households with employed persons.

Table 2.3 Output, gross value added, and fixed assets by industries at current prices (ISIC Rev. 3) Education; health and social work; other community, social and personal services (M+N+O)

Series 20: 1968 SNA, Saudi Arabian riyal, Fiscal year beginning 1 July
Series 200: 1993 SNA, Saudi Arabian riyal, Western calendar year

Data in millions

	2001	2002	2003	2004	2005	2006	2007	2008	2009	2010	2011	2012
Series	**20**			**200**								
Output, at basic prices	...	...		...	...	...	...	...	...	...	...	...
Less: Intermediate consumption, at purchaser's prices	...	...		...	...	...	...	...	...	...	...	...
Equals: VALUE ADDED, GROSS, at basic prices	23064.0	24124.0		26666.0	27877.0	29284.0	30996.0	33021.0	35207.0	37767.6	41892.5	46509.0
Compensation of employees	...	...		...	...	...	...	...	...	...	...	...
Taxes on production and imports, less Subsidies	...	...		...	...	...	...	...	...	...	...	...
OPERATING SURPLUS, GROSS	...	...		...	...	...	...	...	...	...	...	...
MIXED INCOME, GROSS	...	...		...	...	...	...	...	...	...	...	...
Gross capital formation	...	...		...	...	...	...	...	...	...	...	...

Table 4.1 Total Economy (S.1)

Series 200: 1993 SNA, Saudi Arabian riyal, Western calendar year — **Data in millions**

		2001	2002	2003	2004	2005	2006	2007	2008	2009	2010	2011	2012
Series			**200**										
I. Production account - Resources													
Output, at basic prices (otherwise, please specify)			1137111.0	1246166.0	1427087.0	1720099.0	1909488.0	2062625.0	2474758.0	2054136.0			
Less: Financial intermediation services indirectly measured (only to be deducted if FISIM is not distributed to uses)			...	...	...	...	...	...	...	...			
Plus: Taxes less Subsidies on products	a		7386.0	8087.0	8825.0	10115.0	11025.0	11801.0	14940.0	12895.0			
Plus: Taxes on products	a		7386.0	8087.0	8825.0	10115.0	11025.0	11801.0	14940.0	12895.0			
Less: Subsidies on products			...	...	...	...	...	...	...	...			
I. Production account - Uses													
Intermediate consumption, at purchaser's prices			434610.0	446069.0	494242.0	545297.0	582224.0	629264.0	701564.0	652474.0			
GROSS DOMESTIC PRODUCT			709888.0	808184.0	941670.0	1184917.0	1338289.0	1445161.0	1788134.0	1414557.0			
Less: Consumption of fixed capital			65839.0	76287.0	78683.0	82356.0	90257.0	98742.0	113453.0	109457.0			
NET DOMESTIC PRODUCT			644049.0	731897.0	862987.0	1102561.0	1248031.0	1346419.0	1674681.0	1305100.0			
II.1.1 Generation of income account - Resources													
GROSS DOMESTIC PRODUCT			709888.0	808184.0	941670.0	1184917.0	1338289.0	1445161.0	1788134.0	1414557.0			
II.1.1 Generation of income account - Uses													
Compensation of employees			228247.0	247493.0	269951.0	299058.0	323557.0	333650.0	351167.0	388524.0			
Taxes on production and imports, less Subsidies			18583.0	17437.0	13691.0	19096.0	24103.0	23249.0	22562.0	21980.0			
Taxes on production and imports			22932.0	24374.0	25447.0	26783.0	29478.0	29204.0	34083.0	32152.0			
Taxes on products	a		7386.0	8087.0	8825.0	10115.0	11025.0	11801.0	14940.0	12895.0			
Other taxes on production			15546.0	16287.0	16622.0	16668.0	18453.0	17403.0	19143.0	19257.0			
Less: Subsidies			4349.0	6937.0	11756.0	7687.0	5375.0	5955.0	11521.0	10172.0			
Subsidies on products			...	...	...	...	...	...	...	...			
Other subsidies on production			4349.0	6937.0	11756.0	7687.0	5375.0	5955.0	11521.0	10172.0			
OPERATING SURPLUS, GROSS			456906.0	536689.0	650594.0	858342.0	981344.0	1077777.0	1402527.0	991873.0			
MIXED INCOME, GROSS			6151.0	6565.0	7434.0	8421.0	9284.0	10487.0	11878.0	12180.0			
II.1.2 Allocation of primary income account - Resources													
OPERATING SURPLUS, GROSS			456906.0	536689.0	650594.0	858342.0	981344.0	1077777.0	1402527.0	991873.0			
MIXED INCOME, GROSS			6151.0	6565.0	7434.0	8421.0	9284.0	10487.0	11878.0	12180.0			
Compensation of employees			219329.0	239177.0	262326.0	297167.0	321462.0	331487.0	349163.0	386395.0			
Taxes on production and imports, less Subsidies			18583.0	17437.0	13691.0	19096.0	24103.0	23249.0	22562.0	21980.0			
Taxes on production and imports			22932.0	24374.0	25447.0	26783.0	29478.0	29204.0	34083.0	32152.0			
Taxes on products	a		7386.0	8087.0	8825.0	10115.0	11025.0	11801.0	14940.0	12895.0			
Other taxes on production			15546.0	16287.0	16622.0	16668.0	18453.0	17403.0	19143.0	19257.0			
Less: Subsidies			4349.0	6937.0	11756.0	7687.0	5375.0	5955.0	11521.0	10172.0			
Subsidies on products			...	...	...	...	...	...	...	...			
Other subsidies on production	b		4349.0	6937.0	11756.0	7687.0	5375.0	5955.0	11521.0	10172.0			
Property income			127484.0	187535.0	199991.0	279623.0	271573.0	291183.0	408823.0	225980.0			

	2001	2002	2003	2004	2005	2006	2007	2008	2009	2010	2011	2012
Series		**200**										
II.1.2 Allocation of primary income account - Uses												
Property income		113688.0	176440.0	184362.0	276113.0	255117.0	265049.0	372449.0	191452.0			
GROSS NATIONAL INCOME		714767.0	810962.0	949674.0	1186536.0	1352651.0	1469132.0	1822503.0	1446956.0			
II.2 Secondary distribution of income account - Resources												
GROSS NATIONAL INCOME		714767.0	810962.0	949674.0	1186536.0	1352651.0	1469132.0	1822503.0	1446956.0			
Current taxes on income, wealth, etc.		118895.0	174256.0	236599.0	341917.0	443245.0	398023.0	710690.0	322901.0			
Social contributions		23173.0	25063.0	27309.0	30204.0	32596.0	33631.0	35427.0	39022.0			
Social benefits other than social transfers in kind		24690.0	26458.0	28567.0	31538.0	37026.0	43671.0	48284.0	50904.0			
Other current transfers		135567.0	112046.0	108339.0	74145.0	90004.0	149362.0	220795.0	232030.0			
II.2 Secondary distribution of income account - Uses												
Current taxes on income, wealth, etc.		118895.0	174256.0	236599.0	341917.0	443245.0	398023.0	710690.0	322901.0			
Social contributions		23173.0	25063.0	27309.0	30204.0	32596.0	33631.0	35427.0	39022.0			
Social benefits other than social transfers in kind		24690.0	26458.0	28567.0	31538.0	37026.0	43671.0	48284.0	50904.0			
Other current transfers		218962.0	186691.0	182600.0	129519.0	152848.0	213232.0	307089.0	335802.0			
GROSS DISPOSABLE INCOME		631372.0	736317.0	875413.0	1131162.0	1289807.0	1405262.0	1736209.0	1343184.0			
II.4.1 Use of disposable income account - Resources												
GROSS DISPOSABLE INCOME		631372.0	736317.0	875413.0	1131162.0	1289807.0	1405262.0	1736209.0	1343184.0			
Adjustment for the change in net equity of households on pension funds		...	...	...	...	...	...	...	...			
II.4.1 Use of disposable income account - Uses												
Final consumption expenditure		447738.0	471664.0	510403.0	578010.0	668703.0	745909.0	844040.0	903704.0			
Individual consumption expenditure		278512.0	287641.0	303692.0	330545.0	375280.0	444052.0	522919.0	581278.0			
Collective consumption expenditure		169226.0	184023.0	206711.0	247466.0	293423.0	301857.0	321121.0	322426.0			
Adjustment for the change in net equity of households on pension funds		...	...	...	...	...	...	...	...			
SAVING, GROSS		183634.0	264653.0	365011.0	553152.0	621104.0	659353.0	892169.0	439480.0			
III.1 Capital account - Changes in liabilities and net worth												
SAVING, GROSS		183634.0	264653.0	365011.0	553152.0	621104.0	659353.0	892169.0	439480.0			
Capital transfers, receivable less payable		0.0	0.0	0.0	0.0	0.0	0.0	0.0	0.0			
Capital transfers, receivable		4767.0	5421.0	6592.0	13754.0	12296.0	30548.0	12680.0	9304.0			
Less: Capital transfers, payable		4767.0	5421.0	6592.0	13754.0	12296.0	30548.0	12680.0	9304.0			
Equals: CHANGES IN NET WORTH DUE TO SAVING AND CAPITAL TRANSFERS		117794.0	188365.0	286327.0	470797.0	530848.0	560611.0	778717.0	330023.0			
III.1 Capital account - Changes in assets												
Gross capital formation		139109.0	159473.0	180156.0	215687.0	250102.0	309365.0	395961.0	360900.0			
Gross fixed capital formation		128066.0	148098.0	156347.0	195632.0	233065.0	295400.0	348011.0	335328.0			
Changes in inventories		11043.0	11375.0	23809.0	20055.0	17037.0	13965.0	47950.0	25572.0			
Acquisitions less disposals of valuables		...	...	...	...	...	...	...	...			

	2001	2002	2003	2004	2005	2006	2007	2008	2009	2010	2011	2012
Series		**200**										
Acquisitions less disposals of non-produced non-financial assets		...	...	...	...	...	...	...	...			
NET LENDING (+) / NET BORROWING (-)		44525.0	105180.0	184855.0	337465.0	371002.0	349988.0	496208.0	78579.0			

[a] Import duties only.
[b] Refers to all subsidies on production and imports

Table 4.2 Rest of the world (S.2)

Series 200: 1993 SNA, Saudi Arabian riyal, Western calendar year **Data in millions**

	2001	2002	2003	2004	2005	2006	2007	2008	2009	2010	2011	2012
Series		**200**										
V.I External account of goods and services - Resources												
Imports of goods and services		168114.0	194041.0	243322.0	328678.0	425038.0	544434.0	662568.0	607759.0			
Imports of goods		121089.0	138435.0	177659.0	222985.0	261402.0	338089.0	431753.0	358290.0			
Imports of services		47025.0	55606.0	65663.0	105693.0	163636.0	206345.0	230815.0	249469.0			
V.I External account of goods and services - Uses												
Exports of goods and services		291155.0	371088.0	494433.0	719898.0	844522.0	934321.0	1210701.0	757711.0			
Exports of goods		271741.0	349665.0	472490.0	677144.0	791338.0	874403.0	1175552.0	721152.0			
Exports of services		19414.0	21423.0	21943.0	42754.0	53184.0	59918.0	35149.0	36559.0			
EXTERNAL BALANCE OF GOODS AND SERVICES		-123041.0	-177047.0	-251111.0	-391220.0	-419484.0	-389887.0	-548133.0	-149952.0			
V.II External account of primary income and current transfers - Resources												
EXTERNAL BALANCE OF GOODS AND SERVICES		-123041.0	-177047.0	-251111.0	-391220.0	-419484.0	-389887.0	-548133.0	-149952.0			
Compensation of employees		8918.0	8316.0	7625.0	2243.0	2491.0	2626.0	2815.0	2933.0			
Taxes on production and imports, less Subsidies		...	...	...	...	...	...	...	...			
Taxes on production and imports		...	...	...	...	...	...	...	...			
Taxes on products		...	...	...	...	...	...	...	...			
Other taxes on production		...	...	...	...	...	...	...	...			
Less: Subsidies		...	...	...	...	...	...	...	...			
Subsidies on products		...	...	...	...	...	...	...	...			
Other subsidies on production		...	...	...	...	...	...	...	...			
Property income		132.0	70.0	413.0	15090.0	22400.0	30133.0	43435.0	38739.0			
Current taxes on income, wealth, etc.		...	...	...	...	...	...	...	...			
Social contributions		...	...	...	...	...	...	...	...			
Social benefits other than social transfers in kind		...	...	...	...	...	...	...	...			
Other current transfers		83395.0	74645.0	74261.0	55374.0	62844.0	63870.0	86294.0	103772.0			
Adjustment for the change in net equity of households on pension funds		...	...	...	...	...	...	...	...			
V.II External account of primary income and current transfers - Uses												
Compensation of employees		0.0	0.0	0.0	352.0	396.0	463.0	811.0	804.0			
Taxes on production and imports, less Subsidies		...	...	...	...	...	...	...	...			
Taxes on production and imports		...	...	...	...	...	...	...	...			

	2001	2002	2003	2004	2005	2006	2007	2008	2009	2010	2011	2012
Series		**200**										
Taxes on products		...	...	...	...	...	...	...	...			
Other taxes on production		...	...	...	...	...	...	...	...			
Less: Subsidies		...	...	...	...	...	...	...	...			
Subsidies on products		...	...	...	...	...	...	...	...			
Other subsidies on production		...	...	...	...	...	...	...	...			
Property income		13929.0	11164.0	16042.0	18600.0	38857.0	56267.0	79808.0	73267.0			
Current taxes on income and wealth, etc.		...	...	...	...	...	...	...	...			
Social contributions		...	...	...	...	...	...	...	...			
Social benefits other than social transfers in kind		...	...	...	...	...	...	...	...			
Other current transfers		...	...	...	...	...	...	...	...			
Adjustment for the change in net equity of households on pension funds		...	...	...	...	...	...	...	...			
CURRENT EXTERNAL BALANCE		-44525.0	-105180.0	-184854.0	-337465.0	-371002.0	-349988.0	-496208.0	-78579.0			
V.III.1 Capital account - Changes in liabilities and net worth												
CURRENT EXTERNAL BALANCE		-44525.0	-105180.0	-184854.0	-337465.0	-371002.0	-349988.0	-496208.0	-78579.0			
Capital transfers, receivable less payable		0.0	0.0	0.0	0.0	0.0	0.0	0.0	0.0			
Capital transfers, receivable		...	...	...	...	...	...	...	...			
Less: Capital transfers, payable		...	...	...	...	...	...	...	...			
Equals: CHANGES IN NET WORTH DUE TO SAVING AND CAPITAL TRANSFERS		-44525.0	-105180.0	-184854.0	-337465.0	-371002.0	-349988.0	-496208.0	-78579.0			
V.III.1 Capital account - Changes in assets												
Acquisitions less disposals of non-produced non-financial assets		...	...	...	...	...	...	...	...			
NET LENDING (+) / NET BORROWING (-)		-44525.0	-105180.0	-184854.0	-337465.0	-371002.0	-349988.0	-496208.0	-78579.0			

Table 4.3 Non-financial Corporations (S.11)

Series 200: 1993 SNA, Saudi Arabian riyal, Western calendar year **Data in millions**

	2001	2002	2003	2004	2005	2006	2007	2008	2009	2010	2011	2012
Series		**200**										
I. Production account - Resources												
Output, at basic prices (otherwise, please specify)		883951.0	974520.0	1126587.0	1372350.0	1508010.0	1644609.0	2027291.0	1588643.0			
I. Production account - Uses												
Intermediate consumption, at purchaser's prices		352960.0	362663.0	398603.0	425590.0	433338.0	473028.0	532043.0	500800.0			
VALUE ADDED GROSS, in basic prices		530991.0	611857.0	727984.0	946760.0	1074672.0	1171581.0	1495248.0	1087844.0			
Less: Consumption of fixed capital		50844.0	60402.0	62530.0	65761.0	72576.0	80331.0	93954.0	90012.0			
VALUE ADDED NET, at basic prices		480146.0	551454.0	665454.0	880999.0	1002096.0	1091250.0	1401293.0	997831.0			
II.1.1 Generation of income account - Resources												
VALUE ADDED GROSS, at basic prices		530991.0	611857.0	727984.0	946760.0	1074672.0	1171581.0	1495248.0	1087844.0			

	2001	2002	2003	2004	2005	2006	2007	2008	2009	2010	2011	2012
Series		**200**										
II.1.1 Generation of income account - Uses												
Compensation of employees		98151.0	102033.0	108741.0	116425.0	120640.0	125443.0	133235.0	137530.0			
Other taxes less Other subsidies on production		10610.0	8735.0	4264.0	8420.0	12342.0	10780.0	6891.0	8384.0			
Other taxes on production		14959.0	15672.0	16020.0	16107.0	17717.0	16735.0	18412.0	18556.0			
Less: Other subsidies on production		4349.0	6937.0	11756.0	7687.0	5375.0	5955.0	11521.0	10172.0			
OPERATING SURPLUS, GROSS		422229.0	501089.0	614979.0	821915.0	941690.0	1035359.0	1355122.0	941929.0			
II.1.2 Allocation of primary income account - Resources												
OPERATING SURPLUS, GROSS		422229.0	501089.0	614979.0	821915.0	941690.0	1035359.0	1355122.0	941929.0			
Property income		9864.0	11894.0	13257.0	19677.0	14164.0	15694.0	15023.0	15738.0			
II.1.2 Allocation of primary income account - Uses												
Property income		94458.0	155405.0	161637.0	248212.0	228618.0	235777.0	340974.0	163729.0			
BALANCE OF PRIMARY INCOMES		337635.0	357577.0	466600.0	593380.0	727236.0	815275.0	1029170.0	793938.0			
II.2 Secondary distribution of income account - Resources												
BALANCE OF PRIMARY INCOMES		337635.0	357577.0	466600.0	593380.0	727236.0	815275.0	1029170.0	793938.0			
Social contributions		...	...	...	...	...	...	...	...			
Other current transfers		...	...	...	...	...	...	...	...			
II.2 Secondary distribution of income account - Uses												
Current taxes on income, wealth, etc.		117772.0	172882.0	235063.0	339573.0	441619.0	396217.0	708992.0	321112.0			
Social benefits other than social transfers in kind		...	...	...	...	...	...	...	...			
Other current transfers		110221.0	85221.0	78221.0	40221.0	52584.0	109977.0	167721.0	192531.0			
GROSS DISPOSABLE INCOME		109642.0	99474.0	153316.0	213586.0	233034.0	309081.0	152457.0	280296.0			
II.4.1 Use of disposable income account - Resources												
GROSS DISPOSABLE INCOME		109642.0	99474.0	153316.0	213586.0	233034.0	309081.0	152457.0	280296.0			
II.4.1 Use of disposable income account - Uses												
Adjustment for the change in net equity of households on pension funds		...	...	...	...	...	...	...	...			
SAVING, GROSS		109642.0	99474.0	153316.0	213586.0	233034.0	309081.0	152457.0	280296.0			
III.1 Capital account - Changes in liabilities and net worth												
SAVING, GROSS		109642.0	99474.0	153316.0	213586.0	233034.0	309081.0	152457.0	280296.0			
Capital transfers, receivable less payable		-2420.0	-2958.0	-3779.0	-5356.0	-6205.0	-6883.0	-9434.0	-5893.0			
Capital transfers, receivable		2005.0	2080.0	2225.0	2377.0	2477.0	2599.0	2741.0	2872.0			
Less: Capital transfers, payable		4425.0	5038.0	6004.0	7733.0	8682.0	9482.0	12175.0	8765.0			
Equals: CHANGES IN NET WORTH DUE TO SAVING AND CAPITAL TRANSFERS		56377.0	36113.0	87007.0	142469.0	154253.0	221866.0	49068.0	184390.0			
III.1 Capital account - Changes in assets												
Gross capital formation		114024.0	128187.0	140105.0	151689.0	182704.0	216407.0	270818.0	236679.0			
Gross fixed capital formation		104228.0	118321.0	119404.0	133935.0	167474.0	203700.0	229136.0	214443.0			
Changes in inventories		9796.0	9866.0	20701.0	17754.0	15230.0	12707.0	41682.0	22236.0			
Acquisitions less disposals of valuables		...	...	...	...	...	...	...	...			

	2001	2002	2003	2004	2005	2006	2007	2008	2009	2010	2011	2012
Series		**200**										
Acquisitions less disposals of non-produced non-financial assets		...	...	...	...	...	...	...	...			
NET LENDING (+) / NET BORROWING (-)		-6803.0	-31671.0	9432.0	56541.0	44124.0	85790.0	-127796.0	37723.0			

Table 4.4 Financial Corporations (S.12)

Series 200: 1993 SNA, Saudi Arabian riyal, Western calendar year **Data in millions**

	2001	2002	2003	2004	2005	2006	2007	2008	2009	2010	2011	2012
Series		**200**										
I. Production account - Resources												
Output, at basic prices (otherwise, please specify)		37276.0	38999.0	42226.0	45707.0	48751.0	51730.0	54918.0	58565.0			
I. Production account - Uses												
Intermediate consumption, at purchaser's prices		6973.0	8146.0	11467.0	14147.0	14084.0	13372.0	11232.0	12044.0			
VALUE ADDED GROSS, at basic prices		30303.0	30853.0	30759.0	31560.0	34667.0	38358.0	43686.0	46521.0			
Less: Consumption of fixed capital		1653.0	1797.0	1812.0	1968.0	2159.0	2433.0	2857.0	2602.0			
VALUE ADDED NET, at basic prices		28650.0	29057.0	28947.0	29592.0	32508.0	35926.0	40829.0	43919.0			
II.1.1 Generation of income account - Resources												
VALUE ADDED GROSS, at basic prices		30303.0	30853.0	30759.0	31560.0	34667.0	38358.0	43686.0	46521.0			
II.1.1 Generation of income account - Uses												
Compensation of employees		8394.0	8727.0	8873.0	9135.0	9798.0	11156.0	12050.0	12610.0			
Other taxes less Other subsidies on production		244.0	257.0	251.0	234.0	307.0	279.0	305.0	292.0			
Other taxes on production [a]		244.0	257.0	251.0	234.0	307.0	279.0	305.0	292.0			
Less: Other subsidies on production		0.0	0.0	0.0	0.0	0.0	0.0	0.0	0.0			
OPERATING SURPLUS, GROSS		21665.0	21870.0	21634.0	22191.0	24562.0	26923.0	31332.0	33618.0			
II.1.2 Allocation of primary income account - Resources												
OPERATING SURPLUS, GROSS		21665.0	21870.0	21634.0	22191.0	24562.0	26923.0	31332.0	33618.0			
Property income		44538.0	45227.0	46587.0	47592.0	50890.0	53312.0	56232.0	52694.0			
II.1.2 Allocation of primary income account - Uses												
Property income		9862.0	11517.0	13177.0	17996.0	16412.0	19171.0	21667.0	20273.0			
BALANCE OF PRIMARY INCOMES		56342.0	55579.0	55044.0	51787.0	59040.0	61064.0	65897.0	66039.0			
II.2 Secondary distribution of income account - Resources												
BALANCE OF PRIMARY INCOMES		56342.0	55579.0	55044.0	51787.0	59040.0	61064.0	65897.0	66039.0			
Social contributions		23173.0	25063.0	27309.0	30204.0	32596.0	33631.0	35427.0	39022.0			
Other current transfers		1965.0	2122.0	2227.0	2279.0	2358.0	2489.0	3568.0	5378.0			
II.2 Secondary distribution of income account - Uses												
Current taxes on income, wealth, etc.		1123.0	1375.0	1536.0	2345.0	1626.0	1806.0	1698.0	1790.0			
Social benefits other than social transfers in kind		22014.0	23810.0	25944.0	28694.0	30966.0	31949.0	33655.0	37071.0			
Other current transfers		6521.0	6867.0	7511.0	7910.0	8388.0	8892.0	9751.0	2670.0			
GROSS DISPOSABLE INCOME		51820.0	50713.0	49589.0	45322.0	53013.0	54537.0	59787.0	68909.0			

	2001	2002	2003	2004	2005	2006	2007	2008	2009	2010	2011	2012
Series		**200**										
	II.4.1 Use of disposable income account - Resources											
GROSS DISPOSABLE INCOME		51820.0	50713.0	49589.0	45322.0	53013.0	54537.0	59787.0	68909.0			
	II.4.1 Use of disposable income account - Uses											
Adjustment for the change in net equity of households on pension funds		...	...	...	...	...	...	...	...			
SAVING, GROSS		51820.0	50713.0	49589.0	45322.0	53013.0	54537.0	59787.0	68909.0			
	III.1 Capital account - Changes in liabilities and net worth											
SAVING, GROSS		51820.0	50713.0	49589.0	45322.0	53013.0	54537.0	59787.0	68909.0			
Capital transfers, receivable less payable		-342.0	-358.0	-388.0	-420.0	-448.0	-466.0	-505.0	-538.0			
Capital transfers, receivable		0.0	0.0	0.0	0.0	0.0	0.0	0.0	0.0			
Less: Capital transfers, payable		342.0	358.0	388.0	420.0	448.0	466.0	505.0	538.0			
Equals: CHANGES IN NET WORTH DUE TO SAVING AND CAPITAL TRANSFERS		49824.0	48558.0	47389.0	42934.0	50406.0	51639.0	56426.0	65769.0			
	III.1 Capital account - Changes in assets											
Gross capital formation		3733.0	4242.0	4398.0	4469.0	4494.0	4972.0	6171.0	5842.0			
Gross fixed capital formation		3647.0	4138.0	4183.0	4310.0	4369.0	4885.0	5737.0	5611.0			
Changes in inventories		86.0	104.0	215.0	159.0	125.0	87.0	434.0	231.0			
Acquisitions less disposals of valuables		...	...	...	...	...	...	...	...			
Acquisitions less disposals of non-produced non-financial assets		...	...	...	...	...	...	...	...			
NET LENDING (+) / NET BORROWING (-)		47745.0	46113.0	44803.0	40432.0	48070.0	49099.0	53112.0	62529.0			

[a] Refers to net taxes on production.

Table 4.5 General Government (S.13)

Series 200: 1993 SNA, Saudi Arabian riyal, Western calendar year

Data in millions

	2001	2002	2003	2004	2005	2006	2007	2008	2009	2010	2011	2012
Series		**200**										
	I. Production account - Resources											
Output, at basic prices (otherwise, please specify)		190564.0	206180.0	229599.0	270936.0	319626.0	331178.0	354993.0	366683.0			
	I. Production account - Uses											
Intermediate consumption, at purchaser's prices		66078.0	66251.0	74228.0	94585.0	123240.0	130872.0	145715.0	125636.0			
VALUE ADDED GROSS, at basic prices		124486.0	139929.0	155371.0	176350.0	196386.0	200306.0	209278.0	241047.0			
Less: Consumption of fixed capital		12986.0	13702.0	13952.0	14204.0	15058.0	15456.0	16028.0	16284.0			
VALUE ADDED NET, at basic prices		111500.0	126227.0	141419.0	162146.0	181328.0	184850.0	193250.0	224763.0			
	II.1.1 Generation of income account - Resources											
VALUE ADDED GROSS, at basic prices		124486.0	139929.0	155371.0	176350.0	196386.0	200306.0	209278.0	241047.0			
	II.1.1 Generation of income account - Uses											
Compensation of employees		111500.0	126227.0	141419.0	162146.0	181328.0	184850.0	193250.0	224763.0			
Other taxes less Other subsidies on production		0.0	0.0	0.0	0.0	0.0	0.0	0.0	0.0			
Other taxes on production		...	...	...	...	...	...	...	...			

	2001	2002	2003	2004	2005	2006	2007	2008	2009	2010	2011	2012
Series		**200**										
Less: Other subsidies on production		...	...	...	...	...	...	...	...			
OPERATING SURPLUS, GROSS		12986.0	13702.0	13952.0	14204.0	15058.0	15456.0	16028.0	16284.0			
II.1.2 Allocation of primary income account - Resources												
OPERATING SURPLUS, GROSS		12986.0	13702.0	13952.0	14204.0	15058.0	15456.0	16028.0	16284.0			
Taxes on production and imports, less Subsidies		18583.0	17437.0	13691.0	19096.0	24103.0	23249.0	22562.0	21980.0			
Taxes on production and imports		22932.0	24374.0	25447.0	26783.0	29478.0	29204.0	34083.0	32152.0			
Taxes on products [a]		7386.0	8087.0	8825.0	10115.0	11025.0	11801.0	14940.0	12895.0			
Other taxes on production		15546.0	16287.0	16622.0	16668.0	18453.0	17403.0	19143.0	19257.0			
Less: Subsidies		4349.0	6937.0	11756.0	7687.0	5375.0	5955.0	11521.0	10172.0			
Subsidies on products		...	...	...	...	...	...	...	...			
Other subsidies on production [b]		4349.0	6937.0	11756.0	7687.0	5375.0	5955.0	11521.0	10172.0			
Property income		59087.0	113496.0	121301.0	183846.0	186582.0	200089.0	315925.0	135406.0			
II.1.2 Allocation of primary income account - Uses												
Property income		0.0	0.0	0.0	0.0	0.0	0.0	0.0	0.0			
BALANCE OF PRIMARY INCOMES		90657.0	144635.0	148944.0	217146.0	225743.0	238793.0	354515.0	173670.0			
II.2 Secondary distribution of income account - Resources												
BALANCE OF PRIMARY INCOMES		90657.0	144635.0	148944.0	217146.0	225743.0	238793.0	354515.0	173670.0			
Current taxes on income, wealth, etc.		118895.0	174256.0	236599.0	341917.0	443245.0	398023.0	710690.0	322901.0			
Social contributions		...	...	...	...	...	...	...	...			
Other current transfers		5744.0	5886.0	5627.0	6993.0	8411.0	10812.0	11691.0	12243.0			
II.2 Secondary distribution of income account - Uses												
Current taxes on income, wealth, etc.		...	...	...	...	...	...	...	...			
Social benefits other than social transfers in kind		2676.0	2647.0	2623.0	2844.0	6060.0	11722.0	14629.0	13833.0			
Other current transfers		22756.0	20434.0	22139.0	35507.0	42834.0	43007.0	66731.0	53975.0			
GROSS DISPOSABLE INCOME		189864.0	301697.0	366407.0	527706.0	628505.0	592899.0	995536.0	441006.0			
II.4.1 Use of disposable income account - Resources												
GROSS DISPOSABLE INCOME		189864.0	301697.0	366407.0	527706.0	628505.0	592899.0	995536.0	441006.0			
II.4.1 Use of disposable income account - Uses												
Final consumption expenditure		185352.0	199743.0	223197.0	263822.0	312318.0	323237.0	345908.0	357752.0			
Individual consumption expenditure		16127.0	15720.0	16487.0	16356.0	18895.0	21379.0	24787.0	35326.0			
Collective consumption expenditure		169226.0	184023.0	206711.0	247466.0	293423.0	301857.0	321121.0	322426.0			
Adjustment for the change in net equity of households on pension funds		...	...	...	...	...	...	...	...			
SAVING, GROSS		4511.0	101954.0	143210.0	263885.0	316187.0	269662.0	649628.0	83255.0			
III.1 Capital account - Changes in liabilities and net worth												
SAVING, GROSS		4511.0	101954.0	143210.0	263885.0	316187.0	269662.0	649628.0	83255.0			
Capital transfers, receivable less payable		0.0	-25.0	-200.0	-5200.0	-200.0	-600.0	0.0	0.0			
Capital transfers, receivable		0.0	0.0	0.0	401.0	2966.0	20000.0	0.0	0.0			
Less: Capital transfers, payable		0.0	25.0	200.0	5601.0	3166.0	20600.0	0.0	0.0			

	2001	2002	2003	2004	2005	2006	2007	2008	2009	2010	2011	2012
Series		**200**										
Equals: CHANGES IN NET WORTH DUE TO SAVING AND CAPITAL TRANSFERS		-8475.0	88227.0	129058.0	244481.0	300929.0	253606.0	633600.0	66971.0			
III.1 Capital account - Changes in assets												
Gross capital formation		18121.0	23291.0	30386.0	54940.0	58741.0	84042.0	109882.0	112088.0			
Gross fixed capital formation		18121.0	23291.0	30386.0	54940.0	58741.0	84042.0	109882.0	112088.0			
Changes in inventories		...	...	...	...	...	...	...	...			
Acquisitions less disposals of valuables		...	...	...	...	...	...	...	...			
Acquisitions of non-produced non-financial assets		812.0	756.0	1334.0	1542.0	2373.0	2880.0	13348.0	2946.0			
NET LENDING (+) / NET BORROWING (-)		-14421.0	77882.0	111290.0	202202.0	254872.0	182140.0	526397.0	-31780.0			

[a] Import duties only.
[b] Refers to all subsidies on production and imports

Table 4.6 Households (S.14)

Series 200: 1993 SNA, Saudi Arabian riyal, Western calendar year — **Data in millions**

	2001	2002	2003	2004	2005	2006	2007	2008	2009	2010	2011	2012
Series		**200**										
I. Production account - Resources												
Output, at basic prices (otherwise, please specify)		24517.0	25636.0	27787.0	30153.0	32115.0	34101.0	36521.0	39098.0			
I. Production account - Uses												
Intermediate consumption, at purchaser's prices		8139.0	8530.0	9419.0	10403.0	10973.0	11397.0	11968.0	13321.0			
VALUE ADDED GROSS, at basic prices		16378.0	17106.0	18368.0	19751.0	21142.0	22705.0	24553.0	25777.0			
Less: Consumption of fixed capital		329.0	357.0	360.0	392.0	430.0	484.0	568.0	518.0			
VALUE ADDED NET, at basic prices		16049.0	16749.0	18008.0	19359.0	20712.0	22221.0	23985.0	25260.0			
II.1.1 Generation of income account - Resources												
VALUE ADDED GROSS, at basic prices		16378.0	17106.0	18368.0	19751.0	21142.0	22705.0	24553.0	25777.0			
II.1.1 Generation of income account - Uses												
Compensation of employees		9886.0	10183.0	10583.0	11003.0	11428.0	11829.0	12249.0	13189.0			
Other taxes less Other subsidies on production		341.0	359.0	351.0	327.0	429.0	389.0	426.0	408.0			
Other taxes on production [a]		341.0	359.0	351.0	327.0	429.0	389.0	426.0	408.0			
Less: Other subsidies on production		0.0	0.0	0.0	0.0	0.0	0.0	0.0	0.0			
OPERATING SURPLUS, GROSS		...	...	...	...	...	...	...	...			
MIXED INCOME, GROSS		6151.0	6565.0	7434.0	8421.0	9284.0	10487.0	11878.0	12180.0			
II.1.2 Allocation of primary income account - Resources												
OPERATING SURPLUS, GROSS		...	...	...	...	...	...	...	...			
MIXED INCOME, GROSS		6151.0	6565.0	7434.0	8421.0	9284.0	10487.0	11878.0	12180.0			
Compensation of employees		219329.0	239177.0	262326.0	297167.0	321462.0	331487.0	349163.0	386395.0			
Property income		13993.0	16918.0	18840.0	28500.0	19930.0	22084.0	21635.0	22131.0			
II.1.2 Allocation of primary income account - Uses												
Property income		9368.0	9518.0	9548.0	9905.0	10087.0	10101.0	9808.0	7450.0			

	2001	2002	2003	2004	2005	2006	2007	2008	2009	2010	2011	2012
Series		**200**										
BALANCE OF PRIMARY INCOMES		230105.0	253142.0	279051.0	324183.0	340590.0	353957.0	372868.0	413256.0			
II.2 Secondary distribution of income account - Resources												
BALANCE OF PRIMARY INCOMES		230105.0	253142.0	279051.0	324183.0	340590.0	353957.0	372868.0	413256.0			
Social contributions		...	...	...	...	...	...	...	...			
Social benefits other than social transfers in kind		24690.0	26458.0	28567.0	31538.0	37026.0	43671.0	48284.0	50904.0			
Other current transfers		124910.0	100594.0	96332.0	60746.0	75427.0	132343.0	201605.0	209865.0			
II.2 Secondary distribution of income account - Uses												
Current taxes on income, wealth, etc.		...	...	...	...	...	...	...	...			
Social contributions		23173.0	25063.0	27309.0	30204.0	32596.0	33631.0	35427.0	39022.0			
Social benefits other than social transfers in kind		...	...	...	...	...	...	...	...			
Other current transfers		77338.0	71590.0	71485.0	42718.0	46227.0	48675.0	60012.0	83224.0			
GROSS DISPOSABLE INCOME		279195.0	283540.0	305157.0	343545.0	374221.0	447666.0	527319.0	551778.0			
II.4.1 Use of disposable income account - Resources												
GROSS DISPOSABLE INCOME		279195.0	283540.0	305157.0	343545.0	374221.0	447666.0	527319.0	551778.0			
Adjustment for the change in net equity of households on pension funds		...	...	...	...	...	...	...	...			
II.4.1 Use of disposable income account - Uses												
Final consumption expenditure		261583.0	271090.0	286317.0	313235.0	355400.0	421666.0	497097.0	544807.0			
Individual consumption expenditure		261583.0	271090.0	286317.0	313235.0	355400.0	421666.0	497097.0	544807.0			
SAVING, GROSS		17612.0	12450.0	18840.0	30310.0	18821.0	26000.0	30222.0	6972.0			
III.1 Capital account - Changes in liabilities and net worth												
SAVING, GROSS		17612.0	12450.0	18840.0	30310.0	18821.0	26000.0	30222.0	6972.0			
Capital transfers, receivable less payable		1829.0	2488.0	3453.0	9988.0	5630.0	6915.0	8724.0	5454.0			
Capital transfers, receivable [b]		1829.0	2488.0	3453.0	9988.0	5630.0	6915.0	8724.0	5454.0			
Less: Capital transfers, payable		0.0	0.0	0.0	0.0	0.0	0.0	0.0	0.0			
Equals: CHANGES IN NET WORTH DUE TO SAVINGS AND CAPITAL TRANSFERS		19112.0	14580.0	21932.0	39907.0	24021.0	32430.0	38378.0	11908.0			
III.1 Capital account - Changes in assets												
Gross capital formation		3187.0	3704.0	5218.0	4537.0	4110.0	3887.0	9023.0	6225.0			
Gross fixed capital formation		2027.0	2300.0	2325.0	2396.0	2429.0	2716.0	3189.0	3120.0			
Changes in inventories		1160.0	1404.0	2893.0	2141.0	1681.0	1171.0	5834.0	3105.0			
Acquisitions less disposals of valuables		...	...	...	...	...	...	...	...			
Acquisitions less disposals of non-produced non-financial assets		-812.0	-756.0	-1334.0	-1542.0	-2373.0	-2880.0	-13348.0	-2946.0			
NET LENDING (+) / NET BORROWING (-)		17065.0	11989.0	18408.0	37303.0	22714.0	31908.0	43271.0	9147.0			

[a] Refers to net taxes on production.
[b] Refers to capital transfers, net

Table 4.7 Non-profit institutions serving households (S.15)

Series 200: 1993 SNA, Saudi Arabian riyal, Western calendar year | **Data in millions**

	2001	2002	2003	2004	2005	2006	2007	2008	2009	2010	2011	2012
Series		**200**										
I. Production account - Resources												
Output, at basic prices (otherwise, please specify)		803.0	830.0	888.0	953.0	985.0	1006.0	1035.0	1146.0			
I. Production account - Uses												
Intermediate consumption, at purchaser's prices		460.0	479.0	524.0	572.0	588.0	596.0	606.0	672.0			
VALUE ADDED GROSS, at basic prices		343.0	351.0	364.0	381.0	397.0	411.0	429.0	473.0			
Less: Consumption of fixed capital		26.0	29.0	29.0	31.0	34.0	39.0	46.0	41.0			
VALUE ADDED NET, at basic prices		317.0	323.0	335.0	349.0	362.0	372.0	383.0	432.0			
II.1.1 Generation of income account - Resources												
VALUE ADDED GROSS, at basic prices		343.0	351.0	364.0	381.0	397.0	411.0	429.0	473.0			
II.1.1 Generation of income account - Uses												
Compensation of employees		317.0	323.0	335.0	349.0	362.0	372.0	383.0	432.0			
Other taxes less Other subsidies on production		0.0	0.0	0.0	0.0	0.0	0.0	0.0	0.0			
Other taxes on production		...	...	...	...	...	...	...	...			
Less: Other subsidies on production		...	...	...	...	...	...	...	...			
OPERATING SURPLUS, GROSS		26.0	29.0	29.0	31.0	34.0	39.0	46.0	41.0			
II.1.2 Allocation of primary income account - Resources												
OPERATING SURPLUS, GROSS		26.0	29.0	29.0	31.0	34.0	39.0	46.0	41.0			
Property income		2.0	0.0	6.0	8.0	7.0	4.0	8.0	11.0			
II.1.2 Allocation of primary income account - Uses												
Property income		0.0	0.0	0.0	0.0	0.0	0.0	0.0	0.0			
BALANCE OF PRIMARY INCOMES		28.0	29.0	35.0	39.0	41.0	43.0	54.0	52.0			
II.2 Secondary distribution of income account - Resources												
BALANCE OF PRIMARY INCOMES		28.0	29.0	35.0	39.0	41.0	43.0	54.0	52.0			
Social contributions		...	...	...	...	...	...	...	...			
Other current transfers		2948.0	3444.0	4153.0	4126.0	3808.0	3719.0	3932.0	4544.0			
II.2 Secondary distribution of income account - Uses												
Current taxes on income, wealth, etc.		...	...	...	...	...	...	...	...			
Social benefits other than social transfers in kind		...	...	...	...	...	...	...	...			
Other current transfers		2125.0	2579.0	3244.0	3164.0	2815.0	2681.0	2874.0	3402.0			
GROSS DISPOSABLE INCOME		851.0	893.0	944.0	1002.0	1035.0	1080.0	1111.0	1194.0			
II.4.1 Use of disposable income account - Resources												
GROSS DISPOSABLE INCOME		851.0	893.0	944.0	1002.0	1035.0	1080.0	1111.0	1194.0			
II.4.1 Use of disposable income account - Uses												
Final consumption expenditure		803.0	830.0	888.0	953.0	985.0	1006.0	1035.0	1146.0			
Individual consumption expenditure		803.0	830.0	888.0	953.0	985.0	1006.0	1035.0	1146.0			
Adjustment for the change in net equity of households on pension funds		...	...	...	...	...	...	...	...			

	2001	2002	2003	2004	2005	2006	2007	2008	2009	2010	2011	2012
Series		**200**										
SAVING, GROSS		48.0	63.0	56.0	49.0	50.0	74.0	76.0	49.0			
III.1 Capital account - Changes in liabilities and net worth												
SAVING, GROSS		48.0	63.0	56.0	49.0	50.0	74.0	76.0	49.0			
Capital transfers, receivable less payable		934.0	853.0	914.0	988.0	1223.0	1034.0	1214.0	978.0			
Capital transfers, receivable [a]		934.0	853.0	914.0	988.0	1223.0	1034.0	1214.0	978.0			
Less: Capital transfers, payable		0.0	0.0	0.0	0.0	0.0	0.0	0.0	0.0			
Equals: CHANGES IN NET WORTH DUE TO SAVING AND CAPITAL TRANSFERS		956.0	887.0	941.0	1006.0	1239.0	1070.0	1245.0	985.0			
III.1 Capital account - Changes in assets												
Gross capital formation		43.0	48.0	49.0	51.0	51.0	57.0	67.0	66.0			
Gross fixed capital formation		43.0	48.0	49.0	51.0	51.0	57.0	67.0	66.0			
Changes in inventories		...	...	...	...	...	...	...	...			
Acquisitions less disposals of valuables		...	...	...	...	...	...	...	...			
Acquisitions less disposals of non-produced non-financial assets		...	...	...	...	...	...	...	...			
NET LENDING (+) / NET BORROWING (-)		939.0	868.0	921.0	987.0	1222.0	1051.0	1223.0	961.0			

[a] Refers to capital transfers, net

Senegal

Source

The National Accounts of Senegal that were published in September 2008 were compiled by the Division for National Accounting, Syntheses and Analytical Studies of the National Agency for Statistics and Demography (NASD) of Senegal. They represent the final accounts for 2005, semi-final accounts for 2006 and the provisional accounts for 2007.

In 2002, the former Directorate of Forecasts and Statistics (DFS) published the revised provisional national accounts for 1996-2001 with the aim of both clearing the significant backlog and applying the new methodology using a different base year, in accordance with 1993 SNA. With that publication, it was possible to clear the backlog built up by national accounts in the past and, at the same time, to adapt to the new rules for national accounts that are being progressively adopted in most of the States members of the West African Economic and Monetary Union. A CD was prepared in order to disseminate those accounts.

Subsequently, DFS, in collaboration with a certain number of technical directorates and international institutions and, in particular, the Economic and Statistical Observatory for Sub-Saharan Africa (AFRISTAT) and the French Cooperation Agency, undertook a revision and retroactive compilation of national accounts for 1980-2003, using 1999 as the base year. Those accounts were published in March 2005.

National accounts publications are divided into three main sections. The first analyses changes in the principal aggregates and ratios of national accounts; the second presents the various tables of the revised national accounts; and the third provides a concise summary of the methodology. The main tables (macroeconomic indicators, gross domestic product (GDP) and its uses, and aggregates by branch) are disseminated in printed form, accompanied by an analytical note on the outcomes.

The data are also available on the NASD website at www.ansd.sn. More detailed results may be obtained from the NASD Division for National Accounting, Syntheses and Analytical Studies.

General

1993 SNA was adopted in Senegal at the time of the compilation of the revised interim national accounts for 1996-2001 that were published in December 2002. A retroactive compilation of national accounts since 1980 has also been formulated on the basis of 1993 SNA.

The process of compiling those accounts involves seven major stages, as follows:
(a) Review of sources of information and classification. An inventory is made of all available statistics and common classifications are defined. That stage was conducted at the time of the compilation of the revised national accounts for 1980-2003;
(b) Adoption of common classifications. That stage made it possible to reconcile all sources of data through the formulation of conversion tables for the changeover to the Classifications of Activities of AFRISTAT Member States as adapted for use by Senegal, and operations classifications;
(c) Fine-tuning of production. Once the common classifications had been adopted, production was possible using several sources. An initial series of adjustments is conducted in order to set a production value;
(d) Establishment of preliminary resource-use balances;
(e) Compilation of production accounts by branch of activity;
(f) Compilation of preliminary input-output table;
(g) Compilation of final input-output table. After the preliminary table has been compiled, production is fine-tuned by being adjusted to use by branch of activity. Detailed components of production accounts are also processed.

Activities are classified on two levels (42 branches and 93 sub-branches). The classification of products, taken together with the classification of activities, consists of three levels which include 232 products at the most detailed level.

Methodological notes on the compilation of national accounts that described those stages in detail were prepared in 2005 and updated in 2006. The most significant corrections related to the evaluation of agricultural production (rural production n/n+1 is currently applied to year n) and of Government agencies (consumption of fixed capital and all foreign aid is incorporated). The new classifications that are used are adapted from the classifications of activities and products recommended by AFRISTAT member States.

The synoptic tables that are normally published are the following:
- macroeconomic indicators;
- Gross Domestic Product and its uses;
- aggregates by product at current prices and constant prices for 1999.

It should be noted that the fiscal year used is the calendar year.

Methodology:

Overview of GDP Compilation

GDP is calculated using three approaches: production, expenditure and income. The two first are obtained from the supply and use table.

Firstly, supply and use balances and branch accounts for each of the 41 branches of the Classifications of Activities of AFRISTAT Member States, as adapted for use by Senegal, are compiled. Indirectly Measured Financial Mediation services have been assigned to a forty-second, fictitious branch.

Expenditure Approach

GDP equals the sum of net final use (final consumer expenditure by households, general government and non-profit institutions serving households plus gross fixed capital formation plus exports minus imports plus changes in inventories).

The final consumption expenditure of general government and non-profit institutions serving households is derived from production estimates calculated using data obtained from various sources. Non-market general government Final consumption expenditure is obtained by calculating the difference between total production and market production. Final consumption expenditure is divided into individual and collective non-market categories.

Household final consumption expenditure is of two types, namely, market and non-market. The sources of data that have been used heretofore vary. Final merchandise consumer expenditure is estimated for the majority of products on the basis of budget consumer surveys, in particular: (i) Priority survey, 1991; (ii) Survey on household expenditure in the capital, 1996; (iii) the Senegalese household surveys No. 1 and 2, carried out in 1995 and 2002 respectively; and (iv) follow-up survey on poverty in Senegal, 2005-2006. Annual population growth rates and the harmonized consumer price index are used in order to determine final consumption at constant and current prices for a given year.

Non-market final consumption is estimated on the basis of own-consumption rates provided by household surveys.

Private sector gross fixed capital formation (GFCF) reflects the value of acquisitions, less the disposal of fixed assets. It covers the following specific capital assets: livestock products; timber sector products; mining and hydraulic equipment, building and public works equipment, machinery and appliances, and transport and handling equipment and vehicles.

Information on GFCF of imports is obtained by applying a structure that breaks down the use of each imported product.
Public sector GFCF is derived by using data on the performance of State capital and operation budgets, the State

financial transaction table, the financial statements of various central Government agencies, the operating accounts of local administrative bodies (regions, communes and rural communities), and the financial statements of social security funds.

Figures for the imports and exports of goods and services are derived from customs and balance of payment statistics. A conversion table has been prepared in order to convert the foreign trade data, which are presented under with the Harmonized Commodity Description and Coding System, to national accounts product classifications. Separate analysis of the price and volume indices by subsample and year has made it possible to calculate a volume index. Balance of payments statistics have been used in order to determine price trends. The balance of payments is worked out by the Central Bank of West African States, and a conversion table has been established in order to reconcile its classifications with those of national accounts.

Income Approach

Information on the compensation of employees and tax less subsidies on the production of financial and non-financial corporations is derived from company statistical and tax declarations.

With respect to general government, the same data are obtained from monthly payrolls, the table of State financial operations and the accounting records of local communities and public establishments.

As regards households, the information is derived from survey data on the informal sector.

Gross operating surplus and mixed income is estimated from the balance between the value added from the production account of each institutional sector.

Production Approach

GDP is equal to the sum of total value added and net taxes on products.

With respect to total value added, data on merchandise and non-merchandise production are derived from several sources, while those on intermediate consumption are determined using a technical coefficient matrix based on the 2001 input-output table.

Data on the production of subsistence and industrial export crops is derived from the statistics of the Directorate of Analysis, Forecasting and Statistics. They are calculated using prices supplied by the Food Security Commissariat through the market information system.

Data on livestock and fish are provided by the Directorate of Animal Husbandry and the Directorate of Marine Fisheries, respectively.

Forestry production data are provided by the Directorate of Water, Forests, Hunting and Soil Conservation.

Data on mining and manufacturing industry production are obtained from the statistical and tax declarations of companies in that sector.

Data on the production of banks are obtained by using questionnaire data provided by the Central Bank of West African States. Such data include the various services rendered to customers; income from fixed assets; and bank service charges, which in 1993 SNA are called financial intermediation services indirectly measured (FISIM). The value added of the sector to which FISIM has been allocated has the opposite sign to intermediate consumption. Microfinance institution production is determined by using their financial statements.

Data on insurance company production are obtained from the annual report prepared by the Directorate of Insurance. Production equals the difference between gross premiums and net premiums.

General government production is calculated by costs, namely, employee compensation, intermediate consumption, and consumption of fixed capital. Such data is derived from various public institution records.

Informal sector production is determined by using Senegalese household survey No. 1 of 1995 and the survey of the informal sector that was conducted for the 2006 input-output table.

Estimated production for 1996 is projected using price indices for each branch of activity and trends in the economically active population by branch.

Information on net taxes on products is provided by the General Directorate of Public Accounts and Treasury through the State financial transaction table.

Overview of the Compilation of the Integrated Economic Accounts

Following Senegal's undertaking to adhere to the Special Data Dissemination Standard, NASD has formulated the accounts of the institutional sectors and the table of integrated economic accounts. In that regard, it has benefited from technical assistance provided by the Africa Technical Assistance Centre (AFRITAC) for West Africa and financial assistance provided by the African Development Bank, which made it possible to produce the integrated economic accounts for 2001-2005. However, NASD intends to share the results of its work with partners, including the Central Bank and the General Directorate of Public Accounts and Treasury, before they are finally approved and published. Therefore, those data are not presented in this questionnaire.

Table 1.1 Gross domestic product by expenditures at current prices

Series 100: 1993 SNA, CFA franc, Western calendar year — **Data in billions**

	2001	2002	2003	2004	2005	2006	2007	2008	2009	2010	2011	2012
Series	**100**											
	Expenditures of the gross domestic product											
Final consumption expenditure	3241.1	3466.3	3594.6	3861.2	4175.7	4539.7	5037.7	5696.4	5718.7	5924.3	6271.8	
Household final consumption expenditure	2790.4	2973.1	3076.3	3290.1	3565.0	3871.5	4270.6	4890.0	4857.7	4995.9	5293.8	
NPISHs final consumption expenditure	7.5	8.5	11.1	11.8	12.9	13.6	14.5	15.3	16.3	17.2	18.3	
General government final consumption expenditure	443.2	484.7	507.2	559.3	597.8	654.5	752.6	791.1	844.8	911.1	959.7	
Individual consumption expenditure	142.7	155.3	159.9	185.9	211.2	228.6	263.8	276.8	305.3	339.4	350.1	
Collective consumption expenditure	300.5	329.4	347.3	373.4	386.6	425.9	488.9	514.2	539.5	571.7	609.6	
Gross capital formation	657.5	638.5	875.1	917.5	1125.0	1208.9	1582.0	1874.7	1333.2	1443.1	1709.5	
Gross fixed capital formation	812.5	922.7	857.4	944.1	1071.4	1279.7	1414.1	1607.6	1386.2	1430.0	1611.4	
Changes in inventories	-155.0	-284.2	17.6	-26.6	53.6	-70.9	168.0	267.1	-53.0	13.1	98.0	
Acquisitions less disposals of valuables	...	...	...	...	...	...	...	...	...	...	...	
Exports of goods and services	1027.1	1061.3	1061.3	1151.5	1240.8	1254.0	1376.2	1566.3	1471.8	1592.6	1736.0	
Exports of goods	735.3	743.4	730.6	797.5	832.4	833.5	802.2	987.9	990.1	1071.9	1200.4	
Exports of services	291.8	318.0	330.7	354.0	408.4	420.6	574.0	578.4	481.7	520.7	535.7	
Less: Imports of goods and services	1350.3	1448.6	1544.2	1687.3	1948.4	2109.0	2587.6	3142.9	2490.3	2577.8	2950.5	
Imports of goods	1047.1	1111.4	1200.4	1318.5	1523.8	1669.9	1995.5	2510.4	1947.8	2022.4	2354.1	
Imports of services	303.2	337.2	343.8	368.8	424.6	439.1	592.1	632.5	542.5	555.4	596.4	
Equals: GROSS DOMESTIC PRODUCT	3575.5	3717.6	3986.8	4242.8	4593.1	4893.5	5408.3	5994.5	6033.4	6382.3	6766.8	

Table 1.2 Gross domestic product by expenditures at constant prices

Series 100: 1993 SNA, CFA franc, Western calendar year **Data in billions**

	2001	2002	2003	2004	2005	2006	2007	2008	2009	2010	2011	2012
Series	**100**											
Base year	**1999**											
	Expenditures of the gross domestic product											
Final consumption expenditure	3032.4	3160.3	3317.5	3466.2	3643.7	3815.8	4016.8	4215.2	4365.3	4441.4	4516.0	
Household final consumption expenditure	2604.8	2717.6	2862.8	2986.1	3137.9	3284.4	3446.9	3641.2	3781.5	3846.0	3901.6	
NPISHs final consumption expenditure	7.9	8.9	9.5	9.7	10.2	10.7	11.2	11.8	12.2	12.4	12.6	
General government final consumption expenditure	419.6	433.8	445.2	470.4	495.6	520.7	558.7	562.3	571.5	583.0	601.8	
Individual consumption expenditure	150.0	162.6	174.3	186.1	196.8	206.0	225.2	230.6	235.6	242.7	248.4	
Collective consumption expenditure	269.7	271.3	270.9	284.3	298.8	314.7	333.5	331.6	335.9	340.3	353.3	
Gross capital formation	667.1	570.5	719.7	728.3	897.0	878.1	1101.5	1045.1	874.8	844.8	930.1	
Gross fixed capital formation	760.7	781.3	809.5	886.3	940.0	1063.9	1143.0	1235.5	1182.5	1206.0	1339.7	
Changes in inventories	-93.6	-210.8	-89.7	-157.9	-43.0	-185.8	-41.5	-190.4	-307.8	-361.2	-409.6	
Acquisitions less disposals of valuables	...	...	...	...	...	...	...	...	...	...	...	
Exports of goods and services	879.1	910.7	970.3	1036.0	1057.3	1022.9	1022.1	1041.0	1105.5	1177.5	1234.4	
Exports of goods	574.3	585.9	654.1	744.4	704.6	696.5	687.1	625.2	717.6	752.4	836.4	
Exports of services	304.8	324.8	316.2	291.7	352.6	326.4	335.0	415.7	387.9	425.1	398.0	
Less: Imports of goods and services	1160.8	1201.2	1337.9	1345.0	1493.8	1511.7	1727.7	1726.0	1659.4	1577.8	1693.4	
Imports of goods	1012.2	1057.2	1124.3	1144.7	1200.2	1172.8	1345.6	1362.8	1286.9	1231.4	1332.9	
Imports of services	148.6	144.0	213.5	200.3	293.6	338.9	382.1	363.3	372.5	346.4	360.5	
Equals: GROSS DOMESTIC PRODUCT	3417.8	3440.2	3669.7	3885.6	4104.1	4205.1	4412.7	4575.2	4686.1	4886.0	4987.0	

Table 1.3 Relations among product, income, savings, and net lending aggregates

Series 100: 1993 SNA, CFA franc, Western calendar year **Data in billions**

	2001	2002	2003	2004	2005	2006	2007	2008	2009	2010	2011	2012
Series	**100**											
GROSS DOMESTIC PRODUCT	3575.5	3717.6	3986.8	4242.8	4593.1	4893.5	5408.3	5994.5	6033.4	6382.3	6766.8	
Plus: Compensation of employees - from and to the rest of the world, net	26.7	29.8	31.2	31.4	32.3	33.9	34.3	37.6	38.4	38.1	38.6	
Plus: Compensation of employees - from the rest of the world	33.0	33.3	36.4	36.8	37.9	39.0	40.8	43.8	45.7	46.3	47.0	
Less: Compensation of employees - to the rest of the world	6.3	3.5	5.2	5.4	5.6	5.2	6.5	6.2	7.2	8.3	8.4	
Plus: Property income - from and to the rest of the world, net	-103.6	-120.4	-110.5	-100.5	-79.5	-67.0	-69.7	-59.0	-118.6	-109.4	-118.3	
Plus: Property income - from the rest of the world	16.2	13.6	32.9	45.9	71.2	52.6	55.8	86.4	35.2	55.5	77.8	
Less: Property income - to the rest of the world	119.7	134.1	143.4	146.4	150.8	119.7	125.5	145.4	153.8	164.8	196.2	
Sum of Compensation of employees and property income - from and to the rest of the world, net	-76.8	-90.6	-79.3	-69.1	-47.2	-33.2	-35.4	-21.4	-80.1	-71.3	-79.7	

	2001	2002	2003	2004	2005	2006	2007	2008	2009	2010	2011	2012
Series	**100**											
Plus: Sum of Compensation of employees and property income - from the rest of the world	49.2	47.0	69.4	82.7	109.1	91.7	96.6	130.1	80.9	101.8	124.9	
Less: Sum of Compensation of employees and property income - to the rest of the world	126.0	137.5	148.6	151.8	156.4	124.9	132.0	151.6	161.0	173.1	204.6	
Plus: Taxes less subsidies on production and imports - from and to the rest of the world, net[a]	134.6	162.0	63.0	62.2	18.9	-113.3	-63.7	-28.8	2.3	9.3	-80.9	
Equals: GROSS NATIONAL INCOME	3633.3[b]	3789.0[b]	3970.5[b]	4235.9[b]	4564.7[b]	4747.1[b]	5309.2[b]	5944.3[b]	5955.6	6320.3	6606.2	
Plus: Current transfers - from and to the rest of the world, net	220.0	256.9	308.3	333.9	397.6	437.5	618.0	754.4	695.6	767.5	774.2	
Plus: Current transfers - from the rest of the world	259.2	288.8	346.2	377.8	453.2	509.1	746.4	889.3	829.6	928.0	936.5	
Less: Current transfers - to the rest of the world	39.2	31.9	37.9	43.9	55.6	71.7	128.4	134.9	133.9	160.5	162.3	
Equals: GROSS NATIONAL DISPOSABLE INCOME	3853.3	4046.0	4278.8	4569.8	4962.3	5184.5	5927.3	6698.6	6651.2	7087.8	7380.3	
Less: Final consumption expenditure / Actual final consumption	3241.1	3466.3	3594.6	3861.2	4175.7	4539.7	5037.7	5696.4	5718.7	5924.3	6271.8	
Equals: SAVING, GROSS	612.2	579.6	684.2	708.6	786.6	644.9	889.6	1002.2	932.5	1163.5	1108.5	
Plus: Capital transfers - from and to the rest of the world, net	106.9	88.5	87.6	396.4	105.6	1185.9	95.2	107.8	145.1	151.6	118.7	
Plus: Capital transfers - from the rest of the world	106.9	88.5	87.6	396.4	105.6	1185.9	95.2	107.8	145.1	151.6	120.7	
Less: Capital transfers - to the rest of the world	0.0	0.0	0.0	0.0	0.0	0.0	0.0	0.0	0.0	0.0	2.0	
Less: Gross capital formation	657.5	638.5	875.1	917.5	1125.0	1208.9	1582.0	1874.7	1333.2	1443.1	1709.5	
Less: Acquisitions less disposals of non-produced non-financial assets	0.3	-0.0	-0.2	-0.2	-0.4	-1.9	64.3	-0.6	-1.0	-2.1	0.0	
Plus: Statistical discrepancy [c]	-134.4	-154.9	-63.1	-62.4	-19.2	125.4	128.0	28.2	-3.3	-11.4	80.9	
Equals: NET LENDING (+) / NET BORROWING (-) OF THE NATION [d]	-73.1	-125.3[e]	-166.1	125.4	-251.6	749.2[e]	-533.6	-735.9	-257.9	-137.3	-401.3	
	Net values: Gross National Income / Gross National Disposable Income / Saving Gross less Consumption of fixed capital											
Less: Consumption of fixed capital	387.2	426.4	459.3	478.4	526.1	567.1	627.2	695.6	699.7	726.1	640.3	
Equals: NET NATIONAL INCOME	3246.1	3362.6	3511.2	3757.6	4038.6	4180.0	4682.0	5248.7	5255.8	5594.2	5965.9	
Equals: NET NATIONAL DISPOSABLE INCOME	3466.2	3619.5	3819.5	4091.5	4436.2	4617.5	5300.0	6003.1	5951.5	6361.7	6740.1	
Equals: SAVING, NET	225.1	153.2	224.9	230.3	260.5	77.8	262.3	306.7	232.8	437.4	468.3	

[a] Refers to adjustment for balance of payment plus Acquisitions less disposals of non-produced non-financial assets.
[b] Includes the adjustment for balance of payments
[c] Refers to adjustment for balance of payments
[d] Excludes Acquisitions less disposals of non-produced non-financial assets
[e] Discrepancy between components and total.

Table 2.1 Value added by industries at current prices (ISIC Rev. 3)

Series 100: 1993 SNA, CFA franc, Western calendar year

Data in billions

	2001	2002	2003	2004	2005	2006	2007	2008	2009	2010	2011	2012
Series	**100**											
	Industries											
Agriculture, hunting, forestry; fishing	584.4	506.3	602.4	581.4	671.1	633.1	642.6	838.1	919.2	978.6	872.1	
Agriculture, hunting, forestry	524.1	436.4	529.8	507.1	586.8	554.3	549.7	745.5	820.7	877.0	749.7	
Agriculture, hunting and related service activities	498.9	409.4	499.5	474.9	551.1	515.7	500.4	694.6	763.5	818.2	688.5	

	2001	2002	2003	2004	2005	2006	2007	2008	2009	2010	2011	2012
Series	**100**											
Forestry, logging and related service activities	25.2	27.0	30.3	32.3	35.7	38.5	49.3	50.8	57.3	58.8	61.1	
Fishing	60.3	69.9	72.7	74.3	84.2	78.8	93.0	92.6	98.5	101.6	122.4	
Mining and quarrying	40.4	44.8	47.5	45.4	44.1	52.1	51.6	50.7	101.7	118.2	141.0	
Manufacturing	533.4	562.1	559.8	595.1	601.1	609.7	675.2	737.9	739.9	775.8	868.4	
Electricity, gas and water supply	72.8	80.2	91.0	95.5	102.6	115.1	136.3	154.3	153.2	171.4	189.4	
Construction	127.5	143.4	156.2	185.8	196.0	234.5	262.1	262.9	244.2	246.4	271.9	
Wholesale, retail trade, repair of motor vehicles, motorcycles and personal and households goods; hotels and restaurants	661.3	699.8	727.5	781.7	821.5	886.5	983.4	1092.1	1054.1	1101.6	1199.7	
Wholesale, retail trade, repair of motor vehicles, motorcycles and personal and household goods	625.6	662.4	689.5	741.9	780.8	842.0	936.1	1043.4	1007.7	1052.8	1147.5	
Hotels and restaurants	35.7	37.4	38.1	39.8	40.7	44.5	47.2	48.7	46.5	48.9	52.2	
Transport, storage and communications	261.9	278.3	330.1	394.0	452.7	525.7	591.6	668.2	641.8	666.6	719.1	
Land transport; transport via pipelines, water transport; air transport; Supporting and auxiliary transport activities; activities of travel agencies	127.6	134.6	161.0	180.5	189.6	209.9	226.1	261.5	227.9	241.1	281.5	
Post and telecommunications	134.3	143.7	169.0	213.5	263.1	315.8	365.5	406.8	413.9	425.5	437.6	
Financial intermediation; real estate, renting and business activities	395.9	430.3	454.9	486.5	512.9	550.9	616.4	689.9	672.0	718.1	768.5	
Financial intermediation	22.2	24.6	36.5	47.6	50.2	47.7	48.8	55.9	49.7	62.9	72.6	
Real estate, renting and business activities	373.6	405.7	418.4	438.8	462.8	503.3	567.7	634.0	622.3	655.2	695.9	
Public administration and defence; compulsory social security	233.1	254.0	261.9	268.5	291.3	296.2	331.6	361.7	368.9	373.8	395.6	
Education; health and social work; other community, social and personal services	246.1	261.6	269.4	281.1	299.1	328.2	374.8	403.6	412.0	434.6	458.8	
Education	121.0	128.2	126.8	148.4	159.6	175.2	206.1	216.5	222.9	239.0	256.8	
Health and social work	58.0	57.3	61.0	48.5	50.4	59.1	67.0	77.4	78.8	81.5	84.2	
Other community, social and personal services	67.1	76.0	81.6	84.1	89.0	93.8	101.8	109.7	110.3	114.1	117.8	
Private households with employed persons	...	...	...	...	...	...	...	...	...	...	...	
Equals: VALUE ADDED, GROSS, in basic prices	3156.7	3260.8	3500.6	3715.0	3992.4	4232.0	4665.6	5259.5	5307.0	5585.1	5884.5	
Less: Financial intermediation services indirectly measured (FISIM)	...	...	...	...	...	...	...	...	...	...	...	
Plus: Taxes less Subsidies on products	418.7	456.9	486.2	527.8	600.7	661.6	742.8	735.0	726.4	797.2	882.3	
Equals: GROSS DOMESTIC PRODUCT	3575.5	3717.6	3986.8	4242.8	4593.1	4893.5	5408.3	5994.5	6033.4	6382.3	6766.8	
Memorandum Item: FISIM, if distributed to uses	71.2	75.1	74.1	86.7	94.7	103.3	109.9	132.5	133.1	133.2	133.2	

Table 2.2 Value added by industries at constant prices (ISIC Rev. 3)

Series 100: 1993 SNA, CFA franc, Western calendar year — **Data in billions**

	2001	2002	2003	2004	2005	2006	2007	2008	2009	2010	2011	2012
Series	**100**											
Base year	**1999**											
Industries												
Agriculture, hunting, forestry; fishing	548.5	426.5	502.5	514.5	571.1	523.2	492.9	589.1	665.9	704.7	602.7	
Agriculture, hunting, forestry	488.2	371.2	446.1	459.3	510.4	468.6	434.2	533.0	605.2	642.7	538.4	
Agriculture, hunting and related service activities	464.9	347.3	421.7	434.7	484.3	442.3	406.6	505.4	576.1	612.0	506.4	
Forestry, logging and related service activities	23.4	24.0	24.4	24.6	26.1	26.3	27.6	27.6	29.1	30.6	32.0	
Fishing	60.3	55.2	56.4	55.1	60.8	54.6	58.6	56.2	60.7	62.0	64.4	
Mining and quarrying	36.9	41.8	47.6	50.5	41.6	34.8	32.6	33.6	50.9	54.3	58.8	
Manufacturing	489.6	506.4	517.5	536.3	544.8	529.3	561.1	546.9	576.6	598.4	640.8	
Electricity, gas and water supply	76.9	82.8	92.6	94.7	100.3	104.9	113.8	118.4	113.0	121.2	118.8	
Construction	113.3	126.9	131.9	155.6	171.0	193.3	211.5	210.2	200.8	210.3	230.2	
Wholesale, retail trade, repair of motor vehicles, motorcycles and personal and household goods; hotels and restaurants	652.2	662.4	693.5	723.0	736.8	764.9	795.7	809.1	827.0	843.4	873.7	
Wholesale, retail trade, repair of motor vehicles, motorcycles and personal and household goods	620.7	629.9	662.5	691.6	704.0	730.0	760.5	774.5	795.0	809.2	838.5	
Hotels and restaurants	31.5	32.5	31.0	31.4	32.7	34.8	35.2	34.6	32.0	34.2	35.2	
Transport, storage and communications	252.7	283.4	326.6	380.9	434.9	503.7	561.8	609.9	618.1	662.4	692.7	
Land transport; transport via piplines, water transport; air transport; Supporting and auxiliary transport activities; activities of travel agencies	118.3	125.7	146.2	162.5	170.4	176.7	181.9	185.5	165.1	175.5	191.5	
Post and telecommunications	134.5	157.7	180.4	218.4	264.5	327.0	379.9	424.4	453.0	486.9	501.2	
Financial intermediation, real estate, renting and business activities	354.7	383.9	407.2	437.3	461.2	469.6	494.9	509.0	505.0	536.5	565.6	
Financial intermediation	21.2	22.7	32.8	41.2	43.8	41.0	41.2	47.5	44.8	56.3	64.3	
Real estate, renting and business activities	333.5	361.2	374.4	396.1	417.4	428.6	453.7	461.6	460.2	480.2	501.3	
Public administration and defence; compulsory social security	215.8	217.4	216.7	227.3	240.8	251.6	266.0	264.1	266.9	270.7	281.0	
Education; health and social work; other community, social and personal services	239.7	254.7	264.9	277.8	290.6	299.5	325.6	334.1	338.4	345.1	352.8	
Education	117.8	122.0	123.0	131.5	138.8	143.4	157.4	163.3	166.0	168.0	172.6	
Health and social work	56.9	60.7	65.6	68.5	70.2	72.3	80.3	82.2	83.3	85.5	87.9	
Other community, social and personal services	65.0	72.0	76.4	77.8	81.6	83.8	87.8	88.5	89.0	91.6	92.3	
Private households with employed persons	...	...	...	...	...	...	...	...	...	...	...	
Equals: VALUE ADDED, GROSS, in basic prices	2980.3	2986.2	3201.0	3398.0	3593.2	3674.7	3855.8	4024.5	4162.6	4346.9	4417.1	
Less: Financial intermediation services indirectly measured (FISIM)	...	...	...	...	...	...	...	...	...	...	...	
Plus: Taxes less Subsidies on products	437.5	454.0	468.7	487.6	510.8	530.4	557.0	550.8	523.5	539.1	569.9	

	2001	2002	2003	2004	2005	2006	2007	2008	2009	2010	2011	2012
Series	**100**											
Base year	**1999**											
Equals: GROSS DOMESTIC PRODUCT	3417.8	3440.2	3669.7	3885.6	4104.1	4205.1	4412.7	4575.2	4686.1	4886.0	4987.0	
Memorandum Item: FISIM, if distributed to uses	67.7	68.9	66.9	75.8	82.1	88.4	92.5	109.0	108.6	110.7	124.8	

Table 2.3 Output, gross value added, and fixed assets by industries at current prices (ISIC Rev. 3) Total Economy

Series 100: 1993 SNA, CFA franc, Western calendar year

Data in billions

	2001	2002	2003	2004	2005	2006	2007	2008	2009	2010	2011	2012
Series	**100**											
Output, at basic prices	6003.0	6277.2	6694.1	7227.8	7710.9	8154.1	9126.5	10329.2	10212.6	10887.9	11792.6	
Less: Intermediate consumption, at purchaser's prices	2846.3	3016.4	3193.4	3512.8	3718.4	3922.2	4460.9	5069.7	4905.6	5302.8	5908.2	
Equals: VALUE ADDED, GROSS, at basic prices	3156.7	3260.8	3500.6	3715.0	3992.4	4232.0	4665.6	5259.5	5307.0	5585.1	5884.5	
Compensation of employees	664.4	729.2	758.2	824.0	963.5	1018.4	1165.8	1279.7	1337.8	1403.1	1336.4	
Taxes on production and imports, less Subsidies	87.4	91.8	98.9	139.8	125.3	135.4	159.2	174.0	178.3	196.8	189.2	
Taxes on production and imports	93.4	98.3	105.4	146.4	133.7	144.8	170.0	186.1	191.0	210.1	198.1	
Taxes on products	...	...	...	...	...	...	...	...	...	...	...	
Other taxes on production	93.4	98.3	105.4	146.4	133.7	144.8	170.0	186.1	191.0	210.1	198.1	
Less: Subsidies	6.1	6.5	6.4	6.6	8.3	9.4	10.9	12.1	12.7	13.2	8.8	
OPERATING SURPLUS, GROSS [a]	2404.9	2439.8	2643.5	2751.2	2903.6	3078.2	3340.6	3805.8	3790.9	3985.1	4358.8	
MIXED INCOME, GROSS	...	...	...	...	...	...	...	...	...	...	...	
Less: Consumption of fixed capital	387.2	426.4	459.3	478.4	526.1	567.1	627.2	695.6	699.7	726.1	640.3	
OPERATING SURPLUS, NET [b]	2017.8	2013.4	2184.2	2272.9	2377.4	2511.1	2713.4	3110.2	3091.2	3259.0	3718.6	
MIXED INCOME, NET	...	...	...	...	...	...	...	...	...	...	...	
Gross capital formation	657.5	638.5	875.1	917.5	1125.0	1208.9	1582.0	1874.7	1333.2	1443.1	1709.5	
Gross fixed capital formation	812.5	922.7	857.4	944.1	1071.4	1279.7	1414.1	1607.6	1386.2	1430.0	1611.4	
Changes in inventories	-155.0	-284.2	17.6	-26.6	53.6	-70.9	168.0	267.1	-53.0	13.1	98.0	
Acquisitions less disposals of valuables	...	...	...	...	...	...	...	...	...	...	...	
Employment (average, in 1000 persons)	3156.8	3232.1	3300.6	3406.3	3519.3	3632.0	3750.5	3869.6	3999.9	4134.4	4281.8	

[a] Includes Mixed Income, Gross.
[b] Includes Mixed Income, Net.

Table 2.3 Output, gross value added, and fixed assets by industries at current prices (ISIC Rev. 3) Agriculture, hunting, forestry; fishing (A+B)

Series 100: 1993 SNA, CFA franc, Western calendar year — **Data in billions**

	2001	2002	2003	2004	2005	2006	2007	2008	2009	2010	2011	2012
Series	**100**											
Output, at basic prices	752.5	658.5	775.7	757.2	874.6	822.8	846.0	1080.1	1182.5	1264.8	1146.9	
Less: Intermediate consumption, at purchaser's prices	168.1	152.2	173.3	175.8	203.5	189.7	203.4	242.0	263.3	286.2	274.9	
Equals: VALUE ADDED, GROSS, at basic prices	584.4	506.3	602.4	581.4	671.1	633.1	642.6	838.1	919.2	978.6	872.1	
Compensation of employees	4.9	5.9	6.0	5.8	7.8	6.9	8.2	8.5	9.8	10.0	8.1	
Taxes on production and imports, less Subsidies	1.9	2.2	2.2	4.2	3.6	3.3	4.4	4.0	4.9	5.5	4.3	
Taxes on production and imports	2.5	2.9	3.0	4.9	4.5	4.1	5.3	5.3	6.3	6.9	5.1	
Taxes on products	...	...	...	...	...	...	...	...	...	...	...	
Other taxes on production	2.5	2.9	3.0	4.9	4.5	4.1	5.3	5.3	6.3	6.9	5.1	
Less: Subsidies	0.6	0.7	0.7	0.6	0.9	0.8	0.9	1.2	1.4	1.4	0.8	
OPERATING SURPLUS, GROSS [a]	577.6	498.2	594.2	571.3	659.7	622.9	630.0	825.6	904.6	963.2	859.7	
MIXED INCOME, GROSS	...	...	...	...	...	...	...	...	...	...	...	
Less: Consumption of fixed capital	8.3	6.9	8.2	8.7	10.2	9.0	9.7	10.8	12.5	13.5	10.7	
OPERATING SURPLUS, NET [b]	569.3	491.3	586.0	562.6	649.5	613.9	620.3	814.8	892.1	949.6	848.9	
MIXED INCOME, NET	...	...	...	...	...	...	...	...	...	...	...	
Gross capital formation	68.9	-42.6	64.8	17.2	53.0	-38.5	-30.7	102.0	51.2	109.4	-78.7	
Gross fixed capital formation	8.4	7.2	3.3	3.6	4.7	8.5	4.6	7.9	6.4	8.5	6.6	
Changes in inventories	60.5	-49.8	61.5	13.6	48.3	-47.0	-35.3	94.1	44.8	100.9	-85.3	
Acquisitions less disposals of valuables	...	...	...	...	...	...	...	...	...	...	...	
Employment (average, in 1000 persons)	1737.7	1768.3	1792.3	1825.9	1860.2	1895.1	1930.7	1967.0	2004.0	2041.7	2080.2	

[a] Includes Mixed Income, Gross.
[b] Includes Mixed Income, Net.

Table 2.3 Output, gross value added, and fixed assets by industries at current prices (ISIC Rev. 3) Agriculture, hunting and related service activities (01)

Series 100: 1993 SNA, CFA franc, Western calendar year — **Data in billions**

	2001	2002	2003	2004	2005	2006	2007	2008	2009	2010	2011	2012
Series	**100**											
Output, at basic prices	603.6	488.9	598.1	573.2	664.7	619.9	601.5	832.7	915.9	987.2	827.5	
Less: Intermediate consumption, at purchaser's prices	104.7	79.5	98.6	98.3	113.5	104.2	101.1	138.0	152.4	169.0	139.0	
Equals: VALUE ADDED, GROSS, at basic prices	498.9	409.4	499.5	474.9	551.1	515.7	500.4	694.6	763.5	818.2	688.5	
Compensation of employees	0.5	0.5	0.6	0.5	0.7	0.6	0.6	1.0	1.2	1.2	0.7	
Taxes on production and imports, less Subsidies	-0.3	-0.3	-0.4	-0.2	-0.4	-0.3	-0.3	-0.6	-0.6	-0.6	-0.2	
Taxes on production and imports	0.2	0.2	0.2	0.3	0.3	0.2	0.3	0.4	0.4	0.5	0.3	
Taxes on products	...	...	...	...	...	...	...	...	...	...	...	
Other taxes on production	0.2	0.2	0.2	0.3	0.3	0.2	0.3	0.4	0.4	0.5	0.3	

	2001	2002	2003	2004	2005	2006	2007	2008	2009	2010	2011	2012
Series	**100**											
Less: Subsidies	0.5	0.5	0.5	0.4	0.6	0.6	0.6	0.9	1.1	1.1	0.5	
OPERATING SURPLUS, GROSS [a]	498.6	409.1	499.2	474.5	550.8	515.4	500.1	694.2	762.9	817.6	688.1	
MIXED INCOME, GROSS	...	...	...	...	...	...	...	...	...	...	...	
Less: Consumption of fixed capital	3.8	1.7	2.7	3.3	3.8	2.9	2.4	3.4	4.4	5.3	2.9	
OPERATING SURPLUS, NET [b]	494.8	407.5	496.4	471.3	547.0	512.5	497.7	690.8	758.5	812.3	685.2	
MIXED INCOME, NET	...	...	...	...	...	...	...	...	...	...	...	
Gross capital formation	66.6	-45.5	63.1	14.2	53.0	-38.3	-31.5	104.2	48.7	107.5	-80.3	
Gross fixed capital formation	8.4	7.2	3.3	3.6	4.7	8.5	4.6	7.9	6.4	8.5	6.6	
Changes in inventories	58.2	-52.7	59.8	10.6	48.3	-46.8	-36.1	96.3	42.3	99.0	-86.9	
Acquisitions less disposals of valuables	...	...	...	...	...	...	...	...	...	...	...	
Employment (average, in 1000 persons)	1570.9	1602.3	1627.4	1658.1	1689.4	1721.3	1753.8	1787.0	1820.8	1855.3	1890.4	

[a] Includes Mixed Income, Gross.
[b] Includes Mixed Income, Net.

Table 2.3 Output, gross value added, and fixed assets by industries at current prices (ISIC Rev. 3) Forestry, logging and related service activities (02)

Series 100: 1993 SNA, CFA franc, Western calendar year — **Data in billions**

	2001	2002	2003	2004	2005	2006	2007	2008	2009	2010	2011	2012
Series	**100**											
Output, at basic prices	38.8	41.6	46.4	49.4	55.1	59.2	75.7	78.4	87.9	90.9	94.5	
Less: Intermediate consumption, at purchaser's prices	13.6	14.6	16.1	17.2	19.4	20.7	26.4	27.5	30.6	32.1	33.4	
Equals: VALUE ADDED, GROSS, at basic prices	25.2	27.0	30.3	32.3	35.7	38.5	49.3	50.8	57.3	58.8	61.1	
Compensation of employees	0.0	0.0	0.0	0.0	0.0	0.0	0.0	0.0	0.0	0.0	0.0	
Taxes on production and imports, less Subsidies	0.0	0.0	0.0	0.0	0.0	0.0	0.0	0.0	0.0	0.0	0.0	
Taxes on production and imports	0.0	0.0	0.0	0.0	0.0	0.0	0.0	0.0	0.0	0.0	0.0	
Taxes on products	...	...	...	...	...	...	...	...	...	...	...	
Other taxes on production	0.0	0.0	0.0	0.0	0.0	0.0	0.0	0.0	0.0	0.0	0.0	
Less: Subsidies	0.0	0.0	0.0	0.0	0.0	0.0	0.0	0.0	0.0	0.0	0.0	
OPERATING SURPLUS, GROSS [a]	25.2	27.0	30.3	32.3	35.7	38.5	49.3	50.8	57.3	58.8	61.1	
MIXED INCOME, GROSS	...	...	...	...	...	...	...	...	...	...	...	
Less: Consumption of fixed capital	0.8	0.8	0.9	1.0	1.1	1.2	1.5	1.5	1.7	1.8	1.8	
OPERATING SURPLUS, NET [b]	24.4	26.2	29.4	31.3	34.6	37.4	47.8	49.3	55.5	57.0	59.3	
MIXED INCOME, NET	...	...	...	...	...	...	...	...	...	...	...	
Gross capital formation	1.9	2.3	1.7	3.0	0.0	-0.2	0.8	-2.3	2.6	1.9	1.6	
Gross fixed capital formation	...	...	...	...	...	...	...	...	...	...	...	
Changes in inventories	1.9	2.3	1.7	3.0	0.0	-0.2	0.8	-2.3	2.6	1.9	1.6	
Acquisitions less disposals of valuables	...	...	...	...	...	...	...	...	...	...	...	
Employment (average, in 1000 persons)	86.0	87.6	89.3	91.0	92.7	94.5	96.3	98.1	100.0	101.9	103.9	

[a] Includes Mixed Income, Gross.
[b] Includes Mixed Income, Net.

Table 2.3 Output, gross value added, and fixed assets by industries at current prices (ISIC Rev. 3) Fishing (B)

Series 100: 1993 SNA, CFA franc, Western calendar year — **Data in billions**

	2001	2002	2003	2004	2005	2006	2007	2008	2009	2010	2011	2012
Series	**100**											
Output, at basic prices	110.1	128.0	131.3	134.6	154.9	143.7	168.9	169.1	178.8	186.7	224.9	
Less: Intermediate consumption, at purchaser's prices	49.8	58.1	58.6	60.3	70.6	64.8	76.0	76.5	80.3	85.1	102.5	
Equals: VALUE ADDED, GROSS, at basic prices	60.3	69.9	72.7	74.3	84.2	78.8	93.0	92.6	98.5	101.6	122.4	
Compensation of employees	4.4	5.3	5.4	5.3	7.0	6.3	7.6	7.5	8.6	8.8	7.4	
Taxes on production and imports, less Subsidies	2.2	2.5	2.6	4.4	4.0	3.7	4.7	4.6	5.5	6.1	4.6	
Taxes on production and imports	2.3	2.7	2.8	4.6	4.2	3.9	5.0	4.9	5.8	6.4	4.8	
Taxes on products	...	...	...	...	...	...	...	...	...	...	...	
Other taxes on production	2.3	2.7	2.8	4.6	4.2	3.9	5.0	4.9	5.8	6.4	4.8	
Less: Subsidies	0.2	0.2	0.2	0.2	0.2	0.2	0.3	0.3	0.3	0.3	0.2	
OPERATING SURPLUS, GROSS [a]	53.8	62.1	64.7	64.5	73.3	68.9	80.6	80.5	84.4	86.7	110.4	
MIXED INCOME, GROSS	...	...	...	...	...	...	...	...	...	...	...	
Less: Consumption of fixed capital	3.7	4.4	4.5	4.5	5.4	4.9	5.8	5.8	6.3	6.5	6.0	
OPERATING SURPLUS, NET [b]	50.0	57.6	60.2	60.0	67.9	64.0	74.8	74.7	78.1	80.2	104.4	
MIXED INCOME, NET	...	...	...	...	...	...	...	...	...	...	...	
Gross capital formation	0.4	0.7	0.0	0.0	0.0	0.0	0.0	0.0	0.0	0.0	0.0	
Gross fixed capital formation	...	...	...	...	...	...	...	...	...	...	...	
Changes in inventories	0.4	0.7	0.0	0.0	0.0	0.0	0.0	0.0	0.0	0.0	0.0	
Acquisitions less disposals of valuables	...	...	...	...	...	...	...	...	...	...	...	
Employment (average, in 1000 persons)	80.9	78.4	75.6	76.8	78.0	79.3	80.5	81.8	83.2	84.5	85.9	

[a] Includes Mixed Income, Gross.
[b] Includes Mixed Income, Net.

Table 2.3 Output, gross value added, and fixed assets by industries at current prices (ISIC Rev. 3) Mining and quarrying (C)

Series 100: 1993 SNA, CFA franc, Western calendar year — **Data in billions**

	2001	2002	2003	2004	2005	2006	2007	2008	2009	2010	2011	2012
Series	**100**											
Output, at basic prices	76.9	85.5	89.3	85.8	84.6	99.1	97.6	96.5	192.5	226.6	270.3	
Less: Intermediate consumption, at purchaser's prices	36.5	40.7	41.8	40.3	40.5	46.9	46.1	45.8	90.8	108.4	129.2	
Equals: VALUE ADDED, GROSS, at basic prices	40.4	44.8	47.5	45.4	44.1	52.1	51.6	50.7	101.7	118.2	141.0	
Compensation of employees	11.0	12.9	13.2	12.3	13.9	15.7	16.0	15.5	33.5	38.7	32.2	
Taxes on production and imports, less Subsidies	0.5	0.5	0.5	0.8	0.7	0.8	0.8	0.8	1.8	2.3	1.7	
Taxes on production and imports	0.5	0.5	0.5	0.8	0.7	0.8	0.8	0.8	1.8	2.3	1.7	
Taxes on products	...	...	...	...	...	...	...	...	...	...	...	
Other taxes on production	0.5	0.5	0.5	0.8	0.7	0.8	0.8	0.8	1.8	2.3	1.7	

	2001	2002	2003	2004	2005	2006	2007	2008	2009	2010	2011	2012
Series	**100**											
Less: Subsidies	0.0	0.0	0.0	0.0	0.0	0.0	0.0	0.0	0.0	0.0	0.0	
OPERATING SURPLUS, GROSS [a]	28.9	31.4	33.7	32.2	29.5	35.7	34.8	34.4	66.4	77.2	107.1	
MIXED INCOME, GROSS	...	...	...	...	...	...	...	...	...	...	...	
Less: Consumption of fixed capital	8.5	9.7	10.0	9.1	9.0	10.1	10.0	10.0	20.5	23.5	20.0	
OPERATING SURPLUS, NET [b]	20.4	21.6	23.6	23.1	20.5	25.5	24.7	24.4	45.9	53.7	87.2	
MIXED INCOME, NET	...	...	...	...	...	...	...	...	...	...	...	
Gross capital formation	-17.0	-3.0	-10.9	-30.0	84.5	39.3	52.5	167.4	78.8	111.8	29.2	
Gross fixed capital formation	...	...	...	...	...	...	...	...	...	...	...	
Changes in inventories	-17.0	-3.0	-10.9	-30.0	84.5	39.3	52.5	167.4	78.8	111.8	29.2	
Acquisitions less disposals of valuables	...	...	...	...	...	...	...	...	...	...	...	
Employment (average, in 1000 persons)	31.7	32.0	31.0	31.5	32.1	32.7	33.3	33.9	34.5	35.2	35.8	

[a] Includes Mixed Income, Gross.
[b] Includes Mixed Income, Net.

Table 2.3 Output, gross value added, and fixed assets by industries at current prices (ISIC Rev. 3) Manufacturing (D)

Series 100: 1993 SNA, CFA franc, Western calendar year — **Data in billions**

	2001	2002	2003	2004	2005	2006	2007	2008	2009	2010	2011	2012
Series	**100**											
Output, at basic prices	1748.1	1817.4	1893.1	2016.0	2016.0	1982.1	2282.7	2649.8	2500.1	2711.5	3151.1	
Less: Intermediate consumption, at purchaser's prices	1214.7	1255.3	1333.2	1420.9	1414.9	1372.4	1607.5	1911.9	1760.2	1935.8	2282.7	
Equals: VALUE ADDED, GROSS, at basic prices	533.4	562.1	559.8	595.1	601.1	609.7	675.2	737.9	739.9	775.8	868.4	
Compensation of employees	92.7	99.2	101.9	104.4	114.5	112.2	124.9	140.1	140.3	151.9	151.1	
Taxes on production and imports, less Subsidies	22.6	23.4	24.8	35.5	30.8	32.6	37.8	41.2	42.8	49.0	45.4	
Taxes on production and imports	24.6	25.2	26.5	37.0	32.6	34.5	39.9	43.2	45.2	51.5	47.4	
Taxes on products	...	...	...	...	...	...	...	...	...	...	...	
Other taxes on production	24.6	25.2	26.5	37.0	32.6	34.5	39.9	43.2	45.2	51.5	47.4	
Less: Subsidies	2.0	1.8	1.7	1.5	1.8	2.0	2.1	2.0	2.4	2.5	1.9	
OPERATING SURPLUS, GROSS [a]	418.1	439.5	433.1	455.1	455.9	464.9	512.5	556.7	556.7	574.8	671.9	
MIXED INCOME, GROSS	...	...	...	...	...	...	...	...	...	...	...	
Less: Consumption of fixed capital	63.5	68.3	70.3	71.5	73.0	67.7	75.8	86.8	81.4	88.6	87.2	
OPERATING SURPLUS, NET [b]	354.6	371.2	362.8	383.6	382.8	397.2	436.7	469.9	475.3	486.2	584.6	
MIXED INCOME, NET	...	...	...	...	...	...	...	...	...	...	...	
Gross capital formation	216.2	232.7	264.9	264.8	317.5	363.7	581.2	657.5	311.8	328.8	772.8	
Gross fixed capital formation	323.4	372.5	277.2	249.6	318.0	390.4	423.3	583.7	454.2	461.2	546.5	
Changes in inventories	-107.2	-139.8	-12.3	15.2	-0.5	-26.7	157.9	73.8	-142.4	-132.4	226.3	
Acquisitions less disposals of valuables	...	...	...	...	...	...	...	...	...	...	...	
Employment (average, in 1000 persons)	360.9	363.5	366.2	375.7	385.4	395.4	405.8	416.4	427.4	438.8	449.5	

[a] Includes Mixed Income, Gross.
[b] Includes Mixed Income, Net.

Table 2.3 Output, gross value added, and fixed assets by industries at current prices (ISIC Rev. 3) Electricity, gas and water supply (E)

Series 100: 1993 SNA, CFA franc, Western calendar year — **Data in billions**

	2001	2002	2003	2004	2005	2006	2007	2008	2009	2010	2011	2012
Series	**100**											
Output, at basic prices	161.5	178.8	196.1	207.6	231.6	254.0	298.0	336.3	336.3	380.9	419.7	
Less: Intermediate consumption, at purchaser's prices	88.7	98.6	105.1	112.1	129.0	138.9	161.7	182.1	183.1	209.5	230.3	
Equals: VALUE ADDED, GROSS, at basic prices	72.8	80.2	91.0	95.5	102.6	115.1	136.3	154.3	153.2	171.4	189.4	
Compensation of employees	12.1	13.4	14.7	15.5	17.3	19.0	22.3	25.2	25.2	28.5	31.4	
Taxes on production and imports, less Subsidies	6.6	7.3	8.0	8.5	9.4	10.3	12.1	13.7	13.7	15.5	17.1	
Taxes on production and imports	6.6	7.3	8.0	8.5	9.4	10.3	12.1	13.7	13.7	15.5	17.1	
Taxes on products	...	...	...	...	...	...	...	...	...	...	...	
Other taxes on production	6.6	7.3	8.0	8.5	9.4	10.3	12.1	13.7	13.7	15.5	17.1	
Less: Subsidies	0.0	0.0	0.0	0.0	0.0	0.0	0.0	0.0	0.0	0.0	0.0	
OPERATING SURPLUS, GROSS [a]	54.2	59.5	68.3	71.5	75.8	85.7	101.9	115.4	114.3	127.3	140.9	
MIXED INCOME, GROSS	...	...	...	...	...	...	...	...	...	...	...	
Less: Consumption of fixed capital	23.5	26.0	28.6	30.2	33.7	37.0	43.4	49.0	49.0	55.5	61.1	
OPERATING SURPLUS, NET [b]	30.6	33.4	39.8	41.3	42.1	48.8	58.5	66.4	65.4	71.9	79.8	
MIXED INCOME, NET	...	...	...	...	...	...	...	...	...	...	...	
Gross capital formation	...	...	...	...	...	...	...	...	...	...	...	
Employment (average, in 1000 persons)	27.2	28.1	27.1	27.8	28.5	29.2	29.9	30.7	31.4	32.2	32.8	

[a] Includes Mixed Income, Gross.
[b] Includes Mixed Income, Net.

Table 2.3 Output, gross value added, and fixed assets by industries at current prices (ISIC Rev. 3) Construction (F)

Series 100: 1993 SNA, CFA franc, Western calendar year — **Data in billions**

	2001	2002	2003	2004	2005	2006	2007	2008	2009	2010	2011	2012
Series	**100**											
Output, at basic prices	483.6	546.1	580.3	694.9	752.5	885.7	992.0	1021.8	931.9	967.5	1066.0	
Less: Intermediate consumption, at purchaser's prices	356.1	402.7	424.2	509.0	556.6	651.2	729.9	758.9	687.7	721.0	794.1	
Equals: VALUE ADDED, GROSS, at basic prices	127.5	143.4	156.2	185.8	196.0	234.5	262.1	262.9	244.2	246.4	271.9	
Compensation of employees	37.3	43.0	45.8	53.8	63.1	72.2	81.6	83.3	79.8	81.9	77.2	
Taxes on production and imports, less Subsidies	4.3	4.9	5.2	9.9	8.6	10.1	12.4	12.4	12.7	13.9	9.7	
Taxes on production and imports	4.3	4.9	5.2	10.0	8.6	10.1	12.4	12.4	12.8	13.9	9.7	
Taxes on products	...	...	...	...	...	...	...	...	...	...	...	
Other taxes on production	4.3	4.9	5.2	10.0	8.6	10.1	12.4	12.4	12.8	13.9	9.7	
Less: Subsidies	0.0	0.0	0.0	0.0	0.0	0.0	0.0	0.0	0.0	0.0	0.0	
OPERATING SURPLUS, GROSS [a]	85.9	95.5	105.2	122.1	124.3	152.2	168.2	167.2	151.6	150.7	185.1	
MIXED INCOME, GROSS	...	...	...	...	...	...	...	...	...	...	...	

	2001	2002	2003	2004	2005	2006	2007	2008	2009	2010	2011	2012
Series	**100**											
Less: Consumption of fixed capital	18.2	21.2	22.4	25.3	29.3	33.8	38.3	39.3	37.2	37.6	26.6	
OPERATING SURPLUS, NET [b]	67.6	74.3	82.8	96.8	95.0	118.3	129.8	128.0	114.4	113.1	158.4	
MIXED INCOME, NET	...	...	...	...	...	...	...	...	...	...	...	
Gross capital formation	480.8	543.0	576.9	690.8	748.6	880.9	986.2	1016.0	925.6	960.3	1058.3	
Gross fixed capital formation	480.8	543.0	576.9	690.8	748.6	880.9	986.2	1016.0	925.6	960.3	1058.3	
Changes in inventories	...	...	...	...	...	...	...	...	...	...	...	
Acquisitions less disposals of valuables	...	...	...	...	...	...	...	...	...	...	...	
Employment (average, in 1000 persons)	64.0	66.0	70.9	73.5	76.3	79.2	82.2	85.4	88.7	92.3	96.0	

[a] Includes Mixed Income, Gross.
[b] Includes Mixed Income, Net.

Table 2.3 Output, gross value added, and fixed assets by industries at current prices (ISIC Rev. 3) Wholesale retail trade, repair of motor vehicles, motorcycles, etc.; hotels and restaurants (G+H)

Series 100: 1993 SNA, CFA franc, Western calendar year **Data in billions**

	2001	2002	2003	2004	2005	2006	2007	2008	2009	2010	2011	2012
Series	**100**											
Output, at basic prices	1108.0	1174.7	1211.9	1303.8	1377.8	1483.3	1645.2	1840.0	1782.8	1866.8	2025.8	
Less: Intermediate consumption, at purchaser's prices	446.7	474.9	484.4	522.1	556.3	596.9	661.8	747.9	728.7	765.1	826.1	
Equals: VALUE ADDED, GROSS, at basic prices	661.3	699.8	727.5	781.7	821.5	886.5	983.4	1092.1	1054.1	1101.6	1199.7	
Compensation of employees	79.7	86.9	89.2	94.6	108.0	113.6	127.8	141.0	143.5	149.4	136.0	
Taxes on production and imports, less Subsidies	33.2	34.5	36.3	45.9	43.4	46.7	52.5	58.7	58.4	62.3	65.6	
Taxes on production and imports	34.6	36.0	37.7	47.4	45.2	48.8	54.9	61.3	61.0	65.1	67.5	
Taxes on products	...	...	...	...	...	...	...	...	...	...	...	
Other taxes on production	34.6	36.0	37.7	47.4	45.2	48.8	54.9	61.3	61.0	65.1	67.5	
Less: Subsidies	1.4	1.5	1.5	1.6	1.9	2.1	2.4	2.6	2.7	2.8	1.8	
OPERATING SURPLUS, GROSS [a]	548.4	578.4	602.1	641.2	670.2	726.1	803.1	892.5	852.3	890.0	998.0	
MIXED INCOME, GROSS	...	...	...	...	...	...	...	...	...	...	...	
Less: Consumption of fixed capital	36.1	38.9	39.9	41.0	44.8	47.3	52.3	58.1	57.2	59.0	50.9	
OPERATING SURPLUS, NET [b]	512.2	539.4	562.2	600.2	625.4	678.8	750.9	834.4	795.1	831.0	947.1	
MIXED INCOME, NET	...	...	...	...	...	...	...	...	...	...	...	
Gross capital formation	-97.8	-102.7	-19.5	-37.0	-95.8	-56.8	-14.1	-73.7	-43.3	-79.1	-72.0	
Gross fixed capital formation	...	...	...	...	...	...	...	...	...	...	...	
Changes in inventories	-97.8	-102.7	-19.5	-37.0	-95.8	-56.8	-14.1	-73.7	-43.3	-79.1	-72.0	
Acquisitions less disposals of valuables	...	...	...	...	...	...	...	...	...	...	...	
Employment (average, in 1000 persons)	607.5	638.2	678.8	725.5	775.6	829.4	887.2	949.2	1015.7	1087.1	1163.8	

[a] Includes Mixed Income, Gross.
[b] Includes Mixed Income, Net.

Table 2.3 Output, gross value added, and fixed assets by industries at current prices (ISIC Rev. 3) Transport, storage and communications (I)

Series 100: 1993 SNA, CFA franc, Western calendar year **Data in billions**

	2001	2002	2003	2004	2005	2006	2007	2008	2009	2010	2011	2012
Series	**100**											
Output, at basic prices	467.5	506.8	581.4	680.0	788.6	913.6	1029.7	1173.4	1118.0	1174.3	1270.7	
Less: Intermediate consumption, at purchaser's prices	205.6	228.5	251.4	286.0	335.8	388.0	438.1	505.2	476.2	507.7	551.6	
Equals: VALUE ADDED, GROSS, at basic prices	261.9	278.3	330.1	394.0	452.7	525.7	591.6	668.2	641.8	666.6	719.1	
Compensation of employees	96.0	108.9	123.2	141.6	187.5	212.8	248.0	277.7	289.2	297.4	238.1	
Taxes on production and imports, less Subsidies	10.2	10.3	12.6	20.5	17.7	19.4	21.4	24.5	23.0	26.0	28.4	
Taxes on production and imports	12.1	12.5	14.9	23.1	21.1	23.5	26.4	30.1	28.7	32.0	32.3	
Taxes on products	...	...	...	...	...	...	...	...	...	...	...	
Other taxes on production	12.1	12.5	14.9	23.1	21.1	23.5	26.4	30.1	28.7	32.0	32.3	
Less: Subsidies	1.9	2.2	2.3	2.6	3.4	4.1	5.0	5.7	5.8	6.0	3.9	
OPERATING SURPLUS, GROSS [a]	155.7	159.2	194.3	231.9	247.5	293.5	322.2	366.1	329.6	343.2	452.6	
MIXED INCOME, GROSS	...	...	...	...	...	...	...	...	...	...	...	
Less: Consumption of fixed capital	74.5	84.7	95.2	106.7	134.7	155.1	180.0	204.8	208.7	211.7	152.7	
OPERATING SURPLUS, NET [b]	81.2	74.5	99.1	125.1	112.8	138.4	142.2	161.3	120.9	131.5	300.0	
MIXED INCOME, NET	...	...	...	...	...	...	...	...	...	...	...	
Gross capital formation	...	...	...	...	...	...	...	...	...	...	...	
Employment (average, in 1000 persons)	46.6	47.5	43.7	44.4	45.0	45.8	46.5	47.4	48.2	49.1	50.1	

[a] Includes Mixed Income, Gross.
[b] Includes Mixed Income, Net.

Table 2.3 Output, gross value added, and fixed assets by industries at current prices (ISIC Rev. 3) Financial intermediation; real estate, renting and business activities (J+K)

Series 100: 1993 SNA, CFA franc, Western calendar year **Data in billions**

	2001	2002	2003	2004	2005	2006	2007	2008	2009	2010	2011	2012
Series	**100**											
Output, at basic prices	585.5	637.1	667.7	733.7	781.2	839.0	930.8	1059.6	1038.4	1095.6	1182.8	
Less: Intermediate consumption, at purchaser's prices	189.6	206.7	212.8	247.2	268.2	288.0	314.3	369.7	366.4	377.6	414.3	
Equals: VALUE ADDED, GROSS, at basic prices	395.9	430.3	454.9	486.5	512.9	550.9	616.4	689.9	672.0	718.1	768.5	
Compensation of employees	61.6	69.7	74.8	85.8	102.1	104.7	115.1	131.6	135.8	142.0	127.5	
Taxes on production and imports, less Subsidies	3.1	3.5	3.7	6.7	5.6	6.0	7.4	8.1	8.9	9.9	6.7	
Taxes on production and imports	3.3	3.8	3.9	7.0	5.9	6.4	7.9	8.6	9.4	10.4	7.1	
Taxes on products	...	...	...	...	...	...	...	...	...	...	...	
Other taxes on production	3.3	3.8	3.9	7.0	5.9	6.4	7.9	8.6	9.4	10.4	7.1	
Less: Subsidies	0.2	0.2	0.2	0.3	0.3	0.4	0.4	0.5	0.5	0.5	0.3	
OPERATING SURPLUS, GROSS [a]	331.1	357.1	376.4	393.9	405.3	440.2	493.9	550.2	527.3	566.2	634.2	
MIXED INCOME, GROSS	...	...	...	...	...	...	...	...	...	...	...	

	2001	2002	2003	2004	2005	2006	2007	2008	2009	2010	2011	2012
Series	**100**											
Less: Consumption of fixed capital	31.4	35.0	36.2	37.5	41.1	43.3	48.5	54.8	54.7	56.7	47.9	
OPERATING SURPLUS, NET [b]	299.7	322.1	340.3	356.5	364.2	396.9	445.5	495.4	472.6	509.5	586.4	
MIXED INCOME, NET	...	...	...	...	...	...	...	...	...	...	...	
Gross capital formation	6.4	11.1	-1.1	11.7	17.2	20.3	7.0	5.6	9.0	11.8	-0.1	
Gross fixed capital formation	...	...	...	...	...	...	...	...	...	...	...	
Changes in inventories	6.4	11.1	-1.1	11.7	17.2	20.3	7.0	5.6	9.0	11.8	-0.1	
Acquisitions less disposals of valuables	...	...	...	...	...	...	...	...	...	...	...	
Employment (average, in 1000 persons)	116.1	119.9	124.3	127.8	131.7	135.6	140.0	144.8	147.9	152.2	156.6	

[a] Includes Mixed Income, Gross.
[b] Includes Mixed Income, Net.

Table 2.3 Output, gross value added, and fixed assets by industries at current prices (ISIC Rev. 3) Public administration and defense; compulsory social security (L)

Series 100: 1993 SNA, CFA franc, Western calendar year

Data in billions

	2001	2002	2003	2004	2005	2006	2007	2008	2009	2010	2011	2012
Series	**100**											
Output, at basic prices	304.8	334.6	352.1	378.4	395.0	431.6	494.8	520.3	545.8	578.3	616.4	
Less: Intermediate consumption, at purchaser's prices	71.7	80.6	90.2	109.9	103.6	135.4	163.2	158.6	176.9	204.5	220.8	
Equals: VALUE ADDED, GROSS, at basic prices	233.1	254.0	261.9	268.5	291.3	296.2	331.6	361.7	368.9	373.8	395.6	
Compensation of employees	133.7	144.3	141.5	148.4	170.2	164.3	196.2	217.2	228.6	231.5	249.6	
Taxes on production and imports, less Subsidies	...	...	...	...	...	...	...	...	...	...	...	
OPERATING SURPLUS, GROSS	99.4	109.6	120.4	120.2	121.1	131.9	135.3	144.6	140.3	142.3	146.0	
MIXED INCOME, GROSS	...	...	...	...	...	...	...	...	...	...	...	
Less: Consumption of fixed capital	99.4	109.6	120.4	120.2	121.1	131.9	135.7	145.3	142.0	143.1	146.7	
OPERATING SURPLUS, NET	0.0	0.0	-0.0	0.0	0.0	0.0	-0.3	-0.7	-1.7	-0.8	-0.6	
MIXED INCOME, NET	...	...	...	...	...	...	...	...	...	...	...	
Gross capital formation	...	...	...	...	...	...	...	...	...	...	...	
Employment (average, in 1000 persons)	53.0	50.8	51.3	52.8	56.3	58.8	60.5	58.9	61.5	62.3	67.4	

Table 2.3 Output, gross value added, and fixed assets by industries at current prices (ISIC Rev. 3) Education; health and social work; other community, social and personal services (M+N+O)

Series 100: 1993 SNA, CFA franc, Western calendar year

Data in billions

	2001	2002	2003	2004	2005	2006	2007	2008	2009	2010	2011	2012
Series	**100**											
Output, at basic prices	314.7	337.7	346.5	375.1	409.1	442.9	509.6	551.4	584.4	621.6	642.9	
Less: Intermediate consumption, at purchaser's prices	68.7	76.1	77.1	94.0	110.0	114.7	134.8	147.8	172.5	187.0	184.1	
Equals: VALUE ADDED, GROSS, at basic prices	246.1	261.6	269.4	281.1	299.1	328.2	374.8	403.6	412.0	434.6	458.8	

	2001	2002	2003	2004	2005	2006	2007	2008	2009	2010	2011	2012
Series	**100**											
Compensation of employees	135.4	145.0	147.9	161.7	179.2	196.9	225.8	239.7	252.2	271.9	285.2	
Taxes on production and imports, less Subsidies	5.0	5.1	5.7	7.6	5.7	6.2	10.3	10.7	12.0	12.4	10.3	
Taxes on production and imports	5.0	5.1	5.7	7.7	5.7	6.2	10.3	10.8	12.1	12.5	10.3	
Taxes on products	...	...	...	...	...	...	...	...	...	...	...	
Other taxes on production	5.0	5.1	5.7	7.7	5.7	6.2	10.3	10.8	12.1	12.5	10.3	
Less: Subsidies	0.0	0.0	0.0	0.0	0.0	0.0	0.0	0.0	0.0	0.0	0.0	
OPERATING SURPLUS, GROSS [a]	105.7	111.5	115.8	111.7	114.2	125.0	138.8	153.2	147.7	150.2	163.3	
MIXED INCOME, GROSS	...	...	...	...	...	...	...	...	...	...	...	
Less: Consumption of fixed capital	23.6	26.0	28.2	28.1	29.1	31.8	33.6	36.8	36.6	37.0	36.5	
OPERATING SURPLUS, NET [b]	82.1	85.5	87.6	83.6	85.1	93.2	105.2	116.3	111.2	113.2	126.8	
MIXED INCOME, NET	...	...	...	...	...	...	...	...	...	...	...	
Gross capital formation	...	...	...	...	...	...	...	...	...	...	...	
Employment (average, in 1000 persons)	112.1	117.7	115.1	121.4	128.2	130.9	134.5	136.0	140.6	143.5	149.6	

[a] Includes Mixed Income, Gross.
[b] Includes Mixed Income, Net.

Table 3.1 Government final consumption expenditure by function at current prices

Series 100: 1993 SNA, CFA franc, Western calendar year — **Data in billions**

	2001	2002	2003	2004	2005	2006	2007	2008	2009	2010	2011	2012
Series	**100**											
General public services	292.5	321.7	163.2	155.0	165.0	196.6	214.0	237.0	245.0	227.1	...	
Defence	...	...	47.3	44.9	47.8	45.1	46.3	55.4	61.5	70.5	...	
Public order and safety	...	...	16.5	16.1	23.8	21.3	22.9	24.7	27.6	31.0	...	
Economic affairs	...	...	94.7	123.1	123.7	137.1	178.0	165.4	179.5	233.3	...	
Environment protection	...	...	14.5	20.3	13.4	13.7	14.5	18.8	17.9	23.9	...	
Housing and community amenities	4.6	5.2	6.2	6.4	6.6	6.8	7.0	7.2	7.4	7.6	7.9	
Health	30.2	31.7	36.2	32.3	30.6	31.7	37.7	36.9	42.1	44.1	41.4	
Recreation, culture and religion	6.4	7.4	14.0	11.1	13.2	17.5	21.6	21.9	20.3	22.0	22.0	
Education	106.0	116.2	109.7	142.6	167.4	179.4	204.4	218.1	242.4	272.8	286.7	
Social protection	3.4	2.5	4.9	7.6	6.3	5.1	6.2	5.9	6.8	6.3	6.6	
Equals: General government final consumption expenditure	443.2	484.7	507.2	559.3	597.8	654.5	752.6	791.1	844.8	911.1[a]	959.7	

[a] Discrepancy between components and total.

Table 3.2 Individual consumption expenditure of households, NPISHs, and general government at current prices

Series 100: 1993 SNA, CFA franc, Western calendar year — **Data in billions**

	2001	2002	2003	2004	2005	2006	2007	2008	2009	2010	2011	2012
Series	**100**											
Individual consumption expenditure of households												
Equals: Household final consumption expenditure in domestic market	...	...	...	...	...	...	...	...	...	...	...	
Plus: Direct purchases abroad by residents	...	...	...	...	...	...	...	...	...	...	...	
Less: Direct purchases in domestic market by non-residents	...	...	...	...	...	...	...	...	...	...	...	
Equals: Household final consumption expenditure	2790.4	2973.1	3076.3	3290.1	3565.0	3871.5	4270.6	4890.0	4857.7	4995.9	5293.8	
Individual consumption expenditure of non-profit institutions serving households (NPISHs)												
Equals: NPISHs final consumption expenditure	7.5	8.5	11.1	11.8	12.9	13.6	14.5	15.3	16.3	17.2	18.3	
Individual consumption expenditure of general government												
Housing	4.6	5.2	6.2	6.4	6.6	6.8	7.0	7.2	7.4	...	...	
Health	30.2	31.7	36.2	32.3	30.6	31.7	37.7	36.9	42.1	...	...	
Recreation and culture	6.4	7.4	14.0	11.1	13.2	17.5	21.6	21.9	20.3	...	...	
Education	106.0	116.2	109.7	142.6	167.4	179.4	204.4	218.1	242.4	...	...	
Social protection	3.4	2.5	4.9	7.6	6.3	5.1	6.2	5.9	6.8	...	...	
Equals: Individual consumption expenditure of general government	142.7[a]	155.3[a]	159.9[a]	185.9[a]	211.2[a]	228.6[a]	263.8[a]	276.8[a]	305.3[a]	339.4	350.1	
Equals: Total actual individual consumption	2940.6	3136.9	3247.3	3487.8	3789.1	4113.8	4548.8	5182.2	5179.2	5352.6	5662.2	

[a] Discrepancy between components and total.

Table 4.1 Total Economy (S.1)

Series 100: 1993 SNA, CFA franc, Western calendar year — **Data in billions**

	2001	2002	2003	2004	2005	2006	2007	2008	2009	2010	2011	2012
Series	**100**											
I. Production account - Resources												
Output, at basic prices (otherwise, please specify)	6003.0	6277.2	6694.1	7227.8	7710.9	8154.1	9126.5	10329.2	10212.6	10887.9	11792.6	
Less: Financial intermediation services indirectly measured (only to be deducted if FISIM is not distributed to uses)	...	...	...	...	...	...	...	...	...	...	...	
Plus: Taxes less Subsidies on products	418.7	456.9	486.2	527.8	600.7	661.6	742.8	735.0	726.4	797.2	882.3	
Plus: Taxes on products	...	...	...	...	...	...	...	...	...	...	...	
Less: Subsidies on products	...	...	...	...	...	...	...	...	...	...	...	
I. Production account - Uses												
Intermediate consumption, at purchaser's prices	2846.3	3016.4	3193.4	3512.8	3718.4	3922.2	4460.9	5069.7	4905.6	5302.8	5908.2	
GROSS DOMESTIC PRODUCT	3575.5	3717.6	3986.8	4242.8	4593.1	4893.5	5408.3	5994.5	6033.4	6382.3	6766.8	
Less: Consumption of fixed capital	369.9	389.8	414.1	437.2	475.6	522.5	561.3	597.2	596.0	622.2	525.0	
NET DOMESTIC PRODUCT	3205.6	3327.8	3572.7	3805.7	4117.5	4371.0	4847.0	5397.3	5437.5	5760.1	6241.8	

	2001	2002	2003	2004	2005	2006	2007	2008	2009	2010	2011	2012
Series	**100**											
II.1.1 Generation of income account - Resources												
GROSS DOMESTIC PRODUCT	3575.5	3717.6	3986.8	4242.8	4593.1	4893.5	5408.3	5994.5	6033.4	6382.3	6766.8	
II.1.1 Generation of income account - Uses												
Compensation of employees	664.4	729.2	758.2	824.0	963.5	1018.4	1165.8	1279.7	1337.8	1403.1	1336.4	
Taxes on production and imports, less Subsidies	506.1	548.6	585.1	667.6	726.0	796.9[a]	901.9	904.7	994.0	1071.6	...	
Taxes on production and imports	...	...	...	...	...	...	...	...	...	...	...	
Taxes on products	437.5	454.0	468.7	487.6	510.8	530.4	557.0	550.8	523.5	539.1	569.9	
Other taxes on production	...	...	...	...	...	...	...	...	...	...	...	
Less: Subsidies	...	...	...	...	...	...	...	...	...	...	...	
Subsidies on products	...	...	...	...	...	...	...	...	...	...	...	
Other subsidies on production	...	...	...	...	...	...	...	...	...	...	...	
OPERATING SURPLUS, GROSS [b]	2404.9	2439.8	2643.5	2751.2	2903.6	3078.2	3340.6	3805.8	3790.9	3985.1	4358.8	
MIXED INCOME, GROSS	...	...	...	...	...	...	...	...	...	...	...	
II.1.2 Allocation of primary income account - Resources												
OPERATING SURPLUS, GROSS [b]	2404.9	2439.8	2643.5	2751.2	2903.6[a]	3078.2	3340.6	3805.8	3790.9	3985.1	4358.8	
MIXED INCOME, GROSS	...	...	...	...	...	...	...	...	...	...	...	
Compensation of employees	691.2	759.0	789.4	855.4	995.8	1052.3	1200.1	1317.3	1376.2	1441.2	1375.0	
Taxes on production and imports, less Subsidies [c]	640.7	710.6	648.1	729.8	744.9	683.6	838.2	880.2	907.0	1003.3	990.7	
Taxes on production and imports	...	...	...	...	...	...	...	...	...	...	...	
Taxes on products	418.7	456.9	486.2	527.8	600.7	661.6	742.9	...	...	...	...	
Other taxes on production	...	...	...	...	...	...	...	...	...	...	...	
Less: Subsidies	...	...	...	...	...	...	...	...	...	...	...	
Subsidies on products	...	...	...	...	...	...	...	...	...	...	...	
Other subsidies on production	...	...	...	...	...	...	...	...	...	...	...	
Property income [d]	16.2	13.6	32.9	45.9	71.2	52.6	55.8	86.4	35.2	55.5	77.8	
II.1.2 Allocation of primary income account - Uses												
Property income [e]	119.7	134.1	143.4	146.4	150.8	119.7	125.5	145.4	153.8	164.8	196.2	
GROSS NATIONAL INCOME [c]	3633.3	3789.0	3970.5	4235.9	4564.7	4747.1	5309.2	5944.3	5955.6	6320.3	6606.2	
II.2 Secondary distribution of income account - Resources												
GROSS NATIONAL INCOME [c]	3633.3	3789.0	3970.5	4235.9	4564.7	4747.1	5309.2	5944.3	5955.6	6320.3	6606.2	
Current taxes on income, wealth, etc.	...	...	...	...	...	...	...	...	...	...	...	
Social contributions	...	...	...	...	...	...	...	...	...	...	...	
Social benefits other than social transfers in kind	...	...	...	...	...	...	...	...	...	...	...	
Other current transfers	259.2	288.8	346.2	377.8	453.2	509.1	746.4	889.3	829.6	928.0	936.5	
II.2 Secondary distribution of income account - Uses												
Current taxes on income, wealth, etc.	...	...	...	...	...	...	...	...	...	...	...	
Social contributions	...	...	...	...	...	...	...	...	...	...	...	
Social benefits other than social transfers in kind	...	...	...	...	...	...	...	...	...	...	...	
Other current transfers	39.2	31.9	37.9	43.9	55.6	71.7	128.4	134.9	133.9	160.5	162.3	
GROSS DISPOSABLE INCOME	3853.3	4046.0	4278.8	4569.8	4962.3	5184.5	5927.3	6698.6	6651.2	7087.8	7380.3	

	2001	2002	2003	2004	2005	2006	2007	2008	2009	2010	2011	2012
Series	**100**											
II.4.1 Use of disposable income account - Resources												
GROSS DISPOSABLE INCOME	3853.3	4046.0	4278.8	4569.8	4962.3	5184.5	5927.3	6698.6	6651.2	7087.8	7380.3	
Adjustment for the change in net equity of households on pension funds	...	...	...	...	...	...	...	...	...	...	...	
II.4.1 Use of disposable income account - Uses												
Final consumption expenditure	3241.1	3466.3	3594.6	3861.2	4175.7	4539.7	5037.7	5696.4	5718.7	5924.3	6271.8	
Individual consumption expenditure	2940.6	3136.9	3247.3	3487.8	3789.1	4113.8	4548.8	5182.2	5179.2	5352.6	5662.2	
Collective consumption expenditure	300.5	329.4	347.3	373.4	386.6	425.9	488.9	514.2	539.5	571.7	609.6	
Adjustment for the change in net equity of households on pension funds	...	...	...	...	...	...	...	...	...	...	...	
SAVING, GROSS	612.2	579.6	684.2	708.6	786.6	644.9	889.6	1002.2	932.5	1163.5	1108.5	
III.1 Capital account - Changes in liabilities and net worth												
SAVING, GROSS	612.2	579.6	684.2	708.6	786.6	644.9	889.6	1002.2	932.5	1163.5	1108.5	
Capital transfers, receivable less payable	106.9	88.5	87.6	396.4	105.6	1185.9	95.2	107.8	145.1	151.6	118.7	
Capital transfers, receivable	106.9	88.5	87.6	396.4	105.6	1185.9	95.2	107.8	145.1	151.6	120.7	
Less: Capital transfers, payable	...	...	...	...	...	...	...	...	...	...	2.0	
Equals: CHANGES IN NET WORTH DUE TO SAVING AND CAPITAL TRANSFERS	719.1	668.1	771.8	1105.1	892.2	1830.8	987.7	1051.3[f]	...	...	...	
III.1 Capital account - Changes in assets												
Gross capital formation	657.5	638.5	875.1	917.5	1125.0	1208.9	1582.0	1874.7	1333.2	1443.1	1709.5	
Gross fixed capital formation	812.5	922.7	857.4	944.1	1071.4	1279.7	1414.1	1607.6	1386.2	1430.0	1611.4	
Changes in inventories	-155.0	-284.2	17.6	-26.6	53.6	-70.9	168.0	267.1	-53.0	13.1	98.0	
Acquisitions less disposals of valuables	...	...	...	...	...	...	...	...	...	...	...	
Acquisitions less disposals of non-produced non-financial assets	0.3	-0.0	-0.2	-0.2	-0.4	-1.9	64.3	-0.6	-1.0	-2.1	...	
Adjustment entry [g]	134.4	154.9	63.1	62.4	19.2	-125.4	-128.0	-28.2	3.3	11.4	-80.9	
NET LENDING (+) / NET BORROWING (-)	-73.1	-125.3	-166.1	125.4	-251.6	749.2	-533.6	-735.9	-257.9	-137.3	-401.3	
III.2 Financial account - Changes in liabilities and net worth												
Net incurrence of liabilities	...	...	...	...	...	...	...	...	...	...	...	
Currency and deposits	...	...	...	...	...	...	...	...	...	...	...	
Securities other than shares	...	...	...	...	...	...	...	...	...	...	...	
Loans	...	...	...	...	...	...	...	...	...	...	...	
Shares and other equity	...	...	...	...	...	...	...	...	...	...	...	
Insurance technical reserves	...	...	...	...	...	...	...	...	...	...	...	
Financial derivatives	...	...	...	...	...	...	...	...	...	...	...	
Other accounts payable	...	...	...	...	...	...	...	...	...	...	...	
NET LENDING (+) / NET BORROWING (-)	-73.1	-125.3	-166.1	125.4	-251.6	749.2	-533.6	-735.9	-257.9	-224.0	...	
III.2 Financial account - Changes in assets												
Net acquisition of financial assets	...	...	...	...	...	...	...	...	...	...	...	
Monetary gold and SDRs	...	...	...	...	...	...	...	...	...	...	...	
Currency and deposits	...	...	...	...	...	...	...	...	...	...	...	
Securities other than shares	...	...	...	...	...	...	...	...	...	...	...	

	2001	2002	2003	2004	2005	2006	2007	2008	2009	2010	2011	2012
Series	**100**											
Loans	...	...	...	...	...	...	...	...	...	...	...	
Shares and other equity	...	...	...	...	...	...	...	...	...	...	...	
Insurance technical reserves	...	...	...	...	...	...	...	...	...	...	...	
Financial derivatives	...	...	...	...	...	...	...	...	...	...	...	
Other accounts receivable	...	...	...	...	...	...	...	...	...	...	...	

[a] Discrepancy between Total Economy and domestic sectors as one or more data for domestic sectors have not been revised.
[b] Includes Mixed Income, Gross.
[c] Includes the adjustment for balance of payments
[d] Refers to Property income from the rest of the world.
[e] Refers to Property income to the rest of the world.
[f] Data for this year(s) have not been revised. Discrepancy between components and total.
[g] Refers to adjustment for balance of payments

Table 4.2 Rest of the world (S.2)

Series 100: 1993 SNA, CFA franc, Western calendar year **Data in billions**

	2001	2002	2003	2004	2005	2006	2007	2008	2009	2010	2011	2012
Series	**100**											
V.I External account of goods and services - Resources												
Imports of goods and services	1350.3	1448.6	1544.2	1687.3	1948.4	2109.0	2587.6	3142.9	2490.3	2577.8	2950.5	
Imports of goods	1047.1	1111.4	1200.4	1318.5	1523.7	1669.9	1995.5	2510.4	1947.8	2022.4	2354.1	
Imports of services	303.2	337.2	343.8	368.8	424.7	439.1	592.1	632.5	542.5	555.4	596.4	
V.I External account of goods and services - Uses												
Exports of goods and services	1027.1	1061.3	1061.3	1151.5	1240.8	1254.0	1376.2	1566.3	1471.8	1592.6	1736.0	
Exports of goods	735.3	743.4	730.5	797.4	832.4	833.5	802.2	987.9	990.1	1071.9	1200.4	
Exports of services	291.8	318.0	330.8	354.0	408.4	420.6	574.0	578.4	481.7	520.7	535.7	
EXTERNAL BALANCE OF GOODS AND SERVICES	323.2	387.2	482.9	535.9	707.6	855.0	1211.4	1576.6	1018.5	985.1	1214.5	
V.II External account of primary income and current transfers - Resources												
EXTERNAL BALANCE OF GOODS AND SERVICES	323.2	387.2	482.9	535.9	707.6	855.0	1211.4	1576.6	1018.5	985.1	1214.5	
Compensation of employees	6.3	3.5	5.2	5.4	5.6	5.2	6.5	6.2	7.2	8.3	8.4	
Taxes on production and imports, less Subsidies	...	...	...	...	...	...	...	...	...	...	...	
Taxes on production and imports	...	...	...	...	...	...	...	...	...	...	...	
Taxes on products	...	...	...	...	...	...	...	...	...	...	...	
Other taxes on production	...	...	...	...	...	...	...	...	...	...	...	
Less: Subsidies	...	...	...	...	...	...	...	...	...	...	...	
Subsidies on products	...	...	...	...	...	...	...	...	...	...	...	
Other subsidies on production	...	...	...	...	...	...	...	...	...	...	...	
Property income	119.7	134.1	143.4	146.4	150.8	119.7	125.5	145.4	153.8	164.8	196.2	
Current taxes on income, wealth, etc.	...	...	...	...	...	...	...	...	...	...	...	
Social contributions	...	...	...	...	...	...	...	...	...	...	...	
Social benefits other than social transfers in kind	...	...	...	...	...	...	...	...	...	...	...	
Other current transfers	39.2	31.9	37.9	43.9	55.6	71.7	128.4	134.9	133.9	160.5	162.3	

	2001	2002	2003	2004	2005	2006	2007	2008	2009	2010	2011	2012
Series	**100**											
Adjustment for the change in net equity of households on pension funds	...	...	...	...	...	...	...	...	...	...	...	
V.II External account of primary income and current transfers - Uses												
Compensation of employees	33.0	33.3	36.4	36.8	37.9	39.0	40.8	43.8	45.7	46.3	47.0	
Taxes on production and imports, less Subsidies	...	...	...	...	...	...	...	...	...	...	...	
Taxes on production and imports	...	...	...	...	...	...	...	...	...	...	...	
Taxes on products	...	...	...	...	...	...	...	...	...	...	...	
Other taxes on production	...	...	...	...	...	...	...	...	...	...	...	
Less: Subsidies	...	...	...	...	...	...	...	...	...	...	...	
Subsidies on products	...	...	...	...	...	...	...	...	...	...	...	
Other subsidies on production	...	...	...	...	...	...	...	...	...	...	...	
Property income	16.2	13.6	32.9	45.9	71.2	52.6	55.8	86.4	35.2	55.5	77.8	
Current taxes on income and wealth, etc.	...	...	...	...	...	...	...	...	...	...	...	
Social contributions	...	...	...	...	...	...	...	...	...	...	...	
Social benefits other than social transfers in kind	...	...	...	...	...	...	...	...	...	...	...	
Other current transfers	259.2	288.8	346.2	377.8	453.2	509.1	746.4	889.3	829.6	928.0	936.5	
Adjustment for the change in net equity of households on pension funds [a]	-0.1	-6.5	-44.2	0.0	-0.0	1.2	...	...	...	...	...	
CURRENT EXTERNAL BALANCE	180.0	227.4	297.9	271.0	357.2	450.7	628.8	843.7	403.0	288.9	520.0	
V.III.1 Capital account - Changes in liabilities and net worth												
CURRENT EXTERNAL BALANCE	180.0	227.4	297.9	271.0	357.2	450.7	628.8	843.7	403.0	288.9	520.0	
Capital transfers, receivable less payable	-106.9	-88.5	-87.6	-396.4	-105.6	-1185.9	-95.2	-107.8	-145.1	-151.6	-118.7	
Capital transfers, receivable	...	...	...	...	...	...	...	...	...	...	2.0	
Less: Capital transfers, payable	106.9	88.5	87.6	396.4	105.6	1185.9	95.2	107.8	145.1	151.6	120.7	
Equals: CHANGES IN NET WORTH DUE TO SAVING AND CAPITAL TRANSFERS	73.2	139.0	210.3	-125.5	251.6	-735.2	533.6	615.9	...	...	...	
V.III.1 Capital account - Changes in assets												
Acquisitions less disposals of non-produced non-financial assets	-0.3	0.0	0.2	0.2	0.4	1.9	-64.3	0.6	1.0	2.1	...	
NET LENDING (+) / NET BORROWING (-) [b]	73.1	132.5[c]	166.1	-125.4	251.6	-749.2	533.6	735.9	257.9	137.3	401.3	
V.III.2 Financial account - Changes in liabilities and net worth												
Net incurrence of liabilities	...	...	...	...	...	...	...	...	...	...	...	
Currency and deposits	...	...	...	...	...	...	...	...	...	...	...	
Securities other than shares	...	...	...	...	...	...	...	...	...	...	...	
Loans	...	...	...	...	...	...	...	...	...	...	...	
Shares and other equity	...	...	...	...	...	...	...	...	...	...	...	
Insurance technical reserves	...	...	...	...	...	...	...	...	...	...	...	
Financial derivatives	...	...	...	...	...	...	...	...	...	...	...	
Other accounts payable	...	...	...	...	...	...	...	...	...	...	...	
NET LENDING (+) / NET BORROWING (-)	73.1	132.5	166.1	-125.4	251.6	-749.2	533.6	615.9	...	...	...	

	2001	2002	2003	2004	2005	2006	2007	2008	2009	2010	2011	2012
Series	**100**											
	V.III.2 Financial account - Changes in assets											
Net acquisition of financial assets	...	...	...	...	...	...	...	...	...	...	...	
Monetary gold and SDRs	...	...	...	...	...	...	...	...	...	...	...	
Currency and deposits	...	...	...	...	...	...	...	...	...	...	...	
Securities other than shares	...	...	...	...	...	...	...	...	...	...	...	
Loans	...	...	...	...	...	...	...	...	...	...	...	
Shares and other equity	...	...	...	...	...	...	...	...	...	...	...	
Insurance technical reserves	...	...	...	...	...	...	...	...	...	...	...	
Financial derivatives	...	...	...	...	...	...	...	...	...	...	...	
Other accounts receivable	...	...	...	...	...	...	...	...	...	...	...	

[a] Refers to statistical discrepancy.
[b] Excludes Acquisitions less disposals of non-produced non-financial assets
[c] Statistical discrepancy with equivalent item in Table 4.1 (Total Economy).

Table 4.3 Non-financial Corporations (S.11)

Series 100: 1993 SNA, CFA franc, Western calendar year

Data in billions

	2001	2002	2003	2004	2005	2006	2007	2008	2009	2010	2011	2012
Series	**100**											
	I. Production account - Resources											
Output, at basic prices (otherwise, please specify)	2677.1	2933.4	3111.2	3395.3	3588.0	3683.6						
	I. Production account - Uses											
Intermediate consumption, at purchaser's prices	1716.0	1874.3	1933.3	2129.4	2271.7	2307.5						
VALUE ADDED GROSS, in basic prices	961.1	1059.1	1177.9	1265.9	1316.3[a]	1376.1[a]						
Less: Consumption of fixed capital	221.9	249.2	280.7	282.5	313.4	326.3						
VALUE ADDED NET, at basic prices	739.2	809.9	897.2	983.4	1002.9	1049.8						
	II.1.1 Generation of income account - Resources											
VALUE ADDED GROSS, at basic prices	961.1	1059.1	1177.9	1265.9	1316.3	1376.1						
	II.1.1 Generation of income account - Uses											
Compensation of employees	307.0	347.8	396.7	407.5	468.0	488.4						
Other taxes less Other subsidies on production	48.5	52.3	56.1	93.3	72.8	75.3						
Other taxes on production	54.5	58.8	62.5	99.9	80.3	83.5						
Less: Other subsidies on production	6.1	6.5	6.4	6.6	7.5	8.2						
OPERATING SURPLUS, GROSS	605.6	658.9	725.1	765.1	775.5	812.3						
	II.1.2 Allocation of primary income account - Resources											
OPERATING SURPLUS, GROSS	605.6	658.9	725.1	765.1	775.5	812.3						
Property income	...	...	...	...	...	...						
	II.1.2 Allocation of primary income account - Uses											
Property income	...	...	...	...	...	...						
BALANCE OF PRIMARY INCOMES	...	...	...	...	...	...						

[a] Data has not been revised. Discrepancy between Total Economy and domestic sectors.

Table 4.4 Financial Corporations (S.12)

Series 100: 1993 SNA, CFA franc, Western calendar year — **Data in billions**

	2001	2002	2003	2004	2005	2006	2007	2008	2009	2010	2011	2012
Series	**100**											
I. Production account - Resources												
Output, at basic prices (otherwise, please specify)	128.1	136.8	141.8	141.9	141.9	142.0						
I. Production account - Uses												
Intermediate consumption, at purchaser's prices	103.7	109.0	111.0	111.0	111.0	111.0						
VALUE ADDED GROSS, at basic prices	24.4	27.9	30.8	30.9	30.9[a]	31.0[a]						
Less: Consumption of fixed capital	4.3	4.6	4.8	4.8	4.8	4.8						
VALUE ADDED NET, at basic prices	20.1	23.3	26.0	26.1	26.2	26.3						
II.1.1 Generation of income account - Resources												
VALUE ADDED GROSS, at basic prices	24.4	27.9	30.8	30.9	30.9	31.0						
II.1.1 Generation of income account - Uses												
Compensation of employees	26.0	27.8	28.7	28.7	28.7	28.7						
Other taxes less Other subsidies on production	0.2	0.2	0.2	0.2	0.2	0.2						
Other taxes on production	0.2	0.2	0.2	0.2	0.2	0.2						
Less: Other subsidies on production	...	...	...	...	...	...						
OPERATING SURPLUS, GROSS	-1.7	-0.1	1.8	1.9	2.0	2.1						
II.1.2 Allocation of primary income account - Resources												
OPERATING SURPLUS, GROSS	-1.7	-0.1	1.8	1.9	2.0	2.1						
Property income	...	...	...	...	...	...						
II.1.2 Allocation of primary income account - Uses												
Property income	...	...	...	...	...	...						
BALANCE OF PRIMARY INCOMES	...	...	...	...	...	...						

[a] Data has not been revised. Discrepancy between Total Economy and domestic sectors.

Table 4.5 General Government (S.13)

Series 100: 1993 SNA, CFA franc, Western calendar year — **Data in billions**

	2001	2002	2003	2004	2005	2006	2007	2008	2009	2010	2011	2012
Series	**100**											
I. Production account - Resources												
Output, at basic prices (otherwise, please specify)	449.2	491.4	469.0	567.0	599.5	656.0						
I. Production account - Uses												
Intermediate consumption, at purchaser's prices	89.6	100.1	108.1	143.0	144.7	173.7						
VALUE ADDED GROSS, at basic prices	359.6	391.3	360.9	423.9	454.8[a]	482.3[a]						
Less: Consumption of fixed capital	118.2	130.3	128.7	142.8	147.5	158.1						
VALUE ADDED NET, at basic prices	241.4	261.0	232.2	281.1	307.3	324.1						

	2001	2002	2003	2004	2005	2006	2007	2008	2009	2010	2011	2012
Series	**100**											
	II.1.1 Generation of income account - Resources											
VALUE ADDED GROSS, at basic prices	359.6	391.3	360.9	423.9	454.8	482.3						
	II.1.1 Generation of income account - Uses											
Compensation of employees	241.4	261.0	232.2	281.1	307.3	324.1						
Other taxes less Other subsidies on production	...	...	...	...	...	...						
Other taxes on production	...	...	...	...	...	...						
Less: Other subsidies on production	...	...	...	...	...	...						
OPERATING SURPLUS, GROSS	118.2	130.3	128.7	142.8	147.5	158.2						
	II.1.2 Allocation of primary income account - Resources											
OPERATING SURPLUS, GROSS	118.2	130.3	128.7	142.8	147.5	158.2						
Taxes on production and imports, less Subsidies	...	...	...	...	...	...						
Taxes on production and imports	...	...	...	...	...	...						
Taxes on products	...	...	...	...	...	...						
Other taxes on production	...	...	...	...	...	...						
Less: Subsidies	...	...	...	...	...	...						
Subsidies on products	...	...	...	...	...	...						
Other subsidies on production	...	...	...	...	...	...						
Property income	...	...	...	...	...	...						
	II.1.2 Allocation of primary income account - Uses											
Property income	...	...	...	...	...	...						
BALANCE OF PRIMARY INCOMES	...	...	...	...	...	...						

[a] Data has not been revised. Discrepancy between Total Economy and domestic sectors.

Table 4.6 Households (S.14)

Series 100: 1993 SNA, CFA franc, Western calendar year — **Data in billions**

	2001	2002	2003	2004	2005	2006	2007	2008	2009	2010	2011	2012
Series	**100**											
	I. Production account - Resources											
Output, at basic prices (otherwise, please specify)	2741.1	2707.1	2960.9	3111.9	3345.9	3487.0						
	I. Production account - Uses											
Intermediate consumption, at purchaser's prices	935.6	931.5	1038.9	1127.1	1176.4	1202.3						
VALUE ADDED GROSS, at basic prices	1805.5	1775.6	1922.0	1984.8	2169.5[a]	2284.7[a]						
Less: Consumption of fixed capital	42.8	42.3	45.1	48.3	52.0	55.5						
VALUE ADDED NET, at basic prices	1762.7	1733.3	1877.0	1936.5	2117.5	2229.2						
	II.1.1 Generation of income account - Resources											
VALUE ADDED GROSS, at basic prices	1805.5	1775.6	1922.0	1984.8	2169.5	2284.7						
	II.1.1 Generation of income account - Uses											
Compensation of employees	84.0	85.7	91.6	97.2	102.8	113.3						

	2001	2002	2003	2004	2005	2006	2007	2008	2009	2010	2011	2012
Series	**100**											
Other taxes less Other subsidies on production	38.7	39.2	42.6	46.3	48.6	50.9						
Other taxes on production	38.7	39.2	42.6	46.3	48.6	50.9						
Less: Other subsidies on production	...	...	...	...	...	...						
OPERATING SURPLUS, GROSS	1682.9	1650.6	1787.8	1841.3	2018.2	2120.6						
MIXED INCOME, GROSS	...	...	...	...	...	...						
	II.1.2 Allocation of primary income account - Resources											
OPERATING SURPLUS, GROSS	1682.9	1650.6	1787.8	1841.3	2018.2	2120.6						
MIXED INCOME, GROSS	...	...	...	...	...	...						
Compensation of employees	...	...	...	...	...	...						
Property income	...	...	...	...	...	...						
	II.1.2 Allocation of primary income account - Uses											
Property income	...	...	...	...	...	...						
BALANCE OF PRIMARY INCOMES	...	...	...	...	...	...						

[a] Data has not been revised. Discrepancy between Total Economy and domestic sectors.

Table 4.7 Non-profit institutions serving households (S.15)

Series 100: 1993 SNA, CFA franc, Western calendar year — **Data in billions**

	2001	2002	2003	2004	2005	2006	2007	2008	2009	2010	2011	2012
Series	**100**											
	I. Production account - Resources											
Output, at basic prices (otherwise, please specify)	7.5	8.5	11.1	11.8	12.5	13.2						
	I. Production account - Uses											
Intermediate consumption, at purchaser's prices	1.4	1.6	2.1	2.3	2.4	2.6						
VALUE ADDED GROSS, at basic prices	6.1	6.9	9.0	9.5	10.1[a]	10.7[a]						
Less: Consumption of fixed capital	...	...	...	...	...	...						
VALUE ADDED NET, at basic prices	...	...	...	...	...	...						
	II.1.1 Generation of income account - Resources											
VALUE ADDED GROSS, at basic prices	6.1	6.9	9.0	9.5	10.1	10.7						
	II.1.1 Generation of income account - Uses											
Compensation of employees	6.1	6.9	9.0	9.5	10.1	10.7						
Other taxes less Other subsidies on production	...	...	...	...	...	...						
Other taxes on production	...	...	...	...	...	...						
Less: Other subsidies on production	...	...	...	...	...	...						
OPERATING SURPLUS, GROSS	...	...	...	...	...	...						

[a] Data has not been revised. Discrepancy between Total Economy and domestic sectors.